W9-BQJ-876

Outside Readings in
AMERICAN GOVERNMENT

Outside Readings in AMERICAN GOVERNMENT

THIRD EDITION

H. Malcolm Macdonald
THE UNIVERSITY OF TEXAS

Wilfred D. Webb
THE UNIVERSITY OF TEXAS

Edward G. Lewis
UNIVERSITY OF ILLINOIS

William L. Strauss
ARIZONA STATE COLLEGE

THOMAS Y. CROWELL COMPANY · NEW YORK

Library of Congress Catalog Number 56-12626

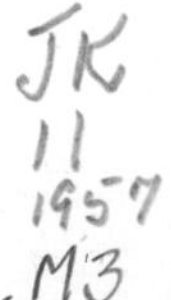

MANUFACTURED IN THE UNITED STATES OF AMERICA

PREFACE TO THE THIRD EDITION

THE PREPARATION of a preface to the third edition of this book is carried out with mixed feelings of satisfaction and frustration. It is a happy and comforting thought that demand for the work has been so great as to justify another edition. On the other hand, what can be said that has not already been written in an earlier preface?

The assignment of collateral readings is one of the established techniques for stimulating student interest and broadening and deepening understanding of a particular field of study. A single volume, in which the student can read the designated articles as readily and systematically as he does his textbook assignments, offers certain advantages over other sources of outside readings. Being at hand the book eliminates trips to the library and checks the tendency of some students to postpone reading outside the textbook. There is also a certain increase in effectiveness when textbook assignments and related articles are read in one sitting. And these advantages are augmented when a broad selection is available at low cost.

The following characteristics of the previous two editions have been retained:

1. Large Size: The volume is large and comprehensive; it provides teachers and students with a broad choice of pertinent selections.

2. Low Cost: The book has been carefully planned to take advantage of all possible economies growing out of modern design and manufacturing methods.

3. Student Motivation: The selections were made primarily for the purpose of quickening student interest in lively issues of the past and present rather than supplying exhaustive documentation.

The editors have also largely retained the original chapter topics and sequence in the belief that experience has shown the arrangement to be both logical and readily adaptable to a variety of approaches to the study of American government. Of the changes made, only a few are in the documentary material and decisions of the Supreme Court of the United States. For example, in Chapter V, "Civil Rights," we have dropped one case (*West Virginia State Board of Education* v. *Barnette*) and added another (*Brown* v. *Board of Education of Topeka*). The most extensive introduction of new material occurs in the area of current problems and issues. Altogether the new selections approximate one third of the original content. It is inevitable, we know from past experience, that not everyone will be satisfied with the alterations made, but we do believe that they improve the book's usefulness for the years ahead.

As we noted in the preface to the second edition, certain articles are strongly slanted in the direction of one point of view and whenever possible these have been counterbalanced with other articles which approach the problem differently. The editors do not necessarily espouse the views presented but justify their inclusion as stimulants to further thought and discussion on the part of the student and teacher.

The editors are grateful to the many persons who have aided by their comments and suggestions in the preparation of the third edition. Special thanks are due to our colleagues in the field who have written us proposing improvements and changes in the book. We regret that it was not possible in this edition to include all of the changes suggested, but in all instances we are grateful for the comments both favorable and unfavorable which we have received. Whatever defects remain are due to the decision of the editors. We are likewise indebted to the publishers and authors who have so generously permitted the reprinting of their work, which, after all, is the entire substance of the book.

H. M. M.
W. D. W.
E. G. L.
W. L. S.

CONTENTS

I. THE FOUNDATION OF AMERICAN GOVERNMENT

II. THE FEDERAL CONSTITUTION

III. THE FEDERAL SYSTEM

IV. STATE CONSTITUTIONS

V. CIVIL RIGHTS

VI. CITIZENSHIP AND SUFFRAGE

VII. POLITICAL PARTIES

VIII. NOMINATIONS AND ELECTIONS

IX. CONGRESS

X. STATE LEGISLATURES

XI. THE FEDERAL JUDICIAL SYSTEM

XII. THE STATE JUDICIAL SYSTEM

XIII. THE PRESIDENT AND THE NATIONAL ADMINISTRATIVE SYSTEM

XIV. THE GOVERNOR AND STATE ADMINISTRATION

XV. LOCAL GOVERNMENT

XVI. GOVERNMENT FINANCE

XVII. COMMERCE AND BUSINESS: THEIR REGULATION AND PROMOTION

XVIII. GOVERNMENT AND LABOR

XIX. AGRICULTURE AND CONSERVATION

XX. SOCIAL WELFARE

XXI. FOREIGN RELATIONS

NOTE TO STUDENTS

THE ACCOMPANYING DOCUMENTS and articles have been chosen by the editors on the basis of their experience as teachers of American Government. The documents and Supreme Court cases have been selected to give you examples of official statements concerning the nature and implications of our governmental system; the articles are intended to point up current and often controversial problems and to vitalize and humanize your study of government. The editors are not always in agreement with the points of view expressed in these selections and anticipate that you also will in some cases dissent from, and in others accede to, the arguments advanced. To the extent that these articles challenge you to a thoughtful evaluation of governmental processes they will have fulfilled our hope and aims.

Each of the selections is preceded by a headnote that places the problem to be discussed in its proper context and serves as a guide for your use prior to the commencement of your reading.

This book is intended to supplement any of the standard textbooks on American government. However, it may profitably be read by any interested person. It is our hope that the selections will help you develop a realistic understanding of the character and problems of our democratic system.

H. M. M.
W. D. W.
E. G. L.
W. L. S.

I

THE FOUNDATION OF AMERICAN GOVERNMENT

1. *Mayflower Compact**

THE MAYFLOWER COMPACT, one of the first documents of American political history, was drawn up and signed by the Pilgrim Fathers while anchored off the coast of New England on the eleventh of November, 1620. In it appear examples of both the contract theory of government and the concept of Divine Right of Kings. Its purpose was, in its own words, to create "a civil body politick" for the governance of the settlers in the New World.

IN THE name of God, Amen. We whose names are under-writen, the loyall subjects of our dread soveraigne Lord, King James, by the grace of God, of Great Britaine, Franc, and Ireland king, defender of the faith, etc., haveing undertaken, for the glorie of God, and advancemente of the Christian faith, and honour of our king and countrie, a voyage to plant the first colonie in the Northerne parts of Virginia, doe by these presents solemnly and mutualy in the presence of God, and one of another, covenant and combine our selves togeather into a civill body politick, for our better ordering and preservation and furtherance of the ends aforesaid; and by vertue hearof to enacte, constitute, and frame such just and equall lawes, ordinances, acts, constitutions, and offices, from time to time, as shall be thought most meete and convenient for the generall good of the Colonie, unto which we promise all due submission and obedience. In witness wherof we have hereunder subscribed our names at Cap-Codd the 11. of November, in the year of the

* William T. Davis, ed., *Bradford's History of Plymouth Plantation* (Charles Scribner's Sons, 1908), p. 107.

raigne of our soveraigne lord, King James, of England, France, and Ireland the eighteenth, and of Scotland the fiftie fourth. An°: Dom. 1620.

2. *Fundamental Orders of Connecticut, January 14, 1639**

The *Fundamental Orders* represents the first written constitution that created a government in America. In 1635-1636 migrations took place from certain eastern communities in Massachusetts to the Connecticut River Valley, among the migrants being the Reverend Thomas Hooker and his congregation of Newtown. Hooker and his associates insisted that the authority of government should rest upon the free consent of the people, and this view is reflected in the document of 1639, that was framed for the common government of the three towns of Windsor, Wethersfield, and Hartford. Even though the term "admitted freemen" was more restrictive in practice than it appears on paper, the establishment of this common government in Connecticut did represent a democratization of the orthodox Puritan theocracy.

Forasmuch as it hath pleased the Allmighty God by the wise disposition of his divyne providence so to Order and dispose of things that we the Inhabitants and Residents of Windsor, Harteford and Wethersfield are now cohabiting and dwelling in and upon the River of Conectecotte and the Lands thereunto adjoyneing; And well knowing where a people are gathered togather the word of God requires that to mayntayne the peace and union of such a people there should be an orderly and decent Government established according to God, to order and dispose of the affayres of the people at all seasons as occation shall require; doe therefore assotiate and conjoyne our selves to be as one Publike State or Commonwealth; and doe, for our selves and our Successors and such as shall be adjoyned to us at any tyme hereafter, enter into Combination and Confederation togather, to mayntayne and presearve the liberty and purity of the gospell of our Lord Jesus which we now professe, as also the disciplyne of the Churches, which according to the truth of the said gospell is now practised amongst us; As also in our Civell Affaires to be guided and governed according to such Lawes, Rules, Orders and decrees as shall be made, ordered & decreed, as followeth:—

* Reprinted with minor editorial changes from *Public Records of the Colony of Connecticut* (Hartford, Brown & Parsons, 1850), I, pp. 20-25.

1. It is Ordered, sentenced and decreed, that there shall be yerely two generall Assemblies or Courts, the on [one] the second thursday in Aprill, the other the second thursday in September, following; the first shall be called the Courte of Election, wherein shall be yerely Chosen from tyme to tyme soe many Magestrats and other publike Officers as shall be found requisitte: Whereof one to be chosen Governour for the yeare ensueing and untill another be chosen, and noe other Magestrate to be chosen for more then one yeare; provided allwayes there be sixe chosen besids the Governour; which being chosen and sworne according to an Oath recorded for that purpose shall have power to administer justice according to the Lawes here established, and for want thereof according to the rule of the word of God; which choise shall be made by all that are admitted freemen and have taken the Oath of Fidellity, and doe cohabitte within this Jurisdiction, (having beene admitted Inhabitants by the major part of the Towne wherein they live.) or the major parte of such as shall be then present.

2. It is Ordered, sentensed and decreed, that the Election of the aforesaid Magestrats shall be on this manner: every person present and quallified for choyse shall bring in (to the persons deputed to receave them) one single paper with the name of him written in yt whom he desires to have Governour, and he that hath the greatest number of papers shall be Governor for that yeare. And the rest of the Magestrats or publike Officers to be chosen in this manner: The Secretary for the tyme being shall first read the names of all that are to be put to choise and then shall severally nominate them distinctly, and every one that would have the person nominated to be chosen shall bring in one single paper written uppon, and he that would not have him chosen shall bring in a blanke: and every one that hath more written papers then blanks shall be a Magistrat for that yeare; which papers shall be receaved and told by one or more that shall be then chosen by the court and sworne to be faythfull therein; but in case there should not be sixe chosen as aforesaid, besides the Governor, out of those which are nominated, then he or they which have the most written papers shall be a Magestrate or Magestrats for the ensueing yeare, to make up the foresaid number.

3. It is Ordered, sentenced and decreed, that the Secretary shall not nominate any person, nor shall any person be chosen newly into the Magestracy which was not propownded in some Generall Courte before, to be nominated the next Election; and to that end yt shall be lawfull for ech of the Townes aforesaid by their deputyes to nominate any two whom they conceave fitte to be put to Election; and the Courte may ad so many more as they judge requisitt.

4. It is Ordered, sentenced and decreed that noe person be chosen

Governor above once in two yeares, and that the Governor be alwayes a member of some approved congregation, and formerly of the Magestracy within this Jurisdiction; and all the Magestrats Freemen of this Commonwelth: and that no Magestrate or other Publike officer shall execute any parte of his or their Office before they are severally sworne, which shall be done in the face of the Courte if they be present, and in case of absence by some deputed for that purpose.

5. It is Ordered, sentenced and decreed, that to the aforesaid Courte of Election the severall Townes shall send their deputyes, and when the Elections are ended they may proceed in any publike searvice as at other Courts. Also the other Generall Courte in September shall be for makeing of lawes, and any other publike occation, which concerns the good of the Commonwelth.

6. It is Ordered, sentenced and decreed, that the Governor shall, ether by himselfe or by the secretary, send out summons to the Constables of every Towne for the cauleing of these two standing Courts, on [one] month at lest before their severall tymes: And also if the Governor and the gretest parte of the Magestrats see cause uppon any spetiall occation to call a generall Courte, they may give order to the secretary soe to doe within fowerteene dayes warneing; and if urgent necessity so require, uppon a shorter notice, giveing sufficient grownds for yt to the deputyes when they meete, or els be questioned for the same; And if the Governor and Mayor [Major] parte of Magestrats shall ether neglect or refuse to call the two Generall standing Courts or ether of them, as also at other tymes when the occations of the Commonwelth require, the Freemen thereof, or the Mayor parte of them, shall petition to them soe to doe: if then yt be ether denyed or neglected the said Freemen or the Mayor parte of them shall have power to give order to the Constables of the severall Townes to doe the same, and so may meete togather, and chuse to themselves a Moderator, and may proceed to do any Acte of power, which any other Generall Courte may.

7. It is Ordered, sentenced and decreed that after there are warrants given out for any of the said Generall Courts, the Constable or Constables of ech Towne shall forthwith give notice distinctly to the inhabitants of the same, in some Publike Assembly or by goeing or sending from howse to howse, that at a place and tyme by him or them lymited and sett, they meet and assemble them selves togather to elect and chuse certen deputyes to be att the Generall Courte then following to agitate the afayres of the commonwelth; which said Deputyes shall be chosen by all that are admitted Inhabitants in the severall Townes and have taken the oath of fidellity; provided that non be chosen a Deputy for any Generall Courte which is not a Freeman of this Commonwelth.

The aforesaid deputyes shall be chosen in manner following: every person that is present and quallified as before expressed, shall bring the names of such, written in severall papers, as they desire to have chosen for that Imployment, and these 3 or 4, more or lesse, being the number agreed on to be chosen for that tyme, that have the greatest number of papers written for them shall be deputyes for that Courte; whose names shall be endorsed on the back side of the warrant and returned into the Courte, with the Constable or Constables hand unto the same.

8. It is Ordered, sentenced and decreed, that Wyndsor, Hartford and Wethersfield shall have power, ech Towne, to send fower of their Freemen as their deputyes to every Generall Courte; and whatsoever other Townes shall be hereafter added to this Jurisdiction, they shall send so many deputyes as the Courte shall judge meete, a resonable proportion to the number of Freemen that are in the said Townes being to be attended therein; which deputyes shall have the power of the whole Towne to give their voats and alowance to all such lawes and orders as may be for the publike good, and unto which the said Townes are to be bownd.

9. It is ordered and decreed, that the deputyes thus chosen shall have power and liberty to appoynt a tyme and a place of meeting togather before any Generall Courte to advise and consult of all such things as may concerne the good of the publike, as also to examine their owne Elections, whether according to the order, and if they or the gretest parte of them find any election to be illegall they may seclud such for the present from their meeting, and return the same and their resons to the Courte; and if yt prove true, the Courte may fyne the party or partyes so intruding and the Towne, if they see cause, and give out a warrant to goe to a newe election in a legall way, either in parte or in whole. Also the said deputyes shall have power to fyne any that shall be disorderly at their meetings, or for not comming in due tyme or place according to appoyntment; and they may returne the said fynes into the Courte if yt be refused to be paid, and the Tresurer to take notice of yt, and to estreete or levy the same as he doth other fynes.

10. It is Ordered, sentenced and decreed, that every Generall Courte, except such as through neglecte of the Governor and the greatest parte of Magestrats the Freemen themselves doe call, shall consist of the Governor, or some one chosen to moderate the Court, and 4 other Magestrats at lest, with mayor parte of the deputyes of the severall Townes legally chosen; and in case the Freemen or mayor parte of the magestrats, shall call a Courte, yt shall consist of the mayor parte of Freemen that are present or their deputyes, with a Moderator chosen by them: In which said Generall Courts shall consist the supreme power of the Commonwelth, and they only shall have power to make lawes or repeale them, to graunt levyes, to admitt of Freemen, dispose of lands

undisposed of, to severall Townes or persons, and also shall have power to call ether Courte or Magestrate or any other person whatsoever into question for any misdemeanour, and may for just causes displace or deale otherwise according to the nature of the offence; and also may deale in any other matter that concerns the good of this commonwelth, excepte election of Magestrats, which shall be done by the whole boddy of Freemen.

In which Courte the Governor or Moderator shall have power to order the Courte to give liberty of speech, and silence unceasonable and disorderly speakeings, to put all things to voate, and in case the vote be equall to have the casting voice. But non of these Courts shall be adjorned or dissolved without the consent of the major parte of the Courte.

11. It is ordered, sentenced and decreed, that when any Generall Courte uppon the occations of the Commonwelth have agreed uppon any summe or sommes of money to be levyed uppon the severall Townes within this Jurisdiction, that a Committee be chosen to sett out and appoynt what shall be the proportion of every Towne to pay of the said levy, provided the Committees be made up of an equall number of each Towne.

3. *The Declaration of Independence--1776* *

IN CONGRESS, JULY 4, 1776
THE UNANIMOUS DECLARATION OF THE
THIRTEEN UNITED STATES OF AMERICA

ON JULY 2, 1776, the Second Continental Congress adopted Richard Henry Lee's motion that the Colonies "are and of right ought to be free and independent states," and formally proclaimed this decision in the Declaration of Independence of July 4. The appearance of the Declaration terminated whatever hope was still entertained of a peaceful reconciliation with England. The document, which is basically the work of Jefferson, affirms the political theory of the Revolution. Intended, in part, as a propaganda document to rally the common people of the colonies and the liberal groups abroad to the support of the revolutionary movement, the Declaration embodies the political and social theories advanced by the more extreme revo-

* Reprinted from *Documents Illustrative of the Formation of the Union of the American States* (Washington, D.C., United States Government Printing Office, 1927), pp. 22-26.

lutionary leaders. Eventual tempering of its liberal implications as the result of the conservative reaction culminated in the states in the Massachusetts Constitution of 1780 and on the national level in the Philadelphia Constitution of 1787.

WHEN in the Course of human events, it becomes necessary for one people to dissolve the political bands which have connected them with another, and to assume among the powers of the earth, the separate and equal station to which the Laws of Nature and of Nature's God entitle them, a decent respect to the opinions of mankind requires that they should declare the causes which impel them to the separation.—We hold these truths to be self-evident, that all men are created equal, that they are endowed by their Creator with certain unalienable Rights, that among these are Life, Liberty and the pursuit of Happiness.—That to secure these rights, Governments are instituted among Men, deriving their just powers from the consent of the governed,—That whenever any Form of Government becomes destructive of these ends, it is the Right of the People to alter or to abolish it, and to institute new Government, laying its foundation on such principles and organizing its powers in such form, as to them shall seem most likely to effect their Safety and Happiness. Prudence, indeed, will dictate that Governments long established should not be changed for light and transient causes; and accordingly all experience hath shown, that mankind are more disposed to suffer, while evils are sufferable, than to right themselves by abolishing the forms to which they are accustomed. But when a long train of abuses and usurpations, pursuing invariably the same Object evinces a design to reduce them under absolute Despotism, it is their right, it is their duty, to throw off such Government, and to provide new Guards for their future security.—Such has been the patient sufferance of these Colonies; and such is now the necessity which constrains them to alter their former Systems of Government. The history of the present King of Great Britain is a history of repeated injuries and usurpations, all having in direct object the establishment of an absolute Tyranny over these States. To prove this, let Facts be submitted to a candid world.—He has refused his Assent to Laws, the most wholesome and necessary for the public good.—He has forbidden his Governors to pass Laws of immediate and pressing importance, unless suspended in their operation till his Assent should be obtained; and when so suspended, he has utterly neglected to attend to them.—He has refused to pass other Laws for the accommodation of large districts of people, unless those people would relinquish the right of Representation in the Legislature, a right inestimable to them and formidable to tyrants only.—He has called together legislative bodies at places unusual, uncomfortable, and distant from the depository of their public Records, for the sole purpose of fatiguing them into compliance with his measures. —He has dissolved Representative Houses repeatedly, for opposing with manly firmness his invasions on the rights of the people.—He has refused for a long time, after such dissolutions, to cause others to be elected; whereby the Legislative powers, incapable of Annihilation, have returned to the People at large for their exercise; the State remaining in the mean time exposed to all the dangers of invasion from without, and convulsions within.—He has endeavoured to prevent the population of these States; for that purpose obstructing the Laws for Naturalization of Foreigners; refusing to pass others to encourage their migration hither, and raising the conditions of new Appropriations of Lands.—He has obstructed the Administration of Justice, by refusing his Assent to Laws for establishing Judiciary powers.—He has made Judges dependent on his Will alone, for the tenure of their offices, and the amount and payment of their salaries.—He has erected a multitude of New Offices, and sent hither swarms of Officers to harrass our people, and eat out their substance.—He has kept among us, in times of peace, Standing Armies, without the Consent of our legislatures.—He has affected to render the Military independent of and superior to the Civil power.—He has combined with others to subject us to a jurisdiction foreign to our constitution, and unacknowledged by our laws; giving his Assent to their Acts of pretended Legislation:—For quartering large bodies of armed troops among us:—For protecting them, by a mock Trial, from punishment for any Murders which they should commit on the Inhabitants of these States:—For cutting off our Trade with all parts of the world:—For imposing Taxes on us without our Consent:—For depriving us in many cases, of the benefits of Trial by Jury:—For transporting us beyond Seas to be tried for pretended offences:—For abolishing the free System of English Laws in a neighbouring Province, establishing therein an Arbitrary government, and enlarging its Boundaries so as to render it at once an example and fit instrument for introducing the same absolute rule into these Colonies:—For taking away our Charters, abolishing our most valuable Laws, and altering fundamentally the Forms of our Governments:—For suspending our own Legislatures, and declaring themselves invested with power to legislate for us in all cases whatsoever.—He has abdicated Government here, by declaring us out of his Protection and waging War against us.—He has plundered our seas, ravaged our Coasts, burnt our towns, and destroyed the lives of our people.—He is at this time transporting large Armies of foreign Mercenaries to compleat the works of death, desolation and tyranny, already begun with circumstances of Cruelty & perfidy scarcely paralleled in the most barbarous ages, and totally unworthy the Head of a civilized nation.—He has constrained our fellow Citizens taken Captive on the high Seas to bear Arms against their Country, to become the executioners of their friends and Brethren, or to fall themselves by their Hands.—He has excited domestic insurrections amongst us, and has endeavoured to bring on the inhabitants of our frontiers, the merciless Indian Savages, whose known rule of warfare, is an undistinguished destruction of all ages, sexes and conditions. In every stage of these Oppressions We have Petitioned for Redress in the most humble terms: Our repeated Petitions have been answered only by repeated injury. A Prince, whose character is thus marked by every act which may define a Tyrant, is unfit to be the ruler of a free people. Nor have We been wanting in attentions to our British brethren. We have warned them from time to time of attempts by their legislature to extend an unwarrantable jurisdiction over us. We have reminded them of the circumstances of our emigration and settlement here. We have appealed to their native justice and magnanimity, and we have conjured them by the ties of our common kindred to disavow these usurpations, which, would inevitably interrupt our connections and correspondence. They too have been deaf to the voice of justice and of consanguinity. We must, therefore, acquiesce in the necessity, which denounces our Separation, and hold them, as we hold the rest of mankind, Enemies in War, in Peace Friends.—

We, Therefore, the Representatives of the united States of America, in General Congress, Assembled, appealing to the Supreme Judge of the world for the rectitude of our intentions, do, in the Name, and by Authority of the good People of these Colonies, solemnly publish and declare, That these United Colonies are, and of Right ought to be Free and Independent States; that they are Absolved from all Allegiance to the British Crown, and that all political connection between them and the State of Great Britain, is and ought to be totally dissolved; and that as Free and Independent States, they have full Power to levy War, conclude Peace, contract Alliances, establish Commerce, and to do all other Acts and Things which Independent States may of right do.—And for the support of this Declaration, with a firm reliance on the protection of Divine Providence, we mutually pledge to each other our Lives, our Fortunes and our sacred Honor.

4. *Articles of Confederation, March 1, 1781**

THE ARTICLES OF CONFEDERATION, which were ratified by the Congress on November 15, 1777, were finally approved by the thirteenth state, Maryland, in January, 1781, and became formally effective March 1 of that year. The legal basis of the central government during the Revolution, they continued in force until the ratification of the federal Constitution. Representing the initial organization of American government on the national level, they were designed to create only enough power to enable the Congress to carry on the Revolution and conclude the peace. After the termination of the Revolution their inadequacy to meet the problems of national integration and economic stabilization occasioned the calling of the Philadelphia Convention.

To all to whom these Presents shall come, we the under signed Delegates of the States affixed to our Names, send greeting.

WHEREAS the Delegates of the United States of America, in Congress assembled, did, on the 15th day of November, in the Year of Our Lord One thousand Seven Hundred and Seventy seven, and in the Second Year of the Independence of America, agree to certain articles of Confederation and perpetual Union between the States of Newhampshire, Massachusetts-bay, Rhodeisland and Providence Plantations, Connecticut, New York, New Jersey, Pennsylvania, Delaware, Maryland, Virginia, North-Carolina, South-Carolina, and Georgia in the words following, viz. "Articles of Confederation and perpetual Union between the states of Newhampshire, Massachusetts-bay, Rhodeisland and Providence Plantations, Connecticut, New-York, New-Jersey, Pennsylvania, Delaware, Maryland, Virginia, North-Carolina, South-Carolina and Georgia.

ARTICLE I. The Stile of this confederacy shall be "The United States of America."

ARTICLE II. Each state retains its sovereignty, freedom, and independence, and every Power, Jurisdiction and right, which is not by this confederation expressly delegated to the United States, in Congress assembled.

ARTICLE III. The said states hereby severally enter into a firm league of friendship with each other, for their common defence, the security of their Liberties, and their mutual and general welfare, binding them-

* Reprinted from *Documents Illustrative of the Formation of the Union of the American States* (Washington, D.C., United States Government Printing Office, 1927), pp. 27-37.

selves to assist each other, against all force offered to, or attacks made upon them, or any of them, on account of religion, sovereignty, trade, or any other pretence whatever.

ARTICLE IV. The better to secure and perpetuate mutual friendship and intercourse among the people of the different states in this union, the free inhabitants of each of these states, paupers, vagabonds and fugitives from justice excepted, shall be entitled to all privileges and immunities of free citizens in the several states; and the people of each state shall have free ingress and regress to and from any other state, and shall enjoy therein all the privileges of trade and commerce, subject to the same duties, impositions and restrictions as the inhabitants thereof respectively, provided that such restriction shall not extend so far as to prevent the removal of property imported into any state, to any other state, of which the Owner is an inhabitant; provided also that no imposition, duties or restriction shall be laid by any state, on the property of the united states, or either of them.

If any Person guilty of, or charged with treason, felony, or other high misdemeanor in any state, shall flee from Justice, and be found in any of the united states, he shall, upon demand of the Governor or executive power, of the state from which he fled, be delivered up and removed to the state having jurisdiction of his offence.

Full faith and credit shall be given in each of these states to the records, acts and judicial proceedings of the courts and magistrates of every other state.

ARTICLE V. For the more convenient management of the general interests of the united states, delegates shall be annually appointed in such manner as the legislature of each state shall direct, to meet in Congress on the first Monday in November, in every year, with a power reserved to each state, to recal its delegates, or any of them, at any time within the year, and to send others in their stead, for the remainder of the Year.

No state shall be represented in Congress by less than two, nor by more than seven Members; and no person shall be capable of being a delegate for more than three years in any term of six years; nor shall any person, being a delegate, be capable of holding any office under the united states, for which he, or another for his benefit receives any salary, fees or emolument of any kind.

Each state shall maintain its own delegates in a meeting of the states, and while they act as members of the committee of the states.

In determining questions in the united states in Congress assembled, each state shall have one vote.

Freedom of speech and debate in Congress shall not be impeached or questioned in any Court, or place out of Congress, and the members of congress shall be protected in their persons from arrests and imprisonments, during the time of their going to and from, and attendance on congress, except for treason, felony, or breach of the peace.

ARTICLE VI. No state, without the Consent of the united states in congress assembled, shall send any embassy to, or receive any embassy from, or enter into any conference, agreement, alliance or treaty with any King prince or state; nor shall any person holding any office of profit or trust under the united states, or any of them, accept of any present, emolument, office or title of any kind whatever from any king, prince or foreign state; nor shall the united states in congress assembled, or any of them, grant any title of nobility.

No two or more states shall enter into any treaty, confederation or alliance whatever between them, without the consent of the united states in congress assembled, specifying accurately the purposes for which the same is to be entered into, and how long it shall continue.

No state shall lay any imposts or duties, which may interfere with any stipulations in treaties, entered into by the united states in congress assembled, with any king, prince or state, in pursuance of any treaties already proposed by congress, to the courts of France and Spain.

No vessels of war shall be kept up in time of peace by any state, except such number only, as shall be deemed necessary by the united states in congress assembled, for the defence of such state, or its trade; nor shall any body of forces be kept up by any state, in time of peace, except such number only, as in the judgment of the united states, in congress assembled, shall be deemed requisite to garrison the forts necessary for the defence of such state; but every state shall always keep up a well regulated and disciplined militia, sufficiently armed and accoutred, and shall provide and constantly have ready for use, in public stores, a due number of field pieces and tents, and a proper quantity of arms, ammunition and camp equipage.

No state shall engage in any war without the consent of the united states in congress assembled, unless such state be actually invaded by enemies, or shall have received certain advice of a resolution being formed by some nation of Indians to invade such state, and the danger is so imminent as not to admit of a delay till the united states in congress assembled can be consulted: nor shall any state grant commissions to any ships or vessels of war, nor letters of marque or reprisal, except it be after a declaration of war by the united states in congress assembled, and then only against the kingdom or state and the subjects thereof, against which war has been so declared, and under such regulations as shall be established by the united states in congress assembled, unless such state be infested by pirates, in which case vessels of war may be fitted out for that occasion, and kept so long as the danger shall continue, or until the united states in congress assembled, shall determine otherwise.

ARTICLE VII. When land-forces are raised by any state for the common defence, all officers of or under the rank of colonel, shall be appointed by the legislature of each state respectively, by whom such forces shall be raised, or in such manner as such state shall direct, and all vacancies shall be filled up by the State which first made the appointment.

ARTICLE VIII. All charges of war, and all other expenses that shall be incurred for the common defence or general welfare, and allowed by the united states in congress assembled, shall be defrayed out of a common treasury, which shall be supplied by the several states in proportion to the value of all land within each state, granted to or surveyed for any Person, as such land and the buildings and improvements thereon shall be estimated according to such mode as the united states in congress assembled, shall from time to time direct and appoint.

The taxes for paying that proportion shall be laid and levied by the authority and direction of the legislatures of the several states within the time agreed upon by the united states in congress assembled.

ARTICLE IX. The united states in congress assembled, shall have the sole and exclusive right and power of determining on peace and war, except in the cases mentioned in the sixth article—of sending and receiving ambassadors—entering into treaties and alliances, provided that no treaty of commerce shall be made whereby the legislative power of the respective states shall be restrained from imposing such imposts and duties on foreigners as their own people are subjected to, or from prohibiting the exportation or importation of any species of goods or commodities, whatsoever—of establishing rules for deciding in all cases, what captures on land or water shall be legal, and in what manner prizes taken by land or naval forces in the service of the united states shall be divided or appropriated—of granting letters of marque and reprisal in times of peace—appointing courts for the trial of piracies and felonies committed on the high seas and establishing courts for receiving and determining finally appeals in all cases of captures, provided that no member of congress shall be appointed a judge of any of the said courts.

The united states in congress assembled shall also be the last resort on appeal in all disputes and differences now subsisting or that hereafter may arise between two or more states concerning boundary, jurisdiction or any other cause whatever; which authority shall always be exercised in the manner following. Whenever the legislative or executive authority or lawful agent of any state in controversy with another shall present a petition to congress stating the matter in question and praying for a hearing, notice thereof shall be given by order of congress to the legislative or executive authority of the other state in controversy, and a day assigned for the appearance of the parties by their lawful agents, who shall then be directed to appoint by joint consent, commissioners or judges to constitute a court for hearing and determining the matter in question: but if they cannot agree, congress shall name three persons out of each of the united states, and from the list of such persons each party shall alternately strike out one, the petitioners beginning, until the number shall be reduced to thirteen; and from that number not less than seven, nor more than nine names as congress shall direct, shall in the presence of congress be drawn out by lot, and the persons whose names shall be so drawn or any five of them, shall be commissioners or judges, to hear and finally determine the controversy, so always as a major part of the judges who shall hear the cause shall agree in the determination: and if either party shall neglect to attend at the day appointed, without showing reasons, which congress shall judge sufficient, or being present shall refuse to strike, the congress shall proceed to nominate three persons out of each state, and the secretary of congress shall strike in behalf of such party absent or refusing; and the judgment and sentence of the court to be appointed, in the manner before prescribed, shall be final and conclusive; and if any of the parties shall refuse to submit to the authority of such court, or to appear or defend their claim or cause, the court shall nevertheless proceed to pronounce sentence, or judgment, which shall in like manner be final and decisive, the judgment or sentence and other proceedings being in either case transmitted to congress, and lodged among the acts of congress for the security of the parties concerned: provided that every commissioner, before he sits in judgment, shall take an oath to be administered by one of the judges of the supreme or superior court of the state, where the cause shall be tried, "well and truly to hear and determine the matter in question, according to the best of his judgment, without favour, affection or hope of reward:" provided also, that no state shall be deprived of territory for the benefit of the united states.

All controversies concerning the private right of soil claimed under different grants of two or more states, whose jurisdictions as they may respect such lands, and the states which passed such grants are adjusted, the said grants or either of them being at the same time claimed to have originated antecedent to such settlement of jurisdiction, shall on the petition of either party to the congress of the united states, be finally determined as near as may be in the same manner as is before prescribed for deciding disputes respecting territorial jurisdiction between different states.

The united states in congress assembled shall also have the sole and exclusive right and power of regulating the alloy and value of coin struck by their own authority, or by that of the respective states—fixing the standard of weights and measures throughout the united states—regulating the trade and managing all affairs with the Indians, not members of any of the states, provided that the legislative right of any state within its own limits be not infringed or violated—establishing or regulating post-offices from one state to another, throughout all the united states, and exacting such postage on the papers passing thro' the same as may be requisite to defray the expenses of the said office—appointing all officers of the land forces, in the service of the united states, excepting regimental officers—appointing all the officers of the naval forces, and commissioning all officers whatever in the service of the united states—making rules for the government and regulation of the said land and naval forces, and directing their operations.

The united states in congress assembled shall have authority to appoint a committee, to sit in the recess of congress, to be denominated "A Committee of the States," and to consist of one delegate from each state; and to appoint such other committees and civil officers as may be necessary for managing the general affairs of the united states under their direction—to appoint one of their number to preside, provided that no person be allowed to serve in the office of president more than one year in any term of three years; to ascertain the necessary sums of money to be raised for the service of the united states, and to appropriate and apply the same for defraying the public expences—to borrow money, or emit bills on the credit of the united states, transmitting every half year to the respective states an account of the sums of money so borrowed or emitted,—to build and equip a navy—to agree upon the number of land forces, and to make requisitions from each state for its quota, in proportion to the number of white inhabitants in such state; which requisition shall be binding, and thereupon the legislature of each state shall appoint the regimental officers, raise the men and cloath, arm and equip them in a soldier like manner, at the expence of the united states; and the officers and men so cloathed, armed and equipped shall march to the place appointed, and within the time agreed on by the united states in congress assembled: But if the united states in congress assembled shall, on consideration of circumstances judge proper that any state should not raise men, or should raise a smaller number than its quota, and that any other state should raise a greater number of men than the quota thereof, such extra number shall be raised, officered, cloathed, armed and equipped in the same manner as the quota of such state, unless the legislature of such state shall judge that such extra number cannot be safely spared out of the same, in which case they shall raise officer, cloath, arm and equip as many of such extra number as they judge can be safely spared. And the officers and men so cloathed, armed and equipped, shall march to the place appointed, and within the time agreed on by the united states in congress assembled.

The united states in congress assembled shall never engage in a war, nor grant letters of marque and reprisal in time of peace, nor enter into any treaties or alliances, nor coin money, nor regulate the value thereof, nor ascertain the sums and expences necessary for the defence and welfare of the united states, or any of them, nor emit bills, nor borrow money on the credit of the united states, nor appropriate money, nor agree upon the number of vessels of war, to be built or purchased, or the number of land or sea forces to be raised, nor appoint a commander in chief of the army or navy, unless nine states assent to the same: nor shall a question on any other point, except for adjourning from day to day be determined, unless by the votes of a majority of the united states in congress assembled.

The congress of the united states shall have power to adjourn to any time within the year, and to any place within the united states, so that no period of adjournment be for a longer duration than the space of six Months, and shall publish the Journal of their proceedings monthly, except such parts thereof relating to treaties, alliances or military operations, as in their judgment require secrecy; and the yeas and nays of the delegates of each state on any question shall be entered on the Journal, when it is desired by any delegate; and the delegates of a state, or any of them, at his or their request shall be furnished with a transcript of the said Journal, except such parts as are above excepted, to lay before the legislatures of the several states.

ARTICLE X. The committee of the states, or any nine of them, shall be authorized to execute, in the recess of congress, such of the powers of congress as the united states in congress assembled, by the consent of nine states, shall from time to time think expedient to vest them with; provided that no power be delegated to the said committee for the exercise of which, by the articles of confederation, the voice of nine states in the congress of the united states assembled is requisite.

ARTICLE XI. Canada acceding to this confederation, and joining in the measures of the united states, shall be admitted into, and entitled to all the advantages of this union: but no other colony shall be admitted into the same, unless such admission be agreed to by nine states.

ARTICLE XII. All bills of credit emitted, monies borrowed and debts contracted by, or under the authority of congress, before the assembling of the united states, in pursuance of the present confederation, shall be deemed and considered as a charge against the united states, for payment and satisfaction whereof the said united states, and the public faith are hereby solemnly pledged.

ARTICLE XIII. Every state shall abide by the determinations of the united states in congress assembled, on all questions which by this confederation are submitted to them. And the Articles of this confederation shall be inviolably observed by every state, and the union shall be perpetual; nor shall any alteration at any time hereafter be made in any of them; unless such alteration be agreed to in a congress of the united states, and be afterwards confirmed by the legislatures of every state.

And Whereas it hath pleased the Great Governor of the World to incline the hearts of the legislatures we respectively represent in congress, to approve of, and to authorize us to ratify the said articles of confederation and perpetual union. Know Ye that we the undersigned delegates, by virtue of the power and authority to us given for that purpose, do by these presents, in the name and in behalf of our respective constituents, fully and entirely ratify and confirm each and every of the said articles of confederation and perpetual union, and all and singular the matters and things therein contained: And we do further solemnly plight and engage the faith of our respective constituents, that they shall abide by the determinations of the united states in congress assembled, on all questions, which by the said confederation are submitted to them. And that the articles thereof shall be inviolably observed by the states we respectively represent, and that the union shall be perpetual. In Witness whereof we have hereunto set our hands in Congress. Done at Philadelphia in the state of Pennsylvania the ninth day of July, in the Year of our Lord one Thousand seven Hundred and Seventy-eight, and in the third year of the independence of America.

*5. Massachusetts Constitution of 1780**

A CONSTITUTION OR FRAME OF GOVERNMENT, AGREED UPON BY THE DELEGATES OF THE PEOPLE OF THE STATE OF MASSACHUSETTS-BAY, -- IN CONVENTION, -- BEGUN AND HELD AT CAMBRIDGE, ON THE FIRST OF SEPTEMBER, 1779, AND CONTINUED BY ADJOURNMENTS TO THE SECOND OF MARCH, 1780.

THE MASSACHUSETTS CONSTITUTION of 1780 embodies the victory of the conservative forces over the radical tendencies that had developed in certain of the states during the Revolution. Returning to the

*Reprinted from *Journal of the Convention for Framing A Constitution of Government for the State of Massachusetts Bay, From the Commencement of Their First*

model of organization set up for a Royal Colony, the constitution provides for a separation of powers, checks and balances, and a restricted franchise. Drawn up and ratified by a popularly elected constitutional convention, the document is truly a "fundamental law" and not the mere creation of the state legislature. The basic governmental framework thus established remains in general effect in Massachusetts today. The constitution as a whole had a profound effect upon subsequent constitutional developments in other states. The sections reproduced below convey the general tone and structure of the document.

PREAMBLE

THE end of the institution, maintenance and administration of government, is to secure the existence of the body-politic; to protect it; and to furnish the individuals who compose it, with the power of enjoying, in safety and tranquillity, their natural rights, and the blessings of life; And whenever these great objects are not obtained, the people have a right to alter the government, and to take measures necessary for their safety, prosperity and happiness.

The body-politic is formed by a voluntary association of individuals: It is a social compact, by which the whole people covenants with each citizen, and each citizen with the whole people, that all shall be governed by certain laws for the common good. It is the duty of the people, therefore, in framing a Constitution of Government, to provide for an equitable mode of making laws, as well as for an impartial interpretation, and a faithful execution of them; that every man may, at all times, find his security in them.

We, therefore, the people of Massachusetts, acknowledging, with grateful hearts, the goodness of the Great Legislator of the Universe, in affording us, in the course of His providence, an opportunity, deliberately and peaceably, without fraud, violence or surprise, of entering into an original, explicit, and solemn compact with each other; and of forming a new Constitution of Civil Government, for ourselves and posterity; and devoutly imploring His direction in so interesting a design, DO agree upon, ordain and establish, the following *Declaration of Rights, and Frame of Government*, as the CONSTITUTION of the COMMONWEALTH of MASSACHUSETTS.

Session, September 1, 1779, To the Close of Their Last Session, June 16, 1780 (Boston: Dutton and Wentworth, Printers to the State, 1832), pp. 222-225; 227-240; 242-244.

PART THE FIRST

A DECLARATION OF THE RIGHTS OF THE INHABITANTS OF THE COMMONWEALTH OF MASSACHUSETTS

ART. I.—All men are born free and equal, and have certain natural, essential, and unalienable rights; among which may be reckoned the right of enjoying and defending their lives and liberties; that of acquiring, possessing, and protecting property; in fine, that of seeking and obtaining their safety and happiness.

II.—It is the right as well as the duty of all men in society, publicly, and at stated seasons, to worship the SUPREME BEING, the great creator and preserver of the universe. And no subject shall be hurt, molested, or restrained, in his person, liberty, or estate, for worshipping GOD in the manner and season most agreeable to the dictates of his own conscience; or for his religious profession or sentiments; provided he doth not disturb the public peace, or obstruct others in their religious worship.

III.—As the happiness of a people, and the good order and preservation of civil government, essentially depend upon piety, religion and morality; and as these cannot be generally diffused through a community, but by the institution of the public worship of GOD, and of public instructions in piety, religion and morality: Therefore, to promote their happiness and to secure the good order and preservation of their government, the people of this Commonwealth have a right to invest their legislature with power to authorize and require, and the legislature shall, from time to time, authorize and require, the several towns, parishes, precincts, and other bodies-politic, or religious societies, to make suitable provision, at their own expense, for the institution of the public worship of GOD, and for the support and maintenance of public protestant teachers of piety, religion and morality, in all cases where such provision shall not be made voluntarily.

And the people of this Commonwealth have also a right to, and do, invest their legislature with authority to enjoin upon all the subjects an attendance upon the instructions of the public teachers aforesaid, at stated times and seasons, if there be any on whose instructions they can conscientiously and conveniently attend.

Provided notwithstanding, that the several towns, parishes, precincts, and other bodies-politic, or religious societies, shall, at all times, have the exclusive right of electing their public teachers, and of contracting with them for their support and maintenance.

And all monies paid by the subject to the support of public worship, and of the public teachers aforesaid, shall, if he require it, be uniformly applied to the support of the public teacher or teachers of his own religious sect or denomination, provided there be any on whose instructions he attends: otherwise it may be paid towards the support of the teacher or teachers of the parish or precinct in which the said monies are raised.

And every denomination of christians, demeaning themselves peaceably, and as good subjects of the Commonwealth, shall be equally under the protection of the law: And no subordination of any one sect or denomination to another shall ever be established by law.

IV.—The people of this Commonwealth have the sole and exclusive right of governing themselves as a free, sovereign, and independent state; and do, and forever hereafter shall, exercise and enjoy every power, jurisdiction, and right, which is not, or may not hereafter, be by them expressly delegated to the United States of America, in Congress assembled.

V.—All power residing originally in the people, and being derived from them, the several magistrates and officers of government, vested with authority, whether legislative, executive, or judicial, are their substitutes and agents, and are at all times accountable to them.

VI.—No man, nor corporation, or association of men, have any other title to obtain advantages, or particular and exclusive privileges, distinct from those of the community, than what arises from the consideration of services rendered to the public; and this title being in nature neither hereditary, nor transmissible to children, or descendants, or relations by blood, the idea of a man born a magistrate, lawgiver, or judge, is absurd and unnatural.

VII.—Government is instituted for the common good; for the protection, safety, prosperity and happiness of the people; and not for the profit, honor, or private interest of any one man, family, or class of men: Therefore the people alone have an incontestible, unalienable, and indefeasible right to institute government; and to reform, alter, or totally change the same, when their protection, safety, prosperity and happiness require it.

VIII.—In order to prevent those, who are vested with authority, from becoming oppressors, the people have a right, at such periods and in such manner as they shall establish by their frame of government, to cause their public officers to return to private life; and to fill up vacant places by certain and regular elections and appointments.

IX.—All elections ought to be free; and all the inhabitants of this Commonwealth, having such qualifications as they shall establish by their frame of government, have an equal right to elect officers, and to be elected, for public employments. . . .

• • • • •

XXX.—In the government of this Commonwealth, the legislative department shall never exercise the executive and judicial powers, or either of them: The executive shall never exercise the legislative and judicial powers, or either of them: The judicial shall never exercise the legislative and executive powers, or either of them: to the end it may be a government of laws and not of men.

PART THE SECOND

THE FRAME OF GOVERNMENT

• • • • •

CHAPTER I

The Legislative Power

SECTION I: *The General Court*

ART. I.—The department of legislation shall be formed by two branches, a *Senate* and *House of Representatives:* each of which shall have a negative on the other.

The legislative body shall assemble every year, on the last Wednesday in May, and at such other times as they shall judge necessary; and shall dissolve and be dissolved on the day next preceding the said last Wednesday in May; and shall be styled, THE GENERAL COURT OF MASSACHUSETTS.

II.—No bill or resolve of the Senate or House of Representatives shall become a law, and have force as such, until it shall have been laid before the Governor for his revisal: And if he, upon such revision, approve thereof, he shall signify his approbation by signing the same. But if he have any objection to the passing of such bill or resolve, he shall return the same, together with his objections thereto, in writing, to the Senate or House of Representatives, in which soever the same shall have originated; who shall enter the objections sent down by the Governor, at large, on their records, and proceed to reconsider the said bill or resolve: But if, after such reconsideration, two thirds of the said Senate or House of Representatives, shall, notwithstanding the said objections, agree to pass the same, it shall, together with the objections, be sent to the other branch of the legislature, where it shall also be reconsidered, and if approved by two thirds of the members present, shall have the force of a law: But in all such cases the votes of both houses shall be determined by yeas and nays; and the names of the persons voting for, or against, the said bill or resolve, shall be entered upon the public records of the Commonwealth.

And in order to prevent unnecessary delays, if any bill or resolve shall not be returned by the Governor within five days after it shall have been presented, the same shall have the force of a law.

III.—The General Court shall forever have full power and authority to erect and constitute judicatories and courts of record, or other courts, to be held in the name of the Commonwealth, for the hearing, trying, and determining of all manner of crimes, offences, pleas, processes, plaints, actions, matters, causes and things, whatsoever, arising or happening within the Commonwealth, or between or concerning persons inhabiting, or residing, or brought within the same; whether the same be criminal or civil, or whether the said crimes be capital or not capital, and whether the said pleas be real, personal, or mixt; and for the awarding and making out of execution thereupon: To which courts and judicatories are hereby given and granted full power and authority, from time to time, to administer oaths or affirmations, for the better discovery of truth in any matter in controversy or depending before them.

IV.—And further, full power and authority are hereby given and granted to the said General Court, from time to time, to make, ordain, and establish, all manner of wholesome and reasonable orders, laws, statutes, and ordinances, directions and instructions, either with penalties or without; so as the same be not repugnant or contrary to this Constitution, as they shall judge to be for the good and welfare of this Commonwealth, and for the government and ordering thereof, and of the subjects of the same, and for the necessary support and defence of the government thereof; and to name and settle annually, or provide by fixed laws, for the naming and settling all civil officers within the said Commonwealth, the election and constitution of whom are not hereafter in this Form of Government otherwise provided for and to set forth the several duties, powers and limits, of the several civil and military officers of this Commonwealth, and the forms of such oaths or affirmations as shall be respectively administered unto them for the execution of their several offices and places, so as the same be not repugnant or contrary to this Constitution, and to impose and levy proportional and reasonable assessments, rates, and taxes, upon all the inhabitants of, and persons resident, and estates lying, within the said Commonwealth; and also to impose, and levy reasonable duties and excises, upon any produce, goods, wares, merchandize, and commodities whatsoever, brought into, produced, manufactured, or being within the same; to be issued and disposed of by warrant, under the hand of the Governor of this Commonwealth for the time being, with the advice and consent of the Council, for the public service, in the necessary defence and support of the government of the said Commonwealth, and the protection and preservation of the subjects thereof, according to such acts as are or shall be in force within the same. . . .

SECTION II: *Senate*

ART. I—There shall be annually elected by the freeholders and other inhabitants of this Commonwealth, qualified as in this Constitution is provided, forty persons to be Counsellors and Senators for the year ensuing their election; to be chosen by the inhabitants of the districts, into which the Commonwealth may from time to time be divided by the General Court for that purpose: And the General Court, in assigning the numbers to be elected by the respective districts, shall govern themselves by the proportion of the public taxes paid by the said districts; and timely make known to the inhabitants of the Commonwealth, the limits of each district, and the number of Counsellors and Senators to be chosen therein; provided, that the number of such districts shall never be less than thirteen; and that no district be so large as to entitle the same to choose more than six Senators. . . .

II.—The Senate shall be the first branch of the legislature; and the Senators shall be chosen in the following manner, viz: There shall be a meeting on the first Monday in April annually, forever, of the inhabitants of each town in the several counties of this Commonwealth; to be called by the Selectmen, and warned in due course of law, at least seven days before the first Monday in April, for the purpose of electing persons to be Senators and Counsellors: And at such meetings every male inhabitant of twenty-one years of age and upwards, having a freehold estate within the Commonwealth, of the annual income of three pounds, or any estate of the value of sixty pounds, shall have a right to give in his vote for the Senators for the district of which he is an inhabitant. And to remove all doubts concerning the meaning of the word "inhabitant" in this constitution, every person shall be considered as an inhabitant, for the purpose of electing and being elected into any office, or place within this State, in that town, district, or plantation, where he dwelleth, or hath his home. . . .

• • • • •

V.—Provided nevertheless, that no person shall be capable of being elected as a Senator, who is not seized in his own right of a freehold within this Commonwealth, of the value of three hundred pounds at least, or possessed of personal estate to the value of six hundred pounds at least, or of both to the amount of the same sum, and who has not been an inhabitant of this Commonwealth for the space of five years immediately preceding his election, and, at the time of his election, he shall be an inhabitant in the dictrict, for which he shall be chosen. . . .

• • • • •

SECTION III: *House of Representatives*

ART. I.—There shall be in the Legislature of this Commonwealth, a representation of the people, annually elected, and founded upon the principle of equality.

II.—And in order to provide for a representation of the citizens of this Commonwealth, founded upon the principle of equality, every corporate town, containing one hundred and fifty rateable polls, may elect one Representative: Every corporate town, containing three hundred and seventy-five rateable polls, may elect two Representatives: Every corporate town, containing six hundred rateable polls, may elect three Representatives; and proceeding in that manner, making two hundred and twenty-five rateable polls the mean increasing number for every additional Representative. . . .

III.—Every member of the House of Representatives shall be chosen by written votes; and for one year at least next preceding his election shall have been an inhabitant of, and have been seized in his own right of a freehold of the value of one hundred pounds within the town he shall be chosen to represent, or any rateable estate to the value of two hundred pounds; and he shall cease to represent the said town immediately on his ceasing to be qualified as aforesaid.

IV.—Every male person, being twenty-one years of age, and resident in any particular town in this Commonwealth for the space of one year next preceding, having a freehold estate within the same town, of the annual income of three pounds, or any estate of the value of sixty pounds, shall have a right to vote in the choice of a Representative or Representatives for the said town. . . .

• • • • •

CHAPTER II

Executive Power

SECTION I: *Governor*

Art. I.—There shall be a Supreme Executive Magistrate, who shall be styled, The Governor of the Commonwealth of Massachusetts; and whose title shall be—His Excellency.

II.—The Governor shall be chosen annually: And no person shall be eligible to this office, unless at the time of his election, he shall have been an inhabitant of this Commonwealth for seven years next preceding; and unless he shall, at the same time, be seized in his own right, of a freehold within the Commonwealth, of the value of one thousand pounds; and unless he shall declare himself to be of the christian religion. . . .

• • • • •

IV.—The Governor shall have authority, from time to time, at his discretion, to assemble and call together the Counsellors of this Commonwealth for the time being; and the Governor, with the said Counsellors, or five of them at least, shall, and may, from time to time, hold and keep a Council, for the ordering and directing the affairs of the Commonwealth, agreeably to the Constitution and the laws of the land.

V.—The Governor, with advice of Council, shall have full power and authority, during the session of the General Court, to adjourn or prorogue the same to any time the two Houses shall desire; and to dissolve the same on the day next preceding the last Wednesday in May; and, in the recess of the said Court, to prorogue the same from time to time, not exceeding ninety days in any one recess; and to call it together sooner than the time to which it may be adjourned or prorogued, if the welfare of the Commonwealth shall require the same: And in case of any infectious distemper prevailing in the place where the said Court is next at any time to convene, or any other cause happening whereby danger may arise to the health or lives of the members from their attendance, he may direct the session to be held at some other the most convenient place within the State.

And the Governor shall dissolve the said General Court on the day next preceding the last Wednesday in May.

VI.—In cases of disagreement between the two Houses, with regard to the necessity, expediency or time of adjournment, or prorogation, the

Governor, with advice of the Council, shall have a right to adjourn or prorogue the General Court, not exceeding ninety days, as he shall determine the public good shall require.

VII.—The Governor of this Commonwealth, for the time being, shall be the commander-in-chief of the army and navy, and of all the military forces of the State, by sea and land; . . . and that the Governor be intrusted with all these and other powers, incident to the offices of Captain-General and Commander-in-Chief, and Admiral, to be exercised agreeably to the rules and regulations of the Constitution, and the laws of the land, and not otherwise. . . .

• • • • •

VIII.—The power of pardoning offences, except such as persons may be convicted of before the Senate by an impeachment of the House, shall be in the Governor, by and with the advice of Council . . .

IX.—All judicial officers, the Attorney-General, the Solicitor-General, all Sheriffs, Coroners, and Registers of Probate, shall be nominated and appointed by the Governor, by and with the advice and consent of the Council; and every such nomination shall be made by the Governor, and made at least seven days prior to such appointment. . . .

• • • • •

XIII.—As the public good requires that the Governor should not be under the undue influence of any of the members of the General Court, by a dependence on them for his support—that he should, in all cases, act with freedom for the benefit of the public—that he should not have his attention necessarily diverted from that object to his private concerns—and that he should maintain the dignity of the Commonwealth in the character of its chief magistrate—it is necessary that he should have an honorable stated salary, of a fixed and permanent value, amply sufficient for those purposes, and established by standing laws: And it shall be among the first acts of the General Court, after the Commencement of this Constitution, to establish such salary by law accordingly.

Permanent and honorable salaries shall also be established by law for the Justices of the Supreme Judicial Court.

And if it shall be found, that any of the salaries aforesaid, so established, are insufficient, they shall, from time to time, be enlarged, as the General Court shall judge proper.

SECTION II: *Lieutenant-Governor*

ART. I.—There shall be annually elected a Lieutenant-Governor of the Commonwealth of Massachusetts, whose title shall be HIS HONOR—and who shall be qualified, in point of religion, property, and residence in the Commonwealth, in the same manner with the Governor: And the day and manner of his election, and the qualifications of the electors, shall be the same as are required in the election of a Governor. . . .

• • • • •

SECTION III: *Council, and the Manner of Settling Elections by the Legislature*

ART. I.—There shall be a Council for advising the Governor in the executive part of government, to consist of nine persons besides the Lieutenant-Governor, whom the Governor, for the time being, shall have full power and authority, from time to time, at his discretion, to assemble and call together. And the Governor, with the said Counsellors, or five of them at least, shall and may, from time to time, hold and keep a council, for the ordering and directing the affairs of the Commonwealth, according to the laws of the land. . . .

• • • • •

CHAPTER III

Judiciary Power

II.—Each branch of the Legislature, as well as the Governor and Council, shall have authority to require the opinions of the Justices of the Supreme Judicial Court, upon important questions of law, and upon solemn occasions. . . .

• • • • •

CHAPTER IV

Delegates to Congress

• • • • •

CHAPTER V

The University at Cambridge, and Encouragement of Literature, &c.

SECTION I: *The University*

ART. I.—Whereas our wise and pious ancestors, so early as the year one thousand six hundred and thirty six, laid the foundation of Harvard-College, in which University many persons of great eminence have, by the blessing of GOD, been initiated in those arts and sciences, which qualified them for public employments, both in Church and State: And whereas the encouragement of Arts and Sciences, and all good literature, tends to the honor of GOD, the advantage of the christian religion, and the great benefit of this, and the other United States of America—It is declared, That the PRESIDENT and FELLOWS OF HARVARD-COLLEGE, in their corporate capacity, and their successors in that capacity, their officers and servants, shall have, hold, use, exercise and enjoy, all the powers, authorities, rights, liberties, privileges, immunities and franchises, which they now have, or are entitled to have, hold, use, exercise and enjoy: And the same are hereby ratified and confirmed unto them, the said President and Fellows of Harvard-College, and to their successors, and to their officers and servants, respectively, forever. . . .

• • • • •

SECTION II: *The Encouragement of Literature, &c.*

• • • • •

CHAPTER VI

Oaths and Subscriptions; Incompatibility of and Exclusion from Offices; Pecuniary Qualifications; Commissions; Writs; Confirmation of Laws; Habeas Corpus; The Enacting Style; Continuance of Officers; Provision for a future Revisal of the Constitution, &c.

• • • • •

6. *Proceedings of Commissioners to Remedy Defects of the Federal Government* *

ANNAPOLIS IN THE STATE OF MARYLAND
THURSDAY, SEPTEMBER 14, 1786

THE ANNAPOLIS CONVENTION was an outgrowth of the Mt. Vernon (Alexandria) Convention of 1785. In both these gatherings the propertied and commercial classes, alarmed at the weaknesses of the central government under the Articles of Confederation, were feeling their way toward the creation of a new and stronger central authority. The importance of the Annapolis Convention lies in the fact that it precipitated the calling of the Philadelphia Convention and the drawing up of the Federal Constitution.

MET agreeable to Adjournment.

The meeting resumed the consideration of the draft of the Report, and after some time spent therein, and amendments made, the same was unanimously agreed to, and is as follows, to wit.

To the Honorable, the Legislatures of Virginia, Delaware, Pennsylvania, New Jersey, and New York—

The Commissioners from the said States, respectively assembled at Annapolis, humbly beg leave to report.

That, pursuant to their several appointments, they met, at Annapolis in the State of Maryland, on the eleventh day of September Instant, and having proceeded to a Communication of their powers; they found that the States of New York, Pennsylvania, and Virginia, had, in substance, and nearly in the same terms, authorised their respective Commissioners "to meet such Commissioners as were, or might be, appointed by the other States in the Union, at such time and place, as should be agreed upon by the said Commissioners to take into consideration the trade and Commerce of the United States, to consider how far an uniform system in their commercial intercourse and regulations might be necessary to their common interest and permanent harmony, and to report to the several States such an Act, relative to this great object, as when unanimously ratified by them would enable the United States in Congress assembled effectually to provide for the same."

That the State of Delaware, had given similar powers to their Com-

* Reprinted from *Documents Illustrative of the Formation of the Union of the American States* (Washington, D.C., United States Government Printing Office, 1927), pp. 39-43.

missioners, with this difference only, that the Act to be framed in virtue of those powers, is required to be reported "to the United States in Congress assembled, to be agreed to by them, and confirmed by the Legislatures of every State."

That the State of New Jersey had enlarged the object of their appointment, empowering their Commissioners, "to consider how far an uniform system in their commercial regulations and *other important matters,* might be necessary to the common interest and permanent harmony of the several States," and to report such an Act on the subject, as when ratified by them "would enable the United States in Congress assembled, effectually to provide for the exigencies of the Union."

That appointments of Commissioners have also been made by the States of New Hampshire, Massachusetts, Rhode Island, and North Carolina, none of whom however have attended; but that no information has been received by your Commisioners, of any appointment having been made by the States of Connecticut, Maryland, South Carolina or Georgia.

That the express terms of the powers to your Commissioners supposing a deputation from all the States, and having for object the Trade and Commerce of the United States, Your Commissioners did not conceive it advisable to proceed on the business of their mission, under the Circumstance of so partial and defective a representation.

Deeply impressed however with the magnitude and importance of the object confided to them on this occasion, your Commissioners cannot forbear to indulge an expression of their earnest and unanimous wish, that speedy measures may be taken, to effect a general meeting, of the States, in a future Convention, for the same, and such other purposes, as the situation of public affairs, may be found to require.

If in expressing this wish, or in intimating any other sentiment, your Commissioners should seem to exceed the strict bounds of their appointment, they entertain a full confidence, that a conduct, dictated by an anxiety for the welfare, of the United States, will not fail to receive an indulgent construction.

In this persuasion, your Commissioners submit an opinion, that the Idea of extending the powers of their Deputies, to other objects, than those of Commerce, which has been adopted by the State of New Jersey, was an improvement on the original plan, and will deserve to be incorporated into that of a future Convention; they are the more naturally led to this conclusion, as in the course of their reflections on the subject, they have been induced to think, that the power of regulating trade is of such comprehensive extent, and will enter so far into the general System of the foederal government, that to give it efficacy, and to obviate questions and doubts concerning its precise nature and limits, may require a correspondent adjustment of other parts of the Foederal System.

That there are important defects in the system of the Foederal Government is acknowledged by the Acts of all those States, which have concurred in the present Meeting; That the defects, upon a closer examination, may be found greater and more numerous, than even these acts imply, is at least so far probable, from the embarrassments which characterise the present State of our national affairs, foreign and domestic, as may reasonably be supposed to merit a deliberate and candid discussion, in some mode, which will unite the Sentiments and Councils of all the States. In the choice of the mode, your Commissioners are of opinion, that a Convention of Deputies from the different States, for the special and sole purpose of entering into this investigation, and digesting a plan for supplying such defects as may be discovered to exist, will be entitled to a preference from considerations, which will occur, without being particularised.

Your Commissioners decline an enumeration of those national circumstances on which their opinion respecting the propriety of a future Convention, with more enlarged powers, is founded; as it would be an useless intrusion of facts and observations, most of which have been frequently the subject of public discussion, and none of which can have escaped the penetration of those to whom they would in this instance be addressed. They are however of a nature so serious, as, in the view of your Commissioners to render the situation of the United States delicate and critical, calling for an exertion of the united virtue and wisdom of all the members of the Confederacy.

Under this impression, Your Commissioners, with the most respectful deference, beg leave to suggest their unanimous conviction, that it may essentially tend to advance the interests of the union, if the States, by whom they have been respectively delegated, would themselves concur, and use their endeavors to procure the concurrence of the other States, in the appointment of Commissioners, to meet at Philadelphia on the second Monday in May next, to take into consideration the situation of the United States, to devise such further provisions as shall appear to them necessary to render the constitution of the Foederal Government adequate to the exigencies of the Union; and to report such an Act for that purpose to the United States in Congress assembled, as when agreed to, by them, and afterwards confirmed by the Legislatures of every State, will effectually provide for the same.

Though your Commissioners could not with propriety address these observations and sentiments to any but the States they have the honor to Represent, they have nevertheless concluded from motives of respect, to transmit Copies of this Report to the United States in Congress assembled, and to the executives of the other States.

By Order of the Commissioners.

7. *Report of Proceedings in Congress Wednesday, February 21, 1787* *

IN PURSUANCE OF the request of the Annapolis Convention, Congress passed a resolution calling for a convention to meet in Philadelphia "for the sole and express purpose of revising the Articles of Confederation." Congress was influenced in its action by the dire condition of the Confederation finances and the hope that the Philadelphia meeting would provide relief in this regard. The emergence of an entirely new governmental structure as a result of the Philadelphia deliberations was more than Congress had bargained for. As a result, Congress forwarded the proposed Constitution to the states for their action only with considerable reluctance.

A MOTION was then made by the delegates for Massachusetts to postpone the farther consideration of the report in order to take into consideration a motion which they read in their place, this being agreed to, the motion of the delegates for Massachusetts was taken up and being amended was agreed to as follows:

Whereas there is provision in the Articles of Confederation & perpetual Union for making alterations therein by the assent of a Congress of the United States and of the legislatures of the several States; And whereas experience hath evinced that there are defects in the present Confederation, as a mean to remedy which several of the States and particularly the State of New York by express instructions to their delegates in Congress have suggested a convention for the purposes expressed in the following resolution and such convention appearing to be the most probable mean of establishing in these states a firm national government.

Resolved that in the opinion of Congress it is expedient that on the second Monday in May next a Convention of delegates who shall have

* Reprinted from *Documents Illustrative of the Formation of the Union of the American States* (Washington, D.C., United States Government Printing Office, 1927), pp. 45-46.

been appointed by the several states be held at Philadelphia for the sole and express purpose of revising the Articles of Confederation and reporting to Congress and the several legislatures such alterations and provisions therein as shall when agreed to in Congress and confirmed by the states render the federal constitution adequate to the exigencies of Government & the preservation of the Union.

II

THE FEDERAL CONSTITUTION

8. *The Virginia Plan, Presented by Edmund Randolph to the Federal Convention, May 29, 1787* *

SEVERAL PLANS of government were placed before the Philadelphia Convention of 1787 for the consideration of the delegates. The chief ones were the Virginia and New Jersey plans and those of Alexander Hamilton (New York) and of Charles Pinckney (South Carolina). The Virginia Plan was drafted by the Virginia delegation under the leadership of James Madison during the period of waiting in Philadelphia for a quorum of the Convention delegates to assemble. It was presented to the Convention by Governor Edmund Randolph of Virginia on May 29. In general the plan represented the views of the large-state group and those who favored a complete revision of the Articles and the creation of a strong national government. The plan, presented as a series of resolutions, is important because it served as the chief basis for discussion and the eventual construction of the new Constitution.

1. Resolved that the Articles of Confederation ought to be so corrected & enlarged as to accomplish the objects proposed by their institution; namely, "common defence, security of liberty and general welfare."

2. Resd therefore that the rights of suffrage in the National Legislature ought to be proportioned to the Quotas of contribution, or to the number of free inhabitants, as the one or the other rule may seem best in different cases.

* Reprinted from *Documents Illustrative of the Formation of the Union of the American States* (Washington, D.C., United States Government Printing Office, 1927), pp. 953-956.

3. Resd that the National Legislature ought to consist of two branches.

4. Resd that the members of the first branch of the National Legislature ought to be elected by the people of the several States every for the terms of ; to be of the age of years at least, to receive liberal stipends by which they may be compensated for the devotion of their time to public service; to be ineligible to any office established by a particular State, or under the authority of the United States, except those beculiarly [*sic*] belonging to the functions of the first branch, during the term of service, and for the space of after its expiration; to be incapable of reelection for the space of after the expiration of their term of service, and to be subject to recall.

5. Resold that the members of the second branch of the National Legislature ought to be elected by those of the first, out of a proper number of persons nominated by the individual Legislatures, to be of the age of years at least; to hold their offices for a term sufficient to ensure their independency; to receive liberal stipends, by which they may be compensated for the devotion of their time to public service; and to be ineligible to any office established by a particular State, or under the authority of the United States, except those peculiarly belonging to the functions of the second branch, during the term of service, and for the space of after the expiration thereof.

6. Resolved that each branch ought to possess the right of originating Acts; that the National Legislature ought to be impowered to enjoy the Legislative Rights vested in Congress by the Confederation & moreover to legislate in all cases to which the separate States are incompetent, or in which the harmony of the United States may be interrupted by the exercise of individual Legislation; to negative all laws passed by the several States, contravening in the opinion of the National Legislature the articles of Union; and to call forth the force of the Union agst any member of the Union failing to fulfill its duty under the articles thereof.

7. Resd that a National Executive be instituted; to be chosen by the National Legislature for the term of years, to receive punctually at stated times, a fixed compensation for the services rendered, in which no increase or diminution shall be made so to as affect the Magistracy, existing at the time of increase or diminution, and to be ineligible a second time; and that besides a general authority to execute the National laws, it ought to enjoy the Executive rights vested in Congress by the Confederation.

8. Resd that the Executive and a convenient number of the National Judiciary, ought to compose a Council of revision with authority to examine every act of the National Legislature before it shall operate,

& every act of a particular Legislature before a Negative thereon shall be final; and that the dissent of the said Council shall amount to a rejection, unless the Act of the National Legislature be again passed, or that of a particular Legislature be again negatived by of the members of each branch.

9. Resd that a National Judiciary be established to consist of one or more supreme tribunals, and of inferior tribunals to be chosen by the National Legislature, to hold their offices during good behaviour; and to receive punctually at stated times fixed compensation for their services, in which no increase or diminution shall be made so as to affect the persons actually in office at the time of such increase or diminution. that the jurisdiction of the inferior tribunals shall be to hear & determine in the first instance, and of the supreme tribunal to hear and determine in the dernier resort, all piracies & felonies on the high seas, captures from an enemy; cases in which foreigners or citizens of other States applying to such jurisdictions may be interested, or which respect the collection of the National revenue; impeachments of any National officers, and questions which may involve the national peace and harmony.

10. Resolvd that provision ought to be made for the admission of States lawfully arising within the limits of the United States, whether from a voluntary junction of Government & Territory or otherwise, with the consent of a number of voices in the National legislature less than the whole.

11. Resd that a Republican Government & the territory of each State, except in the instance of a voluntary junction of Government & territory, ought to be guarantied by the United States to each State.

12. Resd that provision ought to be made for the continuance of Congress and their authorities and privileges, until a given day after the reform of the articles of Union shall be adopted, and for the completion of all their engagements.

13. Resd that provision ought to be made for the amendment of the Articles of Union whensoever it shall seem necessary, and that the assent of the National Legislature ought not to be required thereto.

14. Resd that the Legislative Executive & Judiciary powers within the several States ought to be bound by oath to support the articles of Union.

15. Resd that the amendments which shall be offered to the Confederation, by the Convention ought at a proper time, or times, after the approbation of Congress to be submitted to an assembly or assemblies of Representatives, recommended by the several Legislatures to be expressly chosen by the people, to consider & decide thereon.

9. The Plan Presented by William Paterson (N. J.) to the Federal Convention, June 15, 1787*

THE NEW JERSEY PLAN, laid before the Philadelphia Convention of 1787 on June 15 by William Paterson of New Jersey, is commonly regarded as representative of the views of the small-state group and those delegates who were particularly concerned about the preservation of the "rights" of the states. The plan did not propose, however, a continuation of the weak national government of the Articles but accorded with the general sentiment of the Convention for strengthening and expanding the organs and powers of the central government. Nevertheless, the plan indicated more concern for the organization and operation of national powers with respect to the states than did the Virginia Plan. Although the Convention voted its endorsement of the Virginia Plan on June 19, the nine resolutions of the New Jersey Plan contributed significantly to the final product of the Convention.

1. Resd that the articles of Confederation ought to be so revised, corrected & enlarged, as to render the federal Constitution adequate to the exigencies of Government, & the preservation of the Union.

2. Resd that in addition to the powers vested in the U. States in Congress, by the present existing articles of Confederation, they be authorized to pass acts for raising a revenue, by levying a duty or duties on all goods or merchandizes of foreign growth or manufacture, imported into any part of the U. States, by Stamps on paper, vellum or parchment, and by a postage on all letters or packages passing through the general post-office, to be applied to such federal purposes as they shall deem proper & expedient; to make rules & regulations for the collection thereof; and the same from time to time, to alter & amend in such manner as they shall think proper: to pass Acts for the regulation of trade & commerce as well with foreign nations as with each other: provided that all punishments, fines, forfeitures & penalties to be incurred for contravening such acts rules and regulations shall be adjudged by the Common law Judiciaries of the State in which any offence contrary to the true intent & meaning of such Acts rules & regulations shall have been committed or perpetrated, with liberty of commencing in the first instance all suits & prosecutions for that pur-

* Reprinted from *Documents Illustrative of the Formation of the Union of the American States* (Washington, D.C., United States Government Printing Office, 1927), pp. 967-970.

pose in the superior common law Judiciary in such State, subject nevertheless, for the correction of all errors, both in law & fact in rendering Judgment, to an appeal to the Judiciary of the U. States.

3. Resd that whenever requisitions shall be necessary, instead of the rule for making requisitions mentioned in the articles of Confederation, the United States in Congs be authorized to make such requisitions in proportion to the whole number of white & other free citizens & inhabitants of every age sex and condition including those bound to servitude for a term of years & three fifths of all other persons not comprehended in the foregoing description, except Indians not paying taxes; that if such requisitions be not complied with, in the time specified therein, to direct the collection thereof in the non complying States & for that purpose to devise and pass acts directing & authorizing the same; provided that none of the powers hereby vested in the U. States in Congs shall be exercised without the consent of at least States, and in that proportion if the number of Confederated States should hereafter be increased or diminished.

4. Resd that the U. States in Congs be authorized to elect a federal Executive to consist of persons, to continue in office for the term of years, to receive punctually at stated times a fixed compensation for their services, in which no increase or diminution shall be made so as to affect the persons composing the Executive at the time of such increase or diminution, to be paid out of the federal treasury; to be incapable of holding any other office or appointment during their time of service and for years thereafter; to be ineligible a second time, & removeable by Congs on application by a majority of the Executives of the several States; that the Executives besides their general authority to execute the federal acts ought to appoint all federal officers not otherwise provided for, & to direct all military operations; provided that none of the persons composing the federal Executive shall on any occasion take command of any troops, so as personally to conduct any enterprise as General or in other capacity.

5. Resd that a federal Judiciary be established to consist of a supreme Tribunal the Judges of which to be appointed by the Executive, & to hold their offices during good behaviour, to receive punctually at stated times a fixed compensation for their services in which no increase or diminution shall be made, so as to affect the persons actually in office at the time of such increase or diminution; that the Judiciary so established shall have authority to hear & determine in the first instance on all impeachments of federal officers, & by way of appeal in the dernier resort in all cases touching the rights of Ambassadors, in all cases of captures from an enemy, in all cases of piracies & felonies on the high Seas, in all cases in which foreigners may be interested, in the construction of

any treaty or treaties, or which may arise on any of the Acts for regulation of trade, or the collection of the federal Revenue: that none of the Judiciary shall during the time they remain in office be capable of receiving or holding any other office or appointment during their time of service, or for thereafter.

6. Resd that all Acts of the U. States in Congs made by virtue & in pursuance of the powers hereby & by the articles of Confederation vested in them, and all Treaties made & ratified under the authority of the U. States shall be the supreme law of the respective States so far forth as those Acts or Treaties shall relate to the said States or their Citizens, and that the Judiciary of the several States shall be bound thereby in their decisions, any thing in the respective laws of the Individual States to the contrary notwithstanding; and that if any State, or any body of men in any State shall oppose or prevent ye carrying into execution such acts or treaties, the federal Executive shall be authorized to call forth ye power of the Confederated States, or so much thereof as may be necessary to enforce and compel an obedience to such Acts, or an observance of such Treaties.

7. Resd that provision be made for the admission of new States into the Union.

8. Resd the rule for naturalization ought to be the same in every State.

9. Resd that a Citizen of one State committing an offence in another State of the Union, shall be deemed guilty of the same offence as if it had been committed by a Citizen of the State in which the offence was committed.

10. *Notes of Major William Pierce (Ga.) in the Federal Convention of 1787* *

CHARACTERS IN THE CONVENTION OF THE STATES HELD AT PHILADELPHIA, MAY 1787

THE DELEGATES attending the Philadelphia Convention have been regarded by later generations as men high in the esteem of their countrymen and possessed of an abundance of political talent and sound practical experience. The character sketches of his fellow-delegates by William Pierce of Georgia—evidently made at the Convention or shortly thereafter—support this view. Several of the sketches are reproduced here. With regard to his own character, Major Pierce left it for "those who may choose to speculate on it, to consider it in any light that their fancy or imagination may depict."

MR. GORHAM is a Merchant in Boston, high in reputation, and much in the esteem of his Country-men. He is a Man of very good sense, but not much improved in his education. He is eloquent and easy in public debate, but has nothing fashionable or elegant in his style;—all he aims at is to convince, and where he fails it never is from his auditory not understanding him, for no Man is more perspicuous and full. He has been President of Congress, and three years a Member of that Body. Mr. Gorham is about 46 years of age, rather lusty, and has an agreeable and pleasing manner.

. . . . .

Mr. Sherman exhibits the oddest shaped character I ever remember to have met with. He is awkward, un-meaning, and unaccountably strange in his manner. But in his train of thinking there is something regular, deep, and comprehensive; yet the oddity of his address, the vulgarisms that accompany his public speaking, and that strange new England cant which runs through his public as well as his private speaking make everything that is connected with him grotesque and laughable;—and yet he deserves infinite praise,—no Man has a better Heart or a clearer Head. If he cannot embellish he can furnish

* Reprinted from *Documents Illustrative of the Formation of the Union of the American States* (Washington, D.C., United States Government Printing Office, 1927), pp. 96-98, 100-102, 104-105.

thoughts that are wise and useful. He is an able politician, and extremely artful in accomplishing any particular object;—it is remarked that he seldom fails. I am told he sits on the Bench in Connecticut, and is very correct in the discharge of his Judicial functions. In the early part of his life he was a Shoemaker;—but despising the lowness of his condition, he turned Almanack maker, and so progressed upwards to a Judge. He has been several years a Member of Congress, and discharged the duties of his Office with honor and credit to himself, and advantage to the State he represented. He is about 60.

• • • • •

Colo Hamilton is deservedly celebrated for his talents. He is a practitioner of the Law, and reputed to be a finished Scholar. To a clear and strong judgment he unites the ornaments of fancy, and whilst he is able, convincing, and engaging in his eloquence the Heart and Head sympathize in approving him. Yet there is something too feeble in his voice to be equal to the strains of oratory;—it is my opinion that he is rather a convincing Speaker, that [than] a blazing Orator. Colo Hamilton requires time to think,—he enquires into every part of his subject with the searchings of phylosophy, and when he comes forward he comes highly charged with interesting matter, there is no skimming over the surface of a subject with him, he must sink to the bottom to see what foundation it rests on.—His language is not always equal, sometimes didactic like Bolingbroke's, at others light and tripping like Stern's. His eloquence is not so defusive as to trifle with the senses, but he rambles just enough to strike and keep up the attention. He is about 33 years old, of small stature, and lean. His manners are tinctured with stiffness, and sometimes with a degree of vanity that is highly disagreeable.

• • • • •

Dr. Franklin is well known to be the greatest phylosopher of the present age;—all the operations of nature he seems to understand,—the very heavens obey him, and the Clouds yield up their Lightning to be imprisoned in his rod. But what claim he has to the politician, posterity must determine. It is certain that he does not shine much in public Council,—he is no Speaker, nor does he seem to let politics engage his attention. He is, however, a most extraordinary Man, and tells a story in a style more engaging than anything I ever heard Let his Biographer finish his character. He is 82 years old, and possesses an activity of mind equal to a youth of 25 years of age.

• • • • •

Mr. Governeur Morris is one of those Genius's in whom every species of talents combine to render him conspicious and flourishing in public debate:—He winds through all the mazes of rhetoric, and throws around him such a glare that he charms, captivates, and leads away the senses of all who hear him. With an infinite streach of fancy he brings to view things when he is engaged in deep argumentation, that render all the labor of reasoning easy and pleasing. But with all these powers he is fickle and inconstant,—never pursuing one train of thinking,—nor ever regular. He has gone through a very extensive course of reading, and is acquainted with all the sciences. No Man has more wit,—nor can any one engage the attention more than Mr. Morris. He was bred to the Law, but I am told he disliked the profession, and turned Merchant. He is engaged in some great mercantile matters with his namesake Mr. Robt Morris. This Gentleman is about 38 years old, he has been unfortunate in losing one of his Legs, and getting all the flesh taken off his right arm by a scald, when a youth.

• • • • •

Genl Washington is well known as the Commander in chief of the late American Army. Having conducted these States to independence and peace, he now appears to assist in framing a Government to make the People happy. Like Gustavus Vasa, he may be said to be the deliverer of his Country;—like Peter the great he appears as the politician and the States-man; and like Cincinnatus he returned to his farm perfectly contented with being only a plain Citizen, after enjoying the highest honor of the Confederacy,—and now only seeks for the approbation of his Country-men by being virtuous and useful. The General was conducted to the Chair as President of the Convention by the unanimous voice of its Members. He is in the 52d year of his age.

• • • • •

Mr. Maddison is a character who has long been in public life; and what is very remarkable every Person seems to acknowledge his greatness. He blends together the profound politician, with the Scholar. In the management of every great question he evidently took the lead in the Convention, and tho' he cannot be called an Orator, he is a most agreable, eloquent, and convincing Speaker. From a spirit of industry and application which he possesses in a most eminent degree, he always comes forward the best informed Man of any point in debate. The affairs of the United States, he perhaps, has the most correct knowledge of, of any Man in the Union. He has been twice a Member of Congress, and was always thought one of the ablest Members that ever sat in that Council. Mr. Maddison is about 37 years of age, a Gentleman of great modesty,—with a remarkable sweet temper. He is easy and unreserved among his acquaintance, and has a most agreable style of conversation.

11. *Resolution of the Federal Convention Submitting the Constitution to Congress, September 17, 1787* *

IN CONVENTION, MONDAY, SEPTEMBER 17, 1787

The Philadelphia Convention finally approved the completed constitutional document on September 17, 1787. The Convention had gone beyond the scope of instructions given to most of its members and instead of preparing a revision of the Articles had written a complete constitution that provided for a new form of government. In transmitting the proposed constitution to Congress, the Convention recommended a procedure of ratification that differed from the plan laid down in the Articles and repeated in the resolution of Congress calling the Philadelphia Convention (see Selections 4 and 7). In most textbooks the student will find a brief statement of the probable reasons that influenced the Convention to recommend an unauthorized procedure, one that was certainly bold and, in the light of later events, politically practical.

PRESENT

The States of

New Hampshire, Massachusetts, Connecticut, Mr Hamilton from New York, New Jersey, Pennsylvania, Delaware, Maryland, Virginia, North Carolina, South Carolina and Georgia. Resolved,

That the preceeding Constitution be laid before the United States in Congress assembled, and that it is the Opinion of this Convention,

* Reprinted from *Documents Illustrative of the Formation of the Union of the American States* (Washington, D.C., United States Government Printing Office, 1927), pp. 1005-1006.

that it should afterwards be submitted to a Convention of Delegates, chosen in each State by the People thereof, under the Recommendation of its Legislature, for their Assent and Ratification; and that each Convention assenting to, and ratifying the Same, should give Notice thereof to the United States in Congress assembled.

Resolved, That it is the Opinion of this Convention, that as soon as the Conventions of nine States shall have ratified this Constitution, the United States in Congress assembled should fix a Day on which Electors should be appointed by the States which shall have ratified the same, and a Day on which the Electors should assemble to vote for the President, and the Time and Place for commencing Proceedings under this Constitution. That after such Publication the Electors should be appointed, and the Senators and Representatives elected: That the Electors should meet on the Day fixed for the Election of the President, and should transmit their Votes certified, signed, sealed and directed, as the Constitution requires, to the Secretary of the United States in Congress assembled, that the Senators and Representatives should convene at the Time and Place assigned; that the Senators should appoint a President of the Senate, for the sole Purpose of receiving, opening and counting the votes for President; and, that after he shall be chosen, the Congress, together with the President, should, without Delay, proceed to execute this Constitution.

By the Unanimous Order of the Convention

G° WASHINGTON Presid^t

W. JACKSON Secretary

12. *Resolution of Congress of September 28, 1787, Submitting the Constitution to the Several States* *

UPON RECEIPT of the proposed constitution and the resolution of the Convention, the Congress after some discussion adopted a resolution providing for transmission of the document to the states. The Congress made no comment or recommendation other than that contained in this resolution.

* Reprinted from *Documents Illustrative of the Formation of the Union of the American States* (Washington, D.C., United States Government Printing Office, 1927), p. 1007.

FRIDAY SEPT. 28, 1787

CONGRESS assembled present Newhampshire Massachusetts Connecticut New York New Jersey Pennsylvania Delaware Virginia North Carolina South Carolina and Georgia and from Maryland Mr Ross

Congress having received the report of the Convention lately assembled in Philadelphia

Resolved Unanimously that the said Report with the resolutions and letter accompanying the same be transmitted to the several legislatures in Order to be submitted to a convention of Delegates chosen in each state by the people thereof in conformity to the resolves of the Convention made and provided in that case.

13. *The Federalist: No. X* *

(MADISON)

RATIFICATION of the new Constitution was easily and promptly accomplished in a few states; the process was marked by bitter controversy and a veritable war of words in others. Throughout the fall and winter of 1787 and the spring and summer of 1788 the debate was sustained through newspaper articles, pamphlets, and letters. Opposition to the Constitution was well organized in New York. As a contribution to the campaign for ratification in that state, the papers collectively known as *The Federalist* were printed anonymously in New York City newspapers in the winter of 1787-1788. The chief authors of the eighty-five articles were Alexander Hamilton and James Madison, with some help from John Jay. These papers probably did not exert great immediate influence; nonetheless, they are regarded today as the classic exposition and defense of the American Constitution. The following paper deals with the problem of controlling factions, the most common and durable source of which "has been the various and unequal distribution of property." It is an able and penetrating statement of the economic basis of politics.

To the People of the State of New York:

Among the numerous advantages promised by a well-constructed Union, none deserves to be more accurately developed than its tendency

* Reprinted from the *New York Packet*, Friday, November 23, 1787.

to break and control the violence of faction. The friend of popular governments never finds himself so much alarmed for their character and fate as when he contemplates their propensity to this dangerous vice. He will not fail, therefore, to set a due value on any plan which, without violating the principles to which he is attached, provides a proper cure for it. The instability, injustice, and confusion introduced into the public councils, have, in truth, been the mortal diseases under which popular governments have everywhere perished; as they continue to be the favourite and fruitful topics from which the adversaries to liberty derive their most specious declamations. The valuable improvements made by the American constitutions on the popular models, both ancient and modern, cannot certainly be too much admired; but it would be an unwarrantable partiality, to contend that they have as effectually obviated the danger on this side, as was wished and expected. Complaints are everywhere heard from our most considerate and virtuous citizens, equally the friends of public and private faith, and of public and personal liberty, that our governments are too unstable, that the public good is disregarded in the conflicts of rival parties, and that measures are too often decided, not according to the rules of justice and the rights of the minor party, but by the superior force of an interested and overbearing majority. However anxiously we may wish that these complaints had no foundation, the evidence of known facts will not permit us to deny that they are in some degree true. It will be found, indeed, on a candid review of our situation, that some of the distresses under which we labour have been erroneously charged on the operation of our governments; but it will be found, at the same time, that other causes will not alone account for many of our heaviest misfortunes; and, particularly, for that prevailing and increasing distrust of public engagements, and alarm for private rights, which are echoed from one end of the continent to the other. These must be chiefly, if not wholly, effects of the unsteadiness and injustice with which a factious spirit has tainted our public administrations.

By a faction, I understand a number of citizens, whether amounting to a majority or minority of the whole, who are united and actuated by some common impulse of passion, or of interest, adverse to the rights of other citizens, or to the permanent and aggregate interest of the community.

There are two methods of curing the mischiefs of faction: the one, by removing its causes; the other, by controlling its effects.

There are again two methods of removing the causes of faction: the one, by destroying the liberty which is essential to its existence; the other, by giving to every citizen the same opinions, the same passions, and the same interests.

It could never be more truly said than of the first remedy, that it was worse than the disease. Liberty is to faction what air is to fire, an aliment without which it instantly expires. But it could not be less folly to abolish liberty, which is essential to political life, because it nourishes faction, than it would be to wish the annihilation of air, which is essential to animal life, because it imparts to fire its destructive agency.

The second expedient is as impracticable as the first would be unwise. As long as the reason of man continues fallible, and he is at liberty to exercise it, different opinions will be formed. As long as the connection subsists between his reason and his self-love, his opinions and his passions will have a reciprocal influence on each other; and the former will be objects to which the latter will attach themselves. The diversity in the faculties of men, from which the rights of property originate, is not less an insuperable obstacle to a uniformity of interests. The protection of these faculties is the first object of government. From the protection of different and unequal faculties of acquiring property, the possession of different degrees and kinds of property immediately results; and from the influence of these on the sentiments and views of the respective proprietors, ensues a division of the society into different interests and parties.

The latent causes of faction are thus sown in the nature of man; and we see them everywhere brought into different degrees of activity, according to the different circumstances of civil society. A zeal for different opinions concerning religion, concerning government, and many other points, as well of speculation as of practice; an attachment of different leaders ambitiously contending for pre-eminence and power; or to persons of other descriptions whose fortunes have been interesting to the human passions, have, in turn, divided mankind into parties, inflamed them with mutual animosity, and rendered them much more disposed to vex and oppress each other than to co-operate for their common good. So strong is this propensity of mankind to fall into mutual animosities, that where no substantial occasion presents itself, the most frivolous and fanciful distinctions have been sufficient to kindle their unfriendly passions and excite their most violent conflicts. But the most common and durable source of factions has been the various and unequal distribution of property. Those who hold and those who are without property have ever formed distinct interests in society. Those who are creditors, and those who are debtors, fall under a like discrimination. A landed interest, a manufacturing interest, a mercantile interest, a moneyed interest, with many lesser interests, grow up of necessity in civilised nations, and divide them into different classes, actuated by different sentiments and views. The regulation of these various and interfering interests forms the principal task of modern legislation, and involves the spirit of party and faction in the necessary and ordinary operations of the government.

No man is allowed to be a judge in his own cause, because his interest would certainly bias his judgment, and, not improbably, corrupt his integrity. With equal, nay, with greater reason, a body of men are unfit to be both judges and parties at the same time; yet what are many of the most important acts of legislation but so many judicial determinations, not indeed concerning the rights of single persons, but concerning the rights of large bodies of citizens? And what are the different classes of legislators but advocates and parties to the causes which they determine? Is a law proposed concerning private debts? It is a question to which the creditors are parties on one side and the debtors on the other. Justice ought to hold the balance between them. Yet the parties are, and must be, themselves the judges; and the most numerous party, or, in other words, the most powerful faction must be expected to prevail. Shall domestic manufacturers be encouraged, and in what degree, by restrictions on foreign manufacturers? are questions which would be differently decided by the landed and the manufacturing classes, and probably by neither with a sole regard to justice and the public good. The apportionment of taxes on the various descriptions of property is an act which seems to require the most exact impartiality; yet there is, perhaps, no legislative act in which greater opportunity and temptation are given to a predominant party to trample on the rules of justice. Every shilling with which they overburden the inferior number is a shilling saved to their own pockets.

It is in vain to say that enlightened statesmen will be able to adjust these clashing interests, and render them all subservient to the public good. Enlightened statesmen will not always be at the helm. Nor, in many cases, can such an adjustment be made at all without taking into view indirect and remote considerations, which will rarely prevail over the immediate interest which one party may find in disregarding the rights of another or the good of the whole.

The inference to which we are brought is, that the *causes* of faction cannot be removed, and that relief is only to be sought in the means of controlling its *effects*.

If a faction consists of less than a majority, relief is supplied by the republican principle, which enables the majority to defeat its sinister views by regular vote. It may clog the administration, it may convulse the society; but it will be unable to execute and mask its violence under the forms of the Constitution. When a majority is included in a faction, the form of popular government, on the other hand, enables it to sacrifice to its ruling passion or interest both the public good and the rights of other citizens. To secure the public good and private rights against the danger of such a faction, and at the same time to preserve the spirit and the form of popular government, is then the great object to which our inquiries are directed. Let me add that it is the great desideratum by which this form of government can be rescued from the opprobrium under which it has so long laboured, and be recommended to the esteem and adoption of mankind.

By what means is this object obtainable? Evidently by one of two only. Either the existence of the same passion or interest in a majority at the same time must be prevented, or the majority, having such co-existent passion or interest, must be rendered, by their number and local situation, unable to concert and carry into effect schemes of oppression. If the impulse and the opportunity be suffered to coincide, we well know that neither moral nor religious motives can be relied on as an adequate control. They are not found to be such on the injustice and violence of individuals, and lose their efficacy in proportion to the number combined together, that is, in proportion as their efficacy becomes needful.

From this view of the subject it may be concluded that a pure democracy, by which I mean a society consisting of a small number of citizens, who assemble and administer the government in person, can admit of no cure for the mischiefs of faction. A common passion or interest will, in almost every case, be felt by a majority of the whole; a communication and concert result from the form of government itself; and there is nothing to check the inducements to sacrifice the weaker party or an obnoxious individual. Hence it is that such democracies have ever been spectacles of turbulence and contention; have ever been found incompatible with personal security or the rights of property; and have in general been as short in their lives as they have been violent in their deaths. Theoretic politicians, who have patronised this species of government, have erroneously supposed that by reducing mankind to a perfect equality in their political rights, they would, at the same time, be perfectly equalised and assimilated in their possessions, their opinions, and their passions.

A republic, by which I mean a government in which the scheme of representation takes place, opens a different prospect, and promises the cure for which we are seeking. Let us examine the points in which it varies from pure democracy, and we shall comprehend both the nature of the cure and the efficacy which it must derive from the Union.

The two great points of difference between a democracy and a republic are: first, the delegation of the government, in the latter, to a small number of citizens elected by the rest; secondly, the greater number of citizens, and greater sphere of country, over which the latter may be extended.

The effect of the first difference is, on the one hand, to refine and enlarge the public views, by passing them through the medium of a chosen body of citizens, whose wisdom may best discern the true interest of their country, and whose patriotism and love of justice will be least likely to sacrifice it to temporary or partial considerations. Under such a regulation, it may well happen that the public voice, pronounced by the representatives of the people, will be more consonant to the public good than if pronounced by the people themselves, convened for the purpose. On the other hand, the effect may be inverted. Men of factious tempers, of local prejudices, or of sinister designs, may, by intrigue, by corruption, or by other means, first obtain the suffrages; and then betray the interests, of the people. The question resulting is, whether small or extensive republics are more favourable to the election of proper guardians of the public weal; and it is clearly decided in favour of the latter by two obvious considerations:

In the first place, it is to be remarked that, however small the republic may be, the representatives must be raised to a certain number, in order to guard against the cabals of a few; and that, however large it may be, they must be limited to a certain number, in order to guard against the confusion of a multitude. Hence the number of representatives in the two cases not being in proportion to that of the two constituents, and being proportionally greater in the small republic, it follows that, if the proportion of fit characters be not less in the large than in the small republic, the former will present a greater option, and consequently a greater probability of a fit choice.

In the next place, as each representative will be chosen by a greater number of citizens in the large than in the small republic, it will be more difficult for unworthy candidates to practise with success the vicious arts by which elections are too often carried; and the suffrages of the people being more free, will be more likely to centre in men who possess the most attractive merit and the most diffusive and established character.

It must be confessed that in this, as in most other cases, there is a mean, on both sides of which inconveniences will be found to lie. By enlarging too much the number of electors, you render the representative too little acquainted with all their local circumstances and lesser interests; as by reducing it too much, you render him unduly attached to these, and too little fit to comprehend and pursue great and national objects. The federal Constitution forms a happy combination in this respect; the great and aggregate interests being referred to the national, the local and particular to the State legislatures.

The other point of difference is, the greater number of citizens and extent of territory which may be brought within the compass of republican than of democratic government; and it is this circumstance principally which renders factious combinations less to be dreaded in the former than in the latter. The smaller the society, the fewer probably will be the distinct parties and interests composing it; the fewer the distinct parties and interests, the more frequently will a majority be found of the same party; and the smaller the number of individuals composing a majority, and the smaller the compass within which they are placed, the more easily will they concert and execute their plans of oppression. Extend the sphere, and you take in a greater variety of parties and interests; you make it less probable that a majority of the whole will have a common motive to invade the rights of other citizens; or if such a common motive exists, it will be more difficult for all who feel it to discover their own strength, and to act in unison with each other. Besides other impediments, it may be remarked that, where there is a consciousness of unjust or dishonourable purposes, communication is always checked by distrust in proportion to the number whose concurrence is necessary.

Hence, it clearly appears, that the same advantage which a republic has over a democracy, in controlling the effects of faction, is enjoyed by a large over a small republic—is enjoyed by the Union over the States composing it. Does the advantage consist in the substitution of representatives whose enlightened views and virtuous sentiments render them superior to local prejudices and to schemes of injustice? It will not be denied that the representation of the Union will be most likely to possess these requisite endowments. Does it consist in the greater security afforded by a greater variety of parties, against the event of any one party being able to outnumber and oppress the rest? In an equal degree does the increased variety of parties comprised within the Union increase this security? Does it, in fine, consist in the greater obstacles opposed to the concert and accomplishment of the secret wishes of an unjust and interested majority? Here, again, the extent of the Union gives it the most palpable advantage.

The influence of factious leaders may kindle a flame within their particular States, but will be unable to spread a general conflagration through the other States. A religious sect may degenerate into a political faction in a part of the Confederacy; but the variety of sects dispersed over the entire face of it must secure the national councils against any danger from that source. A rage for paper money, for an abolition of debts, for an equal division of property, or for any other improper or wicked project, will be less apt to pervade the whole body of the Union than a particular member of it; in the same proportion as such a malady is more likely to taint a particular county or district, than an entire State.

In the extent and proper structure of the Union, therefore, we behold a republican remedy for the diseases most incident to republican government. And according to the degree of pleasure and pride we feel in being republicans, ought to be our zeal in cherishing the spirit and supporting the character of Federalists.

PUBLIUS

14. *Objections to the Proposed Federal Constitution* *

IN HIS DIARY (September 17, 1787) George Washington wrote that the Constitution ". . . was subscribed to by every member present except Governor Randolph and Colonel Mason from Virginia, and Mr. Gerry from Massachusetts." George Mason was a leader of the opposition to the ratification of the Constitution in the Virginia Convention. In a pamphlet of October, 1787, which was addressed to the Citizens of Virginia, Mason stated his objections to the proposed Constitution. It is instructive to reflect upon the effect of upward of 150 years of intense political development on these criticisms.

THERE IS no declaration of rights: and the laws of the general government being paramount to the laws and constitutions of the several states, the declarations of rights, in the separate states, are no security. Nor are the people secured even in the enjoyment of the benefit of the common law, which stands here upon no other foundation than its having been adopted by the respective acts forming the constitutions of the several states.

In the House of Representatives there is not the substance, but the shadow only of representation; which can never produce proper information in the legislature, or inspire confidence in the people.—The laws will, therefore, be generally made by men little concerned in, and unacquainted with their effects and consequences.

* George Mason. Reprinted from *Pamphlets on the Constitution of the United States*, Paul Leicester Ford, ed. (Brooklyn, N. Y., 1888), pp. 329-332.

The Senate have the power of altering all money-bills, and of originating appropriations of money, and the salaries of the officers of their appointment, in conjunction with the President of the United States— Although they are not the representatives of the people, or amenable to them. These, with their other great powers, (viz. their powers in the appointment of ambassadors, and all public officers, in making treaties, and in trying all impeachments,) their influence upon, and connection with, the supreme executive from these causes, their duration of office, and their being a constant existing body, almost continually sitting, joined with their being one complete branch of the legislature, will destroy any balance in the government, and enable them to accomplish what usurpations they please, upon the rights and liberties of the people.

The judiciary of the United States is so constructed and extended, as to absorb and destroy the judiciaries of the several states; thereby rendering laws as tedious, intricate, and expensive, and justice as unattainable by a great part of the community, as in England; and enabling the rich to oppress and ruin the poor.

The President of the United States has no constitutional council (a thing unheard in any safe and regular government); he will therefore be unsupported by proper information and advice; and will generally be directed by minions and favorites—or he will become a tool to the Senate—or a council of state will grow out of the principal officers of the great departments—the worst and most dangerous of all ingredients for such a council, in a free country; for they may be induced to join in any dangerous or oppressive measures, to shelter themselves, and prevent an inquiry into their own misconduct in office. Whereas, had a constitutional council been formed (as was proposed) of six members, viz., two from the eastern, two from the middle, and two from the southern states, to be appointed by vote of the states in the House of Representatives, with the same duration and rotation of office as the Senate, the executive would always have had safe and proper information and advice; the president of such a council might have acted as Vice-President of the United States, *pro tempore*, upon any vacancy or disability of the chief magistrate; and long continued sessions of the Senate would in a great measure have been prevented. From this fatal defect of a constitutional council, has arisen the improper power of the Senate, in the appointment of the public officers, and the alarming dependence and connexion between that branch of the legislature and the supreme executive. Hence, also, sprung that unnecessary officer, the Vice-President, who, for want of other employment, is made President of the Senate; thereby dangerously blending the executive and legislative powers; besides always giving to some one of the states an unnecessary and unjust pre-eminence over the others.

The President of the United States has the unrestrained power of granting pardon for treason; which may be sometimes exercised to screen from punishment those whom he had secretly instigated to commit the crime, and thereby prevent a discovery of his own guilt. By declaring all treaties supreme laws of the land, the executive and the Senate have, in many cases, an exclusive power of legislation, which might have been avoided, by proper distinctions with respect to treaties, and requiring the assent of the House of Representatives, where it could be done with safety.

By requiring only a majority to make all commercial and navigation laws, the five southern states (whose produce and circumstances are totally different from those of the eight northern and eastern states) will be ruined: for such rigid and premature regulations may be made, as will enable the merchants of the northern and eastern states not only to demand an exorbitant freight, but to monopolize the purchase of the commodities, at their own price, for many years, to the great injury of the landed interest, and the impoverishment of the people: and the danger is the greater, as the gain on one side will be in proportion to the loss on the other, Whereas, requiring two-thirds of the members present in both houses, would have produced mutual moderation, promoted the general interest, and removed an insuperable objection to the adoption of the government.

Under their own construction of the general clause at the end of the enumerated powers, the Congress may grant monopolies in trade and commerce, constitute new crimes, inflict unusual and severe punishments, and extend their power as far as they shall think proper; so that the state legislatures have no security for the powers now presumed to remain to them; or the people for their rights. There is no declaration of any kind for preserving the liberty of the press, the trial by jury in civil cases, nor against the danger of standing armies in time of peace.

The state legislatures are restrained from laying export duties on their own produce—the general legislature is restrained from prohibiting the further importation of slaves for twenty odd years, though such importations render the United States weaker, more vulnerable, and less capable of defence. Both the general legislature, and the state legislatures are expressly prohibited making ex *post facto* laws, though there never was, nor can be, a legislature, but must and will make such laws, when necessity and the public safety require them, which will hereafter be a breach of all the constitutions in the union, and afford precedents for other innovations.

This government will commence in a moderate aristocracy; it is at present impossible to foresee whether it will, in its operation, produce a monarchy, or a corrupt oppressive aristocracy; it will most probably vibrate some years between the two, and then terminate in the one or the other.

15. *Ratification of the Constitution by New York**

ON JUNE 21, 1788, the ninth state (New Hampshire) ratified the Constitution. Presumably the approval of these nine states was sufficient to make the Constitution effective. However, neither New York nor Virginia was among them; and it was widely recognized that their participation in the new government would be essential to its success. In both states there was strong opposition to the Constitution and it was not at all certain that approval would be given. On June 25, 1788, Virginia ratified by a vote of eighty-nine to seventy-nine; and on July 26, 1788, the New York Convention also voted its approval, thirty to twenty-seven. The decision was not easily won in either state, however. The resolution that follows indicates the nature of conciliatory gestures made toward the opposition in New York.

We the Delegates of the People of the State of New York, duly elected and Met in Convention, having maturely considered the Constitution for the United States of America, agreed to on the seventeenth day of September, in the year One thousand Seven hundred and Eighty seven, by the Convention then assembled at Philadelphia in the Common-wealth of Pennsylvania (a Copy whereof precedes these presents) and having also seriously and deliberately considered the present situation of the United States, Do declare and make known.

That all Power is originally vested in and consequently derived from the People, and that Government is instituted by them for their common Interest Protection and Security.

That the enjoyment of Life, Liberty and the pursuit of Happiness are essential rights which every Government ought to respect and preserve.

That the Powers of Government may be reassumed by the People, whensoever it shall become necessary to their Happiness; that every Power, Jurisdiction and right, which is not by the said Constitution clearly delegated to the Congress of the United States, or the departments of the Government thereof, remains to the People of the several

* Quoted from *Documents Illustrative of the Formation of the Union of the American States* (United States Government Printing Office, Washington, D.C., 1927), pp. 1034-1038.

States, or to their respective State Governments to whom they may have granted the same; And that those Clauses in the said Constitution, which declare, that Congress shall not have or exercise certain Powers, do not imply that Congress is entitled to any Powers not given by the said Constitution; but such Clauses are to be construed either as exceptions to certain specified Powers, or as inserted merely for greater Caution.

That the People have an equal, natural and unalienable right, freely and peaceably to Exercise their Religion according to the dictates of Conscience, and that no Religious Sect or Society ought to be favoured or established by Law in preference of others.

That the People have a right to keep and bear Arms; that a well regulated Militia, including the body of the People *capable of bearing Arms*, is the proper, natural and safe defence of a free State;

That the Militia should not be subject to Martial Law except in time of War, Rebellion or Insurrection.

That standing Armies in time of Peace are dangerous to Liberty, and ought not to be kept up, except in Cases of necessity; and that at all times, the Military should be under strict Subordination to the civil Power.

That in time of Peace no Soldier ought to be quartered in any House without the consent of the Owner, and in time of War only by the Civil Magistrate in such manner as the Laws may direct.

That no Person ought to be taken imprisoned or disseised of his freehold, or be exiled or deprived of his Privileges, Franchises, Life, Liberty or Property but by due process of Law.

That no Person ought to be put twice in Jeopardy of Life or Limb for one and the same Offence, nor, unless in case of impeachment, be punished more than once for the same Offence.

That every Person restrained of his Liberty is entitled to an enquiry into the lawfulness of such restraint, and to a removal thereof if unlawful, and that such enquiry and removal ought not to be denied or delayed, except when on account of Public Danger the Congress shall suspend the privilege of the Writ of Habeas Corpus.

That excessive Bail ought not to be required; nor excessive Fines imposed; nor Cruel or unusual Punishments inflicted.

That (except in the Government of the Land and Naval Forces, and of the Militia when in actual Service, and in cases of Impeachment) a Presentment or Indictment by a Grand Jury ought to be observed as a necessary preliminary to the trial of all Crimes cognizable by the Judiciary of the United States, and such Trial should be speedy, public, and by an impartial Jury of the County where the Crime was committed; and that no person can be found Guilty without the unanimous consent of such Jury. . . . And that in all Criminal Prosecutions, the Accused ought to be informed of the cause and nature of his Accusation, to be confronted with his accusers and the Witnesses against him, to have the means of producing his Witnesses, and the assistance of Council for his defense, and should not be compelled to give Evidence against himself.

That the trial by Jury in the extent that it obtains by the Common Law of England is one of the greatest securities to the rights of a free People, and ought to remain inviolate.

That every Freeman has a right to be secure from all unreasonable searches and seizures of his person his papers or his property, and therefore, that all Warrants to search suspected places or seize any Freeman his papers or property, without information upon Oath or Affirmation of sufficient cause, are grievous and oppressive; and that all general Warrants (or such in which the place or person suspected are not particularly designated) are dangerous and ought not to be granted.

That the People have a right peaceably to assemble together to consult for their common good, or to instruct their Representatives; and that every person has a right to Petition or apply to the Legislature for redress of Grievances—That the Freedom of the Press ought not to be violated or restrained.

That there should be once in four years an Election of the President and Vice President, so that no Officer who may be appointed by the Congress to act as President in case of the removal, death, resignation or inability of the President and Vice President can in any case continue to act beyond the termination of the period for which the last President and Vice President were elected.

That nothing contained in the said Constitution is to be construed to prevent the Legislature of any State from passing Laws at its discretion from time to time to divide such State into convenient Districts, and to apportion its Representatives to and amongst such Districts.

That the Prohibition contained in the said Constitution against ex *post facto* Laws, extends only to Laws concerning Crimes.

That all Appeals in Causes determineable according to the course of the common Law, ought to be by Writ of Error and not otherwise.

That the Judicial Power of the United States in cases in which a State may be a party, does not extend to criminal Prosecutions, or to authorize any Suit by any Person against a State.

That the Judicial Power of the United States as to Controversies between Citizens of the same State claiming Lands under Grants of different States is not to be construed to extend to any other Controversies between them except those which relate to such Lands, so claimed under Grants of different States.

That the Jurisdiction of the Supreme Court of the United States, or of any other Court to be instituted by the Congress, is not in any case to be encreased enlarged or extended by any Fiction Collusion or mere suggestion;—And That no Treaty is to be construed so to operate as to alter the Constitution of any State.

Under these impressions and declaring that the rights aforesaid cannot be abridged or violated, and that the Explanations aforesaid are consistent with the said Constitution, And in confidence that the Amendments which shall have been proposed to the said Constitution will receive an early and mature Consideration: We the said Delegates, in the Name and in the behalf of the People of the State of New York Do by these presents Assent to and Ratify the said Constitution. In full Confidence nevertheless that until a Convention shall be called and convened for proposing Amendments to the said Constitution, the Militia of this State will not be continued in Service out of this State for a longer term than six weeks without the Consent of the Legislature thereof;—that the Congress will not make or alter any Regulation in this State respecting the times places and manner of holding Elections for Senators or Representatives unless the Legislature of this State shall neglect or refuse to make Laws or regulations for the purpose, or from any circumstance be incapable of making the same, and that in those cases such power will only be exercised until the Legislature of this State shall make provision in the Premises;—that no Excise will be imposed on any Article of the Growth production or Manufacture of the United States, or any of them within this State, Ardent Spirits excepted; And that the Congress will not lay direct Taxes within this State, but when the Monies arising from the Impost and Excise shall be insufficient for the public Exigencies, nor then, until Congress shall first have made a Requisition upon this State to assess levy and pay the Amount of such Requisition made agreably to the Census fixed in the said Constitution in such way and manner as the Legislature of this State shall judge best, but that in such case, if the State shall neglect or refuse to pay its proportion pursuant to such Requisition, then the Congress may assess and levy this States proportion together with Interest at the Rate of six per Centum per Annum from the time at which the same was required to be paid.

Done in Convention at Poughkeepsie in the County of Dutchess in the State of New York the twenty sixth day of July in the year of our Lord One thousand Seven hundred and Eighty eight.

By Order of the Convention.

GEO: CLINTON President

16. The Movement for the Constitution *

ONE of the continuing debates of American political history has involved the question: To what extent did the framers of the Federal Constitution, during the process of writing that document, subordinate the general welfare to the particular economic advantage of the interest groups to which they belonged? Although the excerpt here from the writings of the late Charles A. Beard does not answer this question, it does reveal clearly the economic status and interests of the delegates. It may be said that the delegates were fully aware of the importance of conflicting economic interests in the American society and the necessity of erecting the new government on a firm economic foundation.

DID the system of government prevailing in the United States in 1787 affect adversely any of the economic interests enumerated in the preceding chapter? Furthermore, were the leaders in the movement which led to the adoption of the Constitution representatives of the interests so affected?

Fortunately, it is not necessary to devote any considerable attention to the first of these questions. It is answered in part above, and all of the standard treatises show conclusively that the legal system prevailing at the opening of 1787 was unfavorable to the property rights of four powerful groups above enumerated. That system was, in brief, as follows. There was a loose union of thirteen sovereign states under the Articles of Confederation. The national government consisted of a legislature of one house in which the states had an equal voting power. There was no executive department and no general judiciary. The central government had no power to regulate commerce or to tax directly; and in the absence of these powers all branches of the government were rendered helpless. Particularly, money could not be secured to pay the holders of public securities, either their interest or principal. Under this system, the state legislatures were substantially without restrictions or judicial control; private rights in property were continually attacked by stay laws, legal tender laws, and a whole range of measures framed in behalf of debtors; and in New England open rebellion had broken out.

That the economic groups in question looked to a new national

* Charles A. Beard, *An Economic Interpretation of the Constitution of the United States* (The Macmillan Company, 1913), pp. 52-63, 149-151, 237-238, 290-291, 324-325. Reprinted by permission of Mrs. Beard and the publisher.

government as the one source of relief and advantage, is shown in a hundred contemporary pamphlets and newspaper articles. It was in fact the topic of the times.

For example, a letter from Philadelphia, under date of August 29, 1787, sums up concisely the interests which were turning to the new Constitution: "The states neglect their roads and canals, till they see whether those necessary improvements will not become the objects of a national government. Trading and manufacturing companies suspend their voyages and manufactures till they see how far their commerce will be protected and promoted by a national system of commercial regulations. The lawful usurer locks up or buries his specie till he sees whether the new frame of government will deliver him from the curse or fear of paper money and the tender laws. . . . The public creditor, who, from the deranged state of finances in every state and their total inability to support their partial funding systems, has reason to fear that his certificates will perish in his hands, now places all his hopes of justice in an enlightened and stable national government. The embarrassed farmer and the oppressed tenant, who wishes to become free . . . by emigrating to a frontier country, wait to see whether they shall be protected by a national force from the Indians."

A final answer to the second question propounded above would require an exhaustive analysis of the "movement for the Constitution," in the following form:—

1. A study of the economic forces in the Revolution and particularly in the Continental Congress that drafted the Articles of Confederation.

2. An inquiry into the first signs of discontent with the prevailing system, their geographic distribution, and their economic sources.

3. An examination of the several attempts in the Congress under the Articles of Confederation to secure the power to regulate commerce and establish a revenue for discharging the debt.

4. A description of the economic interests of all the members who were most active in these attempts.

5. A description of the economic forces in the communities whose representatives in Congress were zealous in securing a revision of the Articles.

6. A study of the nature and distribution of the several legislative attacks on private rights in property between 1783 and 1787.

7. A minute study of the personnel of the movement for revision and the economic interests of the leading spirits in Congress and the state legislatures and outside of legislative chambers.

Any one superficially acquainted with the sources of American history will see at once the nature of the work which must be done to secure the raw materials for such a study. The enormous mass of unprinted papers of the Continental Congress in the Library at Washington would have to be thoroughly searched; proceedings in state legislatures during the years under consideration would have to be scrutinized; local archives and newspapers would have to be examined.

In the present state of our historical materials, therefore, all that can be attempted here is a superficial commentary on some of the outward aspects of the movement for the Constitution which are described in the conventional works on the subject. Many of the eminent men prominently identified with the events which led up to the Convention of 1787 were themselves members of that Assembly, and their economic interests are considered below in Chapter V. But it is not without significance to discover that some of the leading men outside of the Convention who labored for an overthrow of the old system were also directly interested in the results of their labors.

As early as January, 1781, General Philip Schuyler moved in the senate of New York "to request the eastern states to join in an early convention, which should form a perpetual league of incorporation, subservient, however, to the common interest of all the states; invite others to accede to it; erect Vermont into a state; devise a fund for the redemption of the common debts; substitute a permanent and uniform system for temporary expedients; and invest the confederacy with powers of coercion." General Schuyler was a large holder of depreciated securities.

In February, 1781, Congress recommended to the states that they vest in the national legislature a power to levy a duty to pay the principal and interest of the debt. In April, 1783, Congress again appealed to the states for authority to lay duties for the purpose of supplying a revenue with which to discharge the debt. Among the leaders in Congress who favored this increase in power were Gorham, Higginson, Ellsworth, Dyer, Boudinot, Fitzsimons, Williamson, Izard, Johnson, and King, all of whom held securities which were daily depreciating under the failure of the government to meet its just obligations.

In 1785, Governor Bowdoin, of Massachusetts, in his inaugural address urged the necessity of a stronger union with larger powers, and recommended a convention to deliberate upon the whole matter. Governor Bowdoin was a large holder of public securities. The legislature of the commonwealth, thereupon, resolved that the Articles of

Confederation were inadequate, and directed the representatives in Congress to take steps looking toward a strengthening of the union; but they failed to act.

Men less eminent than Bowdoin and Schuyler were being educated in Federalism by the march of events. In Boston merchants were petitioning Congress for relief from British discriminations; in the Virginia legislature the representatives of the commercial interests were learning their lessons; the demands for positive action were increasing daily in number. Every failure to find a remedy under the Articles of Confederation only served to augment the ranks of those who were ready for a complete reconstruction of the prevailing system.

A few illustrations will serve to show how the demand for reform was being fostered and also the connection between the leaders in the agitation and the personnel of the public bodies which later achieved the great work of framing and ratifying the Constitution. Even before the war was over and the Articles of Confederation tested in a time of peace, the inability of the government under it to afford defence to commerce on the high seas was deplored by merchants whose vessels were falling prey to the British. In April, 1782, a number of prominent merchants presented a petition to Congress in which they lamented the British depredations on American trade and the want of adequate naval protection at sea. Among the signers of this petition were several men who were later known as warm supporters of a strong federal government. One of them, Thomas Fitzsimons, was a member of the Convention which drafted the Constitution; another, John Barclay, was a member of the Pennsylvania convention and voted in favor of the ratification of the new system of government.

Six years before the Convention met in Philadelphia, the disordered financial system under the Confederation was the subject of protest by interested parties. In 1781, "divers inhabitants of the state of Pennsylvania," were petitioning Congress to take some action designed to put the credit of the country on a sound basis. Thus runs the petition: "Humbly sheweth that whereas you thought fit heretofore in the course of your wisdom to emit bills of credit for good and great purposes, but the same depreciating to such an amazing degree beyond the expectation of all living did therefore lay open wide door for the most monstrous and absurd injustices by fraudulent payments which we conclude is directly contrary to your good and great purposes in emitting the same, we therefore, not only firmly relying on the extraordinary clearness of the circumstances of our agrievances, but likewise on the uprightness of your understandings, Do therefore presume to pray your honors would be pleased to recommend to the several states to adopt such measures as they may think most likely to afford a safe and effectual redress to all such agrievances. . . ." Among the signers of this petition are Thomas Bull, John Hannum, and Thomas Cheyney, who six years later as members of the Pennsylvania convention had the pleasure of voting for the ratification of an instrument of government that put an end to the evils against which they had so earnestly protested.

The failure of repeated attempts in Congress to secure an amendment authorizing the laying of impost duties, the refusal of the states to pay the requisitions made by Congress, and the obvious impossibility of gaining their ends through the ordinary channels of ratification by state legislatures, drove the advocates of these measures to desperation. Republican government, as it had been tried out, had failed to secure for personality that protection and opportunity for advancement which it enjoyed under monarchy. The despair of the representatives of the property interests thus jeopardized and their readiness for some heroic measures were fully manifest in the correspondence of the time.

Washington, who was not given to undue alarms, wrote to John Jay from Mount Vernon, on August 1, 1786, to the effect that men of leadership were ready for drastic action: "What astonishing changes," he said, "a few years are capable of producing. I am told that even respectable characters speak of a monarchical form of Government without horror. From thinking proceeds speaking, thence to acting is often but a single step. But how irrevocable and tremendous! What a triumph for our enemies to verify their predictions—what a triumph for the advocates of despotism to find that we are incapable of governing ourselves, & that systems founded on the basis of equal liberty are merely ideal & fallacious! Would to God that wise measures may be taken in time to avert the consequences we have but too much reason to apprehend."

Later in that year, General Knox, who was a holder of public securities, wrote to Washington in the following strain: "The people who are the insurgents [Shaysites] have never paid any, or but very little taxes—But they see the weakness of government; They feel at once their own poverty, compared with the opulent, and their own force, and they are determined to make use of the latter, in order to remedy the former. Their creed is 'That the property of the United States has been protected from the confiscations of Britain by the joint exertions of all, and therefore ought to be the common property of all. And he that attempts opposition to this creed is an enemy to equity and justice, and ought to be swept from off the face of the earth.' In a word they are determined to annihilate all debts public and private and have agrarian Laws, which are easily effected by means of unfunded paper money which shall be a tender in all cases whatever—

"The numbers of these people may amount in Massachusetts to about one fifth part of several populous counties, and to them may be collected, people of similar sentiments, from the states of Rhode Island, Connecticut, and New Hampshire so as to constitute a body of 12 or 15000 desperate & unprincipled men—They are chiefly of the young and active part of the community, more easily collected than perhaps kept together afterwards—But they will probably commit overt acts of treason which will compel them to embody for their own safety—once embodied they will be constrained to submit to discipline for the same reason. Having proceeded to this length for which they are now ripe, we shall have a formidable rebellion against reason, the principle of all government, and the very name of liberty. This dreadful situation has alarmed every man of principle and property in New England. They start as from a dream, and ask what has been the cause of our delusion? what is to afford us security against the violence of lawless men? Our government must be braced, changed, or altered to secure our lives and property. We imagined that the mildness of our government and *the virtue* of the people were so correspondent, that we were not as other nations requiring brutal force to support the laws—But we find that we are men, actual men, possessing all the turbulent passions belonging to that anim[al] and that we must have a government proper and adequate for him. The people of Massachuse[tts] for instance, are far advanced in this doctrine, and the men of reflection, & principle, are determined to endev[or] to establish a government which shall have the power to protect them in their lawful pursuits, and which will be efficient in all cases of internal commotions or foreign invasions—They mean that liberty shall be the basis, a liberty resulting from the equal and firm administration of the laws. They wish for a general government of unity as they see the local legislatures must naturally and necessarily tend to retard and frustrate all general government."

A few months later, Madison, writing to Edmund Pendleton from New York, the seat of the government, corroborated the views expressed by Washington and Knox and set forth what he conceived to be the desperate state of republican government. His letter, dated February 24, 1787, three days after Congress had issued the call for a national Convention, ran as follows: "In general I find men of reflection much less sanguine as to a new than despondent as to the present System. Indeed the Present System neither has nor deserves advocates; and if some very strong props are not applied will quickly tumble to the ground. . . . If the approaching Convention should not agree on some remedy, I am persuaded that some very different arrangement will ensue. The late turbulent scenes in Massachusetts & infamous ones in Rhode Island, have done inexpressible injury to the republican character in that part of the U. States; and a propensity towards Monarchy is said to have been produced by it in some leading minds. The bulk of the people will probably prefer the lesser evil of a partition of the Union into three more practicable and energetic Governments. The latter idea I find after long confinement to individual speculations & private circles, is beginning to show itself in the Newspapers."

A few days after this letter was written by Madison, John Armstrong wrote to Washington from Carlisle that the suppression of the insurrection in Massachusetts had not allayed the fears of leading men in his state. "The alarming flame in Massachusetts," he says, "seems nearly extinguished, but if the subsequent measures of that State respecting the insurgents should be severe, amounting to *death*, Confiscation, or disfranchisement, the consequence may be bad, as tending to reinkindle the flame. Shall I tell you in *confidence*, I have now twice heard, nor from low authority (some principal men of that State) begin to talk of wishing one general *Head* to the Union, in the room of Congress!"

By correspondence such as this just cited, by an increasing recognition of the desperate straights in which they were placed, a remarkable fusion of interested forces was effected. The wealth, the influence, and a major portion of the educated men of the country were drawn together in a compact group, "informed by a conscious solidarity of interests," as President Wilson has so tersely put it.

Having failed to obtain relief through the regular channels of amendment by Congress ratified by the state legislatures, the leaders struck out on a new path. Operating through the Virginia legislature, they secured a resolution inviting the sister commonwealths to send delegates to a convention at Annapolis to take into consideration the trade and commercial system of the United States. The convention duly met, but the attendance was so slim that, as Professor Burgess has put it, "a coup d'état attempted by so small a body could not but fail."

Although the Annapolis convention was ostensibly concerned with commercial regulation primarily, there is no doubt that it was the creation of the men who had been working in Congress and out for a general revision of the whole system. There is no doubt also that it was not regarded as of much significance in itself, but rather as a preliminary to a national convention which would afford an opportunity for reconstructing the government. For this view we have a witness of high authority, James Madison, who in a letter of August 12, 1786, to Jefferson, written a month before the Annapolis conference, said: "Many gentlemen, both within and without Congress, wish to make this meeting subservient to a plenipotentiary Convention for amending the Confederation. Tho' my wishes are in favor of such an event, yet I despair so much of its accomplishment at the present crisis that I do not extend my views beyond a commercial Reform."

Under the influence of Hamilton, the conference at Annapolis contented itself with merely recommending that another convention be called "to devise such further provisions as shall appear to them necessary to render the constitution of the federal government adequate to the exigencies of the Union." Acting on this modest suggestion, Congress, in February, 1787, invited the states to send delegates to a Convention at Philadelphia for "the sole and express purpose of revising the Articles of Confederation."

Certain tentative conclusions emerge at this point.

Large and important groups of economic interests were adversely affected by the system of government under the Articles of Confederation, namely, those of public securities, shipping and manufacturing, money at interest; in short, capital as opposed to land.

The representatives of these important interests attempted through the regular legal channels to secure amendments to the Articles of Confederation which would safeguard their rights in the future, particularly those of the public creditors.

Having failed to realize their great purposes through the regular means, the leaders in the movement set to work to secure by a circuitous route the assemblying of a Convention to "revise" the Articles of Confederation with the hope of obtaining, outside of the existing legal framework, the adoption of a revolutionary programme.

Ostensibly, however, the formal plan of approval by Congress and the state legislatures was to be preserved.

• • • • •

A SURVEY OF THE ECONOMIC INTERESTS OF THE MEMBERS OF THE CONSTITUTIONAL CONVENTION

A majority of the members were lawyers by profession.

Most of the members came from towns, on or near the coast, that is, from the regions in which personality was largely concentrated.

Not one member represented in his immediate personal economic interests the small farming or mechanic classes.

The overwhelming majority of members, at least five-sixths, were immedately, directly, and personally interested in the outcome of their labors at Philadelphia, and were to a greater or less extent economic beneficiaries from the adoption of the Constitution.

1. Public security interests were extensively represented in the Convention. Of the fifty-five members who attended no less than forty appear on the Records of the Treasury Department for sums varying from a few dollars up to more than one hundred thousand dollars. Among the minor holders were Bassett, Blount, Brearley, Broom, Butler, Carroll, Few, Hamilton, L. Martin, Mason, Mercer, Mifflin, Read, Spaight, Wilson, and Wythe. Among the larger holders (taking the sum of about $5000 as the criterion) were Baldwin, Blair, Clymer, Dayton, Ellsworth, Fitzsimons, Gilman, Gerry, Gorham, Jenifer, Johnson, King, Langdon, Lansing, Livingston, McClurg, R. Morris, C. C. Pinckney, C. Pinckney, Randolph, Sherman, Strong, Washington, and Williamson.

It is interesting to note that, with the exception of New York, and possibly Delaware, each state had one or more prominent representatives in the Convention who held more than a negligible amount of securities, and who could therefore speak with feeling and authority on the question of providing in the new Constitution for the full discharge of the public debt:

Langdon and Gilman, of New Hampshire.

Gerry, Strong, and King, of Massachusetts.

Ellsworth, Sherman, and Johnson, of Connecticut.

Hamilton, of New York. Although he held no large amount personally, he was the special pleader for the holders of public securities and the maintenance of public faith.

Dayton, of New Jersey.

Robert Morris, Clymer, and Fitzsimons, of Pennsylvania.

Mercer and Carroll, of Maryland.

Blair, McClurg, and Randolph, of Virgina.

Williamson, of North Carolina.

The two Pinckneys, of South Carolina.

Few and Baldwin, of Georgia.

2. Personalty invested in lands for speculation was represented by at least fourteen members: Blount, Dayton, Few, Fitzsimons, Franklin, Gilman, Gerry, Gorham, Hamilton, Mason, R. Morris, Washington, Williamson, and Wilson.

3. Personalty in the form of money loaned at interest was represented by at least twenty-four members: Bassett, Broom, Butler, Carroll, Clymer, Davie, Dickinson, Ellsworth, Few, Fitzsimons, Franklin, Gilman, Ingersoll, Johnson, King, Langdon, Mason, McHenry, C. C. Pinckney, C. Pinckney, Randolph, Read, Washington, and Williamson.

4. Personalty in mercantile, manufacturing, and shipping lines was represented by at least eleven members: Broom, Clymer, Ellsworth, Fitzsimons, Gerry, King, Langdon, McHenry, Mifflin, G. Morris, and R. Morris.

5. Personalty in slaves was represented by at least fifteen members: Butler, Davie, Jenifer, A. Martin, L. Martin, Mason, Mercer, C. C. Pinckney, C. Pinckney, Randolph, Read, Rutledge, Spaight, Washington, and Wythe.

It cannot be said, therefore, that the members of the Convention were "disinterested." On the contrary, we are forced to accept the profoundly significant conclusion that they knew through their personal experiences in economic affairs the precise results which the new government that they were setting up was designed to attain. As a group of doctrinaires, like the Frankfort assembly of 1848, they would have failed miserably; but as practical men they were able to build the new government upon the only foundations which could be stable: fundamental economic interests.

• • • • •

CONCLUSIONS ON THE PROCESS OF RATIFICATION

Two states, Rhode Island and North Carolina refused to ratify the Constitution until after the establishment of the new government which set in train powerful economic forces against them in their isolation.

In three states, New Hampshire, New York, and Massachusetts, the popular vote as measured by the election of delegates to the conventions was adverse to the Constitution; and ratification was secured by the conversion of opponents and often the repudiation of their tacit (and in some cases express) instructions.

In Virginia the popular vote was doubtful.

In the four states which ratified the constitution with facility, Connecticut, New Jersey, Georgia, and Delaware, only four or five weeks were allowed to elapse before the legislatures acted, and four or five weeks more before the elections to the conventions were called; and about an equal period between the elections and the meeting of the conventions. This facility of action may have been due to the general sentiment in favor of the Constitution; or the rapidity of action may account for the slight development of the opposition.

In two commonwealths, Maryland and South Carolina, deliberation and delays in the election and the assembling of the conventions resulted in an undoubted majority in favor of the new instrument; but for the latter state the popular vote has never been figured out.

In one of the states, Pennsylvania, the proceedings connected with the ratification of the Constitution were conducted with unseemly haste.

• • • • •

CONCLUSIONS WITH RESPECT TO THE ECONOMICS OF THE VOTE ON THE CONSTITUTION IN THE STATE RATIFYING CONVENTIONS

Inasmuch as the movement for the ratification of the Constitution centred particularly in the regions in which mercantile, manufacturing, security, and personalty interests generally had their greatest strength, it is impossible to escape the conclusion that holders of personalty saw in the new government a strength and defence to their advantage.

Inasmuch as so many leaders in the movement for ratification were large security holders, and inasmuch as securities constituted such a large proportion of personalty, this economic interest must have formed a very considerable dynamic element, if not the preponderating element, in bringing about the adoption of the new system.

The state conventions do not seem to have been more "disinterested" than the Philadelphia convention; but in fact the leading champions of the new government appear to have been, for the most part, men of the same practical type, with actual economic advantages at stake.

The opposition to the Constitution almost uniformly came from the agricultural regions, and from the areas in which debtors had been formulating paper money and other depreciatory schemes.

• • • • •

GENERAL CONCLUSIONS ON THE ECONOMIC NATURE OF THE MOVEMENT FOR A NEW CONSTITUTION

The movement for the Constitution of the United States was originated and carried through principally by four groups of personalty interests which had been adversely affected under the Articles of Confederation: money, public securities, manufacturers, and trade and shipping.

The first firm steps toward the formation of the Constitution were taken by a small and active group of men immediately interested through their personal possessions in the outcome of their labors.

No popular vote was taken directly or indirectly on the proposition to call the Convention which drafted the Constitution.

A large propertyless mass was, under the prevailing suffrage qualifications, excluded at the outset from participation (through representatives) in the work of framing the Constitution.

The members of the Philadelphia Convention which drafted the Constitution were, with a few exceptions, immediately, directly, and personally interested in, and derived economic advantages from, the establishment of the new system.

The Constitution was essentially an economic document based upon the concept that the fundamental private rights of property are anterior to government and morally beyond the reach of popular majorities.

The major portion of the members of the Convention are on record as recognizing the claim of property to a special and defensive position in the Constitution.

In the ratification of the Constitution, about three-fourths of the adult males failed to vote on the question, having abstained from the elections at which delegates to the state conventions were chosen, either on account of their indifference or their disfranchisement by property qualifications.

The Constitution was ratified by a vote of probably not more than one-sixth of the adult males.

It is questionable whether a majority of the voters participating in the elections for the state conventions in New York, Massachusetts, New Hampshire, Virginia, and South Carolina actually approved the ratification of the Constitution.

The leaders who supported the Constitution in the ratifying conventions represented the same economic groups as the members of the Philadelphia Convention; and in a large number of instances they were also directly and personally interested in the outcome of their efforts.

In the ratification, it became manifest that the line of cleavage for and against the Constitution was between substantial personalty interests on the one hand and the small farming and debtor interests on the other.

The Constitution was not created by "the whole people" as the jurists have said; neither was it created by "the states" as Southern nullifiers long contended; but it was the work of a consolidated group whose interests knew no state boundaries and were truly national in their scope.

17. A Criticism of the Economic Interpretation*

Charles A. Beard's book *An Economic Interpretation of the Constitution,* from which the previous selection (16) has been taken, was first published in 1913. It aroused much controversy throughout the country, and strong opinions were expressed both in praise and in condemnation of the work. In dealing with the relationship of politics and economics during a critical period in American history, the author touched upon a subject that was to become increasingly significant in American life following World War I. Hence his work has continued to arouse lively interest and controversy. The selection by Professor Edward S. Corwin presented here was written in 1914 as a review of Beard's book, and is one of the most balanced criticisms of that period. For Beard's reaction to this and other discussions of his book, the student is referred to the 1935 edition, issued under the original title.

Under the somewhat misleading title [An Economic Interpretation of the Constitution of the United States], Prof. Beard has brought together a summary statement of the "economic" causes of the framing and adoption of the Constitution. The volume itself will be apt to be misleading to most lay readers. . . .

The longest chapter in the volume and the one in which the writer brings forward considerable new material of his own exhuming, from the records of the Treasury Department at Washington, is Chapter V. In this chapter we are furnished with an account of the property interests of the members of the Philadelphia Convention, but the matter especially emphasized is their holdings of public securities. In brief, Prof. Beard finds that, of the 55 members of the Convention, no fewer than 40 appear at one time or other on the records of the Treasury Department, for the twenty years between 1779 and 1799, for sums varying from a few hundred dollars up to more than one hundred thousand dollars, and amounting in the aggregate, if we leave out of account the probable holdings of Robert Morris, whose ordinary business was that of banker and broker, to perhaps $450,000. He thereupon concludes (pp. 149-50) that "public security interests were extensively represented in the Convention," that with one or two exceptions, "each State had one or more prominent representatives in the Convention who held (*sic*) more than a negligible amount of

* Edward S. Corwin, *History Teachers Magazine*, V (February, 1914), pp. 65-66. Reprinted by permission of the author.

securities, and who could therefore speak with feeling and authority on the question of providing in the new Constitution for the full discharge of the public debt" (p. 150). These conclusions and the conclusions that are reasonably implied thereby invite scrutiny, but it will be seen—scarcely survive it.

In the first place, even if we suppose, for the sake of the argument, that members of the Convention were holders in 1787 of public securities to the face value of $450,000, the probability would be that at least one-third of such securities were evidences of State indebtedness, the payment of which by the National Government the Constitution in no wise suggests. Again of the remaining $300,000 worth, in nominal value, nearly two-thirds would have been, by Mr. Beard's own showing, the holdings of five men, McClurg, Dayton, Gerry, Johnson and Langdon—two of them decidedly inconspicuous figures and one finally an opponent of the Constitution—while the holdings of the five admitted leaders of the Convention, Hamilton, Madison, Gouveneur Morris, Wilson and Charles Pinckney, would have been, save those of Pinckney, who is said to have funded some $14,000 worth of securities "early in the history of the new system" (p. 139), practically nil. But again, even the heaviest holder of securities in 1787 could have obtained but a minimum benefit, we will not say merely from the action of the Convention, but even from the adoption of the Constitution and its going into effect. Thus Mr. Beard himself quotes from Callender (p. 35, foot-note) a statement to the effect that Hamilton pumped into the domestic debt of the Confederation, by his funding proposition of 1790, fully five-eighths of its value, an assertion which is well borne out by Prof. Dewey's statement (Financial History, 1st ed. p. 91) that upon the publication of Hamilton's Report of January 14, 1790, recommending the discharge of this debt at face value, "certificates went up to fifty cents on the dollar." But certainly this debt was worth something before the Convention met. But if this be admitted, and it be further admitted that Hamilton was responsible for five-eighths of its eventual value, what margin remains to represent a gain from the going into effect of the Constitution,—to say nothing of its mere framing?

But the fact of the matter is that Professor Beard's whole argument rests upon a totally unallowable assumption. "It is here assumed," he writes in a foot-note on page 75, "that when a member of the Convention appears upon the funding books of the new government he was a public creditor at the time of the Convention. Of course, it is possible that some of the members who are recorded as security holders possessed no paper when they went to Philadelphia, but purchased it afterward for speculation. But it is hardly to be supposed that many of them would sink to the level of mere speculators." With all due respect, this is the most unmitigated rot. Why should not former members of the Convention have invested their money in public securities in 1790 and the years following, when they saw these rising in value and becoming safe sources of income. By his loose use of the word "speculation," Mr. Beard abstracts all the poison from it. Perhaps three men who were members of the Convention of 1787 deserve the epithet "speculator" in any odious sense of the term, because of their connection with public securities; namely, Gerry, Dayton of New Jersey, and Fitzsimons of Pennsylvania. But at any rate, to return to the main point, so far as Mr. Beard's evidence shows, precisely seven members of the Convention—again excepting Robert Morris—had held public securities anterior to the meeting of the Convention; namely, Baldwin of Georgia, Blair of Virginia, Brearley of New Jersey, Gilman of New Hampshire, Gerry and Strong of Massachusetts, Mifflin of Pennsylvania, and Read of Delaware; and the total holdings of these men were apparently less than $90,000 in nominal value. Furthermore, of this amount fully two-thirds was the property of Elbridge Gerry, who, however, was so little influenced by this consideration that he refused to sign the Constitution and opposed its adoption!

But the case of Gerry is worth a little further investigation, as it turns out. On page 98, in a foot-note, Prof. Beard alludes to Ellsworth's charge, after the Convention, that Gerry finally turned against the Constitution because the Convention had refused to adopt a motion of his to saddle the proposed government with the obligation of redeeming the old continental currency. Of this charge Prof. Beard says: "It does not appear in Farrand's Records that any such motion was made in the Convention." This vindication of Gerry, however, as Mr. Beard should have been aware from his perusal of the Records, is but a technical one against a charge that was faultily worded. For the motion that Gerry stood sponsor for was the motion of Gouveneur Morris (who held no public securities) that "the legislature shall discharge the debts," etc., of the United States. The objections to this motion were pointed out by Mason, as follows: "The use of the term "shall" will beget speculations and increase the pestilential practice of stock-jobbing." Furthermore, "What he particularly wished was to leave the door open for buying up the securities, which he thought would be precluded by the term 'shall' as requiring nominal payment." Gerry followed Mason with a strong defense of stock-jobbing, notwithstanding which Randolph's alternative motion, making the obligations of the Confederation the legal obligations of the proposed Government, but otherwise leaving the creditors in statu quo, was adopted by a vote of ten States to one (Pennsylvania). In other words, not only did the Convention not determine the basis on which the United States was to meet the obligations of the Confederation, but it deliberately avoided doing so. Nevertheless, as we have seen, Prof. Beard describes the members of the Convention as speaking "with feeling and authority on the question of providing in the new Constitution for the full discharge of the public debt."

Prof. Beard is upon safer ground when he asserts that a leading purpose of the Convention was to secure the rights of property against the sort of attacks that these rights had been undergoing at the hands of the State legislatures. The purpose was frankly avowed by the supporters of the Constitution. "To secure the public good and private rights," wrote Madison in the Federalist, against interested majorities, "and at the same time to preserve the spirit and the form of popular government, is the great object to which our inquiries are directed." On the other hand, it was only in the rarest instances that "the interested majorities" whose malignant courses had been so important in bringing the Convention together found any defenders, even among those opposed to the Constitution. It may be noted too, in passing, that this motive of the framers of the Constitution is very fully and adequately recognized by Bancroft (History VI, 167 ff. last revision), whose "interpretation" of history Mr. Beard treats with such lofty condescension (pp. 1 and 2).

Some other features of the work are also provocative of criticism. Thus on the strength of some statistics with reference to foreign trade—statistics which are by no means of unambiguous significance (see Channing III, 422 footnote)—Professor Beard would disparage the idea that the situation confronting the country in 1787 was really serious. But certainly the testimony is quite overwhelming that many people of the time thought it was, at least. (See Elliot, 2d ed. III, 65, 71, 91, 123-4, 136, 432-3, 578-9). Again Prof. Beard would seem to countenance the idea that the movement for the Constitution was a species of coup d'etat, sprung upon the country unawares (pp. 62-4). The fact is that this movement began in January 1786 and ended in July 1788, having in the meantime received twice the sanction of the State legislatures and the Congress of the Confederation, besides that of the Convention that framed the Constitution and that of the popularly chosen Conventions that ratified it. But in this later connection we are informed on page 324, that "the propertyless masses under the prevailing suffrage qualifications were excluded at the outset from participation (through representatives) in the work of framing the Constitution." Yet, on pages 242-3, it is admitted that in Massachusetts, for which alone convincing statistics can be shown, probably only one-fifth of the adult males were kept from voting by a property qualification that was certainly not more liberal than that in most other states (See Chap. IV). It must be remembered that the members of the Philadelphia Convention were chosen by the same legislatures that had been voting paper money and stay laws, and that the Constitution was ratified by Conventions chosen by the same electors who had chosen these legislatures (save in New York, where a more liberal rule was adopted). Finally, Mr. Beard assumes to treat the legal view of the Constitution as the ordinance of "the People of the United States" as a hollow formula. Suppose it was a hollow formula in 1789, was it so five years later? Rather it would seem that, once we leave technical ground in the discussion of this question, we are in fairness bound to adopt a broader view of the process of ratification.

Prof. Beard has undertaken in this volume a task well worth doing and has pointed the way in many instances to its more adequate performance. Had he been less bent on demonstrating the truth of the socialistic theory of economic determinism and class struggle as an interpretation of history, his own performance would be less open to criticism. As it is, in his chapters VI and XI, he has furnished essays that are full of suggestion and value.

III

THE FEDERAL SYSTEM

18. *Federalism--Then and Now* *

OUR THINKING on federalism is largely conditioned by our study of the early development of the concept in this country. The usual discussion of this topic is limited to a consideration of the division of power between the national and state governments, with emphasis on a supposed conflict between these two areas. Professor Anderson reviews the developments of the past seventy-five years and argues that, if the problems confronting us are to be solved, a constructive approach to contemporary federalism must stress cooperation between the national and state governments.

AMERICAN federalism as it is today cannot be understood without a complete revision of our ordinary thinking about it. Most of us have learned what we know about it through historical studies. Starting with the 17th century if not farther back our courses and books in American history filled our minds with a mass of facts about Massachusetts and New York, Pennsylvania, Virginia and other colonies that became States and declared their independence. As the story was developed, the stage was so filled with a multiplicity of characters and "props" and there were so many minor and incidental themes and actions that we could not fully master the grand plot or sense the completeness of its culmination in our own day. When we try now to visualize the actual relations between national and state governments as they are today, we find that we have acquired a certain "set" or orientation of mind about them that is still largely 18th century. We know that there have been numerous changes in governmental or-

* William Anderson. Reprinted from *State Government*, XVI (May, 1943), pp. 107-112. Published by The Council of State Governments, Chicago, Illinois.

ganization and policies since independence was declared but we find it hard to view them all at once in their relationships one to another.

It is the thesis of what I am about to say that as a result of many changes American federalism today is different not only in degree but in kind from what it was in the beginning. There has been a virtual revolution in our system of government, an about-face almost as complete as can be imagined. The words we use, and the concepts that lie behind them, are still much the same as they were one hundred and fifty years ago, but the facts have been so drastically altered that nothing short of a complete reorientation will bring us up to date.

This revolution in American federalism is not the only drastic about-face that is crowded into the years since American independence was established. We have had one reversal after another in laws and in policies. From having been dependencies of a foreign land, the thirteen British colonies in America became States, a union of States, and soon a world power with its own dependencies. At one time this union opened its arms to the peoples of all lands. It was the promised land of freedom for the poor and oppressed in every clime. Today it has immigration laws and quota regulations so strict that as a rule the outward flow of people almost or quite exceeds the inward movement. Then, too, there was a period when it was public policy to open nearly all public lands to private settlement and exploitation on very easy terms. In recent years the government's policy has been to discourage unwise settlement, to re-acquire lands for forest and conservation purposes, and to move many settlers off the very land that they and their forefathers acquired from the government. Need we mention other revolutionary changes—the about-face on slavery, the enfranchisement of women, the changed attitude of government toward labor unions, the complete nationalization of our armed forces, the drastic revision of the American tax system within a generation? Some of these and a number of others will inevitably be mentioned in the pages that follow. They appear to be cognate with the changes in federalism that are to be discussed. They are necessary results of the same forces that have been operating to change drastically our whole American way of life.

But it is unfortunate to use the past tense in describing these crucial modifications. "The revolution continues." Even now in this critical time of our direct involvement in the Second World War, one can dimly foresee further changes in policy as being unavoidable. Our foreign policy, for example, once so negative, timid, and isolationist, obviously must become one of positive and bold participation in international controls. What impacts such a program in foreign policy will have, in turn, upon our federal system, still remain to be seen.

The failure of a people, and even of trained scholars and statesmen, to see and to comprehend the changes that have gone on around them is nothing unusual. Such a lag in the comprehension of changes has been noted many times. It has been observed that even third and fourth generation colonists, far removed from the mother country, often continue to use an archaic language that came over with our forefathers, and to think of the home country in greatly outmoded terms. But this is not so surprising as the lag where a people fail to see and to comprehend the very changes that have taken place among themselves. We are linked to and dominated by the past. We remember and apply today as mature men what we learned in childhood. The more conservative our profession the farther back in time we go for our mental hitching posts.

CONCEPTION OF FEDERAL SYSTEM

It was not only Montesquieu, a foreign scholar, who in the mid-eighteenth century failed to understand the British governmental system. Many Americans, even some of the leaders in the federal convention of 1787 misunderstood it, and so no doubt did many Englishmen at the same time. George Washington continued to the end to misunderstand the nature of a party system; his denunciation of faction and party cannot be explained in any other way. Calvin Coolidge when retiring from the Presidency is said to have sensed vaguely that great changes had taken place that he could not comprehend. He is reported to have said, "I have lived beyond my time."

This essay is an attempt to bring the American conception of its own federal system up to date. That it will not succeed perfectly is just as certain as that many men, well informed men, will disagree with its conclusions. It is the writer's prediction that he is more likely to be found to have understated than to have exaggerated the changes that have occurred.

By "federalism" and "the federal system" I mean especially the relations between the National Government and the States. In general the situation faced by the framers of the Constitution in 1787 will be considered as "Then," but in fact the description of Then will be applicable in part to a period of nearly a generation thereafter while the Founding Fathers remained in power. The adoption of the Constitution changed the legal status, but did not at once undo all factors in the previous situation. "Now" will be taken to include the late 1930's and the early 1940's, down to this date. The many events between 1787 and 1942 that brought about the striking contrasts between the two periods can hardly be mentioned in this sketch. My interest is primarily in results. How is our situation today different from what it was then? Omitting details, the changes are as follows:

Then a small area, with a small and sparse population, mainly agricultural and poor. *Now* one of the world's great nations in both area and population, largely urban and highly industrial, with tremendous national wealth.

Then largely a debtor people and an exporter of raw materials. *Now* a great creditor nation and large exporter of manufactured as well as agricultural goods.

Then meager and slow transportation facilities, and even poorer provisions for communication. *Now* an equipment of railroads, steamship lines, highways, trucks and buses, air transport, and communications of all kinds unexcelled by any other nation and undreamed of in the past.

Then state citizenship, state and local loyalties, interstate suspicions and tariffs, localized business, and considerable internal disunity. *Now* a nation, with national citizenship, primarily national loyalties, a nationwide free market, and nationally-organized business, agriculture, labor, professions, press, and political parties.

Then an upstart and divided people, an international weakling, threatened from north and south, with very poor defense arrangements, and looking out over the Atlantic at an essentially hostile world. *Now* a great world power, an international leader, with a powerful army and navy, and with strong friends and interests (as well as enemies) across both the Atlantic and Pacific.

GROWTH OF FEDERAL ACTIVITY

Then, inactive, negative, laissez-faire government with very few functions, and with only business leaders favoring a national government, and they desiring only to give it enough vigor to protect commerce, provide a nationwide free home market, and a sound currency and banking system. *Now* active, positive, collectivist government, especially at the national level, rendering many services with the support of powerful labor and agricultural elements, while many business leaders have reversed their position.

Then local law enforcement with state protection of the liberties guaranteed in bills of rights. *Now* increasing national law enforcement and national protection of civil liberties even against state and local action.

Then practically no employees of the National Government and very few state and local employees. *Now* a national civil service of normally over a million persons reaching into every county of the country, plus extensive state and local civil services.

Then, small public budgets at all levels. *Now* public budgets and expenditures, especially for the National Government, that reach astronomical figures.

Then (before 1789) no national taxes at all and for decades after 1789 only customs and excise taxes on a very limited scale, with state and local governments relying almost entirely on direct property taxes. *Now* tremendously increased and diversified taxes at both national and state levels, with the National Government rising swiftly to a dominating position with respect to all taxes except those directly on property.

Then (before 1788) state grants to the Congress of the United States for defense and debt purposes. *Now* grants-in-aid by the National Government to the States in increasing amounts and with steadily tightening national controls over state action.

SUPPORTERS OF FEDERAL STRENGTH

Permit me to select a few of these profound changes for special emphasis. Those who planned and carried through the unification of the original States under the Constitution were for all practical purposes the business leaders of the time and their professional advisers. It is generally accepted that most farmers and laborers were either indifferent or hostile to the formation of a stronger union. But labor and agriculture, having learned that the States were incapable of satisfying their demands, also turned to the central government to increase their welfare and security and to enlarge their share of the national income. Today organized laborers and organized farmers are among the strongest supporters of the National Government. They have become truly nationalist in their thinking. At the same time many business leaders, resentful of the new national regulations and taxes imposed upon them in the interests of labor and agriculture, preach a return to states' rights.

This partial reversal of positions is closely connected with the recent unparalleled increase in the activities of government, especially at the national level. An inactive government is necessarily a weak one. During the first century under the Constitution national government activities increased but little and the same was true of the States. For the nation the turning point came fifty years ago with the Interstate Commerce and Anti-Trust acts as the first important national regulations of business. Since the days of the Progressive Movement the increase has gone forward at an accelerated pace, and with each increase has come the further tendency toward centralization at the national level. Today, even discounting the fact of war, the National Government is the strongest and most active it has ever been. Wartime controls only accentuate an established fact.

FEDERAL EMPLOYEES

To these we add one more consideration—the existence today of a nationwide and national bureaucracy. In civilian employments alone the National Government now has over a million servants scattered throughout the length and breadth of the land. It has more employees than the forty-eight States combined. These men and women are engaged in rendering a host of services to the people everywhere. Their functions have become an indispensable part of the life of the nation, essential to the welfare of the people. It is almost unthinkable that any national administration, any Congress, or any Supreme Court for many decades to come would dare to undo or even seriously to threaten these national services to the whole population.

One other point. Since the adoption of the first national income tax a generation ago there has been what amounts to a revolution in American public finance. The revenues now available to the National Government under new and old forms of taxation are incalculably greater than anything in the past. While the States have also increased their revenues, they grow increasingly dependent upon the National Government for aid. Even now while state budgets are mostly in balance, state legislatures, under pressure from taxpayers, are proceeding to reduce existing state taxes. This act of retreat, however laudable its motives, is but a recognition by the States of the overwhelming superiority of National Government in the fiscal field.

For nearly one hundred and fifty years the emphasis in discussions of American federalism was on the division of powers between national and state governments. All readers of our history are familiar with the struggles of the States against the seemingly inexorable advance of the National Government. The theory of states' rights was discussed in the press and on the platform, debated in legislative bodies, pleaded in courts, and fought over on the battle field. In spite of all these contrary efforts, the trend toward national control was never really checked. Today it can be said that to debate national *versus* state powers is to raise one of the least important issues in American public life. For all practical purposes that issue has been settled. Numerous and influential sections of the American people—farmers, laborers, transportation interests, and others—have found that only through national action can their claims be satisfied. A nation has arisen that demands national action to meet national needs. Congress and the President have found that in one way or another they can satisfy most of these demands. The National Government is today regulating, promoting, and aiding agriculture, labor, and industry (which are not mentioned in the Constitution) as well as commerce (which is mentioned) in ways and to an extent obviously never visualized by the founders.

NATURE OF UNION MISUNDERSTOOD

And I might add parenthetically that the term "Federal Government" as applied to our central government is today more clearly a misnomer than it was even in the beginning. The Constitution nowhere uses the term "federation" or "Federal Government." It was a *union* that the people created through the Constitution, and as the people have now become fully a nation, their union government has become their National Government.

The way in which the Supreme Court has been brought to the acceptance of the inevitable is indeed a curious history. Even while asserting a right to declare acts of Congress unconstitutional, in its first fifty years the court tended to be strongly nationalist. Meanwhile a theory had been developed that the Supreme Court existed in large part to police the boundaries between state and national powers and to prevent encroachments by either upon the other. The antagonism of national and state governments was assumed. Their interests were supposed to be always in conflict. Someone had to stand watch to prevent even the slightest trespass by either one upon the area marked out for the other.

Domestic as well as foreign publicists developed this idea. "Federalism is legalism," said Dicey. The Supreme Court was the great defender of the Constitution and of the federal system. By its legal decisions it would stop every leak in the dikes. No matter how high the waters of nationalism might rise, by its words it would turn them back.

RELATION OF STATES AND NATION

Then followed that period in the history of the court when it really tried to hold back a nation that was seeking means of national expression. Hamilton had said that "a nation without a national government is an awful spectacle" and so at times it was as the court again and again struck down important acts of Congress. Various theories of the relations of the nation and the States were developed in the court, including that defined by Professor Corwin as the theory of "dual federalism." But the trend of events was inexorable. Acts of Congress once struck down rose up again in new form. It became evident that some of these acts were needed in the public interest. The court began to yield a little, to distinguish one case from another, and finally to overrule its own prior decisions. In the early years of the "Great Depression" the court temporarily stiffened its opposition to new national regulations. It was hard to tell whether it was more interested in upholding states' rights or in protecting the sphere of anarchy that had been left to private business.

In 1937 this period came to an abrupt end. Recent volumes of Supreme Court reports are filled with debris of old decisions that have been overruled by new. To many persons it seems a significant fact that the court has not since 1937 declared unconstitutional a single act of Congress. More important it appears to me are the battlefields from which the court has retreated. It no longer contends that Congress may regulate only commerce and not industry, agriculture, and labor. Quite the contrary is true. Without considering its war powers, the National Government is today in position to control all that is important in the whole economic life of the nation. In addition it may now tax the salaries and wages of state and local employees, may provide for the adjustment of local government debts, and may cooperate with state and local authorities in extensive programs of social legislation. These are but the most important of the national powers recently sustained. As the court says, the National Government is still one of delegated powers, but the delegations are so broadly construed that in effect Congress is now very much like the British Parliament in the extent of its legislative authority.

To speak of the recent reversal of the court's position as a retreat is in a sense to do injustice to its members. It would be more nearly correct to say that the new court since 1937 has had the statesmanship and the broad intelligence to recognize the facts of nationalism to which the old court had closed its eyes. It sees that many of the economic and social issues that confront the whole people cannot be dealt with successfully without national action. Of necessity this means also that the court accepts the need for collective or governmental action in many cases where that need was once denied. It is even willing to go far beyond the old court in upholding the actions of administrative bodies set up by Congress, because its members realize that a government engaged in many activities cannot do everything through the single channel of Congress.

INTEREST OF STATE AND NATION IDENTICAL

The decisions of this court also reveal a new and constructive approach to the question of state and national relations. It rejects the theory of a necessary antagonism or conflict of interests between the States and the National Government. Peering through the fog of words thrown up by the endless and futile debate over states' rights *versus* centralization, it sees that the real interests of the nation and the States are common interests and that they call for cooperation, not conflict. Along with students and practitioners in the field of public administration, they visualize a new type of functional federalism, a relationship between the nation and the States in which the real issue is how best to perform the necessary public services. The old federalism that was legalism is dead. The old assumption that national and state governments are necessarily antagonistic and in perpetual conflict is dead. The old theory of two mutually exclusive spheres of action, one reserved for the States, the other delegated to the national government ("and never the twain shall meet") is also dead. Yes, and the old judicial theory of laissez-faire, that government should be merely negative and inactive, is dead.

The former constitutional barriers to cooperation between the national and state governments exist now only as memories. Both national and state governments have been freed to carry on jointly or separately, as they choose, their essential public functions. Acts of Congress are not struck down, if within the present broad range of express or implied powers, merely because they might conceivably impinge upon some state interest. Likewise the acts of state legislatures are in general not declared invalid merely because they occupy an area that might be, but has not been, covered by some act of Congress. The effort is usually made to sustain both state and national legislation.

This new approach to federalism that is coming to dominate our thinking does not eliminate all difficulties from our system of government. What it does is to change our focus, our point of view, and from this new vantage point we see new questions arising. If federalism is no longer legalism, as I believe to be the case, what about the future role of the Supreme Court? What importance will it have as compared with legislative and administrative authorities? Having in large measure renounced all pretensions to the right to overrule the economic legislation of Congress, can it continue to be, what once it seemed, a sort of continuous constitutional convention?

What about Congress and the state legislatures? Are they so constituted, so organized, and so implemented with procedures and internal restraints as to enable them to perform wisely the enlarged responsibilities that fall upon them in an era of active government and large scale administration? If they are not, must there be a still further shift toward executive leadership in both national and state affairs? Up to now it has been found easier for the President and Governors and administrative officers to cooperate than for Congress and the state legislatures.

FUTURE OF STATES

And finally, what is to be the real future of the States? An increasing dominance of the National Government in matters of policy cannot be seriously questioned. Furthermore, as to its major functions the National Government is free, if it so desires, to ignore the States and to set up its own administration, complete from top to bottom. Its regulations can be made to override those of the States. By its control in the field of taxation and to satisfy its own tremendous needs it might force the States into progressive diminution of their own revenues and a reduction of their activities. That way lies a rapid strangulation or at best a slow atrophy of the States.

It has been suggested that the National Government should lay down general policies and standards in each major field of service, that the state governments should set up the needed administrative organizations, and that the counties or other local governments should perform the necessary services. In times of great emergency like the present war the cooperation of the States in such an unequal partnership can be expected, but hardly so in times of peace and prosperity. State administrations that are not in sympathy with the National Government will cause considerable difficulty; and it is doubtful whether United States Senators will favor administrative methods that give their potential or actual rivals, the state Governors, the power of patronage over national programs in their States.

In short it is one of the tasks of political scientists and statesmen for the next generation to work out a constructive and autonomous role for the States in the work of the nation. The right formula has not yet been discovered. The value to the whole nation of preserving the States can hardly be questioned and need not be elaborated. To keep them alive and strong they must be kept active in the performance of functions over which they have their own control. They should not be allowed to die of sheer inactivity, or to become mere administrative districts of the National Government. The problem is not simply one of maximum dollars and cents efficiency in performing particular services; that might be attained by complete centralization of functions in Washington. The question is: how, without impairing the power of the National Government to achieve all national purposes promptly and effectively, can the essential public services be rendered on a national scale, without undue waste, and in such a way as to preserve the advantages of state and local government?

To prove their value in the future in the face of a powerful national sentiment that has grown impatient with them, the States must show beyond a doubt that they can be effective and economical in their operations. More than this they must also demonstrate that they can be quickly responsive to local needs and sensitive to regional as well as national opinion. In short they must in the face of great odds win back again some of that great public favor that they once had, and recreate in their peoples that sense of regional loyality that the States once represented. This will not be achieved by heated oratory about states' rights, or by legalistic attempts to obstruct the nation's actions. It is too late for that. What is needed is a deliberate reappraisal and demonstration of the role of the States in the national social order that now exists, and an attempt to re-educate the people in the values of self-government in state and local communities.

As de Tocqueville once said: "A democratic people tends toward centralization, as it were by instinct. It arrives at provincial institutions only by reflection."

19. *The States Are in the Middle* *

THROUGHOUT OUR HISTORY there has been much controversy over the constitutional status, rights, and functions of the states. Recently, there has been a considerable expression of concern over the emergence of the national government as the dominant power in our system and the possible adverse effect upon the autonomy of the states. However, there are other opinions which hold that trends at the national level do not, or need not, pose any serious threat to the states. In this article Professor Gaus presents an appraisal at mid-century of our states in the federal system.

* John M. Gaus. Reprinted from *State Government*, XXIII (June, 1950), pp. 138-142. Published by The Council of State Governments, Chicago, Illinois.

AS ONE attempts to make some estimate of the total experiences of the states in the last fifty years, he is apt to challenge some of the conventional ideas about them. One emerges with the impression that the debate over "states' rights" and "centralization" is either a sham battle or a diversion of energy and feeling from significant tasks. One wonders whether we are not moving into a form of government in which the states should be viewed less than in the past as the centers of experiment and origination. Both of these conclusions derive from the changed nature of our federal system. Within the past fifty years it has become not merely a combination of two jurisdictions, national and state, but a complicated mingling of at least three, probably four, and possibly five, levels. The additional three are the local governments, the emerging regional offices and units of jurisdiction and interstate associations between the state and national levels, and the infant international organizations. These changes in structure and procedure are responses to the more fundamental changes in the "raw materials of politics."

Government may usefully be viewed as the response made by people, in the form of public housekeeping arrangements, to the physical and social environment in which they live. If the physical and social environments change, presumably some adaptation to the change should be reflected in government. To understand the present position of the states and their probable tasks for the next generation, and to appraise their adequacy in organization and procedure to perform the tasks, we must note what the average person finds too little time to examine—the fundamental changes that have been taking place among the American people in relation to their environment.

First of all, note the redistributing of our people by age and place. A much larger proportion of our total population than formerly are the more elderly people. This change has taken place at a time when the older family and neighborhood unit has been altered, so that we have adopted governmental policies adapted particularly to elderly people—and we shall have further pressures for more varied programs that reflect their needs, particularly, as in housing.

Probably redistribution by place is more dramatic and raises more difficult problems of governmental change. The proportion of our people who do not live on farms and who do live in cities has increased; and a great increase has come in the proportion who have spilled over into the suburban areas and the "rurban" fringe. Some of the more obvious effects of this must be familiar to readers of these lines who have driven out through a major metropolitan traffic artery on a Sunday afternoon: the great sprawling highways dotted with new, dispersed shopping centers; the new, single story, straight production line type of factory, sometimes standing adjacent to a cornfield; the sense of waste and frustration that one has from recognizing the failure to fit the pieces of this metropolitan sprawl into their organic, needed pattern. The very beauty of certain of the physical structures, such as some of the bridges that man has created, is an ironic underlining of the failure in design of this metropolitan sprawl, also made by man; underlying and concealed in the new network of streets and real estate developments are the governmental jurisdiction boundary lines that have not yet become adapted to metropolitan needs and resources.

Both these changes, in age and place distribution, are reflected in tremendous and continuing migration. We shall be able to judge this better when the current census is completed and interpreted. An item in the *News Letter* of the American Society of Planning Officials of July, 1948, summarizes the tentative findings of the Census Bureau that seventy million of our people moved to new homes between 1940 and 1947, and, of these, twelve million moved from one state to another. There is a competition of area and region and a flexibility of choice that must have very considerable influence on the attitude of a citizen toward his neighborhood and the extent to which he can understand and concern himself with what should be his responsibilities as a citizen.

Paralleling these alterations in the distribution of our population, and both a cause and a result of them, are the changes in our natural resources and our use of them. Within these fifty years we have seen the rise of various conservation movements as our industrial needs have intensified the use of timber, coal, oil, water, and other physical resources. Exhaustion in some areas and opening of new, low cost supplies in others have heightened and intensified the mobility of population. The emphasis on multiple programs in watershed development is a significant product of this physical change and, like the rise of the metropolitan area, makes meaningless most of the phrases about the role of the states which originated in the days of the slavery controversy.

But perhaps most comprehensive of all has been the change in the task of the American people within these fifty years from that of colonizing a substantial portion of a continent—of making "the continent habitable for civilized people," as Henry Adams saw the challenge in 1868—to the greater range and variety of aims, now perceived because we recognize, a little more than before, the richness of human capacity, need, and personality. A hundred years ago and well down into the present century, our minds and thoughts faced west. Now the continent has been settled, and we have spilled out into the Caribbean and the Pacific. We are concerned both by the diversity of tasks and the cultural variety within our borders and the sometimes overwhelming challenge of adjustment to our relations throughout the world. Habits and attitudes fostered by the frontier and colonization period, the extent of whose meaning and influence is in dispute among our scholars, are constantly plowed up by the readjustments forced upon us by this changed situation. Here, again, the influence upon our thinking about states is as complex as the changes in the distribution of our people and in the use of our natural resources.

THE STATES AND THE NEW FEDERALISM

It is out of these fifty years of change, dramatized by two world wars and an extended major depression, that the new federal system has emerged. There are few functions of government that can be said to be the exclusive responsibility of any one level. Our interdependent communications and economy have led us to a system of employing several levels in policy and administration for any one substantive function. In fact, this joint participation goes back through the land-grant system to beginnings earlier than our United States Constitution. It is a principle whose application at the moment is being subjected to reappraisal and debate. But the present fact that will remain an essential part of the government of this country for a long time is the sharing of all major tasks of public housekeeping by the national, the state, and the local governments, including the newer units of a regional type between the national and state governments and between the state and local governments. The principle is well illustrated in the Water Pollution Control Act of 1949.

One does not encounter the recognition, as frequently as I believe should be the case, of the position of the states as in the middle of our system. This is a point which, interestingly enough, was made as early as 1834 by Alexis DeTocqueville when he attempted to describe our federal system to the European reader. To him the system was characterized by the importance, first, of the local governments, in which people learned at first hand of the utility of self-government. To him the states summarized this first-hand local experience, served in a sense as the agents of the local communities, and then, in turn, transmitted experience and authority as might seem wise and necessary to the national government.

The characteristic legislation of the last fifty years has reflected somewhat different tendencies but moves toward a somewhat similar result. The more characteristic movements of this half-century, or at least the more obvious ones, center around special interests or vocations or commodities. Their participants press for programs, and only as a kind of afterthought do they take account of the complexities of the governmental structure and the problems of administration. This tendency is heightened and intensified by the conditions supplied by international relations and our interdependent economy. But, contrary to general belief, even national legislation continues to allocate to the states and to the local governments a major share in the actual realization of the program.

Hence the states are quite literally in the middle of our system, as never before in any like degree. Upon them falls the responsibility for adjusting national policies and resources and interest group programs to detailed application to the citizen in the spot where he resides and works. It may appear that the old function of the states as originators and experimenters has been lost, and that the new practices and ideas come chiefly from national and interest group sources. I am not sure that a detailed analysis of the past fifty years would bear this out. But, certainly, few states have displayed the initiative in recent decades which the theory of their role as originators would call for. Perhaps, however, this is beside the point. Perhaps the major task and opportunity which confronts the states today is that of assimilation and balance and guidance in the middle position. Perhaps the states have their biggest task in widening the base of public understanding and recruiting citizen participation in public policy—policy that must inevitably reflect the international and national setting but also, to be effective and meaningful, must reflect the outlook and problems of citizens where they live and work.

STRUCTURE AND PROCEDURE

How much has this shift of position been mirrored in the structure and procedure of our states in the last fifty years? I think it may be said that the characteristic developments, however inadequately carried into realization, do indicate that the new task can be tackled in the decades ahead. There are gaps to be noted and challenges still to be met. Yet the most typical of the developments do point to meeting this job of policy and administration. They include the short ballot and executive budget movements; establishment of legislative reference, bill drafting, and legislative council institutions; and some advances in personnel administration. The short ballot and executive budget proposals both were aimed at improving policy making. The emphasis current at the time was on the objectives of "economy and efficiency." But it is clear from the statements of such pioneers in the field as Root, Stimson, Lowden, Alfred E. Smith, and various others that the needs both of party and legislative program-making—in order to offer the citizen some reasonably clear-cut alternatives of policy and in order to allocate resources wisely among the functional programs and departments—called for a clearer line of responsibility leading to the governor.

On the whole, the executive budget movement has been much the most successful of these trends. It could build with greater confidence on legislative support because of the tendency of ability and leadership in the legislative branch to be located in the appropriation and taxation committee. It reflected the most obvious needs for a better preparation of estimates, a more careful allocation of limited resources among the programs, and the necessity for continuous oversight and control in spending. There has been, therefore, a great change since the picture presented early in the century by Eugene E. Agger in his account of *The Budget in American Commonwealths.*

Forty years ago almost no political jurisdiction in this country had a rational system or an administrative unit that could perform the essential functions now generally taken for granted as required for budget administration. Here, indeed, some of the states, like some of the cities, were well in advance of the national government. But the movement should not stand still. "Know thyself" is good philosophy for a state as well as an individual; and the conception of the budget as a financial expression of the total work plan of the state, including long-time capital programs and commitments, is rarely realized. The complexities of grants-in-aid to and from the states (often via semi-autonomous agencies) make total and understandable reporting difficult. Nor do our budgets carry a clear picture of the relation of particular operations to the total resources and needs of the people of the state, and measure the progress of work programs toward the achievement of stated goals, whereby the costs of government may be made meaningful in the light of policy. The budget staff and procedure offer us perhaps the most important tool of policy formulation as well as general management, and that importance is all the greater because the conditions of the governorship limit the possibility for continuous activity in administration by the holders of that position.

It must be recognized that the short ballot movement has had limited success and application in that it has been found all but impossible for the average governor to combine effectively the tasks both of political and party leadership and of managerial direction. Recent intensive studies have brought out clearly the fact that most governors must expend their energies on political activity including legislative policy. In many of our states special conditions have been created by the rise of the great metropolitan regions. The fact that states have not redistricted their legislatures in accordance with population changes leaves the governorship as almost the sole point on which the political interests of metropolitan populations can center for expression. In many states—probably in almost all—the party systems are inadequate as instruments for reflecting the needs of our citizens for carefully thought-out, alternative programs of public housekeeping. State "party" activity is a complex of personal, factional, sectional, and interest group associations. Few citizen organizations are focused upon comprehensive analysis of needs and resources of the particular state. This situation places a heavy burden upon the governor's office, if he has a sincere sense of responsibility for formulating, presenting, and urging programs that reflect the needs of the state. Let it be noted again that these programs will be affected by national programs on the one hand and those of the local governments on the other, each program tied to a jealous agency. The reconciliation of these varied parts into a balanced state program is a complex task.

At this point the improvement of state legislative organization and procedure and of administrative organization and personnel are the decisive factors. The role of a legislative council, closely affiliated with the legislative reference and drafting services, is most important. Rival interest group programs, the various programs of national departments, the emerging needs of rural, urban, and metropolitan communities, must be brought into some balance. They must be fitted into some scheme of priorities and standards of economy and administration. The average legislative session hardly permits this task. Moreover, it is a task that runs throughout the year and should be tied to a continuous acquaintance with the administrative operations. The lack of time and energy available to the governor for managerial control was noted above. Balancing the legislative council, therefore, is the need for a strong general staff, covering departmental operations and the problems of integrating departmental policies both in substantive and financial terms. Here progress has been noteworthy in several of our states, but a great area of experiment lies ahead. The state planning boards of the 1930's, on the whole, have not been successfully assimilated into these structures and procedures. Departments of government in our states remain largely autonomous, and with their ties more closely fixed with national and local departments in their substantive fields. Often the state has been far from a comprehensive instrument of policy and administration.

The commission movement of the early part of the present half-century warrants reexamination in the light of this situation. Perhaps those of us who have been concerned about the relative autonomy among the departments have been blind to some inherent necessity for relating particular governmental agencies most closely to the interests they most directly affect. I believe that we must reexamine this question as fairly as we humanly can; I cannot accept the view, however, that we can afford to leave all of the burden of adjusting the many departmental programs to the overburdened appropriation committees and legislature.

PERSONNEL

Although there have been advances in state personnel policy during the half-century, it is in this field that some fresh experimentation needs to be done. As one who has taught in several of our state universities, I can speak from first-hand experience of the waste of first-rate human quality which now results from the failure of the state governments to offer a fair, competitive channel between the educational institutions of the state and the departments of government.

Some first-rate young men and women going through those institutions, under a substantial subsidy from the people of the state, should be able to pay back in their ability and their enthusiasm some of the wealth which the people have invested in their education. This is all the more important when one sees the need in state administration for a regular flow of junior recruits, not to safe and secure positions, but to a pre-entry kind of apprenticeship. By means of such a flow department heads could get a line on some of these young people, who have already completed a selective process in the educational system and who, as a result of the apprenticeship, would be able to compete for junior administrative and professional positions. Even if a large proportion of apprentices were to go on into private professional and business careers, the state still would be the gainer from having such people in possession of a more realistic view of the state's government and problems. Generally speaking, our departments are undermanned in the junior positions; most important of all in many respects is the fact that some of the valuable civic spirit which these young people possess is lost to the state by failure to offer them a practical and concrete point of competitive recruitment as they approach the ends of their academic careers. The states may well learn and improve on the lesson which is available in the experience of the United States Civil Service Commission with this type of recruitment.

My final comment on the personnel question is that the development of such apprentice training and other related in-service programs is most urgent if we are to have the kind of people who can approach understandingly the problem of better coordination between departments of the state government and between the state, the national, and the local governments. The most efficient handling of these problems of inter-governmental relationship can be achieved only by conscious and deliberate effort to acquaint public officials early in their careers with the interdependence of the various functions and organizations of government.

CONCLUSION

As we look forward into the next fifty years of state government, we can see the continuance of the long-established functions of the states in the providing of specialists' services in physical and mental health, education, social insurance, highways, natural resources, and the maintenance of minimum standards of various employments and occupations. We will see an extension of tendencies of the last forty years whereby the states offer to the local governments a kind of "holding company" facility and service in research, information, the provision of specially trained personnel, and the protection of some minimum standards in various fields—as is now done in public health, agriculture, and forestry. And I believe the states will be called upon to perform more boldly, with greater conscious effort at balanced and comprehensive policy, the service of middle-man and interpreter between the national and local governments, and among the various powerful, functional, and interest divisions of government, from national to local, as well as the groups that cluster around each division.

To perform these tasks successfully the states will need to draw upon their already accumulated experience in the development of the budget procedure and administrative organization. They will need to push ahead with better policy formulation through legislative councils and staffs and various administrative policy and staff organizations. This will best be accomplished through quiet, steady, day-to-day work rather than through the more dramatic, over-all reorganization projects, although the latter probably will continue to have their place from time to time. I am inclined to list as the most urgent need (I believe there already are some experiences in New York and North Carolina—and perhaps other states—on which we can draw) a provision for the regular review and analysis of the relation between dynamic population shifts and the areas and functions of government. Such a program has been well outlined and persuasively argued by James W. Fesler in his *Area and Administration*. The problems of our states are so difficult and their opportunities so great that we need to have a just basis of political representation, which we do not now possess, so that we may tap every type of resource of energy and understanding among our people. If the basis of representation and functions and units of local government are out of adjustment with the facts of location of our people, our whole structure and procedure of government suffers.

This appraisal of our states clashes with the widely prevailing view that they have declined in importance and that all important political functions and decisions have passed to the national government. I believe the fact is that the national government itself has become dependent as never before, even in the successful prosecution of its national and international duties, upon the wisdom of state and local governments. Similarly, the need for adequate public housekeeping in our local governments, with the dramatic increase in the proportion of the urban population and the importance of the functions of rural government, has made the state governments, as their creators, of more vital concern to them. It remains for us to adapt the states better to their great responsibility and opportunity.

20. *McCulloch v. Maryland*

SUPREME COURT OF THE UNITED STATES, 1819 (ERROR) 4 WHEATON 316

This case illustrates Chief Justice Marshall's molding of our constitutional system in the direction of increased Federal power and independence at the expense of the states. The questions before the Court were: (1) Can the Federal government, in the absence of delegated power, charter a bank; and (2), if so, can the state of Maryland tax such a Federal agency? In answering the first question in the affirmative, Marshall developed the doctrine of Federal implied power based on the "necessary and proper clause" as a supplement to the delegated power formally conferred by the Constitution. In answering the second question in the negative, Marshall laid the foundation of the principle of intergovernmental immunity from taxation, a doctrine subject to subsequent modification by the Court. In both holdings the independent authority of the central government was affirmed as against the states, thus serving to define the respective spheres of Federal and state authority during the formative period of our Federal system.

Opinion of the Court.

MR. CHIEF JUSTICE MARSHALL delivered the opinion of the Court:

In the case now to be determined, the defendant, a sovereign state, denies the obligation of a law enacted by the legislature of the Union, and the plaintiff, on his part, contests the validity of an act which has been passed by the legislature of that State. The constitution of our country, in its most interesting and vital parts, is to be considered; the conflicting powers of the government of the Union and of its members, as marked in that constitution, are to be discussed; and an opinion given which may essentially influence the great operations of the government. No tribunal can approach such a question without a deep sense of its importance, and of the awful responsibility involved in its decision. But it must be decided peacefully, or remain a source of hostile legislation, perhaps of hostility of a still more serious nature; and if it is to be so decided, by this tribunal alone can the decision be made. On the Supreme Court of the United States has the constitution of our country devolved this important duty.

The first question made in the cause is, has Congress power to incorporate a bank? . . .

In discussing this question, the counsel for the State of Maryland have deemed it of some importance, in the construction of the constitution, to consider that instrument not as emanating from the people, but as the act of sovereign and independent States. The powers of the general government, it has been said, are delegated by the States, who alone are truly sovereign; and must be exercised in subordination to the States, who alone possess supreme dominion.

It would be difficult to sustain this proposition. The convention which framed the constitution was indeed elected by the state legislatures. But the instrument, when it came from their hands, was a mere proposal, without obligation, or pretensions to it. It was reported to the then existing congress of the United States, with a request that it might "be submitted to a convention of delegates, chosen in each State by the people thereof, under the recommendation of its legislature, for their assent and ratification." This mode of proceeding was adopted; and by the convention, by congress, and by the State legislatures, the instrument was submitted to the people. They acted upon it in the only manner in which they can act safely, effectively, and wisely, on such a subject, by assembling in convention. It is true, they assembled in their several States; and where else should they have assembled? No political dreamer was ever wild enough to think of breaking down the lines which separate the States, and of compounding the American people into one common mass. Of consequence, when they act, they act in their States. But the measures they adopt do not, on that account, cease to be the measures of the people themselves, or become the measures of the State governments.

From these conventions the constitution derives its whole authority. The government proceeds directly from the people; is "ordained and established" in the name of the people; and is declared to be ordained, "in order to form a more perfect union, establish justice, insure domestic tranquillity, and secure the blessings of liberty to themselves and to their posterity." The assent of the States, in their sovereign capacity, is implied in calling a convention, and thus submitting that instrument to the people. But the people were at perfect liberty to accept or reject it; and their act was final. It required not the affirmance, and could not be negatived, by the State governments. The constitution, when thus adopted, was of complete obligation, and bound the State sovereignties.

. . . The government of the Union, then (whatever may be the influence of this fact on the case), is, emphatically, and truly, a government of the people. In form and in substance it emanates from them. Its powers are granted by them, and are to be exercised directly on them, and for their benefit.

This government is acknowledged by all to be one of enumerated powers. The principle, that it can exercise only the powers granted to it, would seem too apparent to have required to be enforced by all those arguments which its enlightened friends, while it was depending before the people, found it necessary to urge. That principle is now universally admitted. But the question respecting the extent of the powers actually granted, is perpetually arising, and will probably continue to arise, as long as our system shall exist. . . .

If any one proposition could command the universal assent of mankind, we might expect it would be this: that the government of the Union, though limited in its powers, is supreme within its sphere of action. This would seem to result necessarily from its nature. It is the government of all; its powers are delegated by all; it represents all, and acts for all. Though any one State may be willing to control its operations, no State is willing to allow others to control them. The nation, on those subjects on which it can act, must necessarily bind its component parts. But this question is not left to mere reason: the people have, in express terms, decided it by saying, "this constitution, and the laws of the United States, which shall be made in pursuance thereof," "shall be the supreme law of the land," and by requiring that the members of the State legislatures, and the officers of the executive and judicial departments of the States shall take the oath of fidelity to it.

The government of the United States, then, though limited in its powers, is supreme; and its laws, when made in pursuance of the constitution, form the supreme law of the land, "anything in the constitution or laws of any State to the contrary notwithstanding."

Among the enumerated powers, we do not find that of establishing a bank or creating a corporation. But there is no phrase in the instrument which, like the articles of confederation, excludes incidental or implied powers; and which requires that everything granted shall be expressly and minutely described. Even the 10th amendment, which was framed for the purpose of quieting the excessive jealousies which had been excited, omits the word "expressly," and declares only that the powers "not delegated to the United States, nor prohibited to the States, are reserved to the States or to the people"; thus leaving the question whether the particular power which may become the subject of contest has been delegated to the one government, or prohibited to the other, to depend on a fair construction of the whole instrument. The men who drew and adopted this amendment had experienced the embarrassments resulting from the insertion of this word in the articles of confederation, and probably omitted it to avoid those embarrassments. A constitution, to contain an accurate detail of all the subdivisions of which its great powers will admit, and of all the means by which they may be carried into execution, would partake of the prolixity of a legal code, and could scarcely be embraced by the human mind. It would probably never be understood by the public. Its nature, therefore, requires, that only its great outlines should be marked, its important objects designated, and the minor ingredients which compose those objects be deduced from the nature of the objects themselves. . . .

Although, among the enumerated powers of government, we do not find the word "bank" or "incorporation," we find the great powers to lay and collect taxes; to borrow money; to regulate commerce; to declare and conduct a war; and to raise and support armies and navies. The sword and the purse, all the external relations, and no inconsiderable portion of the industry of the nation, are entrusted to its government. It can never be pretended that these vast powers draw after them others of inferior importance, merely because they are inferior. Such an idea can never be advanced. But it may with great reason be contended, that a government, entrusted with such ample powers, on the due execution of which the happiness and prosperity of the nation so vitally depends, must also be entrusted with ample means for their execution. . . .

But the constitution of the United States has not left the right of congress to employ the necessary means for the execution of the powers conferred on the government to general reasoning. To its enumeration of powers is added that of making "all laws which shall be necessary and proper, for carrying into execution the foregoing powers, and all other powers vested by this constitution, in the government of the United States, or in any department thereof." . . .

But the argument on which most reliance is placed, is drawn from the peculiar language of this clause. Congress is not empowered by it to make all laws, which may have relation to the powers conferred on the government, but such only as may be "necessary and proper" for carrying them into execution. The word "necessary" is considered as controlling the whole sentence, and as limiting the right to pass laws for the execution of the granted powers, to such as are indispensable, and without which the power would be nugatory. That it excludes the choice of means, and leaves to congress, in each case, that only which is most direct and simple.

Is it true that this is the sense in which the word "necessary" is always used? Does it always import an absolute physical necessity, so strong that one thing, to which another may be termed necessary, cannot exist without that other? We think it does not. If reference be had to its use, in the common affairs of the world, or in approved authors, we find that it frequently imports no more than that one thing is convenient, or useful, or essential to another. To employ the means necessary to an end, is generally understood as employing any means calculated to produce the end, and not as being confined to those single means, without which the end would be entirely unattainable. . . .

We admit, as all must admit, that the powers of the government are limited, and that its limits are not to be transcended. But we think the sound construction of the constitution must allow to the national legislature that discretion, with respect to the means by which the powers it confers are to be carried into execution, which will enable that body to perform the high duties assigned to it, in the manner most beneficial to the people. Let the end be legitimate, let it be within the scope of the constitution, and all means which are appropriate, which are plainly adapted to that end, which are not prohibited, but consist with the letter and spirit of the constitution, are constitutional. . . .

After the most deliberate consideration, it is the unanimous and decided opinion of this court that the act to incorporate the Bank of the United States is a law made in pursuance of the constitution, and is a part of the supreme law of the land. The branches, proceeding from the same stock, and being conducive to the complete accomplishment of the object, are equally constitutional. . . .

It being the opinion of the court that the act incorporating the bank is constitutional, and that the power of establishing a branch in the State of Maryland might be properly exercised by the bank itself, we proceed to inquire:—

Whether the State of Maryland may, without violating the constitution, tax that branch? . . .

That the power to tax involves the power to destroy; that the power to destroy may defeat and render useless the power to create; that there is a plain repugnance, in conferring on one government a power to control the constitutional measures of another, which other, with respect to those very measures, is declared to be supreme over that which exerts the control, are propositions not to be denied. . . .

If the States may tax one Instrument, employed by the government in the execution of its powers, they may tax any and every other Instrument. They may tax the mail; they may tax the mint; they may tax patent-rights; they may tax the papers of the custom-house; they may tax judicial process; they may tax all the means employed by the government, to an excess which would defeat all the ends of government. This was not intended by the American people. They did not design to make their government dependent on the States. . . .

If the controlling power of the States be established; if their supremacy as to taxation be acknowledged; what is to restrain their exercising this control in any shape they may please to give it? Their sovereignty is not confined to taxation. That is not the only mode in which it might be displayed. The question is, in truth, a question of supremacy; and if the right of the States to tax the means employed by the general government be conceded, the declaration that the constitution, and the laws made in pursuance thereof, shall be the supreme law of the land, is empty and unmeaning declamation. . . .

The court has bestowed on this subject its most deliberate consideration. The result is a conviction that the States have no power, by taxation or otherwise, to retard, impede, burden, or in any manner control the operations of the constitutional laws enacted by congress to carry into execution the powers vested in the general government. This is, we think, the unavoidable consequence of that supremacy which the constitution has declared.

We are unanimously of opinion that the law passed by the legislature of Maryland, imposing a tax on the Bank of the United States, is unconstitutional and void. . . .

Reversed

21. *United States v. Curtiss-Wright Export Corp. et al.*

SUPREME COURT OF THE UNITED STATES,
1936 (APPEAL) 299 U.S. 304

THE IMPORTANCE of this case lies in the fact that the decision constituted an expansion of the constitutional doctrine as to the nature and extent of the foreign affairs power of the President. By distinguishing Federal power over internal affairs from Federal power over external relations, the Court reached the conclusion that the President's authority in foreign relations is not dependent on any affirmative grant of power in the Constitution but arises from the sovereign power of the United States as a member of the international community. This leads to the development of the doctrine of "inherent" power in the Federal government, at least as far as foreign relations are concerned. The case is likewise significant in its discussion of the nature of the sovereignty possessed by the states in the Federal union and the legitimacy of delegation of legislative authority to the President in the conduct of foreign affairs. The implications of the case for American government are further developed in *U.S.* v. *Belmont* (301 U.S. 324), which deals with the validity of Executive agreements, and *U.S.* v. *California* (332 U.S. 19), which relates to the question of control over "tidelands."

Opinion of the Court.

MR. JUSTICE SUTHERLAND delivered the opinion of the Court:

On January 27, 1936, an indictment was returned in the court below, the first count of which charges that appellees, beginning with 29th day of May, 1934, conspired to sell in the United States certain arms of war, namely fifteen machine guns, to Bolivia, a country then engaged in armed conflict in the Chaco, in violation of the Joint Resolution of Congress approved May 28, 1934, and the provisions of a proclamation issued on the same day by the President of the United States pursuant to authority conferred by § 1 of the resolution. In pursuance of the conspiracy, the commission of certain overt acts was alleged, details of which need not be stated. . . .

Appellees severally demurred to the first count of the indictment. . . .

It is contended that by the Joint Resolution, the going into effect and continued operation of the resolution was conditioned (a) upon the President's judgment as to its beneficial effect upon the reestablishment of peace between the countries engaged in armed conflict in the Chaco; (b) upon the making of a proclamation, which was left to his unfettered discretion, thus constituting an attempted substitution of the President's will for that of Congress; (c) upon the making of a proclamation putting an end to the operation of the resolution, which again was left to the President's unfettered discretion; and (d) further, that the extent of its operation in particular cases was subject to limitation and exception by the President, controlled by no standard. In each of these particulars, appellees urge that Congress abdicated its essential functions and delegated them to the Executive.

Whether, if the Joint Resolution had related solely to internal affairs it would be open to the challenge that it constituted an unlawful delegation of legislative power to the Executive, we find it unnecessary to determine. The whole aim of the resolution is to affect a situation entirely external to the United States, and falling within the category of foreign affairs. The determination which we are called to make, therefore, is whether the Joint Resolution, as applied to that situation, is vulnerable to attack under the rule that forbids a delegation of the law-making power. In other words, assuming (but not deciding) that the challenged delegation, if it were confined to internal affairs, would be invalid, may it nevertheless be sustained on the ground that its exclusive aim is to afford a remedy for a hurtful condition within foreign territory?

It will contribute to the elucidation of the question if we first consider the differences between the powers of the federal government in respect of foreign or external affairs and those in respect of domestic or internal affairs. That there are differences between them, and that these differences are fundamental, may not be doubted.

The two classes of powers are different, both in respect of their origin and their nature. The broad statement that the federal government can exercise no powers except those specifically enumerated in the Constitution, and such implied powers as are necessary and proper to carry into effect the enumerated powers, is categorically true only in respect of our internal affairs. In that field, the primary purpose of the Constitution was to carve from the general mass of legislative powers *then possessed by the states* such portions as it was thought desirable to vest in the federal government, leaving those not included in the enumeration still in the states. *Carter* v. *Carter Coal Co.*, 298 U.S. 238, 294. That this doctrine applies only to powers which the states had, is self evident. And since the states severally never possessed international powers, such powers could not have been carved from the mass of state powers but obviously were transmitted to the

United States from some other source. During the colonial period, those powers were possessed exclusively by and were entirely under the control of the Crown. By the Declaration of Independence, "the Representatives of the United States of America" declared the United [not the several] Colonies to be free and independent states, and as such to have "full Power to levy War, conclude Peace, contract Alliances, establish Commerce and to do all other Acts and Things which Independent States may of right do."

As a result of the separation from Great Britain by the colonies acting as a unit, the powers of external sovereignty passed from the Crown not to the colonies severally, but to the colonies in their collective and corporate capacity as the United States of America. Even before the Declaration, the colonies were a unit in foreign affairs, acting through a common agency—namely the Continental Congress, composed of delegates from the thirteen colonies. That agency exercised the powers of war and peace, raised an army, created a navy, and finally adopted the Declaration of Independence. Rulers come and go; governments end and forms of government change; but sovereignty survives. A political society cannot endure without a supreme will somewhere. Sovereignty is never held in suspense. When, therefore, the external sovereignty of Great Britain in respect of the colonies ceased, it immediately passed to the Union. . . .

It results that the investment of the federal government with the powers of external sovereignty did not depend upon the affirmative grants of the Constitution. The powers to declare and wage war, to conclude peace, to make treaties, to maintain diplomatic relations with other sovereignties, if they had never been mentioned in the Constitution, would have vested in the federal government as necessary concomitants of nationality. Neither the Constitution nor the laws passed in pursuance of it have any force in foreign territory unless in respect of our own citizens (see *American Banana Co.* v. *United Fruit Co.*, 213 U.S. 347, 356); and operations of the nation in such territory must be governed by treaties, international understandings and compacts, and the principles of international law. As a member of the family of nations, the right and power of the United States in that field are equal to the right and power of the other members of the international family. Otherwise, the United States is not completely sovereign. The power to acquire territory by discovery and occupation (*Jones* v. *United States*, 137 U.S. 202, 212), the power to expel undesirable aliens (*Fong Yue Ting* v. *United States*, 149 U.S. 698, 705 *et seq.*), the power to make such international agreements as do not constitute treaties in the constitutional sense (*Altman & Co.* v. *United States*, 224 U.S. 583, 600-601; Crandall, Treaties, Their Making and Enforcement, 2d ed., p. 102 and note 1), none of which is expressly affirmed by the Constitution, nevertheless exist as inherently inseparable from the conception of nationality. This the court recognized, and in each of the cases cited found the warrant for its conclusions not in the provisions of the Constitution, but in the law of nations.

In *Burnet* v. *Brooks*, 288 U.S. 378, 396, we said, "As a nation with all the attributes of sovereignty, the United States is vested with all the powers of government necessary to maintain an effective control of international relations." *Cf. Carter* v. *Carter Coal Co., supra*, p. 295.

Not only, as we have shown, is the federal power over external affairs in origin and essential character different from that over internal affairs, but participation in the exercise of the power is significantly limited. In this vast external realm, with its important, complicated, delicate and manifold problems, the President alone has the power to speak or listen as a representative of the nation. He *makes* treaties with the advice and consent of the Senate; but he alone negotiates. Into the field of negotiation the Senate cannot intrude; and Congress itself is powerless to invade it. As Marshall said in his great argument of March 7, 1800, in the House of Representatives, "The President is the sole organ of the nation in its external relations, and its sole representative with foreign nations." . . .

It is important to bear in mind that we are here dealing not alone with an authority vested in the President by an exertion of legislative power, but with such an authority plus the very delicate, plenary and exclusive power of the President as the sole organ of the federal government in the field of international relations—a power which does not require as a basis for its exercise an act of Congress, but which, of course, like every other governmental power, must be exercised in subordination to the applicable provisions of the Constitution. It is quite apparent that if, in the maintenance of our international relations, embarrassment—perhaps serious embarrassment—is to be avoided and success for our aims achieved, congressional legislation which is to be made effective through negotiation and inquiry within the international field must often accord to the President a degree of discretion and freedom from statutory restriction which would not be admissible were domestic affairs alone involved. Moreover, he, not Congress, has the better opportunity of knowing the conditions which prevail in foreign countries, and especially is this true in time of war. He has his confidential sources of information. He has his agents in the form of diplomatic, consular and other officials. Secrecy in respect of information gathered by them may be highly necessary, and the premature disclosure of it productive of harmful results. . . .

In the light of the foregoing observations, it is evident that this court should not be in haste to apply a general rule which will have the effect of condemning legislation like that under review as constituting an unlawful delegation of legislative power. The principles which justify such legislation find overwhelming support in the unbroken legislative practice which has prevailed almost from the inception of the national government to the present day. . . .

The judgment of the court below must be reversed and the cause remanded for further proceedings in accordance with the foregoing opinion.

Reversed

(Mr. Justice McReynolds dissents; Mr. Justice Stone absent and not participating.)

22. *Ordinance of 1787 (July 13, 1787)* *

AN ORDINANCE FOR THE GOVERNMENT OF THE TERRITORY OF THE UNITED STATES NORTHWEST OF THE RIVER OHIO

THE NORTHWEST TERRITORY was ceded to the United States by the several states claiming western lands, as a result of the efforts to secure ratification of the Articles of Confederation. The Congress had the problem, therefore, of providing a government for the territory. Several plans were developed, among them one by Thomas Jefferson. This plan, somewhat altered, was adopted in 1784, but was never put into effect. In 1785 Congress adopted the Land Ordinance, which, until the passage of the Homestead Act of 1862, established the basis of the public land system of the United States. The Ordinance provided for the survey and sale of land in the territories, the reservation of one lot in every township for the maintenance of public schools, and the retention of a portion of the mineral rights by the government. While the Philadelphia Convention was in session, the Congress passed the Northwest Ordinance of 1787, which was based on Jefferson's Ordinance of 1784. The new Ordinance established a policy for the government of territory of the United States not yet incorporated as states and —significantly—expressly indicated that territorial status was tem-

* Reprinted from *Documents Illustrative of the Formation of the Union of the American States* (Washington, D.C., United States Government Printing Office, 1927), pp. 47-54.

porary and that statehood would follow when population warranted. This policy was continued by the government under the new Constitution for all contiguous territory acquired on the continent—an indication of the significance of the Ordinance.

SECTION 1. *Be it ordained by the United States in Congress assembled,* That the said Territory, for the purpose of temporary government, be one district, subject, however, to be divided into two districts, as future circumstances may, in the opinion of Congress, make it expedient.

SEC. 2. *Be it ordained by the authority aforesaid,* That the estates both of resident and non-resident proprietors in the said territory, dying intestate, shall descend to, and be distributed among, their children and the descendants of a deceased child in equal parts, the descendants of a deceased child or grandchild to take the share of their deceased parent in equal parts among them; and where there shall be no children or descendants, then in equal parts to the next of kin, in equal degree; and among collaterals, the children of a deceased brother or sister of the intestate shall have, in equal parts among them, their deceased parent's share; and there shall, in no case, be a distinction between kindred of the whole and half blood; saving in all cases to the widow of the intestate, her third part of the real estate for life, and one-third part of the personal estate; and this law relative to descents and dower, shall remain in full force until altered by the legislature of the district. And until the governor and judges shall adopt laws as hereinafter mentioned, estates in the said territory may be devised or bequeathed by wills in writing, signed and sealed by him or her in whom the estate may be, (being of full age,) and attested by three witnesses; and real estates may be conveyed by lease and release, or bargain and sale, signed, sealed, and delivered by the person, being of full age, in whom the estate may be, and attested by two witnesses, provided such wills be duly proved, and such conveyances be acknowledged, or the execution thereof duly proved, and be recorded within one year after proper magistrates, courts, and registers, shall be appointed for that purpose; and personal property may be transferred by delivery, saving, however, to the French and Canadian inhabitants, and other settlers of the Kaskaskies, Saint Vincents, and the neighboring villages, who have heretofore professed themselves citizens of Virginia, their laws and customs now in force among them, relative to the descent and conveyance of property.

SEC. 3. *Be it ordained by the authority aforesaid,* That there shall be appointed, from time to time, by Congress, a governor, whose commission shall continue in force for the term of three years, unless sooner revoked by Congress; he shall reside in the district, and have a freehold estate therein, in one thousand acres of land, while in the exercise of his office.

SEC. 4. There shall be appointed from time to time, by Congress, a secretary, whose commission shall continue in force for four years, unless sooner revoked; he shall reside in the district, and have a freehold estate therein, in five hundred acres of land, while in the exercise of his office. It shall be his duty to keep and preserve the acts and laws passed by the legislature, and the public records of the district, and the proceedings of the governor in his executive department, and transmit authentic copies of such acts and proceedings every six months to the Secretary of Congress. There shall also be appointed a court, to consist of three judges, any two of whom to form a court, who shall have a common-law jurisdiction and reside in the district, and have each therein a freehold estate, in five hundred acres of land, while in the exercise of their offices; and their commissions shall continue in force during good behavior.

SEC. 5. The governor and judges, or a majority of them, shall adopt and publish in the district such laws of the original States, criminal and civil, as may be necessary, and best suited to the circumstances of the district, and report them to Congress from time to time, which laws shall be in force in the district until the organization of the general assembly therein, unless disapproved of by Congress; but afterwards the legislature shall have authority to alter them as they shall think fit.

SEC. 6. The governor, for the time being, shall be commander-in-chief of the militia, appoint and commission all officers in the same below the rank of general officers; all general officers shall be appointed and commissioned by Congress.

SEC. 7. Previous to the organization of the general assembly the governor shall appoint such magistrates, and other civil officers, in each county or township, as he shall find necessary for the preservation of the peace and good order in the same. After the general assembly shall be organized the powers and duties of magistrates and other civil officers shall be regulated and defined by the said assembly; but all magistrates and other civil officers, not herein otherwise directed, shall, during the continuance of this temporary government, be appointed by the governor.

SEC. 8. For the prevention of crimes, and injuries, the laws to be adopted or made shall have force in all parts of the district, and for the execution of process, criminal and civil, the governor shall make proper divisions thereof; and he shall proceed, from time to time, as circumstances may require, to lay out the parts of the district in which the Indian titles shall have been extinguished, into counties and townships, subject, however, to such alterations as may thereafter be made by the legislature.

SEC. 9. So soon as there shall be five thousand free male inhabitants, of full age, in the district, upon giving proof thereof to the governor, they shall receive authority, with time and place, to elect representatives from their counties or townships, to represent them in the general assembly: *Provided,* That for every five hundred free male inhabitants there shall be one representative, and so on, progressively, with the number of free male inhabitants, shall the right of representation increase, until the number of representatives shall amount to twenty-five; after which the number and proportion of representatives shall be regulated by the legislature: *Provided,* That no person be eligible or qualified to act as a representative, unless he shall have been a citizen of one of the United States three years, and be a resident in the district, or unless he shall have resided in the district three years; and, in either case, shall likewise hold in his own right, in fee-simple, two hundred acres of land within the same: *Provided also,* That a freehold in fifty acres of land in the district, having been a citizen of one of the States, and being resident in the district, or the like freehold and two years' residence in the district, shall be necessary to qualify a man as an elector of a representative.

SEC. 10. The representatives thus elected shall serve for the term of two years; and in case of the death of a representative, or removal from office, the governor shall issue a writ to the county or township, for which he was a member, to elect another in his stead, to serve for the residue of the term.

SEC. 11. The general assembly, or legislature, shall consist of the governor, legislative council, and a house of representatives. The legislative council shall consist of five members, to continue in office five years, unless sooner removed by Congress; any three of whom to be a quorum; and the members of the council shall be nominated and appointed in the following manner, to wit: As soon as representatives shall be elected the governor shall appoint a time and place for them to meet together, and when met they shall nominate ten persons, resident in the district, and each possessed of a freehold in five hundred acres of land, and return their names to Congress, five of whom Congress shall appoint and commission to serve as aforesaid; and whenever a vacancy shall happen in the Council, by death or removal from office, the house of representatives shall nominate two persons, qualified as aforesaid, for each vacancy, and return their names to Congress, one of whom Congress shall appoint and commission for the residue of the term; and every five years, four months at least before the expiration of the time of service of the members of the council, the said house shall nominate ten persons, qualified as aforesaid, and return their names to Congress, five of whom Congress shall appoint and commission to serve as members of the council five years, unless sooner removed. And the governor, legislative council, and house of representatives shall have authority to make laws in all cases for the good government of the district, not repugnant to the principles and articles in this ordinance established and declared. And all bills, having passed by a majority in the house, and by a majority in the council, shall be referred to the governor for his assent; but no bill, or legislative act whatever, shall be of any force without his assent. The governor shall have power to convene, prorogue, and dissolve the general assembly when, in his opinion, it shall be expedient.

SEC. 12. The governor, judges, legislative council, secretary, and such other officers as Congress shall appoint in the district, shall take an oath or affirmation of fidelity, and of office; the governor before the President of Congress, and all other officers before the governor. As soon as a legislature shall be formed in the district, the council and house assembled, in one room, shall have authority, by joint ballot, to elect a delegate to Congress, who shall have a seat in Congress, with a right of debating, but not of voting, during this temporary government.

SEC. 13. And for extending the fundamental principles of civil and religious liberty, which form the basis whereon these republics, their laws and constitutions, are erected; to fix and establish those principles as the basis of all laws, constitutions, and governments, which forever hereafter shall be formed in the said territory; to provide, also, for the establishment of States, and permanent government therein, and for their admission to a share in the Federal councils on an equal footing with the original States, at as early periods as may be consistent with the general interest:

SEC. 14. It is hereby ordained and declared, by the authority aforesaid, that the following articles shall be considered as articles of compact, between the original States and the people and States in the said territory, and forever remain unalterable, unless by common consent, to wit:

ARTICLE I

No person, demeaning himself in a peaceable and orderly manner, shall ever be molested on account of his mode of worship, or religious sentiments, in the said territory.

ARTICLE II

The inhabitants of the said territory shall always be entitled to the benefits of the writs of *habeas corpus*, and of the trial by jury; of a proportionate representation of the people in the legislature, and of judicial proceedings according to the course of the common law. All persons shall be bailable, unless for capital offences, where the proof shall be evident, or the presumption great. All fines shall be moderate; and no cruel or unusual punishment shall be inflicted. No man shall be deprived of his liberty or property, but by the judgment of his peers, or the law of the land, and should the public exigencies make it necessary, for the common preservation, to take any person's property, or to demand his particular services, full compensation shall be made for the same. And, in the just preservation of rights and property, it is understood and declared, that no law ought ever to be made or have force in the said territory, that shall, in any manner whatever, interfere with or affect private contracts, or engagements, *bona fide*, and without fraud previously formed.

ARTICLE III

Religion, morality, and knowledge being necessary to good government and the happiness of mankind, schools and the means of education shall forever be encouraged. The utmost good faith shall always be observed towards the Indians; their lands and property shall never be taken from them without their consent; and in their property, rights, and liberty they never shall be invaded or disturbed unless in just and lawful wars authorized by Congress; but laws founded in justice and humanity shall, from time to time, be made, for preventing wrongs being done to them, and for preserving peace and friendship with them.

ARTICLE IV

The said territory, and the States which may be formed therein shall forever remain a part of this confederacy of the United States of America, subject to the articles of Confederation, and to such alterations therein as shall be constitutionally made; and to all the acts and ordinances of the United States in Congress assembled, conformable thereto. The inhabitants and settlers in the said territory shall be subject to pay a part of the Federal debts, contracted, or to be contracted, and a proportional part of the expenses of government to be apportioned on them by Congress, according to the same common rule and measure by which apportionments thereof shall be made on the other States; and the taxes for paying their proportion shall be laid and levied by the authority and direction of the legislatures of the district, or districts, or new States, as in the original States, within the time agreed upon by the United States in Congress assembled. The legislatures of those districts, or new States, shall never interfere with the primary disposal of the soil by the United States in Congress assembled, nor with any regulations Congress may find necessary for securing the title in such soil to the *bona-fide* purchasers. No tax shall be imposed on lands the property of the United States; and in no case shall non-resident proprietors be taxed higher than residents. The navigable waters leading into the Mississippi and Saint Lawrence, and the carrying places between the same, shall be common highways, and forever free, as well to the inhabitants of the said territory as to the citizens of the United States, and those of any other States that may be admitted into the confederacy, without any tax, impost, or duty therefor.

ARTICLE V

There shall be formed in the said territory not less than three nor more than five States; and the boundaries of the States, as soon as Virginia shall alter her act of cession and consent to the same, shall become fixed and established as follows, to wit: The western State, in the said territory, shall be bounded by the Mississippi, the Ohio, and the Wabash Rivers; a direct line drawn from the Wabash and Post Vincents, due north, to the territorial line between the United States and Canada; and by the said territorial line to the Lake of the Woods and Mississippi. The middle State shall be bounded by the said direct line, the Wabash from Post Vincents to the Ohio, by the Ohio, by a direct line drawn due north from the mouth of the Great Miami to the said territorial line, and by the said territorial line. The eastern State shall be bounded by the last-mentioned direct line, the Ohio, Pennsylvania, and the said territorial line: *Provided, however,* And it is further understood and declared, that the boundaries of these three States shall be subject so far to be altered, that, if Congress shall hereafter find it expedient, they shall have authority to form one or two States in that part of the said territory which lies north of an east and west line drawn through the southerly bend or extreme of Lake Michigan. And whenever any of the said States shall have sixty thousand free inhabitants therein, such State shall be admitted by its delegates, into the Congress of the United States, on an equal footing with the original States, in all respects whatever; and shall be at liberty to form a permanent constitution and State government: *Provided*, The constitution and government, so to be formed, shall be republican, and in conformity to the principles contained in these articles, and, so far as it can be consistent with the general interest of the confederacy, such admission shall be allowed at an earlier period, and when there may be a less number of free inhabitants in the State than sixty thousand.

ARTICLE VI

There shall be neither slavery nor involuntary servitude in the said territory, otherwise than in the punishment of crimes, whereof the party shall have been duly convicted: *Provided always*, That any person escaping into the same, from whom labor or service is lawfully claimed in any one of the original States, such fugitive may be lawfully reclaimed, and conveyed to the person claiming his or her labor or service as aforesaid.

Be it ordained by the authority aforesaid, That the resolutions of the 23d of April, 1784, relative to the subject of this ordinance, be, and the same are hereby, repealed, and declared null and void.

Done by the United States, in Congress assembled, the 13th day of July, in the year of our Lord 1787, and of their sovereignty and independence the twelfth.

23. *Interposition--A Proposed Resolution of the Legislature of Texas* *

GROWING CONCERN in Southern states over what some conceive to be a usurpation of authority by the Supreme Court in the *Segregation Cases* has led to the revival of the theory of interposition. This development has been further encouraged by the decisions of the Supreme Court holding producers of natural gas to be subject to Federal regulation under the commerce clause (discussed in the article below), as well as by other rulings of the Court that have invalidated state sedition laws and state "right to work" statutes

* Prepared by John Ben Shepperd, Attorney General of Texas, February, 1956, for consideration in the regular legislative session of 1957.

as the latter apply to labor contracts negotiated with railroad unions (these rulings have also triggered interposition discussions in the Northern states where the Segregation decision did not provoke widespread controversy).

The doctrine of interposition relates back to the concept of nullification as expressed in the Virginia and Kentucky Resolutions and the political writings of John Calhoun. Based upon the theory that the Tenth Amendment reserves to the states and people thereof all sovereignty not granted to the Federal government, it asserts that if the Federal government encroaches upon the reserved state field, the states are entitled to seek nullification of the Federal act through Congress and, if necessary, by constitutional amendment. In its extreme form, interposition represents a return to a constitutional theory long thought settled by the War between the States; and in a milder statement, to a variant of the Dual Federalism in vogue prior to the New Deal. While the majority of contemporary supporters of the doctrine deny that it means nullification in the sense of state refusal to enforce Federal regulations within their boundaries and contend that it is merely a constitutional protest by the states and a demand for lawful remedy of their grievances, a minority interpret it as implying nullification in the fullest sense. If this latter position is maintained, it is hard to see how the implication of secession as the ultimate sanction can be avoided. This revival of interposition and its corollary of nullification in our times indicates the fear of Federal centralization felt by certain sections and groups in the United States. Should the doctrine gain wide support, it would entail a drastic revision of our concept of federalism as it has evolved since 1789. Involved also would be a re-evaluation of the role of the Supreme Court, for the interpositionists hold that the Court is not to be viewed as the final voice in federal problems because this power ultimately rests in the states operating through Congress or by constitutional amendment.

SENATE CONCURRENT RESOLUTION
OR
HOUSE CONCURRENT RESOLUTION

Interposing the sovereignty of Texas against encroachment upon the reserved powers of this State and appealing to sister states to resolve the question of contested power relating to natural resources.

WHEREAS, the Tenth Amendment to the Constitution of the United States reserves to the States respectively, or to the people, powers not delegated to the United States by the Constitution nor prohibited by it to the States; and

WHEREAS, regulation of the conservation and production of the natural resources within this State is nowhere granted to the Federal Government in the Constitution, nor is such regulation prohibited therein to the States; and

WHEREAS, the Congress of the United States by its enactment of the Natural Gas Act of 1938 (52 Stat. 821, 15 U.S.C. Sec. 717 et seq.) exempted from its provisions the production and gathering of natural gas, and this enactment specifically states that it "shall not apply to . . . production or gathering of natural gas"; thereby recognizing the rights of the States to regulate their intra-state commerce; and

WHEREAS, by its decision of June 7, 1954 in *Phillips Petroleum Company* v. *Wisconsin*, 347 U.S. 672, the Supreme Court of the United States placed an interpretation upon the Natural Gas Act having the effect of an amendment thereto, and which this Legislature disapproves, wherein the opinion of the Court was predicated upon a finding that independent producers were engaged in interstate commerce when in truth and in fact such gas was sold at the well head making transactions of independent producers completely intrastate in nature and not subject to Federal regulation; and

WHEREAS, with the Supreme Court's decision and this resolution by the Legislature of the State of Texas, a question of contested power has arisen and the Natural Gas Act as construed by the Supreme Court of the United States constitutes a dangerous attempt by the Federal Government to usurp powers reserved to the States; and

WHEREAS, the State of Texas was admitted into the Union pursuant to the Articles of Annexation for annexing Texas to the United States and joined the Union while a free and independent nation upon an equal footing with other States and with certain additional reservations; and

WHEREAS, the Legislature of the State of Texas again asserts the fundamental principle that whenever the Federal Government attempts the dangerous exercise of powers not granted, the States who are parties to the compact under which the Union of States operates have the right and are in duty bound to interpose and to preserve the authorities, rights and liberties appertaining to them; and that the failure on the part of the State of Texas to assert its clearly reserved powers would be indicative of tacit consent and in the end lead to the surrender of all powers and inevitably to the obliteration of the sovereignty of the States contrary to the sacred compact under which this Union of States operates; and

WHEREAS, the Legislature of the State of Texas does hereby express a determined resolution to maintain and defend the Constitution of the United States and the Constitution of this State against attempts to undermine the fundamental principles in our basic laws by which the sovereignty of the States has been protected and assured; and

WHEREAS, it is declared that the powers of the Federal Government result solely from the compact of which the States are parties and that the powers of the Federal Government in all its branches and agencies are limited by the terms of the instrument under which the compact operates and by the plain sense and intention of its provisions; and that this compact may only be amended in the manner provided by Article V of the Constitution and that no such power is vested in any Court; and

WHEREAS, the very nature of this basic compact is that the ratifying States have agreed voluntarily to surrender certain of their sovereign rights to the Federal Government and that all powers not delegated to the United States by the Constitution have been reserved to the States or to the people; and

WHEREAS, the State of Texas has at no time surrendered to the Federal Government its right to regulate the conservation and production of the natural resources of this State believing that the imposition of Federal controls would greatly impair the proper development of this State's natural resources; on the contrary, by retaining all its public lands, in the Treaty of Annexation Texas indicated a clear intent to protect all its interest, title and rights; and

WHEREAS, the Legislature now asserts the right and authority of the Railroad Commission of Texas to regulate the natural resources of this State without Federal usurpation or interference with that right, this being a governmental power reserved to the States; now therefore

BE IT RESOLVED BY THE HOUSE OF REPRESENTATIVES OF THE STATE OF TEXAS, THE SENATE CONCURRING: (or vice versa)

The Legislature of the State of Texas directs that the Railroad Commission reassert with all the authority at its command its supervision, conservation and regulation of the natural resources of this State forthwith and exercise full control and operation over them.

BE IT FURTHER RESOLVED that the Legislature of the State of Texas appeals to her sister States for that decision which only they are qualified under our mutual compact to make, requesting them to join her in making proper application to the Congress, which application is made on Texas' part hereby for the purpose of calling a convention pursuant to Article V of the Constitution which convention would consider and propose an amendment designed to settle the issue of contested power by allowing the individual States to regulate the conservation, production and gathering of their oil, gas and other minerals herein asserted.

BE IT FURTHER RESOLVED that until the question here asserted is settled by clear constitutional amendment, it is our firm intention to take all appropriate measures, honorably, legally and constitutionally available to us to resist the illegal encroachment upon the sovereign powers of this State and to urge our sister States to exert their prompt and deliberate efforts to check this and further encroachment by the Federal Government upon the reserved powers of the States.

It is requested that a copy of the foregoing resolution be transmitted to the Governors of each of the other States, to each of the Senators and Representatives of this State in Congress and to the members of the Railroad Commission of Texas.

24. *The Constitution and the Territories* *

FROM THE TIME of passage of the Northwest Ordinance of 1787 until the present century it has been generally understood that territorial government is a prelude to state government. This was true of all the territory ceded to the United States by Great Britain in 1783, the territory included in the Louisiana Purchase, and all other continental territory acquired in the westward expansion of the United States. While it may be correct to assume that, despite delays, Hawaii and Alaska will also become states, other overseas possessions of the United States do not have territorial governments that are likely to be followed by state governments. The organization and operation of territorial government in these areas has, according to Professor Wormuth, altered the traditional constitutional development in this field. In this article he explains the nature of what he calls a "rupture of our tradition" and its influence on our domestic institutions and those of the territorial peoples.

ONE OF THE PROBLEMS implicit in the creation of what Chief Justice Marshall liked to call "the American empire" confronted the Chief Justice himself. In 1820 he said, in upholding a Congressional tax on the District of Columbia, that taxation without representation was not necessarily tyranny: not in the case of the District, which "voluntarily relinquished the right of representation"; nor in the case of the terri-

* Francis D. Wormuth, *Current History*, XXIX (December, 1955), pp. 337-342. Reprinted by permission of the author and the publisher.

tories, which were "in a state of infancy advancing to manhood, looking forward to complete equality so soon as that state of manhood shall be attained."

The acquisition of the American empire has raised other questions. Upon what terms may new states be admitted to the Union? Is there a constitutional right to acquire new territory? Is it proper to acquire territory with no intention of granting statehood—that is, to acquire a colonial empire? Does the Constitution apply in such colonial areas? What is the status of the inhabitants of newly acquired territories: do they constitute an inferior class of nationals who lack the rights of citizens?

The line of judicial decision on these questions has been wavering and uncertain, but in the end has followed the course most favorable to territorial aggrandizement. The federal structure has shown itself well suited to the enlargement of the nation by the addition of states, and the law of statehood has faithfully maintained the original pattern. But the law of territories and the law of citizenship which have been developed to meet the needs of empire entail radical departures from the original system.

The government of territories and the admission of new states confronted the framers of the Constitution as immediate problems. Beginning with New York in 1781, the northern states with claims to the Northwest Territory had transferred their rights to the United States. North Carolina offered the Tennessee territory in 1784 and the cession was completed in 1790. The framers granted to Congress exclusive jurisdiction to govern the proposed District of Columbia, and provided that Congress might "dispose of and make all needful rules and regulations respecting the territory or other property belonging to the United States."

Apprehension was expressed concerning the admission of new states. Elbridge Gerry of Massachusetts proposed that the number of new states be limited "in such a manner that they shall never be able to outnumber the Atlantic states." Gouverneur Morris of Pennsylvania argued that Congress should be permitted to admit new states on unequal terms: "It is impossible to discourage the growth of the western country, but we should not throw the power in their hands."

Concern over expansion was not merely selfish; it was widely believed that an extensive country could not maintain a republican form of government. In the end, however, no limit was placed on the admission of new states. No express provision was made with regard to equality. Congress in the enabling act permitting a territory to qualify for statehood has often imposed requirements upon new states which do not apply to other states. Of course, Congress may withhold admission to the Union on any condition it pleases; but the Supreme Court has held that a condition which deprives a new state of political equality with the older states is not enforceable, since the word "state" in the Constitution contemplates equality among the member units.

There have been few decisions on the question, none of them of great moment. A number of the political restrictions have not been litigated, as for example the "perpetual ordinance" which Utah was obliged to enact forbidding the practice of polygamy.

On the other hand, Congress may impose valid restrictions which will survive admission to statehood. These are said to be of a private or proprietary as contrasted with a political character. When Ohio, Louisiana, Indiana and Illinois were admitted, Congress required the acceptance in each case of an ordinance renouncing the right to tax, for a period of five years after the sale, any public lands sold by the United States, and a similar limitation on Minnesota was upheld by the Supreme Court in 1900.

POLITICAL EQUALITY

Ordinarily the enforcement of the rule of political equality has been to the advantage of new states, since the enabling act has attempted to fix conditions of admission less advantageous than those enjoyed by states admitted earlier. But it is also true that a state may not be admitted on conditions more favorable than those enjoyed by the older states. The joint resolution by which Texas was admitted in 1845 provided that Texas was to stand "on an equal footing with the original states in all respects whatever," but that Texas should retain "all the vacant and unappropriated lands lying within its limits."

As a sovereign state Texas had claimed the seabed of the Gulf of Mexico three leagues from land. But the Supreme Court held in the case of California that the right to license extraction of oil in the marginal seas belonged to the United States rather than to the states, and in 1950 the Court applied the rule of equality to hold that Texas had necessarily surrendered its claim to the oil in its marginal seas to the United States. To the argument that what was involved here was property rather than one of the political rights to which the rule of equality applies, the Supreme Court replied that the international aspect of the marginal seas made this "an instance where property interests are so subordinated to the rights of sovereignty as to follow sovereignty."

The territory concerning which needful rules and regulations were to be made, and from which new states were to be created, was that ceded by Great Britain in 1783. Thomas Jefferson, at least, believed that the acquisition of further territory was not permitted by the Constitution, and asked for a constitutional amendment ratifying the Louisiana

Purchase. The Federalists shared his misgivings, but the nation accepted the annexation without the formality of amendment, and since that date it has been assumed that the United States has a constitutional power to acquire new territory.

Various legal instruments have been employed: treaties, in the case of territories acquired from France, Spain, Mexico, Russia, Panama and Denmark; occupation conjoined with a treaty with Great Britain, in the case of the Oregon territory; joint resolutions, since the two-thirds majority in the Senate required for a treaty could not be obtained, in the case of Texas and Hawaii; occupation under the authority of a statute, in the case of the Guano Islands; and executive annexation, with subsequent implied or express Congressional ratification, in the case of Midway and Wake Islands, the eastern Samoan Islands, and the Trust Territory of the Pacific Islands—although this last is not, strictly speaking, annexed to the United States.

For a very long time it was assumed that, whatever the legal instrument used, the only constitutional purpose for which territory could be acquired was eventual admission to statehood. In the Dred Scott Case, Chief Justice Taney asserted that "no power is given to acquire a Territory to be held and governed permanently in that character," a proposition which led him to the conclusion that the power of Congress over the territories was severely limited.

In the debate over the annexation of the Philippines, Senator Hoar of Massachusetts declared that:

> I have been unable to find a single reputable authority more than twelve months old, for the power now claimed for Congress to govern dependent nations or territories not expected to become States. The contrary, until this war broke out, has been taken as too clear for reasonable question.

However, since the United States has acquired permanent dependencies it is usual to rest the power to annex territory upon the legal instrument employed—occupation, war, statutes or treaty—without reference to the power to admit states.

Inevitably there has arisen the question of the extent of the power of Congress, and more particularly of the applicability of the Bill of Rights and other constitutional prohibitions to Congressional acts for the territories. In the Dred Scott Case, Chief Justice Taney declared that Congress had only a trusteeship over territories while preparing them for statehood, and that all acts of Congress were subject to the Constitution: specifically, that forbidding slavery in the territories violated the due process clause of the Fifth Amendment.

Except for two trifling dicta in the intervening period, it was uniformly held until the Spanish-American War that the Constitution governed all acts of Congress for the territories. After 1898, however, Congress adopted policies which apparently contravened the Constitution. It levied import duties upon goods entering the United States from Puerto Rico, although the Constitution requires that "all duties, imposts and excises shall be uniform throughout the United States"; and it ignored the constitutional requirement of trial by jury in the Philippines.

THE INSULAR CASES

In a series of decisions called the Insular Cases the Supreme Court contrived to uphold these actions. Four judges, to be sure, dissented. Four of the majority distinguished between territory which had been "incorporated" in the United States by act of Congress (here the Constitution applied in full) and territory which had been annexed but not incorporated. Here Congress was not subject to the Constitution, except for unspecified "fundamental" provisions. The ninth judge, Justice Brown, regarded all territories (except the District of Columbia) as unincorporated and protected only by the "fundamental" guarantees of the Constitution.

This complex of opinions led Finley Peter Dunne's Mr. Dooley to observe that Justice Brown wrote the decision of the Court, eight judges dissenting. In 1905, in *Rasmussen* v. *United States*, seven of the nine judges adopted the incorporation theory and held that the treaty of annexation and the legislation concerning Alaska constituted incorporation so that the inhabitants were entitled to jury trial.

The doctrine of the Insular Cases is logically incoherent. How can Congress have legal power outside the bounds of the Constitution which creates Congress and simultaneously confers and limits its power? If Congress has such extra-constitutional power, why should "fundamental" provisions of the Constitution apply to it? The rationale of the Insular Cases is to be found in the logic of imperialism rather than the logic of law. Constitutional provisions which presuppose a free society, such as jury trial, cannot be applied in an unfree dependency. Constitutional privileges which even a despot can allow, such as due process, are "fundamental" and may be extended to a subject people.

At the same time, however, it would not do to underrate the significance of the protection of the due process clause. Applying this provision of the Fifth Amendment, the Supreme Court held in 1926 that the Philippine legislature might not forbid a Chinese merchant to keep his books in Chinese, and in 1927 that the Hawaiian legislature might not put unreasonable restrictions upon foreign language schools.

Hawaii was incorporated in 1900. The Philippines were never incorporated, and Puerto Rico, Guam, Samoa, the Virgin Islands and the miscellaneous naval bases in the Pacific (Midway, Wake and lesser islands) have not been incorporated. Puerto Rico, the Virgin Islands and Guam have, however, like the incorporated territories, been given a considerable measure of self-government. Congress has extended important constitutional rights to Puerto Rico and Guam. Midway, Wake and the other Pacific outposts are under no civilian jurisdiction except that of the United States District Court for Hawaii, which has been empowered to deal with their civil and criminal matters under its admiralty jurisdiction.

One of the most important consequences of the doctrine of the Insular Cases is economic. Currently imports into the United States from Guam, Samoa and the Virgin Islands are, subject to certain provisos, dutiable as foreign imports. But even the incorporated territories may be subjected to discrimination. Congress has placed a quota on the importation of refined sugar from Puerto Rico and Hawaii for the benefit of continental refiners. With regard to Puerto Rico there is a readily available justification, since imports from unincorporated territory may be treated as foreign commerce; with regard to Hawaii the action must be rested on the assumption that Congress has a plenary power over all territories.

Within the national government final power over the territories belongs to Congress; but the Supreme Court has held that the President may govern territory occupied in war until Congress acts. The Trust Territory of the Pacific Islands is still under almost exclusive executive control. These islands were formerly Japanese mandates and were captured during World War II; by agreement between the United Nations and the United States, approved under the authority of a joint resolution of Congress, they were made a United Nations trusteeship administered by the United States in 1947. Congress makes appropriations for administration and has asserted the power of audit.

CITIZENSHIP

Of course the annexation of territory raises problems as to the status not only of the territory but also of the inhabitants. Indians living in tribal organizations within the United States were originally neither citizens nor aliens; they were, Chief Justice Marshall said in 1831, "in a state of pupilage." By a series of acts culminating in a statute of 1924 all American Indians were given United States citizenship. Freed Negroes posed a similar problem. In 1822 the Court of Appeals of Kentucky opined that they were subjects rather than citizens, and most state courts which passed on the question took the same position.

In 1857, in the Dred Scott Case, the majority of the United States Supreme Court declared that even if a state conferred state citizenship upon a freed Negro this did not convey national citizenship or the right to the privileges of citizenship in any other state. This decision was abruptly overruled by the Civil War. An opinion by Attorney General Bates in 1862 declared that all freedmen of color born in the United States were citizens of the United States and of the state in which they resided, and denied that there was any intermediate status between citizenship and alienage. The Fourteenth Amendment, which was ratified in 1868, clearly adopted the first proposition, and no doubt the framers of the Amendment intended the second; but they did not make it impossible for the Supreme Court to revive the idea of an intermediate status.

Only persons "born or naturalized within the United States" are citizens by operation of the Fourteenth Amendment, and if the unincorporated territories are not within the United States, a collective naturalization statute, or individual naturalization, is necessary to confer citizenship upon their inhabitants. At least, the Supreme Court has drawn this moral. The natives of such territories owe allegiance to the United States but are not citizens. The term "non-citizen national" has been adopted as less offensive than the word "subject" to describe the members of this class.

All treaties of annexation entered into by the United States prior to 1898 automatically naturalized the inhabitants of the ceded territories. The treaty with Spain by which Puerto Rico, Guam and the Philippines were acquired, however, left the status of the inhabitants to be determined by act of Congress. In 1900 the citizens of Hawaii were made citizens of the United States; those of Puerto Rico, in 1917. The citizens of the Virgin Islands acquired United States citizenship by an act of Congress passed in 1927. The natives of Guam were given citizenship in 1950.

Filipinos continued to be non-citizen nationals throughout the period of United States ownership of the Philippines, and the natives of Samoa are still non-citizen nationals. Presumably inhabitants of the Trust Territory of the Pacific Islands are in no sense nationals of the United States, but they are entitled to the protection of the United States.

The Spanish-American War and the consequent Insular Cases marked a watershed in American constitutional law, the significance of which was not exhausted in the law of territories and the law of citizenship. Concern over the course of manifest destiny was not confined to sympathy for the natives of conquered territory. There was widespread apprehension for the future of freedom in the United States.

The famous political scientist, John W. Burgess, declared that the

Insular Cases made the government of the United States, "in such territory, simply despotism, benevolent and beneficent, perhaps—yes, probably—but a despotism, stripped of every bit of constitutional hypocrisy and standing there bald and bare and unmistakable." This was bound to have domestic repercussions. For the United States as well as for the territories the Insular Cases ushered in "a new political system."

> There is nothing now to prevent the Government of the United States from entering upon a course of conquest and empire. . . . We are by no means a peaceably inclined people. . . . In fact, besides being belligerent and boastful, we are restless, nervous, and at times hysterical. We have just the qualities to answer the call of a Napoleon in the Presidency.

Of course this is an extravagant forecast. There are factors that urge the United States toward imperialism, but there are also factors that work in the opposite direction. The Philippines were emancipated because their resources were regarded as a positive disadvantage by important groups in this country—organized labor and sugar producers. Having failed in the attempt to exclude Filipino immigration and Philippine imports by act of Congress, these groups succeeded in passing in 1934 the Philippine Independence Act which took effect in 1946.

And the word despotism is a little strong to describe the present condition of the territories. A considerable degree of self-government has been extended to all the territories which have a native population except the Samoan Islands. Alaska and Hawaii will sooner or later achieve statehood. The effect of the Insular Cases has been reduced by the action of Congress in granting citizenship to the inhabitants of all our possessions save Samoa, and in extending the protection of important provisions of the Bill of Rights to Puerto Rico and Guam. Moreover, it must be remembered that the fundamental provisions—of which due process is certainly one—apply by operation of the Constitution itself to all possessions except the Trust Territory.

On the other hand, none of the territories has achieved political equality with the states, and some never will. Some Puerto Ricans bitterly resent their status. It is incontestable that the acquisition of overseas possessions has involved a rupture of our traditions, and it is probable that the rationalizations which the Supreme Court supplied have contributed to the attrition of constitutional government.

IV

STATE CONSTITUTIONS

25. *An Ideal State Constitution* *

IN THIS ARTICLE Professor Munro lists several propositions that in his opinion should guide the development of an "ideal state constitution." Before offering his propositions he notes that "There never has been an ideal state constitution in America, and perhaps there never will be." Nevertheless, because the development of constitutions has deeply concerned Americans, they have given a great deal of attention to the "ideal" since the early efforts of Thomas Jefferson. In modern times the most influential ideal constitution has been the *Model State Constitution* of the National Municipal League. First published in 1921, this constitution has undergone several revisions. The League's constitution and several state constitutions now in use are excellent companion pieces to Professor Munro's discussion.

WE ARE all idealists, for man is born to act, and he cannot act without consciously or unconsciously affirming the worth of some ideal. There have been idealists in politics since the days of Plato, undismayed by the seeming impossibility of transmuting their dreams into realities. The vision of a great community, governed to perfection in all its parts, is one of the oldest in human history. The literature of statesmanship, from Moses to Mussolini, is saturated with it. And in spite of doubts and dogmas, there will always be those who choose to speculate on what government might be if people would only follow the light.

* William B. Munro, *The Annals of the American Academy of Political and Social Science*, 181 (September, 1935), pp. 1-10. Reprinted by permission of the author and the publisher. All footnotes omitted.

There has never been an ideal state constitution in America, and perhaps there never will be. Certainly no constitution would be uniformly ideal for all the forty-eight states in our imperial area. Montesquieu was right when he averred that the best constitution is the one which best suits the genius and the traditions of the people who live under it. Massachusetts and Mississippi are under the same flag, and speak (more or less) the same language; but they have little else in common. There is no good reason why they should require the same body of fundamental law. That is the difficulty which one encounters in any attempt to frame a "Model Constitution" suitable for any or all of the forty-eight commonwealths. In such an enterprise one must start with the assumption that there is a fair approach to uniformity in the needs, the traditions, and the political orientation of all the states, which is far from being the case. Nevertheless the effort is worth while, if only to set up a standard to which the wise and honest may repair, with due allowance for variations in local circumstances.

AMERICAN EXPERIENCE WITH CONSTITUTIONS

America is the classic land of constitutions. We have probably had more experience with the making and unmaking of them than all the rest of the world put together. Forty-nine formal constitutions, together with the organic laws upon which the governments of the insular territories are founded, have provided us with abundant scope for adventures in constitutionalism. Hardly a year goes by but constitutions are amended, revised, or replaced. The Constitution of California, for example, has been amended nearly two hundred times during the past half-century. Thus the United States has been doing service as the world's chief laboratory for experiments in constitution-making.

It is difficult to determine when Americans began to be familiar with the idea of a constitution as a fundamental instrument of government. Some of the colonies had charters which were in effect written constitutions. They set bounds to the powers of the colonial authorities. In all the colonies, moreover, the common law of England was regarded as the bulwark of individual liberty, a compendious bill of rights which protected the people against the exercise of arbitrary power on the part of their rulers. Prior to the Revolution, therefore, the inhabitants of the thirteen colonies had acquired a considerable familiarity with the idea of a higher law which established the frame of government and safeguarded the natural rights of men.

The Revolution involved the necessity of transforming colonial governments into state governments. In some cases this was an easy task. Rhode Island and Connecticut merely made a few changes in their colonial charters and let it go at that. Other colonies gave the matter more thought and took more time. The Continental Congress, in advising the establishment of new state governments, proffered no counsel as to the form which these should take or the basis upon which they should rest. Accordingly, each of the newly independent states took its own course, but as they were all permeated by much the same general political philosophy, the results were not widely different when they got through.

EARLY POLITICAL PHILOSOPHY

This political philosophy enshrined a number of principles, of which two stand out most prominently. The first was the idea that government is at best a necessary evil. The people of all the colonies had been well schooled in this point of view by those two stalwarts of philosophic liberalism, Thomas Paine and Thomas Jefferson. Paine wrote:

> Since the end of government is freedom and security, it follows that whatever form of government appears most likely to insure these objectives, with the least expense and greatest benefit, is preferable to all others . . . . The more perfect a civilization is, the less occasion it has for government.

The natural-rights philosophy, to which Jefferson gave allegiance, placed its emphasis on the individual, not on the community. In the belief of the Great Virginian, mankind did not get its rights from constitutions, charters, or governments; these things had their sole justification in a capacity to guard natural rights which the citizen already possessed.

The second outstanding tenet in the political philosophy of this constitution-making era was a corollary from the first. If government is to be effectively restrained from an excess of activity, it must be kept close to the people. Not only must it rest on their consent, but this consent must be frequently renewed. Consequently all officers should be elected for short terms. Nine of the earliest state constitutions provided a one-year term for the governor, and in six of them there was a stipulation that both branches of the state legislature must be renewed annually. The point was pressed so far in Rhode Island and Connecticut that provision was made for the election of the lower house every six months. All these early constitutions betrayed the prevailing fear of governmental autocracy, particularly at the hands of the executive. Leadership was regarded as potential tyranny, so the legislatures were equipped with no provision for it.

This distrust of executive leadership was a product of colonial experiences. The royal governors, being agents of the home administration, had to carry out instructions which were sometimes extremely offensive to the people. So the framers of the new state constitutions exalted the legislatures and reduced the governors to "mere ciphers," as James Madison phrased it. On the other hand, they were not prepared to trust the legislatures overmuch; hence most of the constitutions contained bills of rights limiting the powers of the legislative bodies with respect to the life, liberty, and property of the citizen.

In summary, then, the original state constitutions attempted to set up governments which would do very little governing and keep close to the people, with weak executives, and legislatures firmly bound by bills of rights. They were short documents because they dealt only with fundamentals. The Virginia Constitution of 1776 used only 1,500 words. The people of the post-Revolutionary era did not attempt to enact a code of laws under color of framing a constitution.

CONSTITUTIONAL EXPANSION

From all this, however, we have drawn steadily away. Constitution-makers during the past hundred and fifty years have greatly elaborated the provisions relating to the frame of government. They have developed the habit of specifying in minute detail the powers which the various organs of government are to exercise and the procedure which they must follow. The idea that state governments shall confine themselves to a minimum of activity has long since passed into the discard. It has given place to the doctrine that these governments should busy themselves with all sorts of regulatory functions in the interests of the collective citizenship, no matter how much they may constrain the freedom of the individual. The old natural-rights philosophy has faded from the public mind and has been replaced by the doctrine which was embodied in the Roman maxim: *Salus populi suprema lex esto.*

Bills of rights have also undergone a relentless expansion. To a considerable extent these guarantees and limitations merely repeat the first ten amendments to the National Constitution, although in much more prolix phraseology. In addition, many of the newer state constitutions contain numerous supplementary guarantees, most of them either superfluous or meaningless. They assure to the citizen various rights which under the terms of the National Constitution could not be taken away from him. In fact it has become an American habit to find place in the state constitution for a whole series of primordial platitudes concerning human equality, the rights of man, the duty of law observance, the inviolability of private property, the dignity of labor, the value of education, and the sanctity of every citizen's home.

Sometimes the constitutions go even further. The Constitution of California, for example, guarantees to every citizen "the right to fish," which of course means less than nothing in these days of private ownership and closed seasons. The Constitution of Maryland declares that "monopolies are odious and should not be suffered," thus disregarding the palpable fact that some public services are natural monopolies and cannot be economically provided except as such. Looking through the declarations of rights in other constitutions, one finds provisions relating to all sorts of irrelevancies such as pensions, lotteries, duels, divorces, attainders, lobbying, and contempt of court.

This discursiveness prefigures the abandonment of old ideas as to the purpose which a constitution is meant to serve. The Constitutions of Oklahoma and Louisiana, for example, now cover more than a hundred pages each. These pages are cluttered with statutory provisions. Whole chapters are devoted to the system of public education, the management of the state university, the powers of the public utilities commission, the inheritance of property, and the conduct of elections. Even the methods of lawmaking at the hands of the state legislature are minutely prescribed—the way in which votes shall be taken and counted, the length of the legislative session, and various restraining provisions such as the stipulation that not more than one topic shall be included in any single measure. Likewise, in more than one third of the states the constitution contains elaborate provisions for the use of the initiative and referendum.

Nor is this all. The salaries of various state officers are frequently embalmed in the constitution, likewise the conditions upon which persons may be admitted to practice law or medicine, the payments to be made by the state in support of local schools, the apportionment of gasoline taxes for road-building, the exemption of certain property from taxation, and the terms on which companies may drill oil wells on state lands. The Constitution of Oklahoma gets down into such administrative minutiae as to require that domestic science shall be taught in all the public schools of that state.

REASONS FOR AMPLIFICATION

Of course there are plenty of reasons for this amplification of constitutional provisions. One is the fact that state functions are expanding, and to a certain extent constitutions must expand with them. But the lengthening of state constitutions also betrays a waning public confidence in the wisdom and the integrity of legislators. Makers of state constitutions are more and more inclined to look upon these documents as safeguards against legislative incapacity, favoritism, and corruption. They represent an endeavor to keep legislative bodies and public officials from doing the wrong thing, on the assumption that this is what would happen if constitutional provisions did not stand in the way.

Likewise, the elaboration of these constitutions is due in some degree to public dissatisfaction with the decisions of the courts. Provisions are frequently inserted in the attempt to make sure that statutes relating to particular matters shall not be shattered on the rocks of unconstitutionality. Special interests of various kinds—labor organizations, the farmers, the banks, the public utility companies, the cities, the school teachers, and so on—endeavor to obtain constitutional security against the taking away of what they believe to be their rights. The inclination in many instances is to look upon the state constitution as a means of keeping the courts from nullifying laws which can be put through the legislature by group pressure in derogation of other people's rights.

At any rate, we have almost completely lost sight of the fact that a state constitution is supposed to be an organic document, a basis of government, not a series of legislative enactments. It is intended to facilitate sound administration rather than to place checks upon it. When details are crowded into a constitution, they shackle the hands of the public authorities. The more voluminous a constitution, the more quickly it loses touch with the social and economic needs of a rapidly growing community. The more precise and elaborate its provisions, the greater are the obstacles to the reform of abuses. Litigation thrives on constitutional verbosity.

PROPOSED IMPROVEMENTS

How can this situation be improved? What changes in the form and the content of state constitutions are desirable in order to bring them nearer to the ideal of what such documents ought to be? The answer given to this question cannot, of course, be a short and simple one, nor will it satisfy every one. On the other hand, unless the existing state governments are deemed to be beyond improvement (which no one believes), any man's honest answer to such an important question is entitled to a hearing. Thomas Jefferson, in 1783, set forth his conception of an ideal state constitution. It was promptly consigned to oblivion by his contemporaries. Any revisionist of today whose proposals share the same fate will at least have the consolation of being in good company. So here are some propositions which for clarity are set forth in categorical form:

I. *A state constitution should confine itself to fundamentals.* This of course begs a question as to what one means by "fundamentals." True enough, it is hard to define, but everybody knows what it means. Or, if any one does not, he need only read the Constitution of the United States to acquaint himself with an organic document which comes measurably near fulfilling the requirement. The *Model State Constitution* of the National Municipal League, although one may disagree with its individual provisions, is likewise a document which confines itself (save in a few minor matters) to the fundamentals of government. It is only by strict adherence to such a policy that a constitution can be kept from eventually becoming a code of laws with no constituent earmark except its name.

II. *The bill of rights should be reduced to a minimum.* It seems to be taken for granted that unless individual rights are constitutionally guaranteed and rendered enforceable by the courts, they are certain to be infringed. Such has not proved to be the case in other countries. There are no bills of rights in the constitutions of Australia or Canada, yet the liberties of the citizen are quite as well respected in these dominions as in any of the American states. In some ways they are more secure because they do not depend for their scope or efficacy upon the formularies of judicial interpretation, but are grounded upon popular tradition and a sense of fair play. Freedom of speech and of the press exist in Canada, but not because there is any constitutional barrier to their infringement. It is because the people would turn out of office any government that ventured to interfere with them except for very urgent reasons.

In many of the American states, on the other hand, the broad guarantees of civil liberty embodied in bills of rights have been either circumvented or whittled down by resort to juridical sophistry. Take, for example, the provision which requires "due process of law." Innumerable decisions have been made by the courts in the endeavor to make clear what constitutes due process. Whole books have been written about it. But even at that, no one can tell you what it means. "Few phrases in the law are so elusive of exact apprehension as this," said the Supreme Court of the United States on one occasion. A provision which is "elusive of apprehension" even at the hands of such an august tribunal can hardly be looked upon as a dependable bulwark of protection against the deprivation of life, liberty, or property.

Due process, as a matter of fact, does not guarantee judicial process. It does not avail to prevent deprivations of property in the exercise of the police power. It has not prevented arbitrary action by public officials in the levying of special assessments or the sale of property for delinquent taxes.

On the other hand, it is worthy of note that some constitutional provisions which are not subject to judicial enforcement have been reasonably well observed by the public authorities. An illustration is at hand in the case of the rules relating to the interstate rendition of fugitives from justice. The National Constitution stipulates that such fugitives, on proper demand, "shall be delivered up" by the governor of the state to which they have fled. Many years ago, however, the Supreme Court decided that it would not intervene to enforce compliance with this provision on the part of any recalcitrant governor. The extradition of fugitives is thus purely a matter of executive discretion. A governor may refuse a requisition for any reason or for no reason at all. This constitutional provision, accordingly, is devoid of any judicial sanction. Nevertheless it is almost universally respected by governors. Only in the rarest cases is there the slightest reluctance to comply with it.

All of which goes to prove that where a course of action is clearly dictated by the general well-being, it will be followed irrespective of constitutional compulsion. By the same token, when the governing authorities are compelled by constitutional requirements, judicially enforced, to follow policies or procedures which are not generally regarded as being in the public interest, they will seek and usually find means of evasion. The provision in the National Constitution with reference to Negro enfranchisement has furnished us with an illuminating lesson on this point.

So it has been suggested that a bill of rights ought to contain precepts, not guarantees. It should set forth a creed of individual liberty, a series of things which the public authorities are expected (but not compelled) to do or not to do, as the case may be. These precepts would not operate as ironclad mandates or restrictions, to be scrupulously observed under all circumstances, on penalty of having legislative actions declared unconstitutional. This would transfer the responsibility from the courts to the legislature and from the legislature to the electorate, where it belongs. The ill-starred Weimar Constitution of the German Reich incorporated such an arrangement, but owing to the vicissitudes of Teutonic politics, it never received a fair trial. "The house of every German is his sanctuary and is inviolable," this constitution declares. Then there is added the qualification that "exceptions are permissible only under the authority of law."

But the replacement of guarantees by precepts in American state constitutions would be unwise at this stage. It might well be regarded as an invitation to do some of the things which legislatures have hitherto been prevented from doing by the mandatory character of constitutional phraseology. The American tradition in this matter is strong, and a precipitate departure from a well-established governmental usage often results in more harm than good. The goal, if it is desirable, should be approached by gradual stages. It would seem to suffice for the present if bills of rights could be shortened, clarified, and made more specific in their individual provisions. Instead of stipulating that the legislature shall pass no law abridging the freedom of speech or of the press, for example, it is better to provide, as the Nebraska Constitution does, that "every person may freely speak, write and publish on all subjects, being responsible for the abuse of that liberty."

III. *The framework of state government should be simplified.* State legislatures are too large. They should be considerably reduced in size. Many reputable political scientists believe that every state legislature should be reduced to a single chamber, and Nebraska has made provision for the inauguration of a unicameral legislative body in 1937. The usual argument is that a single chamber will serve the ends of economy, simplify procedure, provide a greater concentration of responsibility for legislation, and secure the election of better men as representatives. The two-house arrangement was designed as a check on hasty and ill-considered lawmaking; but with the rise of the party system, it is argued, this purpose is no longer served. When both chambers are controlled by the same party, one does not in reality serve as a check on the other. When they are controlled by different parties, the result is a series of deadlocks from which important legislation cannot emerge except through the making of unsatisfactory compromises.

It is contended, moreover, that the executive veto has become a much more efficient check on legislative impetuosity than it was expected to be when the bicameral system was adopted, and that the judicial review of legislation affords an additional protection. Finally, in many of the states there is a provision for invoking the referendum against laws which any kind of legislature might enact hastily or without giving due consideration to the public interests involved. In a word, it is suggested that the executive, judicial, and popular checks upon legislative action are now sufficient to warrant the abolition of the bicameral system in the states.

Even if one admits the cogency of these various considerations, however, there seem to be reasons why the bicameral plan ought not to be lightly abandoned, at any rate by some of the states. First among these is the deep-seated popular conviction that areas as well as people have diverse interests and ought to be represented in the process of lawmaking. Single-chamber legislatures may be desirable for Nebraska, Wyoming, Montana, or Mississippi, where the population is relatively uniform in its distribution; but it does not follow that the same is true of New York, Illinois, Pennsylvania, California, or other states which have a sharp differentiation between the rural and urban elements of their electorates. In not a few instances, a single chamber based upon population would be controlled by the large cities; in some cases, by a single metropolitan community. In all matters on which there is a cleavage of interest between urban and rural, the former would decide the outcome. The strongest practical reason for the continuance of the double-chamber system in some of the states is the rural conviction that any other plan would spell urban supremacy in state government.

This suggests a pertinent question, namely, whether the divergence between rural and urban interests is as great as it is commonly alleged to be. Do rural and urban legislators, as a matter of fact, vote on opposite sides of important questions, or do they usually split among themselves? No reliable data, so far as is known to me, have been gathered on this point, but casual observation engenders a suspicion that the urban-versus-rural conflict in legislative halls may be one of the numerous myths of American politics. Nevertheless, a belief in the divergence of interest between the two branches of the electorate is firmly grounded in many of the states and must be taken into account whether it squares with the facts or not.

In any event, the quality of state government does not depend upon the question whether there are two legislative chambers or one. Most of the advantages claimed for the unicameral system can be obtained by reducing the existing legislatures in size, giving the members longer terms, simplifying the procedure, having joint committees (as in Massachusetts), and making better provision for leadership in the process of lawmaking. Without leadership, a single chamber is not likely to function much better than two. The point is sometimes made that the Canadian provinces get along very well under a single-chamber system, but this is irrelevant to the issue. The Federal Parliament of Canada has two chambers and does quite as well, or better. The reason in both cases is the fact that the Canadian system provides the legislative bodies with definite, recognized, responsible, executive leadership, which the American system of state government does not.

IV. *The powers of the executive should be increased.* To the end that effective leadership in legislation may be provided, the governor should be given the right to introduce bills in the legislature and to take the floor in support of such measures. The heads of state departments should likewise have the right to sit in the legislature and take part in the discussion, but without the right to vote. One and all of these department heads should be appointees of the governor, without the necessity of confirmation, and should be removable by him at any time. To provide their work with unity, they should constitute a cabinet as in the Federal system. The governor's term should be fixed at four years, with provision for his recall at mid-term but at no other time. He should be made responsible for the preparation of the budget, and no changes in the budget should be permitted, nor should any other appropriation be valid, without the governor's recommendation, unless passed by a three-fourth's vote of the legislature. On matters other than appropriations, the governor's veto should be subject to the usual two-thirds rule.

These various provisions would enable the governor to assume the active responsibilities of legislative leadership. In all likelihood they would secure most of the advantages of the "responsible executive" system without running counter to what has become a strong tradition in America, namely, the independent selection of both governors and legislators by direct vote of the people.

V. *The judges of all the state courts should be appointed by the governor for long terms.* The superiority of an appointive judiciary has been amply demonstrated in the Federal system of courts. And in those states where the judges are appointed by the governor there is less criticism of the courts than in most of the other states, where they are elected by the people. Appointive judges should be subject to removal by the governor, but only on the basis of a resolution setting forth the reasons and passed by a two-thirds majority of both chambers of the legislature. This is the existing rule in Massachusetts. The organization of the courts, with provision for a judicial council, should follow the general lines laid down in the excellent report made some years ago by the American Judicature Society. This plan provides for a unification of the state judiciary, and restores to the courts a control over their own procedure which should never have been taken away from them.

VI. *A large number of matters now incorporated in the state constitution should be transferred to an administrative code.* In this category are such topics as the methods of registering voters, making nominations, and conducting elections, the provisions relating to the organization of local government (including the home-rule provisions), the duties of administrative officers including the heads of departments, the scope and methods of taxation, the procedure in public borrowing, the organization, powers, and functions of the public utilities commission and other regulatory bodies, the rules relating to state supervision of the public schools including the state university, the acquisition of property for public use, the civil service system, and the auditing of accounts.

All such matters ought to be prescribed in a more formal manner than by ordinary statute, but this does not mean they must be embodied in the state constitution, thus expanding that document to inordinate dimensions and making even slight changes a matter of serious difficulty. Rather, the constitutional convention should prepare, and submit to the people along with the constitution, an administrative code covering the broad range of affairs above indicated.

Such a code, on its adoption, would become subject to amendment in the way that the constitution is amended, but there should also be a simpler procedure, namely, that on recommendation of the governor the administrative code would be amendable by a two-thirds vote of the legislature. This latter provision would give the code a greater flexibility than the constitution, while keeping it on a different plane from the usual run of statutes. The code, in a word, would represent an organic enactment, standing midway between constituent and ordinary legislation. To my mind, an arrangement of this kind would do more than anything else to abbreviate and dignify the constitution.

VII. *Provision should be made for direct legislation.* The use of the initiative and referendum should be permitted, under proper safeguards, with respect to constitutional amendments, changes in the administrative code, and statutes. In addition, all statutory enactments except emergency measures, and all changes in the administrative code when made by the legislature, should be subject to the referendum in case an adequate petition were properly filed. But the details relating to the filing of petitions, the verification of signatures, the framing of questions on the ballot, the issue of publicity pamphlets, and all such things should go into the administrative code, not into the constitution.

A suggestion worth considering is that the number of names now customarily required on petitions for the initiative or for the referendum should be considerably reduced, but with the provision that all persons signing such petitions must affix their signatures at designated public offices. This would eliminate what is now a highly objectionable feature of the direct legislation process, namely, the unseemly scramble for signatures on the part of hired canvassers who are paid so much per name.

VIII. *The Constitution should provide alternative methods of amendment.* It should permit amendments to be proposed by initiative petition, by a two-thirds majority of the legislature, or by a majority vote in two successive legislatures. Ratification should be in all cases by popular vote at a regular election. Provision should be made that any proposal submitted to the people and rejected by them may not be resubmitted in substantially the same form for at least three years.

Subject to this provision the legislature should have power, by majority vote, to submit at any time the question of electing a convention to revise the constitution. If the people vote in the affirmative, the number of delegates to the convention and the procedure in electing them should be in accordance with provisions already established in the administrative code.

ESSENTIAL REFORMS

The foregoing propositions are not put forth as matured conclusions; in fact, I should be unwilling to go to jail as a martyr for any or all of them. They are offered merely as a basis for discussion, in the hope that attention can be focused upon the essential improvements which are needed in state constitutions. These essential reforms would seem to be, first of all, a return to the original philosophy of the constitution as an embodiment of the fundamental law. This, it is believed, could be facilitated by the setting up of an administrative code which would serve as a carryall for the miscellaneous provisions of a non-fundamental character which are now incorporated in state constitutions. Second, there should be a simplifying of the legislative organization, with forthright provision for effective leadership. The latter could be most readily accomplished by increasing the powers and privileges of the governor, making him prime minister as well as titular chief executive. Even with this extension of executive authority and responsibility, however, the attainment of high standards in state administration is not to be counted upon so long as subordinate offices are filled by those who owe both their appointments and their promotions to considerations of party service and influence. All such posts should be filled on a merit basis, the incumbents given adequate security of tenure, promotions made on the basis of efficiency records, and the service of the commonwealth raised to the dignity of a profession. Such provisions, however, are not appropriate in the constitution but in the administrative code—and what would constitute an ideal administrative code is another story.

26. *Public Relations and State Constitutions* *

MANY CONSTITUTIONS have been written and adopted in the American states, and many others have been drafted and rejected. Why should the voters of one state reject a constitution that was every bit as good as one adopted at about the same time by another state electorate? The answer based on the investigation of a specific case would undoubtedly reveal a combination of factors, some dominant and others less significant. However, it is increasingly apparent in our time that one very common factor is that of public relations. Mr. Keith here reviews this aspect of constitutional revision in several states that have within recent years adopted new constitutions.

CHARLTON Chute who took a leading part in the revision movement in Missouri has written the subsequent paragraph which typifies the experience of those who have participated in constitutional revision campaigns:

> Probably no state constitution will be either amended or rewritten until a large share of the people believes that there is need for change. This is fundamental. It underlies the whole procedure of constitutional revision. In Missouri, where a new constitution was adopted in 1945, an informed electorate was at the very heart of success.

In every case in which a state has attempted to revise its constitution in the last fifteen years the need for a campaign to develop public sentiment has been felt. What can be learned about public relations from other states that have modernized their constitutions?

The few states that have been successful in revising their constitutions in recent years, New York in 1938, Georgia and Missouri in 1945, and New Jersey in 1947, have all profited from public relations efforts of concerned citizens. As might be expected, the extent and strength of the publicity had a direct bearing on the results of the revision endeavor. Despite its supreme importance, very little information exists on the publicity campaigns conducted in these states. From what information does exist, certain deductions can be drawn. These deduc-

* John P. Keith, *Public Relations Program for a Citizen Committee* (Austin: Bureau of Municipal Research, The University of Texas, 1950), pp. 62-71. Reprinted by permission of The University of Texas.

tions serve to point out how others handled problems similar to those which your citizen committee now faces.

NEW YORK

In New York the constitution specifies that the people shall vote on the following question at least once in every twenty years: "Shall there be a Convention to revise the Constitution and amend the same?" Under the terms of this requirement, in 1936 Governor Lehman signed a bill which authorized a popular referendum on the question. Although both political parties were luke-warm to the idea of a convention, the voters approved the call.

After a convention ridden with the strife of party politics, a revised constitution draft was submitted to the people in a series of nine amendments, six of which were approved in November, 1938. The National Municipal League made the only organized effort to inform the citizenry about the issues which were involved in this move to revise the fundamental law of New York State. The League established a constitutional committee composed of forty college presidents and the heads of most of the state-wide civic organizations. Despite the activities of this committee, a perusal of O'Rourke and Campbell's study of the convention will convince the reader that the average voter was only partially informed about the basic issues which were being considered by the convention.

Because of his lack of information, the voter was disinterested in the proceedings at the convention. This is not a healthy condition for the future of democracy. The lesson for those who are embarking on an effort to secure an improved state constitution is this: unless a definitive public relations program is developed and a strenuous publicity campaign is undertaken well in advance of the call for a convention, special interests are likely to take advantage of the uninformed electorate to further their own ends. Perhaps this is the best argument against incorporating a clause in a constitution requiring a vote on constitutional revision at stated periods. A large majority of citizens must be intelligently aroused about the subject before constitutional revision is contemplated; otherwise, the whole attempt is apt to fail of its purpose. The only worthwhile convention is the one that results from the pressure of genuine public interest.

GEORGIA

Georgia's revised constitution was written by a commission established for that purpose. The draft was subsequently approved by the legislature and by the people as a single amendment to the then existing document. Two citizen groups, The League of Women Voters and the Citizens' Fact-Finding Movement of Geogia, were instrumental in watching over the drafting process and in publicizing the results. The newspapers of the state, especially the *Atlanta Journal* and the *Atlanta Constitution*, performed yeoman service in centering public attention on the proposed document.

The Georgia experience offers one extremely important observation. Governor Ellis Arnall was carrying on his famous fight with Eugene Talmadge at the time. The adoption of the new constitution in 1945 was a significant victory for the Arnall forces. It was the strength of the governor's personality and his sincere desire to see the Georgia constitution brought up-to-date that inspired the adoption of the revised document. The chances for success of a constitutional reform movement are considerably enhanced if it has strong political leadership, preferably from the administration in power. A governor or a party leader can't do the job alone, but he can help make citizen toil bear fruit.

MISSOURI

Previous to the campaign of 1941-1945 which culminated in success, Missouri had experienced several abortive attempts to revise the state constitution, as have many of her sister states. In fact, many people were convinced that another revision attempt was futile. More has been written on how the citizens of Missouri accomplished their task than on the work of the citizen groups in the other states. . . .

Two campaigns were conducted; the second being a reorganized extension of the first. In 1941 the Statewide Committee for the Revision of the Missouri Constitution was formed. The committee was composed of two delegates and two alternates from each of the state's thirty-four senatorial districts and a number of delegates at large, chosen to represent various business, labor, and civic groups. The total membership approximated one hundred and fifty. Each of these persons was a man of considerable importance in his community. The committee's purpose was to arouse public sentiment for the calling of a constitutional convention.

The activities of the Missouri committee were supervised by a steering committee and six standing committees: press, radio, finance, speakers and meetings, research and publications, and a subcommittee to co-ordinate the efforts of other interested organizations. In addition, local committees were organized in each senatorial district and active support of all state-wide groups was sought. A woman lawyer

(Democrat), with campaign experience, served as full-time paid director of the revision committee. Assisting her was a lawyer with extensive political experience (Republican). Ten field men were employed. Each was assigned from ten to twelve rural counties. These men reached the voters in practically every precinct by seeing that an active organization was established in every county.

The committee used every means available to inform the people of the necessity for revising the constitution. A manual on county organization, which also set forth methods of raising money, went to each delegate. Editorials were sent regularly to over seven hundred newspapers. Six hundred thousand pamphlets were distributed through the Chamber of Commerce and local political committees. Billboard space was obtained gratis. Voters' guides were placed in street cars and busses. Statements of support were secured from ex-governors, mayors, and businessmen; the political parties adopted planks in their platforms favoring constitutional revision; every clergyman in the state received a letter asking him to endorse the project from his pulpit; luncheon clubs set aside constitution days; every major organization in the state was asked to pass an identical resolution supporting constitutional revision; free radio time was engaged; editorial space was procured in house organs; many groups assigned speakers to the speakers' bureau which scheduled over five thousand speeches and was composed of some one hundred and seventy persons; and finally, in the closing hours of the campaign, a group of women conducted a telephone drive to get out the vote.

This overwhelming cannonade of publicity resulted in an affirmative vote for a constitutional convention. After the convention concluded its deliberations, a new committee called the Missouri Committee for the New Constitution was organized, and it conducted with renewed vigor the campaign for adoption of the revised constitution. Together the campaigns are estimated to have cost approximately one hundred thousand dollars.

NEW JERSEY

The representatives of the Committee for Constitutional Revision and the close liaison between that group and the New Jersey Constitution Foundation has already been described. In addition to these noteworthy achievements, New Jersey's campaign offers several other important object lessons.

A small group of New Jersey citizens were agitating for constitutional revision as early as 1940. In 1941, the legislature established a commission to draft a new constitution but failed to act on the commission's recommendations when they were submitted a year later. By good fortune, in 1943, a bill to provide for a referendum on the question of having the legislature act as a convention passed the legislature, and at the referendum the people of the state signified their acceptance of the plan. But in November, 1944, the proposed constitution as written by the legislature was decisively defeated. During that campaign, the Hague machine is estimated to have spent over a half million dollars in order to prevent a favorable vote.

Governor Driscoll, newly elected in 1946, made the question of revision the foremost item on his agenda, as had his predecessors, Edison and Edge. Again a referendum was successful and this time the document drafted during the summer of 1947 was adopted at the polls by a sizable majority. All the hard work that had gone into the various campaigns during the intervening years had laid the foundation for victory. The whole effort was characterized by the perserverance of the citizens of New Jersey in carrying through the project to completion.

There is nothing so effective as organization in the voting districts. At first the New Jersey committee placed reliance almost solely on newspaper publicity and mailing lists. It was doorbell pushing that finally carried the day. As one delegate to the convention expresses it:

> No campaign carried on from one central office can be as effective as an organization reaching down into each county and town. The story of revision, to reach the people, must be brought to them at home, by direct contact, as well as by all available advertising media.

This same delegate, Mrs. Jane Barus, has two other thoughts from her experience in participating in the New Jersey revision. The first is to provide for differences of opinion within the citizen committee. New Jersey's committee was made up of representatives of various state organizations as well as individuals. Unless all the constituent organizations belonging to the committee were on record as favoring a particular policy with respect to rewriting the constitution, the committee did not make a recommendation thereon. This left each organization free to support its own ideas on items upon which agreement could not be reached and as Mrs. Barus expresses it, "This wise provision made it possible for widely differing groups to work together (the Taxpayers' Association and the CIO, for example), and to present a solid front on a substantial number of proposals." Her second observation provides an appropriate closing note for this study of a public relations program for a citizen committee, "A revision campaign is an expensive affair. It requires an office, executive and clerical staff, and substantial sums for printing, mailing, radio and newspaper advertising—and above all organization."

27. *Charter for Last Frontier* *

RECENTLY a convention in the territory of Alaska submitted to the people of that territory a proposed constitution for the hoped-for state of Alaska. While Congress has repeatedly refused to grant statehood to Hawaii and Alaska, both territories have now prepared constitutions against the day of admission. They hope thus to dramatize their positions as seekers of and suppliants for statehood and spur Congress to favorable action on the dormant statehood bills. The problems of constitution-making and admission to statehood are recurring ones in our history. Alaska has been able to draw upon the past experience of all other states in this attempt to solve its own. The members of the convention are convinced that as a result they have avoided many of the mistakes of their predecessors and incorporated many of the best features of the more recent advances in modern constitution-making.

AN ERA IN American history ended at 9:59 A.M., Alaska standard time, February 6, 1956. At that hour the Alaska Constitutional Convention adjourned after three months of work on a constitution for the fondly conceived state of Alaska. Neither snow, nor ice fog at 55 below zero, nor the long Arctic nights had delayed any meeting of the convention or diverted the members for a moment from their appointed task. Thus, 164 years after a convention in Kentucky wrote the constitution for the first frontier state to be admitted to the original Union of thirteen, the people of "the last frontier" on the American continent laid a similar basis for admission as the 49th or 50th state.

A sense both of history and of destiny sat with the 55 delegates throughout their deliberations at Constitution Hall on the campus of the University of Alaska at College, just a few miles west of Fairbanks. Many factors contributed to this: the number 55, chosen in emulation of the 55-member Philadelphia convention of 1787; the belief of

* John E. Bebout, *National Municipal Review*, XLV (April, 1956), pp. 158-163. Reprinted by permission of the *National Municipal Review*.

Alaskans in the limitless future of their vast land and their pride in being the last of the pioneers of the old tradition; the personal dedication evidenced by the members of the convention; and the university setting which was conducive to the remarkable industry and concentration which they devoted to their work.

The constitution, which will be voted upon by the people of Alaska on April 24, preparatory to submission to the Congress, represents the blending of the classic and the modern in American constitutional practice. "A Report to the People of Alaska," issued at the direction of the Constitutional Convention, states that in writing the constitution the convention had been determined that:

1. It should embody the best of America's 180 years of experience in self-government;
2. It should fit the special needs and traditions of Alaska;
3. It should be short and flexible, to allow for the great changes that the future will bring to Alaska;
4. It should provide for a government that is energetic in fostering the growth and development of the whole state and the welfare of all the people;
5. It should respect and guard the equal rights and dignity of all citizens.

"To accomplish these ends," the report continues, "the convention prepared a simple plan of state government that is characteristically American." This "simple plan" calls for "a legislature composed of a Senate of 20 members elected for four-year terms and a House of Representatives of 40 members elected for two-year terms"; an integrated state administration headed by a governor elected for a four-year term and eligible to succeed himself once; and a unified court system substantially on the New Jersey model, with judges selected by the governor, as in Missouri, on nomination of a judicial council composed of representatives of the bar and the lay public.

SIMPLE DESIGN

The report explains that "This system in its essential features is very similar to that of the national government in Washington. This is because the convention found that the state governments that worked best were those that conformed most closely to the simple design given to the government of the United States by the convention that met in Philadelphia in 1787."

The members of the convention were well equipped for their work. Every stateside consultant observed that the average of competence, intellectual integrity and devotion to the common cause was very high for a deliberative body of its size.

The convention was the most representative assembly ever elected in Alaska. Election of the members of the territorial legislature at large from each of four vast districts has resulted in underrepresentation of the scattered population outside the cities. The law providing for the convention avoided this by setting up smaller representative districts. The result was that while 31 of the delegates came from Anchorage, Fairbanks and Juneau, the remaining 24 were divided among nineteen communities ranging from Kotzebue, "the Eskimo capital" of the northwest, to Ketchikan, "the fishing capital" of the southeast. Other places represented include Nenana, a city of about 400 people on the Tanana River southwest of Fairbanks; Nome; Unalakleet, a native village on Norton Sound; Dillingham, fishing center for the Bristol Bay area; Kodiak, site of the first Russian settlement; Seward and Homer on the Kenai Peninsula; Valdez, seaport for central Alaska; Palmer, in the Matanuska Valley; Sitka, long-time capital of Alaska. This distribution not only brought to the convention knowledge of the problems involved in tailoring government to all parts of an area more than twice as large as Texas but also helped every member of the convention develop a more comprehensive understanding of Alaska as a whole.

The geographical distribution was matched by a wide variety of occupational experience. There were thirteen lawyers, nine store owners, four mining men, four fishermen, three housewives, two ministers, two pilots, two freighting operators, two hotel men. Other occupations included news distributor, city planner, editor, architect, homesteader, real estate dealer, banker, publicity man, photographer.

Several of the delegates, including Chairman William Egan, Valdez storekeeper, had served in one or both houses of the territorial legislature, while others had held other territorial or local offices. Few deliberative assemblies have been so fortunate in their choice of chairman. Mr. Egan presided with a combination of firmness, fairness and humor that had much to do with welding a group of comparative strangers, inclined to be suspicious of one another, into a body of friends and coworkers united by mutual respect and common purpose.

Many of the delegates have lived in Alaska all or most of their lives. A number of these, as well as others who had come more recently from the states, had derived from stateside education or experience considerable understanding of the operation and problems of state and local governments.

COMMITTEE MAKES PLANS

A careful job of advance planning for the convention was done by the Alaska Statehood Committee. Public Administration Service was engaged to prepare a series of constitutional studies. These were substantially similar in coverage to studies made for state constitutional conventions in recent years but they were fresh in approach and were specifically oriented to Alaskan conditions. A small but good working library was assembled for the use of the convention and PAS served as hiring agent for a number of stateside consultants selected by the convention to work with it and its committees for limited periods of time while it was in session.

The convention made good use of the documentary and personal assistance available to it. Its committees drove themselves and their consultants hard. Committee members showed that they had studied the PAS papers and other materials available to them carefully and to good effect. The *Model State Constitution* of the National Municipal League, the 1947 New Jersey constitution and the proposed constitution for the state of Hawaii were constantly referred to and used as sources of language, ideas and argument.

Other state constitutions were resorted to both for models and for horrible examples of what the convention wished to avoid. The convention was particularly conscious of such defects of older state constitutions as the long ballot, detailed provisions affecting county and other local governments, inclusion of inappropriate and restrictive legislative material, and failure to provide effective self-executing provisions for legislative reapportionment, for local home rule or for future constitutional conventions. The determination not to import unnecessary governmental baggage from the older states was perhaps best displayed in the local government article, the first section of which reads:

> The purpose of this article is to provide for maximum local self-government with a minimum of local government units, and to prevent duplication of tax-levying jurisdictions. A liberal construction shall be given to the powers of local government units.

"COUNTY" RULED OUT

So convinced was the convention of the weaknesses common to county governments that it sought to rule out even the name county by providing in section 2 that "all local government powers shall be vested in boroughs and cities." The boroughs correspond roughly in area and function to counties in the older states but the provisions of the local government article are designed to avoid major weaknesses that plague county governments: rigid, immovable boundaries; a multiplicity of elected officials and independent agencies; inadequate fiscal and other powers.

The convention recognized that much of Alaska would not need two layers of local government, at least for a long time to come. Consequently, it provided that while the whole state should be divided into boroughs, borough governments should be organized only as needed. Special districts are discouraged by providing that "the state may delegate taxing powers to organized boroughs and cities only" but service areas may be established by the government of an organized borough or by the legislature in an unorganized borough.

Self-executing home rule is provided for first-class cities and boroughs and the legislature is authorized to extend similar home rule powers to others. Coordination between a borough government and the governments of the major cities within it is facilitated by requiring that first-class cities shall be represented on the governing body of the borough by selected members of their councils.

Boundaries of cities and boroughs are to be subject to change in accordance with procedures prescribed by a local boundary commission to be established by law in the executive branch of the state government, or by order of such commission subject to reversal by a concurrent resolution of the legislature. The importance of technical assistance to local government is recognized by the provision that "an agency shall be established by law in the executive branch of the state government to advise and assist local governments."

By these provisions the convention sought to leave future state legislatures free to develop a system of local government adapted to the needs of the people of Alaska, subject only to constitutional guide lines designed to prevent the disorderly, unplanned accumulation of local authorities with which most of the older states are burdened.

Evidence of similar thinking with respect to the good and the bad in stateside experience is to be found in many other parts of the constitution. The executive article, for example, calls for the independent election of the governor only. It avoids even an independently elected lieutenant governor by providing that the legal stand-in and replacement for the governor shall be the secretary of state, whose election is tied in with that of the governor. The governor will be chief executive in fact as well as in name, with effective power to reorganize state administration.

Special care was given to the article on natural resources. Members of the convention were mindful of the failures of older states with respect to the conservation and development of their resources. They were also acutely conscious of the inability of Alaskans under territorial rule to persuade the national government to take or permit certain kinds of action which they regard as necessary to the proper development and protection of the resources of the country. Relying upon the provisions of the latest enabling act considered by the Congress, it is assumed that when statehood is granted a substantial fraction of the public lands now held by the United States will be turned over to the state of Alaska, subject to certain safeguards set forth in the act. Accordingly, article 8 of the proposed constitution seeks to provide for a balance between maximum current use of natural resources and the preservation and expansion of them for future generations. Where practicable the same area is to be subject to development concurrently for different purposes, while replenishable resources belonging to the state are to be so administered as to sustain, not to exhaust, the yield.

The structure of the legislature and the apportionment of its members naturally caused a great deal of soul-searching and debate. Early in the convention a strong plea was made for a unicameral legislature. The proposal was defeated by a decisive vote although there is indication that this was influenced partly by the feeling that the Congress might view a unicameral legislature with some misgivings. Attachment to the unicameral idea is indicated in a number of provisions for action by the two houses sitting together as one body, as, for example, to consider vetoes by the governor.

APPORTIONMENT PROBLEM

In most of the older states the central problem of legislative apportionment is how to provide fair representation to the growing cities. The Alaska convention faced the opposite problem of how to mitigate the urban domination which has impaired the effectiveness of territorial legislatures. The representative pattern of the convention itself actually provided a starting point for a rather complicated solution. Representation is given to all parts of the territory, substantially in accordance with population, in the lower house. In the upper house area is given primary consideration by providing that each of four major socio-economic divisions, roughly corresponding to the four existing judicial and representative divisions, shall always have a certain amount of representation. Substantial reapportionment of the lower house and limited revision of district lines for the upper house are to be carried out every ten years by the governor, subject to the advice of a reapportionment board. The members of the convention were very clear that reapportionment should not depend on action by the legislature itself.

No one pretended to know just how the system of representation, particularly in the Senate, would work out. However, if population growth is such that the Senate becomes painfully unrepresentative of the interests of the state as a whole, it is reasonable to suppose that the system will be altered by a future constitutional convention.

The delegates felt that revision of the constitution should not be at the mercy of future state legislatures. Consequently, the people are to be permitted to vote at least once every ten years on whether or not to have a constitutional convention. Unless both houses of the legislature agree to a law providing for a different basis of representation, the next convention will be based upon substantially the same representative districts as was the recent convention, a plan which guarantees that any convention held within the reasonable future cannot be too unrepresentative of the people of Alaska.

Unlike a convention in an established state, the Alaska convention had a double problem. It had to consider not only what would be acceptable to the people of Alaska but also how it could best advance the cause of statehood. This influenced to some extent specific provisions of the constitution but led also to the adoption of the so-called Alaska-Tennessee Plan. George Lehleitner of New Orleans called this plan to the attention of the prospective delegates to the convention even before they were elected. It is based upon a precedent first set by Tennessee, the first state after Kentucky to be admitted to the new Union, and later followed successfully by six other territories. Under this plan, when the people vote on the constitution they will vote separately on whether or not they want to elect two United States senators and a representative to go to Washington next January and apply for seats in the Congress. This revival of an old method of dramatizing and expediting the objective of statehood is quite in keeping with the spirit with which the convention went about its whole task. Alaskans apparently believe that it is just as logical to use a short-cut toward membership in the Union and representation in the Congress in the air age as it was in the stage coach era.

V

CIVIL RIGHTS

28. *Gitlow v. New York*

SUPREME COURT OF THE UNITED STATES,
1925 (ERROR) 268 U.S. 652

Gitlow was convicted in a New York court for violating the state Criminal Anarchy Act. His specific offenses were the writing of the "Left Wing Manifesto" and the printing, publishing, and distribution of the "Revolutionary Age," both publications allegedly advocating the overthrow of government by force. Following his conviction in the state courts, Gitlow appealed to the Supreme Court, challenging the Act as contrary to the due process of law clause of the Fourteenth Amendment.

Although the Court upheld the conviction of Gitlow, the case has significance because, in agreeing to pass on the constitutionality of the state law, the Court established for the first time that freedom of speech and the press, protected against Federal action by the First Amendment, were also "fundamental liberties," protected against state attack by the word "liberty" in the Fourteenth Amendment. The effect of this decision was to begin the "nationalization" of the First Amendment of the Bill of Rights that had previously been resisted by the Supreme Court in *Barron* v. *Baltimore* (7 Peters 243) and in *The Slaughterhouse Cases* (16 Wallace 36). The extent of "nationalization" under the liberty clause has, however, been limited by the Court to the protection of the "substantive" rights included in the First Amendment and has not included procedural ones (see Selection 29, *Palko* v. *Connecticut*). Federal protection of procedural rights has been approached independently of the Gitlow doctrine by interpretation of the "equal protection of the laws" clause and the "due process of law" clause of the Fourteenth Amendment (see Selection 30, *Norris* v. *Alabama*).

Opinion of the Court

MR. JUSTICE SANFORD delivered the opinion of the Court:

. . . .

The indictment was in two counts. The first charged that the defendants had advocated, advised, and taught the duty, necessity, and propriety of overthrowing and overturning organized government by force, violence, and unlawful means, by certain writings therein set forth, entitled, "The Left Wing Manifesto"; the second, that the defendants had printed, published, and knowingly circulated and distributed a certain paper called "The Revolutionary Age," containing the writings set forth in the first count, advocating, advising, and teaching the doctrine that organized government should be overthrown by force, violence, and unlawful means.

. . . It was admitted that the defendant signed a card subscribing to the Manifesto and Program of the Left Wing, which all applicants were required to sign before being admitted to membership; that he went to different parts of the state to speak to branches of the Socialist party about the principles of the Left Wing, and advocated their adoption; and that he was responsible for the Manifesto as it appeared, that "he knew of the publication, in a general way, and he knew of its publication afterwards, and is responsible for its circulation." . . .

There was no evidence of any effect resulting from the publication and circulation of the Manifesto.

The precise question presented, and the only question which we can consider under this writ of error, then, is whether the statute, as construed and applied in this case by the state courts, deprived the defendant of his liberty of expression, in violation of the due process clause of the Fourteenth Amendment.

The statute does not penalize the utterance or publication of abstract "doctrine" or academic discussion having no quality of incitement to any concrete action. It is not aimed against mere historical or philosophical essays. It does not restrain the advocacy of changes in the form of government by constitutional and lawful means. What it prohibits is language advocating, advising, or teaching the overthrow of organized government by unlawful means. These words imply urging to action. . . .

The Manifesto, plainly, is neither the statement of abstract doctrine nor, as suggested by counsel, mere prediction that industrial disturbances and revolutionary mass strikes will result spontaneously in an inevitable process of evolution in the economic system. It advocates and urges in fervent language mass action which shall progressively foment industrial disturbances, and, through political mass strikes and revolutionary mass action, overthrow and destroy organized parliamentary government. It concludes with a call to action in these words: "The proletariat revolution and the Communist reconstruction of society—*the struggle for these*—is now indispensable. . . . The Communist International calls the proletariat of the world to the final struggle!" This is not the expression of philosophical abstraction, the mere prediction of future events: it is the language of direct incitement.

. . . That the jury were warranted in finding that the Manifesto advocated not merely the abstract doctrine of overwhelming organized government by force, violence, and unlawful means, but action to that end, is clear.

For the present purposes we may and do assume that freedom of speech and of the press—which are protected by the First Amendment from abridgment by Congress—are among the fundamental personal rights and "liberties" protected by the due process clause of the Fourteenth Amendment from impairment by the states. . . .

It is a fundamental principle, long established, that the freedom of speech and of the press which is secured by the Constitution does not confer an absolute right to speak or publish, without responsibility, whatever one may choose, or an unrestricted and unbridled license that gives immunity for every possible use of language, and prevents the punishment of those who abuse this freedom. 2 Story, Const. 5th ed. section 1580, p. 634. . . . Reasonably limited, it was said by Story in the passage cited, this freedom is an inestimable privilege in a free government; without such limitation, it might become the scourge of the republic.

That a state, in the exercise of its police power, may punish those who abuse this freedom by utterances inimical to the public welfare, tending to corrupt public morals, incite to crime, or disturb the public peace, is not open to question. . . .

. . . And a state may penalize utterances which openly advocate the overthrow of the representative and constitutional form of government of the United States and the several states, by violence or other unlawful means. . . . In short, this freedom does not deprive a state of the primary and essential right of self-preservation, which, so long as human governments endure, they cannot be denied. . . .

By enacting the present statute the state has determined, through its legislative body, that utterances advocating the overthrow of organized government by force, violence, and unlawful means, are so inimical to the general welfare, and involve such danger of substantive evil, that they may be penalized in the exercise of its police power. That determination must be given great weight. Every presumption is to be indulged in favor of the validity of the statute. . . . That utterances inciting to the overthrow of organized government by unlawful means present a sufficient danger of substantive evil to bring their punishment within the range of legislative discretion is clear. Such utterances, by their very nature, involve danger to the public peace and to the security of the state. They threaten breaches of the peace and ultimate revolution. And the immediate danger is none the less real and substantial because the effect of a given utterance cannot be accurately foreseen. The state cannot reasonably be required to measure the danger from every such utterance in the nice balance of a jeweler's scale. A single revolutionary spark may kindle a fire that, smoldering for a time, may burst into a sweeping and destructive conflagration. It cannot be said that the state is acting arbitrarily or unreasonably when, in the exercise of its judgment as to the measures necessary to protect the public peace and safety, it seeks to extinguish the spark without waiting until it has enkindled the flame or blazed into the conflagration. It cannot reasonably be required to defer the adoption of measures for its own peace and safety until the revolutionary utterances lead to actual disturbances of the public peace or imminent and immediate danger of its own destruction; but it may, in the exercise of its judgment, suppress the threatened danger in its incipiency . . .

We cannot hold that the present statute is an arbitrary or unreasonable exercise of the police power of the state, unwarrantably infringing the freedom of speech or press; and we must and do sustain its constitutionality. . . .

It is clear that the question in such cases is entirely different from that involved in those cases where the statute merely prohibits certain acts involving the danger of substantive evil, without any reference to language itself, and it is sought to apply its provisions to language used by the defendant for the purpose of bringing about the prohibited results. There, if it be contended that the statute cannot be applied to the language used by the defendant because of its protection by the freedom of speech or press, it must necessarily be found, as an original question, without any previous determination by the legislative body, whether the specific language used involved such likelihood of bringing about the substantive evil as to deprive it of the constitutional protection. In such cases it has been held that the general provisions of the statute may be constitutionally applied to the specific utterance of the defendant if its natural tendency and probable effect were to bring about the substantive evil which the legislative body might prevent. Schenck v. United States, 249 U.S. 51; Debs v. United States, 249 U.S. 215. . . .

And finding, for the reasons stated, that the statute is not in itself unconstitutional, and that it has not been applied in the present case in derogation of any constitutional right, the judgment of the court of appeals is affirmed.

MR. JUSTICE HOLMES, dissenting:

Mr. Justice Brandeis and I are of opinion that this judgment should be reversed. The general principle of free speech, it seems to me, must be taken to be included in the Fourteenth Amendment, in view of the scope that has been given to the word "liberty" as there used, although perhaps it may be accepted with a somewhat larger latitude of interpretation than is allowed to Congress by the sweeping language that governs or ought to govern the laws of the United States. If I am right, then I think that the criterion sanctioned by the full court in *Schenck* v. *United States*, 249 U. S. 47, applies:

"The question in every case is whether the words used are used in such circumstances and are of such a nature as to create a clear and present danger that they will bring about the substantive evils that [the state] has a right to prevent."

It is true that in my opinion this criterion was departed from in *Abrams* v. *United States*, 250 U. S. 616, but the convictions that I expressed in that case are too deep for it to be possible for me as yet to believe that it and *Schaefer* v. *United States*, 251 U. S. 466, have settled the law. If what I think the correct test is applied, it is manifest that there was no present danger of an attempt to overthrow the government by force on the part of the admittedly small minority who shared the defendant's views. It is said that this manifesto was more than a theory, that it was an incitement. Every idea is an incitement. It offers itself for belief and if believed it is acted on unless some other belief outweighs it or some failure of energy stifles the movement at its birth. The only difference between the expression of an opinion and an incitement in the narrower sense is the speaker's enthusiasm for the result. Eloquence may set fire to reason. But whatever may be thought of the redundant discourse before us it had no chance of starting a present conflagration. If in the long run the beliefs expressed in proletarian dictatorship are destined to be accepted by the dominant forces of the community, the only meaning of free speech is that they should be given their chance and have their way.

If the publication of this document had been laid as an attempt to induce an uprising against government at once and not at some indefinite time in the future it would have presented a different question. The object would have been one with which the law might deal, subject to the doubt whether there was any danger that the publication could produce any result, or in other words, whether it was not futile and too remote from possible consequences. But the indictment alleges the publication and nothing more.

29. *Palko v. Connecticut*

SUPREME COURT OF THE UNITED STATES
1937 (APPEAL) 302 U.S. 319

THIS CASE involves double jeopardy and the extent to which the Federal Bill of Rights protects citizens from state action in this regard. The Court noted in its decision that the double jeopardy clause of the Fifth Amendment is applicable only to the Federal government. Accordingly, a state statute allowing appeal in criminal cases by the state, under certain conditions and for the correction of error, is constitutional and does not constitute a denial of due process by the state under the Fourteenth Amendment. The Court viewed the Fourteenth Amendment as extending protection to "substantive rights" endangered by state action but not to "procedural rights," such as protection against double jeopardy. The importance of the case lies in its clearer delineation of the character of the "nationalization" concept developed in *Gitlow* v. *New York* (268 U.S. 652), presented in the preceding selection.

Opinion of the Court

MR. JUSTICE CARDOZO delivered the opinion of the Court:

A statute of Connecticut permitting appeals in criminal cases to be taken by the state is challenged by appellant as an infringement of the Fourteenth Amendment of the Constitution of the United States. Whether the challenge should be upheld is now to be determined.

Appellant was indicted in Fairfield County, Connecticut, for the crime of murder in the first degree. A jury found him guilty of murder in the second degree, and he was sentenced to confinement in the state prison for life. Thereafter the State of Connecticut, with the permission of the judge presiding at the trial, gave notice of appeal to the Supreme Court of Errors. This it did pursuant to an act adopted in 1886 which is printed in the margin. Public Acts, 1886, p. 560; now § 6494 of the General Statutes. Upon such appeal, the Supreme Court of Errors reversed the judgment and ordered a new trial. *State*

v. *Palko*, 121 Conn. 669; 186 Atl. 657. It found that there had been error of law to the prejudice of the state (1) in excluding testimony as to a confession by defendant; (2) in excluding testimony upon cross-examination of defendant to impeach his credibility, and (3) in the instructions to the jury as to the difference between first and second degree murder.

Pursuant to the mandate of the Supreme Court of Errors, defendant was brought to trial again. Before a jury was impaneled and also at later stages of the case he made the objection that the effect of the new trial was to place him twice in jeopardy for the same offense, and in so doing to violate the Fourteenth Amendment of the Constitution of the United States. Upon the over-ruling of the objection the trial proceeded. The jury returned a verdict of murder in the first degree, and the court sentenced the defendant to the punishment of death. The Supreme Court of Errors affirmed the judgment of conviction. . . .

1. The execution of the sentence will not deprive appellant of his life without the process of law assured to him by the Fourteenth Amendment of the Federal Constitution.

The argument for appellant is that whatever is forbidden by the Fifth Amendment is forbidden by the Fourteenth also. The Fifth Amendment, which is not directed to the states, but solely to the federal government, creates immunity from double jeopardy. No person shall be "subject for the same offense to be twice put in jeopardy of life or limb." The Fourteenth Amendment ordains, "nor shall any State deprive any person of life, liberty, or property, without due process of law." To retry a defendant, though under one indictment and only one, subjects him, it is said, to double jeopardy in violation of the Fifth Amendment, if the prosecution is one on behalf of the United States. From this the consequence is said to follow that there is a denial of life or liberty without due process of law, if the prosecution is one on behalf of the People of a State. . . .

We have said that in appellant's view the Fourteenth Amendment is to be taken as embodying the prohibitions of the Fifth. His thesis is even broader. Whatever would be a violation of the original bill of rights (Amendments I to VIII) if done by the federal government is now equally unlawful by force of the Fourteenth Amendment if done by a state. There is no such general rule.

The Fifth Amendment provides, among other things, that no person shall be held to answer for a capital or otherwise infamous crime unless on presentment or indictment of a grand jury. This court has held that, in prosecutions by a state, presentment or indictment by a grand jury may give way to informations at the instance of a public officer. *Hurtado* v. *California*, 110 U.S. 516; *Gaines* v. *Washington*, 277 U.S. 81,

86. The Fifth Amendment provides also that no person shall be compelled in any criminal case to be a witness against himself. This court has said that, in prosecutions by a state, the exemption will fail if the state elects to end it. *Twining* v. *New Jersey*, 211 U.S. 78, 106, 111, 112. . . . The Sixth Amendment calls for a jury trial in criminal cases and the Seventh for a jury trial in civil cases at common law where the value in controversy shall exceed twenty dollars. This court has ruled that consistently with those amendments trial by jury may be modified by a state or abolished altogether. . . .

On the other hand, the due process clause of the Fourteenth Amendment may make it unlawful for a state to abridge by its statutes the freedom of speech which the First Amendment safeguards against encroachment by the Congress. . . . In these and other situations immunities that are valid as against the federal government by force of the specific pledges of particular amendments have been found to be implicit in the concept of ordered liberty, and thus, through the Fourteenth Amendment, become valid as against the states.

The line of division may seem to be wavering and broken if there is a hasty catalogue of the cases on the one side and the other. Reflection and analysis will induce a different view. There emerges the perception of a rationalizing principle which gives to discrete instances a proper order and coherence. The right to trial by jury and the immunity from prosecution except as the result of an indictment may have value and importance. Even so, they are not of the very essence of a scheme of ordered liberty. To abolish them is not to violate a "principle of justice so rooted in the traditions and conscience of our people as to be ranked as fundamental." *Snyder* v. *Massachusetts*, [291 U.S. 97] . . . Few would be so narrow or provincial as to maintain that a fair and enlightened system of justice would be impossible without them. What is true of jury trials and indictments is true also, as the cases show, of the immunity from compulsory self-incrimination. *Twining* v. *New Jersey, supra*. This too might be lost, and justice still be done. . . .

Our survey of the cases serves, we think, to justify the statement that the dividing line between them, if not unfaltering throughout its course, has been true for the most part to a unifying principle. On which side of the line the case made out by the appellant has appropriate location must be the next inquiry and the final one. Is that kind of double jeopardy to which the statute has subjected him a hardship so acute and shocking that our polity will not endure it? Does it violate those "fundamental principles of liberty and justice which lie at the base of all our civil and political institutions?" *Hebert* v. *Louisiana*, [272 U.S. 312]. The answer surely must be "no." What the answer would have to be if the state were permitted after a trial free from error to try the accused over again or to bring another case against him, we have no occasion to consider. We deal with the statute before us and no other. The state is not attempting to wear the accused out by a multitude of cases with accumulated trials. It asks no more than this, that the case against him shall go on until there shall be a trial free from the corrosion of substantial legal error. *State* v. *Felch*, 92 Vt. 477; 105 Atl. 23; . . . This is not cruelty at all, nor even vexation in any immoderate degree. If the trial had been infected with error adverse to the accused, there might have been review at his instance, and as often as necessary to purge the vicious taint. A reciprocal privilege, subject at all times to the discretion of the presiding judge, *State* v. *Carbetta*, 106 Conn. 114; 127 Atl. 394, has now been granted to the state. There is here no seismic innovation. The edifice of justice stands, its symmetry, to many, greater than before.

2. The conviction of appellant is not in derogation of any privileges or immunities that belong to him as a citizen of the United States. . . .

The judgment is

Affirmed

(Mr. Justice Butler dissents.)

30. *Norris v. Alabama*

SUPREME COURT OF THE UNITED STATES
1935 (CERTIORARI) 294 U.S. 587

THE ADMINISTRATION OF JUSTICE to the Negro in the South has long presented a serious problem. In this case the Supreme Court reviewed a state conviction of a Negro on the charge of rape. The point at issue was the lawfulness of the procedure in the state court, in view of the fact that no Negro had been seated on the trial jury. The Court held that the systematic and arbitrary exclusion of Negroes from a jury list in a case in which a Negro was on trial constituted a denial by the state to the Negro of equal protection of the laws under the Fourteenth Amendment. The case is an instructive example of the use of the equal protection of the laws clause by the Supreme Court to protect the civil liberties of a minority group. In practice the Court decision has resulted in many Southern states deliberately including at least one Negro on a jury panel when one of that race is on trial. In order to invoke the ruling of the Court the exclusion of Negroes must be shown to have been "systematic and deliberate."

Opinion of the Court

MR. CHIEF JUSTICE HUGHES delivered the opinion of the Court:

Petitioner, Clarence Norris, is one of nine Negro boys who were indicted in March, 1931, in Jackson County, Alabama, for the crime of rape. On being brought to trial in that county, eight were convicted. The Supreme Court of Alabama reversed the conviction of one of these and affirmed that of seven, including Norris. This Court reversed the judgments of conviction upon the ground that the defendants had been denied due process of law in that the trial court had failed in the light of the circumstances disclosed, and of the inability of the defendants at that time to obtain counsel, to make an effective appointment of counsel to aid them in preparing and presenting their defense. *Powell* v. *Alabama*, 287 U.S. 45.

After the remand, a motion for change of venue was granted and the cases were transferred to Morgan County. Norris was brought to trial in November, 1933. At the outset, a motion was made on his behalf to quash the indictment upon the ground of the exclusion of Negroes from juries in Jackson County where the indictment was found. A motion was also made to quash the trial *venire* in Morgan County upon the ground of the exclusion of Negroes from juries in that county. In relation to each county, the charge was of long continued, systematic and arbitrary exclusion of qualified Negro citizens from service on juries, solely because of their race and color, in violation of the Constitution of the United States. The State joined issue on this charge and after hearing the evidence, which we shall presently review, the trial judge denied both motions, and exception was taken The trial then proceeded and resulted in the conviction of Norris, who was sentenced to death. On appeal, the Supreme Court of the State considered and decided the federal question which Norris had raised, and affirmed the judgment. 229 Ala. 226; 156 So. 556. We granted a writ of certiorari. 293 U.S. 552.

First. There is no controversy as to the constitutional principle involved. That principle, long since declared, was not challenged, but was expressly recognized, by the Supreme Court of the State. Summing up precisely the effect of earlier decisions, this Court thus stated the principle in *Carter* v. *Texas*, 177 U.S. 442, 447, in relation to exclusion from service on grand juries: "Whenever by any action of a State, whether through its legislature, through its courts, or through its executive or administrative officers, all persons of the African race are excluded, solely because of their race or color, from serving as grand jurors in the criminal prosecution of a person of the African race, the equal protection of the laws is denied to him, contrary to the Fourteenth Amendment of the Constitution of the United States. . . .

The question is of the application of this established principle to the facts disclosed by the record. That the question is one of fact does not relieve us of the duty to determine whether in truth a federal right has been denied. When a federal right has been specially set up and claimed in a state court, it is our province to inquire not merely whether it was denied in express terms but also whether it was denied in substance and effect. If this requires an examination of evidence, that examination must be made. Otherwise, review by this Court would fail of its purpose in safeguarding constitutional rights. Thus, whenever a conclusion of law of a state court as to a federal right and findings of fact are so intermingled that the latter control the former, it is incumbent upon us to analyze the facts in order that the appropriate enforcement of the federal right may be assured. . . .

Second. The evidence on the motion to quash the indictment. In 1930, the total population of Jackson County, where the indictment was found, was 36,881, of whom 2688 were Negroes. The male population over twenty-one years of age numbered 8801, and of these 666 were Negroes.

The qualifications of jurors were thus prescribed by the state statute (Alabama Code, 1923, § 8603): "The jury commission shall place on the jury roll and in the jury box the names of all male citizens of the county who are generally reputed to be honest and intelligent men, and are esteemed in the community for their integrity, good character and sound judgment, but no person must be selected who is under twenty-one or over sixty-five years of age, or, who is an habitual drunkard, or who, being afflicted with a permanent disease or physical weakness is unfit to discharge the duties of a juror, or who cannot read English, or who has ever been convicted of any offense involving moral turpitude. If a person cannot read English and has all the other qualifications prescribed herein and is a freeholder or householder, his name may be placed on the jury roll and in the jury box." See Gen. Acts, Alabama, 1931, No. 47, p. 59.

Defendant adduced evidence to support the charge of unconstitutional discrimination in the actual administration of the statute in Jackson County. The testimony, as the state court said, tended to show that "in a long number of years no Negro had been called for jury service in that county." It appeared that no Negro had served on any grand or petit jury in that county within the memory of witnesses who had lived there all their lives. Testimony to that effect was given by men whose ages ran from fifty to seventy-six years. Their testimony was uncontradicted. It was supported by the testimony of officials. . . .

That testimony in itself made out a *prima facie* case of the denial of the equal protection which the Constitution guarantees. . . . The case thus made was supplemented by direct testimony that specified Negroes, thirty or more in number, were qualified for jury service. Among these were Negroes who were members of school boards, or trustees, of colored schools, and property owners and householders. It also appeared that Negroes from that county had been called for jury service in the federal court. Several of those who were thus described as qualified were witnesses. . . .

The question arose whether names of Negroes were in fact on the jury roll. The books containing the jury roll for Jackson County for the year 1930–31 were produced. . . . On the pages of this roll appeared the names of six Negroes. They were entered, respectively, at the end of the precinct lists which were alphabetically arranged. The genuineness of these entries was disputed. It appeared that after the jury roll in question had been made up, and after the new jury commission had taken office, one of the new commissioners directed the new clerk to draw lines after the names which had been placed on the roll by the preceding commission. These lines, on the pages under consideration, were red lines, and the clerk of the old commission testified that they were not put in by him. The entries made by the new clerk, for the new jury roll, were below these lines.

The names of the six Negroes were in each instance written immediately above the red lines. An expert of long experience testified that these names were superimposed upon the red lines, that is, that they were written after the lines had been drawn. The expert was not cross-examined and no testimony was introduced to contradict him. In denying the motion to quash, the trial judge expressed the view that he would not "be authorized to presume that somebody had committed a crime" or to presume that the jury board "had been unfaithful to their duties and allowed the books to be tampered with." His conclusion was that names of Negroes were on the jury roll.

We think that the evidence did not justify that conclusion. The Supreme Court of the State did not sustain it. . . .

As we have seen, there was testimony, not overborne or discredited, that there were in fact Negroes in the county qualified for jury service. That testimony was direct and specific. After eliminating those persons as to whom there was some evidence of lack of qualifications, a considerable number of others remained. The fact that the testimony as to these persons, fully identified, was not challenged by evidence appropriately direct, cannot be brushed aside. There is no ground for an assumption that the names of these Negroes were not on the preliminary list. The inference to be drawn from the testimony is that they were on that preliminary list, and were designated on that list as the names of Negroes, and that they were not placed on the jury roll. There was thus presented a test of the practice of the commissioners. Something more than mere general asseverations was required. Why were these names excluded from the jury roll? Was it because of the lack of statutory qualifications? Were the qualifications of Negroes actually and properly considered?

The testimony of the commissioner on this crucial question puts the case in a strong light. That testimony leads to the conclusion that these or other Negroes were not excluded on account of age, or lack of esteem in the community for integrity and judgment, or because of disease or want of any other qualification. The commissioner's answer to specific inquiry upon this point was that Negroes were "never discussed." . . .

We are of the opinion that the evidence required a different result from that reached in the state court. We think that the evidence that for a generation or longer no Negro had been called for service on any jury in Jackson County, that there were Negroes qualified for jury service, that according to the practice of the jury commission their names would normally appear on the preliminary list of male citizens of the requisite age but that no names of Negroes were placed on the jury roll, and the testimony with respect to the lack of appropriate consideration of the qualifications of Negroes, established the discrimination which the Constitution forbids. The motion to quash the indictment upon that ground should have been granted. . . .

In *Neal* v. *Delaware*, [103 U.S. 370], decided over fifty years ago, this Court observed that it was a "violent presumption," in which the state court had there indulged, that the uniform exclusion of Negroes from juries, during a period of many years, was solely because, in the judgment of the officers, charged with the selection of grand and petit jurors, fairly exercised, "the black race in Delaware were utterly disqualified by want of intelligence, experience, and moral integrity, to sit on juries." Such a presumption at the present time would be no less violent with respect to the exclusion of the Negroes of Morgan County. And, upon the proof contained in the record now before us, a conclusion that their continuous and total exclusion from juries was because there were none possessing the requisite qualifications, cannot be sustained.

We are concerned only with the federal question which we have discussed, and in view of the denial of the federal right suitably asserted, the judgment must be reversed and the cause remanded for further proceedings not inconsistent with this opinion.

Reversed

(Mr. Justice McReynolds not participating.)

31. *Declaration of Constitutional Principles* *

THE FOLLOWING STATEMENT, issued over the signatures of nineteen Senators and eighty-one Representatives, was presented in both houses of Congress on Monday, March 12, 1956. It is indicative of the resentment felt in the Southern states as a result of the Supreme Court's decision on segregation. (It should be read in conjunction with Selections 23 and 32.)

THE UNWARRANTED DECISION of the Supreme Court in the public school cases is now bearing the fruit always produced when men substitute naked power for established law.

The Founding Fathers gave us a Constitution of checks and balances because they realized the inescapable lesson of history that no man or group of men can be safely entrusted with unlimited power. They framed this Constitution with its provisions for change by amendment in order to secure the fundamentals of government against the dangers of temporary popular passion or the personal predilections of public officeholders.

We regard the decision of the Supreme Court in the school cases as a clear abuse of judicial power. It climaxes a trend in the Federal judiciary undertaking to legislate, in derogation of the authority of Congress, and to encroach upon the reserved rights of the states and the people.

The original Constitution does not mention education. Neither does the Fourteenth Amendment nor any other amendment. The debates preceding the submission of the Fourteenth Amendment clearly show that there was no intent that it should affect the systems of education maintained by the states.

* Reprinted from the *Congressional Record*, March 12, 1956, p. 3948 (the same, p. 4004).

The very Congress which proposed the amendment subsequently provided for segregated schools in the District of Columbia.

1868 CONDITIONS NOTED

When the amendment was adopted in 1868, there were thirty-seven states of the Union. Every one of the twenty-six states that had any substantial racial differences among its people either approved the operation of segregated schools already in existence or subsequently established such schools by action of the same law-making body which considered the Fourteenth Amendment.

As admitted by the Supreme Court in the public school case *(Brown v. Board of Education)*, the doctrine of separate but equal schools "apparently originated in *Roberts* v. *City of Boston* (1849), upholding school segregation against attack as being violative of a state constitutional guarantee of equality." This constitutional doctrine began in the North—not in the South—and it was followed not only in Massachusetts but in Connecticut, New York, Illinois, Indiana, Michigan, Minnesota, New Jersey, Ohio, Pennsylvania and other northern states until they, exercising their rights as states through the constitutional processes of local self-government, changed their school systems.

In the case of *Plessy* v. *Ferguson* in 1896 the Supreme Court expressly declared that under the Fourteenth Amendment no person was denied any of his rights if the states provided separate but equal public facilities. This decision has been followed in many other cases. It is notable that the Supreme Court, speaking through Chief Justice Taft, a former President of the United States, unanimously declared in 1927 in *Lum* v. *Rice* that the "separate but equal" principle is . . . within the discretion of the state in regulating its public schools and does not conflict with the Fourteenth Amendment.

This interpretation, restated time and again, became a part of the life of the people of many of the states and confirmed their habits, customs, traditions and way of life. It is founded on elemental humanity and common sense, for parents should not be deprived by Government of the right to direct the lives and education of their own children.

Though there has been no constitutional amendment or act of Congress changing this established legal principle almost a century old, the Supreme Court of the United States, with no legal basis for such action, undertook to exercise their naked judicial power and substituted their personal political and social ideas for the established law of the land.

CHAOS AND CONFUSION

This unwarranted exercise of power by the court, contrary to the Constitution, is creating chaos and confusion in the states principally affected. It is destroying the amicable relations between the white and Negro races that have been created through ninety years of patient effort by the good people of both races. It has planted hatred and suspicion where there have been heretofore friendship and understanding.

Without regard to the consent of the governed, outside agitators are threatening immediate and revolutionary changes in our public school systems. If done, this is certain to destroy the system of public education in some of the states.

With the gravest concern for the explosive and dangerous condition created by this decision and inflamed by outside meddlers:

We reaffirm our reliance on the Constitution as the fundamental law of the land.

We decry the Supreme Court's encroachments on rights reserved to the states and to the people, contrary to established law and to the Constitution.

We commend the motives of those states which have declared the intention to resist forced integration by any lawful means.

We appeal to the states and people who are not directly affected by these decisions to consider the constitutional principles involved against the time when they, too, on issues vital to them may be the victims of judicial encroachment.

Even though we constitute a minority in the present Congress, we have full faith that a majority of the American people believe in the dual system of government which has enabled us to achieve our greatness and will in time demand that the reserved rights of the states and of the people be made secure against judicial usurpation.

We pledge ourselves to use all lawful means to bring about a reversal of this decision which is contrary to the Constitution and to prevent the use of force in its implementation.

In this trying period, as we all seek to right this wrong, we appeal to our people not to be provoked by the agitators and troublemakers invading our states and to scrupulously refrain from disorder and lawless acts.

32. *Brown et al. v. Board of Education of Topeka et al.*

SUPREME COURT OF THE UNITED STATES, 1954
(APPEAL), 347 U.S. 483

IN THIS CASE the Supreme Court dealt a fatal blow to the practice of segregation in public educational institutions. In doing so the Court specifically overruled its decision, in *Plessy* v. *Ferguson* (163 U.S. 537, 1896), establishing the doctrine of "separate but equal" facilities that had been the constitutional foundation for the practice of segregation up until 1956. The decision had been foreshadowed in previous cases in which the Court had prohibited segregation in interstate transportation as imposing an undue burden on interstate commerce, and in a series of other decisions in which segregation in public educational institutions had been progressively attacked on the grounds that the facilities provided for Negroes and whites were not in fact "separate but equal.". In the present case the Court went much further than before by affirming that even if educational facilities were "separate and equal," educational segregation nevertheless violated the equal protection clause of the Fourteenth Amendment. In reaching this decision the Court held that segregation of children in public schools imposed a psychological handicap on minority groups that in effect deprived them of the equal protection of the laws. Because of this line of reasoning the decision has been attacked by pro-segregationists on the grounds that the Court came to its decision on the basis of sociological theories rather than on a legal construction of the meaning of the Constitution.

In reading this decision the student should note Chief Justice Warren's discussion of the Fourteenth Amendment and the necessity of construing it in terms of contemporary conditions. Note also that the implementation of the decree was specifically suspended until after arguments thereon could be heard by the Court. The decision produced bitter resentment in the Southern states and led to the issuance of the Declaration of Constitutional Principles (Selection 31) and to theories of interposition and nullification (Selection 23). Although the decision is specifically limited to the area of public education, there is no doubt that it has overturned for good the doctrine of "separate but equal" and that every effort will be made to extend the new principle to all public facilities—playgrounds, municipal buses, etc. The decision has profoundly affected the social patterns of large sections of our nation, and its implementation in practice will be both slow and difficult.

MR. CHIEF JUSTICE WARREN delivered the opinion of the Court.

These cases come to us from the States of Kansas, South Carolina,

Virginia and Delaware. They are premised on different facts and different local conditions, but a common legal question justifies their consideration together in this consolidated opinion.

In each of the cases, minors of the Negro race, through their legal representatives, seek the aid of the courts in obtaining admission to the public schools of their community on a nonsegregated basis. In each instance they had been denied admission to schools attended by white children under laws requiring or permitting segregation according to race. This segregation was alleged to deprive the plaintiffs of the equal protection of the laws under the Fourteenth Amendment. In each of the cases other than the Delaware case, a three-judge federal district court denied relief to the plaintiffs on the so-called "separate but equal" doctrine announced by this Court in *Plessy* v. *Ferguson*, 163 U.S. 537. Under that doctrine, equality of treatment is accorded when the races are provided substantially equal facilities, even though these facilities be separate. In the Delaware case, the Supreme Court of Delaware adhered to that doctrine, but ordered that the plaintiffs be admitted to the white schools because of their superiority to the Negro schools.

The plaintiffs contend that segregated public schools are not "equal" and cannot be made "equal," and that hence they are deprived of the equal protection of the laws. Because of the obvious importance of the question presented, the Court took jurisdiction. Argument was heard in the 1952 Term, and reargument was heard this Term on certain questions propounded by the Court.

Reargument was largely devoted to the circumstances surrounding the adoption of the Fourteenth Amendment in 1868. It covered exhaustively consideration of the Amendment in Congress, ratification by the states, then existing practices in racial segregation, and the views of proponents and opponents of the Amendment. This discussion and our own investigation convince us that, although these sources cast some light, it is not enough to resolve the problem with which we are faced. At best, they are inconclusive. The most avid proponents of the post-War Amendments undoubtedly intended them to remove all legal distinctions among "all persons born or naturalized in the United States." Their opponents, just as certainly, were antagonistic to both the letter and the spirit of the Amendments and wished them to have the most limited effect. What others in Congress and the state legislatures had in mind cannot be determined with any degree of certainty.

An additional reason for the inconclusive nature of the Amendment's history, with respect to segregated schools, is the status of public education at that time. In the South, the movement toward free common schools, supported by general taxation, had not yet taken hold. Education of white children was largely in the hands of private groups. Education of Negroes was almost nonexistent, and practically all of the race were illiterate. In fact, any education of Negroes was forbidden by law in some states. Today, in contrast, many Negroes have achieved outstanding success in the arts and sciences as well as in the business and professional world. It is true that public school education at the time of the Amendment had advanced further in the North, but the effect of the Amendment on Northern States was generally ignored in the congressional debates. Even in the North, the conditions of public education did not approximate those existing today. The curriculum was usually rudimentary; ungraded schools were common in rural areas; the school term was but three months a year in many states; and compulsory school attendance was virtually unknown. As a consequence, it is not surprising that there should be so little in the history of the Fourteenth Amendment relating to its intended effect on public education.

In the first cases in this Court construing the Fourteenth Amendment, decided shortly after its adoption, the Court interpreted it as proscribing all state-imposed discriminations against the Negro race. The doctrine of "separate but equal" did not make its appearance in this Court until 1896 in the case of *Plessy* v. *Ferguson*, *supra*, involving not education but transportation. American courts have since labored with the doctrine for over half a century. In this Court, there have been six cases involving the "separate but equal" doctrine in the field of public education. In *Cumming* v. *County Board of Education*, 175 U.S. 528, and *Gong Lum* v. *Rice*, 275 U.S. 78, the validity of the doctrine itself was not challenged. In more recent cases, all on the graduate school level, inequality was found in that specific benefits enjoyed by white students were denied to Negro students of the same educational qualifications (*Missouri ex rel. Gaines* v. *Canada*, 305 U.S. 337; *Sipuel* v. *Oklahoma*, 332 U.S. 631; *Sweatt* v. *Painter*, 339 U.S. 629; *McLaurin* v. *Oklahoma State Regents*, 339 U.S. 637). In none of these cases was it necessary to re-examine the doctrine to grant relief to the Negro plaintiff. And in *Sweatt* v. *Painter*, *supra*, the Court expressly reserved decision on the question whether *Plessy* v. *Ferguson* should be held inapplicable to public education.

In the instant cases, that question is directly presented. Here, unlike *Sweatt* v. *Painter*, there are findings below that the Negro and white schools involved have been equalized, or are being equalized, with respect to buildings, curricula, qualifications and salaries of teachers, and other "tangible" factors. Our decision, therefore, cannot turn on merely a comparison of these tangible factors in the Negro and white schools involved in each of the cases. We must look instead to the effect of segregation itself on public education.

In approaching this problem, we cannot turn the clock back to 1868 when the Amendment was adopted, or even to 1896 when *Plessy* v. *Ferguson* was written. We must consider public education in the light of its full development and its present place in American life throughout the Nation. Only in this way can it be determined if segregation in public schools deprives these plaintiffs of the equal protection of the laws.

Today, education is perhaps the most important function of state and local governments. Compulsory school attendance laws and the great expenditures for education both demonstrate our recognition of the importance of education to our democratic society. It is required in the performance of our most basic public responsibilities, even service in the armed forces. It is the very foundation of good citizenship. Today it is a principal instrument in awakening the child to cultural values, in preparing him for later professional training, and in helping him to adjust normally to his environment. In these days, it is doubtful that any child may reasonably be expected to succeed in life if he is denied the opportunity of an education. Such an opportunity, where the state has undertaken to provide it, is a right which must be made available to all on equal terms.

We come then to the question presented: Does segregation of children in public schools solely on the basis of race, even though the physical facilities and other "tangible" factors may be equal, deprive the children of the minority group of equal educational opportunities? We believe that it does.

In *Sweatt* v. *Painter, supra,* in finding that a segregated law school for Negroes could not provide them equal educational opportunities, this Court relied in large part on "those qualities which are incapable of objective measurement but which make for greatness in a law school." In *McLaurin* v. *Oklahoma State Regents, supra,* the Court, in requiring that a Negro admitted to a white graduate school be treated like all other students, again resorted to intangible considerations: ". . . his ability to study, to engage in discussions and exchange views with other students, and, in general, to learn his profession." Such considerations apply with added force to children in grade and high schools. To separate them from others of similar age and qualifications solely because of their race generates a feeling of inferiority as to their status in the community that may affect their hearts and minds in a way unlikely ever to be undone. The effect of this separation on their educational opportunities was well stated by a finding in the Kansas case by a court which nevertheless felt compelled to rule against the Negro plaintiffs:

> Segregation of white and colored children in public schools has a detrimental effect upon the colored children. The impact is greater when it has the sanction of the law; for the policy of separating the races is usually interpreted as denoting the inferiority of the negro group. A sense of inferiority affects the motivation of a child to learn. Segregation with the sanction of law, therefore, has a tendency to [retard] the educational and mental development of negro children and to deprive them of some of the benefits they would receive in a racial[ly] integrated school system.

Whatever may have been the extent of psychological knowledge at the time of *Plessy* v. *Ferguson*, this finding is amply supported by modern authority. Any language in *Plessy* v. *Ferguson* contrary to this finding is rejected.

We conclude that in the field of public education the doctrine of "separate but equal" has no place. Separate educational facilities are inherently unequal. Therefore, we hold that the plaintiffs and others similarly situated for whom the actions have been brought are, by reason of the segregation complained of, deprived of the equal protection of the laws guaranteed by the Fourteenth Amendment. This disposition makes unnecessary any discussion whether such segregation also violates the Due Process Clause of the Fourteenth Amendment.

Because these are class actions, because of the wide applicability of this decision, and because of the great variety of local conditions, the formulation of decrees in these cases presents problems of considerable complexity. On reargument, the consideration of appropriate relief was necessarily subordinated to the primary question—the constitutionality of segregation in public education. We have now announced that such segregation is a denial of the equal protection of the laws. In order that we may have the full assistance of the parties in formulating decrees, the cases will be restored to the docket, and the parties are requested to present further argument on Questions 4 and 5 previously propounded by the Court for the reargument this Term. The Attorney General of the United States is again invited to participate. The Attorneys General of the states requiring or permitting segregation in public education will also be permitted to appear as *amici curiae* upon request to do so by September 15, 1954, and submission of briefs by October 1, 1954.

It is so ordered

33. *The Fifth Amendment**

RECENT ATTEMPTS by Congressional investigating committees, operating primarily in the field of Communism but in other areas as well, to compel reluctant witnesses to answer questions relating to their previous activities and associations has once more brought into focus the protection against self-incrimination extended to witnesses by the Fifth Amendment. The question as to how far a person may go in refusing to answer on the grounds that he might incriminate himself is a difficult one. In this selection Dean Griswold of the Harvard Law School traces the legal history of the doctrine and comes out strongly for a strict construction of its meaning; other scholars have argued for a narrower meaning and would limit the right to criminal cases only. Congress has endeavored to meet the situation by providing immunity under certain conditions for witnesses who might otherwise plead the Fifth Amendment. The contention is that if the witness is assured that his testimony will not be used against him in a future criminal action in a Federal court, he may not continue to plead his privilege under pain of contempt of Congress.

OLD FRIENDS are good friends. Yet even with the best of friends problems sometimes arise. I have the feeling that that is in a sense the situation we find ourselves in with respect to the Fifth Amendment. It has been with us a long time. It is rather comforting to have around. Yet in the past few years it has come to our consciousness as it rarely has before, and it has been troublesome to many members of the public. It has seemed to me worth while, therefore, to undertake a review of the Fifth Amendment with the thought that ordinarily the better we understand something in human experience, the less fearsome it becomes.

Before going further it may be well to introduce our old friend itself. The Fifth Amendment contains a number of provisions which are commonplace. It is the source of our constitutional rule that serious criminal charges must be made by indictment of a grand jury. It provides that no person shall be twice put in jeopardy for the same offense, that no person shall be deprived of life, liberty or property without due process of law, and that private property shall not be taken for public use without just compensation. Along with these other provisions is

* Reprinted by permission of the publishers from Erwin N. Griswold, *The Fifth Amendment Today*, Cambridge, Mass.: Harvard University Press, Copyright, 1955, by The President and Fellows of Harvard College, pp. 1-30.

the phrase which has currently come to the fore: "No person . . . shall be compelled in any criminal case to be a witness against himself." Similar provisions have long been included in the constitutions of nearly every state. We are not dealing with either an alien or a novel doctrine.

Historians can trace the origin of this privilege back to the twelfth century. Apparently it began in controversies between the king and the bishops. The bishops sought to examine people about a wide variety of alleged offenses, and the king sought to limit the bishops to purely ecclesiastical subjects. By the sixteenth century the idea had been reduced to a Latin maxim which was rather frequently voiced, but which does not seem by any means to have reflected the practice of that period. This maxim is *Nemo tenetur prodere se ipsum*—or, in English, No one should be required to accuse himself. As early as 1589, the young Coke apparently obtained a writ of prohibition against proceedings in the spiritual courts, on this ground (*Cullier and Cullier*, Cro. Eliz. 201 [1589]). But the maxim was then little more than an idea. Over the next fifty years, it was apparently standard practice not only to make suspected persons give evidence against themselves, but also to use torture to make sure that the accused would speak. Indeed, it appears that Coke himself at times participated in the administration of torture for this purpose. As we think of the development of the privilege as it has continued to this day, we should not overlook the fact of its close connection with the struggle to eliminate torture as a governmental practice.

It seems quite clear that we owe the privilege of today primarily to "Freeborn John" Lilburne. He was a cantankerous person, the sort to whom we owe much for many of our basic rights. One of his contemporaries said that "if all the world was emptied of all but John Lilburne, Lilburne would quarrel with John and John with Lilburne." Like most contentious people, he was stubborn. In 1637, he was haled before the Star Chamber on a charge of having imported certain heretical and seditious books. He refused to take the oath to answer truly, and the Council of the Star Chamber condemned him to be whipped and pilloried, for his "boldness in refusing to take a legal oath," without which many offenses might go "undiscovered and unpunished." And in 1638 the sentence was carried out.

But Lilburne persisted. He filed a petition with Parliament, and in 1641 the House of Commons voted that the sentence was "illegal and against the liberty of the subject." Later, the House of Lords concurred with this view, and ordered an indemnity paid to him in the amount of £3,000, which was a very large sum in those days.

This event seems to have been enough to establish the privilege against self-incrimination as a part of the common law. By the latter half of the seventeenth century, we find many occasions when the privilege was recognized by the English courts, and it has been recognized ever since. Indeed, it is still a matter of common law in England. But it is very deeply imbedded in the common law.

Thus, the privilege came to this continent as a part of the legal heritage of our early settlers. Some trace of the privilege is found in Massachusetts as early as 1637, in the trials of Anne Hutchinson and John Wheelwright. For example, a contemporaneous account of Wheelwright's trial contains the following passage:

> He demanded whether he were sent for as an innocent person, or as guilty? It was answered neither, but as suspected onely; Then he demanded, who were his accusers? It was answered, his Sermon; (which was there in Court) being acknowledged by himselfe they might thereupon proceed, ex *officio:* at this word great exception was taken, as if the Court intended the course of the High Commission.

The High Commission was, of course, the Star Chamber.

The privilege was also recognized in the other colonies, although the evidences are rather scarce. For one clear case, however, let me read to you a record which has come down to us from Pennsylvania in 1689. In that year, William Bradford was summoned before the Governor and Council of the Province of Pennsylvania. Bradford was the man who introduced the art of printing to the middle provinces of America. He was about twenty-six years old when this episode occurred.

At the instance of one of the citizens of Pennsylvania, Bradford had printed the Charter of the Provinces so that people could see their rights. He had not put his name on the pamphlet, apparently anticipating some trouble. Here is the examination, chiefly by the Governor. You may want to consider whether you have ever heard anything like it before.

> GOVERNOUR. Why, sir, I would know by what power of authority you thus print? Here is the Charter printed!
>
> BRADFORD. It was by Governour Penn's encouragement I came to this Province, and by his license I print.
>
> GOVERNOUR. What, sir, had you license to print the Charter? I desire to know from you, whether you did print the Charter or not, and who set you to work?
>
> BRADFORD. Governour, it is an impracticable thing for any man to accuse himself; thou knows it very well.

GOVERNOUR. Well, I shall not much press you to it, but if you were so ingenuous as to confess, it should go the better with you.

BRADFORD. Governour, I desire to know my accusers; I think it very hard to be put upon accusing myself.

GOVERNOUR. Can you deny that you printed it? I do know you did print it, and by whose directions, and will prove it, and make you smart for it, too, since you are so stubborn.

JOHN HILL. I am informed that one hundred and sixty were printed yesterday, and that Jos. Growden saith he gave 20s for his part towards the printing it.

BRADFORD. It's nothing to me, what "Jos. Growden saith." Let me know my accusers, and I shall know the better how to make my defence.

Little is heard about self-incrimination during the eighteenth century. This may well have been because the privilege was generally recognized in the colonies after it had become established as a part of the common law of England. Violation of the privilege did not figure as one of the major grievances of the colonists, although there are occasional references to "Inquisitional Courts," and there was complaint about the roving jurisdiction of the admiralty courts during the controversy over the Stamp Act. The privilege was included in the Virginia Bill of Rights of 1776 drafted by George Mason, and, apparently largely because of its presence there, it made its way, in various forms, into the constitutions of six or seven of the original states. When the Federal Constitution was ratified, a number of the states proposed amendments, and the privilege against self-incrimination was specifically mentioned. Accordingly, it was included in the proposals made by Congress which became the Fifth Amendment in 1791, and it has been there unchanged ever since. It is truly an old friend, with an ancient and I believe useful history.

A good many efforts have been made to rationalize the privilege, to explain why it is a desirable or essential part of our basic law. None of the explanations is wholly satisfactory. I am going to offer my own attempt to express the reason for the Fifth Amendment, and why I think it is a sound provision of our basic laws, both federal and state.

I would like to venture the suggestion that the privilege against self-incrimination is one of the great landmarks in man's struggle to make himself civilized. As I have already pointed out, the establishment of the privilege is closely linked historically with the abolition of torture. Now we look upon torture with abhorrence. But torture was once used by honest and conscientious public servants as a means of obtaining information about crimes which could not otherwise be disclosed. We want none of that today, I am sure. For a very similar reason, we do not make even the most hardened criminal sign his own death warrant, or dig his own grave, or pull the lever that springs the trap on which he stands. We have through the course of history developed a considerable feeling of the dignity and intrinsic importance of the individual man. Even the evil man is a human being.

If a man has done wrong, he should be punished. But the evidence against him should be produced, and evaluated by a proper court in a fair trial. Neither torture nor an oath nor the threat of punishment such as imprisonment for contempt should be used to compel him to provide the evidence to accuse or to convict himself. If his crime is a serious one, careful and often laborious police work may be required to prove it by other evidence. Sometimes no other evidence can be found. But for about three centuries in the Anglo-American legal system we have accepted the standard that even then we do not compel the accused to provide that evidence. I believe that is a good standard, and that it is an expression of one of the fundamental decencies in the relation we have developed between government and man.

As that old tartar Mr. Justice Stephen J. Field said [in *Brown* v. *Walker*, 161 U.S. 591, 637 (1896)]: "The essential and inherent cruelty of compelling a man to expose his own guilt is obvious to every one, and needs no illustration." And in words which he approved, the privilege is the "result of the long struggle between the opposing forces of the spirit of individual liberty on the one hand and the collective power of the State on the other."

Where matters of a man's belief or opinions or political views are essential elements in the charge, it may be most difficult to get evidence from sources other than the suspected or accused person himself. Hence, the significance of the privilege over the years has perhaps been greatest in connection with resistance to prosecution for such offenses as heresy or political crimes. In these areas the privilege against self-incrimination has been a protection for freedom of thought and a hindrance to any government which might wish to prosecute for thoughts and opinions alone.

But the privilege is broader than that. It is applicable to any sort of crime, even the most sordid. Don't we go too far in giving this protection to criminals? Isn't the claim of the privilege the clearest sort of proof that the person who claims it is guilty of a crime? This has been asserted by high authority, but I do not believe it is true.

Apart from its expression of our view of civilized governmental conduct, another purpose of the Fifth Amendment is to protect the innocent. But how can a man claim the privilege if he is innocent? How can a man fear he will incriminate himself if he knows he has committed no crime? This may happen in several ways. A simple illustration will show the possibility.

Consider, for example, the case of the man who has killed another in self-defense, or by accident, without design or fault. He has committed no crime, yet his answer to the question whether he killed the man may well incriminate him. At the very least it will in effect shift the burden of proof to him so that he will have to prove his own innocence. Indeed, the privilege against self-incrimination may well be thought of as a companion of our established rule that a man is innocent until he has been proved guilty.

In this connection let me quote from a Supreme Court decision written long before our present troubles. In *Burdick* v. *United States*, 236 U.S. 79 (1915), Mr. Justice McKenna wrote,

> If it be objected that the sensitiveness of Burdick was extreme because his refusal to answer was itself an implication of crime, we answer, not necessarily in fact, not at all in theory of law.

Now let us turn to an area which is closer to that which has recently been of concern. I am going to ask you to assume two sets of facts. You may think that both of the sets of facts are unlikely, and that they do not correspond with any case you have ever heard of. All I ask is that you assume the facts. I am simply putting a hypothetical case; and the facts are not the facts of any specific case.

Here is Case 1. A man is a college teacher. He is an idealist and perhaps slow to recognize realities, as idealists sometimes are. He has a great urge for what he regards as social reform. He is native born, went to American schools, and loves his country despite what he regards as its imperfections. You may not agree with his ideas but you would respect his honesty and sincerity. He believes himself thoroughly attached to the country and the Constitution, and he abhors anything involving force and violence. He is a good teacher and works hard on his subjects. He has always believed that as a good citizen he should be interested in politics. Neither of the established political parties provided what he wanted. In the relatively calm period of the past middle 1930's, on the solicitation of a friend, he went to a communist meeting and soon joined the Communist Party. At that time the Communist Party was perfectly legal, and regularly appeared on our ballot. He thought he was simply joining a political party. One of the reasons that led him to join was that he regarded fascism as highly immoral and a great danger to the world, and he felt that the communists were fighting fascism in Spain at this time. His interest was not merely in protecting Spain, but, because the danger which many men then feared most was that of the spread of fascism, he thought that fighting fascism in Spain was an important means of guarding against such a danger here.

Now you may say that this is all very unlikely. To this I reply that I am, for the moment, only assuming a hypothetical case, and I should be able to assume any hypothetical case I want. So these are the facts I put before you. You may feel that such a man must have been very naive or lacking in intelligence. To that I would make two replies: First, that conclusion rests on a large amount of hindsight. A man's actions at any time should be evaluated on the basis of the facts then available to him, and the state of his own mind—on the basis of what he actually knew, and not by facts we learn later that were not known to him. And my second reply would be that the man may have been naive or obtuse. I would say that he was at least misguided and unwise. But I would point out that being obtuse or naive is a very different thing from being a traitor or a spy.

Let me add a few more facts, assumed by me as before. Our teacher was in a communist cell, with other teachers. The communists had great plans for this group. They wanted to use it to infiltrate American education. However, the communist command was canny. They knew that many or all of the members of this cell of teachers were politically innocent, and that they would recoil quickly from any proposals for sabotage or the use of force and violence. So they treated this group with great care. The group was never subjected to the rigors of communist discipline. It was a study group, and its discussions were kept on a high intellectual plane. The more sordid features of the communist doctrine were kept thoroughly in the background. Our teacher never engaged in espionage or sabotage or anything like that, and never saw or heard of any such activities by any member of his group. He would have been horrified by any such actions.

Nevertheless, there were things from time to time which he did not like. He rationalized them in various ways: nothing can be perfect; the thing to do is to stay inside and work against excesses; and so on. Besides, he was a stubborn fellow. Once having started out on something he thought was good, he did not lightly give it up. But he became troubled; and after the war he slowly drifted away from the group. He never formally resigned. He just turned away. By the time of the Korean invasion in 1950, he was thoroughly disgusted and saw that he had been used as a dupe. But he was also convinced in his own heart of the rectitude of his actions, if not of their wisdom; and he did not doubt that many of the people who had been associated with him in the venture were just as innocent of wrongdoing as he was sure he was.

Remember, I am doing the assuming. You may feel that these facts do not fit an actual case. But I am not trying to state an actual case. I am just assuming a hypothetical case, which is one of the ancient rights of any law teacher.

Now let me turn to Case 2. This man is also a college teacher. He never joined the Communist Party. He never thought of joining the Communist Party. He knew a good deal about the realities of communism, and he was thoroughly opposed to it. He was, however, a man who was interested in causes. His father had been a minister, who had dedicated his life to helping people. He himself had a great urge to participate in activities which he felt would help to alleviate suffering or contribute to social progress. In fact he was a sucker for almost any kind of an appeal. He contributed modest amounts to China Relief. He had always had a warm feeling for the Chinese. Sometimes he found himself on some of the letterheads of some of these organizations as a sponsor. He was not sure that he remembered giving permission to use his name this way; but the cause, as indicated by the attractive name of the organization, was one that appealed to him, and he did not bother himself much about it. After a while he heard some rumblings that there might be some communist influence in these organizations, but he was slow to believe that that could be true. In some of the organizations, he had been on committees with thoroughly respectable fellow citizens. He did not want to pull out, because he felt that this would let his friends down. Eventually he heard that some of these organizations had been ruled to be subversive by the Attorney General. But he, too, was a stubborn fellow. He believed in the stated objectives of these organizations. He was also a freeborn American, proud of his country's great traditions, and he allowed his name to be used by some of these organizations, as has been said in a recent article, "as a gesture of opposition to the procedure of proscribing organizations without giving them the right to be heard."

Well, that is the end of my assuming. Let us see what happens to these two individuals. Remember that both of these individuals feel that they are innocent of any wrongdoing. Each one is pure in heart, and perhaps a little too certain of his own rectitude. Each one may now regret some of the things he did, but he does not think that they were wrong. Each one is certain that he is morally innocent of any crime.

We can consider Case 1 first. He is the man who was a member of the Communist Party. He is summoned to appear before a Congressional committee, and is asked whether he is a communist. He answers truthfully: "No." Then he is asked whether he ever was a communist. He is now surely subjected to a substantial risk, even though he honestly believes that he has committed no crime. He knows that a number of communists have been convicted under the Smith Act of 1940, and more have been indicted. Our teacher perhaps magnifies his own predicament. He sees the jail doors opening up if he himself gives the evidence that he was once a communist. Interestingly enough, Section 4(f) of the Internal Security Act of 1950 (commonly known as the McCarran Act) provides specifically that "neither the holding of office nor membership in any communist organization by any person shall constitute per se a violation of . . . this section or of any other criminal statute." But this was enacted after his period of Party membership. It has been declared to be a crime to be a communist in Massachusetts since 1951, but there may be some possible room to question the effectiveness of this statute in view of the provision of the federal Act.

After much internal torment, the witness finally decides to claim the privilege of the Fifth Amendment with respect to the question of his past membership in the Communist Party. Putting aside the question of his wisdom in doing this, can there be any doubt that the claim is legally proper? Past membership in the Communist Party is not a crime in itself; but admitting such membership may well be a link in a chain of proof of a criminal charge against him. Persons have been prosecuted under the Smith Act for membership in the Communist Party plus something else. If he supplies the proof of his own membership in the Party, he does not know what other evidence may then be brought against him to show that he has committed a crime. Thus, an answer to the question will definitely incriminate him, that is, provide evidence which could be used in a prosecution against him. Yet, remember that he thoroughly believes that he is not guilty of any crime; and on the facts I have given he is not guilty of a crime.

There are other factors that influence his conclusion. His own experience is an ordeal. He does not want his friends to be subjected to it. He believes in their innocence of any crime. If he thought that they had committed crimes, he would promptly tell the proper officers of the government. By claiming the privilege against self-incrimination, he can refrain from naming any of his associates. He feels a strong sense of loyalty to them. He feels a strong sense of loyalty to his country, too; but since he is convinced that neither he nor his associates have in fact done anything wrong, his desire to protect them from having to experience his own predicament seems to him to have prevailing weight in the actual circumstances.

He claims the privilege. He cannot be prosecuted on the basis of any evidence he has provided. There can be no doubt, I believe, that his claim of privilege is legally justified. Yet, note that on the facts I have assumed he is not guilty of any crime. Of course his claim of privilege as to his membership in the Communist Party means that he must also claim the privilege as to all other questions which relate in any way to what he did, or to his associates in the activity. For if he answers any of those questions, it will clearly connote his own communist activity.

There is one small point which might be brought in here. It is sometimes said that the privilege may only be rightly claimed if the answer to the incriminating question would be "Yes." I do not believe that is true. Our man in Case 1 has testified that he is not now a communist. He claims the privilege as to a question which asks him if he ever was a member of the Communist Party. He is then asked: "When did you cease to be a member?" He must claim the privilege as to this, or else his answer will disclose that he once was a member, as to which he has legitimately claimed the privilege. Then the examiner starts a new line. He says: "Were you a member of the Communist Party yesterday?" Now the answer is "No." But the witness who has taken this line cannot answer that question. For if he does, the questions will be continued: "Were you a member of the Party last year?—two years ago?—three years ago?" If he answers any of these accurately with a "No," he will come to the place where he must claim the privilege if he is to maintain his basic position. In this way, the date of his withdrawal could be pinpointed, thus giving valuable information for a possible prosecution. Moreover, he may not be sure just when he withdrew; it was a gradual process. And he may have legitimate fears that an honest answer he might give to a question relating to the transitional period might get him involved in a prosecution for perjury. At any rate, it seems clear that questions of this sort are an illustration of a type of question as to which the privilege may be legitimately claimed, as far as the law is concerned, even though the answer to the question would be "No."

Let us turn to Case 2, which we can dispose of briefly. You will remember that that was the man who had lent his name to causes, and had contributed money; and the causes have now turned out to be communist fronts, although they were attractively named, and many good Americans were, at one time or another, associated with them. But he was never a member of the Communist Party.

This man likewise is summoned before a Congressional investigating committee. The mere fact that he is summoned shows that he is suspected of something rather serious, and he is badly worried. He is asked whether he is now a member of the Communist Party; and he answers "No." Then he is asked whether he ever was in the past.

The answer is in fact "No," as we have seen. But he is now in great fear. If he says: "No," then he may be subjecting himself to a real risk of prosecution for perjury. He may rightly fear that proof of the fact of his joining and contributing to so many agencies which have turned out to be front organizations might lead a jury to believe that he actually was a communist.

Now it is probably true that fear of a prosecution for perjury for an answer given to a question is not a proper basis for a claim of the privilege. If it was, almost any witness could claim the privilege as to any question. But our man is in a somewhat different situation. If he says "No" to the question of communist membership, then in his own interest he may have to undertake to state and explain his membership and activities in the various front organizations. The net result may be that he will have to give much evidence which could be used against him in an attempt to prove that he was a member of the communist conspiracy. It would appear, therefore, that he can properly claim the privilege even though his answer to the question as to Communist Party membership at any time would honestly and rightly be "No."

In both of the cases I have put, the privilege may be claimed although the individual was guilty of no crime. In the second case it may be claimed although the person was never a member of the Communist Party. In each case, there may be a "natural" inference from the claim of the privilege, and in each case that inference would in fact be unwarranted. The claim of the privilege is surely a serious business, but it is equally surely not the equivalent of an admission of criminal conduct.

There are other reasons why a person may claim the privilege in a particular case. He might get bad advice; but I do not want to press that, as I think that in many of these cases the individual's troubles are caused in part by the fact that he chooses to make his own decisions and does not accept sound advice. But we should not forget that a person on the witness stand may be badly frightened, even though he is wholly innocent. For example, the Supreme Court of the United States has said, in *Wilson* v. *United States*, 149 U.S. 60, 66 (1893):

> It is not every one who can safely venture on the witness stand though entirely innocent of the charge against him. Excessive timidity, nervousness when facing others and attempting to explain transactions of a suspicious character, and offences charged against him, will often confuse and embarrass him to such a degree as to increase rather than remove prejudices against him. It is not every one, however honest, who would, therefore, willingly be placed on the witness stand.

A witness lost in fear and confusion might turn to the privilege as a means of sanctuary from a situation which he feels himself incompetent to handle. Consider also how much the chance of a witness losing his calm and collected demeanor is enhanced by such things as television, radio microphones, movie cameras, flashing flash bulbs, and procedures which may not seem to him to be based upon the finest spirit of fairness. In connection with this I might mention the recent decision of the United States Court of Appeals for the Sixth Circuit in *Aiuppa v. United States*, 201 F.2d 287, 300 (1952), where we find the following language in the opinion:

> But, in concluding, we think it may not be amiss to say that, notwithstanding the pronouncements of the committee chairman as to intended fairness, the courts of the United States could not emulate the committee's example and maintain even a semblance of fair and dispassionate conduct of trials in criminal cases.
>
> Despite the enjoyment by millions of spectators and auditors of the exhibition by television of the confusion and writhings of widely known malefactors and criminals, when sharply questioned as to their nefarious activities, we are unable to give judicial sanction, in the teeth of the Fifth Amendment, to the employment by a committee of the United States Senate of methods of examination of witnesses constituting a triple threat: answer truly and you have given evidence leading to your conviction for a violation of federal law; answer falsely and you will be convicted of perjury; refuse to answer and you will be found guilty of criminal contempt and punished by fine and imprisonment. In our humble judgment, to place a person not even on trial for a specified crime in such predicament is not only not a manifestation of fair play, but is in direct violation of the Fifth Amendment to our national Constitution.

Ordinarily when the privilege of the Fifth Amendment is exercised, it is in a criminal trial. There a specific charge has been made, and the prosecution has by evidence established a prima facie case of guilt of the particular crime charged in the complaint or indictment. Under such circumstances there is much more than the mere claim of the privilege on which to rest an inference of guilt.

In investigations, however, there are no carefully formulated charges. Evidence to support such charges has not been introduced and made known to the witness before he is called upon to answer. He has no opportunity for cross-examination of other witnesses, and often little or no opportunity to make explanations which might have a material bearing on the whole situation. In the setting of an investigation, therefore, the basis for the inference from a claim of privilege against self-incrimination is much less than it is when the privilege is exercised in an ordinary criminal trial.

There are two more matters to which I should like to make brief reference. The first of these is the rather technical legal doctrine known as waiver of the privilege. A clear instance of waiver occurs when a defendant in a criminal case voluntarily takes the stand. He then becomes subject to cross-examination, and must answer relevant questions. So far as witnesses at investigations are concerned, our current learning on this is based largely on the Supreme Court's decision in *Rogers* v. *United States*, 340 U.S. 367 (1951). In that case, a witness testified that she had been treasurer of a local Communist Party, had had possession of the records, and had turned them over to another person. She then declined to name the person to whom she had given them, claiming the privilege under the Fifth Amendment. The Supreme Court held that by giving the testimony she did she had waived the privilege, and that she was guilty of contempt for refusing to answer the further questions. There was a dissenting opinion by Justices Black, Frankfurter, and Douglas.

My own view is that this decision was not soundly reasoned, and that it has led to unfortunate results. To me the analogy of an adversary proceeding is not apt when applied to an investigation. As a consequence of this case, witnesses who have legitimate fears of prosecution, but who might be willing to cooperate as far as they could, are induced (if not actually compelled) to refuse to answer any questions at all. For if they do answer a single question, it may be contended that they have waived the privilege so that thereafter they may be compelled to testify against themselves. This threat of waiver is not an imaginary matter. It may be found frequently in the transcripts of the proceedings of Congressional committees.

My guess as to the law is that the *Rogers* case applies only where the witness has given an incriminating answer to a prior question. I do not think it would apply if a witness was asked if he had been a member of the Communist Party in 1945, and he said "No." By the latter answer he has not opened up anything which he refuses to explain. Nevertheless, it will take a Supreme Court decision to provide this clarification of the *Rogers* case; and counsel advising a client may well hesitate to make his client bear the risk and expense of taking a case all the way to the Supreme Court. With the *Rogers* case on the books, the only safe advice may be to claim the privilege at the earliest possible moment, so as to be sure to avoid a charge of waiver.

This doctrine of waiver is, I believe, the true explanation of the refusal of some witnesses to answer such questions as "Have you ever taught communist doctrine in your classroom?" or "Have you ever solicited students to join the Communist Party?" These refusals have been deeply disturbing to the public. Yet, the answer to these questions may be "No"; but the witness nevertheless fears that he cannot give that answer without its being said that he has waived the privilege as to questions about other sorts of communist activity. Here again we have a situation where the obvious inference from the refusal to answer the question may be completely unwarranted.

Finally, I would like to make reference to one more problem which is collateral to that of the Fifth Amendment. Suppose a witness is summoned before an investigating committee. He does not claim a privilege against self-incrimination, and talks freely about himself, answering all questions about his own activity. He takes the position, however, that he will not answer questions about others. Or suppose a person first refuses to answer virtually all questions, claiming the Fifth Amendment privilege, but he later decides to waive the privilege as to himself. However, he refuses as a matter which he regards as one of principle to identify other persons. What should be the situation with respect to such a person?

There have been a number of people who have been summoned before investigating committees and taken this position from the outset. They have answered all questions about themselves, and have refused to identify others. As far as I know, no academic person who has done this has been cited for contempt; nor has any such person lost his job. Should it be any different where the witness has first relied on the Fifth Amendment, but has later changed his position, waiving the privilege as to himself, but still refusing to answer as to others?

The problem is undeniably a difficult one. So long as the witness was claiming the privilege, it could be argued that he had done no wrong. If he had committed any crime, the evidence should be brought forth in the proper way and tried out in court. His refusal to answer was not evidence of any crime. This argument, however, is not available where he waives the privilege but refuses to answer questions relating to other persons. Then his Fifth Amendment privilege is wholly gone, and his situation presents new and rather different problems.

Whether he has committed a crime by his refusal to testify may be extremely difficult to tell. Even if he is cited by the legislative body, it will still be for the grand jury to decide whether to indict; it will remain to the courts to decide such questions as whether the committee was properly constituted, and whether the question asked was relevant to the inquiry. We should not forget that a prosecution for contempt was set aside within the past year by the Supreme Court on the ground that the questions asked the witness—as to the identity of his contributors—were not relevant to the particular inquiry. *United States* v. *Rumeley*, 345 U.S. 41 (1953).

However such questions go, though, would it not seem that such a person is at least in no worse a position morally than he was when he stood on the Fifth Amendment? He should not be worse off for being willing to speak fully and frankly about himself than he was when he would not talk at all. His refusal to tell on his friends may be both contrary to valid law and unwise. Nevertheless, it may be based on strong grounds of conscience.

Let me do a little more assuming: Let us assume that the witness feels positive in his own mind that the persons with whom he was associated did no wrong to our country. They did not engage in espionage or sabotage or anything like that. They were merely hopeful but misguided people, as he was. Let us assume, too, that this is all far in the past. The persons in question are in other work. They have families to support. If their names are disclosed, they will surely lose their jobs. He must then resolve for himself the question whether he will give their names and subject them to the same sort of ordeal he has been through in order to save himself from further difficulty and possible prosecution. He may be wrong if he decides that he should not protect himself by sacrificing them. I recognize the legal obligation to testify as to others, and the general importance of this both in trials and in investigations. But can it be said clearly that his action is always immoral?

Of course he may be wrong in his judgment of these other people. They may be worse than he thinks they are. But we all have to use judgment on such things. A man may honestly feel that he cannot bring suffering to others in order to save himself. To a considerable extent such questions can only be resolved in a man's own conscience. We are a society which has long depended on and applauded the virtues of the rugged individualist.

I do not justify the past or present conduct of anyone. I seek only to explain. Because some members of university faculties have claimed privilege under the Fifth Amendment and refused to answer questions, many members of the general public have come to have fear of our educational institutions and general mistrust of academic people. I firmly believe that these fears are unwarranted. I have tried here to show how some of the things that have happened could have happened without there being anything rotten in the universities. It may be a serious error of judgment for an academic person to claim the privilege of the Fifth Amendment, or to refuse to answer questions; but the conduct, regrettable as it is, does not show the existence of treason, espionage, sabotage, or any other serious crime.

The great misfortune from all this, I believe, is that charges are made against our universities and other educational institutions, and more or less believed by some segments of our people. I think myself that it is easy to overestimate the extent of that belief, but it cannot be denied that there is disagreement, uneasiness, and even fear in some quarters. As I have said, I think these fears are not soundly based. It is an injustice not only to the faculty members of our great universities but to the country to allow any conclusion to stand that they are not good Americans or that they do not serve their country well.

As conservative a judge as Pierce Butler once wrote [in *Sinclair* v. *United States*, 279 U.S. 135, 178 (1927)]:

> It has always been recognized in this country, and it is well to remember, that few if any of the rights of the people guarded by fundamental law are of greater importance to their happiness and safety than the right to be exempt from all unauthorized, arbitrary or unreasonable inquiries and disclosures in respect of their personal and private affairs.

On this matter some final observations may be in order, based on our traditional practices and rules. In our criminal courts, we would never think of requiring an accused person to answer questions. He doesn't have to take the stand at all, and if he does so, he has the protection of an impartial judge, and the right to have his counsel speak in court in his behalf.

Why should it be so different in a legislative inquiry, when the information that is sought relates to the witness' own conduct? I recognize fully the power of the Senate and the House of Representatives, the lineal descendants of the Houses of Parliament. These are deliberative bodies, and all points of view are usually represented among their members. Their actions are taken after debate, and represent the judgment of many people from all parts of the country.

I recognize also that these bodies have to operate through committees. A committee in the common acceptance of the term is a group of persons, usually appointed to represent various points of view. Its actions reflect collective judgment taken after consideration and deliberation. In this light, I ask a question: Should these broad investigative powers ever be held by a single person, even though he is formally clothed with the title of a subcommittee?

The more I think about this, the more it seems to me to be an unsound practice. There is nothing about the nature of membership in the Senate or the House of Representatives which should give each member a general commission to go through the length and breadth of the land, far from his own state or district, far from the seat of the general government, making inquiry about any subject, even on formal delegation to him from his House or one of its committees. Committees I am willing to accept. Subcommittees of one give me pause. It may well be that only the Houses of Congress can effectively deal with this problem, but I respectfully commend it to them for their consideration.

34. *Civil Rights--But Not Conspiracy* *

THE ACCOMPANYING ARTICLE by Norman Thomas, six times Socialist candidate for the Presidency, deals with the pressing problem of Communism and our civil liberties. Although Mr. Thomas maintains his traditional position as a staunch defender of civil rights, he concludes that the Communists represent an organized conspiratorial group subject to foreign domination and therefore as individuals they are unqualified for governmental or academic posts. Although taking a forthright stand against the Communist movement, Mr. Thomas warns against hysteria in dealing with it. Basically his article is an appeal to the American people to maintain a sense of balance and moderation while eradicating Communism in those areas in which it represents a basic challenge to the American way of life.

A VITAL aspect of our grim struggle against an aggressive totalitarian communism relates to the preservation of those civil liberties which are so basic a part of our American heritage. In this country, from the time when Jefferson and his political supporters repealed the Alien and Sedition Laws of John Adams' Administration until the coming of the Communist threat, the friends of civil liberty had a philosophy well settled in their own minds and fairly well established in American practice. Its application was relatively simple. It was a theory which had been expressed in eloquent terms by John Milton, John Locke and John Stuart Mill in Britain, and by Jefferson himself and other of the Founding Fathers in America. It was embodied in the Bill of Rights of the Federal Constitution; it inspired the movement which led to the end of chattel slavery and to the Thirteenth, Fourteenth and Fifteenth Amendments; it survived two world wars.

* Norman Thomas, *The New York Times Magazine*, January 7, 1951, pp. 11, 41-42, 44. Reprinted by permission of the author and the publisher.

This historic doctrine of civil liberties rested on two pillars: the first, that man was something less than man unless he were possessed of the right to fair trial and to freedom of conscience, communication, assemblage and association; the second, that society itself was most secure when ideas had their chance to win or lose in the full competition of the marketplace. Jefferson himself thus stated this position in his First Inaugural: "If there be any among us who wish to dissolve this Union or to change its republican form, let them stand undisturbed as monuments of the safety with which error of opinion may be tolerated where reason is left free to combat it."

In the hysteria of World War I and its ugly aftermath, it seemed for a time that the American Government and people had forgotten or forsaken their heritage. But the body politic was sound enough successfully to resist the infection of tyranny. With the subsidence of the war hysteria and the virtual collapse of the infamous Ku Klux Klan, American civil liberties made real progress, especially in the field of race relations and the rights of labor. World War II was notably free from any anti-libertarian frenzy.

The reason was less the strength of the American faith in civil liberty than the fact that, thanks to the Japanese attack at Pearl Harbor, this was the first war in American history to which there was no *political* opposition. There were, however, conscientious objectors on religious and philosophical grounds who did not fare as well as their comrades in Great Britain. And the terrible precedent was set of the evacuation of citizens of Japanese ancestry on the West Coast into concentration camps without trial or hearing. This assertion, that the interest of the state as interpreted by the Commander in Chief of the Army was the supreme law, was unfortunately validated by the Supreme Court in complete contradiction of the Anglo-American theory that each man is entitled to be judged on the basis of his own deeds. But the concentration camps were humanely run; the evacuees were eventually allowed to return to their homes; and some arrangements were made to compensate them for their losses. (How different was the fate of the millions whom the Russian dictators dispossessed!)

In the first World War the extreme Jeffersonian theory of civil liberty was modified by the Supreme Court's adoption of the principle that the Government might properly act to prevent or punish meetings, speech or writing in which might lie clear and present danger to the national security. This qualification came to be generally accepted by supporters of civil liberty, even by those who, like myself, strongly challenged Justice Holmes' first application of it against Eugene Victor Debs and others of his sort in World War I.

It is plain enough that there is an important difference between saying that sometime under certain circumstances it may be the right or the duty of men to use force and violence against injustice, and saying "Let us gather in the dark of the moon to march on the Capitol in Washington." Obviously, between these two extremes there is a large area in which courts must use sober judgment in estimating clear and present danger. As Judge Learned Hand has pointed out, history and the conscience of mankind may determine that a certain revolution was right. But no society or government can include the right to revolution among its civil liberties to be protected by law.

Before the Communists injected a new element into the situation there was need for vigilance to protect civil liberties. I was one of the founders of the Civil Liberties Bureau in World War I which became the American Civil Liberties Union. In all these years we have exercised our rights in frequent and lively discussion of concrete problems of civil liberty. But I am not unfairly telling tales out of school when I admit that in recent times there has been an unprecedented confusion in the counsels of the board of the Civil Liberties Union as it faced the problems presented by Communist tactics.

The new thing which the Communists have injected into the discussion of civil liberties in America is not their advocacy of force and violence. Emma Goldman and her school of anarchists did a lot of talking about the right to use force before World War I. Thomas Jefferson himself had held that the tree of liberty might better flourish if occasionally watered by blood. Nevertheless, history had proved that his theory of freedom greatly reduced any need or excuse of a terrible watering of the tree of liberty by blood. Emma Goldman and her friends generally abstained from the practice of the violence which theoretically they glorified. So, too, have the Communists thus far in America.

The new element which the Communists have injected into the picture is their assertion of a right to the protection of laws which in power they would abolish, a right to do in the American community that which they would punish by slavery or death if they should come to power. They challenge the community as an organized conspiriatorial group under disciplined control of Stalin, the head both of the mighty Soviet Union and of a world-wide movement intent upon achieving universal power over the bodies, minds and souls of men. These Communists are the first dissenting group in American history to make a virtue of lies and deceit, the first to reduce all social ethics to the appalling simplicity of the commandment: "Thou shall at all times obey party orders. There is no other moral law."

There was a time when stanch defenders of civil liberty were inclined to say that Communists were by no means as bad as my statement has implied; that their intentions toward the American Government did not include a use of force and violence; that whatever might seem to be the logic of Communist texts, in practice they were not guilty of overt offenses against American security. Their tactics, in short, did not present a clear and immediate danger. Hence we had time to combat the error of Communist ideas by truth. This theory was especially popular during our honeymoon with our Russian allies in World War II and immediately thereafter.

For thoughtful men it was, however, soon destroyed by facts. Abroad there was the relentless march of communism, the Czechoslovak coup, and cumulative evidences of Communist conspiracy in the use of the big lie and force. At home there was the Hiss case. If we Americans escape or survive a third world war, the story of Alger Hiss will inspire not only further historical inquiry but psychological analysis and perhaps some creative literature of tragedy.

Few men in history whose original intentions were probably good have done so much to imperil that basic confidence in mutual good faith upon which any decent defense of liberty must depend. The verdict in the Hiss case was buttressed by the confession of Henry Julian Wadleigh. It was followed by the arrest and confession of Klaus Fuchs in Britain and some of his confederates in America. These things made it forever impossible to say that the Communist menace to our freedom had only an imaginary or at most a theoretical basis.

The disruptive tactics of the Communists and the methods by which they obtain dominance were not only illustrated in the events to which I have referred but in the experience of the American labor movement which felt compelled to take drastic action to maintain its freedom from the outside dictation of a conspiratorial party.

What should believers in the Jeffersonian doctrine of civil liberties do when confronted with these facts? Jefferson himself had acted vigorously enough against Aaron Burr whom he regarded as a traitor. Would he have expected us to apply his faith in the power of truth in the face not of flamboyantly honest rebels of the older pattern but of a conspiratorial party?

Obviously, the answer is that no Government face to face with conspiracy can fail to act for its own security. But how? A strong but by no means conclusive case can be made that no man is entitled to the freedom which in power he would ruthlessly deny to others. The disgusting hypocrisy of Communists in their role as defenders of civil liberties has had one more striking illustration in their treatment of their deposed leader, Earl Browder. For their sake, he refused to answer questions in a Congressional inquiry and was indicted for contempt. The Communists, through their friends, supporters and front organizations nominally devoted to "liberty," saw to it that all others who had been similarly indicted in their behalf were furnished with bail. But not the heretic Browder.

Him they would treat as they treated the Trotskyist heretics whose conviction they applauded when it was won under the same Smith Law under which their own leaders, for far better reasons, were found guilty in Judge Medina's court. Nevertheless, it is not Communist hypocrisy but conspiracy which chiefly plagues us.

There are protagonists of civil liberties who say, in spite of the conspiratorial nature of the Communist party: "The good old Anglo-American principle must apply. There should be no such thing as guilt by association. Each man must be judged by his own specific acts."

It would, indeed, be a tragedy for justice and freedom were America to accept guilt by association as a basic concept. On the other hand, it is a highly legalistic notion which would hold that there is no element of guilt in the act of accepting the discipline of a conspiratorial and subversive organization.

It is true, at least as matters stand today, that mere membership in the Communist party should not send a man to jail. There is a clause in the Smith Act of 1940, heretofore unused by the Government, which would make it illegal and subject to punishment for anyone to join or remain in an organization which is held to advocate the overthrow of the Government by force and violence. The Supreme Court, possibly with that clause in mind, unanimously upheld the right of a witness, a Mrs. Patricia Blau, to refuse to answer an inquiry as to her membership in the Communist party on the grounds that she might incriminate herself.

This may argue that the Supreme Court is getting ready to uphold the complete validity of the Smith Act. Even if the Supreme Court should find that act wholly constitutional, and even if you think it logical to make it a crime knowingly to belong to a conspiratorial organization, the dangers and disadvantage of proscribing a whole political party which to a large extent operates like other political parties are many and weighty. The attempt to do it suggests hysteria, and hysteria spreads. If the F. B. I. is on the job, it must know the people whom it needs to watch without resorting to a wholesale proscription which would jeopardize one of the most ancient of American liberties.

It is, however, fantastic to say that the right to stay out of jail implies a right to Government employment in places where that employment might easily jeopardize national security or the integrity of the democracy in which we want to bring up our children. It is absurd to say that we ought to trust a man in the State Department until we catch him imitating Alger Hiss or in the schools until he openly teaches sedition to our children. So far as schools are concerned, the guilt of surrending one's freedom of mind and inquiry to a conspiratorial party should be enough to bar a person from a teacher's chair.

Our problem would still be difficult, but it would be much simpler, if we were always or usually able to deal with men and women who admit their Communist affiliations or whose Communist affiliations can easily be proved. The precise opposite is the case. The necessary processes of investigation and inquiry into the beliefs and actions of a conspiratorial group require us to use procedures in police work and investigation which, in their very nature, as all history shows, can easily be subverted to the immense hurt of the innocent and the whole concept of freedom. It is far easier to catch the innocent and honest dissenter whose expression of opinion is entitled to protection than it is to catch the conspirator. The contagion of repression, the zeal for enforced conformity, easily spreads in government and the mob.

Already, there are alarming evidences of pressure to deny access to the radio or television to anyone who voices opinions which an exceedingly vociferous minority would stampede the mob into regarding as Communist. For example, the National Broadcasting Company received from Los Angeles some 350 calls of protest following its documentary in praise of the American Bill of Rights, put on in cooperation with the American Civil Liberties Union. The protesting patriots were completely unaware that they were acting entirely in the Communist spirit. In the struggle against communism, democracy in general and our own national freedom in particular can be lost by military defeat. They can also be lost by imitation of the enemy for the sake of victory.

To protect the national security, the rights of the individual, and the orderly processes of democracy at one and the same time against conspiratorial Communists and despotic police power is not a matter to be solved by exclusive emphasis on liberty or physical security. Constitutions and courts, state and Federal, may greatly serve us but they are not infallible. Liberty is not derived from a Bill of Rights but protected by it. No written document can take the place of a national will for freedom.

Hence, specific problems involving the application of high standards of freedom must be solved by a common sense balance of rights and interests and not automatically arrived at by devotion to any single precept. A law may be found constitutional by a court; its professed purpose may be commendable or at least defensible (as is the case with the McCarran Act) and yet it may in action be enormously hurtful.

To use a homely illustration: rats have no right in a farmer's barn, but he would be an awful fool to burn down the barn to get rid of the rats. Most of our current legislation—the stupid and insulting exaction of special loyalty oaths, the McCarran Act and the various state imitations of it—belong to the barn-burning type of legislation.

It is quite likely that the Communists have in training specialists in sabotage and particular types of sedition. Of course, they aren't going to step up and register. It is doubtful if the most dangerous of them are registered even on the party rolls. They are more likely to be posing as patriots, vociferous members of the American Legion. The processes of the McCarran Act in respect to the admission of aliens have lessened our safety by arousing contempt and irritation abroad. The provisions concerning registration of Communist and Communist-front organizations have not even efficiency to recommend them. Their only advantage is to provide indefinite assurance to the legal profession against unemployment. They will catch the innocent rather than the guilty. Of themselves, these provisions and the fear they create will tend to paralyze honest thinking and speaking on public questions of grave importance.

The passage of the McCarran Act and the way it was passed must be a warning to believers in civil liberty of the extraordinary difficulty in the struggle that lies before them.

The so-called loyalty tests present a different situation. Some examination there must be in the interest of national security. That is an unhappy fact which must be accepted. The American Civil Liberties Union and other organizations and individuals have suggested methods of inquiry, many of which have been adopted, which in action very substantially reduce the danger to individual right and dignity. The Government itself suffers in the process of clumsy screening by alienating able men from its service just as special loyalty oaths alienate highly qualified professors from our colleges.

Labor unions have their own problems of balance. The basis of membership in an American labor union, especially when the union is demanding a union or a closed shop, cannot fairly be political opinion. It must be simply the fact that a man works on the job. Only overt acts—and those acts should not include criticism of a union's leaders or decisions—should bar a man from membership. In the light of present experience, there is more danger to the true interests of the unions themselves in hunting out Communists or those alleged to be Communists than there is in continuing the usual practice which does not bar Communists from membership. Especially is this true where membership is the price of a job.

On the other hand, it has been found that in some unions Communists as officers can so control the union in the Communist interest as to destroy its freedom. It may not sound logical for a union to say: "We shall not bar Communists from membership, but we shall bar them from office." Nevertheless, in some cases, it may be the best balance of respect for individual freedom, regard for union security and practical common sense that can be reached.

Not all problems of balance arise from the Communist menace. There is no greater denial of civil liberties than when the state, through conscription, takes control over a man's whole life. The continuing practice of military conscription in Europe helped to pave the way psychologically for acceptance of the totalitarian state. Conscription for the awful business of war is especially oppressive since a considerable number of individuals are conscientiously opposed to it. Yet it is the well-nigh unanimous conviction of our democracy that the business of war or preparation for it on any large scale requires conscription as a matter of equity and for efficiency. The best that believers in civil liberties can do is to urge respect for the rights of sincere conscience, to insist that conscription must be limited to emergency, and that our goal must be a society in which it will forever be without excuse of necessity.

This article lays down no blueprint for freedom. Rather it pleads the necessity of remembering in these times of trouble the liberty which is our crowning glory and the primary reason for our unrelenting opposition to Communist aggression. Just because we cannot settle our problems by easy appeal to any libertarian scriptures, we must be the more careful lest in the name of fighting communism or any other totalitarianism we lay its foundation in America.

35. *Are We Afraid of Freedom?* *

Throughout the country and for the past several years, state and private institutions of higher learning have been under fire from legislatures and "Citizens Committees" as being hotbeds of Communism and anti-Americanism. Only Harvard's great prestige has exempted it from direct attack, and even in her case vigilant alumni have protested to the Board of Overseers against certain public actions of the university faculty. In the accompanying article Laird Bell replies to these charges on behalf of the University of

* Laird, Bell, Chairman, Board of Trustees, The University of Chicago, April 11, 1949.

Chicago. He demonstrates by citation after citation that freedom of speech and opinion are a basic and fundamental part of the American tradition. He notes also that of all institutions a university has the greatest claim to be known as the "Market Place of Free Ideas." In fact, freedom of opinion and investigation combine to form the lifeblood of the academic body, without them it atrophies and dies. The attempt to confine the speculations of free men can result only in the establishment of democracy's great enemy, totalitarianism. To paraphrase Mr. Bell, are we that afraid of freedom?

A SERIOUS question is raised by an investigating committee of the Illinois Legislature. The question is fundamental to democracy. It underlies all scholarship and all thoughtful inquiry. Therefore, it underlies the very purpose of a great university. The question is this: In these troubled times are we afraid of freedom?

ONCE AGAIN

In 1935 the Legislature of the State of Illinois empowered a committee to investigate alleged seditious activities at the University of Chicago. Charges were made. Damaging surmises were printed in the public press. The work of the University was interrupted. At the conclusion of the investigation the committee wrote in its report:

> Has the University of Chicago or any of its professors violated either the letter or the spirit of our laws? The answer to this question must be in the negative. . . . *Nothing in the teachings or schedule of the school can be held to be subversive of our institutions or the advocation of the communist form of government as a substitution for the present form of government of the United States.*
>
> MAJORITY REPORT ISSUED BY SENATORS GRAHAM AND BARBOUR
> June 26, 1935 (Italics ours.)

The committee cleared the University. But a university is dependent on the public's appraisal of its contribution, and harm had already been done. Even the generosity of Mr. Walgreen, who contributed five hundred and fifty thousand dollars to the University after the investigation was closed, did not remove the impression created by the headline charges.

This year on March 1, 1949, a group of students from Illinois universities, including a number of students from the University of Chicago, traveled to Springfield to protest the five bills introduced into the state legislature by Senator Paul Broyles. This they had the right to do. If they were disorderly, we disapprove of their conduct. Immediately following this student protest, House Joint Resolution No. 21 was passed calling for an investigation of the University and stating: "It appears that these students are being indoctrinated with Communistic and other subversive theories contrary to our free systems of representative government. . . ." This resolution was passed within a few minutes, without customary hearings or referral to committee.

So, once again apparently the University is to be "investigated." Once again statements harmful to the University's reputation have been made. We think that the people who have made these statements do not know the facts. Most of the statements are untrue. But the newspaper reader is likely to assume that "where there's smoke, there's fire." Therefore, this statement is being made. The truth does not lie somewhere between the allegations of irresponsible individuals and our statement of it. The facts spell the truth, and the truth is the opposite of the charges.

There is no Communist professor at the University of Chicago. There is no Communist indoctrination at the University of Chicago in any course or program in its curriculum.

We know that there is a Communist Club at the University—one of some two hundred student organizations. We know also that its membership comprises one-tenth of 1 per cent of the total student body, about one out of every thousand. The Board, which controls and directs the affairs of this University, could refuse to recognize that organization. But we believe with Mr. Justice Oliver Wendell Holmes that "with effervescent opinions . . . the quickest way to let them get flat is to let them get exposed to the air."

Communism is a term which is used loosely by different people to mean different things. Not everyone who advocates change is a Communist. In times when there is fear of Communist infiltration many persons are afraid of any criticism of things as they are. There is a tendency at such times to put a "red" label on anyone with whose opinions one may not agree. Universities have as much duty to defend the free expression of opinion within the bounds of legality as they have to prevent what is illegal. If such defense subjects the University to the harassment of a legislative investigation and to the possibility of inadequate or distorted reports of it, we shall nevertheless defend the University's principles with all the vigor we can command.

The Trustees and Administration of this University are against communism. They are against it because, among other reasons, it is contrary to our free tradition. Communism suppresses ideas. We oppose communism as we oppose all efforts to undermine our constitutionally guaranteed free speech, free press, and free assembly. We oppose communism because we believe in the tradition of individual freedom which men throughout the centuries have fought to preserve. This tradition has been stated by many men in many ways. A few of these statements follow:

JOHN MILTON, *Areopagitica* (1644):

Give me the liberty to know, to utter, and to argue freely according to conscience, above all liberties. . . . And though all the winds of doctrine were let loose to play upon the earth, so Truth be in the field, we do injuriously by licensing and prohibiting to misdoubt her strength. Let her and Falsehood grapple; who ever knew Truth put to the worse, in a free and open encounter?

THOMAS JEFFERSON, "First Inaugural Address" (1801):

If there be any among us who wish to dissolve this union, or change its republican form, let them stand undisturbed, as monuments of the safety with which error of opinion may be tolerated where reason is left free to combat it.

JOHN STUART MILL, *On Liberty* (1859):

This, then, is the appropriate region of human liberty. It comprises, first, the inward domain of consciousness; demanding liberty of conscience, in the most comprehensive sense; liberty of thought and feeling; absolute freedom of opinion and sentiment on all subjects, practical or speculative, scientific, moral or theological.

WOODROW WILSON, "Message to Congress" (1919):

The only way to keep men from agitating against grievances is to remove the grievances. An unwillingness even to discuss these matters produces only dissatisfactions and gives comfort to the extreme elements in our country which endeavor to stir up disturbances in order to provoke Governments to embark upon a course of retaliation and repression. The seed of revolution is repression.

OLIVER WENDELL HOLMES, *Abrams* v. *United States* (1919):

But when men have realized that time has upset many fighting faiths, they may come to believe even more than they believe the very foundations of their own conduct that the ultimate good desired is better reached by free trade in ideas—that the best test of truth is the power of the thought to get itself accepted in the competition of the market. . . .

LOUIS D. BRANDEIS, *Gilbert v. Minnesota* (1920):

The right of a citizen of the United States to take part, for his own or the country's benefit, in the making of federal laws and in the conduct of the government, necessarily includes the right to speak or write about them; to endeavor to make his own opinion concerning laws existing or contemplated prevail; and to this end, to teach the truth as he sees it. . . . Like the course of the heavenly bodies, harmony in national life is a resultant of the struggle between contending forces. In frank expression of conflicting opinion lies the greatest promise of wisdom in governmental action; and in suppression lies ordinarily the greatest peril.

CHARLES EVANS HUGHES, Letter to Speaker Sweet of the New York State Legislature, reported in the *New York Times*, January 10, 1920:

If public officers or private citizens have any evidence that any individual or group of individuals are plotting revolution and seeking by violent measures to change our Government, let the evidence be laid before the proper authorities and swift action be taken for the protection of the community. Let every resource of inquiry, of pursuit, of prosecution be employed to ferret out and punish the guilty according to our laws. But I count it a most serious mistake to proceed, not against individuals charged with violation of law, but against masses of our citizens combined for political action, by denying them the only resource of peaceful government: that is, action by the ballot box and through duly elected representatives in legislative bodies.

ALFRED E. SMITH, in his message vetoing the Lusk Laws, which sought to license schools and to require teachers' oaths (1919):

Its avowed purpose is to safeguard the institutions and traditions of the country. In effect, it strikes at the very foundation of one of the most cardinal institutions of our nation—the fundamental right of the people to enjoy full liberty in the domain of idea and speech. To this fundamental right there is and can be under our system of government but one limitation, namely, that the law of the land shall not be transgressed, and there is abundant statute law prohibiting the abuse of free speech. . . . The profound sanity of the American people has been demonstrated in many a crisis, and I, for one, do not believe that governmental dictation of what may and may not be taught is necessary to achieve a continuance of the patriotism of our citizenship and its loyal support of the government and its institutions.

THE TRADITION CONTINUES

Opinions such as these are often unpopular, especially when they are spoken in times of stress. But they have been stated again and again by men who were not isolated thinkers but men of action. It is fortunate that in the midst of our present apprehensions and alarms America does not lack men of the courage to continue the democratic tradition.

ROBERT A. TAFT, "The Battle against Communism," address to the Executives Club of Milwaukee, May 8, 1948:

There has been a good deal of talk of outlawing the Communist Party. Of course, under our Constitution, we cannot and should not make it illegal for an American citizen to think communism or express his opinions as long as he does not advocate a violent overthrow of the government. We cannot afford, if we are going to maintain freedom in this country, to violate the Constitution. We would be killing the very liberty which it is the purpose of our whole policy to preserve against totalitarian attack.

DWIGHT D. EISENHOWER, Installation Address as President of Columbia University, the expression of his administrative policy, October 12, 1948:

There will be no administrative suppression or distortion of any subject that merits a place in this University's curricula. The facts of communism, for instance, shall be taught here—its ideological development, its political methods, its economic effects, its probable course in the future. The truth about communism is, today, an indispensable requirement if the true values of our democratic system are to be properly assessed. Ignorance of communism, fascism or any other police-state philosophy is far more dangerous than ignorance of the most virulent disease.

Who among us can doubt the choice of future Americans, as between statism and freedom, if the truth concerning each be constantly held before their eyes? But if we, as adults, attempt to hide from the young the facts in this world struggle, not only will we be making a futile attempt to establish an intellectual "iron curtain," but we will arouse the lively suspicion that statism possesses virtues whose persuasive effect we fear.

WILBUR J. BENDER, Dean of Harvard College, in the March, 1949, issue of the *Harvard Alumni Bulletin* answered those who criticized Harvard for permitting Gerhart Eisler to speak before the John Reed Society:

I know of no faster way of producing communists than by making martyrs out of the handful of communists we now have. Forbidding them to speak would be not only treason to the ancient traditions of Harvard and America: It would be proof that we have something to hide, that we have lost faith in our principles and in our way of life. It would be accepting communist practices in the name of Americanism. . . . . I devoutly hope that the time will never come when we are faced with the sorry spectacle of a great University and a great country trembling timorously in fear of the words of a communist or of a demagogic commentator.

WHAT ABOUT SPIES?

Today, some men devoted to freedom are worried about spies. They would "get rid of all the reds" to eliminate the possibility of espionage. We, too, are against spies. But not everyone who is called "red" is a spy. And, more important, not all spies announce themselves as "reds." The danger, if any, does not exist with the noisy agitators. The University of Chicago is engaged in secret projects of vital importance to national defense. The University is under surveillance of professional investigators, agents of the F.B.I. and of the military intelligence units. This, we think, is the way to look for spies. The general suppression of "reds" is too simple, too amateurish to be effective. J. Edgar Hoover, head of the F.B.I., is against it.

THE ATOMIC BOMB

"The Italian navigator has landed in the New World, and the natives are friendly."

In this cryptic message, so legend has it, the news of Enrico Fermi's successful operation of the atomic "pile" under the grandstand of Stagg Field at the University of Chicago was flashed to Washington on December 2, 1942. It meant that the chain reaction worked, and the first unleashing of atomic energy was under control.

The chain reaction made possible the most terrible weapon in history. It created the greatest economic fact of our time. It opened up endless new vistas for scientific accomplishment.

The work on the atomic bomb took great scientists. It also took great courage. Had it failed, the University might have been charged with the most spectacular boondoggle of all time. Or without the adequate calculations and protections which its scientists provided, the University might have been responsible for blowing up the northern end of Illinois.

The chain reaction is in a sense only a symbol of the working of freedom in ideas. It is no accident that the world's leading scientists wish to work in the free atmosphere provided by a great university. Freedom is the necessary condition of learning and progress.

Its contribution to the successful production of the atomic bomb was but one facet of the University's wartime activity. Its alumni and its staff served valiantly. It provided numerous trained individuals for positions of grave responsibility. Its facilities were mobilized and its activities ranged from interpretation and training in Chinese dialects and the prediction of weather in the Arctic region to the development of numerous protective measures for armed forces personnel. The University of Chicago has been honored by the Secretary of War for "contributing materially to the successful conclusion of World War II."

THE MARKET PLACE OF FREE IDEAS

This University was founded and rose to international prominence under circumstances which are possible only in a free and democratic state. Free interchange of ideas, free research, and the right of its faculty members to engage without restraint in the activities dictated by their judgment and their conscience have been protected and encouraged. Out of this freedom have come the renowned contributions of this University to the humanities and to the physical sciences, the social sciences, and the biological sciences.

The galaxy of Midwest state universities—Illinois, Michigan, Minnesota, Iowa—could scarcely have come to their current high standards without the compelling influence of the University of Chicago.

EDWIN R. EMBREE, *Harper's Magazine*, March, 1949

It was in an atmosphere of freedom that A. A. Michelson, earliest American physicist to win the Nobel Prize, measured the diameter of a star for the first time; James H. Breasted, America's first professor of Egyptology, furthered the understanding and reconstruction of ancient society; Robert A. Millikan won the Nobel Prize for measuring the charge of the electron; Edgar J. Goodspeed achieved the status of the nation's foremost New Testament scholar; Arno Luckhardt discovered ethylene gas, used as an anesthetic in millions of operations; Frank Billings demonstrated that teeth and tonsils can be focal centers for the spread of infection; Arthur H. Compton won the Nobel Prize for his pioneer work on X-rays; Charles Merriam rose to eminence as a scholar and teacher of American political thought; Arthur J. Dempster isolated uranium 235, the atomic explosive—these men and the host of their distinguished colleagues produced the achievements which have placed this University among the foremost in the world.

Some day I would like to take a year off, return to Chicago, and write a book about the University of Chicago, which by any reckoning is one of the three or four most outstanding in the world.

JOHN GUNTHER, *Inside USA*

It is in that freedom that the men of the University work today to find a cure for cancer, to harness atomic energy for peaceful productive use, to widen our knowledge of the social, political, and cultural forces in all human experience, and to train the teachers, the scientists, the scholars, and the enlightened citizens of tomorrow. It is upon that freedom that the future promise of the University is dependent. As Norman Cousins, editor of the *Saturday Review of Literature*, wrote in an editorial:

> For it is that environment rather than any dogma that represents the real Chicago Story. It is impossible to spend any time on the campus without sensing the vitality of true academic freedom—not the academic freedom which limits itself (instead of being limited from without) to stump speeches or political activity, but the academic freedom which Holmes used to call the open market place of ideas. The spirit of independence, particularly as it applies to research . . . gives Chicago both its dominant characteristics and its chief claim on the future.

To be great, a university must adhere to principle. It cannot shift with the winds of passing public opinion. Its work is frequently mystifying and frequently misunderstood. It must rely for its support upon a relatively small number of people who understand the important contributions it makes to the welfare of the community and the improvement of mankind; upon those who understand that academic freedom is important not because of its benefits to professors but because of its benefits to all of us.

Today our tradition of freedom is under attack. There are those who are afraid of freedom. We do not share these fears. The University of Chicago needs the support of those who believe as we do.

36. *Eugene Dennis et al. v. United States*

SUPREME COURT OF THE UNITED STATES,
1951 (CERTIORARI) 341 U.S. 494

IN OCTOBER, 1949, Judge Medina of the New York Federal District Court sentenced to jail eleven top leaders of the U. S. Communist Party for violation of the Smith Act of 1940. The trial attracted wide interest because it involved both the fate of the eleven leaders and the constitutionality of the Smith Act itself. On appeal the Supreme Court of the United States in a 6-2 decision sustained the holding of the District Court. In doing so, the Court both upheld the constitutionality of the Smith Act and found the defendants guilty of conspiring to teach and advocate the overthrow of the government by force and violence. Justices Reed, Burton, and Minton concurred in the decision and found, in addition, that the defendants had engaged in a conspiracy that created a "clear and present danger" of overthrowing the government by force and violence. Justices Black and Douglas dissented, and Mr. Justice Clark took no part in the case. The decision did not declare the Communist Party of the U.S.A. to be illegal but the Department of Justice is now instituting procedures against the party under the Internal Security Act of 1950 with the view of compelling it to register as a foreign-controlled agency. The Court's decision is indicative of the temper of the times in regard to the danger of Communism and represents the furthest advance yet made by the present Court in the direction of curtailment of individual liberties. As Mr. Justice Frankfurter pointed out in his concurring opinion, the decision contains implications dangerous to our traditional concept of freedom of speech, long the hallmark of our democratic system.

MR. CHIEF JUSTICE VINSON announced the judgment of the Court and an opinion in which MR. JUSTICE REED, MR. JUSTICE BURTON and MR. JUSTICE MINTON join:

Petitioners were indicted in July, 1948, for violation of the conspiracy provisions of the Smith Act, 54 Stat. 671, 18 U. S. C. (1946 ed.) par. 11, during the period of April, 1945, to July, 1948. The pretrial motion to quash the indictment on the grounds, *inter alia,* that the statute was unconstitutional was denied, United States v. Foster, 80 F. Supp. 479, and the case was set for trial on January 17, 1949. A verdict of guilty as to all the petitioners was returned by the jury on

October 14, 1949. The Court of Appeals affirmed the convictions. 183 F. 2d 201. We granted certiorari, 340 U. S. 863, limited to the following two questions: (1) Whether either par. 2 or par. 3 of the Smith Act, inherently or as construed and applied in the instant case, violates the First Amendment and other provisions of the Bill of Rights; (2) whether either par. 2 or par. 3 of the Act, inherently or as construed and applied in the instant case, violates the First and Fifth Amendments because of indefiniteness.

Sections 2 and 3 of the Smith Act, 54 Stat. 671, 18 U. S. C. (1946 ed.) pars. 10, 11 (see present 18 U. S. C. par. 2385), provide as follows:

> Sec. 2.
>
> (a) It shall be unlawful for any person—
>
> (1) to knowingly or willfully advocate, abet, advise, or teach the duty, necessity, desirability, or propriety of overthrowing or destroying any government in the United States by force or violence, or by the assassination of any officer of such government;
>
> (2) with intent to cause the overthrow or destruction of any government in the United States, to print, publish, edit, issue, circulate, sell, distribute, or publicly display any written or printed matter advocating, advising, or teaching the duty, necessity, desirability, or propriety of overthrowing or destroying any government in the United States by force or violence;
>
> (3) to organize or help to organize any society, group, or assembly of persons who teach, advocate, or encourage the overthrow or destruction of any government in the United States by force or violence; or to be or become a member of, or affiliate with, any such society, group, or assembly of persons, knowing the purpose thereof.
>
> (b) For the purposes of this section, the term 'government in the United States' means the Government of the United States, the government of any State, Territory, or possession of the United States, the government of the District of Columbia, or the government of any political subdivision of any of them.
>
> Sec. 3. It shall be unlawful for any person to attempt to commit, or to conspire to commit, any of the acts prohibited by the provisions of . . . this title.

The indictment charged the petitioners with wilfully and knowingly conspiring (1) to organize as the Communist Party of the United States of America a society, group and assembly of persons who teach and advocate the overthrow and destruction of the Government of the United States by force and violence, and (2) knowingly and wilfully to advocate and teach the duty and necessity of overthrowing and destroying the Government of the United States by force and violence.

The indictment further alleged that par. 2 of the Smith Act proscribes these acts and that any conspiracy to take such action is a violation of par. 3 of the Act.

The trial of the case extended over nine months, six of which were devoted to the taking of evidence, resulting in a record of 16,000 pages. Our limited grant of the writ of certiorari has removed from our consideration any question as to the sufficiency of the evidence to support the jury's determination that petitioners are guilty of the offense charged. Whether on this record petitioners did in fact advocate the overthrow of the Government by force and violence is not before us, and we must base any discussion of this point upon the conclusions stated in the opinion of the Court of Appeals, which treated the issue in great detail. That court held that the record in this case amply supports the necessary finding of the jury that petitioners, the leaders of the Communist Party in this country, were unwilling to work within our framework of democracy, but intended to initiate a violent revolution whenever the propitious occasion appeared. Petitioners dispute the meaning to be drawn from the evidence, contending that the Marxist-Leninist doctrine they advocated taught that force and violence to achieve a Communist form of government in an existing democratic state would be necessary only because the ruling classes of that state would never permit the transformation to be accomplished peacefully, but would use force and violence to defeat any peaceful political and economic gain the Communists could achieve. But the Court of Appeals held that the record supports the following broad conclusions: By virtue of their control over the political apparatus of the Communist Political Association, petitioners were able to transform that organization into the Communist Party; that the policies of the Association were changed from peaceful cooperation with the United States and its economic and political structure to a policy which had existed before the United States and the Soviet Union were fighting a common enemy, namely, a policy which worked for the overthrow of the Government by force and violence; that the Communist Party is a highly disciplined organization, adept at infiltration into strategic positions, use of aliases, and double-meaning language; that the Party is rigidly controlled; that Communists, unlike other political parties, tolerate no dissension from the policy laid down by the guiding forces, but that the approved program is slavishly followed by the members of the Party; that the literature of the Party and the statements and activities of its leaders, petitioners here, advocate, and the general goal of the Party was, during the period in question, to achieve a successful overthrow of the existing order by force and violence.

I

It will be helpful in clarifying the issues to treat next the contention that the trial judge improperly interpreted the statute by charging that the statute required an unlawful intent before the jury could convict. More specifically, he charged that the jury could not find the petitioners guilty under the indictment unless they found that petitioners had the intent "to overthrow the government by force and violence as speedily as circumstances permit."

Section 2 (a) (1) makes it unlawful "to knowingly or wilfully advocate, . . . or teach the duty, necessity, desirability or propriety of overthrowing or destroying any government in the United States by force or violence. . ." Section 2 (a) (3) "to organize or help to organize any society, group or assembly of persons who teach, advocate or encourage the overthrow. . . ." Because of the fact that par. 2 (a) (2) expressly requires a specific intent to overthrow the Government, and because of the absence of precise language in the foregoing subsections, it is claimed that Congress deliberately omitted any such requirement. We do not agree. It would require a far greater indication of congressional desire that intent not be made an element of the crime than the use of the disjunctive "knowingly or wilfully" in par. 2 (a) (1), or the omission of exact language in par. 2 (a) (3). The structure and purpose of the statute demand the inclusion of intent as an element of the crime. Congress was concerned with those who advocate and organize for the overthrow of the Government. Certainly those who recruit and combine for the purpose of advocating overthrow intend to bring about that overthrow. We hold that the statute requires as an essential element of the crime proof of the intent of those who are charged with its violation to overthrow the Government by force and violence. See Williams v. United States, 341 U. S. 97, 101-102 (1951); Screws v. United States, 325 U. S. 91, 101-105 (1945); Cramer v. United States, 325 U. S. 1, 31 (1945).

Nor does the fact that there must be an investigation of a state of mind under this interpretation afford any basis for rejection of that meaning. A survey of Title 18 of the U. S. Code indicates that the vast majority of the crimes designated by that Title require, by express language, proof of the existence of a certain mental state, in words such as "knowingly," "maliciously," "wilfully," "with the purpose of," "with intent to," or combinations or permutations of these and synonymous terms. The existence of a *mens rea* is the rule of, rather than the exception to, the principles of Anglo-American criminal jurisprudence.

See American Communications Assn. v. Douds, 339 U. S. 382, 411 (1950).

It has been suggested that the presence of intent makes a difference in the law when an "act otherwise excusable or carrying minor penalties" is accompanied by such an evil intent. Yet the existence of such an intent made the killing condemned in *Screws, supra,* and the beating in *Williams, supra,* both clearly and severely punishable under state law, offenses constitutionally punishable by the Federal Government. In those cases, the Court required the Government to prove that the defendants *intended* to deprive the victim of a constitutional right. If that precise mental state may be an essential element of a crime, surely an intent to overthrow the Government of the United States by advocacy thereof is equally susceptible of proof.

II

The obvious purpose of the statute is to protect existing Government, not from change by peaceable, lawful and constitutional means, but from change by violence, revolution and terrorism. That it is within the power of the Congress to protect the Government of the United States from armed rebellion is a proposition which requires little discussion. Whatever theoretical merit there may be to the argument that there is a "right" to rebellion against dictatorial governments is without force where the existing structure of the government provides for peaceful and orderly change. We reject any principle of governmental helplessness in the face of preparation for revolution, which principle, carried to its logical conclusion, must lead to anarchy. No one could conceive that it is not within the power of Congress to prohibit acts intended to overthrow the Government by force and violence. The question with which we are concerned here is not whether Congress has such *power,* but whether the *means* which it has employed conflict with the First and Fifth Amendments to the Constitution.

One of the bases for the contention that the means which Congress has employed are invalid takes the form of an attack on the face of the statute on the grounds that by its terms it prohibits academic discussion of the merits of Marxism-Leninism, that it stifles ideas and is contrary to all concepts of a free speech and a free press. Although we do not agree that the language itself has that significance, we must bear in mind that it is the duty of the federal courts to interpret federal legislation in a manner not inconsistent with the demands of the Constitution. American Communications Assn. v. Douds, 339 U. S. 382, 407 (1950). We are not here confronted with cases similar to Thornhill

v. Alabama, 310 U. S. 88 (1940); Herndon v. Lowry, 301 U. S. 242 (1937); and DeJonge v. Oregon, 299 U. S. 353 (1937), where a state court had given a meaning to a state statute which was inconsistent with the Federal Constitution. This is a federal statute which we must interpret as well as judge. Herein lies the fallacy of reliance upon the manner in which this Court has treated judgments of state courts. Where the statute as construed by the state court transgressed the First Amendment, we could not but invalidate the judgments of conviction.

The very language of the Smith Act negates the interpretation which petitioners would have us impose on that Act. It is directed at advocacy, not discussion. Thus, the trial judge properly charged the jury that they could not convict if they found that petitioners did "no more than pursue peaceful studies and discussions or teachings and advocacy in the realm of ideas." He further charged that it was not unlawful "to conduct in an American college and university a course explaining the philosophical theories set forth in the books which have been placed in evidence." Such a charge is in strict accord with the statutory language, and illustrates the meaning to be placed on those words. Congress did not intend to eradicate the free discussion of political theories, to destroy the traditional rights of Americans to discuss and evaluate ideas without fear of governmental sanction. Rather Congress was concerned with the very kind of activity in which the evidence showed these petitioners engaged.

III

But although the statute is not directed at the hypothetical cases which petitioners have conjured, its application in this case has resulted in convictions for the teaching and advocacy of the overthrow of the Government by force and violence, which, even though coupled with the intent to accomplish that overthrow, contains an element of speech. For this reason, we must pay special heed to the demands of the First Amendment marking out the boundaries of speech.

We pointed out in *Douds, supra,* that the basis of the First Amendment is the hypothesis that speech can rebut speech, propaganda will answer propaganda, free debate of ideas will result in the wisest governmental policies. It is for this reason that this Court has recognized the inherent value of free discourse. An analysis of the leading cases in this Court which have involved direct limitations on speech, however, will demonstrate that both the majority of the Court and the dissenters in particular cases have recognized that this is not an unlimited, unqualified right, but that the societal value of speech must, on occasion, be subordinated to other values and considerations.

No important case involving free speech was decided by this Court prior to Schenck v. United States, 249 U. S. 47 (1919). Indeed, the summary treatment accorded an argument based upon an individual's claim that the First Amendment protected certain utterances indicates that the Court at earlier dates placed no unique emphasis upon that right. It was not until the classic dictum of Justice Holmes in the Schenck case that speech *per se* received that emphasis in a majority opinion. That case involved a conviction under the Criminal Espionage Act, 40 Stat. 217. The question the Court faced was whether the evidence was sufficient to sustain the conviction. Writing for a unanimous Court, Justice Holmes states that the "question in every case is whether the words used are used in such circumstances and are of such a nature as to create a clear and present danger that they will bring about the substantive evils that Congress has a right to prevent." 249 U. S. at 52. But the force of even this expression is considerably weakened by the reference at the end of the opinion to Goldman v. United States, 245 U. S. 474 (1918), a prosecution under the same statute. Said Justice Holmes, "Indeed (Goldman) might be said to dispose of the present contention if the precedent covers all *media concludendi*, but as the right to free speech was not referred to specially, we have thought fit to add a few words." 249 U. S. at 52. The fact is inescapable, too, that the phrase bore no connotation that the danger was to be any threat to the safety of the Republic. The charge was causing and attempting to cause insubordination in the military forces and obstruct recruiting. The objectionable document denounced conscription and its most inciting sentence was, "You must do your share to maintain, support and uphold the rights of the people of this country." 249 U. S. at 51. Fifteen thousand copies were printed and some circulated. This insubstantial gesture toward insubordination in 1917 during war was held to be a clear and present danger of bringing about the evil of military insubordination.

In several later cases involving convictions under the Criminal Espionage Act, the nub of the evidence the Court held sufficient to meet the "clear and present danger" test enunciated in Schenck was as follows: Frohwerk v. United States 249 U. S. 204 (1919)—publication of twelve newspaper articles attacking the war; Debs v. United States, 249 U. S. 211 (1919)—one speech attacking United States' participation in the war; Abrams v. United States, 250 U. S. 616 (1920)—circulation of copies of two different socialist circulars attacking the war; Schaefer v. United States, 251 U. S. 466 (1920)—publication of a German-language newspaper with allegedly false articles, critical of capitalism and the war; Pierce v. United States, 252 U. S. 239 (1920)—circulation of copies of a four-page pamphlet written by a clergyman, attacking the purposes of the war and United States' participation therein. Justice Holmes wrote the opinions for a unanimous Court in Schenck, Frohwerk and Debs. He and Justice Brandeis dissented in Abrams, Schaefer and Pierce. The basis of these dissents was that, because of the protection which the First Amendment gives to speech, the evidence in each case was insufficient to show that the defendants had created the requisite danger under Schenck. But these dissents did not mark a change of principle. The dissenters doubted only the probable effectiveness of the puny efforts toward subversion. In Abrams, they wrote, "I do not doubt for a moment that by the same reasoning that would justify punishing persuasion to murder, the United States constitutionally may punish speech that produces or is intended to produce a clear and imminent danger that it will bring about forthwith certain substantive evils that the United States constitutionally may seek to prevent." 250 U. S. at 627. And in Schaefer the test was said to be "one of degree," 251 U. S. at 482, although it is not clear whether "degree" refers to clear and present danger or evil. Perhaps both were meant.

The rule we deduce from these cases is that where an offense is specified by a statute in nonspeech or nonpress terms, a conviction relying upon speech or press as evidence of violation may be sustained only when the speech or publication created a "clear and present danger" of attempting or accomplishing the prohibited crime, e. g., interference with enlistment. The dissents, we repeat, in emphasizing the value of speech, were addressed to the argument of the sufficiency of the evidence.

The next important case before the Court in which free speech was the crux of the conflict was Gitlow v. New York, 268 U.S. 652 (1925). There New York had made it a crime to "advocate . . . the necessity or propriety of overthrowing . . . the government by force. . . ." The evidence of violation of the statute was that the defendant had published a Manifesto attacking the Government and capitalism. The convictions were sustained, Justice Holmes and Brandeis dissenting. The majority refused to apply the "clear and present danger" test to the specific utterance. Its reasoning was as follows: The "clear and present danger" test was applied to the utterance itself in Schenck because the question was merely one of sufficiency of evidence under an admittedly constitutional statute. Gitlow, however, presented a different question. There a legislature had found that a certain kind of speech was, itself, harmful and unlawful. The constitutionality of such a state statute had to be adjudged by this Court just as it determined the constitutionality of any state statute, namely, whether the statute was "reasonable." Since it was entirely reasonable for a state to attempt to protect itself from violent overthrow the statute was perforce reasonable. The only question remaining in the case became whether there was evidence to support the conviction, a question which gave the majority no difficulty. Justices Holmes and Brandeis refused to accept this approach, but insisted that wherever speech was the evidence of the violation, it was necessary to show that the speech created the "clear and present danger" of the substantive evil which the legislature had the right to prevent. Justices Holmes and Brandeis, then, made no distinction between a federal statute which made certain acts unlawful, the evidence to support the conviction being speech, and a statute which made speech itself the crime. This approach was emphasized in Whitney v. California, 274 U. S. 357 (1927), where the Court was confronted with a conviction under the California Criminal Syndicalist statute. The Court sustained the conviction, Justices Brandeis and Holmes concurring in the result. In their concurrence they repeated that even though the legislature had designated certain speech as criminal, this could not prevent the defendant from showing that there was no danger that the substantive evil would be brought about.

Although no case subsequent to Whitney and Gitlow has expressly overruled the majority opinions in those cases, there is little doubt that subsequent opinions have inclined toward the Holmes-Brandeis rationale. And in American Communications Assn. v. Douds, *supra*, we were called upon to decide the validity of par. 9 (h) of the Labor-Management Relations Act of 1947. That section required officials of unions which desired to avail themselves of the facilities of the National Labor Relations Board to take oaths that they did not belong to the Communist Party and that they did not believe in the overthrow of the Government by force and violence. We pointed out that Congress did not intend to punish belief, but rather intended to regulate the conduct of union affairs. We therefore held that any indirect sanction on speech which might arise from the oath requirement did not present a proper case for the "clear and present danger" test, for the regulation was aimed at conduct rather than speech. In discussing the proper measure of evaluation of this kind of legislation, we suggested that the Holmes-Brandeis philosophy insisted that where there was a direct restriction upon speech, a "clear and present danger" that the substantive evil would be caused was necessary before the statute in question could be constitutionally applied. And we stated, "(The First) Amendment requires that one be permitted to believe what he will. It requires that one be permitted to advocate what he will unless there is a clear and present danger that a substantial public evil will result therefrom." 339 U. S. at 412. But we further suggested that neither Justice Holmes nor Justice Brandeis ever envisioned that a shorthand phrase should be crystallized into a rigid rule to be applied inflexibly without regard to the circumstances of each case. Speech is not an absolute, above and beyond control by the legislature when its judgment, subject to review here, is that certain kinds of speech are so undesirable as to warrant criminal sanction. Nothing is more certain in modern society than the principle that there are no absolutes, that a name, a phrase, a standard has meaning only when associated with the considerations which gave birth to the nomenclature. See Douds, 339 U. S. at 397. To those who would paralyze our Government in the face of impending threat by encasing it in a semantic straitjacket we must reply that all concepts are relative.

In this case we are squarely presented with the application of the "clear and present danger" test, and must decide what that phrase imports. We first note that many of the cases in which this Court has reversed convictions by use of this or similar tests have been based on the fact that the interest which the State was attempting to protect was itself too insubstantial to warrant restriction of speech. In this category we may put such cases as Schneider v. State, 308 U. S. 147 (1939); Cantwell v. Connecticut, 310 U. S. 296 (1940); Martin v. Struthers, 319 U. S. 141 (1943); West Virginia State Board of Education v. Barnette, 319 U. S. 624 (1943); Thomas v. Collins, 323 U. S. 516 (1945); Marsh v. Alabama, 326 U. S. 501 (1946); but cf. Prince v. Massachusetts, 321 U. S. 158 (1944); Cox v. New Hampshire, 312 U. S. 569 (1941). Overthrow of the Government by force and violence is certainly a substantial enough interest for the Government to limit speech. Indeed, this is the ultimate value of any society, for if a society cannot protect its very structure from armed internal attack, it must follow that no subordinate value can be protected. If, then, this interest may be protected, the literal problem which is presented is what has been meant by the use of the phrase "clear and present danger" of the utterances bringing about the evil within the power of Congress to punish.

Obviously, the words cannot mean that before the Government may act, it must wait until the *putsch* is about to be executed, the plans have been laid and the signal is awaited. If Government is aware that a group aiming at its overthrow is attempting to indoctrinate its members and to commit them to a course whereby they will strike when the leaders feel the circumstances permit, action by the Government is required. The argument that there is no need for Government to concern itself, for Government is strong, it possesses ample powers to put down a rebellion, it may defeat the revolution with ease needs no answer. For that is not the question. Certainly an attempt to overthrow the Government by force, even though doomed from the outset because of inadequate numbers or power of the revolutionists, is a sufficient evil for Congress to prevent. The damage which such attempts create both physically and politically to a nation makes it impossible to measure the validity in terms of the probability of success, or the immediacy of a successful attempt. In the instant case the trial judge charged the jury that they could not convict unless they found that petitioners intended to overthrow the Government "as speedily as circumstances would permit." This does not mean, and could not properly mean, that they would not strike until there was certainty of success. What was meant was that the revolutionists would strike when they thought the time was ripe. We must therefore reject the contention that success or probability of success is the criterion.

The situation with which Justices Holmes and Brandeis were concerned in Gitlow was a comparatively isolated event, bearing little relation in their minds to any substantial threat to the safety of the community. Such also is true of cases like Fiske v. Kansas, 274 U. S. 380 (1927), and DeJonge v. Oregon, 299 U. S. 353 (1937); but cf. Lazar v. Pennsylvania, 286 U. S. 532 (1932). They were not confronted with any situation comparable to the instant one—the development of an apparatus designed and dedicated to the overthrow of the government, in the context of world crisis after crisis.

Chief Judge Learned Hand, writing for the majority below, interpreted the phrase as follows: "In each case (courts) must ask whether the gravity of the 'evil,' discounted by its improbability, justifies such invasion of free speech as is necessary to avoid the danger." 183 F.2d at 212. We adopt this statement of the rule. As articulated by Chief Judge Hand, it is as succinct and inclusive as any other we might devise at this time. It takes into consideration those factors which we deem relevant, and relates their significances. More we cannot expect from words.

Likewise, we are in accord with the court below, which affirmed the trial court's finding that the requisite danger existed. The mere fact that from the period 1945 to 1948 petitioners' activities did not result in an attempt to overthrow the Government by force and violence is of course no answer to the fact that there was a group that was ready to make the attempt. The formation by petitioners of such a highly organized conspiracy, with rigidly disciplined members subject to call when the leaders, these petitioners, felt that the time had come for action, coupled with the inflammable nature of world conditions, similar uprisings in other countries, and the touch-and-go nature of our relations with countries with whom petitioners were in the very least ideologically attuned, convince us that their convictions were justified on this score. And this analysis disposes of the contention that a conspiracy to advocate, as distinguished from the advocacy itself, cannot be constitutionally restrained, because it comprises only the preparation. It is the existence of the conspiracy which creates the danger. Cf. Pinkerton v. United States, 328 U. S. 640 (1946); Goldman v. United States, 245 U. S. 474 (1918); United States v. Rabinowich, 238 U. S. 78 (1915). If the ingredients of the reaction are present, we cannot bind the Government to wait until the catalyst is added.

IV

Although we have concluded that the finding that there was a sufficient danger to warrant the application of the statute was justified on the merits, there remains the problem of whether the trial judge's treatment of the issue was correct. He charged the jury, in relevant part, as follows:

> In further construction and interpretation of the statute I charge you that it is not the abstract doctrine of overthrowing or destroying organized government by unlawful means which is denounced by this law, but the teaching and advocacy of action for the accomplishment of that purpose, by language reasonably and ordinarily calculated to incite persons to such action. Accordingly, you cannot find the defendants or any of them guilty of the crime charged unless you are satisfied beyond a reasonable doubt that they conspired to organize a society, group and assembly of persons who teach and advocate the overthrow or destruction of the Government of the United States by force and violence and to advocate and teach the duty and necessity of overthrowing or destroying the Government of the United States by force and violence, with the intent that such teaching and advocacy be of a rule or principle of action and by language reasonably and ordinarily calculated to incite persons to such action, all with the intent to cause the overthrow or destruction of the Government of the United States by force and violence as speedily as circumstances would permit.
>
> • • • • •
>
> If you are satisfied that the evidence establishes beyond a reasonable doubt that the defendants, or any of them, are guilty of a violation of the statute, as I have interpreted it to you, I find as a matter of law that there is sufficient danger of a substantive evil that the Congress has a right to prevent to justify the application of the statute under the First Amendment of the Constitution.
>
> This is a matter of law about which you have no concern. It is a finding on a matter of law which I deem essential to support my ruling that the case should be submitted to you to pass upon the guilt or innocence of the defendants. . . .

It is thus clear that he reserved the question of the existence of the danger for his own determination, and the question becomes whether the issue is of such a nature that it should have been submitted to the jury.

The first paragraph of the quoted instructions calls for the jury to find the facts essential to establish the substantive crime, violation of pars. 2 (a) (1) and 2 (a) (3) of the Smith Act, involved in the conspiracy charge. There can be no doubt that if the jury found those facts against the petitioners violation of the Act would be established. The argument that the action of the trial court is erroneous, in declaring as a matter of law that such violation shows sufficient danger to justify the punishment despite the First Amendment, rests on the theory that a jury must decide a question of the application of the First Amendment. We do not agree.

When facts are found that establish the violation of a statute the protection against conviction afforded by the First Amendment is a matter of law. The doctrine that there must be a clear and present danger of a substantive evil that Congress has a right to prevent is a judicial rule to be applied as a matter of law by the courts. The guilt is established by proof of facts. Whether the First Amendment protects the activity which constitutes the violation of the statute must depend upon a judicial determination of the scope of the First Amendment applied to the circumstances of the case.

Petitioners' reliance upon Justice Brandeis' language in his concurrence in Whitney, *supra*, is misplaced. In that case Justice Brandeis pointed out that the defendant could have made the existence of the requisite danger the important issue at her trial, but that she had not done so. In discussing this failure, he stated that the defendant could have had the issue determined by the court or the jury. No realistic construction of this disjunctive language could arrive at the conclusion that he intended to state that the question was *only* determinable by a jury. Nor is the incidental statement of the majority in Pierce, *supra*, of any more persuasive effect. There the issue of the probable effect of the publication had been submitted to the jury, and the majority was apparently addressing its remarks to the contention of the dissenters that the jury could not reasonably have returned a verdict of guilty on the evidence. Indeed, in the very case in which the phrase was born, *Schenck*, this Court itself examined the record to find whether the requisite danger appeared, and the issue was not submitted to a jury. And in every later case in which the Court has measured the validity of a statute by the "clear and present danger" test, that determination has been by the court, the question of the danger not being submitted to the jury.

The question in this case is whether the statute which the legislature has enacted may be constitutionally applied. In other words, the Court must examine judicially the application of the statute to the particular situation, to ascertain if the Constitution prohibits the conviction. We hold that the statute may be applied where there is a "clear and present danger" of the substantive evil which the legislature had the right to prevent. Bearing as it does, the marks of a "question of law," the issue is properly one for the judge to decide.

V

There remains to be discussed the question of vagueness—whether the statute as we have interpreted it is too vague, not sufficiently advising those who would speak of the limitations upon their activity. It is urged that such vagueness contravenes the First and Fifth Amendments. This argument is particularly nonpersuasive when presented by petitioners, who, the jury found, intended to overthrow the Government as speedily as circumstances would permit. . . .

We agree that the standard as defined is not a neat, mathematical formulary. Like all verbalizations it is subject to criticism on the score of indefiniteness. But petitioners themselves contend that the verbalization, "clear and present danger" is the proper standard. We see no difference from the standpoint of vagueness, whether the standard of "clear and present danger" is one contained in *haec verba* within the statute, or whether it is the judicial measure of constitutional applicability. We have shown the indeterminate standard the phrase necessarily connotes. We do not think we have rendered that standard any more indefinite by our attempt to sum up the factors which are included within its scope. We think it well serves to indicate to those who would advocate constitutionally prohibited conduct that there is a line beyond which they may not go—a line, which they, in full knowledge of what they intend and the circumstances in which their activity takes place, will well appreciate and understand. . . . Where there is doubt as to the intent of the defendants, the nature of their activities, or their power to bring about the evil, this Court will review the convictions with the scrupulous care demanded by our Constitution. But we are not convinced that because there may be borderline cases at some time in the future, these convictions should be reversed because of the argument that these petitioners could not know that their activities were constitutionally proscribed by the statute.

We have not discussed many of the questions which could be extracted from the record, although they were treated in detail by the court below. Our limited grant of the writ of certiorari has withdrawn from our consideration at this date those questions, which include, *inter alia*, sufficiency of the evidence, composition of jury, and conduct of the trial.

We hold that pars. 2 (a) (1), 2 (a) (3) and 3 of the Smith Act, do not inherently, or as construed or applied in the instant case, violate the First Amendment and other provisions of the Bill of Rights, or the First and Fifth Amendments because of indefiniteness. Petitioners intended to overthrow the Government of the United States as speedily as the circumstances would permit. Their conspiracy to organize the Communist Party and to teach and advocate the overthrow of the Government of the United States by force and violence created a "clear and present danger" of an attempt to overthrow the Government by force and violence. They were properly and constitutionally convicted for violation of the Smith Act. The judgments of conviction are

Affirmed.

MR. JUSTICE BLACK, dissenting:

Here again, as in *Breard v. Alexandria*, decided this day, my basic disagreement with the Court is not as to how we should explain or reconcile what was said in prior decisions but springs from a fundamental difference in constitutional approach. Consequently, it would serve no useful purpose to state my position at length.

At the outset I want to emphasize what the crime involved in this case is, and what it is not. These petitioners were not charged with an attempt to overthrow the Government. They were not charged with overt acts of any kind designed to overthrow the Government. . . . The charge was that they agreed to assemble and to talk and publish certain ideas at a later date: The indictment is that they conspired to organize the Communist Party and to use speech or newspapers and other publications in the future to teach and advocate the forcible overthrow of the Government. No matter how it is worded, this is a virulent form of prior censorship of speech and press, which I believe the First Amendment forbids. I would hold Section 3 of the Smith Act authorizing this prior restraint unconstitutional on its face and as applied.

But let us assume, contrary to all constitutional ideas of fair criminal procedure, that petitioners although not indicted for the crime of actual advocacy, may be punished for it. Even on this radical assumption, the other opinions in this case show that the only way to affirm these convictions is to repudiate directly or indirectly the established "clear and present danger" rule. This the Court does in a way which greatly restricts the protections afforded by the First Amendment. The opinions for affirmance indicate that the chief reason for jettisoning the rule is the expressed fear that advocacy of Communist doctrine endangers the safety of the Republic. Undoubtedly, a governmental policy of unfettered communication of ideas does entail dangers. To the Founders of this Nation, however, the benefits derived from free expression were worth the risk. They embodied this philosophy in the First Amendment's command that Congress "shall make no law abridging . . . the freedom of speech, or of the press . . ." I have always believed that the First Amendment is the keystone of our Government, that the freedoms it guarantees provide the best insurance against destruction of all freedom. At least as to speech in the realm of public matters, I believe that the "clear and present danger" test does not "mark the furthermost constitutional boundaries of protected expression" but does "no more than recognize a minimum compulsion of the Bill of Rights." *Bridges v. California*, 314 U. S. 252, 263.

So long as this Court exercises the power of judicial review of legislation, I cannot agree that the First Amendment permits us to sustain laws suppressing freedom of speech and press on the basis of Congress' or our own notions of mere "reasonableness." Such a doctrine waters down the First Amendment so that it amounts to little more than an admonition to Congress. The Amendment as so construed is not likely to protect any but those "safe" or orthodox views which rarely need its protection. I must also express my objections to the holding because, as MR. JUSTICE DOUGLAS' dissent shows, it sanctions the determination of a crucial issue of fact by the judge rather than by the jury. Nor can I let this opportunity pass without expressing my objection to the severely limited grant of certiorari in this case which precluded consideration here of at least two other reasons for reversing these convictions: (1) the record shows a discriminatory selection of the jury panel which prevented trial before a representative cross-section of the community; (2) the record shows that one member of the trial jury was violently hostile to petitioners before and during the trial.

Public opinion being what it now is, few will protest the conviction of these Communist petitioners. There is hope, however, that in calmer times, when present pressures, passions and fears subside, this or some later Court will restore the First Amendment liberties to the high preferred place where they belong in a free society.

(Mr. Justice Black and Mr. Justice Douglas dissent; Mr. Justice Clark not participating.)

37. *Who Is Loyal to America?* *

THIS article by Professor Commager could have been titled "What Is Americanism?" True Americanism, he thinks, is something more than unquestioning acceptance of things as they are. It includes a faith in progress; and progress necessarily involves changes in the existing order. The setting of the article is the highly publicized actions of the House Committee on Un-American Activities. That committee acted as if enthusiastic agreement with the free enterprise theory of capitalism were Americanism; any liberal criticism of that theory indicated disloyalty. Those whom the committee regarded as disloyal were put on the public pillory, with scant respect paid to the spirit of the civil liberties clauses of the United States Constitution. Professor Commager underlines anew the importance of safeguarding civil rights. Those rights protect the vital liberty of the individual to advocate peaceful change; peaceful change may be the path to progress.

ON MAY 6 a Russian-born girl, Mrs. Shura Lewis, gave a talk to the students of the Western High School of Washington, D.C. She talked about Russia—its school system, its public health program, the position of women, of the aged, of the workers, the farmers, and the professional classes—and compared, superficially and uncritically, some American and Russian social institutions. The most careful examination of the speech—happily reprinted for us in the *Congressional Record*—does not disclose a single disparagement of anything American unless it is a quasi-humorous reference to the cost of having a baby and of dental treatment in this country. Mrs. Lewis said nothing that had not been said a thousand times, in speeches, in newspapers, magazines, and books. She said nothing that any normal person could find objectionable.

Her speech, however, created a sensation. A few students walked out on it. Others improvised placards proclaiming their devotion to Americanism. Indignant mothers telephoned their protests. Newspapers took a strong stand against the outrage. Congress, rarely concerned for the political or economic welfare of the citizens of the capital city, reacted sharply when its intellectual welfare was at stake. Congressmen Rankin and Dirksen thundered and lightened; the District of Columbia Committee went into a huddle; there were demands

* Henry Steele Commager, *Harper's Magazine*, 195 (September, 1947), pp. 193-199. Copyright, 1947, by Harper and Brothers. Reprinted by permission of the author.

for housecleaning in the whole school system, which was obviously shot through and through with Communism.

All this might be ignored, for we have learned not to expect either intelligence or understanding of Americanism from this element in our Congress. More ominous was the reaction of the educators entrusted with the high responsibility of guiding and guarding the intellectual welfare of our boys and girls. Did they stand up for intellectual freedom? Did they insist that high-school children had the right and the duty to learn about other countries? Did they protest that students were to be trusted to use intelligence and common sense? Did they affirm that the Americanism of their students was staunch enough to resist propaganda? Did they perform even the elementary task, expected of educators above all, of analyzing the much-criticized speech?

Not at all. The District Superintendent of Schools, Dr. Hobart Corning, hastened to agree with the animadversions of Representatives Rankin and Dirksen. The whole thing was, he confessed, "a very unfortunate occurrence," and had "shocked the whole school system." What Mrs. Lewis said, he added gratuitously, was "repugnant to all who are working with youth in the Washington schools," and "the entire affair contrary to the philosophy of education under which we operate." Mr. Danowsky, the hapless principal of the Western High School, was "the most shocked and regretful of all." The District of Columbia Committee would be happy to know that though he was innocent in the matter, he had been properly reprimanded!

It is the reaction of the educators that makes this episode more than a tempest in a teapot. We expect hysteria from Mr. Rankin and some newspapers; we are shocked when we see educators, timid before criticism and confused about first principles, betray their trust. And we wonder what can be that "philosophy of education" which believes that young people can be trained to the duties of citizenship by wrapping their minds in cotton-wool.

Merely by talking about Russia Mrs. Lewis was thought to be attacking Americanism. It is indicative of the seriousness of the situation that during this same week the House found it necessary to take time out from the discussion of the labor bill, the tax bill, the International Trade Organization, and the world famine, to meet assaults upon Americanism from a new quarter. This time it was the artists who were undermining the American system, and members of the House spent some hours passing around reproductions of the paintings which the State Department had sent abroad as part of its program for advertising American culture. We need not pause over the exquisite humor which congressmen displayed in their comments on modern art: weary statesmen must have their fun. But we may profitably remark the major criticism which was directed against this unfortunate collection of paintings. What was wrong with these paintings, it shortly appeared, was that they were un-American. "No American drew those crazy pictures," said Mr. Rankin. Perhaps he was right. The copious files of the Committee on Un-American Activities were levied upon to prove that of the forty-five artists represented "no less than twenty were definitely New Deal in various shades of Communism." The damning facts are specified for each of the pernicious twenty; we can content ourselves with the first of them, Ben-Zion. What is the evidence here? "Ben-Zion was one of the signers of a letter sent to President Roosevelt by the United American Artists which urged help to the USSR and Britain after Hitler attacked Russia." He was, in short, a fellow-traveler of Churchill and Roosevelt.

The same day that Mr. Dirksen was denouncing the Washington school authorities for allowing students to hear about Russia ("In Russia equal right is granted to each nationality. There is no discrimination. Nobody says, you are a Negro, you are a Jew") Representative Williams of Mississippi rose to denounce the *Survey-Graphic* magazine and to add further to our understanding of Americanism. The *Survey-Graphic*, he said, "contained 129 pages of outrageously vile and nauseating anti-Southern, anti-Christian, un-American, and pro-Communist tripe, ostensibly directed toward the elimination of the custom of racial segregation in the South." It was written by "meddling un-American purveyors of hate and indecency."

All in all, a busy week for the House. Yet those who make a practice of reading their *Record* will agree that it was a typical week. For increasingly Congress is concerned with the eradication of disloyalty and the defense of Americanism, and scarcely a day passes that some congressman does not treat us to exhortations and admonitions, impassioned appeals and eloquent declamations, similar to those inspired by Mrs. Lewis, Mr. Ben-Zion, and the editors of the *Survey-Graphic*. And scarcely a day passes that the outlines of the new loyalty and the new Americanism are not etched more sharply in public policy.

And this is what is significant—the emergence of new patterns of Americanism and of loyalty, patterns radically different from those which have long been traditional. It is not only the Congress that is busy designing the new patterns. They are outlined in President Truman's recent disloyalty order; in similar orders formulated by the New York City Council and by state and local authorities throughout the country; in the programs of the D.A.R., the American Legion, and similar patriotic organizations; in the editorials of the Hearst and the McCormick-Patterson papers; and in an elaborate series of advertisements sponsored by large corporations and business organizations. In the making is a revival of the red hysteria of the early 1920's, one of the shabbiest chapters in the history of American democracy; and more than a revival, for the new crusade is designed not merely to frustrate Communism but to formulate a positive definition of Americanism, and a positive concept of loyalty.

What is the new loyalty? It is, above all, conformity. It is the uncritical and unquestioning acceptance of America as it is—the political institutions, the social relationships, the economic practices. It rejects inquiry into the race question or socialized medicine, or public housing, or into the wisdom or validity of our foreign policy. It regards as particularly heinous any challenge to what is called "the system of private enterprise," identifying that system with Americanism. It abandons evolution, repudiates the once popular concept of progress, and regards America as a finished product, perfect and complete.

It is, it must be added, easily satisfied. For it wants not intellectual conviction nor spiritual conquest, but mere outward conformity. In matters of loyalty it takes the word for the deed, the gesture for the principle. It is content with the flag salute, and does not pause to consider the warning of our Supreme Court that "a person gets from a symbol the meaning he puts into it, and what is one man's comfort and inspiration is another's jest and scorn." It is satisfied with membership in respectable organizations and, as it assumes that every member of a liberal organization is a Communist, concludes that every member of a conservative one is a true American. It has not yet learned that not everyone who saith Lord, Lord, shall enter into the kingdom of Heaven. It is designed neither to discover real disloyalty nor to foster true loyalty.

II

What is wrong with this new concept of loyalty? What, fundamentally, is wrong with the pusillanimous retreat of the Washington educators, the barbarous antics of Washington legislators, the hysterical outbursts of the D.A.R., the gross and vulgar appeals of business corporations? It is not merely that these things are offensive. It is rather that they are wrong—morally, socially, and politically.

The concept of loyalty as conformity is a false one. It is narrow and restrictive, denies freedom of thought and of conscience, and is irremediably stained by private and selfish considerations. "Enlightened loyalty," wrote Josiah Royce, who made loyalty the very core of his philosophy, means harm to no man's loyalty. It is at war only with disloyalty, and its warfare, unless necessity constrains, is only a spiritual warfare. It does not foster class hatreds; it knows of nothing reasonable about race prejudices; and it regards all races of men as one in their need of loyalty. It ignores mutual misunderstandings. It loves its own wherever upon earth its own, namely loyalty itself, is to be found.

Justice, charity, wisdom, spirituality, he added, were all definable in terms of loyalty, and we may properly ask which of these qualities our contemporary champions of loyalty display.

Above all, loyalty must be to something larger than oneself, untainted by private purposes or selfish ends. But what are we to say of the attempts by the NAM and by individual corporations to identify loyalty with the system of private enterprise? Is it not as if officeholders should attempt to identify loyalty with their own party, their own political careers? Do not those corporations which pay for full-page advertisements associating Americanism with the competitive system expect, ultimately, to profit from that association? Do not those organizations that deplore, in the name of patriotism, the extension of government operation of hydro-electric power expect to profit from their campaign?

Certainly it is a gross perversion not only of the concept of loyalty but of the concept of Americanism to identify it with a particular economic system. This precise question, interestingly enough, came before the Supreme Court in the Schneiderman case not so long ago—and it was Wendell Willkie who was counsel for Schneiderman. Said the Court:

Throughout our history many sincere people whose attachment to the general Constitutional scheme cannot be doubted have, for various and even divergent reasons, urged differing degrees of governmental ownership and control of natural resources, basic means of production, and banks and the media of exchange, either with or without compensation. And something once regarded as a species of private property was abolished without compensating the owners when the institution of slavery was forbidden. Can it be said that the author of the Emancipation Proclamation and the supporters of the Thirteenth Amendment were not attached to the Constitution?

There is, it should be added, a further danger in the willful identification of Americanism with a particular body of economic practices. Many learned economists predict for the near future an economic crash similar to that of 1929. If Americanism is equated with competitive capitalism, what happens to it if competitive capitalism comes a cropper? If loyalty and private enterprise are inextricably associated, what is to preserve loyalty if private enterprise fails? Those who associate Americanism with a particular program of economic practices have a grave responsibility, for if their program should fail, they expose Americanism itself to disrepute.

The effort to equate loyalty with conformity is misguided because it assumes that there is a fixed content to loyalty and that this can be determined and defined. But loyalty is a principle, and eludes definition except in its own terms. It is devotion to the best interests of the commonwealth, and may require hostility to the particular policies which the government pursues, the particular practices which the economy undertakes, the particular institutions which society maintains. "If there is any fixed star in our Constitutional constellation," said the Supreme Court in the Barnette case, "it is that no official, high or petty, can prescribe what shall be orthodox in politics, nationalism, religion, or other matters of opinion, or force citizens to confess by word or act their faith therein. If there are any circumstances which permit an exception they do not now occur to us."

True loyalty may require, in fact, what appears to the naïve to be disloyalty. It may require hostility to certain provisions of the Constitution itself, and historians have not concluded that those who subscribed to the "Higher Law" were lacking in patriotism. We should not forget that our tradition is one of protest and revolt, and it is stultifying to celebrate the rebels of the past—Jefferson and Paine, Emerson and Thoreau—while we silence the rebels of the present. "We are a rebellious nation," said Theodore Parker, known in his day as the Great American Preacher, and went on:

> Our whole history is treason; our blood was attainted before we were born; our creeds are infidelity to the mother church; our constitution, treason to our fatherland. What of that? Though all the governors in the world bid us commit treason against man, and set the example, let us never submit.

Those who would impose upon us a new concept of loyalty not only assume that this is possible, but have the presumption to believe that they are competent to write the definition. We are reminded of Whitman's defiance of the "never-ending audacity of elected persons." Who are those who would set the standards of loyalty? They are Rankins and Bilbos, officials of the D.A.R. and the Legion and the NAM, Hearsts and McCormicks. May we not say of Rankin's harangues on loyalty what Emerson said of Webster at the time of the Seventh of March speech: "The word honor in the mouth of Mr. Webster is like the word love in the mouth of a whore."

What do men know of loyalty who make a mockery of the Declaration of Independence and the Bill of Rights, whose energies are dedicated to stirring up race and class hatreds, who would straitjacket the American spirit? What indeed do they know of America—the America of Sam Adams and Tom Paine, of Jackson's defiance of the Court and Lincoln's celebration of labor, of Thoreau's essay on Civil Disobedience and Emerson's championship of John Brown, of the America of the Fourierists and the Come-Outers, of cranks and fanatics, of socialists and anarchists? Who among American heroes could meet their tests, who would be cleared by their committees? Not Washington, who was a rebel. Not Jefferson, who wrote that all men are created equal and whose motto was "rebellion to tyrants is obedience to God." Not Garrison, who publicly burned the Constitution; or Wendell Phillips, who spoke for the under-privileged everywhere and counted himself a philosophical anarchist; not Seward of the Higher Law or Sumner of racial equality. Not Lincoln, who admonished us to have malice toward none, charity for all; or Wilson, who warned that our flag was "a flag of liberty of opinion as well as of political liberty"; or Justice Holmes, who said that our Constitution is an experiment and that while that experiment is being made "we should be eternally vigilant against attempts to check the expression of opinions that we loathe and believe to be fraught with death."

III

There are further and more practical objections against the imposition of fixed concepts of loyalty or tests of disloyalty. The effort is itself a confession of fear, a declaration of insolvency. Those who are sure of themselves do not need reassurance, and those who have confidence in the strength and the virtue of America do not need to fear either criticism or competition. The effort is bound to miscarry. It will not apprehend those who are really disloyal, it will not even frighten them; it will affect only those who can be labeled "radical." It is sobering to recall that though the Japanese relocation program, carried through at such incalculable cost in misery and tragedy, was justified to us on the ground that the Japanese were potentially disloyal, the record does not disclose a single case of Japanese disloyalty or sabotage during the whole war. The warning sounded by the Supreme Court in the Barnette flag-salute case is a timely one:

> Ultimate futility of such attempts to compel obedience is the lesson of every such effort from the Roman drive to stamp out Christianity as a disturber of pagan unity, the Inquisition as a means to religious and dynastic

unity, the Siberian exiles as a means to Russian unity, down to the fast-failing efforts of our present totalitarian enemies. Those who begin coercive elimination of dissent soon find themselves exterminating dissenters. Compulsory unification of opinion achieves only the unanimity of the graveyard.

Nor are we left to idle conjecture in this matter; we have had experience enough. Let us limit ourselves to a single example, one that is wonderfully relevant. Back in 1943 the House Un-American Activities Committee, deeply disturbed by alleged disloyalty among government employees, wrote a definition of subversive activities and proceeded to apply it. The definition was admirable, and no one could challenge its logic or its symmetry:

> Subversive activity derives from conduct intentionally destructive of or inimical to the Government of the United States—that which seeks to undermine its institutions, or to distort its functions, or to impede its projects, or to lessen its efforts, the ultimate end being to overturn it all.

Surely anyone guilty of activities so defined deserved not only dismissal but punishment. But how was the test applied? It was applied to two distinguished scholars, Robert Morss Lovett and Goodwin Watson, and to one able young historian, William E. Dodd, Jr., son of our former Ambassador to Germany. Of almost three million persons employed by the government, these were the three whose subversive activities were deemed the most pernicious, and the House cut them off the payroll. The sequel is familiar. The Senate concurred only to save a wartime appropriation; the President signed the bill under protest for the same reason. The Supreme Court declared the whole business a "bill of attainder" and therefore unconstitutional. Who was it, in the end, who engaged in "subversive activities"—Lovett, Dodd, and Watson, or the Congress which flagrantly violated Article One of the Constitution?

Finally, disloyalty tests are not only futile in application, they are pernicious in their consequences. They distract attention from activities that are really disloyal, and silence criticism inspired by true loyalty. That there are disloyal elements in America will not be denied, but there is no reason to suppose that any of the tests now formulated will ever be applied to them. It is relevant to remember that when Rankin was asked why his Committee did not investigate the Ku Klux Klan he replied that the Klan was not un-American, it was American!

Who are those who are really disloyal? Those who inflame racial hatreds, who sow religious and class dissensions. Those who subvert the Constitution by violating the freedom of the ballot box. Those who make a mockery of majority rule by the use of the filibuster. Those who impair democracy by denying equal educational facilities. Those who frustrate justice by lynch law or by making a farce of jury trials. Those who deny freedom of speech and of the press and of assembly. Those who press for special favors against the interests of the commonwealth. Those who regard public office as a source of private gain. Those who would exalt the military over the civil. Those who for selfish and private purposes stir up national antagonisms and expose the world to the ruin of war.

Will the House Committee on Un-American Activities interfere with the activities of these? Will Mr. Truman's disloyalty proclamation reach these? Will the current campaigns for Americanism convert these? If past experience is any guide, they will not. What they will do, if they are successful, is to silence criticism, stamp out dissent—or drive it underground. But if our democracy is to flourish it must have criticism, if our government is to function it must have dissent. Only totalitarian governments insist upon conformity and they—as we know—do so at their peril. Without criticism abuses will go unrebuked; without dissent our dynamic system will become static. The American people have a stake in the maintenance of the most thorough-going inquisition into American institutions. They have a stake in nonconformity, for they know that the American genius is nonconformist. They have a stake in experimentation of the most radical character, for they know that only those who prove all things can hold fast that which is good.

IV

It is easier to say what loyalty is not than to say what it is. It is not conformity. It is not passive acquiescence in the status quo. It is not preference for everything American over everything foreign. It is not an ostrich-like ignorance of other countries and other institutions. It is not the indulgence in ceremony—a flag salute, an oath of allegiance, a fervid verbal declaration. It is not a particular creed, a particular version of history, a particular body of economic practices, a particular philosophy.

It is a tradition, an ideal, and a principle. It is a willingness to subordinate every private advantage for the larger good. It is an appreciation of the rich and diverse contributions that can come from the most varied sources. It is allegiance to the traditions that have guided our greatest statesmen and inspired our most eloquent poets—the traditions of freedom, equality, democracy, tolerance, the tradition of the higher law, of experimentation, co-operation, and pluralism. It is a realization that America was born of revolt, flourished on dissent, became great through experimentation.

Independence was an act of revolution; republicanism was something new under the sun; the federal system was a vast experimental laboratory. Physically Americans were pioneers; in the realm of social and economic institutions, too, their tradition has been one of pioneering. From the beginning, intellectual and spiritual diversity have been as characteristic of America as racial and linguistic. The most distinctively American philosophies have been transcendentalism—which is the philosophy of the Higher Law—and pragmatism—which is the philosophy of experimentation and pluralism. These two principles are the very core of Americanism: the principle of the Higher Law, or of obedience to the dictates of conscience rather than of statutes, and the principle of pragmatism, or the rejection of a single good and of the notion of a finished universe. From the beginning Americans have known that there were new worlds to conquer, new truths to be discovered. Every effort to confine Americanism to a single pattern, to constrain it to a single formula, is disloyalty to everything that is valid in Americanism.

VI

CITIZENSHIP AND SUFFRAGE

38. *Let's Talk about Immigration* *

MR. CORSI wrote this article a few months after he had spent ninety publicity-filled, acrimonious days as a special assistant for refugee and immigration policies to Secretary of State John F. Dulles. In it he criticizes the United States Immigration and Nationality Act of 1952. In his view that law is based on false theories of race; harms the United States by keeping out much-needed, highly skilled workers; and creates ill will among many peoples abroad. Corsi ceased to be Secretary Dulles's assistant after being severely criticized by Representative Francis E. Walter, one of the authors of the immigration act of 1952.

THE CRUCIAL ISSUE of immigration is an old one—about as old as our Republic. The Alien and Sedition Acts, the first manifestation of intolerance and discrimination against immigrants and prospective immigrants, were passed during the Administration of our second President, John Adams, and quickly repealed when Thomas Jefferson took office. What happened later on—the agitations against Irish and Germans, the systematic sowing of fears about "Popish idolatries" and "Jesuit intrigues" in the 1840's and 1850's, the formidable growth of the "Know-Nothing" party before the Civil War—all this is in elementary history textbooks. Unfortunately our present immigration laws serve to remind us that racial and religious bigotry are not just a matter of past history.

In more recent times the flaming crosses of the Ku Klux Klan, revived

* Edward Corsi, *The Reporter*, XII (June 2, 1955), pp. 22-26. Reprinted with permission from *The Reporter*, 136 East 57th Street, New York 22, N. Y.

in 1915, could be considered nothing more than a colorful if brutal item of Americana.

Now we are living in a glass house. Our foreign policy does not express itself exclusively through the declarations of our diplomats and traveling statesmen abroad. Our immigration laws as administered by our consular officials are an essential part of our diplomacy; their impact is felt not just in chancelleries but by the harassed, fearful people whom I saw during my many trips patiently standing in long lines at the doors of American consulates.

It is important to realize, I believe, that whatever our immigration laws may be, good or bad, they are worked out abroad not at the ambassadorial but at the consular level. What the godlike powers of an American consul, whose decisions are beyond appeal, have become these days, I feel incapable of describing. The many-sided artistry of Gian Carlo Menotti has done the job. Some of Menotti's doleful tunes were haunting me while I was visiting American consular establishments. It struck me, however, that there is something new since Menotti composed *The Consul:* The American consul today is a frightened little god who exhausts his energies scrutinizing other people with the same distrustful uneasiness with which he himself is scrutinized by his superior officers back home.

HELP WANTED

The laws the harassed American consul has to apply to the men, women, and children who crowd his office seem primarily designed to keep people away from our shores—whether they are prospective immigrants or merely people who only want visitors' visas. The laws are based on the assumption that some races are inferior to others and that irrespective of race there is evil in the intention and in the character of anyone who for any reason wants to come here. Incidentally, the American public does not know how frequently foreigners who have a good chance of being admitted say "Thank you, no," and walk out of the consulate rather than submit to the endless questioning, fingerprinting, and scrutiny of their pasts that they consider a revolting invasion of their privacy.

The harmful effects of the present immigration law, the McCarran-Walter Act of 1952, which was passed by Congress over President Truman's veto, appear at once when we look at it from the viewpoint of self-interest and see what this law has done to the economy of our country.

Ever since the 1920's our immigration laws have deprived us of the manpower and the skills that our expanding economy require by cutting off immigration from the very countries that can provide these skills. Except during brief periods of recession, our economy has always called for more manpower. This demand used to be met through natural population growth, internal migration of labor—and immigration.

This labor demand is now being met by draining manpower from the farms, by immigration from non-quota countries in the Western Hemisphere, and by importing temporary labor from neighboring lands, much of it smuggled in from Mexico. Like the demand for liquor during the prohibition years, the demand for labor has been satisfied by makeshift and frequently illegal means.

There is at the present time a shortage of manpower in agriculture. Finding local labor to harvest the crops is becoming more and more difficult—sometimes so difficult that fields are left uncultivated.

It is true that as of last January we had 3,347,000 unemployed in the United States. In New York State alone there are now upwards of 266,000 people getting unemployment insurance from the state treasury. Even so, many thousands of extremely important jobs are going begging. Ours is a free society and we cannot force our unemployed to take jobs for which they have no training and no liking.

There are serious shortages of skilled tailors, dressmakers, mechanics, precision workers, watchmakers, cooks, bakers, farmers, domestics, and in other classifications in which many jobs have traditionally been filled by immigrants. David Dubinsky, the head of the International Ladies' Garment Workers' Union and one of the most constructive labor leaders in America, told me recently that if the shortage of skilled workers in the garment industry continues, in ten years it will be hard to find tailors in the United States who can produce a custom-made or fit a ready-made suit. Clothing manufacturers in Rochester are not only having difficulty recruiting trained workers but cannot even find apprentices to train despite the industry's high wages and excellent working conditions.

Restaurants all over America cannot find competent cooks to keep pace with America's growing tendency to eat out rather than at home. The shortage is so acute that the average small restaurant is now relying not on experienced cooks but on ordinary kitchen help improvising at the stove.

These shortages lead to disproportionately high labor costs and to demands for high tariffs to protect goods that cannot be produced competitively here for lack of the necessary skilled labor.

While the McCarran-Walter Act extends preference to workers with high technical training, the numerical limitations of the quota system tend to defeat that purpose.

In this connection, it is important to notice that the traditional antagonism to immigration by organized labor has substantially been abandoned. Needless to say, enlightened and responsible labor leaders like George Meany and Walter Reuther—like every person who has sensibly approached the problem of immigration in our day—are not in favor of a return to the uncontrolled immigration of the early 1900's. But they recognize that a greater flow of immigration—selective and controlled—is needed in order to meet the demands of our expanding economy. Many labor leaders feel that this economy of ours could profitably absorb a quarter of a million immigrants a year—approximately the same number that is proposed in the Lehman-Celler bill now before Congress.

NO SCIENTISTS NEED APPLY

The present law—the McCarran-Walter Act of 1952—fixes a specific annual quota for each of eighty-five countries, the total being 154,657. Any nation's quota is equal to one-sixth of one per cent of the number of persons in our 1920 population who were of that origin. Minimum quotas of one hundred are given to a number of Asian countries that were previously excluded entirely. The quotas allotted each country within this total are neither interchangeable nor cumulative, which means that unless all quotas are filled each year—and this never happens—the unused allottments are forfeited. The United Kingdom, Eire, and Germany are given about 109,000 visas; the remaining 45,000 have to be divided among all the nations of the world. Overpopulated Italy has a quota of 5,645, while the United Kingdom, whose people can emigrate to places within the Commonwealth like Canada and Australia but who are under no great pressure to leave home anyway, has the largest of all quotas—65,361. It is never filled.

Because of the mortgaging of the Greek quota under the Displaced Persons Act of 1948, which allows countries to mortgage up to fifty per cent of their annual quota for an indefinite period, only 154 Greeks can come here each year until 2013. Latvia's quota of 235 is reduced by half for the next 320 years.

The Act provides for non-quota migration from independent countries in the Western Hemisphere. Also, spouses and unmarried children of United States citizens are admitted without restriction. And so are qualified ministers. But professors and scientists, who were admitted outside their countries' quotas under the old Act of 1924, can be admitted under the Act of 1952 only within them.

For example, if someone like the late Enrico Fermi, the refugee Italian scientist who played a major role in the development of the atomic bomb, or the Hungarian Leo Szilard wanted to come to this country for permanent residence today, he would have to do the following: Obtain a clearance from the United States Employment Service, get written statements from some labor organization, submit affidavits from persons having special knowledge of him, assemble clippings of American advertisements calling for the services he claims to be able to render, and produce certified copies of diplomas, school certificates, and similar documents. He would then be placed on a waiting list. Any scientist born in a country to which we have allotted the generous quota of one hundred would have practically no chance at all.

Do the supporters of the McCarran Act think that ours is the only country where refugee scientists and scholars can perform their tasks?

THE RACE MYTH

The reasons for discrimination against certain nations and races and in favor of others were stated quite forcefully by the late Senator McCarran himself in the Senate debate on his immigration bill on May 16, 1952:

". . . the cold, hard truth is that in the United States today there are hard-core, indigestible blocs who have not become integrated into the American way of life, but who, on the contrary, are its deadly enemy." Senator McCarran did not specify from which foreign nations the "hard-core, indigestible blocs . . . deadly enemy" were coming, but . . . we can guess which ones he had in mind.

Many other statements made by our elected representatives during the debate illustrate the climate of opinion which has produced our immigration laws since the early 1920's and still blocks all efforts to liberalize the immigration policy of the United States—an attitude of wholesale mistrust and fear of certain races.

Our lawmakers still lean heavily, whether they know it or not, on the pseudo-scientific theories and baseless fears that went into the writing of the restrictive Acts of 1921 and 1924. These theories first found their expression in the anthropological vagaries and racist myths of Houston Stewart Chamberlain, Madison Grant, Lothrop Stoddard, and other "scientists."

According to these writers, some races are hopelessly wayward; the superior races are the blond Nordics, mainly Anglo-Saxons and Teutons; eastern and southern Europeans, along with Asians, Africans, and the rest of the colored peoples, are to be ruled by their Nordic betters if they know what's good for them.

These now completely discredited theories are still codified in our immigration laws, which provide that preference be extended to the

Germans, the English, and the Celts, whose culture is seen as identical with ours and who are therefore assimilable. The rest of humanity in the quota areas is kept out either by token quotas of one hundred a year—the McCarran-Walter allottment to China, India, the African countries, and other nonwhite areas—or by ridiculously low quotas, as in the case of the Italians, the Greeks, the Poles, and other Europeans.

It is interesting to look back on the writings of these American racists. In *The Passing of the Great Race* (1916), the late Madison Grant of the American Museum of Natural History wrote:

> These new immigrants were no longer exclusively members of the Nordic race as were the earlier ones. . . . The new immigration . . . contained a large and increasing number of the weak, the broken, and the mentally crippled of all races drawn from the lowest stratum of the Mediterranean basin and the Balkans, together with hordes of the wretched, submerged populations of the Polish ghettos . . . the whole tone of American life, social, moral, and political has been lowered and vulgarized by them.

He later wrote:

> Much of the immigration during the last century has been identical with the old British stock in all respects. The English and the Scotch who have came over here, as well as the Scandinavians and most of the Germans, and perhaps some other elements, are to be regarded as reinforcements of the older stock.

In a spirit of lyric exaltation after the Act of 1924 became law, Lothrop Stoddard of Harvard in his book *Re-Forging America* (1927) wrote:

> . . . not since the nation's youthful days before 1850 have America's prospects been so bright as they are right now. We have already seen that the Immigration Restriction Act of 1924 marks the second great turning-point in our national life.

After having quoted the pseudo-scientific rantings of a generation past, it is a relief to be able to report that among a group of internationally respected anthropologists who were consulted in the preparation of a UNESCO pamphlet in 1952:

> There was no delay or hesitation or lack of unanimity in reaching the primary conclusion that there were no scientific grounds whatever for the racialist position regarding purity of race and the hierarchy of inferior and superior races to which this leads.

As to what goes into the racial composition of an American, Sinclair

Lewis gave the classic definition in describing Martin Arrowsmith, the hero of one of his best novels:

Martin was, like most inhabitants of Elk Mills before the Slavo-Italian immigration, a Typical Pure-bred Anglo-Saxon American, which means that he was a union of German, French, Scotch, Irish, perhaps a little Spanish, conceivably a little of the strains lumped together as "Jewish," and a great deal of English, which is itself a combination of Primitive Briton, Celt, Phoenician, Roman, German, Dane, and Swede.

EMBARRASSING QUESTIONS

Although neither reason nor science can furnish any support for the racialist, discriminatory laws of the 1920's, it is not hard to understand how at that particular time the nation turned toward a mythical past and away from Europe. In the revulsion that followed the First World War, any idea that our country had a responsibility of leadership was often rudely or cynically laughed off. What use was there, people asked, in getting further involved with an ungrateful, messy world? It was much better to keep our country isolated and isolationist. The best way to guarantee our freedom in a world tumbling into slavery and chaos was to exert a very strict control over the new blood and the old culture flowing in from Europe.

We cannot go back to that era of wonderful nonsense. Now we are the center of a broad alliance, and our national survival largely depends on the vigor of that alliance. We are frequently and deeply concerned, and rightly so, with elections in nations which our immigration laws still consider inferior and from which we admit only a trickle of immigrants.

When, in 1948, people of Italian descent in the United States embarked on the famous letters-to-Italy campaign urging the defeat of Communism in the Italian elections, the writers laid great stress on the blessings democracy had bestowed upon them in America. The Italian Communists then staged an effective counter campaign of letters to America: What about letting us, people of your own blood, share with you the abundance of American life? they asked. Will your government let us come?

During the hearings before the President's Commission on Immigration and Nationalization in 1952, an American business leader, soldier, and statesman, William H. Draper, summed up the principles that should have guided our lawmakers:

What I am proposing concretely is that we take another close look at our immigration policy and adjust it to the conditions of the world of today and tomorrow and to our place and role in that world. This does not mean that we should remove all barriers and throw our gates open to all and sundry, without control and limits. But it does mean that our policy as expressed in legislation on the statute books should be responsive to our needs and capabilities. We are capable of admitting, absorbing, and assimiliating more newcomers than is permitted under present legislation. We need not tie our hands to national-origin quotas based on legislation enacted over a quarter of a century ago in circumstances which no longer exist and which discriminates undeservedly against some of our own partners in NATO. In endeavoring to strengthen the economic and military defense of the free world, and particularly of the North Atlantic community, we should recognize immigration policy as one of the elements in achieving economic and political stability as well as social equilibrium.

Yet it was not the wisdom typified by General Draper's opinion that prevailed but that of a small, powerful group of politicians, committee chairmen, and "experts," people whose discredited theories are carbon copies of Grant and Stoddard. We find even so reasonable a man as Senator Walter F. George of Georgia, now chairman of the Senate Foreign Relations Committee, saying in May, 1952, on the floor of the Senate, that he had helped frame the 1924 immigration law and "I hope the time has not come when one must apologize for being a hateful Anglo-Saxon. I hope the time has not come when one must apologize for being American."

With due respect for the senior Senator from Georgia, I must say that for its own good our nation must live by the ideals it has professed from the day the Declaration of Independence affirmed that all men—and not just the Anglo-Saxons—are created equal. Certainly of all American ideals none is more genuinely ours or more eloquently proclaimed by our present leaders. Yet it is exactly this American belief in the primacy of the individual as against his membership in any group that our immigration laws now flout. In the 1920's this was a mistake; in the 1950's it may lead to tragedy.

WHAT MUST BE DONE

The first step on the road to sanity is to acknowledge that there can be no return to unregulated, unrestricted immigration. Those who still claim that this is the aim of the opponents of our present immigration laws lie, and they know it. The time when immigrants could come when they themselves decided to seek a new life in America and when each year the total number of arrivals was left to chance—that time is gone forever. It is gone not only because of our immigration laws but also because in every civilized country there are trade unions and in varying degrees all governments feel responsible for the welfare of their citizens. Every government now exerts control over the outflow as well as the inflow of migrants. Our government, because of its position of leadership, must establish its own standards.

Moreover, the problem of displaced persons—there are still distressingly large numbers of them—as well as that of overpopulated countries, cannot be solved by any one nation alone, even with the most humanitarian intentions. These problems must be the object of international negotiations, with each nation that is in no condition to help or in need of help doing its share. There are already several international agencies at work on these problems. The most important of them is the Intergovernmental Committee for European Migration, made up of twenty-six nations. Incidentally, the two American representatives at the recent Geneva meeting of this committee were, of all people, Congressman Walter and Mr. McLeod.

President Eisenhower has stated forcefully on any number of occasions that our immigration policy must be revised. I myself was particularly impressed by his speech at the Alfred E. Smith Memorial Foundation dinner on October 16, 1952, when he said: ". . . we must strike from our own statute books any legislation concerning immigration that implies the blasphemy against democracy that only certain groups of Europeans are welcome on American shores." This was not just campaign oratory. I believe it came straight from the President's heart. Recently when asked at a press conference whether he was satisfied with the way the Refugee Relief Act was administered, the President answered squarely, "No."

The President alone has the power to move from that "No" to positive actions. In my opinion, he should appoint a bipartisan commission, with representatives from both houses and experts of his own choosing, to study the problem thoroughly and propose basic changes in our immigration laws. It may be said that there have been too many such committees, but they have been precommitted and partisan; this one should draw particular authority from the quality of its membership and the President's unflagging support.

INSULTING ENTIRE CONTINENTS

Above all, the commission should make the relevant facts known to the public—facts about the number of immigrants we can put to work and the contribution our country can make in bringing relief to those in dire need of resettlement. There is desperate need that these facts be made known, for the old myths still poison the air. Among the myths, there is that of our people's antagonism to new immigrants. But do the American people really want to shut the door on the rest of the world? Are they really willing to perpetuate this insult to entire continents, Asia and Africa, whose importance in the modern world grows day by day?

Whatever the final solution may be—and there must be a number of acceptable solutions—public discussion is what we need most. For we cannot afford an immigration policy that is inconsistent with both our own economic needs and our position of leadership in the world. There is no reason for us to be afraid of a free and open discussion about immigrants—the very stuff of which this country is made.

39. *Let's Not Get Out the Vote* *

In the November, 1952, presidential election about 37.5 per cent of those eligible to vote did not do so, and in the congressional elections of 1954 about 57.5 per cent stayed at home. Unlike many people, the author of this selection is not unduly depressed by these figures. Mr. Coulson, who is Mayor of Waukegan, Illinois, and active in party politics, attacks the idea that "getting out the vote" necessarily leads to better government. He thinks that uninformed or uninterested voters should stay at home. He prefers voters who make well-considered choices. The opposite and much more widely accepted side of this argument is presented in the next selection, "A Proposal to Tax Those Who Don't Vote."

Three years ago anyone who failed to vote had to face the combined scorn of both political parties, the schoolteachers, boy scouts, war veterans, chambers of commerce, and leagues of women voters. Last year bar associations, girl scouts, tavern keepers, President Eisenhower, radio and TV stations, and junior chambers of commerce joined the

* Robert E. Coulson, *Harper's Magazine,* CCXI (November, 1955), pp. 52-53. Reprinted by permission of the author.

crusade. There is every prospect that in future elections, non-voters will face jail sentences or fines, or be called to testify before investigating committees.

Before this happens, someone should come to their defense. Non-voters are often more intelligent, more fair-minded, and just as loyal as voters. The right not to vote is as basic as the right to. If voting is made a duty, it ceases to be a privilege.

Let's look at the voting behavior of Mr. and Mrs. Whipcord and Mrs. Whipcord's brother Harold, on the day of the local school-board election. Mrs. Whipcord says, "I have studied the candidates and have made up my mind. I will vote for Jones." Mr. Whipcord says, "I know nothing about the candidates or the issues. I will stay home, and allow the election to be decided by the votes of those who have made a study and formed an opinion." Harold says, "I don't know anything about the candidates or the problems, but by golly, I'm going to vote. It's my duty. I'll pick the fellows with the shortest names."

If there is a bad citizen among these three, which one is it? Whose procedure is least likely to bring good government to the school district?

Non-voting, multiplied by the thousands, is said to mean voter apathy, and this is supposed to be a sin. Have we lost our sacred American right to be apathetic? Suppose Mr. Whipcord studied the candidates carefully and concluded that Candidate Jones was a boob and Candidate Smith was a thief. Is it un-American to refuse to choose between them? Or suppose he is satisfied that Jones and Smith are equally qualified, equally able, and that the school's problems are in good hands no matter which man wins. He is not apathetic; he is satisfied. Why should he be forced to choose between candidates on some esoteric basis?

The notion that "getting out the vote" makes for better election results is neither non-partisan, patriotic, nor logical. It is a device to favor the machines of both parties. It handicaps independent candidates, unfairly burdens the party in power, makes elections more expensive to conduct, greatly slows the tallying, and—worst of all—places the emphasis on the ritual of voting rather than the thought behind the vote.

If you fill in all the blank spaces on the ballot, the political machines will steal three-fourths of your vote. Let's see how this works, in a typical primary election.

Here are seven offices to be filled by nomination, with two or three candidates for each office. Citizen Stringfellow is interested in seeing Jones win for Auditor. He has no information about the candidates for

Attorney General, Treasurer, Superintendent of Schools, or the others. He votes for Jones and then looks on down the list. He has been persuaded that it is his duty to vote for *somebody* for each office. So for six of the seven offices, he marks an X opposite the name best known to him, or the name on top, or the name suggested by his committeeman. These are machine candidates, and Citizen Stringfellow has given away six-sevenths of his vote.

After him, comes Citizen Stalwart, who knows the candidates for two of the seven offices. He also fills in all the blanks, letting the machine steal five-sevenths of his vote. One of his blind votes cancels out the intelligent vote cast by Citizen Stringfellow. At this rate, during a day's balloting, the candidates backed by the strongest machines with the biggest publicity budgets will win, even though not a single voter had an intelligent preference for them.

Is this what Thomas Jefferson had in mind?

"Getting out the vote" is always partisan. A calm and dignified effort benefits the party in power. An excited or hysterical effort benefits the party out of power. The Republicans were very happy to use the pressure of "neutral" groups in the 1952 elections. But they had better learn that this is a two-edged sword. Next time, the girl scouts, veterans' groups, radio stations, newspapers, and community funds may be out needling the Republicans with propaganda.

"Vote this time or your vote may be gone forever." "This may be your last chance." "Vote now or never." Anyone who is led to the polls by such arguments is going to vote against whoever brought us to the edge of this crevasse. As the pressure on the public increases, the party out of power is most likely to benefit in direct proportion to it.

All public-opinion surveys show that a certain proportion of the electorate has no opinion about many vital issues, does not know who is running for office, and does not care. A gentle campaign to bring a submissive one-third of the apathetic sheep to the polls gets out a voting majority for the candidates who have had the greatest amount of publicity—who usually belong to the party in power. A rip-snorting effort to get out all the ignoramuses tends to turn them into the rebel column, and thus benefits the outs.

In either event, the girl scouts should wash their hands of it. The job of getting out the vote is a partisan effort which belongs to the professionals.

The silliest idea of all is the notion that it is un-American or unpatriotic not to vote. "A plague on both your houses" is a fair American attitude—all too often a logical one. Stupidity does not become wisdom by being multiplied.

In every election not more than one-third of the people care very much how it comes out. A certain percentage may have some sort of belief or opinion without feeling very strongly about it; another percentage may have studied the matter a little without forming an opinion; another percentage may not even have studied it; and so on, until we come to the people who are not even aware that an election is being held. The more we urge these people to clutter up the polling place, the more delay there is in voting, the more the cost of ballots and clerks, and the slower the returns.

If Candidate Jones would normally have won by 3,000 votes to 1,000, and we corral 10,000 more people into the polling places, won't Candidate Jones still win, by 8,000 to 6,000? Mathematically the last-minute coin-flippers may make the election look close, but what patriotic purpose is accomplished?

And if the coin-flippers should happen to defeat the will of the informed majority, the cause of good government would emphatically not have been served.

Our city had a referendum recently in which the people voted for a tax increase to build an incinerator and against a tax increase to operate it. Every one of your communities has probably known referendums where the voters approved the bonds for a school but disapproved the sites, or voted for the site and against the bonds. All those voters who marked in opposite directions on the same afternoon were unwisely pressured into voting.

You have also seen primary elections where the boob with the catchy name ran away from the able man whose publicity was colorless. You have seen final elections where the straight party voters and the blank fillers smothered any discriminating choices which the thoughtful voters had made. You may have noticed with distress some of the undignified didos, cruel epithets, pompous verbosities, and Shakespearean gestures with which even good men become burdened early in their campaigns. All of these are caused in large measure by "get out the vote" efforts which emphasize putting a cross in half the squares.

Instead of urging people to vote, we ought to be urging them to study and form opinions. If thought and inspection of the candidates do not create a real desire to vote, then the citizen should be encouraged to stay at home on election day. A low vote is part of the public record and itself a significant voter reaction which ought to be preserved. Maybe neither of the candidates was worth voting for.

Certainly the right to vote is important and should not be curtailed. A fool who is willing to walk all the way to the polling place should be given every freedom to record every stupid impulse he feels, for these will tend to cancel each other out. But no one should pretend that marking X in a square is any proof of patriotism or even intelligence. It is not your duty to vote, but, if you choose to, then it should be your duty to be intelligent about it.

40. A Proposal to Tax Those Who Don't Vote *

WHEN WE DISCUSS the problems of suffrage in this country we generally spend a great deal of time talking about restrictions on suffrage, such as the poll tax and various forms of "literacy" tests. We note that many of those who are eligible to vote never exercise their privilege, but we are rarely able to make concrete suggestions that would decrease the percentage of non-voters. Mr. Myers offers such a suggestion in this selection: Tax those who do not vote. He argues that it is just as logical to do this as it is to require compulsory school attendance of children. Although the immediate reaction of most readers to his plan may be unfavorable, the author presents an argument that at least requires a re-examination of traditional attitudes toward voting.

THERE are about 96,000,000 Americans of voting age—American electors. Yet last November only slightly more than half of these electors went to the polls. In the previous Congressional election—in 1946—only about one-third of the electors turned out. In many of our state and municipal elections it has been commonplace to find only 15 to 20 per cent of the potential voters actually voting.

This situation is widely decried. We are told that of all the Western democracies we here in the United States show the poorest record of voting turnout. This was not always so. In Australia, for example, prior to 1925, less than 50 per cent of the electorate habitually turned out for Federal elections. But since then the turnout has usually been between 95 and 99 per cent. Probably the worst record of all was established back in the Eighteen Sixties in Belgium when only 10 per cent of the electorate generally voted. Thirty years later the figures were reversed, and turnouts of between 92 and 95 per cent were being recorded. What happened to bring about these startling changes? Compulsory voting is the answer. Australia adopted a compulsory

* Robert C. Myers, *The New York Times Magazine*, November 6, 1949, pp. 12, 75-76, 78-79. Reprinted by permission of the author and the publisher.

voting law in 1925, and Belgium earlier had incorporated such a law into her 1893 Constitution.

One of the great paradoxes of the twentieth century has been the fervor with which free men everywhere have fought to keep their franchise and to widen their suffrage, and then, having obtained these rights, abstained in large numbers from exercising them. Nowhere is this paradox more clear-cut than in America.

The question that arises is this: Is voting in a democracy a right or a duty? We will here contend that it is both. Unexercised rights are likely to become lost rights. The right to vote has not always existed, and was not easily won. Unless it be considered also to be a duty, it may easily be lost, and democracy with it. Apathetic non-voting on election day stems from a basically perverse attitude which is clearly summed up by the phrase: "Let George do it." If too many of us for too long a time fall into that attitude, then "George" may indeed do it. "George" has been known by many names—sometimes with a VI or an VIII as a suffix; sometimes simply under a pseudonym such as Hitler, or Napoleon, or Franco. Do we really want "George" to do it?

Duties imply sanctions: either rewards for their performance or punishments for their non-performance. We do not believe that a democracy can long survive with an illiterate electorate, and so we have adopted compulsory education. We believe that a democratic government should be supported on the basis of ability to pay, and so we have adopted the compulsory income tax. We do not believe that a democracy should be protected by an army of mercenaries, or that one able-bodied man should serve and another shirk, and so we have adopted selective military service. Yet at the very heart of the democratic philosophy, its very essence, is the belief in a widespread electorate; and here we have no immediately tangible sanction whatsoever. People are able to exercise or evade this duty as they will. Why do we shy away from compulsory voting?

At the present time our poll-tax states apply sanctions *against* voting, not against non-voting. In effect, you pay a fine if you vote, and nothing if you do not vote. The reason why the Government of Mississippi, for instance, would be opposed to compulsory voting is obvious. Those in control of Mississippi apparently have not yet agreed to the basic tenet of democracy: that there should be a widespread electorate.

We hope that this will not always be the case, but since it is the case at the present time we cannot reasonably be expected to include the situation in such states in this discussion. We are discussing reasons why we should not have compulsory voting in a democracy. After all, it is perfectly self-evident why compulsory voting may be opposed in a non-democracy. So we will confine ourselves to those arguments which seem to apply in those states which have no official sanctions *against* voting. Let us briefly review some of them.

COMPULSORY VOTING IS UNDEMOCRATIC

This contention is based upon the theory that people in a democracy do things of their own free will, whereas it is only in totalitarian countries that people are forced or compelled to act in one way or another. Of course, if this were so, we should have no laws at all. And, indeed, every new statute has been attacked by somebody or other as an undemocratic infringement of personal freedom.

Advocates of this argument have fallen into the fallacy of confusing the principles of democracy and anarchy. It is unanarchistic to compel anyone to do anything, but not undemocratic. Democracy is a form of government; not a form of non-government.

A government implies a system of power arrangements whereby people are governed, that is, compelled to do or not to do certain things. The main difference between a democracy and a totalitarian state is that in a democracy the people control the government rather than vice versa. If the people in a democracy want to adopt compulsory voting as in Australia, Belgium and Holland, or compulsory registration as in New Zealand, then they do so. The point is that the electorate freely elects this course, rather than that the measure has been forced on the majority by a powerful minority.

Another fallacy that is commonly involved in the argument that compulsory voting is undemocratic is the tacit assumption that whatever is found in a totalitarian state is ipso facto undemocratic. Thus the fact that compulsory voting existed in Nazi Germany and now exists in Soviet Russia is used to damn the measure as being undemocratic. Of course, compulsory taxes, education and military service also exist in such countries, but these facts are hastily overlooked. The real difference is whether the sanction is imposed from above or adopted from below. And, so far as compulsory voting is concerned, the difference is shown in another characteristic way: In Russia nobody runs against Stalin; in Australia almost anybody may run for Prime Minister every three years.

COMPULSORY VOTING WOULD HERD THE UNINFORMED AND UNCONCERNED TO THE POLLS

This is the effect which the editor of *Public Opinion Quarterly* and a number of other thoughtful citizens fear. Until November, 1948, there was general agreement among pollsters, commentators and other political observers that electors most likely to vote were those with higher incomes and higher education; also that, at least north of the Mason-Dixon line, higher income-education was associated with membership in the Republican party.

Thus, it was argued that the lower the turnout in any election the more likelihood of a Republican victory, and the higher the turnout the more likelihood of a Democratic victory. Even so astute a political statistician as Louis Bean, author of "How to Predict Elections," asserted that Mr. Truman could win in 1948 only if 65 per cent or more of the electorate turned out; that otherwise Mr. Dewey would triumph. Actually, as already noted, the turnout was only slightly over 50 per cent and the experts confessed themselves dumbfounded by the results.

A corollary of this argument contends that under compulsory voting the Republican party might as well disband. Indeed, after the election last fall, one of our prominent pollsters told a predominantly Republican audience: "Any Republican in favor of compulsory voting ought to have his head examined."

Possibly so, but since November there has been a good deal of wailing among Republicans to the effect that their candidate lost because so many of his backers were so sure he was going to win easily that they did not bother to vote. This, of course, is just another of the "Let George do it" type of thinking. At any rate, there are today many Republicans who wish somebody had forced them to the polls last November, and it is no longer safe to assume that everyone in favor of compulsory voting is a Democrat and everyone against it a Republican.

Nevertheless, it is true that a large number of the electors who fail to vote are indifferent to the problems of the day. But it is just as true that many of those who are herded or carted to the polls in chauffeur-driven cars by political machines to help keep themselves in power, as is so often the case today, are equally unconcerned.

The argument also assumes that the same degree of apathy currently shown under voluntary voting would persist under compulsory voting. However, a bit of introspection will show that as a general rule you are more concerned about things you have to do than things you don't have to do. The past twenty-four years of experience with compulsory voting in Australia indicates that people who have to vote, or else pay a fine, are likely to become interested in whom and what they are voting for. It is for this same psychological reason that ever since 1913 the well-to-do in the United States have agitated to have everyone with any income pay an income tax, even if simply a token tax, so that wage-earners as well as the wealthy would concern themselves with the expenditures of the Federal budget.

YOU CAN LEAD A HORSE TO WATER, BUT YOU CAN'T MAKE HIM DRINK

This argument is vigorously upheld by P. H. Odegard and E. Allen Helms ("American Politics: A Study in Political Dynamics") who have paraphrased the old saw in these words: "It may be possible to force citizens into the voting booths, but we cannot force them to think." Let us admit at once that this statement is a truism. But then let us add: "So what?"

Could we not say with equal justice that, "You can force children to go to school, but you cannot force them to learn," as was, in fact, one of the arguments used against compulsory education? The truth of the matter is that children do learn, and that horses do drink—most of the time. It is our feeling that persons who are forced out of their easy chairs to the polling booth on Election Day are more likely to think than persons who are allowed to stay at home in front of their television sets while democracy perhaps dribbles away outside the window.

When writing about this problem twenty-seven years ago in Harper's, Samuel Spring ("The Voter Who Will Not Vote") made an apt comparison between the possible effect of compulsory voting on some electors and the effect of compulsory education on some schoolboys. "The voter," he wrote, "may lag on the way to the polls like the schoolboy; he may creep with snail-like pace * * *." But the main idea is to get the schoolboy to the school, and the voter to the polls.

There are two other arguments closely allied with the present one which should be disposed of here. The first is concerned with the injustice of forcing an elector to vote for a candidate or an issue when he is not favorably disposed toward those which may confront him on his ballot.

This argument is completely specious. If a voter wishes to turn in a blank or "write-in" ballot today, he may do so. No one advocating compulsory voting with the secret ballot (as distinguished from compulsory voting in certain totalitarian states) contemplates that there would be any change in this privilege. What is advocated is that the voter indicate in positive fashion his displeasure with all candidates and issues by casting a blank or "write-in" ballot, rather than in the debatable negative current fashion of some non-voters of simply staying away from the polls.

The second subsidiary argument has to do with primary elections. Compulsory voting in this case would mean in substance that electors were being forced into joining one or another political party. This, we may concede, is a valid contention. All that can reasonably be advocated is that the widest possible publicity should be given to the holding of primaries, so that everybody who wishes may be informed. However, although no useful purpose may be served by compelling attendance at primaries, that is, nominations, we believe that electors would have greater interest in the nominations if they knew that they had later to vote for the candidates who were thus selected. Compulsory voting should then have the effect of increasing interest and activity in nominations, petitions and non-compulsory primaries rather than the opposite. This might make adherents of tight little political machines quite unhappy.

ELECTORS WOULD SELL THEIR VOTES

We are told that under a system of compulsory voting more electors would be tempted to sell their votes than at present. The idea that would supposedly come into prominence runs something like this: "I don't care who wins, but since I have to go to the election booth anyhow I might as well sell my vote to the highest bidder." That this fraudulent idea might occur to some people and be acted upon accordingly cannot be denied.

But before discarding compulsory voting as hopeless because of this apparent defect, let us ponder this fact: A vote always has a market value, whether cast or not, to anybody who wishes to sell his heritage so cheaply. An elector who wishes to sell his uncast vote need only proclaim which candidate he favors, and then accept payment from the opposition not to vote.

Strangely enough, we are told by the historians that this is exactly the situation that developed in Belgium prior to 1893 when as little as 10 per cent of the electorate turned out for some elections. Unsympathetic, or pseudo-unsympathetic electors were being bribed to refrain from voting. After *le vote obligatoire* was adopted in 1893, and turnouts of as high as 90 and 95 per cent were being recorded, it became uneconomical, except in very close elections, for corrupt machines to attempt to buy any useful number of votes. Incidentally, the fine for abstaining from voting was set high enough so that it would also be uneconomical to follow the former practice and bribe people not to vote. Furthermore, non-voting in four elections meant that the elector's name would be forevermore stricken from the voting lists.

So, as already noted, ranged among the opponents to compulsory voting we may expect to find the bosses of many political machines, particularly the small tight-knit ones that today count on a 10 to 25 per cent turnout in municipal elections. Such machines would be confused, to say the least, if non-voters in any number ever tried to sell their non-vote as in pre-1893 Belgium.

The only remaining major argument against compulsory voting has to do with the moral wrongfulness of using fear or terror to bring electors to the polls. These are strong words, but they are bandied about by some critics of compulsory voting because force, compulsion and coercion imply the exploitation of the emotion of fear or terror to guide action in a predetermined direction. There is, however, the matter of the degree of emotion that needs to be aroused to induce any particular action.

To induce most persons to stop at red traffic lights or to refrain from parking their cars beside fire hydrants only relatively modest fines have proved necessary. If you consider that it is fear or terror that deters you from committing minor traffic violations, then you will probably consider that a system of compulsory voting rests on the instilling of fear or terror. Most people, however, would not agree with you. In Australia a turnout of 95 per cent is commonly achieved in Federal elections under the "threat" of paying a fine of $7 if you neglect to vote and cannot convince the local magistrate that you had a "valid and sufficient reason" for staying away.

Many schemes have been adopted or advocated for compulsory voting. The system in Belgium, which we have mentioned, involves the imposition of graduated fines for first, second, third and fourth offense, and then loss of the right to vote. Most of us are familiar with this sort of thing in the use of our automobiles—graduated fines for repeated offenses which may end with revocation of the license to drive. Australia has the flat fine. In Holland, the Electoral Reform Law of 1917 provided that "negligent and recalcitrant" non-voters be fined 3 florins for the first offense and 10 florins for each offense thereafter.

Probably the most complicated scheme ever devised was put into force in Bavaria in 1881. This law decreed that no election was valid unless at least two-thirds of the electorate had voted. In case of an invalid election, the cost of a new election was charged to the electors who had abstained from voting the first time around.

Here at home no state currently has any compulsory voting law on its statutes, although Massachusetts, North Dakota and Oregon have all made motions in that direction. One municipality, Kansas City, Mo,. adopted a compulsory voting ordinance in 1889 which exempted voters from the $2.50 poll tax, thus penalizing non-voters by that amount. This ordinance remained in effect for seven years before being declared unconstitutional by the State Supreme Court. The decision, by some strange twist of logic, called the law an infringement of the "sovereign rights of suffrage."

Among advocates of compulsory voting there are some who believe that a fine of a stated amount would, in its application, be unfair inasmuch as it would tend to work a greater hardship upon the low-income non-voter than upon the one of higher income. In his 1922 article in Harper's, Spring proposed that electors who voted should be exempted from a certain proportion of their property or income taxes, rather than a flat amount. Later, in 1926, Senator Arthur Capper took up the same principle and suggested in the Senate a law that would have imposed a surtax of 1 per cent on the income tax of non-voting electors.

Under compulsory voting we would expect that no extreme faction—either reactionary or radical—would be able continuously to impose its will on the majority. Rather, we would expect to find some kind of moderate liberalism: a readiness to adopt new measures and ways of doing things that were clearly in the public interest. Otherwise no elected officeholder could reasonably expect to hold his office through a new election. In both Belgium and Australia the quality of government today may be characterized as left of center—mildly liberal, but not extreme.

From the point of view of American liberals, Australia would rate high on all counts but one: the stringent racial restrictions on immigration designed to preserve a "White Australia." Traditionally, Australians have long thought of themselves as a white outpost in the midst of a hostile and all-engulfing oriental world. In this one instance, then, compulsory voting has not led to more liberal doctrines (from the American-liberal standpoint) but has simply served to emphasize the fact that Australia's non-white phobia runs through the entire electorate, and has not been imposed from above by a few ruling bigots.

A Constitutional amendment would probably be necessary for the adoption of compulsory voting on a national basis, since our basic law now leaves the regulation of elections to each state, with the exception that no one is supposed to be barred from voting on account of race, color or previous condition of servitude. The controlling attitude being what it is in several Southern states and in those Northern states run by strong-armed political machines, the chances that such an amendment would be ratified satisfactorily are many years distant. Nevertheless, there is a good chance that some individual state might soon see fit to adopt a compulsory voting law as an earnest gesture toward the preservation of democratic principles. If so, the experiment should merit our closest attention and interest.

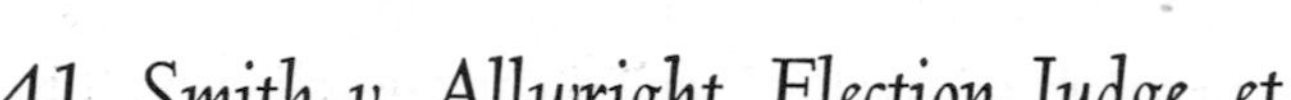

41. *Smith v. Allwright, Election Judge, et al.*

SUPREME COURT OF THE UNITED STATES,
1944 (CERTIORARI) 321 U.S. 649

BECAUSE of the one-party system in the Southern states, the exclusion of Negroes from participation in the Democratic party primary in effect eliminates them from participation in the nomination and election processes in those areas. As long as the Supreme Court was content to view the primary election as a private "party" matter, the exclusion of Negroes therefrom by party action could not be challenged under the Federal Constitution. Commencing with *United States* v. *Classic* (313 U.S. 299), however, the Court began to move from this position and to tie the party primary into the official election structure. In the present case the Court held that primary elections can no longer be viewed as private affairs but have become so intermingled with state activities as to bring them under the protection of the Fifteenth Amendment. Having thus brought the primary within the scope of the Federal power, the Court then ruled that the Democratic party, in its character as an agency of the state, could not exclude citizens from participation in the primary election because of their race or color. The doctrine in this case has been further expanded in *Elmore* v. *Rice* (72, F. Supp. 516, 68 S. Ct. 905), and would seem now effectively to close the door to the revival of the "White Primary," although the possibility of discrimination against the Negro by other means still remains.

Opinion of the Court

MR. JUSTICE REED delivered the opinion of the Court:

This writ of certiorari brings here for review a claim for damages in the sum of $5,000 on the part of petitioner, a Negro citizen of the 48th precinct of Harris County, Texas, for the refusal of respondents, election and associate election judges respectively of that precinct, to give petitioner a ballot or to permit him to cast a ballot in the primary election of July 27, 1940, for the nomination of Democratic candidates for the United States Senate and House of Representatives, and Governor and other state officers. The refusal is alleged to have been solely because of the race and color of the proposed voter. . . .

The Democratic party of Texas is held by the Supreme Court of that State to be a "voluntary association," *Bell* v. *Hill*, 123 Tex. 531, 534, protected by § 27 of the Bill of Rights, Art. 1, Constitution of Texas, from interference by the State except that:

"In the interest of fair methods and a fair expression by their members of their preferences in the selection of their nominees, the State may regulate such elections by proper laws." p. 545. . . .

The Democratic party on May 24, 1932, in a state convention adopted the following resolution, which has not since been "amended, abrogated, annulled or avoided":

> Be it resolved that all white citizens of the State of Texas who are qualified to vote under the Constitution and laws of the State shall be eligible to membership in the Democratic party and, as such, entitled to participate in its deliberations.

It was by virtue of this resolution that the respondents refused to permit the petitioner to vote.

Texas is free to conduct her elections and limit her electorate as she may deem wise, save only as her action may be affected by the prohibitions of the United States Constitution or in conflict with powers delegated to and exercised by the National Government. The Fourteenth Amendment forbids a State from making or enforcing any law which abridges the privileges or immunities of citizens of the United States and the Fifteenth Amendment specifically interdicts any denial or abridgement by a State of the right of citizens to vote on account of color. Respondents appeared in the District Court and the Circuit Court of Appeals and defended on the ground that the Democratic party of Texas is a voluntary organization with members banded together for the purpose of selecting individuals of the group representing the common political beliefs as candidates in the general election. As such a voluntary organization, it was claimed, the Democratic party is free to select its own membership and limit to whites participation in the party primary. Such action, the answer asserted, does not violate the Fourteenth, Fifteenth or Seventeenth Amendment as officers of government cannot be chosen at primaries and the Amendments are applicable only to general elections where governmental officers are actually elected. Primaries, it is said, are political party affairs, handled by party, not governmental, officers. . . .

The right of a Negro to vote in the Texas primary has been considered heretofore by this Court. The first case was *Nixon* v. *Herndon*, 273 U.S. 536. At that time, 1924, the Texas statute, Art. 3093a, afterwards numbered Art. 3107 (Rev. Stat. 1925) declared "in no event shall a Negro be eligible to participate in a Democratic Party primary election in the State of Texas." Nixon was refused the right to vote in a Democratic primary and brought a suit for damages against the election officers under R.S. §§ 1979 and 2004, the present §§43 and 31 of Title 8, U.S.C., respectively. It was urged to this Court that the denial of the franchise to Nixon violated his Constitutional rights under the Fourteenth and Fifteenth Amendments. Without consideration of the Fifteenth, this Court held that the action of Texas in denying the ballot to Negroes by statute was in violation of the equal protection clause of the Fourteenth Amendment and reversed the dismissal of the suit.

The legislature of Texas reenacted the article but gave the State Executive Committee of a party the power to prescribe the qualifications of its members for voting or other participation. This article remains in the statutes. The State Executive Committee of the Democratic party adopted a resolution that white Democrats and none other might participate in the primaries of that party. Nixon was refused again the privilege of voting in a primary and again brought suit for damages by virtue of § 31, Title 8, U.S.C. This Court again reversed the dismissal of the suit for the reason that the Committee action was deemed to be state action and invalid as discriminatory under the Fourteenth Amendment. The test was said to be whether the Committee operated as representative of the State in the discharge of the State's authority. *Nixon* v. *Condon*, 286 U.S. 73. The question of the inherent power of a political party in Texas "without restraint by any law to determine its own membership" was left open.

In *Grovey* v. *Townsend*, 295 U.S. 45, this Court had before it another suit for damages for the refusal in a primary of a county clerk, a Texas officer with only public functions to perform, to furnish petitioner, a Negro, an absentee ballot. The refusal was solely on the ground of race. This case differed from *Nixon* v. *Condon*, *supra*, in that a state convention of the Democratic party had passed the resolution of May 24, 1932, hereinbefore quoted. It was decided that the determination by the state convention of the membership of the Democratic party made a significant change from a determination by the Executive Committee. The former was party action, voluntary in character. The latter, as had been held in the *Condon* case, was action by authority of the State. The managers of the primary election were therefore declared not to be state officials in such sense that their action was state action. A state convention of a party was said not to be an organ of the State. This Court went on to announce that to deny a vote in a primary was a mere refusal of party membership with which "the State need have no concern," *loc. cit.* at 55, while for a State to deny a vote in a general election on the ground of race or color violated the Constitution. Consequently, there was found no ground for holding that the county clerk's refusal of a ballot because of racial ineligibility for party membership denied the petitioner any right under the Fourteenth or Fifteenth Amendment.

Since *Grovey* v. *Townsend* and prior to the present suit, no case from Texas involving primary elections has been before this Court. We did decide, however, *United States* v. *Classic*, 313 U.S. 299. We there held that § 4 of Article I of the Constitution authorized Congress to regulate primary as well as general elections, 313 U.S. at 316, 317, "where the primary is by law made an integral part of the election machinery." 313 U.S. at 318. Consequently, in the *Classic* case, we upheld the applicability to frauds in a Louisiana primary of §§ 19 and 20 of the Criminal Code. Thereby corrupt acts of election officers were subjected to Congressional sanctions because that body had power to protect rights of federal suffrage secured by the Constitution in primary as in general elections. 313 U.S. at 323. This decision depended, too, on the determination that under the Louisiana statutes the primary was a part of the procedure for choice of federal officials. By this decision the doubt as to whether or not such primaries were a part of "elections" subject to federal control, which had remained unanswered since *Newberry* v. *United States*, 256 U.S. 232, was erased. The *Nixon Cases* were decided under the equal protection clause of the Fourteenth Amendment without a determination of the status of the primary as a part of the electoral process. The exclusion of Negroes from the primaries by action of the State was held invalid under that Amendment. The fusing by the *Classic* case of the primary and general elections into a single instrumentality for choice of officers has a definite bearing on the permissibility under the Constitution of excluding Negroes from primaries. This is not to say that the *Classic* case cuts directly into the rationale of *Grovey* v. *Townsend*. This latter case was not mentioned in the opinion. *Classic* bears upon *Grovey* v. *Townsend* not because exclusion of Negroes from primaries is any more or less state action by reason of the unitary character of the electoral process but because the recognition of the place of the primary in the electoral scheme makes clear that state delegation to a party of the power to fix the qualifications of primary elections is delegation of a state function that may make the party's action the action of the State. When *Grovey* v. *Townsend* was written, the Court looked upon the denial of a vote in a primary as a mere refusal by a party of party membership. 295 U. S. at 55. As the Louisiana statutes for holding primaries are similar to those of Texas, our ruling in *Classic* as to the unitary character of the electoral process calls for a reexamination as to whether or not the exclusion of Negroes from a Texas party primary was state action.

The statutes of Texas relating to primaries and the resolution of the Democratic party of Texas extending the privileges of membership to white citizens only are the same in substance and effect today as they were when *Grovey* v. *Townsend* was decided by a unanimous Court. The question as to whether the exclusionary action of the party was the action of the State persists as the determinative factor. In again entering upon consideration of the inference to be drawn as to state action from a substantially similar factual situation, it should be noted that *Grovey* v. *Townsend* upheld exclusion of Negroes from primaries through the denial of party membership by a party convention. A few years before, this Court refused approval of exclusion by the State Executive Committee of the party. A different result was reached on the theory that the Committee action was state authorized and the Convention action was unfettered by statutory control. Such a variation in the result from so slight a change in form influences us to consider anew the legal validity of the distinction which has resulted in barring Negroes from participating in the nominations of candidates of the Democratic party in Texas. . . .

It may now be taken as a postulate that the right to vote in such a primary for the nomination of candidates without discrimination by the State, like the right to vote in a general election, is a right secured by the Constitution. *United States* v. *Classic*, 313 U.S. at 314; *Myers* v. *Anderson*, 238 U.S. 368; *Ex parte Yarbrough*, 110 U.S. 651, 663 *et seq.* By the terms of the Fifteenth Amendment that right may not be abridged by any State on account of race. Under our Constitution the great privilege of the ballot may not be denied a man by the State because of his color.

We are thus brought to an examination of the qualifications for Democratic primary electors in Texas, to determine whether state action or private action has excluded Negroes from participation. Despite Texas' decision that the exclusion is produced by private or party action, . . . federal courts must for themselves appraise the facts leading to that conclusion. . . .

Primary elections are conducted by the party under state statutory authority. The county executive committee selects precinct election officials and the county, district or state executive committees, respectively, canvass the returns. These party committees or the state convention certify the party's candidates to the appropriate officers for inclusion on the official ballot for the general election. No name which has not been so certified may appear upon the ballot for the general election as a candidate of a political party. No other name may be printed on the ballot which has not been placed in nomination by qualified voters who must take oath that they did not participate in a primary for the selection of a candidate for the office for which the nomination is made.

The state courts are given exclusive original jurisdiction of contested elections and of mandamus proceedings to compel party officers to perform their statutory duties.

We think that this statutory system for the selection of party nominees for inclusion on the general election ballot makes the party which is required to follow these legislative directions an agency of the State in so far as it determines the participants in a primary election. The party takes its character as a state agency from the duties imposed upon it by state statutes; the duties do not become matters of private law because they are performed by a political party. The plan of the Texas primary follows substantially that of Louisiana, with the exception that in Louisiana the State pays the cost of the primary while Texas assesses the cost against candidates. In numerous instances, the Texas statutes fix or limit the fees to be charged. Whether paid directly by the State or through state requirements, it is state action which compels. When primaries become a part of the machinery for choosing officials, state and national, as they have here, the same tests to determine the character of discrimination or abridgement should be applied to the primary as are applied to the general election. If the State requires a certain electoral procedure, prescribes a general election ballot made up of party nominees so chosen and limits the choice of the electorate in general elections for state offices, practically speaking, to those whose names appear on such a ballot, it endorses, adopts and enforces the discrimination against Negroes, practiced by a party entrusted by Texas law with the determination of the qualifications of participants in the primary. This is state action within the meaning of the Fifteenth Amendment. *Guinn* v. *United States*, 238 U.S. 347, 362.

The United States is a constitutional democracy. Its organic law grants to all citizens a right to participate in the choice of elected officials without restriction by any State because of race. This grant to the people of the opportunity for choice is not to be nullified by a State through casting its electoral process in a form which permits a private organization to practice racial discrimination in the election. Constitutional rights would be of little value if they could be thus indirectly denied. *Lane* v. *Wilson*, 307 U.S. 268, 275. . . .

Here we are applying, contrary to the recent decision in *Grovey v. Townsend*, the well-established principle of the Fifteenth Amendment, forbidding the abridgement by a State of a citizen's right to vote. *Grovey v. Townsend* is overruled.

Judgment reversed

(Mr. Justice Roberts dissents.)

VII

POLITICAL PARTIES

42. *The Strength of Our Political System* *

He stood a spell on one foot fust
Then stood a spell on t'other,
An' on which one he felt the wust,
He couldn't ha' told ye nuther.

THIS QUOTATION from James Russell Lowell has often been considered a fair characterization of the lack of fundamental differences between the Republican and Democratic parties. Many have decried this similarity and called for the formation of parties, each with a distinctive set of principles. Even though some see evidences of embryonic development along this line in large metropolitan areas, historical developments tend to mold the major parties along similar lines. Far from being a sign of weakness, says Professor Nevins, this is one of the factors that accounts for the strength and stability of our political system.

THE pageantry of the Republican and Democratic conventions is over. Now comes the discipline, the semi-military marshaling of forces and the hard campaign work. It is all distinctively American, and in most respects it is all comparatively new. Though political parties are as old as our Government, the tremendous mechanism of national, state and local party organizations, pivoted upon local, state and national conventions, dates only from the second administration of Andrew Jackson. We have little over a hundred years of history to illustrate the function of fully developed parties in general and the two-party system in particular.

* Allan Nevins, *The New York Times Magazine*, July 18, 1948, pp. 5, 31. Reprinted by permission of the author and the publisher.

Have they a healthy function? Some of the principal leaders of Washington's era (a theoretical era, given to abstract speculation upon government) thought not. They held that parties simply bred factions and discord. Virtuous citizens of the new republic should abjure them, and return to the fine Roman spirit later hymned in Macaulay's Lays: "Then none was for a party, then all were for the state." The unanimous election of Washington as first President seemed to vindicate this ideal. But realities, described by Jefferson in a trenchant passage, sheared through this utopian theorizing. Parties were essential to express political aims, to educate the people, to carry on government, and to criticize the Government. In short, wrote Jefferson, parties were vital to liberty:

"In every free and deliberating society, there must, from the nature of man be opposite parties, and violent dissensions and discords; and one of these, for the most part, must prevail over the other for a longer or shorter time. Perhaps this party division is necessary to induce each other to watch and to relate to the people at large the proceedings of the other."

Probably few Americans realize just how important the instant emergence of parties in the United States was, and how inevitable it was that the division between Federalists and Republicans should follow the two-party model of Great Britain. Our Constitution was so drawn that it might as readily have been given an anti-democratic as a democratic cast; it might long have been the instrument of one-party class control. The electoral college, as first devised, was anti-democratic. The Senate, chosen by the state legislatures (in which property seemed at first supreme) was anti-democratic. The Federalists who, with Washington as nonpartisan head, came into executive power, and who showed a remarkable genius for efficient administration, were anti-democratic. The question whether the Constitution might be given a permanently anti-democratic character had to be settled within ten or fifteen years.

Inevitably, the dominance of the men who wished to see the national Government powerful, well-centralized, and anti-democratic called into existence a counter-party who wished the Government kept weak, uncentralized, and democratic. Washington in the selection of his first Cabinet recognized two parties. On the national and aristocratic side he chose Hamilton for the Treasury and Henry Knox for War; on the democratic side he selected Jefferson for the State Department and Edmund Randolph for Attorney General. The divergence of opinion in Cabinet meetings was paralleled by an even more passionate divergence in the nation at large. Within a few years the two parties were formally reorganized, and every American knew that their struggle would decide the course of constitutional development. Federalist and Republican fought to put Government within their particular molds just as Whig and Tory fought to shape the unwritten British Constitution.

Here was a difference in principle. The dominant purpose of the Federalist party was to place such a construction on the letter of the Constitution as to broaden the powers of the Federal Government and restrict those of the states. The essential purpose of the Jeffersonian party was to interpret the Constitution in such wise as to limit the national and foster the local power. Two rival ideologies were in frontal collision. In France of the period this meant battles and guillotines. In America, however, from the very beginning three factors operated to lessen the violence of the party clash.

What were they? First, principle itself was interpreted with a saving grace of reservations and modifications, and was subject to sudden changes dictated by expediency. Thus Jefferson, once in power, actually made more far-reaching use of the central Government, as in the Louisiana Purchase and the embargo, than John Adams had done, while that good Democrat, Andrew Jackson, proved the sternest nationalist in our history. Second, both parties took up all manner of subsidiary issues, ranging from tariffs and internal improvements to foreign policy; and as they did so, both appealed to a wide variety of constantly fluctuating groups. Third, each party had such a healthy respect for public sentiment that, following the old Anglo-Saxon rule of compromise (undoubtedly the most vital single element in our Government), the majority abstained from abusing its authority, and the minority yielded to the majority on the tacit understanding that no abuse would be practiced.

For a variety of reasons, from Hamilton to Truman the two-party system has perpetuated itself. For one, in a populous democracy the costs of maintaining a party on a national scale, quadrennium after quadrennium, are so great that splinter parties cannot meet them. Also, most great leaders rise to influence within the two main parties. But, above all, the two-party system suits the genius of the people. They want a responsible authority, on which they can count for stability; they want it closely watched by a strong opposition; they want to use its power, but to do so in the spirit of compromise, with a due regard for minority rights.

Is such a party system democratic? "A party," William H. Seward once remarked, "is in one sense a joint stock association, in which those who contribute most direct the action and management of the concern." Accepting this definition, we can see why great parties sometimes fall under an undemocratic control.

Just before the Civil War the Democratic party, as Seward complained, was dominated by a comparatively restricted body of slaveholders who contributed more money, determination and brains to its direction than any other group. After the Civil War the Republican party fell, for a long period, under the domination of big business. But party machinery (through the direct primary, better publicity, restriction of campaign gifts and so on) has been improved to permit of broader controls. If much still remains to be done, as James Reston has pointed out, it *can* be done. And the very heterogeneity of our parties makes for democracy.

If any lesson is written in our history, it is that an undemocratically controlled party sooner or later pays a heavy penalty. Elements of revolt gather within its ranks. Reform groups rise up against the slavery oligarchy, or the Tammany-Bourbon alliance, or the special privilege corporations, or whatever other group has become dominant. They join the opposition party, in such a tremendous accession of "independent" strength as that which in 1884 elected Cleveland over Blaine, for example; or they stage a revolt within their own party, like Bryan's revolt against the Tammany-Ryan combination in 1912; or they organize a third party, as the Progressives did. In one way or another, they strike a decisive blow for a more democratic management of party affairs.

So little is the American system understood that some people are constantly asking: "Why don't the parties stand for hard and fast principles? Why is it so difficult to tell Republican aims from Democratic aims? Why are they so much alike?" Bryce wrote about 1880 that the abiding object of the Democratic party was still to oppose a unitary and much-interfering Government in Washington; but under Woodrow Wilson and Franklin D. Roosevelt the traditional party role on this head seemed reversed.

And so little is the system appreciated that some critics continually repeat the question: "Why can't we have a Conservative party and a Liberal party? Why can't we have parties on economic lines?"

Such statements ignore the cardinal utility of our two great parties. They are an amalgam, not a solvent; their fundamental value in the United States is in pulling together an immensely varied mass of social groups, economic constituencies, racial stocks, and local and sectional interests for the purpose of governing by consent.

The greatest disaster that ever befell the nation in the past resulted from a temporary division of parties along sectional lines. The worst disaster that could possibly happen to it in the near future would be a division along economic and class lines. We have the utmost reason for rejoicing, not for regret, that the Republican and Democratic parties are so much alike that the scepter can pass from one to the other without perceptible shock.

It is of the first importance that each party represent a fair cross-section of the nation, with rich and poor, farmers and city clerks, Catholics, Jews and Protestants, old stock and immigrant stock. Our wide diffusion of property prevents any division between rich and poor. But if we did have a Conservative party of the propertied and a Radical party of the unpropertied we might at last be within sight of the day when the losers in an election would begin throwing up barricades in the streets.

Our type of two-party system has its manifest disadvantages and defects. Obviously, two big, loose, heterogeneous parties are always exposed to schism. Obviously, too, such mammoth parties, making constant compromises within their own ranks, must be guilty of a good deal of time-serving, trimming and hypocrisy. We have seen the spectacle of one Republican Administration after another uttering bright platitudes about Negro equality while courting the "lily whites" in the South. We have seen the Franklin D. Roosevelt Administration preaching noble political ideals while accepting the partnership of Boss Hague and Boss Crump. The alliance of low-tariff Iowa farmers and high-tariff Pennsylvania ironmasters under the Republican aegis, and the alliance of Tammany Hall with Alabama agrarians under the Democratic banner, have not made for political honesty of the austerest type.

At a grave crisis in the Civil War, just after the defeat of Fredericksburg, Lincoln kept the disharmonious Republican party together by obtaining written resignations from Secretary Seward, pet of the conservatives, and Secretary Chase, pet of the radicals; not to be used, but to be balanced against each other. It was an effective stroke, but it did not illustrate the highest kind of political forthrightness.

Nevertheless, the benefits of the existing system far outweigh its drawbacks. We, like the British, and for basically the same reason, find a multi-party system almost unthinkable. Our whole tradition is built on government by a strong and responsible majority, which will wield power effectively but will at the same time respect minority rights. The spectacle of irresponsibility, confusion and intolerance presented by some Continental European nations of multitudinous parties may be exciting, and some of their parties may suggest an intellectual rigor unknown in our politics; but the practical results do not commend themselves to us.

We feel the safer in trusting to two major parties because, unlike the British, we have surrounded minority rights with an elaborate system of checks and balances. We feel the safer because even our strongest Presidents—Jackson, Lincoln, Wilson, the two Roosevelts—have never, despite much short-lived partisan talk to the contrary, shown any really dictatorial tendencies.

Nor are we willing to give up the vast benefits we reap from the fact that the two great parties are ponderous cross-sections of our varied society, representing every element. Third parties have never been that. They have usually been parties of one idea—abolitionism, prohibition, populism—and hence one group. In a nation so large and so variegated in resources and climate, so widely differentiated in economic and social interests, so complex in its stocks and faiths, it is essential that our parties promote unity. In a population which does now and then grow hotly emotional over changing issues, a party organization built on principles of cohesion and compromise is obviously invaluable.

The fundamental character of our political organism has changed astonishingly little between the days of Hamilton and Jefferson, and the days of Truman and Dewey. To that fact we may ascribe much of our national stability.

43. *The Big Hello* *

THIS ARTICLE by Richard H. Rovere offers a lively portrait of an old-fashioned political boss, whose activities are reminiscent of the gaslight era in New York. It presents the favorable side of the type of man who is often characterized as corrupt, living on patronage, and a spoilsman. The career of Peter McGuinness is a case study on the local level of the theory of Harold D. Lasswell that politics is "the study of influence and the influential." It depicts what is sometimes called the social and humanitarian function of the political party.

PART I

PETER J. McGUINNESS, a big, tough, happy, red-faced Irishman who for the past twenty-two years has been the Democratic leader of the section of Brooklyn called Greenpoint, is the first citizen of that community

* Richard H. Rovere, *The New Yorker*, January 12, 1946, pp. 29-34, 36-38; January 19, 1946, pp. 26-32, 34, 39-41. Reprinted by permission of the author and the publisher.

and the last of New York's old-time district bosses. "I'm the boss of Greenpoint," he often says. "What I say there goes." A district boss, unlike the boss of a county or a state, controls none of the actual machinery of government; he cannot, therefore, impose himself upon the community against its will. If he remains boss, he does so either because the voters are largely indifferent to local politics or because he is really popular with them. In McGuinness's case, it is altogether a matter of popularity. Almost no one in Greenpoint, a working-class community in which the Irish tradition is still the dominant one, is indifferent to politics. McGuinness, who was Greenpoint's alderman from 1920 to 1931 and has been its Democratic leader since 1924, has been before the voters of Greenpoint more than thirty times in primary and general elections. On each occasion his showing has been better than the time before. For the past few years no one has even run against him.

Very few New Yorkers today could name the party leaders in the districts in which they live; McGuinness is so well known in Greenpoint that he no longer needs to use his last name on campaign posters. "Vote for Peter," one flyer used in a recent election said. "It's no Wonder that everyone likes him. Peter is the only Politician in the forty-eight States who devotes All his time to the People." To many Greenpointers, McGuinness's name is synonymous with statesmanship in general; the *Weekly Star,* a community newspaper, has frequently reported that schoolboys or first voters, asked to name the Mayor or the Governor, have said he was Peter J. McGuinness. McGuinness is not only Greenpoint's political leader but its social leader and its arbiter of taste. The main social events of the year in Greenpoint are Annual McGuinness Night, a ball that is held in the Labor Lyceum Hall on the first Saturday after Lent and causes a considerable upswing in the hired-tuxedo trade, and the Monster McGuinness Theatre Party, which is held in the late fall in the Meserole Theatre. Possibly the greatest tribute to McGuinness's popularity in Greenpoint is the amount of poetry he has inspired. It may well be that more poetry has been written about McGuinness than about anyone in American politics since Abraham Lincoln. The community newspapers publish an extraordinary volume of poetry, and a large portion of it in the past quarter century has been verse in praise of McGuinness. An example is a ballad of twenty-three stanzas by Maurice Dee, which ends:

> Oh, I could continue writing until this pencil wore down
> About the ways he is loved in this town,
> But the thing we prize most is the fact he is with us,
> Our tall, broad, and handsome Peter McGuinness.

At a time when the public is apt to be cynical about politicians and their motives, such standing as McGuinness enjoys is not easily won or maintained. McGuinness has achieved it because he works hard and loves his work. He tends his vineyard by day and by night. He is probably the only politician in the city who still follows the old custom of holding court on a street corner and greeting passers-by by name. Every Saturday evening and Sunday afternoon, in seasonable weather, he posts himself outside a store on the corner of Manhattan and Norman Avenues, Greenpoint's main intersection, and has a few words with the strollers. "That's when I give me people the big hello," he says. He enjoys giving people the big hello, just as he enjoys everything else about politics. Duties that other men regard as unpleasant chores are to him the main compensations of his career. He likes making speeches, marching in parades, attending weddings and funerals, and running Kiddies' Day outings. He says that the greatest thrill he ever had came during the 1936 Democratic National Convention in Philadelphia, when Jim Farley asked him to read, over a national hookup, the convention resolution thanking the radio companies for their coverage of the convention. "Bejesus," he says, "I stood up there on the platform with the Vice-President of the United States behind me, and senators, and governors from states that are Democratic, and I talked to the whole United States. I'm telling you, you could just see the sweat run down me back. Right then me whole life passed before me eyes."

Next to attending conventions, McGuinness can think of no pleasanter way to spend an evening than to sit behind his desk at his headquarters, the Greenpoint People's Regular Democratic Organization Clubhouse, listening to the requests of constituents and trying to do something about them. "I get a hell of a kick out of that," he says. "Sometimes I even do favors for people in Jersey." A New York district politician who concerns himself with the problems of a New Jersey voter is breaking new ground in human brotherhood, but McGuinness's high regard for his fellow-man extends even beyond Jersey. One Christmas he put an advertisement in the Brooklyn *Citizen* saying "Peter J. McGuinness, Democratic State Committeeman from the Fifteenth Assembly District, Extends Cordial Holiday Greetings to the World."

McGuinness thinks highly of the Jewish holiday Yom Kippur, the day of atonement, on which the pious are supposed to make some charitable gesture toward their enemies. When he first heard of this custom, he sent a memorandum to all the Jewish members of his club telling them to observe the practice and to do something nice for the

Republicans and Socialists. McGuinness is a Roman Catholic, but his favorite man of God was the Protestant evangelist Tom Noonan, who was known as the Bishop of Chinatown and who, until his death, several years ago, ran a Bowery mission. McGuinness respected Noonan because he did favors on such a large scale. Noonan ran a kind of revival meeting on the radio every Sunday, and ended his program with a plea to his listeners for old clothing, eyeglass frames, medicines, and other things needed by his friends on the Bowery and in Chinatown. The response to these appeals was enormous, and McGuinness felt that Noonan, by conceiving the notion of doing favors over the airwaves, had become one of mankind's great benefactors. "Tom Noonan was a most splendid gentleman," McGuinness says. "I never knew of anyone who done so much for the human race of people." McGuinness is probably the only man who ever ran for county sheriff on a program of making life pleasanter for prisoners. In 1935, when he was a candidate for Sheriff of Kings County, he promised in every speech that the prisoners in the county jail would be happy and well fed if he were elected. "Under me they'll get better meenus," he said. He was elected, and his first act was to throw a New Year's Eve party for the prisoners; his second, in fulfillment of his campaign pledge, was to order that beef stew be served twice a week and that hot drinks be handed around before bedtime.

McGuinness is almost always in high spirts. Sometimes he finds it impossible to contain his exuberance. On these occasions, he begins by bouncing up and down in his chair; then he whistles a few bars of jolly music, flicks the dust off the shoulders of his coat with his fingertips, and rises to do a couple of jig steps. "Jeez, I'm feeling spiffy today," he says when this mood is upon him. "Don't mind me, pals. It's just me nature to whistle." He calls everyone "pal," even people he has never met and is talking with for the first time over the telephone. His good nature has endeared him not only to the voters of Greenpoint but to all the professional politicians in town. In the places they most often gather—City Hall, Foley Square, and the Borough Hall section in Brooklyn—no one else is as popular. For the past two decades no social gathering of officeholders or city-news reporters has been considered a success unless McGuinness has attended and done some unusual things with the English language. Before his feet began to bother him a few years ago, he was often chosen to lead contingents of city officials in the annual St. Patrick's Day parade, which he now watches from a place of honor in the reviewing stand. Since 1921, he has been master of ceremonies at the annual outing of politicians and city-news reporters at Travers Island, Whitestone Landing, or wherever.

Among politicians, one good index of a man's standing is the frequency with which he is asked to be an honorary pallbearer for deceased associates. McGuinness is in greater demand for this service than anyone else in the city, sometimes having to decide which of two distinguished corpses he will accompany to the grave on a given morning. He is chairman of the Association of Past Aldermen of the City of New York and an official of half a dozen other societies in which politicians gather to honor themselves. Among those who enjoy paying their respects to him are Mayor O'Dwyer, Fiorello LaGuardia, Jimmy Walker, Samuel Seabury, James A. Farley, Herbert H. Lehman, Newbold Morris, and Robert Moses. Governor Dewey once had a good word for him. The late B. Charney Vladeck, the Socialist leader of the lower East Side and a man who generally classed Democratic officeholders with sweatshop proprietors and exploiters of child labor, was one of his warmest admirers. "That Irishman!" Vladeck used to say. "Sometimes he makes me wish I was a Democrat."

To reciprocate the affection that other men in public life have shown for him, McGuinness honors them by admitting them to the Grand Order of Pork Chops, a fraternal organization of large but uncounted membership, all of it elected by him. Whenever he meets a member, McGuinness says, "Hello, there, me old pork chop!" He started the order some twenty years ago, when he was a member of the Board of Aldermen. "It's just sort of a humorous thing I thought up," he says reluctantly, when asked for an explanation. "What the hell? I had to have *something* to call me very dearest pals. I call them pork chops because all the old aldermen used to like eating pork chops." The Pork Chops have held only one meeting. That was in 1931, upon the occasion of McGuinness's resignation from the Board of Aldermen. The Board adjourned and, after several prominent outsiders had been admitted to the chamber, convened again as the Grand Order of Pork Chops. There were many testimonials to McGuinness, and he was presented with a gold watch, a chain, and a watch charm that he describes as "a gold statue of a pork chop." The Grand Master of the Pork Chops is Isidor Frank, a wholesale butcher who gives Democratic district leaders generous discounts on the turkeys and chickens they distribute to the poor at Thanksgiving and Christmas.

McGuinness is an anachronism. His approach to politics was outdated before he was born. His language went out along with cops in jardinière hats. His exuberance is Dickensian. Even physically, he seems improbable in the twentieth century. Newspaper cartoonists say that they can get a perfect caricature of the old-time Irish ward boss simply by drawing McGuinness as he is; Nast and Keppler, they maintain, never produced anything half so plausible as McGuinness. McGuinness, who is fifty-eight, stands just under six feet and weighs about two hundreds and thirty pounds, which is some forty pounds less than he weighed three years ago, when his doctor advised him to reduce. He has a massive head, clear blue eyes, a complexion that is a shade or two off ripe tomato. His hair is pure white but still plentiful. He parts it neatly in the middle and sometimes scallops it daintly over his forehead in the roach style affected by bartenders fifty years ago. His nose and chin are enormous, granitic affairs that jut far out from their moorings and then tilt sharply upward; they look as if they had been done by a sculptor of noble intentions but imprecise execution. McGuinness can look as benign as Old King Cole or Kriss Kringle in a nursery book or as belligerent as Roughie McToughie, the generic hard guy. He dramatizes his belligerent moods much as he dramatizes his happy ones. He doubles his immense fists, crouches forward in his chair, and starts jabbing sharply in the direction of the nearest wall. "You louse-bound bastard, you," he says to the shadow he is boxing, "who you think you're talking to?" Before he was elected alderman for the first time, in 1919, he had spent fourteen years as a teamster, a lumber-yard worker, and a boss stevedore, and had earned money on the side as a semi-professional boxer, a distance runner, and a bouncer in the barroom of a steamboat that made moonlight pleasure cruises. In those pursuits, he developed a hard, agile body, which has taken on weight without becoming slovenly. McGuinness does not look fat; he looks beefy, powerful, massive, and stately. He is powerful, in fact as well as in aspect. Several months ago, he was the cause of a brief slowdown in war production when he put two obstreperous young shipyard workers on the absentee list for several days. "They got wise with me and called me Pop," he explains. "I give 'em the back of me hand."

He carries his body and his head erect. His walk is slow, lordly, and rather ponderously graceful. Unlike the politicians of the gaslit era to which he is so clearly a throwback, he is conservative in dress, being given to gray tweed suits, white shirts, and patterned blue ties. He does not wear a stickpin, and his only ring is a simple gold one, set with a garnet, which was given to him thirty-five years ago by his wife, Margaret, a handsome woman of proportions nearly as heroic as his own. He addresses her as Maggie and often refers to her as "the old champeen." They have one son, George, an Internal Revenue agent, who is thirty-five and bigger than either of them. The members of McGuinness's club once raised a thousand dollars and bought him a ring with an enormous sparkler, but though they had ordered the largest one in stock, the ring would not fit on any of his fingers, which are as big around as pick handles. "Bless us, but it don't even go on the pinky," he said in his speech at the presentation ceremony, trying to make the best of an awkward situation. He keeps the ring at home and debates with himself the propriety of having the stone set in a ring for Mrs. McGuinness. Perhaps to make up for his lack of jewelry, he bristles with fountain pens, mechanical pencils, and jackknives. His only concessions in dress to the century in which he belongs are his black, hightop shoes and his white cotton socks.

McGuinness has a silver tongue, and he loves to use it. In his twelve years on the Board of Aldermen he missed only two meetings, and he made a speech at every one he attended—generally a long speech. Once he spoke at such length that a fellow-alderman finally crept down the aisle and wrapped a muffler around his head. A cigarette was dangling from one corner of McGuinness's mouth as he spoke, and both he and the muffler were singed. Years of oratory have had a curious effect on him, not unlike the effect that years in the ring sometimes have on fighters. He is speech-drunk. Just as an old pug comes out swinging at the sound of a dinner bell, so McGuinness will break into a speech at the mention of George Washington, Pope Pius XII, Franklin D. Roosevelt, or any of the other names that are hallowed in his kind of politics. Often he will make a speech simply to fill in a gap in conversation. Recently he was conferring with several friends when someone walked in and remarked that a plate of good hot soup was just the thing for the weather that day. Everyone nodded and mumbled agreement. Then, since the subject seemed pretty well covered, an embarrassed silence followed. Before it had gone too far, McGuinness broke it with ten minutes of rhetoric on soup, the underlying theme being that one of the country's weaknesses was a general lack of the kind of nourishing soup made by American womanhood fifty years ago. In ordinary conversation, his voice is low and sometimes scratchy, because of the wear and tear it has had over the years. Often, when he is trying to make a point, he uses a hoarse, confidential whisper, as though he were talking in church. In public speeches, however, or in private ones, his tones are clear and resonant and have a volume comparable to that of the late Joe Humphries. The strength of his vocal cords, like the strength of his muscles, is the subject of tall tales in Greenpoint. One of these is about the time the transmitter went dead while McGuinness was speaking over WNYC. Informed of the mishap, McGuinness just raised his voice a trifle and went on talking. He was heard throughout Greenpoint as well as before.

McGuinness is easily the most successful pork-barrel raider in the city, and many of his accomplishments in this field are the result of his eloquence. His talking has got Greenpoint many millions of dollars' worth of playgrounds and public baths, a hospital dispensary, a nurses' home, one of the two largest public swimming pools in the city, innumerable street pavings, a new high school, and an incinerator. One of his most notable achievements was keeping a ferry line running for thirteen years after it had ceased to pay for itself. Before the Independent Subway reached Greenpoint, this ferry service, which carried passengers from Greenpoint to East Twenty-third Street, provided it with its only direct communication with Manhattan. Chiefly because most people who live in Greenpoint also work there, its patronage declined to the point at which it was no longer used enough to justify its operation. Nevertheless, McGuinness was determined that it should be continued for the few who did commute on it and for those who rode it on summer evenings to keep cool. Every year he appeared before the Board of Estimate to appeal for its continuance, and for thirteen years he was successful. Once, addressing himself to Jimmy Walker, who, as Mayor, presided over the Board meetings, he concluded a long speech by saying, "Please don't take away the old ferry, Mr. Mayor. It would be like separating an old couple that has been together for years to divorce Manhattan and Greenpoint. There would be tears of sorrow in the eyes of the old ferryboats, as there would be tears in the eyes of the people of Greenpoint, if them splendid old boats were put up to rot in some drydock or sold at public auction. Tell me, Mr. Mayor, now tell me that you will love them old ferryboats in December as you did in May." "Peter, you're my favorite alderman," Walker said in return. The ferries kept running.

The next year, when the time came, McGuinness, who has a richly inventive mind, came up with the intelligence that the boats were valuable relics; they had, he claimed he had learned, been used as Union troop transports on the Mississippi in the Civil War. (McGuinness is still fighting the Civil War, in which his maternal grandfather, Major James Fee of the Union Army, was killed. In spite of his loyalty to the Democratic Party, McGuinness dislikes the South, where he spent a few months as a lumber inspector during the first World War. "I never seen anything good down there," he says. "I don't like that Jim Crow they got, and I don't like their goddam white crow neither.") Another year, he said that the ferries would be the only means of escape from Greenpoint in the event of catastrophe. "Listen," he told Mayor O'Brien, "if somebody set fire to Greenpoint and them old boats weren't there, we'd all be roasted alive." The ferries still kept running.

He can use irony as well as sentiment. Once, in the early twenties, his leadership of his district was briefly threatened by the appearance of a college graduate who argued that a forward-looking community should have as its leader a man of culture and refinement, meaning himself. The Higher Learning was enjoying its greatest prestige at the time and the newcomer was impressing a good many voters with his law-school vocabulary. McGuinness, who never got beyond the eighth grade, disposed of the interloper with a line that is a favorite of connoisseurs of political strategy. At the next large meeting McGuinness addressed, he stood silent for a moment, glaring down at the crowd of shirtsleeved laborers and housewives in Hoover aprons until he had their attention. Then he bellowed, "All of yez that went to Yales or Harvards raise your right hands!"

McGuinness is a working politician. By and large, he has been content to leave matters of theory to the professors and platform makers. His concern with political affairs, however, is a good deal less parochial than that of most district leaders, and he has views on a wide variety of subjects. He was, for example, an early opponent of Fascism, and he believes that the Greenpoint People's Regular Democratic Organization was the first political club to pass an anti-Nazi resolution. The resolution, passed early in 1933, took the form of a telegram to President von Hindenburg advising him to yield no further powers to Hitler. The club's protest was made at McGuinness's urging. "Bejesus, I knew what that one was up to," he says. McGuinness has some highly personal theories of history, and among them is the conviction that Hitler himself murdered von Hindenburg. "I'll go to me grave knowing that's so," he says. "That's why I said we should warn the old gentleman." During the North African phase of the war, he had no patience with the policy of dealing with former Vichyites like Admiral Darlan and General Giraud. He held General Giraud personally responsible for the misfortune that occurred to General Mark Clark when, at the secret conferences before the invasion, he lost his pants and the eighteen thousand dollars they contained. "I'm down on the crowd," McGuinness says. "That was a hell of a thing, them letting that happen. Any decent political man, when he gets someone coming into his district, the least he can do is make sure no one rolls him while he's there."

McGuinness has not been a prominent figure in the quarrel between the two Democratic factions during the past decade, but, generally speaking, he is sympathetic to the Left Wing. There are two reasons for this—his dislike of the South, which is almost solidly Right Wing, and his dislike of penny-pinching. During the clamor in Congress and the press on the comparative merits of Henry Wallace and Jesse Jones as guardians of the R.F.C. funds, he sided with Wallace. "Why, you can figure this thing out just from reading the papers," he said.

"They're afraid that if they let Wallace in there, he'll spend the money. What the hell is the money for, anyway? God bless us, we don't want a piker for a job like that." McGuinness's dislike of the South is particularly virulent when it comes to Texas, and he held Jones's Texas background against him. "I'll tell you all about Texas," he said once. "You know what Texas calls itself, don't you? The Lone Star State, that's what it is. Did you ever think what they mean by that? I'll tell you. They want to be all alone down there, they don't want nothing to do with the other forty-seven states. Well, if Texas wants to be the Lone Star State, I'm all for letting her get the hell out of the country. I wouldn't even miss her."

In McGuinness's early days, when the Socialists were politically formidable in Brooklyn, he often campaigned against them, but he was friendly with many of the Socialist leaders and even at times helped to advance their cause. On the old Board of Alderman, he particularly liked B. Charney Vladeck. On several occasions, when Vladeck knew that one of his resolutions would be defeated if it came from a Socialist, McGuinness offered to sponsor it himself, thereby making it a Democratic measure. In this way McGuinness became the author of resolutions expressing sympathy with victims of injustice of whom he had never heard and resolutions protesting abuses for which his own party was responsible. "I loved him like a brother," he says of Vladeck. "The Lord never made a more splendid man than Cheeny. I figured if Cheeny was for something, it was good enough for me. I said to him, 'Cheeny, if you ever got anything you want to slip through here, just give it to me, old pal. I'll make it Irish for you.'" Resolutions sponsored by McGuinness always passed. Two or three years ago, when there was agitation for the release of Earl Browder from the federal penitentiary, McGuinness was asked for his views by a Brooklyn reporter. "I'm for letting him out," he said. "They tell me he's not so bad. He's got a very good job with the Communists. I guess he believes all that stuff, too. You just go back and ask the people who want to keep him in jail how the hell would they like to be there theirselves."

Like most district leaders, McGuinness has managed to keep himself on the public payroll a large part of the time. In addition to being an alderman, he has been Sheriff of Kings County and County Register, and at present he is Assistant Commissioner of Borough Works in Brooklyn. In one sense, his current job is a comedown, since it pays only seventy-nine hundred a year. The shrievalty paid fifteen thousand and the register's job paid twelve. The offices of County Sheriff and Register, however, were abolished three years ago on the ground that they served no useful purpose. On the same day in 1941 that the voters of Kings County elected McGuinness their County Register, the voters of the state adopted a constitutional amendment doing away with the office. McGuinness had to take his present job as the next-best thing. He was appointed to it in 1944, upon the death of the incumbent. "I like this here work pretty good," he says. "It don't keep me tied down none." The Department of Borough Works is charged with the maintenance of streets, sewers, and certain public buildings. It is run by civil engineers and most of its employees are engineers and laborers. McGuinness does not pretend to be an expert on public works—although, having once been in the lumber business, he considers himself an authority on the Coney Island boardwalk—but his job does not seem to require much technical knowledge. In fact, it does not seem to require anything at all except part-time attendance at his office at Borough Hall. He is there two or three hours a day, but most of that time is spent in working on his "contracts"—the politician's term for favors requested of him by his constituents or other politicians. McGuinness has no qualms of conscience about holding a job that involves little work. He feels that his real service to society is the work he does as a political leader in Greenpoint, and he regards his being on the municipal payroll merely a technical device to give him the money to carry on. "The thing of it is," he says thoughtfully, "you got to make jobs like this so a political man can get his work done." Robert Moses, who has given a good deal of thought to matters of this sort, is inclined to agree with McGuinness. "Of course, it's pure nonsense to expect a man like Pete to be an administrator," Moses said recently. "Pete is a leader and one of the best in the city. I've known him and worked with him for twenty years, and whenever I've needed to know anything about Greenpoint I've got more practical help and coöperation from Pete than I could ever have got from a hundred social workers, city planners, poll takers, and all the rest of that trash. No matter what you say about them, men like Pete have held New York's neighborhoods together, and if the reformers ever succeed in driving them out, the city is going to fall apart into racial and religious mobs."

McGuinness's working day is a long and often arduous one. He is up by seven and by eight has started on a long round of errands. Some days he travels by bus, subway, and trolley; some days he is driven around in one of the several limousines at the disposal of the Borough President. He may stop in at a doctor's office or a hospital to arrange for the care of an ailing constituent, attend a funeral or two, pay his respects to the bereaved family, argue with some constituent's landlord about heating problems or unpaid rent, run down a loose-footed husband and try to persuade him to return to his wife, arrange with the head of a city bureau to shift a member of his club from night to day work, and call upon several public agencies to clear up various problems of widows' and veterans' pensions, Social Security, workmen's compensation, service allotments, old-age insurance, and any of the other government business that brings the poor so much closer to their politicians than the well-to-do ever are. McGuinness also visits a good many courts and police stations in his tour. He does not like to say much about what he does there; he considers that when he is acting as lawyer, it is his duty to keep his clients' confidences inviolate. "I never talk about me people's troubles," he says. "But you know how it is. You're walking along the street, and somebody you don't even know bunks into you. You push him away, and he comes back. You give him another shove, and he's back again. One of that kind, you know. You give him a good one, and then some goddam patrolman busts in and takes the both of yez down to the station. *He* don't know who started it, so it's drunk and disorderly, the two of yez. What the hell are you going to do? All the nerves in your body are jumping. You're cold all over. Then it comes to you. 'I'll call Peter McGuinness,' you say to yourself. 'He'll help me out of this.' Bejesus, I *got* to give you a hand on a proposition like that."

Once every week or two, McGuinness simply spends the day in Greenpoint, covering his district on foot. He checks up on such matters of public interest as garbage collection, the efficiency of the Fire and Police Departments, playground administration, compliance with tenement restrictions, and the condition of the pavements. If he sees or hears of anything wrong—a stopped-up sewer, a hole in the pavement, or traffic on a play street—he gets in touch with the authorities. Greenpoint is the most industrialized section of the city, and among its products are soap, varnish, gasoline, and other things whose manufacture is often malodorous. One of McGuinness's many boasts is that he has made Greenpoint smell better. He has forced factory owners to install devices that eliminate objectionable smells and smoke, and he is constantly sniffing for new attempts to pollute the air. As soon as he detects an unpleasant odor on the wind, he calls on the manager of the offending plant and threatens to take him to court for violating a whole series of local ordinances.

The close watch McGuinness keeps on Greenpoint has brought unexpected dividends. During the 1936 campaign, President Roosevelt spoke briefly in Greenpoint. Before he was introduced, he confided to McGuinness that he had been worried by the *Literary Digest* straw vote, in which Governor Landon was well in the lead. "I said to him," McGuinness recalls. "'Mr. President,' I said, 'don't give it another thought. I got that goddam fake figured out.'" The President asked McGuinness what he meant. McGuinness explained that he had recently assigned three of his club members to spy on the city incinerator in his district. Some Greenpointers who lived near the incinerator had complained that horses were being cremated in its furnaces. The McGuinness followers spent several nights hiding in some bushes near the plant to see if horses were being cremated there, and they discovered that every night, after the Sanitation Department trucks had dumped their loads, some men who they knew were Republican party workers were coming there and buying up huge stacks of paper. A little closer snooping showed that they were blank *Literary Digest* ballots. "The people in Brooklyn got them fake ballots," McGuinness told the President, "and they turn them right out. The Republicans come around here and buy them for a nickel apiece. That's why Landon's ahead." The President laughed, and later in the campaign he sent word to McGuinness, through Postmaster Farley, that he was no longer worrying about the straw vote. "You know," McGuinness says, "when you make a man like that feel good, it sends a thrill right through you. It just made me feel cold all over."

McGuinness is in his office in Borough Hall by noon almost every day. He stays there until two-thirty or three, checking up on his contracts, welcoming constituents who find it more convenient to see him then about their troubles, and passing the time with old friends. Early in the afternoon he goes across the street to the press room in the Supreme Court Building, where he spends an hour or so catching up on political gossip, general news, and sitting in on the all-day rummy game there. He leaves not later than five, goes home to dinner, and then walks to the Greenpoint People's Regular Democratic Organization, a made-over three-story frame house just around the corner from his own house, which is very much like it. In a large, gloomy room—decorated only with some blown-up tinted portraits of McGuinness with his arms around Jimmy Walker; a faded pennant bearing the name and portrait of Franklin D. Roosevelt; and a huge picture of McGuinness as a brawny young longshoreman—he sits down at his desk, ready for whatever the evening will bring. Constituents start arriving about six o'clock and wait their turn in straight-backed chairs in a room adjoining his office. These chairs, aside from a couple of small, plain tables and McGuinness's desk, chair, and safe, are the only furnishings in the club. McGuinness, who admires a touch of color in his surroundings, would like his clubrooms to be cheerier, but he says that it would be foolish for the Greenpoint People's Regular Democratic Organization to spend much money on furniture or decorations.

"The fellows that come in here," he says, "talk a lot about baseball and things like that, and sometimes they get to arguing." The club telephone is kept in a padlocked squirrel cage, which McGuinness has to unlock every time the phone rings.

He stays in the club until twelve-thirty or one. He may see anywhere from a dozen to a hundred people before ten o'clock, but not many show up after that. Still, he feels that he should stay. "You never know when there'll be a late straggler," he explains. At about eight-thirty, some of his friends arrive and set up a rummy game, in which he takes a hand whenever he can. Most of the people who come to see him want the kind of routine favors he has done for others earlier in the day; the services McGuinness offers make him a combined attorney, job agent, accountant, and social worker. McGuinness asks no questions and extracts no promises. "A lot of Republicans come in here," he says. "If I can do a Republican a favor, he'll probably go out a Democrat." He also serves as a domestic-relations court. "It's one of the great happinesses in me life," he likes to say, "to think of all the husbands and wives I've kept together." His matrimonial advice to husbands consists of eloquent variations on one theme—"the old girl is always best." There are no statistics on his percentage of success, but McGuinness's way of handling people in trouble is admired by district politicians throughout the city. "None of the rest of us are in it with Peter," one of them said recently. "Sometimes I go out there to play a little rummy with him, and I see him at work. Of course, he always takes people in his office to talk, and he never lets anyone else know what was said. But lots of times you can see the results. One night last winter, I saw something I could hardly believe. A young widow whose husband was killed in the war come in with a lot of papers about pensions and all that for Peter to take care of. She had her kid, a little boy, with her, and the two of them were crying. Peter scooped up the kid and put an arm around the girl and took them both in his office. When they come out—well, it's almost blasphemous to talk about it—but honestly, the two of them was smiling and laughing so, you'd almost think they were happy about what had happened. Just as they were leaving, I heard Peter give them the name of a picture framer and tell them to take the death certificate there. He said to order the very fanciest frame they could get and send the bill to the club." McGuinness, like most men of political influence, is often sought out by distraught relatives of people who have become involved with the law. Since he is considered Greenpoint's leading exemplar of virtue, he is also sought out by parents who simply want him to have a talk with young men and women who show signs of waywardness. His frequent lectures on the upright life are delivered with great solemnity. But he is usually ready to help even when his counsel has not been followed. "Murder, rape, and robbery with a gun I never touch," he says. "But something like housebreaking—what the hell, the first couple times don't prove there's anything wrong with a boy."

McGuinness considers his evening sessions with constituents the pleasantest part of his day. "As the fellow said," he will tell you with quite a show of sentiment, "helping out a pal in trouble—that's all there is in life."

PART II

Peter J. McGuinness, a rotund, robust, perennially high-spirited man who for the past twenty-two years has been Democratic leader in the Greenpoint district in Brooklyn and is today looked upon by many people as the classic American city politician, was born on June 29, 1888, in the section he now bosses. His father was a brass polisher, and there were thirteen children in the family besides Peter, but the McGuinnesses were never poor. The elder McGuinness owned the house the family lived in, and when he died, about twenty years ago, he left an estate of more than twenty thousand dollars, none of which went to Peter, because, he says, his father had wanted him to be a brass polisher and was humiliated by the fact that one of his sons was a politician. "To the old gentleman," McGuinness says reverently, "there was nothing in the world as good as brass polishing. I could never see it that way." McGuinness entered politics at the age of eight, when he became a ward heeler for Senator Pat McCarren, then the boss of Greenpoint and for many years the boss of all Brooklyn. From the time he was five or six, he had worked at odd jobs in the neighborhood, not because his family needed help but because he enjoyed working and wanted pocket money. He ran errands for storekeepers and carried growlers of beer for workingmen; he also sold the eggs of some hens he kept in the back yard. His week-end sideline was serving as standard bearer for a marching society known as the Rinky Dinks. "The Rinks were a lot of young fellows around the Point," he says. "All of them were keeping company with girls, and the girls marched with them. None of them wanted to leave his young lady friend to carry the flag, so they hired me to do it." At his various jobs, McGuinness, who today is on more intimate terms with his constituents than any other district leader in New York, became well known throughout Greenpoint. "I was pals with the whole town," he says. "When I wasn't working or in school, I used to sit in the gutter on Greenpoint Avenue, the corner of Franklin. That way I got to know everybody because everybody came by there. People would come along and say, 'Bejesus, there's Petey McGuinness! Hello, Petey! What are you doing today?' I'd say, 'Oh, I'm fine, thank you, Mr. Flaherty. I was just sitting in the gutter here. How are you today, Mr. Flaherty?' Even in them days I was out there giving them all the big hello." One of McCarren's men, taking note of young McGuinness's politeness and good standing in the community, offered to take him on as a doorbell ringer. On election day of 1896, McGuinness went on the party payroll and made a dollar for getting out thirty or forty votes for Bryan and Free Silver. Each election and primary day he did the same thing, and between elections he was a chore boy for the local Democratic organization, the Jefferson Club. "I liked that kind of work the best of anything," he says. "I was always a great one for anything that had to do with people."

When he was fourteen and in the eighth grade, McGuinness left school, and though he continued to live in Greenpoint and to help out the local Democratic machine, he went to work every day in Manhattan. He was an office boy for R. H. Hoe & Co., printing-press manufacturers; then a runner on the Bowery, delivering Thomas J. Plunkitt's Celebrated Cigars to the Chatham Club, Steve Brodie's, McGurk's Suicide Hall, and other well-known resorts of the period. Everything about McGuinness's speech and appearance suggests the old Bowery, but he never considered himself a Bowery boy. "There were some splendid people on the Bowery in them days," he says, "such as Chuck Connors and Big Tim Sullivan, but I never thought too much of the place. I'm a neighborhood man, and the Bowery wasn't really what I'd call a neighborhood. It wasn't so tough as they say, either. Right now, Greenpoint is a lot tougher than the Bowery ever was, and it's a decent place, too." Later, when he grew old enough for man's work, he became a teamster for S. Brinckerhoff, Hay and Feed, and worked evenings as a bouncer in the barroom of a Hudson River steamboat. For a while he was a promising young middleweight fighter; he fought fifteen bouts in all, of which he lost none and drew two, but he gave up boxing partly because he did not see how it could contribute to his political advancement and partly because, much as he enjoys fighting for fun or honor, he is not the sort to punch people for money. He says that he likes jobs in which he can be of service to his fellow-man, and he sometimes classifies the various political offices he has held according to the opportunities they have provided for social usefulness. Thus, he did not like being Sheriff of Kings County nearly as much as he liked being an alderman. "Being a sheriff and arresting people isn't a very loving thing," he says. "When you sum it all up, I'd say that alderman was about the most loving job I ever had."

Off and on, during this period, McGuinness attended night classes in bookkeeping, but that was the end of his formal education. On the whole, he is sorry he did not get more schooling. He believes in education, particularly in the liberal arts. He was deeply offended a few years ago when, after he had put in a decade of lobbying for a public high school in Greenpoint, the handsome one that was finally built turned out to be the Automotive Trades High School. He feels that there was something undemocratic in this—an assumption, perhaps, that because Greenpoint is a working-class section, it can breed only mechanics. "They think they put something over on me," he says. "Bejesus, now that this war's over, I'm going to get me another high school in here, and this time we're going to get an educational school." In one way he considers it fortunate that his education ended when it did. He had his heart set on a political career, but he wanted to become a district boss as soon as possible and to spend no more time than necessary in the service of some other boss. By making a name for himself, as he later did, outside the machine, he was able to become a full-fledged leader when he was thirty-six, but he feels that if he had gone on to high school or college, he might have been tempted to take a political job immediately upon graduation and then wait his turn for the leadership in the hierarchy of the Jefferson Club, which, like all political hierarchies, was based rather rigidly on seniority. In that case, he might have spent the better part of his life as a time server in a municipal job or perhaps in the State Legislature or Congress. No thought appalls him more. Like most politicians of his school, McGuinness considers congressmen members of an inferior class. To him, the local party bosses, who pick the legislators and tell them what to do, are the élite of politics and congressmen are men who, unable to make the grade as leaders themselves, must serve as legislative secretaries to men who have made the grade. He cannot understand the tendency, comparatively recent in this city, of political bosses to take congressional nominations for themselves. "I've sent plenty of them to Albany and Washington," he says, "but I'd never be such a damn fool as to send meself. Believe me, I'm glad I was never in a fix where anyone else could send me. If a man's a leader in New York, what the hell business has he got in Washington?"

Long before McGuinness became political boss of Greenpoint, he was the boss of its waterfront. In 1908, he gave up his career on the Bowery and started in as a lumber handler and stevedore in the John C. Orr lumber yard in Greenpoint. He was soon a rising figure in Lumber Handlers' Local 955 of the International Longshoremen's Association and was known throughout the section as the toughest of all the dock wallopers. "You could just about say," an associate of those days recalls, "that Peter was the king of this here waterfront right down to the Navy Yard or even Irishtown. He could work better than anyone else, and he could lick anyone else. He would fight anyone, and he licked everyone he fought." McGuinness brought himself to the attention of his fellow-longshoremen by his handling of two union delegates whom he overheard dividing up the dues they had just collected and telling each other their plans for spending the money. He knocked them cold. After he had taken the money away from the delegates and turned back the dues to the men who had trustingly paid the money in, he found that he had several dollars left over, so he bought a few kegs of beer for the next meeting of the local. At that meeting there was a purge and McGuinness got the first of several promotions in the local. He says that his fight with the delegates was the only grudge fight he ever had. "We had fights almost every day," he says, "but they were just for fun. Besides, you had to do that to be boss in them days. The others figured that if they could lick me they'd get to be boss themselves. We had a hell of a lot of fun out of it. Most of the time, we'd fight at lunch hour or just after work. Everybody'd stand around and watch. After the fights, I'd practice oratory for a while. I'd stand up there on a pile of lumber and give them all a hot spiel on something or other. They'd say, 'Bejesus, Peter, you're improving every day. Pretty soon we'll be after sending you to the Board of Aldermen.'"

McGuinness enjoyed the ten years he spent working in the lumber yard, and he regards lumber handling as the most stimulating work he knows of aside from clubhouse politics. He believes that it would be a perfect substitute for peacetime military training. "If they left this conscription thing up to me," he said recently, "I'd have all the kids in the country putting in a year or two in lumber yards. That's where you really get tough and learn to fight. If them Germans or Japs knew they'd be fighting lumber handlers, I don't think they'd ever try anything again."

Today McGuinness is a pillar of Brooklyn Democracy and will tolerate no irregularity, but in his youth he was a seditionist. In 1919, the boss of Greenpoint was James A. McQuade, who enjoyed a brief fame during the Seabury investigation, when he explained his bank deposits of more than half a million dollars by saying that he had borrowed the money to feed "thirty-three starving McQuades." McQuade was a short, squat, and essentially drab Irishman who spent most of his time at the race tracks and in the saloons of Greenpoint, places that Mc-

Guinness never patronized. McGuinness was frank and naturally exuberant; McQuade was inclined to be sly and lugubrious. Nevertheless, McQuade was a reasonably popular leader and was well entrenched. When McGuinness was getting his start in politics, he knew that if he accepted patronage from McQuade, he could not become boss himself until McQuade retired or died, and at the moment either event seemed rather remote. He therefore decided to overthrow McQuade, a job which took him six years and was regarded by those who watched it as a masterpiece of insurrection.

At the beginning of the war between the McQuade and McGuinness forces, Greenpoint was a discontented neighborhood. In the late nineteenth century it had been a community—a town, in fact, and the inspiration for "There'll Be a Hot Time in the Old Town Tonight"—made up of prosperous citizens who worked sedately and industriously, for the most part, in the lumber and ship yards along the waterfront. It was an important shipbuilding center; the Monitor was built there, and in its honor the principal hotel had been named the Yankee Cheesebox. Most of its buildings were row houses, owned by the people who lived in them and amply surrounded by open space. Salt water could be seen from almost any point; shipbuilding had been attracted to Greenpoint in the first place because it was nearly all waterfront. On the west was the East River; on the north and east was Newtown Creek, a salty inlet that is shaped like a scythe; and on the south another inlet, which has since been mostly filled in. But at the start of the new century, Greenpoint began to change, both physically and economically. The city had grown up all around it, so it was no longer a country village but almost the exact geographical center of Greater New York. Its waterfront became too valuable to stay in the hands of minor industries. The ship and lumber yards were replaced by factories and oil refineries, and they brought about an influx of low-wage immigrants, who in turn caused congestion. A hedge of smokestacks rose up along the waterfront, shutting off the view and pouring out upon the residential area clouds of soot, smoke, and smells. Property values went down. People who could afford to leave Greenpoint moved. No investors could be found to finance the replacement or the improvement of old property. The city was reluctant to do much to benefit a community that was degenerating so fast. One of Greenpoint's amateur poets, a woman of insight, wrote in a local paper:

Daily neighbors move to other sections
Where buildings rise in process of erection,
Where bridges close and cars are ever moving,
Where roads and all conditions are improving.

Yet dear Greenpoint, noble town of fame,
Year after year e'er remains the same
Through lack of unity to make a stand,
To fight for the improvements we demand.

Oh, those on high who watch mere mortals act,
Send us a fighter, strong, clean, and intact.
That we may save our fair town from decay
And from the chains of unrest break away.

McGuinness began his attack on the McQuade machine by blaming it for Greenpoint's plight and by becoming the "fighter, strong, clean, and intact," for whom the poet—Julia V. Conlon, who later became his first district co-leader—had called. The press was his first forum. Every time he heard of a new grievance in the community, he wrote a letter to one of the local newspapers blaming McQuade and his organization. He blamed McQuade for Greenpoint's lack of playgrounds, the run-down condition of its streets, the smoke and smells from the factories, the garbage in Newtown Creek, and the fact that livestock was being herded through the streets of Greenpoint to the abattoirs of Long Island City. "These animals," he wrote, "knock over baby carriages with babies in them, and they knock down mothers, and the bulls kick them and knock them down, running into store windows and kicking them and breaking them. Why does Greenpoint have to put up with this? What's our leader McQuade and his Alderman and his Assemblyman doing to stop these beasts?" Other neighborhoods, he said, were getting public baths and showers, but Greenpoint, which was short on domestic plumbing, was not. "What's the matter with Park Avenue Jim McQuade? Don't he think his own people are good enough to have these baths and showers? What we need around here is fighting leaders. Why shouldn't Greenpoint be right up there with Flatbush and places like that?" McGuinness also attacked John McCooey, the Kings County boss, who was supporting McQuade against McGuinness. Like all good politicians, McGuinness pretended to be scornful of politicians in general and presented himself merely as a long-suffering private citizen who had been driven to action by corruption and abuse. "I have to laugh," he wrote to the editor, "when I think of these big bluffs of politicians coming into this district around election time, getting on the platform and telling the people what they will give them, and when elected you never see the old blowhards again. If you ask me, all this is McCooey's work. Now, I say, let Mr. McCooey and his officeholders refuse us these improvements and we'll show them what Greenpoint can do. And who is this Mr. McCooey anyway? Does anyone ever see him around Greenpoint? Our motto here should be 'Greenpointers Work for Greenpoint.'"

In 1918, McGuinness felt that the iron was hot enough for striking. He announced that he would run against McQuade's alderman, William P. McGarry, in the next year's Democratic primary. When the Jefferson Club, for which he had worked since childhood, barred him and his followers, then mostly his fellow-lumbermen, he defiantly organized what he called the Open Air Democratic Club and held meetings on convenient street corners. He ran ads in the Greenpoint *Weekly Star*. "The Man of the Hour," most of them said. "Who Is He? Peter J. McGuinness." He continued to write letters to the editor and made himself good copy. Innumerable items appeared about him in the local press: "When you see Greenpoint's fighting candidate for Alderman, Peter McGuinness, ask Peter why he don't eat macaroni. Boy, he's got some answer." Or: "Jim McQuade better watch out. The Stormy Petrel of the North End was down at the Du Tel Pleasure Club one night last week, and the boys say he's on the warpath again." He organized the Peter J. McGuinness Greenpoint People's Regular Democratic Organization, the Peter J. McGuinness Greenpoint Patriotic League, and the Peter J. McGuinness Charity and Welfare Association. The first of these, from whose title his own name has since been docked, still exists. The others were wartime organizations. McGuinness said that McQuade and the Jefferson Club were not doing enough to boost the morale of Greenpoint's soldiers. McGuinness ordered his followers to canvass the neighborhood for money to buy presents for the men going off to war. Naturally, this was a popular cause. In the last war, the drafted men entrained for camp in public. Whenever a batch of Greenpoint boys went, they were given a sendoff by McGuinness and his partisans, carrying the banners of all three McGuinness organizations, and by the Full Military Brass Band of Professor William F. Connolly, a musician who was, and still is, one of McGuinness's most important political allies. Each draftee was presented by McGuinness with a martial bon-voyage kit of food, cigarettes, soap, razor blades, and the like, as well as an inspirational leaflet signed by Peter J. McGuinness. The soldiers continued to receive presents in camp and overseas, and when they returned many of them joined the Greenpoint Labor Veterans' League, Peter J. McGuinness, Honorary President. One local boy, who claimed to be the first soldier from Greenpoint to reach German soil, wrote home a letter that was prominently displayed in the *Star*. "I was thinking of Greenpoint through every minute of it," he said. "In the last few months I've seen a lot of other Greenpoint boys over here. We talk about home all the time.

. . . I find that most of the boys feel about the way I do. They think that Peter J. McGuinness is doing very good work for Greenpoint. We sure hope he keeps it up and that Greenpoint appreciates him." In the next primaries, McGuinness won the Democratic nomination for alderman despite the regular organization's opposition, and he was easily elected that November. He kept his job in the lumber yard until the day before he took office.

McGuinness stayed an alderman until 1931, and for those dozen years he was unquestionably the Board's most celebrated member. Nowadays he seldom gets into the newspapers, largely because, as Assistant Commissioner of Borough Works in Brooklyn, he is not where news is made, but during the twenties he was the subject of almost as many feature stories as Daddy Browning, Admiral Byrd, and Dr. John Roach Straton. A comment by McGuinness on prohibition, the New Woman, or the war debts, frequently accompanied by a picture of the Alderman in an aggressive pose alongside MacMonnies' statue of Civic Virtue in City Hall Park, was almost a regular department in the afternoon papers. He liked to give out statements defending New York against bluenose attacks on the city. When the Board of Temperance, Prohibition, and Public Morals of the Methodist Episcopal Church released one of its periodic denunciations of New York for its profanity, short skirts, and iniquitous theatre, he said in rebuttal, "New York is the cleanest city in the world. You can't find a more moral race of people on earth. The theatres of New York are great educational institutions. There's no more profanity here than anywhere else. New Yorkers may swear on impulse but never from the heart. New York has the healthiest air in the country. What if the girls do go in for few clothes? The good air gets to their bodies and makes them healthier. Look at Adam and Eve. They wore fig leaves. Think how many descendants they had. Good night, there's no harm in women wearing few clothes."

Unlike most aldermen, McGuinness attended every meeting of the Board and almost always had something to say. He probably made more attempts to devise a legal way around prohibition than any other legislator in the country. No epidemic of grippe or head colds could strike the city without McGuinness's petitioning the federal government to release its stocks of seized liquor to the public. "It's a shame," he would declaim, "to allow whiskey to lie idle while people are lying at death's door who could be saved by it." His most generally admired speech, however, was delivered when Mrs. Ruth Pratt resigned from the Board after being elected to Congress. McGuinness, a lover of political ritual, who is today the President of the Association of Past Aldermen of the City of New York, always took charge of the purely ceremonial functions of the Board, and when Mrs. Pratt resigned he delivered a testimonial on behalf of his fellow-aldermen, which ended:

Ruth, all we have to say is that when you go down to Washington you want to take along that beautiful fur coat that your dear husband gave you. You want to wear that coat in Washington, Ruth, because it's very, very cold down there. Washington may be further to the South than New York, but the people there are as cold as ice. They don't love one another the way people here do. Why, you know yourself, Ruth, that here in the Board of Aldermen there isn't a single man who if you were cold and unhappy, he wouldn't put his arms around you and hug you and try to make you feel good. But you'll never in your life find such loving hearts in Washington. I know, Ruthie darling, because I been there and in the coldness down there I nearly froze meself to death. So you'll sure need that fur coat, Ruthie, me darling.

McGuinness feels that his greatest triumph as a legislator was a series of resolutions asking the heads of city departments to give what he calls their "per dime" employees holidays with pay; these resolutions, which were passed in 1921, are the complete negation of the idea of per-diem employment, but McGuinness holds that they were forerunners of such legislation as the Fair Labor Standards Act and the National Labor Relations Act. He often cites them as evidence that his devotion to the New Deal is of long standing. "When you look back on it," he says, "you can see I was working on a lot of them humane matters meself twenty-five years ago."

The best example of McGuinness's resourcefulness as a politician is his campaign for farm gardens for the children of Greenpoint. During the first World War, most of the local war gardening was done in city parks, parts of which were plowed up and parcelled out to amateur vegetable growers. McGuinness found that the children in his district enjoyed working in the gardens, and when the war was over he persuaded the city administration to let them continue. After a few years, however, when McGuinness's skill at legislative maneuvering was getting Greenpoint far more than the district's fair share of appropriations for improvements, the Board of Estimate began to rebel. By persuasive argument, McGuinness headed off several attacks, but finally he was forced to use guile. He got the funds that made the gardens possible by announcing that, to show the Board how much the children appreciated the privilege, he was going to bring six hundred of them to City Hall for the Board's public hearing on the matter. "I knew that would scare the bejesus out of them," he says. He told a functionary that he had chartered several buses to get the children over. "They'll need a lot of room, God bless them," he said, "because I want them to have their little shovels and hoes and rakes along with them to show the Mayor how much they love tilting the soil." The prospect of six hundred youngsters loose in City Hall with garden tools produced immediate assurance from Mayor Hylan that the appropriations would go through.

The next year, McGuinness got money for the gardens by nominating Mayor Hylan for President. He says that he argued before the Board for an hour and knew that he would lose unless he got the support of the Mayor. "I could see he was going to vote against me," he says. "The sweat was pouring down me back. All the nerves of me body was jumping. I could just see them kids when I had to tell them there wouldn't be any more gardens. Then it just come to me. It burst right into me brain. I made it up as I went along." He said:

Mr. Mayor, in the history of our glorious country there have been two great Presidents. One was the Honorable George Washington, who led this nation to freedom, and the other was the Honorable Abraham Lincoln, who freed the poor slaves in 1865. Ever since 1865 a pair of old black shoes have been standing beside the President's desk in the White House. Those shoes are old and worn, but they stay there in the White House because they know that the man who used to walk around in them was loved in the hearts of the poor people of America. And he loved the poor people, too, Mr. Mayor. He was the man who said that God must have loved the poor people because he made so many of them. Now, when they laid Abraham Lincoln away, those shoes came walking back into the White House and put themselves beside his desk, and they've been waiting there ever since for a man who loves the poor people as much as he did to come in and fill them. Today, Mr. Mayor, the City of New York is going to fill those shoes with one of its own, John Francis Hylan, who in his splendid wisdom in voting for these farm gardens is bringing happiness into the lives of the little ones of Greenpoint and is showing his people and the great Democratic Party, which has always fought for the poor people, that he loves them too. John Francis Hylan will be the next President of the United States.

Hylan cast his three votes for the appropriations. The next morning the newspapers ran stories headlined "Hylan-for-President Move Started by Local Democratic Leader" and the like. When reporters called on McGuinness, he ducked most of their questions. "Hylan's a splendid man," he said, "one of the highest-type men in the country today." When he was finally pinned down, however, he said, "What the hell, I don't mind giving out a few nominations if it will help Greenpoint."

After he was elected alderman, McGuinness let four years pass before he ran for county committeeman, thus challenging McQuade for the district leadership. By that time, he had delivered on most of his campaign promises. In 1924, he defeated McQuade for the leadership. After the election, he told McQuade he had better close up the Jefferson Club and join the McGuinness Club. McQuade declined, and the war was really on. McQuade, who was backed by McCooey and the county machine, tried to regain the leadership in 1926, 1928, 1930, and 1932. Each time McGuinness was reëlected by a larger majority. The contests were exciting, nevertheless. "You should have been out here then," one old Greenpointer has said. "You never saw anything like it. There were bands playing all the time and fights on every street corner. The two clubs were right across the street from each other in the early days, and you'd see Pete making a speech in front of Jim's club and Jim making a speech in front of Pete's club and all the torchlights flaring up around them. And Peter's parades—you never saw such parades." McGuinness feels that his parades had a lot to do with his success. "Them and the baskets," he says. "We gave out the biggest Christmas and Thanksgiving baskets in the history of New York State. I don't think you could name a kind of vegetable we didn't put in them baskets, and we always bought the fattest, juiciest turkeys we could find."

McGuinness's parades were generally in celebration of his triumphs in wheedling improvements out of the city. "Almost every time we'd get a new lamppost, there'd be a parade," he says. Since the improvements were for the benefit of the whole community, everybody marched in the McGuinness parades, even McQuade and the handful of Republicans in Greenpoint. But there was no mistaking the fact that it was McGuinness's show. His club members were always first in the line of march, just behind Professor Connolly's band. Sometimes they rode horseback. McGuinness used to borrow dray horses from the John C. Orr lumber yard. "We held the parades at night," he says, "and the horses wasn't working then, so we thought it would be nice to have them in the parades." McGuinness often led the parades, mounted on a white truck horse and wearing a ten-gallon hat.

Along with the parades, McGuinness arranged a good many clambakes and kiddies' outings, as well as an annual event called Ye Olde McGuinnesse Farme Barne Dance Nighte, with Professor William F. Connolly's Hayseede Orchestra. Most of these parties were designed simply to maintain good will in the district, but a few were on a more commercial basis. These "rackets," as politicians, harking back to an early meaning of the word, call the parties, were to raise money for campaign expenses. Part of this money went for some of the most cryptic propaganda in political history. McGuinness believes less in the placards which most politicians put up in store windows and paste on fences than in throwaways the size of calling cards. "With them, they got something they can carry around and think about," he says. He still has some of the cards used during the long war with McQuade. One of them says:

VOTE FOR MCGUINNESS
MCQUADE CANNOT BE TRUSTED
QUINN (FLOPPER) HAS NO PRINCIPLES
ELIMINATE THE SOREHEADS
VOTE FOR MCGUINNESS

Another goes:

DON'T MIND THE DARN FOOLS
THEY DON'T KNOW WHAT IT'S
ALL ABOUT
EVEN THOUGH THEY WOULD BE
NOMINATED THEY WOULDN'T
KNOW WHAT IT IS TO
BE A LEGISLATOR
NOMINATE EXPERIENCED MEN

McQuade's surrender was a magnificent occasion, as solemn and formal as the Japanese surrender to General MacArthur in Tokyo Bay. It came one May evening in 1932. McQuade and an even hundred of his followers met at the Jefferson Club and locked the front door for the last time. Then, with McQuade at their head, they marched slowly down the middle of Manhattan Avenue, the main thoroughfare of Greenpoint, to Norman Avenue, and down Norman Avenue to the new headquarters of the McGuinness Club. McGuinness stood at the head of the flight of stone steps leading to the door. He was flanked by John McCooey, the county leader, who had finally boarded the McGuinness bandwagon, and by James Burns, the Borough President of Brooklyn. McQuade walked up the steps, and McGuinness stepped a few paces forward and took his hand. He then wheeled about and led him inside, where McGuinness, McCooey, and Burns watched McQuade and the hundred followers sign the McGuinness Club roster and give the treasurer their first month's dues. When this was over, McGuinness and McQuade went outside again, where a crowd had gathered for the ceremony that was to follow. McGuinness and McQuade made brief addresses. "Peter J. McGuinness," McQuade said to the audience, "is now the undisputed leader of this district. Let no man say that I am not earnest in my admiration of him. These ugly rumors must stop." "From this day forward," McGuinness said, "Pete McGuinness and Jim McQuade march forward hand in hand like brothers for the benefit of the grand old Democratic Party."

In one of his speeches before the capitulation, McGuinness had said of McQuade, "He is the most despicable man in public life today. He is a man who is not even a man among men." When McQuade died, in 1935, McGuinness spoke at a memorial service. "You could always say of old Jim McQuade," he said, "that he was a man among men."

Most of the time that McQuade was district leader, he was on the public payroll either as Sheriff or as Register, and when McGuinness became leader he succeeded to these jobs, which he held alternately. Both posts were abolished some years ago, and McGuinness has had to be satisfied with being Assistant Commissioner of Borough Works. He can have this job as long as there is a Democratic administration in Brooklyn, but he has one further ambition. He would like to be Borough President of Brooklyn. He has never wanted a job that would take him out of the city or force him to relinquish his leadership in Greenpoint, but he feels that the Borough Presidency would be a fitting climax to his career. He has had his managers do some exploratory work in the past ten years, but he has only once publicly avowed his ambitions himself. Around convention time every year some reporter with a long memory asks McGuinness whether he would accept the nomination, and he is usually indirect in his answers. "I don't think I ought to be saying anything meself," he once replied, "but I will say for me sweetheart that it would make her proud as a bird of paradise." It was in 1937 that he made his one unequivocal announcement on the subject. "The demands," he said on that occasion, reading from a prepared statement, "have been so many and so general that after considerable thought and for the best interests of Greenpoint and my supporters, I have decided to throw my hat in the ring and declare tonight that I am willing to accept this nomination should the County Leader see fit to honor me."

If McGuinness should ever be nominated, the Citizens Union, which keeps a close check on all candidates for public office, would undoubtedly dust off a statement it has been issuing periodically since 1921, which reads, "The record clearly indicates that Mr. McGuinness is not qualified for any public office." Since neither the opposition nor the endorsement of the Citizens Union has been known to affect the outcome of an election, McGuinness has never bothered to defend himself against it. However, he is always ready to talk about his record for honesty, which is impressive. "Bejesus," he says, "they'll never show anyone where Peter J. McGuinness ever stole a single vote or took a nickel from a man for getting him a job." McGuinness has been investigated twice, once by Samuel Seabury, for the Hofstadter Committee, and once by Paul Blanshard, the former Commissioner of Accounts. Both times his affairs were found to be in order. In 1927, his clubhouse was raided because it was quartering bookmakers. McGuinness makes no bones about the matter. This was during the war with McQuade. Some bookmakers approached McGuinness and told him that many good precinct workers, McGuinness followers at heart, were being kept in bondage to McQuade merely by their love of horseflesh. The McQuade club had facilities for betting; the McGuinness club did not. If McGuinness would provide them with space for operations, the bookmakers said, his club's membership would increase. McGuinness thought that their point was well taken, and so it was. When the gamblers came in, membership rose quickly. The police held him briefly after the raid but released him when the play-and-payoff sheets showed that only the reasonable profit of twelve per cent was being made by the bookies and that there was no evidence that McGuinness or any other official of his club had received any of the gambling money.

At the Seabury investigation, McGuinness was the most ingratiating of all the witnesses. Many of the district leaders called upon to testify were sulky on the stand; a number of them refused to sign waivers of immunity. McGuinness was delighted with the whole proceedings. He came accompanied by dozens of Greenpointers and walked briskly to the witness stand, where he signed a waiver with a flourish. "Gentlemen," he said to the attending members of the Hofstadter Committee, "I am glad to present me presence here today. How do you do?" Seabury kept McGuinness on the stand for hours, largely, he said later, because he liked to hear the man talk. He asked McGuinness about his rise in Greenpoint politics. McGuinness responded with the story of his life and his fight with McQuade, who, Seabury had just discovered, had banked a few hundred thousand dollars more than he had earned. Seabury asked McGuinness if he had any such ill-gotten gains on deposit or in one of the celebrated tin boxes. McGuinness pulled out of a pocket a wallet the size of an overnight bag, which he has always used as a filing case for his "contracts," the politician's term for requests for favors. "Judge," he said, "this is the only tin box I got, Look it over, Judge. It's never contained anything but the heartaches of me people, me Jewish *mazuza*, and me father-in-law's front collar button. He was a great old champ, Judge." Now and then, Seabury questioned McGuinness about gambling in his clubhouse and asked if he would accept responsibility for anything that went on there. "Judge," McGuinness said, "there's only one leader of that club.

Right here before you. Shoot, Judge." There was some more aimless questioning about what had for years been a matter of record, and McGuinness finally grew bored with this. "Judge," he said, "what do you say we bury this? Don't let's be talking about it any more. It's dead, and I'm tired of looking at it." Seabury, after a few pleasantries, ended the examination. As he left the stand, McGuinness again addressed the committee. "Gentlemen," he said, "it's been a pleasure, I assure you, having this great pleasure of coming before you. I want to thank Judge Seabury, too, for being so kind and courteous to me. Good afternoon."

At times, McGuinness adopts a great air of virtue about his honesty. "How do you think I'd feel," he says, "if I was to stand on the corner and see some pal coming down the street, and I couldn't look him in the eye without thinking, well, I got five hundred bucks for getting that one the job he has today? Why, I'd feel just awful inside to think I had one nickel that should be going to feed another man's little ones." More often, however, he puts it on a purely pragmatic basis. "There's no percentage in it," he says. "Suppose I tell a precinct captain to use repeaters. He gets away with it in a city election, then a state election. Then he tries it in a federal election and gets caught. He says I put him up to it. Then I'd have to go before a federal judge that I mightn't even know." He also points out that he is never exposed to the temptations that beset other politicians. He lives simply. He has never, he declares, tasted liquor in his life, or seen a horse race, or placed a bet on anything but his penny-a-point rummy games. He is not a prude, but he just has no need for artificial stimulation. McGuinness and his wife live in a four-room apartment which seems to be furnished largely with blue-tinted mirrors, golden-oak chairs and tables, fringed lampshades, and a reproduction of the "Last Supper" done in butterfly wings. Mrs. McGuinness does all the housework. McGuinness seldom takes any time off. He tries to get away from his club one evening a week to meet Mrs. McGuinness in downtown Brooklyn and go to a motion picture. "The wife picks all the shows," he says. McGuinness has not seen a movie he really enjoyed since Marie Dressler died. He used to smoke five packages of cigarettes a day, but his doctor ordered him to give up tobacco four years ago. "Right now," he says, "I don't smoke, drink, chew, nor gamble. And I never go to any of them Jesse James night clubs. As the fellow said, 'If you don't do none of them things, Peter, what the hell do you do?' I say, all I do is take God's beautiful air and sunshine. And I play politics."

44. The Independent Voter Isn't Independent *

SOME STUDIES of political behavior indicate that the great majority of those who vote generally adhere to one or the other of the major parties. The remainder—perhaps 30%—sometimes vote for one party, sometimes another. Of this latter group some are indifferent, unconcerned, and generally apathetic. Others are really interested in the political process, and want to do what they can to foster better and more intelligent governmental activity. These others tend to call themselves independent; they refuse to align themselves with either party. They feel that they make a greater contribution to society by waiting until the parties have made their selections and then choosing between their offerings. As Mr. Bowles indicates in this article, he believes that these people are really just fooling themselves; they are not so independent as they think they are; they have less choice in politics than those who align themselves with one or the other of the major parties.

BEFORE any election votes were cast last Tuesday, or tallied, you or I could have predicted that, with the rarest exceptions, the winning candidates would be either Democrats or Republicans. For whatever we think of it—and I happen to think very highly of it—the two-party system is the inescapable fact of American political life. Every November the Governors, Senators, Congressmen, Mayors, Selectmen, tax collectors and dog catchers we elect are, with few exceptions, members of the two major political parties of the United States.

This is hardly news. The only surprising thing about it is that a very sizable number of the voting population (in my own State of Connecticut nearly half) persist in behaving as if it were not true. I am talking about the "independent" voters, who fail to join a political party.

It is my sincere, if reluctant, conclusion that these "independents" are slowing the development of a dynamic, responsible two-party system in the United States. I will go even further. Unless the two major parties succeed in wooing and winning the "independents" as regular party members, I believe they will continue to be seriously handicapped in their efforts to offer consistently top-level candidates or aggressive, clearly defined programs, or to produce responsible, effective political action.

* Chester Bowles, *The New York Times Magazine*, November 13, 1949, pp. 13, 61-63. Reprinted by permission of the author and the publisher.

I realize that what I say may disturb the complacency of the many well-meaning citizens who feel that by voting for the "best man" (out of two) they do their duty to democracy. I realize that it may also disturb some old-line political machine leaders who feel that as long as they can control "their" candidates, and win some independent votes with them, there's no special value (and some obvious danger to their political power) in letting the "independents" permanently into the fold.

Let me explain, then, why I feel so deeply, and so strongly, that bringing the "independents" into the two-party system is essential to the health and dynamism of that system.

One of the very real obstacles to the growth of strong party platforms, strong candidates committeed to enact them, and clear party responsibility for performance in office is the independent voter—the man or woman who, for one reason or another, fails to join any political party or to share its responsibilities.

Exactly who are the "independents," and why? Certainly, there are some who refuse to affiliate with either party simply because they are not joiners of any organization. There is also a group who for business or purely social reasons feel it unwise to be allied with any specific party. But, as I have seen it, the large majority of "independents" are such because they have, or think they have, a genuine aversion and disdain for "party politics." Yet a bit of honest analysis shows that the "independent" is at the mercy of, and completely dependent on, the party politics and politicians he so disdains.

True, he has the choice between two candidates, and two platforms. But it may often happen that those two candidates may both be third-rate—precisely because the large body of independents exerted no effort to force the selection of a first-rate man. And of the two-party platforms from which the "independent" must choose, neither may offer him exactly what he wants—again, precisely because he has not taken any voice whatever in deciding the policy in the platforms.

What should he do about it? Obviously, he is concerned with the function of government or he would not vote at all. How can he enter into and adopt responsibility for the conduct of his chosen candidate and party in office?

As I see it, there is only one answer: The independent should give up his wholly illusory independence and join a political party.

Many skittish "independents" may feel that joining a political party is like moving into another and probably turbulent world.

Actually, joining a political party can be a very quiet, simple act of faith. As in any organization there will be those who want to take an active part, and those who do not. But for the guidance of both types of reformed "independents," I believe some of the common illusions and fallacies about political parties should be cleared up.

A first and very important fallacy is that, by joining a political party, and especially in taking an active part in public affairs, the "independent" can no longer be "non-partisan," or "above" politics. I think this view needs very thoughtful discussion.

There is certainly nothing in party membership that insists that one leave behind all freedom of conscience. There is nothing that requires anyone, in the privacy of the voting booth, to abandon all honest considered judgment of men or issues. There is nothing that commits the party member to vote for one man or one issue only. Disagreement within parties on both men and issues is common, expected and healthy—as, I believe, are disagreements between parties.

As I have observed it, however, the ardent "nonpartisans" have actually been those people who, for one reason or another, refuse to take a stand on controversial issues. They feel that by agreeing with neither one side nor the other—regardless of who is right—they have maintained their political purity.

True nonpartisanship for either individuals or organizations, as I see it, would consist of supporting—and to the hilt—those policies of *either* party with which one agreed. But for individuals, the opportunities for effective action of this kind are extremely limited—if one is not a member of a political party. *Within* a party, and before an issue gets to the public, one can thrash out, criticize and perfect, in a nonpartisan, open-minded manner, a controversial, difficult problem.

Once the program is agreed upon, there is certainly no cheap partisanship in supporting it wholeheartedly. And there certainly is vastly greater political effectiveness. And there is also far more "independence" of thought and action than in accepting, as *faits accomplis*, programs or issues evolved behind the scenes by parties in which the voter has no voice.

A second and frequent fallacy is that politicians generally are inferior types, not fit companions for gentlemanly believers in good government. Upper-class independents may draw this conclusion when they find that their local representative to the State Legislature is the neighborhood barber. (We have two barbers in Connecticut's Legislature.)

I would like to be very blunt on this score. Let me say at once that I believe anyone sincerely interested in politics had better first become a democrat with a small "d." Politics in this country involves—and affects—the least and the highest. It is not the prerogative of the elite.

I have been repeatedly impressed with the intellectual calibre of people today entering politics. The war, making soldiers and civilians aware for the first time of the need for individual political action, has brought in and developed men and women of outstanding capability and sincerity.

I could name many able lawyers, local school board members, professors of economics, history, political science and of literature, labor, business and farm leaders, college students, and writers and editors who in my own state and party are taking a creative and increasingly active part in political life.

Fallacy number three is important chiefly to those reformed "independents" who would take an active part in party politics. It is that "machine" leaders so tightly control the two parties that newcomers have no voice whatever in deciding policy or candidates. There are certainly some cities where the party "machine" would still rather control its party in defeat than run the risk of losing it in victory. But, however notorious, such cities are extremely rare.

The actual fact is that a surprising number of local organizations are so small and impotent, they may even have no candidates for local elections and support "compromise" candidates put up by the opposition. This is particularly true of parties whose state organization has been beaten year after year and whose local branches have simply atrophied with neglect.

In such groups newcomers can accomplish veritable miracles. Armed with a cause, a candidate and ideas, they can give the town its first rousing election in years—and if they win, its first good government. I can give you many exciting case histories of this kind from my own experiences in Connecticut.

Even in those places where there is a fairly well organized party, control of that party is usually far less tight than the control of the local country club—and a whole lot easier to change. An average citizen would hardly think of walking in and assuming he could immediately seize the administrative reins of a lodge, union or private club. He would expect there to win others to his viewpoint gradually, as he becomes known and learns the ropes. A political organization is much the same.

The novice at politics—and especially the converted "independent" who has so long set such high value on his individual vote—is perhaps too apt to be impatient when his bright schemes are not immediately adopted and cheered by his political elders, particularly when it is clear that his plans are on the side of the future while the professionals are clinging to the past.

I have occasionally seen some "young idealists," after a single grim encounter with a rigged political caucus, become utter and unreasoning cynics. But I feel even more unhappy about those occasional "ex-idealists" who facilely adopt the cheapest political maneuvers as their own on the cynical assumption that fire can only be fought with fire. Such cynicisim, I feel, is itself a confession of poverty of purpose and sincerity.

But those newcomers who are willing to learn and to work, those who can help produce good candidates and lively honest issues, often find themselves, with surprising speed, among the leaders of their newly adopted parties and with an influence in its affairs far out of proportion to their number.

The fourth common delusion is that an "independent" can do more to improve a party's platform, or candidates, from the outside than from within. This is the frequent plea of liberal "independents" who say they like the role of "gadfly" to the political conscience.

It is quite true that great hue and cry from an outside group of citizens for, say, public housing or civil rights, may force a political party to adopt a housing or civil rights plank. But ardent supporters of housing or civil rights working within the party itself are infinitely more effective. They assure that the adopted platform plank is no mere campaign promise.

And further, they will give far greater assurance that the party itself and all its members have been sold on the program *as a party*, not merely for a campaign issue but as a commitment to perform *once elected*. Pressure from within the party, after election, to turn campaign platforms into performance are far more effective than isolated protests. It is, and should be, the basic source of responsible party government.

Let me state finally my own personal views on politics and politicians.

As I see it politics is the mechanics of democratic government. No public issue, no national or international program on which this country ever embarked was accomplished without politics and politicians.

The Constitution of the United States, which some would have us think today came down on a tablet from heaven, was once a heated political issue. It was drafted, endorsed and adopted by politicians. Jefferson, Jackson, Lincoln, Teddy Roosevelt, Wilson and F. D. R. were all politicians—and very able ones at that.

The emancipation of slaves, the abolition of child labor, woman suffrage, public school education—all these revered and noble programs were effectuated solely through the medium of politics, by politicians and usually after bitter political battles.

Mayors, Selectmen, Governors, Congressmen, Senators and Presidents—these men form our Government. They are the instruments through which we as a town, a country, a state or a nation, get our roads built, our laws made, our judges appointed, our mental hospitals neglected or improved, our treaties ratified, our schools built, our anti-discrimination statutes enacted.

These men are also politicians. They are nominated, supported and opposed by political parties.

To assume that any public business can be accomplished without them is naive folly. To refuse to accept responsibility for these men or their actions is, in a very real sense, refusing to accept responsibility for the work of the world and the course of history.

I, for one, am proud to be a "politician." I am proud to be included among the men and women in my own party who have agreed to take their share of responsibility for the conduct of our public life and the course that it should follow. I respect our opponents in the Republican party who are likewise meeting their public responsibility as they see it.

My own party happens to be that which believes that all of us working through our Government have a clear responsibility to "promote the general welfare" of our people in accordance with our Constitution and with laws written by the duly elected representatives of our people. As a party member and practitioner I am willing to take the responsibility that my party continue in this basic belief and act upon it vigorously and consistently while it is in office. The members of my party likewise accept this responsibility.

I hope we will be joined by those "independents" who agree with this view, and that they will give not only their election-day vote, but day by day, year by year creative support. I repeat, that unless they do they will retard the development of a dynamic, responsible, two-party system in America.

I hope very sincerely and for the same reason that those who, after careful thought, believe us to be wrong, will likewise abandon their independent role and join our Republican opponents.

The challenge of our age is almost overpowering. This challenge can be successfully met only by uniting the intelligence of our people behind programs for responsible democratic political action. In the struggle for peace, prosperity, security and increasing freedom for all our people, no thoughtful citizen can remain on the sidelines.

45. *Political Primer for All Americans* *

LARGE NUMBERS of Americans are convinced that politics is evil and that most politicians are dishonest. This conviction becomes their justification for not participating in politics. It is probably safe to say that the politician is no better or worse than those who elect him and that he reflects the standards of his most active supporters. If the politician is ever to become a mirror of the interests of the whole community, then the whole community must participate in politics. This selection is an exhortation and a guide to action.

I. POLITICS AND POLITICIANS

POLITICS is the science of how who gets what, when and why. Politics exists in every civic group, church, labor union, family. The key man is always a politician. He keeps things going, wheels turning. Politicians are good, friendly people. They resolve conflicts, compromise in the best sense. The alternative to our politicians is a dictator, someone who hates life and people.

To the average American, politicians are crooks. "*What's the use of voting?*" asks Mr. Citizen. "*Politicians are all alike!*" The truth is that politicians are no more corrupt than the people who elect them. The people corrupt the politicians. They demand traffic enforcement along with ticket "*fixing.*" They want an efficient, honest police force and civil service so long as their sons and cousins get jobs—and a fine school system with the faculty staffed with relatives. The politician who refuses requests for patronage and spoils is told that he'll not be reelected.

Let's quit blaming the politicians and face the responsibility of full citizenship. Let's go to work where it counts—in the political party of our choice. Let's be sure our organizations do not waste their vote by splitting it. We are strong *if we vote* and vote together.

II. THE REST OF US

The USA is full of people of good will. They want to make this nation a happier place. They seek out the likeminded. An organiza-

* Prepared by the CIO Department of Research and Education; Director, Kermit Eby.

tion is formed. Committees are assigned to study problems. Minutes are kept, resolutions written, petitions circulated. Sometimes letters are written to public officials. If the situation is critical, citizen groups call on the mayor or governor, are received politely, dismissed politely, often ignored politely. And they become discouraged.

Ever more people in our big cities are rootless, unattached to the community. Men with business in the heart of the city commute to the suburbs. Professional workers in crowded schools and offices live in cleaner, more comfortable areas. In May and October, great numbers of people move from one community or neighborhood to another, failing to register and thereby losing their vote.

Leadership is often left to job-holders, corrupt persons on the spot. Independent voters who cannot be controlled do not bother to vote; machine-controlled voters who can be, do. As a result, our futures are decided by those who act under instruction and those who do not act at all.

III. EDUCATION

Americans are brought up to believe that every profession is honorable save politics and public service. Students inherit from parents and teachers a naive conviction that statesmen are born, that their high place in life is due to a combination of idealism and noble character. National offices—the Presidency, Congress, the Supreme Court—are discussed at length in civic classes; local offices—the mayor, the sheriff, the town council—are skimmed over. It is unfortunate that we grow up so well informed about the terms of offices and salaries of national officials, with whom we have the least influence and contact, and so ignorant of the ingredients of their positions.

Boys and girls should be taught that statesmen are first politicians; should be encouraged to enter politics, join the youth organizations of the Young Democrats, Young Republicans, or Labor Party. Unions should assume the responsibility of training their members in effective political action. Everyone interested in practical steps should learn to ring doorbells, crank mimeographs, keep headquarters in order, study names and faces.

To continue functioning as a democracy, we and our children must learn how democracy works in practice. We must rewrite our textbooks. We must emphasize the individual's responsibility not only to vote but to join a political party, to form and voice his considered opinions, to do his share of legwork. In that we may earn true citizenship!

IV. PRECINCT CAPTAINS AND HOW THEY GROW

Action follows membership in a political party. Precinct captains are men of influence and action. They meet people, help them with their traffic tickets, provide access to the school administration, find legal help and clearance with the courts when needed. During the depression, the precinct captain was often the friend in need, who came through with food and shoes when everyone else had failed. Voting for the captain's candidates was the least a grateful voter could do.

The following steps lead to captaincy:

1. Know the number of your ward and precinct.
2. Do anything which needs doing.
3. Become acquainted with the "bosses" and your neighbors.
4. Listen to your neighbor's beef, but don't argue with him.
5. Make out a list of your friends and acquaintances. Call them on the phone, invite them to meetings, introduce them to candidates, keep a list of those who attend.
6. Do whatever favors you can for people.
7. Make yourself heard at meetings, especially on subjects of policy.
8. Start discussions of local politics at social gatherings: bridge parties, afternoon teas, stag affairs.
9. Distribute literature of sympathetic organizations: labor unions, PTA's, religious and liberal groups.
10. Get control of more votes than anyone else in the precinct—and the job's yours.

V. THE CAUCUS

Once you've become a precinct captain, the next important function is to become part of the caucus to select the candidate. The caucus is the "in-group." Nominate a friend as delegate to the convention and have him nominate you. Nominate your wives as alternates. If this shocks you, remember that the choice is between your policy and your man, and the opposition's policy and man.

The operation of the caucus is more important than the primary, perhaps as important as the election itself. The trades which precede the nomination of candidates should be understood. At the caucus the original choices are made. At the primary our choice is reduced to one. At the election we choose the man on our side as against the man on the other side.

VI. LABOR AND POLITICS

Party caucuses select men who are known. Labor must develop men known for their civic leadership, on school boards, park commissions, etc. The statesman of tomorrow is the politician of yesterday. The effective labor leadership of tomorrow will include the whole community. Labor alone can not be secure in an insecure world.

Organized labor should set up political action committees, both in local union and congressional district, on a permanent basis, which can find and work with labor men active in politics, sympathetic friends in racial and nationality groups, friendly newspaper editors and writers, liberal church and civic leaders. Trade unions should coordinate their political activities through their city and state organizations. They should unite, not split the labor vote.

Labor's contribution to the war effort—through its record-breaking production—and to the normal activities of the community—through the strength of its democratic organization—must be understood and appreciated by middle-class America. The constant hammering of the anti-labor press, emphasizing strikes and reporting anti-union speeches, reviling union members and labeling their leaders racketeers, confuses many citizens. The NAM spends millions on such propaganda, which goes to schools and ministers, poisoning the minds of teachers and children, and glibly keeping from them the true state of affairs.

Labor is no longer a minority group, part of the community. In many sections of America, *labor is the community!* It must therefore assume political leadership. Members of the CIO should follow the leadership of the CIO Committee for Political Action. Every union member should be incorporated in the political activity of his union.

All of us must register.
All of us must vote.
All of us must help get out the vote.
All of us must contribute to campaign expenses.

The non-political union is becoming a thing of the past. Government decisions constantly affect labor.

Organized labor and liberals have failed in the past to elect the right men. They will fail again if they don't get busy now and see that the labor vote is organized and ready for the polls.

Labor's rank and file must assume responsibility for decisions referred to them instead of asking their officials, "What are we paying you for?"

VII. FINANCES

Political organizations and their leaders must be supported by the people they serve. Too often has the income come from special interest groups, organized vice at the bottom of the social scale and organized privilege at the top.

One hundred $1.00 contributions are better in a democratic set-up than one $100 gift. Small gifts from thousands of contributors are the next thing to active participation by all those voters. People are inclined to take more interest in causes they support financially.

"He who pays the piper calls the tune." This is particularly true when contributions are large and from a few sources. More small contributions mean more freedom and democracy in the organization.

VIII. POSTWAR PLANS

The postwar world will contain all the elements of the present world. It is up to us to remold them nearer to a working pattern. Blueprints are legion. Now it is time to make sure our kind will be used. Congress makes the decisions. The kind of Congress which passes anti-union legislation, encourages inflation, stalls on social security and follows conservative business leadership on postwar planning is hardly the kind to foster the people's world we have been fighting for.

In a democracy, our national representatives represent either us or our enemies. Leadership standards in the state legislatures are as high as we demand and are willing to work for; so are members of city councils. The survival of modern society depends on the workers. Let's quit blaming the politicians and face the responsibility of full citizenship. Let's go to work making our organizations strong. Let's not scorn politics! Let's become politicians, ourselves!

46. *The Erosion of Sectionalism* *

SINCE THE Civil War, the South has been considered a one-party area—an almost unbreachable stronghold of the Democrats. Yet in both the 1952 and 1956 elections several Southern and border states voted for a Republican President, and a few Republican Congressmen were elected. Professor Key, author of a distinguished work on southern politics, speculates on the likely durability of this trend away from one-party domination in the South. In the long run, he says, industrialization of the South will bring it nearer to the North in interests and hence in party coloration, but the change will come slowly and irregularly primarily because of the sentiment of sectionalism, the Negro problem, and the fact that traditionally the route to a political career in the South has been through the Democratic Party.

A METEOROLOGIST of the Ice Age could predict tomorrow's weather with a high degree of confidence. "Continued cold" usually turned out to be a safe prognosis. Let us pause a moment to marvel, however, at the reputation a primitive weatherman could have made for himself by forecasting the retreat of the ice cap to the polar regions.

The tale is not irrelevant in the discussion of tomorrow's politics. The politics of the South tomorrow will be quite like the politics of the South today. Patterns of political attitude and action have an impressive capacity of self-perpetuation, but they do change. If the observer is to see more than the superficial flurries that perhaps both obscure and reveal the underlying movements, he must, unlike our mythical weather expert, ignore matters of the moment and center attention on the deeper trends.

All this is not to assert that the new politics of the South is traveling into being at a glacial rate of movement, although impatient souls may regard that estimate as correct. Yet the figure properly emphasizes the singular durability of political institutions, alterations in whose basic character tend to be spread over a considerable period of time. If this proposition is true, concern about what will happen in 1956, or in 1960, can be only futile. One must take a longer look ahead. The fulfillment of tendencies now at work will probably require decades rather than years.

* V. O. Key, Jr., *The Virginia Quarterly Review*, XXXI (Spring, 1955), pp. 161-179. Reprinted by permission of the author and publisher.

Offhand reflection about the emerging politics of the South may make the problem of crudely mapping the broad outlines of the future appear to be a simple exercise. Of a certainty, it might seem, the South in its politics will become more like the rest of the United States. One need only extrapolate the basic tendencies of recent years within the South toward the more general American pattern to delineate that which is to come. This plausible mode of prediction has its defects. The practices of the rest of the United States can scarcely be expected to remain the same as they are today. One must, therefore, deduce one unknown from another. Moreover, drastic changes may be in store for the practice of popular government in America. Yet cataclysms usually come upon the human race unannounced, so constricted are our expectations by the images of the present and the past. About all that one can do is to attempt to discern whether modifications already in process seem to be proceeding toward forms with which we are familiar.

A summary balancing of the interplay of the variables at work can only lead to the conclusion that internal cleavages within the South will deepen, that both the sentiment and the reality of sectionalism will decline, and that kindred interests in South and North will become more and more interwoven. On the political front, these tendencies will increasingly strain the ties that hold men together under the Democratic banner, and more and more of a Republican Party will appear in the South. So bold—and perhaps bleak—a picture, however, fails to give weight to those peculiar elements of the Southern political heritage that will affect both the rate at which political change occurs and the nature of what develops. The politics of the South will be Southern—not Midwestern or Northeastern.

The basic social and economic changes occurring within the South may, with a fair degree of confidence, be expected to continue gradually to weaken the foundations of regional cohesion. By almost all the indices of economic growth the rate of Southern development in recent years far exceeds the rates of the North and East. In effect, the South is undergoing the sharp economic reorganization and drastic population relocation that had occurred in the North and East by 1910. The multifarious processes of growth and change find expression in the common denominator of urbanization. Industrialization and all its associated processes manifest themselves in the growth of cities. From 1930 to 1950 Southern population in cities of 50,000 or more increased at three times the rate for the nation as a whole: 74 per cent in contrast with the national figure of 24 per cent. On the other hand, Southern farm population declined in the single decade, 1940-1950, by more than one-fourth. Although the data of the two censuses on this point are not precisely comparable, the statistic remains arresting even if error exaggerates the actuality of change.

The enlargement of the urban middle classes and the increase in the ranks of non-agricultural workers are creating the foundations for a durable alteration in the politics of the South. The principle of politics underlying such an assertion is, of course, the assumption that political cleavages tend to parallel economic differences, a proposition that is only conditionally valid. In our relatively bland politics, without a historical habit of sustained conflict along rigid lines of social class, potential cleavages along economic lines attain fullest political reality only when opened cleanly by the cutting edge of sharp issues of economic policy. A long spell of general prosperity will mute political differences between those who have more and those with less. To suggest that deep economic differences will not recur sooner or later and have their political repercussions would be to envisage a reorganization of economic life of a sort not readily imaginable. The differences in the ways in which people make a living can confidently be expected to continue to have an important bearing on their political orientation. It is probable, given the nature of resources and facilities of social classes for political action, that the new middle classes will be able to exert their full strength before the new working classes can be fully mobilized. Political leaders who seek to activate the emerging industrial working class, black and white, must overcome ingrained habits of nonparticipation in politics as well as the special handicaps to action inherent in most groups low on the ladder of status.

All these economic changes are, of course, already having their effect in the politics of the South. In the 1952 presidential voting in the South, General Eisenhower drew support chiefly from those types of groups that had long been in the North the mainstay of the Republican Party. Within individual Southern states cleavages in Democratic primaries seem more frequently to resemble the lines that separate Republicans and Democrats elsewhere. The transformation of intraparty warfare into interparty conflict in 1952 occurred at the political level at which party attachment is most fragile. Throughout the United States a considerably higher degree of volatility in partisan loyalty prevails in presidential voting than in matters of state and local concern.

The study of the processes of secular, or long-term, political change is a neglected field, yet one difficulty in translating projected social or economic change into its dependent political development seems fairly clear. That is that some types of political change do not follow forthwith after the occurrence of their cause. The full political effects of social change often await the gradual and long-term cumulation of pressure. At some moment a combination of events and issues may stimulate the sudden appearance of a new alignment which in fact had been in formation for a long time. This happened in the Northeastern states in 1928 when Alfred E. Smith brought into the circle of political participants the potential Democrats who had been multiplying in the cities. In the same way 1952 in the South marked the activation of pro-Republican sentiment that had been building up for a couple of decades. Yet that upthrust of Republican strength did not disturb the control of the Southern Democratic Party in congressional and state politics save in a few localities.

From the impact of 1952 it is plausible to contend that in a limited sense a two-party South is already upon us. At any rate any future presidential campaign manager, Republican or Democrat, who omits the South from his strategic calculations will be guilty as charged of obvious incompetence. Yet a good deal of evolution has to occur before the fulfillment of the inner tendencies at work within the South is completed. The rate at which this development will occur will depend on the weight and temporal incidence of more or less imponderable variables. A long continuation of crisis in foreign affairs and of the correlative prosperity sustained by pump priming from the Pentagon could only serve to delay class-based political adjustments. Indeed, the maintenance of the Republic as a garrison could only operate to narrow the range of internal political conflict tolerated on all sorts of issues. On the other hand, a set of circumstances that elevated to first importance issues of domestic economic policy with divisive effects within the South could only accelerate the more or less inevitable political changes within the South. In other words, the Democratic solidarity of the new South probably could not survive another New Deal.

Readjustments in the political system of the South will depend in part on the form and character taken by the party system of the nation as a whole as it unrolls into the decades ahead. To the extent that the relations between Northern Democrats and Republicans are such that the varied needs and aspirations of the South in the nation may be met through the Democratic Party, by a balance of power tactic, by congressional maneuver, or otherwise, to that extent it may be expected that the centrifugal forces within the Southern Democratic system will not strain it beyond the breaking point. In recent decades the experience has been that as tension sharpens between Republicans and Democrats in the North, an intensification of fratricidal conflict among Southern Democrats occurs. This coincidence of conflict has probably been in large measure a function of the special types of issues at stake. Economic issues in the North sharpened differences between Republicans and Democrats. Within the South the same issues split the Democrats and drove one wing toward Republicanism. It is conceivable that at least from time to time issues will come to the fore that do not divide the South and that may even serve to strengthen for the nonce the ties between Northern and Southern Democrats.

From these observations about the character of the interactions of the politics of the South and of the nation, it would be implausible to anticipate political change in the South that could be well represented by a smooth and gradually ascending line. Spasmodic jolts that from time to time jar the Southern system from its ancient mold are more probable. Each disturbance may be expected to be followed by a partial restoration of the older forms, although from each such event some enduring effect may remain. The rather widespread disenchantment that followed the uncritical enthusiasm of 1952 for General Eisenhower, for example, should not be regarded as a reversal of the long-run trends. Undoubtedly the campaign of 1952 left a net accretion to the basic Republican strength in the South.

Nor should the substitution of a bipartisan cleavage for an intraparty battle be expected to take place at a uniform rate throughout the South. The factors conducive to political change, as well as those that operate to maintain the old order, differ enormously from state to state. A new politics seems most likely to emerge earliest in the states around the rim of the South. It is, of course, in these states that the Republicans have the largest reliable vote on which to build and it is also in these states that the degree of economic and social change is perhaps most notable. The effects of Northern immigration to Florida may be expected to cumulate. The oil magnates of Texas, unrestrained by the sentiments of history and mostly untutored in the later-day notions of the responsibilities of wealth, can be counted as the untrustworthy allies of whichever party makes the higher bid. In Virginia the Democratic machine may seem to go on forever, but its political tutelage of the people can serve only to ease the ultimate build-up of Republicanism which is augured by the underlying reorientation of the economic life of the Old Dominion.

A variable that will affect the rate of activation of latent Southern Republicanism consists of the energy and astuteness dedicated to the problem by the Republican national leadership. In truth, the Republican organizations of the South have on the whole been well satisfied with their minority position. In 1952 several of them in fact seemed bewildered by the prospect of the accession of a mass-following and even resented the intrusion of converts. Nor have the efforts of the national leadership to aid in the construction of viable state and local organizations been characterized by either astuteness or perseverance. Some Southern Republican leaders, of course, stand on their own feet independently of support by the national organization. Even these indigenous Republicans are not always displays well calculated to make Republicanism attractive save perhaps to the most profoundly disgruntled Southern Democrat. Consider, for example, the incongruity of a Republicanism made manifest in national propaganda as the party of crusading uplift and moderate progressivism and in East Tennessee as the party of Mr. B. Carroll Reece.

Elements of the total national situation may be developing to make the ineptness of Republican leadership in the cultivation of the South too expensive to be tolerated. The gradual conversion of some areas of Northern Republicanism to the Democrats seems to be making it more urgent that Republicans pick up more Representatives and a few Senators over the South if they are to win congressional majorities commensurate with the strength they can muster in presidential campaigns. If over the long pull the national balance of forces makes a Southern margin of strength more essential to the Republican Party nationally, a more sustained effort to capture the margin should occur. Yet an expectation of action so rational must be spun out from the nature of things rather than from any evidence of superior political intelligence in the record of Republican dealings with the South.

All these remarks take no account of various special characteristics of the Southern situation which may operate both to retard reorientation of political relations with the rest of the country as well as to color the changes that do occur. The elements in the situation conducive to the maintenance of sectionalism include a layer of sentiment and tradition, worn thin by the stream of time and events, yet not without strength. Urbanization and time may be destructive of the old loyalties but the new Southern urbanism will be slow to achieve the metropolitan provincialism of the Northeast.

Among the more material elements of regionalism must be counted an agriculture which, though declining in relative importance and changing in its types of output and organization, may be relied upon for decades to provide the foundation for a separate sectional interest not completely at one with Northern and Western agriculture. The springs of the old agrarian radicalism may be drying up, but Southern farming will place a special impress on Southern politics for a long time. Similarly, the industrialization of the South will not necessarily create an industry that can invariably find congenial political company with Republican heavy industry of the North. The interests of tobacco, of textiles, and of light industries generally are not inevitably bound up with the lot of Northern metals, although petroleum and chemicals may well differ in this respect.

Of all the factors that contribute to Southern regional cohesion in national politics against Northern Democrat and Republican alike, the question of the role and place of the Negro is without much doubt the most influential and the most pervasive. The seer who proposes to sketch out the probable evolution of this issue in detail must possess in large measure either courage or foolhardiness. However the details may develop, the concentration of Negro population in the South will continue to lend unity to the white South so long as the relative status of white and black is a live question. The tone and intensity of debate on the question may change as Negroes move to the cities, South and North, and as their place in the economic system changes, but the discussion will continue. Surely, a sectional party espousing the cause of "white supremacy" is by now a demonstrated futility. The most hopeful expectation is that the sectional position will be not so much about what the rights of Negro citizens are but about who is to manage the redressment of wrong. In this, Southern Democrats and such Southern Republicans as may rise to office may be expected to take much the same position in advocacy of state rather than of national power.

When all the forces and counterforces in Southern politics are taken into account, the more probable line of development diverges markedly from the possibilities sketched in the popular discussion of recent years. Some of the deep thinkers among the Republicans, such as Senator Karl E. Mundt, of South Dakota, have seemed to regard the South as a monolithic entity restrained from a natural and irrevocable alliance with right-wing Republicanism only by an unreasoning attachment to the cause of the Confederacy. In fact, within the South all kinds and sorts of political interests and aspirations exist. Rather than the movement of a single great Southern bloc into the Republican Party, a more plausible expectation is a spotted sort of development. From time to time the electoral vote of some Southern states will be cast for Republican presidential candidates. Here and there a state will, either regularly or on occasion, send a Republican to the Senate. A larger number of patches of fairly reliable Republicanism will appear on the map of Southern congressional districts. Other districts will become doubtful and be warmly contested and Republican candidates will appear on the ballot in districts where the Democratic candidate has been unopposed at general elections for generations. In this sequence of development the areas first to emerge into a world of two-party politics will be those that have had for quite some time the largest minority Republican vote. At any rate this has been the pattern that prevailed with respect to the new areas of congressional and local Republicanism in recent years.

The question of the organization of politics within the Southern states—for state and local purposes—deserves separate attention. A great strength of the Republican Party in the North has been its firm control of state and local governments, which not only provided sustenance for the party faithful but harnessed to the cause of the G.O.P. the career interests of an imposing army of office seekers. In the South the Democratic Party has enjoyed a similar advantage. Over the decades each party from the base of its sectional stronghold could attempt to capture the country, secure in the knowledge that safe places for retreat and regrouping existed for many of the faithful. While the situation has been somewhat altered in the North, it remains substantially unchanged in the South. If the political evolution of the rest of the country provides a reliable guide, it may be expected that Democratic control of Southern state and local governments will manifest an impressive staying power. Changes at this level will probably lag considerably behind alterations in the position of the South in national politics. The basis for these conclusions is the fact that a similar sequence has occurred elsewhere. To a considerable degree the affairs of states possess an independence of the tides and trends that affect the national political scene. In the national Democratic era such states as Iowa, New Hampshire, Kansas, Wisconsin, and even Nebraska from time to time placed their electoral strength on the Democratic side and Democratic senatorial candidates occasionally carried elections in such states. Yet in most such strongly Republican states these Democratic triumphs in national affairs never affected for long Republican dominance of state affairs.

The persistence of the established party in state and local affairs, despite turmoil and turnover in national politics, is, of course, to a degree a matter of form rather than of substance. A dominant state party, be it Republican or Democratic, may differ enormously from time to time. Indeed, that capacity to roll with the punches is one reason why such a party may remain dominant. In any case, the attachment of the mass of the voters to a particular partisan label, and the habituation of groups and interests to the settlement of matters politically affected through a familiar set of channels, all conspire to create a going institutional constellation, which, if not indestructible, is difficult to overthrow.

In some respects the Democratic Party has within the South a much stronger foundation in human habit than has the Republican Party in even the most Republican of Northern states. The practice for over half a century of settling state affairs by the competition of factions and personalities within the Democratic primaries, without a ghost of a chance of reconsideration at the general election, creates folkways that are a strong block to the introduction of alternative modes of action. Apart from the resistance of the customs of a people to modification, the party as an institution—no matter how diverse its membership may be in interest—gains strength from the fact that it is the custodian of the career interests of practically all the public men of the region. So long as the normal route to local and state office and to political leadership in most of the South is the Democratic Party, those attracted to political careers will in the main seek to fulfill their ambitions through Democratic channels. Their strength will be added to that of the existing generation of public men whose lot is that of the Democratic Party. When law school seniors who contemplate the possibility of soon running for the legislature begin to give deliberation to their choice of party affiliation, then a competitive party politics will have arrived in the South.

Divisions over national issues exert a great influence over the organization of political activity for state and local affairs, but the argument has been that Republicanism may be expected to make some headway in Southern federal politics before they make much of an impress on matters state and local. That prognosis is suggested by the fact that Democratic gains in the North in Republican territory tend to follow a similar sequence. The analogy has persuasiveness, but certain peculiarities in the Southern situation create some uneasiness about the conclusion drawn from it. In the North the classes of superior substance and status by and large find the Republican Party congenial to their tastes in both national and state affairs. When the national political battle goes against them, they retire to a second line of defense in the state governments. In the South, on the other hand, the comparable classes have been able to take care of themselves within the states through the Democratic Party but have come to find themselves in an ambivalent position by their attraction to Republican policies nationally. If, however, a liberal Democratic faction should gain unassailable control of a state government—rather than merely intermittent victories—the Democratic Party would lose a good deal of its appeal to the crypto-Republicans.

The position of Governor Shivers of Texas in 1952 points to the essence of the problem. A leader of the right-wing Democratic faction in his state, he supported Eisenhower for President but gained no notoriety as an advocate of the erection of a Republican Party that could dislodge him and his associates from control of the government of the State of Texas. What this sort of conflict means for the long-run fortunes of the Republican Party in the politics of Southern states is by no means clear. In some of the states the upper-bracket leadership could, if sorely enough tried, mightily accelerate the development of formidable state Republican parties.

Unless American national politics is undergoing some drastic changes, it is unlikely that the Shivers type can long continue to have it both ways, although one may be certain that the attempt will be made by a variety of strategies. A national party can accommodate itself to a great range of internal diversity on policy questions, but to bolt the presidential candidate and also to remain in good standing in the lodge must still be regarded as an exceptional—or transitional—achievement. In some places the dilemma of the Democratic professionals even extends to their own survival. By advocacy of a conservative line and by appeals, explicit or otherwise, to Republicans for support in the Democratic primaries, they become dependent on fair-weather friends who will desert them en masse once a passable genuine Republican candidate turns up on the general election ballot.

All in all, there is no more reason for a closely competitive party politics over state matters to develop uniformly in the states of the South than in Northern and Western states. Few indeed are the states with a two-party politics that is regularly and genuinely competitive. More common is the pattern of a major party most infrequently really challenged in its control of state government. Where a genuine two-party politics does prevail, it exists not because of any innate tendency of political communities toward bipolarization but as an expression of competing and dual interests within the community. Not the least of these foundations of politics is the Protestant-Catholic dualism which has in some states operated as a powerful supplement to economics in the maintenance of the party system. Such religious and ethnic cleavages cannot significantly re-enforce party differences in the South, unless by some awful trick of fate the array of political battle became one of white against black. That may be a possibility in a few states but a possibility apparently most remote in time.

Speculation about whether a dual party division will develop within the South is necessarily chiefly a discussion of political forms, which are, of course, of importance in themselves. Such forms are not likely to be seriously altered save under the leverage of issues of substance. The broad concern to this point has been whether economic issues may not be the means for changing the forms of Southern politics. The question remains whether there are sets of regional attitudes or views on questions of broad political philosophy not so closely connected with political forms. If so, what course should we expect them to follow in the changing South?

It is indeed a nice question whether in fact any marked differences now exist between basic policy attitudes among the mass of Southerners and the generality of people in other sections of the country. Certainly there is no single Southern set of attitudes not shared by at least some people outside the South. A sectional difference, if it exists, must take the form of a significantly higher frequency of attachment to one set of beliefs in the South than elsewhere.

With respect to the sorts of attitudes measured by public opinion polls it is difficult to find any set of issues that divides the population of the South as a whole radically differently from the way it splits the people of other sections. It does not take a poll to tell us that the South has some differentiating attitudes on the race question. Yet most great issues already divide the people within the South along with those of all the nation rather than divide the people of the South off from the rest of the nation.

To attribute to the South a set of beliefs preponderant in the region and peculiar to it brings a risk of the charge of myth-making. (To doubt the existence of such sectional philosophy also involves the risk of indictment for myth-breaking.) Yet there may well be sets of basic attitudes with a special strength in the region that can be counted on to have for some time a continuing effect in unifying the section in national affairs. Some of these views may be limited largely to the echelons of political leadership; others may well have been fixed in mass attitudes by the preachings of generations of politicians. In either case, if they have strength, they must be a product of the history and character of the people.

In the light of the record an obvious question is whether the prevailing attitude within the South on foreign policy differentiates this region from others. The South is commonly thought to have a special disposition to face up to the fact that what happens in the rest of the world is of concern to us and has to be dealt with as best as can be. Certainly the South has no monopoly on this outlook, but it may well be that the Southern attitude has a basis stronger than the fact that Democrats have been compelled fortuitously in this century to take this position by the compelling responsibilities of power.

Generations of dependence on world trade, a dependence radically lessened by modern agricultural legislation, had its effects in creating an awareness of the world as well as a doctrine of free trade. That doctrine remains as perhaps something more than a Sunday religion that routinely allows dispensation for the week-day sin of a tariff for a Southern product. Perhaps more important is the dominantly British origin of the white population of the South, a matter which probably has contributed greatly to Southern acceptance of collaboration with Britain. No strong Germanic strain existed, as in the Midwest, to doubt the wisdom of alliance with the British. Nor has a Congressman from Birmingham been under the same temptation to twist the lion's tail as has his colleague from Boston.

The complex of attitudes growing out of all these factors can only persist and have a controlling influence under some circumstances. A severe test of the generality of the South's internationalism will develop as peoples of color come more to dominate our external problems. There is also a glimmer of evidence that latent within the South itself is a considerable body of sentiment, if not isolationist, at least dubious of economic support of foreign powers. The further democratization of Southern political processes will provide an opportunity for this sentiment to establish its dimensions.

Even on domestic economic policy something may be said for the existence of a special Southern role, if not for the prevalence of a regionally differentiating economic philosophy. A common explanation goes to the effect that it has been the function of the agrarian South to moderate both the greed of Northern capital and the rapacity of Northern industrial labor. The hypothesis undoubtedly is overdrawn but it contains enough truth to be of some comfort to Southerners. In the era of Woodrow Wilson Southern Democrats managed with their Northern allies to enact legislation regarded at the time as restrictive of business abuses and protective of the rights of labor. Again in the New Deal, Southern Democrats came into their own and, despite impressions to the contrary, played an important hand in the not inconsiderable legislative product of the New Deal. Later the South helped stop the New Deal dead in its tracks. In this action it may have been performing its balancing function; it may also have been reflecting the fact that the arbitral role cannot be well performed by one who has become a party at interest. Southern agrarian Democrats might very well help mediate the conflicts between Northern capital and Northern labor, but by 1938 Southerners could not take a disinterested view toward the wages and hours act, a piece of legislation with a special bearing on both workers and employers in the South.

The emerging economic developments are destroying the basis for the Southern role of balance, if indeed the role ever existed in a very clear form. The voices of the old Populists of the South, who, reincarnated as Democrats, long outlived their Western brethren, are dying out. Yet some remnants of agrarian unhappiness with the corporation-ordered way of life ought to persist in diminished strength for some time. Southern agriculture, with its special interests and its large proportion of small farmers, will remain a distinct, if less powerful, conditioner of political action. In truth, one may also doubt that an industrial system led by branch managers can, even among the Southern upper classes, quickly dissolve a tradition of obstreperous separatism and replace it by a loyalty to a class, most of whose members are Northeners.

Closely akin to these matters is the question whether the complex of Southern political attitudes embodies any special set of basic notions on human liberty and individual rights, around which matters may well turn one of the great issues of our times. The general estimate of its record on the Negro may make it appear absurd even to raise the question whether the South might have anything useful to say about the liberties of man. Nevertheless, there are elements in the Southern political tradition which will make it easy to look back and understand why if the South does turn out to be a center of resistance to the great assaults on the ancient liberties of man.

Rather considerable differences set off the practices and traditions of governance within the South. The heritage of political leadership of the older South embodies a couple of centuries of experience in governing, an experience not broken by the political discontinuities and diversions flowing from the infusion of great populations of contrasting origins and beliefs. This leadership, originating as a squirearchy, long retained both the prerogatives and the restrained benevolence of that sort of governing class, even though it came to operate as an aristocracy disciplined by a yeomanry rabidly Jacksonian. It absorbed as well as it could the champions of the people and assimilated them into its political system. It had to contend with the Ku Kluxers of the 1920's and in its long string of battles with rabble rousers of the most diverse talents it learned the reality of demagoguery. It was infiltrated by men of business and battered by the critics. Despite all the vicissitudes perhaps something remains to give the region's governing groups a nature peculiarly Southern *viz.*, a tendency to regard the responsibilities of governance more as the guardianship of a patrimony than as the duty of a corporation lawyer—or a walking delegate—to use the means at hand, whether fair or foul, to advance the momentary interests of his client.

To those of the region most genuinely and most consciously the heirs of the Southern governing tradition the course of events must be appalling. The New Deal jolted them but after all it affected, and not fatally, principally property—and Northern industrial and financial property at that. But now come other departures from the well-ordered course of things. They see demagogues spring up beside whom the demagogues in the Southern past seem like harmless buffoons. They see penalties applied by procedures and on the basis of evidence that no man of honor would use even against the meanest Negro in the most backward county of Georgia. They even see perjured testimony paid for from the public treasury, an action which would end abruptly the political career of any Southern county attorney. They see a cruel embellishment of the patronage system whereby men are not only fired to make way for deserving partisans but are also slandered as disloyal.

And those so held up to the disdain of their fellow citizens happen usually to be Democrats. They hear contemptible little parvenus boasting of their Americanism, men so lightly touched by the American tradition that they do not know that only scoundrels proclaim their own patriotism. They see shameless men convert the grave charge of treason into a routine campaign taunt, and a taunt against the Democratic Party, a term that happens to cover Southern Democrats. Surely all this—and there is more—is enough to provide a test of the strength of a tradition that is supposed to contain a large component of honor.

In any case, the Jeffersonian strain of political doctrine runs more strongly in Mississippi than in, let us say, Ohio. After all, Mr. Jefferson served his apprenticeship in what would today be called a Southern county courthouse gang. Perhaps the South has another part to play out before it is finally dissolved into the national mass. ¿Quien sabe?

VIII

NOMINATIONS AND ELECTIONS

47. *Again It Will Be "The Smoke-Filled Room"* *

WRITING in the pre-convention period of the 1948 presidential election year, Arthur Krock undertook to illuminate the actual process behind the nomination of a presidential candidate. Obviously the voters cannot elect a distinguished President unless the nomination process itself produces a distinguished nominee; the nomination process is therefore of crucial importance. And it is the party, not the public, that nominates the candidate. The carefully stage-managed demonstrations on the convention floor are not the conclusive determinants leading to nomination; the real decision is often made in "the smoke-filled room," that is, in the backstage maneuvering of powerful groups in the party, the results of which are shown on the convention floor. Mr. Krock deals with the qualities of leadership produced by the usual partisan nomination process.

SELDOM in this country does the voice of the people break through the wall of professional politics and call on a major party to nominate for President one man and no other. Even then it may be silenced before the event by devices well known to the politicians. And it may be silenced by a statement from the intended beneficiary that he would not accept the nomination if tendered.

Self-elimination has happened very rarely in our history—only twice in the cases of citizens who had never held political office or engaged in politics in any way before the call for them arose. One was, the other is, a general—William T. Sherman in 1880, Dwight D. Eisenhower in 1948.

• • • • •

* Arthur Krock, *The New York Times Magazine*, February 1, 1948, pp. 5 ff. Reprinted by permission of the author and the publisher.

In the meager list of those whose first nominations were by popular demand are Jefferson, Jackson, William Henry Harrison, Ulysses S. Grant and Herbert Hoover. Washington was the unanimous choice of the people and the politicians—the only form of real draft and perhaps the only one Eisenhower would ever have considered, well knowing it has become a political impossibility. Thus five citizens in all have been party nominees by popular choice and then elected, though thirty-two have served as President of the United States.

Jefferson barely defeated Aaron Burr in 1800. Lincoln trod a rough, uphill path to nomination, as did Blaine, Cleveland, McKinley, Wilson, Willkie and others. Franklin D. Roosevelt was in great danger of being rejected by the convention of 1932. His declining fortunes were salvaged only when the late Senator Pat Harrison drove the wavering Mississippi delegation back into line and William Randolph Hearst—uninterested in Ritchie of Maryland, personally bitter against Alfred E. Smith and determined that Newton D. Baker should not be chosen because he was an ardent League of Nations man—permitted the California delegation to go to Roosevelt, a move that was promptly joined by the other Garner group, the delegation of Texas.

Theodore Roosevelt has a strong claim for admission to the list of those whose nominations came through popular demand, because he was the first Vice President in history that had succeeded to the Presidency by death who was nominated to fill it for four years in his own right (1904). In a lesser degree, since T. R. had broken the trail for him, Calvin Coolidge has a similar claim. But neither can be established as firmly as those of the five others can—Jefferson, Jackson, W. H. Harrison, Grant and Hoover. And this must also be the judgment as to Harry S. Truman, whose nomination—if he wants it—is conceded.

For, since Theodore Roosevelt's time, it has become a political axiom that the party which denies renomination to a President who desires it, whether or not he has previously been elected in his own right, enters the campaign with an apology for his record. Mr. Truman may be the overwhelming choice for nomination of the party voters—and this could be true even if Henry A. Wallace should get the delegates of a state or two in the convention of the party he has repudiated. But that cannot and will not be tested in the circumstances.

• • • • •

Willkie entered the Republican convention of 1940 without anything like the popular demand of a majority behind him. That formed only after Taft and Dewey exhausted themselves, and even then it was shrewdly and ceaselessly stimulated by professional organizing work behind the scenes.

The fact is that almost every four years the American people are required to make a selection for President between two men with whose nominations they have had very little to do.

On the other hand, the nominee of minor parties is always the direct choice of those who intend to vote for him. The very surge of protest against the major political groups which results in the decision to put national candidates in the field against them invariably casts up a single leader. The convention in which he is handed the independent party standard is a mere ratification meeting and always genuine, in contrast with those sham demonstrations in which a President is renominated because there is nothing else his party can do with any hope of success at the polls.

Thus Republicans who were disgusted with the first Grant administration in 1872 held a rump session in which no real contender arose against the national voice of that disgust, Horace Greeley. No name except that of Theodore Roosevelt was put forth in 1912, when once again protesting Republicans formed the Bull Moose party. Robert M. La Follette Sr. was the spontaneous choice of the insurgents against the Harding-Coolidge administration in 1924. . . .

• • • • •

"We want Wilson," the battle cry for the successful contender at Baltimore in 1912, came from the throats of college boys. But behind it was a shrewd and patiently formed organization. "We want Willkie" was a popular chorus at Philadelphia in 1940, sincerely uttered by people off the streets among whom the Willkie managers had scattered tickets. But one of the most remarkable publicity jobs in the history of politics preceded it, in which cost was no object. And it was preceded also by expert pressure on key leaders and influential delegates from their home states, pressure engendered by supporters of Willkie who made it their business to find out who listened to whom. Their purpose, which they achieved, was to produce the belief among the delegates that, after the deadlock, only Willkie of all the eligibles could be sure of election.

At Chicago in 1940, while many Democratic delegates and their leaders faltered uneasily at the prospect of a third nomination for F. D. Roosevelt, and the Southern forces were white with anger against the sham "draft," there was heard the famous "voice from the sewer." Uttering each time the name of a different state in his Taurian bellow from underground, this shouter helped to create the psychology the third term managers required. It was a wholly artificial device, supplied by Mayor Kelly and operated by his Commissioner of Sanitation from a loud speaker in the cellar of the convention hall.

Episodes like this moved Senator Vandenburg to declare that there has been no such thing as a real draft since Washington's time.

What qualifications do the people seek in the rare instance when a popular favorite is nominated by their demand instead of by routine political process? The record shows that he is a citizen who has been commander in a victorious war (Washington and Grant); the leader of a new social-economic movement (Jefferson and Jackson); or one whose appeal arises from a humanitarian labor (Hoover). Despite the masterly achievements of Lincoln, Wilson, Cleveland and the Roosevelts, they were not forced on the politicians by the people. Their nominations were products of compromise among the professionals.

What qualifications do these professionals seek before they come to the decision in the smoke-filled room? First of all, they want a winner. Second, they want a practitioner of their own trade who "speaks their language" and with whom they think they can get along. After this they measure the other talents on which the country must eventually depend for its security and progress.

But there are times and conditions when the first qualification of the professionals—the wish for a winner—has the elements of great usefulness in the Presidency. These times are when the nation and the world are flowing in great and dynamic movements, when the political tactician, the pussyfooter and the mediocrity are shouted down by the anxious people. These conditions are when the party long in power seeks to retain it by scattering reckless promises as catch-alls.

Then to have a winner the opposition must produce a commanding and gifted citizen, a man whose character and record can withstand the corrosive of campaign analysis, a man with intelligent and constructive views and the wit and courage to express them. The professionals must accept one on whom they cannot depend to redeem their political debts and those of the party at the expense of good government and the general welfare.

This was the challenge that brought about the nominations of Lincoln, Cleveland, Wilson and Hoover by convention bosses who had other preferences. There are more examples but they are not so well documented.

When, therefore, there is no true draft, the process is choice by negotiation. Then the political bosses either surrender their real preferences, as noted above, because they must do so to win, or, as in the case of Harding, exert these preferences because they feel sure of victory regardless. This process is the usual and familiar one.

Hence it is that, unless a popular uprising nominates and elects a candidate, overwhelming the political machines in so doing, a convention draft is a rare phenomenon. This being so, the people are generally confronted with two Presidential nominees in whose selection they have played no direct part, one of whom they must send to the White House to exercise four years of vast power over their daily lives and the future of their progeny.

The state preference primary arose as part of an effort to register a popular choice over that of the professional politicians. But it is subject to political control in enough instances to weaken its intended effect, and the convention method of choosing delegates in other states weakens it further. Both systems are influenced by the professionals because politics is their business. They work at it every hour and the average citizen operates it as a sideline for a few weeks a year.

The only strong force for popular action is the true draft. For this to be effective in either the Democratic or Republican parties a man must come on the scene who appeals so powerfully to the people as their salvation in a desperate time that they override his wish to remain in private life, or as vigorously support his known or suspected willingness to serve.

The few examples of the draft that have previously been cited establish its rarity.

Almost as rare is the third party movement that has for its objective the election of its Presidential candidate. Nearly always its real purpose is party reorganization so that the independent leader may take control and come to the White House later as a regular nominee.

• • • • •

48. *Letter from a Campaign Train* *

POLITICAL CAMPAIGNS have been variously described. They are sometimes compared, for instance, to a circus; and such a description seems to portray very well the activities aboard the campaign train of a presidential candidate. Richard H. Rovere, who accompanied Mr. Truman on his 1948 campaign tour, tells here of the "beaters" who preceded the presidential train to make the last-minute arrangements, and of the "shills" implanted in the audience to lead the applause at the proper times. He describes the detailed arrangements made by the Secret Service and the railroad

* Richard H. Rovere, *The New Yorker*, October 9, 1948, pp. 69-76, 79.

company for the safety of the presidential party, the arduous grind of the campaign, and the effect of these experiences on campaigners and the public. He also analyzes the reaction of the people to the campaign activity of Mr. Truman.

En Route with Truman:

POLITICS is a branch of show business, and life aboard a Presidential campaign train—a peculiar and somewhat wearing form of existence that I have been sampling on and off during the past couple of weeks—is like life in a fast-moving road carnival. We are always either setting up the show or knocking it down. We play more towns than the World of Mirth or Brunk's Comedians (a carnival overtaken by the Truman train when I was riding on it through Colorado and Utah), and we work longer hours. The average self-respecting carnival stays for a week if a town is good-sized, and for a night in other places, but we seldom stay anywhere more than a few hours, and we frequently play ten-minute stands. Occasionally, we have been in and out of a town within five or six minutes, and have stood still for only two. On some days, we have played fourteen or fifteen places, starting at dawn and keeping at it until just before midnight. Our main concerns as we go along are narrowly professional. We worry about the tenting facilities in the town down yonder, the availability of baths, the friendliness of the law-enforcement organizations, the liquor regulations in the next state, and the size and humor of the crowds. The name of a town we have been in doesn't stand for a plot of earth and a group of buildings; it stands for a particular audience or a particular incident. To a man who has been riding the rails with President Truman, Reno isn't a famous divorce-and-gambling city but the place where our man blew a few of his lines and talked about "Republican mothbags" when he meant to say "Republican mossbacks."

Ours is, to be sure, a carnival of an unusual sort. It has just one act, and the one act is built around just one performer. For an enterprise of its size, it carries entirely too many hangers-on—twenty-odd in the President's party and fifty-odd in the press party. Still, the road-show analogy, at least on the Truman train (which, I understand, runs on a tighter schedule than the Dewey train), holds pretty true all the way down the line. We have our beaters, who travel ahead of us and make arrangements with newspapermen, police, sign painters, and soft-drink concessionaires. We have our shills, who get out in the audience and, by clapping wherever the script calls for it, help to build a good tip, as old carny hands call a large and eager crowd. Some of our beaters and shills are men of distinguished reputation. The chief advance man is Oscar Chapman, Under-Secretary of the Interior, and the boss shill appears to be Brigadier General Wallace Graham, the famous grain speculator and personal physician to the President. He is sometimes assisted by Clark Clifford, Truman's executive assistant and the chief of the ghost-writing department. Then, too, we have our Princess Bright Cloud—Miss Margaret Truman, who, wherever her father's friends have been able to stir up an audience, steps out from behind a blue velvet curtain onto the rear platform of the train to wave and smile at the crowd. This is, theatrically, the high point of the act. True, it is not followed by a spiel urging the people to lay down the tenth part of a dollar to step inside the tent and see the rest of the show. Nor is anyone advised to buy a bottle of Dr. Truman's Old Missouri Tonic. But there is a request to step inside the polling booths on November 2nd and pull the right levers or "x" the circle next to the donkey. "I don't want you to vote for me," the President of the United States has been saying at county seats and railroad division points all across the country. "I want you to get out on Election Day and vote for yourselves. Vote for your own interests, your own part of the country, your own friends." It seems a rather parochial point of view to be encouraging in Americans at this stage of world history, but it is obvious that the President wants very much to stay on in the White House, and he probably feels that educating the masses toward broader perspectives can wait until he gets Governor Dewey off his neck.

It would be going too far to say that the crowds, either in the small towns or in the large cities, respond enthusiastically to his appeals for support. They don't. There is every evidence that they are kindly disposed toward him and that they sympathize with him about his difficult lot in life, but nothing that I have heard him say between Washington, D.C., and Los Angeles has drawn more than a spot of polite applause. Nobody stomps, shouts, or whistles for Truman. Everybody claps. I should say that the decibel count would be about the same as it would be for a missionary who has just delivered a mildly encouraging report on the inroads being made against heathenism in Northern Rhodesia. This does not necessarily mean that the people who come out to hear him intend to vote against him—though my personal feeling is that most of them intend to do exactly that. It may mean only that he is not the sort of man—any more than his opponent is—to provoke wild enthusiasm.

The part of the act that involves the President's daughter is invariably the most effective part, and Truman's management of it displays a good deal of canniness and trouping instinct. She comes on just before the finale at every matinée and evening performance. The show, as a rule, gets under way after "Hail to the Chief" has been rendered by the local high-school band. Next, a local beauty, a local union man, or a local Kiwanis man hands the President, depending on where we are, a bag of peaches, a mess of celery, a miner's hat, or just the key to the city. He has become quite adept at accepting these offerings graciously and then shoving them the hell inside his car. It takes, by my unofficial clocking, one and three-quarters minutes to give the mayor, the governor, and the Democratic candidate for Congress—the two last are likely to ride along with us through their state—their cracks at the audience. Whoever comes at the end of the procession has, as they say, the unparalleled honor and glorious privilege of introducing the President. During the ten-minute layovers, Truman limits his part of the act to five minutes. He begins with local scenery, local industry, local agriculture, and local intelligence; leads from this into a description of the contempt in which the Republican Party holds the region he is passing through; goes on to a preview of the Good Society that he, given another term and the kind of Congress he wants, will create; and, penultimately, makes his plea for votes. Then, with a surer sense of timing than he shows in major addresses, he pauses a moment, looks quizzically at the crowd, smiles, and asks, very humbly, "And now, howja like to meet ma family?" He cocks his head slightly to catch the response; he has the appealing look of a man who wouldn't be surprised if the answer was no but would be terribly hurt. The crowd's desire to meet the Truman women, however, never fails to exceed by a good deal its desire for repeal of the Taft-Hartley Act. When he has caught the favorable response, he says, "First, Mizz Truman," and the First Lady, who, like her husband, is more relaxed before small crowds than before large ones or photographers, parts the curtain and takes her place at his right side. Sometimes, when the crowd is very small and friendly, the President indentifies Mrs. Truman as "the boss" and winks knowingly at the men in the audience. After Mrs. Truman and her admirers have exchanged greetings, the President says, "And now I'd like to have you meet my daughter, Margaret." (I thought it a nice touch that, down in the border states, he said, whether artfully or not I am unable to decide, "And now I'd like for you to meet Miss Margaret") It involves no disrespect for Mrs. Truman to say that her daughter gets a bigger hand than she does; this country may be run by and for mothers, but its goddesses are daughters. Margaret's entrance comes closer than anything else to bringing down the house.

As soon as the Truman womenfolk have flanked the President, a railroad official, generally a vice-president of the line, who sits at a telephone in the car ahead of the President's, calls the locomotive engineer—fifteen cars, or a quarter of a mile, down the track—and tells him to get slowly under way. As the train pulls out from the station, the family waves goodbye. Mrs. Truman and Margaret then go back into the car to fix their hair for the next curtain call, leaving the President alone on the platform until the last switchman in the yards has had his look. I am certain that, no matter what the fate of the Truman administration, millions of Americans will, for the rest of their lives, have framed in their mind's eye a vivid image of the Three Travelling Trumans highballing off into the black nights of Colorado or Arizona, blending with the tall pines in the Sierras, or being slowly enveloped by the dust of the Midwestern plains. It will be a picture to cherish, and it will stand Harry Truman in good stead for the rest of his life. Travelling with him, you get the feeling that the American people who have seen him and heard him at his best would be willing to give him just about anything he wants except the Presidency.

As a rule, the Truman show does better in the small towns than in the large ones. The President is a feed-mill type of talker, and he can be excellent indeed with a small audience. Charles Ross, his press secretary and the sort of man who wouldn't stoop to inventing a literary background for his employer, tells me that Truman has worked hard at his Mark Twain, which contributes no doubt to the raciness of his conversational style and accounts for the pleasant way it falls on the ear. In Dexter, Iowa, he made a long, scolding speech to seventy-five thousand farmers who were on hand to see the final in a national plowing contest that was being held on the farm of a woman named Lois Agg. The farmers, a happy, prosperous crew, some of whom had flown there in their own planes, were in no mood to be scolded, but they listened courteously, and applauded every now and then. A couple of hours later, after the President had inspected the plowing and some tractor exhibits, and after he had refreshed himself with some pieces of prize-winning cakes and pies, he returned to the platform, to talk informally about his early days on a farm. He carried on for quite a while about the differences between mules and machines. He was delightful, and the people were delighted. When he speaks without a script, as he always does unless he is making a major campaign address, he inflicts considerable damage on the English language, but anything he does on his own is not one-tenth as deplorable as what his ghost-writers do for him. One can choose between, on the one hand, "gluttons of privilege" and "only an appetizer for an economic tapeworm," both of which are creations of his belles-lettres division, and, on the other hand, a Trumanism such as "I'm goin' down to Berkeley to get me a degree." The language of the academy seems to jinx him every time. "I'm only a synthetic alumni," he said modestly when, in Grinnell, Iowa, he was introduced by a professor as the most distinguished graduate of the local college. It can be said of Trumanisms, though, that they are genuine, that they almost always make sense, and that they occasionally, as in the line about Berkeley, have an engaging lilt.

Truman's detailed knowledge of the small towns is unexpected and remarkable. The impression one gets is that he has acquired, in his sixty-four years, a spoonful or two of information about every community west of the Mississippi and about a good many of those east of it. Of course he is briefed, by people on the other side of the blue velvet curtain, on current local problems and local interests before he hits a place in which he is going to speak, but he is always able to throw in something from his own stockpile on its remote or recent past. If he hasn't been there before himself, the chances are that Mrs. Truman or some relative has, and that if no living Truman has connections in town, a dead Truman once had. His maternal grandfather, Solomon Young, drove wagon trains in the West a century ago, and the old gentleman went through an extraordinary number of towns. According to a Pennsylvania Railroad representative on the Truman train, this campaign trip is just about the most elaborate tour ever made of this country. I suspect that he is referring only to railroad trips and has conveniently overlooked, for the sake of rail propaganda, those wagon-train trips made by Grandfather Solomon Young.

In the big cities, the show loses a lot of its fun. One civic auditorium is pretty much like the next one, chicken-and-peas dinners are the same everywhere, and so are Democratic committeemen and committeewomen. Even Los Angeles, from which something out of the way might be expected, put on a drab show for the President. True, there were thirty-two searchlights, but they merely showed up the bare spots in the grandstand. This is a Dewey year in the movie colony, as it probably is almost everywhere else. By the time the Truman people got around to renting a place for the President to speak in, the Dewey crowd had leased the Hollywood Bowl for the evening he was scheduled to talk, in order, as they put it, to "rehearse" the lighting effects for the Governor's appearance the following night. (When one sees the lighting effects at a Hollywood rally, to say nothing of the neon signs in Hollywood and Los Angeles, one can easily understand why federal power projects are so essential to California's welfare.) The Democrats had to be satisfied with a place called Gilmore Stadium. The unfortunate thing about Gilmore Stadium was not that it is smaller than the Hollywood Bowl but that it is larger. Neither Dewey nor Truman drew capacity crowds in Hollywood; as a matter of fact, they drew about the same number of people. But the vacant seats at Truman's meeting were more numerous, because the number of seats was greater.

Almost the only color in the big-city productions is provided by the automobiles in which we ride. Like a circus, we start off with a parade, and though our parades are less animated than those of most circuses, they are as musical and, thanks to the cars, have just as much glitter. Before I started on this trip, I did not realize the odd role played by the automobile in national politics. The Truman party was driven from Dexter, Iowa, to Des Moines, approximately forty miles, in a fleet of thirty-five brand-new cars, all of them convertibles with the top down. I didn't stop to wonder how so many new convertibles came to be at the disposal of the Party of the Workingmen, in Iowa, of all places. Then, riding in Car No. 30, through downtown Des Moines, I began to think it strange that the crowds that had seen the President, riding in Car No. 1, five minutes earlier, did not disperse. They were looking just as hard at the carloads of rumpled and unsmiling reporters as they must have looked at the celebrities up forward. "Sure they're beautiful," I overheard a middle-aged man say to his companion, "but I guess you have to be a Democrat to get one." "Thing about a Packard," another man said, "you can still tell one when you see it—the old pointed radiator and those red hubcaps. Hasn't changed since I've known it." "Ought to strip all that housing down," a third voter remarked. "Ever try to get a jack under one of those things?"

I didn't have time to inquire into the details of automobile procurement in Des Moines, but I did in Denver, two days later. The Truman train was met by twenty-two Kaisers and Frazers and eight new Fords. I asked our driver if he had lent his car to the President out of party loyalty. "Nah," he said. "This isn't my car. I'm just helping out a friend of mine here. He's the Kaiser-Frazer distributor in town—Northwestern Auto Company, they call it—and I guess he come out first in this agency fight. Got mostly Kaisers and Frazers here. Lucky for him. The 1949 models just come in yesterday, and he's getting a chance right off to display them." It was the same everywhere. There was a tie-in with the dealers in every city we visited: free transportation in exchange for free advertising. The new cars were seen by the President's admirers, and the President was seen by admirers of new cars. So far, the struggle has been mainly between Ford and Kaiser-Frazer. The Ford people seem to me to be leading by about three to two. Denver was the only place where Kaiser-Frazer was plainly in the political ascendancy. If the crowds have been, for the most part, pleased with the new models, the Secret Service men guarding the President have not. In Los Angeles, they rebelled. They refused to let him ride through that unpredictable city in anything without running boards for them to stand on. A search for something with running boards was made, and a 1934 Lincoln touring car was found. It belonged to Cecil B. De Mille, who plans to vote for Dewey but whose patriotic impulses are stronger than his party loyalty.

As a piece of railroading, the handling of the Truman train is a work of art. Any Presidential campaign train demands considerable ingenuity and planning by the railroad people, but if the man already in office is a candidate to succeed himself, the trip is particularly difficult to organize. The problems of security are greater, and so are those of communication. The President's train must be a mobile White House as well as a mobile hustings. I talked about the train with Mr. Dewey Long, a Civil Service employee who for fifteen years has been the White House transportation and communications officer, and to Mr. Harry Karr, who is division passenger agent for the Pennsylvania Railroad in Washington, D.C. Both men have been on the Presidential train from the beginning. A good part of Mr. Long's worries were over by the time the train began to roll, but Mr. Karr, who has been on the job of running Presidents around the country ever since the days of Harding, has to think about each Presidential train constantly until it pulls back into the Union Station, in Washington. Mr. Karr is a slight, tense man, physically and emotionally a sort of Ernest Truex, and he says that his job has left its mark on him. "I may not look it from the outside," he says, "but inside I'm a nervous wreck. It's been real high-tension stuff all along—from Harding and Coolidge on down." We were riding, as we talked, through the Royal Gorge of Colorado, where the cut in the Rockies made by the Arkansas River is only thirty feet wide at some points. "Just look out the window," he said. "Makes you sweat blood even to think of taking a President through here. Let a few boulders roll down that thing and we'd all be shooting the rapids. Believe me, we thought long and hard before we agreed to bring this train down through here."

When the President and his political advisers have decided on a trip, they call in Mr. Long and sketch out for him the route they wish the train to travel, the places they wish to visit, and the approximate timetable they wish to keep. The White House tries to alternate between the Pennsylvania and the Baltimore & Ohio out of Washington for western trips, so whichever line is due for its turn gets it. This last time, it was the Pennsylvania, which is why Mr. Long, after getting his first instructions, called Mr. Karr in on the job. Mr. Karr put the Pennsylvania's Special Movement Bureau to work, and the Bureau, in coöperation with the Rock Island, the Denver & Rio Grande Western, the Union Pacific, and other lines over whose track the train was to go, worked out the schedule. "When we're told about a deal of this kind," Mr. Karr said, "we flash the code word 'POTUS' to every line along the way. It stands for 'President of the United States,' and it means that when the time comes, they have to be ready to do a number of things. Every grade crossing has to be manned when the train passes, and I just can't tell you how many switches have to be spiked until we've moved on." To arrange all this spiking and fit the schedule of a Presidential train into train schedules all across the country and back is, naturally, a fairly involved problem, but on this trip it was done almost without a hitch. According to Mr. Karr, only one regular train has been seriously delayed by the transcontinental movement of the President up to now. This was a Rock Island express running between Kansas City and Denver. The superintendent of one division of the line wanted to sidetrack the Truman train, which on this part of the journey was pulling up wherever two or three were gathered together, at a certain point and let the express pass it, but it was decided, after a Sunday conference of railroad officials in Kansas City, not to let the train by. "There was just the tiniest chance that a piece of flying steel or something like that might have hit the President's train," Mr. Karr told me. "Of course, nothing could have hurt the President, in his armored car." At that, the express was only forty-five minutes late getting into Denver.

The train that Mr. Karr had to assemble for the current trip is a heterogeneous assortment of rolling stock. Not counting the pilot train—usually a locomotive and a single car—which runs five miles ahead to see that no anarchists have torn up the track, it is seventeen cars long and includes, in addition to Pullmans, diners, lounges, and a car in which the press can work, a communications car, operated and staffed by the Army Signal Corps, and the Ferdinand Magellan, the President's special car, which belongs to the government and was used by President Roosevelt throughout the war. The communications car, which is just behind the locomotive, contains two Diesel engines to generate power for its radio teletype and other electrical equipment. The radio teletype makes it possible for the President to keep in constant touch with Washington and, through Washington, with the rest of the world. News, most of it in code, is received in the communications car and phoned back to the President's car. The communications car can also transmit messages. Telephone lines are kept open from the White House and the State Department to the towns the President's train goes through. He can pull up at any whistle stop in the country and hold a long-distance Cabinet meeting, provided he can find his Cabinet members.

The Ferdinand Magellan, which has four staterooms, a galley, a dining room, and an observation platform, is, of course, the last car on the train, and brings the over-all length up to the maximum legal length for most states. In effect, it is not only a seventeenth car but an eighteenth, for it weighs two hundred and sixty-five thousand pounds, or about twice as much as the average Pullman. The extra weight of the car is accounted for mainly by the armor plate, partly by the three-inch bulletproof glass in the windows, and partly by the extra equipment it carries, including a couple of escape hatches and the blue velvet curtain.

49. *High Cost of Politics* *

POLITICAL CAMPAIGNS in the United States cost money—often a great deal of it. Campaign money is essential for the office-seeking politician, and most of it must come from others. Money is available, but what of the conditions? Who does give money for campaigns? What do they get, or expect to get, for it? How pertinent are our current statutes? These and other questions are discussed in the following selection.

WE FACE problems that involve life and death for all of us. Yet we insist on having the lowest sort of opinion of the very people we entrust with those problems and we force them to operate under conditions which do everything to repel decent men.

Who are these people who bear this great responsibility and whom we treat so stupidly? They are, of course, the politicians. They include Dwight D. Eisenhower, Adlai Stevenson, 96 senators, 435 congressmen, 48 governors, the 750,000 other elective officials, and the cabinet officers and tens of thousands of appointive officials and political workers who must live under our existing system of politics. These are the people whose day-by-day actions will largely determine the greatest conflict in the history of the world. Yet how do we tell them we regard them? We tell them that we consider them just a little above outlaws. Thus this spring, in a nation-wide Gallup poll, seven out of ten people with an opinion stated they would not like to see their children enter politics as a life's work.

Let us suppose that instead of running a great nation we were run-

* Philip L. Graham, *National Municipal Review*, XLIV (July, 1955), pp. 346-351. Reprinted by permission of the *National Municipal Review*.

ning a pickle works and that our pickle sales were dropping every month. Clearly we would not begin by telling our sales department that all salesmen were stupid and crooked and unnecessary. Yet we do treat problems which are rather more urgent than pickle sales in just that fashion. And if we continue to do so, we probably have as much chance of survival as the buggy manufacturers had of licking Henry Ford.

It will be obvious that fundamental problems call for fundamental solutions. And truly the problems presented by our present system of politics are fundamental. They are not going to be solved by palliatives. It will do us no good at all to resolve that for the next 30 days we shall never place the word "dirty" directly next to the word "politician." It will do us no good to make speeches or to write editorials saying we need better men and women in politics and a higher public regard for politicians.

Yet there is something—something fundamental and lasting—that can be done about the present situation. It is possible; it is urgently necessary; and it is eminently practical. Moreover, if this thoroughly "doable" thing is indeed done, it should constitute the single most important political reform of our time. But before we discuss the solution, let us diagnose the basic problem in a bit more detail. For the problem is deeper than merely a question of public attitudes. While it is a serious matter that politicians rank close to felons in the popularity polls, it is a much more serious matter that we force politicians to live in a system which goes a long way toward depriving them of self-respect.

CAMPAIGN CONTRIBUTIONS

The fundamental defect in our present system of politics has specifically to do with our habits regarding contributions for political campaigns. Even putting the best possible face on the situation, it can only be described as morally squalid, ethically shocking and spiritually revolting. As of 1955 the principal characteristics of our system of political finance can be accurately described in the following manner: (1) We maintain a bold-faced, official lie about the cost of political campaigns and the amounts of political contributions; (2) we almost universally fail to respond to—or even to recognize—the duties of the individual citizen in a free society; (3) we consequently force politicians to live in close connection with the filthy power of gangsters and the acquisitive power of special interest groups and favor seekers.

First, let me briefly expand on the way we maintain an official lie about political expenditures. We do this by having a federal law which limits expenditures by a candidate for Congress to a maximum of $5,000, by a candidate for the Senate to $25,000 and by a national political committee to $3,000,000. Now a senator, even in a small state, cannot run for $25,000 and in a state like Illinois he cannot run for $250,000. But the law remains on the books, the myth is maintained by a series of long-practiced manipulations and evasions. So we force the able man entering politics to launch his career with an initial act of blatant hypocrisy—and to endure this indignity every time he runs again.

In fact, few if any people actually know what modern political campaigns do cost. One of the most respected members of the Senate has told me that in his state (about the size of Illinois) over $3,000,000 was spent in a recent gubernatorial election. But the existing system perpetuates the fraudulent impression that political expenditures are but a fraction of what they are. Thus, in the 1952 presidential campaign a total of $17,500,000 was reported by the national committees of the two major parties. Some students of the matter estimate that actual expenditures came closer to $100,000,000. The limitations of $25,000 for the Senate and $5,000 for the House are patently laughable. For there are counties in this country where even a sheriff's race costs from ten to twenty times more than $25,000.

Next, let us look at how seriously the average person defaults in his duties as an individual citizen. And in doing so let us remember that with the new American economy—with our new wide distribution of wealth—we have a society wherein the average voter is in fact financially able to meet his obligations of citizenship. We can examine the default of the citizenry by studying the 1954 congressional elections. There were 1,054 congressional candidates. Expenditures officially reported totalled $13,700,000, and we can be sure actual expenditures were much higher.

SOME CONTRIBUTORS

After that campaign the Gallup poll asked people whether they had made a political contribution, not only in congressional races but for any of the many other campaigns that year. Assuming that such contributions would be made on a family basis, the answers were computed by families. This showed that only one family out of twenty had made any political contribution. If the answers were computed in terms of individual citizens, this would mean that only about two out of every hundred citizens made any contribution.

Since the default of the individual is so obvious, let us see what forces have rushed in to fill the vacuum. No tidy compilation of statistics is available, but anyone at all familiar with politics can document the situation. There are three major sources of political funds:

(1) The underworld. The sums raised by the gangsters are much larger than anyone imagines. In 1948, for example, it was reported to the *Washington Post* that the numbers operators in Washington had raised $100,000 to be spent against two senators who had tried to investigate local gambling. One of the most profitable businesses in the United States is the illegal race wire service to illegal horse betting establishments. It makes millions every year, has survived every sort of attempt to break it up, and clearly must be the largest single source of political funds in the country.

(2) The second important source of political funds can broadly be called special interest groups. This includes the vast array of individuals and organizations who have something direct to gain from government. They are far different from the underworld in that their aims and purposes are wholly legitimate, if sometimes a bit acquisitive or selfish. So important is this source of funds that it is practically impossible to find any congressman or senator, however high-minded, who has not lost his freedom of decision in some particular area. When one realizes that $100,000 carefully spent in a few small states can place a sizeable proportion of the United States Senate under obligation, it is easy to understand the temptation that exists for all special interest groups.

(3) The third group of established political contributors probably contributes the least in total amount, though their contributions are still important. They can be described as "the hopefuls." They are people who contribute in the expectation of receiving high public office. Their existence explains to a large extent why in the 1954 election less than 1,000 people contributed more than one-fifth of the total amount reported by both major national political committees. Their total gifts represented $1,850,000. And although the law—that same unenforced, hypocritical law—limits individual contributions to $5,000 to any one candidate or committee, it is believed that some resourceful contributors have managed to locate or create enough committees to permit contributions of over $100,000 in a single campaign.

So dominating is the need for political money, that this form of outright sale of positions of public trust is universally accepted. It had to be practiced by that old professional, President Truman, and it has also had to be practiced by that idealistic amateur, President Eisenhower. In bygone days this particular practice probably did little harm. Government was then relatively unimportant and a rich knucklehead here or there in high office could do little harm. Today, of course, this is radically altered. There are few unimportant high public posts. And both this administration and its predecessor have been weakened by the system which we average citizens have forced upon political leaders.

The over-all problem, I would like to repeat, is both serious and simple. We need the highest possible sort of people in politics because of the awesome decisions they must make. And we shall not have this until we get rid of the rotten financial foundation upon which our political system now rests, and thus begin to demonstrate toward politicians some of that decent concern which practitioners of the arts of free government deserve. The political financial problem, we should realize, is going to grow in size. This is inevitable because of our growth in population and growth in power of communications. Obviously politics will be expensive in a nation of 165,000,000 with rapidly widening suffrage. We are many, many years away from 1789 when our constitution was ratified by fewer than 100,000 people—by only some 2 per-cent of the population.

CAMPAIGN COSTS

How to deal with this growing problem is a matter of mounting concern. To give you an idea of its dimensions let me point out that to put a presidential candidate on just one TV network for a single half-hour costs between $50,000 and $100,000. To some these costs indicate only that modern mass communications are expensive. But that is not in fact the case, if we judge them on a per capita basis. Using mass media a candidate today probably spends much less to reach the individual voter than it cost Thomas Jefferson to feed all those horses that pulled his stagecoach, or even Theodore Roosevelt to pay for his campaign train.

The high cost of politics is a direct result of a high population and an expanding right of suffrage. And superficial attempts to solve the problem by having politicians pass rules as to what other politicians can get free TV time are only going to create new problems. Even stronger lauguage can be employed against the suggestion, now 50 years old but constantly revived, that the government should appropriate funds for this purpose.

There is one step toward reform now being studied by the Senate which deserves support and encouragement. That is the effort by a committee, headed by Senator Hennings of Missouri, to write more realistic laws about political contributions. This is the 60th congressional committee to review this subject in the last 50 years. In so far as they are working toward full and honest accounting of all political contributions, they are working toward a desirable end. However, although present limits on expenditures will be considerably raised, the Senate hearings so far indicate that the new limits will still invite evasions by being unrealistically low. In any event, the work of Senator Hennings and his colleagues represents some of the most constructive work in many years. And success in their labors will be a stepping-stone toward better government.

HOW RAISE MONEY?

But the major problem still remains. That is, how can we raise enough honest, untainted money to permit our politicians to run for office without becoming obligated to corrupt or selfish forces? And in doing this, how can we help to create a higher regard for the importance of politics in the American future?

The answer is, I think, not too difficult. . . . Here are the basic facts. In the Gallup poll referred to above, only one family out of twenty made any political contribution in 1954. But Gallup also put this question: If asked, would you give five dollars to the party you prefer? Thirty-three per cent of the families—about 16,000,000—said "Yes." A little over half said "No," while some 13 per cent had no views. Now five dollars from 16,000,000 families equals $80,000,000 and even a fraction of that amount of new, untainted money would revolutionize American politics. Moreover, it is ridiculously defeatist to assume that the other 66 per cent of our families cannot be convinced of their proper obligations of good citizenship.

The problem, then, is how to convince millions of Americans of an obvious fact—that good citizenship requires political contributions by each individual to the party or candidates of his choice. Good citizenship requires this just as much as it requires contributions to one's church, one's community fund, the Red Cross or other causes. The weak at heart may tell us that even such an obvious truth cannot be quickly taught. That is nonsense.

Let's take a parallel though perhaps more difficult problem—the threatened European grain famine after World War II. The ravages of war and a severe drought had destroyed much of the European grain supply. Obviously millions of people were going to starve to death within six months. And almost everyone knew that nothing could be done about it. The only possible rescue was to get us to eat less wheat in America, and this seemed impossible because rationing controls could not be imposed in the short time available. But a few people were unresigned to failure. They assumed that the American people would respond to duty if they only knew what their duty was. So through a barrage of public service advertising, conducted by the Advertising Council, the people were informed. Early in 1946 a Gallup poll showed that almost nobody knew of the need to save grain. By April, 1946, almost nine out of ten Americans knew of the problem. And most of them were doing their duty. As a result our grain shipments reached unprecedented totals and reached them quickly. And not a single European died from famine that summer.

PUBLIC SERVICE ADVERTISING

The use of public service advertising is now so widespread that most of us forget it is a new and vitally useful social tool. In the past twelve years it has been an essential part of the savings bond program, has reduced traffic accidents, prevented forest fires, created blood banks for the armed services and aided a hundred other causes. In 1952 public service advertising told Americans over and over again of their duty to register and vote and helped set new records for registration and voting.

One does not have to be an Einstein to see how great a function public service advertising could perform in helping to build a new and decent foundation under our system of political finance. Through television, magazines, radio, newspapers, billboards, car cards, even match boxes, the average decent American could be reminded and reminded again of the importance of good government; of how good government depends on each citizen's supporting, as he can, the party or candidate of his choice. And by doing this we can gain the larger objective of giving public recognition to the fact that there should be no more noble calling in a free society than that of public life.

A complete, well-coordinated campaign of public service advertising can create proper citizen support for political campaigns. It can do so quickly. By doing so it can, as I have said, create the most important political reform of the century. What is needed to make this happen? What is needed to make it work? Nothing more than the support of decent citizens.

This country has in the Advertising Council a non-profit, non-partisan, public service group that annually administers $100,000,000 worth of public service advertising donated by American business. The Advertising Council could provide a practical means for conducting such an educational campaign. It can be a campaign to further good government by reminding every citizen of his duty to support the party and candidates of his choice.

For my part I hope it is done. For the common concern of this country, we must end the fantastic system under which we treat our politicians as unsavory characters while at the same time we charge them with preserving our very civilization.

50. *Can Government Be "Merchandised"?*

IN RECENT YEARS the public relations expert has come to be an important figure in the administration of major political campaigns; the techniques developed for business have been adapted to politics. What is the significance to American democracy of this development? Is it a practice to be first denounced and then regulated or allowed to develop freely? An answer to this and other related questions is reserved for the future, awaiting the accumulation of reliable data and the firming of public attitudes. Mr. Miller's discussion of certain recent instances of political merchandising is both interesting and enlightening and a contribution to public awareness of the new techniques.

A PROMINENT MEMBER of the "Dewey team" complained after the Governor's first eighteen-hour television show, in 1950, that it was disgraceful that the distinguished Governor of a great state (I think that's the way it goes) should have to appear in such a public-relations stunt. An advertising man who helped to arrange the "telethon" quoted Jimmy Durante in reply: "Dem's da conditions dat prevail."

Da conditions seem now to prevail even more, for public-relations men and their close relatives, advertising men, have moved into politics in a big way. Their activities, which hitherto have included tasks like creating memorable headgear for candidate Kefauver, devising such edifying slogans as "You never had it so good" and "The voluntary way is the American Way," and figuring out new places to print the

* William Lee Miller, *The Reporter*, IX (October 27, 1953), pp. 11-16. Reprinted with permission from *The Reporter*, 136 East 57th Street, New York 22, N.Y.

phrase "I Like Ike," have now come to include the planning of entire campaigns and even, most recently, the conduct of government.

Governor Dewey may owe an extraordinary debt to such professional public relations, for it is said that after his defeat in 1948 an exhaustive investigation of his public personality by an advertising agency led to the redesigning of his mustache. Whether it was this singular service or the hundred thousand votes he admitted the telethon had gained for him, something plainly ended whatever scruples he may have had about public relations in politics, for in 1952 he used all kinds of props and all kinds of twists and hammed it up on each new television production number his advertising agency worked out for him. His question-and-answer programs with prearranged questions from selected ordinary people, his comedy programs about "Harry's Haunted House," and his commentary programs on which he was Deeply Shocked each week at what the Democrats had done showed how thoroughly the distinguished Governor of a great state was willing to accept the admen's judgment as to the conditions that prevail.

SIMPLE, BASIC, DRAMATIC

A public-relations man may defend his new role in politics by saying that he just takes good political ideas that haven't gone across and makes them go across. The editor of *Tide*, an advertising and sales trade publication, remarked during the past campaign, ". . . advertising . . . demonstrated beyond question that it can sell a good idea as successfully as it can sell a good product."

But this statement omits the rather important fact that it can do the same for a *bad* idea. And advertising is not simply neutral as to whether the idea is good or bad, but has a bias within it. I don't mean whatever biases there may be in advertising men and agencies as a result of their relation to the business community and its politics. I mean the bias in the nature of advertising itself. It is this bias of which some public-relations men in politics seem most spectacularly unaware. They seem not to see that the media over which you say something and the devices by which you say it alter what you say.

The advertising man tells the politician to make the argument quick and simple, without any unpleasant complexities. ("VOICE: Mr. Eisenhower, what about the high cost of living? EISENHOWER: My wife, Mamie, worries about the same thing. I tell her it's our job to change that on November 4th.") He says the appeal must be basic and unmistakable. ("The farmer's farming every day, making money and that ain't hay. Clap! Clap! Don't let 'em take it away!")

Qualifications must be carefully subordinated to clear, positive, unequivocal promises. ("VOICE: Mr. Eisenhower, can you bring taxes down? EISENHOWER: Yes. We will work to cut billions in Washington spending, and bring your taxes down.") The opposition between the two parties must be made dramatic and absolute. ("They'll promise you the sky! They'll promise you the earth! But what's a Republican's promise worth?") Fearful and tragic events are to be associated with the Opposition. ("VOICE: General, the Democrats are telling me I never had it so good. EISENHOWER: Can that be true when America is billions in debt, when prices have doubled, when taxes break our backs, and we are still fighting in Korea? It is tragic. It is time for a change.") Familiar symbols of home and prestige must be associated with the client. ("The Democratic Party took apples off the streets and put apple pie on the table. Whenever history puts them to the test, Americans will always choose the best.") The advertiser tells the politician that examples should be memorable, whether or not they are illuminating or representative. ("VOICE: General, just how bad is waste in Washington? EISENHOWER: How bad? Recently, just one government bureau actually lost four hundred million dollars and not even the FBI can find it. It's *really* time for a change.")

Clem Whitaker, partner in the California advertising firm of Whitaker and Baxter, which conducted the American Medical Association's successful multi-million-dollar campaign to eliminate national health insurance ("socialized medicine") from the alternatives politically available to the American people, is one of the most outspoken of the new public-relations men in politics. Whitaker has drawn up an apparently definitive list of the grand strategies of political campaigns built on public-relations techniques: ". . . you can interest voters if you put on a fight. No matter what the fight, *fight for something*. . . . You may wonder if that is the only technique in campaigning. It isn't the only one. There are two. The average American also likes to be entertained. . . . He likes the movies and he likes fireworks and parades. So if you can't fight, put on a show!"

A public-relations man in politics may say he is only doing better what politicians have always done. But though the "old-style" politician often did oversimplify and sloganize and appeal to fear and greed, he does not seem to have done this quite so systematically or so effectively as the modern advertisers in politics. He did not have the dominating control of the sources of opinion that the modern national "mass media" advertiser can enjoy. And he had a restraining set of pressures on him to which some of the political advertising men do not seem to be subject; at least he had to pay some attention to facts. His campaigns may have lacked moxie, but he had to deal with interests of his constituents, which were real and which were independent of his manipulation. He could not, as a memorandum from one public-relations firm advised its agents to do, create situations of reality; he had to fit his actions to a reality that already existed. He could not engage in what public-relations man Edward L. Bernays has described as the "engineering of public consent"; he had to let the public engineer its own consent.

But Clem Whitaker has said that managing campaigns, now becoming "a mature, well-managed business, *founded on sound public relations principles*, and using every technique of modern-day advertising," is "no longer a hit-or-miss business, directed by broken-down politicians."

It's hard to see just how the public will be helped when a "broken-down" politician is rebuilt by Mr. Whitaker's 10,000,000 pieces of printed matter, 650 billboards, and 18,000 smaller posters.

And these new PR men themselves may not necessarily be an improvement over even the "broken-down" politicians. No politicians, for instance, could have the adman's freewheeling auxiliary relationship to politics, thinking up slogans at "brainstorm meetings" for clients with the money to pay for them. The politicians were potential public officials and as such had to shape their relationship to the public to some extent in accord with their ability to act as a part of a government. Many of them, in their quaint, broken-down way, have had a genuine interest in public policy. Occasionally one could even discern, in some of them, an honest conviction. They rarely approached the immaculate amorality of the political public-relations man who, admitting that his candidate did not know anything about anything said, "Let's consider this campaign clinically. After all, you don't criticize a brain surgeon's technique just because he operates on a criminal."

"PUBLIC SENTIMENT IS EVERYTHING"

The public-relations man tends to work backwards, from desired effect to technique to content. If present tendencies continue, we may get political campaigns tailored to fit the requirements of public relations and then government tailored to fit the requirements of the campaign.

Clem Whitaker has a consoling thought to offer on this score: ". . . . whatever technique we use, in the end we always come back to Lincoln's fundamental—public sentiment is everything. If sometimes we go to extremes to create that sentiment, we can recall that some of the greatest statesmen in American history went to extremes, too." Going to extremes has testimonials from top-brand-name statesmen, and never mind whether Mr. Whitaker's extremes are quite the same as Mr. Lincoln's.

It is a bit hard to tell at this distance just what Lincoln meant by his statement "public sentiment is everything," but it is clear what Whitaker, who quotes it fondly, means. He means that public sentiment is *everything.* Other facts of the political world, such as the structure of Congress, the size of armies, the location of oil, national beliefs that run deeper than the mood of the moment—these are not very important, and can easily be controlled by the proper manipulation of public sentiment.

Even a new character for a candidate can be created synthetically, by a nickname, a slogan, the right profile, or a redesigned mustache. Unfortunately for the public-relations man, however, the realities behind the illusions he builds sometimes do break through to spoil things. The candidate's character cannot always be entirely concealed by his public-relations man. This exasperates Mr. Whitaker: ". . . an automobile . . . can't object to your sales talk, and if you step on the starter, it usually runs. A candidate, on the other hand, can and does talk back —and can sometimes talk you out of an election, despite the best you can do in campaign headquarters."

Mr. Whitaker explains that public-relations campaigners like himself have a problem with a candidate's "willingness or unwillingness to hew to the line on the plan of strategy which has been worked out . . . his ability or inability to measure up to the character you give him by your carefully-prepared build-up." Apparently some old-fashioned candidates still want to hew to their own line rather than the adman's, and present to the public the character God gave them rather than that given by Mr. Whitaker's "carefully-prepared build-up."

IDEALS AND ALL THAT SORT OF THING

Some public-relations men in politics tend to substitute illusions of their own devising for existing facts. Then, too, they may hold the view of the public's role in politics exemplified by this statement of Leone Baxter, Mr. Whitaker's partner in "Campaigns, Inc.":

> It's because the public relations profession, and its allied professions, know something about presenting abstract ideas, in attractive form, to masses of people who are too occupied with their daily lives to think analytically on their own account, that the average man today is in a position to know more about the trends of human affairs than ever in history. . . . You are helping him to understand your clients and their problems, their ideals. You are helping him to be a better citizen.

The techniques by which some public-relations people help us to be better citizens now include the saturation radio-TV spot campaign, brought to the service of the nation in the [1952] Republican campaign. The plan for this operation, HOW TO INSURE AN EISENHOWER VICTORY IN NOVEMBER, listed these advantages of concentrating the spot announcements in the last three weeks: "(1) It gives maximum effectiveness of pentration and recall without becoming deadly to the listener and viewer; (2) it delivers the maximum just before the election; (3) it occurs at too late a date for effective Democratic rebuttal." (Since this memorandum makes the regrettable slip of calling the Democratic Party by its name, it must have been another agency which struck a blow for decency in government by deciding that Republican orators should henceforth call the Democratic Party the "Democrat" Party.) The spot-campaign people were concerned with higher things, a "special, all out effort to switch forty-nine counties in twelve states and with it the election to Eisenhower." When I asked the head of the advertising agency that handled the Democratic Party's account about this saturation spot campaign, he seemed worried only that I might think the Republicans had stolen a march on him. "We had the idea for a saturation spot campaign long before the Republicans," he protested, "but we couldn't get the money."

Another way the public is brought to understand the client's ideals is by hearing them whether it wants to or not. For example, the Republican advertisers are well satisfied that they made a net gain [in 1952] over the Democrats by purchasing the higher-priced time already allocated to top TV performers. A man who arranges such political programs explained it to me: "A viewer tunes in to see Arthur Godfrey, but in place of Godfrey there is our program, and since there *are no top programs opposite Godfrey* he has to come back to us!" Thus is the public "delivered" to be taught about trends in human affairs.

To one outside public relations and its allied professions, capturing, delivering, and saturating the public would appear to be rather the opposite of helping it to know human affairs and understand ideals. In a way it would seem that the better the public relations, the wider the gap between the public's emotional approval of the client and the public's rational understanding of the reasons *why* it approves of the client. The advertising man's habit and purpose is to go beneath the reason to build strong emotional attachments to what he is selling, by associating it with all good symbols, relevant or not. Thus, it seems from the pictures in the advertisements that toothpaste has not only brightened the young lady's teeth but also papered the walls, straightened the room, and introduced her to a smashingly handsome young man. The advertiser's victim automatically calls the toothpaste's name when she goes to the drugstore.

An advantage of such techniques to the candidate is that he can now do "scientifically" what politicians have always had to do in fumbling, uncertain ways. He can say something without saying it. His advertising can systematically create an impression that goes well beyond any direct claim he would make and have to stand by. The most striking example of such public relations is the treatment of the Korean War by the Republicans last year, and in particular Mr. Eisenhower's "I-will-go-to-Korea" speech. In millions of American homes, voters had a deep and emotional *impression* that Eisenhower would end the Korean War, but the Eisenhower forces could rightly say that they never directly made any such claim. It was a triumph of the manipulation of public sentiment.

If public sentiment continues to be manipulated in this way, the public may choose world policies simply because they are recommended by some telegenic personality who has a good-looking, cloth-coated wife, born on St. Patrick's Day, and a little dog named Checkers.

The public-relations man says these are the conditions that prevail, and we might as well accept them. But it is possible that the conditions are not quite that prevalent. In the 1952 campaign the Republicans were selling the public something which it very much wanted to "buy," a change and a hero. By evoking distaste in some quarters, the "Ike" advertising may even have helped the Opposition. In the face of the overwhelming odds, the significant evidence about public relations from the 1952 campaign may come from the other side, on which an unknown, running against the hero and against the tide, still managed to gain a respectably large vote. And he did that without a big public-relations ballyhoo.

The two most remarkable appearances of that campaign, an acceptance speech and a concession of defeat, were made without benefit of advertising. No format was tested at an agency, no gimmicks were devised for audience effect. There were no make-up men to arrange each eyebrow, no production men to supervise the camera angles, no charts to tell the audience when to laugh or cry. The words that were spoken were the speaker's and the feelings that he evoked were real and spontaneous, for there is no public relations that can take the place of the honest words of an honest man.

THE BIGGEST CLIENT

The Eisenhower movement, born and nurtured in the smooth new world of public relations, is the biggest client yet persuaded of the prevailing conditions. Not only from Governor Dewey and his team but also from the alert businessmen who flocked to the banner, the crusade came to understand how tough a "selling" job the Republicans had, and how useful modern "scientific" selling practices could be for such a tough job. During the primary campaign Senator Taft complained that some top executives, even against their own inclination, were supporting Eisenhower on the advice of their corporations' public-relations men. Of the convention at which Mr. Eisenhower was nominated, *Tide* wrote in its snappy, underlined newsletter: "The *Republican convention* next week will almost be *a convention of advertising and public relations men.* An amazing number are attending . . ." A group of public-relations men, called the "Eisenhower-Nixon Research Service," takes credit for the first big Eisenhower victory, for it gave the "Fair Play" amendment its felicitous name and planned the triumphantly successful build-up of public support of the Eisenhower side in that crucial convention fight.

During the campaign the same group chose, named, and pushed the "captive candidate" theme against Stevenson, but this was only one of many public-relations groups working for Eisenhower. Three advertising agencies had a hand in the campaign: the Kudner agency, which was originally given the Republican account; Batten, Barton, Durstine & Osborn, which joined the crusade early in September and came to handle all radio and TV for the General; and the Bates agency, one of whose executives thought up the much-debated saturation spot campaign.

But the Eisenhower movement did not stop its use of public-relations techniques on Election Day; the "conditions" apparently "prevail" not only for campaigns but also for governments. An article on "The GOP's 'PR'" in *The Wall Street Journal* late in February said: ". . . the Eisenhower forces already have a fair claim to the title of the most-public-relations-conscious-administration in history. . . . This heavier-than-ever accent on 'scientific' public relations techniques crops up all over the place. . . ."

The *Journal* story concentrated on the Eisenhower-Nixon Research Service, now renamed the Research Associates, and their proposal of a "carefully-calculated, Government-wide effort to cultivate the public" with methods which the *Journal* reporter said were "reminiscent of those employed by a private company . . ." The plan was presented in a "fascinating brochure . . . handsomely gotten up in a black loose-leaf notebook, with cellophane-covered pages, a gaudy lay-out, and the word 'Confidential' stamped on the front," which was reported to have found its way to the bedside table of the President and also to Vice-President Nixon and Postmaster General Summerfield.

A more recent story in *The Wall Street Journal* reported that "Eisenhower & Co. have opened a new sales department right in the White House. The new division of the Republican Administration is headed by a man President Eisenhower privately calls 'the greatest salesman in the world'—the Seattle mortgage banker, Walter Williams . . ." Mr. Williams, who is also Under Secretary of Commerce, will try in this new job "to 'sell' the President's policies to the public—and tout his achievements." As the *Journal* story observed. ". . . the Eisenhower forces, a lot of them former businessmen, simply believe in a little salesmanship.

JUST ONE BIG HAPPY FAMILY

This salesmanship was nowhere more evident than in the President's TV report in June to the people of the nation he governs. It was planned, rehearsed, and presented under the graciously donated professional supervision of B.B.D.&O.

Tide reports that Bernard C. Duffy, head of B.B.D.&O., said of the [1952] campaign that Republican strategy centered on merchandising Eisenhower's frankness, honesty, and integrity, his sincere and wholesome approach. The strategy by which the candidate was "merchandised" was used again in June to "merchandise" the President. B.B.D. &O.'s best techniques of television advertising were employed to bring the President and his Cabinet to the people, to tell them about how the roof was not leaking. It was as though, having created during the campaign the TV character Likeable Ike, his sponsors found it expedient to continue the installments of his adventures. *Advertising Agency* magazine quoted Mr. Duffy's satisfied comment: "One of our best shows."

This adman's "show" did not insist that the public make the hard and controversial decisions about world policy. Instead the implied view of the public was that of a docile, harmonious family, waiting to be told a few fascinating facts about its government by Likeable Ike and his swell friends. Government appeared as a merely technical and administrative matter: "What you're concerned about is that the house is in good order"—about which there is, of course, harmonious agreement. "Now, everybody helps to do that, everybody in the family." Yes, everything is being well handled by these dandy people we have in government: "Since government is just people, you have seen the kind of people that are trying to solve these things for you."

There was no suggestion that there might be at stake profound problems of value about which the public had to decide. Herb and George, and Mr. Benson, who was a farmer himself, and Mrs. Hobby, whose job was a woman's in the home, read their lines, sometimes going into detail about the problems selected for discussion, but the detail served more to show their seriousness and competence and perhaps the romance of government than to provide a genuinely illuminating discussion.

All through these edifying discourses ran the homey advertising gimmicks—the basket of mail from which "we get our ideas"; a letter from a lady in Pawtucket; 8 to 1 approval of the entire program; a chart showing Mr. Benson's travels; a mention of Derby, Kansas, and Limestone, Maine. The "points of interest" described so chattily were all assumed to be completely under control by the genial and efficient new managers of the business—"I'm going over to Bermuda to meet with some of our friends and talk over these things"; "Well, now, of course, George, we know we're going to stop this"—and the public can rest easy, assured that "We've done something and are now doing things to repair the holes in the roof and keep the fences mended." All that was left for the viewing public to do was to say, "How nice!"

Bill Tyler, who writes a column in *Advertising Agency* magazine called "Copy Clinic," had the following illuminating comment:

> Undoubtedly the most effective commercial of the month was the President's TV appearance around the first of June. . . . it closely followed the pattern of an agency new-business solicitation. The President let each department head, armed with slides, present the story of his branch of the business. Then he wrapped the whole thing up in a masterful manner and asked for the order. As a TV salesman, we think you will agree, Dwight Eisenhower has few peers. . . .

Members of the Eisenhower Administration themselves sometimes seem to conceive the relationship of the government to the people in advertising terms. *The Wall Street Journal* quoted this statement from a high official, which the President is said to endorse, explaining the new White House sales office: "We all suddenly realized we were busy manufacturing a product down here, but nobody was selling it." One of the President's top aides sent a memorandum to all government personnel who deal with foreign policy just before the President's important April 16 speech to the American Newspaper Publishers Association. The memorandum described an elaborate plan to publicize the speech around the world, and it called this promotion of a major address of the President of the United States "merchandising-in-depth."

The differences between selling a product in a market and choosing public policies in a democracy may not be immediately apparent to some advertising people. The consumer acts as an individual and can defend himself against high pressure and the gullibility of his neighbor —by consumer resistance or buying different products. But the citizen *must* live under the government that he helps to select, and it can make ultimate claims upon him. The political issue is the health and direction of the whole community, not just the satisfaction of an individual consumer's desire.

It remains to be seen how much the Eisenhower Administration will continue to "sell" its policies with carefully devised "new," "positive," and "dynamic" slogans, even though the policy may be old (our "dynamic" European foreign policy), negative (cutting the Air Force budget to get "more defense"), actually confused ("trade, not aid"), or nonexistent (the "liberation" of eastern Europe). At first the crusade seemed to have taken advertising techniques even into the formulation of national policy itself, as in the remarkable trust our new foreign affairs people had for a while in "psychological warfare." Somebody needed to explain to the new Administration that advertising and public relations had to be secondary to real political action. Apparently the committee headed by William Jackson did just that for the foreign-policy information field.

What we may now need is a similar criticism of the Eisenhower Administration's relations to the American people. It might say to the Republican Party that what is needed (if I may try my hand at a little sloganizing) is not a better selling job but a better doing job.

51. *The Battle of Athens, Tennessee* *

IN THIS ARTICLE Mr. White gives a vivid description of a rural political machine, how it operates and how it is unseated, in contrast to Rovere's "The Big Hello" (Selection 43), which provides a somewhat sympathetic view of an urban machine. In Athens, Tennessee, the more usual characteristic of machine politics is emphasized—a determined, unscrupulous, corrupt group keeping itself in control by violence if necessary. With the ballot boxes regularly stuffed with illegal ballots, the only means of removing the machine seemed to be by violence. The old residents of the county were loath to use force; but the returning G.I.s, accustomed to violence by their war experiences, overcame this reluctance, and thus unseated the old machine. It was fortunate, indeed, that it was the passion for democracy which unleashed the violence in an essentially revolutionary situation.

THE Sweetwater River, a pleasant mountain stream that falls into the basin of the Tennessee, cuts through McMinn County beneath a canopy of high tension wires. The people of McMinn County, like the taut, coppery wires, hum with subdued peaceful activity until they are disturbed; and then, like the wires, they snap in a shower of sparks and violence. It took several killings, ten years of extortion and thuggery, a world war and an official invasion by legal gunmen to bring on the violence of August 1, 1946, and the bloody siege of the Athens jail. But when it was over, democracy was firmly established and authority once again rested with the citizenry.

The people of McMinn County are God-fearing men and women. When the Robert E. Lee highway climbs out of the Shenandoah Valley, which can take its religion or leave it, into east Tennessee on the road to McMinn the highway is sprinkled with signboards telling the godless wayfarers that "Jesus is coming soon" or warning them "Prepare to Meet God." McMinn itself is relatively free of such shrieking witnesses to faith; McMinn's religion is Methodist and Baptist, quiet, bone-deep, and sober. On Saturday afternoon when farmers throng the town, preachers are allowed to call sinners to repentance in the shade of the courthouse at the county seat. But most of McMinn meets God in the serenity of Sunday morning at the red brick or white

* Theodore H. White, *Harper's Magazine*, 194 (January, 1947), pp. 54 ff. Reprinted by permission of Ann Watkins, Inc.

board house of worship in peace and devotion. The church-goers have made liquor illegal, and Sunday movies are unlawful, too.

Next to religion, politics is the most important thing. But until 1946, religion absorbed so much of the spirit of right-thinking people that politics fell automatically to the bad. First, it was the Republicans. They had McMinn County for years and years. The Republicans would let a Democrat get elected now and then, but the sheriff was theirs and they held tight to the county trustee who disbursed funds and issued poll-tax certificates. Then, from 1936, when Paul Cantrell won the election and established an eastern outpost of the Crump machine, it was ten years of Democrats.

Paul Cantrell, state senator from the McMinn area and boss of the county, was a medium-sized, bespectacled man of sallow complexion, a big head, and little neck. Cantrell loved two things: money and power. He had a nervous, fidgety way about him; he rarely looked directly at a man when he talked to him; towards the end, an armed deputy accompanied Cantrell as guard when he strolled through Athens, the county seat. Pat Mansfield, his sheriff, was a tall, handsome man from Georgia. Pat was kind to his family and gave money to his church. He might have been popular but many people resented the sour troop of plug-uglies he had recruited to be his deputy sheriffs. Pat did Cantrell's bidding.

The Cantrell forces were hard, well-connected people. Cantrell was allied with Burch Biggs in neighboring Polk County; the pair were tied tight to the Crump machine, and Crump ran all of Tennessee. They were so close to the Crump machine that George Woods, who represented McMinn in the state legislature, was speaker of the house in the legislature of the State of Tennessee.

The machine bossed the county with a rough hand. The sheriff had sixteen regular deputies and about twenty or thirty other men he would deputize in "emergencies." Three of the deputies had served penitentiary terms. One of them had been convicted of taking a little girl out and violating the age of consent. It wasn't rape, but then it wasn't good, either; and God-fearing people like those who farmed and worked in McMinn didn't like it. When the deputies arrested a man they often slugged him until he was sensible. Nobody talked back much in public because it wasn't safe. The deputies threatened to kill people they didn't like. They were brutal men, ready to beat, blackjack, or bully anyone. One GI who was home on leave during the war was shot and killed by a deputy at a public entertainment house near Athens; a sailor home on leave was killed at the other end of the county.

The gambling joints and bootleggers were all tied to the machine. They paid off the proper people and operated punchboards and slot machines, sold liquor, did as they pleased. As a matter of fact, if someone was in the pen the best way to get him out was to work through the small-time racketeers to get the machine to go easy.

The take from the bootleggers and gamblers wasn't the only source of revenue for the machine. The county was directed by fee-grabbers. A tourist comes riding down the highway; maybe he has a bottle of beer. The deputies arrest him and take him to court. In the court is a little man, called "the informer," who says he is a lawyer. He advises the tourist to plead guilty, pay his fine, and go his way. Sixteen dollars and a nickel. No one will ever know how many people paid their sixteen dollars and a nickel, over and over again, to support the sheriff and his deputies. The sheriff was paid five thousand dollars a year and expenses, but he got seventy-five cents a day for every man in jail that had to be fed. When a drunk was arrested, he was put back on the street next day with a clear head and an empty stomach, but the charge to the county was two days' food at seventy-five cents each. In ten years, county expenses for the sheriff's office had run to over three hundred thousand dollars. McMinn has an audit committee working on the books now.

There was nothing that could be done about it, because you couldn't vote the machine out of office. The machine had taken the county from the Republicans by a famous vote-grab in 1936; some people still tell how the last ballot box from a normally Republican precinct was fixed to show just enough lead to carry the county.

From then on, no matter how people voted, the machine counted the votes. In the key districts when the polls closed the deputies took the ballot boxes to jail, or another safe place, and counted them without any opposition watchers present. Then they would announce the results and always the Cantrell men won. There was nothing that could be done about that either. Appeal to the courts was useless; the Republicans tried that but no suit-at-law was ever won by the opposition.

Things had been that way for a long time when the war came, taking thirty-five hundred boys from McMinn homes and flinging them across the face of the earth. Folks kept writing to their sons about affairs in McMinn County; sometimes the boys would visit on furlough and then write to their friends in camps all around the world. There were four years to think about McMinn County, and Ralph Duggan, who was a lieutenant in the Navy, says he thought a lot more about McMinn County than he did about the Japs. Many were thinking as Ralph did

—that if democracy was good enough to put on the Germans and Japs, it was good enough for McMinn County, too. It got to be a saying in Athens: "Wait till the GI boys come home."

By spring of 1946, the GI boys were trickling back to McMinn from France and Germany and Italy and the Pacific. The people of McMinn say there is nothing but what some good doesn't come of it, and what happened afterwards in McMinn came from the war. The boys learned a lot about fighting and more about patriotism in the Army; when they came home they were ready to do something about democracy in Tennessee.

In February they set to planning. They met secretly because the Cantrell forces had the guns, the blackjacks, and the law; and the deputies could make life hell for anyone they could catch. Once in the summer campaign, they seized one boy, locked him up, took his poll-tax receipt from him, and then, threatening his life, made him sign a statement that no such incident had ever taken place. There were five GI's and one civilian in on the first secret meetings. They decided that in the summer election for sheriff and county officials the GI's would put up a complete slate of their own. Mansfield, Cantrell's sheriff, was going out of office and Cantrell was running for sheriff himself.

The veterans sounded out general feeling and in May they called a mass meeting. To get into the GI meeting you had to show your discharge papers, or your membership card in the American Legion or VFW. The veterans picked a non-partisan slate: three Democrats, two Republicans. Knox Henry, a tall handsome boy who had been hurt in North Africa and ran a filling station, was the man for sheriff. He was Republican, but the county trustee was to be Frank Carmichael, a farmer and a Democrat. Carmichael had been a major in the war and was badly wounded at Saint Lô. The other candidates were GI boys, too, except Charlie Pickel who had been in the first World War and had returned with his wounds to be a carpenter. Jim Buttram, a sturdy, solid chunk of combat infantryman, was to be campaign manager. Jim's family had a grocery store in Athens and Jim was new to politics.

With the slate chosen, the campaign picked up speed. Ralph Duggan, who had come back from the Navy to his law practice, was legal adviser and they pored over the Tennessee Code to see what the laws allowed them. The business men who feared the Cantrell forces contributed money secretly. They were afraid to give openly because the machine could raise the taxes, or arrest them, or generally make life hard. But eight thousand dollars came into the campaign fund and soon loudspeaker trucks were rolling over the hill roads, the *Daily Post-*

Athenian was carrying campaign ads, and the local radio station was putting out fifteen minutes of talk a day. Up and down the pockets and roads went GI's calling meetings in evenings at schoolhouses or homes, begging, urging, pleading with everyone to get out and vote. It wasn't hard to pin scandal on the Cantrell forces; McMinn County had lived with the scandal for almost ten years. Nothing had been done about it for two reasons: first, the only alternative was the old Republicans; and second, it did no good to vote because the Cantrells always counted themselves to victory anyway. So over and over, like the beating of a drum in the darkness, the GI campaign chanted its theme: "Your vote will be counted as cast, your vote will be counted as cast."

"Everybody knew we were trying to do the right thing," said Jim Buttram. "We had twelve public meetings and we knew they were damned good. About three weeks before elections we knew we had won the votes and the hearts of the people of McMinn County. But the hardest thing to do was to build an organization to help us see we got a fair count on election day."

The GI's asked the governor for help; but the governor was elected with Crump backing and was silent. They asked the Attorney General in Washington for help; he did nothing. They made contact with the FBI office in Knoxville; the FBI agent said he couldn't do anything unless Washington told him to, and Washington wasn't telling. The GI's were on their own.

II

Election day dawned sweet and clear over McMinn County. McMinn numbers twelve voting precincts but the decisive vote is cast in two townships, Etowah and Athens. Etowah is some ten miles in the hills from the main highway, but Athens, the county seat, is dead center. Athens sprawls fragrant and green about the old white courthouse; the Robert E. Lee hotel sits on one side, Woolworth's and a movie house on another, stores and offices on the other two sides. One block up from the courthouse lies the red brick county jail. Maple trees and green lawn surround the courthouse; old people sun themselves on the benches, children romp on the grass, blue-denimed farmers stroll casually about buying supplies for home and land.

Election day saw Athens an armed camp. As the voters came to the polls, they found the Cantrell machine in ominous demonstration of force. Almost two hundred armed deputies strutted about, pistols and blackjacks dangling from their belts, badges gleaming. The deputies were strangers. Mansfield claims he asked the governor for National

Guardsmen to help him, and the governor authorized him to get deputies where he could. The machine had turned up a sodden gang of plug-uglies, most of them from foreign counties, some from as far as Georgia. Fred Puett, the Chamber of Commerce secretary, said that they looked as though they were drugged; their eyes seemed as cold and arrogant and hard as those of a band of Nazis.

By the Tennessee Code of Law, each polling place must be staffed with watchers from both parties, and the GI's had chosen boys of the best families, with the best war records, to stand as their representatives at each place. As the polls opened in Etowah, one of the GI watchers asked to see the ballot box opened and demonstrated empty as required by law. "Hell, no," said one of the deputies; an argument sputtered, a highway patrolman was summoned and Evans, the GI poll watcher, was hauled off to jail.

At 9:30 trouble flickered in Athens; the machine charged Walter Ellis, a GI watcher, with an unspecified federal offense, took him from his appointed place at the polls and put him in jail, too. At three in the afternoon Tom Gillespie, a colored man, appeared at the eleventh precinct complete with poll-tax receipt. "You can't vote here," said the machine watchers.

"He can too," contradicted the GI spokesman.

"Get him," yelled one of the deputies and someone slugged Gillespie. Gillespie broke for the door and ran down the street. As he ran, a deputy at the door drew his pistol and shot him in the back. Gillespie was taken to the hospital. Fifteen minutes later, Bob Hairell, another GI watcher at the twelfth precinct, was in trouble. The machine wanted to vote a nineteen-year-old girl; Hairell objected. One of the deputies settled the argument by pulling his blackjack and laying Hairell's head open. Hairell was off to the hospital. The *Daily Post-Athenian* sent a reporter to get the story on Hairell. He, too, was slugged and told not to ask questions.

At four, the polls closed. In the eleventh precinct, the two GI watchers, Charles Scott, Jr. and Ed Vestal, were thrust to one side as the machine prepared to count the vote. Through the plate glass door of the polling place, the people could see the two boys penned in their corner of the large room. By this time, Jim Buttram, the campaign manager, had decided that the vote of the eleventh precinct wasn't worth trading off against the lives of two of his men. Twelve armed deputies had cleared the sidewalk in front of the eleventh precinct polling place, but hundreds of people stood on the opposite side. They watched Jim and Mr. Scott, father of Charles Scott, cross the street to speak to Mansfield, the sheriff.

Mansfield was sitting in a red 1946 Dodge. There were six men in the car. Buttram offered to give him the precinct in return for the release of the watchers.

"Are you trying to tell me how to run this election?" asked Mansfield. "You go over and get them yourself if you want them."

"You wouldn't want me to get shot, would you?" said Jim. A deputy sitting beside Mansfield lifted his thirty-eight from his lap and said: "Buttram, I ought to shoot you right now, you're the son-of-a-bitch who started the whole thing."

Mansfield knocked Moses' gun down and told him to shut up, he was doing the talking.

Mr. Scott leaned over and said: "If you won't let my boy out of there and anything happens to him, you'll have to pay for it."

Pat grabbed his gun, snarled, "Let's settle this right now," and started to open the door of the car. Buttram slammed the door on him, and he and Scott hastily made their way back to the cover of the crowd.

A few minutes later Neal Ensminger, the editor of the local paper, strode over to the precinct door to see if he could get a tabulated count. As he asked one of the deputies a question, the two GI's in the polling place broke for safety. With his shoulder down, young Scott burst the door and pounded out, followed in a moment by Vestal. Bleeding, they ran across the street to the crowd as the deputies trained their guns on the boys. By this time women were screaming, children were crying, and the veterans—still unarmed—stood cursing and shouting from the opposing pavement. The deputies held their fire as the two boys slipped among the people.

It was five now, and following their practice the Cantrell forces removed the ballot boxes of the eleventh and twelfth precincts to the security of the jail for counting.

III

The GI's had promised to get the vote counted as cast, and they gathered at their campaign headquarters around the corner to confer. As they stood in the street, two Mansfield deputies approached to break up the group. Otto Kennedy was watching from his tire store as the deputies walked up the street. With Otto was his brother Oley Kennedy, just out of the Navy, and his brother J. P. "Bull" Kennedy, just out of the Army.

"Pat Mansfield said he was going to give us a fair and square election," said Kennedy, "and then we saw those sons-of-bitches from Georgia, walking around with their guns and badges, telling us to kiss their neck. They'd put our boys in jail, they were running all over us.

I stepped up to the door. I saw them coming. I just couldn't take it. I said to my brother: 'Bull, let's get them.' "

As the deputies stepped into the crowd, the GI's closed about them. They hit hard and high and low. The guns were taken and distributed among the GI's. Three more deputies, then two more walked into the crowd. All were disarmed and the guns handed out. The deputies were loaded on cars, taken to the woods, stripped of their clothes, and left to walk their way out.

The GI's were still indecisive and the Kennedys became cautious. They had struck the first blow; they were vulnerable. Otto decided to go home, telling the veterans that if they decided to do anything the Kennedys were ready to come back; otherwise they were staying away. Dusk was settling and the vets talked. A city policeman walked by to say that Mansfield was coming with tommy-guns and tear gas. Then something happened.

From dusk to dawn, the story of the siege of Athens dissolves into anonymity. The people had voted the GI ticket, trusting the GI guarantee of a fair count. Five districts which had been fairly tabulated by evening had already given the GI's almost a three-to-one lead. But the ballot boxes of the eleventh and twelfth precincts were being counted in the jail. Tomorrow the Cantrell forces would have victory and no one would be safe. On the one hand, the Common Law says that every citizen has the right to prevent a crime or felony from taking place; on the other hand, to take the jail by storm against the lawfully deputized thugs seemed perilously close to insurrection. A very fine point of law is involved and Crump still runs Tennessee. Therefore, no man knows or tells who played precisely what role in Athens on the night of Thursday, August 1, 1946.

Down the highway from Athens is one of the armories of the National Guard. By eight o'clock rifles and machine guns were held by dozens of the veterans. It was a quiet movement. There was no raving or shouting. They collected at their headquarters and gravely, under cover of darkness, walked the two blocks to the jail where the sheriffs had taken the ballot boxes. Behind the jail is a barbed wire enclosure. Facing it, across the street, is a low hill covered with vines and several houses and buildings. The deputies had made a mistake that the battle-wise GI's recognized immediately: they had concentrated forty or fifty of their number in jail and left no reserves in town. The GI's deployed in the darkness in a semicircle above the jail, on the hill behind the cover of vines, on rooftops. A veteran strode into the street and yelled at the silent jail a demand for the ballot boxes and the release of the GI prisoners.

A voice answered, "Are you the law?"

The GI yelled back, "There isn't any law in McMinn County."

A lone shot went off from within the jail. The man that answered from the hill answered with a tommy-gun.

There were several hundred veterans in the semicircle and hundreds of boys and civilians. Some had rifles, a few had tommy-guns, others had bird guns and hunting pieces. The fusillade rose and fell above the night, echoing into the suburbs and hills. Bullets spattered the Chamber of Commerce and the newspaper office a block away. A block down the road, a man standing on the corner of the courthouse square was nicked in the arm.

The local radio station had sent a reporter with a microphone to cover the action; up and down the county farmers tuned in to the running account. Some of them put their clothes on, got their guns, came to join in the shoot. Boys too young to cock a rifle came down to see the fun and remained to learn how to shoot in the night.

The deputies were safe behind the thick brick wall of the jail, and the bullets of the GI's could do no more than cut out chunks of the wall. As the sporadic shooting dragged on hour after hour, the veterans realized with a sick feeling that night was wearing away and, with daylight, state patrolmen—perhaps even the National Guard—might be called in to reinforce the garrison of deputies. Defeat would mean that McMinn County would never be safe again for any man who had taken part in the night's firing. It was go through with it, or get out of town.

At midnight a detachment went over to the county farm where a case of dynamite was located. During a lull, the veterans yelled that unless the ballot boxes and prisoners were released in twenty minutes they would blast the jail. An hour went by and the jail made no answer. Somebody fitted a cap to a stick of dynamite and tossed it into the street. A second stick followed. On the third throw, two sticks were tied together and thrown across to the sidewalk of the jail. The fourth throw of two sticks landed on the porch of the jail and tore it wide apart. Somebody had learned about demolition in the war; for the last try they decided to prepare a homemade satchel charge of the rest of the case and place it under the jail wall. But before the charge could be placed, the jail was yelling surrender. It was 3:30 in the morning.

"We're dying in here," came a call. "Don't use any more dynamite, we're giving up."

No one was dying. Four of the deputies were pretty badly hurt and required hospitalization; ten of the GI's were wounded in the day's action but the war was over.

The vets ordered the deputies to march into the courtyard with their hands up, leaving their guns behind. As they marched out, the crowd gathered round, yelling, cursing, and booing. Someone in the crowd reached out with a razor and slashed at one of the deputies, laying his throat open. Duggan tried to stop the man; the man explained that that deputy had arrested him before, taken him to jail and kicked in four of his ribs. Duggan tried to reason with him, but he made another razor pass. Then Duggan slugged him into obedience and led the deputy off to the hospital. Behind them a file of deputies, guarded by GI's, paraded through the street to the courthouse and back so that the people might see and taunt their unthroned impotence.

By this time dawn was lighting the county and the radio station, broadcasting the victory, was bringing farmers in from all the hills to see what was happening. The state capital had been alerted and the State Commissioner of Public Safety, Lynn Bomar, called up to locate a GI to negotiate. Ralph Duggan answered the phone and spoke to George Woods at the state capital. Woods, who was Election Commissioner of the county, promised—if given a safe conduct—to return to Athens on Monday and certify the election of the entire GI slate. Duggan announced the victory to the crowd at six in the morning and then went home.

Violence flickered on for several more hours. The GI's had had their fill, but the civilians and boys were carrying on. They smashed in windows of the deputies' automobiles, turned them over, burned cars indiscriminately. It was the GI's now who had to restrain the civilians and protect their prisoners. By ten o'clock, however, the fury had spent itself and the GI's were carefully escorting their prisoners out of town. At three, a giant mass meeting was held in the courthouse, men jamming the assembly hall, overflowing onto the steps and the lawn. The Reverend Bernie Hampton read the twenty-third psalm and asked the body of citizens what their will was. Someone suggested the appointment of a three-man committee to administer the county till things settled down. The three-man committee was elected immediately and from Friday to Monday it conducted the county's affairs on a volunteer basis.

It summoned the county court—the local legislative body—to a meeting on Monday morning. The county court declared vacant the offices held by machine contestants in the elections and declared the GI slate duly elected. Six of the twelve precincts' votes were thrown out entirely, for no fair count had been given there. When the GI's broke into jail they found that some of the tally sheets marked by the machine had been scored fifteen to one for the Cantrell forces. Where the GI's witnessed the count, the margin was three to one GI. Thus it was decided that only in those precincts where both parties had watched should the count be accepted. By Monday afternoon, Knox Henry was sheriff of McMinn County and the law was safe.

IV

McMinn is quiet and peaceful again. The courthouse has been painted for the first time in years, and the big clock has been fixed so that it strikes the hours loud, clear, and free over the entire town. The jail has been repaired but it is curiously empty. Within a month Henry was running McMinn County with eight youthful GI deputies. Saturday night no longer filled the cells with fifty or sixty men waiting to be fined; by the end of the month, Saturday night found only three men in jail. The four city policemen had been fired and replaced by veterans. Pat Mansfield was back in Georgia, working as a fireman on a railway. Paul Cantrell was in Nashville and didn't want to come back.

The gambling joints have been closed down, the bootlegging ring has been smashed, fee-grabbing ended. There are no more slot machines or punchboards. Henry has pledged the new regime that the sheriff will live on his lawful salary.

The GI party, too, has been disbanded, but a Good Government League has succeeded it. The Good Government League has branches in fifteen different communities of the county and is the public whip. The county court still has a majority of old Cantrell men, but they don't come up for election till next summer. Meanwhile the Good Government League suggests various actions to it, and the court pays heed.

The first thing the county court was persuaded to do was to establish an audit committee. The Good Government League wants to see what resources are available for the two most pressing local problems: schools and roads. Schools are pretty bad in McMinn. Pay for teachers is so poor that all the best teachers are leaving. In some places in McMinn, teachers get eighty-five dollars a month for the eight months they work; that averages less than fifteen dollars a week, year-round, as take-home pay. Even a waitress at the hotel makes more than that. Highest pay is at the high school and that comes to only thirty dollars a week for a teacher with a master's degree. The Good Government League wants to divert money from the sheriff's heavy budget to the education budget. When the schools and school buses are fixed, they want to do something about the roads. Maybe after that the League will move on to such long-range plans as a permanent county-manager system and a new structure of government.

The GI's like McMinn and they think they can keep it healthy. There will always be bootlegging unless the church people let the county make liquor legal. But now the government will be master of the bootleggers instead of the bootleggers masters of the government. The GI's say they aren't interested in "issues"; they aren't interested in unions or poll-tax laws or running the country. This was a McMinn matter, strictly a battle to give McMinn fair and square elections and force Boss Crump back to Shelby County.

It is true, of course, that Crump still runs the rest of Tennessee and that Crump helped send back to Washington a man named Kenneth McKellar. And until November 1946, McKellar was president of the Senate of the United States of America, called the greatest deliberative body in the world.

IX

CONGRESS

52. *Can a Congressman Serve 900,000 People?* *

AFTER EACH CENSUS Congress—and the rest of us for that matter—ponders the question: How big ought a legislature to be? It is obvious that the more individuals a Congressman represents the more tenuous becomes the relationship between Congressman and constituent. Yet it is obvious that if each Congressman were to represent only a few thousand people the size of the House of Representatives would be increased beyond all bounds of effective action. Congressman Celler indicates approval of retaining the present size of the House, but he thinks that Congress could eliminate some of the time-consuming activities in which it engages, leaving more time for its important legislative and representative functions.

ONCE again the size of the House of Representatives is up for consideration by Congress—as it has been every ten years since the First Congress met in New York City in 1789. This is because, under our Constitution and the laws made to carry out its provisions, House seats must be reapportioned among the states every ten years to reflect population shifts shown by the decennial census. Inevitably, unless the House is enlarged, some states stand to lose one or more seats; and, inevitably, those states wage a battle to maintain their representation by providing more seats.

The President, in a special message to Congress on Jan. 8, listed seven states which will gain and nine states which will lose, a total of fourteen House seats, as a result of gains or losses in population, actual

* Emanuel Celler, *The New York Times Magazine*, March 11, 1951, pp. 13, 29-30. Reprinted by permission of the author and the publisher.

or relative, between 1940 and the census of 1950. Notice of these changes has now been transmitted to the states affected. They will take effect automatically with the Congress to be elected next year—unless the present Congress takes affirmative action to raise the ceiling on the size of the House that has stood at 435 seats since 1911.

Already states which stand to lose seats are vigorously agitating for a larger House to preserve their present numerical representation, and bills have been introduced in Congress to achieve that end. One proposal would reduce the individual losses and increase the compensating gains by enlarging the House to 450 members. Another would save the seats of all present members and reward the faster-growing states by adding seventy-four seats to make a total of 509.

Well, how big *should* the House be?

Any answer entails a choice—or compromise—between conflicting answers to two more basic questions: How many people can a Representative really represent? How large can a national Legislature become before it becomes too unwieldy to get its work done?

• • • • •

For specific suggestions as to the practical range within which a compromise might be worked out we can look to our own history and to the varying choices that have been made by other democracies of the world.

The Constitution set the size of the House temporarily at sixty-five seats and provided that thereafter "the number of Representatives shall not exceed one for every thirty thousand" people. The Second Congress, accepting that figure as an approximate maximum as well as a strict minimum on the population of any Congressional district, increased the membership of the House following the first census in 1790, to 106: one for every 33,000 of population.

Through 1910, as the country grew and new states were admitted to the Union, the House was enlarged every ten years (except in 1840, when a mathematical peculiarity resulted in reducing the number of seats despite an increase in population). Even so, the average member's constituents grew to 210,000.

Since then the country has grown another 60 per cent, but the House has remained at the statutory limit of 435 set forty years ago. With the population now standing at 150,687,361, according to last year's census, the average House member represents almost 350,000 people, and because of inequities within the states the actual population of single districts ranges up to more than 900,000. At the 1790 ratio, the House today would have some 4,560 members.

In a dozen other countries with democratic governments and two-house national legislatures the figures run like this:

	Membership of legislative assembly	Average constitu-ency
Australia	121	66,000
Belgium	202	42,000
Britain	625	81,000
Canada	262	52,000
France	619	66,000
India	500	684,000
Israel	120	11,000
Italy	574	80,000
Mexico	147	166,000
Netherlands	100	100,000
Sweden	230	30,000
Switzerland	194	24,000

Two generalizations stand out: In all but four of those countries the membership of the so-called "lower house" of the national legislature is smaller than ours. But in all except one—gigantic India—each member represents far fewer people.

• • • • •

The argument for enlarging Congress starts with the obvious fact that the House—which the Founding Fathers held should be close to the people—has not grown up with the country. A hundred and sixty years ago a Congressman could actually maintain a personal relationship with a good portion of his constituents. Plainly, a Congressman today cannot maintain that same intimate relationship with a constituency that has grown tenfold. The Congressman, according to those who favor enlarging the House, has become less and less accessible to the people who elected him and less and less responsive to their interests.

Besides having more people to represent, it is argued, the Congressman is further impeded in the opportunity to consult them by the increased burden of his work, which has grown even faster than the number of his constituents. In the First Congress, a century and a half ago, 142 bills were introduced in the House; for an average Congress of the last ten years the flood of bills has risen to more than 5,000. Laws finally passed in a session have gone up at least ten times.

Moreover, bills today are frequently technical and extremely complicated in their economic ramifications. More and more time must be spent studying them in committee as well as threshing out complex issues on the floor. The length of annual meetings has more than doubled from four or five months to almost continuous sessions during the crisis-ridden past decade. The time available for grass-roots refreshment and home-town contacts has steadily lessened almost to the vanishing point.

At the same time, the demands of individuals for special services and of pressure groups for immediate decisions on pending issues have been intensified immeasurably. One member of the House testified before a Congressional reorganization committee a few years ago that his work as Washington errand boy for the folks back home was consuming up to 80 per cent of his time. A Congressman's mail may run from 200 letters a day up to 1,000 when some critical issue is being debated. A member who kept track of telephone calls to his office for a week reported an average of eighty-two a day. Another counted forty-eight callers who sought interviews with him in a single day—forty-six of them on matters not even related to legislation!

Several years ago Representative Luther Patrick of Alabama made a speech in the House that still stands as only a slightly exaggerated listing of some of a Congressman's extra-Constitutional duties:

> A Congressman [said Representative Patrick] has become an expanded messenger boy, an employment agency, getter-out of the Navy, Army, Marines; ward heeler, wound healer, trouble shooter, law explainer, bill finder, issue translator, resolution interpreter, controversy oil pourer, glad-hand extender, business promoter, convention goer, civil ills' skirmisher, veterans' affairs adjuster, ex-serviceman's champion, watchdog for the underdog, sympathizer with the upper dog, namer and kisser of babies, recoverer of lost baggage, soberer of delegates, adjuster of traffic violators, voters straying into Washington and into the toils of the law; binder up of broken hearts, financial wet nurse, good samaritan, contributor to good causes—there are so many good causes—cornerstone layer, public building and bridge dedicator, ship christener. To be sure, he does get in a little flag waving—and a little Constitution hoisting and spread-eagle work, but it is getting harder every day to find time to properly study legislation—the very business we are primarily here to discharge and that must be done above all things.

In an effort to keep in touch with the people of their districts, and to fulfill their reciprocal responsibility for informing public opinion, Congressmen conduct postcard surveys, subscribe to scores of community newspapers, provide letters from Washington free to local editors. They mail out copies of their speeches and Government documents by the bushel. Many maintain offices in their home districts to which constituents who can't get to Washington may bring their complaints, suggestions and requests for assistance.

Indeed, the cartoon of the old-fashioned Congressman enjoying his leisure in Washington, or on his front porch back home, is today a myth. This I can vouch for on the basis of twenty-eight years in Congress. The average Representative is a hard worker. He puts in long hours under severe tension. His responsibilities—and, more, his chores—weigh upon him. His arduous tasks make him a poor insurance risk.

• • • • •

The argument against enlarging Congress also starts with the obvious: that the House would have to be expanded beyond all reasonable bounds to restore the intimate contact with his constituents which each member enjoyed in the early years of the republic.

But even in its present size the House is generally considered by its more experienced members to be too unwieldy, and it has been criticized for lack of orderliness. Those criticisms were cited when the present ceiling was adopted and when a proposal to add thirty-five seats was defeated following the census of 1920.

If the habit of enlarging the membership with each ten-year increase in population were resumed, where would the trend ever end? Imagine, if you can, the effect on the expedition of important business of seventy-four more members—and perhaps another seventy-four after 1960—making speeches for the record to impress the folks back home. Or, contrariwise, the increased frustration of an individual member striving to make his voice heard on the determination of a critical issue.

The British and French Parliaments are sometimes cited as horrible examples of what might be in store for us. In the House of Commons, with its 625 members, many on the back benches (when they can get seats at all) must endure enforced silence during the sessions; because of their great number they cannot effectively participate in debate. Similarly, the very size of the French National Assembly (formerly Chamber of Deputies), with its 619 members, diminishes the value and power of each member. The equivalent of our Speaker in the French lower house does not use a gavel to keep order. He has a huge bell. The great number of members makes it difficult to quell disorder. If the continued ringing of the bell fails to stop the tumult, the presiding officer puts on his hat as a warning that, if the turbulence continues, he will leave the chamber. If after these warnings order is not restored, he clamps on his hat, strides out of the chamber in high dudgeon and calls it a day.

Already the House of Representatives must rigidly curb debate, in comparison to the opportunity for full discussion allowed in the Senate, with its ninety-six members. Sometimes even members of the House committee handling a bill do not have sufficient time to discuss the issues as thoroughly as might be desirable. Often freshmen Congressmen receive no opportunity to speak on bills of great interest.

To the question of the proper size for an efficient legislative assembly, Winston Churchill offered one expert's answer—an arbitrary one, to be sure—in arguing against enlarging the chamber of the bombed-out House of Commons when it was rebuilt after the war. To preserve the intimacy and conversational form of debate conducive to carefully deliberated yet expeditious action, he urged, successfully, that the chamber be held to its pre-war accommodations for only 437 of its 625 members. Perhaps it is worth noting that our lower House comes remarkably close to that figure at its present size of 435.

• • • • •

Is it true, moreover, that increased pressure of work has made the Congressman less accessible to the people who elected him and less responsive to their interests? And, admitting the pressure, does an increase in the number of members offer the only—or even the best—means of alleviating it?

Few public officials and certainly few private business executives are, in my opinion, more accessible or more responsive to the people than the members of the House of Representatives. Most Congressmen still manage, somehow, to keep their office doors open to any importunate constituent or visiting fireman who chooses to walk in. No Congressman who wants to stay in office ignores letters from his voters. Few fail to follow the editorial pages of the influential newspapers of their districts.

Faster means of travel and communication makes it easier for a Congressman to keep in touch with his district than it was in 1790. Administrative assistants, increased clerical staffs and the resources of the Legislative Reference Service of the Library of Congress have made it possible for conscientious members to avoid becoming engulfed by the detailed demands of their offices.

Additional possibilities for relieving the burden—more practical, it seems to me, than enlarging the membership of the House—have been suggested: elimination of the private calendar of bills for the payment of small claims against the Government, which could be handled by administrative agencies; home rule for Washington, D. C., which is now governed directly by Congress; electric voting machines in the House, which could tabulate a roll-call in a few seconds instead of half an hour; fewer and smaller committees; delegation of minor law-making authority to administrative agencies and regional authorities; delegation of some Congressional investigative missions to *ad hoc* public committees such as the new Nimitz commission on security and civil liberties.

A more drastic solution was proposed by Representative Robert Ramspeck of Georgia on the eve of his retirement from Congress in 1946. He suggested splitting the Congressman's job into two parts: the legislative part, to be handled by elected representatives in Congress; the administrative, or errand-running, part by elected representatives before the executive branch of the Government. The House of Representatives, under the Ramspeck plan, would have been reduced to half its present size, and its members would have been prohibited by law from contacting the executive branch except in regard to legislation.

• • • • •

There was, and is, no realistic possibility of any such plan being adopted—as Mr. Ramspeck himself knew best, after seventeen years in Congress. The thought behind it, however, is pertinent today to the decennial discussion of the size of the House of Representatives.

That part of the Congressman's job which has become most burdensome with the increasing size of his constituency, and the only part of it which enlargement of the House might somewhat reduce by distributing it among more members, is his job as Washington lobbyist for the special political, economic, social and cultural interests of the individuals in his district. His primary job, which is to participate in the shaping of wise policies and the writing of sound laws for the general welfare of the nation, could only be impeded by enlarging the House to still more unwieldy proportions.

The question—Should the House be enlarged?—comes down, then, to this basic issue: Whether the Congress shall be organized as a lobby serving a diversity of local interests or as an efficient national legislature, placing the good of the whole country above favoritism to any of its parts. If this issue is seen clearly by the American people, and by their representatives in Congress, there can be no doubt of the choice that will be made.

53. *Excerpts from a Filibuster* *

THE LIBERTY of unlimited debate in the Senate has been abused by filibustering tactics from time to time. The closure rule, adopted in 1917, has not been effective in putting an end to the efforts of Senators to talk bills to death. Various amendments to the closure rule, all designed to end the practice of filibustering, have since been introduced in Congress but without success. It may be doubted, moreover, that the end of this dilatory tactic is likely in the near future. That filibustering may descend to the level of cheap vaudeville is only too evident in this extract from the one-man filibuster of the late Senator Huey P. Long.

• • • • •

MR. LONG resumed his speech. After having spoken for about 5 hours, he yielded to MR. THOMAS of Oklahoma, and the following debate ensued:

MR. THOMAS of Oklahoma. Mr. President, will the Senator yield?

MR. LONG. I yield.

MR. THOMAS of Oklahoma. I suggest the absence of a quorum.

MR. HARRISON. Mr. President, I did not understand the request.

MR. THOMAS of Oklahoma. I suggested the absence of a quorum.

MR. HARRISON. Of course, I do not want to interfere with the speech of the Senator from Louisiana, but I will have to insist upon the rules with reference to the speech, that no Senator shall be permitted to speak more than twice in one day on the same subject matter.

MR. LONG. Mr. President, that gives me another speech after this one.

MR. HARRISON. I do not raise the point of order. I am just stating the rule of the Senate in respect to that matter.

MR. LONG. It has never been the rule of the Senate that a quorum call shall be interpreted as bringing a speech to a conclusion, as I understand. That has never been the rule of the Senate. If the Senator invokes such a rule he invokes something which has never been done before.

MR. GORE. Mr. President, a parliamentary inquiry.

THE PRESIDING OFFICER. The Senator will state it.

* Delivered by Senator Huey P. Long, who was speaking against the National Recovery Act (N.R.A.) on June 12, 1935. Reprinted from *Congressional Record*, Vol. 79, Part 8 (Washington, D.C., United States Government Printing Office, 1935), pp. 9090-9091, 9122-9124, 9129-9130.

MR. GORE. Cannot the Senator from Louisiana yield for the purpose of a quorum call without losing his status?

THE PRESIDING OFFICER. Under the rules of the Senate he can yield.

MR. GORE. For the purpose of another Senator raising a point of no quorum?

THE PRESIDING OFFICER. Yes.

MR. HARRISON. Mr. President, a parliamentary inquiry.

THE PRESIDING OFFICER. The Senator will state it.

MR. HARRISON. If the Senator yields for a point of no quorum to be made, does the Chair rule that he can continue his speech under the rule of the Senate that no Senator can speak more than twice on the same subject matter on the same day?

THE VICE PRESIDENT. Is there a parliamentary question before the Senate?

MR. HARRISON. I made a parliamentary inquiry, Mr. President.

THE VICE PRESIDENT. The Senator will state it.

MR. HARRISON. The inquiry is, If the Senator yields for the point of no quorum to be made, will that be construed, under the rules of the Senate, as not coming under the rule which provides that a Senator cannot speak more than twice on the same subject in the same day?

THE VICE PRESIDENT. Under the practice of the Senate a Senator yielding for the purpose of giving another Senator an opportunity of raising the point of no quorum does not yield the floor. That is the universal practice of the Senate.

MR. HARRISON. What if he should yield twice?

THE VICE PRESIDENT. It does not terminate his speech.

MR. LONG. Very well.

THE VICE PRESIDFNT. That is the practice of the Senate. The Chair is so advised by the parliamentary clerk, who has been here longer than has the Chair. The clerk will call the roll.

MR. CLARK. Mr. President, what business has been transacted since the last quorum call?

THE VICE PRESIDENT. There has been none, so far as the Chair knows.

MR. LONG. Mr. President, the Senate refused to table the motion of the Senator from Oklahoma. That question has been voted on.

THE VICE PRESIDENT. That was done before the Senator from Louisiana took the floor.

MR. CLARK. That roll call, Mr. President, developed the quorum.

MR. LONG. There has been business transacted since the last quorum call.

MR. CLARK. I make the point of order that there has been no business since the last quorum call.

MR. LONG. Mr. President, there has been plenty of business transacted since the last quorum call.

THE VICE PRESIDENT. The Chair is advised that the Senate voted on a motion, and the vote on that motion developed a quorum, and under the practice of the Senate that does not count as a quorum call.

The clerk will call the roll.

• • • • •

MR. LONG. . . . I have spent a number of evenings acquainting people with how to prepare oysters. I had a bucket of oysters sent to me from Louisiana the other night, and I was asked by a very fine bunch of my friends if I would not drop around with the New Orleans oysters and fry some of them for them in good Louisiana style and way. So, Mr. President, I bought a frying pan about 8 inches deep. I bought the frying pan because I was afraid they would not have a frying pan there in which I could fry the oysters. I bought a frying pan, as I said, 8 inches deep and about 17 inches in diameter.

MR. TYDINGS. Mr. President, will the Senator yield?

MR. LONG. I yield.

MR. TYDINGS. When the Senator fries oysters, is potlikker one of the concomitants?

MR. LONG. No; that does not go in with the oysters. I will come to that later. I am coming to that because I am going to have my remarks taken down and a copy made and sent out to the several places where I was supposed to go this evening in order that these recipes and directions may be had by those people, and I will ask the stenographer that as soon as possible he give me at least seven extra copies of these recipes which I dictate into the RECORD so that I may have them for ready circulation in case we do not have an early adjournment.

As I was going to illustrate, Mr. President, about these oysters that I got from New Orleans. I bought this frying pan 8 inches deep and 14 to 16 inches or 17 inches in diameter, and I bought a 10-pound bucket of cottonseed-oil lard, but I forgot to get a strainer, and when I got to the place to fry the oysters I had everything there except the meal and the strainer.

The lady had some meal, but she did not have any salt to salt the meal with, and that was the only bad thing about it. The strainer which they had was not the best strainer in the world, but I could use it all right. However, they had no salt for the meal, but I took the oysters, Mr. President, the way they should be taken, and laid them out on a muslin cloth, about 12 of them, and then you pull the cloth over and you dry the oysters. You dry them, you see, first with a muslin cloth, and then you take the oysters, after they have been dried, and you roll them into a meal which is salted. I did not have it salted this night, but it should have been salted. [Laughter in the galleries.]

Mr. President, you roll these oysters in the dry meal. You do not want to cook the meal or put water in the meal at any time or anything like that. Just salt the meal and roll the oysters in it. Then, let the grease get boiling hot. You want the grease about 6 inches deep. Then you take the oysters and you place the oysters in the strainer, and you put the strainer in the grease, full depth down to the bottom. Then, you fry those oysters in boiling grease until they turn a gold-copper color and rise to the top, and then, you take them out and let them cool just a little bit before you eat them.

Now, Mr. President, most people cannot tell when an oyster is done. They do not know when it has been fried enough. You wrongfully put them on the bottom of a skillet. You have got to have them totally submerged and you wait until they rise to the top, and when they rise to the top, a golden-copper color, then the oyster is cooked just exactly right, and then you take the strainer up out of the grease in the dish and the oysters are there and you let them drip for a little while and allow them to cool a little and then you eat them.

MR. TYDINGS. Mr. President—

THE PRESIDING OFFICER. Does the Senator from Louisiana yield to the Senator from Maryland?

MR. LONG. I yield.

MR. TYDINGS. Does the Senator realize when he describes how these oysters are cooked and how appetizing they seem to be, that those of us who are listening are being inhumanly punished? [Laughter.]

MR. LONG. I had forgotten that. I was trying to make the Senator from Mississippi [MR. HARRISON] hungry, but he was raised in a part of the country where they do not understand the science of eating anyway. He has left the Chamber. I am afraid I made him hungry.

That is the way to cook oysters. If every Member of the Senate will clip out of the Record tomorrow what I have said today and not give it to his wife, but go and do it himself and then teach his wife—learn how to do it himself and then teach his wife—he will know how to fry oysters better than most families in Washington.

There is no telling how many lives have been lost by not knowing how to fry oysters, but serving them as an indigestible food. Many times we hear of some man who was supposed to have had an acute attack of indigestion or cerebral hemorrhage or heart failure, and the chances are the only thing that was the matter with him was that he had swallowed some improperly cooked oysters. [Laughter.]

It is very important that what I say here shall be correctly printed in the Congressional Record and that it shall be taken to heart and learned by every Member of the Senate.

Now, I come to potlikker. Now, I will give my recipe for potlikker. First let me tell Senators what potlikker is. Potlikker is the residue that remains from the commingling, heating, and evaporation [laughter] —anyway, it is in the bottom of the pot! [Laughter.]

Here is how potlikker is made. First you get some turnip greens. You have to wash turnip greens many times. One of the principal reasons why people do not like turnip greens is that they never do get them clean. "You have to wash them lots of times," said Cato, "lots of times." They always call him "Cato." [Laughter.]

Take the ordinary green, turnip greens or mustard greens, though turnip greens are better than mustard greens. Turnip greens contain more manganese than do mustard greens. The trouble with turnip greens is that most people never get the greens washed clean. Sand is always in them. You have to wash them and wash them and wash them, particularly if you have not any flowing water. If you have good flowing water to shower them with, you can wash them more easily. But you have to wash them plenty of times. In order to get every vestige of dirt and sand and grit out of the greens you have to wash them many, many times.

That is the first thing you do—wash the greens. You wash the turnip with the greens or you can cut the turnips off and peel them and wash them by themselves, and then wash the greens by themselves if you want to do it that way.

All right this far! Then you take the greens and turnips and put them in the pot. Remember this: Do not salt them. Do not put any salt, do not put any pepper, do not put any mustard, do not put any kind of seasoning in the pot with them. Put the greens in the pot. Cut up the turnips. The turnip greens could be cut up a little, too. Put them all in there together.

Then when you get them all in the pot together, put in a sizable quantity of water, I should say about as much water as you have of turnip greens. Then put in there a piece of salted side meat. I would say if you had a pot of turnip greens about two-thirds the size of this wastebasket which I hold in my hand, or perhaps three-fourths that much, you ought to put about a 1-pound hunk of side meat that is sliced, but not clear through, just down to the skin part. Put about a pound of side meat in there. That side meat is just salty enough and has just salt enough in it that it will properly temper the turnip greens when it has been cooked enough. That will be all the seasoning that is needed.

When you have cooked the greens until they are tender and the turnips until they are tender, then you take up the turnips and the greens, and the soup that is left is potlikker. [Laughter.]

That brings on the real question of the art of eating potlikker, the matter of consuming potlikker. You draw off the potlikker and you eat it separately from the turnip greens.

(At this point MR. LONG yielded to MR. McCARRAN, who suggested the absence of a quorum, and the roll was called.)

MR. LONG. Mr. President, the quorum call discloses a majority of the Members here, and I am glad they are here. Now, I wish to conclude what I am sending out to the neighborhood in general on the recipe.

I was at the point where I explained the cooking of oysters. I was just down to the preparation of potlikker, and had gotten through the first stages of the explanation of how to prepare potlikker. I had explained everything except to tell that the turnip greens must be cooked long enough. One great trouble here is that they never cook the turnip greens long enough. Do not cook them too long but cook them long enough. Do not steam them. You have to boil them.

I have stated those recipes for the Record this afternoon so that they may be had by all Members of the Senate and by the public at large tomorrow. Now that so many Senators have returned, I am no longer talking for the benefit of the Record. I am talking now for the benefit of the Senate because I have Senators here. I was speaking to the country a moment ago. The remarks I made were intended more for the country than for the Senate. Of course, I intended them for the Senate, too, but I intended them more for the country than I did for the Senate.

Now, I am talking to the Senate, to the Members here only. I am not concerned with whether or not the country hears about it. I want the Senate to get it. I want each and every Member of the Senate to make himself ready to stay here for several hours, until I get through, and if I can do so without having to yield the floor, I should like to propound a parliamentary inquiry.

Would it be possible to call the roll and ask every Senator who will sit here and listen to me to indicate that he will stay here, and those who will not let them indicate that they will not do so? I would just like to find out how many of my friends in the Senate are really and genuinely interested in what I am saying. I do not want them to deceive me; I want to know how many Members of the Senate are genuinely glad to listen to me here today.

THE VICE PRESIDENT. Does the Senator from Louisiana propound a parliamentary inquiry?

MR. LONG. I wanted to know whether or not I could, by unanimous consent, have the clerk call from the desk the names of Senators and have them respond. I will put it in this way: Could I ask unanimous consent, without losing the floor, to have the clerk propound an inquiry to every Member of the Senate as to whether he is willing to stay here and listen to me or whether he really does not care about it?

THE VICE PRESIDENT. The Chair will say to the Senator that he would have to yield the floor if that were done; but the Chair would suggest to the Senator that he can see the Senators sitting around him and he might ask them individually as to their sentiments.

MR. LONG. Give me the list. I should like to find out if Senators really want to listen to me. The first name on the list is that of the Senator from Colorado [MR. ADAMS]. I should like to know if the Senator from Colorado really wants to stay here and listen to me this evening?

MR. LA FOLLETTE. Mr. President, I make the point of order that the Senator from Louisiana cannot yield except for a question.

THE VICE PRESIDENT. The point of order of the Senator from Wisconsin is well taken.

MR. LONG. Very well.

THE VICE PRESIDENT. Any time the Senator from Louisiana yields for anything but a question he loses the floor.

MR. LONG. Very well. I will not yield it, but I was hoping that, by unanimous consent, we could find out about it. I want to find out how popular I am in this body. [Laughter.] I want to know. If it should get back to Louisiana that the Senators are sitting here this evening listening to me, after I had been speaking for 7 hours—

• • • • •

MR. LONG. The violation in this case [*Schechter*] was this: They sent a coop of chickens, I think, from New Jersey to New York. In that coop there were some "dominicker" roosters, a plymouth rock, a buff cochin, white leghorns, and some common chickens that nobody knows by any name except chickens, hill-billy chickens, and various other kinds of chickens. When this coop of chickens got to New York a man opened the coop; the chickens began to flutter around, and he looked into the coop and said to himself, "I believe I like that pullet right over there, that frying-size pullet. I believe I will take that one." The man in charge said, "Hold on there; wait a minute there; before you pull out that pullet hold on a minute; let us get down the N.R.A. rule book and look through it and see what the rule is before you take a chicken out of the coop, because these chickens come in here in interstate commerce and you have got to follow the rule book." So they got down the rule book, volume 6, or whatever volume it was of the code affecting chickens.

I presume there are about 16 or 20 volumes; I do not know as to that; there may not be so many; but let us say, for the purpose of the argument, they got down volume 6 and looked on page 631 of section 4, subsection (z), subdivision 2, and it said there that no man could reach into a coop of chickens and pick out any particular chicken; that he had to blindfold himself and reach in and take whichever chicken came to hand. [Laughter.] That is in the code; that is a part of this wonderful thing that we are sitting here to reenact after a few minutes as soon as I get through talking. Just so soon as I get through speaking that will be the next order of the day.

The rule book of the code said that a man could not reach into a coop of chickens and take whichever one he wanted. "Well," the chicken purchaser said, we will say for the sake of the argument, "that chicken there has got pin feathers that I do not like," or, "I do not want a hen; I want that rooster," or, "I do not want a rooster; I want a frying-size chicken," or, "I want a yellow-legged chicken; I do not want a buff cochin; I want a white leghorn." People are funny that way; they think there is some difference in chickens. As a matter of fact, there is not much difference in chickens; chickens are nearly about the same. Take them up and take them down, a chicken is a chicken, and you cannot make anything else out of it. However, this code said the purchaser had to take whatever chicken he found. He would not do that. So he proceeded to get the chicken that he wanted, regardless of the law and the code. He took the chicken home and put it in his pot, made some dumplings—probably, in violation of the law, being made too big. [Laughter.] So they indicted the poor devil and ordered him sent to the penitentiary because he got out of the coop the kind of a chicken he wanted. He made the dumplings. He fried some dumplings and probably boiled the gizzard, when he should have roasted it. Mr. President, a gizzard is better roasted than boiled. I found that out years ago. Always roast a gizzard; never fry a gizzard. When he got through with the chicken the man was ordered to jail. Of course a man does not like to go to jail if he can help himself. I have been there myself. I was there one time because I did not have any other place to go and another time because they did not want me to go any other place. But this man decided that he would not go to jail. So he went to court. He hired a lawyer. The case was tried and he lost the case.

The judge called him up and said, "Sorry, old man; you violated the law." The defendant asked, "What law?—the law that Congress passed?" The judge said, "No; you violated a law that the rule maker under this chicken-coop case made, which is found in rule book, volume 6, page 641, paragraph Z, subdivision 2, which provides that a purchaser has to take chickens as they come; that he cannot discriminate between chickens." [Laughter.] I remember a poem about that:

> Chickens, chickens, what makes you roost so high?
> Chickens, chickens, they are going to get you before you die.

This fellow then gets a lawyer, pays him his cash, and gets convicted. He appeals the case to the circuit court of appeals. That is the next court up. For the benefit of the laymen of the Senate, I will state that a defendant is first tried in the district court. No; I am wrong as to that.

The first thing is that the rule maker, the man in charge of handling it, comes around and passes on the case. Then you appeal to the code authority of that particular industry, and they pass on the case. If they pass on it against you, you can appeal to the district court. That is the third court to which you get. When this man got to that court they convicted him, and he went to the circuit court. This man came here to the Supreme Court of the United States asking for a writ of certiorari directed to the circuit court of appeals to dissolve the whole case and to annul the sentence. The order would have to be from the Supreme Court to the circuit court of appeals requiring them to set aside the judgment of the district court, as I take it. We use the term "certiorari" in Louisiana. Certiorari is one of our writs, and I suppose it would be about the same procedure as that found in the courts here.

The Supreme Court finally passed on the case. It is a case of very great importance. It is one of the most far-reaching cases of jurisprudence in the country. It is more important than anything since the days of the Roman Empire.

Who knows what the Supreme Court held in that case? This is what they held, that a man has the right to any kind of a chicken he wants to eat.

• • • • •

54. The Chaos of Congress *

THE REORGANIZATION ACT of 1946 was designed to streamline the business and increase the efficiency of Congress. Examining Congress after several years of operation under this Act, Mr. Warner is not impressed with the improvements, which he considers to be meager. He finds major faults in the manner in which Congress handles money bills, in the seniority principle for the selection of committee chairmen, in the duplication of testimony before House and Senate committees, and in the rule of unlimited debate that operates in the Senate.

THREE and a half years ago a congressional reorganization law "modernized and streamlined" Congress. Now it is all too easy to see that nothing was done to improve either chassis or engine. Some chromium and a couple of bug-eye headlights may have been superimposed, but it is still the same old Model-T rattletrap.

One might almost say that the only tangible result of the congressional reorganization act was to raise the pay of congressmen and to provide retirement pensions for them. In all fairness, certain improvements and reforms were made; but they are less conspicuous than the creaking and swaying of the lumbering congressional vehicle.

Take, for instance, the utter lack of financial responsibility in Congress. The last session demonstrated it appallingly. So complete was the financial chaos that the average congressman in the week before adjournment had no idea how much of a government-spending program he was voting, or whether the deficit would be two or twelve billion dollars.

The reorganization law of 1946 had attempted to set up a legislative budget. It directed that the appropriating and tax-raising committees in Congress were to estimate on February 15 of each year the total projected expenditures for the next fiscal year and the total expected revenue. In 1947 and 1948 a Republican Congress gave this provision of the law a half-hearted and disdainful recognition. The Democrats of the 81st Congress threw it in the ash-can. They considered it unworkable, and perhaps it was, in part; but at any rate even the spirit of the law was flouted.

Appropriations bills came along by fits and starts. A chamber would

* Albert Warner, *Harper's Magazine*, 200 (March, 1950), pp. 60-65.

economize one day and go on a spending spree the next. It would cut out three million dollars for a fair in the District of Columbia to celebrate the sesquicentennial of the capital city, and then authorize forty million dollars for the construction of new post offices or federal buildings in every congressman's district, whether needed or not. And the scales were so loaded against economy that the friends of the District Fair could come back three times to the House of Representatives—and make the grade the third time. The House reversed itself and gave the money.

The old back-slapping process, you-help-me-and-I'll-help-you, operated without hindrance on the time-honored pork-barrel bill for rivers and harbors and flood control. The House approved a generous appropriation of 593 million dollars; then the members of the House rushed over to the other side of the Capitol to join their senators at committee hearings and urge still bigger appropriations, till when the bill passed the Senate it had reached 751 million dollars.

The old congressional system of first authorizing a program entailing the spending of money, and then in separate action making the appropriation, lent itself to confusion as usual and played into the hands of the spendthrift. Representative Clarence Cannon, chairman of the House Appropriations Committee, sought to stop an appropriation for drawing up plans for a small dam at Gavins Point on the Missouri River. The dam, he said, should not be built for thirteen years and might never be needed—depending on the effectiveness of other dams under construction. But the House is always sensitive to local projects, and the theory that it was already committed to this one carried the day: the blueprinting of the dam was upheld.

It would have been reasonable to expect all the appropriation bills for the new fiscal year to pass before it began, on July 1. But so dilatory was Congress that it had to adopt five stop-gap resolutions to allow government payrolls to be met while it continued to fumble over bills for weeks after the deadline. On October 1, when a quarter of the fiscal year had elapsed, five appropriation bills were still stuck in the works; and not until October 17 was the vital defense appropriation bill passed—more than three and a half months late!

Not only did the average legislator during the session have no idea of what the appropriations were totaling—according to Representative Mike Monroney, the able Oklahoma Democrat who fathered the reorganization law—but when the session was over even the financial leaders of Congress differed as to what they had done. Representative Cannon, House Appropriations chairman, and Representative John Taber, ranking Republican member of the committee, were about two billion dollars apart on the total of the appropriations they said had been voted.

It is evident that in fiscal matters Congress at the outset of a session doesn't know where it is headed, during the session doesn't know where it is, and at the end doesn't know where it has been.

II

It was the optimistic thought of the sponsors of the reorganization law that they were improving the committee system of Congress. It is true that they reduced the number of standing committees, equipped them with professional staffs, and put a brake on the creation of special committees. But consider the duplication and confusion that still remain.

The duplication of testimony before congressional committees is an indecent waste of time and of officials' energy. The House Foreign Affairs Committee holds hearings on the bill to extend the Marshall Plan for another year. Then the Senate Foreign Relations Committee hears the same men and raises the same questions. Next the House Appropriations Committee, and after it the Senate Appropriations Committee, go over the same well-beaten ground. The joint Congressional Watchdog Committee delves into the same operations. Paul Hoffman, the administrator of the Marshall Plan, spent nine days before the Senate Appropriations Committee alone, being heckled about every export detail from brooms to wigs; and during the past session Louis Johnson, the Secretary of Defense, had to testify before ten different committees or subcommittees of Congress. In one month he made no less than fifteen appearances!

Compounding confusion, the Appropriations Committees are beginning to take over the making of policy also. The Foreign Relations Committee of the Senate was willing to go along with the State Department on policies affecting Franco Spain; but Senator Pat McCarran, as chairman of the Appropriations sub-committee, said to the Secretary of State, "I am not in favor of your policy with reference to Spain and until that policy is changed I am going to examine your appropriations with a fine-tooth comb." And the influence of Senator Sheridan Downey, exercised through the Senate Appropriations Committee, held up the pay of Reclamation Commissioner Michael Straus for five months because the Senator did not like Mr. Straus's policies.

For all the virtues of the reorganization bill, it left untouched the biggest evil of the present committee system: the hoary system of seniority that sits upon the committees like an old man of the sea. The chairmen of committees are those who have grown old coming from safe districts. Ability, effectiveness, knowledge, even political shrewdness—which is sometimes needed to get things done—have nothing to do with the selection of a committee chairman. The oldest man in point of service gets the job.

A committee chairman appoints the personnel of subcommittees. He sets the dates for meetings. He directs what bills are to be considered and when. Because of the traditional deference to him he can practically smother legislation which fails to meet with his personal approval.

The result is that several of the most important committees of Congress have been kept in a state of disorganization. Chairman John Lesinski of the House Committee on Education and Labor began a notable career of ineptness at the outset of the past session by trying to install a committee counsel whom not even his Democratic colleagues on the committee would swallow. Later he so fumbled the Administration's effort to repeal or drastically modify the Taft-Hartley Act that the Administration was humiliated on the floor and saved face only by sending the measure back to committee. The bill for federal aid to education, handled so smoothly by the Senate that it passed with scarcely a ripple, was allowed to fall into a needlessly bitter row in this House committee, and was stranded there, its friends unable to muster a committee majority to consider it. Finally, the chairman used his arbitrary power to abolish several sub-committees. Representative Andrew Jacobs, Indiana Democrat, bitterly protesting, spent the last three weeks of the session trying to have the full committee called together. The chairman by seniority said "no." In the non-democratic committee system of Congress, a chairman's "no" is effective.

Then there is Chairman John E. Rankin of the House Veterans' Affairs Committee—chairman, of course, by virtue of seniority. After giving his committee members only a few minutes to look over a new version of a bill to cost 125 billion dollars for veterans' pensions, he railroaded it to the floor of the House over the shrieks of protesting Democrats. It took not only good sense but considerable political fortitude for the House to send the bill back to committee, because it is considered political suicide to vote against anything for veterans.

At the other end of the Capitol, Senator McCarran, chairman of the Judiciary Committee, secure in his seniority, defied his own party leadership and a majority of both parties of the Senate for one entire session over the bill to revise the displaced-persons law. He did so by just prolonging indefinitely public hearings on the bill. The Senate, always deferential to committee chairmen, had authorized $135,000 for immigration inquiries, which gave scope to protracted study.

III

Much of the unedifying spectacle of congressional dawdling, fumbling, and obstructionism is caused by slow motion in the Senate, and this results from the rule of unlimited debate and the rule of unanimous consent. One dissenter holds up action; and, because there is no requirement that speeches be germane to the issue before the Senate, the discussion of a housing program may be stalled for four hours by a speech on milk for Hottentots. There is value in deliberation and full debate, but the result of such latitude is boredom and a snail's pace. In the past session it was only when summer had crept into fall and the House had taken a conspicuous vacation that the Senate finished what could easily have been completed three months earlier.

During last winter and spring it became standard practice for the Senate to spend two or three weeks on every major bill. Any reasonable men, untrammeled by the habits of the Senate, could have resolved each of those issues in four days with full discussion.

Real filibusters are not frequent, but there are always long, long speeches carried well beyond the point of weariness. While one or two men harry a point for days, the rest of the senators are working in their offices or off home for a visit. Sometimes the speeches are a form of political blackmail. Just to get rid of the talks, the Senate accepts what they demand.

In the midst of the debate over a change in the Senate rules last year, up rose Senator Harry Cain, the Washington Republican, and delivered himself for six and a half hours of his low opinion of Mon Wallgren, whom the President was trying to appoint as chairman of the National Security Resources Board. The senator brought along an extra pair of shoes for the talkathon, changing from one to the other to relieve weary feet. The bored listeners got no such attention.

Incidentally, in the House a roll call takes forty minutes; in the Senate, fifteen. Electrical voting equipment would eliminate this droning ritual. But Congress will have none of it.

IV

Some of the causes of congressional inefficiency appear to be insoluble. For instance, the greatest source of distraction to congressmen in the efficient conduct of their legislative work is their individual constituents. The non-legislative workload of errands and chores takes eighty per cent of the time of some members of Congress. The gamut of these worries runs from jobs, pension troubles, railroad retirement and social security cases, veterans' affairs, and RFC loans, to defense installations and river-and-harbor projects for their home districts.

Mr. Monroney recalls that someone ironically suggested that half of Congress should be legislators and half should be representatives of the districts. The only trouble is that the representatives of the districts would be the ones re-elected.

As if it were not enough that congressmen should be laden with errands for their districts, they are also imposing upon themselves a new load of publicity activity. They are writing weekly columns for their local newspapers and weekly radio talks by transcription to their local radio stations. And now Congressman Gerald R. Ford, Michigan Republican, is setting what may become a ghastly precedent. He has become the actor-star in a Washington travelogue to be sent to clubs and schools back home, a movie full of the Washington monument, the Lincoln Memorial, the Potomac, the chambers of Congress, and Congressman Ford. God alone knows what the demands of television will be!

Perhaps there is no way of curbing such outside activity on the part of our legislators. But some of the other scandalous conditions that I have been discussing can be remedied.

(1) *The chaos in finances.* There is at least a faint hope that this situation will be bettered in the present session by the introduction of a single, comprehensive appropriation bill, lumping together all appropriations. This will give congressmen a chance to look at the total of what they are voting to spend. The appropriations of the previous year will be set in juxtaposition to the omnibus measure, and the same accounting plan will be used for each year. This plan, pushed by Senator Harry F. Byrd, Virginia Democrat, could at least show Congress what it is doing.

To let Congress cope with the administrative departments on more even terms, the Appropriations Committees need a professional staff of perhaps a hundred members—accountants and budgetary experts delving into operations as the budget is made up.

(2) *The demoralizing rule of congressional committees by seniority.* It would be a relatively simple change to have the committee chairmen chosen either by the elected majority leaders of the Senate and the House or by the members of the committees. All that is needed is enough nerve on the part of enough legislators to push through the change; the country would applaud.

(3) *The rules of the Senate which provide for unlimited debate and unanimous consent.* Even a mild limitation of debate, invokable only in extremities, and a standing requirement that speeches must

be germane to the subject before the Senate, would bring improvement.

The old Model-T was a good car but the roads are slicker now and the traffic fast and heavy. The ancient congressional jalopy needs some fundamental rebuilding.

55. *A Senator's Vote: A Searching of the Soul* *

SENATOR PAUL DOUGLAS here analyzes the process by which a conscientious legislator decides how to vote on pending legislation. Lawmakers are sensitive to public opinion as expressed in letters from, and in direct contacts with, the voters in their home state, and are often swayed by the opinions and attitudes of other legislators for whom they have respect. However, Senator Douglas feels that the majority of decisions are made by the individual legislators on the basis of their convictions and evaluation of the matter at hand. To illustrate this point, he discusses the formulation of his own decision on such controversial issues as Federal aid to education and the Slum Clearance Bill. In doing this, he shows the reader some of the practical factors in the legislative "give and take" that have to be considered before making a decision. Senator Douglas' frank account of his own mental processes goes far to humanize the legislator and his problems for the average citizen.

THERE were 226 roll-call votes in the Senate last year. As the clerk called our names, those of us on the Senate floor had to answer either "aye" or "no." Many times we wished an issue had never arisen. Many times the issue itself was not clear. Many times we felt that the truest answer was neither "aye" nor "no" but "maybe." Still, we could not stall by repeating the truth that there was much to be said on both sides. In the Senate, when our names are called, the time for objectivity ends. We must answer with a categorical "aye" or "no."

What lies behind the words that are spoken? What leads one Senator to vote "aye" and another "no"? This question is not only of absorbing interest to a gallery that includes all of America. Men on the Senate floor also ask the same question. "How," we ask, "did we

* Paul H. Douglas, *The New York Times Magazine*, April 30, 1950, pp. 9, 38, 40, 42, 44. Reprinted by permission of the author and the publisher.

get that way and how did the fellow next to us or on the other side of the room reach the same or an opposite conclusion?"

The "realists," as always, have a simple answer. They explain that a Senator either votes according to the weight of his mail or by a rule-of-thumb estimate of how political forces are balanced in the home state. The more cynical among the realists add that a Senator votes the way some political boss, some utility or banking magnate, or some labor leader wants him to vote. In this view, a Senator is a moral puppet who responds more or less automatically to external pressures exerted on him by organized groups in the community at large.

Now, there may be Senators who cast votes in this manner. But if there are such, I do not know them. All Senators, of course, are sensitive to the climate of opinion. They must be. How else could representative government function? All Senators, too, read their mail. They are quick to spot and give special weight to unprompted, open-hearted letters, whether they are scratched on rough paper or written on embossed stationery. They all make tabulations on how the spontaneous mail runs when a controversial issue is approaching a vote.

But experience has taught them that the volume of mail is no true index to public opinion; that the most articulate are often those who have a concentrated special interest; that the great mass of the public, with its diffuse general interest, would, if pressed, frequently state views contrary to those voiced by the "disciplined letter-writers."

In itself, of course, there is nothing virtuous or evil about "disciplined letter-writing." Saints and sinners alike have used the device for ends both good and bad. Anyone has a right to use this device to influence public policy. Moreover, there is no difference between a thousand identical letters or postcards sent in by individual members of an organization, or a thousand signatures on a document sent in by the secretary of the organization. Both are aspects of the right of petition.

But the question here is how the *best* soundings of public opinion can be made by a Senator. In a great state every group interest divides itself into an infinite number of conflicting internal parts, so much so that the differences within groups are often greater than the differences between them. To whom, then, should a Senator listen? I believe his most accurate sounding of public opinion comes about in an almost subjective way.

The Senator, returning to his home state, throws himself open to a tidal wave of voices, of heavings and pullings this and that way. Gradually, and almost unobtrusively, the clamor of many voices somehow yields a consensus that is clearly identifiable to him. Whether he agrees with that consensus or whether he tries to change it is another matter. Bill Herndon used to explain this to Abraham Lincoln by saying that "he felt things in his bones." And Lincoln, in reply, would comically refer to this as "Herndon's bone philosophy." Yet Herndon was closer to the truth than Lincoln suspected.

Some Senators, overburdened with the routine of office work, are often unable, or forget, to return to their point of origin. Others who make these returns for political soundings expose themselves to the charge that they are neglecting their duties in Washington. But the quality of their decisions inevitably becomes better or worse according to the degree to which they can immerse themselves in the bath of genuine public opinion. Apart from these immersions, a Senator has certain selected points of contact which enter into the complex of forces that shape his vote.

There are people in America of experience, objectivity, a devotion to the common good, and a unique skill in making prudent decisions regarding public matters. No one elected them to their posts of opinion-makers. They are that by the sheer force of their arguments. Most generally, they are content to express their viewpoint to a Senator over the telephone or by a brief call at his office. But whether they do it this way, or invite the nation to eavesdrop, they command enormous attention. These devoted servants of the common good may not make up a Senator's mind on how he should vote. But what these men and women say must be answered by a Senator before he casts his vote.

In this connection it is America's good fortune that there are several of these aristocratic democrats who are members of the present Senate. One, whom we all deeply respect, is the man whose name is called first at voting time. He is Senator George D. Aiken, Republican of Vermont, who can neither be bought nor bluffed, fooled nor frightened. I openly confess that there have been times in the Senate when my mind has been in great doubt right up to the voting time.

And then Senator Aiken's name would be called. And I, for one, have often been influenced by the character of his sturdy response to the clerk. Like the rest of us, he may err on an issue of fact. But, like his Democratic counterpart, Senator Frank P. Graham of North Carolina, he has never, to my knowledge, erred on a moral principle.

Is there any thread that runs through a series of separate votes cast by a Senator? At first glance the answer seems to be a negative one. Yet the appearance of pure pragmatism in Senate voting is highly deceptive. For all the wide range of matters on which they cast their votes, in one way or another, all Senators have repeatedly asked and answered the basic questions in politics.

What, for instance, should be the relationship between the One and the Many? What should be the relationship between the leaders and the people? What should be left to the operation of custom and what should be made the subject of law? Which body of practices should be institutionalized and which ones should be left in a free-floating state? At what point must the system of rights be made to intersect with the system of duties? What is the area in which the right of dissent can operate without subverting the will of the majority? These are timeless questions, asked everywhere. In each vote on a particular measure the Senators also vote on a general principle. Indeed, it is the operation of the general principle on their thoughts which gives a discernible inner unity to most of their decisions.

At the same time, while the general principle can be stated and examined objectively, its application to a particular case is often undertaken in a mood of emotional stress. A politician, no less than a surgeon, is commonly reluctant to describe these inner stresses. It is not because his motives are base, or because an open statement of his own struggle would disturb the patient with whose life he is entrusted. It is due more to the reluctance of Americans in all walks of life to expose their inner thoughts and deepest values.

But it so happens that I have been a Quaker of sorts for many years and have painfully acquired the habit of open confession. If I reveal the factors which lay behind my own votes on several matters of current interest, perhaps I can speak for a number of my more reticent colleagues in the Senate.

The first difficult decision I faced was on the problem of Federal aid to education. I believed in the principle of Federal aid because the average income per school child in most of the Southern states is only about one-half the national average and only a third of that in the most prosperous states. The result is that though the South taxes itself for education at a level above the national average, the yield does not produce enough money for decent schooling, whether the children are white or Negro, since its taxable resources are low. Federal aid, representing a levy on the taxable resources of the nation as a whole, is needed if the average Southern child is to have a decent chance in life.

But I soon found that the real conflict was not so much on the program of Federal aid itself as on the relation of the private and parochial schools to it. Some people wanted to specify that Federal money could not be used in any way for private schools. Catholic groups, on the contrary, felt that such moneys should be provided to the private schools, not for religious instruction, but for collateral services such as health, transportation and non-religious books, and that if state laws prohibited this, then the Federal Government should withhold the proportionate funds earmarked for such states and should, on its own, distribute money directly to the private schools.

These two views appeared irreconcilable, though the sincerity of their respective proponents could not be questioned. But if either view became public policy, the effect would be to engender a bitter and divisive religious controversy. I was deeply disturbed by such a prospect and hoped a way could be found which would heal an imminent breach. One avenue of approach suggested itself.

Whether children are in public or private schools, and whether they are Protestant, Catholic or Jewish, children present a uniform health problem, and what is done to improve their health has a beneficial effect upon the community as a whole. In consequence, it appeared to me that a distinction could be drawn between health services on the one hand and transportation and books on the other; that Federal aid for these health services should be furnished to all children, whether they were in private or public schools. Under this view, the schoolhouse at certain hours in the term would have the status of a convenient neighborhood dispensary.

I helped, therefore, to prepare a bill appropriating $35,000,000 for health services to children in all schools, which, when enlarged by local funds, would make available a minimum yearly average of $2.40 for each child. I should note that the measure, although a supplement to the Federal aid bill then under discussion, was kept apart from it so that a vote for the supplemental bill could proceed on its merits alone.

Having gained the approval of the Senate Committee on Labor and Public Welfare for this measure, I thought with its members that the question of using Federal funds for transportation of private school students could best be left to the decision of the people in the various states and localities. By localizing decisions on the transportation features of the education bill, I hoped that the nation as a whole could be spared a religious controversy.

The Thomas Federal Aid to Education Bill, as reported out to the Senate, embraced this principle. It gained the overwhelming approval of the Senate which, by a roll-call vote of 63 to 3, defeated an amendment which would have confined all Federal funds to the public schools. At the other pole, the Senate, by a voice vote, defeated an amendment requiring that these funds must be furnished for auxiliary services to all private schools.

But, as is now known, the House rejected the formula proposed to it by the Senate. It sent the school health bill to the Committee on Interstate Commerce, while the education bill was sent to the Committee on Labor, where it was referred to a subcommittee on education headed by Congressman Barden of North Carolina. In due course, Congressman Barden offered a bill which explicitly denied Federal aid to any private school.

The ensuing bitter discussion has thus far prevented agreement over a formula which would permit this much-needed legislation to pass. I still feel confident, however, that the Senate has pointed the way to gain what is needed.

A similar problem came up in connection with the public housing and slum clearance bill. As matters developed on the Senate floor, those of us who were devoted both to the principle of low-cost housing and slum clearance and to the principle of civil rights, were jockeyed into a heart-rending position. My friends, Senators Maybank of South Carolina and Sparkman of Alabama, had introduced a measure providing $1,000,000,000 over five years to help clear slums. It also guaranteed the interest on local housing bonds sufficient to construct 810,000 housing units, to the immeasurable benefit of at least 3.5 million persons, or about one-quarter of our slum-dwelling population. I was privileged to work with these men in helping to draft the measure, and in the process I came to wish that more of my Northern friends could appreciate the public spirit and devotion of these sons of the South.

Then came a body blow which was all the more telling because it was in the form of an amendment which dealt with a problem of elemental importance to all Americans. Senator Bricker of Ohio proposed an amendment to the housing bill providing that all public housing projects in every city must be thrown open to Negroes and whites. Every liberal-minded Senator wanted to vote for that amendment. But the problem of choice took on a different shape when the amendment was placed in its legislative setting.

To begin with, Senator Bricker was the spokesman for some twenty-five Republican Senators who were openly opposed to public housing. Secondly, these same men had shown little interest in an earlier effort to liberalize Senate rules so that civil rights legislation could be passed. On the contrary, most of them had joined the forces which made those rules all the more restrictive.

What then was the purpose of their civil rights amendment? The answer was perfectly clear. It was to get Northern and Western Senators, like myself, who were for housing but against segregation, to join in support of the Bricker amendment. But what would happen next? The passage of the amendment would then influence some twenty Southern and border state Senators who were for public housing to abandon that support because of the Bricker "civil rights" amendment. Once the housing measure as a whole came up for a vote, they would vote against it—which is what this group had wanted all along. We would then wind up with no slum clearance and no low income homes. No one on the Senate floor was really deceived by the move.

I chose housing, as did virtually every Senator who was also a vocal supporter of civil rights. We voted for housing and against the Bricker amendment, knowing all the while that we exposed ourselves to sharp attack from fellow supporters of civil rights elsewhere who were not familiar with the legislative picture. I felt it to be of the utmost importance that the character of the choice before the Senate should be explained to the country as a whole. Nearly all my political friends urged me not to do this, saying that the subject was so delicate and so highly charged with emotion that anything anyone said would be misunderstood and attacked.

Still, I felt confident that discussion would clear the air. I pointed out that on the basis of past experience Negroes would probably occupy one-third of the units built and that, therefore, about 270,000 families, or over a million and a quarter members of that race, would be provided with decent housing. I furthermore pointed out that most of the public housing projects in the North and West would explicitly bar segregation by local ordinance and that the civil rights principle would be extended rather than curbed.

If, on the contrary, the Bricker amendment was passed, we would have a vacuous assertion of civil rights but no homes in which they could be asserted. Virtually all Northern and Western liberals re-echoed this same view and the housing bill was passed without the Bricker amendment. We all felt that we had the right to choose the ground on which we could fight for civil rights as a measure in itself.

I might mention one more inner struggle between my heart and my head, between my sympathies and my reason, which gave me a few bad days. The first appropriation bill to come up last year was that for the Department of Labor and Federal Security. I was more interested in these agencies than probably any others because I had campaigned for the causes they represented in their formative days over two decades ago. I had actively fought for old-age pensions and unemployment insurance and had played a modest part in getting them adopted into Federal and state laws. Moreover, as an early advocate of public employment offices, and as one who has constantly used price and wage statistics of the Bureau of Labor Statistics, I knew the importance of these two branches of Government work. I wanted all of these agencies to be adequately financed so that they could do effective work.

But I also knew most Government agencies were overstaffed, and from personal experience with the labor agencies I was quite certain that they were not immune from this occupational disease of officialdom. I felt the staffs of these agencies could be pruned with profit and that this was especially necessary in view of the big impending Government deficit.

The Republican leadership was proposing a 5 per cent cut in the administrative expenses of these agencies. As the hour for voting approached, I was torn emotionally by a strong conflict. My inner conflict was made even more intense because I knew that many conservatives wanted to cut the welfare agencies to the bone while at the same time they would later defend wasteful subsidies granted those economic groups that didn't need them. "Why," I asked myself, "should I play into their hands?"

During the last hour of the debate, I left the Chamber and sought the quiet of the Senate reading room. As I sat there alone, it became clear that even though it meant disappointing my friends and my party, I must at all costs vote my convictions. If I were to urge prudence in the way the taxpayers' money was spent I must apply economy even to those agencies and causes in which I was deeply concerned.

As I debated the issue with myself, I resolved it in the conviction that in time fair-minded people would see that economy was also a virtue and that to be a liberal one did not have to be a wastrel. I thereafter went back into the Senate and voted for the cut. The incident was crucial. It forced me thereafter to relate a zeal for prudent expenditure with a desire for human welfare. Having tried to apply the pruning knife on causes which were close to my heart, I was free to seek economies elsewhere with good grace.

Yet all the foregoing does not really explain how and why a Senator casts his vote this way instead of that. When the committee hearings and the important books and articles on a proposal are read; when the mail has been appraised; when the briefs and arguments have been weighed; when the wise men, living and dead, have been consulted, the Senator still faces the task of moving his own lips to say yes or no. On the clerk's list, his name stands out in all its solitude. And that is the way he must vote.

It is also, I believe, the primary way in which he decides beforehand how he is going to vote. His hour of decision is not seen by the outer world. It can come in the dead of night, in periods of reverie in one's office after the day's work is done, over the breakfast or dinner table with one's family, or in a taxicab ride to or from the Capitol. It is at these times, I believe, that the final decisions which affect the life of the nation are generally made. The tension of the roll-call merely expresses the decisions which ninety-six widely differing men, with different background, have already made in the quiet of their individual consciences.

56. *The Farm Bureau* *

THE FARM BUREAU FEDERATION undoubtedly maintains one of the most effective lobbying organizations in Washington. This case study of lobbying describes the growth and development of the Federation—its aims, its officials, and their methods.

THE farmer has learned that to be strong in Washington he needs more than a good cause. He also needs a good lobby. The American Farm Bureau Federation is the best lobby he ever had and probably the best lobby in the business. In the rousing spring days of 1933 it helped pass the first Agricultural Adjustment Act. During the next ten years over $7 billion was distributed for special farm legislation; Bureau President Ed O'Neal, more than anyone else, nursed the necessary appropriations through Congress. During the same years Ed made parity—that generous and arbitrary formula for deciding where farm prices should be—the national synonym for a square deal for the farmer. In 1941, at the behest of the Bureau, Congress guaranteed a minimum price of 85 per cent of parity for the great farm staples; a few months later, the Bureau got a prohibition on price ceilings below 110 per cent of parity. The figure has since been reduced 10 per cent, but the floors have been raised. If a majority of Congress could override a presidential veto, the Farm Bureau would long ago have eliminated consumer subsidies. The Farm Bureau nearly always gets what it goes after.

The Farm Bureau is not the only representative of the farmer in Washington; indeed, one reason for the public's meager knowledge of the farm lobby is the large number of farm lobbyists. The urban American has heard a little about more organizations than he can remember. There are free-lance lobbyists—a scrofulous collection of inexpensive mercenaries who serve anyone with a grievance and a checkbook. Their stock in trade is a close familiarity with the Capitol, an exceptional faculty for secondhand emotion and third-rate oratory. They are an unsightly appendage of democratic government but fortunately they are unimportant.

There are also scores of farm-commodity organizations—one for virtually everything made, grown, or produced by American farms. They are active—the day is long past when they confined themselves to staging a National Apple Week or promoting essay competitions on the food value of cheese. Producers of walnuts, peaches, turpentine,

* J. K. Galbraith, *Fortune*, 29 (June, 1944), pp. 156-160, 188-196. Reprinted by special permission of the Editors.

lemons, grapes, and many other products have negotiated highly profitable deals with the Department of Agriculture for the purchase of surpluses or their conversion into byproducts, and for the stabilization of prices. Sheepmen can—and do—thank their organization for getting special preference for domestic wools in Army clothing purchases. Organized dairymen have worked hard to stamp out traffic in oleomargarine, a commodity they deem injurious to the public health and their own butter market. But the commodity men serve only their own commodity; they do not speak on the great issues of farm policy. Just as numerous business lobbies appeared to pick tariff plums when these were the greatest gift in the giving of the U. S. Government, so the commodity organizations have appeared to pick those plums provided by the farm program of the thirties.

The great issues of farm policy—price and wage stabilization, parity loans, marketing quotas, soil conservation, manpower, steel for farm machinery—are the business of the Farm Bureau. To be sure, even in this field it has competitors—or allies. There is the National Grange, the oldest and (because it admits both farmer and his wife to membership) also the largest of the general farm organizations. However, the modern Granger has little of the militancy of the great railroad baiters of the seventies. The leaders are hesitant, worried, and profoundly conservative. Rather than striking out for themselves, they line up with the Farm Bureau. So also does the National Council of Farmer Cooperatives. This is an organization of organizations—a holding company of the federations into which dairy, poultry, citrus, and other marketing and farm-supply cooperatives are grouped. Both leaders and members of the Co-op Council are more concerned with their near $4 billion merchandising operation than with legislation.

The Farm Bureau's only notable opposition is the Farmers Union—officially the Farmers Educational and Cooperative Union. The leaders of the union are young and aggressive and closely allied with organized labor and the Administration. They are not conservative; the Bureau considers them wildly radical. But the union's membership is small and sparse and until recent years it was badly rent by internal strife. Its leaders would concede that compared with the Bureau they are still small potatoes.

THE GOVERNMENT BUILDS A LOBBY

Among farm organizations and among lobbies, the Farm Bureau is unique. It is, as its detractors never tire of pointing out, a private lobby sponsored and supported by the government it seeks to influence. The Bureau locally is the official and unofficial sponsor of the federal-state Extension Service—more briefly the county-agent system. And this accounts for a good deal of its strength and a great deal of its permanence.

The whole thing came about rather innocently. When the first county agents were appointed, state governments feared that farmers might look this new gift horse in the mouth. To make sure that farmers really wanted an adviser badly enough to use him, it was commonly specified that farmers of the county must first club together and agree to pay part of the expenses of the new office. The county agent soon proved himself one of the county's most useful citizens; farmers organized rapidly to obtain his help. By way of clubbing together, they organized bureaus; then to keep their agents they had to keep their bureaus. In 1914 the federal government began matching dollar for dollar the money spent by states and localities for extension work. By doing so it underwrote with federal funds the tie between local bureaus and the county agent. Five years later, in 1919, these local bureaus had banded into state federations or bureaus, and the state federations were meeting in Ithaca, New York, to form themselves into a national organization, the American Farm Bureau Federation. The local bureaus were ready to come to Washington as the country's first semi-official lobby.

In several states farmers must still organize a bureau to obtain the services of a county agent and the corps of specialists backing him up. In these states the grass-roots organization of the Farm Bureau is especially secure; membership brings to the county not only the best (and most expensive) technical and educational aids available to farmers anywhere in the world, it also brings a skilled organizer in the person of the county agent. The Farm Bureau works very closely with the Extension Service even in states where there is no official tie between the two. The county agent finds that members of the Bureau are good clients; he uses local bureau meetings as a forum for presenting and discussing new methods, new farm programs, and the effect of new laws and regulations. The state bureaus are alert to see that the state legislatures keep the Extension Service well supplied with funds.

Their official and common-law marriage with the Extension Service the Farm Bureau leaders neither publicize nor disguise. But they know well what it means to their organization. Farmers are scattered, hard to organize, and harder to keep organized. The fruits of organization—benefit checks and higher prices—are shared by both those who belong to the organization and those who do not. Farm leaders have no collective-bargaining agreement around which to rally their members and no closed-shop agreement to hold the backsliders. During the past hundred years farm organizations have mushroomed time and again only to disappear a year or so later because the rank and file stopped paying dues. The tie with the Extension Service keeps the local or county farm bureaus alive and strong—and on these the strength of the national organization depends.

There is another thing in the Bureau's favor. It appeals to the prosperous farmers—those who do not need to count their pennies when they pay their dues. The Bureau leaders would like to think that they represented all men of the land; they are often accused of being the organization of the great land barons. The truth is in between. There are not enough great landlords in the U.S. to make a successful organization. Still, the Farm Bureau does not speak for the small owner or tenant. Its 690,000 members who pay dues ranging from $2 a year in Georgia to $15 in Illinois are the larger commercial farmers, who understand most readily the benefits of organization.

The special privileges of the Bureau have not gone unchallenged. In the last few years New Deal agencies—Triple A, Farm Security, Rural Electrification, and the Soil Conservation Service—have brought a whole new corps of officials into farm counties. These are independent of the Extension Service. The county agent has been dwarfed by his now numerous competitors and the local bureau has shared in the partial eclipse. Both Bureau and county agent have found the large number of competing meetings and committees especially exasperating. The national officers of the Bureau are deeply concerned. Since 1940 they have been talking about legislation to give the state directors of Extension Service a large hand in the farm programs of the Department of Agriculture.

The other farm organizations are jealous. The Grange, which relies on community fellowship and a ritual to hold its members, would like to see the Bureau divorced from the Extension Service. The liberal Farmers Union, which is built on cooperative elevators and liberal ideas, vigorously assails the "Farm Bureau-Extension Axis." State legislatures, under this pressure, have occasionally considered separating the two. It has also been suggested that federal funds be withdrawn from states that allow these funds to strengthen so potent a federal lobby. However, the franchise of the Bureau is probably secure. Self-preservation is the first plank in its platform. It would be a poor lobby if it could not protect its own privileges.

None of this means that the Farm Bureau can take things easy; no farm organization can do that. Active and continuous organization work is essential. Even more essential is a supply of issues to keep membership interest alive. Many have wondered why the Farm Bureau has continued to battle for higher farm income at a time when farmers are making record returns. Others have been puzzled by the vigor with which the Bureau has opposed consumer subsidies. The principle of using such subsidies is surely debatable, but the Farm Bureau is hardly their natural foe on grounds of principle; it has sponsored farm subsidies by the billions. Part of the answer is that the Bureau, because it is a farm organization, must do battle over something. Were it to make peace in times of high farm income, it would give the appearance of somnolence and decay. It would lose its reputation for militant farm leadership and with its reputation would go its members.

THE CORN AND COTTON COALITION

Six states provide nearly half of the membership of the Bureau and a good deal more than half of the leadership. Three of these—Alabama, Mississippi, and Arkansas—are in the cotton belt and three—Illinois, Iowa, and Indiana—in the corn belt. Four of them are represented on the eighteen-man Board of Directors of the national organization; the other two, Alabama and Illinois, supply the President and Vice President. The border states—Kentucky, Tennessee, and Missouri—where commercial farming follows the pattern of either corn belt or cotton belt, have moderate-sized state bureaus, and Tennessee is also represented on the Board of Directors. Few of the remaining state federations (there are forty-three state bureaus in all, plus one in Puerto Rico) are influential in the national organization. The large and efficient California federation devotes itself mainly to state affairs. The Bureau is strong in New York and moderately so in Ohio, Vermont, and New Hampshire, but chiefly as the sponsor of farm purchasing cooperatives, cheap insurance, and the Extension Service. In the south Atlantic states, the Pacific Northwest, and most of the mountain states the state federations are small and weak. Texas, leading farm state of the union, has never supported a strong Bureau. Kansas is the only strong Farm Bureau state on the Great Plains.

The American Farm Bureau Federation in brief is a coalition of corn and cotton farmers. As such it represents farmers of the two most populous agricultural regions of the land. From these regions come the legislators who have few industries and little or no labor vote to worry about. They can work full time for the farmer. By themselves corn or cotton farmers would be a political force to be reckoned with; in partnership they become one of the nation's most powerful groups. The job of the Farm Bureau is to preserve that partnership.

Keeping peace between corn and cotton is what Ed O'Neal calls "keeping agricultural unity" and it isn't easy. There are differences in temperament. The Southerners accuse the cornbelt leaders of identifying all agriculture with the corn belt and being unable or unwilling to understand the special problems of cotton. Corn-belt leaders on the other hand think Southerners have an inborn tendency to substitute passion for plain common sense. There are political differences. Southern farm leaders are Democrats; they are now at odds with the Administration but they have never thought of voting Republican. This blind party regularity, northern leaders believe, elects too many legislators who, in the pinches, follow the President rather than the Farm Bureau. The corn-belt leaders are rock-ribbed Republicans; those that strayed briefly with Henry Wallace are again back in the fold. The Southerners dislike Republicans on principle; and they have never been sure the Republican party approved of the Agricultural Adjustment Act and related measures. The Southerners do.

The hardest job is to reconcile the strictly economic differences between corn farmer and cotton planter. History is (or was) against any bargain between the two, and for nearly a century after the Ohio Valley was settled none was struck. The South wanted low tariffs, an international market in which to sell cotton and buy cheap supplies. The new corn-belt lined up with northeastern industry and plumped for a protected market at home. Farmers of the two regions believed they had little or nothing in common.

They continued to think of different solutions until the long agricultural depression of the twenties. This common disaster forced an agreement on some method for raising farm prices above competitive levels; for the South it meant separating itself from the world market and surrendering its ancient faith in free trade. The first peace treaty between the farmers of the two regions, the McNary-Haugen bills, was twice vetoed by Coolidge. Campaigning in Topeka in 1932 Mr. Roosevelt made it clear that he was of a different mind, and the Agricultural Adjustment Act was the new and enduring bargain. It provided a common formula for raising prices and incomes for both the North and South; farmers of the two regions could get together without discussing high principles.

It still wasn't easy to legislate or administer legislation and treat North and South alike. Bureau leaders had a deep and influential interest in the way parity (farm subsidy) appropriations were divided. Meetings to consider the division between the two regions were occasionally long and bitter. Southern leaders wanted to plant corn on some of the acres diverted from cotton by Triple A. Corn-belt leaders stoutly opposed any increase in corn acreage outside what they termed the "natural corn area."

In 1940 Bureau leaders abandoned their policy of requesting large appropriations for direct (parity) payments by government check, a feature of the farm program to that time. Instead they voted for a government guarantee of farm prices to be made effective through commodity loans with the collateral passing to the government should the price fall below the loan level. The cotton leaders wanted loans at full parity price—then about 18 cents. The corn belt was opposed. Except in the purely cash corn areas, corn is marketed as pork. High corn prices only yield high returns after the price of hogs has had time to adjust upward. In the meantime, under the new policy, the corn farmer would not get his benefit check. The corn market, moreover, might be damaged were corn to rise too suddenly while other feeds remained cheap. However, Farm Bureau leaders have learned the value of compromise. A compromise eventually was reached on loans at 85 per cent of parity with parity payments making up the rest. Congress ratified the deal and the President accepted it.

Of late the most troublesome problem for the peacemakers has been inflation. Among some southern leaders fear of inflation is tempered by the possibility that it might mean 25-cent cotton. The corn belt is more cautious. Leaders remembered the World War I sequence of boom and disaster and do not want another. Last year some Bureau leaders joined a bandwagon movement in support of the Pace bill, which would have included farm labor costs in the parity formula and forced higher ceilings. However Earl Smith of Illinois declined to go along and so did the Congressmen from Illinois. The Iowa Farm Bureau followed Smith's lead. As a result the Pace bill was stopped —and the Bureau leadership had an impressive lesson on the importance of keeping peace in the coalition.

So long as the present leaders remain in office the coalition will continue. They remember the days when the North and South could not agree and what it cost in power. Under these leaders farm policy in the U.S. will be made not by and for farmers at large but by and for the producers of corn, hogs, and cotton. For the farm policy and farm politics of the U.S. this is a fact of first-rate importance.

THE HIGH COMMAND

Farm organizations of the past have too often disguised the qualities of a racket with the trappings of a crusade. The leaders have been petty larcenists who preached the ancient injustices of the farmer to provide themselves with a job. Farmers developed a healthy suspicion of their self-appointed messiahs. But the leaders of the Farm Bureau are mostly bona fide farmers or farm owners; few of them depend on the organization for a livelihood.

The two most influential men in the organization are President

O'Neal and Vice President Smith. The Board of Directors . . . meets quarterly with the officers. Emergency sessions have been frequent ever since the beginning of the New Deal. Once a year a resolutions committee, headed by Earl Smith, meets to hammer out a platform for the next twelve months. Afterward this is approved at a full-dress convention of delegates from the member states. As a guide to forthcoming farm legislation it merits considerably closer study than the convention platforms of the major political parties. If the officers find it expedient to modify the established *line* they do so, but rarely without first consulting the Directors or an executive committee of the Board. Individual Directors, particularly if they represent coalition territory, can usually count on a sympathetic hearing for their views.

The Farm Bureau has escaped management by job-hungry promoters but from another classic weakness of farm organizations it has not escaped. That is weakness in staff. Whatever money farm-organization leaders had in the past they have either paid to themselves or used to recruit new members. To impress legislators and their own members they depended on a few physiocratic clichés and a great deal of hot air. Facts were an expensive luxury with which they dispensed. The Farm Bureau staff is better than most farm organizations but far inferior to those of business and labor organizations. In the Chicago headquarters (Bureau doctrine holds that a Washington head office would lead to a warped and urban personality) a small research staff has recently been established. Under the guidance of Bureau Secretary and Treasurer Roger Corbett, until last year head of the Maryland Agricultural Experiment Station, it is likely to grow. And in the three-man Washington office the Farm Bureau has William Raymond Ogg.

It is the tireless Ogg who more than anyone else has kept the staff weakness of the Bureau from being fatal. Thin, low-voiced, unprepossessing, and terribly serious, Ogg is one of the hardest-working men in all Washington. From nine in the morning until ten at night, he digs information out of official reports or government departments, prepares statements for committee hearings and memorandums for Congressmen, confers on legislative strategy with Bureau allies on the Hill, helps draft bills and amendments, and attends meetings called by executive agencies. On minor legislation he appears on behalf of the Bureau to testify. He is constantly on the watch for unauthorized legislation on Capitol Hill, undesirable programs in the Department of Agriculture, and subversive price ceilings from the Office of Price Administration. On all of these matters he reports by long-distance telephone to President O'Neal in Chicago; if things look serious Ed, in turn, will call for a reservation on the Capitol Limited.

But on few things in Washington can the work or views of the inexperienced man be trusted; in spite of the faithful Ogg, the Bureau has paid heavily for its failure to develop and use an expert staff. Bureau legislation is often superficial and badly drafted; on occasion it has missed entirely the purpose for which it was planned. The Bureau was sharply reversed on amendments to the OPA appropriations bill during the summer of 1942 because, unwittingly, it asked for the virtual repeal of the price-control law. Both Ed O'Neal and Earl Smith are capable of great anger; occasionally they have conducted legislative sorties based on emotion untempered by reasoned study.

THERE IS NO FARM BLOC

Speaking at the annual convention of the Farm Bureau last December, Congressman Everett Dirksen gave the main reason for the existence of a farm lobby. Said he, "There is no farm bloc unanimity in the Congress. It is everybody thinking for himself." He was right; the notion that there is a closely knit, well-disciplined band of farm legislators, who think and vote alike on farm issues, is a popular fiction. There is no such organization in Congress; that is why the Farm Bureau exists.

The literal-minded farm legislator comes to Washington, not as a friend of an idea, but as the representative and protector of his own cotton, wheat, or dairy farmers. To do his job well he must, on occasion, be free to oppose the conflicting interests of other farm areas. So he sticks to his own knitting. Senator Bankhead, often styled the farm leader of the Senate, concerns himself largely with cotton. He knows better than to try to represent dairy farmers who favor taxes on oleomargarine, a derivative of cottonseed oil. Bankhead is a leader only because the cotton Senators and Congressmen he commands are the largest farm group in Congress. Senators Gillette of Iowa and Lucas of Illinois represent the midwest corn and hog producers; neither of them would think of speaking for eastern dairy and poultry producers who buy corn. An ancient rift divides the range-cattle producers protected by Senator O'Mahoney (Wyoming) from cattle feeders represented by Senator Butler (Nebraska). Cattlemen in general have never been friendly to the Triple A. Corn and cotton farmers are its staunch supporters.

In the House of Representatives the situation is the same. No member presumes to speak for farmers as a whole; none would be taken very seriously if he tried.

If legislation is to pass it must be planned so as to enlist the support of these diverse and sometimes conflicting groups. Congressmen who cannot be fully satisfied must be made to see that a half cake is better than none at all. A good deal of explanation and persuasion is necessary. Trades must be arranged. Above all, the legislation must be nursed through a Congress that, although it starts many bad laws, has the great virtue of finishing very few of them. All this is done both by the Farm Bureau and by the Department of Agriculture, which has always pleaded the farmer's case before Congress. Sometimes they work together; frequently, in recent years, they have been at odds. The Bureau works through its own special allies—Congressmen Cannon, Dirksen, and Wolcott, Senator Bankhead, Senator Lucas, and a few others. The Department uses the official leadership and a considerable number of special friends of its own. The Department has the higher batting average on completed bills. But it passes few bills over the objection of the Bureau.

THE ROLL CALL IS THE PAY-OFF

Anthony Trollope, one of the shrewdest political observers as well as one of the best novelists of his time, remarked, "A man in the right relies easily on his rectitude, and therefore goes about unarmed!" The Farm Bureau is certain of its rectitude and of the strength that inheres in virtue. Contrasting the tactics employed by the opposing forces in one of its recent legislative battles, the Bureau house organ *Nation's Agriculture* recently reported: "Against this avalanche of propaganda, prejudice, and misrepresentation, agriculture relied mainly on the simple justice of its case." Nevertheless the Bureau does not enter the lists unarmed—or equipped only with that triple armament classically associated with just causes. It has a number of tried methods of getting votes. Five are important:

First. The Bureau rewards its friends with reelection, without trying too hard to punish its enemies. To campaign against a candidate means a dangerous opponent should he be elected, and an angry one if he is defeated. Electioneering is conducted partly by formal endorsement of favored candidates, partly by the weekly newsletter that tallies the votes of Senators and Representatives and makes clear which is right or wrong by Bureau standards. No farm Congressman likes to have his district told he is voting against the best interests of the farmer.

However, direct participation by Bureau leaders in state and local politics is far more important than this scorekeeping. In the key Bureau states—Illinois, Alabama, Iowa, and a few others—the state and local leaders are influential politicians in their own right. Under their guidance state and local bureaus go powerfully to the support of candidates who deserve election and against those who do not. Thus, in Alabama where the small electorate lends itself well to Bureau methods, the state federation is an important cog in one of the quietly efficient political machines of the country. Compact support is given Alabama's John Bankhead and, with his advice and consent, to the members of the congressional delegation who are good friends of the farmer. In Alabama the relation between the Bureau and the Extension Service is very close. The Extension Service is theoretically above politics, but the people of Alabama are accustomed to quiet political activity by public servants. The Alabama Farm Bureau is a great comfort to any legislator who works faithfully for larger appropriations or their modern equivalent, which is higher prices.

Nevertheless the number of Senators and Congressmen whom the Farm Bureau has elected or could defeat is not large. Even in Alabama, John Bankhead is stronger than the Bureau; he has consistently supported the Farm Security Administration, which by Bureau standards is the greatest of all legislative crimes. What the Farm Bureau can do in many cases is turn a sure thing into a horse race, or make unimportant opposition serious. More frequently the Bureau is just one of the organizations that a candidate needs to have on his side if he is to have the best possible chance at the polls.

Second. The Farm Bureau makes masterful use of the conventional lobbying methods. After the Farm Bureau has convened and formulated its platform for the year, a full-dress presentation is made before the House Appropriations Committee and the agricultural committees of the House and Senate. The presidents of the state federations, all skilled in down-to-earth politics, come to Washington for the hearings and to hold private conferences with their own state delegations. Every farm Congressman is thoroughly informed on what the Bureau wants and why. When important legislation is up, Ed O'Neal calls the officers back. Meetings to persuade reluctant or backsliding legislators follow in the Capitol, in the Senate Office Building, or downtown at the Raleigh Hotel. These meetings, it should be said, are almost always friendly; the Bureau leaders talk a great deal about putting on the pressure but they use persuasion rather than threats. At all times Ed and the permanent Washington staff work quietly with friends of the Bureau at the Capitol. All members of Congress receive a steady flow of mimeographed explanations, protests, and denunciations. Few of these reach the public, for, unlike every other official or unofficial agency in Washington, the Farm Bureau issues few press releases.

In emergencies the Farm Bureau asks the officers to wire the members of their congressional delegation. At rare intervals—usually when the prestige of the organization is at stake—the same request is made of the rank and file. Last January *Nation's Agriculture* reported that convention delegates "voted unanimously to barrage the Senate immediately with all the power they could muster in their states, and to carry the fight on to the bitter end." In some states orders to apply pressure to Congressmen are transmitted to local bureaus through the federally aided county agents. This gets results. Congressmen know that a farmer who writes a letter about something is likely to remember the subject until the next election. Nevertheless the Farm Bureau uses such pressure sparingly. Congress will not respond if the appeals are too frequent.

Third. The Farm Bureau has become a powerful supporter of the legislative branch of the government against the executive. In the early New Deal the Farm Bureau defended the programs of Henry Wallace and the appropriations for his department (many people in the Department of Agriculture still believe that the Farm Bureau is a better ally than the President). But those days are gone. The Bureau now fights along with Congress against suspected encroachments by the executive on legislative powers; it has become a spectacular critic of the bureaucrats, including those of the department. A year ago a columnist reported with horror that a congressional sub-committee had given copies of an investigation of the Farm Security Administration to Ed O'Neal and had denied copies to officials of the agency itself. Farm members of the committee saw nothing remarkable about this; Farm Bureau friendship means votes.

Fourth. The Farm Bureau offers prominence and publicity to the legislators who are its friends. Those with some seniority in committees or in the service of agriculture can expect to have their names attached to legislation the Bureau is supporting. Bureau support ensures that there will be hearings and a better than average chance of enactment. Through the house organs and particularly through the thousands of meetings that it conducts, the Farm Bureau advertises its friends. After his fight on subsidies early this year, John Bankhead was publicly thanked by the Bureau and its allies and described as "able and brilliant . . . valiant . . . unwavering," a source of "inspiration and courage." Other friends of the Bureau can expect the same.

This last method of winning friends is probably to be explained by the Irish ancestry of Edward A. O'Neal. Blarney has many uses, as Ed knows. On no person has he used it more lavishly than on Clarence Cannon, chairman of the House Committee on Appropriations. Three years ago Chairman Cannon received the Farm Bureau award for distinguished service to American agriculture. Many who had watched the farm appropriation bills of preceding years believed he had earned the honor.

Fifth. Votes are obtained by skillful trading. In the early years of the New Deal, Ed O'Neal was able to work out many an arrangement with labor by which farm support for relief appropriations and labor legislation was exchanged for urban support of Farm Bureau measures. Numerous arrangements for reciprocal support are also made between the corn and cotton coalition and farmers from those parts of the country where Farm Bureau influence is slight.

Except for trading between farm groups, this method of getting votes is of markedly less importance now than it was a decade ago. For one thing the rift between the Farm Bureau and the unions has widened to the point of open warfare between the two. Bureau leaders believe labor has profited unduly from the war. Labor is blamed for subsidies, which the Bureau has now decided are downright shameful. But more important, the Bureau in recent years has been strong enough to pass legislation without logrolling. Resort to logrolling by a lobby is the result of weakness not strength.

As matters now stand, few things in politics are as certain as Ed O'Neal's ability to get votes. In the House of Representatives, Bureau friends head the Committee on Appropriations and, until the death of Congressman Steagall last year, the Committee on Banking and Currency. They are influential in the Committee on Agriculture. Nearly all farm legislation comes before one or another of these committees; the Bureau can count on a favorable report from any one of them. On the floor of the House of Representatives the Farm Bureau can pass or stop any *farm* measure on which it makes a determined fight. This does not mean that the Bureau controls a majority of the members. But in a showdown with the Administration (the strongest opposition it encounters) it can depend on the help of enough of the Republican minority to win. And the farm allies of the Bureau in Congress stay in Washington and stick to business while the urban members, on which the White House depends, are chronic absentees. The Bureau has met some defeats in the past two years but not in the House.

In the Senate, normally more sensitive to farm issues than the House, the Bureau is not so powerful. Members of the Senate have more political strength in their own right, and the Administration is stronger than in the House. In a pitched battle the Bureau cannot always win in the Senate. However, not all farm legislation requires a fight; and many a good half cake comes out of a conference committee.

The farmers—the kind of farmers who belong to the Bureau—are well represented in Washington.

57. *Some Lobbies Are Good* *

Everyone is aware that lobbying is an important phase of the governmental process, but few have any knowledge of the techniques of lobbyists. Too many of us think lobbyists are reprehensible characters engaged in shady, underhanded tactics. Mr. La Follette, a former Senator from Wisconsin and an acute student of the Washington scene, here presents a favorable picture of the lobbyist and his techniques.

The lobbyists in Washington are out in full force. The reason is self-evident. The Congressional calendar is jam-packed with controversial legislation which affects the pocketbooks and general welfare of millions of businesses, trade organizations, labor unions, professional societies and individual citizens. Lobbying with respect to Federal legislation is a multi-million dollar enterprise and seemingly increasing.

Public housing, labor legislation, Government subsidies, public power development, universal military training, legislation pertaining to oil, railroads and airlines—whatever the decisions may be by Congress on these and other pending issues, they will vitally affect the lives and fortunes of many.

The extent, methods and influence of lobbying activities in the nation's Capitol are not easy to evaluate. Not all of the activity that exists is discernible on the surface—notwithstanding the lobbying registration provisions enacted in conjunction with the Legislative Reorganization Act of 1946. On the other hand, exaggerated opinions are easily conjured in the absence of more complete facts. This much is certain: lobbying with respect to Federal legislation—and this does not necessarily mean attendance in Washington—is a major activity and has developed in recent years to the point where all the intricate and elaborate techniques known to the arts of advertising and public relations are frequently involved.

The fundamental aspects of lobbying are nothing new. In fact, the concept of trying to influence legislation by contacting legislators stems directly from a fundamental right in our democracy—the right of petition. The term itself, which is peculiar to the United States and not used generally elsewhere, apparently has its origins from the practice of seeking contact with legislators in the waiting rooms or lobbies, near the legislative chamber where the public is permitted. It is pic-

* Robert M. La Follette, Jr., *The New York Times Magazine*, May 16, 1948, pp. 15, 54, 56-58. Reprinted by permission of the author and the publisher.

turesque, just as the associated term to "buttonhole" a legislator, which is duly listed in Webster's Dictionary with the definition: "to hold by the button or buttonhole, as for conversation." It is doubtful how effective the literal application of the term may be; but "buttonholing" in the more general sense is in fact lobbying in its simplest and sometimes most effective form.

The practice of lobbying undoubtedly has been stimulated over the years as a result of the greater role assumed by Government in dealing more and more with the everyday activities of its citizens. For better or for worse, gone are the days of laissez-faire, caveat emptor and rugged individualism. The Government, and especially the Federal Government, has become an interested party in all manner of human relationships, economic organization, and with respect to the entire fabric of society.

Undoubtedly, lobbying has been stimulated too by the improved facilities of communication and transportation, whereby the public is enabled to keep tab on every step in the legislative process and to register reactions before it is too late. News and reaction on a large scale can be registered now in a period of a few hours, as against days, weeks or months a century ago. It is possible now, as we saw a few months ago, for a Senator to begin a filibuster speech and express a hope that a public reaction will set in before he finishes that very speech!

Also, lobbying is directly related to the complexity of the legislation under consideration. The more complex or technical a bill may be, the more need there is for expert advice and assistance on details. Often the persons directly affected can give the best information on practical application, as contrasted with the academic approach of the public administrator less familiar with details, even though such "practical" opinion often needs to be discounted to eliminate personal bias or generalized to meet a broader application. Tax legislation most certainly falls in this category.

Lobbying may be a pernicious evil at one extreme or an indispensable part of the legislative process at the other, depending on the circumstances and the methods of lobbyists. Few if any legislators would hold a brief for the avaricious, anti-social or unscrupulous tactics to which some special interests sometimes resort; but even fewer would be willing to abolish lobbying and cut off essential sources of information in exchange for "protection" against the unscrupulous.

The cloud of suspicion and the connotation of evil associated in the public mind with respect to lobbying is probably due primarily to three factors: (1) some lobbying activities do embrace undesirable methods or are working toward objectives which are inimical to the public welfare; (2) an element of secrecy often surrounds lobbying and is conducive to undesirable activities; and (3) there have been instances, which are now rare, when contacts for lobbying purposes were frequently associated with the giving and taking of bribes.

The latter situation was brought within the purview of the criminal code of the United States as far back as 1852 and has been strengthened by several major enactments since then, which provide for heavy fines and imprisonment plus forfeiture of public office and disqualification for holding thereafter any office of honor, trust or profit under the Government of the United States.

It is generally accepted that cases of outright bribery connected with lobbying are rare in Washington nowadays. I have been on the scene and close to many news sources in the Capitol for many years and my own observations confirm this opinion. The distribution of gifts of products or commodities to members of Congress is not uncommon, but there is no evidence that the practice has influence on legislation.

Efforts to curb the abuses of lobbying have been directed generally at the objective of full disclosure of sponsorships and expenditures. The force of public opinion, it is reasoned, will then be brought to bear on its abuses. That is the theory, too, on which most of the state laws on lobbying have been based. Massachusetts passed the first lobbying law in 1890 and about thirty-five states now have such laws, with varying provisions and varying degrees of enforcement.

The Federal Government's general lobbying act went on the statute books less than two years ago as a part of the Legislative Reorganization Act of 1946. Although lobbying on specific issues had been investigated on various occasions, and although legislation was passed on a few random aspects—such as the prohibition on the issuance of free railroad passes to legislators, and the special provisions directed against lobbying by the public utilities and shipping interests (in 1935 and 1936)—the enactment of general legislation had been frustrated for the primary reason that proposed legislation always followed too closely after disclosures of flagrant abuses. This tended to paint all lobbyists with the same black paint. It was naturally resented and opposed even by those who had nothing to fear from disclosure.

Fortunately, the 1946 act was not an aftermath of any lobbying scandal. It was sold to the Seventy-ninth Congress for what it is—an act to reveal the activities of lobbyists, not necessarily to curb or pass judgment thereon, and certainly not to interfere with the rightful access of citizens to their Congress.

As to the effectiveness of the present law in providing disclosures, it is generally agreed that considerable activity goes unreported, much of it under the interpretation that lobbying is not a "principal" activity of the organization or person. The Department of Justice, which is currently investigating compliance with the law, takes the position that any lobbying for compensation which is more than incidental activity must be reported, whether it be by an organization, its agents, or individuals. Until recently very few national trade organizations made reports as such, although their representatives did file reports of their own particular activities; and labor unions took the same course under the law. It remains to be seen what interpretation the courts will place on this section of the act, but already the action of the department has spurred many new registrations on the part of organizations as well as their agents.

The techniques of the lobbyists are many, varied and ingenious. They change and develop as conditions change and develop. The system of deluging Congress with thousands of communications obtained by "pressing a button" and giving the signal to the "faithful" back home to write or telegraph (without their knowing necessarily what the facts and issues are) is a comparatively recent development in Congressional annals. Yet, in the opinion of many, this technique is already outdated and has lost much of its effectiveness. Trade associations, labor unions and public utilities have pushed this device to the limit in past years—to say nothing of the officials in the executive departments who have used it to gain legislative ends or to stave off impending cuts in appropriations, notwithstanding the prohibition in law against using appropriations for such purposes.

A variation of this technique, that of sending large delegations to call in person on members of Congress, has proved to be a liability in some cases. Delegations of this sort are usually not adept in the art of lobbying and, by the very nature of their trek to Washington, they are usually keyed up to the point where almost inevitably they greet Members in an emotional, belligerent or threatening manner which can more easily alienate than win a vote.

However, the situation becomes different if it is apparent that the correspondent or visitor has a reasonable personal knowledge of the issue under consideration or has a viewpoint that is his own; or, if for some other reason the correspondent or visitor is well known and respected by the Congressman. Some of the simplest and most effective lobbies are built around the friendship and respect which is naturally accorded a capable man who represents a responsible organization in an open and above-board manner; who lays his cards on the table before the legislator and is in a position to commit his organization to performance on which they will deliver. Some of the farm organizations and railroad brotherhoods are noted for this technique.

Sometimes the contacts are made in a way that has been called "grass roots" lobbying. An organization which has branch offices or membership throughout the country can apply pressure through friends and associates of the Congressman in his own district—after the persons of influence back home have been properly approached, briefed on the situation and persuaded to make the contact and representation. This technique is often very effective and can be done without undue commotion or show of lobbying activity in Washington. The technique is well adapted for national organizations such as the railroads, labor unions, public utilities, real estate boards, used-car dealers and the like.

The use of the press, radio, or special propaganda publications to influence both the public and the Congress is still another medium for the lobbyist. There has been a growing realization in recent years that winning the support of public opinion is a tremendous asset in influencing legislation. Hence, it is not uncommon to use public-relations techniques to secure favorable opinions in the public prints or on the air. Information on articles or editorials "caused to be published" is required to be reported under the Federal Lobbying Act. Only about one in every eight or ten registered lobbyists acknowledges in his reports any attempts to lobby in this fashion, and then usually the articles are in the trade journals of his industry.

More recently it has become a customary procedure for lobbying organizations to try their own cases in advertisements in the press or in attractive pamphlets and documents intended to influence public opinion—and the Congress. In the controversy over the Taft-Hartley bill, for example, large sums were spent on both sides of the issue for radio and newspaper advertising. It appears that many expenditures for subtle public relations and advertising to influence legislation are charged to routine advertising and legal costs, without ever being reported under the Lobbying Act.

There is a type of lobbying known as "plush-horse" lobbying. This involves social entertainment. Social life is an important part of the Washington scene, and there is no doubt that lobbyists utilize this technique. Usually members of Congress are invited, not to discuss business but to make or maintain the lobbyist's contacts or to add prestige both to the social affair and to the reputation of those who arranged the party. How effective such non-business affairs may be to a lobbyist is a moot point, and it often is difficult to draw any definite line of demarcation between social activity for its own sake and entertainment designed to influence legislation. In any event, to the extent that the costs of such entertainment can be charged off as business expense, the entertainment is a good time for all and the tax collector is the heaviest loser.

So much for some of the techniques of the lobbyists. What about the extent of lobbyists' activities and the purposes for which they lobby?

In sheer numbers there are more registered lobbyists than members of Congress. More than 1,000 have registered under the lobbying law, although not all of these are currently reporting. A tabulation based on current registrations and quarterly statements reveals that the reported expenses and compensation are at a rate which exceeds $4,000,000 per year.

Of this amount, business and trade lobbies account for almost $3,000,000. Prominent in this group are the public utilities, the railroads and other transportation agencies; the N. A. M. and Chambers of Commerce; fiduciary institutions; sugar interests; and construction and real estate organizations. This group includes many of the higher paid individuals, ranging up to $65,000 per year for compensation. Almost 100 current registrants in this group receive compensation and expenses exceeding the rate of $10,000 per year.

The next largest group, labor organizations, accounts for about $400,000. Various professional societies, including those of doctors, dentists, nurses, libraries, teachers, osteopaths, chiropractors, optometrists, architects and insurance agents, account for about $250,000. A score of "public" lobbies, including various citizens' committees, womens' leagues, etc., total a similar amount. Lobbyists for the various farm organizations have reported expenditures aggregating about $150,000; and the veterans' organizations about $80,000.

Some of the subjects that are or have been under consideration by this Congress and which produced the major portion of lobbying activities are: rent control, public housing, reduction of taxes, amendments to administrative features of the tax law, taxation of cooperatives and insurance companies; long-range agricultural policies embracing price support, land use, soil conservation and the contest between butter and oleomargarine; railroad legislation such as the Bulwinkle bill granting exemption from certain provisions of the anti-trust laws; public utilities, including amendments to the Natural Gas Act, TVA and the California Central Valley project; sugar, labor, health, Federal aid to education, veterans; and foreign policy.

In summary, anyone who examines Federal lobbying will be impressed by the amounts of energy and dollars which are devoted to an effort to influence legislation. Some of it is useless. Some of it is wasteful. Some of it is contrary to the public interest. By and large, however, lobbying reflects the complexity of our society and Government. The bulk of it is a representation of viewpoints and interests which should be and are considered in the legislative process.

The legislators and the public must properly evaluate each lobby. Pressures exerted are not necessarily proportionate to the strength of an organization or to the merits of its position. Similarly, a "compromise" piece of legislation which satisfies various pressure groups does not necessarily make it good legislation. Legislative "log-rolling" (you support my proposition and I'll support yours) is one form of compromise which is indefensible.

The lobbying law relies upon publicity to accomplish its objectives. In this connection, three points should be emphasized:

(1) A stigma should not be attached to lobbying *per se* or to registration under the present lobbying act. The facts of full disclosure should speak for themselves without prejudice.

(2) Better compliance with the present lobbying law will be forthcoming when the law is further clarified by the courts and improved by the Congress.

(3) The Federal lobbying law is a step in the right direction. It is not the number of lobbyists in Washington that is most important, but rather what they are doing and how they are spending their money. It is in the public interest for the people and the Congress to have this information.

58. *Can the President and Congress Cooperate?* *

THE PRESIDENT and Congress are constitutionally coequal. Probably the framers of the Constitution intended the President to execute the legislative policy formulated by Congress, although—intent on an elaborate system of checks and balances—they did not clearly separate the two functions. As the living Constitution has developed, the President has become in a very real sense Chief Legislator as well as Chief Executive. Incumbents of the office have assumed this role more and more because the President is the only elected official with a truly national constituency. The internal structure of Congress and the decentralized character of our political parties have inhibited the rise of real leadership in Congress; thus, if legislative leadership is to exist, it must come from the President. As a legislator, however, the President comes into conflict with a Congress that is intensely jealous of its prerogatives. Failure of the President and Congress to cooperate results in governmental stale-

* Robert K. Carr, *The New York Times Magazine*, February 27, 1955, pp. 9, 26, 28, 30. Reprinted with the permission of the author; *The New York Times*; and Rinehart & Company, Inc., publisher of *American Democracy in Theory and Practice* (rev. ed. 1955), by Robert K. Carr and others, from Chapter 22 of which the present article was drawn in large part.

mate. Professor Carr explains why the President must attempt to lead Congress—a difficult and delicate undertaking—and what might be done to make cooperation more likely.

ABOUT A YEAR AGO, President Eisenhower held a press conference. A few days before, the Eighty-third Congress had convened for its second and final session and already one message after another had gone "to the Hill" outlining the President's legislative wishes concerning such diverse subjects as the farm problem, labor, social security and foreign policy. This was a sharp change from the preceding year in which Mr. Eisenhower had submitted very few legislative recommendations to Congress—so few that political commentators were recalling "weak Presidents" of the past and speculating whether Mr. Eisenhower intended to follow in their footsteps. And now at this press conference the following exchange took place between a reporter and the President:

Q. Mr. President, could you say what percentage of your recommended proposals . . . you would expect to be passed at this session?

A. The President said, Look, he wanted to make this clear. He was not making recommendations to Congress just to pass the time away or to look good. . . . He was going to work for their enactment. Make no mistake about that. That was exactly what he was in the White House for and what he intended to do.

Thus did the President, after one year in office, come to the realization that history judges "strong Presidents" by the caliber of their legislative proposals concerning the great policy issues of their times, and, what is more, by the success they enjoy in persuading Congress to enact these proposals into law. In the months following this press conference, Mr. Eisenhower, like other Presidents before him, learned that it is far easier to submit legislative proposals to Congress than it is to bring about their acceptance. Some seven months later when the Eighty-third Congress adjourned *sine die*, much of the Eisenhower legislative program either had been killed outright or had not been acted upon.

Now with so many pressing issues confronting the nation, the complex means by which the President and the Congress together control the making of national policies deserves new study. The fact that both Houses of the present Congress are controlled by the opposition party has some bearing on the issue, but it is not the fundamental factor. There are more basic reasons that make it hard for two branches of the National Government to work together.

These are the questions that need to be answered:

1. Why must a President do his best to lead Congress in the making of policy?

2. Why does he find this a very difficult thing to do?

3. What, if anything, can or should be done to convert the President and Congress to a smoother working team?

There is, first of all, an elementary reason why the President must try to impose his will on Congress. The President must lead Congress because Congress is not capable of leading itself. It is an inescapable fact that there is insufficient power in any one office or combination of offices inside Congress to produce vigorous, powerful leaders among the 531 members of that body. It is true that certain Congressmen, through the posts they hold, through their party seniority, and through the force of their personalities and abilities, are able to exercise influence over their colleagues. This is sufficient to provide Congress with a form of "collective leadership." But such leadership is seldom able to bridge the gap between House and Senate. Moreover, even within either House it is extremely unstable.

Experience shows that these leaders are seldom able to work together as a team for any period or to keep rank-and-file Congressmen continuously in line. Every Congressman's role as an "ambassador" to Washington from his home district takes precedence over his membership on a national "legislative team." Whenever district interests or personal inclinations clash with the team position, he does not hesitate to quit the team.

One illustration will suffice. The Senate majority floor leader in the Eighty-third Congress, William Knowland of California, made no effort to lead the fight against the Bricker Amendment when it was being considered by the Senate in 1954, in spite of the fact that President Eisenhower earnestly hoped that Republican Senators would vote against it. He not only refused to lead the opposition to the amendment; he insisted upon voting for it. The President himself had to throw off reserve and dignity and take charge of the beleaguered forces in the Senate that were trying to hold the line against the unwanted amendment.

The nature of the times is the second reason why it is absolutely essential that the President lead Congress. The world over, in democratic and non-democratic countries, the technical character of problems of policy determination compels legislative bodies to defer more and more to the ideas and recommendations of executive authority in government. In the areas of foreign policy and national defense, Congress is particularly dependent on the President. Getting along with foreign nations and safeguarding our own nation against attack have become complex undertakings. The President has direct access to the advice and knowledge of professional experts in these fields, and as Chief Executive he alone is in a position to weigh the data and recommendations of the experts and to suggest policies to Congress.

Congress may jealously guard its right to scrutinize and revise these recommendations, but it is forced to recognize its own inability to make the initial study of a problem or to originate a policy. What is true of foreign policy and national defense is true in only slightly less degree of such domestic issues as the farm problem, tax policy or labor-management relations.

The third reason for Presidential leadership is that the President alone represents the nation at large, because he alone is chosen in an election in which national issues, and alternatives as to national policy, are brought into reasonably sharp focus. The President can claim to speak for a majority of the people; the Congressman, however informed or renowned, occupies no such exalted position. Only the voters back home have passed judgment on him, or will determine his fate when Election Day comes again. No wonder then that the task of leadership falls to this one man who has the confidence and approval of the people, not just of Massachusetts or Texas, but of the entire nation.

Why does the President find it hard to lead Congress? Why do a President and his advisers have to assume that Congress will be difficult to handle, whether or not his party has working majorities in both Houses? Why do they have to remind themselves continuously that it takes shrewd, untiring effort to win that measure of executive-legislative cooperation essential to the success of any administration? Several factors have a bearing upon the answers to these questions.

Separation of powers makes it difficult for the President and Congress to work together harmoniously in the achievement of common goals. Each derives its authority directly from the Constitution; each is fully aware of the independent position it has always enjoyed in American history; each is impressed by its own importance; each jealously guards its power and prestige. Separation of powers may be a bulwark against tyranny; but it is not conducive to smooth teamwork.

At the same time that the election of President and Congressmen by different constituencies makes it necessary for the President to try to lead Congress, it renders that task difficult. Because the President has received the support of 30,000,000 or more voters in a national election, he finds it natural to think and act in terms of the grand strategy of national policy, or to serve, as Theodore Roosevelt put it, as "the steward of the people."

The Congressman, on the other hand, is often a hostage of powerful groups back home. His inability to resist the pressures brought upon him by these groups may cause him to resent the relative ease with which the President ignores such a factor in calling for enlightened national legislation, to stiffen his loyalty to the home state or district, and to criticize the President as a visionary, a "do-gooder" more concerned about saving the world than with wheat prices in Kansas or unemployment in Detroit.

The sense of antagonism between the President and Congress is further heightened by the fact that more often than not the President favors a positive attack upon social problems while Congress frequently takes a let-well-enough-alone attitude. Because Congressmen are often caught in the crossfire of rival pressure groups, they are prone to operate by the rule, "When in doubt vote no." Because he represents the nation at large, the President can keep his eyes fixed on the larger issues confronting the country and try to tackle them head-on without making concessions to local interests to a point where national policy ceases to be positive or forthright.

The President is also apt to have superior access to information. He may be, as is President Eisenhower, a conservative person, disinclined to approve vigorous or broad exercise of the power of government. But when his subordinates brief him concerning the facts of a social problem, the case for positive action by government often becomes compelling to him. Congressmen do not have such direct access to data, and do not find it so compelling when it reaches them second-hand.

The most important handicap under which the President operates in trying to lead Congress is the character of our national political parties. These parties are so poorly disciplined and so highly decentralized that they fail to serve as the means by which an administration's adherents in Congress can be welded into a smooth-running machine. The President is thus denied democracy's most effective tool for executive control of a Legislature—the responsible, disciplined party.

Far more often than not, the President is able to persuade Congress to accept his recommendations only by means of bipartisan majorities. The failure of the party groups in Congress to function as cohesive voting factions is illustrated again and again in every session of Congress.

A striking example was supplied in the Eighty-third Congress in the vote on the Bricker Amendment. The amendment, which required a two-thirds majority for approval, was defeated at the end in a watered-down version by the narrow margin of one vote, the final line-up being sixty in favor and thirty-one opposed. Thirty-two Republicans and twenty-eight Democrats voted for the proposal and fourteen Republicans, sixteen Democrats and one Independent voted against it. The party groups were thus split right down the middle.

This weakness of the party groups leaves the President with the problem of overcoming the divisive effects of the group struggle in

Congress. He can usually count on his own party for a hard core of support. But this will seldom be enough, and he must laboriously try to piece together a coalition that includes a majority of the participants, in what Bertram Gross calls "the legislative struggle," if a controversial bill is to be enacted.

Among these participants are the President himself, the two party organizations, and the powerful pressure groups—in particular, those representing business, labor and agriculture. We are here face to face with one of the central problems of American government. Given widespread but necessarily vague public support for governmental action on a social problem, and given intelligent understanding of the problem by the President, which leads him to advocate a policy that takes into account "national interest" considerations, how can Congress be persuaded to take any action at all, and then to take action that will not be so hopelessly compromised by concessions to particular interests that it will not serve the national welfare?

What can be done to convert President and Congress into a smoother working team? Many answers to this question have been suggested in recent years. They run all the way from the belief that we must continue to try to make the present system work, to drastic programs for constitutional reform looking toward the adoption of some form of parliamentary government as in Great Britain.

Proposals in the latter class vary, but they provide for either the replacement of the President by a Prime Minister who would be directly responsible to Congress, or the election of the President, Senators and Representatives for simultaneous terms with provision for dissolving the Government in case of a deadlock and calling a new election.

A proper regard for reality compels recognition of the fact that no startling changes in the basic character of American government are likely to be made in the foreseeable future. If our national salvation depends upon the adoption of far-reaching constitutional changes, the battle is almost certainly already lost. For such changes will not come in time to help us solve the problems of the present world crisis or of our dynamic domestic system.

In avoiding the illusion of salvation through constitutional change, we must also recognize that in good measure the inability of the President and Congress to work together is deeply rooted in the character of our nation. Ours is a great industrial society, characterized by geographic, cultural and economic diversities greater than those that have ever been found in any other society. No mere streamlining of our political machinery will ever enable us to avoid the necessity of seeking a constant compromising of these diverse interests, or of continuously searching for a satisfactory balance in our national policies between representation of group interests and the national welfare.

In a very real way the group interests have their innnings in Congress, whereas the national welfare finds its defender in the President. Thus a substantial measure of conflict between these two is both inevitable and desirable. It is the price we pay for wanting both unity and diversity—for trying to maintain a united nation in which 165 million people are permitted to develop highly varied and individual interests.

Constitutional change may be out. But there are more modest proposals for change that might make it easier for President and Congress to work together. One is the oft-suggested executive-legislative cabinet which calls for the adding of ten Congressional leaders to the heads of the ten Executive departments to constitute the top policy-planning agency of a National Administration.

Members of Congress would thereby be given a formal role in the initiation of a President's legislative program, and there is good reason to suppose that this might result in a friendlier reception for the President's recommendations when they reached Congress. Not the least attractive aspect of this proposal is that it could be put to a trial without even the necessity of passing a law. The present Executive Cabinet rests on a customary basis only; custom could easily henceforth provide for a Cabinet containing legislators as well as administrators.

Another proposal is that all of the Congressional candidates of both parties in all forty-eight states be nominated in a single primary election on the same day—say, the first Tuesday in September in election years. Advocates of this proposal assert that such a plan would help to focus attention on national issues in the selection of Congressional candidates and to strengthen party discipline in Congress. The nomination and election of Congressmen is bound to remain a highly *local* undertaking in a nation as large as ours, but the possibility that a national Congressional primary might alter the balance ever so slightly toward a greater concern for national considerations is very real. Moreover, it would take only an act of Congress to put the proposal into effect.

Finally, there are numerous proposals for internal changes in Congressional procedure designed to strengthen party discipline, and thereby to make it easier for President and party leaders to work for the adoption of a legislative program.

Among the most promising of these proposals are abolition of the seniority rule for the selection of committee chairmen in favor of some system that would place a greater premium upon party regularity in the assignment of these important posts; curbing unlimited debate in the Senate to allow passage of bills which have majority backing in that body; and supplanting the Rules Committee in the House of Representatives with a steering committee truly responsible to the majority party. All of these changes could be made by the simple expedient of amending the House and Senate rules.

It seems likely that the pressure to find ways of achieving more efficient teamwork between the Executive and Legislative branches will continue to increase. Whether we will try one of the plans discussed above, or find some other means of smoothing out the difficulties that now plague the President and Congress in their efforts to work together, is not easy to say. In the long run, this is surely an area of American government where the flexibility and change that have so often characterized our past political development will be strongly needed in the future.

In the meantime a President must do what he can to lead Congress.

X

STATE LEGISLATURES

59. *The State Legislator: Two Views*

MR. AND MRS. NEUBERGER have been members, respectively, of the Oregon Senate and House of Representatives. Mr. Neuberger, now United States Senator from Oregon, recounts experiences in his own political fishbowl, showing the types of tribulations that face modern state legislators. Although he is critical of some of the activity of the state legislature, he understands, appreciates, and defends those politicians whom T. V. Smith has called "the patron saints of American life." Mrs. Neuberger writes about the "lady legislator" and discusses some of the problems of women in politics.

A. TRIBULATIONS OF A STATE LEGISLATOR*

MY COLLEAGUES and I are typical state legislators. We enact the laws that set speed limits on the highways; we specify minimum salaries for classroom teachers; we fix the content of butterfat in Grade A milk; we draw up the rules governing the purity of drinking water; and we determine whether a citizen convicted of murder in the first degree shall be gassed, hanged, shot, electrocuted, or merely clapped behind iron bars.

Amendment 10 of the Constitution, added by Madison and his fellow States' Righters in 1791, says:

> The powers not delegated to the United States by the Constitution . . . are reserved to the States respectively.

This constitutional responsibility may not be carried out wisely or too well, but there are many extenuations. We are underpaid, under-

* Richard L. Neuberger, *The Reporter*, II (January 31, 1950), pp. 31-33. Reprinted by permission of the author and the publisher.

staffed, and perennially short of time. We are so accessible to every pressure group that we barely can push our way through the marble corridor for coffee and sandwiches at lunch time.

I sit in the Oregon senate, where I represent the state's largest city. In one morning we passed fourteen bills. The longest ran to forty-two pages and contained eleven thousand words. We were told by the sponsors that it raised the fees on all motor vehicles. Only after the bill had gone to the governor did we discover that, while doubling the toll on passenger sedans, it also contained a section that substantially reduced highway fees for large trucks and trailers.

Was there venality in this? I am doubtful. Our committees have no research staffs, and no investigators. We cannot even take testimony under oath. If I want to check something at the state library, I put on overshoes and slosh over there through the snow. The air is good for my physical well-being, but I dare not go often. What if a bill of paramount interest to my urban constituents should come up while I am away from the floor?

We direct the spending of $300,000,000 in state revenue, and a legislative session costs a fraction of one per cent of this: $790,000. Our daily pay during the session amounts to $4.12. This just about takes care of the rent for the modest auto court where my wife and I live.

At least half the senators, unable to get by on $4.12, add an extra eight dollars to their exchequers by hiring their wives as secretaries. Few of the wives are trained to type, take shorthand, or even keep track of documents. On one occasion we voted an amendment into a Columbia River barge-line bill, but it was lost by one member and never showed up in the law.

The United States Congress is generous with funds for its own patronage and perquisites. Why are we of the legislature so contrastingly stingy? Largely because we function under more careful surveillance from the voters, who peer over the gallery rail and buttonhole us on our way to our lodgings. One visiting grade-school class, for instance, took home to parents an unfavorable report about me—I had my feet on the desk during a senate session.

Life in this political fishbowl makes for amusing timidity on the part of the occupants. In a way, the legislature is like Uncle Wilbert Robertson's description of a minor-league baseball club—"full of has-beens and would-bes." Near me sit several state senators who have aspired repeatedly, without success, to the governorship or the U. S. Senate. Salted among these political relics are a number of young members whom the press regards as certain for the big-time. Ambition sticks out on these men like whiskers. They never move without counting risks. Occasionally they duck a controversial roll call.

Despite the wage scale, most legislators are not poverty-stricken. The per-capita income of the people of our state is $1,302, but a veteran capital correspondent estimates that of the average legislator at $10,000.

"Who else," he asks, "could afford to leave his job or business for the munificent sum of $4.12 a day?"

We keep in touch with other legislatures, and find we are not too far out of line in respect to salaries. Rhode Island pays five dollars a day, Florida ten, and Kentucky fifteen. But wealthy New York pays the men and women who make its laws five thousand dollars a year. Some of our full-time state department heads do not get so handsome a sum.

Are most legislators honest? I am certain the state doubts that we are, which is one big reason why the voters disapprove of more adequate legislative salaries. Yet I believe few members would take an outright bribe. Occasionally we feel some senator is tied by financial tethers to a slot-machine ring or liquor lobby, but such men are readily marked, and their effectiveness is questionable.

Subservience to interests and lobbies is of a subtler sort, and does not involve currency changing hands behind a convenient pillar or cloakroom door. As a British versifier once remarked of his country's press:

> You cannot hope to bribe or twist,
> Thank God, the British journalist;
> But seeing what the man will do.
> Unbribed, there's no occasion to.

Practically every one of us has his eye on a more heavily-braided political epaulet. Campaign funds are important to this goal. It took a treasury of $50,623 to elect one of our colleagues to the governorship in 1948. A state legislator who has favored keeping ax and saw away from timberlands reserved for school revenues is hardly apt to have his gubernatorial dream financed by sawmill proprietors.

Today a new political factor has intruded. Since 1940 the population of Oregon has gone up fifty-nine per cent. The state was predominantly rural a decade ago; now most of the people live inside city limits, and thousands of them belong to trade unions. No longer are the lobbyists for power and lumber, with their overflowing treasuries, the only ones to call the tune. Union representatives sit in the galleries and write down names as the roll calls proceed.

After a vote on industrial accident benefits, the square-jawed CIO secretary said to a man who had sat in the senate for a good number of years: "I believe you'll regret your *nay* on that, my friend."

The remark was passed without malice, but when I came back from lunch the senator was still slumped in his chair, his face the color of the linen handkerchief which protruded from his pocket. Perhaps he was totting up the number of CIO loggers and longshoremen in his district.

The legislature generates its own social life, its rivalries for preeminence in the receiving line, and its own intrigues. Two downtown hotels in the capital, a city of fifty thousand inhabitants, house most of the members, although a few save money by doing their own cooking at motor courts. Barely a week of the session has gone by before the gossip is fully stabilized.

Everyone knows which senator cannot hold his liquor, and which lonely representative has formed a comfortable friendship with a fortyish old maid in one of the state agencies, whose deep-cut neckline at the Governor's Ball showed what some man had been missing.

Yet the legislators' conduct on the whole is decorous. These men work hard—as they must to possess even a fragmentary knowledge of the bills being considered. Our state, for example, has an obscure statute exempting from the corporate income tax all businesses deriving ninety-five per cent of their receipts from property rentals, a strike of truly Klondike proportions for the real-estate trade. Someone didn't catch that joker.

Since 1932 the country has been decisively Democratic in every Presidential election and in every Congressional election except one, but throughout that time the Republicans have made a far stronger showing in the states. Legislatures in the Northern and Western states have been preponderantly Republican, but the national totals of Republican and Democratic state legislators are pretty even, because of such legislatures as Alabama's, in which one hundred forty Democrats and one Republican sit.

The G.O.P.'s power in the states is partly explained by the fact that most legislatures have failed to reapportion their districts in conformity with population shifts. Oregon's state constitution requires a redistributing of the legislature every ten years, yet the senate has not been reapportioned since 1909. Although people since have migrated to the city to drive trucks and build ships, the legislature continues to represent an agrarian population pattern that has largely vanished.

My urban district has eighty-one thousand residents. A few chairs away is a senator from a backwoods constituency with eight thousand inhabitants. His vote can cancel mine on any issue, and we are poles apart on virtually all social and economic questions. Why should he try to understand a bill providing for slum clearance? In his realm the ranches are measured by horizons rather than acres.

The whole senate chamber tingles with mistrust of the big city. I even encountered suspicion when I sponsored a bill which would have diverted city tax revenues to improve rural schools. Mayor William Devin of Seattle recently pointed out that his community cannot install parking meters or improve civil service without first getting the permission of the hinterland senators and representatives who rule the state legislature.

A distinguished member of the U. S. Senate once said to me:

> You get a little better perspective on things three thousand miles from home. The voters aren't looking right down your throat all the time. And it's a little more difficult for a handful of people to make it look like they represented the whole universe.

I now know exactly what he meant. Recently I put my name to a bill which would limit the numbers of the billboards that make garish corridors out of our highways. A few men were naturally stung on what Justice Brandeis once called "the pocket nerve." They were soon able to make it seem as if the entire state was up in arms against the proposed law.

Although I had a perfect voting record on the AFL scoresheet, the head of the Signpainters Union called me an "enemy of labor," and claimed that I wanted to throw hundreds of men out of work. Then the "widows and orphans" began to appear: forlorn families which would become public charges if they no longer could rent their roadside property to the signboard companies. The state advertising club sent an impressive delegation, which accused me of being a foe of the Bill of Rights: The advertising men would lose their "freedom of speech" if their billboards were barred from the countryside.

Although the bill had been suggested to me by a wealthy old woman who loved scenery and did not like to see it defaced, my proposal was denounced by these delegations as being of Communist origin. Presently several senators came to me shamefacedly and revoked their pledges to vote for the measure.

Put to a public referendum, I imagine the bill would have passed by at least five to one. These few small pressure groups were able to induce the legislature to reject it overwhelmingly. I still marvel at the fact that the billboard owners themselves never once appeared during the entire operation. One can admire an enemy's technique even while being victimized by it.

B. FOOTNOTES ON POLITICS BY A LADY LEGISLATOR*

I AM the only woman in a House of Representatives of sixty members. In recent weeks, we have debated such issues as the price of milk, tenure for school teachers, the legality of yellow margarine, and where to establish homes for wayward children. These are questions which primarily concern women, yet they have been decided by a legislative body overwhelmingly made up of men.

What if the situation were exactly reversed?

We also have debated hunting and fishing regulations, a tax on cigars, employment preference for Korean war veterans, penalties for fixing athletic contests, and the pay of policemen and firemen. These questions primarily involve men. I can only imagine what the male population of our state would think if they had been decided by fifty-nine women and one lone man!

The Bureau of the Census has just announced that women now outnumber men for the first time in United States history. Yet out of 7,234 members of the legislatures of forty-eight states, only 235 are women. This is a negligible 3 per cent.

The simple fact is that every time men enact a law today, more women than men are affected by the result. But there are other, equally compelling reasons why there should be more women in our legislative halls. Where educational matters are being decided, they can represent the viewpoint and hopes of the child more accurately than any man could hope to do. Most women have a humanitarian approach to social problems that is a healthy antidote to practical politics.

And, to climax the argument, a lawyer who lobbies in all eleven of our Western states said to me: "I've met some men legislators who had their hands out, but I've never yet even heard of a woman in public life who wasn't impeccably honest."

In view of this, isn't it time to consider "equal representation" for women?

Demagoguery ill suits a woman. A male politician may get by with stem-winding speeches that sound like a steam calliope. Such a performance from a woman would be regarded as practically a vaudeville act. Her contribution must be the short, pithy observation which gets right down to brass tacks. Equivocation may promote the ambitions of the male officeholder, but the woman is best off when she speaks her mind.

* Maurine B. Neuberger, *The New York Times Magazine*, May 27, 1951, p. 18. Reprinted by permission of the author and the publisher.

In politics, long considered a realm exclusively for males, the woman intruder is most effective when she is seen but rarely heard. This does not mean she should be a cipher—far from it. But she must make every verbal missile count If she even remotely confirms the legend of the clacking female, her usefulness is at an end.

Most male politicians believe, in their smug superiority, that women know nothing of politics. This has its advantages, for the woman. She can make a statement which would be looked upon as heresy coming from an elective official in trousers, yet in her is attributed to naïveté or lack of "experience."

For example, the dairy interests long have been practically sacrosanct in our state. Both our United States Senators, including the intrepid Wayne L. Morse, opposed removal of the punitive Federal tax on butter's cheaper competitor, oleomargarine. After I had risen to my feet in the State Assembly and cited figures to show that Oregon dairy farmers were robbing the housewife with their abnormal fees for milk poundage, one of my awed male colleagues confided to me: "What you said is true, but only a woman could make such a statement in this Capitol building—and get away with it."

In politics, the woman's mission is to champion the particular aspirations of her sex, but to expect no quarter in doing so. She is in for a grim awakening if she enters public life thinking her male associates will defer to her opinions merely because she is a woman. Superficial amenities she will receive by the score, but these often will cloak the grimmest kind of opposition to her cherished legislative proposals.

My fifty-nine male associates bow and scrape when merely the social graces are at stake. I am "our fair and lovely colleague" or "the gentlewoman from Multnomah County." I sit by common consent at the head table at banquets. No one lets me carry my own briefcase through the marble corridors. Representatives rise when I enter the members' lounge. On the surface, my every wish is a command.

I thought so, too—at first.

Then, one emotion-fraught afternoon, I appealed from a ruling of the chair. Someone had to second my appeal to carry the issue to a vote.

Robert's Rules of Order later proved to be on my side, but the fifty-nine males in the chamber, Republicans and Democrats alike, sat on their hands and stilled their voices. The danger flags were flying. No longer was I a mere female in a fluffy blouse and sheer hose. This was womankind challenging man's inherent right to rule. And chivalry died right then and there.

The woman who enters politics must be feminine, yet firm. Without sacrificing any of the qualities which make women attractive in men's eyes, she must stand by her convictions and uphold the interests of her sex. And when questions involving economic dominance and political power are at issue, not only will she receive no preference because of her sex, but she probably will be considered fair game for that reason.

This has been demonstrated in greater political arenas than the Oregon State Legislature. Not even Senatorial seniority kept Margaret Chase Smith of Maine from losing an important committee assignment as a result of her rebuke to Senator McCarthy. And one of the most bitter campaigns of vilification in the annals of the Pacific Coast helped bring about the defeat of Helen Gahagan Douglas for the Senate in California last November.

Gossip, much of it malicious, has been the servant of politics from time immemorial. If, to a man, it can be an annoyance and matter of concern, to a woman it can be far worse. Because my photograph appeared in a local paper in a swimming suit, it has been whispered by some that I am everything from a nudist to a nautch dancer.

Out of 164 legislative nominees in our state last fall, only four were women. I personally know of many qualified women who would have run had they been able psychologically to steel themselves to the inevitable slurs. In a way, the scurrilous attack on Mrs. Anna Rosenberg last winter may have salutary effects.

That episode has shown that a woman can endure a Gethsemane of abuse and yet emerge stronger and more respected for it. Her confirmation by the Senate to be Assistant Secretary of Defense was unanimous.

Politics are as close as we come to war in our normal peacetime lives. The "killer instinct" to destroy an adversary is rarely suspended because the adversary happens to wear skirts and bear children. In a nice, smiling sort of way, the American woman in politics must not let herself be pushed around.

After I had written to the daily paper in a near-by city questioning the vote of the local legislator on an issue of interest to women, he came to me with the clipping in his hand. "I'm getting lots of mail from housewives because of your letter," he said angrily. "I don't think that was a very ladylike thing for you to do."

"Perhaps it wasn't," I replied sweetly. "But if you were a gentleman, would you have voted against a lady's bill?"

That stopped him.

60. *Those Dinosaurs--The State Legislatures* *

MR. DESMOND, a member of the upper house of the New York legislature, refers to legislatures as dinosaurs. Dinosaurs may be extinct, but legislatures definitely are not. Mr. Desmond would not, of course, remove legislatures from the governmental scene as no longer useful or worthy to survive. He recognizes that legislatures perform a vital function in our democracy. The organization, committee structure, lack of staff, limited sessions, and other deficiencies inherited from a simpler society deprive legislatures of the opportunity to function efficiently—or even democratically in some instances—in the present day. If they are to regain their rightful place in modern government, reform is necessary. Mr. Desmond describes the nature and practices of existing legislatures and suggests changes to improve their performance.

NEW YEAR this year rang in the lawmaking season for some 6,500 state legislators in forty-two states (the others meet in the spring or in even-numbered years). January is the month most state representatives (or assemblymen) and senators leave their farms, insurance offices and law practices to gather at their state capitols for the opening of the 1955 legislative sessions.

It is a time of joyous reunion for the lawmakers. In the thirty-four states and Alaska that have biennial sessions in odd-numbered years, many have not seen each other in two years (in eight states it is only a one-year absence). As they thumped each other's back in hearty welcome and inquired with genuine solicitousness about each other's health, there was much of the gay spirit which prevails at a college reunion.

But if the legislators greeted the opening of the sessions with happy heart, they were virtually alone. The convening of the legislatures is greeted with less than enthusiasm by the public. Business shudders. Labor holds its breath. Farmers shrug their shoulders. Governors wince at the chore of keeping a rein on lawmakers. In many states the sessions are deemed somewhat as a recurrent, unavoidable public calamity.

Nor is this apprehension new. Thoreau, when informed the Massachusetts legislature was about to convene, is reported to have told a neighbor, "I must go downtown to buy a lock to put on my back door."

* Thomas C. Desmond, *The New York Times Magazine*, January 16, 1955, pp. 15, 56, 58. Reprinted by permission of the author and publisher.

In 1912 the newsmen who covered the state capitol at Albany sang this meaningful ballad:

> The Capitol's a funny place,
> Where statesmen congregate to legislate,
> They come to "cure" the people's ills,
> And bring along a ton of bills;
> But when the real work comes along
> And the session's end is nigh,
> You see them flag the people's bills
> To let their own get by. For——
>
> Every honest statesman has some interests of his own,
> Every legislator wants his good things left alone;
> And all the hot air and agitation
> Over water and conservation
> And Niagara's illumination
> Has a meaning all its own.

The fact is that state legislatures lumber about their business with all the grace and efficiency of a dinosaur. January is given over to a leisurely oiling of the lawmaking machinery. Leaders are picked, committee chairmen designated, patronage allocated, staff people hired. And behind each task may lie days of backroom wrangling and trading by party leaders in and out of the legislatures, and in some states by powerful lobbyists who dangle lawmakers like charms on a woman's bracelet.

In February, the wheels begin to move. Bills are winnowed and weeded. Committee hearings are held; budgets passed; appropriations authorized, and measures reported out for debate and vote. At the end of February or mid-March, with a final roar and in a hectic nerve-racking last-minute burst of energy, the legislatures will drive themselves to a fury of activity and grind out mountains of laws. Most are non-controversial; many are passed at the rate of one a minute.

Based on past records, some 100,000 bills will be introduced during this legislative season. About 25,000 will become law. All this within sixty days in Arkansas and Nevada, in ninety days in Minnesota and North Carolina. New York legislators can continue at work indefinitely but customarily finish toward the end of March; Illinois lawmakers, by July 1.

The 1955 sessions will attempt again the endless quest for a solution to the dilemma of trying to reduce taxes while increasing services. Desegregation will occupy the limelight in Southern legislatures. Right-to-work and utility anti-strike legislation will be pressed in states that do not have strong unions. Ohio will consider creating an office of public defender to protect consumers from utility "rate-gouging." Arkansas will debate going into the wholesale liquor business. Bingo will win major attention in New York, while old-age pensions will give California its recurrent headache. Nearly every state will find new highway appropriations looming up high on the lawmakers' priority list.

Legislatures will have their quotas of bills to shorten or lengthen the season for taking alewives, a protected species of fish, or to legalize some forgetful village clerk's failure to advertise bids for a snow plow in the local weekly paper. All will poke their official noses into a thousand minor details of government. But to emphasize the wearisome or ludicrous minutiae which occupy much of the time of the legislators is to present a distorted view.

Our lawmakers are engaged in one of the most colorful and important dramas of our time. In our legislatures labor is pitted against management, farmers versus consumers, liberals against conservatives. Here is the clash of men and groups seeking power or profit. Here the dislocations in our society are bared.

The state legislatures are the training ground for future Governors, Congressmen and Presidents. Here, much like baseball managers at winter training camps, party leaders test the loyalty of promising prospects, size them up under pressure. Franklin D. Roosevelt learned the political arts in the New York senate at Albany. Abraham Lincoln gained self-confidence at Springfield. Sherman Adams, assistant to President Eisenhower, was tutored in government in the New Hampshire legisature. Theodore Roosevelt sharpened his wits, tongue and political skills in the New York assembly.

But even in moments of epic achievement, the halo of heroism does not fall on state legislators. It is the governor who is cast in the hero's mold. He is the dashing quarterback; the lawmakers are the unimaginative beefy line-men. The activities of lawmakers are shrouded in technicalities and obscured by legalistic procedures which hide the sheer drama of lawmaking.

Perhaps more importantly, the history of our state legislatures has been studded with too many shameful examples of venality, corruption and irresponsibility. The tough South Side of Chicago has sent to the Illinois legislature members reputed to have been allied with the Capone mob. The liquor lobby in California, the dog-track mob in Massachusetts, the oil interests in Texas, to name but a few examples, have contributed to the shame of the state legislatures.

But the substantial accomplishments of the lawmakers tend to be overlooked. The state legislatures have adopted some of the most far-reaching social advances of our time. They instituted workmen's compensation systems. They started relief for the indigent long before the Federal Government stepped into the field. They took the first steps to wipe out child labor. They established public schools and state universities. They promoted disease research facilities. For every legislature that meekly obeyed the whims of a Huey Long or a Frank Hague, there have been others, as in Wisconsin, which pioneered in social legislation.

Virtually all phases of modern life come within the realm of statutes passed in our state legislative chambers. Laws that tax you and laws that command you and laws that often don't mean a thing; laws that deal with the mortgage on your home and the electrical wiring in your apartment; laws that regulate the marketing of the clothes you buy, the purity of the water you drink.

But the legislatures have far more important duties than manufacturing statutes. They furnish a forum for release of the socio-economic tensions in our society. They provide an outlet for the pent-up feelings of the disgruntled, the trapped, the under-dogs and the top bananas. So long as the drys and wets, the tenants and landlords, workers and bosses, have a way, through the legislature, of obtaining a fair hearing, democracy avoids violence or disruptive direct action.

Actually, lawmakers rarely initiate laws; they simply affirm or disapprove solutions developed by others. The legislatures are not adept at problem-identification nor at problem-solving. They are too big, averaging forty members in the senates, and 120 in the lower chambers. They are too unwieldy; Georgia has sixty-three standing committees in its house of representatives alone. So they handle current problems with all the deftness of a bulldozer; at best, they lunge at a few main issues, and toss most of the others into the laps of experts in state agencies or technicians hired by the lobbies.

One of the most significant aspects of lawmaking is that it is a group process. An unsolved mystery about our legislatures is that while the lawmakers are generally better educated, more economically secure, at least as intelligent as their constituents, and not infrequently are quite able, earnest men, the group product is far below the expected quality, based on individual capacities. Somehow, one lawmaker plus one lawmaker equals one-half a lawmaker. Much of the weakness of our legislatures stems from the fact that operating as a group appears to dilute the effectiveness and integrity of the individuals within it.

Both the textbooks and state constitutions are silent on the numerous significant interrelationships which are a vital part of the lawmaking process. For example, a rap on the gavel and a message from the Governor charting his legislative program officially opens the sessions. But they actually convene, though unofficially, on the Diesel expresses and Convairs that carry the lawmakers to the capitols. "Charlie," one will say, "if you don't need your season pass to the trotting races in my district, I'd appreciate your giving it to me; I can make some votes with it."

Another lawmaker will buttonhole a colleague and say, "Joe, I've got a rotten bill I'll have to sponsor in the Assembly for my hometown Mayor; when it comes over to your side in the Senate, I'd appreciate it if you'd kill it for me."

Like any club of adolescents, legislatures have an unwritten strictly enforced code of conduct. The first commandment is: "Thou shalt be loyal to thine own party and party leaders, lest thy days be numbered as a lawmaker." Thus a Democratic legislator looks with horror, not admiration, upon a Republican colleague who votes against the Republican party line. Independence is scorned. Conformity is expected. The legislator who votes his own convictions against party wishes is deemed untrustworthy, unreliable.

Other basic elements of the code are:

1. Attacks on a fellow-legislator, his patronage or activities, whether or not he is of the same party, are banned.
2. An attack on a fellow-lawmaker, regardless of party, by any outsider is to be considered an attack on all legislators.
3. On non-party measures, vote "with the boys," trade votes if it will help a colleague.

Violations of the code will usually bring swift retaliation. A few of the weapons used to enforce the code include ostracism, stripping a member of patronage, denying him committee chairmanships, closing up sources of outside income, or putting pressure on his home organization to deny him renomination.

It is this feeling of "one for all and all for one" that has made the legislatures refuse to ban members from accepting campaign contributions from liquor interests, Government contractors, race-track groups and lobbies. Few legislatures have taken steps to dry up the "hidden salaries" of members, the lush insurance contracts, the big legal fees that come from these same interests.

The legislatures are not only highly structured groups but war veterans who serve in a legislature tend to form unofficial but powerful groups within the two chambers. Members from the same region tend to associate in area cliques. Similarly, bankers, lawyers, farmers and other occupational groups in the legislature organize influential "cells" which wield great influence on legislation within their own fields.

One characteristic of a group is for individuals within it to assume roles that either fit their own personalities or are thought by them to be the roles the others expect them to play. The legislature is no exception. Every legislature has its member who prides himself on being "the great compromiser" or "practical, behind-the-scene manipulator." There is always one who aspires to be cast in the toga of "the great liberal." And you will find usually a member who fancies himself a silver-throated orator although usually the silver is somewhat tarnished.

Legislative chambers are shaped for demagoguery, not decision-making. They are houses designed for The Great Harangue. Today, oratorical fireworks change few votes and are aimed mainly to impress the press or the galleries. A Republican majority leader one day was assailing the Democrats for fully half an hour with all the modulation of a hog-caller, when he whispered to the Democratic minority leader across the aisle, "How am I doing?" "Good," was the hushed response, "but you'd better quit now; it's my turn." Whereupon the majority leader yielded the floor to permit his ostensible mortal enemy to condemn the Republicans. Like TV wrestling matches, the vocal tilts of legislators are often more in the nature of exhibitions than contests.

Until we learn how groups such as the legislatures can encourage the individuals within it, how they can promote idealism, can turn out a product worthy of democratic assemblies, can promote freedom of thought and even freedom of the group, we shall continue stumbling along, permitting circumstance and strong governors and even stronger lobbies to shape our destinies.

Out of such new knowledge may come encouragement for small, one-house legislatures or smaller two-chamber bodies, new designs for legislative chambers, new techniques for promoting legislative deliberations, new controls over visible and invisible lobbies. Perhaps then we shall be able to attract to lawmaking more men of judgment and character who will not cower before the group but will help weld it into a team working in the public interest.

In a world in which decisions bearing on the future of man are being made in groups—in the United Nations, in Parliaments, in executive-legislative relationships—it becomes vital that free men everywhere have all available knowledge on how man as lawmaker acts in such groups.

61. *How the Farmer Rules Your City* *

Although most state constitutions require legislative reapportionment after each decennial census, the constitutional mandate may be ignored with impunity. Even where it is followed, it does not usually result in equitable representation for rural and urban areas. In 1790 approximately 95 per cent of the population lived in rural areas. Legislative representation logically reflected that fact. Currently only 36 per cent of the population resides in rural areas, but present-day legislative apportionment does not reflect the change. Rural areas continue to be grossly overrepresented in our legislative halls. Cities are therefore at the mercy of legislatures dominated by rural interests. In this selection Mr. Bendiner enumerates and illustrates the problems thus created for metropolitan governments, and indicates certain procedures for adjusting the difficulties described.

In the United States today 54,000,000 country slickers have 96,000,000 city suckers securely under their collective green thumb. Bit by bit it is dawning on the urban easy marks of the nation that if they are not altogether the victims of taxation without representation, they are very close to it, with rural legislatures playing the role of the tyrant.

The mayor of Milwaukee, one of the many city officials who welcomed my invitation to unburden himself on this subject, tilted his hat back on his head and thrust out his chin. "I'm burned up about it," he said. "If there's a second-class citizen in the United States today, it's the man who lives in the large urban center. If the states don't begin to do justice to their cities, then the cities are justified in going to Washington and asking to be made wards of the federal government."

The Honorable Frank P. Zeidler may be unique in his approach, but in spirit he is at one with fellow mayors from Seattle to Miami, with town and city newspaper editors of all political shadings, and with a growing number of city dwellers who are just beginning to appreciate the extent to which their country cousins have taken them in.

Latest official census figures show that 64 per cent of Americans now live in urban communities. But thanks to hoary state constitutions, and to the blandly lawless refusal of legislatures to reapportion their memberships, this great majority of our population is governed by lawmakers it does not elect and over whom it has virtually no control.

The United States Conference of Mayors estimates that almost three fourths of all the state legislators in the country are elected by one third

* Robert Bendiner, *Collier's*, CXXXII (November 27, 1953), pp. 34-36, 38, 40-41. Reprinted by permission of the author.

of the people—those who live on farms and in tiny villages. Often they have little interest in the great metropolitan areas of their states and even less knowledge of a city's complex problems. And not infrequently they retain a countryman's suspicious hostility for cities that harks back to the days of Sodom and Gomorrah.

Yet every year our mayors must go begging to these rural legislators (usually in vain) for a fair share of the revenues their cities contribute to the state's treasury. Only with the consent of these farm-minded men can most cities levy taxes of their own and in other respects manage their affairs like responsible units of government.

Men who never saw a subway in their lives pass on New York's vastly complicated transit problems, and the most picayune questions of local government are decided by the same remote control. In Frederick County, Maryland, local officials had to go to the legislature at Annapolis for permission to reduce the license fee for unspayed dogs from $5 to $2. The giant metropolis of Chicago, which has more people than 36 of the 48 states, was forced to go humbly to the legislators at Springfield to permit the selling of peanuts on a municipal pier. Between city and state, the courts have long held, "The state is supreme, and its legislative body, conforming its action to the state constitution, may do as it will. . . ."

Today our cities find themselves in a tightening three-way squeeze. Federal and state governments have grabbed off the choicest sources of revenue. Meanwhile, "daytime citizens," pouring in from the surrounding metropolitan areas, sop up the cities' facilities and services but pay their local taxes in the suburbs where they sleep.

And now mayors from coast to coast are in a fever at the prospect that the present administration, true to its campaign pledges, will return to the states many of the functions assumed by the national government in the last twenty years. Federal aid for municipal airports has already faded away, leaving cities with new construction plans stopped cold. Will slum clearance, road construction and aid to schools and hospitals be similarly shifted to the states? If so, Mayor Zeidler recently told a convention of municipal officials, "American cities will be in a financial strait jacket. . . . If you go to the Federal government for grants-in-aid, you will be told to go to your state legislature but how can you go to your state legislature when you have hardly any voice in it?"

And there's the rub, for there is nothing regional about the rotten borough system that afflicts our state legislatures. It's a nation-wide custom. Do you live in Atlanta? Then it takes 63 of your fellow townspeople to earn political representation equal to that of a farmer in rural Echols County. No matter how large Atlanta grows, the Georgia constitution says Fulton County will never rate more than three representatives in the legislature's lower house, while four swamp counties—whose total population is one thirty-seventh of Atlanta's—will have four.

Do you live in Hartford, Connecticut? If so, you have two members in the state House of Representatives to stand up for your city's 177,400 people. Colebrook, population 600, also has two representatives, solely because it was incorporated before 1818. Cities and towns over 20,000 make up about two thirds of Connecticut's population, but they get fewer than one sixth the representatives. The 700,000 people who live in the state's five largest cities can be outvoted by representatives from six towns with a total population of 10,000.

THE PLIGHT OF LOS ANGELES COUNTY

Suppose you live in Los Angeles. Your county, with more than 4,000,000 people, sends a single senator to Sacramento, California's state capital. So does tiny Kings County, with just a shade more than one per cent of that population (its largest town, Hanford, has 10,000 people). Even worse, the cactus counties of Mono, Inyo and Alpine, with a population of 14,000 among them, have the same senatorial representation as Los Angeles County—a disparity of about 300 to one. Many Americans, thinking of the Federal Congress, assume that state senates are, and should be, based on geographical divisions, while lower houses rest on population. But mayors and municipal experts with whom I talked feel strongly that the comparison with Congress is farfetched.

The composition of that body was a necessary, even painful, compromise between two powerful groups that created the Constitution. One side put all the emphasis on the sovereign states, the other on the nation as a whole. A Senate for the states and a House of Representatives for the people was the formula that emerged. But there is no comparable situation within the states, where counties and senatorial districts are purely artificial divisions, with no faint pretense to sovereignty. They exist solely for convenience and can be combined or abolished at the whim of the state legislatures.

So far as our cities are concerned, it makes little difference whether it is the state senate or the house that is stacked for what Mayor Zeidler likes to call the "areacrats." The effect is the same. To quote the pained understatement made to me by Mayor Norris Poulson of Los Angeles, "This is a problem of major proportions." Under his state's top-heavy arrangement California's billion-dollar budget, requiring a two-thirds vote, can be vetoed by 14 senators representing 7 per cent of the state's people.

New Yorkers get a better break in proportions but not enough better to give them control of their city's destinies. "Our trouble in addition to inflation," Mayor Vincent R. Impelliteri recently complained, "is the medieval financial relationship that makes this great city the vassal of the state. . . . We have 8,000,000 of the state's population. The rest of the state has 7,000,000. Yet we have 92 legislators. Upstate has 114."

Chicagoans are even worse off. With more than half of the state's population, Cook County (which encompasses Chicago) enjoys little more than one third of the representation at Springfield. In Portland, Oregon, State Senator Richard Neuberger says: "I speak for 85,000 urban residents; the state senator at the desk next to mine represents 8,000 rural residents. Yet each of us should have the same number of constituents."

So it goes throughout the country. In New Jersey the eight counties that hold three fourths of the state's people have eight senators, while the thirteen with the remaining fourth of the population have thirteen. An authority on the subject testifies that Ohio is less representative today than when it was created in 1803.

A CAUSE OF NATIONAL UNREST

Choose your city at random—Detroit, Baltimore, St. Louis, Minneapolis, Denver, Wilmington, New Orleans, Oklahoma City, Des Moines, Birmingham, Butte—the story is similar everywhere. "We do not have truly representative government in the 48 states," says the Conference of Mayors. "It is the cause of more national trouble and unrest than any other one thing. And until it is driven out, we can expect those troubles to increase."

How has it come about that where government affects our daily lives on the most intimate level—health, transportation, schooling, housing, protection from crime and fire—citizens have become subordinate to acres . . . even where those acres are little more than swamp, forest, sagebrush or sand dunes? And, more important, what are the consequences?

How it came about is relatively simple. When the country was new, the farmers got into the saddle because they belonged there. The first census, in 1790, showed that as a nation we were 95 per cent rural; such cities as we had were regarded by leaders like Thomas Jefferson as unwholesome congregations of riffraff, with politics to match. Similarly, all the states that subsequently joined the Union were predominantly rural. In time the majority of the national population drifted to town—but the legislatures did not. For one or both houses, 42 state constitutions provide for periodic reapportionment—but the legislatures blithely ignore the law for decades at a stretch. Many states haven't reapportioned since President Hoover's day; Louisiana and Indiana not since Harding's. Minnesota's setup dates back to 1913, Delaware's to 1897, and Mississippi's to 1890. Connecticut's lower house is made up today on the basis of a law that was passed 135 years ago.

In states where periodic reapportionment is mandatory, the duty is generally laid upon the legislature. But the constitutions rarely provide for enforcement, and the courts consider themselves powerless to coerce an equal branch of government. It should be noted that rural legislators are not alone in their allergy to reapportionment. City representatives, once in office, sometimes show the same reluctance to upset the apple cart. True, reapportionment might shift the center of power from country to city—but it might also move it from one end of the state to another or (dread thought) from one party to another, affecting rural and city representatives alike.

Granted that our legislatures are preposterously out of joint, do they really affect the day-to-day life of the city dweller? They do, to a far greater extent than many an urbanite imagines.

For the most part our major cities are treated like mental incompetents. Boston's police commissioner is chosen not by the government of the city he is charged with protecting, but by the governor of Massachusetts. Once in his office, it's the commissioner who is judge of his department's personnel and financial requirements; the city of Boston is permitted to do little more than pay the bill. The same system prevails in the three largest cities of Missouri. Kansas City, with a clean local government, for years bore a national reputation as the gangster haven of the Midwest, scene of the notorious Binaggio murder. But few outsiders knew that its police department was operated by remote control from Jefferson City, the state capital.

Not only Boston's police, but its harbor, its transportation system and its airport are all run from the Statehouse, and its elected mayor may be arbitrarily removed by the legislature without so much as a hearing. As in many other states, the legislature fixes the hours of city policemen and firemen, occasionally lowering them without providing any means whatever for the additional revenue required.

Chicago has to have state approval for the location of its traffic lights. In last year's session, the Illinois rural legislature also considered whether the city's municipal courts should be open over week ends, whether Chicago might regulate the lighting of stairways and vestibules in buildings and in what form its municipal journal should be kept. State dictation is so strict that although the city has a surplus in its fund for removing dead trees, it can't use the money for sorely needed playgrounds. Except for a few streets, all exits south from the Loop are blocked by railroad yards—but, an alderman told me, the city cannot break the bottleneck by consolidating its terminals so long as the legislature withholds the power to condemn railroad property.

In some states the very form of your city's government can be changed by people who wouldn't live there, as they say, if you gave them the place. The citizens of Knoxville, Tennessee, switched in 1923 to the city-manager plan—only to have the legislature some years later override them and restore the political mayoralty without consulting the city in any way. Year after year, Chicagoans are refused the right to reorganize their patchwork municipal government, set up mostly under a Cities and Villages Act passed by the legislature in 1872. The city of Memphis was once abolished altogether by legislative fiat in order to keep it out of the bankruptcy courts. Only a few months ago some Florida legislators tried (unsuccessfully) to merge Miami with the rural areas of Dade County, the whole irrational unit to be governed by county commissioners.

STATE TYRANNY IN NEW ORLEANS

Undoubtedly the worst example in modern times of state tyranny over a city occurred five years ago in Louisiana. In New Orleans they still refer bitterly to Earl Long as "the hillbilly governor who hated the city and tried to destroy it." Earl promised to "improve on everything Huey did" and came close to succeeding.

Through Earl Long's pliant legislature went some 200 bills intended to strip New Orleans of more than 25 per cent of its revenues, change its form of government into an unworkable administrative hodgepodge, seize control of its port facilities, increase its financial obligations to the point of bankruptcy, restore the spoils system and permanently reduce the mayor to the status of a figurehead. "I don't know of anything else that can be done," said young Mayor de Lesseps S. Morrison, "except throw us into the lake."

Fortunately, some of Long's "improvements" called for constitutional amendments, and had to be voted on at the polls. The worst of them were beaten after mass demonstrations at the Capitol and after Mayor Morrison had stumped Louisiana, pointing out everywhere that what was poison for New Orleans was poison for the state.

But the effects of the ripper legislation were crippling, if not killing. Eventually the aroused city, aided by special bond issues, private contributions and even legacies, climbed out of the financial pit the legislature had dug for it. Morrison was overwhelmingly re-elected. With a new Home Rule charter to go into effect next year, he enjoys cordial relations with the current administration at Baton Rouge, where Earl's men once called him "little smart aleck"—just as Huey habitually addressed the mayor of New Orleans in his day as "Old Turkeyhead."

If few cities offer as melodramatic an example as New Orleans, most of them suffer stolidly, year in and year out. Legislators from Wappingers Falls and Owls Head can tell New York City, with a bigger budget than any of the 48 states, how to conduct its finances. In the legislative file at Albany you can find state laws graciously authorizing the nation's biggest city to get rid of its old schoolbooks, giving Buffalo the go-ahead to spray its trees, and permitting Syracuse to use substances other than water for cleaning its streets.

Rural legislators at Madison only recently permitted Milwaukee to use parking meters, though other cities in Wisconsin have been allowed to for years. Theoretically, Ohio cities have home rule, but they were unable to establish day nurseries for working mothers when their masters at Columbus refused to give the word. State legislative calendars everywhere are choked with bills that by every rule of reason, efficiency and democracy should be solely in the province of city councils—permission to keep bicycles off the sidewalks of a North Carolina town, authorization to an Iowa city to buy new uniforms for its policemen, sanction for the town of Revere, Massachusetts, to extend its dogcatcher's term of office.

But cities feel the lack of representation most acutely in the field of taxation. As recently as 1929, local units of governments collected 56 per cent of the total tax dollar. Twenty years later, according to Allen E. Pritchard, Jr., who directs the Ohio Municipal League, they were down to 17 per cent. Today they are even worse off. Mayor Zeidler estimates the present division as 75 per cent for Federal, 15 for the states and a miserable 10 per cent for local governments, which must either maintain a life line to Washington or get along with whatever sources of revenue their state legislatures choose to leave them.

"GRABS" OF TWO CITIES' TAXES

Mayor William B. Hartsfield told me with some heat how the Georgia legislature a few years ago deprived Atlanta of $900,000 in revenue at a single swipe and, in the same session, seriously debated putting the city's firemen on a 40-hour week, at an additional cost of some $400,000. When Fiorello H. La Guardia was mayor of New York, he devised three successful local taxes—on cigarettes, public utilities and retail sales. As soon as they proved their worth, the state took over two thirds of the utilities and all of the cigarette taxes—and refrained from grabbing the city's sales tax only for fear of being accused of driving business into the border towns across the state line.

What infuriates most mayors is that they never get back anything like a share proportional to their population or their contribution to the state treasury. The California Citizens' Committee for Equal Representation found several years ago, as one result of the cities' under-representation at Sacramento, that for every dollar which empty Mono County paid into the state treasury, it got back $6.21 in appropriations, while Los Angeles got back 60 cents on the dollar and San Francisco 41 cents.

Examples of this sort can be cited by the dozen. Mayor Zeidler told me that Milwaukee foots 35 per cent of Wisconsin's bills and gets back 12 per cent of its benefits. Minnesota's Twin Cities of Minneapolis and St. Paul, with well over a quarter of the state's population, contribute 45 per cent of the state school fund and get back less than 20 per cent.

One of the most striking ways in which the cities are hornswoggled by their country brothers is in highway construction. Fully half the nation's total annual travel is concentrated on city streets, making virtually every one of the metropolitan areas in the nation a chronic traffic bottleneck. Yet as recently as 1940, 28 states distributed no motor-vehicle revenues whatever to their cities for local streets and 22 spent no money whatever on vital links that would have made the state highways genuinely state-wide instead of rural systems interrupted by urban nightmares.

The situation has improved in the last few years, but is still fantastically unfair. In Ohio, to cite a typical case, approximately 52 per cent of the vehicle-miles traveled are in urban areas, but less than 17 per cent of the registration and gasoline taxes collected are made available directly to the cities for construction and maintenance. Most cities, moreover, aren't able to tax motor vehicles on their own score to make up the cost to the community.

"GOLD HIGHWAY LAW" RECALLED

On the other hand, rural areas that have long had adequate farm-to-market roads go right on getting the lion's share of highway appropriations. The classic case is the "gold highway law," in force in Connecticut until five years ago. The hamlet of Canaan paid $6,000 a year toward the state highway fund, while the city of Waterbury, with about 100 times its population, paid $1,000,000. Under the law Canaan and Waterbury each received $26,000 a year in aid. As the irate Waterbury *Republican* pointed out editorially, Canaan made a profit of 430 per cent, which it salted away, while Waterbury got back less than a third of what it cost to oil its streets, fill in its worst holes, and sweep away the rubbish. Underrepresentation is expensive.

In the competition for taxes, New Jersey's Governor Alfred E. Driscoll says, "The national government is fishing with a seine, the states with a hook and line, and the localities, in many instances, are forced to fish with a bent pin." It's small wonder many of them have been driven to inequitable forms of revenue like New York's gross-business tax, or to freakish and piddling levies.

Some cities in Washington State require municipal licenses for everything from bicycles, cats and bathhouses to delicatessens, pinball games and street telescopes.

Little Rock a few years ago slapped a tax on the sale of sliced watermelon sold in restaurants that pay no other license fee.

Domino, checker and dart games are taxed in some cities when played in public parlors. And Hood River, Oregon, five years ago dreamed up a tax on jugglers.

Citizens of Lansing reasonably grumbled at the irony of paying a tax to the State of Michigan on gasoline consumed when Lansing's fire trucks put out a blaze in the state Capitol.

IN CHRONIC NEAR BANKRUPTCY

Considering that our cities are caught in what the Conference of Mayors calls a "chronic condition of near bankruptcy," it is a miracle that they function as efficiently as they do. Up to now, most authorities agree, they have been saved by Federal funds in the form of grants-in-aid. "However much one may like or dislike concentration of power in the Federal government," the conference people say, "it has doubtless been driven there by our gerrymandered states themselves." This sentiment finds echoes even in the deep South, where one might least expect to hear them. "As a rule, the most laggard government in our nation is state government," says Atlanta's Mayor Hartsfield, who is the president of the American Municipal Association. "State politicians cry in Washington for State rights, but never mention state responsibilities and obligations."

A TYPICAL MUNICIPAL PROTEST

The city of West Palm Beach made the same point four years ago in a letter to the Florida legislature. It is worth quoting, in part, as a summary of what American municipalities have been going through.

> . . . the fire protection we furnish is with antiquated equipment; our streets are in disrepair; sidewalks and street lamps oftentimes are an exception rather than the rule; ancient sewers collapse under the burden of increased traffic. . . .
>
> [But] we lay the blame at your door—not ours! . . . You have tapped all sources [of revenue] first and you drain them to the dregs. . . . If our state fails to provide "CITY RIGHTS," we may be constrained to view state rights as a mere historical anachronism.

Among the city officials and municipal experts I talked with, there is little expectation that Federal aid will be continued in its present volume, much less increased. A tug of war is going on in Washington right now. City interests—represented by such vigorous groups as the American Municipal Association and the United States Conference of Mayors—are naturally wary of changes that might weaken direct Federal-City relationships, while the governors want all Federal funds for local purposes funneled through the states. The feeling of the mayors so far is that this is a "governors' administration"; that the President, after a lifetime in the Army, prefers to have things go through channels.

Nevertheless, at President Eisenhower's suggestion, Congress has created a Commission on Intergovernmental Relations, and city officials hope that the hearings at least will give the public some idea of what they are up against. The time allotted for the study is short, however, and there is lively fear in some quarters that the whole project will serve largely to increase state power at the expense of Federal, but without added responsibility. The hungry cities would still be on the outside looking for handouts.

Where else is there to turn? Milwaukee is planning to have another go at the courts. The Conference of Mayors has for some time been flirting with the idea of lawsuits on the part of underrepresented cities to compel equal representation in the legislatures under the Fourteenth Amendment, which forbids a state to "deny to any person within its jurisdiction the equal protection of the laws."

FANNING SPARKS OF REBELLION

It may be too strong to say, as one observer has, that our "cities are openly talking rebellion," but there have been rebellious sparks. As far back as the twenties, Chicago's city council instructed municipal attorneys to outline the legal steps necessary for secession from the state, and the Cook County Board of Commissioners attempted to withhold state taxes. New York, Detroit and other cities periodically hear talk in high places of petitioning for separate statehood. A former mayor of Grand Rapids has suggested that "perhaps a few Boston Tea

Parties might serve a useful purpose." And an Alabama grand jury two years ago recommended refusal by petit or grand juries to enforce the tax laws until the state was reapportioned.

Since no secession may take place without the sanction of the very legislatures that are causing the trouble, most of this defiance has more to do with arousing public opinion than with pointing to a solution. Yet in the long run public opinion will force a change.

THE SUBJECT MUST BE TALKED UP

Except for those engaged in politics, comparatively few people are aware of the extent to which the democratic process has bogged down at this vital level of government. As the Fort Wayne *News-Sentinel* put it a few years back, "The subject will have to be talked about in homes, on street corners, in organization meetings, in business, professional and labor circles."

When that happens, governors and party leaders, who depend on the votes of cities as well as of farms, may develop a certain persuasiveness with their legislatures in the matter of reapportionment. In the states where citizens have the power of thc initiative, they will use that device, as some already have, not only to bring their legislatures up to date, but to provide for automatic reapportionment in the future—at stipulated intervals and by an administrative agency that is clearly subject to control by the courts. In the same way they will compel the granting of city home-rule charters which are not so loosely worded that a legislature may interpret them to death.

Fair representation will not cure the ills of our cities and by itself usher in an era of metropolitan glory. But without it, it is clear, there can be no bright future for the communities where almost two thirds of the American people have chosen to live.

XI

THE FEDERAL JUDICIAL SYSTEM

62. *The Law**

Lord Chancellor:
The Law is the true embodiment
Of everything that's excellent,
It has no kind of fault or flaw,
And I, my lords, embody the Law.
—Iolanthe

63. *The Job of a Supreme Court Justice***

MR. JUSTICE FRANKFURTER, who, after twenty-five years as a professor at the Harvard Law School, was named Associate Justice of the United States Supreme Court by President Roosevelt in 1939, here describes the qualities of mind a judge should possess. This is a deeply philosophical yet highly important question. Frankfurter says that a judge should try to interpret the law so as to reflect the views and feelings of the community. A judge's decisions are inevitably influenced by his own background, experience, and philosophy. But, in reaching his decision the judge must cut himself

* By W. S. Gilbert. From *Authentic Libretti of the Gilbert and Sullivan Operas*, p. 55. Copyright 1939 by Crown Publishers. Reprinted by permission of Crown Publishers.

** Felix Frankfurter, *The New York Times Magazine*, November 28, 1954, p. 14. Reprinted by permission of the author and publisher.

off from any narrow self-interest or bias. He should be "in the grip of his function." He is no longer a corporation lawyer, a law school professor, a partisan politician; instead he is an arbiter of the destinies of the people of the nation.

A JUDGE should be compounded of the faculties that are demanded of the historian and the philosopher and the prophet. The last demand upon him—to make some forecast of the consequences of his action—is perhaps the heaviest. To pierce the curtain of the future, to give shape and visage to mysteries still in the womb of time, is the gift of imagination. It requires poetic sensibilities with which judges are rarely endowed and which their education does not normally develop. These judges must have something of the creative artist in them; they must have antennae registering feeling and judgment beyond logical, let alone quantitative, proof.

Judge Learned Hand bears quoting:

> I venture to believe that it is as important to a judge called upon to pass on a question of constitutional law, to have at least a bowing acquaintance with Acton and Maitland, with Thucydides, Gibbon and Carlyle, with Homer, Dante, Shakespeare and Milton, with Machiavelli, Montaigne and Rabelais, with Plato, Bacon, Hume and Kant, as with the books which have been specifically written on the subject.
>
> For in such matters everything turns upon the spirit in which he approaches the questions before him. The words he must construe are empty vessels into which he can pour nearly anything he will. Men do not gather figs of thistles, nor supply institutions from judges whose outlook is limited by parish or class. They must be aware that there are before them more than verbal problems; more than final solutions cast in generalizations of universal applicability. They must be aware of the changing social tensions in every society which make it an organism; which demand new schemata of adaptation; which will disrupt it, if rigidly confined.

The decisions in the cases that really give trouble rest on judgment, and judgment derives from the totality of a man's nature and experience. Such judgment will be exercised by two types of men, broadly speaking, but of course with varying emphasis—those who express their private views or revelations, deeming them, if not *vox dei*, at least *vox populi*; or those who feel strongly that they have no authority to promulgate law by their merely personal view and whose whole training and proved performance substantially insure that their conclusions reflect understanding of, and due regard for, law as the expression of the views and feelings that may fairly be deemed representative of the community as a continuing society.

Judges are men, not disembodied spirits. Of course a judge is not free from preferences or, if you will, biases. But he may deprive a bias of its meretricious authority by stripping it of the uncritical assumption that it is founded on compelling reason or the coercive power of a syllogism. He will be alert to detect that though a conclusion has a logical form, it, in fact, represents a choice of competing considerations of policy, one of which for the time has won the day.

It is asked with sophomoric brightness, does a man cease to be himself when he becomes a Justice? Does he change his character by putting on a gown? No, he does not change his character. He brings his whole experience, his training, his outlook, his social, intellectual and moral environment with him when he takes a seat on the Supreme Bench.

But a judge worth his salt is in the grip of his function. The intellectual habits of self-discipline which govern his mind are as much a part of him as the influence of the interest he may have represented at the bar, often much more so. For example, Mr. Justice Bradley was a "corporation lawyer" *par excellence* when he went on the Court. But his decisions on matters affecting corporate control in the years following the Civil War were strikingly free of bias in favor of corporate power.

To assume that a lawyer who becomes a judge takes on the bench merely his views on social or economic questions leaves out of account his rooted notions regarding the scope and limits of a judge's authority. The outlook of a lawyer fit to be a Justice regarding the role of a judge cuts across all his personal preferences for this or that social arrangement.

Need it be stated that true humility and its offspring, disinterestedness, are more indispensable for the work of the Supreme Court than for a judge's function on any other bench? These qualities alone will not assure another indispensable requisite. This is the capacity for self-searching. What Jacques Maritain said in another connection applies peculiarly to members of the Supreme Court. A Justice of that court cannot adequately discharge his function "without passing through the door of the knowing, obscure as it may be, of his own subjective."

This is not to say that the application of this view of the judge's function—that he is there not to impose his private views upon society, that he is not to enforce personalized jusice—assures unanimity of judgments. Inevitably there are bound to be fair differences of opinion. And it would be pretense to deny that in the self-righteous exercise of this role obscurantist and even unjustifiable decisions are sometimes rendered.

Why should anyone be surprised at this? The very nature of the task makes some differences of view well nigh inevitable. The answers that the Supreme Court is required to give are based on questions and on data that preclude automatic or even undoubting answers. If the materials on which judicial judgments must be based could be fed into a machine so as to produce ineluctable answers, if such were the nature of the problems that come before the Supreme Court and such were the answers expected, we would have IBM machines doing the work instead of judges.

Mr. Chief Justice Hughes summed it up this way:

> How amazing it is that, in the midst of controversies on every conceivable subject, one should expect unanimity of opinion upon difficult legal questions! In the highest ranges of thought, in theology, philosophy and science, we find differences of view on the part of the most distinguished experts—theologians, philosophers and scientists. The history of scholarship is a record of disagreements. And when we deal with questions relating to principles of law and their application, we do not suddenly rise into a stratosphere of icy certainty.

The core of the difficulty is that there is hardly a question of any real difficulty before the Court that does not entail more than one so-called principle. Anybody can decide a question if only a single principle is in controversy. Partisans and advocates often cast a question in that form, but the form is deceptive.

This contest between conflicting principles is not limited to law. Recently I came across this profound observation in The London Times Literary Supplement: "When, in any field of human observation, two truths appear in conflict it is wiser to assume that neither is exclusive, and that their contradiction, though it may be hard to bear, is part of the mystery of things."

But judges cannot leave such contradiction between two conflicting "truths" as "part of the mystery of things." They have to adjudicate. If the conflict cannot be resolved, the task of the Court is to arrive at an accommodation of the contending claims. This is the core of the difficulties and misunderstandings about the judicial process. This, for any conscientious judge, is the agony of his duty.

64. *Judicial Self-Restraint* *

PROFESSOR ROCHE and Mr. Justice Frankfurter (Selection 63) have similar views on the role of the Supreme Court in our society. Both agree that the Constitution and the laws are often changed as they are applied by judges to solve particular controversies. Supreme Court judges, therefore, are major political policy makers in our society, neither directly restrained by nor directly responsible to the voters. Both authors agree that the judges restrain themselves. Mr. Justice Frankfurter says that the judge should not write into the law or the Constitution his personal views but rather should try to reflect the views and feelings of the community. Professor Roche looks at the opposite side of the coin—not at the principles a judge should apply in interpreting the law, but instead at the ways in which a judge can avoid making difficult political decisions—another form of judicial self-restrait. After describing legal techniques that have been used to avoid difficult decisions, Professor Roche considers the conditions in which these techniques are used.

EVERY SOCIETY, sociological research suggests, has its set of myths which incorporate and symbolize its political, economic, and social aspirations. Thus, as medieval society had the Quest for the Holy Grail and the cult of numerology, we, in our enlightened epoch, have as significant manifestations of our collective hopes the dream of impartial decision-making and the cult of "behavioral science." While in my view these latter two are but different facets of the same fundamental drive, namely, the age-old effort to exorcise human variables from human action, our concern here is with the first of them, the pervasive tendency in the American political and constitutional tradition directed towards taking the politics out of politics, and substituting some set of Platonic guardians for fallible politicians.

While this dream of objectivizing political Truth is in no sense a unique American phenomenon, it is surely true to say that in no other democratic nation has the effort been carried so far and with such persistence. Everywhere one turns in the United States, he finds insitutionalized attempts to narrow the political sector and to substitute allegedly "independent" and "impartial" bodies for elected decision-makers. The so-called "independent regulatory commissions" are a classic example of this tendency in the area of administration, but unquestionably the greatest hopes for injecting pure Truth-serum into

* John P. Roche, *The American Political Science Review*, XLIX (September, 1955), pp. 762-772. Reprinted with permission from *The American Political Science Review.*

the body politic have been traditionally reserved for the federal judiciary, and particularly for the Supreme Court. The rationale for this viewpoint is simple: "The people must be protected from themselves, and no institution is better fitted for the role of chaperone than the federal judiciary, dedicated as it is to the supremacy of the rule of law."

Patently central to this function of social chaperonage is the right of the judiciary to review legislative and executive actions and nullify those measures which derogate from eternal principles of truth and justice as incarnated in the Constitution. Some authorities, enraged at what the Supreme Court has found the Consitution to mean, have essayed to demonstrate that the Framers did not intend the Court to exercise this function, to have, as they put it, "the last word." I find no merit in this contention; indeed, it seems to me undeniable not only that the authors of the Constitution intended to create a federal government, but also that they assumed *sub silentio* that the Supreme Court would have the power to review both national and state legislation.

However, since the intention of the Framers is essentially irrelevant except to antiquarians and polemicists, it is unnecessary to examine further the matter of origins. The fact is that the United States Supreme Court, and the inferior federal courts under the oversight of the high Court, have enormous policy-making functions. Unlike their British and French counterparts, federal judges are not merely technicians who live in the shadow of a supreme legislature, but are fully equipped to intervene in the process of political decision-making. In theory, they are limited by the Constitution and the jurisdiction it confers, but, in practice, it would be a clumsy judge indeed who could not, by a little skilful exegesis, adapt the Constitution to a necessary end. This statement is in no sense intended as a condemnation; on the contrary, it has been this perpetual reinvigoration by reinterpretation, in which the legislature and the executive as well as the courts play a part, that has given the Constitution its survival power. Applying a Constitution which contains at key points inspired ambiguity, the courts have been able to pour the new wine in the old bottle. Note that the point at issue is not the legitimacy or wisdom of judicial legislation; it is simply the enormous scope that this prerogative gives to judges to substitute their views for those of past generations, or, more controversially, for those of a contemporary Congress or President.

Thus it is naive to assert that the Supreme Court is limited by the Constitution, and we must turn elsewhere for the sources of judicial restraint. The great power exercised by the Court has carried with it great risks, so it is not surprising that American political history has been sprinkled with demands that the judiciary be emasculated. The really startling thing is that, with the notable exception of the McCardle incident in 1869, the Supreme Court has emerged intact from each of these encounters. Despite the plenary power that Congress, under Article III of the Constitution, can exercise over the appellate jurisdiction of the high Court, the national legislature has never taken sustained and effective action against its House of Lords. It is beyond the purview of this analysis to examine the reasons for congressional inaction; suffice it here to say that the most significant form of judicial limitation has remained self-limitation. This is not to suggest that such a development as statutory codification has not cut down the area of interpretive discretion, for it obviously has. It is rather to maintain that when the justices have held back from assaults on legislative or executive actions, they have done so on the basis of self-established rationalizations such as Justice Brandeis' famous "Ashwander rules."

The remainder of this paper is therefore concerned with two aspects of this auto-limitation: first, the techniques by which it is put into practice; and, second, the conditions under which it is exercised. It might be noted that no judgment will be entered on the merits of judicial action: the American people, however wisely or foolishly, have incorporated the notion of judicial supremacy in their social myths; I accept that fact as a constant in the equation. Furthermore, there seems to be little question of principle in the long-standing argument over the legitimacy of judicial legislation. On the contrary, it appears that all hands have been in favor of judicial restraint when it operates on their behalf, and in favor of judicial intervention when such action forwards their objectives. From the Jeffersonians, who maintained that the judiciary should declare the Sedition Act of 1798 unconstitutional, to President Franklin D. Roosevelt, who kept to himself his view that a section of the Lend-Lease Act was unconstitutional to avoid embarrassing his congressional lieutenants, American politics has demonstrated little abiding concern with "principles of jurisprudence." An analyst may be devoted to such principles, but he should not permit his ideological "aprioris" to dominate his presentation of descriptive data.

TECHNIQUES OF JUDICIAL SELF-RESTRAINT

The major techniques of judicial self-restraint appear to fall under the two familiar rubrics: procedural and substantive. Under the former fall the various techniques by which the Court can avoid coming to grips with substantive issues, while under the latter would fall those methods by which the Court, in a substantive holding, finds that the matter at issue in the litigation is not properly one for judicial settlement. Let us examine these two categories in some detail.

PROCEDURAL SELF-RESTRAINT

Since the passage of the Judiciary Act of 1925, the Supreme Court has had almost complete control over its business. United States Supreme Court *Rule* 38, which governs the certiorari policy, states that discretionary review will be granted only "where there are special and important reasons therefor." Professor Fowler Harper has suggested in a series of detailed and persuasive articles on the application of this discretion that the Court has used it in such a fashion as to duck certain significant but controversial problems. While one must be extremely careful about generalizing in this area, since the reasons for denying certiorari are many and complex, Harper's evidence does suggest that the Court in the period since 1949 has refused to review cases involving important civil liberties problems which on their merits appeared to warrant adjudication. As he states at one point: "it is disconcerting when the Court will review a controversy over a patent on a pin ball machine while one man is deprived of his citizenship and another of his liberty without Supreme Court review of a plausible challenge to the validity of government action." That this restraint is not wholly accidental is suggested by Professor Pritchett's recent study of the general attitude of the Vinson Court towards civil liberty issues.

Furthermore, the Supreme Court can issue certiorari on its own terms. Thus in *Dennis* v. *United States*, appealing the Smith Act convictions of the American Communist leadership, the Court accepted the evidential findings of the Second Circuit as final and limited its review to two narrow constitutional issues. This, in effect, burked the basic problem: whether the evidence was sufficient to demonstrate that the Communist party, U.S.A., was *in fact* a clear and present danger to the security of the nation, or whether the Communists were merely shouting "Fire!" in an empty theater.

Other related procedural techniques are applicable in some situations. Simple delay can be employed, perhaps in the spirit of the Croatian proverb that "delay is the handmaiden of justice." The case of *Duncan* v. *Kahanamoku*, contesting the validity of military trials of civilians in Hawaii during the war, is a good instance of the judicial stall: Duncan was locked up in August, 1942, and only succeeded in bringing *habeas corpus* action in the District Court in April, 1944. In November, 1944, the Ninth Circuit affirmed the denial of the writ, and Duncan immediately applied to the Supreme Court for certiorari—which was granted in February, 1945. The Supreme Court studied the case carefully while the war ended, and then in February, 1946, determined that Duncan had been improperly convicted. The Japanese-Americans, attempting to get a judicial ruling on the validity of their detainment in relocation centers, met with the same Kafka-esque treatment. However, the technique of procedural self-restraint is founded on the essentially simple gadget of refusing jurisdiction, or of procrastinating the acceptance of jurisdiction, and need not concern us further here.

SUBSTANTIVE SELF-RESTRAINT

Once a case has come before the Court on its merits, the justices are forced to give some explanation for whatever action they may take. Here self-restraint can take many forms, notably, the doctrine of political questions, the operation of judicial parsimony, and—particularly with respect to the actions of administrative officers or agencies—the theory of judicial inexpertise.

The doctrine of political questions is too familiar to require much elaboration here. Suffice it to say that if the Court feels that a question before it, e.g., the legitimacy of a state government, the validity of a legislative apportionment, or the correctness of executive action in the field of foreign relations, is one that is not properly amenable to judicial settlement, it will refer the plaintiff to the "political" organs of government for any possible relief. The extent to which this doctrine is applied seems to be a direct coefficient of judicial egotism, for the definition of a political question can be expanded or contracted in accordian-like fashion to meet the exigencies of the times. A juridical definition of the term is impossible, for at root the logic that supports it is circular: political questions are matters not soluble by the judicial process; matters not soluble by the judicial process are political questions. As an early dictionary explained, violins are small cellos, and cellos are large violins.

Nor do examples help much in definition. While it is certainly true that the Court cannot mandamus a legislature to apportion a state in equitable fashion, it seems equally true that the Court is without the authority to force state legislators to implement unsegregated public education. Yet in the former instance the Court genuflected to the "political" organs and took no action, while in the latter it struck down segregation as violative of the Constitution.

Judicial parsimony is another major technique of substantive self-restraint. In what is essentially a legal application of Occam's razor, the Court has held that it will not apply any more principles to the settlement of a case than are absolutely necessary, e.g., it will not discuss the constitutionality of a law if it can settle the instant case by statutory construction. Furthermore, if an action is found to rest on erroneous statutory construction, the review terminates at that point: the Court will not go on to discuss whether the statute, properly construed, would be constitutional. A variant form of this doctrine, and a most important one, employs the "case or controversy" approach, to wit, the Court, admitting the importance of the issue, inquires as to whether the litigant actually has standing to bring the matter up.

But while on the surface this technique of limitation appears to be quasi-automatic in operation, such is not always the case. For example, the Court held in the United Public Workers and the Alaskan cannery workers cases that the plaintiffs could not get adjudication until the laws they challenged had been employed against them; it also agreed to review the constitutionality of the New York Teacher Loyalty statute *before* anyone had been injured by its operations. Similarly, the Court for years held that a state government had no standing to intervene *parens patriae* on behalf of the interests of its citizens, but changed its mind in 1945 to permit Georgia to bring action under the antitrust laws against twenty railroads.

A classic use of parsimony to escape from a dangerous situation occurred in connection with the evacuation of the Nisei from the West Coast in 1942. Gordon Hirabayashi, in an attempt to test the validity of the regulations clamped on the American-Japanese by the military, violated the curfew and refused to report to an evacuation center. He was convicted on both counts by the district court and sentenced to three months for each offense, the sentences to run *concurrently*. When the case came before the Supreme Court, the justices sustained his conviction for violating the *curfew*, but refused to examine the validity of the evacuation order on the ground that it would not make any difference to Hirabayashi anyway; he was in for ninety days no matter what the Court did with evacuation.

A third method of utilizing substantive self-restraint is particularly useful in connection with the activities of executive departments or regulatory agencies, both state and federal. I have entitled it the doctrine of judicial *inexpertise*, for it is founded on the unwillingness of the Court to revise the findings of experts. The earmarks of this form of restraint are great deference to the holdings of the expert agency usually coupled with such a statement as "It is not for the federal courts to supplant the [Texas Railroad] Commission's judgment even in the face of convincing proof that a different result would have been better." In this tradition, the Court has refused to question *some* exercises of discretion by the National Labor Relations Board, the Federal Trade Commission, and other federal and state agencies. But the emphasis on *some* gives the point away: in other cases, apparently on all fours with those in which it pleads its technical *inexpertise*, the Court feels free to assess evidence *de novo* and reach independent judgment on the technical issues involved. Without getting involved in the complexities of the *Ben Avon* case, *Crowell* v.

Benson, or *FPC* v. *Hope Natural Gas Co.*, we need only cite the instance of *N.L.R.B.* v. *Highland Park Manufacturing Co.*, in which the Court overruled the N.L.R.B. The Board had held that the C.I.O. was not a "national union" within the meaning of the Taft-Hartley Act, but was rather a confederation of labor unions, but Justice Jackson announced for the Court that "the C.I.O. . . . is certainly in the speech of people a national union, whatever its internal composition." Justices Frankfurter and Douglas dissented, suggesting that the Supreme Court was not qualified to replace the Board.

In short, with respect to expert agencies, the Court is equipped with both offensive and defensive gambits. If it chooses to intervene, one set of precedents is brought out, while if it decides to hold back, another set of equal validity is invoked. Perhaps the best summary of this point was made by Justice Harlan in 1910, when he stated bluntly that "the Courts have rarely, if ever, felt themselves so restrained by technical rules that they could not find some remedy, consistent with the law, for acts . . . that violated natural justice or were hostile to the fundamental principles devised for the protection of the essential rights of property."

This does not pretend to be an exhaustive analysis of the techniques of judicial self-restraint; on the contrary, others will probably find many which are not given adequate discussion here. The remainder of this paper, however, is devoted to the second area of concern: the conditions under which the Court refrains from acting.

THE CONDITIONS OF JUDICIAL SELF-RESTRAINT

The conditions which lead the Supreme Court to exercise autolimitation are many and varied. In the great bulk of cases, this restraint is an outgrowth of sound and quasi-automatic legal maxims which defy teleological interpretation. It would take a master of the conspiracy theory of history to assign meaning, for example, to the great majority of certiorari denials; the simple fact is that these cases do not merit review. However, in a small proportion of cases, purpose does appear to enter the picture, sometimes with a vengeance. It is perhaps unjust to the Court to center our attention on this small proportion, but it should be said in extenuation that these cases often involve extremely significant political and social issues. In the broad picture, the refusal to grant certiorari in 1943 to the Minneapolis Trotskyites convicted under the Smith Act is far more meaningful than the similar refusal to grant five hundred petitions to prison "lawyers" who have suddenly discovered the writ of habeas corpus. Likewise, the holding that the legality of congressional apportionment is a "political question" vitally affects the operation of the whole democratic process.

What we must therefore seek are the conditions under which the Court holds back *in this designated category of cases.* Furthermore, it is important to realize that there are positive consequences of negative action: as Charles Warren has implied, the post-Civil War Court's emphasis on self-restraint was a judicial concomitant of the resurgence of states'-rights. Thus self-restraint may, as in wartime, be an outgrowth of judicial caution, or it may be part of a purposeful pattern of abdicating national power to the states.

Ever since the first political scientist discovered Mr. Dooley, the changes have been rung on the aphorism that the Supreme Court "follows the election returns," and I see no particular point in ringing my variation on this theme through again. Therefore, referring those who would like a more detailed explanation to earlier analyses, the discussion here will be confined to the bare bones of my hypothesis.

The power of the Supreme Court to invade the decision-making arena, I submit, is a consequence of that fragmentation of political power which is normal in the United States. No cohesive majority, such as normally exists in Britain, would permit a politically irresponsible judiciary to usurp decision-making functions, but, for complex social and institutional reasons, there are few issues in the United States on which cohesive majorities exist. The guerrilla warfare which usually rages between Congress and the President, as well as the internal civil wars which are endemic in both the legislature and the administration, give the judiciary considerable room for maneuver. If, for example, the Court strikes down a controversial decision of the Federal Power Commission, it will be supported by a substantial bloc of congressmen; if it supports the FPC's decision, it will also receive considerable congressional support. But the important point is that either way it decides the case, there is no possibility that Congress will exact any vengeance on the Court for its action. A disciplined majority would be necessary to clip the judicial wings, and such a majority does not exist on this issue.

On the other hand, when monolithic majorities do exist on issues, the Court is likely to resort to judicial self-restraint. A good case here is the current tidal wave of anti-communist legislation and administrative action, the latter particularly with regard to aliens, which the Court has treated most gingerly. About the only issues on which there can be found cohesive majorities are those relating to national defense, and the Court has, as Clinton Rossiter demonstrated in an incisive analysis, traditionally avoided problems arising in this area irrespective of their constitutional merits. Like the slave who accompanied a Roman consul on his triumph whispering "You too are mortal," the shade of Thad Stevens haunts the Supreme Court chamber to remind the justices what an angry Congress can do.

To state the proposition in this brief compass is to oversimplify it considerably. I have, for instance, ignored the crucial question of how the Court knows when a majority *does* exist, and I recognize that certain aspects of judicial behavior cannot be jammed into my hypothesis without creating essentially spurious epicycles. However, I am not trying to establish a monistic theory of judicial action; group action, like that of individuals, is motivated by many factors, some often contradictory, and my objective is to elucidate what seems to be one tradition of judicial motivation. In short, judicial self-restraint and judicial power seem to be opposite sides of the same coin: it has been by judicious application of the former that the latter has been maintained. A tradition beginning with Marshall's *coup* in *Marbury* v. *Madison* and running through *Mississippi* v. *Johnson* and *Ex Parte Vallandigham* to *Dennis* v. *United States* suggests that the Court's power has been maintained by a wise refusal to employ it in unequal combat.

65. *Marbury v. Madison*

SUPREME COURT OF THE UNITED STATES,
1803 (ORIGINAL) 1 CRANCH 137

THIS CASE should be read against the background of the Federalist-Jeffersonian conflict. Unless this struggle is kept in mind, it is not possible to appreciate the skill with which Marshall escaped from the political dilemma in which Marbury's request had placed the Court. The facts of the case are that Marbury, a "midnight" judicial appointee of the outgoing Federalist administration, having been refused delivery of his commission by the new Secretary of State Madison, petitioned the Supreme Court for a writ of mandamus to compel Madison to deliver. Marbury based his petition on Section 13 of the Judiciary Act of 1789, which purported to authorize the Supreme Court to issue such writs. Chief Justice Marshall decided the issue by holding Section 13 unconstitutional on the grounds that it constituted an improper augmentation of the original jurisdiction of the Supreme Court as laid down in Article III of the Constitution. By thus refusing to issue the writ on jurisdictional grounds, Marshall escaped from the dilemma of either issuing a writ that the Jeffersonian administration would probably have ignored, or seeming to dismiss the petition out of fear of the new administration. At the same time Marshall enunciated the principle of the independence of the judiciary from improper interference by other branches of government.

Although Marshall's refusal to issue the writ appeared on the surface to be a Jeffersonian victory, the establishment of the principle of judicial review was to prove to be a formidable instrument for the imposition of Federalist ideas upon the new national government. Aside from the immediate decision on the issuance of the writ, the importance of the case lies in this: that the Court for the first time invalidated a Federal statute, thus establishing the power of judicial review as a proper function of the Court and a permanent feature of our Federal system.

Opinion of the Court.

MR. CHIEF JUSTICE MARSHALL delivered the opinion of the Court:

• • • • •

In the order in which the court has viewed this subject, the following questions have been considered and decided.

1st. Has the applicant a right to the commission he demands?

2d. If he has a right, and that right has been violated, do the laws of this country afford him a remedy?

3d. If they do afford him a remedy, is it a *mandamus* issuing from this court?

• • • • •

It is then the opinion of the Court.

1st. That by signing the commission of Mr. Marbury, the President of the United States appointed him a justice of peace for the county of Washington, in the District of Columbia; and that the seal of the United States, affixed thereto by the Secretary of State, is conclusive testimony of the verity of the signature, and of the completion of the appointment; and that the appointment conferred on him a legal right to the office for the space of five years.

2d. That, having this legal title to the office, he has a consequent right to the commission; a refusal to deliver which is a plain violation of that right, for which the laws of his country afford him a remedy.

It remains to be inquired whether,

3d. He is entitled to the remedy for which he applies. This depends on,

1st. The nature of the writ applied for; and,

2d. The power of this court. . . .

[The appropriate remedy was a writ of mandamus, and the question was, "Whether it can issue from this court."]

The act to establish the judicial courts of the United States authorizes the supreme court "to issue writs of *mandamus* in cases warranted by the principles and usages of law, to any courts appointed, or persons holding office, under the authority of the United States."

The secretary of state, being a person holding an office under the authority of the United States, is precisely within the letter of the description, and if this court is not authorized to issue a writ of *mandamus* to such an officer, it must be because the law is unconstitutional, and therefore absolutely incapable of conferring the authority, and assigning the duties which its words purport to confer and assign.

The constitution vests the whole judicial power of the United States in one supreme court, and such inferior courts as congress shall, from time to time, ordain and establish. This power is expressly extended to all cases arising under the laws of the United States; and, consequently, in some form, may be exercised over the present case; because the right claimed is given by a law of the United States.

In the distribution of this power it is declared that "the Supreme Court shall have original jurisdiction in all cases affecting ambassadors, other public ministers and consuls, and those in which a State shall be a party. In all other cases, the Supreme Court shall have appellate jurisdiction." . . .

When an instrument organizing fundamentally a judicial system, divides it into one supreme, and so many inferior courts as the legislature may ordain and establish; then enumerates its powers, and proceeds so far to distribute them, as define the jurisdiction of the supreme court by declaring the cases in which it shall take original jurisdiction, and that in others it shall take appellate jurisdiction; the plain import of the words seems to be, that in one class of cases its jurisdiction is original, and not appellate; in the other it is appellate, and not original. If any other construction would render the clause inoperative, that is an additional reason for rejecting such other construction, and for adhering to their obvious meaning.

To enable this court, then, to issue a *mandamus*, it must be shown to be an exercise of appellate jurisdiction, or to be necessary to enable them to exercise appellate jurisdiction.

It has been stated at the bar that the appellate jurisdiction may be exercised in a variety of forms, and that if it be the will of the legislature that a *mandamus* should be used for that purpose that will must be obeyed. This is true, yet the jurisdiction must be appellate, not original.

It is the essential criterion of appellate jurisdiction, that it revises and corrects the proceedings in a cause already instituted, and does not create that cause. Although, therefore, a *mandamus* may be directed to courts, yet to issue such a writ to an officer for the delivery of a paper, is in effect the same as to sustain an original action for that paper, and, therefore, seems not to belong to appellate, but to original jurisdiction. Neither is it necessary in such a case as this, to enable the court to exercise its appellate jurisdiction.

The authority, therefore, given to the supreme court, by the act of establishing the judicial courts of the United States, to issue writs of *mandamus* to public officers, appears not to be warranted by the constitution; and it becomes necessary to inquire whether a jurisdiction so conferred can be exercised.

The question, whether an act, repugnant to the constitution, can become the law of the land, is a question deeply interesting to the United States; but, happily, not of an intricacy proportioned to its interest. It seems only necessary to recognize certain principles, supposed to have been long and well established, to decide it.

That the people have an original right to establish, for their future government, such principles, as, in their opinion, shall most conduce to their own happiness is the basis on which the whole American fabric has been erected. The exercise of this original right is a very great exertion; nor can it, nor ought it, to be frequently repeated. The principles, therefore, so established, are deemed fundamental. And as the authority from which they proceed is supreme, and can seldom act, they are designed to be permanent.

This original and supreme will organizes the government, and assigns to different departments their respective powers. It may either stop here, or establish certain limits not to be transcended by those departments.

The government of the United States is of the latter description. The powers of the legislature are defined and limited; and that those limits may not be mistaken, or forgotten, the constitution is written. To what purpose are powers limited, and to what purpose is that limitation committed to writing, if these limits may, at any time, be passed by those intended to be restrained? The distinction between a government with limited and unlimited powers is abolished, if those limits do not confine the persons on whom they are imposed, and if acts prohibited and acts allowed, are of equal obligation. It is a proposition too plain to be contested, that the constitution controls any legislative act repugnant to it; or, that the legislature may alter the constitution by an ordinary act.

Between these alternatives there is no middle ground. The constitution is either a superior paramount law, unchangeable by ordinary means, or it is on a level with ordinary legislative acts, and, like other acts, is alterable when the legislature shall please to alter it.

If the former part of the alternative be true, then a legislative act contrary to the constitution is not law: if the latter part be true, then written constitutions are absurd attempts, on the part of the people, to limit a power in its own nature illimitable.

Certainly all those who have framed written constitutions contemplate them as forming the fundamental and paramount law of the nation, and, consequently, the theory of every such government must be, that an act of the legislature, repugnant to the constitution, is void.

This theory is essentially attached to a written constitution, and, is consequently, to be considered, by this court, as one of the fundamental principles of our society. It is not therefore to be lost sight of in the further consideration of this subject.

If an act of the legislature, repugnant to the constitution, is void, does it, notwithstanding its invalidity, bind the courts, and oblige them to give it effect? Or, in other words, though it be not law, does it constitute a rule as operative as if it was a law? This would be to overthrow in fact what was established in theory; and would seem, at first view, an absurdity too gross to be insisted on. It shall, however, receive a more attentive consideration.

It is emphatically the province and duty of the judicial department to say what the law is. Those who apply the rule to particular cases, must of necessity expound and interpret that rule. If two laws conflict with each other, the courts must decide on the operation of each.

So if a law be in opposition to the constitution; if both the law and the constitution apply to a particular case, so that the court must either decide that case conformably to the law, disregarding the constitution; or conformably to the constitution, disregarding the law; the court must determine which of these conflicting rules governs the case. This is of the very essence of judicial duty.

If, then, the courts are to regard the constitution, and the constitution is superior to any ordinary act of the legislature, the constitution, and not such ordinary act, must govern the case to which they both apply.

Those, then, who controvert the principle that the constitution is to be considered, in court, as a paramount law, are reduced to the necessity of maintaining that courts must close their eyes on the constitution, and see only the law.

This doctrine would subvert the very foundation of all written constitutions. It would declare that an act which, according to the principles and theory of our government, is entirely void, is yet, in practice, completely obligatory. It would declare that if the legislature shall do what is expressly forbidden, such act, notwithstanding the express prohibition, is in reality effectual. It would be giving to the legislature a practical and real omnipotence, with the same breath which professes to restrict their powers within narrow limits. It is prescribing limits, and declaring that those limits may be passed at pleasure.

That it thus reduces to nothing what we have deemed the greatest improvement on political institutions, a written constitution, would of itself be sufficient, in America, where written constitutions have been viewed with so much reverence, for rejecting the construction. But the peculiar expressions of the constitution of the United States furnish additional arguments in favour of its rejection.

The judicial power of the United States is extended to all cases arising under the constitution.

Could it be the intention of those who gave this power, to say that in using it the constitution should not be looked into? That a case arising under the constitution should be decided without examining the instrument under which it arises?

This is too extravagant to be maintained.

In some cases, then, the constitution must be looked into by the judges. And if they can open it at all, what part of it are they forbidden to read or to obey?

There are many other parts of the constitution which serve to illustrate this subject.

It is declared that "no tax or duty shall be laid on articles exported from any State." Suppose a duty on the export of cotton, of tobacco, or of flour; and a suit instituted to recover it. Ought judgment to be rendered in such a case? Ought the judges to close their eyes on the constitution, and only see the law?

The constitution declares "that no bill of attainder or ex *post facto* law shall be passed."

If, however, such a bill should be passed, and a person should be prosecuted under it; must the court condemn to death those victims whom the constitution endeavors to preserve?

"No person," says the constitution, "shall be convicted of treason unless on the testimony of two witnesses to the same overt act, or on confession in open court."

Here the language of the constitution is addressed especially to the courts. It prescribes, directly for them, a rule of evidence not to be departed from. If the legislature should change that rule, and declare one witness, or a confession out of court, sufficient for conviction, must the constitutional principle yield to the legislative act?

From these, and many other selections which might be made, it is apparent, that the framers of the constitution contemplated that instrument as a rule for the government of courts, as well as of the legislature.

Why otherwise does it direct the judges to take an oath to support it? This oath certainly applies in an especial manner, to their conduct in their official character. How immoral to impose it on them, if they were to be used as the instruments, and the knowing instruments, for violating what they swear to support!

The oath of office, too, imposed by the legislature, is completely demonstrative of the legislative opinion on this subject. It is in these words: "I do solemnly swear that I will administer justice without respect to persons, and do equal right to the poor and to the rich; and that I will faithfully and impartially discharge all the duties incumbent on me as , according to the best of my abilities and understanding agreeably to the constitution and laws of the United States."

Why does a judge swear to discharge his duties agreeably to the constitution of the United States, if that constitution forms no rule for his government—if it is closed upon him, and cannot be inspected by him?

If such be the real state of things, this is worse than solemn mockery. To prescribe, or to take this oath, becomes equally a crime.

It is also not entirely unworthy of observation, that in declaring what shall be the supreme law of the land, the constitution itself is first mentioned; and not the laws of the United States generally, but those only which shall be made in pursuance of the constitution, have that rank.

Thus, the particular phraseology of the constitution of the United States confirms and strengthens the principle, supposed to be essential to all written constitutions, that a law repugnant to the constitution is void; and that courts, as well as other departments, are bound by that instrument.

The rule must be discharged.

66. *Should People Distrust Lawyers?* *

MR. ASPELL, a lawyer, defends his profession against those who malign it. Lawyers, whose function is to know the law and, when they become judges, to apply it to individuals, are the guardians of

* William P. Aspell, *The Saturday Review*, XXXVIII (December 17, 1955), pp. 7-8, 37-38. Reprinted by permission of the author and publisher.

the law. Law embodies the rules that hold society together and keep it running more or less smoothly. Thus, lawyers are the guardians of society. We should not forget, however, that lawyers who make and apply the law are human beings who are subject, as all of us are, to human frailties.

OUR TIMES glorify speed, efficiency, the flamboyant stroke. The law seems the antithesis of these things, an antique relic society has not yet had the courage to store in the attic beside the oil lamp and the spinning wheel. Its cumbersome processes irritate people. Unrest is aggravated on emotional occasions such as the Rosenberg appeals, the Hiss trials, sensational criminal proceedings like the Jelke vice trials and the Sheppard murder case; but even without such artificial stimulation the law is ever scorned.

Nor is public dissatisfaction with the law a new development. The cry of reformers and revolutionaries has always been loud against lawyers. Bench and bar have furnished villains for books and plays as far back as the Bible itself. Undoubtedly this hostility has its roots in a common aversion to a group which maintains itself upon the disputes and imperfections of other men. Certainly it is inevitable that those who cannot be aided will be disgruntled. And it is a commonplace of legal folklore that the victorious client seldom has a sense of gratitude. He is, after all, one of the elect receiving his due (after a totally unnecessary delay). But as for "those lawyers" who attached themselves to the cause like so many parasites?—people say that sensible men could have handled matters with greater speed and less expense. The law is truly an ass.

Although unexpressed, another cause for these hostile feelings is probably the human desire for a scapegoat. Those involved in the law seldom make its acquaintance under pleasant conditions. If the law is not responsible for their difficulties, the bitter family quarrel over Uncle Harry's will, the petty bickerings of the divorce courts, then the parties must accept the blame themselves. For all but the most mature this is difficult to do. Accordingly, in self-exculpation, they mutter loudly against the evils of the system designed to bring their problems to solution.

It must be frankly and sorrowfully admitted that the law and many of its practitioners are full of faults. We humans are a tainted race. With too many of us an opportunity for profit will always appear more attractive than the preservation of moral standards. Lawyers, in the nature of things, are often in positions from which they can profit unfairly; being human, sometimes they do. Because of the kind of work they do, also, lawyers are often incited to wrongdoing by their clients, a temptation some of them do not always resist.

Public distrust of the bar, therefore, has some justification in the acts of attorneys who have been false to their trust. No defense is offered for these men or against the hostility they bring upon themselves. The disturbing element of the criticisms is the inability of many detractors to make the necessary and important distinction between the errors of individual lawyers and awesome accomplishments of The Law.

Perhaps some would better grasp this distinction if a few of the law's important services in a democratic society were restated in nonlegal terms. President Griswold of Yale recently said, "The American people do not sufficiently understand the rule of law because it has never been properly explained to them." If this is true, certainly an attempt should be made. The logical starting point is a definition of law, but the winds of controversy howl so strongly around that subject that it seems unwise to take it on in a discussion of what law *does*. Therefore the term will not be defined; if this be chaos, make the most of it. Though the subject is left uncrystallized, the concept is yet sufficiently definite for a broad look at its place in society. Let us say merely that the law embodies all the general rules of civilization, represented by constitutions, statutes, court decisions, and legislative regulations, which channel the daily lives of the citizens and control their relations with the state and with each other.

Aside from religious authority or historical justification, what are the law's claims to the respect of society? First of all, it must be acknowledged that a sense of stability, the state of a community which permits intelligent planning for the future on the part of its citizens, is essential to freedom. There is nothing more typical of despotic government than the sudden midnight arrest; the unlooked-for, unexplained swerve of public policy by which the hero of yesterday becomes the traitor of today; the hopeless plight of the average man who cannot tell what his job, his money, or his life will be worth in the morning. The cataclysmic downfall of Lavrenty Beria and his henchmen, with its rumble of tanks and convictions to the Lubyanka and death, was a characteristic scene of despotism at work.

On the other hand, it is a commonplace of democratic life that tomorrow will be much like today, so that an intelligent (or, at least, honest) approach to current problems will bring rewards in relative freedom from the problems of the future. No President of the United States has yet been executed, or even much harassed, by his successor. Law is the partition between these two ways of living. Of course, tyrannies and dictatorships have their statutes, but there law is the whim of the rulers, altered or ignored at convenience. In a free society the law is something more; it is an entity to which the ruler must submit, a free acting force.

But not all legal operations are on the heights where governing monarchs sit; it is in this area of stability and permanence that most of the ordinary business laws of the community make their contribution. A stable system of law reassures the investor that his corporation will not be seized if it becomes profitable, as the juicy plums of German industry were confiscated by Nazi leaders. It is law which gives the sense of confidence necessary to accept a check, purchase a house, own life insurance, save money, retire on a pension, buy an automobile, make the hundreds of simple commitments to the future which constitute so great a part of daily life. If law did nothing else, this function alone would justify its claim to being a useful vocation.

A democratic society also implies protection of the individual against the power of the state. Our conception of a tyranny has always included the helpless prisoner whipped to death in a torture cell; the old man fading through the years, imprisoned without a trial; innocent families uprooted from their homes and marched in agony to distant barracks with neither explanation nor pity. Typical of this degradation of human dignity by a state turned against its own citizens were Belsen, Buchenwald, the other German concentration camps with their lampshades of human skin and piles of salvaged wedding rings.

Among the democracies such things are incredible. Even in a Rosenberg trial or a Hiss trial, where the deepest emotions are inflamed, we would be shocked if orderly procedures for the defense of the individual were ignored or bypassed, or a vicious and inhuman punishment imposed. Yet all that prevents these events are the concepts of fair trial and governmental responsibility, enforced through the much maligned "legal technicalities" of newspaper reports. The writ of *habeas corpus*, a "legal technicality" if there ever was one, requires the government to produce its prisoners in court and explain why they are being held. If the state has no reasonable grounds (again a "legal technicality"), they must be released. If there is justification for holding them, other "legal technicalities" force a speedy and public trial. At that trial the government cannot compel the accused to testify against himself, or introduce his confession without corroborating evidence or—in any event—if it is shown to be the result of force or fraud. Because of "legal technicalities" hearsay evidence cannot be introduced, so that the defendant may have the benefit of cross-examining in public the person or persons who accuse him of crime.

Violation of these rules can be appealed to the higher courts. If the appeal is sustained it results in annulment of the conviction. Thus law, through the specific rules it provides for doing things, called "legal technicalities," directs the machinery of a democratic government against itself as a control upon excesses of power.

Of course, the idea of one part of a state restraining another is a logical absurdity, like lifting yourself by your bootstraps, but the proof of experience is that it can be made to work. The full explanation of its success is not easily come by, but it is evident that the arrangement is effective in large part because of the climate created by the traditions of honor, integrity, and independence which judges and lawyers of the democratic world have preserved for generations, symbolized in the magistrate's black robe and the ceremonials attending the arrival of a judge in his courtroom.

A further necessary aspect of democracy is equality between persons. Once again the law renders the theoretical concrete. Our own times are seeing this in the Supreme Court litigation concerning segregation in the public schools. Where, even in a democracy, could a peaceful solution for such a controversial problem be reached except through the operation of an antiseptic judicial system which permits, indeed almost compels, each side to set forth the best arguments available in support of its thesis? The end result of these decisions is not yet fully apparent, but it would be a rash man who would say that they have not been a major contribution to the advancement of the democratic ideal. The credit rests directly with the judges and attorneys involved, not to mention the lawyers and jurists of the past whose devoted efforts erected a system of law capable of dealing with such a crisis.

In more mundane instances, too, the legal system preserves and cultivates the equality which has been postulated as the reason for our national existence. The conduct of drab automobile negligence cases, the murky complications of a shareholders' derivative suit, the instructions and advice to clients given in thousands of quiet law offices—through all these the bland, generalized philosophy of our government is transmuted, sometimes with a deplorable excess of heat, into the firm directions applied to specific issues which make equality a throbbing, vital thing.

One of the most valiant of the attempts to translate equality into law is the Internal Revenue Code. Its complications are as much evidence of the good intentions of the drafters as they are monuments to the difficulty of the task. Irritating and unsatisfactory though the end result is, anyone with a thorough knowledge of world history will acknowledge the tremendous improvement in fairness and equity which it represents over the means of collecting government revenue which have held favor in the past, most of which, in theory or in fact, relied largely upon arbitrary confiscation.

Yet another attribute of a free society is its capacity for orderly change. Unlike despotisms, where the death or decline of a Stalin, Hitler, or Mussolini brings on violence and unrest, democracies, when truly served, reject old names and embrace new policies with relative calm and deliberation. Labor unions, for example, were once regarded by the American people as criminal conspiracies against the rights of property. Ultimately the majority changed its mind, and began to consider it a basic right of laborers to be free to bargain collectively. A more complete reversal of ideas is difficult to imagine, yet, guided by a series of progressive statutes and court decisions, we stepped across the social chasm from one view to the other without a slip. It was the concept of law, and respect, which rendered this peaceful change possible.

There is, after all, nothing inevitable in orderly change. Spain has proven that. So, too, have Germany, Italy, France, Russia, England, even our own country at various times. Peaceful change requires the satisfaction of the people with the tools of reform at their disposal. In our society these tools are laws, brought into action by legislators, judges, lawyers. The concept of a secret ballot, for example, basic to orderly elections, is an absurdity without an agency to guarantee secrecy. So, too, are the ideas of popular government and freedom of speech, if there are no methods to preserve them against the efforts of prejudice, force, and fraud. In a practical sense, at least, Oliver Wendell Holmes was correct when he said that rights had no existence outside a system of law; it is a sad truth about human nature that without means of enforcement "rights" would receive short shrift.

One of the greatest contributions of law to democracy is the satisfactory, nonphysical method it provides for the discharge of hostile feeling and the settlement of violent differences. Originally men enforced their wishes by axe or club. The first step away from violence, and the first step toward law, was the introduction of formalized duels between hired champions who took up with their arms the task of determining the righteousness of opposite points of view. Even in modern law, where money damages substitute for physical blows, the essential idea of conflict and retribution still prevails. A discontented wife can denounce her husband from the witness stand, instead of assaulting him in his sleep; the defrauded creditor can bring his debtor into court, instead of thrashing him in an alley; the general public can watch the slow progress of the law drawing a rapist to judgment rather than lynching him in haste, in horror, and perhaps in error.

This function of law reaches its highest level in the great public cases, like the Triangle Shirtwaist fire case of fifty years ago from which sprang much of our anti-sweatshop legislation; or the Scopes evolution trial in Tennessee. The proceedings on such occasions become a medium for the molding and expression of public opinion. Through them the public learns the other side of controversial issues, becoming better equipped to deal with them. And in this type of litigation there is much to be said for the law's slow pace, in spite of the fuming of the impatient, since the deliberation serves both as a dramatic device to focus attention and as a reinforcement of the ultimate cathartic effect.

All this is beneficial to the public peace. Since the energy involved is turned to constructive purposes, the process is good also for the long-range welfare of society. How much better it would have been if Alexander Hamilton and Aaron Burr had settled their differences in a courtroom, rather than snuffing out the life of the one and the reputation of the other in a savage outburst of violence. Negatively, then, a function of law is the conclusion of disputes without murder. Positively, one function is to bring further accretions of strength to the coral reef of habit and tradition which make up the framework of civilized society.

When the law falters, or is not invoked, as in the occasional lynchings and riots which have defaced our history, as well as the parodies of court proceedings which have sometimes passed for Congressional investigations, we can glimpse the snake-pit into which so many nations have fallen. Once—in the Civil War—we went through that terrifying experience ourselves. But if we are as sensitive to the rarity of these events as we are to their ugliness, we can gain a new appreciation of the protecting net, silent and elastic, the law has woven between us and anarchy.

Let those who doubt the contribution of law to society take note of the special attention tyrants and foreign conquerors, from the Romans to the Communists, have always paid to the legal systems of the land they despoil. The most prominent lawyers, the finest judges, are the first members of society to find themselves behind the fences of a concentration camp, or to be left bloody in a ditch, because tyrants know it is essential that the law be bent to their will. Or observe the results of anarchy on the international scene, where without a sure, enforceable rule of law among nations there is no stability, equality, or orderly change; where, rather than the peaceful settlement of disputes, the ultimate concern of mankind appears to be with the apocalypse of hydrogen-bomb war.

While the law is not perfect, there is no other system for the governing of men except violence. The difference between an alley-fight and a debate is law. The same legal technicality which frees a burglar can also free a patriot. It is exasperating, sometimes, that the writs are used so often in behalf of the burglars, but how much more comforting it is to know that even a burglar's rights have weight than it would be to feel sure that every criminal in the nation was safe behind bars, but that with them were thousands of citizens innocent of any wrong.

Perhaps, if our people grasped that fact as firmly as they should, they would appreciate the relative unimportance of the shoddy and dishonest elements in the bar. Perhaps they would come to an awareness that shysters are mere scum on the waters, witnesses to the fallen nature of man rather than to the profession which they have chosen to deface. Perhaps, also, people would be more aware of their own responsibilities toward the law, recognizing the importance of their attitudes toward such matters as fixing motor-vehicle arrests and bringing false personal-injury claims, when considered against the importance of a harmonious and equitable system of law to the preservation of our society. Then, at last, we all might understand how important a contribution to our progress toward the democratic ideal has been made by the generations of lawyers and jurists down the years, and develop that reverence for law which is the only safeguard of our way of life.

XII

THE STATE JUDICIAL SYSTEM

67. *Elected Judges--Or Appointed?* *

FOR YEARS a controversy has raged over the best means of selecting judges. Should they be appointed with legislative confirmation, as in the Federal judiciary, or elected, as in three fourths of the states? A few states have a hybrid form in which judges are appointed by the governor from a list of names drawn up by a partly lay and partly professional commission, with periodic voting on the question, "Shall Judge Blank be retained in office?" It is said that an appointed judge serving during good behavior is independent, while an elected judge is more responsive to the popular will. Professor Berle, in this selection, says that both the appointive and elective systems are in reality much alike. In both forms the party leaders nearly always choose the judge. The check against abuse of the system, says Mr. Berle, is public opinion.

HOW SHOULD judges be chosen? The only honest answer is that the method is less important than the true source of the appointment. Here is one method now in use:

Dwight D. Eisenhower, President of the United States of America, to all to whom these presents shall come, GREETINGS:

KNOW YE that, reposing special trust and confidence in the integrity, prudence and ability of John Doe, I . . . etc. . . . do appoint him a Judge of the District Court of the Federal District Court for the Southern District of New York. . . .

John Doe, being fully confirmed by the Senate, thereupon holds his judgeship for life. This is the appointive system; the Federal Govern-

* Adolf A. Berle, Jr., *The New York Times Magazine*, December 11, 1955, pp. 26, 34, 37-38, 40. Reprinted by permission of the author and publisher.

ment has it, and also a number of states, notably, Massachusetts.

Here is the second method:

We, the undersigned, the members of the Board of Election in The City of New York, having canvassed the whole number of votes cast at the Election on [such-and-such a date] according to the original statements of said votes filed with us in the manner directed by law, do hereby *certify* that Richard Roe, of 10 West 76th Street, New York, N. Y., was duly elected a Justice of the Supreme Court . . . etc.

This is a judgeship obtained by election in an open campaign. A majority of states uses this system for some, and New York uses it for all, of its higher court judges. In New York the term is commonly for fourteen years. The judge was nominated by a political party or group, he financed and carried on a campaign for election, and so got the job.

Both methods have had their advocates in a long-standing public debate, and both are now being considered by the Temporary Commission on the Courts which is preparing a report on judicial reform for submission to the 1956 Legislature. Offhand, you might assume that the two systems are as different as possible. You would be wrong. The two systems are in ultimate analysis almost the same.

Factually, both the appointive and elective methods really mean that judges are chosen by the chieftains of the political parties involved. Your judge will be just as good as the political leadership of the area involved—state, judicial district, county, as the case may be. There seems to be no escape from this. Let us look behind the formal procedure and see what really happens.

Take the appointive system, prescribed by the Constitution of the United States with regard to all Federal judges. The idea was that judges should be as far removed from political pressure as possible; so they are appointed by the President (in state systems like Massachusetts, by the governor). Once appointed, they cannot be removed except by impeachment. Their salary cannot be cut; neither legislature nor executive can do anything to them. But behind the certificate of appointment, a quite different drama goes on.

A Federal judge is to be appointed, let us say, for the Southern District of New York. The President (unless he happens to come from that area) cannot possibly know the men who should hold judicial office. His principal law officer is the Attorney General of the United States. It is a recognized part of the Attorney General's job to recommend judicial appointments. Except in the case of his own district, he does not know the men either. So he expects, and the fact is, that the Republican state chairman of New York (assuming a Republican Administration) will make a recommendation, commonly in conjunction with the Republican Senator or Senators, if any, from the state. The Attorney General knows perfectly well that none of these men will recommend except after consultation with the county Republican leader who handles patronage in the district. That county leader has a group of hungry district leaders; they want credit for giving out the job (if they do not want the job themselves); indeed, they have been eying the particular vacancy for a good while. Probably several contesting leaders urge their pet candidates. The county leader has to resolve the question.

When, as in the case of the Federal judicial districts, the district covers more than one county, and even crosses state lines, he has to work it out with other leaders. Quite likely there has been a considerable ruckus—probably the continuation of ruckuses of previous years—resulting in a prior understanding about whose turn it is to get the next vacancy. The individuals who want the job have been busy as beavers lining up political support all the time.

County leaders, if they are any good, weed out the obviously impossible candidates. They finally arrive at an understanding that John Doe has the background necessary to be a judge, and decide that his appointment will satisfy the district leader who is entitled to it. All hands having been squared, a recommendation goes up. The local United States Attorney has probably been in on the discussions; he is likely to be asked by the Attorney General whether the man is all right. Not, you understand, whether he is the best possible man for judge, but whether his character, standing and so forth, are such that his appointment will not excite controversy.

The views of the state chairman have been ascertained. Consultation with the party United States Senator is usually essential; he is a political power himself; if the man is obnoxious to him, he can block confirmation by the Senate. (The most cruel Congressional prerogative is that of "courtesy of the Senate"—a polite way of saying that if a Senator objects to a Presidential appointment from his party in his state, all other Senators will vote against confirmation.)

By now, the "way is cleared," as politicians say. The recommendation goes forward to the Attorney General. He gets reports. The F.B.I. has investigated and discovers the man never joined the Communist party or murdered his mother-in-law. The local bar associations have reported him "qualified" for the job. The United States Attorney's Office has indicated that the man will do (not infrequently the United States Attorney is himself a candidate for the job). The party National Committee agrees because the party state chairman has agreed.

The Attorney General thereon takes or sends the whole dossier with favorable recommendation to the President, who sends up the name of the prospective judge to the United States Senate. The appointment goes promptly to the committee on Judiciary; unless the man has made important enemies, this body after reviewing the file reports recommending confirmation; the Senate confirms; the Presidential certificate of appointment is issued; a new judge mounts the bench in the United States Courthouse in Foley Square.

On analysis, the real choice was made by the party leader or leaders in the unimpressive setting in which political parties act.

How about elective judges? The power of choice is in the same hands, though the stages are somewhat different. The Constitution of the State of New York says that the justices of the Supreme Court (which in New York is not "supreme" but is a trial court) and the county judges shall be elected for a term of fourteen years. But, if an elective judge serves out his term with even moderate competence, the salutary and unbreakable custom in New York is that he shall have renomination by *all* parties, thus guaranteeing re-election.

For practical purposes, therefore, election is for life or until retirement age. He can only be displaced by a two-thirds vote of both houses of the legislature on charges of misconduct. True, judges are nominated not by ordinary party convention, but by special judicial district conventions which are naively supposed to mean that the ugly hand of politics is somewhat removed from their choice. In practice, a judicial convention consists of a slate of delegates put up by the district leaders. Invariably they nominate the candidates arrived at by the county leader and his district leaders in the same way as are candidates recommended for appointment by the President.

But, at least, isn't there an election? A Republican does run against a Democrat, so that the people have something to say? No. Or at least, frequently not. There are few "doubtful" judicial districts in most states—very few, indeed, in New York. The Democrats know absolutely that they have control in most districts in the city; the Republicans have exactly the same control upstate. In the "safe" districts, the county leader's nod is equivalent to nomination and election.

When the election is in doubt, the practice increasingly has been for the leaders of both parties involved to get together. Not infrequently when three judges are to be elected, you find two Democrats and one Republican, or two Republicans and one Democrat, all nominated by *both* parties. The rival party leaders have sat down together, figured out the relative possibilities of the situation, agreed that one should nominate two judges and the other should have the third, canvassed their district leaders, decided on the deal and put through the nominations. For practical purposes in that case, one of the judges has been picked by the Republican county leader; two have been picked by the Democratic county leader; as there is no contest, the election is a form. From time to time, of course, there are real contests. They are relatively rare.

So for practical purposes, ultimate power to choose every judge, elected or appointed, rests in the hands of the county machines of the two major political parties. There are exceptions, but so few that they rather prove the rule.

At this point one conjures up visions of a crooked, politically influenced bench. Has this been the fact? No, it has not. Surprisingly, the results in this strange and unpredictable working of the American political system have been good. The level of the New York elective bench rates as "good"; the level of the Federal appointive bench falls just short of continuous excellence.

If you examine the grimy surrounding circumstances, you would swear that it could not happen. Politics fairly burgeons in the selective process, frequently of the least savory kind. In nominating a man for the bench, a county leader frequently considers what kind of campaign contribution the candidate will make to the party war chest. At one time in New York City no one could expect a Democratic judicial nomination unless he was prepared to lay down $20,000 as a "contribution" to the campaign fund; frequently the quotation has been higher. When several men want the job (this is usually the case), they may even bid against each other.

One justice of the New York Supreme Court was widely known as the "$100,000 Judge" because he or his friends reportedly laid that contribution on the line. He got the job—and, having got it, did a remarkable piece of work. He was assigned to resolve the endless chaos resulting from the failure of the guaranteed mortgage companies in 1933; and he succeeded.

Powerful party figures often want judgeships for their relatives. The late Samuel Untermeyer had amassed a legal fortune. He was a thumping power in Tammany councils. He arranged to have two of his sons, Alvin Untermeyer and Irwin Untermeyer, named to the bench. Both turned in outstanding records.

The old Brooklyn boss, John McCooey, had his son put on the New York Supreme Court; a relative of the late Ed Flynn of the Bronx has quite recently got similar recognition. The old Manhattan Republican county leader, Sam Koenig, was represented on the Supreme Court bench by his brother, Morris Koenig.

Occasionally the nomination can be useful for other reasons: a party stalwart may have aspirations to be Mayor, and the organization can conveniently remove him from the situation by putting him on the bench. Yet the fact is that most of these men, once there, do an honest and effective job.

Politics does not quite end with appointment or election. A judge does have a considerable amount of patronage to distribute. In the Federal courts he can appoint trustees in bankruptcy, receivers, referees, and so forth. In the state courts he can appoint special guardians and other court officers. Both sets of judges have at least one very important appointment, namely, a law clerk or law secretary. It surprises almost no onc to find that a Democrat invariably appoints Democrats to these jobs—not infrequently lists of suggestions are given him by the party which nominated him. His secretary is quite usually an aspiring lawyer with a good record for party fidelity.

But by now our judge is on, not off the bench, and he is thinking of his own reputation. If there is anything conspicuously wrong with the party follower he is asked to appoint as receiver, special guardian, referee, or the like, he knows the onus falls on him, and will find a way of appointing someone else. His law clerk on whom he must rely for continuous legal research has to be pretty competent, else the judge is in trouble.

Everything considered, the results have been paradoxically satisfactory. I have seen a Tammany judge, under the heaviest political pressure, decide squarely against his party organization in a proceeding to invalidate a nomination, the case involving construction of the election law. It did not hurt his career.

There have been scandals occasionally. They have been rare. One judge whose appointment was at least partly forwarded by the famous underworld character, Frank Costello (at all events, the judge thought so), has turned in an unexceptionable record of judicial probity.

Still, one asks, is this rational? When choosing a judge we ought to be looking for the highest level of character and legal ability; we ought not to be dredging the party machines. Cannot better ways be found? Unquestionably, while the system has worked reasonably well, many men who should be on the bench never get there. Really first-rate lawyers rarely reach the bench. It looks like tempting Providence to expect figs from political thistles.

A number of possibilities have been suggested. One has been that all appointments to the state courts should be made by the Governor for life. This merely makes the Federal method of appointments general throughout the country. As we have seen, this merely means a political recommendation to him, instead of a political nomination for election.

A much discussed Western proposal has been that the bar association in each area shall make up a panel of names from which appointments or nominations for election, as the case may be, shall be drawn. In theory this is splendid: a bar association should be arbiter of legal ability, guardian of professional ethics, setting standards for the bench as well as for the bar.

In practice it is not so simple. Bar associations fulfill all these functions as long as, and only so long as, they stay out of politics. If at any time bar associations obtain power to name candidates for judgeships, would politics stay out of bar associations? Not probably. Most politicians are lawyers, and politics is one of the standard ways by which lawyers become known in their community. (On one occasion, even the Association of the Bar of the City of New York—blue ribbon organization of the country—was pressured into endorsing an individual for election. Its president, Harrison Tweed, a friend of the man in question, delivered a smashing rebuke, and in New York such an incident is not likely to be repeated.) What a bar association can do is to invite consultation with it before candidates are nominated for election or proposed for appointment, but only on a single issue: is the candidate of good character and professionally fit for the job?

Bar associations can—and do—issue reports to their members and to the public, stating that all of the candidates are of good character and are professionally fit to be judges—or the contrary, if any of them are not. Such verdicts have influence only. They may help to guide voters. In New York City, they frequently do not. Possibly such reports would have more influence on a governor urged to appoint an unfit man.

But if the bar association ever is endowed with power to choose judges, or to make the panel from which judges are chosen, you can bet your last dollar that every political machine will suddenly take an enormous interest in seeing the bar association has the right president and picks the right committee on judiciary.

Political influence will be present in practically any system which can be devised. It will be there if judges are chosen by the legislature instead of by the governor, or by the Congress instead of the President. It will be there if they are chosen by a non-political council. It will get out of hand in every case where public opinion does not demand that judges be of good quality.

American public opinion is the reason why, in the main, American judges, Federal and state, have been good; it is the controlling reason; and it is the only safeguard. The American public unquestionably reveres its bench. A governor or President who has appointed a bad judge hears of it in the newspapers, from his political opponents, and at the next election. He transmits his annoyance at once to the Attorney General and through him to the district leader who urged the appointment.

Next time around, recommendations from that source get bad treatment. Even county and district leaders dislike a bad reputation. Their other activities are likely to come in for more careful and wholly unwanted scrutiny if they have produced men who affront the desire of practically everyone for incorruptible and capable courts.

The crookedest politician knows that; and he can estimate very closely the extent of public interest. Public opinion, as a rule, has little interest in choosing who should be judges. But it is wholly clear that it wants good judges and someone's scalp if they are not. If that public opinion ever flags, the standards of acceptability used by political leaders and the quality of judges, however chosen, will promptly drop. Whenever the public and the press show interest in the subject, politicians will move up their standards and even "bosses" will request that the men proposed be top quality.

68. *What Makes Up the Juror's Mind* *

The jury system has long been regarded as a palladium of our liberties. Developed in England after the Norman conquest as an instrument for centralizing administration under the Crown, it came to be looked upon as the chief safeguard of the citizen against arbitrary judicial process. In recent years in England and America it has been under attack but still remains the distinctive characteristic of our criminal proceedings at Common Law. Mr. Curran, a former Judge of the Special Sessions Court of New York, discusses in the accompanying article some of the factors that influence the juror in "making up his mind" on the case presented to him. Among these factors Mr. Curran gives special attention to the judge, the attorneys, and the witnesses.

The oddest job in the world, perhaps, is to be a juror. Unsung, unheeded, unheard—except when the verdict comes in—he homeward plods his weary way after hours and days of sitting and listening, and even his family often looks upon him as no more than an amiable and stationary contemplator of the universe.

To be sure, he is heard when the verdict comes in—just that once—and the defendant in a criminal case will cock his ears well at that

* Henry M. Curran, *The New York Times Magazine*, November 27, 1949, pp. 17, 66-67, 69-70. Copyright, 1949, by The New York Times Company. Reprinted by permission of the author and the publisher.

moment; but beyond that the general impression is that the less said about jurors the better. In the same vein we leave paving blocks and coal holes out of our conversation, looking upon them as necessary but not really reeking in glamour. The juror is the true forgotten man. If the juror be a woman, she is the true forgotten woman.

And yet the whirligig of fate does strange things. From time to time it scratches up out of obscurity some humble fellow who has saved a life, or put to flight a stick-up man, or has done some act of bizarre but instinctive kindness which puts him in the news for a whole day. He is the same good man he was the day before, and he will be the same good man the day after, when the little candle of his unsought fame has flickered out, but he has had his moment.

So it is with jurors just now for a few months, and their candles are still burning, for three recent criminal cases involving as many varieties of treason are still with us, still on the tip of every tongue. There are or have been the two Judith Coplon trials, the two Hiss trials and the trial of the eleven Communist leaders. In such cases there comes a moment when the jury alone holds the spotlight—the moment the jurors return to the courtroom from their deliberations and the world waits on tiptoe for their verdict.

Now, what about these jurors whom we take so easily for granted? How do they come to a decision that may mean the difference between freedom and jail? What influences them?

Well, there is nothing abstruse about it, nor yet simple. It is not easy to be a juror, to know the impact of the restless trinity of judge and lawyers and witnesses, to assay them all, discount and ponder them, to cast aside any shred of prejudice, to guess, then change one's mind and guess again, and then decide.

I have had some experience of it in a different way, for the two courts in which I served as a judge for a good many years are so contrived that the judge decides on the facts as well as the law. The minor crimes and offenses, as they are called, go through those courts—minor in the statutory gradation of crime, not minor in the anguish, the puzzle, the pathos of how men and women get into trouble, and what to do about them. But, the facts? They are hard to find out. They never stop being hard; and there are definite elements that influence the determination of them.

With a jury the most unexpected influence is the judge. The juror keeps close track of him, as close as a driver's eyes peering through city traffic. He will be quick to detect prejudice or weakness, or to sit back comfortably in the realization of fairness and strength on the bench. He will know the judge, inside out, before the case is over; silent and impersonal, one of a dozen in a jury box, he will know; and his wish to follow the judge as a good leader will be a pathetic thing to see, as moving as a good dog, born wordless in a world of speech, trying to understand what his human friend is saying to him.

Especially, the juror will watch the effect of testimony on the judge. No judge ever lived who could disguise his own impression of witnesses, his own idea of the facts. He will show it unconsciously, in a dozen different ways, and the juror will take note, weighing it with other influences, and with respect. It is the juror who must decide, not the judge, but the influence is there. Directly, of course, the judge's impartial charge, when the case is over, will be obeyed.

As to the lawyers, those Lancelots of the courtroom who take the case, prepare and present it, then joust it through to a finish, I think the juror appreciates their indispensable service, but is influenced not at all by their forensic outbursts. They are advocates. They must give their clients the best of it they can, trying to put in testimony through a second door if the judge has closed the first door, straining at gnats, never letting up, until it is over. But jurors dislike waving of arms and pounding of tables, bear up unhappily under Hollywood eloquence, sigh under loudness. Oratory is less welcome than it used to be. When it comes, the juror cannot protest. He must just "take it."

I remember a judge who used to help the helpless juror in this respect. When the lawyer became long and loud, perhaps not realizing it, the judge would gently lift a hand.

"Would you mind speaking a little louder?" he would ask, innocently and respectfully. "I cannot hear."

It worked, every time. The lawyer came back to earth, and the jury was grateful.

The juror is afflicted too by the lawyer who does not know what to do with his hands, and so puts them in his pants pockets, sticks out his stomach and feels better. It is a sorry sight to see.

"Is there something the matter with your hands?" the judge would ask, sympathetically, anxiously, almost tearfully.

The lawyer, alarmed, invariably took his hands out of his pants, examined them nervously, then saw the point. One such lawyer protested hotly that he had a right to put his hands where he liked, the same as any other free American, that there was nothing against it in the canons of ethics.

"Ah, yes, you have the right," the judge observed, "but have you thought how we suffer who have to look at you!"

The hands stayed out. The jury perked up.

Those are little things, but it is the little foxes that spoil the vines. When it comes to browbeating a witness who appears to be honest, the juror, like any of us, will favor the witness. Conversely, he will favor the lawyer who finds the witness tricky but plays fair himself. Jurors are human. To most lawyers they will accord a ready respect, despite oratory and eccentricities, for they see clearly the difficulties and pitfalls of advocacy in a criminal court, and they like a man who fights, with fairness, skill and courage, to the last inch.

Witnesses are different from both judge and lawyer, different among themselves, a kaleidoscopic parade of human nature, with the jury in the reviewing stand. The juror keeps step with them, misses nothing, compares their conflicting stories and personalities, builds his own house of facts. He is more influenced by witnesses than by anything else in the world—and sometimes not so much by what they say as by the way they say it.

Naturally the few perfect witnesses wield the strongest influence. Telling only what they know, telling it truthfully and clearly, and stopping when it is time to stop, they are a boon to the bewildered juror. They are rare birds.

It is the imperfect witness who provides the puzzle. Like all Gaul he falls into three parts, and the least objectionable of these is the witness of slight intellect, of sloppy observation or poor memory. For this type of witness is honest and fair, although he helps but slightly in building the story. He will tell just what happened as he remembers it, but though the telling be understandable and coherent, the juror cannot feel that he is hearing the facts.

Even with average men and women, the stories of an identical incident will disagree. A few weeks ago I saw the aftermath of a stick-up in a jewelry store just across the street, just across Fifth Avenue. From a window on the hither side I saw the thief run down the avenue, with a man running after him. At the corner he ran into the cop, who with pistol drawn stopped him, frisked him, made him lie down on the sidewalk and meanwhile fired two shots at the conferedate who was running away through the side street. I saw and heard it and so did two or three others in the next window. Twenty minutes later we were telling totally different stories of what happened, and yet we all saw the same thing. Of course my own story was the correct version!

And yet the juror is required to piece the stories together the best he can, and then decide what really happened. But the "dumb" witness will be the least of his troubles.

The prejudiced witness gives greater concern and has less influence. He will try not to show his prejudice. He will try conscientiously if he is honest, artfully if he is not. In either case he will show the prejudice just the same, and the juror will discount his story accordingly.

A robust witness once told me about an automobile accident.

"Where were you when you saw something happen?" I asked.

"Your honor, I was standin' on the corner where I seen the defendant comin' fast through the red light."

"Strike out the red light," I observed. "We'll take that up later. Where was the defendant when you saw him?"

"Your honor, he was comin' hell bent down the avenue through the red light."

"Stop. Did you see him driving the car?"

"Yes, your honor, I seen him comin' bloody murder through the red light."

The witness, it seemed to me, was just a little bit tinged with prejudice against the defendant, and so, to my sorrow, his influence waned.

And now we come to the most difficult of the three general varieties of witness, the one who least influences the juror. He is the liar—but you have to find that out, and it is not always easy. The juror has no yardstick for it. He must guess, with all the shrewdness he can muster, just as you and I do as we go through life, when we suspect that somebody is not telling the truth.

Just how do you spot a liar? There is no rule. He takes the oath to tell "the truth, the whole truth and nothing but the truth" without a quiver of eyelash and with raised hand. He starts clear. Then, perhaps, he will seem just a little too glib in his answers, a little quick in a desire to show how true his story must be, because it ripples along so easily.

Or he will hesitate overmuch, striving to avoid an answer that may be inconsistent with another answer of a few minutes before, or wondering uneasily if the jury has somehow discovered that he is lying. He may lose his nerve, and put up his guard against dangerous questions by resorting to the impenetrable "I don't know" or "I don't remember." Or he may sweat about the forehead at just the moment when he is most anxious that no telltale sign of inner disturbance be given.

The keen juror will watch, too, the witness's hands, and especially his feet. A quick, unconscious closing of the feet will sometimes indicate that the witness suddenly finds himself more or less concerned. The hands can do anything, despite the wish of the witness that they do nothing. There are innumerable other signs. The juror will read all of them that he can see, studying personality as best he may. He will be none the less quick to reverse an unfavorable impression if he becomes convinced that the witness is not lying but is just scared to death. It is not easy to know when someone is lying, although there is a lot of it going on.

Of course the witness may tell the truth in some respects and lie in others. There may be just one thing that he wants to cover up.

There are many degrees of lying. Good cross-examination, inexorable and without heat, will disclose much. Sometimes the witness has undergone so keen a previous cross-examination by his own lawyer before the trial that the rehearsal has taught him what is dangerous to put in or leave out, and he testifies accordingly.

So there are three general varieties of witness, with their different kinds of evidence and their different measures of influence upon the jury. Whatever they say and however they say it, their stories will disagree. If there were complete agreement, there would be nothing for a jury to decide, and so there would be no jury. We have not yet reached that millennium. We have to have juries.

I suppose that a juror is influenced as much by human nature as by logic. He must study both, and sometimes his heart will lock horns with his mind. He will be like all the rest of us in quick sympathy for undeserved hard luck, for the one sharp lapse in life that made all the trouble for the defendant, or for the grievous hurt of a complainant who was without fault. He will be influenced by his own feeling as well as by the facts. So are we all.

In the jury room, where the twelve go to decide, the conflicting results of their study comes out with a downright forthrightness which sometimes leaves the disputants in a frame of mind where it is good for the public peace if they never see one another again. One stubborn juror holding out against his eleven colleagues may cause a conflagration of exasperation that will warm the walls of even the bleakest jury room —and jury rooms are bleak. The bare four walls and floor, the prim chairs ranged around the long bare table do not tempt to dalliance.

The foreman at the end of the table will usually call at once for a vote, and then, if there be disagreement, the last influence of all comes into play, the influence of juror upon juror. It brings out the truth. Especially, it reveals prejudice. A juror may have developed so strong a dislike for a witness or a lawyer that his distaste colors his estimate of the facts. "Why, that man just lied!" he will often exclaim. "I wouldn't believe a word he says."

Or an unrealized prejudice against the whole nature of the prosecution or of the defense may become apparent to a juror's colleagues, if not to himself. The thing will out, whatever it is, and the discussion will take account of it. The gradual approach to an agreement will come mostly by way of jurors whose power of personality, fairness and mind are the greater; their influence will decide. It is usually an orderly process; the little flames of feeling are the exception.

In this alchemy of the blending of opposite opinion, the women are especially helpful. They want peace—and they are keen jurors. When the law first brought them into jury duty they sprang a few surprises of inexperience. One woman held out for an hour against her male colleagues, insisting on going off into a corner alone in order that she might consult the spirits who would tell her, through the ring on her finger, what to do. When she came back, it appeared that the spirits were in accord with the rest of the jury, which helped a lot.

Another woman, a social worker, agreed with the eleven men that the defendant was clearly guilty of peddling narcotics to addicts but she thought he ought to be reformed instead of sent to jail. She finally agreed that it was the judge's job to send him to jail or not, the jury's job to decide only between innocence and guilt. The peddler went to jail, where he belonged.

The men want peace, too, but there were three famous farmers who voted against the accused railroad because, as they frankly admitted, the railroad had been mean to them. They held out. "I'll sit here till hell freezes over," their spokesman finally announced, "before I'll vote for that railroad." The other nine jurors had to give up.

These rare little sparks are the fireflies which illuminate the general day in, day out grind of jury duty well done. Jurors work very simply for justice. They work hard and well for it. Throughout this labyrinth of conflict there is just one towering fact, and that is the certainty that the juror's lot is not a happy one. There are few opportunities for solace. One of the best is the quest of the double negative. The philosophical juror will watch for them, take them to his heart and be comforted. On one occasion a doorkeeper, accused of letting a stranger into a hilarious club, was testifying.

"Did you let the man in?" asked the lawyer.

"No, sir, I don't never let nobody in that don't belong."

It was a quintuple negative! Solace, happiness, quintuple peace in the breast of the philosophical juror!

The oddest job in the world, then, to be a juror? I think so. Service, public service it is, of high devotion, but taken for granted, save for that one moment of climax—when the verdict comes.

An old trial lawyer once said: "When we have the verdict, the facts become immaterial."

The verdict! That comes from the juror, from nobody else.

69. *The Press and the Administration of Justice* *

THIS SELECTION is based on a speech delivered by Mr. A. T. Burch, associate editor of the Chicago *Daily News*, before a meeting of chief justices of state courts in Chicago. The author deals with a much-debated question—how free should newspapers be in pretrial reporting? He describes major United States Supreme Court decisions applying to this issue. A "trial by newspapers" before or during court proceedings may make it difficult for the judge and jury to be impartial. Part of this selection deals with a proposed solution to this difficulty—placing a severe limitation on pretrial reporting, as is done in England. Mr. Burch opposes this proposal.

A NEWSPAPERMAN could not address the Chief Justices of so many states without feeling an obligation to thank them for their part in maintaining the freedom of the press on the firm foundation where it now stands.

This freedom helps all newspapers to stay in business and some of them to make money. But you have not honored the press on that account. The right of the newspaper is no different from that of any other organization or individual to write, speak, print, or crank a mimeograph machine. You have upheld it, not primarily for the benefit of the writers, printers, and speakers, but for the good of the whole people. You have wanted the people to have access to every kind of information and to choose freely among the doctrines circulating in our times.

Until 1925 your courts had by far the largest share of responsibility for maintaining these liberties under the constitutions and laws of the states, among which there was some variation. In that year the United States Supreme Court asserted its jurisdiction over restraints on public expression imposed by state law. It decided that the Fourteenth Amendment of the Federal Constitution required it to apply the standards of the First Amendment to state cases restraining the press.

Since then, the United States Supreme Court has relieved a few newspapermen from penalties that you or your predecessors had inflicted on the home grounds. California, Texas, and Florida courts, for instance, have been denied the privilege of punishing editors for

* A. T. Burch, *State Government*, XXVII (November, 1954), pp. 227-231, 236. Reprinted by permission of the author and publisher.

contempt in a series of cases extremely interesting to us potential defendants.

Today it is rather difficult for a newspaper editor to get himself jailed for contempt of court by mere publication. This state of affairs is generally convenient, though it has deprived editorial writers of some opportunities for pay raises, promotion, and national publicity. These used to be the customary rewards for a contempt citation. Now a newspaper may have to defy a judge's order not to take a picture, or (as in Cleveland) forge a divorce decree to win celebrity by contempt.

It was in 1941 that the Supreme Court of the United States really deflated contempt by publication in deciding two cases with one opinion. Both arose in California. One involved Harry Bridges, the much litigated left-wing labor leader. The other involved a newspaper, the Los Angeles *Times*.

The *Times* had written an editorial demanding that a judge impose a severe sentence on two union truck drivers who had just been convicted of assaulting a nonunion truck driver.

In the other case, Harry Bridges' union had lost a court decision in a fight with an A.F. of L. union over bargaining jurisdiction. With a motion for a new trial pending, he threatened to call a longshoremen's strike and tie up every Pacific Coast port if the court's original order was enforced. He made this threat in a telegram addressed to the Secretary of Labor. The court held this communication privileged. But he made the telegram available to the press, which was not privileged. Though verdicts had been reached in both cases, they had not been completely wound up in all respects.

In both cases, five members of the Supreme Court held there was no clear and present danger that the course of impartial justice would be swerved by these declarations. Four members held the contrary. Justice Black wrote the majority opinion; Justice Frankfurter the minority. Justice Frankfurter took the view that Bridges had explicitly threatened the court in an effort to get it to change its verdict. He found an implied threat in the language of the Los Angeles *Times* editorial. It was captioned, "Probation for Gorillas?" and said in part:

"Judge A. A. Scott will make a serious mistake if he grants probation to Matthew Shannon and Kennan Holmes. This community needs the example of their assignment to the jute mill." The "jute mill" meant the state penitentiary.

If I might be permitted to testify as an expert on the psychology of editorial writers, I would say that a threat was not necessarily intended in the *Times*' strong expression of opinion, even though, as Justice Frankfurter noted, Judge Scott had to seek re-election next year. The editorial page is a running comment on public affairs. A newspaper often supports on his total record a public official whom it may have criticized on some occasions. An implied threat to criticize would not necessarily be a threat to defeat.

The issues in the case involved the psychology of judges as well as editorial writers. Justices Black and Frankfurter both might be presumed to be experts on this; but as experts often do, they differed. Justice Frankfurter took the low view that judges are human, particularly if they are elective, and that they might be swayed from their duty by raucous coaching from the sidelines. Justice Black, however, regarded it as an insult to the bench to assume that judges would be influenced by the words either of the Los Angeles *Times* or of Harry Bridges. It would, he declared, "impute to judges a lack of firmness, wisdom or honor—which we cannot accept as a major premise."

In 1947 Justice Douglas gave a picturesque expression to this doctrine in a Texas case, when he said "Judges are supposed to be men of fortitude able to thrive in a hardy climate."

In this line of decisions it may seem that your virtues absolve our vices. If you gentlemen miss the fun of throwing editors in jail, you can at least console yourselves by the high court's compliment to the unassailability of your honor and the thickness of your hides.

It is a credit to the good sense and self-restraint of the press generally that it has not pushed its practice to the full limit of its apparent privilege under the rule of *Bridges* v. *California*. It is certainly not customary for newspapers to tell judges what sentences they ought to impose on convicted criminals. Though they might not be punished for it, they would ordinarily consider it improper. There are few editors indeed that wish to usurp the functions of the courts. The prevailing practice is to withhold editorial comment on judicial actions until after the event. We respect the Constitution, and we know that a fair and impartial trial as well as a free press is guaranteed by the Bill of Rights.

Even if a newspaper imposes on itself a strict rule against commenting before and during the first trial of a case, how long after the verdict may the case be said to be pending? It is surely not reasonable to ask that comment be withheld on a matter of intense public interest until every last possible step has been taken to get the judgment appealed or modified. In the Los Angeles *Times* case, Justice Black said:

> An endless series of moratoria on public discussion, even if each were very short, could hardly be dismissed as an insignificant abridgement of freedom of expression. And to assume that each would be short is to overlook the fact that "pendency" of a case is frequently a matter of months or even years rather than days or weeks.

Not only in the case of *Bridges* v. *California*, but in others, Justice Frankfurter has been the chief advocate on the United States supreme bench of firmer restrictions on the press. In his dissenting opinions in freedom of the press cases, he has repeatedly castigated "trial by newspaper."

This has been the subject of a good many articles in the law journals. It was recently debated before the New York State Bar Association, after having been broached by the Association of the Bar of New York City. The object of this agitation is not merely to restrict newspaper *comment* before or during a trial, but the reporting of certain kinds of facts, as well. After full debate, the New York state bar refused to support a gag law, and contented itself with a warning to lawyers to restrain their own statements to the press before and during trials.

Maryland, so far as I know, is the only state ever to experiment with penalties on pretrial reporting. A Baltimore court adopted a rule forbidding publication of a confession before the confession was presented in open court. It also forbade publication of the prior criminal record of an accused man.

This rule was declared invalid by the Maryland Court of Appeals in 1949, after a lower court citation of a Baltimore radio station for violating it in a rape-murder case. The station broadcast that the accused man had confessed to the crime. It listed his long criminal record. It said he went to the scene of the crime, re-enacted the killing, and dug up the knife with which he had killed his victim. The broadcast was not challenged on the ground that it was false, but on the ground that it was prejudicial to a fair trial.

The Supreme Court of the United States was asked to review the case, but refused to do so. Justice Frankfurter noted that his court had expressed no opinion on the validity of the Baltimore rule. He then reviewed a long list of English cases, illustrating the strict rules prevailing in that country on pretrial reporting as well as comment. There, too, it is illegal to report a confession before trial, or the criminal record of an accused man. But the British restraints go far beyond that. Virtually nothing may be published between the arrest of a suspect and his trial except the fact of his arrest, a plain statement of the charge against him, and such bald data as the time set for hearing.

The English courts have punished newspapers for assigning their own men to investigate a case and report the results of their investigation. The penalties imposed for printing prejudicial facts or comments have ranged from a few pounds to thousands of pounds; publishers and editors have been sentenced to jail for terms of several months.

In theory, at least, the English restraints are not intended solely to protect the defendant, but the orderly process of justice. This was illustrated in the case of a man arrested when he was found carrying a pistol close to the person of the present Duke of Windsor just before that dignitary became king. One editor was fined because his paper referred to the man as an assassin. Another was fined because his paper reported that the man seemed to be a harmless crank. Both statements were regarded as prejudicial to a fair trial. Now if all judges really are the kind of men, full of fortitude, wisdom, and honor, that they are presumed to be by Justices Black and Douglas, they surely would not be swayed by any such reporting.

The real question about pretrial reporting is the possible effect, not on judges, but on juries. No one would assert that all jurors have the magnificent detachment attributed to judges. They have not had years of training in distinguishing between the relevant and the irrelevant, the competent and the incompetent. The problem of public opinion would exist in some degree, however, even if there were no newspapers, radio stations, or television. With all the sensationalism that may be charged to the press, it almost never equals the virulence of word-of-mouth gossip, uncorrected by any printed record.

The law has never wholly made up its mind about the functions of the jury, anyhow. In its earliest beginnings it was not even supposed to be unprejudiced. It was made up of men who best knew the prisoner and the circumstances. That, of course, has not been the conception for centuries past. Impartiality is the key thought of the Bill of Rights guarantee of a fair trial. Nevertheless, we retain the jury system precisely because it has been believed that some element of common garden variety public opinion ought to be interposed between a man accused of a crime and a strictly mechanical application of the law to a set of facts. It is hardly an exaggeration to say that we have juries to prevent the conviction of guilty men if their crimes do not offend the moral sense of the community.

Notwithstanding the exposure of juries to all the influences of press, radio and television, does the jury system, on the whole, operate for or against the interests of defendants? The question can be answered by asking another. Do criminal lawyers advocate the abolition of the jury system? The ones I know certainly do not.

Trial by newspaper takes place in big cities, at least, only in a small minority of sensational cases. The press does create a problem in its treatment of these events. But does anyone imagine that the British people, including prospective jurors, do not talk to each other about a celebrated crime before its perpetrator is tried?

The literature on trial by newspaper dwells on the difficulty of getting a jury to adhere to instructions as to the prejudicial matter that a jury should disregard. But perhaps we underestimate the capacity of jurors in this respect.

What does a newspaper ever say about a case that is more prejudicial than the fact that a man has been arrested, has been indicted, has been led into the court room under custody to be tried? The judge instructs the jury that the man is presumed to be innocent until proved guilty beyond a reasonable doubt. This almost amounts to saying that the jurors should believe that the police, the prosecuting attorney, and the grand jury, through malice, ignorance, or incompetence, may be trying to perpetrate a monstrous injustice. This may actually be true, but surely it is more natural for a juror to start out believing that the prisoner wouldn't be there if he hadn't done it. Notwithstanding the difficulty, the jurors do seem, for the most part, to comprehend in its truer sense the judge's instruction to withhold judgment until the evidence is in. For they certainly do not convict every defendant—certainly not in Chicago.

Chicago newspapers, however, have some very diligent crime reporters. Several times in the last year, acquittals here in both the Federal and county courts have brought upon juries the ferocious denunciation of presiding judges—a practice, by the way, which the Chicago Bar Association has reproved by formal resolution. Pretrial reporting had certainly not damaged the defendants in these cases.

I have not made the foregoing observations to deny totally any risk that justice may miscarry through "trial by newspaper." I have merely attempted to put the problem into some kind of perspective.

The Supreme Court of the United States has reversed convictions by state courts because the trial took place in the actual presence of intimidating mobs. A newspaper can be the leader of a mob, and, God forgive us, I am afraid that newspapers sometimes have been.

The Supreme Court of the United States has reversed at least one conviction because a newspaper published a purported confession which was never introduced in the trial. It has reversed the conviction of a United States collector of revenue on the ground that publicity made it impossible for him to get a fair trial at the time and place where he was tried. He had asked for a delay, and it had been refused.

I am sure the state courts you gentlemen represent have ordered retrials under some such circumstances when justice so required.

There is, therefore, some remedy available to the defendant if the press endangers him—at least once in a while. The remedy might, unfortunately, be slow and costly, like so many other remedies at law.

Those who favor the English system want to reduce this jeopardy by putting criminal penalties on papers if they talk too much about a pending case. There was a time when at least one great American paper favored this. The Chicago *Tribune* demanded a law to restrain itself and its competitors on July 23, 1924, on the aftermath of the Loeb and Leopold convictions, referred to in the *Tribune* as the Franks case. In an editorial captioned "Justice and Publicity" it said in part:

> Criminal justice in America is now a Roman holiday. The courts are in the Colosseum. The state's attorney's office is an open torture room of human souls. Exposure of the processes of justice, originally a public safeguard, has been perverted into a public danger. . . .
>
> The Franks case has been a three months' moral pestilence imposed upon our people before the trial. It is an aggravated instance of what has happened with increasing frequency for two decades since the Thaw trial and before. There is reason for the statement by the chief justice of the United States that the product of our judicial machine is a national disgrace. It has been turned into a public show.
>
> The injury to justice is in *publicity before* the trial. Newspaper trials before the case is called have become an abomination. The dangerous initiative that newspapers have taken in judging and convicting out of court is journalistic lynch law. It is mob murder or mob acquittal in all but the overt act. It is mob appeal. Prosecuting attorneys now hasten to the papers with their theories and confessions. Defense attorneys do the same. Neither dare do otherwise. Half-wit juries or prejudiced juries are the inevitable result.
>
> The *Tribune* has its share of blame in this. No newspaper can escape it. They have met demand, and in meeting it stimulated public appetite for more. . . .
>
> Papers that refuse to accept this harsh discipline of public demand will die. Many have died. A debased currency always will displace a sound currency.
>
> The slide downhill is inevitable. Who can deny that it is founded on authentic human nature? General reform must be undertaken or none at all. The nation's press must act together.
>
> There is one remedy. Drastic restriction of publicity before the trial must be imposed by law. . . .

The editorial goes on, however, to call for the fullest possible reporting of the actual trial, including broadcast of the proceedings by radio in important cases. Television had not been invented. This editorial was printed thirty years ago. The *Tribune* has not in recent years repeated its demand for a law to restrain pretrial publicity, and, I understand, would oppose one now. It has often repeated its insistence on the right of full reporting of the actual proceedings by any means which does not disturb them.

The restraints imposed on picture-taking, broadcasting and televising in courtrooms will be fully and competently debated before a section of the American Bar Association next week. In my opinion it is perfectly correct to prohibit them when they would create a disturbance. A mob of photographers banging away with flash bulbs does create a disturbance. So does the cumbersome machinery ordinarily used in broadcasting and televising. Cameras and films, however, have been so improved that a still picture can be taken even indoors without disturbing anybody. If it is done this way, there is no reason to forbid it. The hall of the United Nations has been provided with glassed-in side galleries where even moving pictures and television may operate without disturbing anybody; the very presence of the machines and their operators is not easy to detect from the floor. Similar equipment could be provided in new courtrooms to be built or remodelled hereafter. To thrust a television camera directly into the face of a witness would surely increase the chances of error in his testimony by confusion and embarrassment.

I had to stand up all one afternoon in the press alcove to hear arguments before the Supreme Court of the United States in the School Segregation case. Only a few could find standing room. Had the courtroom been equipped like the United Nations, a great public service would have been performed by telecasting this session of the Court. To deny this, it seems to me, is to deny some of the basic premises of democracy.

Existing restraints in this field should be modified, and I predict they will be, step by step, with the improvement in the arts involved and provision of off-stage facilities for them. If there were in the archives motion pictures with sound recordings of Aaron Burr's trial for treason or the Supreme Court's hearing of the Dred Scott case, would your dignity or that of those old courts be degraded by attending a showing? This generation could make such contributions to history and the education of the next generation's youth. Why should it not do so?

To return to the danger (not very clear or present) that some bar association will persuade some state to adopt a pretrial law on the British model. It doesn't seem to me there is a serious chance that such a law would be upheld by the United States Supreme Court. Since *Bridges* v. *California,* it has not lowered its estimate of the high value to be given press freedom. The vote was 5 to 4 in that case. It was unanimous in *Pennekamp* v. *Florida.* There were only two dissenters in *Craig* v. *Harney,* which came up from Texas. Justice Frankfurter is the only one of the dissenters in *Bridges* v. *California* still serving. All but one of the original majority are still on the bench. The English example would not be persuasive to those who joined with Justice Black in this declaration: "No purpose in ratifying the Bill of Rights was clearer than that of securing for the people of the United

States much greater freedom of religion, expression, assembly and petition than the people of Great Britain had ever enjoyed." I might add—*have* ever enjoyed.

But if they were constitutional, would the English restraints be desirable?

The English practice assumes a police and court system functioning with almost automatic precision. It does work with an efficiency that presents an amazing contrast with our own. England is a country where perfect order is preserved by policemen who carry no weapon more deadly than a billy club. The police never torture suspects, and even the traffic cops are polite. Are the British so law-abiding because their criminal procedure is so effective? Or is their procedure so effective because the people present it with few and simple problems?

It does not work with absolute infallibility. Last year they hanged John Christie for murdering six women over a period of years. He confessed all these crimes and the court believed him. The trouble is that the British had already hanged another man for killing two of these women. England, remember, is a country where an editor can be fined for assigning his own men to investigate a case and publishing the findings after a suspect has been arrested. It is quite possible that, if some enterprising crime reporters had worked on the case, they wouldn't have hanged the wrong man before they hanged the right one. In the United States, certainly, many an innocent man owes his liberty or even his life to the enterprise of investigating reporters.

Endless statistics could be cited to illustrate the difference between the crime problem in England and the United States. One will suffice. I am indebted for it to Virgil W. Peterson, Operating Director of the Chicago Crime Commission.

In 1952 there were only nineteen armed robberies in all of London and its suburbs, though Britishers were complaining about the breakdown of moral standards after the war. Chicago, with considerably less than half the population of London, had 4,400 armed robberies in the same year. Throughout the nation, only a third of such crimes result in indictments. In Chicago, Mr. Peterson wrote in the *Atlantic Monthly*, there have been approximately 700 gang murders during the past twenty-five years. He notes that the number of persons convicted in connection with these slayings could be counted on one's fingers. Notwithstanding the evil reputation Chicago gained in the old Capone days, Chicago's crime rates are no worse than those of other big cities.

Are the newspapers to stand passively by, mere spectators of this awful anarchy? It is not merely their privilege but their duty to combat it, by every legitimate means in their power. The real complaint that should be made is that they do not fight it hard enough or *effectively* enough. The arrogance of organized crime is a provocation not only to honest indignation but (human nature being what it is) to blind rage. The newspaper doing its duty should stay angry, but it should not go blind.

The noblest services of American newspapers to their readers have been their exposures of public corruption and politically protected crime. In the course of these crusades they have printed some matter prejudicial to potential defendants. Sometimes—and you should be grateful for it—they have used their columns to prove the guilt of public enemies by evidence so indisputable that no shyster was slick enough, no prosecutor weak enough, no machine-kept judge crooked enough, to refute it or evade it.

It is the newspaper's duty to print facts, not to try them. That is the duty of the courts. We want them to do it thoroughly and fairly. We do not want to threaten them or coerce them or influence them improperly. We want every defendant to have the benefit of due process—the whole treatment, with all the trimmings. But we see too much of the undue processes that help armies of dangerous malefactors to escape conviction, indictment, or even arrest.

If we seem to "usurp" the investigating functions of the police and the prosecutor's aides once in a while, it is because they are not doing the job themselves. Actually, it has never been a usurpation of anything for a citizen to holler "stop thief" when he sees a pocket being picked or to yell "bloody murder" when one takes place before his eyes. We mean to keep on hollering.

Some day the American people may become so law-abiding that newspapers can lay down their arduous and expensive duty to investigate everything. Then they can give more of their effort to such topics as the irreconcilable conflict between Christian Dior and Marilyn Monroe.

But if we are going to make it a crime for newspapers to investigate crime, let's wait until some year when there are only nineteen armed robberies in Chicago.

70. *Probation and Parole--The Pay-Off* *

MR. TRAMBURG, who at the time he wrote this selection was Director of the State Department of Public Welfare of Wisconsin, describes the Wisconsin probation and parole program. Under it many a criminal offender after careful screening is returned to the community under close supervision. This is both a treatment and a test. The offender is treated because while working in the community he is actually being rehabilitated. He is also tested, because he must demonstrate by his actions that although he has already failed once, he has now learned to adapt himself to ordinary community existence. Only twenty per cent of the parolees or probationers fail this test—an impressive demonstration of the success of the program.

LAST JANUARY 1, some 2,946 men and women who, under other circumstances, would have been "doing time" in one of Wisconsin's three institutions for adult offenders, were living relatively normal lives in the community, supporting themselves and their families, finding for themselves a suitable niche in society. Of these, 1,063 were parolees from those three institutions, and 1,883 were offenders who had been placed on probation by the courts of the state. On that same date a total of 2,235 individuals were confined in the Wisconsin State Prison, the State Reformatory and the Home for Women.

Figures may make dull reading, but there is a dynamic significance in those figures for Wisconsin and for other forward-looking states. There is social significance in the fact that far more than half of the total number of offenders can be trusted in the community, do not need confinement. There is economic significance in the fact that these offenders, while paying their debt to society for their infractions, likewise are making some productive contribution to the community, even though in the individual case it may be small. There is financial significance in the fact that, were it not for this program, the state would be faced with the great cost of building more prisons to house them and the greater costs of caring for them while in custody.

Wisconsin has long been keenly aware of the social values implicit in these things, and over the course of many years has made steady progress toward their development, progress which has been greatly accelerated in the last few years. The state likewise is committed to the ideal of a unified, coordinated program of treating the offender

* John W. Tramburg, *State Government*, XXVIII (June, 1955), pp. 125-127, 140. Reprinted by permission of the author and publisher.

and the law violator, one which will bring to bear all its resources—the courts, the institutions, the community itself—on the rehabilitation or restoration of the faltering individual. Wisconsin recognizes and accepts probation and parole as important tools for the accomplishment of these objectives.

For the purpose of our present discussion, it may be worth while to see how they are integrated into the over-all program.

Words have different meanings in different places. This is as true of the words "probation" and "parole" as it is of many others. In some jurisdictions they are used interchangeably; in others they are regarded as synonymous or overlapping. Since, in Wisconsin, there is legal as well as administrative differentiation, it may be well for reasons of clarity to point up the distinction.

Probation, in its initial application to the individual case, is a judicial function. Under the law the judge of the trial court, and only the judge, can decide whether the facts in the case warrant giving the offender "another chance." If the judge so decides he can suspend sentence or withhold sentence entirely and return the offender to his place in society with an opportunity to prove that he can get along. At the discretion of the court, the probationary period may be either with or without supervision, although in practice it is usual to provide for supervision. Probation, then, is in a sense a short cut in the process of rehabilitating the offender. In its initial application, at least, it bypasses the institutional agencies of the state to place on the individual—and, in a sense, the community—responsibility for his return to grace. Only in case of violation of probation, and again at the discretion of the court, is the institution called into play.

Parole, on the other hand, is an administrative function. It involves the release of an offender from the correctional institution to which he has been committed by the court, prior to completion of the term to which he was sentenced.

In Wisconsin, the Director of Public Welfare is the sole paroling authority. Neither the courts nor the law enforcement agencies nor the institution has a voice in the action. Within the statutory limitations governing the time for application by the prisoner, parole is granted only when the individual by his actions, bearing and attitude offers evidence that he may be ready to return to society as a useful, law-abiding citizen, reasonably unlikely to offend again and capable of demonstrating, under trained supervision, that he can meet the responsibilities of day-to-day living on the "outside."

Parole, thus administered, obviously is not clemency, since clemency, the sole prerogative of the Governor, may be granted or withheld as an act of authority with no necessary relationship to the character of the individual receiving it. Rather, parole is a period for readjustment to normal life in society, for demonstration of good intentions and good faith on the part of the individual concerned, and for acceptance by the community and by society.

Parole, in Wisconsin, is not easy to get nor easy to serve. From the time he enters the institution until he makes his first—or subsequent—parole appearance, the prisoner is not only under constant surveillance by the custodial staff but is studied and appraised by the psychiatric, medical, educational and other professional staff members. When he appears for his parole hearing, a board of three permanent civil service members, appointed by the Director of Public Welfare to hear the applications and make recommendations for action, has before it all the records of these studies, all the reports bearing on the prisoner's conduct and attitude, all the information that has been assembled concerning him.

The hearing itself is perhaps unique in that there are no participants except the prisoner and the board members—no lawyers, no friends, no institution officials. There is no retrial of the case nor rehashing of the offense except as the board members may seek information for their guidance. The proceedings are informal in the fullest sense of the word. The prisoner, we may presume, has only one desire—to put his best foot forward—and he is given the opportunity to do so; the board has only one purpose—to arrive at a proper conclusion as to the prisoner's readiness for return to society. It is a testing process, and the nature of the test may be indicated by the fact that recommendations for "grants" average only about 35 per cent at the State Prison, slightly higher at the State Reformatory and the Home for Women.

Nor is the prisoner "out of the woods" when he has been granted parole. He goes out only to a place and a job that have been arranged by the field agent who will supervise him, and which he cannot leave without permission; he must maintain regular contact and make regular reports to his officer; he must be normally diligent and regular in his work habits; he must manifest a reasonable sense of social responsibility as well as decent behavior and deportment. He will serve out his term, withal, knowing that his parole, as an administrative act, can be rescinded—revoked—at any time for any reason by the paroling authority, and he can be returned to the institution to continue serving his time "in the walls."

There is, of course, another side to the coin. While he is on parole the prisoner has the guidance, counsel and help of his supervising agent, who is familiar with his problems and will help him over the rough spots. In general, he will find a social and community climate conditioned by experience to be accepting of his efforts and ready to lend a helping hand. He will be given every opportunity and every help in making good.

Nevertheless, we submit, making good on parole, like making parole in the first place, is a test—and not an easy test at that. While perhaps not so designed, it calls for the development or at least the demonstration of character, capacities and capabilities on the part of the parolee which had not been manifested previously. In a sense, therefore, it may be regarded not only as a test but as a treatment process, as well.

In view of the fact that in parole, and perhaps to a lesser extent in probation, we are dealing with notoriously fallible material—human beings—and dealing, moreover, with individuals who have failed in society at least once, the records of the Wisconsin Bureau of Probation and Parole show a very considerable degree of success. From 80 to 90 per cent of those placed under supervision complete their probation or parole periods without mishap. A failure rate of 20 per cent seems a not unreasonable allowance for mistakes of human judgment or the mischances of ordinary community living.

Thus we see probation and parole, dissimilar in their genesis but alike in their purpose and practice, playing double roles in the handling of the offender and law violator: First, they are tools to be used in the rehabilitation or attempted rehabilitation of the man or woman who has gone astray, tools sufficiently flexible to be adaptable to the individual case and able to draw on a variety of official and social resources for assistance or implementation. Second, they are means for testing or measuring the individual and his social responses even while the treatment is in progress.

In this dual role, probation and parole are justified by experience, even if they stand alone. As elements of a unified, integrated corrections program, however, they have still another important part to play.

No one questions, of course, that the primary purpose of a corrections program is the protection of the community; indeed, one may make the statement even more broadly that that is the sole function of such a program. But differences, sometimes sharp differences, of opinion arise when we try to decide just what constitutes protection —real long-term protection—for society. These differences become even wider when methods of providing this protection are brought into the picture. There are, on the one hand, proponents of the "lock-'em-up-and-forget-'em" theory, who believe that the only effective way of dealing with the offender is to punish him—the more severe the punishment the more effective the "treatment." This out-of-sight-out-of-mind theory is still more prevalent than many of us would like to believe. At the other extreme are those who insist that the idea of punishment, any sort of punitive treatment, is not only outmoded but futile; that prisons, for instance, are outworn social anachronisms; that treatment methods can be applied effectively only in the community.

The state of Wisconsin, for many years, has accepted and adhered to a social philosophy falling between these two extremes. It has developed, steadily and consistently, a program and method for penal and corrections administration which not only will provide the protection society rightly demands but at the same time will salvage and preserve individual and social values which might otherwise be lost.

We in Wisconsin agree, at least in part, with the lock-'em-up school in that we concede that a very considerable number of offenders should be imprisoned—kept in custody, if necessary, and as long as necessary to safeguard the community against aggressive and socially undesirable behavior. We agree that the concept of punishment should not be summarily dismissed, at least insofar as the penalty is a measure of society's disapproval of the individual's behavior. But we insist that custody shall be the means to an end, not the end itself; that it be recognized and used as a period during which the individual may be retrained for an early return to society, or may at least be better fitted for his return when the law has run its course.

Likewise we accept, with reservations, the theory of those who decry entirely the need of prisons or custodial institutions. We agree with them that in many cases placing the offender in the community is the best and most effective method of dealing with his problem. But we insist that proper protection of the community welfare requires us to be as sure as humanly possible what direction the offender's development may take; in many cases that calls for custody and an opportunity for study, appraisal and retraining.

In brief, Wiconsin's corrections program calls for custody or confinement, of such degree or such duration as may be necessary in the individual case, as an immediate protection to society. But beyond that it looks to rehabilitation of the offender—within the institution, if necessary, but outside, if possible—as the best long-term safeguard for the interests of the whole community.

As of this date Wisconsin has achieved a fair measure of success in coordinating the activities of the four major agencies of government which are most directly concerned with the problems of law violation and antisocial conduct—the courts, the law enforcement agencies, the penal institutions and the field services embodied in the Bureau of Probation and Parole.

Without seeking in any way to intrude upon the functions or infringe upon the prerogatives of the courts, the Division of Corrections in the Department of Public Welfare has found ways to be useful to the courts through presentence investigations, case studies and other means. Thus the treatment technique frequently is applied in the first stages of an individual's career as an offender.

Likewise, law enforcement officers and agencies, usually the first and often the last public contact with the law violator, have found broad areas in which they can work to forestall delinquency in the first place or combat it in a later stage.

In our institutions steady progress has been made in the development of treatment programs. Insofar as possible, all the techniques of psychiatry, education, trade-training, individual and group counseling and other means of training or retaining offenders for useful living in free society are being used in larger and larger degrees.

More and more, in every facet of the corrections program, emphasis is being shifted to preparation of the offender for successful return to normal living, not only—or even so much—for his sake, but as the best safeguard for the community against repeated misbehavior.

And so, in somewhat roundabout fashion, we come back to probation and parole and the dual part they play in the over-all program. We have already seen them as useful tools for refitting the offender for his niche in society, and likewise for testing his readiness for restoration to the normal status of a free citizen. Another role remains for them—they are, actually, the final test of the whole program!

Have our estimates of this man's character been correct, and is it best to put him back into society without sending him to prison? We may think so, but we cannot know until we try him.

Have we helped this man by teaching him a useful trade in prison? We can hope so, even believe so, but our hope and faith must still be justified.

With all our emphasis on treatment, despite all our efforts at character rebuilding, the only measure of the efficacy of our efforts to change offenders for the better is their successful adjustment in the community. The big test of all our programs, the only way we can know what they have done or what they have failed to do, comes when the offender is tried "on his own." Only probation or parole can provide this test.

Truly, they are the pay-off!

71. *The Courts and Juvenile Delinquency* *

JUDGE COOPER, Chief Justice of the Court of Special Sessions of New York City, deals with the great moral and material cost of juvenile delinquency and suggests a partial remedy. He reminds us that crime is an outgrowth of the thoughts and actions of the community, not something unconnected with it. Each of us is in some degree responsible. The difficult question for the judge is to know which offenders can be returned to the community under a probation program and which must be kept apart from it in jail or a juvenile home. If more courts could afford to hire professional probation officers to conduct a pretrial investigation of each offender, the judge would be better able to answer this crucial question. The value of such professional services is demonstrated in Selection 70.

IT IS generally agreed that no higher professional service can be rendered by the courts than the protection of individuals in the possession and exercise of vital liberty—to be untrammeled in thought, activity, and movement within such areas as the community, through law, guarantees. This involves a double obligation: to protect the individual against the community as well as the community against the individual.

As populations have increased and the tools of modern life have become power-driven, even split-second irresponsibility can have lethal consequences. Standards of accountability have been raised to levels that prove uncomfortable to many.

The immense spread in the range of criminal acts has increased tremendously the nature and number of cases appearing on the calendars of our criminal courts. These jurisdictions no longer deal largely with depraved and/or degenerate individuals—that is, with persons congenitally or by habit unable or unwilling to conform to community minimums of behavior. A large proportion of today's criminal cases concern defendants involved in strictly contemporary situations, the full outlines of which many of them do not understand, and—even more important—situations so new and uncharted that the legislatures and administrative bodies which pronounce the prohibited acts and establish regulations regarding them have not been in a position to think them through.

In his *Autobiography*, William Carlos Williams tells this story:

* Irving Ben Cooper, *The American Scholar*, XXIII (Autumn, 1954), pp. 459-466. Reprinted by permission of the author and *The American Scholar*.

An old friend of my father's once said to me when I was one day raving against a flagrant miscarriage of justice in our local courts, "Willie, what do you think you can get in a court of law?"

"Why the least you can ask for," I said, "is common justice."

"Oh no," he replied, "you won't get justice, that's impossible. All you'll get is the best that is made available in your locality."

While it must always remain the function of the community through its representatives to define the areas of vital liberty, since these are the gifts of the community to itself, the testing ground of regulations is their effect on the whole social structure. Effects are to be discovered only by the patient and meticulous examination of results. The scientist can make his ten-thousandth experiment in the laboratory previous to announcing his formula or equation. In contrast, legislatures first publish the formula, after which courts are the test tubes. Society has great need for the assistance of its best legal talents to study the situations with which statutes are devised to deal. The law, like other arts, lags behind the inventiveness of matter and of human nature. It is only by returning to situations that a professional person can escape the net of his professional procedures. It is easier to fall back on his pharmacopoeia than it is to study the social structure.

When a justice begins to fear that a sentence he is about to impose cannot, in view of the known facts, be appropriate or fitting, his professional sense is outraged. Insofar as a sentence is a prescription for remedial treatment of the crime as a given personality syndrome, judges need information about the constitution of the delinquent and the extent of his moral involvement. This is particularly true for the first offender. How normal, in physical health, mentality, emotional stability and capacity for sustained effort, is he? What were the provocations provided by the complainants and by the community in which he was reared and which set the behavior patterns after which he molded himself? Were strife and thievery, as with the Spartans, the "mode" of the neighborhood—a black eye a decoration and not a reproach? What of the cultural and civic resources of the neighborhood: the religious institutions in which moral values and codes are taught, exemplified and highlighted with festival? the schools, playgrounds, political clubs, public libraries, police, sanitary and other services? What effect do these have upon him now? What capacity for sound living has he shown to date? What is his ability to learn to integrate new experiences? What is his moral potential? What resources will be needed to free this potential? Who stands ready to help him? Can he learn faster in the community or does he need to be withdrawn from associations and conditions in which his character has been formed? What kind of community will give him the support he must have? What incentives can it provide to help energize his will?

The juvenile offender has been with us since the day of Cain and Abel. The biochemistry of youth is keyed to lust, violence, acquisitiveness, tempestuous and ill-considered actions. Among the costs of carrying youth over the decade of transition from childhood into the beginning of responsible maturity is an incalculable mass of material and social wreckage—demolished family cars, increased insurance rates, wanton destruction of household, commercial and community property, medical bills growing out of carelessness and foolhardy exploits, irresponsible pregnancies and births. Families, relatives, friends and neighbors absorb a major share of these costs. This situation is age-old, and the community, in effect, has adapted itself. Crime is that one eighth of the iceberg of human cussedness whose ravages are put down and added up in police and court records.

For every first offender brought before the court, a presentence investigation ought to be a routine aspect of treatment, regardless of the degree of the crime. The objection cannot be allowed that this kind of investigation is so costly that there is no hope of its being generally applied. Lack of it costs millions in money and untold years of human suffering and community apprehension. It must be attempted, and attempted on a national scale, because only so, at this stage of our understanding of human behavior, can society acquire the kind of knowledge that will enable it to heal itself of lesions set up by cherished social habits of waywardness, greed and irresponsibility.

I do not believe that the average citizen senses the role that crime plays as a national problem. It exists on a scale so enormous that it is difficult to grasp. It can reasonably be estimated that $20 billion annually is the cost of crime in this country. This represents a cost of $495.00 for each family in the United States; for every $1.00 spent on education, $1.82 goes to crime; for every $1.00 donated to churches, $10.00 goes to crime.

As for figures concerning youth in crime, of the 1,110,675 persons arrested in 1953, 7.8 per cent were under 18 years of age; 13.3 per cent were under 21 years of age; and 23.1 per cent were under 25 years of age. The group under 18 years of age accounted for 19.4 per cent of all robberies, 36.9 per cent of all larcenies, 47.8 per cent of all burglaries, 52.6 per cent of all auto thefts. Nearly one half of the persons arrested for crimes against property involved people who were under 21 years of age.

One of the real problems presented constantly to these courts is to be able to recognize the innate potential of individual offenders for moral rehabilitation, and the kind and extent of family and community support available to them in their efforts to re-establish themselves. There is often little difference in the offenses and the superficial attitudes of persons who are widely different in their human needs. Though rounded up by the same department-store detective for the same offense, the little stenographer who is excited about giving up her job for marriage and a family; the erratic and superficially charming woman whose act is the culmination of a long and progressive series of impositions and thefts against family, relatives and friends; and the sheltered widow who, until the death of an indulgent husband, has never had a possessive impulse thwarted, represent far from identical situations.

The establishment of degree of legal culpability will not solve the problem of how these three persons are to be assisted to manage themselves and to establish a sound position in the community. Until the extent of character deterioration is known and the probable nature of the remedial measures needed to meet the condition is determined, the court cannot complete its mission with assurance.

The great mass of offenders consists of persons who have not made very good use of their opportunities and who are prone to give vent to their feelings at slight provocation. They accept the easiest way out of trying situations. They have never really faced up to life as a challenge.

A common factor in most of these cases is that, set against the life situation, the criminal charge lacks major importance. Where there is so much deep-seated misery, one additional increment does not seem to matter too much. The life situation may inhere in the defendant's relations to his mother or father, to his family tradition, to his neighborhood associates, to the social situation of his school or shop or other place of employment, to the standards of the community as these are reflected in magazines, papers, movies, actions of important people, envy of others. Treatment involves dealing with these primary causes.

The need of these defendants for the help of society and the court is greater than that of the morally sensitive and the family-bolstered individuals. For these misguided defendants are in great peril—the peril of rejecting and being rejected by the community.

An important consideration in the search for a remedy is the public attitude toward crime. People deny it in themselves, turn away from anyone accused or suspected, are willfully ignorant of its varieties or treatments, and prefer to believe that it does not exist. To consider crime by youth as something foisted on an innocent community, rather than as an aspect of its own thought of itself and its own action, is to be naive beyond sanity.

The community's attitude toward youthful offenders, like its treatment of youth generally, is a mixture of softheartedness, exasperation, wounded resignation and sadistic pleasure in punishment. Once a complaint is issued against the young offender, the good forces about him shrink and evil forces are alerted. Those he has injured are naturally outraged; the parents of susceptible children become fearful; the godly draw their garments around them; the evil-minded, anxious for social support, welcome a convert; and the police close in.

For his part, the slow learner will not be convinced only by statistics about proportions of good men and good women, and the availability of jobs, recreation, straight-shooting and loyal pals and friends, honorary membership in community institutions and affairs. He must experience these values—and the invitations must meet him a little more than half way. He is easily rebuffed, easily scared off, easily bored. Only as he is brought into relations of responsibility with people and institutions, and so gains a realistic acquaintance with actual social norms, can he start to build on his new evaluation of society.

The court must command his attention through the period required for him to revise his image of himself and to gain a working foothold in the community's life. The court that through its probation department can carry a young first offender to the point where he is ready to meet life's challenges "on his own" has "saved a life." This kind of working on the foundations is not done cheaply. It costs blood and money. It very seldom costs as much as one year in a reform school or a penitentiary, surely a bargain in moral healing. Over-punishment is particularly useless in dealing with youth. Ineptitude in the treatment of young offenders can easily mis-educate an entire generation.

A delinquent is usually very well aware that he has made a mess of at least one situation, and, he suspects, of others. The botched situation once was rosy with promise. But he cannot live in it any longer; he must move out into another compelling dream. A famous Scottish divine once preached a sermon entitled "The Expulsive Power of a New Affection." What the delinquent needs above all else is that "new affection." No one, least of all a disappointed delinquent, can desire forgiveness or crave "reinstatement" for more than a little while. What he wants is job status, a sweetheart, wife, children, a house and garden. These dreams, once lighted, have a steady incandescence.

The health of the community lies in the absence of disease, rather than in its resources for isolating the sick and providing for their cure. Crime is beginning to be understood as an aspect of man's mental-emotional-moral nature. This nature, assailed by many forces both within and without his bodily frame, is susceptible to many infections.

Some are capable of destroying their victim, and more important still, of infecting others. Public health authorities have learned to follow a typhoid or other "carrier" from state to state, even across the nation, once they have become aware of his existence. We follow the determined offender through his fingerprints, but not the youth in his most infectious stage.

Juvenile crime is crime at the source. The youthful criminal may be self-infected, but he has frequently been infected by another, or he may have been conditioned by the mores of his gang or his neighborhood or even his family. He may even be so naive and unacquainted with morality as not to be aware of his entrance into the age of responsibility.

It is in the courts that the dramas behind the figures presented in the annual reports of the Federal Bureau of Investigation, and in the local police reports on which the national profile is based, that the significance of these figures unfolds and takes on life. And it is from the court records that cities, towns and villages might, if they wish, learn what kind of crimes are committed, who are committing them, the conditions that breed or facilitate certain crimes, and the community prophylaxis called for to prevent them by promoting the community's moral health and capacity to resist evil temptations.

Unfortunately for many courts, the law now provides the tool, but not the motor and the "juice" to run it. We have a one-half where we should have a ten horsepower motor. In other words, the law does not make it mandatory upon the community to provide the resources needed to make valid its instinct to help.

The pity of it is that there is ample good will in our states and cities to authorize the necessary appropriations. For it is not at all inaccurate to say that communities, like parents, are as yearningly afraid of youthful offenders as offenders are of them. The youth has not altogether repudiated the community, and the community has not altogether disowned him. Both are on the defensive. The youth needs assurance that he has worth and the power to compensate for his fault. The community needs assurance that the offender understands he has been out of step and that he wants to get back into line. For the community, in the shape of the parents with adolescent children, is all too conscious of the narrow line that separates its own youngsters from the youthful lawbreaker. This insight can change the community's attitude toward the court's functions and needs.

Not until courts throughout the nation are adequately staffed with the professional skills I have pleaded for will we be able to distinguish the youthful offender with good moral potential, who can be safely returned to the community to line up with the orderly citizens, from the hair-trigger, perverted or psychopathic first offender, who needs institutionalized care. Yes, "Possibilities of murder and desperate love are inside all the least likely skulls." As things stand now, the courts can do little to minimize recidivism; they cannot complete their mission with assurance.

It is high time we translated into overt action that prophetic utterance by Chief Justice Charles Evan Hughes:

> The Supreme Court of the United States and the courts of appeal will take care of themselves. Look after the courts of the poor, who stand most in need of justice. The security of the Republic will be found in the treatment of the poor and ignorant; in indifference to their misery and helplessness lies disaster.

A judge speaks out with equal candor when he warns that we continue the present ineffective approach to these throbbing issues only at our great peril. How true the warning of 125 years ago from the *London Times:*

> The greatest tyranny has the smallest beginnings. From precedents overlooked, from remonstrances despised, from grievances treated with ridicule, from powerless men oppressed with impunity, and overbearing men tolerated with complacence, springs the tyrannical usage which generations of wise and good men may hereafter perceive and lament and resist in vain. At present, common minds no more see a crushing tyranny in a trivial unfairness or a ludicrous indignity, than the eye uninformed by reason can discern the oak in the acorn, or the utter desolation of winter in the first autumnal fall. Hence the necessity of denouncing with unwearied and even troublesome perseverance a single act of oppression. Let it alone and it stands on record. The country has allowed it and when it is at last provoked to a late indignation it finds itself gagged with the record of its own ill compulsion.

XIII

THE PRESIDENT AND THE NATIONAL ADMINISTRATIVE SYSTEM

72. *Power and Administration**

THE BEGINNING STUDENT of public administration will be introduced quite early in his study to the concept of principles of organization. He will learn of the chain of command, hierarchy, span of control, unifunctional departments, and so on. In this article Professor Long touches only incidentally upon these organizational precepts. The kind of organization that draws his attention here is the structure of power that "encloses each significant center of administrative discretion." He notes that the power resources of an administrator or agency are only one consideration in administration; yet "the lifeblood of administration is power," and the student and practitioner can ill afford to neglect this subject. Professor Long's comments upon the nature and source of administrative power in our system afford an opportunity to grasp a bit of the realities of administration, an opportunity to penetrate a bit behind the lines of the organization chart.

I

THERE is no more forlorn spectacle in the administrative world than an agency and a program possessed of statutory life, armed with executive orders, sustained in the courts, yet stricken with paralysis and deprived of power. An object of contempt to its enemies and of despair to its friends.

The lifeblood of administration is power. Its attainment, maintenance, increase, dissipation, and loss are subjects the practitioner and student can ill afford to neglect. Loss of realism and failure are almost

* Norton Long, *Public Administration Review*, IX (Autumn, 1949), pp. 257-264. Reprinted by permission of the author and the publisher.

certain consequences. This is not to deny that important parts of public administration are so deeply entrenched in the habits of the community, so firmly supported by the public, or so clearly necessary as to be able to take their power base for granted and concentrate on the purely professional side of their problems. But even these islands of the blessed are not immune from the plague of politics, as witness the fate of the hapless Bureau of Labor Statistics and the perennial menace of the blind 5 per cent across-the-board budget cut. Perhaps Carlyle's aphorism holds here, "The healthy know not of their health but only the sick." To stay healthy one needs to recognize that health is a fruit, not a birthright. Power is only one of the considerations that must be weighed in administration, but of all it is the most overlooked in theory and the most dangerous to overlook in practice.

The power resources of an administrator or an agency are not disclosed by a legal search of titles and court decisions or by examining appropriations or budgetary allotments. Legal authority and a treasury balance are necessary but politically insufficient bases of administration. Administrative rationality requires a critical evaluation of the whole range of complex and shifting forces on whose support, acquiescence, or temporary impotence the power to act depends.

Analysis of the sources from which power is derived and the limitations they impose is as much a dictate of prudent administration as sound budgetary procedure. The bankruptcy that comes from an unbalanced power budget has consequences far more disastrous than the necessity of seeking a deficiency appropriation. The budgeting of power is a basic subject matter of a realistic science of administration.

It may be urged that for all but the top hierarchy of the administrative structure the question of power is irrelevant. Legislative authority and administrative orders suffice. Power adequate to the function to be performed flows down the chain of command. Neither statute nor executive order, however, confers more than legal authority to act. Whether Congress or President can impart the substance of power as well as the form depends upon the line-up of forces in the particular case. A price control law wrung from a reluctant Congress by an amorphous and unstable combination of consumer and labor groups is formally the same as a law enacting a support price program for agriculture backed by the disciplined organizations of farmers and their congressmen. The differences for the scope and effectiveness of administration are obvious. The Presidency, like Congress, responds to and translates the pressures that play upon it. The real mandate contained in an Executive order varies with the political strength of the group demand embodied in it, and in the context of other group demands.

Both Congress and President do focus the general political energies of the community and so are considerably more than mere means for transmitting organized pressures. Yet power is not concentrated by the structure of government or politics into the hands of a leadership with a capacity to budget it among a diverse set of administrative activities. A picture of the Presidency as a reservoir of authority from which the lower echelons of administration draw life and vigor is an idealized distortion of reality.

A similar criticism applies to any like claim for an agency head in his agency. Only in varying degrees can the powers of subordinate officials be explained as resulting from the chain of command. Rarely is such an explanation a satisfactory account of the sources of power.

To deny that power is derived exclusively from superiors in the hierarchy is to assert that subordinates stand in a feudal relation in which to a degree they fend for themselves and acquire support peculiarly their own. A structure of interests friendly or hostile, vague and general or compact and well-defined, encloses each significant center of administrative discretion. This structure is an important determinant of the scope of possible action. As a source of power and authority it is a competitor of the formal hierarchy.

Not only does political power flow in from the sides of an organization, as it were; it also flows up the organization to the center from the constituent parts. When the staff of the Office of War Mobliza-tion and Reconversion advised a hard-pressed agency to go out and get itself some popular support so that the President could afford to support it, their action reflected the realities of power rather than political cynicism.

It is clear that the American system of politics does not generate enough power at any focal point of leadership to provide the conditions for an even partially successful divorce of politics from administration. Subordinates cannot depend on the formal chain of command to deliver enough political power to permit them to do their jobs. Accordingly they must supplement the resources available through the hierarchy with those they can muster on their own, or accept the consequences in frustration—a course itself not without danger. Administrative rationality demands that objectives be determined and sights set in conformity with a realistic appraisal of power position and potential.

II

The theory of administration has neglected the problem of the sources and adequacy of power, in all probability because of a distaste for the disorderliness of American political life and a belief that this disorderliness is transitory. An idealized picture of the British parliamentary system as a Platonic form to be realized or approximated has exerted a baneful fascination in the field. The majority party with a mandate at the polls and a firmly seated leadership in the Cabinet seems to solve adequately the problem of the supply of power necessary to permit administration to concentrate on the fulfillment of accepted objectives. It is a commonplace that the American party system provides neither a mandate for a platform nor a mandate for a leadership.

Accordingly, the election over, its political meaning must be explored by the diverse leaders in the executive and legislative branches. Since the parties have failed to discuss issues, mobilize majorities in their terms, and create a working political consensus on measures to be carried out, the task is left for others—most prominently the agencies concerned. Legislation passed and powers granted are frequently politically premature. Thus the Council of Economic Advisers was given legislative birth before political acceptance of its functions existed. The agencies to which tasks are assigned must devote themselves to the creation of an adequate consensus to permit administration. The mandate that the parties do not supply must be attained through public relations and the mobilization of group support. Pendleton Herring and others have shown just how vital this support is for agency action.

The theory that agencies should confine themselves to communicating policy suggestions to executive and legislature, and refrain from appealing to their clientele and the public, neglects the failure of the parties to provide either a clear-cut decision as to what they should do or an adequately mobilized political support for a course of action. The bureaucracy under the American political system has a large share of responsibility for the public promotion of policy and even more in organizing the political basis for its survival and growth. It is generally recognized that the agencies have a special competence in the technical aspects of their fields which of necessity gives them a rightful policy initiative. In addition, they have or develop a shrewd understanding of the politically feasible in the group structure within which they work. Above all, in the eyes of their supporters and their enemies they represent the institutionalized embodiment of policy, an enduring organization actually or potentially capable of mobilizing power behind policy. The survival interests and creative drives of administrative organizations combine with clientele pressures to compel such mobilization. The party system provides no enduring institutional representation for group interest at all comparable to that of the bureaus of the Department of Agriculture. Even the subject matter committees of Congress function in the shadow of agency permanency.

The bureaucracy is recognized by all interested groups as a major channel of representation to such an extent that Congress rightly feels the competition of a rival. The weakness in party structure both permits and makes necessary the present dimensions of the political activities of the administrative branch—permits because it fails to protect administration from pressures and fails to provide adequate direction and support, makes necessary because it fails to develop a consensus on a leadership and a program that makes possible administration on the basis of accepted decisional premises.

Agencies and bureaus more or less perforce are in the business of building, maintaining, and increasing their political support. They lead and in large part are led by the diverse groups whose influence sustains them. Frequently they lead and are themselves led in conflicting directions. This is not due to a dull-witted incapacity to see the contradictions in their behavior but is an almost inevitable result of the contradictory nature of their support.

Herbert Simon has shown that administrative rationality depends on the establishment of uniform value premises in the decisional centers of organization. Unfortunately, the value premises of those forming vital elements of political support are often far from uniform. These elements are in Barnard's and Simon's sense "customers" of the organization and therefore parts of the organization whose wishes are clothed with a very real authority. A major and most time-consuming aspect of administration consists of the wide range of activities designed to secure enough "customer" acceptance to survive and, if fortunate, develop a consensus adequate to program formulation and execution.

To varying degrees, dependent on the breadth of acceptance of their programs, officials at every level of significant discretion must make their estimates of the situation, take stock of their resources, and plan accordingly. A keen appreciation of the real components of their organization is the beginning of wisdom. These components will be found to stretch far beyond the government payroll. Within the government they will encompass Congress, congressmen, committees, courts, other agencies, presidential advisers, and the President. The Aristotelian analysis of constitutions is equally applicable and equally necessary to an understanding of administrative organization.

The broad alliance of conflicting groups that makes up presidential majorities scarcely coheres about any definite pattern of objectives, nor has it by the alchemy of the party system had its collective power concentrated in an accepted leadership with a personal mandate. The conciliation and maintenance of this support is a necessary condition of the attainment and retention of office involving, as Madison so well saw, "the spirit of party and faction in the necessary and ordinary operations of government." The President must in large part be, if not all things to all men, at least many things to many men. As a consequence, the contradictions in his power base invade administration. The often criticized apparent cross-purposes of the Roosevelt regime cannot be put down to inept administration until the political facts are weighed. Were these apparently self-defeating measures reasonably related to the general maintenance of the composite majority of the Administration? The first objective—ultimate patriotism apart—of the administrator is the attainment and retention of the power on which his tenure of office depends. This is the necessary pre-condition for the accomplishment of all other objectives.

The same ambiguities that arouse the scorn of the naive in the electoral campaigns of the parties are equally inevitable in administration and for the same reasons. Victory at the polls does not yield either a clear-cut grant of power or a unified majority support for a coherent program. The task of the Presidency lies in feeling out the alternatives of policy which are consistent with the retention and increase of the group support on which the Administration rests. The lack of a budgetary theory (so frequently deplored) is not due to any incapacity to apply rational analysis to the comparative contribution of the various activities of government to a determinate hierarchy of purposes. It more probably stems from a fastidious distaste for the frank recognition of the budget as a politically expedient allocation of resources. Appraisal in terms of their political contribution to the Administration provides almost a sole common denominator between the Forest Service and the Bureau of Engraving.

Integration of the administrative structure through an over-all purpose in terms of which tasks and priorities can be established is an emergency phenomenon. Its realization, only partial at best, has been limited to war and the extremity of depression. Even in wartime the Farm Bureau Federation, the American Federation of Labor, the Congress of Industrial Organizations, the National Association of Manufacturers, the Chamber of Commerce, and a host of lesser interests resisted coordination of themselves and the agencies concerned with their interests. A Presidency temporarily empowered by intense mass popular support acting in behalf of a generally accepted and simplified purpose can, with great difficulty, bribe, cajole, and coerce a real measure of joint action. The long-drawn-out battle for conversion and the debacle of orderly reconversion underline the difficulty of attaining, and the transitory nature of, popularly based emergency power. Only in crises are the powers of the Executive nearly adequate to impose a common plan of action on the executive branch, let alone the economy.

In ordinary times the manifold pressures of our pluralistic society work themselves out in accordance with the balance of forces prevailing in Congress and the agencies. Only to a limited degree is the process subject to responsible direction or review by President or party leadership.

The program of the President cannot be a Gosplan for the government precisely because the nature of his institutional and group support gives him insufficient power. The personal unity of the Presidency cannot perform the function of Hobbes' sovereign since his office lacks the authority of Hobbes' contract. Single headedness in the executive gives no assurance of singleness of purpose. It only insures that the significant pressures in a society will be brought to bear on one office. Monarchy solves the problem of giving one plan to a multitude only when the plenitude of its authority approaches dictatorship. Impatient social theorists in all ages have turned to the philosopher king as a substitute for consensus. Whatever else he may become, it is difficult to conceive of the American president ruling as a philosopher king, even with the advice of the Executive Office. The monarchical solution to the administrative problems posed by the lack of a disciplined party system capable of giving firm leadership and a program to the legislature is a modern variant of the dreams of the eighteenth century savants and well nigh equally divorced from a realistic appraisal of social realities.

Much of administrative thought, when it does not assume the value of coordination for coordination's sake, operates on the assumption that there must be something akin to Rousseau's *volonté générale* in administration to which the errant *volonté de tous* of the bureaus can and should be made to conform. This will-o'-the-wisp was made the object of an illuminating search by Pendleton Herring in his *Public Administration and the Public Interest.* The answer for Rousseau was equivalent to the latter is the resultant of the relevant pressures, as enlightened dictatorship or counting the votes. The administrative Herring shows. The first alternative seems to require at least the potency of the British Labour party and elsewhere has needed the disciplined organization of a fascist, nazi, or communist party to provide the power and consensus necessary to coordinate the manifold activities of government to a common plan.

Dictatorship, as Sigmund Neumann has observed, is a substitute for institutions which is required to fill the vacuum when traditional institutions break down. Force supplies the compulsion and guide to action in place of the normal routines of unconscious habit. Administrative organizations, however much they may appear the creations of art, are institutions produced in history and woven in the web of social relationships that gives them life and being. They present the same refractory material to the hand of the political artist as the rest of society of which they form a part.

Just as the economists have attempted to escape the complexities of institutional reality by taking refuge in the frictionless realm of theory so some students of administration, following their lead, have seen in the application of the doctrine of opportunity costs a clue to a science of administration. Valuable as this may be in a restricted way, Marx has more light to throw on the study of institutions. It is in the dynamics and interrelations of institutions that we have most hope of describing and therefore learning to control administrative behavior.

III

The difficulty of coordinating government agencies lies not only in the fact that bureaucratic organizations are institutions having survival interests which may conflict with their rational adaptation to over-all purpose, but even more in their having roots in society. Coordination of the varied activities of a modern government almost of necessity involves a substantial degree of coördination of the economy. Coordination of government agencies involves far more than changing the behavior and offices of officials in Washington and the field. It involves the publics that are implicated in their normal functioning. To coordinate fiscal policy, agricultural policy, labor policy, foreign policy, and military policy, to name a few major areas, moves beyond the range of government charts and the habitat of the bureaucrats to the market place and to where the people live and work. This suggests that the reason why government reorganization is so difficult is that far more than government in the formal sense is involved in reorganization. One could overlook this in the limited government of the nineteenth century but the multi-billion dollar government of the mid-twentieth permits no facile dichotomy between government and economy. Economy and efficiency are the two objectives a laissez faire society can prescribe in peacetime as over-all government objectives. Their inadequacy either as motivation or standards has long been obvious. A planned economy clearly requires a planned government. But, if one can afford an unplanned economy, apart from gross extravagance, there seems no compelling and therefore, perhaps, no sufficiently powerful reason for a planned government.

Basic to the problem of administrative rationality is that of organizational identification and point of view. To whom is one loyal—unit, section, branch, division, bureau, department, administration, government, country, people, world history, or what? Administrative analysis frequently assumes that organizational identification should occur in such a way as to merge primary organization loyalty in a larger synthesis. The good of the part is to give way to the reasoned good of the whole. This is most frequently illustrated in the rationalizations used to counter self-centered demands of primary groups for funds and personnel. Actually the competition between governmental power centers, rather than the rationalizations, is the effective instrument of coordination.

Where there is a clear common product on whose successful production the sub-groups depend for the attainment of their own satisfaction, it is possible to demonstrate to almost all participants the desirability of cooperation. The shoe factory produces shoes, or else, for all concerned. But the government as a whole and many of its component parts have no such identifiable common product on which all depend. Like the proverbial Heinz, there are fifty-seven or more varieties unified, if at all, by a common political profit and loss account.

Administration is faced by somewhat the same dilemma as economics. There are propositions about the behavior patterns conducive to full employment—welfare economics. On the other hand, there are propositions about the economics of the individual firm—the counsel of the business schools. It is possible to show with considerable persuasiveness that sound considerations for the individual firm may lead to a depression if generally adopted, a result desired by none of the participants. However, no single firm can afford by itself to adopt the course of collective wisdom; in the absence of a common power capable of enforcing decisions premised on the supremacy of the collective interest, *sauve qui peut* is common sense.

The position of administrative organizations is not unlike the position of particular firms. Just as the decisions of the firms could be coordinated by the imposition of a planned economy so could those of the component parts of the government. But just as it is possible to operate a formally unplanned economy by the loose coordination of the market, in the same fashion it is possible to operate a government by the loose coordination of the play of political forces through its institutions.

The unseen hand of Adam Smith may be little in evidence in either case. One need not believe in a doctrine of social or administrative harmony to believe that formal centralized planning—while perhaps desirable and in some cases necessary—is not a must. The complicated logistics of supplying the city of New York runs smoothly down the grooves of millions of well adapted habits projected from a distant past. It seems naive on the one hand to believe in the possibility of a vast, intricate, and delicate economy operating with a minimum of formal over-all direction, and on the other to doubt that a relatively simple mechanism such as the government can be controlled largely by the same play of forces.

Doubtless the real reasons for seeking coordination in the government are the same that prompt a desire for economic planning. In fact, apart from waging war with its demand for rapid change, economic planning would seem to be the only objective sufficiently compelling and extensive to require a drastic change in our system of political laissez faire. Harold Smith, testifying before the Senate Banking and Currency Committee on the Employment Act of 1946, showed how extensive a range of hitherto unrelated activities could be brought to bear on a common purpose—the maintenance of maximum employment and purchasing power. In the flush of the war experience and with prophecies of reconversion unemployment, a reluctant Congress passed a pious declaration of policy. Senator Flanders has recorded the meager showing to date.

Nevertheless, war and depression apart, the Employment Act of 1946 for the first time provides an inclusive common purpose in terms of which administrative activities can be evaluated and integrated. While still deficient in depth and content, it provides at least a partial basis for the rational budgeting of government activities. The older concept of economy and efficiency as autonomous standards still lingers in Congress, but elsewhere their validity as ends in themselves is treated with skepticism.

If the advent of Keynesian economics and the erosion of laissez faire have created the intellectual conditions requisite for the formulation of over-all government policy, they do not by any means guarantee the political conditions necessary for its implementation. We can see quite clearly that the development of an integrated administration requires an integrating purpose. The ideals of Locke, Smith, Spencer, and their American disciples deny the need for such a purpose save for economy and efficiency's sake. Marx, Keynes, and their followers by denying the validity of the self-regulating economy have endowed the state with an over-arching responsibility in terms of which broad coordination of activities is not only intellectually possible but theoretically, at least, necessary. Intellectual perception of the need for this coordination, however, has run well ahead of the public's perception of it and of the development of a political channeling of power adequate to its administrative implementation.

Most students of administration are planners of some sort. Most congressmen would fly the label like the plague. Most bureaucrats, whatever their private faith, live under two jealous gods, their particular clientele and the loyalty check. Such a condition might, if it exists as described, cast doubt on whether even the intellectual conditions for rational administrative coordination exist. Be that as it may, the transition from a government organized in cilentele departments and bureaus, each responding to the massive feudal power of organized business, organized agriculture, and organized labor, to a government integrated about a paramount national purpose will require a political power at least as great as that which tamed the earlier feudalism. It takes a sharp eye or a tinted glass to see such an organized power on the American scene. Without it, administrative organization for over-all coordination has the academic air of South American constitution making. One is reminded of the remark attributed to the Austrian economist Mises; on being told that the facts did not agree with his theory, he replied "*desto schlechter für die Tatsache.*"

IV

It is highly appropriate to consider how administrators should behave to meet the test of efficiency in a planned polity; but in the absence of such a polity and while, if we like, struggling to get it, a realistic science of administration will teach administrative behavior appropriate to the existing political system.

A close examination of the presidential system may well bring one to conclude that administrative rationality in it is a different matter from that applicable to the British ideal. The American Presidency is an office that has significant monarchical characteristics despite its limited term and elective nature. The literature on court and palace has many an insight applicable to the White House. Access to the President, reigning favorites, even the court jester, are topics that show the continuity of institutions. The maxims of LaRochefoucauld and the memoirs of the Duc de Saint Simon have a refreshing realism for the operator on the Potomac.

The problem of rival factions in the President's family is as old as the famous struggle between Jefferson and Hamilton, as fresh and modern as the latest cabal against John Snyder. Experience seems to show that this personal and factional struggle for the President's favor is a vital part of the process of representation. The vanity, personal ambition, or patriotism of the contestants soon clothes itself in the generalities of principle and the clique aligns itself with groups beyond the capital. Subordinate rivalry is tolerated if not encouraged by so many able executives that it can scarcely be attributed to administrative ineptitude. The wrangling tests opinion, uncovers information that would otherwise never rise to the top, and provides effective opportunity for decision rather than mere ratification of prearranged plans. Like most judges, the Executive needs to hear argument for his own instruction. The alternatives presented by subordinates in large part determine the freedom and the creative opportunity of their superiors. The danger of becoming a Merovingian is a powerful incentive to the maintenance of fluidity in the structure of power.

The fixed character of presidential tenure makes it necessary that subordinates be politically expendable. The President's men must be willing to accept the blame for failures not their own. Machiavelli's teaching on how princes must keep the faith bears re-reading. Collective responsibility is incompatible with a fixed term of office. As it tests the currents of public opinion, the situation on the Hill, and the varying strength of the organized pressures, the White House alters and adapts the complexion of the Administration. Loyalties to programs or to groups and personal pride and interest frequently conflict with whole-souled devotion to the Presidency. In fact, since such devotion is not made mandatory by custom, institutions, or the facts of power, the problem is perpetually perplexing to those who must choose.

The balance of power between executive and legislature is constantly subject to the shifts of public and group support. The latent tendency of the American Congress is to follow the age-old parliamentary precedents and to try to reduce the President to the rolе of constitutional monarch. Against this threat and to secure his own initiative, the President's resources are primarily demagogic, with the weaknesses and strengths that dependence on mass popular appeal implies. The unanswered question of American government—"who is boss?"—constantly plagues administration. The disruption of unity of command is not just the problem of Taylor's functional foreman, but goes to the stability and uniformity of basic decisional premises essential to consequent administration.

It is interesting to speculate on the consequences for administration of the full development of congressional or presidential government. A leadership in Congress that could control the timetable of the House and Senate would scarcely content itself short of reducing the President's Cabinet to what in all probability it was first intended to be, a modified version of the present Swiss executive. Such leadership could scarcely arise without centrally organized, disciplined, national parties far different from our present shambling alliances of state and local machines.

A Presidency backed by a disciplined party controlling a majority in Congress would probably assimilate itself to a premiership by association of legislative leadership in the formulation of policy and administration. In either line of development the crucial matter is party organization. For the spirit of the party system determines the character of the government.

That the American party system will develop toward the British ideal is by no means a foregone conclusion. The present oscillation between a strong demagogic Presidency and a defensively powerful congressional oligarchy may well prove a continuing pattern of American politics, as it was of Roman. In the absence of a party system providing an institutionalized centripetal force in our affairs, it is natural to look to the Presidency as Goldsmith's weary traveler looked to the throne.

The Presidency of the United States, however, is no such throne as the pre-World War I *Kaiserreich* that provided the moral and political basis for the Prussian bureaucracy. Lacking neutrality and mystique, it does not even perform the function of the British monarchy in providing a psychological foundation for the permanent civil service. A leaderless and irresponsible Congress frequently makes it appear the strong point of the republic. The Bonapartist experience in France, the Weimar Republic, and South American examples nearer home, despite important social differences, are relevant to any thoughtful consideration of building a solution to legislative anarchy on the unity of the executive.

The present course of American party development gives little ground for optimism that a responsible two party system capable of uniting Congress and Executive in a coherent program will emerge. The increasingly critical importance of the federal budget for the national economy and the inevitable impact of world power status on the conduct of foreign affairs make inescapable the problem of stable leadership in the American system. Unfortunately they by no means insure a happy or indeed any solution.

Attempts to solve administrative problems in isolation from the structure of power and purpose in the polity are bound to prove illusory. The reorganization of Congress to create responsibility in advance of the development of party responsibility was an act of piety to principle, of educational value; but as a practical matter it raised a structure without foundation. In the same way, reorganization of the executive branch to centralize administrative power in the Presidency while political power remains dispersed and divided may effect improvement, but in a large sense it must fail. The basic prerequisite to the administration of the textbooks is a responsible two party system. The means to its attainment are a number one problem for students of administration. What Schattschneider calls the struggle for party government may sometime yield us the responsible parliamentary two party system needed to underpin our present administrative theory. Until that happy time, exploration of the needs and necessities of our present system is a high priority task of responsible scholarship.

73. *Our Super-Government--Can We Control It?* *

THIS ARTICLE, which, like the one preceding it, (72), deals with controlling the enormous machinery of the United States government, was inspired by the Hoover Commission report that exposed how much overlapping and confusion exists among executive agencies. Professor Burns points out that the bigness of the United States government is based on the many services it performs for its citizens; he shows that the Hoover Commission did not suggest reducing the services, but rather said that they should be performed more efficiently. Most of such an increase in efficiency can come about only if Congress passes laws allowing the executive departments to be reorganized, for under the constitutional principle of separation of powers the President executes the laws, but the machinery that he must use is created by Congress.

DURING a campaign talk in 1920 Warren G. Harding said airily that "government is a simple thing." A year in the White House was enough to change his mind. "I can't make a damn thing out of this tax problem," he exploded to a secretary one day. "I listen to one side and they seem right—and the—God!—I talk to the other side and they seem just as right, and here I am where I started. God, what a job!"

Stronger Presidents than Harding have had trouble managing "the toughest job on earth." Much of the difficulty has stemmed from the creaking machinery, the fuzzy organization and the sheer bulk of the executive branch of the National Government. For decades our Chief Executives have been trying to overhaul and modernize the administrative apparatus, which Franklin D. Roosevelt once termed a "higgledy-piggledy patchwork of duplicate responsibilities and overlapping powers." Since McKinley's time distinguished committees have been appointed, elaborate studies made, reforms recommended. But our administrative structure has remained sadly out-of-date; the Chief Executive's job has become more grueling than ever.

Guided by an ex-President who had wrestled with the problem in his

* James MacGregor Burns, *The New York Times Magazine*, April 24, 1949, pp. 7, 28,30-33. Reprinted by permission of the author and the publisher.

own day, the latest excursion into the Dark Continent of the national bureaucracy is now coming to an end. The reports of the Hoover Commission on Organization of the Executive Branch indicate that our Federal Government has become the most colossal and complicated enterprise on earth. It employs over two million persons. It spends over forty billions a year—more than the total income of all Americans hardly a generation ago. It employes over half the types of skills found in all private enterprise. It owns one-fifth of the area of the United States.

The Government is big because its jobs are big. The Treasury Department handles almost fifty million individual income tax returns every year, the Postoffice Department almost forty billion pieces of mail. The Veterans Administration manages about forty billion dollars of insurance policies. Sometimes work failures come in proportion to work accomplished. A medium-sized agency confessed to the Hoover Commission last year that it had on hand a backlog of over a quarter-million cubic feet of wartime records that had not yet been processed.

Many Americans eye this burgeoning giant with suspicion, if not with open repugnance. Some of them look eagerly to the day when large parts of it can be dismantled. But the extraordinary fact seems to be that the commission on organization—headed by Herbert Hoover himself and sprinkled with conservative business men and Congressmen—has supplied the most convincing evidence we have yet had that our super-Government is here to stay.

In setting up the commission Congress emphasized an interest not only in economy and efficiency but also in "abolishing services, activities and functions not necessary to the efficient conduct of government." Here was a mandate to the commission to track down the hundreds of worthless bureaus that—according to popular notion—make up a large part of the National Government. But the commission took no such tack. Its efficiency experts found waste, duplication of effort, lack of order, poor control. It has urged the consolidation of activities and the adoption of sweeping reforms. But after sixteen months of exhaustive investigation the commission has not recommended the abolition of any significant function. Indeed, the commission has urged the expansion of a number of Government services.

How can this result be explained? The answer is that the commission and its staff carefully studied the facts of governmental life instead of contenting themselves with generalities about "bureaucracy rampant." They discovered—if they did not already know—that government is not a single entity that can be easily deflated like a balloon. It is a collection of hundreds of separate agencies, rendering a tremendous variety of services to "clients" who depend heavily on those services. It is a collection of human beings with many tasks: a hoof-and-mouth disease inspector in Texas; an economist in Washington; a weather forecaster in New York; a veterans' counselor in Seattle; an expert on Korean affairs in the Pentagon, and thousands of others.

Very few of these functions compete with private enterprise; on the contrary, almost all of them are responses to needs that only government can meet. It has long been agreed that our Government should deliver the mail, wage war, regulate interstate commerce, take the census, and the like; few seriously argue that such tasks could or should be turned over to private individuals.

Our super-Government, in short, has become a fixed part of the "American way of life." It has become a vital instrument for social progress. But its very size and importance make it a costly and dangerous instrument if not properly managed. It is precisely on this point that the Hoover Commission, while recognizing that big government is here to stay, has raised storm warnings.

The American people directly hire and fire only one person—the President—out of the two million in the Executive branch. The Chief Executive must serve as a firm link between the people and their bureaucracy. His office is the funnel through which their needs and urges are translated into administrative action. Everything depends on the responsiveness of the bureaucracy to the President's—and hence to the people's—direction.

That is where the troubles lies. By far the most significant finding of the Hoover Commission is that the Chief Executive does not have full control of his own establishment. Authority is scattered about; lines of control are tangled and broken. Broad policy does not flow from the White House to the agencies as clearly as it should, but is confused and dissipated.

For one thing, the agencies are not set up in well-defined, cohesive groupings. President Truman has shown visitors a huge chart on his office wall picturing well over 100 officials required by law to report to the Chief Executive alone, and has complained that "I cannot even see all these men, let alone actually study what they are doing." Even if the President were able to ignore his legislative, political and ceremonial duties and concentrate wholly on administration—which he cannot do—he would have only a few minutes a week to meet with these officials.

With an adequate staff the Chief Executive might give a measure of direction and coordination to this labyrinth of departments and commissions. But he is lacking some of the indispensable tools of good management. Control of personnel is not fully in his hands, and he lacks the means to check on the performance of the agencies. The

President cannot choose his own staff as freely as he would like. Nor can he rely on his Cabinet for disinterested advice, because the members are concerned mainly with their departmental duties and often represent warring factions in the party. A dozen years ago President Roosevelt's Committee on Administrative Management summed up the situation simply: "The President needs help." The need is even greater today.

The strong chain of command that should tie the bureaucracy to the President and thus to the people is broken at other points. Subordinate officials have been given power by law to act independently of the Chief Executive. For example, the Secretary of the Interior can control the sale of helium to foreign nations, and the Army Chief of Engineers can prepare river development plans without referring to superior authority. Independent boards make vitally important decisions that are beyond Presidential reach. The Maritime Commission's control of shipping can sharply affect our foreign relations. Yet the President must negotiate with the Maritime Commissioners almost as with foreign plenipotentiaries.

The chain of command is also weakened at the departmental level. Often the departments are mere "holding companies" for semi-independent bureaus that go their own way. Such a situation breeds administrative slackness and aloofness, and what Pendleton Herring called "quiet sabotage by unsympathetic technicians and genteel blackmail by high policy officials." Delay and fumbling are hard enough to curb under any conditions. Harry Hopkins complained during the war, according to Robert E. Sherwood, that after important decisions had been reached by Mr. Roosevelt and Mr. Churchill and by the generals and admirals, months-long delays would occur—"and then you start investigating and it takes you weeks to find out that the orders have been deliberately stalled on the desk of some lieutenant commander or lieutenant colonel down on Constitution Avenue."

If failures of top control are serious in the civilian agencies, they are positively dangerous in the military. Traditionally, Americans have had a healthy fear of military cliques and of the "man on horseback." Knowing something about military oppression, the framers of the Constitution carefully put the Army and Navy under civilian control. The safeguards they provided are all the more important under conditions of modern war, whether of the atomic, bacteriological, or "push-button" variety. The fact that the per capita cost of defense is now $100 annually has given taxpayers a tremendous stake in the efficiency of the military as well as its responsibility.

On this score, too, the Hoover Commission has uttered an urgent warning. It reports that centralized civilian control "scarcely exists." It has found a weak link in the chain of command between the Secretary of Defense and the service departments—the Army, Navy and Air Force. The basic trouble here arises from the manner in which the new military establishment was tacked together as a federation of competing services rather than as a unified, integrated system with clear control in the hands of the President and the Secretary of Defense. The Joint Chiefs of Staff—composed of military chiefs—are virtually a law unto themselves.

To clear up the disorganization and irresponsibility in both the civilian and military parts of the Executive branch, the Hoover Commission has proposed some old-fashioned remedies. Among these are intelligent grouping of agencies in major departments, centralization of authority in the President, clear lines of command and accountability, and adequate staff services. These suggestions are, indeed, so obvious that the question arises: Why is it that after a decade or two of big government we are still trying to apply first principles to the running of our administrative machinery?

If our Chief Executives had had the power to manage the Executive branch as they wished, they long ago would have applied these first principles in an effort to lighten their own heavy burdens. But the Constitution, while vesting the "executive power" in the President, does not give him exclusive authority over his own branch of government. Under our system of checks and balances Congress has considerable control of administration, just as the President in turn takes part in law-making through his veto and other powers.

Congress determines whether a new function of government will be placed firmly under the President or will be somewhat independent of him. It can give the President a good deal of leeway in setting up agencies, or it can specify provisions that bind the President at every turn. Congress, in short, has the power to organize the Executive branch—and to reorganize it. Even more important, the Senate and House of Representatives hold the "power of the purse" through their appropriations committees.

Along with these constitutional powers are others that have grown up by custom and usage. The House and Senate have expanded their investigating power into strong tools for influencing administrators. Sometimes the probes are full-dress committee inquiries conducted amid exploding flash bulbs; sometimes they are quiet "fishing expeditions" by one or two Congressmen with special interests. In any event, they help to make the harassed administrator watchful of his Congressional relationships. Finally, Congress has considerable weight in the selection of officials. Under the Constitution the Senate must confirm major appointments; moreover, the President, by the unwritten rule of "Senatorial courtesy," must clear thousands of selections with interested Congressmen.

Inevitably Congress has come to wield day-to-day influence over large parts of the Executive branch. Inevitably, too, the bureaucrat has come to look not simply to the White House for orders and support, but also to Capitol Hill. Administrators are quick to see that Presidents may come and go, political parties may rise and fall, but the committee chieftains in Congress seem to go on forever.

What is the result? Not only is control of the bureaucracy divided between President and Congress. In Congress it is further divided among Senate, House, legislative blocs, committees, sub-committees and individual members. As a result of this fragmentation of power in Congress one finds lines of authority running horizontally from committee or Congressman to department or bureau chief, so that authority is shifted from the President and dispersed throughout the bureaucracy.

Under such conditions any hope of pinning responsibility for mistakes or achievements on the proper officials often becomes forlorn indeed. The source of administrative direction often seems to be far underground, lost in a maze of subterranean channels among President, administrators, Congressional blocs and committees. "There is no danger in power," Woodrow Wilson said, "if only it be not irresponsible. If it be divided, dealt out in shares to many, it is obscured; and if it be obscured, it is made irresponsible."

The Hoover Commission wants to pin on the President as much executive responsibility as the Constitution will allow, and thus to make him strictly accountable to Congress *as a whole* and to the people. Its pleas for a stronger chain of command from the President downward stem from its conviction that singleness of control is the essence of both responsibility and efficiency.

Unhappy experience indicates, however, that any move to reorganize the Executive branch will run head-on into the opposition of the groups that profit from the present state of affairs. Every major function of government is carried on amid intense pressures from the interests affected. Agency heads are often caught squarely in the storm center of labor politics, farm politics, transportation politics, medical politics, as the case may be. They cultivate close ties with interests they promote or regulate. Sometimes they find it hard to mediate between the national welfare and the interest of a particular group.

Congress as a whole genuinely favors responsibility and efficiency in government. But individual Congressmen and blocs in each chamber are likely to demand that their own agencies be left out of any plan for firmer control by the President. They prefer the agencies to be more vulnerable to Congressional control, to be more responsive to the affected interests. The Congressmen cannot be blamed for holding such views, for they too are under pressure from the groups dominant in their states and districts. The Hoover Commission had only to suggest the shift of some public works functions from the Corps of Engineers to the Interior Department for a storm of protests to descend on Capitol Hill.

A sizable group of Congressmen opposed to reorganization can logroll the proposals to death. The process is much like the traditional handling of tariff bills, when Congressmen forgot their free-trade principles in their zeal for protection for the "folks back home" and busily swapped concessions with one another. The only remedy for such logrolling is to delegate extensive power to the President to draw up proposals. In 1912 Congress granted President Taft power to make reorganization changes without referring back to the Legislative branch.

More recently Congress has been niggardly in giving the President reorganization powers. Changes proposed by Presidents Coolidge and Hoover failed in the face of stout resistance. In 1937, after hearing the advice of his Committee on Administrative Management, President Roosevelt asked Congress for broad reorganization authority. Along with specific changes he proposed that the President have the power to draw up reform proposals; these would become law unless disapproved by both Senate and House within sixty days.

This proposal provoked a great hue and cry from groups that feared the effect of the plans on their favorite agencies. Although Taft had received far greater reorganization power, the President's bill was soon dubbed the "dictator bill." The violent fight over the Supreme Court reform proposal had just taken place, and many Americans swallowed the charge that the reorganization bill was but another move toward executive tyranny. Deluged by telegrams, the House killed the bill. In 1939 a far weaker act was passed, later to be renewed in about the same form until 1948.

President Truman recently asked Congress to re-enact and broaden the power to initiate reorganization plans. The Hoover Commission heartily supports this request. It has warned, moreover, against putting limitations on the President's power, for "once the limiting and exempting process is begun," the commission says, "it will end the possibility of achieving really substantial results." No safeguard is necessary other than the right of Congress to veto Presidential reorganization plans as a whole.

The renewal of the Reorganization Act—and the form in which it is renewed—will be one of the important issues facing Americans during the immediate years ahead. Already a sharp battle seems to be shaping up. Last January Congressional leaders told President Truman flatly that no reorganization bill could pass unless several independent commissions were exempted. More "grasshopper bites," as Chairman Hoover called them, were taken out of the bill before it passed the House. Recently Congressmen have complained of lobbying against proposed reforms by pressure groups and even by agency heads.

Much will depend on the ability of Americans to understand that granting the President more power over the Executive branch is a move not toward dictatorship but toward more responsible government. Years ago Lincoln stressed the need of maintaining a Government strong enough to fulfill its obligations but not too strong for the liberties of the people. A Chief Executive accountable to people and Congress and firmly in control of the bureaucracy is a first step in meeting that need. For in the age of super-government, nothing can last very long without skillful and responsible management—not even our own democracy.

74. *Survival in the Bureaucratic Jungle* *

ONE OF THE first tenets advanced by the late nineteenth century pioneers, of whom Woodrow Wilson was one, in the development of American public administration was that administration is a field of business and politics is well—politics. Although the emphasis upon the separation of administration and politics perhaps contributed to the development of more efficient administrative techniques, to understand public administration in modern government we must recognize, as Mr. Cleveland puts it, "that government is a mixture of politics and administration, accommodation and logic, consent and decision."

ABOUT ELEVEN YEARS AGO I was sitting against the wall of a Senate committee room, watching two political executives sell a Lend-Lease appropriation to the greatest, or at least the most deliberative, body in the world. My capacity on this occasion was as a briefcase carrier—one

* Harlan Cleveland, *The Reporter*, XIV (April 5, 1956), pp. 29-32. Excerpted from a paper delivered at the Woodrow Wilson Centennial Conference on "The Political Executive in the National Government," held at Princeton University. Reprinted with permission from *The Reporter*, 136 East 57th Street, New York 22, N. Y.

of those anonymous civil servants who sit behind government witnesses at these affairs, handing them scribbled calculations and bits of advice on scraps of paper. The witnesses were Leo Crowley, the Wisconsin politician who headed the Foreign Economic Administration, and his deputy Oscar Cox, who as one of the New Deal's brightest lawyers had drafted that extraordinary piece of legislation, the Lend-Lease Act.

The scene was a study in contrast. Crowley seemed more senatorial than the Senators, a languid, paunchy man with a mane of white hair, a florid complexion, and a deceptively benign expression. Cox was thin and efficient, his jerky gestures matching his crisp and factual eloquence. He was easy to carry a briefcase for; he already knew its contents by heart.

Most of the questions were taken by Cox. Before a Senator had finished asking his question, Cox was way ahead of him, guessing what was on his mind and starting to reply in impressive, uncompromising detail. Crowley leaned back, utterly relaxed, sometimes putting in a comment or telling a joke to keep things moving. Finally a Senator asked Crowley a question about one of the most intricate features of the Lend-Lease program, and I learned an important lesson.

"Well, I'll tell you, Senator," Crowley said in his Middle Western accent, "I've always wondered how that works, too. Let's see if Oscar can explain it to us."

Soon the hearing was over, the lesson complete. Two or three of the Senators were clapping Crowley on the back, saying what a fine presentation he had made. Cox, who had made it, was alone at the other end of the room, stuffing his papers back into his efficient-looking briefcase.

THE JUNGLE HE INHABITS

A discussion of that political animal, the government executive, should start with some picture of the jungle in which he lives and works and, if he is fit enough, survives. We can agree, I am sure, that government is a mixture of politics and administration, accommodation and logic, consent and decisions—a blend, in short, of Crowley and Cox.

We instinctively demand that our Presidents be "double firsts"—that they be great politicians and great administrators, too. Of course they don't usually succeed on both counts. Franklin Roosevelt, who is possibly unsurpassed in this century as a builder of consent in war and peace, was as casual an administrator as ever hit Washington. Harry Truman, whose reputation and training were in politics, proved himself an able and orderly administrator, but when it came to building consent for a government program he can hardly be rated better than fair. President Eisenhower, whose forte was military administration, has combined a remarkable talent for evoking consent with an equally remarkable tendency to appoint as administrators of his policies men who disagree with them.

Yet if we seldom or never get quite the perfect Presidential blend, we continue to pine for that rare amalgam—the man who can run the Executive Branch and still get along with most of the other Americans, in and out of Congress, who think *they* are anointed to run the government, too.

What is not so clear in much of the literature of public administration is the fact that every official of the Executive Branch must in some measure combine the two qualities we look for in a President—the ability to manage and the talent to build political support for what is managed. Government is a mixture of administration and politics all the way up and down the line, not merely at something called the political level where people called political executives get jobs by a process called political appointment.

THE DIFFUSION OF POWERS

What is it about our government that makes it so political a jungle? The standard explanation is the Constitutional separation of powers, the built-in checks and balances, the fact that everybody is in every act but nobody seems to be in charge of the performance.

Woodrow Wilson called this "administration by semi-independent executive agents who obey the dictation of a legislature to which they are not responsible." He was sure that Congress ran the show, described legislation as "the originating force," and complained that the "blind processes" resulting from the division of power made that power irresponsible. But Wilson was too pessimistic about the ability of the government to function in spite of this division of power and purposes—or better, perhaps, because of it. He was certainly overimpressed with the power of the legislature in his academic days, though as President he later underestimated its veto power when it came to getting the League of Nations ratified. The legislature is powerful and can do a massive job of wreckmanship, as we know from our own recent history. But the men who wrote our Constitution were clear about the "dangers from legislative usurpations." "One hundred and seventy-three despots would surely be as oppressive as one," Madison said in one of the Federalist papers. ". . . An elective despotism was not the government we fought for."

Despite the periodic flurries of legislative usurpation, we don't have an elective despotism. But we do have a Congress that participates with appalling vigor in the task of running the Executive Branch of the government. We have, indeed, a system that not only separates the general Constitutional powers but diffuses the power of decision on quite specific matters. One of the very first things I ever had to do in Washington, as an "intern" in the office of Senator "Young Bob" La Follette, was to stand in for the Senator at a hearing in the Veterans Administration on a compensation case. I recall being struck at the time by the distortion of functions thus dramatized: Here I was, a legislative bureaucrat, horning in on the efforts of executive bureaucrats to perform a judicial function.

Each official in each branch of the government has a chance to exercise two (and occasionally even three) of the Constitutional powers at once; and by the same token, each of the three branches gets a crack at nearly every major public issue.

The result of this diffusion of power is not merely, as Odegard says, that "Congress has . . . found ways and means for interposing itself between the President and his executive subordinates and thus confusing the clear line of bureaucratic responsibility." Each executive official, whether politically appointed or not, has to spend an unconscionable amount of his time and energy telling Congress what he is doing, and why. In my last year with the Mutual Security Agency, I figure that I spent the equivalent of six months out of the twelve preparing and presenting on Capitol Hill the detailed exposition of the program I was supposed to be helping "administer."

Nor is it enough for an administrator to defend a program from political attack. He finds himself actively promoting a political coalition in its support. For our Congress, which I have heard described to a group of visiting Frenchmen as a model of party discipline, is of course as choice an example of coalition government as the notorious French Assembly.

If there is any doubt that Congress is managed by complex, *ad hoc* coalitions which shift with every issue, look for a moment at the record of the Eighty-third Congress. In this supposedly Republican Congress, the fluctuating balance of power swung against the Administration on foreign aid and public housing, but supported the President on farm price supports and (by one vote) the Bricker Amendment. A coalition majority could be put together for confirming the New Deal, reducing taxes, cutting slightly the funds for defense, continuing the 1950 version of U.S. foreign policy, and allowing some of its committees to trample on Executive toes. On hardly any of these issues could one party get its way solely with the votes it could deliver from its own side of the aisle.

We see the same pattern operating in the Eighty-fourth Congress, which is theoretically led by the Democrats. There was an excellent example in the Senate when thirty-one Republicans and twenty-two Democrats beat twenty-four Democrats and fourteen Republicans and sent the natural-gas bill to Thomasville, Georgia, to be vetoed by a Republican President.

Because Congress is the way it is, every executive must help splice together the particular coalition that will pass *his* appropriation and protect *his* program and *his* reputation from damage. (His coalition may be very different from another one being fashioned for a different purpose by a colleague in the next office.) If every executive has Congressional relations as an important segment of his duties—even though he may not himself carry a bulging briefcase up Pennsylvania Avenue to "the Hill"—every executive has to have some of the instincts of a politician.

It is usually said that there are seven to eight hundred "political executives" in the national government. But by my definition there are thousands of government executives engaged in "politics." Under our Constitutional diffusion of powers, the Federal government would hardly operate at all if they were fewer.

THE INSIDE TRACK

Many distinguished writers have pondered whether the American Congress adequately represents the American people, but this is an academic question about which I have never been able to get excited. For the American people do not limit their representation in Washington to electing half a thousand Congressmen. The people are directly represented in the Executive Branch, too.

When I say "the people," I mean what David Riesman intends by the phrase "veto groups." In *The Lonely Crowd*, Riesman observed that political leadership has passed from businessmen as a class to "a series of groups, each of which has struggled for and finally attained a power to stop things conceivably inimical to its interests and, within far narrower limits, to start things. . . . Among the veto groups competition is monopolistic; rules of fairness and fellowship dictate how far one can go." The tidelands group refrained from going too far; the natural-gas lobby, consisting of some of the same people, so outraged the public conscience that a President thought to be favorable to its objectives had to turn against the natural-gas bill. The farm group's effective power is enormous; the smaller effectiveness of the labor group may be traced, at least in part, to the fact that it overplayed its hand during the New Deal.

What Riesman did not mention is the fact that the power of these new-style lobbies can be roughly measured by the strength of their surrogates *within* the Executive Branch of the government. The Department of Agriculture has long been regarded, both by the farm organizations and the rest of the government, as a farmers' defense league inside the Federal bureaucracy. Organized labor, particularly the CIO, substantially controlled the National Labor Relations Board during the period (in the 1930's) when the Board was clearing the way for the rapid expansion of the CIO. The housing program, created by the New Deal for the purpose of getting houses built, placed itself in the hands of the speculative builders and the savings-and-loan associations to such an extent that moral corruption shaded over into pecuniary corruption. The organized veterans have their own preserve in the Veterans Administration. The Commerce Department has for some years had a Business Advisory Council whose function, in effect, is to bring to bear on internal government decisions an organized business opinion. Defense contracts are habitually given out by men recruited from the businesses that are getting the business, and regulations are drafted by surrogates of the industries to which they apply. The National Recovery Act was declared unconstitutional early in the New Deal, but "self-government of industry" is an established practice with a venerable tradition behind it.

During the Korean War, as John Corson has said,

> The Office of Price Stabilization official in charge of price regulations for the apparel industry [in 1951] was borrowed from a leading firm in this industry. His aide, who specializes in women's woven underwear, is "on loan" from Barbizon, one of the principal competing manufacturers in this field. A succession of five or more chiefs of the Iron and Steel Division in the National Production Authority have been loaned by their companies, the major companies in the steel industry. The acting director of the Equipment and Materials Division of the Defense Transport Administration for most of 1951 was on loan from the American Car and Foundry Company. He actively promoted, for the Defense Transport Administrator, a plea that the NPA make available sufficient steel to build ten thousand freight cars a quarter; his firm . . . is engaged in the production of freight cars.

From time to time this sort of thing gets out of bounds, as in the recent cases of Air Force Secretary Talbott and Chairman Hugh Cross of the Interstate Commerce Commission, both of whom admitted error in using their official positions to advance their private interests. Much more often, there is no formal "conflict of interest." It is considered normal and natural for a steel man to lubricate with government contracts the growth of steel production; for a housing man to get more housing built by having the government absorb a good part of the risk;

for a farmers' representative to promote aid for farmers from inside the Department of Agriculture; for a labor organizer temporarily in the government to promote the right of labor to organize. We have institutionalized the inside track.

The political executive consequently has to do more than run his shop and deal with Congress. He has to maintain a complex network of horizontal relations with the veto groups whose interests his actions may affect, with others who think their interests might be affected, and with the surrogates of these groups in *both* the Executive and Legislative branches of the government.

I am trying hard not to pass any moral judgment on this system, but merely to describe how it seems to work. Given the nature of our society, it is almost bound to work this way. The government is, after all, the least bureaucratic of the major interest groups with which it has to deal. Turnover of government personnel is high, especially at the top. Even if this were not true for other reasons, we make sure of it by having reasonably frequent elections. The same is not true of the major aggregations of veto power outside: In business, labor, agriculture, and a good many other categories, elections are often a façade for maintaining the same leadership from year to year and even from decade to decade. If you don't like the President of the United States, you can vote against him every four years. If you don't like the president of General Motors or the head of a labor union, you can only wait for him to die.

This difference in tenure between government and outside interest groups is critical. If the outside leaders know more about the subject than their opposite numbers inside the government, if they are providing key experts, advisers, and sometimes even the political executives themselves, the views of the regulated are likely to be pretty influential with the regulators. In the United States, the road to the riskless society that Europeans call socialism is paved with the incestuous intention of nearly every major economic interest to bring in the government as the risk-taking partner.

Where, in this picture, does the "public interest" appear? Not, certainly, through the organized political parties, which inflate like balloons at election time and are of small consequence in governmental decision making the rest of the time. No, the defense of the public interest rests in the hands of the people as a whole, who can't do anything much about it, and of the President they elect, who can.

THE BUCK PASSES UP

Whether, under our system, the government ultimately serves the public interest, or merely obliges the private and sectional Trojan horses encamped inside the walls of the Federal bureaucracy, depends on the President to an extraordinary and alarming degree. He is the chief mediator among the veto groups, the one political executive whose whole job is to consider the situation as a whole. He is the one remaining safety man available to stop a specialized interest which breaks through the normal line of checks and balances and threatens to gain too much yardage at the expense of other groups.

In a revealing passage of his autobiography, Mr. Truman regarded it as quite natural that nobody should consider the public interest but the President.

> I was always aware, [he wrote] of the fact that not all of my advisers looked at the . . . problem in the same manner I did. This was nothing unusual, of course. It is the job of the military planners to consider all matters first and always in the light of military considerations. The diplomat's approach is—or in any case should be—determined by considerations of our relations to other nations. The Secretary of the Treasury thinks in terms of budget and taxes. Except for the members of his personal staff, each Presidential adviser has and should have a departmental outlook.

Though we sometimes make gods or supermen of our Presidents, they have not generally been more moral than most of us. The difference is that in the White House they are compelled to stand a little higher on the mountain than anybody else, and they consequently see farther at the horizon. It is this unique and lonely vantage point that lends grandeur to the American Presidency.

Yet the President's high rank does not necessarily mean that he makes more "decisions" than other political executives below. Indeed it is arguable that in our government, the higher one's rank the fewer decisions one makes. The man who buys paper clips makes a number of unreviewed decisions without consultation—what size and shape of paper clip, from whom to buy, at what price. As you go up the ladder of authority each official is beset with more committees, more horizontal clearances, more veto groups and political personalities whose views must be reconciled or discounted before the "final decision" is reached.

I once tried to get this important idea across to a very bright businessman who had just been appointed a division director and had promptly started to operate as if he were solely responsible for the program coordinated by that division. One day, months after he had taken office, I knew he would survive the transition to becoming a public servant. For he came to me and said: "I'm director of this program, but that doesn't mean I direct anybody, does it? I mean I don't make any *decisions*. I'm really a sort of broker, I guess."

The President's role as chief broker makes possible a certain order in the bureaucratic jungle. It is no accident that matters that frequently get to the White House are often better handled than matters that do not. The Housing Agency worked off in a corner by itself for years, dealing direct with the housing industry and hardly ever creating a crisis requiring Presidential attention. As a result, corrupt practices like "mortgaging out" under Section 608 came to be regarded by some as the natural order of things until Congress finally made a political scandal of them. The foreign-aid program, on the other hand, has spent more than $50 billion since the Second World War, with hardly a trace of scandal. Why? Could it be because so many departments and agencies were always fighting for the right to manage foreign aid that the program was a matter of monthly, even weekly, concern to the President himself?

The saving grace of our Executive bureaucracy, then, is that nearly everybody in it works for the President. To be sure, each political executive is also responsible horizontally to four or five Congressional committees; he has to deal with several outside interest groups whose leaders feel the executive is answerable to *them*; and within the Executive Branch he is constantly evading his own responsibility by burying it in collective decisions by interdepartmental committees. But when the chips are down on any one issue, all political executives are accountable to the President—which is another way of saying that if they get into a tight spot, they can generally pass the buck to him.

The buck passes *up:* Many of the most serious crises in our government's operations come from temporary lapses in following this first law of the jungle. Many elements of the present Federal security system—a major subject in itself when it comes to considering why it is so hard to get and keep good political executives—is a travesty of this principle. For the system legitimizes the downward passing of the buck, and even prepares ahead of time an endless file of scapegoats for administrative error and sacrificial lambs for periodic Congressional slaughter. It encourages a reversion to the old English principle that the king can do no wrong: If the government errs, it must be some spy in the ointment.

One lesson of our recent madness is clear—legislative usurpation generally takes the form of trying to find the disloyal official down the line on whom the blame for bad policy can be laid. The depth of the Army-McCarthy crisis was revealed when it became clear that Secretary Stevens, Counsel John Adams, and General Zwicker were to be left standing out in the rain without the umbrella of Presidential backing. The natural-law reply to that insistent question "Who promoted Peress?" was always plain: "The President did. Want to make something of it?"

Government is politics, but the Executive Branch has to be run by executives. And in government, as in other hierarchies, the buck can travel in one direction only—up.

75. *Let's Abolish the Government**

MEMORANDUM FOR SOME FUTURE HOOVER COMMISSION

THIS ARTICLE was written when the Hoover Commission report on the existing disorganization and need for reorganization of the executive branch of the government was being discussed from one end of the United States to the other. Mr. Catton satirically reminds us that some of the disorganization and inefficiency is caused by the very nature of government itself, and, indeed, that some of it is probably desirable. He bases these conclusions on his "Law of the Progressive Ossification of Structure," by which he means that in any organization, after a time, the way a job is done becomes more important than what is done. He points out that ideas are even more important than smoothly running machinery.

Gentlemen:

BY DIRECTION of the President and Congress, and at some expense, you have been called together to make studies and recommendations that will bring about a truly efficient and economical organization of the executive branch of the United States government.

* Bruce Catton, *Harper's Magazine*, 199 (August, 1949), pp. 97-98. Copyright, 1949, by Harper and Brothers. Reprinted by permission of the author and the publisher.

That is a fine idea and everybody seems to be in favor of it. The only trouble is that it just can't be done. For the immutable fact is that all government agencies, of any kind whatsoever, become completely unmanageable soon after they are born and stay that way forever. Neither the President, Congress, nor anyone else can control them; they can only give them things to do—and, unfortunately, government departments and agencies are quite unable to do anything whatever unless it happens to be something that they have been doing all along. Therein lies your problem, and your present method of approach won't even come close to solving it.

To help you out, I am submitting my own plan for remodeling the executive branch of government. It is very simple, and it is also the only plan on earth that will do any good. Briefly, it is as follows:

Let there be a constitutional amendment under which, once in every decade, the entire organization of government (except for the Presidency, Congress, and probably the Supreme Court) is automatically abolished, from the loftiest department down to the tiniest inter-agency committee. At high noon on a given day everything would vanish. There would be no State Department, no Department of Agriculture, no Federal Trade Commission, no nothing; the monumental buildings would remain, but they would for the moment be tenantless.

It would then be up to the President and Congress to set up a new government—new departments, agencies, boards, commissions, and whatnot. They would start from absolute scratch. They would not be reorganizing; they would be organizing afresh.

Obviously, they would have to think up some way to keep the physical assets of government—its airplanes, warships, dams, postage stamps, and so on—from being dissipated or stolen during the interim. That is a detail, and we won't go into it now. It could be done and I assume it would be done. My point is that only by a clean sweep such as I propose can the real problem of government organization be solved.

For my plan is the only one that recognizes the root of the evil—the great, fundamental law of government which for convenience (if that is the word) I have called the Law of Progressive Ossification of Structure. Under this law, the mechanism by which government actions are taken must, in the long run, become more important than the actions themselves, so that an agency reaches full manhood and relatively complete impotence simultaneously. It is as inexorable as the second law of thermodynamics, and there is no escape from it.

One little illustration will make the whole thing clear. A veteran government administrator remarked the other day that whenever he proposed that his own bureau take any positive action, he had to clear his proposal with at least twenty other people, any one of whom could block the action but no one of whom could make it possible. This man's bureau was originally set up to *do* things, of course; but this man (like every single one of his confrères) has found that he can actually make it do things only at the risk of getting stomach ulcers, acquiring a number of personal enemies, and ultimately getting unfrocked for heresy. Consequently, this man does as little as possible, in the most dignified way imaginable. He keeps quite busy at it, too.

You think you will solve all this simply by getting at and removing those twenty people? Gentlemen, that is the one thing you cannot possibly do. They *have* to be there. Look what you're up against. To get rid of them, you must abolish the Civil Service Commission, the Bureau of the Budget, the General Accounting Office, all of the personnel, budget-control, and supervisory sections of the individual departments, the right of Congress to control the purse-strings, the President's right to boss the executive branch, and the general theory that it ought to be impossible for anyone to steal or to waste public funds.

That's where those twenty obstructionists come from, and they are the people who make the Law of Ossification effective. You can't buck them. All you can do is get around them, by wiping the slate clean every so often and forcing everybody to start all over again. (What is in your favor, you see, is the fact that the fabulous twenty have to follow all of their own rules; hence it takes them a few years to get operating, and that's where you get your leeway.)

It was doubtless a dim awareness of this fact that led the New Dealers to set up so many new agencies instead of relying on the old-line Departments to carry out their program. The new agencies could operate while they were still new; the bloom began to go off the rose about the time those new agencies got into the inevitable groove and became concerned with orderly administration rather than with action. As of that moment, the New Deal became a historical item.

The objections to my proposal (and there are only two) can be met with ridiculous ease. The first one is that the whole business would be very rough on government workers, who would lose their jobs every ten years. But it wouldn't really be much worse than the strain and uncertainty that comes over them with every Presidential election; and anyway, by all our current traditions, government workers are unworthy people who *ought* to have it rough. This objection, you see, disappears at once.

The other objection is that my plan would make for inefficiency in government. That may well be true. I hope that it is true. That would be the greatest single argument in its favor. For the simple fact is that we don't really want our government to be very efficient. Its one saving grace, down through the years, has been its inefficiency. Democracy lives because of the lost motion in Washington. Eliminate the lost motion, and democracy is apt to die.

Have we over-lapping, duplication, and cross-purposes in government? Indeed we do—and we are all better off for it. It means that government can experiment, can proceed by trial and error, can try several approaches to the same problem, can reverse itself in mid-flight, and can accomplish something really big only when the public as a whole is back of it pushing—all of which is exactly what the government of a democracy ought to be like. Our government is so big that its hand rests upon all of us; the looseness of its grip is all that makes it tolerable.

No, gentlemen: you must not try to bring about true efficiency in government. It doesn't just happen that democratic governments are inefficient; the fact that they are so is what keeps them democratic. Of all totalitarianisms on earth, that of a genuinely efficient career-class of permanent-status civil servants would unquestionably be the worst, for it would be the one totalitarianism without any vestige of an ideology; a state which, in the end, ran things simply for the sake of obeying the rules of good administration.

All we really want is to have government put back within our reach and made moderately responsive, set up in such a way so that when we really want it to do something it can do it. Give us that, but don't give us efficiency. (You can't give us efficiency anyway, but we would not like it if you did, so forget it.) The Law of Progressive Ossification is your one valid target. It can be hit only by the Program of Decennial Abolition.

76. *"Gobbledygook"**

THIS SHORT EXCERPT explains itself. Former Congressman Maury Maverick issued the instructions to his employees in the hope of insuring that they would write or say what they meant in plain, straightforward English. He wanted them to avoid covering up a simple idea with fancy language—a standard practice in Washington and elsewhere.

* Maury Maverick, *Public Administration Review,* IV (Spring, 1944), p. 151. Reprinted by permission of the author and the publisher.

BE SHORT and use Plain English.

Memoranda should be as short as clearness will allow. The Naval officer who wired "Sighted Sub—Sank Same" told the whole story.

Put the real subject matter—the *point*—and even the conclusion, in the opening paragraph and the whole story on one page. Period! If a lengthy explanation, statistical matter, or such is necessary, use attachments.

Stay off gobbledygook language. It only fouls people up. For the Lord's sake, be short and say what you're talking about. Let's stop "pointing-up" programs, "finalizing" contracts that "stem from" district, regional or Washington "levels." There are no "levels"—local government is as high as Washington Government. No more patterns, effectuating, dynamics. Anyone using the words "activation" or "implementation" will be shot.

77. *Let's Go Back to the Spoils System**

REFORM of the civil service has been well described as the "romance" of the merit system, a reform desperately fought for and most necessary. Since the Pendleton Act of 1883 the merit system of filling government positions by competitive, non-political examinations has been held by some to be the continuing panacea for the ills of government. Efficiency could be produced only by freeing the administration from politics. Mr. Fischer's satirical article is a counter-irritant to this view. One of the unfulfilled recommendations of the President's Committee on Administrative Management was that the Civil Service Commission should be reconstructed under one head directly accountable to the President. Mr. Fischer urges that this recommendation be adopted. By this method he thinks that the devotion of the Civil Service Commission to keeping politics out of the federal service and its worship of personnel regulations could be harnessed to the larger task of efficient management of the federal service. In spite of its title Mr. Fischer's article is a plea for strengthening the merit system instead of abandoning it.

THE good citizens slapped each other on the back on the evening of January 16, 1883, and their hosannahs were heard throughout the land.

* John Fischer, *Harper's Magazine*, 191 (October, 1945), pp. 362-368. Reprinted by permission of the author and the publisher.

A reluctant Congress had just passed the Civil Service Act, which would guarantee an honest, efficient, and economical government forevermore. The corrupt political bosses finally had been routed; their thieving henchman would be shooed away from the public trough; and from then on federal jobs would be filled strictly on merit by the ablest men the country could produce. It was a major victory for Righteousness, Liberalism, and Good Government.

But somehow, in the sixty-two years since that glad day, the Great Reform has gone sour. Today Washington is filled with good citizens who lie awake nights thinking up new and sulphurous curses to hurl at Civil Service. Nearly every agency pays a large staff to figure out ingenious schemes for carrying on the public business in spite of Civil Service regulations. (These rules and regulations, couched in language that would gag a Philadelphia lawyer, fill a 524-page book, plus 46 pages of reference tables. Probably no living man wholly understands them; but they govern every waking hour of the three and a half million people in the federal service, including—*especially* including—their behavior off the job.) Thousands of typists, who might be doing useful work in a hand laundry, waste their dreary lives filling out stacks of Civil Service forms, usually in quintuplicate. A responsible executive officer in the War Department recently offered (very privately) his considered judgment that the Civil Service system had been the greatest single obstacle to the war effort.

Even Congress finally has recognized the failure of Civil Service. Whenever our lawmakers want to set up a really effective and businesslike agency—for example, TVA or the Federal Farm Mortgage Corporation—they always provide that it shall operate "without regard to the provisions of Civil Service."

II

What's gone wrong with Civil Service is easy enough to find out. You can get the story, in almost identical terms, from anybody who has ever held an executive job in Washington.

First of all, it's too slow. If you were an administrator in urgent need of a new assistant, you might hope to get somebody on the job—with luck and infinite finagling—in six or eight weeks. (He wouldn't be the man you want, of course.) In wartime the pace was a little faster—there were even cases in which a man was hired within a week—but even then par for the course was at least a month. If you wanted to beat that, you had to "hand process" the appointment, personally carrying the sheaf of papers through the maze of the agency personnel office and the Civil Service Commission, and mobilizing all the pressure you could, including telephone calls from the applicant's congressman.

When you want to fire a man, the procedure naturally is more tedious. In theory, it is as easy to get rid of an incompetent in the government service as it is in private industry; in practice, the ordeal may drag on for six or eight painful months. If you are an experienced administrator, you will never try to fire anybody—you will foist him off on some unsuspecting colleague in another bureau, or transfer him to the South Dakota field office, or reorganize your section to abolish his position.

I once spent a whole winter trying to "terminate," as Civil Service puts it, an elderly female clerk who had become so neurotic that no other woman could work in the same room with her. This involved written charges, interviews with my tearful victim, protests from her senator, indignant union delegations, and formal hearings before a panel of personnel experts. In the end I gave up and arranged for her transfer, with a raise in pay, to the staff of a trusting friend who had just joined the government. She is there to this day, chewing paper clips, frightening secretaries, and muttering to herself as she misfiles vital documents; I think of her every time I pay my income tax. My friend, who no longer speaks to me, is trying to get her transferred to the Veterans Administration, before General Omar Bradley learns how Washington works.

Even worse than the Civil Service Commission's leisurely gait is its delight in harassing the operating officials who are responsible for running the government. The typical administrator may spend as much as a third of his time placating the commission and the hordes of minor personnel specialists who infest Washington. He draws organization charts, argues with classification experts, fills out efficiency ratings, justifies the allocation of vacancies, and listens to inspiring lectures on personnel management until he has little energy left for his real job. He may search for hours for those magic words which, properly recited in a job description, will enable him to pay a subordinate $4,600 instead of $3,800. (The phrase "with wide latitude for exercise of individual initiative and responsibility" is nearly always worth $800 of the taxpayer's money; but it took me two years to find that out.)

No bureaucrat can avoid this boondoggling. If he fails to initial a Green Sheet or to attach the duplicate copy of Form 57, the whole machinery of his office grinds to a halt. If he deliberately flouts the established ritual, or neglects to show due respect for the personnel priesthood, his career may be ruined and his program along with it. In a thousand subtle ways the personnel boys can throw sand in the gears. They can freeze appointments and promotions, block transfers, lose papers, and generally bedevil any official who refuses to "co-operate." If they bog down a government project in the process, that is no skin off their backs—nobody can ever hold them responsible.

Nor can the administrator escape the Civil Service investigators, who drop in once or twice a week to question him about the morals, drinking habits, and possibly treasonable opinions of some poor wretch who has applied for a federal job. These investigators often are amusing fellows. I got well acquainted with one who formerly had been a small-town private detective; he had an uncommonly prurient mind, which led him to handle every case as if he were working up adultery charges for a divorce suit. Nearly all of them operate on the theory that anybody willing to work for the government must be a scoundrel, probably with Communist tendencies, who could never hold a job anywhere else. They have a boundless appetite for gossip, and they waste a lot of other people's time. What purpose they serve is obscure, because their investigations often are not completed until five or six months after the new employee starts work. If he actually were as villainous as they seem to suspect, he would have plenty of time to sell the country's secrets to a sinister foreign power before the investigators caught up with him.

These are minor indictments, however. The really serious charge against the Civil Service system is that it violates the most fundamental rule of sound management. That rule is familiar to every businessman: when you hold a man responsible for doing a job, you must give him the authority he needs to carry it out. Above all, he must be free to hire his own staff, assign them to tasks they can do best, and replace them if they don't make good.

In peacetime, at least, no agency operating under the trammels of Civil Service has this authority. Suppose, for example, that Congress sets up a special Flood Control Agency, with urgent orders to harness the rampaging Ohio River. The new FCA administrator, full of zeal, asks the Civil Service Commission to give him the best chief engineer the merit system can supply.

After some argument whether a first-class engineer—capable of earning $30,000 a year in private practice—is worth $6,500 to the government, the commission finally tells the administrator to take his choice of three men. They head its list of people who once took a Civil Service engineering examination. All the best men on the list have already been snapped up by other agencies, of course, because the last examination was held five years ago. And it wasn't a very good list in the first place, because few people in the profession knew that such an examination was being held. (It had been announced in a bulletin, printed in the kind of type used for Bible footnotes and displayed on postoffice notice boards between the Marine recruiting posters and the FBI photos of escaped kidnappers.)

Of the three "referrals," one turns out to be a professor at Freshwater Academy who never poured a yard of concrete in his life. The second is afflicted with a personality which makes it impossible for him to work in any organization. The third actually has had some practical experience—he once designed a garbage disposal plant—but he has no sympathy with the flood control program; he is a firm believer in Free Enterprise and non-interference with acts of God. The administrator has to take him anyway, although he personally knows a dozen better-qualified men who are eager to tackle the job.

During the next six months, while the administrator tries desperately to recruit the rest of his staff from Civil Service registers, the chief engineer surveys the Ohio River. He reports that flood control is neither practical nor desirable, and that in any case it should be left to private industry. Meanwhile, a flood wipes out Cincinnati, Louisville, and Paducah. With one voice the press denounces the administrator as a bungling bureaucrat, and a Senate investigating committee demands his head.

The Civil Service Commission, of course, is unperturbed. It has done its duty in preserving the merit system free from all taint of patronage. The sacred regulations have been kept intact. If a few thousand unfortunates have been drowned in the Ohio Valley, that is none of its concern.

Fantastic? Not in the least. In the past twelve years a number of government programs have been hobbled in precisely this fashion.

III

Although the defects of Civil Service are plain enough, the reasons for them are not so easy to find.

By no means all the blame rests on the Civil Service Commissioners. They are three earnest, well-meaning people, who grieve sincerely over the flaws in their organization.

The chairman of the commission is Harry B. Mitchell, a ruddy-faced Montana rancher and publisher, who once served as mayor of Great Falls. His health is none too robust, he has had no special training in large-scale management problems, and even his admirers do not describe his leadership as dynamic. Perhaps his chief interest has been the improvement of the retirement system for decrepit government employees. Appointed in the early months of the Roosevelt regime at the suggestion of the late Senator Tom Walsh, he serves—like his colleagues—

at the pleasure of the President. Since his son recently was elected senator from Washington, no one doubts that the President will be pleased to keep him on indefinitely.

The other Democratic member is Mrs. Lucille Foster McMillin, widow of a former congressman and governor of Tennessee. Her husband was the boon friend and political mentor of Cordell Hull, and she herself once represented Tennessee on the Democratic National Committee. So long as Hull's influence is felt in the Administration, her seat presumably is safe. A Southern gentlewoman of the old school, Mrs. McMillin devotes much of her energy to the protection of the federal working girl. Every fresh outbreak of rape in the Washington parks fills her with alarm, and she labors tirelessly to improve housing and working conditions for women.

Paradoxically, the commission actually is run by its lone Republican member, Arthur S. Flemming, the youngest, most progressive, and best qualified of the three. Roosevelt drafted him six years ago from the American University School of Public Affairs, which Flemming had directed with marked ability. To him belongs the credit for most of the wartime improvements in the commission's operations.

His major reform was a temporary relaxation of the regulations to give the war agencies considerable freedom in recruiting their own staffs, subject to a review of each appointment by the commission. He also has decentralized a good deal of responsibility to the field offices, brought in a number of able assistants, improved the techniques of examination, and cleaned out most of the witch-hunters and hayseed dicks from the investigation staff.

In these and other efforts to shore up their rickety machine, Flemming has won the assent of his Democratic colleagues by the exercise of unmeasured patience and tact. They now leave to him the day-to-day chores of management, and even permit him to speak for the commission before congressional committees. He has had less success, however, in gaining the support of the commission's permanent staff—the most inbred, tradition-ridden clique in Washington.

These veteran bureaucrats know that their bosses come and go, while they endure forever. They are skilled in the art of passive resistance, and they have no intention of letting any upstart commissioner tamper unduly with their time-hallowed procedures. Their idol is Theodore Roosevelt, the only Civil Service commissioner who ever attained national prominence—his desk is enshrined in the central hall of their F Street lair—and they look with grave suspicion on any ideas which he did not sanction in 1895.

The tight inner circle of the permanent staff is made up of men who started with the commission as messengers or clerks some twenty years ago, and rose to positions of power on the seniority escalator. Few of them have had any experience in private business or other government departments; they have little conception of the problems of an operating agency.

They have two guiding principles. The first is Keep the Rascals Out. Civil Service, in their view, is a kind of police force designed to keep political patronage appointees from creeping into federal jobs. This they do well—but they rarely feel any responsibility for positive action to make the government work, or to persuade the best possible men to enter the federal service.

The second aim of the commission bureaucracy is to increase the dignity and power of the personnel profession. To this end, they have developed a special jargon which no outsider can understand, plus an elaborate structure of regulations, red tape, and ritual which can be mastered only after years of study. They demand of the whole government what Dr. Floyd W. Reeves, professor of administration at the University of Chicago, has described as "an almost idolatrous worship" of the commission's "detailed and antiquated rules."

It is hard to blame them for this—after all, they are only doing what the legal and medical professions did centuries ago. The result, however, is a vested interest in complexity and formalism which is largely responsible for the ill-repute of the Civil Service system.

But the greatest share of guilt falls on Congress. Lacking any real enthusiasm for the Civil Service idea, it has never bothered to work out comprehensive legislation for a modern, effective system of personnel administration. Instead, over the course of years it has encrusted the original act of 1883 with scores of piecemeal amendments and special statutes. This has resulted in a legal patchwork which would baffle even the ablest and most aggressive commissioners. One law, for example, sets up special qualifications for coal mine inspectors; another provides that employees of the Farmers' Home Corporation must be residents of the states where they work; a third specifies that superintendents of national cemeteries must be disabled Army veterans—no sailors or Marines need apply. All of these laws, and many more like them, undermine the principle that the best man ought to get the job; each one is intended to confer special preference on some particular group of job-hunters. They are simply devices for legalizing favoritism and patronage on a large scale.

In addition, Congress has steadfastly refused to give the commission enough money to hire a proper staff or to run its business efficiently. (Until a few years ago, one of the field offices got along with a single telephone and borrowed chairs from the federal jail whenever it had to hold an examination.) Nor have there ever been funds to develop scientific testing methods, or to keep the registers fresh with frequent examinations.

It is true, of course, that the commission seldom fights aggressively for the money it needs, and that it sometimes has actually encouraged Congress to pass bad legislation. Only a few months ago, for example, the commission managed to have written into law one of its most hampering regulations—the so-called "Rule of Three," which limits choice in appointments to the three names at the top of the register. Dr. Reeves, a leading authority in the field of public administration, characterized this step as "a major disaster."

Nevertheless, such blunders would be impossible if Congress took an intelligent interest in the problems of federal employment. Of all the present congressmen, only one—Robert Ramspeck of Georgia—has shown such an interest. The attitudes of the rest range from indifference to frank contempt. As a result, government pay scales are notoriously low, and any bill designed to harass or discriminate against government workers is almost sure to pass with whoops of glee.

Worst of all, Congress has perpetuated the basic flaw in the original Civil Service Act. The commission is still an independent agency, entirely divorced from the normal structure of government. Although it wields great power it is responsible to no one. It serves only as a kind of decrepit watch-dog, which growls at the regular departments, but seldom tries to help them get their job done.

IV

It can be argued, in all seriousness, that Congress would do well to wipe out Civil Service, hide, horns, and tallow, and go back to the old-fashioned spoils system.

Any political party which believes intensely in its program presumably would choose the ablest men in its ranks to put that program into effect. Each administrator would be in sympathy with the project he is assigned to run, and he could expect loyal support from every subordinate. Moreover, he could count on fast action; no ward heeler could survive unless he handled appointments more promptly than the present Civil Service machinery.

Naturally every congressman would slip a few of his maiden aunts and broken-down henchmen onto the public payroll. But they could hardly be more useless or expensive than the thousands of personnel men now roosting in Washington. Indeed, the treasury might well save a few millions, since most political hacks are harmless creatures, who merely draw their pay and don't bother anybody, while personnel experts take great zest in pestering the working officials.

And if the party in power should ever load the payroll with too many thieves and incompetents, then a healthy democracy would throw out the whole gang at the next election. The constant threat of a change in administration would help keep all government employees on their toes; they would never dare sink into the smug mediocrity which now afflicts so many civil servants who are sure of indefinite tenure.

Such a forthright return to the patronage system would, however, be a pretty drastic step—probably more drastic than is actually necessary. Before junking Civil Service entirely, maybe Congress should consider replacing the 1883 jalopy with a 1945 model.

The blueprint for a modern and workable Civil Service is already at hand. It was drawn up in 1937, after months of careful study, by a group of experts from outside the government known as the Committee on Administrative Management. The committee's suggestions were warmly endorsed by most of the recognized authorities in this field, and the President urged Congress to put them into effect immediately. As usual, Congress wasn't interested, and nothing happened.

These proposals are still as sensible as they were eight years ago and even more urgently needed. They call for four major reforms:

1. The present commission should be abolished, along with its whole collection of red tape and the senescent bureaucrats who weave it. (These gentlemen should be permitted to leave Washington quietly, in spite of a widespread demand among other government workers that they be tarred, feathered, and ridden out of town on their own filing cabinets.)

2. Each agency should be permitted to hire its own help. They should be chosen strictly on merit, with all political influence ruled out, on the same basis which TVA now is using so successfully. Every department would then be able to get a competent personnel staff to replace its present herd of second-raters—it could attract good men because it could give them real responsibility.

3. A single Federal Personnel Administrator, responsible directly to the President, would lay down over-all policies for the various agencies, and see to it that they are carried out. (He would *not* try to enforce a multitude of petty rules.) His office also could carry on the few functions of the present commission which really need to be centralized —such as handling retirement funds, arranging transfers, and pooling the recruitment of minor employees.

4. A part-time, unpaid, non-political board should be set up to keep a wary eye on the administrator and on the personnel operations of the agencies. From time to time it might suggest general policies or standards. Its main job, however, would be to look out for the public interest, and make sure that the new, decentralized merit system actu-

ally worked with a minimum of political interference. (It would of course be impossible, and probably undesirable, to get a scheme which would be entirely free of politics. The present setup certainly is not —the whims of a senator now are treated with religious deference by nearly all Washington personnel men, from the commission down.)

These changes, plus a number of minor reforms suggested by the Committee on Administrative Management, should result in an immediate and substantial saving for the taxpayer. By eliminating the present overlapping and duplication between the functions of the Civil Service Commission and those of the agency personnel offices, it should make possible a sharp reduction in the total number of personnel men in Washington. What Dr. Reeves describes as the "elaborate, time-consuming, and costly reports" now prepared at the commission's behest could be dispensed with; every week, according to my rough estimates, this should save 1,328,772 forms, Green Sheets, affidavits, and classification charts, thus releasing from bondage whole regiments of typists. Moreover, many an expensive subterfuge could be abandoned. A department could put a new man on the regular payroll the day it needed him, for example, instead of hiring him as a "temporary consultant" at $25 a day during the months it takes for his appointment papers to trickle through the commission.

Far more important, however, would be the gains in speed and efficiency throughout the entire government. Offices no longer would be demoralized by the annual ordeal of efficiency ratings. Transfers and promotions might come through on schedule. Administrators could spend their time administering, instead of practicing the mumbo-jumbo of the Civil Service liturgy. Men of stature might then be more willing to enter the public service, and the machinery of government perhaps could cope a little more adequately with the unprecedented loads which are being thrust upon it.

It is too much, of course, to hope that Congress will do anything to improve the Civil Service on its own initiative. But President Truman already has asked Congress for authority to undertake a sweeping reorganization of all federal agencies. His request presumably will be acted upon early in the present session. If Congress does not exempt the Civil Service Commission from the reorganization—as it did when Roosevelt made a similar request—Truman will have a chance to give the merit system its first thorough overhauling. It may also be his one best chance to save his program from being marred, as Roosevelt's so often was, by inexcusable failures in administration.

78. *A New Look at the Vice Presidency* *

THE VICE PRESIDENCY was long regarded as a political dead end, an office of little consequence (see, for instance, George Mason's comments of 1787 in Selection 14). From time to time there would be a flurry of interest, but it was quick to abate. The following discussion is concerned not only with the history of the office but also, and primarily, with the "new look" in Vice Presidents. What are the problems and prospects of this office? Is it to assume a new significance in our governmental system?

ONCE AGAIN the nation has become achingly aware of the heartbeat on which the Presidential succession depends. Once again the national spotlight has swung to the Vice Presidency—the most neglected office in America.

Four times now in the last four decades Presidents have died in office or, like Woodrow Wilson in 1919 and Mr. Eisenhower today, have become too ill for a time to carry the grinding burden of the office. Three Presidents before that were assassinated, and two met natural deaths. Each of these occasions has aroused a flurry of interest in the Vice Presidency. Each time the interest has quickly died away.

Small wonder, for Americans like to joke about the office rather than think about it. The office was not two years old when a Senator suggested "His Superfluous Excellency" as the occupant's title. A wag of the Eighteen Nineties, watching Adlai E. Stevenson (grandfather of the present one) pass by, said, "There goes the Vice President of the United States with nothing on his mind except the health of the President." One Vice President likened his condition to that of a man in a cataleptic fit—conscious of all that goes on but unable to speak, move or even suffer pain.

In recent years the office has taken on a decided "new look." Vice President John Nance Garner helped put the New Deal through Congress and later helped slow it down. Henry A. Wallace ran some key war programs. During Alben W. Barkley's tenure the Vice President became a member of the National Security Council. Mr. Eisenhower, more than any President before him, has deliberately elevated and strengthened the Vice Presidential office. Richard M. Nixon has become one of the most publicized Vice Presidents in the history of the office.

* James MacGregor Burns, *The New York Times Magazine*, October 9, 1955, pp. 11, 67-70. Reprinted by permission of the author and publisher.

Will this "new look" continue? What did the framers of the Constitution want the office to be? Why did it become a piddling and comical job? What must be done to make the office of lasting use to the nation?

The Founding Fathers did not expect the Vice Presidency to be impotent. They saw its occupant as truly the second citizen of the land next to the President; some of them, indeed, feared that both as an Executive official and as President of the Senate he might wield a dangerous combination of powers. The first two Vice Presidents, John Adams and Thomas Jefferson, lived up to the framers' highest hopes. Each was a leading political figure; each went on to become President.

Then the office steadily deteriorated. Why?

One reason was a change in the method of choosing the Vice President. Originally he was the man who won next to the most votes for President in the Electoral College. Such a person must be a major figure in his own right. But the Twelfth Amendment, adopted in 1804, changed this. Henceforth electors chose between two slates, a Presidential and a Vice Presidential candidate on each.

The Vice Presidency might still have been a considerable post, but now a second factor came into play. The American party system began to take on the peculiar shape that it still has today. National party politicians, trying to win votes in a nation of checkered interests, sections and ideas, used the Vice Presidential nomination as a way of giving "balance" to the ticket. Sometimes this practice meant nominating for Vice President an ambitious factional leader hostile to the Presidential candidate. Sometimes it meant choosing some dignified old party warhorse whose only virtue was that he had antagonized nobody.

It is not surprising that the office lost its standing. There were, to be sure, occasional occupants of the stripe of John C. Calhoun or Andrew Johnson. But the names of many others have sunk into oblivion: Daniel D. Tompkins, Richard M. Johnson, George M. Dallas, Henry Wilson, William A. Wheeler. It was an office, wrote Gideon Welles in 1868, "without responsibility, patronage, or any duty worthy of honorable aspiration."

The main importance of the Vice Presidency during most of its existence was as a stepping stone to the White House. Since adoption of the Twelfth Amendment, only one occupant—Martin Van Buren—ever moved directly from the Vice Presidency into the Presidency by winning election to it. But in the amazingly short span of sixty years between 1841 and 1901, two Presidents died of illness and three by assassination. In several cases, however, fate played a deserved trick on the parties: representing a different party faction, the new President played ducks and drakes with his predecessor's appointees and policies. By the same token, the first four of these five "Presidents by chance" were unceremoniously dumped by their party and denied renomination at the end of their term. Only in the case of Theodore Roosevelt did the new President gain re-election.

The shots that killed McKinley projected into the White House a man who would not be content to serve the rest of the dead President's term and then fade from the limelight. Displaying his usual drive and gusto, Theodore Roosevelt steadily drew into his own hands the strings of party power. When he easily won the Republican nomination in 1904 and then the Presidential race, he demolished the tradition that a Vice President entering the White House by chance could not stay there on his own. Both Calvin Coolidge and Harry S. Truman duplicated this feat, and the office gained considerably in political prestige.

The main reason for the Vice Presidents' heightened stature, however, lies in the deliberate efforts of recent Presidents to give them added duties and powers. The Presidential office itself has become loaded down with heavy responsibilities, and Chief Executives have had to look for help where they could find it. Thus Franklin Roosevelt turned again and again to Garner for help in winning votes in both the House and Senate for New Deal bills. It was significant that in 1940 Roosevelt chose for his next running mate an experienced administrator, Henry A. Wallace, and for his third, a Senator, Harry S. Truman, who, it was hoped, could help put through crucial postwar legislation.

Later, President Truman had good reason to feel keenly that the Vice President should be in close touch with key affairs of state. As he has said recently in his memoirs, as Vice President he had not known about vital diplomatic and military developments, including the plans for the atomic bomb. During his second term the Vice President was made formally a member of the National Security Council with the result that Barkley had a voice in such important decisions as the defense of South Korea against invasion and the recall of Gen. Douglas MacArthur as Far Eastern commander.

It is under President Eisenhower that the Vice Presidency has come into its own. The President from the start wanted to strengthen the office; right after they both were nominated in Chicago in 1952, he told Senator Nixon that he did not want him to be a "Throttlebottom." In the first glow of enthusiasm, other Presidential nominees have made the same promise to their running mates, only to ignore them later on, but President Eisenhower stuck to his word.

The record is impressive. Mr. Eisenhower during his absences from Washington has put Vice President Nixon formally at the head of both the Cabinet and the National Security Council, thus outranking the highest officials in the Executive branch. The President has sent him on noteworthy goodwill trips to Asia and Latin America. Especially since Senator Robert A. Taft's death in August, 1953, Mr. Eisenhower has turned to his Vice President for help in putting his legislation program through Congress. He has asked him to appear for him at party rallies and to take the Administration's case to the country.

Mr. Nixon has played his part well. Only 39 when he took office, relatively inexperienced, and willing to be trained into his job, he has made the most of the President's sponsorship. He has also made the necessary adjustments. He considers his executive role far more important than his legislative job, he told this writer recently. His first loyalty is to the President; if an issue arises between the President and the Senate he acts as an agent of the former in trying to work out a compromise.

So thoroughly has the President built up the Vice Presidential office and so willingly has Mr. Nixon fit the office that the Vice Presidency today, in the words of Irving G. Williams, has gone into "a kind of second blooming of a century plant."

Must it take another hundred years or so for this century plant to bloom again? The answer to this question depends in the first instance on the President or Presidential candidate himself, and ultimately on the people as a whole. If it is initially the President who makes a strong office out of the Vice Presidency, what can we expect from future Presidents on this score?

The Chief Executive needs all the support and assistance he can get in managing his gigantic job. But obviously he will not turn for help to a Vice President who differs with him. It would be unprofitable and even dangerous to do so. Some Presidents have been on frigid terms with their Vice Presidents because they had little in common politically or personally. Thrown together on a hybrid ticket at the end of a long convention, they were at opposite poles in their party.

The problem, then, is to choose Presidential tickets each composed of men who will work in harmony if elected, the President giving big jobs to the Vice President and the latter willing to subordinate himself to his chief.

This problem would seem to be easy to solve, for it is well known that Presidential nominees ordinarily choose their running mates, and the convention merely ratifies his selection. In fact, though, the matter is not so simple.

The nominee may be politically in debt to state leaders who threw him some votes at the crucial moment, and he may pay off this debt with the Vice Presidential nomination, as did Roosevelt and Farley in the case of Garner in 1932. Or the nominee may be under heavy pressure to "reunite the party" by tossing the nomination as hush money to some faction disgruntled over losing the main contest. It takes a man of some vision to resist these immediate pressures and foresee his needs in the White House—if he gets there. He is likely to think almost entirely of the exacting campaign coming up, and to hope that things will work out later on. That is why we have so often ended up with an internationalist and an isolationist as Republican running mates, and with a liberal and a conservative on the Democratic ticket.

If, then, we cannot always depend on the Presidential candidate to exercise judgment on this score, the job ultimately will fall on the parties and on the voters. National convention delegates will have to discard the old idea that only a hybrid ticket can win. To be sure, they will want to keep the traditional balance, in the sense of pairing an Easterner with a Westerner, a younger man with an older man, a Senator from a rural state with a Governor from an urban state, and so on.

But balance in the sense of nominating men of opposing ideology is unnecessary and dangerous. The delegates should remember that the very mechanics of the convention, which cast aside party extremists in favor of moderates, insure that the convention's Presidential choice will represent the party consensus on major political issues.

After all, there is little evidence that hybrid tickets gain many votes. People tend to choose between Presidential tickets almost wholly in terms of the men at the head of the slate. It is doubtful that McNary won many votes for Willkie in 1940, or Bricker for Dewey in 1944; it is even more doubtful that a Knowland would help an Eisenhower Republican in 1956, or that a conservative Democrat would help Stevenson. On the contrary, voters may be more attracted by a Presidential ticket that in the case of a President's death, would elevate a man pledged to carry on the policies that a majority had backed at the polls.

In view of all this, we have good reason to hope for a continuation of the recent practice of nominating political running mates who, if elected, would make close executive teammates in the fullest sense. If these hopes are realized, the question arises as to whether the Vice Presidency as an office should be further strengthened in order to help the President handle his tasks. Concerned about this problem, a number of Congressmen and other officials in Washington are considering a four-point program to make the Vice President an "assistant" or even an "associate President":

1. *Give the Vice President more staff.* Mr. Nixon today has less staff than a Senator from California, yet he must make speeches to, answer letters

from, and consider himself a representative of a constituency of 160,000,000. Like any other important public official, he needs help on research, correspondence, public relations, speech-writing and the like.

2. *Provide the Vice President with an official residence and an adequate entertainment allowance.* Mr. Nixon today—and this may be even more true of his successors—finds himself in the awkward position of being entertained royally and officially on his trips to foreign lands and then, when his hosts pay him a return visit to Washington, finding it necessary to entertain them at a private club. Blair House has been suggested for the Vice Presidential residence.

3. *Equip him with an airplane, more office space, and other facilities that a modern executive needs.* At present, the Vice President has a rather small office in the Capitol. Since his job is and ought to be tied in closely with the Presidency, perhaps he should have space in the White House and his own secretariat should be integrated closely with that of the President.

4. *Clear up the confusion over Presidential disability.* When is an ill President unable to perform his constitutional duties? Woodrow Wilson's stroke in 1919 left him partially paralyzed and unable to carry the full Presidential load. The Cabinet was in confusion, and Vice President Thomas R. Marshall later commented bitterly that he did not dare even to ask about Wilson's health lest someone accuse him of longing for his place. Some historians believe that if Marshall had been able to take over, he might have prevented Senate rejection of the League of Nations.

Today Mr. Eisenhower's illness reminds us that another such dangerously chaotic situation could come at any time. Congress should provide for a permanent committee on Presidential disability, which, with the assistance of a panel of physicians of its own choice, would have power to authorize the Vice President to take over, and if conditions later permitted, to authorize the President to resume office.

Since vital matters might be at stake, such a committee should represent all three branches of government; it might well be composed of the Secretary of State and the Attorney General, the Vice President himself (who would thus have a voice, but not a final one, in the matter) and the Speaker of the House, and the Chief Justice of the United States as chairman.

It must be stressed again that the desirability of building up the Vice Presidential office by these and other means must be judged in terms of its impact on the Presidency. To strengthen an arm of the President is one thing. To create a stronger office for a Vice President who stands for some party element or party philosophy contrary to the President is something else—its effect would be to strengthen one more of the many centrifugal forces that already divide government and reduce its effectiveness in formulating and directing great programs at home and abroad.

Indeed, increasing Vice Presidential power outside the Presidential orbit in the long run would be dangerous for the Vice Presidency itself, since it would make the office and its powers a political football.

In that event, something far more radical might seem necessary—complete abolition of the office. John Randolph of Roanoke urged such drastic surgery when the office was only a few decades old; appalled by Vice Presidents' uselessness and capacity for mischief, students of politics have been advancing similar proposals ever since. Under these proposals the Senate would elect its own President.

If the Presidency became vacant for any reason, Congress would choose a temporary President until a new President could be selected at the time of the mid-term Congressional elections or at the usual four-yearly interval. Such a change, it is believed, would not require a Constitutional amendment, for it lies within the present powers of Congress.

Unfortunately, the plan has severe drawbacks. It would help only if Presidential death or disability occurred during the first fifteen months of his term, since at least six months are necessary for the complex process of choosing national convention delegates, holding conventions, and campaigning across the country. Hence Congress might be selecting "temporary" Presidents who would actually serve for two years or more.

Such Presidents would usually lack direct popular backing; they would doubtless owe their office to a coalition of powerful factions in Congress; they might be forced to mark time until another popular mandate was registered. This is a recipe for Presidential weakness—something that this country can least afford.

The Vice Presidency is here to stay. President and people, working together, have it in their power to make the incumbent a strong left arm for the man in the White House, and a trained and worthy successor if the office falls vacant. If these efforts fail, the office might best be allowed to return to its past impotence, when the Vice President's most important job was presiding over the Senate and his most significant policy statement was the deathless remark of Vice President Marshall that "what this country needs is a good 5-cent cigar."

79. *Youngstown Sheet & Tube Co. et al. v. Sawyer*

SUPREME COURT OF THE UNITED STATES,

1952 (CERTIORARI) 343 U.S. 579

THIS CASE is included as an interesting example of a discussion of the limits on executive power in our system of government. President Truman's seizure of the steel mills was declared null and void by the Court on grounds that neither was there statutory authorization for it nor could it be justified on the basis of the President's authority as Commander in Chief. The decision also illustrates the vitality of the separation of powers theory in our government, for the Court pointed out that President Truman's act, had it been allowed to stand, would have been an invasion of the legislative authority of the Congress.

MR. JUSTICE BLACK delivered the opinion of the Court.

We are asked to decide whether the President was acting within his constitutional power when he issued an order directing the Secretary of Commerce to take possession of and operate most of the Nation's steel mills. The mill owners argue that the President's order amounts to lawmaking, a legislative function which the Constitution has expressly confided to the Congress and not to the President. The Government's position is that the order was made on findings of the President that his action was necessary to avert a national catastrophe which would inevitably result from a stoppage of steel production, and that in meeting this grave emergency the President was acting within the aggregate of his constitutional powers as the Nation's Chief Executive and the Commander in Chief of the Armed Forces of the United States. The issue emerges here from the following series of events:

In the latter part of 1951, a dispute arose between the steel companies and their employees over terms and conditions that should be included in new collective bargaining agreements. Long-continued conferences failed to resolve the dispute. On December 18, 1951, the employees' representative, United Steelworkers of America, C.I.O., gave notice of an intention to strike when the existing bargaining agreements expired on December 31. The Federal Mediation and Conciliation Service then intervened in an effort to get labor and management to agree. This failing, the President on December 22, 1951, referred the dispute to the Federal Wage Stabilization Board to investigate and make recommendations for fair and equitable terms of settlement. This Board's report resulted in no settlement. On April 4, 1952, the Union gave notice of a nation-wide strike called to begin at 12:01 A.M. April 9. The indispensability of steel as a component of substantially all weapons and other war materials led the President to believe that the proposed work stoppage would immediately jeopardize our national defense and that governmental seizure of the steel mills was necessary in order to assure the continued availability of steel. Reciting these considerations for his action, the President, a few hours before the strike was to begin, issued Executive Order 10340. . . . The order directed the Secretary of Commerce to take possession of most of the steel mills and keep them running. The Secretary immediately issued his own possessory orders, calling upon the presidents of the various seized companies to serve as operating managers for the United States. They were directed to carry on their activities in accordance with regulations and directions of the Secretary. The next morning the President sent a message to Congress reporting his action (*Cong. Rec.*, April 9, 1952, p. 3962). Twelve days later he sent a second message (*Cong. Rec.*, April 21, 1952, p. 4192). Congress has taken no action.

Obeying the Secretary's orders under protest, the companies brought proceedings against him in the District Court. Their complaints charged that the seizure was not authorized by an act of Congress or by any constitutional provisions. The District Court was asked to declare the orders of the President and the Secretary invalid and to issue preliminary and permanent injunctions restraining their enforcement. Opposing the motion for preliminary injunction, the United States asserted that a strike disrupting steel production for even a brief period would so endanger the well-being and safety of the Nation that the President had "inherent power" to do what he had done—power "supported by the Constitution, by historical precedent, and by court decisions." The Government also contended that in any event no preliminary injunction should be issued because the companies had made no showing that their available legal remedies were inadequate or that their injuries from seizure would be irreparable. Holding against the Government on all points, the District Court on April 30 issued a preliminary injunction restraining the Secretary from "continuing the seizure and possession of the plants . . . and from acting under the purported authority of Executive Order No. 10340."

• • • • •

The President's power, if any, to issue the order must stem either from an act of Congress or from the Constitution itself. There is no statute that expressly authorizes the President to take possession of property as he did here. Nor is there any act of Congress to which our attention has been directed from which such a power can fairly be implied. Indeed, we do not understand the Government to rely on statutory authorization for this seizure. There are two statutes which do authorize the President to take both personal and real property under certain conditions. However, the Government admits that these conditions were not met and that the President's order was not rooted in either of the statutes. The Government refers to the seizure provisions of one of these statutes (201 (b) of the Defense Production Act) as "much too cumbersome, involved, and time-consuming for the crisis which was at hand."

Moreover, the use of the seizure technique to solve labor disputes in order to prevent work stoppages was not only unauthorized by any congressional enactment; prior to this controversy, Congress had refused to adopt that method of settling labor disputes. When the Taft-Hartley Act was under consideration in 1947, Congress rejected an amendment which would have authorized such governmental seizures in cases of emergency. Apparently it was thought that the technique of seizure, like that of compulsory arbitration, would interfere with the process of collective bargaining. Consequently, the plan Congress adopted in that Act did not provide for seizure under any circumstances. Instead, the plan sought to bring about settlements by use of the customary devices of mediation, conciliation, investigation by boards of inquiry, and public reports. In some instances temporary injunctions were authorized to provide cooling-off periods. All this failing, unions were left free to strike after a secret vote by employees as to whether they wished to accept their employers' final settlement offer.

It is clear that if the President had authority to issue the order he did, it must be found in some provision of the Constitution. And it is not claimed that express constitutional language grants this power to the President. The contention is that presidential power should be implied from the aggregate of his powers under the Constitution. Particular reliance is placed on provisions in Article II which say that "The executive Power shall be vested in a President . . ."; that "he shall take Care that the Laws be faithfully executed"; and that he "shall be Commander in Chief of the Army and Navy of the United States."

The order cannot properly be sustained as an exercise of the President's military power as Commander in Chief of the Armed Forces. The Government attempts to do so by citing a number of cases upholding broad powers in military commanders engaged in day-to-day fighting in a theater of war. Such cases need not concern us here. Even though "theater of war" be an expanding concept, we cannot with faithfulness to our constitutional system hold that the Commander in Chief of the Armed Forces has the ultimate power as such to take possession of private property in order to keep labor disputes from stopping production. This is a job for the Nation's lawmakers, not for its military authorities.

Nor can the seizure order be sustained because of the several constitutional provisions that grant executive power to the President. In the framework of our Constitution, the President's power to see that the laws are faithfully executed refutes the idea that he is to be a lawmaker. The Constitution limits his functions in the lawmaking process to the recommending of laws he thinks wise and the vetoing of laws he thinks bad. And the Constitution is neither silent nor equivocal about who shall make laws which the President is to execute. The first section of the first article says that "All legislative Powers herein granted shall be vested in a Congress of the United States. . . ." After granting many powers to the Congress, Article I goes on to provide that Congress may "make all Laws which shall be necessary and proper for carrying into Execution the foregoing Powers, and all other Powers vested by this Constitution in the Government of the United States, or in any Department or Officer thereof."

The President's order does not direct that a congressional policy be executed in a manner prescribed by Congress—it directs that a presidential policy be executed in a manner prescribed by the President. The preamble of the order itself, like that of many statutes, sets out reasons why the President believes certain policies should be adopted, proclaims these policies as rules of conduct to be followed, and again, like a statute, authorizes a government official to promulgate additional rules and regulations consistent with the policy proclaimed and needed to carry that policy into execution. The power of Congress to adopt such public policies as those proclaimed by the order is beyond question. It can authorize the taking of private property for public use. It can make laws regulating the relationships between employers and employees, prescribing rules designed to settle labor disputes, and fixing wages and working conditions in certain fields of our economy. The Constitution does not subject this lawmaking power of Congress to presidential or military supervision or control.

It is said that other Presidents without congressional authority have taken possession of private business enterprises in order to settle labor disputes. But even if this be true, Congress has not thereby lost its exclusive constitutional authority to make laws necessary and proper to carry out the powers vested by the Constitution "in the Government of the United States, or any Department or Officer thereof."

The Founders of this Nation entrusted the lawmaking power to the Congress alone in both good and bad times. It would do no good to recall the historical events, the fears of power and the hopes for freedom that lay behind their choice. Such a review would but confirm our holding that this seizure order cannot stand.

The judgment of the District Court is

Affirmed

(Mr. Chief Justice Vinson, with whom concurred Mr. Justice Reed and Mr. Justice Minton, rendered a dissenting opinion.)

XIV

THE GOVERNOR AND STATE ADMINISTRATION

80. *An Effective Chief Executive**

The enormous increase in national government functions in recent years has been duplicated on a smaller scale in state governments. Yet state governmental machinery, following the attitudes of state constitution builders of the second half of the last century was elaborately and inflexibly designed to check any possibility of abuse of power by state governmental agencies. The fear of abuse went so far that even the possibility of effective action by state governments was made exceedingly difficult. The standard restrictions hedging the office of state governor are a fair example of the restrictive tendency. All the governors were given official families of independently elected officials through whom to exercise their executive functions. The problem of coordinating the exercise of the functions of state government is almost insoluble under the existing state constitutions. Yet the business of managing state government is becoming increasingly complex. One of the solutions, put forward in Minnesota, was the creation of the office of commissioner of administration, who was responsible, under the governor, for the business management of the state, leaving the governor free to set general policies, and carry on his political functions. Mr. Gravlin describes how the office of commissioner of administration operated at its inception.

Not many years ago the governorship of Connecticut was regarded as a part-time job. The state's chief executive could comfortably dispose of

* Leslie M. Gravlin, *National Municipal Review*, 36 (March, 1947), pp. 137-141. Reprinted by permission of the author and the publisher.

his work within the few hours he spent daily in his office at the capitol. His annual salary was a pittance, no doubt because it was thought he earned no more.

Connecticut had not yet entered the struggle to get itself out of the mud nor had it embraced far-reaching programs of health and social welfare. It carried on with a small budget and few taxes. State employment then was small.

Able leaders in business were active in the guidance of the various departments where they served on part-time boards, and the state's operations were not so complex that close managerial direction from the top was an imperative. We could say the same thing about many other states in that era before the states began to assume a place of greater importance in the governmental scene. In a lesser degree much the same condition applied to our cities.

But it remained for the cities to blaze a trail which is not sufficiently appreciated in this country. Daring to strike out in new directions they first brought into being the commission form of government, trying to establish in government the principle of a small policy-determining body comparable to the board of directors so common in the world of business. When it became apparent that in too many instances this produced a headless organization they ventured to adapt the system to a council-manager plan in which the basic principle of separated powers is observed but in which there is an executive trained in public administration. They found the answer to making the executive more effective.

The idea of a manager, which finds growing acceptance in our cities, towns and counties, cannot, and I do not say that it should, be reproduced in its entirety in our systems of state or federal government. Yet it is significant that at least one state has borrowed liberally from it and there has been more and more talk about management at the federal level. Recently Congressman Monroney proposed the election of two vice presidents, one of them to be in effect a federal business manager. The congressman's proposal would, of course, require a constitutional amendment. In Minnesota the change was possible without altering the constitution.

Minnesota's now proven experiment, and the kind of thinking propounded by one of the leaders in congressional reform, may indicate a new trend in our concept of the executive, not alone in state government but in national as well. Perhaps we are now ready to recognize the tremendous burden which we place on our governors and presidents. But these remarks will be confined to observations drawn from my experience as an administrator serving a governor.

Let us assume that we are thinking about an elected chief executive

—a governor chosen by the people. That is the pattern set by our state constitutions and there is no reason to believe that the people would consider giving up their choice of the state's chief executive to have an appointive manager. So long as there are important issues on which the desires of voters may be in conflict we can expect the people to want to elect their governor. At the local level, where the cleavages of public opinion on basic issues are absent, we have a different picture. Therefore, a mayor limited to political leadership and a manager to direct administration are wholly in keeping with recognized democratic principles.

Consider a governor, however, who has to campaign for office, see thousands of people who feel they must talk to him, consult with party leaders and workers, guide legislative programs to which he or his party are pledged, serve on a pardon board, pass on extradition matters, make innumerable speeches, greet distinguished visitors, and always be planning for the next election. Somehow, in between that trip to the far-off corner of the state to address the crowd at the county fair and the next day's conference with the delegation that wants its teachers' college made into a branch of the state university, he must, in the absence of some device to meet the situation, attend to that question about making the welfare appropriation do to the end of the year.

EXECUTIVE POWERS LIMITED

Also consider the limitations of executive power that prevail so widely under our state constitutions. We must recognize the fact that a governor's authority may be seriously modified by the executive power shared by elected auditors, secretaries of state and attorneys general, who may even be of an opposing political persuasion. How can a governor faced with such restrictions, if not actual obstacles, not to mention a sprawling mass of boards and commissions largely appointed by predecessors, effectively direct the administration of state affairs?

The series of state governmental reorganizations that followed the first world war were predicated on the assumption that the governor himself could fulfill the function of administrator if the host of boards, commissions and independent agencies could be regrouped into a few major departments whose heads would in effect be a governor's cabinet.

Undoubtedly great good has come from the consolidation of state agencies. The reduced span of executive control is in itself a gain. But in too many instances the expected results did not follow.

Such a reshuffling still leaves a managerial responsibility which few if any governors can effectively discharge. Minnesota's success with its department of administration, even under an organizational plan which did not proceed as far as it might have in the direction of consolidation, confirms this belief.

As a leader in legislation and the head of the state government who must be in constant touch with the public, the executive must be freed from all but the most important problems of state management. The Minnesota plan has met this requirement. At the governor's right hand is the commissioner of administration, who has come to be more commonly known as the state business manager. He is the governor's alter ego in matters of administration.

GOVERNOR LAYS DOWN POLICY

Only management problems which clearly must be settled by the governor—generally matters of a policy type—take up the time of the governor. As an illustration let us take the budget. Under Minnesota's law there is definitely an executive budget. But the time-consuming task imposed on some governors who are required to sit patiently through long hearings in preparing the budget is eliminated. The governor merely lays down the over-all polices and the commissioner of administration with his staff conduct the budget conferences, after which the completed budget is submitted to the governor for final consideration. It then goes to the legislature together with the governor's budget message.

In a similar way the governor establishes the policy to be used in cutting back allotments when falling revenues make it necessary to take such action. In the first two years under the system spending of appropriations had to be curbed. Aside from a few basic decisions such as the amount to be saved, and exceptions to be made such as state school aids, the details were left to the discretion of the commissioner. The governor was periodically informed of the financial condition of the state through quarterly reports from the commissioner's office and occasionally by special memoranda.

Both of these provisions as to budgeting were, of course, prescribed by law.

Obviously, no law can prevent department heads from going to the governor with their worries but in my own experience there was exceedingly little of that. In this connection it might be pointed out that an important instrument in promoting direct relations between the commissioner and the various departments was the cabinet meeting which was held at frequent intervals. At such conferences, presided over by Governor Stassen, the policies to be carried out through the commissioner of administration were clearly outlined for department heads. Thus the governor relieved himself of many individual meetings with the administrators of the operating agencies.

But the real advantage of such a reorganization lies in the constant attention that the commissioner of administration can give to operating problems. The governor, whose calendar of appointments is always filled, leaving no idle hours to extract from talk and tables the facts that are essential to wise administrative decisions, is not equipped to do such a job well.

If the executive must rely on several officials to provide data on any given question of administration, he must sift out the facts and piece them together himself. But if he can turn to one official, who is clothed with adequate authority and provided with a qualified staff, to keep him informed, his effectiveness is increased immeasurably. Minnesota's unsuccessful reorganization plan of 1925 failed to heed this fact, and the commission of administration and finance then created soon exhibited the weaknesses of board control. By and large it added little to the effectiveness of the chief executive.

COORDINATION UNDER MANAGER

Like so many administrative boards it quickly apportioned spheres of influence so that the business of the purchasing commissioner, for instance, became none of the business of the budget commissioner. The reorganization act of 1939, in which the department of administration with a single head was created, brought an end to this lack of coordination. The commissioner of administration, appointed for a term coinciding with that of the governor, was vested with most of the powers previously entrusted to the "Big Three." Ex-officio he was budget director and purchasing agent.

The importance of this linking of related functions under one man definitely answerable to the governor cannot be overestimated in evaluating it as a device for increasing the effectiveness of the executive. Great importance attaches also to the power of the commissioner of administration over salary schedules and salary adjustments granted to employees of the civil service. Here we have a practical example of how a governor can assume his expected responsibility for expenditures because he knows that all the elements affecting those expenditures can be managed at one point.

It may be demonstrated by example just how purchasing was made to play its part in wiping out Minnesota's inherited deficits of 1939. Knowing that we had to get out of the red and also prevent any current deficits we overlooked no opportunities to achieve success. A competent purchasing agent was no small factor.

An illustration is the saving made in the purchase of liquor and beer tax stamps. Prior to 1939 they had been bought from one company and without open competitive bidding. The state had been paying $110,000 per year for the stamps. Open competitive bidding reduced the contract to about $17,000.

We were, of course, in a buyers' market which increased the possible savings, but the development of specifications contributed very definitely to reduced expenditures for supplies, materials and equipment. While establishing good standards for foods and other items for state institutions we at the same time cut expenditures for such purposes about 10 per cent the first year. This accomplishment was not alone the result of coordinated efforts of the commissioner of administration and his subordinate, the purchasing agent. It also meant close cooperation with the director of institutions.

The governor was not left in the position of uttering pious hopes about preventing deficits and then leaving it to chance that several agencies would achieve such a result. His policies were effectively executed by a centralized authority employing simple managerial procedures. And certainly no executive can be effective who cannot produce the fiscal results expected of him by the public.

Moreover the lessons distilled out of the continuing experience of such an executive agency as a department of administration lay the foundation for the success of future governors.

VARIED TASKS OF MANAGER

The aspects of state management are so varied that one can do no more than sketch them briefly here. Minnesota's consisted of much more than preparing budgets and allotting funds and controlling their expenditure. To cite a few, there was the work with the highway department and the attorney general's office to establish sound and abuse-proof policies in the rental of equipment, our assistance in developing a practical annual-wage plan for certain classes of highway labor, and setting up property inventories and transferring unused equipment from one agency to another. The department also organized central agencies for the distribution of office supplies and the maintenance of typewriters. All but a few agencies with special problems were required to use a central duplicating division.

The tasks of management in state government are beset on the one hand by the diffusion of authority among the numerous departments, boards, bureaus and commissions and, on the other, by the acute sense of independence that many of them develop from having their own funds. The lush spending of one well heeled department and the starvation diet of another depending on the generosity of a legislature for its support impose a difficult task on an official responsible for the budgetary control of both. Yet it was found possible to enforce somewhat similar standards of operation on both, using the authority of the comprehensive budget control law. Stimulation of careful programming was sought.

Experience no doubt will disclose refinements that will be necessary in the organization and scope of the Minnesota plan. It is unfortunate that the original act did not coordinate the state's accounting with its budgeting by putting the two functions together in the department of administration. But as a tool for making the chief executive more effective it has solidly established itself.

81. *Administration in State Governments* *

IN THIS selection, one of a group of papers prepared for a conference on the role of the states in our governmental system, Professor Willbern is primarily concerned with the traditions of American state administration, the reorganization movement of this century, and the major issues of today. The federal system, as we know it, assumes a vital and significant role for the states. They are today challenged as never before to act this role effectively. All parts of state government are involved, but certainly administration—the very embodiment of today's big government—has a leading part.

STATE ADMINISTRATION IS A BIG OPERATION

MORE THAN a million people are employed directly by state governments in the United States. Local units of government, which are created and supervised by the states, employ nearly four million more. Together, state and local governments employ twice as many civilian employees as does the national government.

In 1953 state government expenditures amounted to almost $17 billion. Local governments spent over $21 billion. In the same year, the national government spent over $80 billion, but state and local expenditures combined were considerably in excess of those Federal expenditures not related to national defense and security. In fact, state

* From "Administration in State Governments" by York Willbern in *The Forty-eight States: Their Tasks as Policy Makers and Administrators*, December, 1955, published by The American Assembly, Columbia University, as background papers for participants in the Eighth American Assembly. With permission of The American Assembly.

governments alone spent nearly the same amount as the national government on non-war-connected activities.

Among the three chief levels of government in the United States—national, state, and local—state government ranks third as measured by expenditure and number of personnel. Expenditures aggregating $17 billion and employees totaling over one million indicate, however, very large and sweeping operations. Note, too, that state expenditures and state employment rolls have been expanding at a more rapid rate in the ten years since World War II than have those of either the national government or local governments.

The management of this many employees and this much money would be a challenge to any business enterprise. To be sure, we are talking about 48 state administrations. In some of them the scale of operation is quite modest. But in each of the 10 states with over half the nation's population, the operation is large, involving expenditures from $430 million in North Carolina to $2 billion in California.

State administration is big in other ways less measurable than money and employees. It is big in significance to the people. Education, highway transportation, public welfare, public health, industrial safety, regulation of utilities, banks, insurance, professions—these are not light responsibilities. State administration is big, too, in terms of complexity. It has its own problems of complexity because its functions are so diversified. These, though, are compounded by the need to link what it does with what the national and local governments are doing in the same fields. Not the least of the problems grows out of the fact that, since all local units of government are ultimately creatures of the state government, there is a sort of reserve power in each state to supervise or control their functions. In Phenix City, Alabama, when the breakdown of local law enforcement agencies became notorious, the governor of the state took over the police function through the state militia, and the state attorney general sent in state prosecutors and investigators. Less extreme situations regularly command less dramatic state interest and action.

ORGANIZING THE ADMINISTRATION

THE INHERITED PATTERN

In the earliest days of American state government, executive or administrative activities were dominated by the legislatures. The American Revolution had been a war as much against colonial governors as against British rule—the two were hardly separable in the minds of the people. The first state constitutions provided for a separation of powers, but the legislatures completely dominated the government.

As the legislature gradually lost its pre-eminence during the nineteenth century, it was replaced largely by the electorate rather than by the executive. When the original constitutions began to be revised, the chief impelling motive was the extension of the suffrage and increased participation by the electorate. Not only was the governor to be independently elected, but judges and the other executive officers were also subjected to popular choice.

This process of increasing the scope of popular election continued well into the twentieth century. It produced the "long ballot," common in many states. In recent years, in a few states, there has been a slight reduction in the number of elected officials. Yet, in 1950 the number of elected state executives and administrative officials in each state averaged about 13. The range was from 2 in New Jersey (after its new constitution) to 37 in Nevada.

It is proper to say that most American states have a plural executive, in one sense, although the elected officials do not form a collegial body.

Despite some evidences of distrust, Americans have not hesitated to use government in a great many ways. When a social problem of any consequence appears, the reaction of the people frequently is "Let there be a law" on the subject. Soon thereafter, and sometimes at the same time, the reaction is "Let there be an agency." Although there have been some reductions in number of agencies in some states, the tendency to create new administrative agencies is far from halted. . . .

Not only should the total number of state agencies be noted, but the number of major departments indicated is worth special notice. To have as many as 54 (Texas) or 78 (Oregon) major departments indicates a highly fragmented view of the responsibilities of the state government.

The development of such a great number of separate agencies has been a cause for concern by many observers of state government. The job of holding 30, or 50, or 70, or 100 state agencies separately responsible, either to the legislature or to the electorate, seems an impossible task. Many persons have been, and are, worried about the possibility of overlapping and duplication. There seems no doubt that, in housekeeping matters at least, many of these agencies are trying to do separately what can be done better jointly.

DEMANDS FOR CHANGE

While the tendencies and pressures for further "administrative sprawl" have continued, there has been since about 1910 a substantial contrary tendency. This is generally called the state reorganization movement. While there were of course germinating ideas at an earlier time, the beginning of the modern period of administrative reorganization in the United States may be connected to President Taft's Commission on Economy and Efficiency in the national government, in 1911. In the early years of that decade, studies and proposals were made in Oregon, Wisconsin, Massachusetts, and New Jersey. In New York, a carefully studied and comprehensive set of proposals was made in 1915. The first sweeping administrative reorganization took place in Illinois in 1917 under the leadership of Governor Lowden. In a new civil administrative code, Illinois consolidated about 54 independent agencies into 14; the heads of nearly all of these new departments were made subject to appointment by the governor.

Illinois was followed by many other states. By 1925, 15 states had had substantial reorganization, including most of the leading industrial states. The reorganization movement continued, with various slowdowns and speed-ups through the 1920's and 1930's. By the beginning of World War II, about 30 states had had substantial reorganizations, and nearly every state had had studies and proposals looking in that direction. Some states had been reorganized twice, or even three times. A substantial business was conducted by several management survey and public administration consulting firms, making studies and proposals for the reorganization of state administrative systems.

Since the war, and particularly since 1947, there has been a striking rash of reorganization studies and proposals.

LITTLE HOOVER COMMISSIONS

Reorganization study commissions in the states were similar to, and frequently patterned after, the national Commission on Organization of the Executive Branch of the Government, of which former President Herbert Hoover was chairman. They were generally known as, and sometimes formally named, Little Hoover Commissions. Since 1947 approximately 32 of the 48 states have had official studies accompanied with recommendations concerning their administrative organization. The study commissions varied in size from 4 to 41 members; most of them had some 7 to 13 members. They were chosen in various ways, and had differing relations with the governors and legislatures.

Altogether, the studies constituted an impressive display of consideration of the state administrative machinery. The amount of financial support varied considerably, and the intensity and quality of the study efforts also had wide variations, but there were many instances of thorough, searching investigation and careful consideration of the recommendations.

The results of the series of postwar investigations have been very modest, if we reckon them in terms of legislative enactment of commission recommendations. In 1953, after 24 states had completed their studies and given state legislatures one session or more in which to consider commission recommendations, the legislative response in only 2 of the 24 states—New Hampshire and New Jersey—was pronouncedly positive. An evaluation made primarily by Professor Karl A. Bosworth, concluded that in 9 of the 24 states the legislative reception was either completely negative or so slight as to be regarded as a "soundly negative response," while in the other 13 there was some 30 to 50 per cent adoption of the commission proposals. Events since the publication of this study do not indicate that the pattern of generally negative response has changed. It is still appropriate to remark on "such meager accomplishment from so much effort."

GUIDING PRINCIPLES OF THE REORGANIZATION MOVEMENT

With rare exceptions and minor qualifications, all the state reorganization movements of the last 40 years have been dominated by the same assumptions or "principles." Many years ago, Arthur E. Buck, one of the most active of the reorganizers, put them this way:

1. Concentration of authority and responsibility
2. Departmentalization, or functional integration
3. Undesirablity of boards for purely administrative work
4. Coordination of the staff services of administration
5. Provision for an independent audit
6. Recognition of a governor's cabinet

Support for the sixth of these principles has not been as uniform or as widespread as for the others, but the other five could be stated as the credo of most of the commissions.

In 1949, The Council of State Governments sponsored a conference of representatives of twenty state reorganization commissions which were then active. The consensus of their deliberations was summarized as follows:

> In general it was felt that reorganization movements should result in strengthening the office of the governor; reducing the independent agencies and administrative boards and commissions and grouping them into major departments; extending the gubernatorial power of appointment and removal of department heads; and strengthening executive controls over budgeting, accounting, purchasing, state property, etc. At the same time, it was pointed out, it is of the utmost necessity to revise legislative procedures in the direction of greater efficiency, and to provide the legislature with more effective reporting and auditing controls—in order that the executive may be held to proper accountability.

The Commission on Intergovernmental Relations, in its report of June, 1955, said that there was "substantial agreement" that these arrangements "if generally applied, would greatly strengthen state administration."

Perhaps the most basic of the reorganization "principles," and the one most difficult of realization in practice, is that of the unity of the executive branch under the governor. The state reorganization commissions have consistently urged the general principle of executive unity, although the recommendations of many have stopped short of complete adherence. Concentration of authority and responsibility, it was argued, is essential both to good management and to democratic control of policy.

The grouping of related agencies into a few major departments has also been considered essential. The most frequently used summaries of the effect of reorganization programs have been comparisons of the number of independent agencies existing after the reorganization with the number existing before; the most successful reorganization was the one which found the largest number of agencies and reduced this to the smallest number.

The substitution of single administrators for boards or commissions at the heads of agencies has been another goal for the reorganizers. The multiplication of boards and commissions has been one of the most significant and notable features of the growth of state administration in the last 80 or 90 years. Studies by the Little Hoover Commissions found, for example, that Nevada had 73 boards and commissions, Washington had 56, Mississippi had 50 boards and commissions appointed by the governor and numerous others chosen in other ways.

Many of these boards and commissions, of course, have comparatively minor and unimportant responsibilities. But there remain a number of major departments that are also headed by boards or commissions, and that thus disregard a canon of the reorganizers' creed.

It is true, of course, that boards have not been universally or completely condemned by reorganization surveys. Advisory boards, without the power of decision, have frequently been suggested. Furthermore, boards have been conceded to be useful for "quasi-legislative" and "quasi-judicial" work, although the exact definition of these types of work, as distinguished from other "administrative" work, has not been too clear. It is when boards, instead of single individuals, are made the heads of major departments of state administration that reorganizers protest.

The most widely accepted feature of the reorganization programs has been the provision of certain central staff services and controls. In considerable measure these central staff services have been of the housekeeping variety: central purchasing of materials and supplies, including the rental of state property; operations of central warehouses; maintenance of central records on state property; maintenance and general control of buildings and grounds; supervision of public printing; operation of a central motor pool; central mailing, messenger, and telephone service. The provision of a central personnel agency has been partly for economy in housekeeping, but is intended more particularly to improve and maintain a higher quality of personnel. In some of the reorganization proposals, consideration was given to a state planning agency, to provide for coordinated forethought about various state activities and programs.

Probably the most important, and certainly the most widely adopted, of the central staff services and controls is that of a unified budget. Associated with the budget are various types of controls of expenditure, after appropriations are made.

Last of the commonly accepted "principles of reorganization" is that of an independent audit. There has been some confusion between the function of *approval of expenditure* and that of *examination of expenditure*. The proposals have generally suggested that approval of expenditure is an administrative control which should not be performed independently of the elected chief executive, but that examination of expenditure, with a report, usually, to the legislature, should be completely independent. The standard phrases are "an *executive* budget" and "a *legislative* audit."

FRAGMENTATION OF THE EXECUTIVE BRANCH

PRESSURES FOR SEPARATISM

The central tendency followed by all the reorganization surveys has been that of concentration of authority and responsibility. These proposals for administrative integration have not, however, been overwhelmingly successful. There have been many forces and pressures leading to dispersion of administrative activity among separate and independent agencies. Some of these pressures may be suggested:

1. *"Normal" drive for agency autonomy.* It seems to be an innate characteristic of administrative agencies to desire independence. The Mississippi Legislative Fact-Finding Committee on Reorganization of State Government summarized the uniform response of agency heads to the Committee's proposals for integration; the typical agency head wrote:

> I think this is one of the very best things that has ever been done in the State of Mississippi and I have long been of the opinion that this work should have been accomplished in the past. However, my department is of a type, character and kind that cannot be consolidated with any other agency, as its duties and functions are unique, and a reduction of personnel or a transfer of any duties of this department would work a hardship and

prevent certain citizens from receiving benefits to which they are entitled.

2. *Historical background of separate responsibility to the electorate.* Most of our present state constitutions were written during the two or three generations when the strength of Jacksonian democracy was at its highest. This was the period when the standard prescription for the ills of democracy was more democracy. It was felt that the way to assure responsiveness to popular wishes was to provide for popular elections. Some of the most important of the early officials of state government, such as the attorney general, the secretary of state, and the treasurer were subjected to popular election. Then as some of the other functions of state government increased in importance, the heads of the agencies administering these functions were also made elective. While the long ballot has grown so shockingly long that this tendency to add elective offices has been largely stemmed, it is very difficult, often impossible, to "lower" an agency head from elective to appointive status.

In the first place, the voters have become accustomed to voting for that office, and have a tendency to feel that it is appropriately elective. Second, the appeal of "direct responsibility to the people" is difficult to overcome. Third, the incumbent of an elective post has, by definition, a political following of some consequence, and his position of independence will not be tampered with lightly by knowledgeable legislators. Finally, there is some political advantage to a party or a faction in having a long ballot; particular sections or racial groups or individual leaders can be appeased or courted by being given one of the elective slots.

3. *"Reform" movements for special functions.* The political process is not always spotless. When spots appear in some sensitive place, interested, indignant, and outraged citizens frequently attempt to haul an activity which seems important to them out of the political process. In Alabama, when scandals, or alleged scandals, developed in the prison system, the remedy applied by the legislature and widely endorsed by the press was to set up an independent board of corrections and institutions to replace the politically appointed head of the department. It has seemed to many thoughtful citizens who are sincerely interested in effective performance of certain functions that the only escape from the petty, particularistic, discriminatory, and sometimes even corrupt administration by low-grade politicians was complete independence for the function, in order that it might be cleaned up and boosted to a higher level of operation.

4. *Clientele and interest group attitudes.* The American society is largely a pluralistic one. Most individuals have stronger loyalties to particular groups of which they are members than to the community

as a whole, or at least these special loyalties are much more clearly discernible. The Farm Bureau wants the Extension Service subject to its control, not subject to general control by the governor and legislature. The Parent-Teachers Association feels that the Education Department should be sacrosanct and untouchable by "political" hands. If a reorganization commission tries to tamper with a fish and game bureau, the organized sportsmen are likely to raise enough furor to make the commission wonder what happened to it.

Not only do the clientele groups want their agencies separate; they also want their money separate. The motorists' associations have been instrumental in getting constitutional amendments forbidding the "diversion" of gasoline tax revenues. The education associations insist that new taxes be earmarked for schools. Every group which has set up a governmental licensing program wants the license fees kept out of the general fund.

Each interest group, identifying the public interest with its own, feels that it can best insure that its affairs are properly considered by keeping the agency and funds involved "independent"—meaning independent of everyone but the particular interest concerned. For general, ballot-box politics there is substituted the politics of special influence, often with the highest of motive.

5. *Professionalism.* One of the most significant and sweeping developments in the public service, particularly in this century and this generation, has been the rise of many strong professions. Teaching, social work, highway engineering, tax assessing, purchasing, librarianship, forestry, penology, and many others, as well as the traditional professions of law and medicine, are deeply involved in the public service. These professions have organized bodies of knowledge, generally available only to members; group standards of training and performance; codes of ethical conduct; and, particularly, close group ties and associations.

The growth of professionalism has promoted respect for and recognition of technical expertness, facilitated communication and the spread of new developments, and produced a degree of group loyalty and discipline and satisfaction that have been tremendous assets to public administrative agencies. The development has been enthusiastically welcomed by many observers and participants in the administrative process. The 1936 *Municipal Year Book* suggested that professionalization of public officials was "the key opening the door to effective democracy." If legal and political controls of administrative officials are inadequate, as they obviously are, the self-control and self-stimulation of professional organization and activity might fill the gap.

Professionalism, however, produces particularly strong tendencies toward separatism.

Sometimes the special insistence on professional independence can be traced in some measure to the resistance made by the traditional political structure to the development of the special training, security of tenure, and personal mobility inherent in the growth of professions. Stronger, probably, is the fact that a profession is necessarily set apart by the possession of a special lore, and the members of the profession have a strong group consciousness which leads them to insist on being distinct from the common herd. This desire for independence is one of the most powerful disintegrating forces acting upon governmental organization. In bringing a particular professional group very closely together, it tends to shatter general political control. For social workers and teachers, professional ties may become stronger than ties to political superiors.

Professionalization, as a disintegrating force, is closely related to the pressures of special clientele groups and to functional links to other levels of government—all separatist in tendency.

6. *Functional links to national government.* The various governmental functions are no longer, if they ever were, divided sharply between the various levels of government in this country. In many fields of activity in which there is a state governmental program, there is also a national program. There are a great many interrelationships between the national and state programs. These tend to link national activities with state activities in each specific function, but they make it difficult to associate the various programs at the state level together.

The strongest link between national and state governments is the grant-in-aid. The Commission on Intergovernmental Relations tabulated 61 different programs under which Federal grants were made to state and local governments in fiscal 1955. A very few of these were made directly from the Federal government to local governments, but the overwhelming majority were made to or through state government agencies.

In fiscal 1953 national grants-in-aid and the state funds required to match them constituted 25 per cent of the total expenditures of the 48 states, and rose to 46 per cent in Missouri.

The conditions accompanying the grants tend to destroy central political control at the state level. True, the state can refuse to accept the national grants, but this is not a practicable alternative. The program area itself is specified; sometimes the specification is rather narrow, leaving no room for political choice at the state level. Grants for vocational education, for example, are subdivided into 13 categories, including such restricted objects as teachers' salaries in part-time schools for trades and industries. Through matching requirements, the grant-in-aid programs require the use of state funds for specified purposes which might be used in another way, narrowing still further the range of political control at the state level. In some instances, the terms of the national grant specify particular types of administrative arrangements or agencies. In three of the grant programs, as an extreme, the national funds are available only if a state earmarks certain revenue sources specifically for those programs.

In all instances, the procedures and manner of administration of the grant programs are subject to some degree of control from Washington. State agencies' work plans, financial accounting arrangements, and rules for disbursing funds must meet national requirements, even if these administrative arrangements or procedures do not mesh with those in use in the state. Even more important, in grant-in-aid programs, there is built up a continuing and close relationship between the national agency and the state agency involved in the particular program. This relationship tends to supersede or weaken any relationship of responsibility to the state governor through a political department head.

There can be little doubt that the national grant-in-aid system, and most of the links to national agencies, have improved the quality of administration of the particular programs involved at the state level. The Commission on Intergovernmental Relations, with surprisingly little dissent among its 25 distinguished members of varying backgrounds, endorsed the continuation of grant-in-aid arrangements on essentially the same basis as that on which they have been conducted, although the Commission recognized that the system had various complexities and that it tended to divide, and offer opportunity to dodge responsibility. Not only did the Commission endorse the grant-in-aid system, but it suggested that the trend had been and would continue to be "toward sharper definition of objectives, closer attention to conditions and requirements, more extensive administrative supervision. . . ."

If grants-in-aid and other forms of national-state cooperation continue to expand, and if there is closer attention to conditions and more extensive administrative supervision, there are significant implications for state administration. The important pressures will be put on the national government as the source of funds and initiator of policies, and the state agencies will become more and more the administrative field services of nationally developed programs. The need in these circumstances will be for increasingly professional state services, able and willing to cooperate in the national programs, rather than for increased political responsibility at the state level.

7. *Desire to insulate special types of programs.* There have been widespread and frequently very influential beliefs that special kinds of governmental programs exist which should be kept in some measure apart from the political process.

One of these special types consists of the regulatory activities, particularly those which involve determinations upon the basis of evidence presented through a formal hearing process. The independence of the judiciary has been one of the cornerstones of the English-American tradition. In agencies like the Interstate Commerce Commission at the national level and the railroad and the public service commissions at the state level, procedures resemble those of the judiciary so much that there has been great reluctance to subordinate them to the direction of a political chief executive. The agencies have most frequently been headed by boards or commissions, and they have generally had substantial protection against central political control.

It is also suggested that there are certain especially "controversial" areas in which freedom from political control permits a higher degree of objectivity. The promotion of fair employment practices, the control of alcoholic beverages, the equalization of property tax assessment are examples. This argument says, in effect, that some things are just too political to be given to the politicians.

Related are activities considered to be experimental in character. In some states, for example, special agencies have been set up to combat juvenile delinquency, or to pioneer programs of stream pollution control. Frequently it is felt that new ground is more likely to be broken by a new and independent agency than by part of the regular bureaucracy.

Trading agencies are also frequently exempt from many of the central controls. The corporate device has been used at the state as well as at the national level to provide the kind of flexibility and continuity that seemed to be desirable in commercial type enterprises. While many of these advantages can be attained without freedom from political control, the wish to have the trading agency exempt from particular controls on finances and personnel has been added to doubts about the desirability of political determination to bring an insistence on administrative independence. The liquor monopolies present in some states, the state docks systems in others, state insurance funds, retirement systems with many attributes of an insurance system, and similar programs have been entrusted to corporations, or boards, or authorities, which are separated to considerable degree from the regular administrative structure. The growth of special authorities for the administration of toll roads and other transportation facilities is contributing further to the rapid multiplication of independent agencies.

8. *Political division between legislature and governor.* In spite of what seems to be a growing amount of political leadership in the governor's office, the American system of separation of powers does not always produce the highest degree of mutual trust between the legislature and the governor. In many states, the governor is the choice of an electoral majority largely urban in character, while the legislature is

chosen on an apportionment basis practically guaranteeing rural control.

When it is at odds with the governor, or even restive under gubernatorial leadership, the legislature, being responsible for the basic outlines of administrative organization, will normally feel it can keep control of an activity better if the activity is administratively independent of the governor. Or, it may feel that an activity is better off free from any central political control rather than subject to the control of the governor. This is true not only in the initial organization of new agencies, for which the legislature is responsible, but also in any reorganization proposals which suggest the subjection of heretofore independent or partially independent agencies to gubernatorial control.

9. *Dissatisfaction with central political processes.* Underlying many of the various pressures for separatism outlined above is a considerable degree of distrust of the political systems of our state governments. Many people feel that the state political systems do not produce qualified and responsible leaders. This leads them to prefer, for programs which they consider important, professional responsibility, clientele and interest group influences, boards of unpaid citizens, and national prescription of program and administration to the kind of central leadership actually produced by the political process.

A paragraph from a resolution passed by a group of leading citizens in Birmingham, Alabama, opposing a bill which would have increased the governor's control over the state department of public welfare, is typical of this attitude:

> The hundreds of thousands of recipients of public assistance in the State of Alabama require the most thoughtful, considerate, humane and knowledgeable service the state and counties can provide. This means that no political considerations whatsoever should be permitted to intrude in the administration of such services. Under the proposed Bill, the selection of public welfare staff, from the State Commissioner down to the subordinate employees in every county department, is wide open to political manipulations. This could result in trafficking in human misfortune.

This objection to integration, of course, goes to the heart of the matter. The basic assumption of the proponents of reorganization is that the popular will is satisfactorily expressed through the political process of electing the legislature and, in particular, the governor. Many persons, on the other hand, feel that state politics as presently conducted is based upon lack of attention to issues, upon excessive attention to personality, and so is not properly organized to produce any real consensus as to governmental programs. They prefer, then, to trust the narrower, special, and concealed politics of influence which is brought to play upon administrative agencies largely independent of central political control. They do not believe, in other words, that the forces which combine to produce a majority of those voting in a state election are the best forces to which the conduct of state programs can be entrusted. The tendency produced by this belief would be, and has been, to make state election politics a sort of game with comparatively limited stakes, with most of the activities actually administered at the state level exempt from this central political game and left instead to the diverse forces of a highly pluralistic society.

DEVICES FOR SEPARATISM

In various ways an agency can be held out of the main administrative structure, and in various degrees it can be made independent.

One of the oldest and most deeply embedded devices for preserving administrative independence is popular election of the agency head. Even where officials are appointive, limitations are made upon the appointment power. Sometimes the officials are appointed by other persons than the governor. Sometimes there are narrowly limiting qualifications for office, prescribed either by statute or by the circumstances and forces surrounding an administrative operation. When terms of office do not coincide with that of the governor, control by him is much more difficult. Limitations on the power of removal also make it more difficult to exercise supervision from the chief executive's post.

Boards or commissions as heads of administrative agencies limit central political control, regardless of the method of appointment. This is particularly true where terms of office are long and not coterminous with that of the governor.

The earmarking of revenue sources for specific functions or agencies is another device promoting administrative separatism. Earmarking is frequently very extensive, and over-all budgetary control limited greatly by it.

One of the most sophisticated of the devices for administrative independence is the government corporation, an institutional device which appears to be growing.

These formal arrangements for administrative separatism are not always the really determinative criteria as to the degree of central political control. Sometimes elected or other apparently independent agency heads are closely tied in to the central political machinery, chiefly where party or factional organization is strong, and the elected official is part of the same "organization" as the governor. In other instances, where the agency head is subject to gubernatorial appointment, the strength of a particular clientele group or profession may be so great that there is, in reality, a very high degree of administrative independence. This may be true, for example, in the public health department, or in a game and fish agency, where the professional or the interest group may be potent enough to ward off any attempt by the governor to influence program, or level or manner of expenditures.

SEPARATISM VERSUS INTEGRATION

Should state administrations be reorganized into streamlined pyramids of hierarchical authority and responsibility? Should the "executive branch" of state government be a unity, with the office of governor at the top? Should the dozens and scores of administrative agencies be grouped into a few departments subject to gubernatorial authority, and assisted and controlled by central staff agencies for budgeting, purchasing, personnel, and so on? Or should agencies dealing with specialized functions keep their close ties to their clientele, develop their own professional specialization, cultivate their connections with national and local agencies, and avoid contacts with "politics" of the type usually practiced by state governors and their cohorts?

There need be no single answer to this central question of state administrative organization. There should, however, be thoughtful consideration of the implications of the question and, perhaps, commitments to certain tendencies or directions of movement.

THE CASE FOR INTEGRATION

Two basic arguments for administrative integration are apparent and these are closely related.

The first of the arguments is the desirability of coordinating state administrative activities. The activities of the government should be consistent; and the more independent agencies, the more possibilities for inconsistencies. An integrated, systematic, and rational program of activities for state government calls for an integrated, systematic, and rational arrangement of administrative agencies.

Some question arises as to how real the need for coordination of state programs is. Historically, and perhaps still in many states, the activities of state government have been confined to a number of areas having no particular relationship to each other. State government was, and may be yet, multipurpose without being comprehensive. This has been one of the reasons why governors' cabinets have not been widely used or effective. Between the state superintendent of education and the state highway director was little common ground, to use as examples the two biggest functions of state government. Areas in which there were impingements, such as a school health program, could easily be "coordinated" informally by negotiation between the departments affected.

Coordination, however, involves more than the reconciliation of occasional program overlappings. Coordination also involves the economies possible through joint housekeeping activities. The purchase of supplies, the use of transportation facilities, the use of state buildings and land offer obvious opportunities and needs for consideration from the standpoint of all of state government, rather than from that of a single agency. It is in this type of "coordination" that the reorganization proposals have had greatest success.

Even more important is the budgetary aspect of coordination. Any state government has limited financial resources, and choices must be made as to the comparative desirability and urgency of the various programs. Informed and rational choice between alternative ways of using limited funds is possible only if there is some vantage point from which all the varying programs can be studied and evaluated.

This vantage point could be the legislature. But the legislature has obvious shortcomings in this regard. It meets for limited and infrequent sessions, is composed of part-time amateurs, and cannot adequately supervise the necessary staff. Most states have realized for a quarter to a half century that for the whole of state government only the governor is in a position to prepare an adequate budget, subject to criticism, amendment, and change by the legislature. This was thought by many to be the task of a chief administrator, but it is now recognized more clearly that, to the degree that they can be separated, preparation of the budget is much more a political than an administrative task. The governor seems best equipped for this key *administrative* function because he is ordinarily the chief *politician* of the state.

The other basic argument for integration is that responsibility to the people is furthered if there is a single focus for the whole governmental program.

The great numbers of people doing the actual work of state government can be responsible to the citizens of the state through two chief channels: First, through control over administrative programs and actions by an elective legislature and an elective chief executive; second, through the diverse and complex paths of influence which can be exerted upon specific administrative individuals and agencies through direct contacts, group associations, pressures of specific opinion channels, and the myriad interrelationships which connect people working at specific jobs with the persons whom those jobs interest and affect. The assumption of the proponents of administrative integration is that the simpler, clearer, cleaner, and more wholesome lines of responsibility lie in the main channel of the elective process, that is, through the responsibility of the legislature and the governor to the people.

The first Hoover Commission put it this way:

The President, and under him his chief lieutenants, the department heads, must be held responsible and accountable to the people and the Congress for the conduct of the executive branch.

Responsibility and accountability are impossible without authority—the power to direct. The exercise of authority is impossible without a clear line of command from the top to the bottom and a return line of responsibility and accountability from the bottom to the top.

If the word *governor* be substituted for *President,* and *legislature* for *Congress,* the most important axiom of most students of state administrative organization would be clearly stated.

Thoughtful persons will realize that it is a great oversimplification to expect, in any arrangement of public institutions, a single line of responsibility. Administrative agents will be guided in their decisions by many and intricate lines of influence. They will be responsive to the law, as they read it; to the courts, for all American officials live in the shadow of the courthouse; to administrative superiors of various kinds; to their office and professional associates, for following and upholding socially accepted standards; to public and group opinion; to their consciences, formed by their education and experiences going back to childhood.

Some of these "lines of responsibility" can be emphasized and strengthened in relation to others, however. It seems likely that a general responsibility to a general public interest may be better achieved through the main line of political responsibility, focused on the legislature and the governor, than through the limited, specific, hidden responsibilities involved in some of the other relationships.

The great body of the public is a poor enough competitor with the organized groups who are especially interested in the activities of an agency, even when the agency has an overriding responsibility to the popularly elected chief executive. In a health department controlled by doctors, for example, the doctors will protect the public interest *as they see it,* even though at times they will inevitably confuse their own interests with the public interests. If a board to control the price of milk is controlled by the producers and distributors of milk, the consumers' interest may be given lip service rather than real service. Much justification exists for the basic assumption that the dominant and overriding line of responsibility should be to the public as a whole, through the ballot box. And there is much reason for the view that the clearest line of responsibility to the whole public at the ballot box is through the election of the governor.

Furthermore, if visibility is a desirable characteristic for the operations of government in a democratic society, it seems likely that public scrutiny and attention will be better focused upon operations conducted in the main political channels than upon those conducted in their own separate, independent, and sometimes concealed channels of political influence and control.

QUALIFICATIONS TO THE CASE FOR INTEGRATION

The validity of these basic arguments for integration—the need for coordination of governmental programs and the likelihood that a higher degree of responsibility to the whole population can be achieved through integration—appears to depend upon two fundamental conditions: First, are the state governments actually engaged in programs of real consequence to the whole people? And, second, does the central political system operating in the states provide a real responsibility to the whole people for the conduct of these programs? The two conditions are of course interrelated.

If state programs do not in actuality impinge substantially upon the lives of the majority of the people, there is no substantial reason why the limited clientele groups involved or the qualified professional groups should not run the programs. And if the actual operation of the political system does not present the public with significant and meaningful program alternatives, and the legislative and gubernatorial elections are determined on the basis of personality attributes unrelated to program, or upon irrational campaign appeals, or upon arrangements between political leaders more interested in petty spoils than in program goals, there will be appropriate reluctance to substitute a sham political responsibility for a real professional or clientele or intergovernmental responsibility.

As this reasoning suggests, the desirability of systematic administration depends upon the existence of systematic politics. If the major portion of the population does not use the state political process to secure consequential governmental programs, the ground is removed from the arguments for a rationally organized administration.

We are confronted with a chicken-and-egg proposition, however. A chief reason why state governments have not been entrusted with larger program responsibilities is doubt as to the competence of an irrational and disorganized administrative system. Furthermore, if the governor were actually in the driver's seat of the state government, the stakes of the political game would be so increased as to make serious participation by a serious citizenry much more likely. Responsibility is the great developer of men.

We should recognize, though, that separatism and integration are not opposites without middle ground. Neither is ever absolute. Even with an agency that appears completely independent, the governor may have much influence simply because he has produced a majority of the popular votes, has influence with the legislature, and has public prestige and constitutional responsibilities. And even in an agency over which the governor appears to have complete control, the influence of a special clientele, of the group connections and thought habits of the employees, of interested legislators and legislative committees, and of intergovernmental relationships all will be of incalculable importance. Agencies will be grouped all along the spectrum from nearly complete independence to nearly complete subordination to central political control. The essential question of public policy is the direction in which agencies and activities should be shifted, and the degree of shift which should be encouraged.

It may be that some agencies need to be much further along the road to integration than others. All states have, in fact, made this determination, linking some agencies much more closely into the hierarchy than others. It may be doubted, however, that the calculations upon which the respective decisions were based have been completely rational and thoughtful, or that the decisions should be left undisturbed. The basic calculation involved, a highly complex one, involves the weighing of the actual need for coordination and for responsiveness to central political control against any valid pressures for independence.

In some cases, budget and financial tools will provide enough central control; in others, as great subordination as possible may seem indicated; in still others, a high degree of autonomy may be permitted.

The continuing resolution of the conflict must be made, it seems, in each of the states in view of its own political situation, history, and program needs. It would seem not to be an accident, for example, that the governor of New York is much more the chief administrator than is the governor of New Mexico.

CRUCIAL ROLE OF THE GOVERNOR

It has been implicit in all these discussions of administrative organization that the key figure in the administrative process is the governor. The governor is, and will be, the chief administrator of the state because he is, and to the extent that he is, the chief politician of the state.

If the governor is a substantial political leader, or if he represents a real political leadership, and if he has been chosen governor by the majority of the people in order to produce a particular program or tendency in government, the pressures will be very strong to give him the tools with which to produce that program or tendency. If he is chosen on the basis of "irrelevant" (irrelevant to a political scientist, but obviously relevant to the electorate) personal considerations, or if he is the instrument or spokesman of a group interested primarily in the patronage and contract (as contrasted to program) spoils of office, or if it is the tradition of the state that the governor not concern himself much with important public matters, the pressures for independent boards and clientele representation and similar devices for separatism will be very strong.

An interesting question may be raised as to the correlation between a man's ability to produce an electoral majority and his ability to administer a large organization. At the level of the national government, there appears to be a very high correlation, provided primarily by the nominating process and only secondarily by the actual election process. A man with the characteristics to satisfy the widely diverse elements in one of our great modern parties, and with the ability to work with "the organization"—a requisite for nomination and election—will almost certainly have in large measure the high politico-administrative skills required at the top of a government. At the state level are some of the same tendencies, but exceptions are much more likely. In many of our states, the political system is so disorganized that individuals without organizational ties or without acceptability to divergent groups can be elected by purely personal feat. The supplanting of convention nominations by the direct primary has made this possibility more likely. Such a "maverick" may secure and retain popularity at the polls without having any real understanding of how to lead an organization such as a political party or an executive branch.

While the position of the governor as political leader and chief of administration is largely a function of the pattern of political life of the state, a few aids to gubernatorial responsibility might be mentioned.

Use of a four-year rather than a two-year term, and indefinite eligibility for re-election would seem to be important in providing a context for more effective and responsible gubernatorial leadership. The quality of the administrative machinery of a state can be changed comparatively little in two years. Only if a governor is in a position to concern himself about a considerable future is he likely to be motivated to much of an interest in improved administration, and only if administrative officials must reckon with the possibility of a continuing influence from the governor will his leadership be very effective. Much of the same regard for the future can be obtained, of course, in a well-organized and closely knit party or political faction with a real prospect of continuing in office for considerable time. Where the governor is merely a bird of passage, however, central leadership and concern about general administrative improvement are not to be expected, although, of course, specific agencies with effective functional responsibilities may have enough stability to generate within themselves a concern about improved administrative quality.

The battery of powers available to the governor is also closely related to the effectiveness with which he is likely to conduct his administrative tasks. Obviously this applies to appointment and removal powers, control over finance and personnel, and similar direct administrative controls. It applies also to legislative powers. If the governor has the item veto, or power to reduce items in appropriation bills, his influence over the administration will be vastly increased. And the larger his legislative role, then the larger his responsibility for program, and the greater the degree to which he will be required to concern himself about the administration of the various programs.

Finally, with relation to the governor, it should be said that, while the political and executive responsibility rests on a single individual, the office must be institutionalized if it is really to play an important role.

One form of institutionalization is purely political. In some states the governorship is in the hands of a group or faction for which the governor himself is merely chief spokesman.

Another form of institutionalization is the development of staff for the governor. In many states an important reason why the governor has limited influence and control is that he has too small a staff. The governor requires staff assistance in his relationship with the legislature and with the public, and he also needs help in his relationship to administrative agencies. Only if the governor has a personal staff able to discover matters of administrative importance and to advise him on them can he be effectively responsible for what goes on.

• • • • •

SOME MAJOR ISSUES

1. Perhaps the chief issue of state administrative organization is the desirability of integration under the governor. Should an increasing portion of the administrative machinery of the states be responsible to the people through the governor? Or should the various functions of state government be administered through agencies as independent of election politics as possible, depending upon relationships to clientele groups and development of professional integrity rather than upon political control?

If the answer is in favor of increased gubernatorial control, a grouping of agencies into fewer departments will be a necessary corollary, to permit effective central supervision.

2. Related closely to this central issue are many more. Should

strong efforts be made to reduce the number of elective administrative officials in each state? Should limitations upon the power of the governor to appoint and remove administrative officials be decreased? Should administrative terms of office be synchronized with the term of the governor?

In what circumstances should boards or commissions be used to head administrative agencies? Should board members have overlapping terms?

What is sound policy with regard to creation of independent "authorities" and "corporations" for new governmental activities?

3. In considering state administration it is impossible to escape the problem of intergovernmental relations. Should the national government be encouraged to assume increasing portions of the fiscal and program-determining responsibilities of many administrative programs, even though this means transferring the major political concern and much of the administrative supervision of the activities from state to national government? If this is an inevitable development, should not chief reliance for quality of state administrative performance be placed on the establishment of national standards and on professionalization rather than on state political responsibility?

4. Are there special types of administrative agencies for which independence from gubernatorial control is more necessary or more justified than for other agencies? If so, what are the criteria for identifying the agencies to be set apart?

5. Should the tendency toward stronger chief executives be continued? Should governors' terms be lengthened? Should limits on eligibility for re-election be removed? Should governors have the power to veto or reduce items in appropriation bills?

6. How comprehensive and how strong should the state budget be? Should all incomes of the state be subject to the budget and regular appropriation process? What grounds are there for exceptions?

Should preparation of the budget be an exclusively executive matter, or should legislative staffs or key members of the legislature be involved in the major steps in its development? Is it proper for heads of administrative agencies to continue to press for appropriations higher than those recommended in the budget?

7. Is the problem of political spoils still a central one in state administration? Can governors be trusted with control of personnel administration? Is a single personnel director responsible directly to the governor to be preferred to an independent personnel board? Within the framework of what organizational arrangements is there most likely to be a development of high morale and devotion to the job on the part of state civil servants?

8. In what circumstances and with the support of what forces are improvements in state administration feasible? How can reorganization surveys be made more realistic and effective? Is the development of management improvement staffs a promising prospect?

9. Most important, are the competence and quality of state administrative institutions improving rapidly enough to assume larger burdens of responsibility?

82. *Why I Want to Get Rid of My Job**

MR. CROSBY advances the idea that the office of lieutenant governor be abolished in Nebraska because its real functions are few and unimportant. Others have made the same suggestion, but the states have given little heed to the proposal. However, the ten states that have no lieutenant governor have experienced no difficulty, thereby giving weight to Mr. Crosby's argument.

"BOB, why do you want to abolish your office?"

So many of my friends have been throwing that question at me that I have undertaken to put the answer on paper.

It all began in February of this year when a bill was introduced in the Nebraska Legislature which suggested that the office of Lieutenant Governor be abolished. Yes, that is the office to which I was elected last year. The bill was introduced by Senator C. Petrus Peterson, a former Speaker of the Legislature. I had asked him to introduce the bill.

In the Government Committee of the Legislature the bill was approved by a vote of seven to two. Later the bill was rejected on the floor of the Legislature, largely on the grounds that this is not a propitious time to submit a Constitutional Amendment of this sort to the people and also on the grounds that this sort of proposition could be better handled at a Constitutional Convention.

Although many people seem amazed at the suggestion that the Lieutenant Governor can be dispensed with, I discovered when I began a careful study of the office after being elected that there is nothing new about the idea.

* Robert B. Crosby, *State Government*, XX (Chicago, the Council of State Governments, July, 1947), pp. 193-194, 204. Reprinted by permission of the author and the publisher.

For many years, eleven states have gotten along nicely without electing a lieutenant governor. They are not confined to any particular section of the nation. In the East are Maine, New Hampshire, Maryland, and New Jersey. On the west coast Oregon's governor manages somehow without a lieutenant. Other western states without lieutenant governors are Wyoming (our neighbor), Arizona, and Utah. The South is represented by Florida, Tennessee, and West Virginia.

Nor by any means am I the first in Nebraska to favor such a proposal. Former Governor Sam R. McKelvie in 1920 recommended to members of the Constitutional Convention that the office of lieutenant governor be omitted from the new constitution. In a recent letter to me he said, "It should have been done long ago." By the way, Governor McKelvie is himself a former lieutenant governor, serving in 1913-15.

The group which in 1934 drafted the amendment creating our unicameral (one house) legislature was in favor of deleting the office, but did not propose it for fear of obscuring the main issue. It will be recalled that Senator George W. Norris conceived the idea of having only one legislative chamber with non-partisan membership and regarded its adoption in Nebraska as one of his proudest achievements.

A political writer for Nebraska's largest daily is said to have stated in 1944 that the office might well be abolished.

Even the members of the 1943 Nebraska legislature are reported to have been "evenly divided on the wisdom of replacing the Lieutenant Governor as a presiding officer with a president elected by the legislature."

Incidentally, the recollection of this sentiment in the 1943 legislature, when I was Speaker, is one of the chief reasons for my proposal to this legislature. Remember that the lieutenant governor presides over the legislature. Even if the members of the legislature felt that his office ought to be abolished, it would be embarrassing to undertake such legislation if their presiding officer resented it.

It is my purpose to give the legislature a free choice in the matter. I shall not be troubled by its decision, whether favorable or not.

What does a lieutenant governor do in Nebraska? Just two things: stand by as a "spare tire," and act as parliamentarian when the legislature meets.

The "spare tire" function is performed when a vacancy occurs in the office of Governor. Then the lieutenant governor becomes acting governor. Did you know that never in the history of Nebraska has a Governor died in office? Taking the country as a whole the mortality rate of Governors has been surprisingly low. Worse luck for aspiring lieutenant governors! A vacancy did occur once in Nebraska in 1901 when our U.S. Senator died, and Governor Dietrich resigned in order to permit the lieutenant governor, having thus become acting governor, to appoint Dietrich to the unexpired term in the Senate.

Some folks think that the lieutenant governor "pinch-hits" when the Governor is out of the state or away from Lincoln. Our Supreme Court dispelled that notion in 1942 when it held that "mere temporary absence from the state . . . does not vacate the office of governor and instate the lieutenant governor therein. . . ."

So, the lieutenant governor just stands by.

It has been suggested that the lieutenant governor should be given the direction of an executive department to keep him busy and a salary commensurate with full-time employment. (I now draw $1,744 per year.) In 1933 they tried this in Indiana. The lieutenant governor was made the head of the Department of Commerce and Industries, and a member of three governing boards. Can you guess what happened? Everything went smoothly until 1940 when the Governor was a Democrat but the Republicans elected the lieutenant governor. You can hardly blame the Democrats' Governor for not liking a Republican at the head of some of his departments. When the dust settled the Indiana Supreme Court had declared that it is unconstitutional for a lieutenant governor "to exercise any executive powers or functions whatever" except in case of a vacancy in the office of Governor. Incidentally, twice in Nebraska during the last fifteen years the lieutenant governor has belonged to a different party from the Governor's.

Suppose the Governor and the lieutenant governor both die. Who then acts as Governor? Under our Constitution the Speaker of the Legislature does. It follows that if the office of lieutenant governor is eliminated, the Speaker is first in line to succeed to a vacancy in the office of Governor.

The above fact has caused consternation in two camps. The political parties do not like the idea of the Speaker being first in line of succession because he is non-partisan. As already indicated, our legislators, like Minnesota's but unlike any others, are elected on "non-political" ballots and actually serve in a non-partisan spirit (I can vouch for this, having been a legislator). To make it worse this year, when every state executive in Nebraska is Republican, the Speaker of our Legislature is, in private life, a member of the Democratic party.

Many members in this legislature feel it would be unwise for their Speaker to be first in succession to the Governorship because it would inject party-politics into the legislature. In other words, the members in such case would elect their Speaker with an eye to his private political faith.

Another angle disturbs many, including myself. It is that the

Speaker has been elected to the Legislature by just the voters in one of the 43 legislative districts. We like to think of our chief executive, even tho' he be an acting governor, as being the choice of the people at a state-wide election.

Just one thought in defense of the Speaker being first in line: excepting myself, the Legislature has shown excellent judgment in choosing outstanding men to the Speakership. Considering the small membership, it is submitted that this will almost certainly continue to be true; in a group of 43 men (no woman has yet been elected to our unicameral legislature) faults of character and ability are quickly discovered.

Of course, this matter of succession really presents no problem. We need only designate one of our other elected state officers to fill a vacancy in the Governor's office if one should ever occur. In Nebraska we elect five other executive officers every two years besides the Governor and Lieutenant Governor.

In three of the states which now have no lieutenant governor it is provided that the Secretary of State shall succeed the Governor. Instead of trying to "make" work for the lieutenant governor, as Indiana did, it is much more sensible to pick for our "spare tire" an official who now performs a useful function. If, for instance, the Secretary of State should succeed to the Governorship the manner of filling the resulting vacancy in the Secretary of State's office is now provided by our Constitution.

Any office chosen as successor to the Governorship would for that reason gain in prestige and receive even more careful consideration from the voters.

Besides awaiting a vacancy, the lieutenant governor's only other duty is to preside over the legislature. Before 1937, when we had two houses in our legislature, the lieutenant governor presided over the Senate and the Speaker presided over the House. Now that we have only one house (a respect in which we are unique among the states) our legislature is still required to elect its Speaker. But he doesn't preside; the lieutenant governor does that. Having once been Speaker myself perhaps I can say the following more gracefully than could another: The Speakership is an office of high honor without any corresponding duties or authority.

Why shouldn't the legislature be permitted to choose its own chairman? The legislators themselves are the best judges of the qualities they desire in their presiding officer. The Speaker should be what his name implies: the presiding officer.

Haven't you been struck with the absurdity of having a Republican or Democrat serve as chairman of our non-partisan legislature? That is what I, elected on the Republican ticket, am doing.

One of the consequences of this mismating is that the lieutenant governor cannot have any influence on legislative issues. Oil and water do not mix. The non-partisan legislators do not want a party politician intruding into their deliberations.

It follows that our lieutenant governor, if he intends to be popular, will act solely as a parliamentarian. In states having partisan legislatures the lieutenant governor is a leader of his party in the Senate and takes an active part in the legislative program. Thus he has some real usefulness.

One argument favoring my proposal is so apparent it hardly needs to be mentioned. The ever-mounting cost of government causes most of my constituents to put on a wry face at tax-paying time. Elimination of the lieutenant governor would save the expense of operating that office.

In Nebraska, as in most states, the voter is plagued at elections by a long list of candidates for state office. There are never less than seven offices to be filled in Nebraska. It is my experience during campaigns that even the county leaders of my party are hard put to remember the names of all their candidates for minor offices, much less know something about their qualifications. Removal of one set of candidates by abolishing the lieutenant governor's office will assist in simplifying the task of the average voter.

Now a word of caution which can be said more tactfully by quoting Arch Mandel of the Detroit Bureau of Governmental Research. He said in 1921, "so long as the office of lieutenant governor carries with it nothing but an empty title, and is a blind alley politically, men of capacity and ability, men of large affairs who aspire to public service, will not seek the office nor will they have it thrust upon them."

If the office is a blind alley politically in other states it should be doubly so in Nebraska. This is because of our peculiar constitutional provision making the lieutenant governor ineligible to be a candidate for any other office during his term. The practical effect of this is that he must remain out of state office for two years in order, for instance, to become a candidate for Governor.

Let no one think from what has been said that I set a low value on my election as lieutenant governor. It is the highest honor that has ever been accorded me. I am proud of it, almost to excess perhaps. But pride of office should not obscure the facts nor prevent a regard for the best interests of the state.

Permit me one final argument in a lighter vein. Elimination of the office would save my constituents a lot of embarrassment. The title "lieutenant governor" is quite a mouthful. Some call me "Governor" which is a form of flattery that I enjoy, but it really isn't correct. Some call me "lieutenant" which is what I answered to in the Navy, but it revives my inferiority feeling about Commanders. Why not be done with it and abolish the title entirely?

XV

LOCAL GOVERNMENT

83. *County Pattern for the Future* *

SINCE THE END of World War II, renewed interest in the improvement of local government has developed. County government, long referred to as "the dark continent of American politics," is in serious need of reform for the sake of increased efficiency and the preservation of democracy. Professor Mauck indicates reasons for, and suggests means of, making desirable changes.

AFTER the hiatus of the past years of world conflict, the interests of the people of the United States are turning once more to their normal peacetime institutions. Some of those institutions have been permanently modified as a by-product of the war; others are resuming their prewar characteristics. In the field of local government, most institutions have quickly sloughed off their battle dress. In a remarkably short time they divested themselves of all activities relating to selective service, civilian defense, price control, rationing and other wartime functions.

Another postwar development in local affairs is the resumption of interest and participation in improvement of government structure and procedures by local community groups and civic leaders.

The evidence is unmistakable that sentiment for reform in local government is developing rapidly and extending to all parts of the United

* Elwyn A. Mauck, *National Municipal Review*, 36 (February, 1947), pp. 83-88. Reprinted by permission of the author and the publisher.

States. For the forces of good government it cannot and will not be a losing battle! The institutions of local government must advance in conjunction with other social developments; there are no alternatives.

It is not to be blithely assumed that the advocates of county reform "know all the answers." They can merely formulate plans, on the basis of all available evidence, which will serve to guide the development of our institutions in order to have them serve our best interests. In the present momentous transitional period through which we are passing, no one can foretell precisely where the transition will lead us.

The shaping of things to come, however, does lie most definitely in the hands of the people in a democratic nation. Our government is exactly what we make it. It will suffer from our neglect or it will flourish as a result of our attention. If we are to retain our democratic institutions we cannot afford to assume the complacent attitude of the woman who, in answer to a question by a Gallup poll-taker, declared, "No, I have never voted in my life. Thank God, I am not responsible for that mess down in Washington."

The fate and future of county government are by no means clear. Some persons are prepared to sing a requiem for the county; but others are inclined to believe it will continue to exhibit an entirely satisfactory degree of life and vitality. To maintain a healthy condition, however, it is obvious that the county must continue to perform desired functions with an acceptable degree of efficiency. Otherwise it will atrophy and disappear like the vestigial organs of the human body.

Strong local government requires active participation by civic leaders in the community. An apathetic attitude can be as destructive to good government as outright opposition. If we relax our vigilance democracy will disappear at the grass roots, and our recent military victory over the authoritarian form and theory of government will have been in vain. What the people of the United States have won for themselves by force of arms must be preserved by virtue of popular insight and understanding of modern government. Any lesser course is unthinkable.

COUNTY SERVICES

County government provides essential services for practically all our people. In rural areas it frequently is the major unit of local government; only in urban areas is it sometimes of lesser importance. Almost everywhere it levies its taxes and, in return, performs specified services for its residents. Many of the important services it renders go unheralded. It records our birth, issues our marriage license, registers our title to real property (including all our mortgages on it), and it takes appropriate notice of our death. It might even investigate should we die under mysterious circumstances. If we want to own a dog or go hunting or fishing, county officials will issue the appropriate license. The county builds and maintains our roads, keeps the peace, cares for the poor, and provides for the administration of justice.

In addition, modern American counties have expanded their functions into many other fields of activity. They now have established health, medical and recreational services; they provide streets, water, lights, fire protection and sewerage systems; they plan and zone; they build houses, auditoriums and airports; and their war programs included participation in activities such as selective service, price control, commodity rationing, civilian defense and aids to service men.

What do the prophets of doom predict for the county? They point to the trend toward centralization as proof that the county is an outmoded unit. They ridicule its weak, disintegrated structure of government. They urge us to destroy the "court house gang." They declare that the needs of modern society require that we by-pass the county for the sake of efficiency.

The true friends of counties, however, also have been in the vanguard of those who have publicized the evils in county government. They recognize that only in eradication of the evils does there lie hope for thriving county government. Hence they have outlined the evils in order to point the way to reform. With reform the county should experience a renewal of strength.

Without reform, the county has been experiencing a gradual drain of power and authority to larger units of government. The trend toward centralization is a reality and to some degree it is inevitable and desirable. We cannot oppose the trend merely because it means that local governments lose their powers to states, states to the nation, and perhaps the nation to the United Nations. Local self-government, states' rights and national sovereignty are values which must be considered in conjunction with other values which may contain points of conflict. We must look to the values to be gained as well as the values sacrificed by every such trend or transfer of powers.

The trend toward centralization must be evaluated from points of view in addition to that of hypothetical administrative efficiency. The value of democracy is not open to question in this discussion. Assuming its virtue, there is little doubt that the most effective training ground for democracy lies in the field of local self-government. This is a factor that must be weighed along with factors of efficiency when one analyzes the effects of the transfer of functions to larger units of government.

HOW SECURE EFFICIENCY?

The standards of efficiency and democracy are less likely to be in conflict with each other when the problem involves local government consolidation. Much has been written about consolidation of counties, city-county consolidation, and functional consolidation. Developments on occasion appear to be filled with promise, but satisfactory results have been meager. Several sparsely populated counties in western states have voted in favor of dissolution of their county governments and amalgamation of their areas with adjoining counties. No city-county consolidation has been effected for decades, although in numerous communities it is a topic of current discussion. Functional consolidation between municipality and county or between other local units has been adopted in many metropolitan communities, and almost without exception it has been an instantaneous success. In numerous other communities, some form of consolidation is being actively debated, and it is safe to assume that there will be further progress in the not too distant future.

The manager plan continues to be one of the most promising developments in the field of county government. Although less than a dozen of the country's 3,000 counties have a manager as recognized by the International City Managers' Association, many have some modified form of a manager plan which alleviates the worst features of the usual disintegrated type of county government. During recent decades the county manager plan has been the subject of vote and debate in many communities, and the number of manager counties gradually is increasing.

Home rule for counties also has been the subject of more discussion than action, although recent developments indicate that a revival of activity may be in prospect. The two new state constitutions of Missouri and Georgia contain county home rule provisions, and several counties in each state have initiated action to secure home rule charters. Also counties in other home rule states have indicated a revival of interest in securing home rule charters. In some states in which constitutional home rule has not been achieved, the counties are seeking to secure a degree of autonomy through statutory home rule.

A survey I completed recently for the Consultant Service of the National Municipal League serves to illustrate many of the problems and some of the solutions proposed with specific application to a given county. Wicomico County, Maryland, is located on the eastern shore, and probably can be described as a typical county in its area. It is a rural county devoted to truck gardening, although Salisbury, the county seat, contains several small industries and approximately half the county's population. There were no unusual governmental problems, no crises, nothing to set Wicomico apart from other Maryland counties. Its problems were those of most counties which cling to outmoded forms of government.

"FOURTEEN POINTS" FOR REFORM

The recommendations resulting from the survey can be summarized in fourteen points:

1. Adopt the county manager plan, if possible in cooperation with similar action by the city of Salisbury;
2. Adopt a modern budget system, including a long term capital budget, and consider changing the fiscal year;
3. Join with the city and board of education in centralized purchasing;
4. Integrate financial functions, including collection of taxes, in a division of finance;
5. Install modern personnel procedures;
6. Join with the city of Salisbury in all activities which prove adaptable to cooperative effort;
7. Investigate possibility of securing more favorable formulas for allotment of state welfare and road money;
8. Consider possibility of securing the return from the state of greater jurisdiction over services such as health, welfare, county roads and assessment of property;
9. Establish a planning and zoning board to provide controls for the orderly development of the county;
10. Develop and integrate the recreational services which have been initiated;
11. Investigate further the need for a county police force, with full consideration of existing state and city facilities;
12. Take necessary action to have control over the liquor dispensary transferred to the county;
13. Provide desired services for unincorporated communities by the establishment of special districts;
14. Seek codification, simplification and clarification of the statutory and constitutional authority under which the county operates, with a view to permitting more effective home rule in all matters of primarily county concern.

The problems of powers, organization and structure have been discussed to the exclusion of problems of functions because the functions will continue to be entrusted to counties only if they prove themselves appropriately organized and competent to retain or undertake such functions. They are being given an unprecedented opportunity at the present time to play a significant role in developing governmental services for which there is an acute need. Many counties have appointed veterans service officers, and other counties are currently announcing the appointment of such officers. They will assist in all problems of veteran readjustment to civilian life including vocational counselling, housing, securing of government surpluses, loans for business or continuing the veteran's education, and similar matters. Although new housing at present is primarily an aid to veterans, the problem permeates every aspect of community life and has its impact on everyone in the community.

NEW JOBS FOR THE COUNTY

Counties are being given a renewed opportunity in highway construction and maintenance. Roads have been allowed to deteriorate and new construction has been deferred during the course of the war. Hence an unprecedented demand has accumulated. Federal legislation requires that counties be consulted in the expenditure of federal grant-in-aid funds for highway construction purposes. The extent and effectiveness of such consultation depends ultimately upon the vigor with which counties assert their legal rights.

Airport construction and maintenance constitutes another field in which counties may assume a prominent role. It is obvious that we are now entering the air age. Commercial air transportation is expanding at a remarkable rate, and the large air lines are being supplemented constantly by smaller feeder lines. Unscheduled commercial flying and private business and recreational flying also are in their early developmental stages. The construction of airport facilities, airport zoning, and other aspects of development and regulation fall appropriately within the sphere of county jurisdiction.

There remains the question of the means to be employed to attain the objective of reform in county government. Organization, public education and the usual electoral processes furnish the answer. On this matter I may allude also to the exceptional means adopted recently by the citizens of a county in Tennessee. A group of ex-soldiers in McMinn County resolved to rid themselves of their local boss-ridden machine. They organized their own political party for county offices, but on election day they were able to secure an honest count only after a six-hour siege and exchange of gunfire with the election and other county officials. The count then showed that the GI party had won an overwhelming victory.

The action of the GI party cannot be either unqualifiedly endorsed or condemned. As a precedent it is undoubtedly dangerous. Illegal violence cannot be condoned under any but exceptional circumstances, and violent revolution must necessarily be suppressed by existing government. Violent means can be equally useful for good and evil ends, and in that lies its danger. The recent establishment of the fascistically-minded Columbians, Inc., in Atlanta, Georgia, amply illustrates this danger.

On the other hand, the vigor and determination of the GI party adherents to secure fairness and honesty in the election must command the admiration of all persons also interested in honesty in government. For philosophic justification they can find ample support in the writings of Thomas Jefferson. In the case at issue, apparently the majority will could be secured only through violent seizure of the governmental machinery from corrupt officials. The uneasy question must continue to plague many of us, "How many times is the will of the majority defeated only because a minority has a stranglehold on the election process?"

I believe we are safe in assuming that such conditions of extreme corruption are exceptional, although that they exist elsewhere there can be no doubt. In the vast majority of cases orderly processes can and must be followed, and illegal violence must be suppressed by duly constituted authority. As a first step, the forces for good government must organize inside or outside of existing party or civic associations. The organization must be built on a permanent basis, for the battle will never be entirely won. The necessary research must be undertaken, the program adopted, and the battle lines drawn. Temporary defeat must be regarded merely as an opportunity for re-evaluation and elimination of mistakes. Under such a program eventual victory for good government is inevitable. Only under such a program will we participate adequately in shaping our future and insuring the safety of our democratic institutions.

84. *Too Many Jobholders**

Since the first settlements along the Atlantic seaboard, we have been engaged in weaving, by the establishment of boundary lines, a pattern of local units of government. By this process we have laid across the entire country a network of lines that establish the political jurisdiction of the county, the municipality, the New England town, the school district, and other local units. In general, each such unit of government has certain functions to perform and certain tax-gathering powers. In many areas, unit has been piled upon unit to such an extent that the citizen is anxious and bewildered about the future of his local government and the political scramble for a share of his financial resources. Mr. Brownell here comments upon several of the characteristics and problems of these local governmental units.

There are 155,000 local governments in the United States today. That is 152,500 too many. Your bank balance, and the country as a whole, would be better off if 61 out of 62 of our present counties, cities, villages, townships, school districts, and special districts were wiped off the map. That's the conclusion to be drawn from the report of a nation-wide investigation just completed by the Council of State Governments.

By streamlining local government, say the experts, we Americans could save nearly $2,000,000,000 on our local tax bill—equivalent to a saving of about 20 per cent to the average taxpayer.

We hear a lot about getting rid of government waste and government inefficiency and duplication. The papers are full of proposals for pruning the federal administration in order to save money and reduce taxes; every day somebody suggests lopping off another needless Washington board or bureau. We don't hear so much about pruning local government; and yet the chances are that the setup right in your home town cries out for the ax and saw at least as loudly as the federal government.

The vast majority of our local units are too small in area, contain too few people, and lack sufficient tax resources. What's more, they overlap one another to form a crazy quilt of competing—and oftentimes conflicting—authorities.

Take the situation in Cook County, Illinois. Cook County, em-

* Frederick G. Brownell, *The American Magazine*, 143 (May, 1947), pp. 23, 110-113. Reprinted by permission of the author and publisher.

bracing Chicago and its environs, contains no less than 413 independent local tax-collecting agencies, each one with its own staff, ranging in size from a few dozen to several thousand salaried employees.

Or consider School District No. 1, Town of Brighton, Monroe County, just outside Rochester, N. Y. Within that one school district there are 64 units of local government. These 64 districts overlap in such a way as to form 114 different tax zones, the people in each zone paying taxes at a different rate to a different combination of authorities.

Your local government touches your life more intimately and at more points than either the state or the federal government. It educates your children, safeguards your health, maintains your streets, provides pure water, protects you from robbers, and keeps your house from burning down. That is why it shouldn't be made a sinecure for a bunch of political jobholders.

Local governments throughout the United States today employ upward of 2,500,000 people. That's more people than are to be found on the civilian pay rolls of all the federal agencies and departments and the 48 state governments combined. At least half a million of these jobs are probably unnecessary and could be eliminated if local government were to be reorganized and brought up to date.

In normal times we shell out considerably more money to support our state and local governments than we pay to Washington. In 1940, state-local tax collections amounted to 11 per cent of the total national income—11 cents out of every dollar we earned. Local governments are responsible for two thirds of all state-local expenditures. It takes six times as much money to run local governments today as it did a half-century ago.

In many cases local taxes meet only a minor fraction of the total bill; the states have been forced to step in and make up the difference. More recently the federal government, too, has been drawn into the picture. To find out whether this money was being wisely spent, and what, if anything, should be done to improve the situation, the Council of State Governments recently undertook a comprehensive survey of state-local relations. A distinguished committee, including four state governors, worked two years on the report. Outstanding among their findings, is that there are far too many units of local government: one for every 850 people and every 19 square miles.

Our counties, townships, and school districts were laid out at a time when travel was difficult and communications were erratic. It was important for every citizen to be within reach of his schoolhouse, town hall, and county seat. The functions of government then were simple and expenses small. Local officials were usually unpaid and the tax rate was low.

But the horse-and-buggy days are over. Automobiles and telephones have collapsed space. Meanwhile, the functions of local government have multiplied in number and complexity, calling for the services of full-time salaried officials. What's more, since human abilities and material wealth are not distributed according to geography, certain local units now find themselves unable to supply either the talents or the financial resources necessary to maintain essential services.

Today every state is cursed with too many subdivisions, according to the report. The bramble patch of local government extends from the granite coasts of Maine to the golden sands of California. Some states, moreover, are worse off than others. In numbers, Illinois leads the list with 15,854 units, as against 54 in Rhode Island. Population-wise, South Dakota heads the parade, with one local government unit for every 131 inhabitants, compared with one for every 10,554 people in Massachusetts. Big-city areas in all parts of the country are overgrown with local governments. For example, the metropolitan region of New York contains no less than 1,039 separate units.

For extreme instances of fragmentation, however, you have to turn to rural districts. At the time of the last census the villages of Eagle Harbor, Maryland, and Ophir, Colorado, had 2 inhabitants apiece. Among townships, Cedar, South Dakota, had a population of 7; Perkins Plantation, Maine, 9; and Jones, Kansas, 10. Loving County, Texas, had 285 residents; and Alpine County, California, 323.

Government experts will tell you that it takes a minimum of 25,000 population to maintain a reasonably effective school system or to support an adequate program of public works, public health, or public welfare. For the most efficient operation, they insist, a population of 50,000 is desirable.

Local governments not only are too small; they also overlap. Units are piled on top of units like canned goods in a grocer's window. Although one layer of local government is all any district needs, or should be called on to support, a large part of the country is buried under three or more layers. In Illinois, four layers of local government (county, township or road district, municipality, and school district) blanket most of the state; areas of five overlapping districts are quite common; while nearly 900 communities groan under the burden of supporting 6, 7, 8, or even 9 separate levels of tax-levying authority. And Illinois is not by any means unique. Until recently the village of Baxter Estates in Nassau County, New York, was footing the bills of 11 independent taxing agencies.

In other parts of the country the local tax situation has become a sort of progressive piggyback, with John Q. Citizen supporting a horde of little government units, on whose backs has clambered a bigger horde of littler government units, which, in turn, support a still bigger horde of still littler units.

Because of small size and duplication, you and I pay too much and receive too little from our local governments, say the authors of this survey. Half the population of the United States now lives in 140 metropolitan areas, each consisting of a central city of 50,000 or more, surrounded by a ring, or rings, of suburbs. Political boundaries, cutting through such a metropolitan area and splitting it into administrative fragments, make it difficult to cope with area-wide problems.

Police protection is a case in point. The police department of the central city usually maintains a detective bureau, a homicide squad, a crime-detection laboratory, and other specialized divisions geared to meet the menace of organized crime. But the jurisdiction of the city police force ends at the city limits. Suburban cops are often few, poorly equipped, and untrained in combating criminals. Mobsters, operating freely across political boundaries, enjoy a big advantage over police who must stay within them.

Or take fire protection. Fires are easier to localize than crime. However, smaller and poorer suburbs frequently can't afford the type of fire protection the central city could supply if political barriers didn't interfere. On the other hand, well-heeled suburbs often maintain expensive fire-fighting equipment for which they alone have little use. In the case of San Francisco, it's been figured out that an integrated fire-fighting system would give the city and nine satellite communities better protection than they now get, with 31 fewer companies than they have at present.

Water supply is another example. The cost of maintaining watersheds, reservoirs, aqueducts, purification plants, pumping stations, and other expensive installations is multiplied when the central city and a dozen of its suburbs all go their separate ways.

Or take health. Disease is no respecter of political barriers. The negligence of a single public-health agency can endanger the population of an entire area. Nevertheless, there is often a wide spread between the health standards of the dozens of municipalities that make up a single metropolitan region. Some communities analyze their drinking water daily; others, only once a month. Some treat their sewage; others dump it raw into adjacent water courses.

If you live in the central city, you'll find that your tax problem is still further complicated by the ease with which thousands of your neighbors each year escape paying for city services by moving to the suburbs. To offset this loss of revenues, cities like New York and New Orleans have found it necessary to impose a tax on retail sales; others, like Philadelphia, have resorted to a tax on incomes earned within the city limits.

Piling one local government on top of another inside the metropolitan area also results in excessive overhead and needless inefficiency. Listen to what Prof. Charles Merriam has to say after an exhaustive study of the Chicago situation:

"The financial structure of the region offers no encouragement to those who are concerned about the prudent management of public finance—no central reporting system, no accounting system, no budget or budgetary control, no co-ordinated financial plan looking either to the present or the future, no unification of personnel, no advantage taken of central purchasing, or pooling of credits, or handling of deposits, or dealing with debts. Nearly all the canons of sound financial administration are violated."

How long, one wonders, would any private business continue to exist if it operated this way? And yet the welter of competing agencies that afflicts Chicago is quite typical of other American cities. Within the metropolitan district of Peoria, Illinois, for example, there are 316 independent units of local government—or an average of 1 unit for every 514 inhabitants.

What can be done to improve the present situation?

Co-operated effort has been suggested as one way out of the financial chaos now stifling community progress. Two or more governmental units may get together for the performance of some specific function. In Virginia, you'll find several counties banded together for the purpose of providing better health, welfare, and school services than they could separately afford. The Metropolitan Water District of Southern California is a second example of functional integration; not an independent government unit, it represents, instead, an actual union of scores of municipalities for the purpose of securing to each an adequate water supply.

Or one unit may agree to provide service to another in return for a fee. Communities in and around Los Angeles County, California, have entered into more than 200 such service contracts, covering highway maintenance, sewage disposal, library service, fire protection, and public health. In some instances the county provides the service; in others, the City of Los Angeles.

Sometimes these intergovernmental contracts produce curious results. For instance, 33 suburban communities buy water from Chicago. Five of them resell part of that water to other communities at a higher price.

Recently, Chicago taxpayers woke up to the fact that they were selling water to Harvey at 6.8 cents a thousand gallons, which Harvey, in turn, sold to Markham for 19 cents, and Markham retailed to the Cook County Infirmary for 25 cents. As most of the cost of running the Infirmary comes out of the pockets of Chicago taxpayers, the effect was that Chicagoans were buying their own water back at 3½ times the selling price.

Functional integration is not enough, the report insists. Local government throughout the United States is ripe for a drastic structural reorganization. What we need is not a tidying-up, but a complete house-cleaning—including the wiping out of thousands of little units and many thousands of unnecessary political jobholders, and their replacement by a few larger and more efficient units.

Some slight progress has been made. During the decade before the war New York State managed to rid itself of 3,000 small school districts through consolidations. And Oklahoma abolished all 969 of its townships, transferring their functions to the counties.

On the other hand, special districts dealing with soil conservation, sewage disposal, airports, and public housing are still on the increase. Unfortunately, experience has proved that it is generally easier to create new districts for such purposes than it is to persuade the legislature to enlarge the powers of an existing unit. Then, too, as a matter of practical politics, the creation of a new district means more jobs and more patronage for the local party in power.

If we are going to do a thorough job of reorganization, according to the experts, we've got to aim at more than merely consolidating a few school districts and eliminating a few townships. Real reorganization means wiping out *all* overlapping authorities and leaving but one unit of local government in a given area. Furthermore, the resulting units must be large enough in population for efficient operation and rich enough in taxable resources to pay for a substantial portion of their own services. As far as possible, each should cover a single integrated community—as, for example, an entire metropolitan region.

What is the logical unit of government under such a plan? For urban areas, it is the city. For rural areas, it is the county. All other units should go.

As we have seen, the difficulties that beset big cities arise, first, from the sandwiching of many communities within a single area; and, secondly, from the piling of scores of independent governments on top of one another. In reorganizing a metropolitan area, our aim should be to bring all the people who live in that area under a single local government.

Outside big-city areas, the county comes closest to meeting the standards of size, wealth, and population necessary for efficient operation. All school and special districts ought to be abolished and their duties turned over to the county. Townships, too, have outlived their usefulness and should be tossed onto the trash heap. This doesn't apply to the larger New England towns, which function more like cities.

Moreover, it would be well, say the experts, if all over the United States the smaller cities, towns, and villages were to turn in their charters and let the county government take over. Cities over 25,000, but not part of a metropolitan area, should have the choice of combining with their counties or setting up as separate city-counties of their own. Finally, one fourth of all the counties in the country have too few inhabitants, and should be merged with others.

After such a reorganization, what would we have left? There would be:

140 metropolitan city-counties, ranging from New York City (11,690,000) to Pueblo, Colorado (62,000)
260 other city-counties of more than 25,000 population
2,100 rural counties ranging in size from 10,000 to 75,000

—or a total of 2,500 local government units. There would be just one level of local government throughout the United States; and the average state would have 52 units to look after, instead of 3,200 as at present. Of the 155,000 units now in existence we should have eliminated 152,-500, including 109,000 school districts, 8,300 special districts, 19,000 townships, 16,000 cities and villages, and 700 counties.

Obviously, this is a goal for us to shoot at, not a program for immediate adoption. No such comprehensive overhaul of local government is going to be accomplished next week—or next year. Legislative consent, and possibly constitutional amendment, in each one of the 48 states will be required first. Metropolitan areas like New York and Kansas City, which occupy parts of two or more states, may never achieve complete integration.

However, it's worth noting that reorganization and consolidation along the lines just discussed would entail drastic revision of the present system of local government only in the states west of New York to Montana, and south from Minnesota to Missouri. The New England, Southern, and Far Western States would have to do considerably less pruning.

Several states—notably Virginia and New Hampshire—have already made a start in helping local governments to streamline themselves through simplification and consolidation. But all the state can do is to foster needed changes; the motive power for reorganization must come from the local community itself.

In every city, town, and district you'll find people who are opposed to any change. In rural areas, opposition centers primarily in two groups: local office-holders who would lose their jobs in the consolidation; and well-meaning but parochial-minded citizens who, despite the inefficiency of the present setup, insist that only they and their neighbors should have a say in running their community. In metropolitan regions, the chief defenders of the *status quo* are suburban property owners who fear their taxes would go up if their municipality were annexed to the big city. They are joined by pious folk in all the small towns throughout the region who look upon the metropolis as a modern Babylon, and who shudder at the prospect of being bossed by an "alien" and possibly corrupt political machine.

Nevertheless, in any fair-minded appraisal, the material benefits of consolidation far outweigh its drawbacks. Nobody knows how much money could be saved to taxpayers by a complete reorganization of local government throughout the United States. Professor Merriam has estimated that Cook County, Illinois, alone would profit to the extent of $140,000,000. For the country as a whole, a cut of at least 20 per cent in operating costs would appear not unreasonable. This would amount to the tidy sum of $1,700,000,000.

But a reduction of 20 per cent in costs doesn't necessarily imply a cut of 20 per cent in the local tax rate. It is more likely to result in proportional expansion of the services performed by local government.

Fifty years ago, the service feature of local government in many states was virtually non-existent. Instead of the county's keeping up roads, the owners of adjoining farms were "warranted" (that is, ordered) to make repairs. This they either did themselves, or else hired the work done and paid for it out of their own pockets. The few free public schools that then existed were charity affairs, maintained for the benefit of boys and girls whose parents were too poor to send them to any of the private academies and seminaries which provided the bulk of the education. Health services were a joke; diphtheria scourged the countryside in winter and malaria and typhoid in summer.

Within 50 years we have taken this thing we call local government and transformed it into an agency for collective housekeeping. Today, 85 cents out of every tax dollar you pay to your locality and your state goes for the support of public works, public education, public health, public welfare, and public safety—five types of community service that either did not exist at all, or existed only in the most rudimentary form a half-century ago.

What's more, our demands for service are increasing. Today, we expect our communities to provide airports, playgrounds, ambulance service, tuberculosis clinics, smoke abatement, mosquito control, and free school lunches. Who knows what we'll ask them to provide tomorrow? To perform these services efficiently and at reasonable cost, local governments have simply got to be bigger and better organized than they are today.

Consolidation plans are sure to be attacked on the ground that they threaten local self-government and constitute a denial of democracy. According to the experts, both these arguments are specious.

Local self-government rests on local competence and local efficiency. When units are too small or weak to provide adequate service at reasonable cost, local autonomy breaks down and the state is forced to intervene. The best way of assuring continued local self-government is by making units large enough and strong enough to guarantee their functioning effectively.

Local government has been called the schoolroom of democracy. At present that schoolroom sadly needs a new curriculum and a new teacher. In thousands of communities the setup is so complex that the average citizen can't make head or tail of it. All too often, as the election figures show, he doesn't even bother to cast his ballot unless there are state or national issues to be decided. One large local unit of government, simply organized, with fewer elective officials, would make it easier for voters to exercise their franchise intelligently on local issues—and also to make their influence felt between elections.

Government, in the last analysis, is largely *local* government. In these days, when rival ideologies are competing for supremacy throughout the world, it's more important than ever to make our form of government work. Reorganizing local units is the best way of assuring that the tree of democracy will continue to flourish at its roots.

85. *Hope for "Suburbanitis"**

ONE of the special and more complex problems of American local government is that of the metropolitan area. Political scientists, sociologists, planning engineers, and others have for years been engaged in diagnosing the social and political maladies infecting the metropolis and prescribing remedies. Curative courses have been laid down, but the patient has been reluctant to accept them. So the problem has dragged on. In 1945 Professor Herbert A. Simon

* Thomas H. Reed, *National Municipal Review*, 39 (December, 1950), pp. 542-553. Reprinted by permission of the author and the publisher.

stated that "There are no new solutions to the problem of metropolitan organization. . . . If any recent trend can be noted it is a growing apathy toward the endless discussion of these alternatives and a growing hopelessness that anything really fundamental can be done to remedy the situation."† In this article Dr. Reed offers some hope for a solution to the political problems of the metropolitan area.

THE Buffalo *Evening News* a few weeks ago coined a new word—"suburbanitis"—to describe a disease which is crippling Buffalo and its environs. Let me reassure Buffalo at once. It is in no danger of catching it. It has it already. It is endemic in every urban community in the United States and Canada and almost everywhere else for that matter. It is not a new disease. Students of municipal administration have been recording and analyzing its symptoms and suggesting means for its cure for a generation. It was discussed for the first time on a National Municipal League program in a paper I read at the 1925 meeting in St. Louis, and it has been on the League's program almost every year since.

Many better and wiser city planners and political scientists than myself have poured out millions of words by tongue, pen and typewriter on the same theme, but frankness requires me to say that so far we have accomplished little more than a world's record for words used in proportion to cures effected. This appears like a pretty sorry performance. Can it be improved? I think it can.

A glance at the nature of suburbanitis will show why it is so hard to cure. Cities have always grown at their peripheries. Growth has to take place where there is room for it. The outward movement of city population until very recently, however, has been held severely in check first by the necessity for defensive walls and later by the absence or inadequacy of transportation facilities. Two great names stand out in the story of urban decentralization, Roger Bacon, whose invention of gunpowder made walls useless, and Henry Ford, whose perfection of the popular priced automobile has made it possible for masses of men and women to live anywhere within a radius of 30 miles or more of the office, shop or factory where they work.

Urban expansion, which throughout most of human history was deliberate enough to permit the slow processes of political change periodically to catch up with it, has in the past forty years become an avalanche which has left those responsible for local government dizzy and bewildered. Population has spread all over the countryside around

† "Planning for Organization and Management," *Public Management*, April, 1945, p. 108.

large cities with utter disregard of existing political boundaries. Nucleus cities have lost many of their best citizens and have been obliged to meet ever-increasing governmental costs with withering revenues. Counties have had thrust on them functions they are ill organized to carry out.

A vast demand has arisen for the extension of water, sewers, highways and other public works which the minor municipalities, except in rare instances, have neither the energy nor the resources to provide. New schools have had to be built while old schools in the nucleus city stood empty. The whole metropolitan area has suffered intensely from the almost entire absence of planning in this vast and unruly growth. This is "suburbanitis," a disease not peculiar to any unit of the metropolitan area but affecting every nook and corner of it.

SURGERY CALLED FOR

It is easy to see why so little progress has been made toward the cure of suburbanitis. A genuine cure calls for drastic surgery on the present scheme of local government. For a complete cure many of the existing organs—cities, counties, towns and villages—must be removed and the body sewed together again so that it will function successfully. Most local politicians would as soon consent to the removal of their right arms as to such an operation. Simple private citizens are appalled at the prosepect of changes so drastic in a matter so complex and, unable to visualize the beneficial results of the operation, assume an attitude of obstinate negation. The combined opposition of the politicians and people of any substantial number of the units of local government in a metropolitan area is usually enough to put a dead stop to any thorough readjustment of the number and relationships of such units. A nucleus city like Buffalo cannot of its own motion put over city-county consolidation. It must have strong cooperation from county, town and village sources.

The single example of a successful attempt at city-county consolidation in the last generation—Baton Rouge and East Baton Rouge Parish (County)—is only an apparent exception to this rule. The new plan of government in this case was violently opposed by the parish politicians. In the referendum the portion of the parish outside Baton Rouge voted against the plan of government. In this case, however, the amendment to the state constitution authorizing consolidation provided for a vote in the parish as a whole, including the city of Baton Rouge which voted heavily for the plan. Success, therefore, was due in large measure to the shrewdness of those who drafted the amendment and the unusual lack of alertness on the part of the parish politicians who let it get through the legislature.

It is not at all surprising, in fact, that public opinion has not yet welcomed the idea of metropolitan unification. To do so requires the acceptance of a wholly new conception of the city, not as a compactly built-up area in which water, sewers, paved streets, lights, police patrol and fire protection are provided, in sharp contrast to the rural areas outside, but as a great sprawling macropolis covering hundreds of square miles where farms and pastures mingle with intense residential developments, factories and shopping centers.

Just such a transformation is rapidly taking place, but the nature and governmental implications of the change are hardly noticed except by professional students of urbanism. Ordinary man is just too busy living to realize the character of the drama in which he plays a part. I see no reason for discouragement in the fact that a single generation has not sufficed to bring about general recognition that new social and economic conditions require a readjustment of the areas of local government. It is natural that such a reform, inevitably leading to the abolition of jobs, the destruction of vested interests and the abandonment of long cherished traditions, should take longer of accomplishment than improvements in the internal organization and procedures of existing units of government. I believe that the next ten years will see startling progress toward metropolitan integration.

That is assuming that we go about it intelligently. In the first place, nothing can be gained by promoting antagonism between the city and the suburbs. The motives which have induced people to seek homes in the suburbs are laudable—cheaper land, lower taxes, more room for the children, purer air, less smoke and dirt, healthier living, a larger share in community life, a new home in place of the old one become shabby and obsolete. Suburbanites are man for man just as good as city people and entitled to every bit as much consideration. To array the city against the suburbs is to court defeat. The objective in every successful campaign against suburbanitis must be the welfare of the whole metropolitan area—the greater city of tomorrow.

An intelligent approach to the problem of suburbanitis also calls for the most careful study of the facts of each situation. Although suburbanitis is present in more or less aggravated form in every large urban concentration, each such area has its own peculiarities which must be taken into account in determining the methods to be adopted in combatting the disease. I personally prefer to take my medicines on a doctor's prescription and, in my opinion, the same principle applies to governmental changes. The attempt to cram down the throats of Community A a dose of reform on the sole ground that a similar dose has produced favorable results in Community B decreases the chance of the dose being swallowed by A and increases the chance that if the dose is taken it will produce an unfortunate reaction. To be of real value the study must be impartial. To be generally accepted it must also appear to be impartial. The best course is to have it sponsored by a committee as broadly representative of all conflicting interests as possible.

LOOK FOR COMPLETE CURE

Such a study should consider first what remedy is necessary for a complete cure rather than half measures and palliatives. It does not necessarily follow, however, that if a complete cure—out-and-out city-county consolidation let us say—is bound to be defeated, that all hope of progress must be surrendered. A choice must be made between the relative advantages of the uphill fight over a period of years, in successive elections and before successive sessions of the legislature, and some immediately achievable gain. The uphill fight may be the shortest road to ultimate victory, and the history of local government reform is full of instances in which brave men and women have fought doggedly through defeat after defeat to win in the end. The adoption of half measures or palliatives, moreover, has served to delay real integration. The very success of the state controlled Massachusetts Metropolitan Commission has blocked for nearly three-quarters of a century a self-governing Greater Boston. I do not favor any plan for selling out local self-government for a mess of metropolitan district pottage, no matter how well seasoned the dish may be.

THE BOROUGH PLAN

There are, however, steps short of complete consolidation which may properly be taken if the opposition to going the whole way seems too overwhelming. One of these is the so-called borough plan in which the functions of local government in the area are divided between a central metropolitan government and the existing municipal units. Such a plan avoids some at least of the usual opposition from suburban units. In fact, the only time that a complete charter providing for such a plan has been presented to the voters of a metropolitan area it was accepted by a majority of the voters in the central city and outside as well.

This was the plan proposed by the Pennsylvania Commission to Study Municipal Consolidation in Counties of the Second Class (Allegheny) in 1929. It preserved, indeed froze in forever, Pittsburgh and the other 121 cities, boroughs and townships of Allegheny County, with all their functions except the few which were transferred to the county under the name of "City of Pittsburgh." It is usual to pass this plan off with the statement that it failed at the polls. It did but only because of the peculiar method of ratification required by the enabling constitutional amendment, to wit, by a two-thirds majority in a majority of the cities, boroughs and townships of the county. It is usually forgotten that while it got a two-thirds majority in four less than a majority of the 122 units concerned, it not only carried in Pittsburgh by better than a two-thirds vote but had a majority of the votes cast in two-thirds of all the units outside. It actually was approved by the people, as votes in America are usually counted, not only of the city of Pittsburgh but the remainder of Allegheny County as well. The vote, moreover, came after a long and hard fought campaign in which the issues were clearly presented to the public.

Only two other borough schemes have been put to vote in any form, the St. Louis plan of 1930 and the Miami-Dade County plan of 1948. In both instances the test came on the adoption not of a charter but of an enabling constitutional amendment. The St. Louis amendment was defeated in a statewide referendum at the earnest behest of the County Court of St. Louis County where the vote was also in the negative. The Dade County amendment which would have consolidated Miami and some small municipalities with Dade County while leaving the larger suburban places in *status quo* was voted down in a preliminary referendum in Dade County at the May primary in 1948. The Miami-Dade County plan, on which 38,000 out of 90,000 of those voting in the primary failed to vote at all, is significant of the difficulty of selling a metropolitan pig in a poke.

It will be worth the while of a community afflicted with suburbanitis to consider the merits of a plan of metropolitan organization which received popular endorsement in its one clear-cut presentation to the public in recent years. I must warn you, however, that the only municipal organization of the kind now in existence is the administrative county of London. New York, it is true, has boroughs, but they are in no sense autonomous units of local self-government. They are the districts from which members of the Board of Estimate and Apportionment are elected. Certain public works activities are organized on a borough basis under the direction of the borough president. These activities aggregate but a minor fraction of the total city budget in which they are included. Like the Paris arrondissements, the New York City boroughs merely provide a means for some deconcentration of an administration which would otherwise be wholly centralized.

It should also be pointed out that the great disparity in size and character between the cities, towns and villages in any large metropolitan area, and in New York State especially where villages are superimposed on towns, presents difficulties in the way of adoption of the borough plan. The reorganization of the area into boroughs of something like equal size might prove every bit as difficult to sell as an out-and-out consolidation. The possibilities of the borough plan should be canvassed but without any commitment in advance that the plan will prove feasible.

FUNCTIONAL CONSOLIDATION

Most of the progress toward the integration of metropolitan areas which has actually taken place has been in the direction of what for lack of a better term is called "functional consolidation." I would prefer to eliminate from this discussion functional consolidation effected by the creation of *ad hoc* authorities. They complicate the already too complex picture of local government. Where they are not responsible to the local electorate they are a threat to local self-government. I would not for a moment think of belittling the credit that is due to some of these authorities (especially some of those furthest removed from popular control) for the outstanding services they have rendered. Where an international or state line cuts the area to be served the only practicable device is an *ad hoc* authority based on treaty and concurrent legislation. For matters within the jurisdiction of a single state, however, there is seldom any excuse for increasing the number of local units.

Functional consolidation in practice usually has been limited to transferring to a county functions hitherto performed by the smaller municipal units such as cities, towns and villages. Where the metropolitan area covers the whole or parts of several counties such transfers fall a good deal short of providing metropolitan integration. Even in such cases, however, its result is to reduce the number of units struggling with a particular function and, where the county corresponds fairly well with the metropolitan area, actual integration for that particular function, at least, is accomplished.

The Buffalo metropolitan area broadly conceived lies in both Canada and the United States and includes both sides of the Niagara River for its entire length. I take it, however, that Erie County is the maximum area in which as a practical matter we can expect definite progress toward integration in the reasonably near future. Already considerable progress has been made in the way of functional consolidation in Erie County as contrasted with most counties in this country. Health, hospitals, libraries and welfare—including all forms of poor relief, usually wholly or partly municipal functions, are in the Buffalo area attended to exclusively by Erie County. It is obvious that, to the extent that other municipal functions are transferred to the county, they will be administered and paid for on a metropolitan area-wide basis.

Here is the line of least resistance which by-passes for the time at least the question of duplications as between towns and villages, and which avoids any frontal attack on the existence of any unit. Such functional consolidation can be carried to the point where it amounts practically to the borough form of consolidation except for a few points of greater or lesser importance. The Pittsburgh borough plan gave the name "City of Pittsburgh" to Allegheny County. This had a certain prestige value for Pittsburgh businessmen. Especially in a city which has ceased to show any population increase, extending its name over the rapidly growing suburbs is the easiest way in which its chamber of commerce and other business leaders can show the world what a big and thriving place it really is.

GIVE COUNTY CONTROL

Moreover, the effects of suburbanitis cannot be removed unless the county not only takes over services but also controls. It is not only important to repair the ravages of the disease but to prevent its recurrence. As a matter of fact, the tendency for population to seek the outer reaches of the metropolitan area is even stronger today than it was ten or twenty years ago. It was held in check somewhat by the restrictions on building activity during the war and postwar periods, but in the last two or three years the floodgates have opened again. To what extent the flow may be restrained by new regulations no one can say, but one can say that with the removal of the new regulations the outward movement will go on with increased velocity.

The mere words "atomic bomb" suggest a motive to the dispersion of urban population more powerful than any which has preceded it. If the vastly expanded and less dense urban areas of the future are not to become sprawling jumbles of inconvenience in which proper works and services can be furnished only at impossible cost, their growth must be regulated. European cities have to a considerable extent escaped the worst consequences of suburbanitis because they generally forbid sub-division of outlying lands until vacant lands contiguous to developed areas have been built up.

We cannot do this by direct command under our constitutional system but a great deal can be accomplished by vigorously enforced zoning based on comprehensive and intelligent plans. By making lot sizes in outlying areas large—as large perhaps as two to five acres—and by requiring that the necessary services be installed in all sub-divisions before the plat can be accepted for filing, a strong curb can be placed on the premature development of thickly built-up sections far from the sources of water supply and sewage disposal facilities. Such planning and zoning powers are not ordinarily possessed by counties but, if suburbanitis is to be attacked by transferring functions beyond the capacity of cities, towns, and villages to the county, such strong planning and zoning powers must be entrusted to the unit which has jurisdiction over the whole area.

A frequent motive for settlement in the outlying parts of a metropolitan area is that less stringent building regulations permit the construction of cheaper homes. This means not merely that a few build their own homes in their off hours—an exhibition of American initiative with which we have natural sympathy—but the building of homes wholesale by unscrupulous contractors who foist their jerry-built work on unsuspecting customers. A sound building code on a county-wide basis is a necessary corollary of zoning in securing ordered and substantial development. Power over this matter too ought to be extended to the county if it is to be able effectively to combat suburbanitis.

MILLIONS FOR HIGHWAYS

The outward movement of population has been stimulated further by the widely current policy of spending millions to make the central city more accessible to the suburbs, while little or nothing is done to improve or rehabilitate the declining quarters of the city itself. I am not suggesting that arterial highway developments are not in many instances necessary. I am suggesting that making it ever easier to live outside and work inside the city while nothing is done to retain or restore the attractiveness of close-in areas is not the way to cure suburbanitis. It is obvious that if this aspect of the problem is to be grappled with effectively a single metropolitan-wide agency—the county if the attack is along functional lines—must be given planning and public works powers broad enough to deal with both horns of the dilemma.

There is an unwarranted stimulus to the outward movement of population which is beyond the reach of any local authority—the policy of the federal agencies which have to do with housing and the guaranteeing of mortgages. Those dealing with the encouragement of low-rent housing have often sought cheap land in the suburbs for their projects without much regard to future problems of service and administration. The FHA has consistently put the weight of its enormous credit resources behind the development of new projects in outlying sections. It does not do much good to integrate local government within a defined area if immediately thereafter vast housing projects or speculative building developments are to be set up under federal authority just over the border. The federal authorities will say that they conform to the local planning and zoning regulations, but if this means of control is to be at all effective the regulations must apply in the area in which the project or development is projected. This is a further argument for the planning and zoning powers of the county being extended over the whole metropolitan area.

REORGANIZE COUNTY STRUCTURE

The greatest single obstacle to the progress of functional consolidation as a cure for suburbanitis is that county government is not organized to handle to the best advantage such extensive powers of policy control and administration. I want to make it clear in what I have to say on this subject that I am not impugning the character or motives of any county official anywhere. I have no hesitation, however, in saying that county government under large boards of supervisors, as in New York and Michigan, is peculiarly unadapted to the job of performing functions of the kind necessary for the cure of suburbanitis. County government, except in a very few counties which have been reorganized in recent years, has no head. Its powers are distributed between a county board and a number of elective officers whose duties are narrowly defined by state law. This board, as a rule, works through a variety of officers and commissions without the benefit of any centralized executive authority. It is a system well enough adapted to the conditions of a simple agricultural economy but hopelessly inadequate to manage the complex affairs of a populous metropolitan area.

Reorganization of the county government along modern municipal lines is therefore a condition precedent to a permanent and constructive plan of metropolitan integration, even one which leaves existing cities, towns and villages with a considerable part of their present responsibilities.

Reorganization of county government is a tough job, especially where it is accompanied by extension of its powers into the municipal field. Take Cuyahoga County (Cleveland), Ohio, for example. Reorganization and consolidation have been in the public mind for years. A charter which included nothing in the way of consolidation won a popular victory more than a decade ago but was put to death on a technicality by the Ohio Supreme Court. For most of 1950 a second charter commission toiled and wrangled, coming up with a document which provided for a county board of nine elected at large and an elective county administrator with broad executive powers. It provided also for transferring to the county from Cleveland and other municipalities functions most of which Erie County already handles—hospitals, charitable and correctional institutions, poor relief, public health, airports, enforcement of minimum standards for building construction and the intermunicipal aspects of sewers, water and similar matters. It required a special referendum before the county could take over Cleveland's transportation system. No one could say it was a revolutionary measure, but it went down before a substantial popular majority on the seventh of November.

There are enough examples of reorganized county governments to give encouragement to Buffalonians. Monroe County, New York, has a county manager, while Westchester and Nassau Counties, New York, have elective county executives. All have administrative organizations which compare favorably with the best governed cities of the state. County home rule is already established in the constitution and laws of New York and reorganization in Erie County only waits upon action by its citizens. County managers are also to be found in several large counties in Virginia, California, Georgia and other states.

SELL IDEA TO CITIZENS

I think I have said enough to indicate the types of reform which can be attempted with reasonable chance of success in eradicating or at least mitigating suburbanitis. When, however, a reasonable plan, adapted to the needs of the particular community, has been selected after careful and impartial study, there remains the job of selling it to the people, for unless you can sell it to the people the politicians at the courthouse and in the legislature can hardly be expected to do much about it. There are, of course, all sorts of devices for selling ideas to the public. We in Connecticut have just had a deluge of them in the political campaign of 1950: comic strips, singing "politicals," television programs, speakers arriving (or not) in helicopters, as well as the older inducements of quartettes, bands, sound trucks, transparencies and billboards. You can get plenty of better advice than mine on the form of presentation of the case for the selected cure for suburbanitis. Whatever the method, what has to be got to the people are the facts. They must be presented persistently but good humoredly.

We have mentioned the importance of the group which sponsors the study being representative of all elements in the metropolitan area. It is just as important that the campaign be similarly sponsored. The city and its officials cannot wage war on the county and its officials and the lesser municipalities and their officials and win anything but self-approbation and defeat. In these matters I am a believer in citizen action under the leadership of a citizen group without personal axes to grind. The cure of suburbanitis, even its substantial amelioration, requires action of a kind which politicians rarely take except under some form of compulsion. Their personal and party interests are too deeply involved for it to be otherwise.

The task of convincing the public is by no means a hopeless one. The facts looked at from a long-range point of view will do the job. I do not blame home owners in the suburbs for reacting on first impression against the idea of absorption by a neighboring big city. They have gone to the outskirts in the hope of cheaper and better living. They may not have found it. The construction, maintenance and operation of a well and a septic tank, higher fire insurance rates, the fee paid to the garbage collector and other costs incident to semi-rural life, not infrequently balance the lower price of the lot and the lower taxes. All the more reason why they should balk at the higher taxes of a large city on top of these investments. You can't talk them out of their opposition by calling them parasites, chisellers or leeches. They may to some extent be getting a free ride on the backs of city taxpayers but they just can't be expected to see that without some very careful and tactful explanation.

The fact is, however, that suburbanitis is catching up with them. As the suburban population grows, wells and septic tanks become unsatisfactory. They need waterworks and sewer systems. The little towns and villages which a dozen years ago were run satisfactorily on an amateur or part-time basis, at low cost to the taxpayer, have become large towns and villages and have to pay for what they get at the same wages and prices as prevail in the neighboring city. The surge of wartime babies now pouring into the lower grades of the schools has finally demonstrated the inadequacy of the school plant everywhere, and the town and village districts, like the city districts, are going to pay through the nose to make up for the building deficiencies of the last two decades.

Suburban taxes, real taxes—the rate times assessed valuation—have been for some time on the climb and are apparently destined to scramble up so fast that the differential the suburbs have enjoyed will soon be a thing of the past. The plight of the poorer suburbs which never had low taxes except at the sacrifice of needed services will be particularly forlorn in the years ahead. These are facts which can be demonstrated to any citizen with a grammar grade education.

ENCOURAGE UNITY

The suburbanite usually feels, and often with justification, that his suburban government is more honest, efficient and responsive than that of the big city or the embracing county. To the extent that this is illusion it will be eliminated by the rising costs of the era on which we are all embarked. To the extent that the belief is well founded I can suggest no way out but the improvement of city and county government. A city which feels the need of integration in its metropolitan area must approach the matter with clean hands. Complete asepsis is rightfully demanded of those who would operate on a metropolitan community for suburbanitis.

Every incidental thing should be done that can be done to encourage a sense of metropolitan unity. Community Chest, Red Cross, March of Dimes and other drives should be if possible on a county-wide basis, with full participation in the honors as well as the work for the suburbanites. Civic organizations, luncheon clubs, all manner of voluntary citizen activities, should also be on at least a county-wide basis. Obviously, Chamber of Commerce and Advertising Club publicity should at all times emphasize the idea of the greater city in whose pride and prosperity all can share. In other words, take the suburbanites into partnership. It often happens that many of the best and most active business and professional men of the city by day are suburbanites by night.

A RECENT PROBLEM

All this takes some doing but it can be done. It will take time but the world was not made in a day and the essential institutions of mankind, among which local government is rightly numbered, cannot be changed, unless by violence, in many many days of effort and debate. That is why democracy is the most stable of all forms of government. It makes superficial changes rapidly, it alters the course of its deeper currents very slowly indeed. We are here dealing with a change in the basic outline of local self-government. We should not be disheartened because a problem which emerged only 30 years ago has not been solved.

There has been a lot of nonsense talked about the optimism of youth and the pessimism of old age. Youth is full of animal vigor which takes risks lightly but it is easily discouraged when hope is deferred. In old age personal hopes and ambitions may fail but faith in the future of a good cause grows stronger because progress can be measured against the perspective of a long distant past. It is now just 50 years since I was a senior at Harvard, getting my first bite of a course which dealt in part with local government. There were not then a dozen colleges in the country which thought the subject worth teaching at all. There was no textbook on American local government for student use. The proceedings of the National Municipal League's Conferences on

Good City Government, then in their seventh year, contained most of the material in print on the subject.

At that time neither the commission nor the manager plan of government had been heard of. There was no such thing as a merit system for the employees of any city except those in New York and Massachusetts. Every change in party control made a clean sweep of city halls and courthouses. The word "budget" was only a recent importation from Europe, scarcely applicable to anything in the United States. Municipal accounting was concerned only with the inflow and outflow of cash in the sometimes vain attempt to keep the hands of politicians out of the till.

There was no such thing as a nonpartisan municipal ballot. In fact, there was no such thing as a well regulated partisan primary. Nominations for local office were made by caucus and convention, in which the outsider or independent had no chance. There was scarcely a good registration system in the country. In close elections the names on the very tombstones were voted. There were no limitations on election expenditures, no restrictions on political contributions by city or county employees. Reform waves were always sporadic because reform candidates could be elected only by an effort too prodigious to be repeated frequently. In short, Bryce's dictum of thirteen years before, that municipal government was our "one conspicuous failure," was still true and accepted with fatalistic resignation by 99 per cent of those who should have been fighting for reform.

I have seen all this change. American politics is by no means spotless but let no one tell you that it is not incomparably cleaner, and American local government infinitely more honest and efficient than it was 50 years ago. When I was a senior at Harvard the subject we have been discussing today had not even been heard of except as it had already affected such great cities as London and New York. Buffalo, Cleveland, Pittsburgh, Atlanta, Birmingham, and a hundred other communities in which suburbanitis is acute today were not even aware that there could be such a disease. The conception of the greater city of to-morrow had not even dawned on the minds of dreamers. I am confident that as we have solved so many other problems of organization and procedure in local government, in spite of the intense opposition of the politicians and the deadening pessimism of the public, we shall in good time—not too far off—conquer suburbanitis.

86. *Fellow Citizens and Taxpayers**

DR. BROMAGE, a professor of political science at the University of Michigan, has taught courses and written extensively in the field of American local government. In the spring of 1949 he was elected city councilman in Ann Arbor. In this article he takes a look at citizen interest in municipal government—a subject with which he has dealt in the past as teacher and scholar. His views are no doubt influenced by his participation in city politics.

"I AM a citizen and a taxpayer." How many times, as a city councilman in Ann Arbor, Michigan, have I heard this sentence—at a public hearing, on the sidewalk, in the corridor, or over the telephone. This is the battlecry of democracy, the bugle call before the citizen charges the citadel of city hall. When Mr. Average Citizen drives homeward, and his purring, elegant motor car encounters a chuck-hole in the black-top pavement, he says in his subconscious: "I am a citizen and a taxpayer." Such an affront ought not to happen to any citizen, and certainly not to a taxpayer!

Any conversation which begins with this stinging sentence puts me on aldermanic guard. I know that something has happened. A traffic ticket has been issued by a misguided police department. The garbage has gone uncollected for several days. Heavy rains have caused "sanitary" sewage to back up in someone's basement. A barking dog in a neighborhood has barked once too often. The snow wasn't cleared from all the arterial streets by 8 a. m. The zoning ordinance is about to be amended at the wrong corner. It may be anyone of 57 different varieties of problems which can cause citizen reaction to that target building known as city hall.

One belligerent citizen (who, incidentally, wanted to violate a city ordinance) said he would turn the city hall upside down and get to the bottom of things. He promised to fight it out along that line, if it took all winter. It didn't take all winter, and his problem was solved by the aldermen before the city hall was turned topsy-turvy. I have some idea how a city hall looks to the citizen, but I sometimes wonder if the citizen and taxpayer ever considers how he looks from inside city hall.

* Arthur W. Bromage, *The Municipality*, 45 (July, 1950), pp. 141, 154-155. Reprinted by permission of the author and the publisher.

THE DISINTERESTED CITIZEN

One of the mysteries of our democracy is the disinterested citizen, who is also a taxpayer. For those of us who labor at city hall, it is startling to analyze the election returns. We can estimate that one out of four will vote in the primary, and only one out of three will participate in the general election—that is, of the registered voters! In how many cities and for how many years is this a fair prognostication of voting habits? It covers a lot of wards and years in my town and your town.

In December, 1949, I went around ward 6 in Ann Arbor collecting not less than 12 and not more than 48 signatures to renominate one of my colleagues on the city council. In one rainy Saturday afternoon, when it would have been more comfortable before an open fire, I collected 24 signatures, enough to place this candidate in the Republican primary. No one ran against him in that primary, so he was nominated without opposition. In the April, 1950, general election this Republican candidate polled 381 votes to 275 for his Democratic opponent, with more than 2,000 registered voters on the list. Where were the other voters? They couldn't possibly have all been ill, too busy to vote or vacationing in Florida. One can only conclude that most of them just weren't interested enough in their local democracy to vote.

I tried to explain this to some visiting German students at the university, but I failed, as did the voters. They weren't impressed with my theory that many of the voters may have been too well satisfied with things as they were to vote.

These same non-voting Americans have time to make a living in our democracy, to raise a family, to drive around in automobiles and to belong to clubs and associations. In an emergency, they would spring to arms overnight to defend democracy. How can we persuade them that democracy needs also to be defended, year in and year out, at the polls; that ballots as well as bullets count?

From the council table at city hall one looks at vacant chairs behind the rail. The public space can seat only 100 citizens and taxpayers—out of the 18,000 odd registered voters. Yet, standing room is never at a premium. The attendance is unlikely to go over 25, unless a high-school civics class has been mustered out or a pressure group is seeking specific action or inaction from city hall.

One long-time alderman told his ward forum meeting in 1950 that he was tired of seeing the public seats in city hall filled by interest groups. Where were the objective citizens with a general interest in the affairs of the city? He got no answers from the audience. Any old-time alderman can spot the issue at a council meeting by looking at the audience. He knows that many citizens are apathetic; that the group in attendance is for or against a specific question; that they will go home after that item is passed on the agenda. Scanning the civic horizon from city hall, too many of the citizens have a vacant look.

THE BELLIGERENT CITIZEN

The belligerent citizen likes to sound off to his councilman. One of my friends told me he supposed some one would have to be killed at a certain intersection, before the council would put in a traffic light. We are allegedly so deadened to the public interest that tragedy alone can goad us into action. As a matter of fact, this traffic intersection is studded with stop signs; can not legally be entered from any direction without stopping, and is illuminated by a flashing signal. I once asked a visiting chief of police who knew something about traffic if he considered the intersection to be adequately controlled. He observed the intersection and cross walks for a long time. He thought our police had used the best solution in view of the heavy pedestrian traffic.

Looking through my telephone card file, I find recorded some of the things which belligerent citizens say. The police should not arrest adult citizens and taxpayers for speeding; let them get after the high school boys who tear around town. The city should not amend the zoning ordinance to permit a large apartment house for that is unfair to existing landlords. The police should not prohibit parking on the north side of a certain street to facilitate traffic flow because the neighbors can't find a place to park. The city shouldn't hire more rookies because too many police are already regulating the citizens. The city should pass an ordinance to regulate sale of specified milk products since outside competitors are invading the local market. The public health standards are too severe, in view of the high cost of new equipment for drugstores and restaurants.

No one expects everything to be always "lovely-lovely" in this best of all possible democracies. Society is full of frictions and aldermen are supposed to do something about them, whether they derive from human beings, dogs, or rats. For every regulation, someone is regulated, unless selective enforcement, alas, finds a course midway between the law and social custom. Part of being a councilman is to know how to handle the belligerent, as well as the reasoning citizen.

It is an old saying around city hall that the irate citizen must be allowed to talk himself or herself out. Until this pent-up, emotional steam has been vented, no amount of reasonable counter-argument will prevail. Only after belligerence has waned can reason begin to take over. The only acceptable answer to the fuming citizen, who has ceased to fume, is that other people get fined the same amount for the same infraction; that other assessments are equitable in relation to his assessment, and that other citizens suffer from the same defects in operation because the city doesn't have enough money to go around.

Often the belligerent citizen and taxpayer is more to be admired than the complacent. At least, he expects something he isn't getting, or he gets something he isn't expecting. He reacts, and by his reactions, he may point the way to necessary changes in policy or in administration. With tactful handling, he can sometimes be turned around (but not always) to be as staunch in fighting for city hall, as he has been in fulminating against it.

THE ACTIVE AND REASONABLE CITIZEN

Fortunately for city aldermen, most of the active citizens are reasonably tolerant of city hall. They appreciate that all issues are not cut-and-dried "Yes" and "No" answers. They do not ask for favoritism, but for justice as they see it. They present their complaints and suggestions in a relatively quiet manner, and do not begin with the basic assumption that the city councilor or administrator is always wrong, or trying "to do in" the citizens. They will listen to explanations concerning the "why and wherefore" of regulations. They come before a board of review, a board of appeals, or the council itself with the underlying belief that they will get a fair hearing and that approximate justice, rather than favoritism, will prevail.

Although active and reasonable citizens will protest stoutly against a certain sign in the neighborhood, they will accept the intruder if you can prove that the sign is legal. Rather than vowing on the telephone to turn city hall upside down they will come to the appropriate public hearing and protest earnestly, but not belligerently, against a change in zoning which affects their neighborhood. They may ask for a traffic light at a certain intersection but they do not become obnoxious when told that it cannot be installed for several years. They can be persuaded that traffic counts and accident statistics should be used in determining priorities in installing signals. They pay traffic fines without calling an alderman to berate him. They pay taxes willingly, if not gladly.

Reasonable citizens appreciate the obvious fact that many city councilmen serve without salary or for a nominal honorarium. They comprehend that election does not make a person a magician. They do not expect the master plan for city improvements to be implemented in a few years. They realize that the local tax rate can only span a certain amount of police, fire, and public health protection; a specific number of park and recreational facilities, and a limited amount of construction and maintenance of public works. They understand that the water filtration plant and the sewage treatment plant can't be expanded without an increase in the rates charged for municipally owned utilities. They don't expect a silk purse in public administration to be made out of a sow's ear in taxes.

Fortunately for Ann Arbor aldermen, most of the active citizens are of this reasonable variety. They meet city hall on the level. It is not a citadel to be stormed in angry surges. It is not a political pest house to be avoided by failing to vote or to take any intelligent interest in whatsoever. It is their city hall. They built it and they determine who shall go there and how long councilmen shall stay. They will even vote extra tax dollars to establish a retirement system for municipal employes who have served the community faithfully for many years.

It takes all kinds of citizens and taxpayers to make a community: the disinterested, the belligerent, and the active and reasonable. More power to the last but not the least of these citizens. May they live long and may their number increase if democracy is to survive! Democracy in your town and my town is not won by pushbuttons. Like the old-fashioned automobile, it has to be cranked by someone for every primary, every election, every ordinance and every achievement in public administration. In our local democracies we could use more civic crankers and fewer arm-chair critics. The citizen cranker will vote, observe and suggest, taking as much pride in his own community as he does in his own home and business. Without the active and reasonable citizen, the councilman falls prey to the disinterested and the belligerent.

87. *Significant Trends in Municipal Politics**

MR. MERRIAM, former Alderman from the Fifth Ward, City Council, City of Chicago, and a political scientist as well as a politician, discusses "trends" primarily in relation to the modern problems of government in the metropolitan areas, where over half of us live today. Our cities are vastly better governed now than in the late nineteenth century when Lord Bryce found this to be our great failure in government. The problem of government today involves not only *the city* but also the cities, towns, villages, and other units of government in the metropolitan areas. How, now, do we meet this challenge?

I WOULD LIKE to look with you at some of the problems of our cities and our municipal governments. We live in a world of unbelievable change, and our cities are a product of that change. Few of us recall that when our national constitution was written, 95 per cent of our ancestors were rural dwellers and only 5 per cent were living in the 24 urban centers, as compared to 4,000 urban areas today. Over half our population today—84,671,000 people to be almost exact—live in just 168 concentrated built-up agglomerations that we call metropolitan areas.

—14 of these metropolitan areas exceed 1,000,000 population.
—7 of them contain more than 50 per cent of their respective states' population.
—One state, Ohio, has 10 metropolitan areas that contain over 60 per cent of the entire state population.
—While the total United States population increased 14 per cent in the decade 1940-1950, the metropolitan areas increased by 21 per cent, and within the metropolitan areas (but outside the central cities) this figure rose to 34 per cent.
—Your metropolitan area, Detroit, grew by 27 per cent in the decade, with the areas outside the central city expanding 55 per cent while the central city grew only 14 per cent.

These metropolitan centers of today, of course, are the best measure of our industrial prowess. The productive might and industrial genius, of which this metropolitan area is the greatest symbol, represent, far

* Robert E. Merriam, *Vital Speeches of The Day*, XXII (March 1, 1956), pp. 316-320. An address delivered before The Economic Club of Detroit, Michigan, December 12, 1955. Reprinted with permission from the publishers of *Vital Speeches*.

more than any new weapons, the deterrent to Communist aggression.

The metropolitan area is the product of our increased specialization, both industrial and agricultural, and the development of the modern means of transportation—for which Detroit is the great symbol. The telephone and the automobile are the prime movers in the vast centrifugal movement which is throwing population further and further out, away from the center of the metropolitan area.

The effect of all this on government is staggering. Our national constitution makes no provision for organizing the subdivisions of the states, because no problem existed in 1787 when there were only 24 urban centers. Most state constitutions were written or rewritten before the urban phenomenon became a real thing. And we all know that state legislatures today still are dominated by the rural sections. However, certain common forms of local government were adopted by the states. Most states were divided into counties, and counties were divided into townships. Towns or incorporated places, including cities, were created where clusters of people gathered. To handle the education of the young, school districts were created and generally were superimposed on top of the county-township organization. And finally, a series of special districts were created, including everything from mosquito-abatement districts to transit authorities, sanitary districts, park districts, and housing authorities. Many of these special districts were formed on what I believe is the mistaken notion that the more governments and elected officials there were, the more democratic one became. Sometimes these new governmental units were formed because citizens, incensed over corruption or graft in their existing local governments, would hope to avoid this corruption by setting up a new special district to bypass the discredited city government. Sometimes new governmental units were piled on top of the existing structure because of state constitutional or statutory limitations on taxing or bonding power which restricted the ability of established local governments to meet new needs. Sometimes they came about because of national legislation authorizing aid for specific tasks, on the condition that special agencies would be created to do the job. Part of the proliferation just happened—like Topsy, the urban governments just growed.

Whatever the cause, here is what we find today:

—16,210 separate governments exist in these 168 metropolitan areas—an average of 96 per area.

But some do much worse . . .

—New York metropolitan area—1,071 governments.

—Chicago—960.

—Philadelphia—702.

—Pittsburgh—616.
—St. Louis—420.
—Oakland—372.
—and Detroit—355 governments in the metropolitan area.

What do we find as a result?

—city-suburb jealousies.

I had a debate one day with the mayor of a suburban town in the Chicago area about whether there was a metropolitan problem. I must say that I felt somewhat frustrated when we even had to debate the premise of the argument.

—police work hampered by jurisdictional problems.

In Cook County, the home county of Chicago, there are 101 different police forces just in that one county. Because there are 101 police forces a very heinous murder of 3 youths that occurred in a no man's land of responsibility is being badly bungled; no one knows exactly who is responsible for doing what. So these aren't merely theoretical problems that we are talking about.

—transportation needs not integrated.

—planning in most areas almost non-existent on an area basis (although I hope you know that your metropolitan area is a welcome exception to this case).

—problems of water supply, sewage and drainage, to mention a few of the many problems from the proliferation of governments.

—a long ballot—sometimes called—in Chicagoland at least—the bed-sheet ballot because of its size.

—so many elected officials one never knows whom to blame when things go wrong. Chicagoans elect 389 officials, to give you an example of the problem one area faces.

And all this time the problems of these metropolitan areas have been multiplying.

. . . The central areas of cities have been deteriorating; we are just beginning to learn the technique of harvesting a new crop of houses and buildings in an old city.

. . . Transportation needs create problems of undreamed magnitude —whether it be that hour's ride from an airport, the problems of a complex network of highways, congestion of cars, the question of whether to build parking garages at a cost of $16,000,000, the problems of an ailing public transportation system; these are only some of the problems of urban life today. (Chicago has 1,000,000 people every day who descend upon and then leave the central downtown area. And they are all in a hurry—both ways. And many of them arrive in their automobiles.)

. . . We are trying to make sense out of land usages which have grown by happenstance rather than reason—industry next to residence, highways cutting up industrial areas, long commercial ribbons, etc.

. . . We have urgent problems of housing standards and decent shelter.

. . . We have health hazards aggravated by congestion; smoke is just one of the many health problems.

. . . We have organized criminal elements preying upon the wealth of these urban concentrations.

. . . We have tremendous educational and recreational needs.

. . . And there are problems of intergroup relations in the urban melting pot.

Any one of these problems is enough to stagger the imagination of even the bold of heart. When added together and then considered in the framework of divided governments and diffused power, they add up to a national crisis.

Take a quick look at the problem of circulating people around a metropolis as an example. Cars are built to go faster and faster on roads that take them slower and slower, and present horrible problems of congestion. An expressway program costing several hundred million dollars helps. But have we adequately provided spaces for cars to park when they arrive at their destination? And can we ever keep up with this insatiable demand for parking space? Yet every public transportation system in the country is having trouble keeping its head above water, and buses on city streets are involved in a vicious cycle: the buses move slowly because they must fight the traffic of private autos; because the buses move slowly even more people drive their own cars; which means more congestion and even slower bus times; which means that even more people drive their cars, leading to even more congestion; which leads to an even further loss of bus riders; which means a fare raise to make up for the loss of revenue; which results in even fewer riders; and so the cycle goes. But we are only beginning to talk about monorails or other modern transportation media that might move the huge volume of passengers that need to get somewhere within the metropolitan area (not just the city)—and usually, as I say, in a hurry.

Or take the problem of the urban melting pot. The central city has always been the receiving center for the newest migrants to the city. The successive waves of European migrants—the Irish, Italians, Poles—have now been succeeded by the last remaining market of unskilled and semi-skilled labor—the southern Negro. This migration is necessary if our industry is to continue to expand. A committee on which I served, studying racial tensions in Chicago, heard testimony which upset some wishful thinkers who were hoping for a return to what they liked to call "the good old days." A student of population movement said,

"The day migration from the South ends is the day you should begin to worry. It will mean that your industry has stopped growing." The eyes of some tough-minded citizens of Chicago were opened by this comment.

Politically, this migration presents added problems. The Negro does not blend into the life of the community as rapidly as did his predecessor migrants—his skin is a different color, even if his problems are the same. And so he is pressed more closely together—many times in unbelievable living conditions—subject to the prey of unscrupulous demagogues who want to exploit him for personal power or gain. Block voting of any kind is dangerous and blind. A hemmed-in population living in crowded, congested quarters, bound together by the pressure from a hostile society, presents even more problems.

The urban Negro can present a block of votes of unparalleled power. In my home town (where we have partisan national politics at the local level), the Negro—who overwhelmingly supports the Democratic Party—gets the worst services as thanks for his support; he has the least police protection and garbage collection; and the most illegal conversions of buildings. The dominating powers in the government get away with it only because they know, because of party labels and allegiances, that they *can* get away with it.

I don't pretend to know the answer to this problem. The answer lies deep in the souls of men. But I do know that we can't get away from the problem simply by fleeing to the suburbs or living in an ivory tower. You who are in industry—and who need the labor supply to keep your factories going—most certainly have a grave responsibility to help find some answers. The solution does not lie in abandoning as beyond redemption the central city—which after all is the nerve center of every metropolitan area.

I have thrown at you fast and furiously some of the headaches of metropolitan life, and I have barely scratched the surface at that. When we look at these and many other things that local governments do, we begin to ask ourselves how anyone can ever say that these things are unimportant.

We have been the most inventive society the world has yet known—in our governmental as well as in our industrial life. We have painfully built up the only truly effective decentralized government in the world. We have devised and made work a system of divided powers between these levels of government—national, state, and local—and within the levels as well, with the courts, the legislatures and the executive branch.

Is it asking too much that we now turn greater attention to making that which we have developed really work? Are we to say that these vast, urban agglomerations cannot be so organized to provide effectively and rapidly that which people demand.

The metropolitan area is here to stay—as are its problems, and the problems have only begun. The task before us is to develop, at the metropolitan level, governmental mechanisms which can meet present-day problems.

In terms of governmental structure, there are some possible remedies to these metropolitan ailments. The growing urban centers once solved these problems of expansion by annexing the new urban territory. Without this procedure, most of the large central cities of today would not be in existence. But around the turn of the century this trend slowed down, again partly because of widespread corruption in municipal governments, partly because suburbanites thought they could avoid the problems of the central city by politically divorcing themselves from it, partly because they thought they could avoid expanding tax burdens by remaining independent. Today we are burdened with the results of this philosophy. Some cities, like Detroit, have special problems created by the end of annexation with cities completely within the central city. (Such a situation leads to some special headaches when expressways are being located, to mention just one example.) None of the above stated reasons for independent communities are as valid today; congestion in schools, double shifts, and high tax rates are metropolitan-wide problems, not just city-wide. We have found that corruption is not associated with bigness as much as it is with disinterest (which can be as prevalent in the suburb as in the central city). And with the movement of industry ever outward, problems of plant location are area-wide, not just central-city wide. The plain fact is that there is no way to escape the problems of urbanism, short of leaving the urban area—and this just isn't going to happen.

But the psychological block to annexation is so great as to preclude that method as a practical solution to metropolitan problems. As an alternative, some have urged the strengthening and fortifying of county government. Yet most county governments are headless wonders, with large boards and no central executive responsibility. City-county consolidations have been tried with some success in a few urban areas, but there has been no general enthusiasm for this technique. In some metropolitan regions, area-wide authorities have been established to cope with specific problems.

What happens is that usually when there is agreement that there is a metropolitan problem, somebody suggests another new government —for sanitation, or highways, or water, or the like. To the extent that such an authority provides services on an area basis, it may be good. But the net result is a further growth in the number of independent governments, the number of elected or appointed officials, the diffusion of authority, and the fragmentalization of responsibility.

A quick calculation shows that the authorities in the Detroit area have a total of 128 members all told; just to examine a map of their differing jurisdictions makes me dizzy. If carried to its ultimate extreme, we would end up with a metropolitan authority for each functional activity of government, and we might be worse off than before. Some such units may be helpful. For instance, a really effective metropolitan planning unit (like the one in Detroit) can be a real assist in area development. And I don't mean to imply by my remarks that all such authorities are bad, or that they don't do a good job in and of themselves.

It seems clear to me, however, that the only effective answer lies in the development of some kind of integrated metropolitan government. An improved county structure with a county manager or similar responsible executive authority might be one possibility. A federation of governments, on the Toronto pattern, is another possibility, with the over-all metropolitan government being given certain area-wide responsibilities and certain individual local units retaining administration of those services which can still be carried out effectively on a small-scale basis. New York's borough system is an example of this, and has worked well, but it covers only a part of that metropolitan area.

Whatever the particular scheme, somehow we have to produce a governmental structure which is able to provide services and at the same time develop the political structures and processes that are comprehensible and accountable to the electorate.

Of one thing I am very certain, however: the near breakdown of governmental services will never be solved by some easily found gimmick or panacea. We Americans are great on this and we traditionally look for short-cuts. In government, when a problem finally is identified and recognized we usually look for that easy answer. Create a new authority! Change the election laws! Bring in voting machines! Get a new charter! These are the traditional chants of the well-intentioned short-cut artist.

Some of these proposals are good, but as a means not an end. None solves the basic problems. Effective metropolitan government must be simply organized, the responsibilities must be clearly allocated, and it must be able to cope with all the problems of all of the area.

And I am certain of one other fact: the answer to this, what ails us, will never be found in Washington. The greatest contribution of our society to government was the federal system with wide areas of local autonomy. Before running to Washington with our problems we ought to ask ourselves: "If we had the will could we perform this function ourselves?" In far too many instances, had the question been asked, the answer would have been yes.

I am one who believes that states' rights should be more than a political slogan. But like everything else, it must be worked at to succeed. States' wrongs rather than states' rights may be our problem. And the same applies to local governments. In my office at the Bureau of the Budget in Washington a steady stream of visitors, including many businessmen, come wanting the national government to do something for them.

Many of the activities they come to talk about are important—but can we really talk about states' rights or against encroachment by the national government if we continue to follow the easy trail to Washington? And must we admit that these services will be better performed if done by the national government?

The Bureau of the Budget is now finalizing its recommendations to the President for the 1957 fiscal year. The size of our operations staggers me, I'm frank to admit, and makes me understand more than ever why states and local governments must assume every possible legitimate function of government within their responsibility. Do you want your local problems to get bogged down in this:

—a budget of over $60 billion.
—a payroll of over $10 billion.
—civilian personnel totaling over 2,000,000.
—programs ranging from development of new crop seeds to the H-bomb.
—pressures for new programs, beyond belief.

Our budget experts tell me that without batting an eyelash, for legitimate programs, things which someone should do, we could easily expand our national budget by 30 to 40 per cent. And yet how easy it seems to be to run to Washington to "get a law passed." New York City is now talking about trying to get the national government to underwrite the cost of their subway system, believe it or not. Chicago wants the national government to break ice on the river. Memphis wanted us to build a steam plant for it at everyone's expense. And so it goes. These are things that local governments can and should do. But think of the things they can't do—thirty-four billion dollars for our defense establishment:

—$200 million to build an aircraft carrier.
—$3 million just to replace its defective propeller shafts.
—or $110,000 to build one modern tank.
—$9 million to build one B-52.

These are some of the legitimate functions of the national government. Nobody else can do these things. Let's leave the national government free to perform the things it is best equipped to do, and at the same time strengthen state and local governments so they will do the things they could and should. (But let's not use this states' rights argument, either, may I add, as a camouflage to hide attacks on necessary national programs for social betterment.)

We come then, as we always must in talking about politics in government, to the greatest problem of all: How to get people interested in helping to solve urban problems. It seems strange that this is a problem in a democracy, and yet the history of municipal politics is one of active disinterest on the part of too many people.

A Gallup poll at the end of World War II asked the mothers of returning servicemen what they wanted their sons to do when they got home from the service. As might be expected, there was no agreement on this subject, except in a negative sense—over three quarters of the mothers wanted their sons to have nothing to do with politics.

Eight years as a member of Chicago's City Council taught me the bitter facts about this feeling. Not only is it hard to get people interested in politics—it is hard enough to get them to vote. "What's the use?"; "they're all corrupt"; or "what's the difference?" are standard responses to those who ask why more people aren't participating.

A vicious cycle sets in. Which comes first makes little difference, but the net effect is lack of participation—the three negative N's of politics, nonvoting, noninterest, and nonparticipation, replace the teachings of the civics class. Nationally our voting habits are bad enough, but at the local level they are atrocious. In Chicago, which in this example is no different from most other communities, 600,000 registered voters stayed away from the polls on a sunny April day this spring when a new mayor was being selected. (And although I'm convinced that all of those 600,000 would have voted for me, I'll have a hard time ever proving it. My only consolation is that this turnout was about par for the municipal course.)

Some of my supporters were curious as to why these 600,000 registered voters stayed home, and they hired an outstanding national opinion-taking organization to conduct a post-election survey to see if they could get any real insights into nonvoting patterns. The results were interesting, although both encouraging and discouraging. At one end of the spectrum they found about 25 per cent of the voting population who vote religiously in practically every election—their voting habits were instilled early in life, most frequently, interestingly enough, by parental example. At the other end of the spectrum was a block of about 10 per cent of the population who never vote. Their answers ran something like this: "lack of interest;" "ignorance of politics;" "lack of time;" or sometimes "politics is crooked," etc. The remaining two thirds of the potential voters have fluctuating voting records. They will vote when they think there is something important at stake: in the 1952 Presidential election over 90 per cent of Chicago's voters came to the polls; but consistently they have not gotten as excited about local elections.

The bright side of the survey was the indication that although only a fraction of the potential voting population actively participate in election campaigns (something like 5 per cent of eligible voters), once active they usually remain active and seldom backslide into the non-voting category. Surprisingly enough, one of the things the survey dug up was that there are definite indications that older persons participated more than the younger generation. (In the Chicago election, three quarters of the persons aged 50-64 voted as compared with less than half of the persons 21-34. And the surveyors were prompted to note that perhaps we should spend more attention getting the young voters who now have the franchise to vote, and less attention on the question of what the initial voting age should be.)

If you will forgive a continuing use of a personal example, the really encouraging thing about the Chicago mayoralty election of this year was that about 3,000 citizen-politicians actively worked precincts (most of them for the first time) in the Citizens for Merriam organization which was a genuine fusion effort with Republicans, Democrats, and Independents, nationally, uniting in an effort to smash the dominant local Democratic machine. And although we lost the battle, I think we eventually will win the war because those 3,000 citizens got a taste of political activity, and even today many of them are girding themselves for the next round in this never-ending fight against a powerfully entrenched machine.

Three attitudes hindered our efforts to build a better city government. First, was the indifference I have just mentioned. Second, was the cynicism about politics which we find all too often. The poison of corruption can, and does, spread noiselessly through an entire community, often without people being aware of what is happening. In Chicago, alliances between police and politicians and the underworld, so open and brazen as to astound the outsider, were taken for granted. It was accepted that contracts are meant for the friendly (and that latter word does not mean just a smile on their faces). One of your fellow townsmen went through the "treatment" when he was audacious enough to bid on some business he wasn't supposed to get. His story is a story of jungle politics at work. The fact that he finally got the contract with my help is, I think, perhaps my proudest moment in

Chicago politics. I had never known the man before, but the two of us—and we were literally all alone—licked a system just by standing up and fighting.

But there are, unfortunately, all too few businessmen or others who will stand up and fight. I have seen industrial giants—national firms—ignominiously knuckle under to peanut politicians because it seemed to be the "easy" thing to do. It was common gossip in Chicago, for example, that price lists were posted for the granting by some aldermen of permits to break the curb. For eight years businessmen would tell me of their payments, and pat me on the back for refusing to "charge." But not one of them would, in that entire time, publicly come forward to tell his story—and so the practice very probably still goes on.

And the third paralyzing attitude was a blind acceptance of the need for national partisan politics at the local level. I may very immodestly say that I would be Mayor of Chicago today were it not for this attitude and the state election laws prohibiting a candidate from having his name on the ballot under more than one party label. One of our pre-election polls showed that the voters wanted Merriam 2 to 1, but also wanted the Democrats to win 2 to 1. When these conflicting forces met head on, the party loyalty overcame the personal choice. The only effective argument the Democratic machine used was that they had to keep Chicago Democratic to help elect a President in 1956. I hope you will understand that it is not just personal pique that makes me suggest—paraphrasing the famous railroader's comments—that "this is a hell of a way to run a municipality."

Now let me say right here that I am a firm believer in the two-party system of national politics. I think with all their faults (yes, bickerings and compromises, too), in this vast, complicated land with diverse regions and peoples, the two-party system has worked well.

But what about the arguments for national party politics at the local level? Usually when all the verbiage is stripped aside, its purpose is to make available to the dominant party the machinery of local government, including jobs for party faithful, to assist that party in its efforts to get votes for its national candidates. Now in itself perhaps this is no sin. But what are the results:

1. Patronage, overplayed, leads to ineffective if not corrupt government.

2. The use of favoritism to special cliques, be they industry, labor, or gambling syndicates, can wreck a government.

Detroit is fortunate in having a unique municipal election law—the nonpartisan election of mayor and a small at-large city council. Believe me, take it from one who has been through the mill of a partisan city council and city government! I think you probably do not know how fortunate you are. You have something which you should guard zealously and vigorously, because I defy anyone to show me the Republican or Democratic way of collecting garbage or policing the streets. Partisan local politics—using a city government as a chessman in national issues—can, and usually does, mean bad local politics. Hundreds of cities and towns have gotten away from this, and have found that they are better able to consider their problems as a result.

This is a quick overview of some metropolitan problems. I wish I could give you simple answers to all of these problems. I would say very simply, however, that in politics and government nothing is easy —unless we decide we really want to do something about it. Those great men who drafted our Constitution 168 years ago gave us the finest political document ever written—and the best means yet discovered by which man can govern himself. That flexible document has enabled us to withstand the strain of—

—civil war
—two world wars
—a world depression
—an unbelievable industrial revolution

A country of less than 4,000,000 rural inhabitants, has become the most powerful nation in the world—165 million of us, with national income of $300 billion a year; total governmental expenditures of nearly $100 billion a year.

The descendants of Paul Revere's minute men became the citizen-soldiers of those world wars we fought. What we now need, I submit —desperately—are citizen-politicians: you and you and you. Who else has a greater stake in his community, a greater opportunity to be of help, a greater chance to see progress: If you don't take the lead, someone else will, because of one thing I am sure—we must and we will break the log-jam of indifference and jealousy which has clogged the stream of metropolitan progress.

XVI

GOVERNMENT FINANCE

88. *An Economist's Viewpoint on Tax Policy* *

In a letter to M. Leroy in 1789 Benjamin Franklin commented that "Our Constitution is in actual operation; everything appears to promise that it will last; but in this world nothing is certain but death and taxes." Our Constitution continues to give promise that it will last, and we citizens hold firmly to the conviction that taxes are certain. In the present article Mr. Shere provides an interesting analysis of factors that he considers important in the development of a tax policy. As the title indicates, the article represents the viewpoint of an economist; a politician or a businessman, for instance, might differ with Mr. Shere on a number of points.

Tax policy in America is adrift. The finances of government are not effectively organized to help maintain prosperity. They will not steer the economy away from the danger zones of instability.

The present Federal, state, and local system is the product of slow growth. It is partly a conglomerate of inadvertently accumulated tax provisions and techniques, and many of its salient characteristics were forged on the anvil of emergency during World War I, the Great Depression, and World War II. Some features of the inherited system are outmoded; others, sired by misguided tax policy, never have effectively promoted a prosperous America. If the welfare of the public is to be served, both tax policy and tax structure must be modernized to fulfill the needs of a dynamic America.

In taxation as elsewhere, inertia and complacency are the great obstacles to reform. Natural tendencies to adhere to old procedures must

* Louis Shere, *The Annals of the American Academy of Political and Social Science*, 266 (November, 1949), pp. 166-173. Reprinted by permission of the author and the publisher.

be surmounted. New ideas must be embraced and put into effect before, not after, the defects of present tax arrangements become patent to the least imaginative segment of the population and its legislative representatives.

It is not necessary to make any revolutionary changes in the American tax system, but several major adjustments are urgent The need for tax reform has been obscured by the extraordinary financial experiences of government under the exceptional circumstances of a wartime and postwar inflated economy. Under more typical peacetime conditions, the lethargic approach to tax and fiscal problems cannot expected to remain harmless.

SIZE OF GOVERNMENT

Government has grown enormously, both absolutely and in relation to the economy. The impact of government on business and all phases of economic life is now very much more important than it was at the beginning of World War II. The huge amounts of revenue collected and of public funds spent leave their marks on the levels and patterns of investment, production, consumption, employment, and every critical index of economic activity. The gloomier observers have witnessed this process of government expansion in painful fear for the survival of the private enterprise system.

Basically the situation is by no means a desperate one; at least it is far less desperate than the counselors of despair depict it. Strangely afflicted with myopia when peering into the future, and hyperopia when contemplating the past, each wave of public expenditure induces in the modern Canutes a vociferous command to retreat. But instead, public expenditures persist on an upward course.

This upward trend has been characteristic of democratic governments for decades the world over, and it will not be reversed by the deterioration of or improvement in the fortunes of any political party. The growth in government is permanent. Economies can and should be effected. The healing of international wounds would permit the reduction of military expenditures by billions. Except temporarily, however, the absolute cost of government will continue to rise as the public insists now on one costly program and then on another. Effective leadership in matters of tax and fiscal policy hinges in large part upon the clear recognition of this datum.

Government cannot be shrunk to the size of any favored past period. The struggle to accomplish such a goal would be both futile and prejudicial to prosperity and economic development.

More important for the preservation of the free enterprise system and democratic government than the absolute size of government is its size relative to the national economy. This should shrink. It can shrink despite increasing public expenditures if economic policies in general are skillfully directed to realize the potential increase in production which inheres in a steadily growing labor force. The tax burden can be lightened and demands for necessary public services can be met as well, only if the vitality of the American free enterprise system is preserved and the rate of growth of production outruns the growth of government.

This does not mean that America cannot be kept free and prosperous with some enlargement of government relative to the economy. It is easier, however, to be specific than to be informed on precisely where to draw the boundary line between democratic free enterprise and a regimented economic system. In the United States, government now accounts for about 25 per cent of economic activity. Some pretend to see that this constitutes an outside limit of safety. As evidence that the American situation is far from alarming, the more discerning point to the substantial variation and greater role of government among the democracies with which America is associated for the preservation of a way of life.

BROAD OBJECTIVES OF TAXATION

Superficially, the broad objectives of tax policy seem well defined, and there appears to be a large measure of agreement on the criteria of a desirable tax system. Actually, the semblance of harmony is attained either by abstinence of thought or by permitting different schools of thought to read conflicting meanings into the same words. This becomes evident once an attempt is made to apply the criteria of desirable tax policy to specific tax measures.

Subject to the foregoing qualifications, acceptable principles of taxation were well described in Secretary of the Treasury Snyder's statement to the Ways and Means Committee on May 19, 1947:

> The tax system should produce adequate revenue. It should be equitable in its treatment of different groups. It should interfere as little as possible with incentives to work and to invest. It should help maintain the broad consumer markets that are essential for high-level production and employment. Taxes should be as simple to administer and as easy to comply with as possible. While the tax system should be flexible and change with changing economic conditions, it should be possible to achieve this flexibility without frequent revisions of the basic tax structure.

The huge tax load is inevitably forcing to the surface, for scrutiny, every tax measure that is suspect as regards its effect upon production and a just distribution of the burden.

FISCAL POLICY

Effective fiscal policy may be expected to be tardy in its development. It is directed to stabilize an economic system of great complexity, the operation of which is but imperfectly understood by the experts, let alone the public, and yet appropriate fiscal policies cannot be pursued without the support of an enlightened public opinion. The major instruments of fiscal policy evade general comprehension. Few understand the mysterious interconnections between debt management, tax policy, public expenditures, and monetary policy, and the articulated effects of all in combination upon the economy. Even in recent years, when one may expect greater sophistication than in past decades, it is not difficult to find outstanding examples of incongruous and conflicting objectives heatedly pursued on the general domain of fiscal policy.

It is recognized that the major instruments of fiscal policy frequently have not been properly articulated. At no time, however, have the experts been able to agree as to which parts were at fault. While there is no disposition to decry the prevalence of intellectual independence in economic investigation, it should not be shocking to the more ardent economic practitioners to find that disagreement among the experts is confusing to the legislators charged with final responsibility for the implementation of fiscal policy.

Fortunately, a complete public understanding of fiscal policy is not essential for American prosperity. It would be a major achievement if, at the policy and legislative level, agreement could be reached on the fundamental principle that, irrespective of the size of the public debt, taxes in relation to public expenditures should be higher in periods of rising and high business activity than in periods of declining and low business activity; for stability in revenue can be attained only at the cost of economic instability and a higher level of public debt. Even this limited application of acceptable fiscal policy encounters major obstacles which are based on an exaggerated conception of human frailty. The fear is that spending would not be as enthusiastically curbed, and taxes imposed, in prosperity, as expenditures would be stimulated, and taxes lightened, in depression, and thus the size of government and the public debt would constantly increase.

This gloomy appraisal of human nature has stimulated a search for automatic economic correctives as a substitute for or an aid to fiscal policy, which so far has yielded only tentative blueprints for a variety of safety valves, gongs and whistles, to be installed in strategic places.

Structural changes in the monetary and tax systems doubtless are needed to attain greater countercyclical flexibility. However, automatic economic correctives are not a substitute for responsible fiscal policy. Ultimately, it is essential to trust the integrity and intelligence of the public and its elected representatives to operate the finances of a democratic government in a manner compatible with the public welfare. Economic mechanisms that facilitate the achievement of clearly discerned objectives are desirable; laws that bind the human intelligence are not.

The extent of fiscal policy manipulation required to support a program of economic stability is directly related to the quality of the basic tax structure. The laissez faire approach to fiscal policy is most feasible when the tax system is flexible in its adjustment to changing economic conditions, is equitable, and is balanced to minimize the repressive effects upon production and consumption. Fiscal policy tinkering should be avoided, for while it is human to err, business expectations are easily disrupted, and business planning for expansion would fall an easy prey to unessential minor adjustments, even if they are founded upon accurate appraisals, and certainly if they are not. Fiscal policy action should be reserved to resist the development of major economic swings.

INTERGOVERNMENTAL FISCAL RELATIONS

Some major changes in the American tax system are needed to make it function satisfactorily even under strong fiscal policy direction.

Intergovernmental fiscal relations are antiquated. Tax reform can be but limited, without action in the field of intergovernmental fiscal relations. An adequate factual background of the intergovernmental flow of funds by source and functions is not yet available. Still, the salient facts are known.

Local governments, and to some extent the states too, are hard pressed for revenue to match their costly functions. Federal grants are flowing in growing volume to the states and are spilling over state barriers in the direct channels to local governments. After a period of substantial growth, state grants and shared taxes are encountering resistance at both the giving and the receiving ends. The financial responsibilities for expanding governmental costs are being thrown back in large measure to the local units of government. The states are implementing this policy by endowing their subdivisions with new taxing powers which, however, do not encompass the relaxation of property tax limitations.

UNWISE POLICIES

Thus under enormous financial pressure and gross misguidance, a big step backward was taken in intergovernmental fiscal relations and reform of the American tax system. Thousands of local units of government have enacted many more thousands of undesirable consumption and miscellaneous business and other taxes. Problems of tax compliance and administration, of tax barriers, tax migration, and multiple taxation, of equity, of market and incentive effects, and of flexible fiscal policy, all loom more than proportionately larger in the bigger three-deep tax model of the postwar period than in the two-deep model of prewar days.

The retrogressive policies now being pursued in intergovernmental fiscal relations are unbelievable. They are overwhelmingly naive and dangerous, politically and economically. They are sponsored by proclaimed friends of home rule and states' rights, but it would be difficult to conceive plans fundamentally less compatible with either, unless it be the hoary and bankrupt separation of sources, the extreme opposite of the current local duplication of state and Federal taxes. Either approach leads to failure, and failure ironically leads to centralization, the bogey from which these unimaginative plans seek to escape.

NEW SYSTEM NEEDED

Wisdom in the field of intergovernmental fiscal relations begins with the discard of the pragmatic approach, if this is interpreted to be identical with the famed British muddling-through technique. Americans do not appear to be skillful muddlers. A comprehensive plan of action is essential. Such a plan transcends taxation. Shrinkage of the number of governmental units and reallocation of the functions of government must proceed simultaneously and be articulated with the tax reforms. The whole job of reorganizing government and its finances cannot be accomplished in one swoop. However, each change must be put in place in accordance with an over-all plan in order to attain desired objectives. The step-by-step implementation of a comprehensive plan is vastly different from the pragmatic approach which proceeds with the attainable without clear conception of the role of each change in the complex whole.

Even after the governmental units have been reorganized and the functions reallocated, state and local government will not have adequate tax resources to meet their expenditure needs. Governmental revenues may be more centralized than expenditures for reasons of efficiency, interpersonal equity, inter-regional equalization, and fiscal policy. The intergovernmental flow of funds can be expected to be more rather than less significant in the future, because it is being increasingly recognized that there is a joint responsibility of all levels of government for the provision of minimum standards in a growing number of functions irrespective of regional financial capacity.

There are definite limits, however, to the extension of the grant system. Grants have been resisted by the recipient governments in fear of their independence, and by the disbursing governments in fear of stimulating wasteful and extravagant expenditures. Grants without prescribed standards and effective controls would constitute a wasteful equalization technique without assuring the accomplishment of the disbursing government's objectives. The extreme sensitivity to controls, however reasonable, places a definite limit on the potentialities of grants-in-aid and shared taxes as an instrument of intergovernmental fiscal co-ordination.

TAX RESERVES

New methods of co-ordination must be developed to supplement grants if the state and local governments are to be supplied with adequate revenue under variable economic conditions without loss of their fiscal autonomy. The most promising device, substantially untried, appears to be the use of tax reserves. Briefly, the plan is to have each state set up for itself, and separately on behalf of its larger subdivisions, a tax reserve into which would be paid the excess of tax receipts or from which would be drawn the excess of expenditures over scheduled amounts based on a system of tax rates designed to balance the budgets over a period of five or six years, which normally would embrace years of both estimated prosperity and depression. The funds could be invested in United States Government securities in the same manner as the trust funds for the state unemployment compensation system.

The use of tax reserves would make feasible greater employment of unstable tax sources at the state and local levels of government, and this would contribute substantially to the stability of their tax systems as well as to economic stability. It would buttress a sound system of grants, for while Federal grants can be supported easily in bad times as well as good through the exercise of the borrowing power, state grants and shared taxes must rely upon the taxing power, and can be maintained in depression, if at all, only by boosting tax rates, in conflict with stabilizing fiscal policy. A tax reserve system would be a bulwark against the need for emergency grants of the type that bulked so large during the depression of the thirties.

TAX SUPPLEMENTS

The fiscal independence of state and local governments can be strengthened also by the use of tax supplements. Too little is known about the costs of compliance and administration, but their unnecessary duplication in cases where the different levels of government use the same tax is wasteful of resources. Duplication of such costs can be as effectively eliminated by supplements as by tax sharing, with the important difference that under supplements local responsibility is assumed for the tax, and the tax can be tailored to fit the variable fiscal requirements of the different sizes and types of governmental jurisdictions.

However, the supplement imposes certain limitations on the independent determination of tax. Since uniformity of the tax base is essential, powers must be delegated to the collecting level of government to settle numerous controversial conceptual issues. In the case of the income tax, for example, questions of how to handle capital gains and losses, tax-exempt securities, the integration of corporate profits and individual incomes, percentage depletion, accelerated depreciation, inventory valuation—to mention but a few of the more perplexing problems among a host of more technical and minor ones—would need to be resolved. In addition, the collecting level of government would need to acquire complete control over jurisdictional disputes as regards the source of tax, the allocation of business profits, and the domicile of individual taxpayers.

On the whole, what needs to be relinquished, by abridging independent determinations, is of small magnitude in relation to the fiscal freedom which potentially can be acquired. The Federal Government and the states are eminently better equipped to assume the additional tasks of administration implied in a system of supplements than the smaller units of government are to handle an extensive array of duplicating taxes.

It would be more profitable to sponsor a fiscal commission to explore the potentialities of some new and promising co-ordinating techniques and to submit a program of action, than to rail against the Federal Government and sponsor outmoded intergovernmental fiscal arrangements which inevitably must lead to greater centralization than is compatible with the degree of local self-government upon which the American system is founded.

MAJOR AREAS OF TAX REVISION

The blueprint for a correlated Federal, state, and local tax system should call for a substantial de-emphasis on miscellaneous state and local business taxes, and a reduction in their variety. At least in substantial part, these taxes are shifted to consumers. Their burden is inequitably distributed. They constitute unwarranted barriers to the free flow of investment. They promote unfair competition. They distort the pattern of consumers' choice. In general, they accomplish an uneconomic allocation of economic resources.

Substantially the same complaints can justly be made with respect to many of the Federal, state, and local sales and excise taxes. Together with the shiftable business taxes, the sales and excise taxes constitute an unhealthy burden on consumption. They tend to shrink the markets. Under less favorable economic conditions than those prevailing during the extraordinary past decade, these taxes, if retained at a comparable relative level, could easily retard secular economic growth and contribute in a major way to economic instability.

Reform in the area of business and consumption taxes calls for a substantial shift away from the regressive types to further use of the income tax. At the Federal level, this would involve replacing the worst excises with additional revenue derived in part from the transformation of the corporation income tax in excess of 20 or 25 points into an undistributed-profits tax applicable to profits after basic tax in excess of $50,000, or in excess of one-quarter of such profits if greater than $50,000. A portion of the replacement revenue would thus be derived from the larger distribution of corporate profits, and a portion directly from the corporations. At the state and local levels, corresponding remedial steps would require that existing statutory and constitutional prohibitions against the income tax be swept aside; for without freedom of legal action, little can be accomplished in many areas of American taxation that bear the stamp of antiquity.

The debilitation of the property transfer taxes, at death and *inter vivos*, and of the more important general property tax, constitutes two of the more amazing chapters in the history of American tax policy.

Economic and equity considerations point to a broadening of the estate and gift tax base, perhaps to the point of doubling the revenue yield. In the area of intergovernmental fiscal relations, these taxes have played a role out of all proportion to their fiscal importance. The accumulation of sizable estates usually transcends regional sources. It would seem that this consideration, rather than who got there first—and with which law books—should have an important bearing on the issue of which level of government should collect the revenue.

PROPERTY TAX

The general property tax has been progressively de-emphasized to the point where it no longer plays an adequate role in the American tax system. Tangible and intangible personal property is substantially exempt, and where not exempt, taxes extend primarily to the questionable categories of business personal property and are readily shifted to consumers. The real estate base has been riddled by excessive homestead exemptions, by governmental, charitable, religious, and similar exemptions, and by a callous and inequitable system of under assessment. Superimposed on an inadequate base is a complex system of protective rate limitations.

Moreover, while some of the excluded categories of property are taxed under a chaotic system of in-lieu taxes, including income taxes, the property tax on the whole is not properly integrated with the income tax. Both equity and incentive considerations point to the need for better integration of these two taxes. Such integration might require a complete departure from the present method of assessing the property tax to the possessor of the property on the basis of capital valuations which take no account of the owner's equity in the property. It would seem to require also more complete accounting of imputed income based on a conception that is much more extensive than has been customarily recognized. Imputation of current income is appropriate with respect to investment in all noncash-income-yielding property.

NEED FOR NEW ATTITUDE TOWARDS TAX INCENTIVES

In the past it has been customary to discuss the need for tax incentives in terms of specific partial or complete exemptions. The revenue requirements of government now and in the future are likely to be so large as to render impracticable tax incentives that reduce the revenue. The tax incentives worth considering for the future are those that take the form of specific additions in areas that are prejudicial to risky investment.

Times were when substantial debate centered on the stalling effects upon the economy flowing from the existence of a relatively small volume of funds that found a tax-free haven in tax-exempt securities. Funds are now permitted to flow into many more areas without the cash or imputed income being brought to current account. These privileges must be abridged in the interests of equity, revenue, and a stable but dynamic economy.

Moreover, in re-examining a large array of technical tax matters, such as the taxation of capital gains and losses, depreciation, depletion, inventory valuation, tax-exempt securities, federally owned property, and lesser items, the criteria of desirable taxation and fiscal policy will be more harmoniously attained if a new emphasis is given to completeness and currency instead of exemption and postponement.

89. *Federal Grants-in-Aid* *

FEDERAL GRANTS of money to aid states in performing governmental functions are now an accepted part of our governmental pattern. Historically grants-in-aid were instituted to stimulate the states to perform certain desired functions. Another factor has been the feeling that the Federal government can raise the necessary revenue with greater ease than the individual states whose tax resources vary widely. Also it has sometimes happened that interested groups found a single concerted campaign directed toward the government in Washington more fruitful than forty-eight separate campaigns. Each grant to a state must be matched by an agreed proportion of state funds and must be spent in accordance with the rules and regulations specified in the Federal enactments. The Commission on Intergovernmental Relations, appointed to survey the entire field of the interaction of state and Federal governments, has analyzed the present status of Federal grants-in-aid, stated the advantages and disadvantages of the system, and made pertinent suggestions for its improvement.

THE GRANT-IN-AID DEVICE is used by central governments to assist smaller governmental units in practically all political systems, whether Federal or unitary. Grants are found in a wide variety of forms. The common characteristic of all forms is that the central government provides aid without supplanting smaller units as the governments which bring the aided services to the public.

Grants made by the United States Government to the states are usually in the form of money, although the earliest grants were in land and at present some grants of agricultural commodities are being

* Reprinted from the Commission on Intergovernmental Relations, *A Report to the President for Transmittal to Congress* (Washington, D.C., Government Printing Office, June, 1955), pp. 118-131.

made. Most grants-in-aid are continuing arrangements; there have, however, been a few one-time grants. . . .

At first glance existing Federal grant programs look like a hodgepodge. Purposes are not always clearly stated, the choice of activities seems haphazard, apportionment methods and controls vary widely. The Commission's study of past and present Federal grant-in-aid programs showed plainly that the grants do not constitute a system, and indeed that they were never intended to make up a system. Their varied characteristics are largely the natural outgrowth of their varied objectives and piecemeal development. This conclusion becomes apparent in examining the historical development of grants.

EVOLUTION OF THE GRANT-IN-AID

The national government has used the grant-in-aid primarily to achieve some national objective, not merely to help states and local governments finance their activities. Specific objectives have been as varied as getting the farmer out of the mud, assisting the needy aged, providing lunches for school children, and preventing cancer. As a condition of financial assistance the national government establishes requirements and provides administrative supervision.

The trend has been toward sharper definition of objectives, closer attention to conditions and requirements, more extensive administrative supervision, and, recently, greater attention to relative state fiscal capacity.

FEW CONDITIONS IN EARLY GRANTS

The early land grants to the states specified the broad objective for which proceeds from sales were to be used (generally education or internal improvements), but had no other conditions and almost no plan for supervision or control. The Morrill Act of 1862 tightened the definition of objectives and introduced new conditions and some supervision. Each state had to maintain a college with a curriculum emphasizing "such branches of learning as related to agriculture and the mechanic arts." Funds had to be invested in safe securities and only the interest could be spent. State matching was indirectly required since the Federal money could not be used for construction. Annual reports were prescribed.

The second Morrill Act, in 1890, provided an annual cash grant for instruction in the land-grant colleges. The law empowered Federal officials to withhold money from any institution not fulfilling its obligations.

The first provision for Federal audit was in an 1895 amendment to the Hatch Act of 1887, which had authorized grants for agricultural experiment stations as adjuncts of the colleges. The Weeks Law of 1911, authorizing Federal-state cooperation in forest fire protection, and the Smith-Lever Act of 1914, providing for cooperative agricultural extension work between the land-grant colleges and the Department of Agriculture, contained further innovations. These acts introduced apportionment formulas, dollar-for-dollar matching, and the requirement for advance approval of state plans by the national government.

THE GRANT ATTAINS MATURITY

As a result of many developments, the grant has become a fully matured device of cooperative government. Its elements are well established: the objectives are defined; apportionment and matching formulas are laid down; conditions, minimum standards, and sanctions are prescribed; and provisions are made for administrative supervision. The maturing of the grant as a means of stimulating and shaping particular programs, as distinct from a subsidy device, is reflected not only in increasing legislative attention to conditions, standards, sanctions, and methods of supervision, but also in the evolution of national administrative machinery and procedures. The conditions attached to grants have not remained mere verbal expressions of National intent; National agencies have generally had funds and staff to make them effective.

In establishing grant-in-aid programs, the Congress has apparently regarded the disparities in fiscal capacity among the states as a matter of secondary importance. Almost all grants are available to all states, even the wealthiest; the formulas for allotting funds among the states and prescribing their matching expenditures do not usually reflect differences in state resources; and, further, many programs offer relatively small amounts of money.

During the past decade, however, the grant structure has been modified to recognize varying state fiscal capacity. In grants for hospital construction, school lunches, and public health, for example, the national government assumes more of the financial burden in states of lesser fiscal capacity than in more prosperous ones. Thus Mississippi, with the lowest per capita income, receives for hospital construction four and one-half times as much per capita as New York does.

This marks a significant change in the character of grants-in-aid. It appears that relative state fiscal capacity will receive greater attention in future legislation. Even so, there will remain a wide gap between conditional grants, which combine fiscal objectives and the functional objectives of specific programs, and the outright subsidy or subvention type of grant, which is purely a fiscal device. In an evaluation of Federal grants-in-aid, it is helpful to compare these two types.

SUBSIDIES VS. CONDITIONAL GRANTS

Many central governments—including those of the federal systems of Canada and Australia—and some of our state governments make grants in the form of broad subsidies. The Commission has considered whether a similar policy by the national government might be preferable to the use of the conditional type of grant.

It has been argued that a subsidy policy would provide maximum help to the states that most need funds, give all states an opportunity to use money where they feel their need is greatest, preserve for them a larger and more independent governing role, and relieve the national government of administrative burdens and of the difficult task of selecting specific objects of aid. The national responsibility would be limited to the minimum supervision needed to prevent fraud.

Experience with different types of grants, however, suggests that subsidies would not materially relieve pressures for national action for specific objectives. Other factors that are responsible for the establishment of existing grant programs would still remain. Among them are such conditions within the states as the fear of being placed at a competitive disadvantage by fully exploiting their own taxable resources, insufficient interest in certain programs of concern to the nation, and lack of technical skills and information. Even in New York where fiscal capacity has not been wanting, the Temporary Commission on the Fiscal Affairs of State Government found that in many fields Federal grants had helped to stimulate activity and to raise standards.

In short, if a system of subsidies were adopted, there is no assurance that the funds would be used to provide all the services thought necessary by the national government. There would still be pressure for national programs for specific objectives. The end result would be a piling of conditional grants on top of subsidies, as in Canada and Australia, or enlargement of the field of direct national provision of services, or both.

There are other objections to unconditional subsidies. National authorities would have inadequate control over the use of appropriated funds. On the state and local side, a policy of unconditional subsidies with no matching requirements would be likely to undermine the sense of financial responsibility. The tendency would be for states and localities to look more and more to the national government to perform the disagreeable task of extracting money from the taxpayer.

CONTINUED USE OF CONDITIONAL GRANTS

Where aid is determined to be necessary, the national government's conditional grants represent a basically sound technique, despite their piecemeal development and hodgepodge appearance. It is the only technique that is in any sense self-limiting, both as to objectives and amounts of expenditure and as to the extent and nature of national control. When Federal aid is directed toward specific activities, it is possible to observe the effects of each grant, to evaluate the progress of aided activities, and to relate the amount of financial assistance to needs. There is more assurance that Federal funds will be used to promote the nation's primary interests. Finally, the direct control exercised by the national government is confined to limited and well-defined governmental activities, leaving other areas of state and local responsibility relatively unaffected.

While the traditional type of grant-in-aid is to be preferred to the subsidy, substantial improvement is desirable in determining both when and how to use it. The Commission advances the following broad principles for guidance:

1. A grant should be made or continued only for a clearly indicated and presently important national objective. This calls for a searching and selective test of the justification for national participation. The point has been made . . . that existence of a national interest in an activity is not in itself enough to warrant national participation. Related questions are the relative importance of the national interest and the extent to which it may be served by state and local action. Consequently, where the activity is one normally considered the primary responsibility of state and local governments, substantial evidence should be required that national participation is necessary in order to protect or to promote the national interest.

2. Where national participation in an activity is determined to be desirable, the grant-in-aid should be employed only when it is found to be the most suitable form of national participation. It is important to compare the strong and weak points of the grant-in-aid device with those of other forms of national-state cooperation as well as with those of direct national action. It is likewise important to consider the types of objectives and situations for which the grant is best adapted. The probable effect on state or local governments is an important consideration.

3. Once it is decided that a grant-in-aid should be made, the grant should be carefully designed to achieve its specified objective. This requires careful attention to the shaping of apportionment formulas and matching requirements, the prescription of standards and conditions, and

the provision for administrative machinery and procedures. Objectives as varied as cancer control, old-age assistance, highway construction, and forest fire prevention call for imaginative use of varied types of standards, controls, and fiscal formulas. It is more important to shape these elements of the grant to a particular purpose than to achieve complete uniformity among the programs. At the same time, in order to ease the impact of grants-in-aid on state and local government, as much uniformity should be striven for as is compatible with the achievement of specific objectives.

The areas of possible improvement, then, lie in developing more searching tests of the desirability of national participation in activities for which grants are proposed or already being made; in more discriminating understanding of the possibilities and limitations of the grant; and in more conscious and skillful adaptation of legislative provisions and administrative supervision to grant-in-aid objectives. . . .

THE USES AND LIMITATIONS OF THE GRANT-IN-AID

Assuming the desirability of some form of national participation in a governmental program, in what situations is the grant-in-aid device most appropriate?

There are two general considerations to be weighed. One is the degree of national participation required to achieve a given objective. The other is the nature of the activity.

As to the former, the principle of minimal action applies. If, for example, a given national objective can be achieved by supplying information, consultation, research, or some other form of assistance involving a relatively minor assumption of responsibility, a grant-in-aid would be an unnecessary and undesirable extension of national authority. But if the only effective alternative to the grant-in-aid is direct national administration, the grant-in-aid, if appropriate on other grounds, may actually conserve state responsibility. The question is one of the degree of national participation. Assuming the desirability of some form of national action, the grant-in-aid's strong and weak points can be realistically assessed only in the light of the alternatives available.

As to their appropriateness for different types of activities, grants in the past have been used for services rather than for regulatory activities of government. This is illustrated by the six programs that absorb more than 90 per cent of the Federal-aid dollar: public assistance, highway construction, employment security, school lunch, school construction and operation in Federally affected areas, and hospital construction.

There are two reasons why the grant-in-aid has been confined to fields of service. On the positive side, service programs generally cost more than regulatory ones, so that financial aid is a more effective inducement to the states to undertake or increase the desired activity. On the negative side, uniformity—a prime need in regulatory activities—cannot be ensured as adequately by the grant-in-aid. Direct national action can achieve uniformity much more readily than a device that has to depend on the cooperation of 48 states and perhaps thousands of smaller units of government.

GRANTS AS A STIMULATING DEVICE

The grant's widest use has been in stimulating the states to launch or expand services for which state and local governments are generally regarded as primarily responsible. National funds and leadership have stimulated state and local activity in agricultural education and research, welfare services, public health services, and vocational education, to cite some prominent examples. In some of these fields the states or localities had already made a start before the grant was made. Generally, though not always, the grants have produced notable spurts in state and local action, and the proportion of state and local expenditures to Federal aid has shown a steady and substantial overall increase.

Stimulation has been understood by many to imply termination of national aid after a limited period of time. . . . Grant-in-aid legislation does not ordinarily specify a termination date. Some programs may have been initiated with the understanding that national grants would pass out of the picture, but in the absence of a specific expression of intent, there has been little concerted attention in and out of Congress toward bringing to a close those grants which have adequately stimulated state and local activity. In practice, the objectives of stimulation and support have been merged, and continued Federal aid has been claimed necessary in many instances to stimulate states to maintain desired programs. It is sometimes argued that a temporary grant would fail to stimulate state activity, on the ground that many states, particularly those with low incomes, would naturally hesitate to undertake nationally aided programs where the national support is clearly temporary. The Commission recommends, however, that wherever practicable Congress declare in the statute establishing a grant-in-aid the concrete goals which the grant is designed to achieve, provide for periodic evaluation of the progress achieved toward these goals, and indicate the conditions which could justify the termination of the grant.

Where used effectively, the grant not only has increased the volume of state and local services, but also has promoted higher standards both in service and in administration. These gains have come through the conditions attached to the grants and from the administrative leadership and supervision of national agencies. Thus a study made for the Commission on the impact of grants-in-aid in one state concluded:

> Grant-in-aid programs have had a significant effect upon the administrative practices of the State departments***. Personnel management is distinctly better in Welfare, Health, Employment Security and Highways than in the non-federally aided departments. Again, the necessity of preparing annual work programs for the review of Federal agencies has developed a concept of the work program which makes for more effective and better organized administrative performances within those departments. Similarly, the necessity of preparing monthly and annual reports for the review of the responsible Federal agency has improved the reporting practices of the State agencies concerned. This would appear to be in distinct contrast to the rather loose and general reporting practices of the non-federally assisted State agencies.

Comparable findings were reported from other states.

A good illustration of these effects is afforded by the highway grants that were first authorized in 1916. Automobiles were then swarming onto roads designed for the horse and wagon. Federal grants served both to increase the volume of construction and to introduce minimal standards and some interlocking of state systems. One of the major results was the speedy establishment of state highway departments in all states; before the grant became available, only a few states had set up this type of agency. Without the national standards, the states and localities in this early period could hardly have served the national interest in an adequate highway system.

Many of the grants have produced beneficial national-state and national-local cooperation. Both services and administrative relationships have been improved by free exchange of information and ideas and by the provision of technical guidance. Levels of government drawn together in ventures financed by grants have become increasingly aware of the mutuality of their interests. These gains are perhaps as important as more tangible results.

OTHER USES OF GRANTS

The grant-in-aid can be used for purposes other than the stimulation of state activity in fields where states are already at work. It may be used, for example, to transfer an activity from the national to the state or local level. Some of the programs included in the Social Security Act of 1935 provided for state and local operation of grant-aided programs to replace certain emergency activities which had been carried on directly by the national government. Two years later the low-rent housing program was shifted to state and local operation by this method.

Again, a grant may be used to compensate local (and perhaps state) governments for unusual burdens placed upon them as a direct result of national action. When national action imposes on a locality the burden of speedy and substantial expansion of local governmental services, the national government has an obligation to render financial assistance while the locality adjusts itself to the new demands. A grant-in-aid of the type now being made for education in Federally affected areas is one way of discharging such an obligation.

LIMITATIONS OF THE GRANT

Notwithstanding its obvious usefulness, the grant-in-aid is not a panacea. Its limitations should be recognized along with its potentialities.

When only a few states are not providing reasonably adequate services, the grant-in-aid may be a costly way to stimulate these states. The national government has not as yet developed a method of making grants that is flexible enough to meet such a limited objective. In this situation it remains to be explored whether national contractual services or loans or direct national action on a limited basis, may be a preferable alternative to a grant.

Other limitations of the grant-in-aid are inherent in its complexity. It divides responsibility and offers ample opportunity to dodge it. There is joint provision of policy, finances, and administration, but national and state action do not mesh perfectly. The states must wait for Federal appropriations to plan their budgets for grant-aided activities; state policy must be geared to national standards and conditions; and state administrators must accept national supervision. In such a situation some friction cannot be avoided.

EFFECT ON STATE BUDGETS

The Commission notes with concern that a number of state budget officers believe that grants-in-aid have distorted state budgets. Neither the nature nor the extent of the distortion, however, is entirely clear.

Almost of necessity, grants-in-aid in their early stages will induce state and local governments to adopt a pattern of expenditure in which the emphasis is somewhat different from that which would prevail in the absence of grants. Such an effect is indeed one of the major objectives of grants-in-aid, for the grant is intended to stimulate states and their localities to exert greater effort in aided programs than they presumably would exert without financial inducement from the national government.

To say that states are not required to accept grants-in-aid is not a completely satisfactory answer. Although state authorities are not legally required to accept grants, they are under strong practical compulsion to do so.

It is questionable whether any state, today, spends more of its own funds on major activities supported by grants-in-aid than it would were there no Federal support of these activities. However, restrictions attached to the use of some Federal grants, particularly those in the fields of public health, vocational education, and highways, probably do affect the relative support of various special programs in some state budgets. This element of distortion could be eliminated or greatly reduced by giving the states more discretion in the allocation of grant-in-aid funds. . . .

Grants-in-aid may also hamper the budgetary flexibility of the states—their freedom to shift their own resources from one governmental activity to another in response to shifting needs. When Federal grants are made for too narrowly defined objectives, flexibility is still further impaired.

On the basis of reports made to the Commission, it is apparent that the distortion and attendant inflexibility vary from state to state. There is a potential danger that could become serious, particularly for low-income states, in the event of any considerable expansion of grants-in-aid requiring substantial increases in state matching expenditures.

There is unanimous agreement that effective budgeting of grants is hampered by poor timing on the part of Congress and state authorities. States now prepare budgets without being sure how much money they will get from most grant-in-aid programs. They are sometimes embarrassed when Congress fails to vote the anticipated amounts. Much of this trouble would be cured if Congress made more grants for two years in advance, as it does with grants for highway construction.

SUMMARY

To sum up, the grant-in-aid is first of all an instrument used by the national government to reach its objectives. The grant always entails some national control, as well as assistance and cooperation. Because the control is indirect and the execution of the program is given to the states, the impact of a proposed grant on state and local responsibility may not be fully taken into account. The Commission believes that a healthy safeguard here is for the Congress to consult representatives of state governments—those with overall responsibility as well as heads of functional agencies—on the need for and the form of national participation.

Once a determination has been made that national action is desirable for a given objective, however, the fact that the grant-in-aid involves some diminution of state autonomy is not in itself a compelling argument against its use. Against a direct national program that would give the states no role whatsoever, the grant-in-aid may often be preferred.

90. *Are Our Cities Going Broke?**

INFLATION and an increasing demand upon city governments for new and expanded services have created a need for additional revenue in many of our municipalities. This situation has resulted in both an increase in existing taxes and a frantic search for new sources of revenue. This selection outlines what cities are doing to meet their financial problems.

THE nation's cities are confronted with a rapidly developing financial crisis. In their operations, they have come to resemble huge business enterprises. They provide all sorts of services for their citizens. Costs of these services are moving up steadily. And income won't stretch far enough to pay for them. As a result, the cities are in a desperate search for new sources of revenue.

Rising costs are hitting municipal governments from every angle. Schoolteachers, policemen, firemen and other city employes, pinched by the rising costs of living, are demanding higher wages, and often getting them. The prices are rising on all sorts of city equipment. And tremendous backlogs of public works are piling up for the cities to carry out at premium prices for labor and materials.

Property taxes, although being boosted steadily, are proving inadequate as sources of revenue for the cities. All across the country, cities are turning to sales taxes, income taxes, and special charges of all kinds. The search for money has set the cities to charging individual citizens for some of the services that the municipalities perform for their residents.

Behind the crisis stand several factors:

The war years have piled up all sorts of urgent work for the cities. Housing needs have accumulated. City streets have worn out. Public buildings need repairs and expansion. For all of these, both materials and labor costs are up from 25 to 125 per cent as compared with the

* Reprinted from *The United States News*, February 14, 1947, p. 20, an independent weekly magazine on national affairs published at Washington. Copyright 1947, United States News Publishing Corporation.

prewar period. And city revenues show only an infinitesimal increase in comparison.

A *mood for decentralization* is adding to the plight of the cities. More and more persons are moving out into suburban areas where taxes are lower. But, while the suburbanites contribute less to the support of the cities, they still earn their livings there, use streets and other city facilities, and often take their children to city schools. The cities want to tap the suburban source of income.

The historic grip of rural areas upon State legislatures stands in the way of the creation of a realistic relationship between the States and their cities. The cities, their industries and citizens, contribute 90 per cent of all taxes to all levels of government in the United States. But the cities get back only a small portion of this sum. And many forms of revenue are being withheld from the cities by legislatures in which rural members dominate.

Rising costs are standing in the way of many kinds of municipal works.

Municipal workers, from schoolteachers and policemen and firemen all the way through the list, have been hard hit by the higher costs of living. But, in spite of the fact that their pay has not kept pace with the 50 per cent lift in the cost of living that has come about since 1939, municipal pay rolls are more than 30 per cent higher than before the war.

City construction needs have grown into the billions of dollars during the war years when neither materials nor labor were available. Cities have upward of $7,000,000,000 of sewer and sanitary work to do, and need a minimum of $2,000,000,000 of new school buildings. New streets, municipal buildings and fire, police and recreational facilities may raise the total to well over $20,000,000,000.

But inflated costs are holding up these activities. Construction costs are from 20 to 50 per cent higher than before the war. Bids for construction sometimes run as high as 135 per cent above city engineers' estimates of what the costs should be. Even on small items that cities buy, the wholesale prices are up anywhere from 10 per cent on some pieces of equipment to as much as 125 per cent for various textile products.

The combination of higher wages and inflated construction costs is forcing many cities to postpone major public-works projects. Cities such as Austin, Tex.; Berkeley and Long Beach, Calif.; Roanoke, Va.; High Point, N.C., and Muskegon, Mich., have announced such postponements.

In spite of the increased costs, however, the cities steadily are being compelled to expand the number of services that they provide for their citizens. In 1824, Detroit gave its citizens 24 services. It now supplies about 400, including the traditional police and fire protection, public health, hospitals and education, along with such newer things as broadcasting stations and traffic control.

MIGRATION

But the cities must find the money somewhere to pay for these things. And the men and money are moving out of the cities into suburban areas to get away from the crowds and into the fresh air. People commute by automobile, by trains, by subways and otherwise, and pay smaller taxes.

But the suburbanites work and play in the cities and often educate their children there. The cities now are trying to tap the money that the suburbanites earn inside their borders.

The property tax still supplies about 85 per cent of the revenue for the 155,000 local units of government. In spite of all their efforts to increase their receipts from this source, the cities are not getting enough money from it that is to run the big public-service institutions that they maintain.

Valuations and assessments are being pushed upward steadily. Between 1941 and 1946, the assessments in 249 U.S. cities were boosted by 10½ per cent. Seventy-one of these cities now assess property at 100 per cent of its value.

But upward of $20,000,000,000 of the property that lies inside cities is tax exempt for one reason or another. New York City alone has $5,500,000,000 of tax-exempt property in the form of schools, churches and government property.

Thus, while the costs are rising and new jobs are piling up for cities, their time-worn source of revenue is reaching the peak of its producing power, and city debts are rising. The bonded debt of cities over 25,000 slacked off from $7,795,000,000 to $7,492,000,000 during the war years when materials and labor were not available. Now it is beginning to soar again.

NEW SOURCES OF REVENUE

In this situation, the cities are tackling State legislatures for either a share of the revenues collected by the States—of which the cities pay upward of 75 per cent—or for permission to levy taxes on new sources of revenue.

In Illinois, Chicago is asking that the State share its revenues with the municipalities. Cook County revenues have been hard hit by an act of the Legislature that froze assessed valuations for five years at the 1942 level, low point for the war years. This fixed the assessed valuation of Evanston at $47,000,000, compared with $119,000,000 on which it might have collected taxes in 1945. Evanston is finding it necessary to reduce all its personnel by one third.

New York and several other States already have a system by which some of the revenues that are obtained from certain taxes are shared with the cities. In spite of this added revenue, the cities still are compelled to resort to all kinds of special taxes of their own.

Baltimore has received permission from the Maryland Legislature to impose any kind of tax that the State uses. But all of the legislatures keep a tight rein upon their cities and specify what kinds of taxes the cities may use.

All types of taxes are being devised by cities in their efforts to reach the money of suburbanites.

The income tax is being used by St. Louis, Philadelphia and Toledo.

Sales taxes are used by several cities, among them Denver, New York, New Orleans, Atlantic City, San Bernardino and Santa Barbara, Calif., and Huntington, W. Va. Gross-receipts taxes are used by St. Louis and Kansas City. Salt Lake City has a business-franchise tax.

Cigarette taxes are used by Baltimore, Denver, St. Louis, Kansas City and Birmingham.

Other taxes to which cities are turning include amusement taxes, and taxes on hotel rooms, gas, electric and telephone bills, pinball machines, music boxes, vending machines, motorbus mileage, water bills, taxicabs, carnivals, gasoline. In one way or another they are trying desperately to raise the money to keep going. Some cities are charging for garbage collection and for sewer connections, and are operating parking lots. Many are installing parking meters.

The cities are fighting for their municipal lives.

91. *What Ails the Property Tax?**

PROPERTY TAXES no longer account for a major share of tax revenue, but such taxes are important sources of revenue for local units of government. Although only about 11 per cent of our total tax bill is paid through property taxes, the total dollar amount of property taxes currently collected is some ten times greater than it was in 1900. The inequities and weaknesses of the property tax demand attention and correction if this tax is to be maintained, and because it is essential to local government, its reform is directly related to the future effectiveness of local government. Unless reform comes, local governments must look for other sources of revenue—a search that may not be productive—or local governments must depend more than they now do on subventions from state and Federal governments. Mr. Freeman explains the weaknesses of the property tax and makes suggestions for the improvements necessary to make it both lucrative and equitable.

IT HAS BEEN SAID that the property tax is like a mule: no pride in ancestry, no chance of progeny. History records innumerable attempts to make the property tax fair and equitable; few of them succeeded for any length of time. Evasion and inequity have characterized property taxation through the ages.

The principle of *ad valorem* taxation is ancient. The settlers of Massachusetts Bay Colony, 300 years ago, "levied every man according to his estate." They took this concept from Elizabethan forms of taxation which can be traced back as far as William the Conqueror's Domesday Book. The earliest mention seems to be a real estate tax which the legendary Roman King Servius Tullius slapped on his unsuspecting subjects in the sixth century before Christ. The Romans soon after abolished the kings but they were never able to abolish the tax.

In the United States property was undoubtedly burdened with too great a share of the cost of government until about twenty years ago, when property tax collections totalled more than all other taxes—Federal, state and local—together.

The picture changed drastically in the past quarter century: the property tax turned from a major into a minor item on our tax bill. For some years now it has accounted for only 11 per cent of all taxes.

* Roger A. Freeman, *National Municipal Review*, XLIV (November, 1955), pp. 506-511. Reprinted by permission of the *National Municipal Review*.

To be sure, property tax collections have not declined. They mounted from $700 million at the turn of the twentieth century to $5 billion in 1929, and to $9.3 billion in 1953. But other taxes outpaced them. Governments in the United States now derive 63 per cent of their tax revenues from income taxes and 26 per cent from excise taxes.

Property taxes claimed about 5 per cent of our national income in the early part of the twentieth century, took 6 per cent in 1929, jumped to 12 per cent during the depression years and fell back to 6 per cent by 1939. Since then our income has climbed faster than property taxes. In recent years property taxes have equalled about 3 per cent of the national income.

All other taxes totalled 5 per cent of the national income early in the twentieth century and until about 1930; since then they have soared to 25 per cent. This radical shift in the tax burden probably exceeds the fondest hopes of those who fought excessive property taxation some 20 and 30 years ago.

But the property tax still is an essential part of our tax structure. As long as the over-all burden is as heavy as it is, we must of necessity diversify the forms of taxation by which we measure each man's contribution. *Ad valorem* taxes which are gauged by the ownership of property as a major economic resource serve to provide a better balance of the burden of government. No other tax is equally well suited for imposition by local jurisdictions. Land and houses stay put. The continued existence of local government is inextricably tied to the property tax base.

PROPERTY TAX DECLINE

In the past two decades other sources of municipal income have sprung up—sales, business and income or payroll taxes. In 1932 they contributed 3 per cent of the tax revenue of local governments; in 1942, 8 per cent; in 1953, 13 per cent. But 87 per cent of all locally collected taxes still comes from property. Municipal nonproperty taxes will keep growing at a moderate pace. But the property tax will continue to be called upon to supply the bulk of local government revenues.

The relative decline of the property tax was caused by several developments:

1. State government, which used to receive a substantial part of its income from property taxes, virtually withdrew from the field.

2. Several major functions which had been responsibilities of local government were partially or completely shifted to state or Federal governments. This is particularly true of public welfare, roads, and schools.

3. The pastures of state and Federal aid looked greener. State and Federal payments to local governments climbed from $56 million in 1902 to $605 million in 1927 and to $5.7 billion in 1953. In 1902 they equalled 8 per cent of locally collected taxes; in 1927, 14 per cent; and in 1953, 55 per cent. The states in turn started leaning increasingly on the Federal treasury. Federal aid to states rose from $3 million in 1902 to $107 million in 1927 and to $2.6 billion in 1953. In the fiscal year 1955 it exceeded $3 billion.

Looking toward the future we seem to face a choice between two alternatives:

1. We can continue the trend of transferring activities and responsibilities to higher levels of government. We can easily foresee that such a policy will slowly but surely turn local governments—and eventually state governments—into mere field offices of the Federal government.

2. We can strengthen the fiscal powers of local government so that it can cope with its residual responsibilities. This process will inevitably include a program of vitalizing the property tax.

If we are to follow the second alternative we shall need to correct the major shortcomings of the present property tax administration. They are:

1. *Exemptions.* The number of tax exemptions has been increasing to a point where we are dealing less and less with a "general" property tax. Thirteen states grant homestead exemptions, sixteen states veteran exemptions from $500 up to $5,000 assessed value. Because assessed values are only a fraction of current values, far more residential property escapes taxation than was intended. About a dozen states permit the exemption of new industrial property. Eight states do not tax personalty and a number of states make other concessions. Various studies have shown that exemptions are an ineffective and costly method of attracting industrial location. Exemptions are of course popular with the groups for whose benefit they were enacted but it is not sufficiently realized how much of an additional burden they place on nonfavored classes of property owners.

The Federal government enjoys immunity from local taxation. A few agencies make payments in lieu of taxes; e.g., Tennessee Valley Authority, Atomic Energy Commission, Housing and Home Finance Agency. Other departments share revenues with state and local governments (forests, grazing, minerals). Some assistance is given to schools in Federally affected areas. But many of these payments fall short of a fair contribution to local government. What is needed—and was recommended by the Commission on Intergovernmental Relations—is a comprehensive system of payments in lieu of taxes in those cases where the Federal government has acquired land or buildings in recent years and operates facilities which serve essentially national purposes or commercial operations.

Much state and local government property which is used for proprietary operations, particularly in the utilities field, escapes taxation. Its share is shifted to the general taxpayer.

2. *Rate Limitations.* Limitations on property tax rates have been used for almost a century but became more widespread in the early 1930s. Nine states now have over-all rate limitations. Almost all states limit the property taxing powers of their political subdivisions and municipal corporations to a maximum millage. Some states permit these rates to be exceeded by popular vote; others do not.

These millage limitations were established at a time when the scope and standards of public services were much lower than they are today. Debt limits which in almost all states are based on assessed valuations frequently prevent local governments from financing school buildings and other badly needed improvements.

These taxing and bonding limits are often cut to a half, a third or less of their statutory level by the practice of assessing property at a fraction of its full value.

3. *Fractional Assessment.* Constitutional and statutory provisions notwithstanding, property has, with rare exceptions, probably never been assessed at full value. In 1929, real estate assessments in the United States totalled $135 billion. It was estimated at the time that the true value was about twice as high. The value of real estate may now be estimated at between $600 and $700 billion. Real estate assessments in the United States total only $200 billion. In other words, real estate is on the average assessed at less than one third of its current value. That varies, of course, from state to state, the ratio in New York being 65 per cent, in Washington 20 per cent.

Sometimes fractional assessments are rationalized by claiming that current prices are inflated. That is a confusion of terms. What is inflated is not the prices but our currency: we are dealing in 50-cent dollars. The price of real estate is expressed in the same dollars with which we pay taxes and with which cities and schools must pay their salaries and other costs. The statement that assessments are set at "normal" values is an attempt to evade by dialectic means the clear mandate of the law. Appraisals of real estate for other than tax purposes—for banks, insurance, loan companies, prospective buyers—do not seem to be plagued with a concept of "normal" value.

In the 25 states where the state government still receives some share of property tax collections, there is positive encouragement to competitive underassessment as a means of minimizing local contributions. Half the states distribute grants-in-aid on formulas based on local wealth as evidenced by assessed values. This system penalizes correct assessment and rewards underassessment. The so-called equalization ratios used in some states are with few exceptions fictitious. In 37 states local taxes are levied on state-assessed intercounty utility property. The owners of such property are almost universally being overtaxed.

4. *Uniformity of Assessments.* The laws of most states prescribe that property be assessed uniformly (if sometimes by classes). No law is more flagrantly broken. Governor Langlie said in his message to the 1953 and 1955 sessions of the Washington legislature: "Valuations are now a mockery of the uniformity provisions of our state constitution."

John Sly said in his New Jersey property tax study, which he significantly captioned *A Century of Inequities:* "Never has so much money been raised from so many people so inequitably as in the current administration of the local tax on real estate." Uniform treatment, he said, was undiscoverable except in isolated instances. The ratio of assessed to full value varied among the 21 New Jersey counties from 16 per cent to 56 per cent. A Pennsylvania study showed variations from 20 per cent to 78 per cent, a Washington study from 13 per cent to 38 per cent. Variations within counties are even greater than among counties.

Variations among individual pieces of property and omissions are due to incompetence of assessments, to insufficient staffing and to failure to use up-to-date technical aids. Assessors' offices are frequently given inadequate budgets.

Variations among classes are due to a deliberate if illegal policy. The New Jersey study found that commercial property was assessed at an average of 49 per cent, residential property at 29 per cent. In Washington residential property is assessed at an average of 19 per cent, commercial property at 27 per cent to 38 per cent. The reasons for these discrepancies are patent: there are more votes among owners of residential property than of commercial property.

What all this adds up to is a breakdown of local property tax administration. In no other tax could such conditions exist. They can exist in the property tax field only because taxpayers do not know how bad the situation is. Many governors have bitterly criticized the sorry condition of property tax assessments. With rare exceptions, legislatures have closed their eyes to the disgraceful situation or at best have taken half-hearted action.

COURTS HAMPER ACTION

Courts have a record of more often hampering rather than helping attempts to correct these injustices. They seem to have difficulty distinguishing between the appraisal of property, which is a technical process, and the power of taxation, which is a political process. There has been a reluctance to interfere because of a mistaken concept of "home rule." We may wonder whether there is an inherent right of local officials to break the constitution and laws of the state and inflict flagrant injustice under the cloak of home rule. State government has a duty to act if law enforcement breaks down within its borders, if some local units of government are prevented from exercising their legitimate duties by the failure of some officials to uphold the law.

The maladministration of the property tax has probably done more to weaken home rule than anything else. This condition if continued much longer will destroy home rule by ruining the financial integrity of local government. There is in the long run no political independence without fiscal independence.

I have mentioned that there have been many attempts to improve property tax administration. All but eight states have taken some action since the end of World War II to equalize property tax assessments. Ten states have enacted measures toward this end in the past year. In a majority of the states, the results have been modest or disappointing.

Why is it that the property tax is in such bad shape while other taxes seem to be fairly well administered? What distinguishes the property tax from all others?

The property tax in the United States originated long before the others; its organization and methods are hopelessly outdated. In no other tax field do we elect local administrative officials. But the great majority of property tax assessors are elective. It is quite likely that our income tax administration would be in no better shape if the employees of the Internal Revenue Service were locally elected without regard to technical qualifications.

The appraisal of property—just as the verification of income tax or sales tax returns—is a technical job which requires professional skill and knowledge. It is not supposed to be a policy-making job. The employees of the Internal Revenue Service or of the state tax department do not claim the discretion to apply the tax rates to 30 per cent or 50 per cent of a taxpayer's income or sales volume. But property tax assessors exercise such an authority.

The question is sometimes asked what difference it makes whether the size of the tax levy is raised or lowered by manipulating assessments, or by adjusting tax rates. The difference is that in the former case under legal millage limitations the policy decision is shifted from the legislative body—the city council, board of county commissioners, school board—which under the law has the power, to a single official who usurped it. Instead of the representative bodies which are responsible for the operation of their governmental units, it often is the tax assessor who decides how much they can spend.

ASSESSOR SETS RATES

It has been said that the tax assessor has made himself the budget officer for all local governments. That is not quite correct. A budget officer administers a budget but does not set its size or the amount of the tax bill. That power belongs to legislative bodies. The property tax assessor is the only single public official in the United States who can in effect determine tax rates and set the amount of taxes which the residents of a jurisdiction must pay. He exercises that authority not by law but by arrogation. He has made himself in effect a one-man legislature. Often he makes vital decisions about the operations of cities, counties or school districts although he has no responsibility for their activities.

A long and disgraceful record has proven that local property tax administration except in rare circumstances will fail. Sporadic attempts at improvement by local initiative or under state stimulation have at best been temporarily successful. If we want property tax assessments to cease to be a political football then we must put them on a scientific and objective basis. An increasing number of people are coming reluctantly to the conclusion that this will not be accomplished until the appraisal of property is divorced from local administration and made uniform by the same method by which intercounty utility property is appraised in most states: under uniform standards on a statewide basis. Home rule will be more effectively guaranteed by leaving the decision on tax rates in fact as well as in name to locally elected responsible bodies.

It is unlikely that local governments will be able to cope with the task that lies before them in the next decade without a restoration of the property tax. The need for added services and facilities is vast and urgent, present inequities are drastic and widespread. Minor corrections or palliative measures will not do the job.

Now, when Federal taxes have been cut $7.3 billion and may be eased further next year, is the time to make local governments more self-supporting. The only alternative is gradually to transfer more duties to higher levels and to keep local governments nominally alive by increased subsidies. That is what we have been doing for the past twenty years. A continuation of this trend will eventually mean the end of strong, self-propelled local government.

92. *The Art of Taxmanship**

OR HOW TO SAVE MONEY WITHOUT GOING TO JAIL

SOMETIME before April 15 of each year millions of taxpayers struggle long hours in the preparation of their income tax returns for the Federal government. Many have concluded that time and money are saved by hiring tax and accounting experts to perform this chore for them. Some of these experts have discovered an additional source of income: Besides advising their immediate clients they publish guide books for those individual taxpayers who insist on filling out their own forms. These guides explain in considerable detail what can be included as a deductible item and what must be excluded, what is included as income and what revenue may not be income for tax purposes, and how generally and specifically to take advantage of the technicalities of the law. The purpose of these guide books is to maximize tax avoidance. The courts recognize the propriety of tax avoidance because no one should be required to pay more than the law specifies. At the same time the courts and the Revenue Service frown on tax evasion that is patently illegal. Mr. Margolius here delineates the thin line that separates tax avoidance from tax evasion. He also describes how successful tax avoidance stimulates the Revenue Service and Congress to plug the loopholes that the tax experts discover.

IN THESE DAYS of soaring taxes, the strategy of tax avoidance—or taxmanship—has become a new national pastime, second only to baseball in general interest and to none in excitement, because more people can play and all of them play for keeps. To provide for the growing enthusiasm for the game, a sizable new industry—tax experting, the science of "minimizing"—has sprung up with a literature and code all its own. J. K. Lasser's tax guide alone has sold more than thirteen million copies in its eighteen years as the taxpayer's *vade mecum*, and

* Sidney Margolius, *Harper's Magazine*, CCX (March, 1955), pp. 63-67. Reprinted by permission of the author.

this year its sales are running 100 per cent ahead of last. There are also seven other annual guides, and Commerce Clearing House—one of the big professional tax services which ran its presses on three shifts during 1954—is currently building a huge new plant to keep up with the national hunger for tax tips. There is even a Tax Book Club for deduction *aficionados* and a monthly magazine, *Taxes*.

The tax-information industry plays the game itself, and one of its more inspired feats has been to establish that the costs of its literature and services are themselves deductible—as is, no doubt, this issue of *Harper's* if you bought it primarily for this article. And no less an authority than Justice Learned Hand has given his support to the whole performance by finding tax avoidance moral as well as legal. He wrote, in a famous decision: "Taxes are enforced extractions, not voluntary contributions. Nobody owes any public duty to pay more than the law demands."

But—let it never be forgotten—there is a thin but discernible line between tax avoidance, which is legal, and tax evasion, which is not. In tax avoidance, you look for loopholes. You postpone income until a more favorable tax year, or you marry on December 31 to get the tax-splitting advantages of a joint return for the whole year, or you plan to have your children born as close as possible to New Year's Eve to add another last-minute $600 exemption. In tax evasion, you break the law; you fail to report income. Modern practitioners of taxmanship should take care that they recognize this distinction, for the chances that they may be called to account are greater than almost anyone likes to think.

The Bureau of Internal Revenue checks an average of one out of every twenty returns. But the larger your income and the more unusual the deductions you claim, the stronger the chance that your return will be audited. If you are self-employed, the likelihood rises sharply; about one in ten returns from self-employed people come under scrutiny. And if you are self-employed and make more than $10,000, your return has a 50 per cent chance of being investigated.

There is an excellent possibility, therefore, that you will find a polite letter in your mail one of these days, inviting you to drop down to the local Internal Revenue office for a little chat—and to bring all of your canceled checks, receipted bills, and other records along with you. If you are a normal citizen, your first reaction is likely to be:

"This is it. Leavenworth, here I come."

You probably will be pleasantly surprised to find yourself, eventually, talking to a quiet-spoken, reasonable-looking man at one of a long row of desks in a big open room. The course of the conversation will then depend largely on how well you have kept your books. The ideal taxpayer, from the government's point of view, is apparently one who spends most of his evenings humped over a set of big ledgers, jotting down every detail of his fiscal autobiography.

At one such interview recently, a friend of mine was first questioned about a $75 charity deduction for a used sofa he had given to a hospital. The examiner commented, mildly, that he himself had found it necessary to pay someone to cart some old furniture away from his house. Had the taxpayer got an expert appraisal of market value on that sofa?

"Well, no. But it was a good sofa."

"You should at least have asked the hospital for a letter acknowledging its value," the examiner persisted. But he wasn't tough about it. After a little more friendly debate, they compromised on $50.

Then the government man got down to his real gripe. The taxpayer had claimed a $200 deduction for entertaining out-of-town professional contacts at his home. He had no receipts for food or liquor purchases, and in the end he found himself forced to compromise on $150. (The Treasury Department usually tends to slice from one- to two-thirds off a questioned entertainment deduction if it is not backed up by records.) Furthermore the $300 he had deducted as the cost of taking his wife with him to a professional convention was disallowed, even though he insisted that wives were expected to attend.

On the other hand, a ballet teacher who had deducted so many expenses that the government couldn't understand why she was still in business appeared before the examiner with all her records in order —and won her case. It is for reasons like this that one well-known economist and connoisseur of taxmanship refuses to carry cash. He has charge accounts at all restaurants and other places where he conducts various phases of his professional affairs.

Business entertainment and travel expenses are perhaps the grayest area in which ingenious taxpayers hunt deductions. If you count yourself among their number it is well to remember that tax officials generally apply three yardsticks to these: (1) Is the expense necessary to produce income? (2) Are all the expenses listed strictly business or do they conceal some personal expenditures? (3) How do the deductions compare with the usual ones of people in the same income bracket and profession?

Considering the amount of human guile to which they are continually exposed, examiners still get surprisingly emotional about a man who accumulates a half-million dollars while paying only $4,000 of income tax. But they are apt to blink a tolerant eye at a workingman's small deduction for dungarees which he has listed as a special work uniform.

IT PAYS TO HATE GOLF

For it is a signal fact of the art of taxmanship that—as a tax expert pointed out to the dean of a medical school who asked if the cost of the teas he gave for students were deductible—"if you don't take a deduction, you never get it." The original expounder of this significant concept was the late J. K. Lasser, whose policy was always to carry the attack to the government, that is, to deduct first and prepare to argue later if questioned. And shortly before his death in 1953, according to Sydney Prerau, now director of the J. K. Lasser Tax Institute, he scored a major victory in this field in the famous educational-expense controversy.

A Rochester attorney attended Lasser's Institute on Federal Taxation at New York University and, under Lasser's direction, took off his income tax his travel and living expenses while there. The Commissioner and the Tax Court disallowed the deduction. But the Second Circuit Court of Appeals supported it. According to the judges, the attorney had "an immediate, over-all professional need to incur the expenses to perform his work." In time this decision may open the way for other professional people to take similar deductions—provided, of course, they can show similar compelling need to take the courses. Meantime a number of enterprising taxpayers have tried to get away with far less likely expenses.

In one celebrated case, the official of a New England shoe company deducted the $6,000 tab for his daughter's wedding because many of the guests were business contacts. The Tax Court turned him down because no actual business was written during the festivities and anyway the main purpose was to get the girl married. It rejected in like manner the undertaker who tried to deduct the cost of his family groceries because his wife solicited business while she was in the grocery store. But a lawyer who deducted the cost of joining a golf club to make business contacts earned the Court's approval when he testified that he actually hated the game.

The revenue service is also always suspicious of part-time farmers who deduct agricultural losses from business income. But one weekend farmer won in the Tax Court by proving that he handled cattle, planted, and helped with the harvest. "This," declared the Court against the grumbling of the government's attorneys, "can scarcely be called recreation."

Taxmanship has wrought interesting changes in American life. It has swayed the choice of luncheon companions toward those who may legitimately be claimed as business deductions, and it has made the

Dutch treat a thing of the past. It has encouraged the giving of expensive presents to business contacts, for gifts are tax deductible to the giver and not taxable income to the receiver—a taxpayer's dream of heaven. And if one taxpayer is now a fiscal expert to be reckoned with, two are a formidable team. I recently overheard a customer arguing with the proprietor of a stationery store. The customer wanted to pay his bill before the end of the year to take a deduction for business expenses. The stationer wanted to delay receipt of the money until after the first so that he wouldn't have to include it in the year's income. At length they agreed that if the customer mailed out the check on December 31, they both would be satisfied.

PLAYING LEAPFROG WITH CONGRESS

There are literally thousands of devices for minimizing taxes, and somebody thinks up new ones every year. But what keeps taxmanship an alive and challenging sport is that often, as soon as you have discovered an inviting loophole, Congress steps in and blocks it up. Several years ago the movie people—probably the single most tax-conscious group in America—devised the system of setting up corporations to collect the money they made on pictures instead of taking a salary. Subsequently the corporations would disband, and the actors or directors who owned them would cheerfully pay the lower capital-gains tax on corporation profits—and no regular income tax. Congress caught on and forbade collapsible corporations. But meanwhile it had innocently legislated an exemption on income earned out of the country, designed to encourage engineers and Point IV specialists to work abroad. Hollywood seized on the idea with joy and planeloads of actors took off to make movies in Europe and other tax-free oases. By 1953 Congress had caught up with them again and limited the amount of foreign earnings that may be exempted.

Congress has also lately ended one of the small taxpayer's favorite minimizers—the toothpaste deduction. For years the citizens' tax guides listed toothpaste and brushes as a deductible medical expense, and millions of people took it. The tax examiners were annoyed, but the amounts involved were too small to make questioning them worthwhile. Then a year or so ago an Oklahoma couple claimed so many deductions for sales tax, cigarette tax, toothpaste, and other such items that the Treasury Department fought it out with them in the Tax Court. There it was decided that toothpaste is a toilet article, not a medicine. And in 1954 Congress wrote this decision into the law.

In the same year it legislated more than 3,000 other changes, making the 1954 revisions in the tax code the most sweeping since 1942. However, it need hardly be added, almost before the revisions were completed the tax experts had found loopholes in them large enough to wheel a deduction through.

One of the first loopholes they found was in the new dividend credit which exempts the first $50 of dividends from stocks or mutual fund shares and grants a 4 per cent credit on dividends received after July 31, 1954. Virtually as soon as the credit was announced investment firms started sending out notices to customers: their lawyers had discovered ways in which one family could get several credits. Not only could a man and his wife both claim the $50 credit, even on a joint return, if some dividends were held by each or if shares were registered in both names, but if they also registered shares in trust for their children, they could take a dividend credit for each child.

An even wider loophole—and one on which there will be heated arguments before the matter is finally settled—is the new rule on sick pay. Formerly the tax code permitted you to exclude from your taxable income any money received from a sickness-and-accident insurance policy paid for by your employer. The new rules allow you to exclude *any* sick pay received from a wage-continuation plan maintained by your employer. The big question is: Does your regular salary received while you are ill come under this provision? Many tax experts feel that it does, as long as your employer has a uniform policy of continuing to pay employees while they are sick. And the American Federation of Government Employees has scored an early victory by getting at least unofficial confirmation from Internal Revenue officials that government sick-leave pay is exempt.

The new rule may well prove a boon to delicate citizens who will find that they earn more actual take-home pay when they are sick than when they are working. However only up to $100 a week of such pay is exempt, and payments for the first week are taxable unless you are hospitalized for at least a day or your illness is due to an injury. (One business magazine has already suggested seriously to its readers that it will pay them to spend a day of the first week in the hospital.)

The new retirement income credit, which exempts part of the income of older people, opens other interesting possibilities. A son who is sophisticated as well as dutiful will find, for example, that it is more profitable to transfer an income-producing property to his elderly parents than to support them from his own wholly taxable income. A working woman with a child can do even better and couple the retirement-income provision with the new child-care deduction by paying her mother to take care of the youngster. The pay will be deductible to the working wife and tax-free to the grandmother. Although it may not have been one of the authors' objectives, the new credit can profoundly influence America's attitude toward elderly people.

THE TAXMANSHIP WAY OF LIFE

The tax laws are influencing our lives in other ways as well. The rule that has had the deepest social impact of all—according to John Powers, the president of Prentice-Hall, which supports an extensive tax-advisory service—is the 1942 provision allowing employers to set up tax-free pension and trust funds for employees. The government could not order employers to establish benefits for employees, but it offered spectacular tax advantages if they did, and thousands of employers seized the opportunity. Unimpeded by taxes, these funds are growing tremendously. Sears Roebuck's fund, for example, is now the single largest stockholder in that huge enterprise.

The funds have far-reaching effects for employee, employer, and society at large. They have already provided many moderate-income workers with sizable pensions. They have permitted companies to give their employees more real income at less cost. And their vast amounts of money available for investment have become a noticeable influence in raising stock-market prices. Finally, their importance in corporate affairs is growing steadily greater than that of any large individual investor.

The whole recent trend of tax legislation has been to encourage saving and investing. But for the vast numbers of taxpayers who are primarily interested in personal deductions—apart from business expenses—there are still three main avenues of "minimizing":

1. *Planning income* to avoid bunching it in any one year which may put the taxpayer in a higher bracket. A wage-earner who depends chiefly on his salary can, of course, hardly postpone his income until another year unless he has also found a way to postpone eating. But many professional and self-employed people can, and do. And sophisticated investors with stock-market profits from the 1954 boom used a simple technique to nail down their profits late in the year and at the same time avoid including them in their 1954 income: they sold the stocks short while continuing to hold them long.

2. *Bunching deductions in alternate years.* This originated as a high-income strategy, but it is trickling down to the moderate brackets. You plan to take the optional 10 per cent allowance on contributions and expenses one year in order to accumulate costs which you itemize the next. For example, two years' charitable contributions can be combined in one by donating at the beginning and end of the year. Doc-

tors' bills, property taxes, mortgage interest, and the like can be similarly timed.

3. *Securing capital gains.* It is now standard procedure among investors to seek long-term capital gains (only 50 per cent taxable) rather than dividend income, and for executives to take stock options as part of their compensation. Many corporations in which insiders have large holdings deliberately keep dividend payments low, since the value of the shares grows more rapidly if the profits are plowed back into the business. And the new tax code further encourages such hot-house cultivation of share values by putting the burden of proof of excessive accumulation of profits on the government, instead of the burden of defense on the corporation as before.

High-income taxpayers also have yet another minimizer—counting losses. Losses are 100 per cent deductible and long-term gains are only 50 per cent taxable. Thus a loss of $1,000 can wipe out the tax on a $2,000 gain. As Commerce Clearing House explains it, a capital-gains loss is valuable because it erases income in the top bracket.

Armed with these tips and suggestions you should find yourself at least a passable player in the game of taxmanship. But however skillful you become, Congress will always have the last word. When the taxpayers find enough deductions, Congress can simply raise the tax rate a couple of notches. And there is still an iron hand behind such recent public-relations touches as the change of title from "collectors" to "directors" of internal revenue, and from "Bureau " to "Service." As a matter of fact, late in 1954, the "Service" increased its staff of tax-detecting examiners by almost 50 per cent to cope with the intricate maneuvers of the taxpayers on the new Form 1040. Bear this in mind as you sit down to work out your return.

XVII

COMMERCE AND BUSINESS: THEIR REGULATION AND PROMOTION

93. *Government and American Economic Life**

WHAT IS the proper relationship between government and the economic system? Certainly this is one of the fundamental questions that faced the people of this country in the past and, in all likelihood, will continue to do so in the future. It was fundamental in the struggle over the Constitution of 1787, as it was in the period following the Civil War, and as it is today. Mr. Lyons says that at present the government implements private enterprise, protects competition, establishes a plane of competition, and engages in economic production. All of these things it does because some, or all, sectors of the business community have demanded this or that particular activity. Knowledge of what is the present relationship between government and the economy will be of assistance in determining what the future relationship ought to be. Mr. Lyons cautions that "the curse of bigness" may be applicable to government as well as to private industry.

THE proper relationship of government to economic affairs has been a topic of perennial discussion. Plato, not far from 400 B.C., said in the opening book of the *Laws:* "In the next place our business transactions, one with another, will require proper regulation." Almost exactly one hundred years ago John Stuart Mill was writing: "One of the most disputed questions in political science and in practical statesmanship at this particular period relates to the proper limits of the functions and agency of governments."

In the century which has passed since Mill wrote, this problem has

* Leverett S. Lyon, *The Journal of Business of The University of Chicago*, 22 (April, 1949), pp. 83-91. Reprinted by permission of the author and the publisher.

increased rather than diminished in significance. Certainly, during the last two decades, with the growth of fascism, communism, and socialism, which identify government and economic affairs, and with the development of the New Deal in America, all the issues of government in relation to economic life have been intensified.

It is these changes which lead me to the view that the time has passed when business executives can be satisfied with listening to cheers for their own convictions about government and economic affairs. Their convictions may be right, and it is my belief that essentially they are right, but something is happening in the United States which should suggest to businessmen the need for careful thinking. However much we prefer perorations on the perfections of private enterprise, with the pleasant sense of emotional massage which they produce, I believe it is not enough to be satisfied with such appeals.

The traditional American system of organizing economic affairs is in grave danger, and we need to be aware of its dangers and as ready as possible to appraise its deficiencies and to protect its values. Accordingly, I believe it is a good deal more important to help businessmen to be thoughtful than to help them to be cheerful.

This subject of government's relation to American economic life is one of such cosmic proportions that any consideration of it in a short article presents a major problem. It has occurred to me to set down, in the form of ten statements, the things which I believe that thoughtful citizens should have in mind in considering this relationship. For purposes of this paper, I shall call these ten statements "ten precepts for business executives." Thus, while I have no aspiration to pose as Jehovah or even as Moses, this discussion takes the form of a sort of economic decalogue on the subject of government and the American economic system.

PRECEPT NO. I

It is important to realize that the term "economic life" or "economic activity" is more inclusive than "business" and that the economic life of our country is a more fundamental thing than its business life. The economic life of a country consists of all the operations through which its population is kept alive and supplied with whatever is produced to make the whole standard of living. Economic life was just as real in the United States when the country belonged to the Indians—although there were no businessmen—as it is at present. It is as real today in the South Sea Islands or in Communist Russia as it is in our own country. Where economic activity does not exist, a population does not exist because there is no means of making a living.

Business, on the other hand, is only one method of organizing economic affairs. It is a method which, though it has demonstrated unrivaled power to produce, is comparatively new in the world and is a system which is very sensitive to shock and vulnerable to many forms of attack.

PRECEPT NO. II

Government is not something external to our economic affairs. In a democracy, government is a tool which we have invented and use to aid us in carrying on these affairs. Moreover, government is not single but plural. Governments range in size and power all the way from library boards and school districts through municipal councils and state governments to the national government. When we think of "government," we should, I believe, avoid thinking of an abstraction and think instead of very specific lawmaking and law-enforcing bodies, each with jurisdiction in a certain limited area—lawmaking and law-enforcing bodies which consist of people chosen by us and subject to change in personnel, in form, and in policy.

We use governments in many ways in economic life. In fact—as I shall try to make clear a little later—we use government to create or establish the business system and to maintain the very life of that system.

PRECEPT NO. III

It is a great error to assume that there must be a definite and outright choice between sole reliance on governmental agencies for the decisions of economic life and sole reliance on individual or private decisions. We often hear this error expressed in such statements as "America is at the crossroads: we must choose between private enterprise and government ownership," or "America must choose between laissez faire and socialism." The choice is not so simple.

There has never been in the history of civilized nations an economic system in which governments were not used to carry on some economic activities. It is equally true that there has never been one in which some reliance was not placed on the initiative of private individuals. It is possible to conceive of an almost infinite variety of combinations of these divisions of responsibility.

Moreover, no one country has ever continued indefinitely with any one division of responsibility between governmental agencies and private individuals. Nor has there ever been a time when the division of responsibility was alike in all the countries of the world. The result has been, both throughout the course of history and within any one period, a great variety of economic systems. There are at present some modern countries in which responsibility for organizing economic life is primarily in the hands of official governmental agents. There are others—like our own—in which such responsibility rests primarily with individuals. But the choice has never been absolute and is not so now.

PRECEPT NO. IV

The most important single use which can be made of government is in determining the extent to which our economic affairs shall be organized by private individuals and the extent to which they shall be organized by governmental agencies. Since some responsibilities are given to governments and some to individuals, there must be some way of deciding which shall have which. The only way we can do this is by setting it out in law, and this means we must use a governmental agency to make the decision. When, for example, it was decided that the right to coin money shall be a prerogative of the federal government and that this privilege should be denied to private individuals, that decision could be made only through governmental action, the agency being the constitutional convention. When, in the city of Chicago, it was recently decided that the major elements of the local transportation system should no longer remain a matter of private enterprise but should be operated by the municipality, that decision could be made only by a governmental agency, in this instance the city council.

Through governmental agencies we are constantly changing the balance of authority between governments and individuals, giving more or less to one or the other. This is the most important single use that we can make of governmental agencies. It is the use always available to improve the division of responsibility and to correct the mistakes of the past.

PRECEPT NO. V

An outstanding relationship of government to American economic affairs is in government's implementation of private enterprise. It is, indeed, in this implementation that the business system is created. I must make it clear that I am speaking of private enterprise as a human capacity. Private enterprise is the capacity of an individual to make decisions, to exercise judgment, and to use initiative. This capacity is one of the most priceless resources of the human race. But this capacity, as a resource, is as real in present-day Russia or England as it is America. But in neither of these countries is it now implemented with the legal arrangements to permit it to function in the organization and operation of economic affairs.

The most fundamental form which this implementation takes in America is in the legal institution of private property. Without the laws which give rights in property and without the possibility of increasing the possession of such rights through personal effort, private enterprise is valueless in economic matters. It is government which gives and enforces such private rights. The essential difference between business and gangsterism is that in a business system a government authorizes and enforces the rights and transfers of ownership, while in the gangster world such rights and transfers rest on the sawed-off shotgun.

One might carry this further and point out that it is only to the degree that there is private ownership in one's self—a right established in our constitution—that one can direct one's personal talents and abilities to those vocations which one believes will be most advantageous. This legal right is the essence of personal freedom, as distinct from personal slavery.

It sounds elementary to state this fact, but it is only through centuries of legislation and judicial decision that we have arrived at our present principles of private property rights and the principle, for persons, of freedom and of equal justice before the law. Indeed, the current discussion of existing labor legislation and the judicial decisions of the past year make it clear that the determination of rights in one's self is still in process and is—as will probably always be the case—a continuing operation, to be developed and revised by governmental agencies.

No less important than private property as an instrument for implementing individual enterprise is the right of contract. Of what value would be our individual judgments in a business matter if it were not for the right to make a governmentally enforcible contract? Indeed, our whole so-called "private-enterprise system" might well be defined as, in large part, a continuous rearranging of private property rights by means of legally enforcible contracts determined by the decisions of individuals as to what they believe will be personally advantageous.

Of the many illustrations which might be given of the implementation of private enterprise, these two must suffice. But it is through a complicated mechanism of civil law that the great human power to initiate and decide has been made into the system which we call "business."

PRECEPT NO. VI

A further relationship of government to American economic life is the maintenance or protection of competition. It is common knowledge that the so-called "business system" developed in England and that we adopted its major principles as they had been developed there. A part of this history was the struggle to win from such monopolies as the guilds and the chartered companies the right, for individuals, to enter business and to compete against those who had the special privileges of carrying on economic affairs. The history of the rise of business is in no small part the history of the rise of competition. In America public policy has been true to the tradition in which business was born—a public policy of using government to maintain competition and to forbid the making of contracts when there is proof that such contracts would be used to destroy the freedom of contract itself. England followed a somewhat different philosophy, with results which none of us now envy, as we view the antiquated industrial mechanism with which, largely as a result of her cartels, she is presently equipped. Competition has, by contrast, kept American industry modern and vigorous.

More than one level of government has been used to protect competition. We have used state laws, and, in the federal jurisdiction, such legislation as the Sherman Act, the Clayton Act, and the Robinson-Patman Law.

Until well into this century it was thought to be as important to enforce competition in the field of labor as in the field of business enterprise. The common law used the concept of "conspiracies in restraint of trade" as readily in one field as in the other. Declared public policy in the field of labor, however, has shifted during our history from such a viewpoint to an actual tendency to facilitate labor monopoly. This took place first through the Clayton Act modifying the Sherman law, then through the Railway Labor Act and the Norris–La Guardia Act. The change went still further in the National Industrial Recovery Act; and, although this was declared unconstitutional, the National Labor Relations Act reasserted the rights given employees in that law and placed employers in a less advantageous position. The Taft-Hartley Law was the first reversal of this trend. The Labor Relations Act was the most extreme modification of the maintenance of competition thus far seen in our country, with the possible exception of the National Recovery Act.

PRECEPT NO. VII

Government is used to establish a plane of competitive action for private enterprise. Whatever one thinks of a specific regulation, there is no business executive who does not believe in some ethical code for business. Commercial bribery, for example, transgresses the idea of common honesty, as does misrepresentation and fraud. In the early days of business many techniques of the gangster were employed. In the effort to control such forms of competitive action, there has been developed a legal plane upon which it is considered proper for business to operate.

It is often assumed that codes of fair competition are easily constructed. Nothing could be further from the truth. Centuries of development of the common law, the enactment of federal and state statutes throughout our history, and nearly thirty-five years of the Federal Trade Commission have all indicated the fallacy of such a view. The experience of the National Recovery Administration demonstrated it once more. Indeed, the intense, though brief, life of that agency most clearly indicates for all who will analyze its activities that the problem of what is fair in private enterprise is one of the most difficult and complicated with which businessmen and governments have ever tried to deal.

Perhaps the most important federal action affecting the plane of competition was the establishment of the Federal Trade Commission, which was given broad powers to eliminate "unfair methods of competition" in commerce. As is well known, the Federal Trade Commission Act put a new emphasis upon enforcement and gave the commission the power to issue orders to cease and desist, under which it has attacked a wide range of deceptive and obstructive practices by sellers. The Wheeler-Lea Act later strengthened the powers of the commission in this regard. To some degree government regulations make positive requirements, such as those for disclosures of information and quality of products. In such cases the plane of competition consists of "thou shalt" as well as "thou shalt not."

The plane-of-competition concept has also been extensively developed in employer-employee relations. On grounds of public welfare, businessmen have been forbidden to use child labor, even though it would be competitively profitable. A plane of competitive action has also been established regarding maximum hours of work, first for women and then for employees in general.

PRECEPT NO. VIII

It is helpful to realize that governments are extensively used for economic production in America and that businessmen are often strong proponents of such use of governments. A hundred years ago governmental production was comparatively limited. It was used for little except for protection of the peace, for national defense, and, through the courts, for the dispensation of justice. Even education as a public activity was, however, undeveloped, and such common governmental activities as public water supply and public sewage disposal existed only in the larger cities.

How extreme has been the change in such a field as education is realized when we compare our present government provision of education with the condition that prevailed when Governor Berkeley of Virginia is reputed to have said: "Thank God we have no free public schools in this colony."

Numerous factors have, for better or for worse, brought about a greatly increased use of governmental agencies in production. One is urbanization. A century ago a large proportion of our population lived on farms, and there were only four cities of 100,000 or more containing about 4 per cent of the total population. Half our population now lives in such large centers, and only one-fourth in the country. This urbanization has increased the need for joint action and also made such action more practicable. Fire hazards are greater, and central fire departments have become possible. Private wells and individual waste disposal became less satisfactory than the supplying of these services by social action. Urban traffic makes street paving a necessity, which private action is incapable of effecting. It was in urban centers that the use of government as organizer and producer of economic goods first became extensive.

A concomitant of urbanization was an increase in employment, in the sense that livelihood depended on a job as contrasted with dependence on contact with the soil. It was the uncertainties, and to some degree the irregularities, of such employment which forced public thinking toward governmental operations in the field of relief and unemployment insurance.

The widening of suffrage—the right to vote—combined with new concepts in taxation has contributed greatly toward the use of government in productive activities. While for many years the right to vote was restricted in most states by property qualifications, it is now universal. In the meantime, the distribution of income has undergone little change. This has made it possible for voters, particularly through the use of the graduated income tax, to obtain, through government production and distribution, many benefits, the receipt of which has no relation to the incidence of costs. When taxation was primarily on real estate or in the form of excise taxes on products widely used, there was a general awareness of tax burdens. The progressive income tax, however, and such taxes as those on corporation profits and pay rolls, except when the latter are expressly deducted from wages, are not felt as a burden by many of those who benefit from the services which these taxes make possible.

A further factor in promoting governmental production is bureaucratic growth. It is a commonplace to say that few things have more capacity for expansion than a governmental bureau. Once a venture into governmental production is made—wisely or unwisely—the subsequent enlargements seem almost inescapable. Those who are benefited begin to feel a vested interest and organize to protect their gains. Opposition, which may be strong at the outset, weakens, once a general principle is established. Eventually, those who oppose are dubbed "conservative" and "reactionary." Those exercising the power, partly, perhaps, from a desire to extend their own rewards and prestige and partly, perhaps, from an honest intention to extend their work, press for expansion, larger appropriations, and wider responsibility.

Experience throughout the United States in recent years has furnished abundant evidence of this tendency toward bureaucratic growth. When, as of today, we contemplate something close to a $40 billion federal budget, we do not need to remind ourselves that the end of this is not yet.

The final factor in promoting governmental production, with its accompanying expenditure, has been the shift in the international and military situation of the United States. In years gone by the most striking contrast between the American national budget and that of any European country was the fact that our expenditures for military purposes were a minor part of the total. Even World War I involved an expenditure of only some $24 billion. Now, having accumulated our enormous national debt, it can only be with a sense of shock that, in contemplating our currently proposed budget, we realize that 79 per cent is "war related," to use a phrase of the Secretary of the Treasury. This includes, as its largest single item, $11 billion for national defense, over $6 billion for veterans' services and benefits, and over $5 billion for interest on the public debt—most of which is a war debt.

Some persons contend that war expenditures should not be classed as production by government, on the ground that military action is not productive. With this I must disagree. Assuming that national protection is necessary, military expenditures are for a most important form of economic goods.

PRECEPT NO. IX

Businessmen should be alert to the dangers of the increasing tendency to utilize government to regulate the pace of general business activity. This use of government is comparatively new. While there were early efforts in this direction—in which the so-called "protective tariff" might be included and of which central banking policies between World War I and the depression of the thirties are a good example—these efforts, during the depression and since, have become greatly intensified. There have also been important shifts in the character of the measures employed—shifts from the regulation of the supply of currency through the machinery of the Federal Reserve System to the controls through Treasury policies respecting taxation, spending, and lending. Currently, we find much discussion of controlling the vitality of American economic life by policies of "surplus or deficit financing," changes in the incidence of federal taxation with a view to influencing the volume of private expenditure, and, strangest of all, perhaps, the management of the public debt.

This same purpose—the control of the general pace of business activity through governmental management—was also an avowed part of the philosophy of the National Recovery Adiminstration, the Agricultural Adjustment Act, the Labor Relations Act, and the Fair Labor Standards Act.

Governmental action to check inflation in general or to check depression in general—at this moment we are not quite sure which we want to do—usually results also in the creation of new public agencies, such as administrations, commissions, and authorities. To these—as in the case of the National Recovery Administration and the labor boards—there is delegated an unusual degree of responsibility. Such governmental activities also lead to special insistence by pressure groups, of which we had perhaps the most extreme example in the Labor Relations Act and its administration.

Is it possible to summarize what has been occurring in the United States and to make specific suggestions? As to summary, I believe, first, that any objective observer must conclude that our history reflects a tendency toward increased governmental management of economic affairs and, on the part of many sections of the public, a diminished confidence in private enterprise, a confidence, however, which was in part restored by the matchless contribution of business during the war.

Second, there is a growing tendency in the United States for special groups to identify their limited good with the national good and to ask government for subsidy, support, or special protection rather than for laws which increase competitive opportunity.

Third, this growth of group action has tended to restrict the freedom of individuals in the groups concerned, extensively in many cases but nowhere else so much as in the field of labor. The result is diminished independence and less opportunity for initiative.

Fourth, the depression and the war have added greatly to public responsiveness to proposals of extensions of governmental action. The depression did this through fear growing from widespread unemployment. The war did it through a realization that in such an emergency the economy must be totally subservient to military needs.

PRECEPT NO. X

The believers in free enterprise will be effective in restraining undue governmental action and in protecting the business system to the extent that they are aware of the real nature of that system and to the extent that their objectives are actually identified with the general welfare rather than with the furtherance or protection of a personal or group interest. This should be joined with consideration of proposed governmental action in specific terms rather than in broad and unrealistic generalities. When a man says that he does not believe in governmental action, he is saying that he does not believe in public education, in a national army, or in public roads. What we need to consider is always the specific—How large an army is called for? If universal military training is considered, what form should it take, and in what forms, if any, is it worth its costs?

Businessmen believe in public education. The question is: How much? What kinds? What specific extensions at a particular moment can be justified? Businessmen are not opposed to assistance to orphans, to the blind, or to others physically handicapped. Each year they direct and otherwise participate in community fund drives and similar efforts, to which they and the companies they manage are major contributors. The issue is not, therefore, whether one is for or against social security. It is whether a specific form or type of social security or its administration is desirable at a given moment.

I am sure I have conveyed the view that government is a useful tool in economic affairs—useful in direct production—and vital to business—vital to its operation, its maintenance, and the regulation of its competitive action.

But, having said that, I would leave a false impression if I did not conclude by saying that government authority must always be granted with caution and watched with everlasting constancy. "Eternal vigilance is the price of freedom." That ringing phrase was uttered with reference to royal monarchs, but it could well be applied to all political power. The priceless quality of personal initiative, if kept competitive, works for progress, output, and economy. Political position feeds on pay rolls and is always under pressures toward job expansion, nepotism, and technical stagnation. The use of government is inescapable; but where a choice is reasonable—where the decision is close—we can well afford to remember that competitive private enterprise has brought us an unparalleled national income and has given us an industrial equipment more modern than any other in the world. We can also afford to realize that, as we give government control over increasing areas of economic life, the factors which must be taken into consideration in framing public policy become increasingly technical and complicated. To the extent that this is true, it is correspondingly more difficult for officials to foresee them. I speak, I believe, with the attitude of a realist, not that of the reactionary, when I say that it is well to remember that in government, even more readily than in private administration, there can be, in Justice Cardozo's words, "delegation running riot," and that the "curse of bigness," of which Justice Brandeis has written so brilliantly, can blight an industrial empire under the control of government quite as effectively as it can one under the management of private citizens.

94. *What Do You Mean, Free Enterprise?* *

THIS SELECTION, like the one immediately preceding (93), deals with the relationship of government to the economy. If free enterprise means a minimum of government and monopoly influence, then, says Mr. Robertson, we don't have free enterprise in the United States. He points to a variety of governmental activities that interfere with the free operation of the law of supply and demand—for instance, price supports and insurance of bank deposits. He concludes that what we have in this country is more of a safe enterprise system than a free enterprise system. And who supplies the safety? Why, the government, of course, replies the author.

THE United States today is in a condition comparable to that of a man suffering from schizophrenia. A few innocent fancies are safe enough in quiet times, but in a crisis, either the patient gives up his delusions, or society commits him to the firm hold of others. Our national phantasy, fateful in these edgy times, is our belief that we are living in a free-enterprise system. Since reality is quite the reverse, we are in no condition to make rational decisions. It is time to get wise to ourselves.

It is true that we have a free-enterprise system in the sense that if a man has enough money he can go into any work or any business he chooses. In most respects he can run his business to suit himself. He may make money or he may go under, depending upon the circumstances and his own ability. He can get out of one occupation or business and go into another whenever he can afford to.

* Nathan Robertson, *Harper's Magazine,* 197 (November, 1948), pp. 70-75. Copyright, 1948, by Harper and Brothers. Reprinted by permission of the author and the publisher.

But these are only the surface signs. Fundamentally, a free-enterprise system, as spelled out by Adam Smith, the great classical economist, is one in which there is a minimum of government or monopoly interference—in which the natural laws of supply and demand rule. In that kind of system an individual entrepreneur takes all the risks and, as a reward for bearing those risks, is entitled to all the law of supply and demand will permit him to win.

America once had close to—although never completely—a free-enterprise system of that kind. Of course, from almost the beginning, this country had tariffs which interfered with the laws of supply and demand; subsidies to the railroads and to Western pioneers which fell considerably short of Adam Smith's ideal; prohibitions against some businesses regarded as immoral, such as the slave trade; and government competition, such as the postal system in communications.

But except for a few interferences of this kind, the laws of supply and demand were in control, and we had something rather similar to a free-enterprise system. There was little government interference or monopoly. A man could go into any business he chose, pay any wages for which he could get men to work, charge any price he could get, and make as much money as the laws of supply and demand would permit. He could even throw away the nation's basic natural resources in the most profligate manner if he chose to do so in his grab for riches and power. He could make millions—or go bankrupt.

Today we have something quite different. The individual entrepreneur still faces the risk of competition within his own segment of the economy—if he happens to be in an area of business where competition still exists, such as farming or retailing. But in many segments of our industry, competition has been drastically restricted so that the laws of supply and demand no longer operate as they are supposed to. Many of our big manufacturing industries have price-fixing schemes of one kind or another. The steel, cement, and other heavy industries, until very recently, have had the basing-point system for controlling competition, and it is not yet clear to what extent the practice has been abandoned since it was outlawed by the Supreme Court. Price-fixing has extended clear down through the retail trades under the Miller-Tydings Act, which permits manufacturers to fix the price at which their products can be retailed to the public. Patents have been used as the basis for widespread price-fixing.

Even beyond all this, American industry has become so big, with such huge industrial units, that only those with many millions of dollars to risk can enter into many fields of enterprise. This large scale, of course, limits competition. It takes huge aggregations of capital to enter most of the big industries like steel, automobile, machinery, or electrical equipment manufacturing—and even publishing. At least $10,000,000 is needed to launch a metropolitan newspaper today, and even then the chances of making a profit are slim—as Marshall Field can testify.

But a more important factor in changing our economic system is government. Today a business man, whether he is a manufacturer or retailer or farmer, no longer faces the biggest risk of all in a free-enterprise system—the risk of the uncontrolled ups-and-downs of the economy. No one believes that we have completely eliminated the business cycle, but we have today so vast a network of government supports that many economists believe we will never again have anything like the crash of 1929. Some of these economists contend that this is the reason we escaped the postwar depression, which was expected to throw 8,000,000 men out of work after hostilities ceased.

So today, instead of having a nearly-free-enterprise system in this country—as we used to have and as most people still seem to think we have—we are operating under something quite different. It is a drastically revised system—revised by monopoly and by government supports. Partly because we still have not recognized just how different our new system is, no one has yet named it—but it might be called the "safe-enterprise system."

This "safe-enterprise system" is almost as different from the one that Adam Smith talked about or the system we once had as the economy of Nazi Germany or of Soviet Russia. But it is just as American and goes along with democracy and liberty as naturally as the original. In fact, our democracy today is probably more complete than it ever was in the past. We still have free speech and free worship. We still can protest and vote "no" if we want, and more of us have the right to vote "no" than ever before. But we no longer have the freedom to pay workers five or ten dollars a week for a sixty-hour week, or to put millions of people into the breadlines.

The schizophrenic part about all of this is that we still talk and plan as though we had a system of the old kind. Proposals are rejected in Congress day after day because they will "interfere with the free-enterprise system." People tend to confuse the "free-enterprise system" with basic Americanism and put it on the same pedestal as "liberty" or "democracy."

What makes this particularly strange is that we did not even begin to call our system a "free-enterprise system," or to use that phrase as almost synonymous with capitalism, until about ten or fifteen years ago. We had occasionally referred to it earlier as a system of "free competitive enterprise." But the more simple phrase, with the competitive idea eliminated, was popularized by the business interests of this country about ten years ago, when they were fighting off some of the New Deal reforms. One of the bright young men then working for the National Association of Manufacturers is credited with promoting the new phrase.

The slogan had great value in fighting such innovations as the wage-hour law and the Wagner labor act. The business men were afraid that we were going to abolish the "free-enterprise" system which permitted them to pay their workers whatever they could get them to work for individually, and perhaps to regulate how much profit they could make. Actually we did abolish the first of these "rights"—but we never tampered with their profits, except to a limited extent during the war. So far, the changes in the "free-enterprise system" have not hurt business. In fact, profitwise, business is going better today than ever before in history—with profits reaching more than $18,000,000,000 after taxes last year, or more than double what they were in the boom year of 1929.

Business pushed the phrase in speeches, advertisements, and propaganda. Politicians accepted it and won applause with it. Everything indicated that the American people wanted a free-enterprise system, except that by the time the phrase took hold we had moved on to another system without most people realizing it—although they had repeatedly approved the measures which brought the change about.

All the phrase did was to confuse America at a time when it could scarcely afford to be confused. It is important for the people of this country to get over their confusion—their schizophrenia—if they are to run the new system intelligently. Business men need to recognize the nature of the new system in order to adopt workable price policies, labor needs to recognize it to develop sound bargaining programs, and the public needs to recognize it to decide the issues of the day rationally. To decide some of the questions we now face without recognizing where we are or where we are going is like a ship captain trying to chart a course before he knows where he is or what port he wants to reach.

II

Most Americans seem to be in the same boat with the ship captain. Sensible and responsible men who are looking to the best interests of the country frequently take violently opposing stands on the same issues. People speak in the most glowing language about the free-enterprise system and then in almost the same breath show they really do not want it. Recently, for instance, one of the leading critics of the New Deal in Congress, a man who talks volubly about the glories of free enterprise, explained his constant support of the farm program by telling newspapermen that "certain parts of the New Deal have become a part of 'the American way of life.' "

The shape of our economy started to change in the last part of the nineteenth century with the growth of monopolies and the governmental steps to curb them. Actually the first big change came when we decided to place restrictions on some areas of free enterprise: the public utilities and the industries engaged in developing our natural resources. We decided that the railroads and the utilities, because of their subsidies and their monopoly positions, were secure and were not taking as big a risk as other businesses, and so should not be permitted to earn such rich rewards. We set up the Interstate Commerce Commission and the public utility commissions to regulate their profits and the services they provided the public. To protect our national resources, we gradually—and too late—enacted legislation limiting to some extent the aggressions of selfish entrepreneurs in the lumber and other natural resource industries. And as industry grew bigger and more powerful, we enacted the anti-trust laws, though we did not do much to enforce them.

In most areas of business we still maintained a system of comparatively free enterprise until the depression of 1929 shook America and the world to their economic and political foundations. Some governments and economic systems fell, and others came close to it. Desperately we began under Herbert Hoover to pour billions of dollars of government money into the railroads, the banks, and the insurance companies to shore up our economy. Franklin D. Roosevelt came into office and extended the same help to the average citizen.

We were so desperate that we didn't worry too much about abstract theories of government—although the Senate did debate for days over the question of whether we could feed hungry people as well as hungry cattle. There were warnings at the time that we were destroying our freedom, but we ignored them and probably would again under the same circumstances. We voted, or our representatives voted, a lot of changes in our system, piece by piece, in an effort to save various segments of the economy from ruin. These changes added up to a radical revision of the whole. But more important than any one of them, or all of them together, was the new principle of government Hoover and Roosevelt joined in writing into our system at that time—that the government stands back of our economy in time of trouble.

The men who initiated this fundamental change, and the other revisions of our system under the New Deal, believed in the free-enterprise system and were merely trying to save it by correcting isolated abuses or weaknesses. For instance, one of the most fundamental changes of all—the federal insurance of bank deposits—came not from the New Deal but from a conservative Republican, Senator Arthur H. Vandenburg of Michigan, who sponsored it and fought for it in Congress with only tacit approval from the Administration.

The farm program adopted in 1933 as one of the first acts of the Roosevelt Administration, and now accepted by both parties, was a drastic modification of free enterprise. It placed a government cushion, or guarantee, under our biggest industry—an industry which supports directly or indirectly about half the people of the country and vitally affects the rest. With the adoption of that law the "free-enterprise system" went at least half the way out of the window—without protest from anyone in authority except the Supreme Court. And even the Supreme Court changed its mind within a year or two.

In the face of such a law it is silly to talk of free enterprise in agriculture any longer. And yet that is just what the farm spokesmen do when they oppose ceilings on farm prices because they would "interfere with the free enterprise system." Like many of the rest of us the farmers want floors, but no ceilings. The latest crop report points to the possibility of huge surpluses in some of the major crops, which may require the government to put up support money running past the billion dollar mark to hold prices up at a time when many of us would like them to go down. This is not free enterprise, under which prices can drop with a bang.

Our urban economy now has fully as many government cushions under it as the farm economy, although most business men do not feel them because they are more indirect. First there is the social security law, providing floors below which the incomes of our industrial workers cannot fall even during unemployment—and providing continuing income for the aged and infirm. Then, for those who work, the wage-and-hour law provides a floor under wages and a ceiling over the hours of work. What a change this is from the old free-enterprise days when men and women worked in sweatshops and cotton mills for seventy hours a week to earn perhaps seven dollars! These two measures alone protect millions of individuals. Together with the farm income guarantees, they provide a tremendous structure supporting national purchasing power—the foundation stone for our whole industrial prosperity.

Supplementing the social security law is a vast system of retirement plans set up by private industry during the recent war, when taxes were so high that it was almost as cheap to set up a lavish retirement system as to pay taxes on the income. These reserves—estimated to run into many hundreds of millions of dollars—are just as secure a bulwark to the individuals and the economy as the social security benefits.

There are besides a wide variety of government subsidies and cushions for specific industries. The air-transport industry, for instance, is subsidized through airmail contracts, and when the TWA got into financial difficulties it rushed to Washington for a retroactive subsidy to pull it out of the hole. More recently the entire air-transport industry, with the exception of one or two companies, has been under financial strain. Instead of raising rates and competing under the rules of supply and demand the industry appealed to President Truman for help. Amid applause from the airlines, the President directed the RFC, the ever-ready crutch for industry, to study the situation, presumably as a preliminary to government loans. At the same time the Civil Aeronautics Board considered requests from the lines for bigger government subsidies—which would not be Adam Smith's solution to the problem.

The shipping industry has been subsidized by the government in one way or another for many years. Current subsidies to the merchant marine are running close to $100,000,000 a year on top of all the rich benefits provided these companies by the government in the past. Even the nation's press, which is founded on the word "free," is not free of subsidies. Newspapers and magazines enjoy the benefits of mail subsidies totaling many millions of dollars a year. Colonel Robert R. McCormick, of the Chicago *Tribune*, estimated not long ago that mail subsidies represented the entire profit of the prosperous *Time-Life-Fortune* enterprises.

Whether our banking system is subsidized is open to debate, but some economists contend that the banks got close to a billion dollars a year in subsidies during the war for handling the paper war debt. Government research subsidies are now reaching into almost every field of private enterprise and running into many hundreds of millions of dollars a year. They go not only to business concerns and educational institutions in the form of research grants, but even into the pockets of private physicians, the men who seem most determined to avoid government interference with their own profession (these payments come directly from the Public Health Service, which some physicians regard as an arch-enemy).

In some areas the definition of subsidies becomes difficult. Many industries benefit substantially from the government's weather reports, from the trade-promotion activities of the Commerce Department, from the improvements for the benefit of commerce on our rivers and harbors, from flood control expenditures, soil conservation, the establishment and maintenance of air navigation facilities, and a host of similar government operations including the production of cheap hydroelectric power.

Without counting any of these hazy fields, the Budget Bureau reported to Senator James E. Murray of Montana that subsidies to business and agriculture in the fiscal year 1946 totalled $2,247,000,000. The Byrd Economy Committee of the Senate used an even higher figure. This, of course, was in a year of prosperity—when most of the government's guarantees did not cost the Treasury anything. In addition, the federal government paid in various grants to the states that year a total of $971,000,000—much of which eventually went to construction companies, road-building material manufacturers, and others.

Moreover, the huge payments now being made to foreign countries under the Marshall Plan provide a sizable cushion for industry's base of purchasing power. Most of that money is returning to this country for the purchase of goods, and such payments will probably run into the billions of dollars for years to come. But for many years the biggest cushion for business will be military expenditures by the government. They are expected to level off at about $15,000,000,000 a year—which is several times the biggest spending program ever launched by the New Deal.

Government money has become such a major element in the American economy that one out of every six adults in this country now receives some of it in one form or another. Regular payments go to almost 16,000,000 individuals, including veterans and their dependents, members of the armed forces, government employes, federal pensioners, social security beneficiaries, and farmers.

Even more basic than any of these money payments, however, are the guarantees the federal government now offers to our credit structure. In addition to the federal insurance of bank deposits, which has eliminated the national fear of bank runs, the government offers ninety per cent guarantees on farm and urban mortgages. These guarantees, which cover a big segment of the private debt structure, have stabilized the mortgage market as it never was before—and to some extent, at least, have eliminated the wild ups-and-downs that have brought so much disaster in the past.

III

The federal government alone is now pumping into the economic system about $40,000,000,000 annually—most of which will have to continue unless we drastically modify the services our government provides, the military force, benefits to veterans, and foreign aid. This figure, which equals our total national income of only sixteen years ago, is for a period when we have been enjoying boom prosperity. State and local government expenditures swell the total beyond $50,-000,000,000 a year.

Come a depression, the federal government's spending would go far beyond these figures, since it is legally obliged to cushion farm prices, pay unemployment benefits, and make good its guarantees. Furthermore, under the principle of government established by Hoover and Roosevelt in the past depression—that neither business nor people shall be permitted to go under *en masse*—the government would have an obligation to pour billions of dollars into financial and industrial enterprises and into relief of individual need. That it will do so is conceded.

What this all amounts to, in short, is not a free-enterprise system, but a comparatively safe-enterprise system under which our economic health is founded on government credit and government credit is used not only to battle depression but to avoid it. Even in good times the government will act to save an industry—as it did recently for the air-transport companies.

There is still risk in business, particularly in those areas where competition prevails. Many small businesses fail every day. Government does not guarantee a profit to every business man, or even to every farmer. An entrepreneur's rewards still depend considerably on his ability and his luck. But the risks in business today are far more limited than they were in the days when we really had the "free-enterprise system" we talk about so much. . . .

This is a fact with vast implications—for every business man, for every worker, and for every citizen. Certainly every politician must recognize and face up to the new system.

And the American people must admit that the safe-enterprise system under which they live requires certain adjustments. Does this system, for example, warrant such unlimited business profits as in the past, when business men risked all to win all? If business does not make the necessary adjustments in price and profit policies we must decide whether or not a large segment of industry has achieved the relative security of a public utility—a position where limited risks warrant legislation limiting profits. We will have to face up, also, to a permanent budget of $40,000,000,000 or more a year and pay the taxes that such a system of government services and supports require. In good years we will have to pay in taxes considerably more than that, so that the government will be sound enough to meet the extraordinary expenses it faces in bad times.

The old free-enterprise system exists only in our nostalgic imagination, and we have spent more than enough energy defending it. If we want to retain custody of our economic fate, the first step is to admit the facts.

95. *Gibbons v. Ogden*

SUPREME COURT OF THE UNITED STATES,
1824 (APPEAL) 9 WHEATON I

THE DECISION of the Supreme Court in this case invalidated a New York statute granting to certain persons the exclusive right to steamboat navigation in New York waters. The New York Legislature in 1797 had by a statute granted an exclusive right to steam navigation on the territorial waters of the state to one John Fitch for 14 years. The franchise was subsequently revoked and regranted to Robert Livingston and Robert Fulton for a 20-year, and later extended to a 30-year, period. Any person engaging in steam navigation on New York waters without prior license from Livingston and Fulton was subject to forfeiture of his boat. These state provisions conflicted with a federal statute of 1793 regulating the licensing of vessels engaged in coastwise commerce and fishing. Ogden, who claimed to hold the franchise by indirect assignment from the original holder, sought an injunction against Gibbons, alleging the latter to be the operator of two steamboats moving between New York and New Jersey in violation of Ogden's franchise. The injunction having been issued by the New York court, Gibbons defended his position by reference to the federal statute noted above. After being denied relief by the state court, he appealed to the Supreme Court of the United States.

In holding the state statute invalid, Marshall availed himself of the opportunity of giving a broad national interpretation to the commerce clause in the Constitution. Although the nature of commerce has proven to be one of the most difficult concepts with which the Court has had to deal, the decision in *Gibbons* v. *Ogden* set the general pattern for future Court decisions. In essence the decision established a broad interpretation of the word *commerce* itself; as the Chief Justice said, "Commerce undoubtedly is traffic but it is something more, it is intercourse." Further, the Court held that the control of commerce was an exclusive federal power as long as such commerce was interstate or foreign in character. The states were left with authority over purely intrastate commerce. In rendering this decision, Marshall broadened and strengthened his policy of expanding the power of the national government at the expense of the states and opened the way to extensive federal regulation of commerce and its instrumentalities.

Opinion of the Court

MR. CHIEF JUSTICE MARSHALL delivered the opinion of the Court: . . . The appellant contends that this decree is erroneous, because the laws which purport to give the exclusive privilege it sustains, are repugnant to the constitution and laws of the United States.

They are said to be repugnant:—

1st. To that clause in the constitution which authorizes congress to regulate commerce. . . .

As preliminary to the very able discussions of the constitution, which we have heard from the bar, and as having some influence on its construction, reference has been made to the political situation of these States, anterior to its formation. It has been said that they were sovereign, were completely independent, and were connected with each other only by a league. This is true. But when these allied sovereigns converted their league into a government, when they converted their congress of ambassadors, deputed to deliberate on their common concerns, and to recommend measures of general utility, into a legislature, empowered to enact laws on the most interesting subjects, the whole character in which the States appear, underwent a change, the extent of which must be determined by a fair consideration of the instrument by which that change was effected.

This instrument contains an enumeration of powers expressly granted by the people to their government. It has been said that these powers ought to be construed strictly. But why ought they to be so construed? Is there one sentence in the constitution which gives countenance to this rule? In the last of the enumerated powers, that which grants, expressly, the means of carrying all others into execution, congress is authorized "to make all laws which shall be necessary and proper" for the purpose. But this limitation on the means which may be used, is not extended to the powers which are conferred; nor is there one sentence in the constitution which has been pointed out by the gentlemen of the bar, or which we have been able to discern, that prescribes this rule. We do not, therefore, think ourselves justified in adopting it. . . . If, from the imperfection of human language, there should be serious doubts respecting the extent of any given power, it is a well-settled rule that the objects for which it was given, especially when those objects are expressed in the instrument itself, should have great influence in the construction. We know of no reason for excluding this rule from the present case. . . .

The words are: "Congress shall have power to regulate commerce with foreign nations, and among the several States, and with the Indian tribes."

The subject to be regulated is commerce; and our constitution being, as was aptly said at the bar, one of enumeration, and not of definition, to ascertain the extent of the power it becomes necessary to settle the meaning of the word. The counsel for the appellee would limit it to traffic, to buying and selling, or the interchange of commodities, and do not admit that it comprehends navigation. This would restrict a general term, applicable to many objects, to one of its significations. Commerce, undoubtedly, is traffic, but it is something more; it is intercourse. It describes the commercial intercourse between nations, and parts of nations, in all its branches, and is regulated by prescribing rules for carrying on that intercourse. The mind can scarcely conceive a system for regulating commerce between nations, which shall exclude all laws concerning navigation, which shall be silent on the admission of the vessels of the one nation into the ports of the other, and be confined to prescribing rules for the conduct of individuals, in the actual employment of buying and selling, or of barter.

If commerce does not include navigation, the government of the Union has no direct power over that subject, and can make no law prescribing what shall constitute American vessels, or requiring that they shall be navigated by American seamen. Yet this power has been exercised from the commencement of the government, has been exercised with the consent of all, and has been understood by all to be a commercial regulation. All America understands, and has uniformly understood, the word "commerce" to comprehend navigation. It was so understood, and must have been so understood, when the constitution was framed. The power over commerce, including navigation, was one of the primary objects for which the people of America adopted their government, and must have been contemplated in forming it. The convention must have used the word in that sense, because all have understood it in that sense; and the attempt to restrict it comes too late.

If the opinion that "commerce" as the word is used in the constitution, comprehends navigation also, requires any additional confirmation, that additional confirmation is, we think, furnished by the words of the instrument itself. . . .

The word used in the constitution, then, comprehends, and has been always understood to comprehend, navigation within its meaning; and a power to regulate navigation is as expressly granted as if that term had been added to the word "commerce."

To what commerce does this power extend? The constitution informs us, to commerce "with foreign nations, and among the several States, and with the Indian tribes."

It has, we believe, been universally admitted that these words comprehend every species of commercial intercourse between the United States and foreign nations. No sort of trade can be carried on between this country and any other, to which this power does not extend. It has been truly said, that commerce, as the word is used in the constitution, is a unit, every part of which is indicated by the term.

If this be the admitted meaning of the word, in its application to foreign nations, it must carry the same meaning throughout the sentence, and remain a unit, unless there be some plain intelligible cause which alters it.

The subject to which the power is next applied, is to commerce "among the several States." The word "among" means intermingled with. A thing which is among others, is intermingled with them. Commerce among the States cannot stop at the external boundary line of each State, but may be introduced into the interior.

It is not intended to say that these words comprehend that commerce which is completely internal, which is carried on between man and man in a State, or between different parts of the same State, and which does not extend to or affect other States. Such a power would be inconvenient, and is certainly unnecessary.

Comprehensive as the word "among" is, it may very properly be restricted to that commerce which concerns more states than one. The phrase is not one which would probably have been selected to indicate the completely interior traffic of a State, because it is not an apt phrase for that purpose; and the enumeration of the particular classes of commerce to which the power was to be extended, would not have been made had the intention been to extend the power to every description. The enumeration presupposes something not enumerated; and that something, if we regard the language or the subject of the sentence, must be the exclusively internal commerce of a state. The genius and character of the whole government seem to be, that its action is to be applied to all the external concerns of the nation, and to those internal concerns which affect the States generally; but not to those which are completely within a particular State, which do not affect other States, and with which it is not necessary to interfere, for the purpose of executing some of the general powers of the government. The completely internal commerce of a State, then, may be considered as reserved for the State itself.

But, in regulating commerce with foreign nations, the power of congress does not stop at the jurisdictional lines of the several States. It would be a very useless power if it could not pass those lines. The commerce of the United States with foreign nations, is that of the whole United States. Every district has a right to participate in it. The deep streams which penetrate our country in every direction, pass through the interior of almost every State in the Union, and furnish the means of exercising this right. If congress has the power to regulate it, that power must be exercised whenever the subject exists. If it exists within the States, if a foreign voyage may commence or terminate at a port within a State, then the power of congress may be exercised within a State. . . .

We are now arrived at the inquiry—What is this power?

It is the power to regulate; that is, to prescribe the rule by which commerce is to be governed. This power, like all others vested in congress, is complete in itself, may be exercised to its utmost extent, and acknowledges no limitations, other than are prescribed in the constitution. These are expressed in plain terms, and do not affect the questions which arise in this case, or which have been discussed at the bar. If, as has always been understood, the sovereignty of congress, though limited to specified objects, is plenary as to those objects, the power over commerce with foreign nations, and among the several States, is vested in congress as absolutely as it would be in a single government, having in its constitution the same restrictions on the exercise of the power as are found in the constitution of the United States. . . .

It has been contended by the counsel for the appellant, that, as the word "to regulate" implies in its nature, full power over the thing to be regulated, it excludes, necessarily, the action of all others that would perform the same operation on the same thing. That regulation is designed for the entire result, applying to those parts which remain as they were, as well as to those which are altered. It produces a uniform whole, which is as much disturbed and deranged by changing what the regulating power designs to leave untouched, as that on which it has operated.

There is great force in this argument, and the court is not satisfied that it has been refuted.

Since, however, in exercising the power of regulating their own purely internal affairs, whether of trading or police, the States may sometimes enact laws, the validity of which depends on their interfering with and being contrary to, an act of congress passed in pursuance of the constitution, the court will enter upon the inquiry, whether the laws of New York, as expounded by the highest tribunal of that State, have, in their application to this case, come into collision with an act of congress, and deprived a citizen of a right to which that act entitles him. Should this collision exist, it will be immaterial whether those laws were passed in virtue of a concurrent power "to regulate commerce with foreign nations and among the several States," or in virtue of a power to regulate their domestic trade and police. In one case and the other, the acts of New York must yield to the law of congress; and the decision sustaining the privilege they confer, against a right given by a law of the Union, must be erroneous. . . .

In pursuing this inquiry at the bar, it has been said that the constitution does not confer the right of intercourse between State and State.

That right derives its source from those laws whose authority is acknowledged by civilized man throughout the world. This is true. The constitution found it an existing right, and gave to congress the power to regulate it. In the exercise of this power, congress has passed "an act for enrolling or licensing ships or vessels to be employed in the coasting trade and fisheries, and for regulating the same." The counsel for the respondent contend that this act does not give the right to sail from port to port, but confines itself to regulating a pre-existing right, so far only as to confer certain privileges on enrolled and licensed vessels in its exercise. . . .

This act demonstrates the opinion of congress, that steamboats may be enrolled and licensed, in common with vessels using sails. They are, of course, entitled to the same privileges, and can no more be restrained from navigating waters, and entering ports which are free to such vessels, than if they were wafted on their voyage by the winds, instead of being propelled by the agency of fire. The one element may be as legitimately used as the other, for every commercial purpose authorized by the laws of the Union; and the act of a State inhibiting the use of either to any vessel having a license under the act of congress, comes, we think, in direct collision with that act. . . .

Reversed

96. *Romance and Realism in Antitrust Policy* *

THE SHERMAN ANTITRUST ACT, passed in 1890, had as its purpose the curbing of monopoly power. After its passage farmers and small businessmen, who had been among the prime movers for its adoption, hoped for improvement in their economic position, which they felt had been adversely affected by monopoly practices. These high hopes suffered severely when the Supreme Court, in effect, nullified the effectiveness of the act. Although the original act has been amended from time to time, the Department of Justice has not followed a consistent policy regarding enforcement. The reason may be that effective public opinion regarding antitrust action is divided between those who regard monopoly as evil in itself and those who feel that modern technology makes corporate giantism necessary and probably more efficient than numerous competitive units. Professor Dewey reviews current Department of Justice anti-

* Donald Dewey, *Journal of Political Economy*, LXIII (April, 1955), pp. 93-102. Reprinted by permission of the author and publisher, University of Chicago Press.

trust policy and concludes that although the government may nominally win, in terms of the opinions in its antitrust proceedings, the courts' opinions are not translated into appreciable changes by means of effective court decrees.

THE FATE OF THE "NEW" SHERMAN ACT

NEARLY EIGHTEEN YEARS have passed since the Justice Department began the first of the cases that are generally taken to have produced the "new" Sherman Act. For a time in the middle forties, judicial opinion reflecting the "monopoly is sin" bias of the Temporary National Economic Committee investigations was hailed in some circles as evidence that the venerable statute has finally been transformed into a "positive instrument of progress." Most students of the antitrust scene, however, preferred to reserve judgment pending final disposition of the important cases, for it is a commonplace in antitrust work that the government wins the opinions and the defendants win the decrees. Too often in the past, hopes for a trust-busting program had foundered and sunk on the reluctance of the courts to disturb established corporate structures.

By now it is clear that this caution was fully justified, notwithstanding the impressive efforts of the Justice Department to follow up its legal victories with a radical application of dissolution and divestiture. Even the most cursory look at the results achieved by the "big" cases decided, compromised, or abandoned since 1938 suffices to establish that the judicial bias in favor of the corporate status quo remains substantially unchanged. Indeed, only the decrees entered in the Pullman and Paramount cases were ambitious enough to merit consideration as possible exceptions to this conclusion.

If one has embraced the comfortable thesis that economic progress is now the unique product of research in the large corporation, the fate of the new Sherman Act, far from being a matter for concern, is a positive source of satisfaction. For those of us who still prefer to resolve all doubts in favor of workable competition whenever the economic advantages of concentration are not conclusively demonstrated, the defeat of the Antitrust Division would seem to call for a reappraisal of our case.

LEGAL FICTION AS A SOURCE OF CONFUSION

Most of our difficulties follow, I believe, from the "fact" that dissolution and divestiture suits are conducted upon a premise which most judges and laymen really do not accept. Unlike the advocates of strong remedies, they are not convinced that the exercise of monopoly power which has been acquired by means neither actionable nor indictable per se violates the law to an extent justifying its elimination without a sympathetic attention to the position of workers and stockholders whose interests may adversely be affected by trust-busting.

This view does not regard vested interests in monoply as bona fide property rights merely by virtue of their established character. But it does assume, however inarticulately, that possible public gains must be weighed against possible private losses and that, the more problematical the public benefit, the greater the proper conservative bias in favor of private claims. Thus it is one thing for the reasonable judge to order the termination of profitable leasing arrangements to the end that a secondhand market for shoe-making machinery may hasten the introduction of new equipment; it is quite another for him to transform a going concern into three smaller units on the hope that consumers will benefit in ways that the Antitrust Division cannot spell out in concrete terms.

Friends of the Antitrust Division may object that possession of monopoly power alone has never constituted a violation of the Sherman Act; that the courts have always required a showing of power over price plus something more—though admittedly the something more is none too clear. Occasionally (notably in the Alcoa case) the courts have appeared to employ a test for unlawful monopolization that would have satisfied Frank Fetter himself. Nevertheless, it is true that they have generally held back from accepting the economist's definition of monopoly as the touchstone of policy. The history of antitrust litigation, however, may fairly be viewed as a struggle over how much importance is to be accorded to economics in the legal definition of monopoly; that is, as an attempt to strengthen the modest safeguards conferred upon competition by the common law.

In 1890 the position of monopoly power at common law was clear enough. "Unreasonably" restrictive agreements among business rivals for the purpose of inhibiting competition were not enforceable at law or equity; but merchants need not fear indictment or civil liability so long as their actions did not violate the ordinary criminal or civil codes. For example, the deliberate use of below-cost pricing to eliminate competition did not expose one to legal penalties so long as it was "rational" business behavior and not intended to gratify a sadistic desire to humble a fellow-human beyond the requirements of profit maximization.

Since the coming of the Sherman Act, departures from common law treatment of monopoly have followed two main lines. On the one hand, the courts have come to treat the elimination of competition by certain methods as so highly suspect that their illegality is virtually presumed. Thus one may no longer dispose of a troublesome rival by purchasing his facilities at an inordinately high price or force him to terms by pricing below short-run average cost; nor, of course, may one contract with him to share the market or observe fair prices.

On the other hand, the courts have held that the "totality" of the defendant's conduct may be examined in order to determine whether his policies reveal an unlawful "intent" to secure or preserve monopoly power. So far as I know, the courts have never ruled that a firm may not protect itself against the incursion of rivals by producing the better mousetrap or reducing production costs on the existing model. But neither have the courts unambiguously declared that economies of scale in production or research constitute the only valid reasons for permitting the domination of an important industry by a single firm or a handful of firms.

A number of early decisions before the advent of the rule of reason, especially *The Northern Securities Co.* v. *United States*, came close to equating unlawful monopoly with power over price. Since 1940 the courts have seemingly indicated a willingness to jettison the reasonableness test. In the Big Three tobacco case, the Supreme Court implied that unlawful conspiracy could be inferred from parallel action even in the absence of evidence showing overt collusion. In the Alcoa case, Learned Hand's remarkable opinion seemed to convey that, no matter how carefully the defendant has comported himself, the law is violated when he (a) controls too great a fraction of the industry's output and (b) enjoys a size and power that have the effect of frightening off potential rivals. If these two decisions could be taken at their face value—a pitfall to be avoided in the study of antitrust law—Professor Galbraith's "preposterous" conclusion would seem to follow: the very fabric of American capitalism is indeed illegal.

As to the present state of antitrust policy, four observations may be ventured. First, if the court does not accept some version of the textbook definition of monopoly, it must necessarily work with the good-trust—bad-trust dichotomy. This classification is perhaps useful in deciding whether a particular firm should be allowed to strengthen its position by acquiring rivals or important patents. It may also serve to discourage business expansion by particularly antisocial means, notably trade wars. But the reasonableness test leaves the major corporations invulnerable to dissolution or divestiture so long as they forego the cruder methods of dampening competition.

Second, even if the court employs a test for unlawful monopoly more acceptable to most economists, it does not follow that severer remedies will find favor; the court may prove to have some rather surprising notions of what must be done in order to restore "competitive" conditions.

Third, regardless of the legal definition of monopoly implied, the possibility that the elimination of power over price may injure the fortunes of innocent parties is seldom explicitly explored in antitrust suits. It is the "company" that is charged with violating the antitrust laws. If the company has unlawfully suppressed competition in the past (in the Pullman case company records from the 1870's were accepted in evidence), the court is clearly obliged to prescribe action designed to restore competitve conditions. Enforcement of the law cannot be suspended on the plea that the company will suffer if forced to disgorge its ill-gotten gains. Since the corporation is a fictitious person, during the trial the court is under no obligation to take cognizance of the obvious; namely, that the beneficiaries of any successful "attempt to monopolize" are those stockholders, workers, and executives who realized capital gains or higher incomes as a consequence of unlawful business aggrandizement. When the corporation's monopoly power antedates the antitrust suit by more than a few years, the presumption is that most persons currently dependent upon the corporation for an income have not materially profited from its exercise.

Finally, although the interests of these parties cannot openly be pleaded to estop the ending of unlawful monopoly, they nevertheless influence the framing of decrees. The Antitrust Division now finds it fairly easy to convince the courts that the activities of a major firm in some sense "unlawfully" restrain competition; but, unless the company officers have committed acts that blatantly offend against acknowledged canons of decency, the fiction that stockholders and workers have no legitimate stake in corporate power over price will seldom suffice to persuade the courts to follow through with the logical remedies.

THE LIMITATIONS OF PAINLESS TRUST-BUSTING

Defenders of trust-busting will probably object that our preoccupation with its possible effects on the fortunes of innocent parties is quite unnecessary; that the dangers to the interest of workers and stockholders in the plans for corporate reorganization put forward by the Justice Department are much exaggerated; and that, in fact, a dissolution or divestiture decree has not yet discernibly injured owners or employees in a dismembered concern. I cannot believe that writers who give this assurance perceive its implications. For if a court order directing dissolution or divestiture does not hurt workers and stockholders, only the following inferences are possible: (1) the company had no appreciable monopoly power in the first place; (2) the company had previously refrained from making the most profitable use of whatever monopoly power it did possess (*i.e.*, the company was a "good" trust); (3) monopoly power residing in the company was not disturbed by dissolution or divestiture; (4) the unlawful power over price has merely been bequeathed or sold to other corporate units; (5) the fall in income sustained by the company as a consequence of its loss of monopoly power was offset by a fortunate development or concatenation of circumstances unrelated to the antitrust suit—for example, a fall in the cost of raw materials, an increased demand for the firm's output, tax relief, or profitable innovation; the company may have emerged unscathed from its dissection through luck or good management or any combination of the two; and (6) some monopoly power was eliminated by dissolution or divestiture, but such power had previously rested upon so precarious a foundation that it had never been capitalized into appreciably higher security prices or incorporated into established employee expectations.

Hence when the proponents of trust-busting contend that their measures will reduce monopoly power without inflicting a financial loss on hapless stockholders and employees, we can only conclude that they (a) are mistaken, (b) are employing a definition of monopoly power which an economist cannot accept, or (c) are deliberately eschewing attacks on the more formidable enclaves of monopoly power in the economy. And if capitalized monopoly *is* the target, their proposals must be rejected as resting upon a premise that is logically untenable. Not only does the destruction of monopoly power entail the imposition of a financial loss upon hapless parties, but the magnitude of the loss is the measure of "monopoly" eliminated.

In view of the obvious limitations of the legal fiction that makes the present employees and stockholders of a corporation responsible for the unlawful policies of past managements, one may doubt whether the courts would consent to impose harsh remedies even if it were clear that monopoly power could be touched in no other way. In fact, the need for the calculated doing of damage to property values is never made apparent in an antitrust case. On the contrary, federal attorneys, as a matter of trial technique, resolutely deny that their requests for relief will adversely affect the interests of workers and stockholders. Hence they are unable to prevent the defendant from suggesting to the judge that, if his decree *should* harm these groups, *ipso facto* he will have wantonly destroyed the efficiency of a going concern. Actually, the severity of what the courts regard as a "harsh" decree is much more likely to relate to the vagaries and imperfections of the capital market than to any contemplated destruction of monopoly power. Thus, when stock divestiture is ordered, the investor is normally allowed to retain ownership until a "fair" price obtains for his securities—provided voting rights are surrendered to an acceptable trustee. The probable consequences of trust-busting for employee fortunes is a better index of how it promises to affect the firm's power over price; and our tacit assumption that workers are, so to speak, usually disinterested spectators in an antitrust action involving their employer is perhaps the most telling evidence that we do not really expect a decree that will seriously disturb monopoly power.

In fact, once control over price has been capitalized into the value of securities owned by Johnny-come-lately's or incorporated into wage scales, it is, for all practical purposes, safe from judicial attack. Thus, so far as the reduction of monopoly power is concerned, there are only two situations in which trust-busting is worth the trouble and expense of extended litigation.

The first, of course, is where any financial loss will fall upon the persons who have engineered the unlawful suppression of competition. Judges must ever affirm that a court of equity imposes no penalties for past conduct; but, as one would expect, the most severe decrees involving dissolution and divestiture have been returned against companies whose major stockholders have been personally responsible for the castigated policies of their firms. Unfortunately, the separation of legal ownership and effective control in most large and medium-sized corporations is now so complete that the government has not much opportunity to employ trust-busting as a *sub rosa* punishment.

As a second possibility, a dissolution or divestiture suit can be prosecuted with some prospect of success when the target is monopoly power which cannot be captitalized; that is, when it is inseparably bound up with the acumen or charisma of particular individuals. In this circumstance, trust-busting can presumably contribute to freer markets by curbing the power and influence of the objectionable entrepreneurs—by forcing the withdrawal of a Duke or Rockefeller. In short, meaningful anti-monopoly remedies can be anticipated only when it is possible for judges to "personalize" the issues, which is to say that until the courts can bring themselves to impose decrees that seriously menace the interests of innocent parties the Sherman Act can never serve as an instrument to further anyone's program for laissez faire.

THE CASE FOR CONSERVATISM

The libertarian of the Fetter-Simons persuasion would therefore seem to have a choice of three courses of action. He can return undaunted to the battle in the hope that he may yet persuade the courts that dissolution and divestiture designed to injure hapless workers and stockholders falls within the domain of "reasonable" behavior. But, of course, the libertarian cannot elect this alternative unless he has first convinced himself that failure to pursue an aggressive free-market policy will ultimately place the country in dire jeopardy. (Some police-state variety of state socialism is generally made the end of the road for big-business capitalism by the friends of trust-busting.) For better or worse, most of us have not the confidence in our own prescience that this course requires.

As a second possibility, the libertarian can discard the legalistic approach to antitrust problems and acknowledge monopoly power as a bona fide property right, which the state may not destroy without paying compensation. Thus, if the public interest is thought to require dissolution in the aluminum industry, the assets of the member firms could be acquired at their monopoly valuation, and new firms organized and sold for what they will bring as competitive units. To the extent that workers have managed to obtain part of the fruits of the industry's power over price, they too must be guaranteed against any loss of income sustained as a consequence of the compulsory reorganization.

The administrative difficulties that would accompany any effort to carry out a compensated elimination of monopoly require no comment, and they probably explain why it is never seriously proposed. But then if one accepts the reduction of monopoly power as a goal justifying resort to such a program, it is only a short step to the view that the public's great stake in trust-busting makes indemnification unnecessary.

Finally, the libertarian can come to terms with his world by recognizing that dissolution and divestiture on the scale requested by the Antitrust Division is simply not palatable to most legislators and judges. He will recognize that, at this late date, the large corporation is not to be destroyed by a frontal assault, however much one may regret that it was allowed to intrench itself in the first place. And for transforming competition among the giant few into some more acceptable variety, he will place his hopes in unspectacular Fabian tactics—the blocking of doubtful mergers, close scrutiny of the awarding of government contracts and the disposition of surplus federal property, curtailment of the patent privilege, and the harassment of trade associations. Whether defensive measures of this sort will suffice to achieve the libertarian goal is, of course, as yet open to question.

In summary, it is the burden of this paper that the new Sherman Act is rapidly becoming indistinguishable from the old; that this result was "inevitable" given the judicial reluctance to disturb private rights in the interest of promoting nebulous public goals; that in most antitrust cases this conservatism is both understandable and commendable; and that, on balance, ambitious attempts at trust-busting probably do the aims of the Antitrust Division more harm than good. At best, dissolution and divestiture suits tie up the agency's limited means in lengthy battles which will probably be lost. At worst, the occasional securing of a dismembering decree which does not touch monopoly power may delude the friends of antitrust policy into thinking that they are progressing in the right direction.

XVIII

GOVERNMENT AND LABOR

97. *National Labor Relations Board v. Jones & Laughlin Steel Corp.*

SUPREME COURT OF THE UNITED STATES,
1936 (CERTIORARI) 301 U.S. 1

THIS DECISION holds constitutional the National Labor Relations Act of 1935, which guaranteed to labor the right to collective bargaining and protection from specified unfair labor practices by the employer. The constitutional basis of the act was the commerce clause. The Jones & Laughlin Steel Corporation sought to escape from compliance with the act on the ground that its business was intrastate in character and could not be brought under the act. In sustaining the act, the Court emphasized the doctrine that the federal power to control commerce extends also to its protection and advancement. If an action, although seemingly local in character, is such as substantially to affect interstate commerce, then the power of the federal government to regulate such activity is included under the commerce power. The Court held that the act, by providing for collective bargaining and other measures and thus preventing labor disputes in industries engaged in interstate commerce, was directly related to maintaining commerce and therefore constitutional. The case is significant as an example of the broadening of the Court's interpretation of the commerce clause for the purpose of allowing federal regulation, especially when it is set against the Court's previous decisions in the Schechter (*Schechter* v. *U.S.* 295 U.S. 495), and Carter (*Carter* v. *Carter Coal* Co. 298 U.S. 238) cases.

Opinion of the Court

MR. CHIEF JUSTICE HUGHES delivered the opinion of the Court:
In a proceeding under the National Labor Relations Act of 1935, the

National Labor Relations Board found that the respondent, Jones & Laughlin Steel Corporation, had violated the Act by engaging in unfair labor practices affecting commerce. The proceeding was instituted by the Beaver Valley Lodge No. 200, affiliated with the Amalgamated Association of Iron, Steel and Tin Workers of America, a labor organization. The unfair labor practices charged were that the corporation was discriminating against members of the union with regard to hire and tenure of employment, and was coercing and intimidating its employees in order to interfere with their self-organization. The discriminatory and coercive action alleged was the discharge of certain employees.

The National Labor Relations Board, sustaining the charge, ordered the corporation to cease and desist from such discrimination and coercion, to offer reinstatement to ten of the employees named, to make good their losses in pay, and to post for thirty days notices that the corporation would not discharge or discriminate against members, or those desiring to become members, of the labor union. As the corporation failed to comply, the Board petitioned the Circuit Court of Appeals to enforce the order. The court denied the petition, holding that the order lay beyond the range of federal power. 83 F. (2d) 998. We granted certiorari. . . .

We turn to the questions of law which respondent urges in contesting the validity and application of the Act.

First. The scope of the Act.—The Act is challenged in its entirety as an attempt to regulate all industry, thus invading the reserved powers of the States over their local concerns. It is asserted that the references in the Act to interstate and foreign commerce are colorable at best; that the Act is not a true regulation of such commerce or of matters which directly affect it but on the contrary has the fundamental object of placing under the compulsory supervision of the federal government all industrial labor relations within the nation. The argument seeks support in the broad words of the preamble (section one) and in the sweep of the provisions of the Act, and it is further insisted that its legislative history shows an essential universal purpose in the light of which its scope cannot be limited by either construction or by the application of the separability clause.

If this conception of terms, intent, and consequent inseparability were sound, the Act would necessarily fall by reason or the limitation upon the federal power which inheres in the constitutional grant, as well as because of the explicit reservation of the Tenth Amendment. *Schechter Corp. v. United States*, 295 U.S. 495, 549, 550, 554. The authority of the federal government may not be pushed to such an extreme as to destroy the distinction, which the commerce clause itself establishes, between commerce "among the several States" and the internal concerns of a State. That distinction between what is national and what is local in the activities of commerce is vital to the maintenance of our federal system.

But we are not at liberty to deny effect to specific provisions, which Congress has constitutional power to enact, by superimposing upon them inferences from general legislative declarations of an ambiguous character, even if found in the same statute. The cardinal principle of statutory construction is to save and not to destroy. We have repeatedly held that as between two possible interpretations of a statute, by one of which it would be unconstitutional and by the other valid, our plain duty is to adopt that which will save the act. Even to avoid a serious doubt the rule is the same. . . .

We think it clear that the National Labor Relations Act may be construed so as to operate within the sphere of constitutional authority. The jurisdiction conferred upon the Board, and invoked in this instance, is found in § 10 (a), which provides:

"Sec. 10 (a). The Board is empowered, as hereinafter provided, to prevent any person from engaging in any unfair labor practice (listed in section 8) affecting commerce."

The critical words of this provision, prescribing the limits of the Board's authority in dealing with the labor practices, are "affecting commerce." The Act specifically defines the "commerce" to which it refers (§ 2 (6)):

"The term 'commerce' means trade, traffic, commerce, transportation, or communication among the several States, or between the District of Columbia or any Territory of the United States and any State or other Territory, or between any foreign country and any State, Territory, or the District of Columbia, or within the District of Columbia or any Territory, or between points in the same State but through any other State or any Territory or the District of Columbia or any foreign country."

There can be no question that the commerce thus contemplated by the Act (aside from that within a Territory or the District of Columbia) is interstate and foreign commerce in the constitutional sense. The act also defines the term "affecting commerce" (§ 2 (7)):

"The term 'affecting commerce' means in commerce, or burdening or obstructing commerce or the free flow of commerce, or having led or tending to lead to a labor dispute burdening or obstructing commerce or the free flow of commerce."

This definition is one of exclusion as well as inclusion. The grant of authority to the Board does not purport to extend to the relationship between all industrial employees and employers. Its terms do not impose collective bargaining upon all industry regardless of effects upon interstate or foreign commerce. It purports to reach only what may be deemed to burden or obstruct that commerce and, thus qualified, it must be construed as contemplating the exercise of control within constitutional bounds. It is a familiar principle that acts which directly burden or obstruct interstate or foreign commerce, or its free flow, are within the reach of the congressional power. Acts having that effect are not rendered immune because they grow out of labor disputes. . . .

Second. The unfair labor practices in question.—The unfair labor practices found by the Board are those defined in § 8, subdivisions (1) and (3). These provide:

"Sec. 8. It shall be an unfair practice for an employer—

"(1) To interfere with, restrain, or coerce employees in the exercise of the rights guaranteed in section 7."

"(3) By discrimination in regard to hire or tenure of employment or any term or condition of employment to encourage or discourage membership in any labor organization: . . ."

Section 8, subdivision (1), refers to § 7, which is as follows:

"Sec. 7. Employees shall have the right to self-organization, to form, join, or assist labor organizations, to bargain collectively through representatives of their own choosing, and to engage in concerted activities, for the purpose of collective bargaining or other mutual aid or protection."

Thus, in its present application, the statute goes no further than to safeguard the right of employees to self-organization and to select representatives of their own choosing for collective bargaining or other mutual protection without restraint or coercion by their employer.

That is a fundamental right. Employees have as clear a right to organize and select their representatives for lawful purposes as the respondent has to organize its business and select its own officers and agents. Discrimination and coercion to prevent the free exercise of the right of employees to self-organization and representation is a proper subject for condemnation by competent legislative authority. Long ago we stated the reason for labor organizations. We said that they were organized out of the necessities of the situation; that a single employee was helpless in dealing with an employer; that he was dependent ordinarily on his daily wage for the maintenance of himself and family; that if the employer refused to pay him the wages that he thought fair, he was nevertheless unable to leave the employ and resist arbitrary and unfair treatment; that union was essential to give laborers opportunity to deal on an equality with their employer. . . .

Third. The application of the Act to employees engaged in production.—The principle involved.—Respondent says that whatever may be said of employees engaged in interestate commerce, the industrial relations and activities in the manufacturing department of respondent's enterprise are not subject to federal regulation. The argument rests upon the proposition that manufacturing in itself is not commerce. . . .

The congressional authority to protect interstate commerce from burdens and obstructions is not limited to transactions which can be deemed to be an essential part of a "flow" of interstate or foreign commerce. Burdens and obstructions may be due to injurious action springing from other sources. The fundamental principle is that the power to regulate commerce is the power to enact "all appropriate legislation" for "its protection and advancement" (*The Daniel Ball,* 10 Wall. 557,564); to adopt measures "to promote its growth and insure its safety" (*Mobile County* v. *Kimball,* 102 U.S. 691, 696, 697); "to foster, protect, control and restrain." *Second Employers' Liability Cases,* [223 U.S. 1, at p. 47]. *Texas & N. O. R. Co.* v. *Railway Clerks,* [281 U.S. 548]. That power is plenary and may be exerted to protect interstate commerce "no matter what the source of the dangers which threaten it." *Second Employers' Liability Cases,* p. 51; *Schechter Corp.* v. *United States, supra.* Although activities may be intrastate in character when separately considered, if they have such a close and substantial relation to interstate commerce that their control is essential or appropriate to protect that commerce from burdens and obstructions, Congress cannot be denied the power to exercise that control. *Schechter Corp.* v. *United States, supra.* Undoubtedly the scope of this power must be considered in the light of our dual system of government and may not be extended so as to embrace effects upon interstate commerce so indirect and remote that to embrace them, in view of our complex society, would effectually obliterate the distinction between what is national and what is local and create a completely centralized government. *Id.* The question is necessarily one of degree. As the Court said in *Chicago Board of Trade* v. *Olsen,* [262 U.S. 1, at p. 37], repeating what had been said in *Stafford* v. *Wallace,* [258 U.S. 495]: "Whatever amounts to more or less constant practice, and threatens to obstruct or unduly to burden the freedom of interstate commerce is within the regulatory power of Congress under the commerce clause and it is primarily for Congress to consider and decide the fact of the danger and meet it."

That intrastate activities, by reason of close and intimate relation to interstate commerce, may fall within federal control is demonstrated in the case of carriers who are engaged in both interstate and intrastate transportation. There federal control has been found essential to secure the freedom of interstate traffic from interference or unjust discrimination and to promote the efficiency of the interstate service. . . .

The close and intimate effect which brings the subject within the reach of federal power may be due to activities in relation to productive industry although the industry when separately viewed is local. This has been abundantly illustrated in the application of the federal Anti-Trust Act. . . .

It is thus apparent that the fact that the employees here concerned were engaged in production is not determinative. The question remains as to the effect upon interstate commerce of the labor practice involved. In the *Schechter* case, *supra*, we found that the effect there was so remote as to be beyond the federal power. To find "immediacy or directness" there was to find it "almost everywhere," a result inconsistent with the maintenance of our federal system. In the *Carter* case, *supra*, the Court was of the opinion that the provisions of the statute relating to production were invalid upon several grounds,—that there was improper delegation of legislative power, and that the requirements not only went beyond any sustainable measure of protection of interstate commerce but were also inconsistent with due process. These cases are not controlling here.

Fourth. Effects of the unfair labor practice in respondent's enterprise.—Giving full weight to respondent's contention with respect to a break in the complete continuity of the "stream of commerce" by reason of respondent's manufacturing operations, the fact remains that the stoppage of those operations by industrial strife would have a most serious effect upon interstate commerce. In view of respondent's far-flung activities, it is idle to say that the effect would be indirect or remote. It is obvious that it would be immediate and might be catastrophic. We are asked to shut our eyes to the plainest facts of our national life and to deal with the question of direct and indirect effects in an intellectual vacuum. Because there may be but indirect and remote effects upon interstate commerce in connection with a host of local enterprises throughout the country, it does not follow that other industrial activities do not have such a close and intimate relation to interstate commerce as to make the presence of industrial strife a matter of the most urgent national concern. When industries organize themselves on a national scale, making their relation to interstate commerce the dominant factor in their activities, how can it be maintained that their industrial labor relations constitute a forbidden field into which Congress may not enter when it is necessary to protect interstate commerce from the paralyzing consequences of industrial war? We have often said that interstate commerce itself is a practical conception. It is equally true that interferences with that commerce must be appraised by a judgment that does not ignore actual experience. . . .

Our conclusion is that the order of the Board was within its competency and that the Act is valid as here applied. The judgment of the Circuit Court of Appeals is reversed and the cause is remanded for further proceedings in conformity with this opinion.

Reversed

(Justices McReynolds, Van Devanter, Sutherland, and Butler dissent.)

98. *United States v. Darby*

SUPREME COURT OF THE UNITED STATES,
1941 (APPEAL) 312 U.S. 100

THE IMPLICATIONS of the Court's decision in this case are far-reaching. By a unanimous decision the Court held constitutional the Fair Labor Standards Act of 1938. In reaching this conclusion the Court specifically overruled the old child labor case (*Hammer v. Dagenhart*, 247 U.S. 251) and sustained the right of the federal government to prohibit the shipment in interstate commerce of the products of child labor. In addition the Court sustained the power of the federal government under the commerce clause to establish minimum wage and hour regulations for businesses engaged in interstate commerce. In a subsequent case (*Opp Cotton Mills v. Administrator*, 312 U.S. 126) the Court likewise sustained the broad discretionary powers granted the Administrator under the act. This case and subsequent ones further expanding its doctrine dealt a body blow to advocates of states' rights and opened the door to the attainment of the goals of a "social service state," especially in the field of labor relations.

Opinion of the Court

MR. JUSTICE STONE delivered the opinion of the Court:

The two principal questions raised by the record in this case are, *first*, whether Congress has constitutional power to prohibit the shipment in interstate commerce of lumber manufactured by employees whose wages are less than a prescribed minimum or whose weekly hours of labor at that wage are greater than a prescribed maximum, and, *second*, whether it has power to prohibit the employment of workmen in the production of goods "for interstate commerce" at other than prescribed wages and hours. A subsidiary question is whether in connection with such prohibitions Congress can require the employer subject to them to keep records showing the hours worked each day and week by each of his employees including those engaged "in the production and manufacture of goods to wit, lumber, for 'interstate commerce.' "

Appellee demurred to an indictment found in the district court for southern Georgia charging him with violation of § 15 (a) (1) (2) and (5) of the Fair Labor Standards Act of 1938; 52 Stat. 1060, 29 U.S.C. § 201, *et seq.* The district court sustained the demurrer and quashed the indictment and the case comes here on direct appeal . . .

The Fair Labor Standards Act set up a comprehensive legislative scheme for preventing the shipment in interstate commerce of certain products and commodities produced in the United States under labor conditions as respects wages and hours which fail to conform to standards set up by the Act. Its purpose, as we judiciously know . . . is to exclude from interstate commerce goods produced for the commerce and to prevent their production for interstate commerce, under conditions detrimental to the maintenance of the minimum standards of living necessary for health and general well-being; and to prevent the use of interstate commerce as the means of competition in the distribution of goods so produced, and as the means of spreading and perpetuating such substandard labor conditions among the workers of the several states. . . .

The indictment charges that appellee is engaged, in the State of Georgia, in the business of acquiring raw materials, which he manufactures into finished lumber with the intent, when manufactured, to ship it in interstate commerce to customers outside the state, and that he does in fact so ship a large part of the lumber so produced. There are numerous counts charging appellee with the shipment in interstate commerce from Georgia to points outside the state of lumber in the production of which, for interstate commerce, appellee has employed workmen at less than the prescribed minimum wage or more than the prescribed maximum hours without payment to them of any wage for overtime. . . .

The demurrer, so far as now relevant to the appeal, challenged the validity of the Fair Labor Standards Act under the Commerce Clause and the Fifth and Tenth Amendments. The district court quashed the indictment in its entirety upon the broad grounds that the Act, which it interpreted as a regulation of manufacture within the states, is unconstitutional. It declared that manufacture is not interstate commerce and that the regulation by the Fair Labor Standards Act of wages and hours of employment of those engaged in the manufacture of goods which it is intended at the time of production "may or will be" after production "sold in interstate commerce in part or in whole" is not within the congressional power to regulate interstate commerce.

The effect of the court's decision and judgment is thus to deny the power of Congress to prohibit shipment in interstate commerce of lumber produced for interstate commerce under the proscribed substandard labor conditions of wages and hours, its power to penalize the employer for his failure to conform to the wage and hour provisions in the case of employees engaged in the production of lumber which he intends thereafter to ship in interstate commerce in part or in whole according to the normal course of his business and its power to compel him to keep records of hours of employment as required by the statute and the regulations of the administrator.

. . . The appeal statute limits our jurisdiction on this appeal to a review of the determination of the district court so far only as it is based on the validity or construction of the statute. *United States* v. *Borden Co.*, 308 U.S. 188, 193–195, and cases cited. Hence we accept the district court's interpretation of the indictment and confine our decision to the validity and construction of the statute.

The prohibition of shipment of the proscribed goods in interstate commerce. Section 15 (a) (1) prohibits, and the indictment charges, the shipment in interstate commerce, of goods produced for interstate commerce by employees whose wages and hours of employment do not conform to the requirements of the Act. Since this section is not violated unless the commodity shipped has been produced under labor conditions prohibited by § 6 and § 7, the only question arising under the commerce clause with respect to such shipments is whether Congress has the constitutional power to prohibit them.

While manufacture is not of itself interstate commerce, the shipment of manufactured goods interstate is such commerce and the prohibition of such shipment by Congress is indubitably a regulation of the commerce. The power to regulate commerce is the power "to prescribe the rule by which commerce is governed." *Gibbons* v. *Ogden*, 9 Wheat. 1, 196. It extends not only to those regulations which aid, foster and protect the commerce, but embraces those which prohibit it. . . . It is conceded that the power of Congress to prohibit transportation in interstate commerce includes noxious articles . . . stolen articles . . . kidnapped persons . . . and articles such as intoxicating liquor or convict made goods, traffic in which is forbidden or restricted by the laws of the state of destination. . . .

But it is said that the present prohibition falls within the scope of none of these categories; that while the prohibition is nominally a regulation of the commerce its motive or purpose is regulation of wages and hours of persons engaged in manufacture, the control of which has been reserved to the states and upon which Georgia and some of the states of destination have placed no restriction; that the effect of the present statute is not to exclude the prescribed articles from interstate commerce in aid of state regulation as in *Kentucky Whip & Collar Co.* v. *Illinois Central R. Co.*, [299 U.S. 334], but instead, under the guise of a regulation of interstate commerce, it undertakes to regulate wages and hours within the state contrary to the policy of the state which has elected to leave them unregulated.

The power of Congress over interstate commerce "is complete in itself, may be exercised to its utmost extent, and acknowledges no limitations other than are prescribed in the Constitution." *Gibbons* v. *Ogden, supra,* 196. That power can neither be enlarged nor diminished by the exercise or non-exercise of state power. *Kentucky Whip & Collar Co.* v. *Illinois Central R. Co., supra.* Congress, following its own conception of public policy concerning the restrictions which may appropriately be imposed on interstate commerce, is free to exclude from the commerce articles whose use in the states for which they are destined it may conceive to be injurious to the public health, morals or welfare, even though the state has not sought to regulate their use. . . .

Such regulation is not a forbidden invasion of state power merely because either its motive or its consequence is to restrict the use of articles of commerce within the states of destination and is not prohibited unless by other Constitutional provisions. It is no objection to the assertion of the power to regulate interstate commerce that its exercise is attended by the same incidents which attend the exercise of the police power of the states. . . .

The motive and purpose of the present regulation are plainly to make effective the Congressional conception of public policy that interstate commerce should not be made the instrument of competition in the distribution of goods produced under substandard labor conditions, which competition is injurious to the commerce and to the states from and to which the commerce flows. The motive and purpose of a regulation of interstate commerce are matters for the legislative judgment upon the exercise of which the Constitution places no restriction and over which the courts are given no control. . . . "The judicial cannot prescribe to the legislative department of the government limitations upon the exercise of its acknowledged power." *Veazie Bank* v. *Fenno,* 8 Wall. 533. Whatever their motive and purpose, regulations of commerce which do not infringe some constitutional prohibition are within the plenary power conferred on Congress by the Commerce Clause. Subject only to that limitation, presently to be considered, we conclude that the prohibition of the shipment interstate of goods produced under the forbidden substandard labor conditions is within the constitutional authority of Congress.

In the more than a century which has elapsed since the decision of *Gibbons* v. *Ogden,* these principles of constitutional interpretation have been so long and repeatedly recognized by this Court as applicable to the Commerce Clause, that there would be little occasion for repeating them now were it not for the decision of this Court twenty-two years ago in *Hammer* v. *Dagenhart*, 247 U.S. 251. In that case it was held by a bare majority of the Court over the powerful and now classic dissent of Mr. Justice Holmes setting forth the fundamental issues involved, that Congress was without power to exclude the products of child labor from interstate commerce. The reasoning and conclusion of the Court's opinion there cannot be reconciled with the conclusion which we have reached, that the power of Congress under the Commerce Clause is plenary to exclude any article from interstate commerce subject only to the specific prohibitions of the Constitution.

Hammer v. *Dagenhart* has not been followed. The distinction on which the decision was rested that Congressional power to prohibit interstate commerce is limited to articles which in themselves have some harmful or deleterious property—a distinction which was novel when made and unsupported by any provision of the Constitution—has long since been abandoned. . . . The thesis of the opinion that the motive of the prohibition or its effect to control in some measure the use or production within the states of the article thus excluded from the commerce can operate to deprive the regulation of its constitutional authority has long since ceased to have force. . . . And finally we have declared "The authority of the federal government over interstate commerce does not differ in extent or character from that retained by the states over intrastate commerce." *U.S.* v. *Rock Royal Co-operative*, 307 U.S. 533, 569.

The conclusion is inescapable that *Hammer* v. *Dagenhart* was a departure from the principles which have prevailed in the interpretation of the Commerce Clause both before and since the decision and that such vitality, as a precedent, as it then had has long since been exhausted. It should be and now is overruled.

Validity of the wage and hour requirements. Section 15 (a) (2) and §§ 6 and 7 require employers to conform to the wage and hour provisions with respect to all employees engaged in the production of goods for interstate commerce. As appellee's employees are not alleged to be "engaged in interstate commerce" the validity of the prohibition turns on the question whether the employment, under other than the prescribed labor standards, of employees engaged in the production of goods for interstate commerce is so related to the commerce and so affects it as to be within the reach of the power of Congress to regulate it.

To answer this question we must at the outset determine whether the particular acts charged in the counts which are laid under § 15 (a) (2) as they were construed below, constitute "production for com merce" within the meaning of the statute. As the Government seeks to apply the statute in the indictment, and as the court below construed the phrase "produced for interstate commerce," it embraces at least the case where an employer engaged, as is appellee, in the manufacture and shipment of goods in filling orders of extrastate customers, manufactures his product with the intent or expectation that according to the normal course of his business all or some part of it will be selected for shipment to those customers.

Without attempting to define the precise limits of the phrase, we think the acts alleged in the indictment are within the sweep of the statute. The obvious purpose of the Act was not only to prevent the interstate transportation of the proscribed product, but to stop the initial step toward transportation, production with the purpose of so transporting it. Congress was not unaware that most manufacturing businesses shipping their product in interstate commerce make it in their shops without reference to its ultimate destination and then after manufacture select some of it for shipment interstate and some intrastate according to the daily demands of their business, and that it would be practically impossible, without disrupting manufacturing businesses, to restrict the prohibited kind of production to the particular pieces of lumber, cloth, furniture or the like which later move in interstate rather than intrastate commerce. . . .

There remains the question whether such restriction on the production of goods for commerce is a permissible exercise of the commerce power. The power of Congress over interstate commerce is not confined to the regulation of commerce among the states. It extends to those activities intrastate which so affect interstate commerce or the exercise of the power of Congress over it as to make regulation of them appropriate means to the attainment of a legitimate end, the exercise of the granted power of Congress to regulate interstate commerce. . . .

Congress, having by the present Act adopted the policy of excluding from interstate commerce all goods produced for the commerce which do not conform to the specified labor standards, it may choose the means reasonably adapted to the attainment of the permitted end, even though they involve control of intrastate activities. . . .

Our conclusion is unaffected by the Tenth Amendment which provides: "The powers not delegated to the United States by the Constitution, nor prohibited by it to the States, are reserved to the States respectively, or to the people." The amendment states but a truism that all is retained which has not been surrendered. There is nothing in the history of its adoption to suggest that it was more than declaratory of the relationship between the national and state governments as it had been established by the Constitution before the amendment or that its purpose was other than to allay fears that the new national government might seek to exercise powers not granted, and that the states might not be able to exercise fully their reserved powers. . . .

From the beginning and for many years the amendment has been construed as not depriving the national government of authority to resort to all means for the exercise of a granted power which are appropriate and plainly adapted to the permitted end. . . .

Validity of the wage and hour provisions under the Fifth Amendment. Both provisions are minimum wage requirements compelling the payment of a minimum standard wage with a prescribed increased wage for overtime of "not less than one and one-half times the regular rate" at which the worker is employed. Since our decision in *West Coast Hotel Co.* v. *Parrish,* 300 U.S. 379, it is no longer open to question that the fixing of a minimum wage is within the legislative power and that the bare fact of its exercise is not a denial of due process under the Fifth more than under the Fourteenth Amendment. Nor is it any longer open to question that it is within the legislative power to fix maximum hours. . . .

The Act is sufficiently definite to meet constitutional demands. One who employs persons, without conforming to the prescribed wage and hour conditions, to work on goods which he ships or expects to ship across state lines, is warned that he may be subject to the criminal penalities of the Act. No more is required. . . .

Reversed

99. *Will Merged Labor Set New Goals?* *

IN 1935 the American Federation of Labor appointed the Committee on Industrial Organization, which had immediate success in the organization of industrial workers in various fields previously untouched by union influence. The divergence of views between the leaders of the new industrial unions and those of the older craft unions led to a split in labor's ranks. In the following decade efforts to mitigate the cold war between the AFL and the CIO foundered because of ideological and personal differences. When new leaders, represented by Walter Reuther of the CIO and George Meany of the AFL, rose to power in both organizations ideological

* Sidney Lens, *Harvard Business Review,* XXXIV (March-April, 1956), pp. 57-63. Reprinted with permission from the *Harvard Business Review.*

and personal differences were sublimated sufficiently to allow a merger of the two groups. The prospect of a 15,000,000-member labor bloc has caused many to view this merger with considerable alarm. Mr. Lens surveys the new organization in an effort to determine what the future goals of the labor movement will be.

WHAT DOES labor want? The merger of AFL and CIO—the partnership of Meany and Reuther, who headed the two unions when they were separate—has added a new dimension to this question.

Last time the labor movement was united, back in 1935, it was a mere pygmy of some 3 million members. It was quiet, nonpolitical, and stagnant. It opposed such social measures as unemployment compensation with the epithet "dole," and looked upon the New Deal with somewhat jaundiced eyes. But the pygmy has now grown to a giant, 15 million strong, fully one tenth of the population and, if you include dependents, nearly one fourth. It is no longer a weak, futile voice crying in the wilderness. Reunited, it is at the very core of things, a force to be reckoned with in all social and political considerations. The point of doubt seems to be *how much* it intends to modify, or even remodel, the established order.

MATCHING FEARS

In the minds of many the mere unification of the two federations portends major social changes, an eventual labor party, and a definite orientation toward a labor government. One management representative, during a recent debate, visualized labor domination of every political subdivision down to the village hamlet. The terms "merger" and "labor monopoly" have been used interchangeably to signify a dangerous monster, capable of engulfing the whole society—and plotting to do so.

Strangely enough, the fears on management's side of the table are matched in emotional impact by opposite fears in labor circles: that the drift in labor ideology will now be to the right. This is particularly true of those unionists in the secondary echelons who were formerly with CIO. Tempestuous Mike Quill of the transport workers articulated some of these concerns when he accused George Meany, president of the new united AFL-CIO, of being "only slightly to the left of Senator Knowland." Meany's proposal for an industrial peace pact with the National Association of Manufacturers and other employer representatives fed fuel to this fire.

Actually, the fears on both sides of the industrial tracks are a familiar mixture of fantasy and reality common to everyone who steps out on an unknown path. The wedding of labor's goliaths opens up so many possibilities that each observer can fill in with his own wildest private fears. The unregenerate "private enterpriser" sees in it an end to traditional capitalism and the emergence of something like "British Socialism," and the unregenerate "socialist" sees in it a trend away from the hoped-for Labor Party and Labor Government—two opposite points of view based on the same set of facts. Each of these interpretations rests on subjective evaluations—fears, for instance, that a "radical-socialist Reuther" will loom larger than ever before, or that a "conservative Meany" will now dominate the labor scene.

The fact is that, although these men will certainly play important parts in the labor story of tomorrow, in the final analysis it is the objective unwinding of history which will be the primary determinant of labor's goals. To chart these goals for the future one must go beyond the words or dispositions of either Meany or Reuther to the essences of labor unionism.

ESSENCE OF UNIONISM

Samuel Gompers simplified all labor's goals in the one-word dictum: "more." But when you begin to define this "more," it obviously has different meanings in different circumstances. "More" can mean simply "more wages" and nothing else; it can mean "more security" or "more dignity"; and it can also mean "more state power." The exact content is dictated by a complex interweaving of objective and subjective factors.

When capitalism is sick, in depression, labor's goals become more radical, and those leaders who do not ride with this radical tide are swept under. One need only look to the 1930's to see what happened to the many conservative union officials who were engulfed by rising radicals like the Troskyist Dunne brothers in Minneapolis, the Stalinist Harry Bridges, the Wobbly Harry Lundenberg.

On the other hand, when capitalism is vibrant and dynamic, labor is relatively conservative, and its radical forces are buried deep in the secondary echelons. When Walter Reuther today decries the "Marxian theory of class struggle," though this runs completely counter to his former philosophy, he is not insincere; he is altering his thinking to fit new circumstances, and sticking to the helm. If he had remained as radical as he was 20 years ago, it is doubtful that he would have risen as high as he has.

Thus American labor, like labor everywhere, follows a course parallel to that of capitalism. It may be locked in combat with individual capitalists or even with the system as such, but its structure, perspectives, and to some extent ideologies are shaped by the very system which it may be fighting. Each stage of the union movement has meshed with the particular stage of capitalism:

Our first American unions were craft unions because American industry was primitive and had no great division of labor. And our first unions were radical, socialist, and utopian, because our economic system was weak and incapable of the concessions that would moderate labor's goals.

The simple, nonradical unionism of the AFL was finally born in 1886 when industrial capitalism—following the Civil War victory—had achieved a measure of stability. In an era of expansion, when employers could grant significant reforms to skilled employees, it was almost inevitable that union leaders would brush aside the utopian uplift unionists in rapid order in favor of a moderate form of unionism that fitted the economic climate.

Similarly, a half century later, in 1935, CIO was born because the historical prerequisites for this form of unionism were at hand. Industry had become highly diversified, division of labor had replaced individual production, and the economic pendulum had begun to swing upwards from the depths of depression. John L. Lewis and Sidney Hillman made their contribution to this great event, but if the historical soil had not been fertile, their efforts would have been in vain.

Labor's leadership dares not dance too far out of step with the tunes of the times; its interpretation of the word "more" is rigidly circumscribed by the penchants of history. Labor's goals, clearly, are not absolutes. They are responses to particular challenges imposed by the capitalist milieu under which it lives. Let those challenges change, and labor's goals change, too.

THE 1956 PICTURE

With this as our theme we seek a different type of insight into the labor merger. What particular changes in capitalism, 1956 edition, have dictated the unification of the two federations and the goals of the new group?

The fact is that American business has been able to contain American labor and has even begun to roll it back. In the political field, the victory of Eisenhower and the business administration; in the organizational field, the failure to organize the South; and in the legislative field, the failure to amend Taft-Hartley and the increasing barrage of eighteen right-to-work laws—these are symptoms of labor's loss of power. In the period prior to merger there were few overt signs of disintegration, but if these defeats were followed to their logical conclusion, they would lead to severe losses. In the weaker unions the organization would burst asunder and perhaps go out of business.

Labor is certainly not in a crisis. At its hard core—in the organized building trades, teamsters, auto workers, and steel workers—it is at the crest of its strength, solid and formidable. But the tide of progress has been checked. True, since 1935 labor's ranks have swelled sensationally. The united federation is five times as large as the united federation 20 years ago, before it broke in two. In 1933 only 5.4 per cent of the labor force was enrolled in unions. By 1953 this had quintupled, to 26.8 per cent. Yet since the end of the war the drive has definitely been stopped. The percentage figure has remained almost constant and the few increases in labor's ranks have been primarily in already organized companies that have expanded, or in "filling out" through union shop contracts. Few new areas have been organized.

In addition, growing disparities within the industrial system have emerged. A whole group of consumer goods industries are "sick." The number of textile workers in the United States has declined in recent years by 50 per cent, and union membership has shrunk apace. The needle trades are in poor shape. Hundreds of plants have run away to the relatively unorganized and low-wage South, and this poses a danger for the organized unionists in the North. The 1953-1954 figures of the Bureau of Labor Statistics showed that southern factory differentials were approximately 20 per cent below New York rates. In August, 1954, the average wage for workers in sawmills and planing mills in the South was $1.05 per hour, while in the highly unionized West it was $2.23.

In the major industries, policed by strong unions, there is only a token struggle with management today. The recent one-day and two-day strikes in auto plants for the guaranteed annual wage and in steel for higher wages were more symbolic than real. But the two-year resistance of the Kohler Company, the vigorous fight of the Perfect Circle Corporation management, the concerted effort to defeat the long Pittsburgh department store strike, and the violent reactions to the railroad and telephone strikes in the South, all are reflections of the disparity within the ranks of labor, where one third of the working class is organized and the other two thirds are outside the ranks. A part of the working force is becoming secure and middle-class in its approach; a larger part is being forced into militant and often violent action to secure its aims.

In sum, a divided labor has been batting its head against a stone wall this past decade. Prosperity has cushioned that wall somewhat so that its head is not too bloodied, but the obstacles have forced the merger at this historical juncture as a measure to reverse the trend, and the goals set by that merger will also reflect labor's current problems—all against a background of a capitalistic system that is strong enough to make concessions and adaptations.

DIRECTION OF CHANGE

Within the broad limits set by the whole pattern of the times, there remains, naturally, a certain latitude for labor's leadership. For instance, should the threat of technological unemployment become more acute for the auto workers, Reuther, who holds the key post of president of the industrial union department, can respond with one of four distinct goals, two in the economic field and two in the political:

A shorter workweek of 30 or 35 hours established by union contract.

A guaranteed annual wage for 52 weeks or 104 weeks or 156 weeks in the contract.

A shorter workweek of 30 or 35 hours established by government fiat.

Higher state unemployment compensation for longer periods.

Reuther's choice among these alternatives would depend partly on his own attitudes. But he is limited by another factor, which itself is affected by the general climate: the temper of his rank and file and the internal situation in the union. Given the current political lassitude on the part of labor's privates, for instance, its generals would most likely concentrate on the 35-hour or 30-hour week and the longer guaranteed wage in labor contracts. Given more political turbulence, the emphasis might change to the political objectives.

There is no doubt that the internal conditions of the merger itself impose real limitations on Reuther's freedom of action.

TOWARD THE RIGHT

The merger reflects the inability of the more militant CIO, after 20 long years, to win a majority of labor to its side as against the more tepid AFL.

When the first attempt was made at unity, back in 1937, CIO was mushrooming and riding high. It had quadrupled membership in two short years, and its president and founder, John L. Lewis, had visions of a labor federation that would grow within a few years to 20 million and absorb a declining AFL into its fold. But this cherished dream never reached fruition. CIO's dynamo sputtered after the first few years, and AFL recovered its equilibrium to the point where at the time of merger it was more than twice as large as its rival.

AFL had accepted some of the CIO philosophy, such as a partial industrial unionism, moderate political activity through the Labor's

League for Political Education, and considerable organization of the unorganized. But its general approach was still far less aggressive. The two organizations had really fought themselves to a stalemate, each blending toward the other. Now the smaller CIO was in effect submerging into the AFL.

This note of submergence was in evidence throughout the CIO convention which preceded the unified meeting in New York last December. Here was the end of a militant era for the old-time delegates, who had been at the first CIO conventions and were now in their 40's and 50's. Reuther had been forced to move fast and yield ground because the second largest CIO affiliate, David McDonald's steel workers, had threatened to go it alone back into the AFL. The McDonald-Reuther internal schism cut the CIO's bargaining power drastically and commensurately increased that of AFL.

In the honeymoon that followed merger, each of the old antagonists —Meany of the AFL and Reuther of the CIO—was anxious to prove that love was flourishing full-bloom with perfect harmony between the parties; but the specific gravity of labor's leadership had unquestionably swung to the right. While Meany and his coterie are no milquetoasts, they are certainly a few notches more moderate than Reuther and the ex- and neo-socialist group around him.

Labor's goals—and the ability of the leaders to set them—are clearly dependent on the forces at the leaders' disposal. A new type of militant unionism would demand very substantial alterations in the merged organization. As presently constituted, it simply is not capable of the hard-hitting, flexible, unified action that a full-scale drive demands.

AWAY FROM MILITANCY

To start with, an outright conflict requires an internal solidarity which the merger lacks. Members of the press may talk of a powerful labor monopoly, but in the highways and byways of the labor movement there is anxiety lest the merged federation explode to bits through such fratricidal strife as the Beck-Reuther bickerings, or the intrinsic and undimmed conflict over craft versus industrial unionism. The inner circle in the labor world knows that unity has been plagued by scores of problems, any one of which might boil over into a new and fatal schism.

That was why appeasement of both right and left was the order of the day at the unified meeting. Reuther gave assurances to the doubters within CIO by pointing to the vigor of the antidiscrimination policy of the merged federation, the appointment of two Negro vice presidents, and the Ethical Practices Committee which was to police racketeering and communism within the affiliated organizations. Meany gave assurances to die-hards within AFL by his general tone of moderation throughout the sessions. But it was evident to everyone that the course of events would be mixed and perhaps confused—hardly a basis for a strong campaign of any kind.

Any militant campaign would also require that leadership be transferred from the 141 international unions to the pivotal center of the AFL-CIO federation itself. As things stand now, George Meany has no intrinsic power except in the legislative arena and (since the convention) in the organization of the unorganized. His voice in the key sphere of collective bargaining is merely an advisory one; the international unions are still the real power centers in the house of labor. They receive the major funds and give final approval on contracts, strikes, and other internal affairs to the 68,000 local unions. The actual power rests with the Becks, Reuthers, McDonalds, Hayeses, Dubinskys, and Hutchesons—the men who head the teamsters, automobile workers, steel workers, machinists, garment workers, and carpenters.

Meany's predecessor, William Green, yielded to these forces and was next to impotent in directing the destiny of American labor. The new president is far more resolute and balances himself with admirable agility between the contending forces within the federation to assert his own leadership. It is certain that he will attempt to continue this trend further. He will now have at his disposal $7 million or $8 million for organizational efforts, and there is some intelligent speculation that he will use the lure of 20 or 30 paid organizers to various rival international unions to effectuate mergers—in the chemical, paper, retail, and various other fields. This directing force will certainly enhance his own power and tend toward greater centralization.

But centralization has a long and painful row to hoe. In the way stand forceful business unionists like Dave Beck and his teamsters, who aspire to a greater power role themselves, and the democratic unionists, like Woodruff Randolph of the typographical union, who guard autonomy with a jealousy difficult to overcome.

Meany has taken a number of important steps to assert his central authority: expulsion of the racket-ridden longshoremen, temporary expulsion of the air pilots union for strikebreaking, the no-raiding pact, establishment of the Ethical Practices Committee to look into corruption and communism. But these are only steps. It is doubtful that he can domesticate the giants in the building trades, or the teamsters, or the auto workers, or the steel workers; or that he will risk a schism with such potent forces.

Another necessary internal change is in the area of economic power. If unions are to match the strength of employers, they must develop structures that parallel those of management. Such changes are currently being undertaken in some of the larger unions. For instance:

The teamsters have divided geographically into area conferences such as the Western Conference, Central States Conference, Eastern Conference, Southern Conference, and into 15 national industrial divisions such as automotive, bakery, brewery and soft drinks, building materials and construction, cannery, chauffeurs and taxicabs, dairy, and the like. The auto workers have their General Motors, Ford, Chrysler, farm implement, aircraft, and similar departments. Such structures make the individual union more effective within a given field.

But before labor can make many further advances, it will have to set up *interunion* councils covering specific employers or specific industries. Consider the coal and steel industries, for example. They are integrated through the ownership of many key mines by the steel companies. A council of steel workers' representatives and miners would obviously pyramid the power of the two unions far beyond their individual strengths. Similarly, other interunion councils are clearly indicated as a means of enhancing labor's influence on employers who deal with 10 or 20 unions. None of this can take place without structural changes inside the federation and inside each international.

POLITICAL INACTION

Despite the well-advertised activity of CIO's PAC and AFL's LLPE, the fact is that both have been woefully inadequate and highly overrated as instruments of political influence. Meany stated over television on December 11 that in its best year LLPE was able to collect only $700,000 for political activity—only $1 per 15 members. Doorbell ringing and truly sustained political action are even less advanced. Except in special instances, labor simply does not mobilize the vote. That was evident when Taft was elected in Ohio in 1950 even though a combined labor made its major national concentration on this one state. Political analyst Samuel Lubell even noted that innumerable steel workers deliberately voted for Taft just because their leaders had asked them to vote for his opponent, Ferguson.

The lesson to be drawn from this is that the worker's allegiance to his union is on a number of different levels. Ordinarily he gives his local full and almost unquestioned support on economic issues; the benefits to be derived from collective bargaining or a strike are immediate, direct, and crystal-clear. He will seldom cross a picket line, and though he misses most union meetings, he will be present at the one that discusses next year's raise. But political and community action is another matter entirely. The benfits are not direct and are somewhat shrouded by a process and world he knows little about.

In this arena he will support his leaders only if he has thorough confidence in them, if there is some personal rapport between him and them. Unfortunately this is not too frequently the case in the labor movement as currently constituted. In a few unions this confidence exists to a substantial enough degree so that rank-and-file workers and stewards are willing to spend off-hours, at the behest of their officials, canvassing the neighborhood and pasting stamps on political literature. In many auto worker locals in Detroit, in Local 688 of the teamsters in St. Louis, on the South Side in Chicago, in parts of Massachusetts, and in a few other spots, that kind of allegiance is possible. But by and large it is still a hope for the future.

The average unionist will contribute his dollar for PAC, because the dollar means little and it salves his political conscience. But he will not go beyond that; he does not identify himself enough with his union or its "brass" to give more of himself to the common political effort. If he continues to vote for the Democratic Party, it is not because his leaders tell him to do so but because of the leveling traditions of Roosevelt's New Deal and the continuing liberalism of northern Democrats. It is a decision made outside the framework of his union allegiances, and sometimes even in spite of them.

The proof of this fact was evident in 1952, when so many million unionists voted against Stevenson, the choice of most labor leaders. A recent poll estimated that even in the secondary union echelons at least 25 per cent are pro-Eisenhower Republican; down closer to the grass roots the number must be still higher. The organized American worker frequently thinks of himself as a middle-class citizen: he often owns property and stocks, and he has interests that take him beyond his position as a wage worker. If he thinks about the matter at all, the threat of politics affecting his personal welfare usually seems remote—or he may even feel, on occasion, that a more conservative government program is the right one for him in his new status.

Since, then, workers will not participate actively in the union's political goals unless they can identify themselves with the union, the union must be truly representative of its members if it is to enlist their efforts. This means that before there can be a major reorientation of labor's role in politics, some major internal changes in those unions which have become ossified through the years and have drawn apart from their rank and file will be necessary. Those inside the labor movement know that this is no mean task, but one of stupendous proportions.

PROGRAM OF MODERATION

Under pressure from these three forces—the general climate of the times, the temper of the rank and file, and the limitations of the instrument with which they must work—the leaders of the merger will set goals that emphasize tactics and tightening-up. The specific historical challenge will evoke an elaborate response on the part of the merged labor movement, but in its initial stages anyway—until there are new objective pressures and subjective realignments—it will be quite temperate.

The "more" will be limited to a number of important economic and political objectives, but few curtailments of management prerogatives or significant conflicts with the social system as such. Labor's executives will fight for a guaranteed annual wage, but certainly not for codetermination of industry or for nationalization. Labor will work with the Democratic Party for amendment (rather than repeal) of Taft-Hartley and obliteration of the state right-to-work laws, but it certainly will not attempt to establish a party of its own. It will continue to disassociate itself from the doctrine of "class struggle" and will work assiduously to achieve "class collaboration"—to use the classical Marxian terms.

Organizing the unorganized will require a number of important reorientations, the most important on the race question. If the South is to be enrolled and the low-paid workers in unorganized northern industries attracted, a special appeal must be made to the Negro who constitutes so large a portion of this potential field. The AFL-CIO manifested an astute recognition of this fact by electing two Negroes, A. Philip Randolph and Willard Townsend, as vice presidents for the first time in labor history. It also denounced racial discrimination in more vigorous terms than before, particularly insofar as the AFL was concerned. It requested its affiliates to clean house on this score and put an end to Jim Crow organizations. Without such an appeal to millions of Negro workers whose earnings average only 52 per cent of their white brethren's, a dynamic organizing drive is impossible.

Another area of possible change is in the sphere of internal union behavior. Failure of some unions to root out corruption reflects so adversely on labor as a whole that, unless action is taken in this field, organizational efforts in new fields are seriously inhibited. Much depends on the policing efforts of the new Ethical Practices Committee, headed by Al Hayes of the machinists, an unblemished trade union man.

But these are only minor changes in an effort to strengthen organization efforts. William F. Schnitzler, secretary-treasurer of the AFL-CIO, typified the note of moderation in a recent speech and delineated the middle-class philosophy behind labor's goals. He said:

The "living wage" is no longer the primary, single objective for unions. Their goal now includes what might be called a little butter on the bread:

a constantly improved living standard, a level of income that permits workers to buy houses and insurance policies, build up saving funds, and, strange as this may seem coming from a union leader, invest in corporation securities.

Schnitzler also pointed out that the organized worker is earning surplus funds above his basic necessities for the first time in history, and is searching for a way to save or invest them. He urged both minimum wage legislation and union organization to force employers in the low-wage industries to mechanize, to improve productivity, and thereby meet the needs of their employees for decent subsistence.

This is hardly a revolutionary panacea. Adding a number of middle-class goals widens the horizons of labor only infinitesimally. Of the old, established objectives labor merely wants "more of the same." A relatively healthy American capitalism keeps in check radical potentials within labor's leadership. It is only in the sick branches of capitalism —down South and wherever else the lack of unionism decrees low-wage standards—that labor's leaders will stir to a more militant role. But even here it will only be "*somewhat* more," not "*radically* more."

CONCLUSION

The mere agglomeration of the two federations, then, will do little to alter labor goals in itself, for in the final analysis the objectives of unions reflect the process of American capitalism. There will be significant changes and a departure from the present moderate course only if there are major irritants within capitalism that cause such changes. Such irritants could come from a number of sources. For instance:

Antilabor laws which chip away at union security or limit the economic power of the union.

Vicious anti-unionism in the South which is willing to resort to violence and highly restrictive local legislation. (If this continues, it will build up the same kind of pressures which gave birth to the sit-down strike in the mid-1930's. We tend to forget that it was the broken heads on outside picket lines and the activity of organized vigilantes which led labor—spontaneously, in fact—to the sit-down tactic.)

Economic recession which brings unemployment, tends to make segments of labor more radical, and thereby pushes some of the leadership into a more militant stand.

So long as the economic and political ship is stable, however, the goals of labor's leadership will be modified only slightly, and so long as capitalism has safety valves, labor's goals will be narrow. In this connection the statistics on strikes provide a significant point:

American workers strike more often and lose more man-days of work than those of any other country. Of the 28 leading industrial nations in the Free World, the United States, with only one-fourth of the number of workers, loses at least half of the number of man-days of work through strikes. In these last eight years it has stood first in the number of man-days lost per thousand workers five times, and second three times.

Clearly American unionists are among the striking-est in the world, among the most militant on the picket line. Yet they are certainly the least political, the least class-conscious, the least revolutionary. If they can make moderate improvements within the framework of the present social system, they do not raise their sights or alter their goals appreciably. They confine their activity almost exclusively to the economic sector, with only minor innovations from year to year.

By the same token, there will be no labor party unless the Democrats and Republicans fail labor abysmally. Individual unionists may advocate such a program and may gain lesser or greater support depending on their individual qualities as leaders, but right now both major figures—Meany and Reuther—have made it clear that a labor party is definitely not in the blueprint. There can be no doubt that their words are meant as the hard coin. Meany has never publicly advocated such a party, and Reuther's advocacy has moderated from proposing such a party as an immediate goal after the war, through postponing it for some nebulous future date, and finally, in the last two CIO conventions, to complete repudiation of the idea.

Tomorrow, as yesterday, labor's leadership will play an important role in shaping the goals of the labor movement. One kind of leadership will modify those goals one way, while another will predispose them in another fashion; but the major and final determinant will still be the objective situation, the degree of health or sickness in the capitalist system itself.

100. *The Coal Miner Speaks* *

TO LARGE SEGMENTS of the general public union labor is an abstraction or an impersonal force. To some it represents a considerable mass of humanity living at the beck and call of a particular labor leader. Relatively few consider union laborers as

* *Fortune*, 35 (March, 1947), pp. 97-99, 202-206. Reprinted by special permission of the Editors. Copyright by Time Inc.

individuals subject to the average human frailties and responsive to the ordinary demands made upon human beings. This article presents a picture of the life and work of John Allshouse, coal miner and active member of the United Mine Workers. Through an understanding of this union member and others like him, in coal mining and in other industries, the problems, the hopes, and the goals of union labor generally may be more intelligible to others.

"PEOPLE seem to think miners are some kind of animal—underground rats, they call us—but we're just like other people trying to earn a living. Coal mining is all right—but you can't always keep working."

John Allshouse ought to know what he is talking about. His father was killed in a mine, and he has been a Pennsylvania coal miner for thirty-nine years—ever since he was thirteen. He and his wife and seven children have known plenty of bad times and some relatively good times. There have been months of hunger, and winters when it was hard to pay for coal to heat the house. But since 1942 wages have been high and now the Allshouses have meat every Sunday and are buying their own eight-room house. Working conditions were once abominable and Allshouse can still get sore ("With the company, it's production first, safety second"). But mining is no longer the hazard it once was. He is not uncritical of John L. Lewis but he gives him a lot of credit. Worst of all, perhaps, has been insecurity. Since 1942 employment has been steady, but in earlier years Allshouse was lucky if he got as much as 200 days' pay. Always a good union man, he has been through thirty or forty strikes—he can't recall the exact number—and at least as many layoffs. Allshouse feels that his own life is justified, and he expects to go on working in the Pittsburgh Coal Co.'s Westland mine as long as they'll keep him. But he hopes that his two sons will go through high school and stay aboveground. "I want them to get steady jobs even if the pay is lower. They'll thank me someday."

The Westland mine belongs to the Pittsburgh Coal Co., part of the largest commercial coal company in the U.S., Pittsburgh Consolidation, which includes the Fairmont mines in West Virginia, Consolidation in Kentucky, and Hanna in Ohio. Westland, Pennsylvania, is an isolated mining village, or patch, in Washington County, about twenty-five miles southwest of Pittsburgh. The naturally lovely rolling countryside is criss-crossed by railways and power lines, pitted and scarred by strip mines and quarries. The streams run poison-yellow from chemical-plant refuse. Even the sheep on nearby farms are dirty gray from coal smoke, and the smell of smoke hangs over the gray-brown scrubby hills. The mine tipple and beltway to the smoking slate heap dominate Westland as the cathedral spires dominate Chartres. The town itself is nothing more than the mine, the company store, the union hall, fifty or so shingled double houses in bleak rows, a couple of small independent stores and taverns, two schools, and the United Presbyterian Church. About a hundred of the mine's 550 employees live there; the others drive over from Washington, Canonsburg, Hickory, and other nearby towns and villages.

The mine was opened eighteen years ago and there is enough coal left in the Westland reserves (part of the rich bituminous Pittsburgh Seam) to last another fifty or sixty years. John Allshouse has been there since the beginning and is now working in an entry four miles back under the hill, about 350 feet below ground. There is no mine shaft at Westland—the white rock-dusted main haulways and entries run back from the pit mouth in gentle downward slopes, and electric locomotives, not mules, haul the coal cars and "man-trip" (personnel) cars direct from the tipple to the black working face.

Almost all the mine operations are mechanical. Every coal miner is a specialist, a skilled cutter, driller, shooter, loader, engineer or (like Allshouse) tracklayer. An electrically driven machine undercuts the coal to a depth of about nine feet, holes are driven with electric drills for the explosive charge. The men move back around two corners of the entry before the "shooting" (the thud of explosive is little more than familiar dusty pressure and a taste for powder), and then back to the shattered coal on the wet floor. A mechanical loader, with groping steel fingers, moves in, and the mine cars are pushed after it by an electric locomotive.

John Allshouse is steady and reliable, although not quite so fast as some of the younger men. At fifty-two the muscles of his back stand out in hard ridges and he can still drag a 400-pound rail into place, bolt it, and spike it down as well as the next—and do his day-shift job from the time he boards the man-trip cars at the pit mouth at 6:30 A.M. until he comes out and hangs up his lamp at 3:30 P.M. He works with his foreman, young Fred Klink, who first came into the mine as Allshouse's helper, and two or three assistants. He is usually up near the face with the production crew, although he may be installing switches somewhere along the mine's seventy-five miles of track, or repairing ties and rails after a wreck. The floor is covered with water, the shored-up roof is close over his hard-skull cap. The only light is from his cap lamp and he must watch his footing as he drags the heavy rails into position.

There has never been a disaster at the Westland mine, but there is danger in any mine—more, in a way, than when most of the work was done by hand, because carelessness with equipment or machinery can mean sudden injury or death. But the greatest danger at Westland is from falling roof. The slate above the coal seam can break off in great chunks (the timbers used for shoring are chiefly valuable to give warning when they begin to crack). John Allshouse was laid up for thirteen months a few years ago with a broken leg. He and all the other men are required to wear hard hats, hard-toed boots, and goggles.

Aside from the danger of accident, conditions in the mine are not bad. The air is pure enough, although it is dusty at the coal face, and the temperature stays between 50° and 60° all year round. Coal mining is a dirty job—there are no showers at the pit mouth and the men must walk or drive home before they can wash—but there are no special disease hazards. Allshouse, at fifty-two, is not unhealthy, although he is slightly stooped from work and, at the end of the day, his tiredness shows in the slump of his body and the deep lines in his face as he sits in his warm, bright kitchen, still in his hard hat and heavy pit belt, to draw deeply on the first cigarette of the day.

BORN TO THE MINE

John Allshouse's father was a miner and a union man before him (of Scotch-Irish descent, he had been adopted by a German family and taken their name), working in a small privately owned mine in the village of Noblestown, about ten miles from Westland. Allshouse was run over and killed by the mine dilly three months before John was born. His widow worked to support her three children, and by the time John was thirteen and through eighth grade he persuaded the mineowners to take him on (the legal working age was fourteen) to help out his mother.

He went down as a car greaser at $1.25 a day and was later put on the job of coupling cars after the coal was dumped. Almost all the operations were by hand and he did everything from driving mules to pick-and-shovel. During World War I he spent a year overseas in the Signal Corps. ("He doesn't talk about it much," his wife says, "but he saw a lot.") Back home, he tried jobs in a steel mill, on the railroad, in a gas station—but it wasn't long before he was back in the mine as a coal loader. He stayed there until the strike of 1927, when the Noblestown mine shut down for good.

The new Westland mine opened in the fall of 1928 and word went round that there was enough coal there to provide a job for the rest of a man's life. It was the biggest commercial mine in the Pittsburgh area and John Allshouse was one of 1,200 to get work. He was on the tipple, loading railroad cars, at $4.25 a day. Soon after he had come back from the Army he had married Anne Chalmers, one of nine brothers and sisters from a Scotch family in nearby McDonald. He and his growing family (by the time he went to Westland there were two girls, Dorothy and Phyllis) moved into four rooms, half a house, for which he paid the company $8 a month. Food and clothing and supplies were bought at the company store and charged off against his pay check. There were many paydays when the check was only a dollar or so, and on some he owed money at the store.

"The worst was Hoovertime. The mine was down lots of the time and we either had no work or we'd be shifted over to another mine and get paid 75 cents or $1 a day." There were more to feed by that time —Peggy Anne (born in 1929) and William (born in 1931)—and sometimes Mrs. Allshouse's family had to help out. During the thirties Allshouse and the other miners at Westland worked an average of 200 days a year. Often the annual wage was less than $1,000. Many miners were laid off as the operations were mechanized. Today 550 men get out almost as much coal as the original 1,200 employees. The mine produces about 5,000 tons a day, nine tons per man.

After a year on the tipple Allshouse went into the mine as a tracklayer, the job he has held, with one break, ever since. The break came as a result of the New Deal and Section 7a of the NRA, under which labor's right to bargain collectively was secured and John L. Lewis' United Mine Workers began to flourish. Allshouse had been a member of the U.M.W. since he started work in 1908 and he helped organize Local 2026 at Westland. He was elected checkweighman at the mine by the union members. He was paid a regular wage by the company but his job was outside, as the union's checker of daily production. He took an active part in the affairs of the local, as organizer and at various times later as treasurer, vice president, and secretary—a position he held until his resignation last year. As an official he was paid about $15 a month, which helped out on the budget, and he also picked up a few dollars as Democratic committeeman in his precinct. He can always use all the extra cash that comes his way.

In spite of labor legislation and a strong miners' union, there were still strikes, sometimes industry-wide, sometimes local, and also layoffs during periods of overproduction. The Allshouse family was growing: in 1933 the fifth child was born—Norman Robert Allshouse for NRA —and in 1935 the sixth. The older children needed clothes and shoes. There were no savings, and even a week without work meant going in the hole at the store. There was no running water in the house then, no electricity, and not too much food on the kitchen table.

A RADIO BUT NO BATHROOM

Life is better for the Allshouse family now—but still not what they would like it to be. The war brought higher wages and almost continuous employment. Allshouse often made $75 a week when he worked six days, and sometimes had enough to put into war bonds. The oldest girl, Dorothy, went to work for the company store and paid some of the household expenses. The company decided to sell its houses to the miners, and two years ago Allshouse began making purchase payments on the whole double house. He has paid off all but $100 of the $1,200 price and the family of nine (Mary Jane was born in 1939) now have eight rooms instead of four. There is a cold-water tap in the kitchen, but drinking water still comes from a pump a block away and hot water from a teakettle on the stove. There is electricity, gas for cooking, and two coal stoves for heating. Allshouse buys coal from the mine for $2.85 a ton. Dorothy and her mother have papered and painted the whole house and, by constantly battling the sifting coal dust, they keep it neat and clean. The floors are covered with linoleum, the windows with beige lace curtains.

The parlor and dining-living room are seldom used. Usually the family sits and eats and works in the two back rooms, the kitchen and a sort of general workroom where food is kept, coats hung, clothes laundered. In this room are a coal heater, behind which sleep two little whitish mongrels, and a glider on which Mr. Allshouse naps when he comes from work. Upstairs are four bedrooms, each with a double bed and a bureau. Mr. and Mrs. Allshouse sleep in one; the others are shared by Dorothy and Mary Jane, Peggy Anne and Edith, Bill and Bobby. Phyllis recently took a job in a glass factory in Pittsburgh. When she comes home she sleeps in with her two middle sisters.

There is a radio in the house, but no bathroom, no refrigerator, no telephone. The Allshouses do not own a car. They had a dozen chickens last year, but ate most of them during the November strike. They have a vegetable garden in the back yard between the coal shed and the outhouse. The rest of the food comes from the store, where prices are kept level with chainstore prices in neighboring towns. The family eats a big meal with meat and gravy and potatoes (half a peck at a time) and vegetables on Sundays; other days of the week they have sandwiches for lunch and a pot of soup or spaghetti or beans for supper, along with a lot of store-bought bread and pie and cake. Most of the children are fattish, like their mother, and pale, but they are seldom ill.

Mrs. Allshouse is a big cheerful woman, fond of and proud of her family. All the children were born at home with the help of the company doctor. The company deducts $2 a month for the doctor's services and he charges an additional $10 or $15 for a delivery fee. Mrs. Allshouse doesn't take up much of his time. "Two hours before Edith was born I was in the yard hanging out a big wash." The girls help their mother around the house and the boys carry in coal and water and fetch the groceries. All but Dorothy and Phyllis are in school. Peggy Anne and Bill go by bus to high school in Hickory, six miles away, and have difficulty with some of the courses. Peggy Anne, who wants to be a nurse, can't catch on to shorthand. She goes to jukebox dances at the miners' hall, likes to wear her older sisters' clothes, and wants to see New York, particularly the Stork Club and "21." The children spend Sunday morning getting ready for Sunday school, pressing dresses, curling hair, washing at the kitchen sink. Mr. and Mrs. Allshouse seldom go to church, seldom visit their neighbors. "There's too much to do at home, and always lots of us here for company." Sometimes the family plays euchre in the evening, but usually the children have homework to do. Once in a great while they take the bus into Canonsburg and see a movie.

John Allshouse is paid twice a month. At the end of a period of two six-day weeks his pay slip may look like this:

Earnings		
10 shifts at $11.85	$118.50	
2 shifts at $16.00	32.00	
Shift differential	.10	
		$150.60
Deductions		
Federal tax (old age)	$ 1.55	
Withholding tax	2.00	
Assignments (food, clothing, etc., at store)	107.83	
Union dues	1.00	
Doctor	1.00	
House purchase	25.00	
Employees Relief Assn.	.10	
Death fund	1.00	
		$139.48

There is $11.12 left over. There are also bills for electricity ($2), gas ($1.50), water ($1), coal ($1), insurance premiums ($2.50). Often Dorothy pays these bills, but there are always extras—dentist's bills or a high-school ring for Peggy Anne or birthday presents. And sometimes a collection at the mine for the family of a miner who has met bad luck. "Even during the depression, when I only had $1 in my pay check, I'd give 50 cents."

When Allshouse works a five-day week, as he has many times and probably will again, he gets only $59.25 and it is harder to make ends meet. Company officials are willing to run the mine six days, but sometimes orders are slack, sometimes there are no railroad cars available for loading, and for a while this winter the union voted a five-day week. Allshouse would like to work six days every week, even if he gets tired. With time and a half the extra day means an extra $16 a week. Since 1942, Allshouse has made an average of over $3,000 a year, but there is no assurance that his annual wage will stay at that unprecedented level.

"IT'S NOT THE MINERS' FAULT"

Last spring the mine was down for nine weeks during the strike, and last fall for three weeks. The spring strike wasn't so bad. Allshouse could work in the garden and around the house ("It's hard for a miner to loaf, no matter what the papers say") and he still had some war bonds to cash. The union won, too. But the November strike was something else. Westland was down for three weeks because some of the younger men jumped the gun by several days ("One guy hung his lamp on the rack and quit and the others followed. Nobody knew why"). It was cold in the late fall, there wasn't much to do, the war bonds were gone, Christmas was coming. And nothing was gained by the strike. Allshouse was glad to go back to work.

John Allshouse is completely loyal to the United Mine Workers. John L. Lewis, he says, has won for the miners everything they've ever got. "He earns his $25,000 a year." But he is not entirely unthinking or uncritical. He knows that public opinion was against Lewis and the miners last fall ("I hated to read the papers those days") and he thinks Lewis might have been "a little too smart." He knows that every time wages go up prices go up. "Somebody's got to quit sometime. Somebody's got to put things in balance. People say John L. Lewis ought to be shot or strung up, but it wouldn't surprise me if he turned out to be the one to balance things."

Some of the miners, and practically all the miners' wives, griped last fall—but only at home. And they are still for Lewis, ready to follow him out in April if he gives the order. Allshouse blames Truman and the press and the companies for the strike's failure. Lewis had a right to end the contract, he says, and Truman was wrong to bring him to court. The press took the companies' side and scared the public, he says. "People yelled about not having coal, but look what happened—we went back to work, and in a few days some mines began to lay off men. It's not the miners' fault if there isn't enough coal."

Strikes are not what they used to be. In the old days companies tried to keep the mines going. They brought in scabs from West Virginia or someplace, Allshouse says, and turned the strikers out of company houses. There were riots and battles—miners remember the

Herrin (Illinois) Massacre in 1922 when twenty-five men were killed. Now, with coal mining a closed shop, there are no scabs and when the miners walk out the mine is down until they come back. U.M.W. members can do chores at home, go hunting or fishing, or pick up odd jobs. "We don't sit around drinking the way the papers make out," Allshouse says, "though once in a while I walk down to the tavern to have a beer and hear the news."

Even if they wanted to, it would be hard for most miners to find temporary jobs during strikes. There usually are no other jobs in a mining town and a man can't learn a new trade overnight or move away if he has a family. Besides, Allshouse says, you get used to working in an even temperature underground and you can't accustom yourself to cold or heat in a few weeks. Why miners stick to mining as a permanent job is something else again. Not all do, of course—some of the Westland men who went to the war did not come back to the mine, and not every miner's son becomes a miner. On the other hand, many miners' sons, like Allshouse himself, are faced at an early age with family financial troubles and the easiest job to get is in the mine.

Right now Bill says he wants to go into the Navy and Bobby says he wants to be a Marine. There is no guarantee, however, that they won't go into the mine. Already seventeen-year-old Billy Lloyd, next door, is working as a breaker boy, picking coal off the belt leading to the slate heap, making as much as $10 and $12 a day, and he is trying to persuade Bill Allshouse to take a mine job next summer. If John Allshouse should be ill or laid up by an accident, or if he lost his job, the chances are that Bill would take the first work that came along. At Westland it would be on the slate belt or in the mine.

Retiring age for miners is sixty-five. Allshouse has thirteen years to go, if nothing happens to him or to the mine. There is more than enough coal under the Westland hills to keep him in a job, but no one knows what will happen to coal mining as an industry in the next years, or to miners and miners' wages. The President of Pittsburgh Consolidation, George Love, says, "Miners are, and should be, well paid, and we hope they will continue to be." But he goes on to say that in order to continue to pay the miners, production per man-day must be increased through mechanization and efficiency of operation.

Allshouse would not object to increased production if it were achieved through technological advances, but he would if it meant harder work or lower safety standards. State safety laws are strict. The union, however, would like one of its own men as a full-time inspector. Allshouse, chairman of the local's safety committee, may inspect any portion of the mine where danger is reported but has no right to inspect over-all conditions.

Allshouse goes about his work carefully and deliberately, and he does not hurry when the day is over. The younger men rush for seats in the man-trip car and run across the lot to hang their lamps on the rack and start for home. Allshouse is the last to leave the car and walk to the office. He walks home in the sooty winter twilight and into the bright kitchen. While he smokes his cigarette, Mary Jane opens his lunch pail to look for the bit of cake or pie he always saves for her. Mrs. Allshouse tells him there is a notice for him from the Boy Scouts, on whose local committee he sits.

After a short rest Allshouse strips off his coat and shirt and washes at the sink. He takes a look at the paper before supper. He tries to keep up with the news about the United Nations and thinks it is a good thing, but it wouldn't surprise him if there were another war. Roosevelt might have stopped it. Truman isn't much good. "I might like him better if I hadn't liked Roosevelt so much more." He is no radical. He doesn't want to do away with democracy or the capitalist system, but he thinks there will probably be a third party, a Labor party, if Truman is nominated next year. He wishes there were a good general magazine or newspaper to give unbiased labor news to the public. "The press writes us up all wrong when a strike is going on and then forgets about us."

John Allshouse and his wife like their house and love their children. "There's something money can't buy." And they expect to go on living in Westland until he retires from the mine. By that time most of the children will be grown and self-supporting. Allshouse carries $500 life insurance on himself, $400 on each child. He has no savings, does not belong to a pension plan, and will get from his federal old-age insurance only about $75 a month. But, with the children's help, he expects to get along all right in his old age. "We've got a house and good health and food. When you come right down to it, we're a lot better off than some." But John Allshouse wants people to know how things really are. And he does not want his two boys to be miners.

XIX

AGRICULTURE AND CONSERVATION

101. *Mulford et al. v. Smith et al.*

SUPREME COURT OF THE UNITED STATES,
1939 (APPEAL) 307 U.S. 38

THE FEDERAL GOVERNMENT, having been unsuccessful in its attempt to deal with agricultural problems by means of the taxing power (Cf. *U.S.* v. *Butler* 297 U.S. 1), turned to the commerce power and enacted the Agricultural Adjustment Act of 1938. This case involves the constitutionality of that act. In its decision the Court sustained the government's power under the commerce clause to institute a program for the control and regulation of agriculture. It made the distinction between control over marketing, which the Court holds to be within the commerce power, and control over production. Although the effect of the government's regulation of marketing ultimately constituted a regulation of production, the Court refused to consider this point, maintaining that the motive of the government in exercising its authority was immaterial to a decision of the case. The decision indicated the changing attitude of the Court toward New Deal legislation and was expressive of its willingness to accept the new regulatory policies.

Statement of the Case

Appeal from a decree of a three-judge District Court which dismissed the bill in a suit brought by tobacco farmers to enjoin warehousemen from deducting, and remitting to the Secretary of Agriculture, the penalties inflicted by the Agricultural Adjustment Act of 1938 on tobacco sold for the plaintiffs in excess of the quotas assigned to their respective farms. The suit was begun in the Superior Court of Georgia. The defendants removed the case to the federal court. The United States intervened, under the Act of August 24, 1937.

Opinion of the Court

MR. JUSTICE ROBERTS delivered the opinion of the Court:

The appellants, producers of flue-cured tobacco, assert that the Agricultural Adjustment Act of 1938, is unconstitutional as it affects their 1938 crop.

The portions of the statute involved are those included in Title III, providing marketing quotas for flue-cured tobacco. The Act directs that when the supply is found to exceed the level defined in the Act as the "reserve supply level" a national marketing quota shall become effective which will permit enough flue-cured tobacco to be marketed during the ensuing marketing year to maintain the supply at the reserve supply level. The quota is to be apportioned to the farms on which tobacco is grown. Penalties are to be paid by tobacco auction warehousemen for marketing tobacco from a farm in excess of its quota. . . .

The appellants plant themselves upon three propositions: (1) that the Act is a statutory plan to control agricultural production and, therefore, beyond the powers delegated to Congress; (2) that the standard for calculating farm quotas is uncertain, vague, and indefinite, resulting in an unconstitutional delegation of legislative power to the Secretary; (3) that, as applied to appellants' 1938 crop, the Act takes their property without due process of law.

First. The statute does not purport to control production. It sets no limit upon the acreage which may be planted or produced and imposes no penalty for the planting and producing of tobacco in excess of the marketing quota. It purports to be solely a regulation of interstate commerce, which it reaches and affects at the throat where tobacco enters the stream of commerce,—the marketing warehouse. The record discloses that at least two-thirds of all flue-cured tobacco sold at auction warehouses is sold for immediate shipment to an interstate or foreign destination. In Georgia nearly one hundred per cent of the tobacco so sold is purchased by extra-state purchasers. In markets where tobacco is sold to both interstate and intrastate purchasers it is not known, when the grower places his tobacco on the warehouse floor for sale, whether it is destined for interstate or intrastate commerce. Regulation to be effective, must, and therefore may constitutionally, apply to all sales. This court has recently declared that sales of tobacco by growers through warehousemen to purchasers for removal outside the state constitute interstate commerce. Any rule, such as that embodied in the Act, which is intended to foster, protect and conserve that commerce, or to prevent the flow of commerce from working harm to the people of the nation, is within the competence of Congress. Within these limits the exercise of the power, the grant being unlimited in its terms, may lawfully extend to the absolute prohibition of such commerce, and *a fortiori* to limitation of the amount of a given commodity which may be transported in such commerce. The motive of Congress in exerting the power is irrelevant to the validity of the legislation.

The provisions of the Act under review constitute a regulation of interstate and foreign commerce within the competency of Congress under the power delegated to it by the Constitution.

Second. The appellants urge that the standard for allotting farm quotas is so uncertain, vague, and indefinite that it amounts to a delegation of legislative power to an executive officer and thus violates the Constitutional requirement that laws shall be enacted by the Congress.

What has been said in summarizing the provisions of the Act sufficiently discloses that definite standards are laid down for the government of the Secretary, first, in fixing the quota and, second, in its allotment amongst states and farms. He is directed to adjust the allotments so as to allow for specified factors which have abnormally affected the production of the state or the farm in question in the test years. Certainly fairness requires that some such adjustment shall be made. The Congress has indicated in detail the considerations which are to be held in view in making these adjustments, and, in order to protect against arbitrary action, has afforded both administrative and judicial review to correct errors. This is not to confer unrestrained arbitrary power on an executive officer. In this aspect the Act is valid within the decisions of this court respecting delegation to administrative officers.

Third. In support of their contention that the Act, as applied to the crop year 1938, deprives them of their property without due process of law in violation of the Fifth Amendment, the appellants rely on the following undisputed facts.

Tobacco growers in southern Georgia and northern Florida began to arrange for the planting of their 1938 crop in December, 1937, when it was necessary for them to prepare beds for the planting of the seeds. . . . At the date of approval of the Act each of the plaintiffs had planted his seed beds and, about the middle of March, began transplanting into the fields, which were prepared and fertilized at large expense. The plants were thereafter cultivated and sprayed, and harvesting began during June and continued during July, followed by the curing and grading of the tobacco.

All of these activities involved labor and expense. . . .

The marketing season for flue-cured tobacco in Georgia and Florida commences about August 1st of each year. Each of the appellants was notified of the quota of his farm shortly before the opening of the auction markets. Prior to the receipt of notice each of them had largely, if not wholly, completed planting, cultivating, harvesting, curing and grading his tobacco. Until receipt of notice none knew, or could have known, the exact amount of his quota, although, at the time of filing the bill, each had concluded from available information that he would probably market tobacco in excess of any quota for his farm.

The Act was approved February 16, 1938. The Secretary proclaimed a quota for flue-cured tobacco on February 18th and, on the same date, issued instructions for holding a referendum on March 12th. March 25th the Secretary proclaimed the result of the referendum which was favorable to the imposition of a national marketing quota. In June he issued regulations governing the fixing of farm quotas within the states. July 22nd he determined the apportionment as between states and issued regulations relative to the records to be kept by warehousemen and others. Shortly before the markets opened each appellant received notice of the allotment to his farm.

On the basis of these facts it is argued that the statute operated retroactively and therefore amounted to a taking of appellants' property without due process. The argument overlooks the circumstance that the statute operates not on farm production, as the appellants insist, but upon the marketing of their tobacco in interstate commerce. The law, enacted in February, affected the marketing which was to take place about August 1st following, and so was prospective in its operation upon the activity it regulated. The Act did not prevent any producer from holding over the excess tobacco produced, or processing and storing it for sale in a later year; and the circumstances that the producers in Georgia and Florida had not provided facilities for these purposes is not of legal significance.

The decree is

Affirmed

(Mr. Justice Butler and Mr. Justice McReynolds dissent.)

102. *From Agriculture to Agribusiness*

MR. DAVIS contends that one of the basic reasons the "farm problem" has never been solved is that it has never been considered in its relationship to other sectors of our economy. Legislative efforts to improve the condition of the farmer have all been designed as if

* John H. Davis, *Harvard Business Review*, XXXIV (January-February, 1956), pp. 107-115. Reprinted with permission from the *Harvard Business Review*. Chart omitted.

the farms existed in an isolated position rather than actually being a part of a vast complex of interdependent business units: productive, manufacturing, and distributive. Price stability in agriculture can come only, the author argues, if the task is assumed by agribusiness rather than by government. Agribusiness refers to "the sum total of all operations involved in the production and distribution of food and fiber." Mr. Davis analyzes the problems facing agribusiness and the possible solutions, both long-range and short-range.

TODAY rural America is being subjected to terrific forces which are altering its very form and essence. Not only are farming methods and practices changing, but alterations are taking place in our entire rural society—physically, socially, educationally, politically, organizationally, morally, and even spiritually. Literally, nothing is being left untouched. Further amplifying this process of change is the fact that agriculture is a part of a national economy which also is undergoing alteration at a rapid rate.

Powering this great transformation are the forces of research and technology. These great drives, which have been at work for more than a century, today are gaining new momentum and power. This accelerating trend promises to characterize the future as far ahead as one can see. It seems safe to predict that more change will take place in agriculture during the next five years than has taken place in the past ten.

These forces of change are, in large measure, irresistible; we could not stop them even if we wanted to. However, we can exercise some direction over them.

INTERDEPENDENT OPERATIONS

This technological revolution has brought agricultural production and marketing closer and closer together—actually making them interdependent. Thirty years ago agriculture produced 70 to 80 per cent of its own production supplies—buying only 20 per cent to 30 per cent from business. Today agriculture buys from business almost 50 per cent of its production input items in the form of machinery, tractor fuel, commercial fertilizer, mixed feeds and supplements, building materials, and so forth. Currently these purchases are running about $16 billion per year.

Farmers combine these purchased supplies with items from the farm, such as land, management, and labor, in the production of food and fiber, which they then sell to business for an aggregate sum of about $30 billion. Business firms, in turn, assemble, store, process and package these commodities and distribute the end products derived therefrom to the consumer for an aggregate bill of about $75 billion. Synthetic fibers, imports, and seafood items make the consumer total about $90 billion.

The truth is that modern agriculture is inseparable from the business firms which manufacture production supplies and which market farm products. It could not operate for one week if these services were cut off. And, by the same token, the business firms which serve agriculture would exist without purpose except for farmers to buy their supplies or sell commodities to them. Today agriculture and business are highly interrelated and give every promise of becoming even more so. This fact must be taken into account in developing farm policy.

Of late the point frequently has been stressed that one farm worker in 1955 produces enough to feed himself and 17 other persons, whereas a century ago he produced only enough to feed himself and two or three others—as if the fact that we needed proportionately fewer farm workers somehow made agriculture less important. But a comparison limited solely to production on the farm is misleading. In addition to producing food and fiber the farmer of 100 years ago also grew or made most of his own production supplies, provided most of his own storage, and did most of his own processing and selling—functions which today are largely performed by business rather than by farmers.

To contrast the food and fiber picture of today with that of 100 years ago, we need to look not just at production on the farm but at the aggregate of all agricultural purchasing-production-distributing operations. Currently, these combined operations account for about 40 per cent of our economy when measured either in terms of employment or of gross national product. This compares with 50 to 60 per cent in 1855.

Thus, the relative importance of farming, plus manufacturing of farm supplies, plus handling, processing, and distribution of farm products, is not very different from what it was 100 years ago. The big difference is in the nature of functions performed; today operations and end products are much more varied and extensive.

BROAD CONCEPT

Actually, we are so unaccustomed to looking at farm problems in their broad agriculture-business setting that the English language is wholly lacking in a word to describe such a concept. Up to this point, the only way to express the idea has been by a sentence, a paragraph, or even a page—as has been attempted here—which is not only awkward and time-consuming, but also lacking in precision and clarity of meaning. Hence, to enable us to think in terms of this broader concept, I am suggesting a new word—the noun *agribusiness*.

By definition agribusiness means the sum of all farming operations, plus the manufacture and distribution of all farm production supplies, plus the total of all operations performed in connection with the handling, storage, processing, and distribution of farm commodities. In brief, agribusiness refers to the sum-total of all operations involved in the production and distribution of food and fiber—that major component of our national economy which, as we saw above, employs almost 40 per cent of our total work force and accounts for about 40 per cent of our gross national product. . . .

CRUCIAL PROBLEMS

The penetration of government into such an important phase of our national economy cannot fail to raise serious questions in the minds of those who believe strongly in private enterprise. However, if we are to reduce the role of government on the farm front, we will have to do so by transferring to agribusiness the responsibility for basic price stability now borne by government.

The rate of progress in this direction will depend on our success in developing new strength within the agribusiness economy—strength to carry the price stability load and combat the susceptibility of agriculture to periods of low income. Whether or not we ever succeed in completely transferring all of this responsibility to agribusiness, most Americans will agree that it is desirable to move in this direction as rapidly and as far as possible and still achieve our national goals of economic progress and growth.

LAGS IN PROGRESS

Many of the current problems in agriculture grow out of the fact that progress has taken place too much on a piecemeal basis. Certain phases of agriculture have moved forward rapidly while other phases have lagged behind, thus creating pools of stagnation which have grown into farm problems. We have concentrated on research to solve specific problems which have confronted segments of agriculture, and we have neglected certain broader phases essential to assure progress on an even keel. To illustrate:

We have improved livestock and plant characteristics, perfected insecticides, found ways of stimulating the growth of desired plants and retarding the growth of weeds, found better ways of managing soil, developed disease- and drought-resistant plants—the list could be extended almost without limit—and in so doing have created a productive capacity for which there is no comparable market.

We have created a need for larger farm units, and have left over two million farm families stranded on units which are too small.

We have subjected agriculture to more and more rigid production costs without developing corresponding stability in the price structure of farm products.

We have increased the management and technical skills essential for successful operation of an efficient family farm without assuring income opportunities compatible with these requirements.

In brief, we have mixed the new with the old in such a hit-or-miss pattern as to cause serious disorder and maladjustment on the farm front. The result is that today agriculture is being subjected to stresses and strains that push and pull at it with uneven force from various directions.

LACK OF BALANCE

Currently one of the most troublesome problems on the agribusiness front is the imbalance between supply and demand with respect to many farm commodities. Since World War I this problem, more than any other, has pushed us in the direction of federal price supports.

At present, America's capacity to produce food and fiber is roughly half again as big as it was before World War II. Furthermore, there is a sizable backlog of technical know-how already developed and ready for use—a backlog which, if put fully into operation, would expand our agricultural output by another 30 to 40 per cent or more. Under high incentives like those that existed during World War II this vast expansion could take place in a period of only three or four years. Even with moderate incentives, the increase in farm output of many commodities promises to run ahead of market outlets during the next five or ten years—probably longer.

This output potential, then, presents the problem: How can we best utilize our productive capacity? Or, if surpluses continue, how can we bring supply and demand into balance?

A common suggestion is that we drop farm prices to the point necessary to bring supply and demand into balance. Those advocating this measure point out that such reduced prices would attack the problem from both ends by retarding production on the one hand and by stimulating utilization on the other. There is much to commend this solution: it is in the tradition of private enterprise, it reduces the role of government, and it makes us competitive in world markets—all of which are important. However, there is a price we would have to pay:

The reduction in output would be slow; and to a considerable extent it would come about as the result of financial distress and even bankruptcy.

With this would come reduced farm purchasing power, which in turn would be reflected in varying degrees in other segments of the economy. But even though a marked drop in farmer purchasing power today might not shock the economy quite as severely as it would have 25 years ago when agriculture was a relatively larger component of the total economy, still its effect would be felt pronouncedly in terms of our over-all national economic potential. The national total can never be as big when part of the economy is lagging as when all of it is moving forward together.

Another serious aspect to a policy of reducing farm production through low prices is the fact that this, in turn, would tend to slow down the rate of technological progress in agriculture. By such retardation we would be penalizing not only the farmers but also future consumers.

INCOME ANEMIA

When we attempt to balance supply and demand by permitting farm prices to seek their own level during periods of adjustment, such as the present, we subject agriculture to a critical form of "income anemia"—a disease to which most other industries are relatively immune. By this I mean that under completely free markets farm prices frequently tend to get so low as to deplete agriculture of its basic income and risk capital—so essential to its health and progress.

This income anemia is the result of a combination of factors: (a) the inability of farmers to adjust production to demand, (b) the tendency of a small surplus to produce a big drop in price, and (c) the tendency of farm production costs to remain rigid when commodity prices decline.

The inability of agriculture to tailor production to demand means that farmers cannot themselves avoid shortages and surpluses. Surpluses, when they appear, cause commodity prices to drop sharply—adversely affecting farm income. This, coupled with the tendency of farm production costs to remain relatively fixed, often subjects farmers to conditions commonly referred to as the *price-cost squeeze.* This form of income anemia is peculiar to agriculture, largely because farm production is a growth process highly dependent on weather and seasons. In no sense is it evidence that farming is an obsolete industry like buggy making. In general, other industries have not been confronted with such a problem; for, when surpluses develop, industrial management itself can more quickly adjust the supply.

FARM PROGRAMS

The problem of depressed farm income is in no sense a recent one. It has been with us for decades. It was behind the Granger Movement of the 1870's and the Populist and Free Silver movements of the 1890's. Following World War I it was reflected in a drive for co-operative marketing, pressure for McNary-Haugen type legislation, and finally the Agricultural Marketing Act of 1929 which created the Farm Board.

Thus, present farm programs have their roots reaching deep into the past. Income anemia, brought about by price-cost squeezes, has been the prime motivation for price-support programs. While the pressure for such devices has varied with the prosperity of the times, in general it becomes more persistent with the passing years.

Does this mean, then, that we have no choice but to continue farm support programs by government? Certainly there are sound arguments for getting and keeping the government out of the functions of commodity storage and marketing. The several billion dollars of stocks currently owned by the Commodity Credit Corporation constitute a disturbing weight over the market. As a former president of the Commodity Credit Corporation, I can testify to the difficulty of disposing of commodities once the government becomes the owner. The moment seldom comes, outside of wartime, when government stocks can be moved, or even be rumored to move, without injury to sensitive markets.

The truth is that the government is a cumbersome agency when it comes to the development, expansion, or improvement of farm markets. It cannot function as dynamically or expeditiously as can private enterprise.

PRIVATE ENTERPRISE

This fact raises a basic question: In view of the seriousness of income anemia in agriculture during the past 50 years and the limitations of support programs as a means of combating it, why have not farmers joined together to build a counterforce within the private sectors of the economy to offset the inherent weaknesses of agriculture?

The answer is that farmers have tried—but with limited success. The cooperative marketing ventures which received new impetus during the 1920's were of this type. In some instances these efforts have been supplemented by marketing agreements and market orders which, while involving some government participation, do not entail government ownership of stocks. For a few commodities these efforts have been reasonably effective, but for most major commodities this type of program has not provided the answer to the farm price-cost problem. By and large, farmers have lacked the cohesion necessary to solve the problem of income anemia.

A somewhat related question is this: Why has not business, which performs virtually all of the handling, processing, and distributive functions for agriculture, built counterforces to offset the price instability inherent in agriculture?

Actually, business can put up considerable defense for not having assumed greater responsibility on the farm front. In the first place, it can point out that the inability of farmers to adjust supply to demand reflects a weakness in the production rather than the marketing function. Secondly, the production and marketing operations of agriculture have been considered as more or less separate operations—production being a job for farmers and marketing a job for business. Farmers as well as businessmen have shared this view. (For my purposes here, I am classifying farmer cooperatives as business.)

THE REAL SOLUTION

There are 3 million farm families with an annual gross income of less than $2,500—half of them below $1,500. Their plight is serious. Their particular problem is that they have been unable to adjust quickly to progress or take advantage of it. Their plight is more than a matter of temporary or periodic income anemia. The sensible course is to encourage these people to find the most productive and remunerative outlets for their skills. For a majority this will mean turning to off-farm employment, either full time or in combination with limited farming operations. For those who elect to remain full time in agriculture and who give promise of success, we should concentrate on helping them to increase the size of their farms and to catch up with progress in terms of technical and managerial know-how.

For commercial farmers the over-all solution to the so-called farm problem lies in progress. On the whole these farmers still can do much to increase their efficiency by availing themselves of improved equipment, better seed and livestock, better farm management, and improved quality of products. However, in order for this increased farm efficiency to be matched by appropriate expansion of market outlets, it is important that there be corresponding progress throughout the whole agribusiness structure.

Unfortunately, solving farm problems through progress is a long-run task. And, at best, progress will be upsetting to many people. For the older, the less educated, and the physically handicapped, it often means hardship and in some cases even suffering. But for the young, energetic, skilled, and resourceful, it means opportunity—in fact, greater opportunity than that known by any previous generation. Such an objective is not less worthwhile because it is difficult and time-consuming.

Of course, we must begin with what we have if we are to build to something better. With accumulated stocks now piled high, present programs must be kept in effect, at least in modified form, until we dispose of excess stocks and develop improved methods for maintaining basic economic stability for agriculture. Ultimately, we should never be satisfied with methods of maintaining such stability that make it necessary for a government agency like the Commodity Credit Corporation to actually take title to vast quantities of commodity stocks.

AGRIBUSINESS POLICY

The starting point in formulating either agricultural or agribusiness policy which will promote progress is an awareness of our over-all national economic goal. The President has stated this goal in terms of a gross national product in excess of $500 billion by 1965. The Joint Congressional Committee on the Economic Report sets it at $535 billion. Others have suggested goals that are even higher.

Whatever goal we take, we must formulate farm and agribusiness policies consistent with it. This means we must stop tying our goals for farm income to past bench marks such as 1910 to 1914. Instead, we must consider what level of farm income is most conducive to the welfare of the nation in the achievement of our national economic goals. More specifically, this means asking ourselves what level of farm income is essential to provide needed risk capital, to attract sufficient numbers of *capable* farm boys and girls to remain in agriculture, and to assure that rural standards of research and education will be commensurate with the need.

Against the background of our national economic goals we must deal with the food and fiber problems in their total setting. By this I mean we must look at the related operations of agriculture and business as a unified function. We cannot expect to find adequate answers to farm problems by putting a fence between agriculture and business and then in effect saying, "Now we are going to solve the farm problem within this agricultural sector." We have committed that error too often in the past.

This is a big order. How do we do it? How do we begin from where we are and build to where we want to go? We do it by approaching the problem with agribusiness perspective, thus getting the teamwork of producers, warehousemen, processors, distributors, and so on.

RESEARCH AND DISCUSSION

One of the first essentials is to organize research on an agribusiness basis. We must have facts in order to make valid decisions.

Heretofore, agricultural research has been conducted largely on a piecemeal basis, the various phases of a problem being studied more or less independently. But we can never expect to find answers in this way to the complex problems which exist today. We must organize our research on a base that is as broad as the problems we want to solve. For example, when analyzing the problem of what level of farm income is desirable, we cannot expect to find answers by studying farm prices, farm costs, or so-called middlemen's margins as separate factors. Not only must they be examined as related factors, but they must be viewed in the total setting of the agribusiness economy and against the background of our national economic goals.

Don't misunderstand me. I am not suggesting that we drop the research we are doing now. Rather, I am pleading that we reorient it on an agribusiness basis and then, if necessary, add new projects to fill in the gaps which become apparent as we look at the broader picture with proper perspective.

After we have organized research on an agribusiness basis, we must start policy discussions on an agribusiness basis. In this, the leadership of established organizations—both producer and business—can play an important role. Research technicians should be called in to provide essential information and to get instruction as to what additional research is needed.

The agribusiness approach is applicable when dealing with a commodity problem as well as in the formulation of national policy. Here, again, it involves bringing together all related interests dealing with that commodity—producer, handler, processor, and distributor—for the exchange of ideas and formulation of policy. This, of course, necessitates the reorientation of pertinent research to the commodity-wide picture.

Indeed, it is imperative that much of the basic work of formulating an agribusiness policy be done on a commodity basis in view of the great variation in circumstances, commodity by commodity. Only it must also be related to the interests of other commodities, the nation, and to our international responsibilities. The total picture is still the important one.

In addition, the agribusiness approach can give us a clearer idea of the importance of foreign trade in farm commodities and products derived therefrom. This it can do by providing a suitable framework for seeing both the export and the import picture in truer perspective —perspective which puts in proper focus the interests of the farmer, the agribusiness economy, and the total economy.

VERTICAL INTEGRATION

In general the industrial sectors of the economy have achieved greater economic stability than agriculture by means of vertical integration—integration which relates the procurement of raw materials, production, and distribution. This has been achieved by numerous methods, including central ownership, franchises, and other contractual arrangements.

In essence, the job confronting agribusiness today is that of finding techniques and devices which will provide the agribusiness sector of the economy with economic stability comparable to that which industry has achieved through vertical integration. The weakest link in the agribusiness structure, of course, is the one between production on the farm and the processing and distributing functions which are performed by business. As already indicated, the problem of economic stability with respect to agricultural commodities is a tougher undertaking than in the case of most industrial products because of the large number of farming units and the peculiar vulnerability of agriculture to instability and income anemia.

But the toughness of the job must not stop us. To assure economic progress on the agribusiness front and to strengthen our national economy we must find ways and means of building new strength into agribusiness so that gradually it can assume more and more of the stabilizing functions now performed by the Federal government. If real progress is to be made, we must be willing to look for new answers.

In doing so, we need to review the past and glean what good ideas we can from the vast experience of the last 30 years and apply them to current situations—primarily as a springboard to the future. Our real objective must be to evolve new and better courses of action, in the light of what is good for agriculture, good for business, and good for the public. As already indicated, this is an evolutionary process—one of beginning where we are and moving progressively to something better.

COURSES OF ACTION

In the development of a progressive agribusiness policy there are three main alternatives open to us:

1. *Large corporate units.* Copy directly from industry's book and reorganize our farm production on the basis of large corporate units—units big enough to integrate with production the procurement of farm supplies and the storage, processing and distribution of farm products. This might be approached either by the merger of existing farms, with the present owners converting their equity into stock in the new corporations, or by business firms which handle farm supplies or products acquiring land, or both. In the past, corporate farms have gained only limited foothold in American agriculture; at present they account for about 1 per cent of farm units and 6 per cent of farm output.

2. *Farmer cooperatives.* Follow a pattern of promoting efficient-size family farms and integrating them vertically with related operations through cooperative ownership by farmers of the facilities for manufacturing farm supplies and for handling, processing, and marketing farm products. Currently, about 20 per cent of farm supplies and products are handled on this basis through one or more phases of operation. In terms of the total functions involved, farmer cooperatives perform between 5 and 10 per cent of the total. For some products, such as citrus fruits, nuts, and milk in certain milksheds, the cooperatives' share is over 50 per cent.

3. *Enlightened teamwork.* We could achieve the effect of vertical integration without central ownership by means of enlightened teamwork between the producer and the business phases of agribusiness. This type of operation has been gaining momentum in recent years.

The third alternative of enlightened teamwork offers a number of past experiences for us to look at—no one of which has been fully an answer to the farm problem, but each of which has value in terms of ideas and avoids the ownership of stocks by the Commodity Credit Corporation:

Promotion campaigns have been sponsored by such organizations as the American Dairy Association.

Marketing agreements and/or Federal orders are in force for some 25 fruit and specialty crops and in more than 60 milksheds.

The National Cotton Council working closely with textile manufacturers has developed new uses for cotton and boosted the demand for cotton goods. Fully as important, it has served as a forum in which the various sectors of the industry—producer, ginner, crusher, merchant, exporter, and spinner—can exchange views and discuss common problems, with the result that each sees his own problems as a part of the total agribusiness structure rather than just within the scope of the function he performs.

Other voluntary programs, some international in scope, have been developed for sugar, wool, etc.

A noteworthy kind of teamwork is that of the grower groups and the food-distribution trades. Since 1936, about 300 promotions have been conducted on such products as citrus fruits, apples, pears, peaches, cherries, lettuce, cabbage, potatoes, and dairy products. In 1954 alone, 28 food items were given major promotion to increase consumption of foods in heavy supply.

One of the biggest recent campaigns was that aimed at increasing beef consumption:

Action was precipitated in the late spring of 1953. At that time a long drought in the West and Southwest had created a severe shortage of feed crops. The result was an unprecedented movement of cattle to market, and the price of prime steers dropped from around 40 cents per pound to 25 cents.

At this point, under heavy pressure from cattlemen, the Department of Agriculture called a series of meetings which were attended, on the one hand, by cattle raisers, and, on the other, by representatives of the National Association of Food Chains, the National Association of Independent Grocers, the Hotel and Restaurant Association, the Livestock and Meat Board, and the Meat Institute. The outcome of the conference was a beef promotion campaign into which an estimated $50 million was poured by the various private sectors of the economy. The food chains alone spent about $12.5 million advertising fresh beef, plus $1.5 million more for frozen and canned beef.

The results in increased consumption of beef were spectacular. Consumption went up from 61 pounds per person in 1952 to 75 pounds in 1953 (and it has continued to rise, reaching 79 pounds in 1954). And not only did beef consumption increase by 14 pounds in 1953, but the consumption of all meats rose by 10 pounds per capita.

A similar campaign has been in progress during the fall of 1955 to move pork into consumption. It is clear from these experiences that growers and distributors can cooperate effectively when they want to, and apparently to their mutual profit.

It is significant that business has played an important role in all such efforts. It has shown initiative in developing new ideas on both the farm supply and the processing and marketing fronts. To mention a few examples, there has been the work done in improvement of farm machinery, mixed feeds, and chemicals; there has been the development of processes for freezing and concentrating food products; there has also been the vast growth of supermarkets and food chains which have initiated progress in the form of self-service, quality improvement, better displays, mass distribution, convenient customer parking lots, and so on.

The list of campaigns and other efforts worthy of study could be considerably expanded. The point is that there exists a wealth of information on which to begin formulating an improved farm policy designed to strengthen our agribusiness economy and to implement our national economic goals.

IN THE SHORT RUN

Assuming that we keep our traditional freedoms in America, it is likely that in the short run we shall see some further development along the lines of each of the three alternative courses of action that I have indicated.

First, there may be a few phases of agriculture in which corporate farming will show an advantage over the family farm—particularly phases which require large investment for development or large space for economical use of equipment. However, there is little reason to believe this trend will become pronounced.

Second, it is probable that in certain other phases of agriculture further development may take place with respect to cooperative purchasing and marketing. Much will depend on the type of leadership which comes forward in this area and on the willingness of cooperatives to pay the competitive price for good management. The fact that agribusiness did not develop initially on the basis of vertical integration through cooperative ownership, except in the case of a few commodities, means that general conversion to such a plan would entail tremendous reorganization of the present business structure.

Third, and offering great potential, is the opportunity for enlightened teamwork between the various segments of agribusiness for the purpose of achieving the advantages of vertical integration without central ownership. This course of action will require cooperation and statesmanship of a high order. It has the advantage of preserving the existing basic organizational structure of both farms and business units. Also, it has the potential of accomplishing results more quickly than could be done by integration through vertical ownership.

A limiting factor is the inertia which must be overcome in obtaining the essential teamwork when it is on a voluntary basis. Here one possibility worthy of study would be the use of the force of law to impose the will of a two thirds majority on the minority, such as is now done in the case of marketing agreements.

IN THE LONG RUN

One or more of the three alternatives, no doubt, will tend to become dominant—that is, if we succeed in solving so-called farm problems on an agribusiness basis. It is important that the economic and political climate be such as to make possible the emergence of the solution or solutions which are best suited to our future needs. Or stated negatively, it would indeed be unfortunate if, as the result of inertia, bickering, or politics, we artificially tip the scales in favor of second-rate or third-rate answers when first-rate answers are obtainable. In such event the whole country will suffer—the farmer, the businessman, and the consumer.

Should we fail to develop agribusiness answers to present problems, then by default we will have decided to go the route of big government programs to help agriculture. But big government programs for supporting prices do not come within the scope of agribusiness. Instead, they are substitutes for agribusiness in that they involve using the arm of government to achieve ends which we have failed to achieve through private enterprise.

We must not forget, however, that the present large holdings by the Commodity Credit Corporation and the already expanded capacity of agriculture to produce in excess of current needs greatly complicate the undertaking of implementing an agribusiness policy. There will have to be interim measures, as a sort of bridge to the future. Not only will we have to retain modified support programs until sounder policies can be implemented, but we may have to take artificial steps to bring supply and demand more nearly into balance by reducing farm output.

This we might do by a program of transferring selected land not suitable for cultivation to the production of grass or timber. In addition we might find it necessary to divert selected acres of arable land from production for market to use in soil-building practices, thus creating a fertility reserve for the future. Temporarily we would be operating our agricultural plant at something less than total capacity, and simultaneously taking appropriate steps to improve it. This is a policy already widely used by industry. It is a subject which merits serious study on an agribusiness basis.

CONCLUSION

The basic solution of farm problems is progress. This is true equally for the low-income farmers and for the commercial farmers, even though in each case the answers lead in somewhat different directions. Moreover, it is essential that we make progress on an even front, promptly eliminating eddies of lag when they appear. The old idea of trying to solve the farm problem on the farm is outmoded.

Today we are on the threshold of a new era—the atomic era—the potential of which no man knows. One thing, however, is certain: great opportunity lies ahead of us—opportunity far surpassing anything we have ever known. Even now promising research is going on to develop techniques such as the tenderizing of tough meats and the preservation of food through irradiation. These, and scores of other techniques not yet thought of, are certain to be perfected in the decades ahead.

One of the great blessings which accompanies a dynamic, progressive economy is that it contains within itself the power to overcome maladjustment and past mistakes. This is true because it constantly is creating new capital, new jobs, and new business opportunities. In such a climate the weaknesses of any one phase of the economy can be corrected without loss to other phases. On this score America is particularly fortunate among the nations of the world.

In the dynamic era ahead the term "farm problem" will become more and more a misnomer; farm problems will be recognized as being also business problems and vice versa. More precisely, farms problems will be agribusiness problems. Therefore, we must solve them through the agribusiness approach. By this approach we should be able to improve the economic status of agriculture, reduce the role of government on the farm front, enhance the profit opportunities of business, and assure the consumer of high-quality food at reasonable price and with less drudgery of preparation.

All of America stands to benefit by the use of the agribusiness approach to farm problems. Our end objective should be to utilize our vast capacity to produce food and fiber for the further improvement of our own living standard and the implementation of our aims abroad.

103. 200 *Acres in Iowa: "We Need Help Right Now"* *

The possible solution to the "farm problem" discussed by Mr. Davis (Selection 102) was a generalized one in terms of the totality of the situation. Like his article, much of the literature in agricultural economics is written in terms of the total situation. Thus we have discussions of parity pricing, flexible versus fixed price supports, soil bank plans, or crop reduction. All this may be essential to a complete understanding of the agricultural situation, but it does little to explain in concrete terms the problems now facing an individual farmer as he attempts to make a living on a farm. While conditions in Iowa may differ from those in other farm states those differences are not so great as to detract from this vivid picture of Herb Ring as he farms his 200 acres. His welfare and that of the farm population generally are dependent upon a proper solution of the "farm problem" and constitute a prime factor in that solution.

Herb Ring is a stocky, quick-moving man of thirty-eight who farms

* Dale Kramer, *The Reporter*, XIV (February 9, 1956), pp. 34-37. Reprinted with permission from *The Reporter*, 136 East 57th Street, New York 22, N. Y.

two hundred acres near Sigourney in southeastern Iowa. He is spoken of as a "damn good farmer," to distinguish him from simply a good farmer, and he has grown accustomed to think of himself as a success.

As a boy in the early 1930's Herb had been aware of his father's struggle to keep his head above water, and he was prepared to take some ups and downs. But somehow he got the idea "they" wouldn't allow a bad farm slump to happen. By "they" he meant the government people in charge of agricultural programs and the big fellows who run the business economy.

But Newt Ring, Herb's father, never stopped preaching wariness. His memories of the First World War boom, the postwar bust, the loud cries for "farm relief" during the 1920's, then the big bust and the life-saving farm programs were vivid. Old Newt made quite a little money during the Second World War, paid off his indebtedness, and socked all he could into the bank. In his opinion "they" wouldn't act fast enough at the end of the war boom, and he frankly lacked faith in the workability of the law of supply and demand as far as agriculture was concerned.

HERB'S POSTWAR START

Herb came back from the Army late in 1945. Already he was a family man, for he and Evelyn, a neighbor girl, had seen no use in waiting until after the war to marry. They had a three-year-old son. Herb's older brother had taken over the home place, but Newt, on retiring, had been careful to make an even division of assistance among his three children. Herb's share was $7,000. He had $2,000 of his own in the bank, accumulated from prewar savings, the sale of his car before going into service, and what he put aside from his sergeant's pay. Evelyn, living with her parents, had saved $900 from his allotment. So they had a total capital of nearly $10,000.

A 160-acre farm about ten miles from the Ring home place came up for sale, and Herb, wanting to get in a 1946 crop, bought it in a competitive market. Yet the price of $250 an acre was not considered unreasonable. The six-room house and the outbuildings were in good repair. Herb put down $6,000 and an insurance company lent him the $34,000 balance on a twenty-year mortgage at five per cent. This meant that he would have to get up $3,400 in principal and interest at the end of the first year.

Herb figured up what the new machinery he wanted would cost him. The total was more than $6,000. Of course he couldn't afford it, and anyhow not much new equipment was available in the restricted postwar market. Secondhand machinery was high. He paid $800 for an eight-year-old tractor that had cost $1,100 new. He got a three-plow attachment for $200, a set of harrows for $100, disks for $125, a four-row cornplanter for $210, and a couple of wagons at $90 apiece. Altogether, he put $1,900 into secondhand essentials. He would borrow his brother's oats combine, his mechanical cornpicker, and his hay baler. Or, if they should both need the equipment at the same time, he would hire a custom harvester.

The house would have to wait for new furnishings. They bought the former owner's electric range and refrigerator—the Rural Electrification Administration's lines were hooked in—and pieced out the house with borrowings from relatives and things picked up at closing-out sales. A car was a big item in the short market. Herb had to pay $700 for a 1940 Chevrolet that had cost little more than that when it was new.

All told Herb had spent $9,000 of his capital, and there still wasn't a live thing on the place. The cost of putting in a crop had to be met, and there was the cost of operating beyond that. Therefore Herb went after another $5,000 of credit—and got it at the local bank on his note. His security was a second mortgage on the farm, a mortgage on his chattels, and—quite an important item—his father's signature. He paid $100 apiece for thirty brood sows. He gave $375 for three milk cows. Evelyn got three dozen hens from her mother and bought two hundred brood chicks at the hatchery.

The job now was to make a crop. Herb spread lime on forty of the sixty acres he was putting into corn—the major Iowa cash crop, whether marketed directly or fed into pork and beef—but any real soil-building program would have to wait. For seed, tractor fuel, hired help, and other cash operating expenses he set aside $2,000. He would still need some credit for feed, hog vitamins, veterinarians' bills, and the like. Evelyn, who is strong if rather slight, put in a big garden. The weekly check for butterfat and eggs paid most of the grocery bill.

THE FIRST AND SECOND YEARS

Twenty years earlier Herb would have needed the help of a full-time hand to farm the 160 acres. But now, working the tractor all day and part of the night, and with Evelyn doing nearly all the milking, he got by with only $400 in hired labor. The crop year was a good one. The corn averaged sixty bushels to the acre. He saved an average of nearly seven pigs from each of his sows.

Herb was in the government corn program, and he took a loan on most of his corn, getting $4,500 of badly needed capital. After saving twenty of the best young sows from the hog crop, he marketed the balance at an average of $24.15 a hundredweight. His check was for $6,375.

Herb rejected the impulse to lump the two sums, forget a large part of his expenses, and report expansively that he had cleaned up $6,000 or $8,000 during his first year of operation. Being a man who likes to know exactly where he stands, he was keeping records under the guidance of the Iowa State Agricultural College. The system is complicated, taking into account interest, depreciation, taxes, and other more or less hidden costs. But it shows a farmer his net profit above the labor of himself and his family.

Herb figured $45 a week combined wages for himself and Evelyn. His net profit that first year was $2,800. Most of the gross cash income had gone to pay off the bank note and other operating indebtedness. Yet even the net-profit figure was a bit deceptive. He hadn't paid himself interest on his $10,000 investment. And of course there was $3,400 principal and interest to pay on the farm mortgage. When that was subtracted from $5,140—the total of net profit plus family labor—he could see why they had been forced to skimp on their living.

Of course Herb had to borrow again at the bank for his operating expenses. And wanting to get a better return for his corn, he plunged heavily on beef cattle for fattening. In May, 1947, he got some relief by the sale of his fall hog crop. In Iowa hogs are traditionally known as "mortgage lifters." Herb was able to lift his chattel mortgage from everything except the beef cattle, which were for the time being living inexpensively on pasture.

In the fall of 1947, the second year, Herb and Evelyn relaxed. The corn was fine. Prices were rising. Herb was mastering the new farming methods that had been developed under pressure from the government to increase wartime food production. The vitamins and minerals and special seeds were expensive, but Herb was convinced they paid dividends. His cattle and hogs hit top grades. That winter of his second year his checks totaled a fancy $17,000.

Yet he was able to figure only $3,150 as net profit. For one thing, the repair bills on the old machinery had been high. And the prices of all the things he had to buy were skyrocketing. It had been another year of skimpy living.

Herb realized that to afford the new machinery he wanted he would have to find more land so that he could put the equipment to maximum use. Fortunately he was able to rent forty acres nearby, and, feeling confident, he spread himself for the first time since coming home from the Army. The major items were a tractor at $1,700, a cornpicker at $1,500, and a combine at $2,000. With other smaller items the total came to $8,000. He borrowed most of the money.

1948 AND POLITICS

Herb gave little thought to politics. Like most other veterans he was too busy catching up. But in 1948, as prices turned downward, his ears began to open to the warnings of old Newt. The drift of talk among farmers was that if a postwar slump was in the making, then it might be wiser to bank on the Democrats, who at least had a record of acting in a pinch. Herb went along with the majority. It was this wariness of the farmers that carried Iowa for Harry Truman and ousted a Republican Senator, George A. Wilson.

In 1949 prices were on the rise again. Herb's net profit went above $4,000 for the first time. He bought a new Chevrolet—on terms—and Evelyn lavished $1,000 on new furniture. The next year they had a new baby and painted the house and barn and the barnyard fences.

Then came the Korean War and soaring prices. Yet Herb's net profits for 1950 and 1951 did not rise very much. Costs had shot up too fast. He noticed that according to Iowa State College statisticians the cost of machinery and power had increased 400 per cent since 1940. Herb's own figures showed a doubling of operating costs since 1946. He tried to be cautious in buying new machinery, yet he always found himself paying interest on $4,000 or $5,000 of equipment mortgages.

In 1952 Herb liked Ike, even if his father didn't. Newt said Eisenhower's promise of 100 per cent parity was hogwash. Yet certainly Eisenhower wasn't responsible for the pinch that came in the fall and winter of 1952. Both hog and cattle prices broke. Herb's net profit dropped a couple of thousand dollars to what it had been in 1947 when he had only the 160 acres and the old machinery. The situation was better in the years 1953-1954—but Herb wasn't able to get his net profit up to $3,000.

At the beginning of 1955, Herb, while feeling that nine years of hard work ought to have put him further ahead, was not worried. He could look with satisfaction at the reduction of his farm mortgage by $15,300, down to $18,700. The interest load was lighter now. His implement notes were under $4,000. But his standard of living was not really very high. The car was going on six years old. Except for a television set, they had bought no important item for the house in five years. From year to year they had put off installation of running water. They ought to paint again. And the eight-year-old tractor was about due to be traded for a new one.

When the price of hogs, the mortgage lifters, began to slide in the spring, Herb began to worry. In May he sold his fall crop at $17 a hundredweight, or 80 per cent of parity. That was going to pull down his net profit.

LOW ON THE HOG

Then it happened. Hog prices began to spin dizzily to one new depth after another. Down they went to fourteen-year lows, down at last to 55 per cent of parity. Cattle prices sagged.

"I came out about even on my beef," Herb says. "The hogs killed me. I could have stood $18. What I got was under $11. There on the hogs is the way I figured my loss for the year—somewhere close to $4,000."

When Herb says he "lost" $4,000, he doesn't mean his books will show a red figure that large. What has happened is that his usual net profit is wiped out and he and Evelyn have had their joint wages cut from $45 to about $20 a week. And of course he has gained nothing on his investment of some $30,000.

The harsh question staring Herb in the face is this: Where is the money for amortization and interest on his farm mortgage to come from? His 1956 total is $2,635. Heretofore the money had come out of his net profit—with an occasional chunk of his wages thrown in.

Herb isn't broke. Far from it. But he is frankly scared. He wrote to his farm-mortgage holder, asking if he might forgo the $1,700 principal this year, paying only the interest. So far there has been no reply. This is not surprising. There are many thousands of Herb Rings, and the insurance companies and other big investors have a major decision to make on the leniency of their credit policies. If necessary Herb can pay the $1,700. He can refinance his mortgage through the Federal Land Bank, clapping a bigger mortgage on the farm. In effect this would be digging into his savings. Many have already done it. So Herb will still be in business this year. The bank will probably let him have all the operational credit he needs. But he won't buy the new tractor, or replace the 1949 Chevrolet, or paint the house.

According to Herb, he literally trembles when looking at his fixed costs. Land taxes have almost doubled since 1946. In the old days of live horsepower a man could trim expenses in a hurry. Nowadays costs are still mounting. Tractor fuel, repairs, and hired labor will be higher. About the only place to cut is in the standard of living.

Herb is sore. "Evelyn and I have worked like dogs," he says. "Instead of going ahead I've gone back at least a year. That means I've really lost two years. If the market stays down and the price of land drops—why, three or four years will bust me flat."

A couple of his friends have already "busted on the quiet." Not as well capitalized as Herb, they sold out under pressure from creditors. Handbills carrying the opening line "As I am quitting farming, will sell at public auction . . ." are appearing in large numbers.

FLEXIBLE SUPPORTS

For months it has been fashionable to "cuss Benson." Herb is now almost as vociferous as old Newt, who always said big business would use the Eisenhower Administration to smash the farmer. The Secretary of Agriculture's inaction in the face of plummeting prices has been infuriating. But the resentment goes deeper. Farmers are quite willing to admit to overproduction. But not many are convinced that Benson's flexible-support program is the answer.

The flexible method is adjustment of government supports to the supply. If a surplus of, say, corn forces the market down, as happened in 1955, the support will be lowered in the next year. The experts predict that the price of corn will be dropped 15 per cent on the 1956 crop. There are no supports for pork and beef, since the price of feed is supposed to control livestock prices. In theory the farmers, aware of oversupply and facing reduced supports, will cut production.

"Take a look at my case and you'll see why the flexible program won't work," says Herb Ring. "I can't get my fixed costs down. If I knew everybody else was cutting production—why, sure, I would too. But as things stand I'll have to raise every bushel of grain and feed all the livestock I can in order to get the cash I need. Besides, we need help right now."

IKE'S "SOIL BANK"

Herb read the newspaper accounts of President Eisenhower's farm message to Congress, with its emphasis on a "soil bank," and his spirits were not raised. As near as he could make out, the "soil bank" was just another acreage-cutting proposition. At best the compliance payments would not be large enough to do him much good. And there was a real chance of his being damaged further.

The President's suggestion that surplus grain be released to farmers was what bothered Herb. That would mean a greater supply of feed, which in turn would lead to greater livestock production and lower prices. Herb was inclined to agree with the Des Moines *Register* that

President Eisenhower "offered nothing in the way of a direct attack on the problem of low livestock prices."

All evidence indicates that Iowa farmers want production payments. They want prices pegged, with the government making up the difference between the market and the pegged figure. Such a program, they freely admit, is open government subsidization. They argue that other elements of the economy, especially industry, are subsidized. They point to billions spent for armaments and declare that food is every bit as important as weapons. The cry of "regimentation" is seldom raised any more. Most are willing to accept production controls along with payments.

The shift to the production-payments view was well under way in late summer. In September a *Wallace's Farmer* poll reported 63 per cent in favor of pegged hog prices. (By December the number had jumped to 76 per cent.) Significantly, 68 per cent of the younger men spoke out for high supports as compared with 58 per cent of the older men. The Des Moines *Register* has squabbled with the conservative Farm Bureau, which officially backs flexible supports, and is close to backing production payments.

But the most striking proof is in the rise of the National Farm Organization, which had its inception during the early fall in protest meetings in southwestern Iowa. Drought was stirring farmers to quicker action than in other regions. The chief demands were for pegging hogs at $20 and cattle at $30. The movement gained impetus when a former Republican governor, seventy-eight-year-old Dan Turner, joined it and took to the hustings with surprising vigor. Ironically, it was Turner who in the early 1930's sent National Guardsmen to quell the earliest farm-discontent riots. But Turner has roots in the old Populist movement. He is a big farm owner, and when the pinch came he joined the hue and cry after Benson despite his fondness for President Eisenhower.

Politicians waited to see whether the NFO would spread out from the drought areas. In late November and early December it did—sensationally. The organizational method is based purely on spontaneity. A farmer or group of farmers in a county get in touch with the NFO office at Corning, a small town in southwestern Iowa. Dan Turner or an NFO organizer—some ordinary farmer who can spare a little time—goes in to speak at a county-wide meeting. The local farmers then drive through their school districts signing up members. In one Missouri county 1,600 were enrolled in a few days. The response in many Iowa counties was nearly as great. The organization has kept dues down to $1.

In early January the NFO roared into Herb Ring's county. On

three days' notice 800 farmers packed a hall in Sigourney to hear Dan Turner. Five days later 1,005 members—half the farmers of the county—had been enrolled. Only a few of those approached failed to join, and the leaders expect to enroll more than 90 per cent of the farm population.

There is no longer any doubt in the minds of Iowa politicians and most others of the Middle West that the current now flowing is deep and strong. Not long ago Senator Bourke B. Hickenlooper, up for re-election, indicated extreme political panic by suddenly proposing an expensive sow-killing program. Benson brushed it aside. It is difficult for Hickenlooper, who introduced the flexible legislation, to jump all the way to production payments. But most Iowa political observers expect him to manage it, and he has already begun to make some fancy jumping motions.

It can be seen from the example of Herb Ring and his neighbors that the current of protest in the Middle West does not come from poverty. But it is also untrue, as is often charged, that farmers are merely angry over failing to share in the national boom prosperity. They have been hurt. The young men are badly scared. And the older men are concerned with more than investment depreciation and the prospect of working for nothing. They are worried, as Herb Ring is, over the future of their children.

Midwestern farmers are consciously fighting to make a solid place for themselves in the national economy. Not long ago the Des Moines *Register* declared: "Ezra Taft Benson may have served a noble purpose, in the long run, by dramatizing the issues and stirring up the political animals." It is safe to say that the drama has barely opened.

104. *The Transplantability of the TVA* *

THE SUCCESS of the Tennessee Valley Authority has been phenomenal. As a result many believe that the economic and social ills of all river valleys will be magically cured if Valley Authorities are designed for them. Professor Pritchett here outlines the reasons for the success of the TVA; some of the problems that would arise

* C. Herman Pritchett, *Iowa Law Review*, 32 (January, 1947), pp. 327-338. Reprinted by permission of the author and the publisher. All footnotes omitted.

if the TVA pattern were to be applied to the Missouri Valley; and a possible solution of the administrative problems of valley development.

MOST people are now prepared to admit that the Tennessee Valley Authority has been a success. It is hard to dispute that since 1933, the whole face of the region in which the TVA operates has been changed for the better. The energies of its streams have been harnessed, and their destructive potentialities largely brought under control. A "Great Lakes of the South" has been created with tremendous possibilities for recreational devolpment of the area. The immense amounts of power made available at low rates have been responsible for new industries, new patterns of rural living. Educational and demonstration activities have resulted in materially transforming an exploitative agricultural system into one which conserves and promotes both natural resources and human values.

From one point of view, indeed, the TVA may have been too successful. One might well ask, after watching the scores of bills which have been dropped into the congressional hopper since 1933 seeking the creation of similar regional authorities for almost every river valley in the United States, whether the authority device had not been oversold. How many of these bills, one may wonder, have been based on a real understanding of the authority plan? To how many people is the TVA more than a slogan? It was against an unthinking overenthusiasm for transplantation of the Tennessee Valley formula to other areas that Secretary Ickes was fulminating in 1944 when he warned that problems of regional development could not be solved "merely by lighting a candle and intoning, 'TVA, TVA, TVA.'"

THE TVA IDEA

First of all, it is necessary to understand the basic elements in the authority device. David E. Lilienthal considers that there are three essentials in the TVA idea: "(1) a federal autonomous agency, with authority to make its decisions in the region; (2) responsibility to deal with resources, as a unified whole, clearly fixed in the regional agency, not divided among several centralized federal agencies; (3) a policy, fixed by law, that the federal regional agency work cooperatively with and through local and state agencies."

The authority thus differs in several important ways from the regular pattern of federal departmental administration. The basis on which departments are normally established is that of major purpose or function. They are given a single major function to perform, and a wide jurisdiction in which to perform it. Thus the Forest Service is responsible for carrying out its program of forestry development and protection over the entire nation. The jurisdiction of a federal major-purpose organizational unit may of course be less than nationwide, as in the case of the Bureau of Reclamation which operates only in the arid western half of the country, or the Bonneville Power Administration, which carries on its power distribution operations in the Columbia River region. But in such instances the program is still a single-purpose one, with no responsibility for or control over other governmental programs affecting the same area.

The result of the functional plan of organization is that in each geographical area such action programs as the federal government may determine to undertake are in the hands of separate federal bureaus or agencies, each concentrating upon its own field of specialized interest and sharing no responsibility for the program or operations of its neighbors, with whom, in fact, its relations may be those of competition or rivalry rather than cooperation. The approach to regional problems is thus uncoordinated, piecemeal, and segmented.

It is precisely this characteristic of the federal government's action programs in the Missouri Valley, which have been entrusted to such bitter antagonists as the Army Engineers and the Bureau of Reclamation, that has led to the demand for a Missouri Valley Authority. For the regional authority reverses the normal departmental pattern. It is a multiple-purpose agency with jurisdiction limited to a particular geographical area, within which it has broad powers to plan and operate a comprehensive and unified program of resource development. Instead of land and water and forests and minerals and transportation being split up among separate agencies, each jealous of its own domain, the authority can include and interrelate all these elements in its plans. Thus it avoids and ignores the lines which regular federal agencies must draw. If there are conflicting claims, as for water use, they can be adjusted within the confines of a single agency which has a responsibility to the region as a whole, and do not become a bone of contention over which separate administrative agencies quarrel.

But it is not only the multiple-purpose, omnicompetent quality of the regional authority which distinguishes it from the regular government agency. Equally important is the fact that the control and direction of the authority are exercised within the region, in contrast to the normal Washington-dominated bureaus. It is true that regional or field offices are customarily maintained by federal bureaus, and that these locally-situated officials may well appreciate the special problems of their regions and seek to adapt the general national policies of their bureaus to local needs. But these officials are responsible to a bureau chief in Washington, and he takes orders from his department head, so that final decisions may be made on the basis of paper knowledge and by officials motivated principally by a desire to maintain nationally uniform procedures and policies.

A centralized federal bureau is also going to have to fight inherited routines and patterns of thought if it makes significant use of other federal agencies and local government institutions in the various regional programs which it administers. In contrast, a regional authority set up as a corporate entity, outside the regular departmental system, has an unusual opportunity to plan a development program on the basis of regional needs. Its center of gravity lies within the area. Free from departmental jealousies, preconceptions, and administrative routine, it can develop an original approach to the satisfaction of regional needs, can bring a wide variety of functions within the control of a single operating organization, and can hope to secure the cooperation of other public agencies in its program.

Although not one of the characteristics listed above by Lilienthal as an essential value of the authority idea, the adaptability of the regional authority to the administration of self-supporting enterprise functions has been amply demonstrated by TVA experience. Free from the traditions, limitations, and timidities of normal departmental programs and methods, the TVA has been able to build up a gigantic power system, to plan and construct distribution lines, to work out policies on rates, and in general to conduct a large-scale business operation with a considerable measure of managerial freedom. It is difficult to see how a successful operation of this sort could be conducted under more constrained circumstances.

Such freedom, of course, brings its responsibilities as well as its opportunities. As an autonomous financial unit, separate from any other government agency, the authority is forced to stand on its own financial feet and make its own decisions as to rates and other financial matters with the knowledge that it is directly responsible to Congress and to the public for maintaining a satisfactory financial record. Because financial tests can be applied to a government operation which proceeds under these circumstances—tests which are not relevant to ordinary government spending activities—a public authority can be released from some of the financial controls which have to be applied to regular government agencies.

Another aspect of the TVA's administrative freedom has been its exemption from the regular civil service laws. Operating simply under a requirement to select its employees on the basis of "merit and efficiency," the TVA has made what is in many respects the best record in effective and non-political personnel administration ever achieved by a government agency in this country.

THE MVA PROPOSALS

The principal legislative proposals for establishing an MVA seek to follow the pattern developed in the Tennessee region in all these respects. S. 555, as introduced in the 79th Congress by Senator Murray, provided for a unified approach to the planning, development, and control of the water resources of the Missouri Valley. It proposed to set up a single organization, which would see the whole valley as a single problem. No longer would separate departmental agencies be identified with separate sections of the valley, nor could the problems of the different sections be handled by the dubious method of establishing spheres of influence within which each agency would proceed according to its own predilections. The MVA would have to develop and place before Congress a plan which it could defend as constituting the most effective utilization and the fairest possible division of water resources among the various uses and sections that could be devised.

A unified approach would also be achieved in carrying out the plan as developed and approved, and in making the basic decisions with respect to water management and control. The unity typified by a single boss for a single valley might well be instrumental in fostering notions of cohesiveness and cooperation among the people of the different sections of the valley. The authority would furnish an object lesson in the values of taking a wider view, and supply a core around which larger regional loyalties could form. It would dramatize the fact that it is all one river, and that the factors which seem to divide the different sections of the valley are less significant than those which unite them.

The MVA plans have sought the goal of decentralized administration by such means as the provision in S. 555 requiring the MVA to "maintain its principal office at a convenient place in the territory in which its activities are conducted," working in and with the valley. The bill did not require that the three members of the MVA board should be residents of the area, an arrangement which would probably be undesirable since there is a national interest and responsibility involved. But it did set up an advisory committee to assist the board in the discharge of its duties, this committee to include nine persons resident in the area, three each representing the interests of agriculture, commerce, and labor. The committee was to meet in the area not less than once a year, and to receive the annual report of the board. The bill summarized the regional emphasis of the authority philosophy by directing the MVA to "utilize to the fullest possible extent the advice, assistance, and cooperation of the people of the region, and their public and private organizations—local and state. . . ."

Finally, S. 555 sought to give the MVA a degree of corporate administrative freedom sufficient to permit the effective handling of its enterprise functions and business responsibilities. It was not required to turn over all its revenues to the Treasury, but only the net proceeds from its operations after the deduction of all necessary expenses and the withholding of sums for operating capital and new construction. It was given the right to determine its own system of administrative accounts, permitted to have the final word with respect to expenditures questioned by the General Accounting Office, authorized to settle claims brought against it, and exempted from regular civil service requirements.

The MVA plan has thus been founded on the proposition that the regional authority plan which has achieved such notable success in the Tennessee Valley can operate with equal effectiveness in the Missouri Valley. If this proposition is to be denied, it must be either on the ground that there were special circumstances in the TVA experience which enabled it to succeed there which are not present in the Missouri region, or conversely that duplicating the TVA in the Missouri Valley presents problems not previously met. Conclusions as to the transplantability of the TVA must take such considerations into account.

FACTORS FACILITATING TVA SUCCESS

The non-transferable factors which helped to promote TVA success are both personal and organizational in character. The influence of President Roosevelt in the formative years of the TVA was incalculably great. It was his imagination which saw in Muscle Shoals not merely an "opportunity for the Federal Government to do a kind turn for the people in one small section," but rather a chance to experiment with "national planning for a complete river watershed" on a scale that "touches and gives life to all forms of human concerns." While his contacts with the Authority were intermittent, his interest and leadership constantly influenced the direction of the TVA program, dramatized its achievements, and heartened the organization to withstand the attacks made upon it.

Likewise the two great chairmen of the TVA board, Arthur E. Morgan and David E. Lilienthal, though they proved to be mutually incompatible, made contributions of the greatest significance to the TVA. Morgan infused the organization with an idealism, a social consciousness, a resolute resistance to political influences. Lilienthal supplied a somewhat more practical and balanced idealism, a driving energy, an inventively fertile mind, and a compelling devotion to democratic and cooperative procedures. The MVA would be fortunate to find two such talents for its board of directors.

Time, place, and circumstance played an important role in the TVA record of achievement. The emergency conditions prevailing in 1933 had prepared the way for an experiment in planning, had made Congress willing to delegate unusual measures of responsibility to administrative agencies, and had relaxed the normal controls over expenditure of funds. Depression and poverty had dissolved the suspicions and the reluctance that might have been the regional reaction to the incursion of these Yankee-Greeks bearing gifts.

The TVA, with an area four-fifths the size of England stretched out through seven states and comprehending diverse conditions of climate, agriculture, economy, and social life, was nonetheless set in a relatively compact and manageable region, especially when compared with the sprawling mass of the Missouri Valley. In the Tennessee region comparatively few other federal resource development agencies had established themselves on a firm basis. The Department of Agriculture was of course carrying on its agricultural and forestry programs there, and the Corps of Engineers was operating Wilson Dam, maintaining its navigation program, and getting the construction of Wheeler Dam under way. But there was no irrigation or reclamation work, no extensive federal land holdings, few Indians. Thus the TVA's problem of working out its relations with other federal agencies was a relatively uncomplicated one.

The fact that the TVA was the only regional authority on the scene likewise facilitated its operations. There was no problem of coordination with the possibly competing activities or demands of authorities in adjacent regions. Because of the fact that the TVA was the only one of its species, the President could spare the time necessary to advise on its policy or settle its internal disputes, Congress was willing to give it unusual privileges, and the departments did not object to yielding some of their responsibilities to it. It had the advantages of being an only child.

FACTORS COMPLICATING MVA STATUS

A realistic appraisal of the factors relevant to the success of an MVA must immediately recognize that the political milieu is now much less favorable than that in which the TVA got its start. The political temper is, for the time being at least, unreceptive to plans for planning or increased governmental activity. There is no support from a dynamic president. The region involved is one which has been most vociferous in devotion to the neo-Republican doctrine of states' rights, and it has been easy to present the regional authority proposal as a threat to the existing federal-state balance of power. The governors of the states in the area have sought to demonstrate that no change in prevailing patterns of federal resource development programs is needed. The two federal agencies most intimately concerned with water control in the area have concluded a treaty of alliance and mutual assistance aimed at preventing the establishment of an MVA.

Congress, moreover, is at present scarcely in the mood, even in the unlikely event that it would approve an MVA bill, to write into such legislation the types of freedom in program planning and in administration that aided so materially in the accomplishments of the TVA. Congress has indeed already passed the Government Corporation Control Act of 1945, under the restrictive provisions of which a corporate MVA would have to operate, so that much of the speed and flexibility of TVA administration would be simply unobtainable under present legislative standards.

Apart from the changed political climate, there are administrative considerations which would considerably complicate the operations of an MVA. It would be set down in a tremendous geographical area where many strong single-purpose federal agencies, well-rooted in the region and strongly supported from Washington by department chiefs and influential congressmen, are already operating. If a truly regional approach to the problems of resource development is to be worked out, the regional authority must mold these existing departmental programs into an integrated plan of operations. For this result a choice of tactics is available; as the saying goes, the MVA can either beat 'em or join 'em.

The former policy would require the ousting of these bureaus from the region, and assumption by the MVA of sole responsibility for administering the programs they now carry on—affecting reclamation, river development, navigation, power, the public lands, grazing, and other federal resource interests in the region. Such a step would probably have few advocates, not only because of its obvious political inexpediency, but also because of the scrapping of the special competence developed by the existing bureaus in their respective fields, and because of the challenge which such a regional sub-government would constitute to the prevailing pattern of national administration.

But the policy of "joining" the MVA and the bureaus has its own drawbacks. Under such a plan, presumably the bureaus would continue with much the same functions, but would operate under the directives of the MVA in accordance with its over-all plan for the valley. This arrangement would make MVA principally a planning organization, its operating responsibilities perhaps being limited to the field of power distribution. Acting largely through others, would its program hit the Missouri Valley with the impact that was felt in the Tennessee Valley from the TVA program? And would these old, established agencies accept without a fight planning decisions of the MVA which might conflict with their own notions of river development?

The TVA experience demonstrates that it is possible for a regional agency to cooperate with single-purpose federal bureaus, but there can be little doubt that such a program of cooperation would be harder to arrange under the conditions prevailing in the Missouri Valley. S. 555 appeared to leave the way open for the MVA to adopt either the solitary or the cooperative policy. By that bill the President was given power to transfer to the MVA all water control projects in the Valley. But on the other hand the Authority might, "if in its judgment the interests of economy and efficiency will be secured thereby," construct or operate any of the projects called for by the basic plan "through, or in conjunction with, other departments and agencies of the United States, or in conjunction with States or subdivisions or agencies thereof. . . ." Thus the Authority could, if it chose, perform its channel improvement work through the Army Engineers, and carry on irrigation activities through the existing Bureau of Reclamation setup.

Whether to beat 'em or to join 'em is not the only administrative dilemma posed by the MVA proposal. A problem which is perhaps even more difficult concerns the degree of independence from executive controls which the MVA can be permitted to enjoy. The TVA pattern calls for a status entirely outside the departmental system, control responsibilities being vested directly in the President. This characteristic has been regarded as one of the most important factors in preserving the regional integrity of the authority and guaranteeing that regional considerations will dominate in the decisions of the agency. This is the heart of the decentralization, the "grass roots" approach, about which Lilienthal has written so persuasively. Is there any reason why an MVA should not be given similar independence?

There is a reason why this suggestion tends to give pause to persons concerned with over-all federal organization. The independence of the TVA could be dismissed as a special case, but if a second authority is set up on the same pattern, then it begins to become a habit—a habit which has some bad features. A regional authority free from departmental control either will or will not be effectively supervised by the President. If it is not supervised, then it constitutes an area of irresponsibility operating without executive control. It might be guided by pressures and opinions in the region, perhaps channeled through the advisory committee provided for by S. 555. But the authority would have a national as well as a regional responsibility. Congress might keep the MVA under its supervision, especially in connection with its budget and its major regional plans and projects, but administrative supervision and control are not tasks which Congress is fitted to perform.

On the other hand, if the President does undertake to discharge the responsibilities that fall upon him in connection with such an independent agency, the affairs of the MVA must compete with the thousands of other duties which make the Presidency the hopelessly overworked office that it now is. In the crowded budget of his time the President must find a few odd moments to consider the problems of a three-man board located, perhaps, in Omaha—not a fortunate situation for the development of effective administrative relationships.

If it is agreed that effective control by the President is impossible under such conditions, and if it is admitted that there must be some coordination of the work of an authority organized on a regional principal with the programs of the regular federal operating departments across whose respective fields of jurisdiction it cuts, then some thought must be given to providing for such coordination at a level lower than that of the President's office. Particularly would this need seem to be urgent if additional authorities were set up, which might very well, in the pursuance of the interests of their respective regions, develop competitive or conflicting policies which would need prompt attention from a common superior. Former Secretary of the Interior Ickes took the position that in the absence of some central departmental control over regional authorities there would be "confusion and overlapping and headlong adventures in every direction without any central guidance or policy enforced upon all." His candidate for the agency to supply this central guidance was naturally the Department of the Interior. Others saw this suggestion as merely a tactic for capturing the entire development program.

Other suggestions have been heard that the head of a department not so directly concerned with operating programs in the watershed development field, such as the administrator of the Federal Works Agency, might be in a better position to serve as a neutral coordinator. Or possibly coordination through a single department head is too simple, and consideration should be given to a more complicated arrangement, under which various federal agencies would assume coordinating responsibilities for one particular function in each watershed. For example, the Federal Power Commission might be given responsibility over power rates and accounting, while the authority agricultural program would be cleared with the Department of Agriculture

DEPARTMENTAL REFORM AS AN ALTERNATIVE

The more closely this organizational problem is examined, the more it appears that there is no entirely satisfactory method of blending omnicompetent regional organizations in with single-purpose units organized on a national basis. It may well be concluded that the case for the independent regional authority rests not so much on its own inherent strength as on departmental failure to integrate developmental programs at the regional level. It is consequently of the highest importance that every encouragement be given to improving departmental achievements along this line. William Pincus has recently suggested the possibility of gathering together on a national scale the scattered functions and activities concerned with natural resources development around the nucleus of the primary tools which Congress placed in the hands of the TVA—water use and control and incidental power development—and placing them in a revamped or new federal department. Such an organization, Pincus suggests, "might avoid the necessity for exposing this nation to all the problems which the uncoordinated development of various regions would inevitably create in both the administrative and economic fields."

Another suggestion along this same line comes from Charles McKinley, who proposes that existing federal water and power agencies could be brought together in a reconstituted Department of the Interior, thus preserving the traditional functional pattern of national administration, but with the department so set up as to give "as large a degree of regional autonomy to its field representatives as the need for regional variation, celerity of design and construction, and efficient operation might require." Even under this plan, however, he recognizes that related regional functions would still be in the charge of other departments, such as the Department of Agriculture, so that a consistent and comprehensive regional program would still need to be fused and put into effect against the familiar jurisdictional obstacles to cooperative administration operations. Some approximation to common regional boundaries and bureau and departmental field headquarters would also be required.

Departmental reorganizations of this more heroic sort will be correspondingly hard to engineer, so that attention must also be given to experience with various coordinative devices employed under existing departmental arangements. But until the tide for departmental reform begins to run more strongly than it has in the past, the temptation to use the short-cut to regional integration offered by the valley authority will remain a strong one. As one advocate of the device has said: "The valley authority reaches into Washington and puts a big piece of the whole federal government right down into each regional area." It is the most readily available and immediately promising method of breaking through the compartmentalization of federal resource development programs and producing a unified, dynamic attack on regional problems.

There is a price to be paid, however, for its speed and its concentration. There is a real chance that regional autonomy will be achieved at the expense of national control. Regional concentration can develop into a narrow sectionalism. The administrative freedom claimed for a regional authority may extend so far as to undercut executive responsibility. Ways must be found to prevent the valley authority from developing the defects of its virtues, for these are the real limits on the transplantability of the TVA.

105. *One Fourth of a Nation--Public Lands and Itching Fingers* *

THE FEDERAL GOVERNMENT owns some 25 per cent of the land area of the United States. Most of this lies within the eleven Western states. It was the purpose of the government to sell all of the public land to individual buyers or to give it away to encourage public improvements. Selling land in the arid West was not so easy as in the other parts of the country where rainfall was more abundant and the mountain area much less formidable. In 1872 Yellowstone Park in Wyoming was reserved from public sale, and many acres of land have since been added to our developing national park system. Forces favorable to the conservation of natural resources have also succeeded in reserving from public sale vast areas of the public domain for forest reserves, public power sites, watershed preservation, and other conservation reasons.

The early efforts of Gifford Pinchot and Theodore Roosevelt to arouse the public to the need for conservation were built upon the work of Major John Wesley Powell whose *Report on the Lands of the Arid Region* (1878) initiated the movement for conservation. Today the fight to conserve the natural resources of the arid West still continues; the basic issues remain the same; and the arguments

* Wallace Stegner, *The Reporter*, VIII (May 12, 1953), pp. 25-29. Reprinted with permission from the author and *The Reporter*, 136 East 57th Street, New York 22, N. Y. Copyright 1953 by the Fortnightly Publishing Co., Inc.

for and against conservation are still those used when Powell sought the aid of Congressional legislation. Wallace Stegner here reviews the current threat to the dream of Major Powell and present-day conservationists.

HISTORY, like the balance of nature, is all of a piece. Tinker with it anywhere and you must adjust everywhere. That is why the proposed transfer of the offshore oil lands to the states is one of the most explosive issues that the Eighty-third Congress will touch. The policy affecting those oil lands is related to all Federal land and resources policies; a jar to one will be felt through the whole structure. Transfer of the oil lands will threaten the whole public domain. Not simply a policy but the direction of our history is at stake in the oil-lands dispute.

What is the public domain? As of April, 1953, the Federal government owns 458 million acres of the continent proper, and on this land it owns and operates scores of storage and flood-control dams, pumping stations, and power stations. Through a public corporation it owns also the whole vast development of the Tennessee and its tributaries. Through the Forest Service, National Park Service, Bureau of Land Management, and other agencies it administers 139 million acres of national forests, 147 million acres of grazing land, 12 million acres of parks and monuments, 14 million acres of defense installations, and 9 million acres of Indian reservations. It also owns 95 per cent of the total area of Alaska. The acreage in Federal hands in 1951 was 24 per cent of the area of the nation; west of the Rockies, about half of the land was government-owned.

Uncle Sam became his own biggest landlord by necessity, not intention. He tried to give it all away, but homesteaders wouldn't take it all. And if he had succeeded in giving away or selling all his real estate and had bought none back, there would be no TVA, no Columbia Basin or Central Valley projects. Yellowstone and Yosemite and Glacier and the other parks would be logged off; the watersheds would be even more eroded than they are; and there would be annual floods more destructive than that on the Missouri in 1952. Beer halls and dance pavilions would grace the prow of Mesa Verde, and entrepreneurs would be selling Western scenery wherever any was left. And giving the offshore oil to the states would really be what it only seems now to some people—the last act of a long drama of disposal.

There is a brand of states-rightsism that is more Western than Southern, more Republican than Democratic, and based not on history or sentiment but on natural resources of enormous value. And yet the real struggle is not between states and the Federal government but between the public interest and the powerful and persistent private interests that for years have tried to corral the West's land, water, timber, and water power.

More than the resources themselves are involved. Almost as important are the intangible assets: the protection of watersheds and the regulation of stream flow and the control of silt; the conservation of the "biotic layer" of the topsoil upon which all life depends; hunting, fishing, recreation, and the propagation and protection of wild life; and the international security that is based on having adequate oil reserves.

AN OLD STORY

If Federal ownership and management of resources in the public interest is "creeping socialism," then socialism has been creeping for a long time. The first major exception to the policy of complete disposal implicit in the Homestead Act of 1862 was the reservation of Yellowstone National Park in 1872, with the purpose of preserving it from private exploitation. The national forests date back to the Forest Reserve Act of 1891; most of the reservations were established by Presidents Harrison, Cleveland, McKinley, and Theodore Roosevelt, who were fought every step of the way by patriotic Americans eager to "develop" timber resources.

The system of leasing public lands for mineral and oil extraction began with the Mineral Leasing Act of 1920, amended several times since but not altered in its basic assumption that the lands involved were going to remain in government hands. The same lease system was applied to the range land by the Taylor Grazing Act of 1934. That Act, to all intents and purposes, ended the period of disposal and settled us in the policy of local management under Federal ownership.

Of the principal acts of legislation that brought the change about, only the Taylor Grazing Act was passed under the New Deal, and even that was the product of almost sixty years of agitation. It was fathered by a Democratic Congressman from Colorado, Edward Thomas Taylor, who had fought Federal authority over the public lands for years. And while it was on its way through Congress, Washington was visited by the same persuasive force that had converted Representative Taylor: Wind from the Dust Bowl blew across half the nation to sift dust on the streets of the capital itself.

By and large, all Federal assumptions of responsibility for management have come as emergency rescue operations. The Civilian Conservation Corps, the Soil Conservation Service, and other innovations of the 1930's found their work and their justification in a mined-out and eroded public domain. A large part of the Federal land purchases in the past twenty years has been of overgrazed, eroded, or otherwise submarginal land that had either to be retired from use or become desert.

One after another, as its resources began to disappear before exploiters careless of the future, the nation rescued what it could of its wilderness areas, its timber, its water, its essential minerals, and its range. In more than fifty years, the only real breaks in the development of this policy have been two Republican Administrations, Taft's and Hoover's. There are many who think the third, and most dangerous, may be the Administration of Dwight D. Eisenhower.

Gifford Pinchot, never one to minimize his own achievements, gave himself credit for initiating the conservation movement and Theodore Roosevelt credit for selling it to the American people. The record testifies to the effectiveness of both men; but it also testifies that Pinchot himself called William J. McGee "the brains of the conservation movement," and that McGee, in turn, derived most of his ideas from his friend and onetime boss, Major John Wesley Powell, the second director of the U.S. Geological Survey.

Conservation began, actually, with Powell's *Report on the Lands of the Arid Region* in 1878. It hardly had time to raise its head before it was stamped to death by enraged Western Congressmen.

And yet if Congress had accepted and acted on Powell's report, the nation would almost certainly have been spared the worst evils of the Dust Bowl, the incalculable waste of precious topsoil, and the sad failure of thousands of homesteaders on the plains. It would now be farther along with a coherent program of reclamation for the West, and it would have simpler, more workable water laws to deal with. The government would, in fact, own less of the public domain than it does now, for Powell's proposals would have made more land habitable by homesteaders. He suggested yielding to the conditions of the arid West and altering the sacred 160-acre homestead so that an irrigation farmer would get no more than 80 acres, a grazing farmer as much as 2,560 acres. Both farmers would get inseparabale water rights with their land. He called for Federal encouragement of irrigation, at least through surveys, and he pointed out that irrigation in Montana, navigation and flood control on the Missouri-Mississippi, and reclamation of swamps in Louisiana were all involved the moment men began regulating a stream of the Missouri headwaters.

Powell was talking about the multipurpose river-basin development as we know it now, but talking at least sixty years too soon. They called him a revolutionary and they stopped him cold for ten years. Then at the end of the 1880's there began a long, disastrous drought that depopulated whole sections of the plains and drove Congress to action. The most intelligent suggestions at hand were those Powell had made ten years before, and he was empowered to make an irrigation survey of the West.

By a freak of legislative inattention, the enabling law contained an amendment intended to frustrate speculators: It called for the temporary withdrawal from settlement of all potentially irrigable lands in the arid region. No one had bothered to define the arid region, and no one could know what lands were irrigable until the survey was completed. The result was that *all* Western lands were withdrawn, and an enraged Congress found that it had closed the public domain to settlement for the first time in our history as a nation and given Powell unprecedented powers to say when and how it should be reopened.

He had a chance to regulate settlement, discourage the settling of submarginal lands, and steer settlers to those they could actually farm, and he waged a campaign to get public support. He urged the organizing of the new Western states not according to arbitrary county lines but by drainage basins. He pointed out the interdependence of forested mountains, watershed slopes, grazing benchlands, and the lower irrigable lands, and the ways in which water dominated them all. "All the great values of this territory," he told the Montana Constitutional Convention in 1889, "have ultimately to be measured to you in acre feet." Implicit or explicit throughout Powell's argument is the concept upon which all the river-basin plans are built. Every element of modern multipurpose development is in his thinking except hydroelectric power, which he allowed for but whose importance he could not fully foresee.

For his pains the Congressmen stamped Powell down again in 1890, curtailed his powers, and broke up his survey by cutting his appropriations. He retired as head of the Geological Survey in 1894. But one by one, over many years and under the jurisdiction of many bureaus, practically everything he proposed has been enacted into law or built up into cooperative institutions.

In the year of his death, 1902, came the National Reclamation Act, with all its authorizations for water storage, irrigation, stream regulation, and power. Flood control has become, under various rivers and harbors bills, the preoccupation—not to everyone's satisfaction—of the United States Army Corps of Engineers. The hydrographic work that Powell's Irrigation Survey began is now carried on by the Water Supply division of the Geological Survey. Most of the savable forests are reserved. The spirit of the cooperative open range proposed in the 1878 report is achieved by the Taylor Grazing Act—or would be if administration of the act had not been crippled by its enemies.

THE OPPOSITION

While these policies have been developing, opposition has continued virulent and implacable. Senator Pat McCarran's tactics in destroying the Taylor Grazing Act—to investigate and cut appropriations—were precisely the tactics used against Powell by Senator William M. Stewart, also of Nevada, in 1890. Local and special resistance has made some clauses of the Reclamation Act unenforceable. The Forest Service and the Park Service have been under pressure from stockmen, oilmen, and lumbermen—all urging transfer of forest or park lands to private owners or to the states.

Conceivably, concerted attacks at this time could overturn the whole policy of Federal management. They are likely, however, to be only partly successful, to whittle out of government hands the most productive elements now Federally owned or to remove the controls that now prevent great profits by land and power companies and speculators. The grazing lands, including those within the national forests, are in danger; public power is in danger; the 160-acre water limitation within reclamation projects is in danger; and the offshore oil lands are in the most serious danger. Maybe these riches will ultimately be restored, but they will probably return gutted, eroded, and mined out, when they are of no further use to private owners. Then the nation can try to restore them.

It may be taken as gospel that the strongest antagonism to government ownership and management will be found among those who would profit most from their elimination. Whatever the diversionary tactics and political smoke screens, the issue is public interest vs. private profit. If stockmen or landowners grow wrathful about Federal absentee landlordism and call for the "return" of Federal lands to state tax rolls (where they never have been), they do so because a powerful local group can dominate a state government more easily than it can a Federal bureau.

Consider the tactics of the stockmen's attempted raid on the Federal lands in 1946-1947. Following up Senator McCarran's emasculation of the Taylor Grazing Act and working through friendly Western members of Congress such as former Senator Edward V. Robertson and former Representative Frank A. Barrett of Wyoming (now a Senator), the National Livestock Association proposed that all Taylor Grazing District lands be turned over to private ownership. As a second step it wanted reclassification of grazing lands within the national forests, parks, and monuments. Once reclassified, these would be turned over with the Taylor lands to the stockmen. One of the prime objectives was to gobble the Jackson Hole National Monument. Another was to escape government supervision over grazing and the limitations on the animal units per month that could be run on government land.

They might have got the grazing lands alone, for the Grazing Districts were almost helpless and the lands themselves enlist no one's sentiment, as the parks and forests do. But in extending the grab to the parks and forests the stockmen challenged conservationists and vacationers, and these people rose up in such numbers that Representative Barrett's House Committee on Public Lands, which had set out to hold hearings throughout the West, crept home protesting the innocence of its intentions. So violent was the purely Western opposition to the stockmen's proposals that the chief of the Forest Service thought the threat could not arise again for years to come.

But before 1953 was a fortnight old, the Livestock Association was making public noises about "the return of the Federal lands to the tax rolls of the states." Characteristically, it neglected to say that the states on being admitted to the Union gave up any claim to these lands or that in acquiring them the states would saddle themselves with conservation and management costs, expose the lands to overgrazing and erosion again, and reduce the amount of Federal aid for roads and other improvements.

Also before 1953 was a fortnight old, Representative Clair Engle (D., California) had introduced a bill in the House that would authorize California to operate the Central Valley project under Federal reclamation law. He admitted that the state-ownership people would not be fully pleased, but he called state operation a step in the direction of state ownership, and hence a step toward the elimination of the offending acreage and power clauses. His bill paralleled in advance Attorney General Herbert Brownell's suggestion of March 2 that the states manage offshore oil production under continued Federal ownership.

GIMME, GIMME, GIMME

We may expect more pressure for local ownership or local operation, more political support for the Corps of Engineers, whose projects are so opportunely uninhibited, more efforts to have acreage limitations voided on particular projects. The trick of playing off one bureau against another is as old as reclamation itself. Resisting it involves more than a simple defense of the Bureau of Reclamation against the Corps of Engineers, for conservation forces themselves are divided on the wisdom of some projects. Hydroelectric power sites do not last forever; they silt up or suffer impaired flow, and some must be conserved for the future. Moreover, the Hoover Commission's recommendation that Engineers and Reclamation Bureau be fused into one civilian agency meets not only bureau resistance but doubts among the friends of reclamation. The one point on which there is agreement among conservationists is that the Corps of Engineers should be brought under the same organic law, subject to the same restrictions and with the same obligation to enforce them, that the Bureau of Reclamation works under. Otherwise the whole program will be cracked open by political manipulations.

How friendly the Eisenhower Administration will be to the revisionists is still an unanswered question. But there are indications, and some of these have got the conservation people worried.

In San Francisco on January 30 the eleventh annual convention of the National Rural Electric Cooperative Association, representing more than three million farmers, passed a resolution condemning the multimillion-dollar private power lobby that aims at destroying public power and the cooperatives that are associated with it. The convention accused the private power industry of manifesting "the same arrogant disregard for the public interest that it showed in the 1920's," and of obstructing court actions and the "very processes of democratic government." In a companion resolution it asked Congress to reject "a barehanded raid on the commonwealth" threatened by "certain vested interests." That raid, it said, would be calculated to turn over the national forests to private exploitation, sell TVA, the Bonneville Power Administration, and other great government projects to private companies, and kill off the Rural Electrification Administration.

In Cleveland on April 11, former President Herbert Hoover bolstered these fears by urging a program whose object would be to get the Federal government "out of the business of generating and distributing power as soon as possible."

Even more disturbing possibilities were hinted at earlier in January by Drew Pearson's report that Senator Hugh Butler (R., Nebraska) already had an omnibus bill calculated to clear the government out of the West. According to Pearson, Butler's justification for the wholesale transfer will be the transfer of the offshore oil lands, on the reasoning that if the coast states are entitled to these prizes, then the other Western states are entitled to the public lands within their borders.

What does Secretary of the Interior Douglas McKay say in this uproar, which already begins to look like a pitched battle? Before a closed session of Senator Butler's Interior Committee in January he was reported to have said that he (1) disapproved of "some of the efforts to build up Federal controls over electric power and distribution in the Pacific Northwest; (2) favored transfer of the offshore oil lands to the states (this he repeated before the Committee in February); (3)

wanted more control of public lands and electric power at state and local levels instead of in Washington; (4) would not take a definite stand in the jurisdictional dispute between the Departments of the Interior and Agriculture over who should manage the public lands for grazing and lumber production; and (5) approved of continued Federal construction of multipurpose dams, but wanted private power companies to be given a greater share in power distribution and sale. The Secretary seemed to suggest that once government millions had regulated a stream, private power companies might then be allowed to construct power plants at appropriate sites and sell—presumably without wicked government competition—this power to consumers. To one Western conservationist, McKay's program looks like "skim milk for the taxpayer, higher rates for the power user, and cream for the private utilities."

The same dubious construction could be put upon McKay's remarks, early in March, that the continued presence of many thousands of Indians on reservations was an anachronism. Skeptics remember that several Indian reservations have turned out to contain riches in oil, vanadium, and power sites; and history records how Indians have fared when put in private possession of land coveted by white Americans.

DARK CLOUDS GATHERING

The wider the base, said Alexander Hamilton, the better the democratic system will work. The more interests represented, the less danger there is that a single one will be able to dominate. Absentee landlordism of the Federal kind may sometimes suffer from insufficient information, but it is less subject to manipulation or subversion, and in questions of policy it almost invariably will take a broader view than local interests or local government.

The related problems of the public domain dramatize as nothing else can the fundamental differences of philosophy between the Truman and Eisenhower Administrations. If these differences are as great as some people think, the fight over the public domain may be the biggest fight in the Eighty-third Congress. And if the private interests persist in pushing an apparent political advantage against a conservation movement that often sleeps but is a giant when aroused, this issue could cause the Republicans to lose control of the Eighty-fourth Congress.

XX

SOCIAL WELFARE

106. *The Pressing Problem of Old-Age Security* *

PROFESSOR SCHLICHTER begins by pointing out that only half of the men and one tenth of the women over sixty-five years of age are employed; and that of these senior citizens the men may expect to reach seventy-seven; the women, eighty-nine. How can their security be attained? The author finds fault with both employer-instituted and union-negotiated pension systems and criticizes Federal old-age assistance. He favors Federal old-age insurance, but finds it inadequate at present. He recommends that the law be amended to increase considerably the number covered by insurance and that retirement at sixty-five be curtailed. Although the Social Security Act has been amended since this article was written, Professor Schlichter's discussion still poses basic problems of old-age security.

LESS than half of the men and less than one out of ten of the women of sixty-five years of age or over in the United States are at work. A man of sixty-five years of age may expect to live on the average about twelve years longer; a woman nearly fourteen years. How are people going to support themselves for twelve or fourteen years without working? An annuity paying $100 a month for life, if purchased at the age of 65, would cost more than $15,000. If it also provided a payment of $75 a month to a wife who survived her husband and who was about the same age as the husband, it would cost several thousand dollars more. Few persons who reach the age of 65 have savings of $15,000 or more. Consequently, the voluntary savings of individuals can meet only a small part of the need. How retired workers shall be supported is plainly one of the biggest economic problems in the United States.

What should be done about the problem of security in old age? Is the problem being made unnecessarily large and difficult by unwise retirement policies on the part of business? How good are the four principal ways through which the country is now attempting to meet

* Sumner H. Slichter, *The New York Times Magazine*, October 16, 1949, pp. 9, 66-71. Reprinted by permission of the author and the publisher.

the problem—employer-initiated pension plans, union-negotiated plans, the Federal old-age assistance plan, and the Federal old-age pension plan? Do these plans need to be supplemented or superseded by new arrangements? In particular, how good are the pension plans that have been negotiated by trade unions? The fact-finding board in the steel case said that so long as the Government fails to provide security in "an adequate amount, industry should take up the slack." Is this reasonable? Are union-negotiated plans a good way of meeting the problem of old-age security?

The House of Representatives has just passed a bill extending the Federal old-age pension plan to at least 6 million more persons and raising the monthly benefits by roughly 70 per cent. How far would these changes go in meeting the problem of old-age security?

The seriousness of the problem of old-age security is greatly aggravated by the unwise retirement policies of business. Few people retire voluntarily—most retirements occur against the will of the worker at the decision of the employer. The community obviously would be better off if the older persons who were willing to work had jobs and were producing goods. Furthermore, most persons would be happier at work than they are in retirement. Special reasons for early retirement exist, it is true, in the case of executives, technicians and professional people, who hold jobs that require imagination, originality and resourcefulness. These jobs are best held by relatively young men.

For the great majority of jobs, however, the age of 65 is too early for retirement. Hence, the growing practice of retiring all persons at the age of 65 should be decisively halted. Had the rule of retirement at 65 been generally in effect in August, 1949, 3 million fewer people would have been at work in the United States, and the annual output of the economy would have been nearly $11 billion less—except to the extent that the dropping of older workers might have raised the efficiency of younger workers.

Although a higher age of retirement would diminish the size of the problem of old-age security, it would not eliminate the problem. Even at the age of 70 the average male may expect to live nine years longer. An annuity of $100 a month for life at the age of 70 would cost him in excess of $13,000—certainly more than the average worker of 70 would have. Let us look, therefore, at the four principal ways which are now used to provide retired workers with incomes and let us see whether any of them offers a solution for the problem.

I. EMPLOYER-INITIATED PLANS

These plans have been growing by leaps and bounds—from fewer than 200 in 1915 to more than 400 in 1929 and more than 9,000 today.

In the last ten years their growth has been greatly stimulated by the tax laws. More than three-fifths of the employer-initiated plans are non-contributory. Most of the plans were started in order to permit firms to make some overdue retirements. Under the circumstances, managements were hardly able to ask employes to contribute.

Pension plans initiated by private employers have four major deficiencies, and they are clearly not the answer to the problem of old-age security—though they may do much good in the plants where they operate. A primary major deficiency for employer-initiated pension plans is that they will never give adequate coverage. One reason for this is that they do not apply to self-employed persons, of whom there are about 11 million in the United States. They need a source of income after retirement no less than do employes.

Employer-initiated pension plans also fail to give adequate coverage because they are expensive. Hence, only the more prosperous companies will adopt them. Even in the highly prosperous year of 1945, more than one-fourth of all corporations were "in the red." Pensions, depending upon their size, are likely to cost at least 6 to 8 per cent of payrolls. This does not include the special cost of meeting the large accrued liability with which most pension plans start. This special cost is a result of the fact that the plans apply to employes who have worked for the employer for many years and who will soon have reached the age of retirement. No payments have been made before the initiation of the scheme to buy pensions for these employes.

Finally, the employer-initiated plans will not give adequate coverage because they are limited to certain types of employes—usually long-service employes. The present 9,000 employer-initiated plans cover a little more than one-third of the employes of the firms which have the plans.

A second major shortcoming of employer-initiated pension schemes is that they may be abandoned at the will of the employer, leaving the employe without protection. Of 418 plans in existence in 1929, forty-five had been abandoned by 1932.

A third major defect of most employer-initiated pension schemes is that they restrict the movement of workers—a man who leaves one employer to work for another does not ordinarily carry his pension rights with him.

A fourth major defect is the handicap they put on older workers in finding employment. This deficiency is a result of the third one, namely, that employes do not carry their pension rights from one employer to another. Even twenty years' contributions on behalf of a worker will not buy him a very adequate pension unless these contributions are at a high rate. Consequently, a man who is hired at the age of 55 and retired at the age of 65 or 68 would receive a very small pension. Managements do not care to undermine the morale of their workers by giving substandard pensions to employes who are retired, and they avoid this difficulty simply by not taking workers of more than about 45 years of age except for temporary jobs.

II. UNION-NEGOTIATED PLANS

Pension plans negotiated by unions with employers may be less easily abandoned than an employer-initiated plan and they may cover a larger proportion of the employes, but they suffer from the same four major defects as do employer-initiated plans. Consequently, it was a blunder for the fact-finding board in the steel dispute to recommend union-negotiated plans for the various steel companies.

Union-negotiated plans will never give adequate coverage, partly because they do not apply to the self-employed and partly because they can be instituted only in those plants where the employer is making enough money so that he can grant the union demand for pensions, meet the large accrued liability, and hold his own in competition. No matter how strong the union, it cannot impose an adequate pension plan on those employers who are financially weak. The limitation of coverage is especially great when the cost of pensions falls entirely on the employer. Consequently, if union-negotiated plans are established, the workers should contribute part of the cost.

The union-negotiated pension plans which have been established thus far do not, as a rule, permit an employe who leaves an enterprise to carry his pension rights with him to his next job—though some of the stronger unions may be able to correct this defect by negotiating changes in the plans. Union-negotiated pension plans, like employer-initiated plans, discourage employers from hiring older workers and thus handicap older workers in finding jobs.

A special drawback of many union-negotiated pension plans is their financial unsoundness. Many of these plans make no provision for meeting the huge accrued liability with which the plans start. In many cases the cost of the pensions in a decade or so will be so large that the unions will have to consent to a reduction in the pensions in order to gain wage increases. Consequently, the so-called "security" offered by many union-negotiated pension plans is illusory.

The pension fund in the coal industry is a glaring example of an arrangement which provides illusory security because it is financially unsound. No adequate provision has been made to finance the enormous accrued liability with which the scheme started. Nor has the underwriting of the risks been arranged to assure that any part of the payments now being made into the fund will be available to provide pensions ten or twenty years hence for the men who are today counting on getting pensions when they retire. An insurance company which attempted to operate as the miners' welfare fund is being operated would quickly be in trouble with the law.

III. OLD-AGE ASSISTANCE

The old-age assistance program of the Federal Government is the largest single source of income to retired persons. About 2.6 million are drawing old-age assistance, and total old-age assistance payments are roughly twice as large as all of the pension payments made under the Federal old-age pension scheme. More than half of the money now disbursed for old-age assistance comes from the Federal Government, but administration is in the hands of the states.

The old-age assistance program is open to two major objections. One is that it is demoralizing and the other is that it opens the door to grave political abuses. It is demoralizing for people to have to accept charity after a lifetime of work. And since the money comes from general revenues, recipients of aid do not have the satisfaction of knowing that they have made a specific contribution to help finance the payments which they receive.

The fact that payments are based upon a means test makes the plan difficult to administer. Need is difficult to define, and this creates the danger of political favoritism. The danger is aggravated by the fact that payments are made out of general revenue and that most of the states, which administer the scheme, are paying out more Federal money than state money.

During the last ten years the record of old-age assistance strongly suggests that such a scheme cannot be satisfactorily administered. Although unemployment (which tends to be especially high among older persons) dropped from 9.5 million in 1939 to 2.1 million in 1948, payments for old-age assistance increased 2.7 times. There are wide differences between states in the proportion of persons receiving aid, and there are wide variations in average monthly payments even between adjoining states. In Louisiana no less than four out of five persons of 65 years of age or more are receiving old-age assistance—a sudden doubling of the number since June, 1948.

In Oklahoma and Georgia more than half, and in Texas, Colorado, Alabama and Mississippi nearly half of all persons 65 years of age or over are drawing old-age assistance, but in New York and New Jersey the proportion is only one out of ten.

Wide variation also occurs in the size of payments. In Louisiana the average monthly payment has more than doubled between June, 1948, and June, 1949, rising from $22.87 to $47.05. In the two adjoining states of Arkansas and Mississippi the average monthly payment in June, 1949, was $20.95 and $18.80, respectively. Monthly payments in Massachusetts were nearly twice as large as in Vermont and one-third again as large as in Rhode Island.

IV. OLD-AGE INSURANCE

The most satisfactory arrangement for providing income for retired persons is the Federal old-age insurance plan. It avoids the principal weaknesses of the other three schemes. In the first place, it is comprehensive, for it covers all jobs in all plants within the covered industries. It is not limited to the generous and prosperous employers or to the plants where unions are strong. In the second place, it gives enduring protection because it cannot be abrogated at the will of an employer, and employes do not lose their pension rights if their employer goes out of business. In the third place, since employes carry their pension rights with them, the plan does not deter employers from hiring older workers.

In the fourth place, the burden on financially weak employers is limited by the fact that the plan applies alike to all competitors in an industry, by the fact that the accrued liability is met very gradually (as is possible only under a compulsory system), and by the fact that half of the cost falls on employes. In the fifth place, the self-respect of the workers is protected because pensions are given as a matter of right without a means test and are financed, not from general revenues, but from a payroll tax to which both employes and employers contribute equally. Finally, the fact that pensions are paid as a matter of right eliminates the chance for political favoritism.

Although the Federal old-age insurance scheme is basically sound, it has three serious defects—its coverage is inadequate, its eligibility requirements are too strict, and the benefit payments are too low. The coverage is inadequate because the plan does not cover certain important types of workers, such as domestic servants, employes of non-profit institutions, farm employes and the self-employed. All in all, it covers about three out of five jobs. The eligibility requirements are too strict—it takes too long for workers to acquire insured status. As a result, only about one out of five persons of 65 years of age or more is drawing pension benefits or has insured status under the plan. The low benefit payments are indicated by the fact that the average payment for single workers is about $26 a month and for a worker with one dependent, about $40 a month.

The House of Representatives on Oct. 5 passed a bill, H. R. 6,000, which would make substantial improvements in the old-age insurance scheme. The bill would extend the coverage of the act to include nearly one million out of three million domestic service employes, about 200,000 farm laborers, and about 4.5 million urban self-employed. It would extend partial protection, and possibly complete protection, to about 600,000 employes of non-profit institutions.

By voluntary agreement between state governments and the Federal Government, about 3.8 million employes of state and local governments might be covered. The bill would liberalize the eligibility requirements so that newly covered employes would become insured more quickly. Finally, it would raise benefit payments about 70 per cent to an average of between $50 and $60 a month.

The provisions of the bill just passed by the House, though a long step in advance, fall short of the recommendations of the Advisory Council on Social Security appointed two years ago by the Finance Committee of the Senate. This body consisted of seventeen members —six business men, two representatives of organized labor, four persons from the public service, and five persons from university work and scientific research. The council was unanimous in recommending that coverage of the old-age and survivors' insurance be made virtually universal.

For example, the council would cover farmers and professional workers who would not be covered under the recommendations of the Ways and Means Committee. The council was also unanimous in recommending that eligibility requirements be changed so as to permit workers to qualify more promptly for pensions. The council also recommended increases in benefits which would raise the average benefit of a retired worker without dependents from $26 a month to $55 and of a worker with a wife from $40 to $85 a month.

The Federal old-age pension plan, if its coverage were extended to nearly all of the 25 million uncovered jobs and if the average benefits were substantially raised, would provide the country with an adequate plan of old-age security and would limit the dependence of the country upon unsound employer-initiated or union-negotiated plans which tend to tie the worker to one employer and which handicap older workers in obtaining employment.

A comprehensive and adequate old-age insurance plan is the only way of checking the rapidly snowballing old-age assistance payments. The usefulness of the Federal old-age pension plan in relieving the community of dependence on unsound alternative arrangements will depend upon adequacy of benefit payments. Surely it is not unreasonable that the pension of a man with a wife to support should be at least half of his earnings before retirement. In the case of a man who had been earning $300 a month throughout his working life, the recommendations of the Advisory Council would result in a monthly pension of $106.87—a little more than one-third of his monthly earnings.

Although the Federal old-age pension plan can be easily developed to provide adequate protection to retired workers, some employers and some unions may wish to establish supplementary plans. The Federal Government, however, has an obligation to see that supplementary plans really provide the security which they promise, that they do not tie a worker to a given employer, and that they do not encourage employers to discriminate against older workers.

This can be done by requiring that the plans meet certain standards in order for employer contributions to be a deductible expense under the corporate income tax law. These standards should require that the plan be properly underwritten and that the employes who leave the service of an employer take their pension rights with them. In addition, in order to avoid encouraging noncontributory plans in preference to contributory, the Federal Government should permit the contributions of employes to pension plans to be a deductible expenditure under the personal income tax—at least if the employe's contribution is matched by one from his employer.

Can the country afford an adequate scheme of security for old age? With stiff wage demands constantly being made on industry, with large quantities of goods needed for national defense and to provide help to sixteen countries in Europe, can industry produce enough to give decent pensions to retired workers? And are not all schemes by which the community undertakes to provide security for retired workers wrong in principle? Are not such schemes bound to undermine thrift, initiative, self-reliance, and the spirit of independence?

The cost of an old-age pension plan paying benefits moderately more liberal than those included in the bill recently passed by the House or recommended by the Advisory Council on Social Security may be put roughly at 8 per cent of payrolls. In the past, output per man-hour in the United States has increased about 2 per cent a year. If it continues to grow at the rate of 2 per cent a year, it will increase by over 80 per cent in the next thirty years.

Hence, the total cost of a fairly adequate old-age security program would be about one-tenth the increase in production during the next generation—assuming that output per man-hour grows no faster than in the past. The one thing that must be avoided, in order to keep the cost of old-age security within moderate limits, is a further drop in the usual age of retirement. Universal retirement at 65, depriving the community of nearly $11 billion of products a year, would be ten times as costly as the present old-age pension program is today.

The danger that a system of old-age security will undermine thrift is remote. The usual method by which men have provided for their old age has never been thrift—it has been by having plenty of children and expecting the children to help the parents. Certainly pensions which pay 50 per cent more or less than average earnings leave much room for thrift. Furthermore, no one need fear that the incentives to practice thrift are about to disappear—there are many good things which the ordinary person can acquire only by practicing thrift quite rigorously. Any wage-earner who buys a house at present prices will have a good opportunity to be thrifty for years to come.

Nor is old-age security likely to undermine initiative, self-reliance and independence—it is likely to strengthen these qualities. The reason is obvious. The worker, small-business man or high executive who has a minimum of protection for his old age is likely to be willing to take some economic chances which he would not otherwise dare take. The extension of old-age security to small-business men may be particularly useful in making them feel better able to take risks. Certainly if the prospect of a pension is likely to undermine initiative or self-reliance, this probability has been overlooked by the many corporations which have provided generous noncontributory pensions for their executives—the very men who most of all need to have initiative and self-reliance.

One final word of warning. The greatest danger to an adequate old-age security plan is rising prices. A rise of 2 per cent a year in prices would cut the purchasing power of pensions about 45 per cent in thirty years. The greatest danger of rising prices is from wages rising faster than output per man-hour. If unions put up money wages 5 per cent a year and output per man-hour increases 3 per cent a year, prices will have to rise by the difference, or 2 per cent a year. Hence, whether the nation succeeds in providing adequate security for retired workers depends in large measure upon the wage policies of trade unions. If unions push up wages faster than output increases, they undermine the security of all retired workers.

107. *Don't Strangle Your Medicine in Government Red Tape**

THE CONTROVERSY engendered by the recent proposals to amend the Social Security Act to provide for compulsory sickness insurance has produced a vast amount of literature on the subject. This selection and the following one illustrate the tendentious nature of these writings. Dr. E. J. McCormick, a member of the medical profession, indicates what he and many of his fellow physicians and surgeons think of this expansion of the Social Security Act. He defends the existing system of medical care in the United States and argues that the passage of such a measure as the Murray-Wagner-Dingle Bill would seriously undermine the foundations upon which the efficiency of the American system of medical care depends and eventually undermine the foundations of the American governmental system itself. Students of federalism will note his acceptance of state control of public health measures at the same time that he objects to extension of activity on the part of the national government.

WHILE Federal bureaucracies have agitated constantly for expansion of their bureaus and for more and more authority, the American people, under our American system of free enterprise, are continuing to develop plans for providing adequate medical care to workers and their families, and this, too, without paying the price of governmental control and the socialization of medicine.

The chief objection of the American medical profession and most of the people of the United States to the socialization of medicine and its political control by government is the certainty that such a change will definitely lower the quality of medical care now available to the American people. Nowhere in the world in the past 10 years has medicine made the progress that has been made in the United States under our republican system of government.

Physicians are convinced that socialization of medicine such as has been proposed by President Truman, in his national health program, and by Senators Wagner and Murray and Representative Dingell, in the current version of the Wagner-Murray-Dingell bill, will have as its chief effect the building of a new bureau with as many as 200,000 or 300,000 government employes. It will introduce political patronage as

* E. J. McCormick, *The Republican Magazine*, June 1, 1946. Reprinted by permission of the author and the publisher.

the main factor in securing medical service. Such interference will disturb the confidential relationship between doctor and patient that is fundamental in the maintenance of the dignity of the human being. Perhaps worst of all, this communization of medical care will serve to depreciate the quality of medical education which is now higher in the United States than anywhere else in the world and will deter from the study of medicine the type of young man who has come to seek medicine as a distinguished career of service to humanity.

INDIVIDUAL BECOMES SERVILE

Under a proposal such as the Wagner-Murray-Dingell bill, the people, for the sake of an apparent benefit, will surrender control over their lives in health and in sickness to a Federal agency. The constant fear of the loss of benefits that the individual has already paid for will compel his obedience and servility to the bureau that is in power. This very situation prevailed in Germany in all of the years after 1883 when Bismarck first introduced the principles of social security into the German government. These conditions led inevitably to the totalitarianism of Hitler and Goering and Goebbels and led eventually to the destruction of the German government.

In America, the Social Security Act of 1935 provided old age insurance administered by the Federal government and unemployment compensation administered jointly by the Federal and the state governments. Medical care was aided by increased appropriations for health with grants in aid distributed from the United States Public Health Service and the children's bureau to the individual states. These grants in aid served to help mothers and children, to extend the care of the crippled and the blind, and to help others handicapped.

When the Social Security Act was passed, President Roosevelt, after receiving the reports of two special committees which had been appointed to study the subject, did not recommend compulsory sickness insurance, and Congress did not include it in the bill. Nevertheless, the welfare workers and collectivists, who have been trying to gain control of medical science and medical practice for a quarter of a century, have never ceased in the effort to get the Social Security Act amended to include compulsory sickness insurance. There have been three Wagner-Murray-Dingell bills. In each of these measures, Senator Wagner has endeavored to correct some of the faults of the previous legislation. Never, however, has he, nor the group which urges him into these activities, desisted from their desire to put medical care under a Federal bureaucracy.

PATIENT LOSES INITIATIVE

In his statement to the American people, President Truman said that these proposals were not socialized medicine. This is playing with words. If socialization means removal of responsibilities from the individual and division of the responsibilities among groups of people, the bill is socialized medicine. If socialization means taking the initiative away from the patient and from his doctor and putting it in a Federal bureau, this proposal is socialized medicine.

Both President Truman and Senator Wagner insist that this measure grants the free choice of a doctor. This it never does. It grants only the free choice of the kind of doctor who is willing to sink his medical science and his personal responsibility into a government agency and who is willing to engage in that kind of medical service. A recent study, made by investigators who visited thousands of doctors in their offices and in their homes, revealed that more than 90 per cent of the doctors have little, if any, favor for such a system.

The medical profession feels that the enactment of this legislation would undermine and destroy our system of medicine that has developed by gradual evolution. It would make the social security board and the surgeon general of the United States Public Health Service virtual dictators over all American medicine. The surgeon general of the United States Public Health Service could say who is a specialist and who is not. He could tell a doctor how many people he could serve and he could say which hospitals would be entitled to participate.

In the United States, our hospitals have developed out of that fundamental motive that makes the care of the sick one of the highest spiritual obligations. Our great Catholic, Jewish, and Protestant hospitals are intimately associated with religion and with the right of freedom of worship. Even these hospitals might have to modify their practice to meet the dictates of government agencies from which they would derive their principal support.

TELL ALL—GET NOTHING

The government system, proposed by the Wagner-Murray-Dingell bill, would live by the funds taken from the worker and from his employer. However, the worker or any member of his family who wanted to take advantage of his insurance would have to yield to a government agency intimate facts concerning his illness, its causes, the financial situation of his family, and other information which should remain confidential between the doctor and his patient.

The American medical profession and the people of the United States have not been idle in trying to meet the challenge for adequate medical care for all at a price they can afford to pay. Our Blue Cross Hospital plans now provide hospitalization and insurance for 20 million people. Through industries and through our private insurance companies at least 40 million people are protected, either in whole, or in part, against accidents and illnesses. Proposed legislation, such as the Hill-Burton bill and the National Science Foundation measure, and appropriations for the United States Public Health Service and the children's bureau, make certain that the construction of hospitals and health centers will be extended, that facilities for medical research and education will be improved, and that our nation will continue to progress in the provision of medical care.

These activities are in accordance with the scientific method which provides that we must determine the area of need and then apply the remedy generally to that area. We are having surveys made in each of our states to determine the special medical needs that exist, then we will utilize to the fullest extent local, county, and state facilities and funds. We will accept the aid of Federal grants with these and continue to improve the facilities and the quality of medical service. Few people realize that much of our illness is not controllable by anything that medical science can do, but only by maintaining a high standard of living and extending such a standard to more and more people.

The American Medical Association recognizes these facts in its own program for improving the nation's health. We urge a minimum standard of nutrition, housing, clothing, and recreation as fundamental to good health. We urge the provision of preventive medical care by efficient and competent health departments with sufficient equipment to meet fundamental needs. We urge that all the procedures established for the protection of prospective mothers and for adequate medical care in childhood be made available to all at a price that they can afford to pay.

We have always felt, however, that the individual should be able to show his need before he is pauperized by a complacent government.

The child throughout infancy should have proper attention, including proper nutrition, immunization against diseases, and other services included in infant welfare. However, the medical profession knows that such services are best supplied by personal contact between the mother of the child and the individual physician. For all veterans, the medical profession urges the best possible medical care, including hospitalization, wherever the disability can be related to war service. Indeed, every veteran should be provided with adequate medical service if he is unable to provide it for himself.

STATE AID IS ENOUGH

In all of these fields, the medical profession recommends that participation by the Federal government be limited to the provision of the necessary funds to the individual states so that there may be local and state control in all matters related to the public health. It is a fundamental principle, established by those who wrote the Constitution of the United States, that the care of the sick is a matter of state control and not of Federal control. There are decisions of the Supreme Court of the United States that affirm this principle. Every child, in a civics class in high school, learns that all responsibilities and duties, not specifically assigned to the Federal government by the Constitution, are within the provinces of the individual states.

Fundamental to the public health and the alleviation of illness is widespread education about health and disease and the prevention of disease. Such education is a necessary function of all departments of public health, of medical associations, and of school authorities, and, particularly, a function of the father and the mother who teach the child in the home.

The national health program of the American Medical Association will develop a system of medical care consistent with the American system of government. For the people it will maintain the essentials of individual initiative and personal responsibility that are a part of the American spirit—the American way of life.

The Council on Medical Service of the American Medical Association and the board of trustees of the American Medical Association, representing 120,000 members of the medical profession in America, expect to have in operation before the end of the current year voluntary prepayment medical plans in more than 40 states.

VOLUNTARY SYSTEM IS BEST

The evidence at hand plainly indicates that under such a voluntary system the highest type of medical care can be given to the people of the United States, including the indigent. In no instance will the cost of such voluntary prepayment medical care approach the great cost which a Federal plan of socialized medicine or political medicine will demand. It has been pointed out by those who have studied the bills for compulsory health insurance, which have been introduced in Washington, that the cost would not be less than $4 billion a year.

Those who are interested in preservation of this American republic and the Constitution of the United States, which has made this country the greatest country in the world, should give considerable thought to the following statement made by Albert Richie:

> Through expenditure of prodigious sums of public money, and through the conditions the government imposes upon the states before they may receive these funds, American self-government is being destroyed before our eyes.

Will Rogers once said: "We ought not spend money we do not have for things we do not need."

It is the thought of most informed Americans that we have, at present, the best of everything in the United States, including medical service.

It is paradoxical, indeed, that some should feel that we should install in our country any part of the philosophies of the old world. There is nothing in history that would lead anyone to believe that these philosophies and ideologies have, in any instance, been successful when the United States in 150 years, under a republican form of government with opportunity for all, has become the greatest nation in the world.

108. *Letter to a Family Doctor* *

IN THE PREVIOUS ARTICLE (107) a member of the medical profession attacked the proposal for compulsory medical insurance. In this selection Mr. DeVoto, a layman, has not undertaken to defend the system under attack; he has chosen to level his shafts at the methods of the medical profession in attacking the proposed amendments to the Social Security Act and in defending the present system of medical care. Mr. DeVoto has expressed for many of his fellow laymen their doubts concerning the omniscience of the medical profession. That this is a controversial matter need hardly be stated but it is, nevertheless, a problem upon which the American citizen must eventually pass.

DEAR Doctor Jay: My check for $14.45 accompanies this letter. I have taken two deductions from the $15 for which you billed me. The first one, thirty cents, is the 2 per cent for current payment customary in

* Bernard DeVoto, *Harper's Magazine*, 202 (January, 1951), pp. 56-60. Copyright, 1951, by Harper and Brothers. Reprinted by permission of the author and the publisher.

commercial transactions; business ethics, I gather, now govern our relationship. I will explain the remaining twenty-five cents in a moment.

I fully understand why you have been forced to raise your fee for house calls from $10 to $15, though I am not able to adjust my own professional fees so readily to the rise in living costs. I am still being paid for the Easy Chair just what I was getting in June, 1946 when I wrote a piece attacking the anti-vivisectionists for which you and about a thousand other medical men wrote me letters of approval. (Many of them phrased so similarly as to suggest that someone had sent out word to give me a hand.) Still, though my income is not large enough to enable me to pay for my children's education this year without dipping into savings, I realize that it is large enough to put me, statistically, in the topmost 5 per cent of Americans. I am therefore glad to send you the $15, less deductions, as payment for your treatment of my son's cold plus my share of your treatment of others who cannot afford your full fee or perhaps any of it. The 95 per cent of my fellow-countrymen who are less able than I to afford medical treatment thrust themselves on my attention. I will help American medicine take care of them—as long as I can.

I do not know how long that will be. This month the hospital to whose staff you belong asked me to contribute to its endowment drive. The last time it did so I sent what was for me a thumping big check, much larger than I could really afford. I would be glad to contribute now, all the more glad because of the magnificent care I received during the three weeks I spent there last April. But this year I cannot afford to give the hospital a dime. One reason, besides taxes and the inflation, is that the cost of those three weeks, the fee of the surgeon who operated on me, and the loss of income while I was convalescing used up all my margin. The chairman of the drive tells me that it is going to fall far short of its goal; many people on whom it could once depend for contributions can no longer afford them. He, you, and I all know how grave a danger this is to the hospital, to your profession, and to the public. Who is going to pay the hospital's deficits and who is going to support its medical research now that we of the middle class no longer can? I understand your trade association, the AMA, to say that though it cannot answer that question it will not permit the government to pay for them.

I thank you for the publicity matter which you inclosed with your statement. I am especially glad to have the copy of Dr. Elmer L. Henderson's inaugural address, "Medical Progress versus Political Medicine." I understand that in sending me this material you were helping in the crusade which Messrs. Whitaker & Baxter outlined for you in "A Simplified Blueprint of the Campaign against Compulsory Health

Insurance." You must, they tell you there, "do double duty until this issue is resolved." You must, they say, "help in treating the ills of the body politic." But I must tell you that as part of the body politic I do not think you are qualified either to diagnose or to treat such illnesses, and I know that advertising agencies will make any diagnosis asked for on a fee-for-service basis.

Your proprietary advertising reached me opportunely. I was following the ads which you were running in the Boston newspapers. I found them dishonest, and they further annoyed me by the copywriter's assumption that I am a fool. But they harmonized well with the ads on the opposite page, which were trying to sell me water from a radium spring that is guaranteed to cure everything from impotence to cancer. They set out to rouse the same fears to the same ends. Your radio commercials interested me too. Little dramatic sketches presented you as the old family doctor, with the nobility and self-sacrifice which copywriters now have you wearing like a streetwalker's smile, and assured me that you were guarding my health (without fee, the implication was) and simultaneously protecting me from political enslavement. I observed that as soon as you signed off, another little drama came on. There was a woman who was very, very tired. She was so exhausted and suffered so much from backache that she could not greet her husband with the loving eagerness which alone could save their marriage. It turned out that she needed the dollar economy-size of a cathartic which acts painlessly, and I rejoiced that the advertising agencies were saving freedom, monogamy, and peristalsis in the same half-hour.

You and a tobacco company will relieve throat irritation; you and Seneca Snake Oil will get rid of gallstones. Your advertising has already cost you a very great deal of the prestige which the advertising agency told you would put your campaign over. And it has radically changed the relationship between you and me. Your ads speak of the trust between physician and patient, so noble it says here, so sacred, so certain to be destroyed by what the propaganda calls socialism. But I do not like any kind of solicitation that trades on prestige or on such fears and hopes as illness necessarily involves, and I will not tolerate political solicitation in a relationship of trust. Solicitors who call at my house must use the back door.

My second deduction, the twenty-five cents, signifies that I will not help pay for the $25 assessment you sent to the AMA to run these ads and print these pamphlets. I will not help you finance distortion and demagoguery. In an envelope that has your name and degree on it you tell me by way of Dr. Henderson that "all infectious diseases have been brought under effective methods of prevention, control, and treatment." I am to have no more colds, then, and my friend's daughter need not have died of poliomyelitis last summer. Cure guaranteed, Dr. Henderson's ad says in effect, and it was only through inadvertence that he did not mention the great increase in chronic diseases, especially among the elderly, and that he did not point out how our increased longevity makes more medical service necessary, not less. There is much further disingenuousness in his anthem of self-praise but let us pass over it. I am willing to grant him that on the whole "the history of American medicine is a vibrant, continuing story of human progress." But when you follow him into a political agitation that is at once arrogant, insolent, and dishonest, someone has got to call you.

"It is," the two of you say, "the administrative arm of our Government in Washington which has failed us in this generation—a Government which is sick with intellectual dishonesty, with avarice, with moral laxity, and with reckless excesses." You say that to me when you send me his speech, Doctor. You sound like Mr. Vishinsky, and that eloquent rabble-rouser was surely pleased by your allusion to "the totalitarian plan which Washington directs and the people pay for." You and Dr. Henderson are to be highlighted in your nobility against the government's viciousness, and I am to rejoice that, all other moral heroisms having been defeated, yours will keep us free. And the conspiracy, though so powerful, is so small. You tell me that the people who do not stand on the AMA's party line are "a comparatively small group of little men—little men whose lust for power is far out of proportion to their intellectual capacity, their spiritual understanding, their economic realism, or their political honesty." Expert hysterical rabble-rousing, Doctor, and you add, "Their real objective is to gain control over all fields of human endeavor. Their real objective is to strip the American people of self-determination and self-government and make them a Socialist State in the pathetic pattern of the socially and economically bankrupt Nations of Europe which we, the American people, are seeking to rescue from poverty and oppression." You go on to say that the issue is "whether we are to become a Socialist State, under the yoke of a Government bureaucracy, dominated by selfish, cynical men who believe the American people are no longer competent to care for themselves." You and Dr. Henderson and his publicity adviser, from your advertising agency I suppose, appear to believe that the American people are no longer competent to think for themselves. But you make me wonder how competent you are.

Much might be said about this delirious rant, which would have landed Dr. Henderson before the un-American Activities Committee if it had been circulated by a group of excited college boys who had just heard of Marx. One thing is this: you and Dr. Henderson are saying what is not so. Another is this: Dr. Henderson acquires no immunity by wrapping the flag round the vested interest of the AMA's bureaucracy and trustees. Your acquiescence in his claptrap withdraws you from my respect but I take it to be a consequence of the fact that you have not done much thinking about the subject he is misrepresenting. Medicine is your field, not economics, sociology, or government. You come innocent and virginal to social thinking. It is a fair bet that, like thousands of other physicians whose rage Dr. Henderson is whipping up, you have not even read the bills for compulsory payroll deductions for medical insurance which, after all, are what he is talking about. You probably do not know what the bills say, and you had to work so hard on biochemistry at college that you did not learn to detect the propaganda in such phrases as "socialized medicine," "statism," "socialism," and "totalitarianism." With what valorous stupidity you charge head down at those red rags—and all they are concealing is certain bills which would require some people to take out medical insurance. Bills that are an admittedly clumsy attempt to remedy an intolerable situation which your trade association refuses to face realistically and which, it makes clear, must be solved without its help.

You are a busy man, I know. You have not got time to find out for yourself, though every day you see some of the conditions that the bills are trying to alleviate. So you check your intelligence with the AMA, whose refusal to do anything grows more reactionary as conditions grow more alarming. And with your intelligence and your $25 in its pocket, the AMA systematically distorts the facts and misrepresents the conditions to you. You docilely swallow the cure-guaranteed elixir which your propagandists prescribe. And, docile to them but truculent to me, you send me Dr. Henderson's nonsense and forfeit your status.

A friend of mine, a Vermonter, has a useful locution. He does not say, "Joe is a damned fool." Knowing the mixed nature of the human being and the fallibility of human judgment, he says instead, "Joe puts me in mind of a damned fool." What you put me in mind of, Doctor, is a sap.

You had better stop acting like a sap. Our constitutionally elected government, which has to do something about an increasingly alarming social situation that the AMA refuses to deal with at all except on its own long-obsolete terms—do you really think it is what Dr. Henderson says it is? You had better think again, fast and hard. And this pamphlet called "Old Doc Truman's Pink Pills." Have you read it, Doctor? Take the passage that begins on page 27. It equates the Democrats, the party which a majority of our citizens have maintained in power, with Communists, and in doing so it makes some of the most scabrous and feculent statements I have ever seen in print. Its distributors have learned a little caution, but not much, from the public outrage that followed the notorious "Dear Christian Colleague" letter which one of your propaganda organizations sent out. As it describes the plot of various committees and learned foundations to deliver medicine and the United States over to Stalin, it insistently repeats Jewish names. It never quite says right out that the Democrat-Communist plot is a Jewish plot but it is so written as to make many a reader believe that it is. Thus it arrives at a standard technique of totalitarianism: anti-Semitism. Do you accept responsibility for this? You will be held responsible. I got the pamphlet from the office of your State medical society and the girl there said that it was for distribution to patients. You paid the $25 assessment. The noble old family friend has corrupted the relationship of trust with anti-Semitism.

I know that you, personally, do not approve of this, but there it is. Thousands of your colleagues do not, either, and still there it is. Take a tumble to yourself.

And take a tumble to your leaders. Dr. Henderson says that in three more years ninety million people will be enrolled in voluntary health-insurance plans and that "when that number has been reached, the problem will be largely resolved." Even if his wild guess should prove accurate, and even if all those voluntary plans should prove adequate, *will* the problem be "largely resolved"? Dr. Henderson will be satisfied if the remaining 40 per cent of the population are without insurance—will you be satisfied? And are you sure that the AMA will support the voluntary plans which it is now praising? For years it opposed voluntary health insurance as violently as it now opposes payroll deductions. Twenty-six state medical societies, I make it, have sponsored legislation which limits such plans to those that are controlled wholly by physicians. That is, plans in which neither the public nor the subscriber has effective power. Many medical societies have threatened disciplinary action—up to measures which would make practice impossible—against any of their members who participate in any other kind of plan. Some have been convicted of conspiracy in restraint of trade—which is a crime, Doctor—and others are under indictment for such interference with *voluntary* prepayment plans. The AMA has fought hard against comprehensive prepayment plans. It has tried to kill those that have succeeded. On the showing so far, is it honest about voluntary insurance or is it throwing dust in my eyes and yours?

Like a lot of physicians, a lot of us laymen are fed to the teeth with the AMA's methods. With its persistently negative approach to everything. With its unvarying misrepresentation of the efforts other countries are making to solve the problem. With its "crusade" and its "battle" and its vilification of the government, the public, and its own members who speak out. With its uniformly misleading attack on "government medicine." Everyone in the military services is under a system of "government medicine"; so is everyone in a veterans' hospital or receiving out-patient treatment from one. The Public Health Service is "government medicine." Several thousand of your colleagues who have had the best training available are practicing "government medicine." Are they venal, inferior, and suppressed?

One of your ads listed "damage to research" among the ills certain to follow "government domination of the people's medical affairs under compulsory health insurance." What about that? The hospital which asked me for a contribution is carrying out fundamentally important researches that are being paid for by the government. They are entirely in the hospital's hands. How have they been damaged? As a member of a committee of the National Research Council, you regularly go to Washington to appraise projects in medical research for which the government is to pay. Your committee is composed exclusively of medical men who are not in the government service. You decide whether a project is valuable and how much ought to be spent on it; the project then passes to representatives of the government just long enough for them to allocate the money for it; it then passes entirely out of their hands and the government has no more to do with it till private medicine has finished the job. . . . Why do you submit to a patent misrepresentation? Why do you try to deceive me?

The advertising, propaganda, and vilification which the AMA conducts is steadily, and now seriously, undermining your professional standing and prestige. The public very much needs both. The traditional system of medical practice has burst its seams; it is now inadequate and outworn. We are going to have something different. No matter what your propagandists say, it is certain to be not a single system but multiple and mixed. And there is no chance whatever that the AMA will get what it demands—no chance that the mixed system will be developed and administered solely by doctors. This is a public matter, a community and national matter. It requires innumerable skills which medical men simply have not got, and it must be under the unremitting scrutiny of representatives of the public with power to act. Medical knowledge is only one of many kinds of knowledge that are required for social action.

But you and your colleagues can shape the future of American medicine if you will accept the responsibility. If you study the problem and act to solve it, not to prevent its being solved. If you turn back the AMA's headlong opposition to every change not approved by the extremely small group of men who enforce its reactionary policy on its whole membership. (Is there no lust for power on the top level of the AMA? And how much of this policy is designed to secure to a very few men the largest possible incomes while the average income of medical men is smaller than it would be if people could afford to pay their doctors' bills?) If you stop acting like a sap, then you can count on shaping the solution. But time passes, the problem grows more desperate all the time, and a solution will be worked out somehow—with, without, or in spite of you. It had better be with your help.

Desperate social problems have to be solved, Doctor; they are solved as needs must, if it comes to that. Even if we accept Dr. Henderson's figures, 40 per cent of the population will have no insurance protection against medical expense. Of his 60 per cent, only a part will have adequate insurance. Ward service in the hospital that is trying to raise funds now costs $10 a day, the cheapest room $18 a day. Last week in the out-patient department I saw a patient getting a prescription filled at a drug window. It called for six capsules of aureomycin a day for ten days. The hospital was selling him the capsules at cost, forty cents apiece, $24. If his job paid him $40 a week, he could not afford them. In that case the hospital would give them to him, but the hospital had to pay $24 for them—and it can no longer get its deficits paid by contribution. Yet aureomycin is cheap compared to certain other remedies which medical research—in part supported by government appropriation—has developed. How could he afford ACTH, or the hospital afford it for him?

There are other considerations too. You know that, in spite of what your advertising says, the only places where American medicine can fully live up to its possibilities are the teaching hospitals. You know that elsewhere it is not doing as well as it wants to and must. You know that there are many areas inadequately provided with doctors, hospitals, and the proper equipment for tests, treatment, and research. You know that some doctors are not well enough trained—with the cost of training climbing before your eyes—and that some hospitals are not good enough—with the cost of making them better steadily mounting.

You know too that thousands of physicians disapprove of the AMA policy, are alarmed by it, and want to substitute for it one which will enable the profession to grapple successfully with all these problems. And you know that the hard facts of a rapidly changing world are forcing thousands of other physicians into activities—contract practice is one of them—which the AMA condemns. You know that many thousands of your colleagues agree with Dr. James Howard Means, who is not a Communist, who I think is not a Democrat either, but who *is* Chief of Medicine at a great hospital and Professor of Clinical Medicine at a great medical school. "A learned profession has sunk, or been dragged, in its political sphere, to a distressingly low level," Dr. Means wrote, and he went on, "What organized medicine needs . . . is a new and more enlightened leadership."

That puts it up to you, Doctor. For the campaign of what the AMA calls "public education" run by an advertising agency, you had better substitute one of self-education. You had better adopt the scientific attitude and find out what the facts are and what, besides propaganda, can be done about them. You might begin by reminding Dr. Henderson of his oath: "I shall strive constantly to maintain the ethics of the medical profession and to promote the public health and welfare." The public does not consider misrepresentation ethical. The AMA is not promoting public health and welfare by intimidating its members, trying to frighten laymen, lapsing into anti-Semitism, and accusing a government which has also sworn to promote the public welfare, of conspiring with Communists to stamp out freedom in the United States.

You can hold your leadership to proper ends, Doctor, or you can repudiate it. You have that option. But if you are to retain the public respect that has been yours or if you are to do your part in guiding the future of medicine in the United States, you have no other choice.

109. *The White House Conference on Education--Summary Statement* *

AS HAS BEEN KNOWN for some time, the schools in current use and on the drawing boards will not be adequate to house the foreseeable school population; there are not enough teachers to staff the schools properly; the curricula offered do not meet the needs of the community as a whole; and existing tax programs provide insufficient revenue. It has been obvious that a realistic re-evaluation of the purpose and function of American education is essential. In December, 1954, President Eisenhower appointed a Committee for the White House Conference on Education to furnish "the most thorough, widespread, and concerted study the American people have ever made of their educational problems." The governors of the states and territories were asked to call local, regional, and state conferences on education prior to the national meeting, and more

* Reprinted from The Committee for the White House Conference on Education, *A Report to the President*, Washington, D.C., April, 1956, pp. 4-7.

than 3,000 such conferences were held before the White House Conference on Education of November 28–December 1, 1955. A summary of the conference recommendations follows. The magnitude of its recommendations is indicated in the suggestion that funds spent on educational services be doubled within the next decade.

FROM THE WORK of the Committee for the White House Conference on Education, one fundamental fact emerges: schools now affect the welfare of the United States more than ever before in history, and this new importance of education has been dangerously underestimated for a long time.

Some of the reasons for the rapidly increasing importance of the schools have been often noted. Ignorance is a far greater handicap to an individual than it was a generation ago, and an uneducated populace is a greater handicap to a nation. This trend is obviously going to continue and quicken.

An equally important and less frequently mentioned reason for the growing importance of education is the plain fact that the schools have become the chief instrument for keeping this nation the fabled land of opportunity it started out to be. In other decades, the opportunities of America lay primarily in escape from the rigid class barriers of Europe, the availability of free land at the frontier, and the excitement of a violently growing nation, where farms often became villages and villages became cities within the span of one human life. When the frontier was closed, it would have been easy for opportunities to dry up in this Nation, and for rigid class barriers to develop. It has been primarily the schools which have prevented this from happening. As long as good schools are available, a man is not frozen at any level of our economy, nor is his son. Schools free men to rise to the level of their natural abilities. Hope for personal advancement and the advancement of one's children is, of course, one of the great wellsprings of human energy. The schools, more than any other agency, supply this hope in America today. By providing a channel for ambition, they have taken the place of the frontier, and in a highly technical era, have preserved the independent spirit of a pioneer nation. The schools stand as the chief expression of the American tradition of fair play for everyone, and a fresh start for each generation.

It is this fundamental conception of schools designed to give a fresh start to each generation that has broadened the ideals of education in America so much in the past 25 years. It is no longer thought proper to restrict educational programs to the skills of the mind, even though those skills remain of fundamental importance. Schools also attempt to improve children's health, to provide vocational training, and to do anything else which will help bring a child up to the starting line of adult life as even with his contemporaries as native differences in ability permit.

The most practical aspect of this new concept of education is that it calls for the most careful mining and refining of all human talents in the land—it is in itself a kind of law against waste. This new educational ideal represents the fullest flowering of the long western tradition of emphasizing the dignity of the individual. Many difficulties, of course, attend its development, but the members of this Committee believe that in essence it is noble and right, and that in the long run it will prove to be one of the great strengths of America.

It is, of course, obvious that much progress has been made toward realizing this new educational ideal in the United States during the recent past. It is the belief of this Committee, however, that improvement has been nowhere near fast enough. The onrush of science has outstripped the schools. What is even more important, ideals of human conduct have in some areas advanced as rapidly as technology. Many a school which seemed good enough a generation ago now seems a disgrace to the community where it stands.

The schools have fallen far behind both the aspirations of the American people and their capabilities. In the opinion of this Committee, there is growing resolve throughout the Nation to close the gap between educational ideals and educational realities. This Committee therefore makes the following fundamental recommendations:

1. We recommend that school authorities emphasize the importance of priorities in education. This Committee has embraced with enthusiasm the concept of schools which provide a great variety of services designed to do all that is possible to fit children for fruitful adult lives, but there is real danger that in attempting to do everything a little, schools may end by doing nothing well. At present, school funds are limited, and the student's time will always be limited. It is essential that schools pursue a policy of giving children first things first. In the rush for a great quantity of courses, quality must not be lost. The desire to provide education for all American children need not be inconsistent with the need to provide full opportunity for the gifted.

2. We recommend that the American people study carefully their systems of school organization and consider measures to deny funds, other than local, to districts which do not, after reasonable time, organize on an efficient basis. If the American people are asked to make sacrifices for better education, they deserve to have their funds used as efficiently as possible. This cannot be done without a great deal

of reorganization in both rural and urban areas. There is no excuse for the existence of the 8,674 school districts which operate no schools. That is just one dramatic example of the need for reorganization. There is special need for studies of school systems in large cities, where most American children are now congregated. Ways must be found to decentralize large urban school systems to make them more responsive to the will of the people.

3. We recommend that local boards of education quickly assess their school building needs, and give this information to their State departments of education, and that the chief State school officers quickly relay this information to the United States Office of Education. Responsible estimates place the Nation's school building need at from less than 200,000 to nearly a half-million additional classrooms by 1960. Inadequate communication between local school districts and State departments of education is the chief cause for these contradictory figures. This Committee also recommends that every community and every State do all that is economically possible to construct the buildings required, and that during such emergency periods as now exist, Federal funds also be used wherever shown to be necessary. In the richest nation in all history, there is no valid reason for the grimy, dilapidated, and overcrowded school buildings which too many children now occupy. It is an ironic truth that most Americans would not permit their children to live in a house which is as bad as the school buildings which many pupils are forced by law to attend.

4. We recommend that greater inducements of all kinds be offered to attract and retain enough good teachers, and that during the coming decade of teacher shortages, every effort be made to utilize the services of available teachers more effectively. Practical steps must be taken to change the concept of teaching as an impoverished occupation. Teaching must be made a financially comfortable profession. Every effort must be made to devise ways to reward teachers according to their ability without opening the school door to unfair personnel practices. Present salary schedules have the effect of discouraging many able people from entering the profession. Teacher preparation programs have the reputation of requiring needless and repetitious courses. This reputation has the effect of deterring brilliant young people from becoming teachers. Salary schedules and preparation courses should be reexamined and changed where necessary to make the teaching profession more attractive to the most able young men and women. This Committee believes that the next decade and possibly two decades will be emergency periods during which the teacher shortage will grow more acute, but that there is ample reason to hope for sufficient supplies of good teachers in the long run.

5. We recommend that a new look be taken at the entire question of how much money this society should spend on education. In view of the recommendations of this Committee concerning the objectives of education, teachers, and buildings, it seems obvious that within the next decade the dollars spent on education in this Nation should be approximately doubled. Such an increase in expenditure would be an accurate reflection of the importance of education in this society. The exact sources of the necessary funds will be determined more easily when there is more public agreement that the funds must be provided, and more vigorous determination to do something about it. In the opinion of this Committee, money for schools must continue to come from all three levels of government, with a portion of funds for school buildings being made available by the Federal Government on an emergency basis. Good schools are admittedly expensive, but not nearly so expensive in the long run as poor ones.

6. We recommend that every possible step be taken to encourage the interest and activity of all citizens in school affairs. Citizen advisory groups, organizations of parents and teachers, education conferences, and all other means at the disposal of the people of a democracy should be utilized to keep the schools in close contact with the people. In the final analysis, it is only the public which can create good schools and nurture them. In the long run, schools must do what the public wants, and if no strong public will is made known, schools falter. Public interest in education is aroused only by knowledge of problems and intentions, and can continue only if the public can play an active role in school affairs.

7. We recommend that a White House Conference on Higher Education, similar in scope to the program just concluded on the needs of elementary and secondary schools, be held promptly to consider the many complex problems facing, or soon to face, the nation's colleges and universities. This Committee believes there is yet time to acquaint the American people with their imminent needs in higher education, but the time grows shorter and shorter. The flood of students now in the elementary and secondary schools is not far away from the colleges. If the people of the United States expect to attract more and more students into college, they must begin preparing for them now.

XXI

FOREIGN RELATIONS

110. *The Responsibility for Decision in Foreign Policy* *

Dean Acheson, Secretary of State in the Truman Administration, places the responsibility for decision in foreign policy directly on the President. The Congress, he says, is divided into too many wings and blocs to be able to put forth a unified, consistent foreign policy. In making his decision, the President may ask advice of whomever he chooses, but in the field of foreign policy the Secretary of State is especially well fitted because he is supported by the fact-gathering and fact-analyzing agencies of the Department of State. The President, having listened to the expert information, reaches whatever seems to him to be the best solution.

In giving one's reflections on "The Responsibility for Decision in Foreign Policy" two lines of thought occur. One concerns the importance of decisiveness in conducting foreign relations, the effect of indecision, or no decision, or contradictory decisions. The other relates to the body or person upon whom rests the final responsibility for making the decisions which determine our course as a nation, and how this task is or should be performed. Both lines start from a common point—where the responsibility and authority lie.

In our American system the President is the person charged with the heavy duty of giving us the line to follow in our dealings with other nations. But, wholly apart from constitutional and legal considerations, his will is not given unlimited scope. In the first place, he is making

* Dean Acheson, *The Yale Review*, XLIV (Autumn, 1954), pp. 1-12. Reprinted with permission from *The Yale Review*, copyright Yale University Press.

decisions about our relations with foreign nations—countries, areas, peoples outside of the United States where our laws do not govern and our writ does not run, where the preconceptions of American life are not taken for granted—in short, that vast portion of the earth's surface where Americans are foreigners. The very idea requires the enlightenment which came to the old mountaineer who took his first train ride from his Appalachian crossroads to town, with his face pressed against the window. When the train stopped, he heaved a deep sigh and said to his companion, "John, there's a heap of folks between here and home, and I guess, by God, we ain't seen half of 'em."

Here is the beginning of understanding of foreign affairs.

It is amid the manifold complexities of the relations between the external world and our own by-no-means-simple country that the President must lay down the line to follow. Whether we, his fellow citizens, follow it or not is another matter. And this suggests the second factor qualifying the freedom of the President's will in reaching his decisions. He is deciding for this particular country at a particular time and under particular circumstances. So there is involved the kind of country and people he leads—the sort of ideas we have inherited and now hold, our traditions and affiliations, our physical resources and the use to which we are putting them and are capable of putting them. All these elements narrow and affect the course of decisions, as currents, winds, shoals, and land affect the decisions of the mariner.

But to return to our point, the final responsibility for decision lies with the President. Sometimes confusion arises about this. We hear it said that the National Security Council is to make, or has made, some important decision. This is an illusion, and a most troublesome one. The NSC decides nothing. It is merely a mechanism for preparing and presenting matters for the President's decision. The power and the responsibility lie with him. He can accept, modify, reject, or do nothing with recommendations from the Council, which is merely a meeting of certain of his advisers. If he does nothing, no decision is made, or a decision to do nothing is made by default. However much the Council's staff is elaborated, it remains a forum—and one which can be very useful—for determining the main problems which require decision and for presenting recommendations to the President.

Again, one reads from time to time that at some meeting with "leaders on the Hill" this or that matter of foreign policy was "decided." This, too, I believe, involves a misconception. These meetings produce not so much a decision of policy as opinions as to whether or how a particular proposal or decision in which Congressional action will be needed can be carried out. Again the responsibility for deciding whether or how to go ahead rests with the President.

It is placed there by the Constitution and confirmed by a century and three-quarters of experience. The Presidential system supported by the separation of powers is the special American contribution to the science and art of government. It is a contribution which presents its problems, which calls for strong and decisive leadership, but which, given such leadership, has served the country well. Under it the President, the only official in the country elected by all the people, the leader of the dominant political party, the chief magistrate, is the head. His cabinet officers, the chiefs of the departments of government, are selected by him, hold their tenure at his pleasure, and are advisers to him. They can be effective only through him and with his support.

Attempts to graft onto this system institutions and practices drawn from the cabinet of parliamentary systems are usually a mistake and can be mischievous. No good comes from attempts to dilute, share, or usurp the authority and responsibility of the President.

While no good comes from attempts to invade the authority and responsibility of the President, they are continually made and sometimes succeed. This occurs under weak Presidents. The result is Congressional government, which, in turn, results, under twentieth-century conditions, in a negative and vacillating foreign policy, the impairment of our world position, and danger to our national safety. This situation has been described by a former colleague as the "Frenchification" of the Constitution. By this he means government where power is centered in a national assembly as in the four French republican constitutions. Under this system, the Presidency tends to become ceremonial, executive power virtually disappears, and authority is assumed by parliamentarians, undisciplined by any penalty for repudiating the executive, divided into numerous groups no one of which commands decisive power, and unable and unequipped to lead the country in a sustained, complex, and difficult course of action. The foreign policy emerging from such a situation is formed by slogans and emotion; decisions represent the lowest common denominator of the groups in the legislative assembly. The vital issues, which are always painful, are evaded and decision postponed until events decide them.

We are familiar enough with this course of events as it has appeared and reappeared in French history from the First Republic to the Fourth. But perhaps we do not understand how closely our own situation approximates the French when the Presidential powers fall from hands not strong enough to wield them. For these powers are not self-executing. They cannot be exercised by a committee. They reside in and depend upon the quality of one man. This has been stated by one [Harry S. Truman] who held and knew how to use them:

Many diverse elements entered into the creation of the office, springing, as it did, from the parent idea of the separation of powers.

There was the firm conviction of such powerful and shrewd minds as that of John Adams that the greatest protection against unlimited power lay in an executive secured against the encroachments of a national assembly. Then there were the fears of those who suspected a plot to establish a monarchy on these shores. Others believed that the experience under the Confederation showed above all the need of stability through a strong central administration. Finally, there was the need for compromise among these and many other views.

The result was a compromise—a compromise which that shrewd observer, Alexis de Tocqueville, over a hundred and twenty years ago, believed would not work. He thought that the Presidential office was too weak. The President, he thought, was at the mercy of Congress. The President could recommend, to be sure, but he had no power and the Congress had. The Congress could disregard his recommendations, overrule his vetoes, reject his nominations. De Tocqueville thought that no man of parts, worthy of leadership, would accept so feeble a role.

This was not a foolish view and there was much in our early history which tended to bear it out. But there is a power in the course of events which plays its own part. In this case again, Justice Holmes's epigram proved true. He said a page of history is worth a whole volume of logic. And as the pages of history were written they unfolded powers in the Presidency not explicitly found in Article II of the Constitution.

In the first place, the President became the leader of a political party. The party under his leadership had to be dominant enough to put him in office. This political party leadership was the last thing the Constitution contemplated. The President's election was not intended to be mixed up in the hurley-burley of partisan politics. . . . The people were to choose wise and respected men who would meet in calm seclusion and choose a President. The runner-up would be Vice President.

All of this went by the board—though most of the original language remains in the Constitution. Out of the struggle and tumult of the political arena a new and different President emerged—the man who led a political party to victory and retained in his hands the power of party leadership. That is, he retained it, like the sword Excalibur, if he could wrest it from the scabbard and wield it.

Another development was connected with the first. As the President came to be elected by the whole people, he became responsible to the whole people. . . . Our whole people looked to him for leadership, and not confined within the limits of a written document. Every hope and every fear of his fellow citizens, almost every aspect of their welfare and activity, falls within the scope of his concern—indeed, falls within the scope of his duty. Only one who has held that office can really appreciate that. It is the President's responsibility to look at all questions from the point of view of the whole people. His written and spoken word commands national—often international—attention.

These powers which are not explicitly written into the Constitution are powers which no President can pass on to his successor. They go only to him who can take and use them.

We have had Presidents who have not exercised the Presidential power. It will not exhaust the list to mention Presidents Pierce, Buchanan, Grant, Harding, and Coolidge. When Presidential default occurs it is not correct to say that Congress steps into the vacant place. Attempts are made to do so, but they cannot fully succeed since Congress is not designed, organized, or equipped for executive leadership.

Aside from the obvious reason that so large a body, designed to be a check upon action, cannot be the leader in action, there is another reason highly relevant to our present inquiry. It is that our two-party system cloaks a multiparty reality. There is a saying—not wholly accurate—that strict party votes occur only on the organization of the House and Senate. But it is true that strict party votes are rare enough to cause considerable comment. Every newspaper reader knows that across the traditional party lines run perhaps even deeper alignments—the farm bloc, the protectionist bloc, the isolationist group, the Southern group (on certain questions), the "liberal group" (on certain questions), the mountain states (on minerals and wool), the public power group, the economy group, and so on.

The conclusion relevant here is that a party leader in Congress is not a leader, so far as foreign affairs is concerned, qualified to speak for the party which he nominally leads. His view is not accepted as any more important or controlling than that of any other member. In the absence of Presidential leadership, Congressional policy must be evolved by negotiation among the groups and with a high appreciation of short-term electoral approval. These conditions are not favorable to understanding or dealing with fundamental realities and issues or to producing continuity of policy and the sober facing of difficult problems requiring costly sacrifices. The Nye Committee did not provide the country with an understanding of the problems left by the First World War or with policies consistent with the security of the United States. It resulted in a withdrawal into "Fortress America" which was no fortress at all, because the incidence of power pressures occurred outside it. And it is there—where the pressures focus—that the United States must exercise its capacity to mold and shape the future.

So we return to the President as the pivotal point, the critical element in reaching decisions on foreign policy. Now the capacity to decide is not a common attribute of mankind. It becomes increasingly rare as the difficulty of the problems increases. The choice becomes one between courses all of which are hard and dangerous. The "right" one, if there is a right one, is quite apt to be the most immediately difficult one. It was certainly so in reaching a decision regarding Korea in June, 1950. In these cases the mind tends to remain suspended between alternatives and to seek escape by postponing the issue. There are always presuasive advocates of opposing courses. "On the one hand" balances "on the other." The problem itself becomes the enemy.

General Marshall understands this very well. Many a time he would burst out in an interminable discussion with, "Gentlemen, don't fight the question. Decide it." And he has often observed that the rarest of all gifts is the capacity for decision. Many men and some Presidents don't have it. And when this occurs, the consequences are irreparable. It is one of the maladies for which there is no cure, except amputation.

Some years ago a lawyer friend received a call from a man who thanked him for giving him the best advice he had ever received. "You did not take my case," the man explained. "You listened to me, and you said, 'My friend, you are in one hell of a fix.' And," he added, "I was."

So is the country when the function of decision in foreign policy breaks down. For the inescapable result is drift. And it is drift away from the association, the coalition, of free nations which cannot exist without us, and without which we cannot exist as the nation all of us have known. And it is drift in this direction not necessarily from desire—many members of Congress desire quite the opposite—but because policy in association or coalition requires a vast number of coordinated and continuous actions which, for the reasons given, Congress without vigorous executive leadership is not able to provide. This vigorous leadership often involves conflict and competing appeals to the people, the common source of power. This is inherent in the system of separation of powers, the framers of which did not rate harmony between the executive and legislative branches as highly as some of their successors.

Different Presidents have gone about reaching conclusions and decisions for the conduct of foreign relations in different ways. Some have relied heavily on solitary reflection and study. One can see instances of this in Presidents Jefferson, Lincoln, and Wilson. Some have relied substantially upon advisers not in the established chart of organization. Here one might cite the two Roosevelts. Others have been meticulous in sticking to "channels," of whom President Truman is outstanding. But, however he works, the President must be free to choose the methods most suited to him. He cannot be confined. Particularly, he must not be confined by law. Legislation that a

President must consult this, that, or the other person or body will be futile and harmful. He can be given facilities, but he cannot be compelled to use them.

But it can properly be said that some courses are apt to be more successful than others. Successful organization and method will recognize two fundamental truths—the indivisibility of policy and the specialty of the foreign field.

Governmental policy is an integer—political policy, diplomatic, military, economic, fiscal. It is all one. Each depends upon, is stimulated and limited by the others. The history of our government decisions in the year 1950 is a clinic for any who wish to spell out this thesis. But it will hardly be disputed in theory, while it is very apt to be disregarded in practice. And there will always be argument about the hierarchy of importance. Do we cut the pattern according to the cloth or do we cut the cloth according to the pattern? And where do we find the pattern? But the first requirement is that there must be a pattern.

While this is true, it is also true that, despite popular belief, the field of foreign affairs is a field of special competence. Those who have spent their lives in the study of foreign nations and peoples know more about them than those who have not, just as physicians or physicists know more about their fields of special study. They often make mistakes, and bad ones. We are under no compulsion to take their advice. But, where our lives are at stake, as between tossing a coin and consulting the specialists, we would be wise to do the latter.

Now it is an interesting fact that the Secretary of State is the senior member of the Cabinet. He is the senior member because this cabinet office was the first to be created upon the formation of our government. And it was the first to be created because then, as now, our relations with foreign nations were the most pressing of all problems with which our government had to deal. This has not always been true in the years which intervened. But it was true then, and it is true now.

Whatever primacy one attaches to our relations with the world beyond our borders, it is plain that a President needs continuous and knowledgeable advice about them. The Department of State exists for this purpose, is highly competent to perform it, and should be the principal, unifying, and final source of advice and recommendation. Unifying and final in this sense, that reports and recommendations from all sources, official and unofficial, come to the President—some of them good, more of them plausible. All of these should be referred to and reported on by the Department of State, which must live with the problem. Its view may be rejected, but it should be heard.

So far we have spoken of a "department" and about "its" view. But a department is made up of thousands of people. It cannot advise the President. And it rarely has *a* view. Here enters the Secretary of State—an unenviable figure. As Henry Adams pointed out, he is destined to be a pariah with the Congress because he represents problems which the Congress wishes to forget. Votes can be lost but not gained through foreign policy.

Nevertheless he has a place, and an important one, in the making of decisions. It is not the one most photographed and publicized—his exhausting flights to conferences, his greeting of visiting dignitaries, his appearance before committees of Congress and the public as a spokesman for the Administration. His other and essential role concerns both the special knowledge of the foreign field and the synthesis of foreign policy into a unified governmental policy.

In the first aspect he must draw from the Department of State in usable form its full knowledge and wisdom upon the many matters which press for decision. He should distrust conclusions, his own or others', when they provide answers too facile and pat, but should rather spur and encourage his departmental colleagues to bring together all their varied knowledge and points of view so that all possibilities are tested against the most stringent criticism. He must keep them headed into the problem and present to them the other governmental factors involved which fall outside their field of special competence, but which must weigh heavily with the President.

Out of this method of work will come recommendations from the foreign affairs point of view influenced by, but not wholly coordinated with, the limiting factors of our capabilities in the economic, fiscal, military, and domestic political fields. This final reconciliation must be made by the President. He should be kept fully informed of the progress of the work so that issues are not presented to him suddenly and at a late stage when choices have narrowed, and so that the President's thought may be fully reflected in the work of preparation. But, before the matter comes to the President for action, much can be done to assure that all his advisers have understood and considered one another's points of view and the whole scope of limitations and capabilities applicable to the problem.

Much of this is accomplished by consultation between cabinet colleagues and through such valuable interdepartmental machinery as the National Advisory Council on financial matters and the National Security Council on security matters. It would unduly extend this article to go into these established channels for coordinating policy. But one matter should be mentioned which defies formal organization, but which is absolutely essential. It concerns habits of work and confidence and collaboration between officers of different departments.

One of the curious and toughly resistant characteristics of government departments is the tendency of their people to isolate themselves from other departments and to regard persons outside their ranks with something amounting, on occasion, to suspicion and hostility. It may seem extraordinary, but it is nevertheless true, that not until General Marshall's tenure as Secretary of Defense had the Secretary of State and his senior officers met with the Secretary of Defense and the Joint Chiefs of Staff for continuous discussion and development of policy. And yet foreign policy and military policy divorced from one another are both operating in the field of phantasy.

From September, 1950, until January, 1953—I am not informed thereafter—officers of the two Departments worked in the closest and most loyal cooperation and greatly to the public good. This does not happen automatically; it requires constant attention and effort from all concerned and especially from the top. For both Departments have internal differences springing from perfectly proper differences of emphasis and interests, either from the services, in one case, or the geographical divisions, in the other. Both desire to keep their differences within the family. But it is useful and often most productive to bring them out in discussion, provided those in the discussion preserve confidence. The value of these years of common work in mutual enlightenment, confidence, and advancement of policy and action cannot be overstated.

The same relationship existed with the Economic Cooperation Administration and with its successor, the Mutual Security Agency, and to a lesser, but useful, degree with other Departments having functions in the foreign field—Treasury, Commerce, Agriculture, and Labor.

The purpose of all this was not necessarily to get agreed recommendations and papers, but to get understanding; and, where there were differences, to have them brought out, not covered up, and to have them intelligent and intelligible differences. One can always get an agreed paper by increasing the vagueness and generality of its statements. The staff of any interdepartmental committee has a fatal weakness for this type of agreement by exhaustion. But such agreements are no good and of no service to the President, if he has the capacity for decision. What he needs to know are the real issues, honestly presented, with extraneous matter stripped away.

We come back then to where we started—to the President. The decisions are his. Helped by his departmental advisers and their staffs, helped by his own Executive Office—the Bureau of the Budget, the Economic Advisers, and so forth—ultimately he must decide. The volume of work which should be done is appalling. It cannot be got through by listening to oral presentations, or "briefings," or reading one-page memoranda. It has to be sweated out. The facts have to be mastered, the choices and their consequences understood—so far as consequences can be understood; and then upon "judgments and intuitions more subtle than any articulate major premise" the decision made.

111. *The President and National Security* *

MR. ANDERSON, Special Assistant to the President for National Security Affairs, describes how the National Security Council works. This enormously important agency, created in 1947, advises the President on basic policies to be followed for preserving national security. The fundamental policies put into operation by the Department of State in the field of foreign affairs, and by the Department of Defense in the field of military affairs, are most often based on directives worked out by the National Security Council and approved by the President. The Council also considers the domestic aspects which follow from its recommendations. It is no exaggeration to say that this agency is a supercabinet for national security affairs.

IN THE "lucid view that hindsight affords," historians will one day record our country's successes and failures in world affairs during these pregnant middle years of the twentieth century. A hundred years hence, even the most superficial students of the record will be able to assess our progress toward our ultimate goal—just and lasting world peace. This hindsight, of course, is not available to those who must make the present decisions; they must trust to foresight. Hindsight discloses history's lessons, one of which is that history often repeats itself, and another that often history does not; these lessons must be blended rightly with the other elements of foresight if the true course is to be found. Only so, in our role of leader of the free world, can we make a realistic reckoning of probable future developments.

What are these other elements of a clear look ahead? Of what is foresight compounded—foresight that must enter into planning long-range national policy in the foreign field? These parts are vast and

* Dillon Anderson, *The Atlantic*, CXCVII (January, 1956), pp. 42-46. Reprinted with permission from *The Atlantic*.

unbelievably complex. There are all the essential facts, foreign and domestic, which bear upon our posture in the presence of the world and our ability to maintain it: the economic, military, and political policies and capabilities of other nations; the ideologies and aspirations of peoples, and the varying degree of responsiveness of leaders to attitudes of their constituents; the shifts and tendencies in the never static alignments of nations; and the forces at work that presage further changes.

To these historical and factual data there must be applied the techniques of analysis, appraisal, imagination, judgment; then decision on policy objectives and planned courses of action to attain them. The test of the quality of the foresight in such matters can be severe, since the margin for error may not always be a wide one.

Under our Constitution the conduct of affairs affecting the national security is a settled Executive responsibility, though treaties must be approved by the Senate, and enactment by the Congress of appropriate legislation is a vital coordinate. And, of course, Congress alone may declare war. Since 1947, the crucible in which Executive policy in this field has been refined has been the National Security Council.

What is the National Security Council, and what are its origins? How are matters brought before it? How does it function? What does it produce? Since the Council was organized less than ten years ago; since its meetings are not publicized; since its deliberations, and even its agenda, are usually protected for security reasons, the answers to the foregoing questions are for the most part not widely known. There is, however, no secrecy about the mechanism of the National Security Council; and no reason exists why these questions may not be answered, provided there is neither disclosure of information which would prejudice the security of the United States, nor any revelation of the intimate discussions between the President and his advisers, which for obvious reasons must be privileged.

The concept of the Council was formalized during the years which followed World War II. This was a period in which total danger was still continuing; yet it was, at the same time, a period auguring vastly increased well-being for mankind if, in more assured peace, science and technology could provide better plowshares.

Our relatively new pre-eminence in world affairs, the commensurate responsibility for leadership in the free world, and the realization by such thoughtful and patriotic men as James Forrestal that technological advances had created another kind of world—all these combined to convince our leaders in both the Executive and Legislative branches that national policy planning and formulation needed to be brought together at a central point which had to be the peak of government. The natural participants were the heads of the departments and agencies responsible for carrying out various elements of national security programs.

The use of interdepartmental committees for developing integrated policy was, of course, not a new one; many such committees had acted before, although on a more or less *ad hoc* basis. But here was a clear need for something more. In other words, no longer could appropriate military policy on the one hand or supportable foreign policy on the other be formulated in isolation one from the other; and by the same token neither military nor foreign policy could be considered adequately without taking into account the best integrated intelligence estimates of the world situation and the availability of United States resources to support our objectives and commitments with respect to the rest of the world. Moreover, decisions affecting related activities of several responsible departments could no longer be made safely on the ex parte presentation to the President by a single department head.

Thus, to meet the need for the integration of national security policy at the highest level, Congress enacted the National Security Act of 1947. That legislation, together with the 1949 amendments, did four principal things: (1) it created the Department of Defense and brought together under it the Army, Navy, and Air Force; (2) it created a Central Intelligence Agency for the collation and appraisal, at one central point, of world intelligence relating to our national security; (3) it created the National Security Resources Board (now the Office of Defense Mobilization) "to advise the President concerning the coordination of military, industrial and civilian mobilization"; and (4) it established the National Security Council.

The statutory duties of the Council are, in substance, as shown in the following excerpts from the law:

> . . . to advise the President with respect to the integration of domestic, foreign, and military policies relating to the national security so as to enable the military services and the other departments and agencies of the Government to cooperate more effectively in matters involving the national security. . . .
>
> . . . to assess and appraise the objectives, commitments, and risks of the United States in relation to our actual and potential military power. . . .

and

> . . . to consider policies on matters of common interest to the departments and agencies of the Government concerned with the national security, and to make recommendations to the President in connection therewith.

Thus the Congress carefully recognized the presidential prerogatives which follow his constitutional responsibility, the duty of decision. The other Council members are no more than an advisory body. As such, the Council may examine, assess, and advise, but it does not decide; it is limited to making *recommendations* to the President. Thus, with one exception noted later, the Council does not act in a corporate way as a Board of Directors; nor does it conduct operations or issue directives. Only the *President* decides.

The Council has five statutory members, beginning with the President, who presides at its meetings. The other four statutory members of the Council are: the Vice President, the Secretary of State, the Secretary of Defense, and the Director of the Office of Defense Mobilization. The reasons for including these officials are readily apparent. The Vice President is there primarily to ensure Executive continuity, though he also brings to the Council the benefit of his judgment and experience, including that gained as presiding officer in the upper house of Congress. The Secretary of State is present as the President's chief adviser on foreign relations. The Secretary of Defense represents the three combined military services. And the Director of the Office of Defense Mobilization brings to the Council an appraisal of our domestic resources in connection with his responsibilities for formulating plans and programs for industrial mobilization, and for ensuring that we maintain a maximum degree of readiness for emergency in respect to materials, production, and manpower to support our military needs.

Two other statutory agencies also participate in Council affairs: the Central Intelligence Agency, which is represented by its Director, and the Joint Chiefs of Staff, for whom the Chairman is usually spokesman. They are the senior presidential advisers in their respective fields.

In addition to the foregoing, others who now regularly participate in Council meetings are the Secretary of the Treasury, who is the President's chief adviser on how national security dollars are to be provided; and the Director of the Bureau of the Budget, who brings to the President a bird's-eye view of the various claims on the Government's annual income. President Eisenhower's inclusion of these latter two officials as Council participants is indicative of his conviction that one of the most essential elements of the national security is a strong and viable economy to which defense expenditures can be geared for the long pull.

From time to time, other department or agency heads attend Council meetings, by invitation of the President, to participate in matters on the agenda in which they have a particular interest or departmental responsibility. These may include the Ambassador to the United Nations, the Attorney General, the Secretary of the Interior, the Secretary of Commerce, the Secretaries and the Chiefs of Staff of the three Armed Services, the Director of the International Cooperation Administration (formerly FOA), the Federal Civil Defense Administrator, the Director of the United States Information Agency, and the Chairmen of the President's Internal Security Committees. Likewise one or more of the special assistants to the President attend Council meetings on the President's invitation. They include the President's Special Assistant on Atomic Energy (likewise Chairman of the Atomic Energy Commission); on Disarmament; on Foreign Economic Affairs; and on Coordinated Planning.

The Special Assistant to the President for National Security Affairs attends all meetings in carrying out his duties toward the Council—which will be later described. The secretariat function is carried out by the attendance of the Executive Secretary of the Council and his deputy. They attend all meetings.

The NSC functional structure today may be likened to a pyramid with the President and the Council at the apex. Along the base are four supporting elements—two created by statute, and two interdepartmental groups formed by executive order and presidential directive.

As above indicated, the National Security Act set up the Central Intelligence Agency, the affairs of which are managed by a Director. Here is established for the benefit of the Council the integrated Intelligence viewpoint; and through the Director, the Council keeps advised of the current world estimates by the Intelligence community. The Director reports, under the provisions of the statute, to the members of the National Security Council in the only corporate capacity in which the Council acts. In other words, the Council is a statutory Board of Directors for the CIA.

The second element at the base of the Council pyramid is an interdepartmental group which in one form or another has functioned since the organization of the Council. At present this group, operating pursuant to presidential directive, is called the NSC Planning Board, through which policy proposals flow upward to the Council.

Proposed national security policy papers normally are originated in the various departments whose heads are Council members, though the initial stimulus may have been a presidential request for study and recommendations, a similar request made in a Council meeting and approved by the President, or a departmental proposal. After departmental staff study and the contribution there of the specialists by area and subject, the paper goes to the National Security Council Planning Board. That group duplicates, at the Assistant Secretary level, the composition of the Council itself. Thus State, Defense, ODM, Treasury, and Budget have Planning Board members; CIA and JCS have advisers; and observers from Justice, AEC, and other agencies attend as their interests may require. These participants in Planning Board affairs are appointed by the President upon the recommendations of the department heads. The Special Assistant to the President for National Security Affairs presides over these meetings.

It is in the NSC Planning Board that every policy proposal is tested in lengthy discussions against the views of the assistant secretaries of the several participating departments as a sort of preliminary to the discussion which will take place in the Council later on. In this process of distillation the papers are modified, expanded, and generally rewritten.

There may be and often are departmental differences of views. And as the work progresses each Planning Board member is able to keep current with his department's reaction to proposed revisions, and check back with his Secretary between Planning Board meetings. Thus many differences are reconciled, much common ground is found, and many disagreements prove after full discussion to be illusory and not basic differences after all. But if an irreconcilable disagreement arises between the departments represented, the Planning Board must identify clearly the elements of the disagreement and spell out the alternative policy courses and reasons therefor so that they may be presented fully to the National Security Council.

Working in the same area as the Planning Board is the third element of support. It is a small permanent staff provided for by the statute, which serves under the Executive Secretary of the NSC and performs the technical service of digesting, analyzing, and arranging the mass of material flowing in to the Council daily. The work of this staff is independent of the departments whose heads make up the NSC, and its nonpartisan services are of great importance to the Council, to the Special Assistant for National Security Affairs, and to the NSC Planning Board in crystallizing the issues to be presented to the Council.

The most recent addition to the elements of NSC support is the formation of the Operations Coordinating Board (OCB). This is an innovation of President Eisenhower's, and it is designed to round out the policy cycle by gearing departmental action to the achievement of national security objectives. The Board consists of the Under Secretary of State, the Deputy Secretary of Defense, and other departmental representatives who parallel much of the membership of the NSC itself. This group in its regular weekly meetings seeks to ensure that agency programs in the international field are timely, consistent with each other, related each to the other, and best calculated to carry out presidentially approved policies.

The OCB is not an operating agency; its duty is to coordinate. This board receives reports and keeps under continuous review the status of national security programs being carried out by the various departments. It likewise informs the Council, by means of periodic reports, what action is being taken and what progress is being made toward the achievement of each policy objective. This fourth supporting element has provided a most meaningful adjunct to the functioning of the NSC.

What is the relation of the Council to other similar bodies which have existed in the Government from the earliest days? The answer is that they mesh well. The functions of the Council in no way impinge, for example, upon the prerogatives of the Cabinet. The NSC is no super Cabinet. Both bodies are advisory to the President and both have overflowing, but not overlapping, agenda. The degree of overlapping membership prevents conflicting actions. By and large, the Cabinet predominates in domestic affairs—matters relating to Justice; Post Office; Interior; Agriculture; Commerce; Labor; Health, Education, and Welfare; Civil Service; and the like. The Council, on the other hand, deals with national security strategy—and in a very intensive way.

Nor does the Council's work interfere with the operations of the State, Defense, or any other department having "action" responsibility in the broad field of national security. Actually the reverse is true. The result of the Council action is to broaden the base of support for the department which has primary responsibility for carrying out Administration policy. For one thing, the policy has been carefully hammered out and tested by the views of all the Council members. They have participated in its formulation, and there is the assurance that all affected departments in the Executive branch have, after full hearing, been directed by the President to cooperate in the implementation of the Executive policy adopted.

The National Security Council meets regularly in the Cabinet Room at the White House on Thursday mornings. The meetings normally last for about two and one half hours, although they sometimes last much longer.

The Special Assistant for National Security Affairs introduces each item on the Council agenda and gives a brief statement of its background and its relation to other existing national security policies. He states why the policy is up for revision; or, if it is a new proposal, why it has come before the Council, and how the Council has acted on it or related subjects before. He endeavors to make clear what is to be decided, what the alternatives are, any divergences of views, and what action is recommended by the NSC Planning Board.

The President always takes time to become thoroughly familiar with each subject on the Council agenda and all departmental differences which have not been resolved in the NSC Planning Board. This preparation is completed a day or so before each Council meeting in briefing sessions between the President and the Special Assistant for National Security Affairs, frequently attended by the Council's Executive Secretary. Thus, the President is able to make timely calls for additional information, as desired, and to sleep over the problems that are to be dealt with at the upcoming Council meeting. This process is duplicated in the various departments. In other words, the Planning Board members go over the agenda items with their principals who are to sit in the NSC meeting.

Every member of the Council usually speaks in the meetings, and those others who attend are always free to speak—and frequently do. In the concept of President Eisenhower, Council members are not there simply to advocate the narrow departmental view for the special interest of their particular agency; nor are they there to act as rubber stamps. Rather they act as intimate advisers of the President in the last phase of deliberation before he makes decisions of the very greatest importance to the future of our country and of the world. As the President once put it, the function of the Council members "should be to search for and seek, with their background and experience, the most statesmenlike answers to the problems of national security."

The meetings of the Council are informal, and no transcript is taken of proceedings. A Record of Action is all that is made. This is a concise statement of the exact decisions or policy directives upon which the President has settled. After the first draft of the Record of Action has been prepared, it is circulated among all departments participating in Council affairs to give each of them an opportunity to comment and make suggestions. Then it is submitted to the President for his final scrutiny. This record, with such changes as the President may make before he approves it, then becomes national security policy.

Thus when the product of the National Security Council takes written form, it may be the adoption, after Council revision, of a policy paper brought up through the Planning Board; a directive that old policy be reviewed and that recommended revisions thereof be brought back to the Council; or recorded decisions on any one of the many and varied subjects falling in the broad field of national security as defined by the statute.

The way the Council has functioned in recent years, with its frequent and sometimes lengthy meetings, represents a technique for forward policy formulation well calculated to take into account historical experience, to assess our present risks and commitments, and to seek out sound, long-term policy objectives. This is not crystal-ball gazing in any sense; it is a highly organized effort to look ahead realistically and to lay the proper groundwork for our nation's continued ability to discharge its responsibilities to ourselves and to the free world.

The NSC, still a relatively new mechanism in our Government, has become the helm from which the President looks out toward the broad horizon ahead and charts the world course we are to follow. He has, in the process, probed the thinking of his responsible ministers, in his presence, in the presence of one another, and all together; he has assessed their own thinking in the light of their experience, wisdom, and imagination and in the course of their debate; he has made his policy determination against the background of a full and free expression of the views of every minister who has a contribution to make or who will be affected by the action to be taken—all in a thoroughly prepared and intensive effort to bring to the reckoning a clearer foresight into the always murky future.

As a result of this process, there has been accumulated a reservoir of basic policy and forward strategy which today, though not inflexible and always subject to constant review and revision from time to time, nevertheless does represent certain fundamental concepts and contains identified guidelines for those departments in Government which are responsible for action. Such preparation seems well calculated to avoid the necessity for panic decisions.

This reservoir of policy guidance stands the nation in good stead during periods when the President must be away from his office, as President Eisenhower was last fall while recuperating in Denver. The heads of the various departments are in a position to carry on during such times with full knowledge of the continued validity of the broad policy concepts established by the President in the cumulative experience of the NSC. There continues, moreover, the momentum of the Executive team's integrated program in the field of national security affairs, forged in the case of President Eisenhower during more than a hundred weekly NSC meetings.

It might well be observed that the continued functioning of Government in such periods under a body of established policy exemplifies, in a real sense, the principle which John Adams wrote into the Massachusetts Constitution in 1780—that ours is a Government of laws and not of men.

112. *The Faults of American Diplomacy* *

SIR HAROLD NICOLSON, career diplomat and former Member of Parliament, makes a plea for what he calls the old-fashioned French style diplomacy instead of the American style. He is primarily concerned in this selection with the methods that countries use in dealing with each other rather than the results, although he does draw some fundamental substantive conclusions. For example, he feels that great powers are more important than small powers, so that negotiations carried on as if all states were equal are bound to be unreal. He charges that President Wilson, in 1919, started the unfortunate diplomatic revolution by demanding that negotiations between states should be open rather than secret. Whether or not we agree that these changes can properly be called American innovations, we must agree that the author has raised some important and thorny issues.

SINCE THE CLOSE of the first world war, international diplomacy has been dominated—or at least heavily influenced—by what might be called "the American method." It has almost completely replaced the Old Diplomacy—the French method, which was originated by Richelieu and adopted by all European countries during the three centuries that preceded 1919. Yet it would hardly be accurate to speak of a New Diplomacy. I prefer—since the Americans have not yet discovered their own formula—to call it "The Transition between the Old Diplomacy and the New."

The French method, in my opinion, was best adapted to the conduct of relations between civilized states. It was courteous and dignified; it was continuous and gradual; it attached importance to knowledge and experience; it took account of the realities of existing power; and it defined good faith, lucidity, and precision as the qualities essential to any sound negotiation. The mistakes, the follies, and the crimes that during those three hundred years accumulated to the discredit of the Old Diplomacy can, when examined at their sources, be traced to evil foreign policy rather than to faulty methods of negotiation. It is regrettable that the bad things they did should have dishonored the excellent manner in which they did them.

I am not, of course, proposing to scrap all existing machinery and to return to the system of the eighteenth and nineteenth centuries.

* From Sir Harold Nicolson, *The Evolution of Diplomatic Method*, copyright 1955 by the author and used with the permission of The Macmillan Company. Reprinted from *Harper's Magazine*, CCX (January, 1955), pp. 53-58.

The conditions on which the old diplomacy was based no longer exist. I am suggesting only that as a method of negotiation it was infinitely more efficient than that which we employ today.

Let me therefore consider five of the chief characteristics of the Old Diplomacy.

In the first place Europe was regarded as the most important of all the continents. Asia and Africa were viewed as areas for imperial, commercial, or missionary expansion. Japan, when she arose, appeared an exceptional phenomenon. America, until 1897, remained isolated behind her oceans and her Doctrine. No war, it was felt, could become a major war unless one of the five Great European Powers became involved. It was thus in the chancelleries of Europe alone that the final issue of general peace or war would be decided.

In the second place it was assumed that the Great Powers were greater than the Small Powers, since they possessed a more extended range of interests, wider responsibilities, and, above all, more money and more guns.

The Small Powers were graded in importance according to their military resources, their strategic position, their value as markets or sources of raw material, and their relation to the Balance of Power. There was nothing stable about such categories. At one moment Egypt, at another Afghanistan, at another Albania, would acquire prominence as points of Anglo-French, Anglo-Russian, or Slav-Teuton rivalry; at one moment the Baltic, at another the Balkans, would become the focus of diplomatic concern. The Small Powers were assessed according to their effect upon the relations between the Great Powers; there was seldom any idea that their interests, their opinions, still less their votes, could affect a policy agreed upon by the Concert of Europe.

This axiom implied a third principle—that the Great Powers possessed a common responsibility for the conduct of the Small Powers and the preservation of peace among them. The principle of intervention was generally accepted. The classic example of joint intervention by the Concert of Europe in a dispute between the Small Powers was the Ambassadors Conference held in London in 1913, at the time of the Balkan Wars. That Conference—which provides the last, as well as the best, example of the old diplomacy in action—prevented a Small-Power crisis from developing into a Great-Power crisis.

DIPLOMACY BY PROFESSIONALS

The fourth characteristic bequeathed by the French system was the establishment in every European country of a professional diplomatic service on a more or less identical model. These officials representing their government in foreign capitals possessed similar standards of education, similar experience, and a similar aim. They desired the same sort of world. They tended to develop a corporate identity. They had often known each other for years, having served in some post together in their early youth; and they all believed—whatever their governments might believe—that the purpose of diplomacy was the preservation of peace. This professional Freemasonry proved of great value in negotiation.

The Ambassadors, for instance, of France, Russia, Germany, Austria, and Italy, who managed to settle the Balkan crisis of 1913, each represented national rivalries that were dangerous and acute. Yet they possessed complete confidence in each other's probity and discretion, had a common standard of professional conduct, and desired above all else to prevent a general conflagration.

It was not the fault of the professional diplomatists that the supremacy of Europe was shattered by the first world war. The misfortune was that the advice of these wise men was disregarded at Vienna and Berlin, that their services were not employed, and that other, non-diplomatic influences and interests assumed control of affairs.

The fifth main characteristic of the Old Diplomacy was the rule that sound negotiation must be continuous and confidential. It was a principle essentially different from that governing the itinerant public conferences with which we have become familiar since 1919. The Ambassador in a foreign capital who was instructed to negotiate a treaty with the government to which he was accredited was already in possession of certain assets. He was acquainted with the people with whom he had to negotiate; he could in advance assess their strength or weakness, their reliability or the reverse. He was fully informed of local interests, prejudices, or ambitions, of the local reefs and sand-banks, among which he would have to navigate. His repeated interviews with the Foreign Minister attracted no special public attention, since they were taken for granted as visits of routine. Since his conversations were private, they could remain both rational and courteous; since they were confidential, there was no danger of public expectation being aroused while they were still in progress.

Every negotiation consists of stages and a result; if the stages become matters of public controversy before the result has been achieved, the negotiation will almost certainly founder. A negotiation is the subject of concession and counter-concession: if the concession offered is divulged before the public are aware of the corresponding concession to be received, extreme agitation may follow and the negotiation may have to be abandoned. The necessity of negotiation remaining confidential has never been more forcibly expressed than by Jules Cambon—perhaps the best professional diplomatist of this century.

"The day secrecy is abolished," writes M. Cambon, "negotiation of any kind will become impossible."

An ambassador negotiating a treaty according to the methods of the old diplomacy was not pressed for time. Both his own government and the government with whom he was negotiating had ample opportunity for reflection. A negotiation that had reached a deadlock could be dropped for a few months without hopes being dashed or speculation aroused. The agreements that in the end resulted were no hasty improvisations or empty formulas, but documents considered and drafted with exact care. We might cite as an example the Anglo-Russian Convention of 1907. The negotiation between the Russian Foreign Minister and our Ambassador in St. Petersburg occupied a period of one year and three months; and at no stage was an indiscretion committed or a confidence betrayed.

VICES OF THE OLD AMBASSADORS

I trust that my preference for professional to amateur methods of negotiation will not be ascribed solely to the chance that I was myself born and nurtured in the Old Diplomacy. I am fully conscious of the many faults that the system encouraged. The axiom that all negotiation must be confidential did certainly create the habit of secretiveness, and did induce men of the highest respectability to enter into commitments which they did not divulge. We must not forget that as late as 1914 the French Assembly was unaware of the secret clauses of the Franco-Russian alliance or that Sir Edward Grey (a man of scrupulous integrity) did not regard it as wrong to conceal from the Cabinet the exact nature of the military arrangements reached between the French and British General Staffs. Confidential negotiations that lead to secret pledges are worse even than the televised diplomacy that we enjoy today.

Nor am I unaware of the functional defects which the professional diplomatist tends to develop. He has seen human folly or egoism operating in so many different circumstances that he may identify serious passions with transitory feelings and thus underestimate the profound emotion by which whole nations can be swayed. He is so inured to the contrast between those who know the facts and those who do not know the facts, that he forgets that the latter constitute the vast majority and that it is with them that the last decision rests. He may have deduced from experience that time alone is the conciliator, that unimportant things do not matter and that important things settle themselves, that mistakes are the only things that are really effective. He may thus incline to the fallacy that on the whole it is wiser, in all circumstances, to do nothing at all.

He may be a stupid man or complacent; there are few human types more depressing than the self-satisfied diplomatist. He may be of weak character, inclined to report what is agreeable rather than what is true. He may be vain, a defect resulting in disaster to all concerned. And he often becomes denationalized, internationalized, and therefore, an elegant empty husk. A profession should not, however, be judged by its failures.

The speeding up of communications has done much to alter the old methods of negotiation. In former days it took many months before a dispatch could be received and answered, and ambassadors abroad were expected to use their own initiative and judgment in carrying out the policy outlined in the instructions they had received on leaving home. Some ambassadors profited by this latitude to pursue a personal policy.

"I never," wrote Lord Malmesbury, "received an instruction that was worth reading." Other highly gifted ambassadors, such as Sir Hugh Elliott and Sir Henry Bulwer, relished their independence as enabling them to indulge in personal eccentricities and romantic affairs.

Yet these were exceptions. Most ambassadors during the period of slow communications were so terrified of exceeding their instructions or of assuming an initiative that might embarrass their home government, that they adopted a purely passive attitude, missed opportunity after opportunity, and spent their time writing brilliant reports on situations that had entirely altered by the time their dispatches arrived.

Today a Foreign Secretary from his desk in Downing Street can telephone to six ambassadors in the course of one morning or can even descend upon them quite suddenly from the sky. Does this mean that a diplomatist today is no more than a clerk at the end of a line? Such an assumption would be much exaggerated. An ambassador in a foreign capital must always be the main source of information, above all the interpreter regarding political conditions, trends, and opinions in the country in which he resides.

In every democracy, in every cabinet or trade union, power at any given moment rests with three or four individuals only. Nobody but a resident ambassador can get to know these individuals intimately or be able to assess the increase or decrease of their influence. It must always be on his reports that the government base their decision about what policy is at the moment practicable and what is not. That in itself is a most important function and responsibility.

But the ambassador also remains the chief channel of communication between his own government and that to which he is accredited. He alone can decide at what moment and in what terms his instructions can best be executed. Moreover he remains the intermediary who alone can explain the purposes and motives of one government to another. If he be foolish, ignorant, vain, or intemperate, great misunderstandings may arise and damaging indiscretions be perpetrated. Important results may depend upon the relations that he has been able to cultivate and maintain, upon the degree of confidence with which he is regarded, upon his skill and tact even in the most incidental negotiation.

Nor is this all. An ambassador should possess sufficient authority with his home government to be able to dissuade it from a course of action which, given the local circumstances, he knows will prove disastrous. Governments who allow themselves to be represented in foreign capitals by ambassadors to whose judgment and advice they pay no attention are wasting their own time and public money. No newspaper, no banking firm, would consider for one instant being represented abroad by a man in whose opinion they placed no confidence.

I do not agree, therefore, that improvements in means of communication have essentially diminished the responsibility of an ambassador, or to any important extent altered the nature of his functions.

WILSON'S DANGEROUS IDEALS

No, it was not the telephone that, from 1919 onward, brought about the transition from the old diplomacy to the new. It was the belief that it was possible to apply to the conduct of *external* affairs, the ideas and practices which, in the conduct of *internal* affairs, had for generations been regarded as the esentials of liberal democracy.

It was inevitable, after the first world war, that some such experiment should be made. On the one hand, the ordinary citizen—convinced that the masses in every country shared his own detestation of war—attributed the breach of the peace to the vice or folly of a small minority, which must in future be placed under democratic control. On the other hand, when the Americans arrived as the dominant partners in the coalition, they brought with them their dislike of European institutions, their distrust of diplomacy, and their missionary faith in the equality of man.

President Wilson was an idealist and—what was perhaps more dangerous—a consummate master of English prose. He shared with Robespierre the hallucination that there existed some mystic bond between himself and "The People"—by which he meant not only the

American people but the British, French, Italian, Romanian, Yugoslav, Armenian, and even German peoples. If only he could penetrate the fog-barrier of governments, politicians, and officials and convey the sweetness and light of his revelation to the ordinary peasant in the Banat, to the shepherds of Albania, or the dock-hands of Fiume, then reason, concord, and amity would spread in ever widening circles across the earth. He possessed, moreover, the gift of giving to commonplace ideas the resonance and authority of Biblical sentences, and, like all phraseologists, he became mesmerized by the strength and neatness of the phrases that he devised.

During the long months of the Paris Peace Conference, I observed him with interest, admiration, and anxiety, and became convinced that he regarded himself, not as a world statesman, but as a prophet designated to bring light to a dark world. It may have been for this reason that he forgot all about the American Constitution and Senator Lodge.

I have no desire at all to denigrate President Wilson, who was in many ways inspiring and inspired. He assumed a weight of responsibility greater than any single human being is constituted to support, and he was tragically crushed. Yet if we read again the tremendous sermons that he delivered during 1918 we shall find in them the seeds of the jungle of chaos that today impedes and almost obliterates the processes of rational negotiation.

The first of his Fourteen Points of January 8, 1918, provided that in future there should be nothing but "open covenants of peace openly arrived at" and that "diplomacy should proceed always frankly and in the public view." On reaching Paris, President Wilson quickly decided that by "diplomacy" he had not meant "negotiation," but only the results of that negotiation, namely treaties. He also decided that the phrases "openly arrived at" and "in the public view" were relative only and contained nothing that need deter him from conducting prolonged secret negotiations with Lloyd George and Clemenceau—while one American marine stood with fixed bayonet at the study door, and another patrolled the short strip of garden outside. I can well recall how startled I was, on first being admitted to the secret chamber, to discover how original was the President's interpretation of his own first rule. Today, being much older, I realize that the method he adopted was the only possible method which, in the circumstances, could have led to any result.

The general public, however, were not similarly constrained to test the validity of the President's pronouncements against the hard facts of international intercourse. They continued to assume that by "diplomacy" was meant both policy and negotiation, and to conclude that, since secret treaties were demonstrably evil things, negotiation also must never be secret but conducted always "in the public view." This is perhaps the most confusing of all the fallacies that we owe to President Wilson.

In the second of his Four Principles of a month later, the President announced that the system of the Balance of Power was now forever discredited and that subject populations must be granted their independence, irrespective of the wishes of other states. In the Four Ends of the following July he foreshadowed the creation of a League of Nations which would establish, to quote his words, "the reign of law, based upon the consent of the governed and sustained by the organized opinion of mankind."

He failed to realize that the public is bored by foreign affairs until a crisis arises; and that then it is guided by feelings rather than by thoughts. Nor did he foresee that it would be impossible to organize the same opinion in every country simultaneously—or that the conscience of mankind, as a means of sustenance, might prove inadequate when faced by a dictator controlling all means of information.

In the Five Particulars on September 27 he pronounced that the rule of justice which America must achieve would be one that "plays no favorites and knows no standards but the equal rights of the several peoples concerned." This commandment was subsequently misinterpreted to signify that not the rights merely but also the opinions and the votes of even the tiniest country were of a validity equal to that of a Great Power. Egalitarianism was thus for the first time extended to imply equality among nations—an idea which does not correspond to reality and which creates mixed ideas.

If read as a whole, the successive pronouncements made by President Wilson during those months of 1918, constitute a magnificent gospel. They embody conceptions which no man should either ignore or disdain. The misfortune was that the public imagined that what was intended as a doctrine of perfectability was in fact a statement of American intentions. Thus when America repudiated her own prophet, a regrettable dichotomy was created between the realists and the idealists in every country. The former concluded that the whole of the Wilson doctrine was sentimental nonsense, and the latter floated off into vague imaginings that what they wanted to happen was likely to occur. As the latter were in the majority, the practical politician found himself in an invidious position. It was the endeavor to reconcile the hopes of the many with the doubts of the few that brought such seeming falsity to foreign policy in the twenty years between 1919 and 1939.

The Covenant of the League of Nations was none the less a very sensible document which—had it been applied with consistent strength

—might well have established something like the rule of law among nations. The Secretariat created at Geneva was a truly remarkable innovation, which, had general confidence been maintained, might have provided the world with a machine far preferable to that of the old diplomacy. The trouble was that this fine experiment was based upon a view of human nature which, had it been a correct view, would have rendered any League unnecessary. The ordinary peaceful citizen came to suppose that violence could be restrained by reason; it was not until it was too late that he understood that it could only be restrained by force. The old systems of authority—such as the Balance of Power, the Concert of Europe, and the discipline of the Great Powers—had been discredited. The new theory of reason proved incapable of controlling the unreasonable. In place of the old methods of stability, a new method of the utmost instability was introduced.

Two important changes were introduced into diplomatic method in the period that followed the war of 1914-18. The first was the refusal of the American legislature to ratify a treaty negotiated and signed by their own chief executive in person. That assuredly was an innovation of the utmost significance and one that dealt a heavy blow to the sanctity of contract and the reliability of negotiation.

THE CURSE OF CONFERENCES

The second was the increasing practice of indulging in the method of diplomacy by conference. By that I do not mean merely the several *ad hoc* conferences, such as Spa, Cannes, Genoa, Lausanne, Stresa, and so on: some of these were necessary and some were not. I am referring rather to the permanent state of conference introduced by the League system and later by the United Nations.

These conferences do little to satisfy the vague desire for what is called "open diplomacy." But they do much to diminish the utility of professional diplomatists and, since they entail much publicity, many rumors, and wide speculation—since they tempt politicians to achieve quick, spectacular, and often fictitious results—they tend to promote rather than allay suspicion, and to create those very states of uncertainty which it is the purpose of good diplomatic method to prevent.

The defects (or perhaps I should say the misfortunes) of the New Diplomacy are today magnified for us as if on some gigantic screen. The theory that all states are equal, even as all men are equal, has led to lobbies being formed among the smaller countries (as for instance between the Asians and the Latin Americans) the sole unifying principle of which is to offer opposition even to the reasonable suggestions of the Great Powers. The theory that "diplomacy should proceed always frankly and in the public view" has led to negotiation being broadcast and televised, and to all rational discussion being abandoned in favor of interminable propaganda speeches—addressed, not to those with whom the delegate is supposed to be negotiating, but to his own public at home.

I have made but slight reference to the diplomacy of the Soviet Union. Mr. W. P. Potjomkin, in his history of diplomacy, assures us that the Russians possess one powerful weapon denied to their opponents —namely "the scientific dialectic of the Marx-Lenin formula." I have not observed as yet that this dialectic has improved international relationships, or that the Soviet diplomatists and commissars have evolved any system of negotiation that might be called a diplomatic system. Their activity in foreign countries or at the international conferences is formidable, disturbing, compulsive. I do not for one moment underestimate either its potency or its danger. But it is not diplomacy; it is something else. This may be a sad conclusion. But it is not my final conclusion.

It would, in my view, be an error to take as an example of modern diplomatic method the discussions that are conducted in the Security Council and the Assembly of United Nations. We may resent the wastage of time, energy, and money; we may regret that, in transferring to external affairs the system of parliamentary argument, a more efficient type of parliament should not have been chosen as a model. We may deplore that the invectives there exchanged should add to the sum of human tension and bewilderment. Yet it would be incorrect to suppose that these meetings are intended to serve the purpose of negotiation: they are exercises in forensic propaganda and do not even purport to be experiments in diplomatic method. Such negotiation as may occur in New York is not conducted within the walls of the tall building by the East River: it is carried out elsewhere, in accordance with those principles of courtesy, confidence, and discretion which must forever remain the only principles conducive to the peaceful settlement of disputes.

It is not therefore either diplomacy by loud-speaker or diplomacy by insult that we need consider, since these contain a contradiction in terms. It is whether the changes inspired by President Wilson in 1919 do not repeat and emphasize the defects of previous systems and render more difficult what must always remain the chief aim of diplomacy—namely international stability

Woodrow Wilson, with his academic intelligence and missionary spirit, did not realize that foreign affairs are *foreign* affairs, or that a civilization is not a linotype machine but an organic growth. He believed that the misfortunes of mankind are due to the faults of statesmen and experts and that "the people" were always right: he did not realize that, although it may be difficult to fool all the people all the time, it is easy to fool them for a sufficient period of time to compass their destruction. Thus the "Wilsonian," or the "American," method omits many of the merits of the earlier diplomatic systems and exaggerates many of their faults.

WHO HAS THE LAST WORD?

For example, the chief fault of democratic diplomacy as practiced by the Greek City States was its uncertainty. Not only were their diplomatic missions composed of delegates who betrayed each other, but the final decisions rested with an Assembly whose members were ignorant, volatile, impulsive, and swayed by emotions of fear, vanity, and suspicion. No negotiator can succeed unless reasonable certainty exists that his signature will be honored by his own sovereign. If either the conduct or results of negotiation are subject to irresponsible intervention or repudiation on the part of an assembly or even a Congressional Committee—then uncertainty is spread. My first criticism therefore of the American method is that it weakens certainty.

Again, the fault of the method perfected by the Italians of the Renaissance was that it lacked all continuity of purpose and represented a kaleidoscope of shifting combinations. It may be, for all I know, that the President, the State Department, the Pentagon, and Foreign Affairs Committee of the Senate, are unanimous regarding the aim to be achieved; but they are not unanimous as to the means to be adopted. The variability of the diplomatic method employed suggests opportunism rather than continuity; this is an unfortunate impression, a Machiavellian impression, for a great good giant to convey.

The French system possessed the great merit of creating a centralized authority for the formation of foreign policy and a professional service of experts through whom that policy could be carried out. The misfortune of the American system is that no foreigner (and few Americans) can be quite positive at any given moment who it is who possesses the first word and who the last. Although the Americans in recent years have been in process of creating an admirable service of professional diplomatists, these experts do not yet possess the necessary influence with their own government or public. The egalitarian illusions of the Americans—or if you prefer it, their "pioneer spirit"—tempts them to distrust the expert and to credit the amateur. I am not just being old-fashioned when I affirm that the amateur in diplomacy is apt to be suspicious.

"Gullibility," as Sir Edward Grey once said to me, "is in diplomacy a defect infinitely preferable to distrust."

Now that the old disciplines of Pope and Emperor, the old correctives of the Concert of Europe and the Balance of Power, have been dispensed with, it is regrettable that the authority exercised by the United States is not more consistent, convincing, and reliable. Yet I am not pessimistic about the evolution of their diplomatic method. I know that the Americans possess more virtue than any giant Power has yet possessed. I know that, although they pretend to deride the lessons of history, they are astonishingly quick at digesting the experience of others. And I believe that the principles of sound diplomacy—which are immutable—will in the end prevail, and thus calm the chaos with which the transition between the Old Diplomacy and the New has for the moment bewildered the world.

113. *Is War with Russia Inevitable?* *

In this article Mr. Kennan, formerly of the State Department, analyzes one of the pressing problems of our time, namely: Is war with Russia inevitable? In dealing with this problem the author examines the ideological background of Marxian Socialism, the psychological attitude of the Russian people, and the probable effect of the production of atomic bombs by the USSR. In this latter respect it is to be noted that the writing of the article predates President Truman's announcement that the USSR had exploded a second atomic bomb, an occurrence that somewhat modifies Mr. Kennan's position. The conclusion reached in the article is a conservative one tinged with moderate optimism and based on the thesis of the containment of the USSR by diplomatic means and a show of force. The article, published in the State Department *Bulletin*, may be taken as indicative of the mind of our policy makers on the subject, and accordingly gives us a clue to the probable nature of American diplomatic strategy in the future.

Great confusion of thought prevails today with respect to American policy toward the Soviet Union and Russia's real attitude toward us. There is much loose talk going around—on both sides of the ocean—about "preventive war," "the inevitability of the conflict," and "war mongering imperialists."

* George F. Kennan, *The Department of State Bulletin*, 22 (February 20, 1950), pp. 267-271, 303.

Let us ask, and answer, five basic questions—and see if they do not give a pretty clear answer to all this talk of war.

I. ARE THE RUSSIANS PLANNING TO MAKE WAR ON US?

Naturally, only the Soviet leaders themselves could answer this question with certainty. But the following facts are worth remembering.

It is true that Lenin wrote: "The existence of the Soviet Republic side by side with imperialist states for a long time is unthinkable. One or the other must triumph in the end. And before that end comes, a series of frightful clashes between the Soviet Republic and the bourgeois states is inevitable." And this still remains accepted Communist doctrine.

But current Stalinist doctrine does not demand war. On the contrary, it also teaches that eventually capitalism will fall largely of its own weight, i. e., as a result of the inner "contradictions" which the Communists believe it embodies. They see the role of communism as one of hastening the collapse of capitalism and assisting, as a midwife, at the birth of the Socialist order. In theory, they seem inclined to regard this as primarily the task of the native Communists in each country, and not of the Soviet Red Army.

There is nothing in Stalinist doctrine which would make it necessarily the main responsibility of the armed forces of the Soviet Union themselves to overthrow capitalism everywhere by direct military action. This premise would actually seem illogical and improper, from the Communist point of view; for it would imply that capitalism, in the absence of such an attack, would be basically sound and capable of coping permanently with its own "contradictions." But this is exactly what good Marxists do not believe.

So much for doctrine. How about Russian tradition? This factor cannot be ignored; for everyone who knows the Russians is sure that Russia has changed communism more than communism has changed Russia.

Russia has a long history of expansion; but it is generally a history of a sly and cautious expansion, of a readiness to wait patiently for opportunities to extend existing borders without undue risk. Apparent exceptions, such as the Finnish War, seem to have been the results of miscalculations.

The Russians, because of the vastness of their territory and the nature of their geographic position, are land-minded; and this psychology leads them to a preoccupation with their land frontiers and the territories which lie just beyond them. This, on account of their technical and economic backwardness, generally precluded them from ventures which would carry them far afield. They have made it a point to consolidate one newly acquired territory, if they could, before trying to bite off another.

Russian imperialism has generally been a process of nibbling, carefully geared to the capacity of the digestive organs of the Russian State. The experience with the present Eastern European satellites indicates that in this case Soviet imperialism bit off more than it could comfortably chew. The resulting discomfort should make the Kremlin more wary, rather than less, about taking on much bigger bites just at this time.

Finally, we must ask ourselves whether the Soviet leaders would have reason, from the standpoint of their internal interests, to want a world war at this time.

Less than 5 years have elapsed since the termination of the one great war in which the Soviet Union has engaged. For the Russians, that war was terribly wearing and destructive. While steady progress is being made, it will probably be several years before the human and material damages have been entirely remedied.

In addition to repairing the devastations of the war, the Soviet regime is engaged, with deadly seriousness, in implementing a program designed to make the U.S.S.R. a strong and well-rounded industrial state. It will also take several years before some of the basic parts of this program could possibly be completed. World War II set the program back nearly 10 years. Another one could not fail to constitute another serious interruption.

Viewed against the background of doctrine, tradition, and practical realities, therefore, the picture would look something like this: The Russian leaders believe our downfall is inevitable. They would do anything they can to hasten it, but they would not wish to endanger in any major way the security of the world citadel of communism, the U.S.S.R.

In these circumstances, where another world war would obviously involve such dangers, it is hardly likely that the Russians are now charting an early military onslaught on the Western world.

II. HOW DOES RUSSIA'S DEVELOPMENT OF ATOMIC WEAPONS AFFECT THIS SITUATION?

From the evidence available today, Russia's development of the atomic bomb does not affect it very much. The bomb is complicated, costly, and difficult to produce. The raw materials required for its production are still not easy to come by.

Alone, the bomb could not win a total war against a great industrial nation unless it were possible to deliver enough bombs to cripple military resistance at the outset and to compel the government to sue for peace on the attacker's terms. The crippling of resistance would in itself require not just one bomb, successfully delivered, but many. And there are no indications that the Soviet Union now possesses anything like the requisite number of bombs and carriers to achieve this effect on the United States.

In 1946, Stalin said: "I do not believe the atomic bomb would be as serious a force as certain politicians are inclined to regard it. Atomic bombs are intended for intimidating weak nerves, but they cannot decide the outcome of war." There is no reason to believe that the Soviet leaders have departed from this view.

Furthermore, an aggressor would have to take account of the factor of retaliation. In a war where your adversary also has bombs and means of delivery, you have to reflect not only upon what you might do to him, but also upon what he might do to you. A single bomb will not suffice to cripple a great industrial nation; but a single bomb may suffice to wipe out national landmarks and shrines of inestimable value in the hearts and traditions of a citizenry, to say nothing of individuals whose importance to the nation cannot be measured in any material terms. It is one thing to ask an innocent people to bear such blows when they come, unprovoked, from an arrogant aggressor. It is another thing to ask people to bear them when they represent the logical and foreseeable consequence of a policy on which their own government has deliberately embarked.

In the past, aggressors have generally had the hope that their own countries might emerge relatively unscathed from the adventure upon which they were embarking. Weapons being what they were, it was technically possible, if your superiority looked good enough, to have such a hope. Today, if you inaugurate the use of the bomb against civilian-industrial targets and if your adversary also has atomic bombs and carriers, this hope becomes much dimmer. You may do fearful injury to your adversary; conceivably, if you have enough bombs and the ability to deliver them, you may even inflict upon him damage which would wreck for a time his capacity for large-scale, organized resistance; but only two or three of his bombers need get through in order to wreak upon your own country counter-injuries which can make any reports of victories far afield sound to most people like a hollow mockery.

Let us apply these considerations to the purposes and psychology of the men in the Kremlin.

With respect to such retaliation, it is not hard to guess at Soviet reactions. There is no country where the evidences of man's handiwork, both in the cultural monuments of the deep past and in the products of modern industrialization, mean more to people. The cultural monuments are few. They symbolize cultural achievements won with suffering and anguish from the soul of the Russian people. They command deep and general reverence.

The modern industrial plant has also been built up the hard way. Much of it would not compare qualitatively with our own. But to most Russians, regardless of their attitude toward the Communist regime, it symbolizes, again, the potential road of escape from the bondage of Russian backwardness. As for the Russian Communists themselves, it is their outstanding prize and achievement. It was for this, good Communists might privately tell you, that the comfort and the freedoms of at least one generation have been sacrificed.

Now we have already seen that these physical values took a terrible beating in World War II. In these circumstances, further large-scale destruction in Russian cities or industrial communities would constitute a major tragedy, from the standpoint of both the regime and the people. This is not to mention the human values; and not even the Kremlin can be oblivious to these, for manpower constitutes the core of dictatorship as well as of democracy. The idea that the men in the Kremlin, just because they are tough, "wouldn't care" about atomic destruction in Russia, reflects an ignorance of Russian realities.

For the Russians, then, atomic aggression would be an inconclusive and risky venture. It might produce certain momentary favorable effects, but it would also involve considerable dangers. It would begin a war which it alone could not finish. The last two world wars stand as lessons to those who start things they can't finish and particularly to those who attempt to conquer Europe before they have found some means of permanently neutralizing the military-industrial potential of the North American continent.

In an atomic world, total war remains a possibility, inherent in the susceptibility of men to fallacy. But it is now perhaps even less of a probability than before. For it has become potentially more suicidal; and the masters of the Kremlin, in contradistinction to Hitler and the Japanese, are not suicidally inclined.

III. IS WAR POSSIBLE?

Of course it is, and we must unfortunately always think of it as possible as long as we have the sort of world we have today. As Alexander Hamilton once wrote, "Let us recollect that peace or war will not always be left to our option; that however moderate or unambitious we may be, we cannot count upon the moderation, or hope to extinguish the ambition, of others."

There are three main reasons why we must reckon with the possibility of war:

(a) Wars can arise by accident, even though none of the parties really wants them. Considerations of prestige, and the natural nervousness which surrounds the use of armed forces anywhere, mean that nations can become involved in wars accidentally. This risk is perhaps less than it used to be: people are today well aware of the horror of war; and they have calmer nerves than they used to have in dealing with explosive incidents.

The totalitarian states are particularly callous about these matters. In 1938, the Russians and the Japanese fought a full-fledged pocket war, using artillery and aircraft and whole divisions of troops, with scarcely a word about it in their government-controlled newspapers and without any formal complications. The democratic countries, which are more old-fashioned in this respect, are also learning to keep cool nerves in tight situations. But still, when you have military forces operating in such close physical proximity and in such complex conditions as our forces and the Russian forces in Germany and Austria, there is always a danger of incidents.

(b) War can occur because the Russians may think some one is going to attack them. While their ideology does not say that they must attack us, it does not say that we will not sooner or later attack them. On the contrary, the official doctrine is that most non-Communist statesmen are panting to unleash military attacks on the Soviet Union; that they are restrained temporarily by the might of the Red Army and by the great sympathy and respect which, according to the Soviet press, the U.S.S.R. enjoys among the popular masses throughout the world; but that eventually, unless world revolution or some devastating inter-capitalist war intervenes, the attack will come.

The fact that this is nonsense does not make it any the less serious. One of the worst things about totalitarian governments is that they tend to misinform themselves. No one, not even the dictator, can be sure that he is getting honest and reliable information. While we think the Soviet leaders must know that we are neither armed nor aiming for aggressive war, we have absolutely no reason to trust the accuracy of the information about our ultimate intentions which is permitted to reach higher authority by the organs of the Soviet secret police. And we have no reason to trust the ability of that higher authority—cut off as it is from normal contact with the world—to evaluate such information as it receives.

The thesis that the outside world is hostile and deceitful and menacing is essential to the maintenance of the internal power and position of the Soviet secret police. They will do everything they can to uphold that thesis without regard to reality. We can never be entirely sure that they will not, some day, succeed either in convincing themselves and their masters that a capitalist attack is imminent, in which case they might feel that they had to move in order to get the jump on their enemies, or in causing those masters to make further miscalculations similar to those they have occasionally made in the past, with similar results.

(c) This analysis, like any other analysis involving the future of international affairs, may be wrong. Of estimates of this nature, none is foolproof; there are only some that are more likely to be right. The author believes that his is likely to be right, or he would not have written it. But the public should bear in mind, as the author does, that he may be wrong.

These are all reasons why we must regard war as possible. No one of them could be cited, nor all of them together, as a valid reason for regarding war as probable at an early date.

IV. WHERE, IN THESE CIRCUMSTANCES, MUST THE ACCENT OF U. S. POLICY LIE, WITH RESPECT TO THE COMMUNIST DANGER?

It must continue to lie in a vigorous and hopeful foreign policy, which firmly rejects all defeatism about a future war and aims at keeping alive and pursuing vigorously every possibility for solving international differences where possible (and for bearing them where solution is not yet possible) without recourse to war.

The events of the past few months have caused many of us to be concerned primarily with the possibility of military attack on our own territory. But that is not the only way that our security can be menaced. If the Russian Communists should succeed, by means short of war, in bringing progressively under their influence the remaining non-Communist countries of Europe and Asia, our security would be more subtly (but perhaps just as dangerously) undermined than by an atomic attack on our own territory. For the world balance of power would then be turned, at least temporarily, against us.

It is this political expansionism which has been the real Soviet program since the conclusion of World War II. During this period, the Soviet Government has not taken one inch of land by outright military aggression. There are easier, less expensive, and far less risky means of extending power than aggressive war; and it is on these means that the Kremlin appears to have placed its first reliance. There is no reason to believe that this basic relationship will be changed by Russia's possession of the atomic weapon.

Thus, we still have justification for hoping that, by continuing the political struggle known as the "cold war," the worst of our present difficulties can eventually be overcome without another great outbreak of international violence. It means that we must continue to take an intelligent and helpful interest in the efforts of people everywhere to withstand the sort of pressures which are brought to bear against them from the Moscow Communist side. It means that we must continue the policy of throwing our weight into the balance wherever there are relatively good chances that it will be effective in preventing the further expansion of the power of international communism.

This policy has never been guaranteed to be equally successful always and everywhere. There are limits to what a democracy can do in this respect. The result depends invariably not just on what we do but on the interaction between our own policy and the natural powers of resistance which exist among the peoples affected. (No one can force a country to be free which is not itself deeply concerned for its own freedom.) Nothing that has occurred in the recent past has disproved the thesis that such a policy, if resolutely and actively pursued, provides the best chance of carrying us over the peculiar dangers of the present to a more stable and satisfactory condition of international society.

This procedure will not satisfy those impatient spirits who look for some sudden or dramatic solution to the ills which now beset the international community. But these people would find it easier to reconcile themselves to this procedure if they would reflect realistically on the alternatives. There are only two of these: (a) a return to isolation and armed neutrality or (b) war. The first would be accompanied by a disastrous deterioration of conditions in the rest of the world. The second is something which no democratic country could make the objective of its policy.

An attempt at an over-all "agreement" with the Soviet leaders is not really an alternative. The dynamism of world communism would not be seriously affected by such an agreement. Words would still mean different things to the Russians than they mean to us. The agreement would be worth precisely what the realities of world power made it worth at any particular moment. Unless the free world, including ourselves, maintained a vigorous resistance to Soviet Communist political expansion wherever possibilities for such resistance presented themselves, these realities would rapidly deteriorate from our standpoint and with them the value of the agreement. Not to mention that fact that, in any over-all agreement, the Russians would doubtless insist on provisions which would be interpreted everywhere as an acceptance and approval, on our part, of the system of colonial oppression and exploitation which they have imposed upon other peoples in Eastern Europe and elsewhere.

The "cold war" will not be entirely settled in our favor until those whose aims and decisions now keep the international community in a turmoil have been caused to conclude that efforts to maintain or establish political power over other peoples are detrimental to their own selfish interests and that it is inadvisable for them to pursue those efforts further. They will not be brought to this view by oral persuasion. They must come to it in their own manner in the face of a situation of fact which it is our business to help create. Until they do this, no over-all written agreement will really bind them to act as though they had.

It is evident, then, that there is no escape for us from the long hard road on which we have been advancing with a view to bringing about, by peaceful means, a happier and safer and more stable international society. This is the hardest task our country has ever undertaken. It is one unfamiliar to us by experience or tradition. But it has fallen to us by the logic of history and there is no avoiding it.

V. ON WHAT, THEN, DOES OUR NATIONAL SECURITY REALLY REST IN THIS COMING PERIOD?

It might be said that our security rests today in four fundamental points.

First, our security rests in making sure that military aggression remains improbable if not impossible. We should continue to maintain a military posture which, as Theodore Roosevelt once said, will make fighting us "too expensive and dangerous a task to be undertaken lightly by anybody." Let us not be diverted from our task by a morbid preoccupation with what *could possibly happen if.* Let us remember that there is no security in a search for the absolute defense. Security lies in accepting the moderate risks in order that the immoderate ones may be avoided.

Second, our security rests in remembering that the fiber of political resistance among our allies to Moscow Communist pressure will be deeply affected by the extent to which they continue to feel themselves secure in the military sense. Let us give those allies the assurance that we are solidly with them. At the same time, let us help to achieve, for their part, a calm and balanced understanding of the nature of their danger so that their enemies cannot play on false fears.

Third, our security rests in keeping our flag flying high here at home. Few Americans are aware of the intense and skeptical scrutiny to which our domestic affairs are subjected by the outside world and of the beneficial effect produced on both our friends and our enemies by evidences that we are seriously tackling the problems of our own society.

This is not just a question of material prosperity. What the outside world is more eager to know is whether we are capable of coping with the sociological and spiritual strains placed upon us by all this abundance. It is eager to know whether we are going to be able to retain, in a mechanized environment, the individuality, the emotional tone, and the civic vigor of earlier generations of Americans. Naturally, a nation cannot rely on social and spiritual progress for safety any more than it can rely on inoffensiveness. But the connection between these things is closer than most of us would think. We will not convince others, or perhaps even ourselves, that we are protecting something precious unless we cultivate that something as assiduously as we prepare to defend it. To make sure that we can fully respect ourselves remains the best way to hold the respect of others.

Fourth, our security rests in continuing to act in a spirit of justice and good will toward others which will make it possible for us to help a little toward bringing about a general attitude of peaceful cooperation in the world at large. It is here that the present possibilities of the United Nations come into their own.

We should not lose ourselves in vainglorious schemes for changing human nature all over the planet. Rather, we should learn to view ourselves with a sense of proportion and of Christian humility before the enormity and complexity of the world in which it has been given to us to live.

If we do these things, we should be able to go about our international business with our heads high and our eyes clear, untroubled either by overweening ambitions or by panicky anxieties, accepting the risks which are the inevitable concomitant of all real human progress, and keeping our gaze fixed confidently on the distant goals which it is every man's duty always to move toward even though they may never be entirely reached. We will then be doing the best we can in a complex and problematical world. No nation can do more than that.

114. *Blunt Truths about Asia**

AMERICAN RELATIONS with the great continent of Asia are of crucial importance, as the continued presence of American military units and outposts throughout the area demonstrates. Mr. Michener, author of *Tales from the South Pacific*, gives us the "facts of life" in Asia—how the people in the different countries live, eat, pray, and how they are lead. As the author interprets these facts, they must underlie any realistic foreign policy.

ASIA—the mighty continent that for so many decades seemed mute, mysterious and almost impersonally remote to most Americans—has at last become, to these same people, terrifyingly alive and urgent. In November of last year, for the first time in American history, U.S. foreign policy in Asia provided a key issue in a national election, as Republicans raged (rightly enough) that our recent mistakes had stripped us of Asian friends and imperiled our national safety. The return of General Douglas MacArthur this spring effectively took this election issue and converted it into an unprecedented drama of national crisis. No more somber measure of the gravity of the drama is needed than the almost 70,000 American dead, wounded and missing in Korea.

In this way has Asia exploded into the center of American life. Now it will stay there forever. What we do about the fact can make or crush us as a nation .

This sure knowledge makes it all the more frightening for an American to travel in Asia today. Along the entire eastern seaboard the American is utterly unwelcome. In countries like China, Malaya and Indo-China he runs the risk of being murdered. In great cities like Singapore, Saigon and Jakarta wise Americans stay indoors at night. Where he is not hunted, the American is reviled. Never in our national history have we been so feared and despised. Though we encouraged, often helped China, India, Burma and Indonesia to win their national freedom, those very nations today condemn us as reactionary and imperialistic. We, who did most to reclaim Asia from Japanese aggressors, are now ourselves branded as willful aggressors.

That all this may be unfair matters less than the fact that it is so: something has gone badly wrong in our relations with Asia. Nor can it be corrected by either petulance or prideful protestations of inno-

* James A. Michener, *Life*, 30 (June 4, 1951), pp. 96-97, 100, 105-106, 109-110, 115-119, 121. Copyright, 1951, by James A. Michener. Reprinted by permission. Maps and photographs omitted.

cence. The times call for cool, simple, sensible decisions. To make them every American needs to know a lot more about this vast continent than he does at present. This calls for less oratory and more facts in the political fare currently being fed to the public.

For whatever help it may be, I offer a handful of plain and important facts—and some conclusions that seem to me to follow logically.

ASIA IS A BIG AND IMPOSING CONTINENT

It is more than five times as large as the U.S.—16,690,000 square miles to our 3,022,000. It has almost nine times as many people, 1,300,000,000 to our 151,000,000. It is separated from Europe by only a name and some relatively low mountains; from Africa, by only the Suez Canal. Thus it is no wild nightmare to imagine Asia's present enmity spreading across the land masses of the world. If that happened, then—to our east—the Scandinavian and Iberian peninsulas and the British Isles would become daggers pointed at us. To our west we would be beseiged by Siberia and the Kamchatka peninsula. Directly across our Panama life line would be the mighty menace of an alienated Africa. Big as we are, we would then be engulfed. Rich as we are, we would be cut off from many critical raw materials. Strong as we are, we would be doomed.

Six great nations dominate Asia. On the mainland four wield the bulk of power: China (463 million people), India (346 million), Pakistan (74 million) and Russia-in-Asia (50 million). Off the eastern coast stand the other two great nations: Japan (83 million) and Indonesia (80 million).

The importance of these statistics can be measured by the fact that the little-known nation of Pakistan is much larger in population and potential world importance than any nation in Europe save Russia, or any nation in the Americas save the U.S.

ASIA HAS NOT BEEN ABLE TO FEED ITS PEOPLE

If the total food supply were properly distributed, the thousands who yearly starve in Asia might be assured at least of a meager diet. Pakistan, Thailand, Burma, Indo-China and peacetime Korea produce surpluses of food. Starvation does constantly threaten the vast concentration of people in China, India and Japan—the latter saved today solely by American support. And yet Asia is not so heavily populated per square mile as Europe. It has 77 persons to the square mile to Europe's 138. Even Asia's densest nations have fewer people per square mile than comparable areas in Europe or America. Japan has

577 people to the mile, but Belgium has 730. India has 282, but the United Kingdom has 534. China has 123, but the Netherlands has 774. No country of Asia has the population concentration of our state of Rhode Island (674 per square mile).

Asia's real food problem is the common twofold one: turning waste land to use and efficiently distributing its production to deficit areas. In these terms the difficulties of Japan are no different from those of Britain. Both are overpopulated island kingdoms incapable of feeding themselves and hence dependent on manufacturing skill to earn enough for the purchase of food abroad. In this picture there is nothing inscrutable or insoluble. There is no need to blur it with vague visions of "the mysterious east," snared in exotic and exasperating problems. The facts are quite unmysterious.

ASIA IS A BACKWARD CONTINENT

Although it may one day wield greater political and industrial strength than Europe (I am convinced it *will*), Asia today is a distracted and disorganized continent—a place of pain and pathos.

The death rate is shocking. In India life expectancy is 27 years. Men of 40 seem old and worn out. Infant mortality is high. Epidemic diseases sweep across Asia with paralyzing fury.

I remember a typical "water supply" I saw in a Pakistan village. It consisted of a big square hole in the ground called a tank. During the monsoon it filled to overflowing and the water was not bad. In late winter the level was down and was surfaced with green scum. In this water the villagers bathed, urinated, washed their meat for cooking. The children scooped the slime into their mouths.

Rarely is the rest of Asia any better. In Delhi there has been for more than a thousand years a choked and crowded bazaar of silversmiths and cloth merchants, the famed Chandni Chauk. Here on a hot day portions of the renowned street become unbearable, for many of the stores are built over open sewers. The main canals of Jakarta and the side canals of Bangkok serve as spacious, sluggish sewers—and provide the citizens with the water for brushing their teeth and cooking.

Through all Asia the women are still in bondage. Swathed in burlap and cotton from the sight of men, they are denied a fruitful rôle in society. The Begum Liaquat Ali Khan, wife of the Prime Minister of Pakistan, told me that she had been severely criticized for having begged the women of her land to go as nurses among starving and mutilated refugees as they staggered into Pakistan; she was reviled as teaching devout Moslem women shameless behavior.

Almost every intelligent man and woman in Asia hopes this bondage will end. It is quite possible that the first Asiatic nation which does liberate its women will become the leader of Asia.

Illiteracy ranges from 42% in Ceylon, a relatively advanced country, up to 90% in India. The great mass of Asians cannot read, have no radios, have never seen a moving picture. Their native intelligence is high (American agricultural experts testify to this), but their knowledge of the world is abysmal. Not long ago an American journalist, interviewing natives of a village near a major city of India, asked the obvious: "What do you think of America's intervention in Korea?" The first answer was: "What is Korea?"

ASIA IS A VAST OLIGARCHY

Of the six major Asiatic countries only Japan has a directly elected parliament. All the rest, unversed in democracy, have appointed or self-perpetuating assemblies.

To talk seriously of general elections in an area where 90% of the electorate cannot read is to mock the very meaning of democracy. Few educated Asians like or approve this denial of suffrage—there is constant agitation for elections—but power continues to be held by a tiny minority. Often enough this minority is neither stupid nor selfish; it may even rule reluctantly—but rule it must. India is governed by a group of wonderful elderly men: in 1920 they were the leaders of the struggle against Britain; in 1951 they run the country. Pakistan is governed by a younger, dedicated group of Moslem revolutionaries (perhaps a more adaptable group than the Indian leaders). Burma is governed by very young men not yet sure of themselves. China—is Red China.

One typical group of oligarchs is to be found in Indonesia. Most Indonesian leaders are around 40 years of age: the Dutch educated few natives, and those who learned anything about government learned it under the Japanese invasion. Consequently a handful of brilliant and devoted young men rule 80 million people. So conspicuous are youngsters in their 20s that many government bureaus give the impression of a student-government meeting in a large American university. The youthful enthusiasm is admirable—but one shudders to think of these kids governing the sixth largest nation on earth.

These Indonesians know their own problem. One of them, who knows America well, summed it up to me: "If Washington were destroyed, wiping out your entire government, you could go to a city like Des Moines or Denver and find a group of men quite capable of carrying on—someone to handle taxes, another foreign affairs, another national health. Here, if our capital of Jakarta were destroyed, Indonesia could have no government."

Asia, in short, remains today what it has been for centuries, a vast oligarchy. A relatively few leaders—their particular preconceptions, their ambitions, their fears—effectively rule the continent. And yet everywhere are signs of slow change, deep stirrings among vast masses of people—and *their* ambitions and fears number the days of the oligarchs.

THE CITIES ARE THE KEYS TO ASIA

Although most Asians—more than 80%—live in villages, and although ultimately Asia will become a great agrarian economic unit, today the cities control everything: education, political thought and economic power. Vast as it is, the countryside—except where Communist bands rove and terrorize—has not yet found its voice. It is each country's great cities—Tokyo, Shanghai, Manila, Bombay—that set the pitch and purpose of national life, while a few great ports like Singapore and Hong Kong supply enormous inland areas.

Most spectacular are the newer cities of Asia. Before the war Jakarta had a population of 800,000. Today, swollen by tides of refugees fleeing the bandits who ravage the countryside, Jakarta has almost three million. Tempers are short in this teeming capital. I stood not 40 feet from a cyclist who failed to obey a traffic cop. The policeman raised a machine gun, blasted the cyclist and then hauled the body to the side of the road while traffic resumed. Jakarta is a city that might explode against the white man—or against any foreigner—at any moment.

Even more dangerous is Calcutta—recently a city of only two million that today has more than six million people crowding its wildly colorful streets. They came following the 1943 famine, then in another wave after the religious riots. Huge bearded Sikhs roam Calcutta, marked for death if Moslems ever catch them alone. The few Moslems move in perpetual fear, for they are virtual hostages if new religious riots start as a result of trouble in Kashmir. The city's millions of Hindus are nearer than ever to mass starvation since much of Calcutta's rich hinterland was taken from India and given to Pakistan. And Calcutta is the home of the fanatic followers of Subhas Chandra Bose, the nationalist leader who collaborated with the Japanese and died in a plane crash in 1945; today his followers persist in believing he survived and is hiding in Moscow, ready for the right moment to return to lead a new revolution. Be that as it may, here is a city whence, at any moment, riots could explode and shake all India.

The truly astonishing city of Asia is Karachi. A dusty, second-rate seaport of 300,000 before Pakistan's creation, it precipitately became the capital of the new state and a metropolis of 1.3 million, daily swollen by new refugees from India. On its flat plains Karachi encompasses a great number of complete little cities—clusters of mud refugee shacks, tent cities, lean-to cities, cave cities. Through the streets great lumbering camels haul the fabulous riches of this new nation down to the harbor. In the fragile temporary huts that often serve as government offices, young leaders and civil servants work long, dedicated hours with the new and tortuous problems of freedom. In old mosques devout, even fanatical Moslems pray five times each day, offering thanks that they have been able to create the world's foremost religious nation. This is a city that has enough food, much work and enormous sense of purpose.

In all these cities a peculiarly Asiatic phenomenon is the unemployed intellectual. He is a key factor in Asiatic politics, contributing to both the importance and the explosiveness of the crowded cities. What little education Asia has enjoyed has been classical (for many a major job in British India one had to memorize Latin classics). The result has been a plethora of philosophers and a shortage of bricklayers.

Since Asians are naturally gifted in disputation, everyone who could became a lawyer. This was usually a prelude to unemployment and in turn led the young classical scholars right into the middle of some kind of revolution. Gandhi, Jinnah, Soekarno, Bose, Chou En-lai and Madame Chiang Kai-shek represent Asian intellectuals who gained power. It is a dead cinch that today such people—lacking an English or Dutch imperialism to connive against—are plotting against their own governments. A typical recent example is the case of Malaya, which was quite tardy in establishing a university. Once established, it stressed a classical education—and within two years it became a hotbed of Communism. I happened to stumble upon a meeting of the student leaders on the evening of their arrest. Brilliant young men, with no prospect of earning money as philosophers, they had become speculative Communists—while what their nation desperately needed were sewage experts and motor mechanics.

In a sense all these turbulent cities of Asia present the same political paradox as do the oligarchs. For today the cities are much more powerful than the countryside in much the same way as the oligarchs are more politically real and vital than the diffuse popular movements. Yet, as surely as those popular movements must one day prevail, so also is Asia's slumbering peasantry sure to awake with the fury already evident in Red China.

RELIGION IS A CRUCIAL FORCE

Perhaps more than in any other part of the world, events in Asia are directed by religion.

There are exceptions to this, as to any, rule—in this case there are two. In China, Confucianism has always signified no formal religion but rather an ethical system, unweighted with metaphysics or theology; and recent decades have witnessed even a decline in allegiance to Confucianism's social and spiritual precepts. Korea, the second exception, is unique in the world: it has never had a prevailing religion. A 1945 census revealed that in a population of 25 million more than 24 million reported themselves as adhering to no religion; and since Christianity's 500,000 followers constituted the biggest single sect, Korea becomes by default the only "Christian" nation of the Far East mainland.

These exceptions notwithstanding, the rule of religion in Asia holds. Hinduism, the dominant religion of India, is probably the oldest continuing organized religion in the world. It is at once a moral system and a socio-economic system, instructing in such matters as how a wife must obey her husband, how a father must parcel his land among his sons. Tried in other countries with little success, Hinduism in India has withstood assaults by Buddhism, Islam and Christianity. As a result it forms a barrier between India and the rest of Asia. It has already proved a barrier within India, compelling the Moslem minority to feel —rightly or wrongly—that they could live only in a separate state.

Buddhism—initially a reform movement within Hinduism—swept India for a time but slowly receded, only to spread abroad to become at one time or another the principal religion of China, Tibet, Burma, Ceylon, Thailand, Indo-China and Japan. A warm and generous religion, neither nationalistic nor imperialistic, it has little chance of becoming a major force in unifying Asia, for it is fragmented into many sects. Nonetheless it is politically vital today because of its repeated, resolute hostility to Communism.

Of all Asia's religions today, the most striking and significant is Islam. Not only are Pakistan and Indonesia Moslem peoples, but so are almost all countries west of Pakistan, forming a solid belt through the Middle East and across Africa to the Moroccan shores of the Atlantic. Shocked by Israel's victory over the Arabs, all these peoples have recently united into a World Moslem Conference (MOTAMAR). Their cry of "Back to Mohammed"—proclaiming their will for spiritual strength and unity—is sure to ring through Asiatic politics ever more loudly for the next 50 years.

Inamullah Khan, the secretary of MOTAMAR, is a typical Moslem leader. Young, fiery, brilliant, he fled his native Burma to be able to live a wholly Moslem life. He helped found Pakistan itself, then MOTAMAR. Dedicated to bringing all Moslems "back to the Koran, back to our days of glory," he recently helped organize a MOTAMAR conference in Karachi, attended by delegates from 36 nations representing most of the world's 661 million followers of Mohammed.

The aggressiveness of the Moslem forces in Asia is sure to force many crises in the future. Men like Inamullah Khan (who dream of an Islamic "third force" between Communism and the West) deplore violence. But already Moslem fanatics are claiming the southern part of the Philippines. In Thailand they have begun agitating for a separatist state. In Indonesia the government, itself predominantly Moslem, has had to outlaw the fanatic extremists. In Iran the ancient Persian practice of assassination again threatens to rock the whole Middle East.

In this tumultuous world, Christianity is in retreat. Here one finds a heartbreaking and yet wonderful contradiction. Even as Christianity is being driven from Red China, yet its power persists as a major influence on the minds of the leaders of Asia. However few of its leaders may subscribe to Christianity formally, in private they acknowledge with astonishing frequency that they owe much of their education, their attitude toward law and toward the world at large to this same alien religion. It is thus an enormously important legacy that Christian missionaries and Christian teachers have left behind.

To understand Asia's new attitude toward religion, there is no more authoritative source than Miss Fatima Jinnah. She is the beautiful, wraithlike sister of the man whose indomitable will created Moslem Pakistan. She declares emphatically, "We are a democracy in which most of the people happen to be Moslem—and we are determined to remain Moslems. For generations you Christian countries sent missionaries to convert us. We want to be no kind of a theocracy. We want to be left alone to have our kind of nation."

In spite of Miss Jinnah, thousands of Asia's most devout Moslems are equally determined that their nations shall be complete, tightly regimented theocracies. The struggle between these opposing forces has already started, and their contentions may soon stir the whole Moslem world.

ASIA IS READY FOR PROGRESS AND POWER

It is time now to deduce from the plain facts of Asia's past and present some equally plain conclusions about its immediate future.

Common clichés can cripple America's ability to understand Asia.

One such cliché is: "China is a peasant country that can never attain industrial power." Another is: "India is so torn by religious strife it can never achieve the unity to be strong in the modern world."

All such clichés have a common denominator: they deprecate the strength of Asia, its infinite capacity for growth. They also all overlook with singular blindness one mighty fact: modern Japan. It took Japan no more than 60 years to give the lie to all who scorned Asians' ability to become both politically potent and industrially talented.

I wish that any American who clings to such dangerously silly skepticism could have come with me to the city of Morioka in northern Japan. There I experienced a shocking revelation. The streets of Morioka are narrow, and few are paved. Its alleys are thick with mud. The heatless houses are flimsy shacks, the crowded shops without doors. The factories look so dirty and disordered that no American would work in them. Yet it was from shoddy factories like these—from the hands of men living in such squalid hovels—that there came, during World War II, a number of precision weapons to match anything the U.S. could produce. From such places early in the war came torpedoes that greatly exceeded ours in range. They ran true, kept their depth, exploded. Ours didn't.

It is but little more than a half century since this Japan, which almost drove the U.S. from the Pacific, was being glibly tagged with all the empty epithets still currently applied to the rest of Asia. It was "retarded." It was "feudal." It was "rural." The truth is that there is no solid reason why in another 60 years China and India, perhaps Indonesia and Pakistan, cannot progress with the same stunning speed

To match this capacity for power, Asia today is in a mood for power and progress—by its own will. It is resolved to assert its will freely; if necessary, it will do it violently. The shrill dominant note in this mood is nationalism. Imperialism is absolutely finished. And any white men who try to re-establish it will be murdered ruthlessly.

The white man himself is finished in Asia—in any role, however disguised, of local sovereignty. Each Asiatic nation is going to govern itself, in its way and by its own whims. Quite possibly, therefore, American capital will soon be thrown out of Indonesia as peremptorily as British capital is being thrown out of Iran. Wherever this happens, it remains possible that the white man, his money and technical skills, will be invited back on the Asians' terms. If he tries to fight his way back, he will win at best a short and precarious victory.

These are the least pleasant and the most important facts that the nations of the West must accept if they are to make any intelligent decisions about Asia's future or their own.

ASIA IS LEADERLESS

Perhaps the key paradox about Asia is this: though eager for power and competent to attain it eventually, the great continent still contains a huge power vacuum. Russia is making a well-planned effort to fill this vacuum but is almost certain to be thwarted by the same clamoring nationalism that defies any non-Asiatic country. And there is as yet no nation of Asia itself that can offer clear title to the role of continental leader.

In history's long run the leadership of Asia will pretty surely be supplied by one of the three great powers: India, Japan or China. There is an outside chance of some form of Moslem League becoming dominant, but it is more likely that such a league would effectively tip the balance in favor of one of these three.

This contest for power has a plain pattern. It entered a critical phase in 1931 with Japan's assault on Manchuria. It now enters a new, no less menacing phase with China's open excursions into Korea and Tibet, her veiled intervention in French Indo-China and Malaya.

Underlying the inescapable competition among "the big three" is the fact that each of these powers is a rice-deficiency area. India, Japan and China cannot grow enough rice to feed their people. It is the smaller nations, unable to protect themselves, that provide the surplus which the large nations demand. Japan, by World War II, was well on the way to resolving this whole struggle by her own formula: make China absorb her manufacturing surpluses while she commandeered the grain of Korea, Indo-China, Thailand, Burma and eastern India. We smashed this Japanese-German attempt to gather the rice-surplus areas under one leadership. Today we face a Chinese-Russian attempt to do precisely the same thing.

As this struggle continues, it will increasingly affect the war for the world between Communism and the West. And the West must understand in each of the three great Asiatic powers the elements of strength and of weakness.

INDIA'S LEADERSHIP IS LIMITED

The stand of Nehru against the West has won him great popularity. It has tended to underscore dramatically the independence, the spiritual stamina with which India is credited by many Asians. What a young nationalist in Malaya told me was typical of such feelings: "We look to India for guidance. She speaks for the true Asian."

Nonetheless the truth is that the force of India's spiritual leadership is commonly exaggerated, particularly by those whose sentimental allegiance was long ago won by India's fight for freedom. There are powerful factors working against India's permanent leadership. The first is religion. India is Hindu, whereas Malaya and Indonesia are predominantly Moslem; Burma and Ceylon are Buddhist. As Islam becomes even more powerful, India's spiritual leadership will be increasingly challenged.

In the second place, India is now—and will for years remain— susceptible to violent upheavals from within. A famine, failure to solve the cloth problem, an unfavorable outcome of the Kashmir question or the rise of agrarian revolutionists—any of these, in grievous enough form, could topple the government at any time. Both politically and economically India is in perilous balance.

In the third place, India is extremely vulnerable militarily. I found myself in a group of Asians who were discussing the threat of Chinese invasion from the north. An Indian observed sadly, "The sorry truth is that a Chinese or Russian army could march through India like a hot knife cutting through butter." Replied a Burman, "Wrong metaphor. Like a hot knife *falling* through butter."

Finally—and much to India's credit—very few Indians (except perhaps Nehru) aspire to leadership of Asia. They know they have too much work to do at home. Shri Dev Kanta Borooah, a brilliant member of the Indian parliament, told me it would be immoral for India to worry about external problems until she had operated upon her own cancers: education, food supply, roads, elections, health and the status of women. Said Borooah, "If every Indian worked ceaselessly for 10 years we might start to solve some of these problems. We don't ask for a glowing place in the world."

JAPAN IS A QUESTION MARK

In a most important sense Japan was not beaten in World War II. Her seductive motto, "Asia for the Asiatics," has become now the keynote for the policies of all Asiatic countries.

Traveling through Asia today, you hear curiously frank acknowledgment of this fact everywhere. A Malay nationalist told me, "Yes, I worked for the Japs during the war. They did more to awaken my country than all the years of English rule. They showed us what Asians could accomplish." Before the wondering eyes of Malayans, of Burmans, of Asians wherever the Japanese went, whether building bridges or just issuing truculent communiqués, they taught the same lesson in audacious self-reliance.

Nowhere was the lesson better learned than in Indonesia. Sutan

Sjahrir, who at 36 became one of the foremost brains of the new republic, summed it up to me this way: "The Japanese did what the Dutch never did. They showed us how to govern ourselves. It's true the government they set up was intended only to be a puppet, but in operating the puppets we learned to govern. When the Japs left, we retained the government they had given us. With very few changes we still have it." And a brilliant Indonesian newspaperman recalled to me, "Unbelievable as it seems, the Japs were even responsible for our new language. They outlawed Dutch and made us standardize our own language and learn to write it in Roman letters. They were extremely cruel—but they taught us many things."

While all this leaves Japan with a huge potential for Asiatic leadership, Japan herself is today a mixture of strength and weakness hard to measure precisely. The success of the U.S. occupation has been a modern political miracle, attested by the order and discipline of the country even when stripped of U.S. troops by the Korean war. Japan's enormous productive skill has been fortified by her assimilation of American methods. Given a new chance to lead Asia constructively, Japan might well prove successful.

But Japan is far from secure economically. She cannot feed herself. Both agriculturally and industrially she is today sustained only by the dollars America is pumping into the nation. The long-range danger is aggravated by Japan's bewildering fecundity which each year produces more and more people beyond the economic saturation point.

Another question mark must be faced: Japan's present acquiescent posture under military occupation is no automatic guarantee of any abiding affinity for the U.S. She has her own national destiny to pursue. As her own interests cry more loudly for satisfaction in the future, they may be in direct conflict with ours. I remember a cool and sensible remark of a brilliant Japanese soldier, now working as a clerk. I wondered what rank he would now hold if Japan's army had not been disbanded, so I asked, "If Japan had won, what would you be now?" He laughed and said, "I'd be a full colonel in New York, asking you these same questions."

CHINA IS ASIA'S NATURAL LEADER

In size, in economic potential, in command of strategic positions and in prestige among all the peoples of Asia, China is equipped to be the continent's foremost nation. Her present bonds with Russia can damage her repute in time; and yet—military losses in Korea notwithstanding—China's readiness to challenge non-Asiatic powers in Korea fits the mood and excites the mind of most of Asia today.

China has one unique political weapon rarely appreciated by Americans. In almost every nation, every city, every island from Burma eastward to Tahiti there is a Chinese enclave—a minority in some places, in others a majority—which forms a ready-made fifth column in case China runs wild. Precise figures on these alien groups are difficult to obtain. Counting both native-born and those born in China, a responsible estimate for a few countries would be: Thailand, 2.5 million; Malaya, 2.6 million; Philippines, 120,000; Burma, 300,000; Indonesia, 1.9 million. Yet more significant than their numbers is the dominant role played by the Chinese in Asia's economic life. They control nine out of 10 rice mills in Thailand, eight out of 10 in Indo-China and the Philippines. They serve as bankers, wholesale merchants and shippers. Dominating cities like Hong Kong (97% Chinese) and Singapore (77%), they constitute the continent's most powerful entrepreneur class.

In a crisis no one can be sure which loyalty of these people will prevail. As hardheaded, free-enterprising businessmen, they have vast stakes in their communities and a natural antipathy to Communism. But other factors are at work in their minds. There is, for one thing, the effective work of Communist agents among these populations—persistently assuring every Chinese businessman that only his slightly richer neighbor or competitor would suffer from Red rule. And finally there is that perverse kind of pride that enables even rich Chinese capitalists in foreign countries to cheer the sheer audacity of the homeland Communists. As a Bangkok merchant told me tersely, "For 100 years everybody make fun of China. Kick her around. Now China big and tough. People stop making fun of us."

CHINA IS THE TEST OF U. S. POLICY

Only rarely does a nation get a crucial second chance. The United States is lucky: it will. For every nation in Asia is following the main pattern of China's violent experience. This gives America the opportunity to heed and apply the lessons of its fiasco in China.

The essentials of this Asia-wide pattern are fairly simple. The Chinese revolution that, in the 1920s, finished the overthrow of the old order, has since been copied in India, Indonesia, Burma, Ceylon and Pakistan—and is now being followed in French Indo-China, Malaya and Iran. China went one important step further in setting the pattern when it evolved into an oligarchy under Chiang Kai-shek. And this too has been repeated in almost all subsequent revolutions.

It was in grappling with this stage of Asia's revolution that the United States fumbled so badly. We really failed to face the simple facts of life of Asia. This was true in two senses: we failed to realize that Chiang was an inevitable political fact at this point in Asia's growth, indeed was our most important ally; and we also failed to realize that his government must itself inevitably evolve to embrace the ideas of younger men of broader vision. Had we understood that this evolution, with our help and counsel, would surely follow in due time, we could have lived realistically in the present. Instead, we dreamed and we dallied. We did just enough to defeat ourselves on all counts. We refused Chiang enough coherent and effective support to enable him and China to progress—while ambiguously offering just enough to ensure that his Communist enemies could smear him as a tool of American imperialism. This was a classic diplomatic example of self-frustration.

To appreciate the greatness of our loss one must visit Formosa. This island today is the bright spot of Asia. The Nationalist government, shaken to its withers by the debacle on the mainland, has matured astonishingly in the chastisement of defeat. It has established an enlightened commonwealth. Nowhere in Asia is the food problem more fairly handled. Nowhere are justice, human safety and property —those universal measures of good government—so respected and secured. The American cannot visit this island without one lament filling his mind: *this* might have been China today.

Tomorrow it will be India, Pakistan, Indonesia; Burma, Thailand, Iran, the Philippines. Consider India for a moment. Some of her leaders are great men, but most of them are old men, and even were they not mortal, they will prove no more adaptable to new demands and new ideas than China's rulers. *This* oligarchy too will shudder before the attack of new leaders with radically new ideas of land reform or industrialization. And once again the U.S. may elect to pursue either of two ways to ensure defeat for its own interests. One will be to brand indiscriminately all new leaders as Communists (and so drive them into alliance with real Reds). The second will be to play with the fanciful illusion that the real Reds are merely "agrarian reformers" who, for all their loud barking, are really only playfully nibbling at the rights of free men.

In all of Asia the first and perhaps the toughest fact that America must accept is that this world is not made in the American image. This means accepting two specific things. One: it *is* a continent run by oligarchs and, whether or not the idea is congenial to our predispositions, we must deal with them, with all their prejudices and limitations. Two: even when we have made that adjustment to reality, we must not think we have found some permanent formula for political action, for this continent and its oligarchs are going to keep on changing with sometimes bewildering speed. And we will have to change with them.

THERE ARE A FEW RULES FOR OUR ROLE

There can be no pat formulas, no magic keys to success, for our dealings with hundreds of millions of humans in upheaval. But we can set some rules of temper and conduct for ourselves. At worst they can spare us egregious error and the irrevocable loss of more friends. At best they may help Asia to save itself—and ourselves in the process.

I think the most important of these rules of behavior are these.

First: let us keep our normal wits about us. This is not a continent of barbarian hordes or inscrutable evil. It would, in fact, be a most healthy thing if the word "Asia" were never again, in American print, to be prefaced with adjectives like "inscrutable" or "mysterious." They are only fuzzy wraps we throw around our minds when we feel an unpleasant chill of ignorance.

Second: let us apply our keenest brains to the problems. Although the embassies of Paris or London claim more glitter and promise, more frequent front-page mention for aspiring diplomats, Asia cries out for the attention and intelligence of our ablest minds, be they diplomats, soldiers, merchants, technicians or propagandists. Our political reporting from Asia should shine with precision. Our political conduct should be sparked by a flawless sense of timing.

Third: let us banish from our minds the commonest clichés about Asia, for they are often the falsest. They also throw such a smokescreen over serious debate of major issues that both sides find themselves—when the smoke of rhetoric clears a little—firing furiously into positions long since abandoned by their opponents. A good example of a bad cliché is: "You *can't* fight the whole Chinese people." Now —while I do not believe that such a fight could reasonably be called good or necessary today—that statement simply isn't true. The United States most certainly *could* fight the whole Chinese people—and win. Since the time of the Mongols the job has been done more than once. The latest to do it were the Japanese, whose administration of occupied China went pretty much as planned and, without World War II, might have survived indefinitely.

Fourth: let us also purge our thoughts of any lingering illusion that, if things get tough, we can quietly abandon Asia. Last winter, when the Korean war was going badly, a number of cowardly voices (who had hoarsely cheered "police action" a few months earlier) muttered that we had better run to live and fight another day. If trouble is going to soften rather than stiffen our resolve, we simply have to stay out of trouble. Today that's the same thing as planning to stay out of the world.

Fifth: let us be prepared to be disappointed, patient and persistent. Korea is a bitter enough lesson in the fact that it takes time to win. As a people we have to be prepared at times to get licked—and to loathe it. Loathing it enough means staying in the fight. We cannot afford to be thrown off balance by mere irritation, letting petulance parade as a policy. It does not matter whether some Indian leaders are railing wildly against us in public: if it is a good and wise thing to send wheat to India (and it is), we should do it. It is unfair that much of the scorn Asia is heaping upon us is the bitter legacy of a European imperialism in which we played no part ourselves—but this is no time for a debate over 19th Century history. We have to make the best of the facts of our time. If our missionaries are thrown out of China, we must transfer their hospitals and their schools and their churches elsewhere—*in* Asia. If we must close our banks in Hong Kong, we must reopen them in Saigon. If the Communists have devastated Korea by their vicious aggression, we must not only beat them but start rebuilding Korea itself.

Sixth: let us not scorn our European allies in Asia. The costly folly of their colonialism is but part of the truth. The other part is that Great Britain, despite past errors and despite her own failure in China, is widely and deeply respected in many parts of Asia today. By her wise and generous postwar handling of India's demand for freedom Britain saved millions of lives and made possible a Western stand in India on a new footing. As a learned Indian remarked to me, after England was kicked out the front door, she reappeared at the kitchen offering to help do the dishes. Thanks to this, to Britain's wide propagation of her laws, to her evident political experience, Asians today, while they revile Americans, generally remember the English as very decent men.

Finally, let us not, even as we practice the wisdom of forbearance, be beguiled into appeasement. To grovel before Peking's Communists, as British diplomats have found themselves doing, is as futile as it is humiliating. It banishes the last vestige of respect from those it seeks to placate. No Asiatic ally worth having can be bought that way.

The future of the West, in this continent where the white man is so hated, is in terrible doubt. But throughout our history we have won futures, which in dark moments seemed worse than dubious. Here the cost of failure is too staggering to allow us to proceed with anything less than confidence.

CORRELATION TABLES
AND
SUBJECT INDEX

Text Chs.	Anderson and Weidner *American Government,* 4th ed., Henry Holt, 1953	Carr, Morrison, Bernstein, and Snyder *American Democracy: In Theory and Practice,* Revised ed., Rinehart, 1955	Burns and Peltason *Government by the People,* 3rd ed., Prentice-Hall, 1957[1]
	Related Articles in Outside Readings in American Government		
1	—	—	—
2	—	—	1–4, 6–17
3	1, 2	4, 6–17	65
4	3–5, 22	—	20–22, 24
5	6–17	65	18, 19, 23, 89
6	—	18–23, 89	33, 34–37
7	25–27	3, 29, 30	31, 32
8	20, 21, 63–65, 79, 101	28, 34–37	28–30
9	—	31–33	38–41
10	—	—	56, 57
11	—	66	—
12	18, 19, 21, 23, 89	62–65	39, 40, 44
13	—	38	42, 43, 46
14	20	39–41	47–50
15	38	42–46	52
16	28–37	56, 57	53–55
17	—	—	78, 79
18	39–41	47–50	58
19	56, 57	96	72–77
20	42–46	52, 54	62–66
21	51	53, 55	79
22	47-50	58	110, 113, 114
23	—	72–76	112
24	52, 61	78, 79	111
25	54, 60	77	93–100
26	53, 55, 59	93, 94	101–103, 105–109
27	78, 79	88, 92	88, 104
28	80, 82	95	25, 27
29	58	101–105	59–61
30	—	97–100	67–71, 80–82
31	72–76, 81	106–109	83
32	77	112–114	85–87
33	—	110	—
34	88, 90–92	111	84, 90
35	62–66	—	39, 51
36	67–69	—	—
37	—	25–27, 83	—
38	110, 112–114	51, 59–61, 87	—
39	22, 24	80–82, 84, 86	—
40	111	—	—
41	70, 71	89–91	—
42	—	85, 86	—
43	93–100	—	—
44	101–105	—	—
45	106–109	—	—
46	—	—	—

	Ferguson and McHenry *The American System of Government,* 4th ed., McGraw-Hill, 1956[2]	Johnson *American Government: National, State, and Local,* 2nd ed., Crowell, 1955[3]	Johnson *Government in the United States,* 6th ed., Crowell, 1956
Text Chs.	*Related Articles in Outside Readings in American Government*		
1	—	1–4, 66	3, 4, 6, 7
2	1–4	8–17	8–17
3	7–17	20, 65	20, 65
4	65	18, 19, 21–24, 89	1, 2, 5, 25–27
5	18, 20, 21, 23	28–37	18, 19, 22, 24, 89
6	19, 89	38–41	28–37
7	28–37	42–46, 56, 57	38–41
8	38	47	42–46, 56, 57
9	56, 57	48–50	47
10	42–46	78, 79	48–50
11	39–41, 47–51	58	78, 79
12	52, 54	52	58
13	53, 55	53–57	80–82
14	78	62–66	52
15	58, 79	72–76	53–57
16	62–66	77	59–61
17	72–76	88	62–66
18	77	93–96	67–71
19	88, 92	97–100	72–76
20	—	101–105	81, 83–87
21	21, 110	106–109	77
22	112–114	111	88, 92
23	22, 24	110, 112–114	93–96
24	111	—	99–100
25	95	5, 25–27	101–105
26	93, 94, 96	51	106–109
27	104	80, 82	111, 113
28	97–100	59–61	110, 112, 114
29	106–109	67–71	—
30	101–103	81	—
31	105	90, 91	—
32	5, 25–27	—	—
33	59–61	83	—
34	80–82	84–87	—
35	67–71	—	—
36	84–87	—	—
37	83–84	—	—
38	90–91	—	—
39	—	—	—
40	—	—	—
41	—	—	—
42	—	—	—
43	—	—	—
44	—	—	—
45	—	—	—
46	—	—	—

CORRELATION OF THIS BOOK WITH AMERICAN GOVERNMENT TEXTS

	Ogg and Ray *Introduction to American Government,* 11th ed., Appelton-Century-Crofts, 1956[4]	Saye, Pound, and Allums *Principles of American Government,* 2nd ed., Prentice-Hall, 1954	Swarthout and Bartley *Principles and Problems of American National Government,* 2nd ed., Oxford, 1955
Text Chs.	*Related Articles in Outside Readings in American Government*		
1	1, 2	—	—
2	3, 4, 6–17, 65	1–17	1–17
3	18–21, 23, 89	65	65
4	28–37	18–20, 89	18–24, 89
5	38	28–37	38
6	39–41	38	28–37
7	56, 57	39–46	39–41
8	42–46	47–50	42–46
9	51	78, 79	56–57
10	47–50	110–114	52
11	52	72–77	53, 55
12	54, 55	52, 53	54, 58
13	53	24, 54, 55, 93–100	47–50, 78
14	58	62–66	79
15	78, 79	80–87	62–66
16	72–76	—	72–76
17	77	—	77
18	62–66	—	88, 92
19	93–96	—	111, 113, 114
20	97–100	—	110, 112
21	101–103	—	—
22	104, 105	—	95
23	106–109	—	93, 94, 96–100
24	110, 112, 114	—	104, 105
25	111, 113	—	106–109
26	22, 24	—	101–103
27	88, 92	—	—
28	25–27	—	—
29	60, 61	—	—
30	59	—	—
31	80, 82	—	—
32	81	—	—
33	—	—	—
34	91	—	—
35	67–71	—	—
36	—	—	—
37	83	—	—
38	84	—	—
39	86, 87, 90	—	—
40	85	—	—
41	—	—	—
42	—	—	—
43	—	—	—
44	—	—	—
45	—	—	—
46	—	—	—

CORRELATION OF THIS BOOK WITH AMERICAN GOVERNMENT TEXTS

	Gosnell, Lancaster, and Rankin *Fundamentals of American National Government,* McGraw-Hill, 1955	Swisher *The Theory and Practice of American National Government,* Houghton, 1951
Text Chs.	*Related Articles in Outside Readings in American Government*	
1	3, 36	—
2	—	—
3	—	—
4	64, 65, 79	1–4, 6–17
5	18–24, 89	28–41
6	—	42–46
7	1–17	47–50
8	20, 65, 95, 98	51
9	28–41	—
10	42–46, 49	56, 57
11	56, 57	—
12	52	53, 57
13	—	—
14	53-55	55, 58
15	47, 48, 50	78, 79
16	58, 78, 79	—
17	62–66	77
18	72–76	72–76
19	77	62, 66
20	88, 89, 92	63–65
21	93–96	—
22	101–105	88, 92
23	106–109	89
24	110–114	—
25	—	104, 105
26	—	95
27	—	93, 94, 96
28	—	101–103
29	—	97–100
30	—	106–109
31	—	21, 110, 114
32	—	112
33	—	111
34	—	113
35	—	22, 24
36	—	18
37	—	19, 20
38	—	90
39	—	—
40	—	—
41	—	—
42	—	—
43	—	—
44	—	—
45	—	—
46	—	—

Since the following books, limited in scope to the National Government, consist of chapters which correspond to the earlier chapters of the books indicated, the chapter references as given, apply to these also.

[1] Burns and Peltason, *Government by the People: National,* 3rd ed., Prentice-Hall, 1957
[2] Ferguson and McHenry, *The American Federal Government,* 4th ed., McGraw-Hill, 1956
[3] Johnson, *American National Government,* 4th ed., Crowell, 1955
[4] Ogg and Ray, *Introduction to American Government: National,* 11th ed., Appelton-Century-Crofts, 1956

INDEX